# A DICTIONARY OF AMERICAN IDIOMS

**FOURTH EDITION**

Adam Makkai
M. T. Boatner
J. E. Gates

Revised and thoroughly updated by

**Adam Makkai**
Professor of Linguistics
University of Illinois at Chicago

BARRON'S

*All inquiries should be addressed to:*
Barron's Educational Series, Inc.
250 Wireless Boulevard
Hauppauge, NY 11788
**http://www.barronseduc.com**

ISBN-13: 978-0-7641-1982-8
ISBN-10: 0-7641-1982-6

*Library of Congress Catalog Card Number 2003052485*

**Library of Congress Cataloging-in-Publication Data**
A dictionary of American idioms / [edited by] Adam Makkai,
M.T. Boatner, J.E. Gates.— 4th ed. / revised and thoroughly
updated by Adam Makkai.
   p.  cm.
   ISBN 0-7641-1982-6 (alk. paper)
English language—United States—Idioms—Dictionaries.
2. Americanisms—Dictionaries. I. Makkai, Adam. II. Boatner,
Maxine Tull. III. Gates, John Edward.

PE2839.D5    2004
423'.1—dc21                              2003052485

PRINTED IN CANADA
9 8 7

# Contents

# Acknowledgments

This dictionary is the result of the work of many hands. It was first published in 1966 in West Hartford, Connecticut, and later republished in 1969, copyrighted by the American School for the Deaf under the title *A Dictionary of Idioms for the Deaf*, edited by Maxine Tull Boatner, project director, aided by chief linguistic advisor, J. Edward Gates. The consulting committee consisted of Dr. Edmund E. Boatner, Dr. William J. McClure, Dr. Clarence D. O'Connor, Dr. George T. Pratt, Jack Brady, M.A., Richard K. Lane, and Professor H. A. Gleason, Jr., of the Hartford Seminary Foundation. Special editors for various subcategories, such as usage, sport terms, etc., were Elizabeth Meltzer, and E. Ward Gilman; Loy E. Golladay helped as language consultant with reviewing and editing. Definers were Edmund Casetti, Philip H. Cummings, Anne M. Driscoll, Harold J. Flavin, Dr. Frank Fletcher, E. Ward Gilman; Loy E. Golladay, Dr. Philip H. Goepp, Dr. Beatrice Hart, Dr. Benjamin Keen, Kendall Litchfield, Harold E. Niergarth, Ruth Gill Price, Thomas H. B. Robertson, Jess Smith, Rhea Talley Stewart, Harriet Smith, Elizabeth D. Spellman, John F. Spellman, and George M. Swanson, Barbara Ann Kipfer, and Justyn Moulds. The following have cooperated as simplifiers: Linda Braun, Dr. G. C. Farquhar. Carey S. Lane, Wesley Lauritsen, Nellie MacDonald, Ruth S. McQueen, and Donald Moores. In 1975 an edition was prepared for Barron's Educational Series, by the well-known expert on idioms Professor Adam Makkai of the University of Illinois at Chicago Circle.

For the second edition, Professor Makkai deleted obsolete material, updated old entries, and added hundreds of modern idiomatic phrases to the collection. Many of these new entries were of the slang character, originating within recent cultural movements; others reflect the popular usage of specialized areas of endeavor, including computer technology. Professor Robert A. Hall, Jr. of Cornell reviewed the manuscript of the revision and made invaluable suggestions.

In this new, thoroughly revised and updated fourth edition, Professor Makkai added *more than 2,000* new entries, making it the largest dictionary of American idioms available on the market today.

The ever-increasing international demand for more and better dictionaries of American idioms necessitated the inclusion of eight foreign language prefaces explaining what idioms are and how this book works. We wish to acknowledge the help of the following individuals in preparing these foreign language prefaces:

*Arabic:* Hussein, Quwaider, Ph.D., University of Bath.
*Chinese:* Professor Guo Yianzhong, University of Hangzhou, P.R.C.
*French:* Professor Jean-Luc Garneau, Lake Forest College.
*German:* Doris Jutta Glatzl, M.A. (UIC), Department of German.
*Hebrew:* Aya Katz, Ph.D., Rice University, Houston, TX
*Italian:* Professor Marcel Danesi, University of Toronto.
*Japanese:* Richard Goris, Shubun International, Tokyo.
*Russian:* Maya Aleksandrovna Glinberg, M.A., University of Moscow.
*Spanish:* Verónica Cortés, M.A. (UIC), Department of Linguistics.

We also acknowledge with thanks the numerous inquiries and letters from readers of this dictionary. Their questions and suggestions have been a most welcome source of inspiration for further research. Once again we encourage all interested users of this book to jot down any queries, suggestions, and questions that occur. Please send all such correspondence to the Editor, c/o Barron's Educational Series, 250 Wireless Blvd., Hauppauge, NY 11788, USA.

# The Most Useful Dictionary of American Idioms

As you compare this *Dictionary of American Idioms* with similar works, please be aware that you are holding the most comprehensive dictionary of its kind on the market:

- More than 8,000 entries taken from real life and based on actual observations of how Americans use them.
- A dictionary with an international scope that aims at anybody whose native language was not American English. Prefaces written in nine languages help explain what an idiom is, what kinds there are, and how they work.
- A totally revised and updated edition that capitalizes on its astounding past success and brings brand-new idioms from all areas of human endeavor.
- Logical ordering of information that includes the parts of the sentence, clear explanations, enlightening examples, and cross-references in alphabetical order on every pertinent page.

# Introduction

## WHAT IS AN IDIOM?

If you understand every word in a text and still fail to grasp what the text is all about, chances are you are having trouble with the idioms. For example, suppose you read (or hear) the following:

*Sam is a real cool cat. He never blows his stack and hardly ever flies off the handle. What's more, he knows how to get away with things . . . Well, of course, he is getting on, too. His hair is pepper and salt, but he knows how to make up for lost time by taking it easy. He gets up early, works out, and turns in early. He takes care of the hot dog stand like a breeze until he gets time off. Sam's got it made; this is it for him.*

Needless to say, this is not great literary style, but most Americans, especially when they converse among themselves, will use expressions of this sort. Now if you are a foreigner in this country and have learned the words *cool* 'not very warm,' *cat* 'the familiar domestic animal,' *blow* 'exhale air with force,' *stack* 'a pile of something, or material heaped up,' *fly* 'propel oneself in the air by means of wings,' *handle* 'the part of an object designed to hold by hand'—and so forth you will still not understand the above sample of conversational American English, because this basic dictionary information alone will not give you the meaning of the forms involved. An idiom—as it follows from these observations—is the assigning of a new meaning to a group of words which already have their own meaning. Below you will find a 'translation' of this highly idiomatic, colloquial American English text, into a more formal, and relatively idiom free variety of English:

*Sam is really a calm person. He never loses control of himself and hardly ever becomes too angry. Furthermore, he knows how to manage his business financially by using a few tricks . . . Needless to say, he, too, is getting older. His hair is beginning to turn gray, but he knows how to compensate for wasted time by relaxing. He rises early, exercises, and goes to bed early. He manages his frankfurter stand without visible effort, until it is someone else's turn to work there. Sam is successful; he has reached his life's goal.*

Now if you were to explain how the units are organized in this text, you would have to make a little idiom dictionary. It would look like this:

| | |
|---|---|
| *to be a (real) cool cat* | to be a really calm person |
| *to blow one's stack* | to lose control over oneself, to become mad |
| *to fly off the handle* | to become excessively angry |
| *what's more* | furthermore, besides, additionally |
| *to get away with something* | to perpetrate an illegitimate or tricky act without repercussion or harm |
| *of course* | naturally |
| *to be getting on* | to age, to get older |
| *pepper and salt* | black or dark hair mixed with streaks of gray |
| *to make up for something* | to compensate for something |
| *lost time* | time wasted, time spent at fruitless labor |
| *to take it easy* | to relax, to rest, not to worry |
| *to get up* | to rise from bed in the morning or at other times |
| *to work out* | to exercise, to do gymnastics |
| *to turn in* | to go to bed at night |
| *like a breeze* | without effort, elegantly, easily |

| | |
|---|---|
| *time off* | period in one's job or place of employment during which one is not performing one's services |
| *to have got it made* | to be successful, to have arrived |
| *this is it* | to be in a position or in a place, or to have possession of an object, beyond which more of the same is unnecessary |

Many of the idioms in this little sample list can be found in this dictionary itself. The interesting fact about most of these idioms is that they can easily be identified with the familiar parts of speech. Thus some idioms are clearly verbal in nature, such as *get away with, get up, work out,* and *turn in.* An equally large number are nominal in nature. Thus *hot dog* and *cool cat* are nouns. Many are adjectives, as in our example *pepper and salt* meaning *'black hair mixed with gray.'* Many are adverbial, as the examples *like the breeze* 'easily, without effort,' *hammer and tongs* 'violently' (as in *she ran after him hammer and tongs),* and so forth. These idioms, which correlate with the familiar parts of speech, can be called *lexemic idioms.*

The other most important group of idioms are of larger size. Often they are an entire clause in length, as our examples to *fly off the handle,* 'lose control over oneself,' and to *blow one's stack,* 'to become very angry.' There are a great many of these in American English. Some of the most famous ones are: to *kick the bucket* 'die,' *to be up the creek* 'to be in a predicament or a dangerous position,' to *be caught between the devil and deep blue sea* 'to have to choose between two equally unpleasant alternatives,' to *seize the bull by the horns* 'to face a problem and deal with it squarely,' and so on. Idioms of this sort have been called *tournures* (from the French), meaning 'turns of phrase,' or simply *phraseological idioms.* What they have in common is that they do not readily correlate with a given grammatical part of speech and require a paraphrase longer than a word.

Their form is set and only a limited number of them can be said or written in any other way without destroying the meaning of the idiom. Many of them are completely rigid and cannot show up in any other form whatever. Consider the idiom *kick the bucket,* for example. In the passive voice, you get an unacceptable form such as *the bucket has been kicked by the cowboy,* which no longer means that the 'cowboy died.' Rather it means that he struck a pail with his foot. Idioms of this type are regarded as *completely frozen forms.* Notice, however, that even this idiom can be inflected for tense, e.g., it is all right to say *the cowboy kicked the bucket, the cowboy will kick the bucket, he has kicked the bucket,* etc. Speakers disagree as much as do grammarians whether or not, for example, it is all right to use this idiom in the gerund form (a gerund being a noun derived from a verb by adding *–ing* to it, e.g., *singing* from *sing, eating* from *eat,* etc.) in *His kicking the bucket surprised us all.* It is best to avoid this form.

The next largest class of idioms is that of well established sayings and proverbs. These include the famous types of *don't count your chickens before they're hatched* (meaning 'do not celebrate the outcome of an undertaking prematurely because it is possible that you will fail in which case you will look ridiculous'); *don't wash your dirty linen in public* (meaning 'do not complain of your domestic affairs before strangers as it is none of their business'), and so forth. Many of these originate from some well known literary source or come to us from the earliest English speakers of the North American Continent.

Lack of predictability of meaning (or precise meaning) is not the only criterion of idiomaticity. Set phrases or phraseological units are also idiomatic, even though their meanings may be transparent. What is idiomatic (unpredictable) about them is their construction. Examples include *How about a drink? What do you say, Joe?* (as a greeting); *as a matter of fact, just in case; just to be on the safe side,* and many more.

Another important case of idiomaticity is the one-word idiom that occurs when a word is used in a surprisingly different meaning from the original one. Examples include *lemon,* said of bad watches, cars, or machines in general; and *dog,* said of a bad date or a bad exam. *(My car is a lemon, my math exam was a dog.)*

Why is English, and especially American English, so heavily idiomatic? The most probable reason is that as we develop new concepts, we need new expressions for them, but instead of creating a brand new word from the sounds of the language, we use some already existent words and put them together in a new sense. This, however, appears to be true of all known languages. There are, in fact, no known languages that do not have some idioms. Consider the Chinese expression for 'quickly,' for example. It is *mǎ shāng*, and translated literally it means 'horseback.' Why should the concept of 'quick' be associated with the back of a horse? The answer reveals itself upon a moment's speculation. In the old days, before the train, the automobile, and the airplane, the fastest way of getting from one place to the other was by riding a horse, i.e., on horseback. Thus Chinese *mǎ shāng* is as if we said in English *Hurry up! We must go 'on horseback,'* i.e., 'Hurry up! We must go quickly.' Such a form would not be unintelligible in English at all, though the speaker would have to realize that it is an idiom, and the foreigner would have to learn it. However, in learning idioms a person may make an incorrect guess. Consider the English idiom *Oh well, the die is cast!* What would you guess this means— in case you don't know it? Perhaps you may guess that the speaker you heard is acquiescing in something because of the *Oh well* part. The expression means 'I made an irreversible decision and must live with it.' You can now try to reconstruct how this idiom came into being: The image of the die that was cast in gambling cannot be thrown again; that would be illegal; whether you have a one, a three, or a six, you must face the consequences of your throw, that is, win or lose, as the case may be. (Some people may know that the phrase was used by Caesar when he crossed the Rubicon, an event that led to war.)

How, then, having just learned it, will you use this idiom correctly? First of all, wait until you hear it from a native speaker in a natural context; do not experiment yourself with using an idiom until you have mastered the basics of English grammar. Once you have heard the idiom being used more than once, and fully understand its meaning, you can try using it yourself. Imagine that you have two job offers, one sure, but lower paying, and one that pays more, but is only tentative. Because of nervousness and fear of having no job at all, you accept the lower paying job, at which moment the better offer comes through and naturally you feel frustrated. You can then say *Oh well, the die is cast . . .* If you try this on a native speaker and he looks at you with sympathy and does not ask 'what do you mean?'—you have achieved your first successful placement of a newly learned idiom in an appropriate context. This can be a rewarding experience. Americans usually react to foreigners more politely than do people of other nations, but they can definitely tell how fluent you are. If a person always uses a bookish, stilted expression and never uses an idiom in the right place, he might develop the reputation of being a dry, unimaginative speaker, or one who is trying to be too serious and too official. *The use of idioms is, therefore, extremely important. It can strike a chord of solidarity with the listener.* The more idioms you use in the right context, the more at east Americans will feel with you and the more they will think to themselves 'this is a nice and friendly person—look at how well he expresses himself!'

We will now take a look at some practical considerations regarding the use of *A Dictionary of American Idioms.*

## HOW TO USE THIS DICTIONARY

This dictionary can be used successfully by nonnative speakers of English, students, workers, immigrants—in short, anybody who wants to make his English more fluent, more idiomatic. It contains phrases of the types mentioned above, lexemic idioms, phrase idioms, and proverbial idioms, that have a special meaning. When a phrase has a special meaning that you cannot decode properly by looking up and understanding the individual words of which it is composed, then you know you are dealing with an idiom. You may already know some of these idioms or may be able to imagine what they mean. Look in the book for any of the following idioms that you may already know well; this will help you to understand how you should use this book: *boyfriend, girlfriend, outer space, piggy bank, get even, give up, going to, keep on, keep your mouth shut, lead somebody by the nose, look after, show off, throw away, all over, in love, mixed-up, out of this world, throw away, I'll say, both X and Y.*

A dictionary is like any other tool: You must familiarize yourself with it and learn how to use it before it begins to work well for you. Study the directions carefully several times, and practice looking up idioms. That way, searching for an idiom and finding it will become second nature to you. If you hear an idiomatic expression that is not in this book, after using it for a while, you will develop the ability to track down its meaning and write it down for yourself. Keep your own idiom list at home, right beside your regular dictionary. If you read a technical text, or a novel or a newspaper article and do not understand an expression, look it up in your regular school dictionary first; if you do not find it, try this one.

How do you find out if this dictionary can help you understand a hard sentence? Sometimes you can easily see what the phrase is, as with *puppy love, fun house, dog-eat-dog, mixed-up.* If not, pick out an important word from the most difficult part and look for that. If it is the first word in the idiom, you will find the whole phrase, followed by an explanation. Thus the expression *bats in the belfry* is listed in this dictionary under *b,* the word *bats.* If the word you picked is not the first word, you will find a list of idioms that contain that word. For example the word *toe* will be found in entries such as *curl one's hair OR curl one's toes, on one's toes, step on the toes (of somebody).* You may, of course, find that the reason why you do not understand a particular sentence is not because of any idioms in it; in that case your regular dictionary will be of help to you. Also, there are more idioms than listed in this book; only the most frequently occurring in *American English* are included. British English, for example, or the English spoken

in Australia, certainly has many idiomatic expressions that are not a part of American English.

## TYPES OF ENTRY

This dictionary contains four kinds of entry: *main entries, run-on entries, cross reference entries,* and *index entries.* A main entry includes a full explanation of the idiom. A run-on entry is a phrase which is derived from another idiom but would be separated from it if it entered at its own alphabetical place. These derived idioms have been run on at the end of the main entry (e.g., *fence-sitter* at *sit on the fence*) with an illustration and a paraphrase; an extra explanation has been added when understanding the derivative from the main explanation seemed difficult. When an idiom has come to be used as more than one part of speech, a separate entry has been made for each usage.

A cross-reference entry guides you to a definition in another place. Suppose you want to look up *cast in one's lot with.* You can look under *cast,* and under *lot;* but the cross-reference entry will send you to *throw* in the phrase *throw in one's lot with.* The reason for this is that *cast* is a much rarer word nowadays and so the usual, more frequent form of this idiom starts with the verb *throw.*

An index entry directs you to all other entries containing the index word. Thus the word *chin* is followed by the phrases of which it is a part, e.g., *keep one's chin up, stick one's chin (or neck) out, take it on the chin, up to the chin in.*

## PARTS OF SPEECH LABELS

Those idioms that correlate with a well-defined grammatical form class carry a part of speech label. Sometimes, as with many prepositional phrases, a double label had to be assigned because the given phrase has two grammatical uses, e.g., *in commission* can be either adverbial or adjectival. Many prepositional phrases are adverbial in their literal sense, but adjectival in their nonpredictable, idiomatic sense. *v.* stands for verb; it was assigned to phrases containing a verb and an adverb; verb and preposition; or verb, preposition, and adverb. *v. phr.* Stands for 'verbal phrase'; these include verbs with an object, verbs with subject complement, and verbs with prepositional phrase.

## RESTRICTIVE USAGE LABELS

You must pay particular attention to whether it is appropriate for you to use a certain idiom in a certain setting. The label *slang* shows that the idiom is used only among very close friends who are quite familiar with one another. *Informal* indicates that the form is used in conversation but should be avoided in formal composition. *Formal* indicates the opposite; this is a form that people usually do not say, but they will write it in an essay or will state it in a speech or a university lecture. *Literary* alerts you to the fact that people are usually aware that the form is a quotation; it would be inappropriate for you to use these too often. *Vulgar* indicates that you should altogether avoid the form; recognizing it may, of course, be important to you as you can judge a person by the language he uses. *Substandard* labels a form as chiefly used by less educated people; *nonstandard* means that a phrase is felt to be awkward. *Archaic* (rarely used in this book) means that the form is heavily restricted to Biblical or Shakespearean English. *Dialect* means that the form is restricted to its geographical source; e.g., *chiefly British* means that Americans seldom use it, *Southern* means that the form is of much higher currency in the South of the United States than in the North.

*Adam Makkai, Ph.D.*
*Professor of Linguistics*
University of Illinois at Chicago
*Executive Director and Director of Publications,* Emeritus, Linguistic Association of Canada and the United States (LACUS), Inc.,
*Executive Director,* Atlantis-Centaur, Inc.

# مقدمة

## ما هي العبارة الاصطلاحية؟

إن عرفتك لمعنى كلّ كلمة في نص ما مع في الوقت نفسه غير قادر على إدراك فحوى ذلك النصّ فهذا يعني أنك تواجه مشكلةً مع العبارة الاصطلاحية. لنفترض مثلاً أنك تقرأ أو تستمع إلى ما يلي؛ هنا لا يسعنا القول بأن هذا النصّ لا يتسّم بأسلوبٍ أدبيٍ رفيع:

*Sam is a real cool cat. He never blows his stack and hardly ever flies off the handle. What's more, he knows how to get away with things...well, of course, he is getting on, too. His hair is pepper and salt, but he knows how to make up for lost time by taking it easy. He gets up early, works out and turns in early. He takes care of the hot dog stand like a breeze until he gets time off. Sam's got it made; this is it for him.*

ولكنّ معظم الأمريكيين يستخدمون تعابير كهذه لا سيّما في أحاديثهم اليومية. ولو كنت أجنبياً تعيش في أمريكا وتعلّمت مفرداتٍ مثل كلمة cool بمعنى ليس دافئاً جدا وكلمة cat بمعنى قط، ذلك الحيوان الأليف وكلمة blow التي تعني نفث الهواء بشدة وكلمة stack بمعنى كومة من الأشياء المكدّسة فوق بعضها وكلمة fly بمعنى يطير في الهواء مستخدماً جناحيه وكلمة handle بمعنى مقبض، ذلك الجزء الذي يمسك باليد ومع ذلك لن تدرك مغزى النص المدون أعلاه الذي يعتبر نموذجا للغة التخاطب في أمريكا لأن المعلومات الأساسية المعجمية وحدها لن تكفي وبالتالي لن توفر لك معاني التعابير التي يتضمنها النص. إن العبارة الاصطلاحية كما يفهم من هذه الملاحظات تعني استنباط معنى جديدا لمجموعة من الكلمات التي عرفنا لتو معانيها. أدناه تجد ترجمة للنص المدون أعلاه بلغة عربية مبسّطة وذلك بعد أن ترجم إلى لغة إنجليزية/أمريكية عامية أكثر رسمية وخالية من أية عبارات اصطلاحية وذلك على الرغم من أن النص الأصلي يتصف باصطلاحيته الشديدة :

سام شخص هادئ الطبع حقاً. لا يفقد أعصابه مطلقاً ونادراً ما يغضب. أضف إلى ذلك، فهو يعرف كيف يدير عمله جيداً بجودة الى التحايل والدهاء. لقد بدأ يتقدم في السن ومع ذلك يزحف البياض الى شعره الأسود. كما أنه يعرف جيداً كيف يعوّض وقته الضائع بالخلود إلى الراحة وعدم الاكتراث بأي شيء حيث ينهض باكراً ليمارس تمارينه الرياضية ويأوي إلى فراشه مبكراً أيضاً. يمارس عمله في كشك لبيع النقانق بكلّ سهولة ويسر لحين وصول العامل البديل. سام شخص ناجح وقد تمكن من تحقيق هدفه في الحياة.

ولو طلب منا هنا توضيح الكيفية التي تم من خلالها تكوين هذا

النص المترجم فلا بدّ عندئذٍ من إعداد معجم صغير للعبارات الاصطلاحية والذي سيكون على النحو التالي:

| To be a cool cat | شخص هادئ حقا |
| To blow one's stack | يفقد أعصابه |
| To fly off the handle | يغضب |
| What's more | أضف الى ذلك |
| To get away with something | يتملص/يتحايل |
| Of course | طبعاً |
| To be getting on | يتقدم في السن |
| Pepper and salt | شعر أبيض يشوبه السواد |
| To make up for | يعوّض |
| Lost time | الوقت الضائع |
| To take it easy | يأخذ الأمور ببساطة |
| To get up | ينهض من فراشه |
| To work out | يمارس التمارين الرياضية |
| To turn in | يأوي إلى فراشه |
| Like a breeze | بسهولة ويسر |
| Time off | انتهاء نوبة عمله |
| To have got it | يحقق هدفه |
| This is it | الحصول على أكثر مما يبتغيه |

كثير من العبارات الاصطلاحية المدرجة في القائمة أعلاه يمكن أن ترد في هذا المعجم ولكن الأمر المثير للاهتمام بشأن معظم هذه العبارات أنه يمكن التعرف عليها من خلال أقسام الكلام المألوفة لغويا حيث نجد بعضها ذات طبيعة فعلية ( تأخذ شكل الفعل ) مثل get away with, get up, turn in, work out, وبعضها الآخر ذات طبيعة اسمية ( تأخذ شكل الاسم ) مثل cool cat, hot dog بينما نجد عددا آخر على شكل صفة كما في مثالنا pepper and salt بمعنى شعر أسود يشوبه البياض وعدداً مماثلاً ذات طبيعة ظرفية مثل like a breeze بمعنى «بسهولة ويسر» وكذلك hammer and tongs التي تعني «بعنف» كقولنا She ran after him hammer and tongs وهكذا دواليك. هذه العبارات الاصطلاحية التي ترتبط بأقسام الكلام المألوفة يمكن تسميتها العبارات الاصطلاحية المفرداتية أو المعجمية Lexemic idioms أما المجموعة الأخرى من العبارات الاصطلاحية الأكثر أهمية تكون ذات تراكيب أطول حيث تماثل في طولها شبه جملة كما في الأمثلة التي وردت في النص أعلاه مثل عبارة fly off the handle (يفقد السيطرة على أعصابه ) وعبارة blow one's stack (يغضب) حيث نصادف العديد من هذه العبارات في لغتنا الإنجليزية/الأمريكية. ومن أهم هذه العبارات يمكن أن نسوق ما يلي: kick the bucket (يموت) وعبارة to be up the creek (تكون في وضع خطر) وعبارة :

XI

الإنجليزية في قارة أمريكا الشمالية.

والجدير بالذكر أن عدم القدرة على التنبؤ بمعنى العبارة الاصطلاحية أو إن صح التعبير بمعناها الدقيق لا يعد المعيار الوحيد لاصطلاحية تلك العبارة لأن بعض العبارات والوحدات اللغوية التي تتميز بتركيبها الخاصة تكون أيضاً اصطلاحية بالرغم من شفافية معناها والقدرة على إدراكه. كل ما في الأمر أن اصطلاحية تلك العبارات (عدم القدرة على التنبؤ بمعناها) تكمن في تراكيبها ليس إلا. وكمثـال علـى ذلك نسوق العبـارات التـالية: What do you, say, Joe? (مـا قـولك يـا جـو؟) What about a drink? (ما رأيك في كأس؟) وذلك مـن باب التـحيـة. أضف إلى ذلك عبـارة As a matter of fact, just in case. (في الواقع، تحسباً ما يمكن أن يحدث) وعبارة Just to be on the safe side: (حتـى نـكون في الجانب السليم وذلك من باب الاحتيـاط) وغيرها كثير.

وهناك حالة مهمّة أخرى من العبارة الاصطلاحية تتمثّل بوجود عبارة اصطلاحية مكونة من كلمة واحدة وذلك لدى استخدام كلمة ما بمعنى مختلف تماما عن معناها الأصلي. وتعبيرًا عن هذه الحالة يمكن أن نسوق بعض الأمثلة مثل كلمة «lemon» (ليمون) للدلالة على الفشل والإخفاق بشكل عام و للدلالة على رداءة ساعات اليد أو الجيب أو السيـارات ولآليـات عمومـا وهنـاك أيضـا كلـمة «dog» (كلب) للدلالة على موعد غرامي أو امتحان فاشل كقولنا My car is a lemon and my exam was a dog هنا نتساءل: لماذا يا ترى نجد اللغة الإنجليزية عمومـاً والإنجليزية/الأمريكية على وجه الخصوص حافلة بالعبارات الاصطلاحية؟ لعل السبب الذي يبدو أكثر احتمالاً هنا يكمن في كوننا نسعى دائما إلى خلق مفاهيم جديدة وبالتالي نحتاج إلى تعابير جديدة لتوضيح مدلول تلك المفاهيم ولذلك بدلاً من أن نبتدع كلمة جديدة من أصوات اللغة نلجأ إلى استخدام بعض الكلمات الموجودة أصلاً في اللغة وصوفها في عبارة ذات مفهوم جديد. هذا الأمر ينسحب على جميع لغات العالم لأنه لم نسمع عن لغة ما لا تشتمل على العديد من العبارات الاصطلاحية.

فلو أخذنا التعبير الصين mā shāng بمعنى «سريعا» وترجمناه حرفياً لوجدنا أنه يعني «ظهر الحصان». لماذا يربط مفهوم السرعة بظهر الحصان؟ الجواب يعبرّ عن نفسه بلحظة تأمّل سريعة. من المعروف أنّه في قديم الزمان وقبل ظهور وسائل النقل السريعة مثل القطارات والسيارات والطائرات كان الركوب على ظهور الخيل أسرع وسيلة للانتقال من مكان إلى آخر. وعليه يمكننا القـول بأن استخدام العبارة الصينية mā shāng شبيه باستخدام العبارة الاصطلاحية:

Hurry up! We must go on horseback

التي تعني حرفياً «أسرع! يجب أن نذهب على ظهر الحصان». إن عبارة كهذه لن تكون غامضة أبداً في اللغة الإنجليزية رغم إدراك المتحدث بأنها اصطلاحية وأن على الأجنبي أن تعلّم تلك العبارة. من جانب آخر، إن دارس العبارات الاصطلاحية قد يخطئ في تخمينه لمعنى العبارة الاصطلاحية. فلو أخذنا على سبيل المثال هذه العبارة الإنجليزية Oh well! The die is cast التي تعني حرفياً:

To be caught between the devil and the deep blue sea (تختار أهون الشرّين) وكذلك عبارة to seize the bull by the horn (مواجهة المشاكل والتعامل معها بشكل مباشر). هذا النوع من العبارات الاصطلاحية قد أطلق عليه كلمة tournure المأخوذة عن الفرنسية والتي تعني عبارة ذات صفة خاصة أو متميّزة وكذلك تسمية phraseological والتي تعني عبارة غريبة التركيب. ان الصفة المشتركة لهذه العبارات تتمثل في كونها غير مرتبطة بأحد أقسام الكلام المنوه عنها سابقاً وتتطلب معنىً تفسيرياً أطول من مجرد كلمة واحدة. كما أن شكل وتركيب هذا النوع من العبارات الاصطلاحية غير قابل للتعديل أو التغيير. غير أن هناك عدداً محدوداً جداً من هذا النوع يمكن أن يتقبل بعض الإضافات أو التعديلات على شكله وتركيبه دون تشويه معنى العبارة ومع ذلك يبقى أغلبها واقعاً في قوالب جامدة التركيب بحيث تبقى على غموض معنى العبارة وتحول دون ظهورها بأي صورة من الصور. لنأخذ مثلا عبارة kick the bucket التي تعني «يموت» والتي لو قيلت بصيغة المبني للمجهول لحصلنا عندئذٍ على شكل غير مقبول وبعيد عن المعنى الأصلي للعبارة كقولنا The bucket has been kicked by the cowboy التي لم تعد تعني أن راعي البقر قد مات و إنما أصبحت تعني أن راعي البقر قد ركل الدلو بقدمه. وعليه يمكن اعتبار هذا النوع من العبارات الاصطلاحية محدد الشكل وتراكيبه ذات قوالب جامدة تماما. ولكن من الأشياء التي يسمح بها هذا النوع من العبارات تقبله تصريف الفعل الداخل في تركيبه بأن يأخذ صيغة الماضي والمستقبل وغيرها كقولنا :

The cowboy kicked the bucket.
The cowboy will kick the bucket.
The cowboy has kicked the bucket.

لكن يفضل عدم استخدام صيغة المصدر المنتهية بالمقطع (ing) التي يتم اشتقاقها من الفعل المصدر بإضافة المقطع (ing) كاشتقاقنا كلمة singing من الفعل المصدر sing وكلمة eating من الفعل المصدر eat كما هو الحال في العبارة التالية: His kicking the bucket surprised us all وذلك على الرغم من اختلاف الآراء سواء آراء الناطقين باللغة أو آراء النحويين بشأن إمكانية استخدام هذه الصيغة أو عدم استخدامها. وتشكل الأمثال والأقوال المأثورة واحدة من أكبر فئات العبارة الاصطلاحية. ومن أبرز العبارات التي تمثل هذا النوع نذكر عبارة: Don't count your chickens before they are hatched والتي تعني حرفياً «لا تعد أفراخك قبل أن تفقس» بمعنى أننا يجب ألا نتعجل الفرحة بإنجازنا عمل لم يكتمل بعد لأن فشله ممكن في أي لحظة ونبدو عندئذ في وضع لا نحسد عليه. وهناك عبارة: Don't wash your linen in public. التي تعني حرفياً «لا تنشر غسيلك الوسخ أمام الناس» وتعني اصطلاحياً «يجب ألا نطرح مشاكلنا الخاصة أمام الآخرين» لأنه لا شأن لهم بها وهكذا دواليك. وهنا يشار إلى أن العديد من هذه العبارات يرجع في منشأة إلى أصول أدبية أو انتقال إلينا عن طريق الناطقين الأوائل للغة

«أواه! لقد ألقى النرد» واصطلاحياً: لقد فات الأوان أو سبق السيف العذل فهل كان بوسعك تخمين معناها الاصطلاحي إذا كنت لا تعرفه أصلاً؟

وقد يتبادر إلى الذهن بأن المتحدث الذي ينطق تلك العبارة يقبل بشيء ما بسبب وجود الكلمتين !Oh Well في العبارة آنفة الذكر. إن المعنى الاصطلاحي للعبارة كما أشير قبل قليل هو أن المتحدث قد اتخذ قراراً لا رجعة فيه وعليه أن يتقبل النتائج. وبالرجوع إلى العبارة المذكورة يمكننا محاولة إضافة تركيب الصورة التي جرى من خلالها تكوين العبارة الاصطلاحية حيث أن عملية إلقاء النرد في لعبة القمار لا يمكن تكرارها أو إعادتها لأن ذلك غير قانوني، فسواء أشار النرد إلى رقم واحد أو ثلاثة أو ستة عليك أن تتقبل النتائج وتتحمل عواقب رميتك سواء بالربح أو الخسارة. (هناك اعتقاد سائد لدى بعض الناس بأن هذه العبارة قالها يوليوس قيصر لدى عبوره نهر الروبيكون، الأمر الذي ترتب عليه نشوب الحرب)

والآن عزيزي القارىء هل يمكنك استخدام العبارة الاصطلاحية بشكل سليم بعدما تعرفت عليها؟ أولاً وقبل كل شيء عليك التريّث قليلاً لحين سماعك إياها من أحد الناطقين بلغتها ضمن سياق طبيعي وليس مناسباً أن تجرب استخدام أية عبارة اصطلاحية لحين التأكد من إتقانك أساسيات قواعد اللغة. فبعد سماعك العبارة الاصطلاحية وهي تستخدم لأكثر من مرة وإدراكك التام لمعناها ومدلولها يمكنك عندئذ أن تجرب استخدامها بنفسك. تخيّل أن لديك عرضي عمل في وقت واحد، أحدهما مؤكد ودائم ولكنه ضئيل الأجر، والآخر عالي الأجر ولكنه مؤقت. وبسبب توترك وخوفك من ألا تظفر بأي منهما تضطر لقبول العمل الأقل أجراً لأنه مؤكد ولكن بعد ذلك يعرض عليك العمل الدائم الأعلى أجراً أنا! فينتابك الشعور بالندم والإحباط فتقول .Oh well! The die is cast فلو جرّبت النطق بهذه العبارة على مسمع من أحد الناطقين باللغة وأحسست بتعاطفه معك دون أن يسألك ماذا تعني؟ عندئذ يمكنك التأكد بأنك قد نجحت في أول محاولة لاستخدام عبارة اصطلاحية تعلمتها مؤخراً في سياقها المناسب وتكون بالتالي قد حصلت على تجربة مجزية. وعادة ما تكون ردة فعل الأمريكيين تجاه الغرباء أكثر تهذيباً وأدباً من تلك التي تبديها الشعوب الأخرى ولكنهم في الوقت نفسه يبدون رأيهم الصريح حول مدى طلاقتك في التحدث. وإذا كان الشخص المتحدث يستخدم الكلمات الطنانة والأسلوب المتكلف ولا يستخدم مطلقاً العبارات الاصطلاحية في مكانها الصحيح فإن هذا يجعله عرضة للاتهام بأنه متحدث جاف أو أنه جاد ورسميّ أكثر من اللازم.

إن استخدام العبارات الاصطلاحية أمر بالغ الأهمية ويعمل على خلق نوع من التوافق والتواصل مع المستمع. وكلّما أكثر استخدامك العبارات الاصطلاحية في السياق الصحيح ازداد الأمريكيون تعاطفاً معك وازدادوا قناعة في قرار أنفسهم بأنك شخص لطيف وودود انطلاقاً من قناعتهم بأنك تجيد التعبير عن نفسك. والآن سوف نلقي نظرةً عملية على استخدام هذا المعجم.

## كيف نستخدم هذا المعجم

يمكن استخدام هذا المعجم من قبل فئة معينة من الناطقين باللغة الإنجليزية وكذلك الطلاب والعمال والمهاجرين، باختصار من قبل أي شخص يود أن يجعل لغته الإنجليزية أكثر طلاقة وأكثر اصطلاحية. هذا المعجم يشتمل على عبارات من الأنواع التي تم ذكرها أعلاه: عبارات اصطلاحية مفرداتية أو معجمية وعبارات اصطلاحية من أشباه الجمل ومعجمية وعبارات اصطلاحية من الأمثال والأقوال المأثورة والتي لها معنى خاص. وعندما يكون للعبارة معنى خاص ولا يمكنك فك رموزها وشرح معناها عن طريق استخراج معاني مفرداتها المكونة لها من المعجم العادي فهذا يعني أنك أمام عبارة اصطلاحية.

ولعلك عزيزي القارىء تعرف بعض هذه العبارات الاصطلاحية أو يمكنك تخيّل معانيها. فتش في المعجم عن أي من العبارات الاصطلاحية التالية التي ربما تعرفها سلفاً لأن ذلك من شأنه أن يساعدك على فهم طريقة استخدامه. من هذه العبارات نذكر ما يلي:

boyfriend, girlfriend, outer space, piggy bank, got even, give up, going to, keep on, keep your mouth shut, lead somebody by the nose, look after, show off, throw away, all over, in love, mixed-up, out of this world, I'll say, both X and Y.

هذا المعجم يشبه أي أداة أخرى لذا يترتّب علينا أن نتآلف معه ونتعلّم طريقة استخدامه قبل أن يبدأ عمله من أجلنا لذا يتوجب قراءة الإرشادات والتوجيهات بعناية ولعدة مرّات، علاوةً على ممارسة عملية استخراج معاني العبارات الاصطلاحية من المعجم حيث أن هذا الإجراء المتمثّل في البحث عن العبارة في المعجم والاهتداء إلى مكانها يصبح طبيعة ثانية من طبائعنا ولو صادفت تعبيراً اصطلاحياً غير مدرج في هذا المعجم فإن استخدامك المتكرر له سوف يساعدك على إدراك معناه ومن ثم تدوينه في كرّاستك الخاصة حيث أنه من الضروري أن تحتفظ بقائمة للعبارات الاصطلاحية إلى جانب معجمك. ولو قرأت نصّاً فنياً أو رواية أو مقالة صحفية وعجزت عن فهم معنى أحد التعابير فيها حاول أن تبحث عنه أولا في معجمك المدرسي وإن لم تعثر عليه جرّب هذا المعجم.

## كيف يمكنك اكتشاف قدرة هذا المعجم في مساعدتك على فهم جملة صعبة؟

في بعض الأحيان لن تجد صعوبة تذكر في التعرّف على معنى عبارات مثل: dog-eat-dog, fun house, puppy love and mixed-up, etc. ......

فإن عجزت في مسعاك اختر إحدى الكلمات المهمة من أصعب جزء في العبارة وابحث عن معناها في المعجم ولو جاءت تلك الكلمة في بداية العبارة الاصطلاحية ستعثر عندئذ على مجمل العبارة متبوعة بشرح وتفسير هكذا فإن التعبير bats in the belfry (يعني حرفيا: وطاويط في برج جرس الكنيسة واصطلاحيا: الاضطراب العقلي) تجده مدرجاً تحت الحرف «b» في كلمة bats وإذا لم يكن موقع الكلمة المختارة في

XIII

مستهل العبارة، عندئذ ستجد قائمة بالعبارات الاصطلاحية التي تتضمن تلك الكلمة. فعلى سبيل المثال ستجد كلمة «toe» (إصبع القدم) في مداخل مثل: curl one's hair (يجعد شعره أو يوقف شعر رأسه) أو curl one's toes (بمعنى يتسبب في إحراج الآخرين)، step on one's toes (يدوس على رؤوس أصابعه)، on the toes (of somebody) (يدوس على أقدام الآخرين). وبالطبع، تجد في بعض الأحيان أن السبب في عدم فهمك لجملة ما لا يعود دائماً لوجود عبارة اصطلاحية فيها ووقتئذ يمكنك اللجوء إلى أي معجم عادي. أضف إلى ذلك بأن هناك العديد من العبارات الاصطلاحية التي لن تجدها في هذا المعجم لكونه مقتصراً على العبارات المأخوذة من اللغة الإنجليزية/الأمريكية فقط. طبعا هناك العديد من العبارات الخاصة باللغة الإنجليزية/البريطانية وتلك المستخدمة في أستراليا التي لم يتم إدراجها في هذا المعجم.

## أنواع المداخل :

هذا المعجم يتضمن أربعة أنواع من المداخل: المداخل الرئيسية، مداخل العبارات الفرعية المشتقة من العبارات الأساسية، المداخل المرجعية و مداخل الفهرسية. يشتمل المدخل الرئيسي على شرح وافٍ للعبارة الاصطلاحية في حين نجد في المدخل الفرعي تعابير مشتقة من عبارات اصطلاحية أخرى ولكن يتم عزلها عنها إذا ما تم إدراجها هجائيا. لقد جرت العادة على إدراج هذه التعابير المشتقة في نهاية العبارة الاصطلاحية الرئيسية مثل: on the fence) (fence-sitter, sit مع شرح وإضافة صياغة بهدف توضيح المعنى وغالباً ما يكون الشرح مستفيضاً إذا رؤي أن العبارة المشتقة يصعب فهمها. كما أنه اذا كان من الضروري استخدام العبارة الاصطلاحية في أكثر من قسم من أقسام الكلام عندها يتم تخصيص مدخل مستقل لكل استخدام من هذه الاستخدامات. أما المدخل المرجعي فانه يرشدك إلى تعريف في مكان آخر. فلنفترض أنك تود استخراج معنى العبارة: cast in one's lot with التي تعني (يشارك في عمل ما أو يدلي بدلوه) إبحث عن المعنى تحت كلمة «cast»، وكذلك تحت كلمة «lot with» ولكن المدخل المرجعي سوف يأخذك إلى كلمة «throw» الواردة في عبارة: «throw in one's lot with» والسبب في ذلك يعود إلى أن كلمة «cast» أصبح استخدامها نادراً جداً في وقتنا الحاضر لذا يتم التحول إلى كلمة «throw» الأكثر استخداما. إن إيجاد مدخل فهرسي يقودك إلى جميع المداخل الأخرى التي تتضمن الكلمة الفهرسية. وهكذا فان كلمة chin تتبعها مجموعة من الكلمات التي هي جزء منها مثل: Keep one's chin up، stick one's chin (neck out), take it on the chin, up to the chin in.

## علامات تعريف أقسام الكلام :

إن العبارات الاصطلاحية المرتبطة بنوع من الأنماط النحوية المعروفة جيدا تحمل «عبارة تعريف معجمية» من أجل التوضيح. وفي بعض الأحيان عندما تكون العبارة الاصطلاحية مكونة من حرف جر

واسم (مجرور به) يتم عندئذ استخدام عبارة تعريف مزدوجة لأن العبارة تلك لها استخدامان مزدوجان. فلو أخذنا على سبيل المثال عبارة «in commission» نجد أنه من الممكن أن تكون ظرفية أو نعتية في آن معاً وغالباً ما يكون العديد من تلك العبارات ظرفية في معناها الحرفي ونعتية في معناها الاصطلاحي الذي يصعب التنبؤ به. إن حرف (V) يعني الفعل فقط وقد تم تخصيصه للعبارة التي تتضمن فعلاً أو ظرفاً أو فعلاً وحرف جر أو فعلاً وحرف جر وظرفاً. أما الرمز (V Phr) فإنه يعني التعبيرة الفعلية التي تتكون من فعل ومفعول به أو من فعل واسم مكمّل أو فعل مع تعبيرة جرّية (حرف جر + اسم مجرور به).

## علامة تعريفية بالاستخدام المقيد

يتوجب على مستخدم هذا المعجم التأكد مما إذا كان مناسباً أو غير مناسب أن يستخدم عبارة اصطلاحية معينة في وقت معيّن. إن العلامة التعريفية «slang» (عامي) تشير إلى أن استخدام العبارة مقتصراً على الأصدقاء المقرّبين فقط بينما العبارة التعريفية «informal» (ودي أو غير رسمي) تشير إلى أن استخدام العبارة الاصطلاحية مقتصر على المحادثة فقط ولا يجوز استخدامها في المكاتبات الرسمية في حين تشير العلامة التعريفية «formal» إلى العكس، بمعنى أن استخدام العبارة مقتصر على الأعمال الكتابية أو الخطب الرسمية أو المحاضرات الجامعية. وبالنسبة إلى العلامة التعريفية «literary» (حرفي) فإنها تنبّه مستخدم المعجم إلى أنه من غير الملائم استخدام العبارة كثيراً لكون الآخرين غالباً ما يكونوا على علم بأن العبارة «كلام مقتبس». أما علامة «vulgar» (سوقي) فإنها تشير إلى تجنب استخدام العبارة ولو أن استخدامها يساعد على الحكم على لغة الشخص الذي يستخدمها. وبالنسبة إلى العلامة التعريفية «sub-standard» (دون المستوى المعياري) فإنها تشير إلى أن مستخدم العبارة من ذوي الثقافة المتدنّية بينما علامة «non-standard» (غير فصيح) فإنها تدلّ على أن العبارة سمجة وغير لبقة. وفيما يتعلق بعبارة archaic (لفظة مهجورة) (نادراً ما تستخدم في هذا المعجم) فإنها تشير إلى أن العبارة تعود إلى لغة الإنجيل أو لغة شكسبير الإنجليزية. علامة «dialect» (لهجة) تعني أن العبارة ذات مصدر جغرافي مثل chiefly British التي تدلّ على أن الأمريكيين نادراً ما يستخدمونها. أما علامة «southern» (جنوبي) فإنها تبيّن أن العبارة أكثر تداولاً في الولايات الأمريكية الجنوبية منها في الشمالية.

الدكتور آدام مكاي
أستاذ اللسانيات
جامعة إيلينوي في شيكاغو
المدير التنفيذي ومدير المطبوعات لدى

جمعية اللسانيات في كندا والولايات المتحدة الأمريكية

Adam Makkai and Hussein Quwaider

# 序　言

## 一、什麼是成語

在閱讀英語時，如果你明白句子中每一個詞的意義，却不懂整個句子的意思，那很可能是遇到了成語問題。例如，你若讀到或聽到下面這段話，就會遇到這個問題。

*Sam is a real cool cat. He never blows his stack and hardly ever flies off the handle. What's more, he knows how to get away with things . . . Well, of course, he is getting on, too. His hair is pepper and salt, but he knows how to make up for lost time by taking it easy. He gets up early, works out, and turns in early. He takes care of the hot dog stand like a breeze until he gets time off. Sam's got it made; this is it for him.*

毋庸違言，這段話不太文雅，但大都數美國人，尤其是他們自己互相交談時，往往都會這麼說的。如果你是美國的外國人，當你聽到這段話時，儘管懂得那些單詞的意義，例如，cool 意思是"涼的"，cat 意思是"貓" blow 意思是"吹"，stack 意思是"一堆東西"，fly 意思是"飛" handle 意界是"把手"，等等，可是，你仍不明白這段口語體的美國英語到底說的是什麼意思，因為，詞典上所給予的這些單詞的基本含義不能提供上述表達方式的意義。從以上例子的分析，我們就可以知道，所謂成語，是指賦予了新的意義的一個詞組，儘管該詞組中的每個單詞各具其本身獨立的意義。現在，我們把這一段充滿成語而又非常通俗的美國英語"譯"為成語相對較少而又較正式的文體；

*Sam is a really calm person. He never loses control of himself and hardly ever becomes too angry. Furthermore, he knows how to manage his business financially by using a few tricks . . . Needless to say, he, too, is getting older. His hair is beginning to turn grey, but he knows how to compensate for wasted time by relaxing. He rises early, exercises, and goes to bed early. He man-*

*ages his frankfurter dispensary without visible effort until it is someone else's turn to work there. Sam is successful; he has reached his life's goal.*

> 薩姆是個頭腦冷靜的人。他從不失去自控，也很少不發雷霆。而且，他也懂得怎樣玩弄一些小詭計賺錢。……當然，他人也漸漸老了，黑髮中出現了白髮。但他懂得如何把日子過得悠閒些，以贖回虛度的光陰。他早上起得很早，然後鍛煉身體，晚上也很早上床睡覺。他管理自己的那個熱狗攤，顯得輕鬆自如，直到別人接他的班。薩姆很成功。他已經達到了他人生的目標。

如果你想了解這些詞組是怎樣組成的，就得編一個小小的成語詞典。該詞典的樣子大致如下：

| | |
|---|---|
| *to be a (real) cool cat* | 頭腦冷靜的人 |
| *to blow one's stack* | 失去自制 |
| *to fly off the handle* | 大發雷霆 |
| *what's more* | 而且 |
| *to get away with something* | 做成（某壞事或錯事而未被發覺或受處分） |
| *of course* | 當然 |
| *to be getting on* | 變老 |
| *pepper and salt* | （頭髮）黑白參雜的 |
| *to make up for something* | 補償，瀰補 |
| *lost time* | 浪費的時間 |
| *to take it easy* | 休息，不憂慮 |
| *to get up* | 起床 |
| *to work out* | 鍛煉身體 |
| *to turn in* | 上床睡覺 |
| *to take care of sg.* | 照管 |
| *like a breeze* | 毫不費力地 |
| *time off* | 下班時間 |
| *to have got it made* | 成功，達到 |
| *this is it* | 達到了目標 |

上面列出的這些成語都能在本詞典中查到，有趣的是，大多數成語都能與我們所熟悉的語法中詞類相對應。有些成語很

XV

明顯相當於動詞，*get away with, work out, turn in* 等。不少成語具有名詞性質，如 *hot dog* （熱狗，麵包夾香腸）和 *White House* "白宮，美國總統官邸"。還有很多成語相當於形容詞，如 *pepper and salt* "黑白參雜的（頭髮）"；另一些成語又具有副詞性質，如 *like a breeze* "輕鬆自如地"，*hammer and tongs* "拼命地，竭盡全力地"，(*She ran after him hammer and tongs* "她拼命追求他。"）如此等等，不一而足。這些與語法中的詞類相關的成語，稱之爲詞彙成語，即這類成語以詞彙爲單位。

另一類重要的成語組成的單位較大，有時往往有一個子包那麼長。例如 *to blow one's stack* "失去自制" 和 *to fly off the handle* "大發雷霆"就屬此類。在美國英語中，這類成語很多。下面幾個就是大家都熟悉的成語：

| | |
|---|---|
| *to kick the bucket* | 死 |
| *to be up the creek* | 遭到困難 |
| *to be caught between the* | 處於困境 |
|    *devil and deep blue sea* | 進退兩難 |
| *to seize the bull by the horns* | 不畏艱險 |

這類成語曾經被稱之爲 *tournures*（該詞源自法語），意即具有短語的特色，可簡單地稱作 "短語成語"。這類成語的共同特點是，它們並不與語法里的某一詞類相關聯，並且需用不至一個詞才能把意思解釋清楚。

這類成語的形式是固定的，只有少數成語在使用時可以有變化而仍不損其原意。許多成語是完全固定不變的，無論如何不能以別的形式出現。試以成語 *kick the bucket* 爲例。如果把這一成語用在被動語態中，*The bucket has been kicked by the cowboy*，這種用法就不對了。因爲句子的意思不再是 "那牛仔死了"，而是說 "那牛仔用腳踢了那只桶"。這類成語可謂是 "全凍式"，即其形式是完全固定不變的。然而，值得注意的是，即使是這類成語，也可以用在不同的時態中。例如，我們可以說：

*The cowboy kicked the bucket.*
*The cowboy will kick the bucket.*
*He has kicked the bucket.* 等等。

但這類成語是否可以以動名詞形式出現，語法家和普通大衆都莫衷一是，意見不一。我們的建議是最好盡量避免使用動名詞形式。所謂動名詞，就是在動詞後加上 *-ing* 變成名詞。例如，我們應避免使用下面的形式：

*His kicking the bucket surprised us all.*

另一大類成語是人們常用的諺語。例如，大家熟悉的有：*Don't count your chickens before they're hatched.*

別在蛋未孵化之前先數小鷄。

這句話的意思是 "事情未成功以前，別先慶祝，因爲可能會失敗；如果失敗，那就被人笑話了。"意即 "別指望得太早"。

*Don't wash your dirty linen in public.*

別在大庭廣衆面前洗自己的髒被單。

這句話的意思是 "不要在陌生人面前談家醜，因爲跟他們無關"，意即 "家醜不可外揚。"

許多這類成語出自文學名著或早期北美演說家的演講詞。

爲什麼英語，尤其是美國英語，成語這麼豐富呢？最可能的原因是，當新概念形成時，我們需要有新的表達方式。有時，我們不想創造新詞，而是用原有的詞，組成新的意義。這種用已有的詞，組成新的表達方式，在世界各國語言中都是存在的。事實上，就我們所知，沒有一種語言是沒有成語的。例如，在漢語中，表示 "快" 的意思用 "馬上" 這一表達方式。如果其譯成英語，意即 "*horse back*"（在馬背（上）。那麼，"快" 的意思又怎麼會跟 "馬背" 聯系在一起呢？原來，在古代，在火車、汽車和飛機出現之前，從一個地方到另一個地方最快的方法就是騎馬，也就是 "在馬背上"，意思是 "趕快！我們得快走。"這種表達方式在英語里也不是不可理解的，只是說話的人必須知道，這是成語，外國人得學習方能懂得。但在學習成語時，我們往往會猜錯意思。試以英語成語 *Oh well, the die is cast!* 爲例，如果你不知道這一成語，你猜會是什麼意思呢？也許，因爲這句中有 *Oh well* 這兩個詞，你會以爲說話者是在默然同意某件事情。其實，這句話的意思是："我已作了不可挽回的決定，後果如何我也只

能忍受了。"意即"木已成舟"（事已定局，無法挽回了。）現在，再試想一下這個成語是如何來的。想像一下，在賭博時，骰子一擲出就不能再擲了，想拿回來再投就算犯規。不管你投出幾點，是三是六，是輸是贏，你都得接受。可能有人知道，公元前四十九年凱撒越過魯比孔河與羅馬執政龐培決戰時會用過此語。

那麼，學了這個成語後，怎樣才能正確使用呢？首先，你得聽到以英語為母語的人在自然的場合下使用這個成語。在自己沒有掌握成語的基本含義之前，千萬別急於使用。在你多次聽到別人使用這一成語並徹底了解成語的意義之後，才可以自己試着使用。譬如，你找到兩個工作。一個肯定能得到，但薪水低；另一個薪水高，但沒把握得到。由於憂慮和担心什麼工作都找不到，你接受了那份低薪的工作。就在那個時候，那份高薪工作也通過了。你自然感到失望，這時，你就可以說："*Oh well, the die is cast . . .* "如果這句語你是對以英語為母語的人說的，他聽了之後用同情的眼光注視着你，也沒有問你"你是什麼意思？"那就表明，你第一次在適當的場合正確地使用了這一成語。這於你可算是一次有益的經驗。美國人對外國人要比其他國家的人對外國人有禮貌，但他們完全知道你的英語是否熟練。如果一個人老是用文縐縐的、誇張不自然的詞句，而從不使用成語，那別人就會認為他是一個死板的人，一個乏味的人，要不就認為他是太嚴蕭了，太官氣十足了。所以，使用成語是十分重要的。使用成語能使聽話人起共鳴。在適當的場合，你成語使用越多，美國人跟你談話就會越感到自在；他們在心裡越是會這麼想："這個人多好，多友善——看看他自己的思想表達得多好啊！"

下面我們談談這本《美國成語詞典》的使用方法。

# 二、如何使用這本詞典

這本詞典是為非英語民族的學生、工人和移民編寫的。總之，任何人若想學會

說流利而地道的英語，都可使用本詞典。詞典中包括前面所談到的三類成語，即詞彙成語、短語成語和諺語成語。這些成語都有其特定的意義。當一個短語具有特定的意義，光從短語中的單詞的意義你無法解釋整個短語的意思，那你就可能遇到了成語。你也許已經知道了一些成語，也能猜出這些成語的意義。現在，請你在本詞典中查閱一下下列成語的意義，這會幫助你了解怎樣使用這本詞典，儘管其中的有些成語你已知道，但也務必查一下。這些成語是：

*boyfriend, girlfriend, outer space, piggy bank, get even, give up, going to keep on, keep your mouth shut, lead somebody by the nose, look after, show off, throw away, all over, in love, mixed-up, out of this world, I'll say, both X and Y.*

詞典像其他工具一樣，你必須熟悉它，並學會如何使用，才能更好地為你服務。應該反復仔細地研讀使用說明，並練習查成語。只有這樣，你才能得心應手地查出成語，並了解成語的意義。以後，你如果聽到一個習慣的表達方式，但在本詞典中又查不到，在你使用本詞典相當一段時間之後，你就會自己找出那個習慣用語的意義，並自己把它記下來。把自己記下來的這些成語放在家中自己常用的詞典旁邊。在你閱讀科技文章、小說或新聞時，若碰到你不懂的表達方式，先查一下你常用的詞典；若查不到，則可試試查這本詞典。

如何知道這本詞典可以幫助你了解難句呢？有時，你一眼就可以知道一些短語的意思，例如 *puppy love, fun house, dog-eat-dog, mixed up* 等。如果不懂，就找出難住你的那個短語中最重要的詞查一下。如果這個詞是短語中的第一個詞，你就會發現整個短語，短語後面就是解釋。例如，短語 *bats in the belfry* ，在本詞典中就列在字母 *b* 下面的 bats 這一詞下。如果你查閱的詞不是短語中的第一個詞，你就會發現包含這個詞的好幾個成語。例如，在 *toe* 這一詞條下，列出了下列成語：*curl one's hair OR curl one's toes, on one's toes, step on the toes (of somebody)*

當然，有時候你不懂整個句子的意思並不是因爲其中包含的成語的關係，那你就可以查一下普通詞典。當然，也有許多成語沒有列入本詞典，這裡，我們只收入了最常用的美國成語。例如，英國英語或澳大利亞英語中，也有許多習慣表達方式，但那些不屬於美國英語，當然就不包括在本詞典之內了。

## 三、詞條類型

本詞典的詞條包括四種類型，即主詞條，內詞條，參照詞條和索引詞條。主詞條包括對成語完整的釋義。內詞條是指從另一個成語派生出來的短語，若以短語本身的字母排列，就會與這個成語分開，所以把派生的成語附在主詞條之後。例如，*fence-sitter* 附在 *sit on the fence* 之後，並加以解釋；如果光看主詞條的解釋對理解派生的成語有困難，則另加說明如果一個成語可以作不同的詞類使用，也以不同的詞類分別列入詞條。

參照詞條使你能在另一個地方找到釋義。假如，你要查成語 *cast in one's lot with*，你查 *lot* 或 *throw* 詞條，你得到的是 *throw in one's lot with* 這一短語。其原因是，*cast* 一詞現在已很少用了，在這一成語中，現在更常用的是 *throw* 一詞。

索引詞條可使你找到包含該索引詞的其他所有的條目。例如，在 *chin* 一詞後，列出了包含這一詞的所有的短語：*keep one's chin up, stick one's chin (or neck) out, take it on the chin, up to the chin.*

## 四、詞類標記

每條成語凡是與語法中的詞類相關聯的，均標上詞類標記。有的成語有兩種詞類標記，如介詞短語，因爲這類成語能有兩種語法作用。例如，*in commission* 這一短語，既可用作形容詞，也可用作副詞。許多介詞短語其詞面意義往往作副詞用，其不可預測的習慣意義，往往又用作形容詞。V 表示動詞，這類短語包含一個動詞和一個副詞，或一個動詞和一個介詞，或一個動詞，一個介詞和一個副詞。V. phr. 表示動詞短語。這類短語包括動詞及其賓語，動詞及其主語補語，以及動詞及其詞短語。

## 五、慣用法標記

使用成語，需特別注意場合是否合適。現把成語的習慣用法的標記分別說明如下：

*Slang:* 俚語，只用於十分熟悉的好朋友之間。

*Informal:* 非正式用語，用於日常談話中，但應避免使用在書面語中。

*Formal:* 正式用語，與上述非正式用語相反，一般不用於日常談話中，而用於文章中，正式演說中，或大學講課中。

*Literary:* 文學用語，一般都用在引語中，應避免經常使用這類成語。

*Vulgar:* 粗俗語，應完全避免使用這類成語。當然，很重要的一點是，你經常可以從使用的語言判斷一個人。

*Substandard:* 不規範用語，主要用於教育水平不太高的人們之間。

*Nonstandard:* 非標准用語，這類成語使人聽了感到別扭。

*Archaic:* 古體詞，現已不通用。

*Chiefly British:* 主要用於英國英語中，美國人很少用。

*Southern:* 南方英語，指在美國南方用得多，北方很少用。

原序作者：馬亞當教授，
美國芝加哥伊利諾大學語言系
原序翻譯：郭建中教授，
中國杭州大學外語學院

*Adam Makkai/Guo Yianzhong*

# Préface

## QU'EST-CE QUE C'EST QU'UNE EXPRESSION IDIOMATIQUE?

Lorsqu'on comprend chaque mot d'un texte et qu'on n'en arrive tout de même pas à le déchiffrer, dans bien de cas c'est dû à une mauvaise compréhension des expressions idiomatiques. Le texte qui suit illustre ce que je veux dire. Disons que vous lisez (ou entendez) ce qui va suivre:

*Sam is a real cool cat. He never blows his stack and hardly ever flies off the handle. What's more, he knows how to get away with things . . . Well, of course, he is getting on, too. His hair is pepper and salt, but he knows how to make up for lost time by taking it easy. He gets up early, works out, and turns in early. He takes care of the hot dog stand like a breeze until he gets time off. Sam's got it made; this is it for him.*

Il va sans dire que ce texte n'est pas du meilleur style littéraire, mais la plupart des Américains, quand ils bavardent, emploient des expressions de ce genre. Or, si l'on est un étranger dans ce pays, et si l'on a appris les mots *cool* «pas très chaud», *cat* «l'animal domestique familier», *blow* «expulser de l'air avec force», *stack* «un tas de quelque chose» ou «matériel empilé», *fly* «se déplacer dans l'air au moyen d'ailes», *handle* «la partie d'un objet par laquelle on le tient dans la main», ... et ainsi de suite, l'on ne pourra quand même pas comprendre l'échantillon donné ci-dessus, d'anglais américain employé dans la conversation, car ces seuls renseignements de base que fournit le dictionnaire ne vous révéleront pas la signification des formes employées dans le texte idiomatique. Un idiotisme, — comme nous l'indiquent ces observations — consiste à attacher une nouvelle signification à un groupe de mots qui ont déjà leur propre signification. Vous trouverez ci-dessous une «traduction» de ce texte écrit en anglais américain très idiomatique et familier, en une variété d'anglais plus conventionnel et d'où, dans la mesure du possible, les expressions idiomatiques sont absentes.

*Sam is really a calm person. He never loses control of himself and hardly ever becomes too angry. Furthermore, he knows how to manage his business financially by using a few tricks . . . Needless to say, he, too, is getting older. His hair is beginning to turn gray, but he knows how to compensate for wasted time by relaxing. He rises early, exercises, and goes to bed early. He manages his frankfurter stand without visible effort, until it is someone else's turn to work there. Sam is successful; he has reached his life's goal.*

Si l'on voulait expliquer comment les unités sont disposées dans ce texte, il en sortirait un petit dictionnaire d'expressions idiomatiques à l'aspect suivant:

| | |
|---|---|
| *to be a (real) cool cat* | être une personne très calme |
| *to blow one's stack* | perdre son sang froid, se fâcher |
| *to fly off the handle* | se mettre très en colère |
| *what's more* | depuis, d'ailleurs, en outre |
| *to get away with something* | perpétrer un acte illégitime ou rusé, sans répercussion ni mal |
| *of course* | naturellement |
| *to be getting on* | vieillir |
| *pepper and salt* | cheveux noirs ou foncés bariolés de gris |
| *to make up for something* | compenser pour quelque chose |
| *lost time* | temps perdu, temps passé à un travail infructueux |
| *to take it easy* | se détendre, ne pas s'inquiéter |

| | |
|---|---|
| *to get up* | se lever le matin ou à tout autre moment |
| *to work out* | faire de l'exercise, de la gymnastique |
| *to turn in* | aller se coucher le soir |
| *to take care of something* | s'occuper de quelque chose, en prendre soin |
| *like a breeze* | sans effort, élégamment, facilement |
| *time off* | période de temps où l'on ne travaille pas |
| *to have got it made* | avoir du succès, avoir réussi |
| *this is it* | être dans une situation où un endroit, ou posséder un objet à un tel degré qu'en avoir davantage n'est pas nécessaire |

Un grand nombre d'idiotismes contenus dans cette courte liste d'exemples-ci paraissent aussi dans le dictionnaire.

Il est intéressant de remarquer que la plupart de ces idiotismes se laissent facilement classifier sous les rubriques grammaticales bien connues des (parties du discours). Ainsi, certains idiotismes appartiennent clairement à la classe du verbe, tels que *get away with, get up, work out, turn in*, etc. D'autres, tout aussi nombreux, appartiennent à la classe du substantif. Par exemple, *hot dog* «saucisse entre deux morceaux de pain», *White House* «résidence officielle du président des Etats-Unis», sont des noms. Plusieurs sont des adjectifs comme dans notre exemple *pepper and salt*, qui veut dire «cheveux noirs bariolés de gris». Plusieurs sont des adverbes comme dans les exemples *like the breeze* «facilement, sans effort», *hammer and tongs* «viollement» (comme dans l'expression *she ran after him hammer and tongs,)* et ainsi de suite.

Les idiotismes qui appartiennent à une classe grammaticale bien définie peuvent être appelés *idiotismes lexémiques*.

Les idiotismes faisant partie de l'autre groupe le plus important forment des expressions plus longues. Ils sont souvent de la longueur d'une locution entière, par exemple, *to fly off the handle*, «perdre son sang froid» et *to blow one's stack* «se mettre en colère». Il y en a plusieurs de cette catégorie en anglais américain. Parmi les plus célèbres nous trouvons : *to kick the bucket* «mourir», *to be up the creek* «être dans une situation dangereuse », *to be caught between the devil and the deep blue sea* «devoir choisir entre deux situations également peu plaisantes», *to seize the bull by the horns* «faire face à un problème et le résoudre honnêtement», etc. Ces idiotismes portent le nom de tournures (d'après le français) qui veut dire (tours de phrases), ou simplement idiotismes phraséologiques. Ce qu'ils ont tous en commun, c'est qu'il serait difficile de les ranger sous une classe grammaticale donnée (partie du discours) et qu'une paraphrase d'un seul mot ne suffirait pas à les expliquer.

Leur forme est figée et seulement un nombre limité de ces idiotismes phraséologiques peuvent se dire ou s'écrire d'une façon différente sans détruire la signification de l'idiotisme. Il en est beaucoup qui sont complètement figés et qui ne peuvent apparaître sous aucune autre forme que ce soit. Prenons comme exemple l'idiotisme *kick the bucket*. Si l'on met cette expression au passif, le résultat est inacceptable *(the bucket has been kicked by the cowboy)* ce qui ne veut plus dire que «le cowboy est mort» mais qu'il a frappé du pied une chaudière. Les expressions idiomatiques de ce genre sont considérées commes des formes complètement figées. Il est à remarquer cependant, que ces idiotismes portent la marque des inflexions temporelles, e.g., l'on peut dire *the cowboy kicked the bucket, the cowboy will kick the bucket, he has kicked the bucket,* etc. Les sujets parlant tout comme les grammairiens ne s'entendent pas touchant l'emploi de ces idiotismes au gérondif (un gérondif étant un nom dérivé d'un verbe auquel on ajoute la forme *-ing*, e.g., *singing*, de *sing, eating*, de *eat*, etc.) Comme dans *?His kicking the bucket surprised us all?* (Les points d'interrogation placés au début et à la fin de l'expression indiquent qu'il n'existe pas de commun accord sur la grammaticalité ou la non-grammaticalité de cette expression; nous vous conseillons de l'éviter).

La catégorie d'expressions idiomatiques qui se révèle ensuite la plus grande c'est celle bien connue des dictons et des proverbes. Parmi ces idiotismes apparaissent les types célèbres du *don't count your chickens before they're hatched* (ce qui veut dire « ne vous réjouissez pas trop tôt des résultats d'une entreprise, car il est possible que vous échouiez et que vous ayez l'air ridicule ») *don't wash your linen in public* (voulant dire « ne vous plaignez point de vos problèmes de famille devant des étrangers car ça ne les regarde pas »), ainsi de suite. De ces expressions idiomatiques un grand nombre ont vu le jour dans quelque oeuvre littéraire bien connue ou nous viennent des premiers habitants du Continent Nord Américain à parler anglais. Cette littérature avait influencé leur culture linguistique à eux aussi.

Pourquoi l'anglais, et surtout l'anglais américain, sont-ils aussi peuplés d'idiotismes? C'est là un fait intrigant. La raison la plus plausible, c'est que, développant de nouveaux concepts, nous avons besoin de nouvelles expressions pour les exprimer, mais au lieu de créer un mot de toute pièce à partir des sons de la langue, nous employons plutôt des mots déjà en existence et nous les mettons ensemble en leur donnant une nouvelle signification. Il semble que cela serait vrai de toutes les langues connues. Il n'existe, en effet, aucune langue connue qui n'ait au moins quelques idiotismes. Citons l'expression chinoise pour « vite » par exemple. C'est *mǎ shāng*, et traduite littéralement cette expression veut dire « à dos de cheval ». Pourquoi—peut-on se demander—l'idée de « vitesse » devrait-elle être associée au dos d'un cheval? Quelques moments de réflexion ont vite fait de nous révéler la réponse. Dans le bon vieux temps avant l'avènement du train, de l'automobile et de l'avion, c'était le cheval qui fournissait le moyen le plus rapide de se rendre d'un endroit à un autre. L'expression chinoise *mǎ shāng* est donc comparable à ce qu'on pourrait dire en anglais *hurry up! "We must go on horse back"* i.e., « Dépêche-

toi! Nous devons aller vite ». Une telle forme serait tout à fait compréhensible en anglais, bien que le sujet parlant dût se rendre compte que c'est un idiotisme, et que l'étranger dût faire l'effort pour l'apprendre. En disant que ces expressions ne sont pas inintelligibles, je veux dire que « à dos de cheval » et « vite » ne sont pas tellement éloignés l'un de l'autre quant à leur signification: même si l'on n'avait jamais entendu dire que *mǎ shāng* veut dire « vite » il est fort possible qu'on puisse en deviner la signification. Mais il se peut aussi que l'on ne devine pas juste. Prenons l'idiotisme anglais *Oh well, the die is cast!* Quelle en serait la signification selon vous—au cas où vous ne connaissiez pas cette expression? A cause du *Oh well*, il se peut que vous pensiez que le sujet parlant donne son consentement à quelque proposition. L'expression veut dire « J'ai pris une décision sur laquelle je ne peux pas revenir et je dois l'accepter ». L'on peut maintenant essayer de reconstruire l'apparition de cet idiotisme: ce qui apparaît sur les dés jetés au jeu ne peut pas être changé; ce serait illégal; que vous obteniez un un, un trois ou un six, il vous faut accepter les conséquences de votre jeu, c'est-à-dire, gagner ou perdre, selon le cas. (Il y a des gens qui savent peut-être que cette expression a été employée par César au moment où il traversait le Rubicon et que cette action causa la guerre).

Après avoir appris cet idiotisme, comment l'exploierez-vous correctement? Tout d'abord, attendez de l'entendre de la bouche de celui dont l'anglais est la langue maternelle et utilisé dans un contexte naturel; n'essayez pas d'employer un idiotisme avant d'avoir fait l'apprentissage des règles fondamentales de grammaire anglaise. Après avoir entendu l'expression idiomatique plus d'une fois et en ayant compris toute la signification, c'est le moment de l'employer vous-mêmes. Imaginez qu'on vous fait deux offres d'emploi, l'un certain, mais à un salaire moindre et l'autre à un meilleur salaire, mais qui n'est que provisoire. Parce que vous êtes nerveux et que vous avez peur de n'avoir aucun emploi, vous acceptez l'emploi au salaire plus bas. A ce moment la meilleure offre se réalise et vous vous sentez naturellement contrarié. Vous pouvez alors dire *Oh well, the die is cast...* Si vous faites cet essai avec quelqu'un dont l'anglais est la langue maternelle et s'il vous regarde tendrement sans vous demander *"What do you mean?"* «Que voulez-vous dire?»—vous avez réussi à employer votre premier idiotisme avec succès dans un contexte approprié. C'est là une agréable expérience. Les Américains indigènes acceptent les étrangers plus poliment d'ordinaire que les autres nations, mais ils peuvent sans contredit, porter un jugement sur votre connaissance de la langue. Si l'on emploie toujours une expression livresque et recherchée, ne pouvant jamais utiliser un idiotisme en temps et lieu, l'on s'attirera sans doute la réputation d'être un locuteur plat et sans imagination, ou de quelqu'un qui essaie d'être trop sérieux ou trop officiel. *L'emploi d'idiotismes est par conséquent d'une importance extrême. Il peut faire naître de la sympathie chez celui qui vous écoute.* Plus vous utilisez d'idiotismes dans le bon contexte et plus les Américains se sentiront à l'aise avec vous et plus ils se diront « voilà un chic type—regarde comme il s'exprime bien! »

Arrêtons-nous maintenant à quelques considérations pratiques sur notre *Dictionary of American Idioms.*

# COMMENT UTILISER LE DICTIONNAIRE

Ce dictionnaire a été compilé pour les gens dont l'anglais n'est pas la langue maternelle, qu'ils soient étudiants, ouvriers, immigrants, bref pour tous ceux qui veulent améliorer leur anglais et le rendre plus idiomatique. Il contient des expressions appartenant aux catégories dont on a fait mention plus haut, idiotismes léxémiques, idiotismes phraséologiques, et idiotismes proverbiaux, qui ont une signification particulière. Quand une expression a une signification particulière qu'on ne peut pas déchiffrer adéquatement en cherchant dans le dictionnaire et en comprenant chaque mot dont elle est formée, l'on a alors affaire à un idiotisme. Il est possible que vous connaissiez déjà quelques-unes de ces expressions idiomatiques et que vous puissiez en imaginer la signification. Cherchez dans le dictionnaire l'un ou l'autre des idiotismes suivants que vous connaissez peut-être déjà bien: ceci vous aidera à comprendre comment utiliser ce livre: *boyfriend* «ami», *girlfriend* «amie», *outer space* «l'espace», *piggy bank* «tire-lire», *get even* «se venger», *going to* «aller», *keep on* «continuer à», *keep your mouth shut* «taisez-vous», *lead somebody by the nose* «mener par le bout de nez», *look after* «s'occuper de», *show off* «faire parade de», *throw away* «gaspiller», *all over* «partout», *in love* «amoreux», *mixed-up* «troublé», *out of this world* «fantastique», *I'll say* «dites donc», *both x and y* «à la foid x et y».

Il en est d'un dictionnaire comme de tout autre outil: il faut apprendre à le connaître et à s'en servir avant qu'en retour cet outil nous rende service. Etudiez les modes d'emploi avec soin plusieurs fois, et cherchez des idiotismes dans le dictionnaire à plusieurs reprises. De cette manière chercher un idiotisme et le trouver deviendront pour vous seconde nature. Si vous entendez un expression idiomatique qui n'est pas dans ce livre, après l'avoir employée un certain temps, vous pourrez en identifier la signification et l'ajouter vous-même à la liste. Dressez votre propre liste d'idiotismes chez vous, juste à côté de votre dictionnaire usuel. Faites-nous parvenir vos observations et vos remarques. Si vous faites la lecture d'un texte de prose technique, ou d'un roman ou d'un article de journal et que vous ne comprenez pas une expression, cherchez-la dans votre dictionnaire habituel d'abord; si vous ne la trouvez pas, essayez ensuite le dictionnaire que voici.

Comment vérifier que ce dictionnaire peut vous aider à comprendre une phrase difficile? Parfois la locution saute aux yeux, comme dans le cas de *puppy love, fun house, dog-eat-dog, mixed-up.* Si ce n'est pas aussi évident, choisissez un mot important tiré de la partie la plus difficile de l'expression et cherchez-le dans le dictionnaire. Si c'est là le premier mot de l'idiotisme, vous allez trouver la locution entière suivie d'une explication. Ainsi l'expression *bats in the belfry* «araignée au plafond», apparaît dans le dictionnaire sous la lettre *b,* le mot *bats.* Si le mot choisi n'est pas le premier mot, vous trouverez une liste d'idiotismes qui renferment ce mot. Par exemple, le mot *toe* se trouvera sous les entrés *curl one's hair* OU *curl one's toes*, OU *one's toes, step on the toes (of somebody)*. Il se peut, naturellement, que vous découvriez que ce n'est pas à cause de la présence d'un idiotisme dans une phrase que vous ne la comprenez pas; dans ce cas, votre dictionnaire de tous les jours vous viendra en aide. Il y a aussi, il va sans dire, plus d'idiotisme que ce dictionnaire n'en contient: nous ne donnons ici que les idiotismes les plus fréquemment employés en *anglais américain*. L'anglais d'Angleterre, par exemple, ou l'anglais parlé en Australie, renferme, bien sûr, plusieurs idiotismes qui n'existent pas en anglais américain. Un dictionnaire qui contiendrait tous les idiotismes de la langue anglaise où qu'elle se parle, serait un dictionnaire *interdialectal des idiotismes anglais*. Ce livre n'existe pas présentement, mais devrait éventuellement être compilé.

## GENRES D'ENTRÉE

Ce dictionnaire renferme quatre sortes d'entrée: *entrées principales, entrées dérivees, entrées de références* et *entrées d'index*. Une entrée principale contient une explication complète de l'idiotisme. Une entrée dérivée est une locution qui est dérivée d'un autre idiotisme mais qui en serait séparée si elle apparaissait dans l'ordre alphabétique qui lui est assigné. Les idiotismes dérivés ont été placés à la fin de l'entrée principale (e.g., *fence-sitter* à *sit on the fence)* suivis d'une illustration et d'une paraphrase; on a ajouté une explication supplémentaire quand il nous a semblé qu'il serait difficile de comprendre l'explication de la locution dérivée à partir de l'explication de la locution de base. Quand un idiotisme en est venu à être employé sous plus d'une des parties du discours sans changer de forme, on a créé une entré séparée pour chacun. Une entrée de référence vous guide vers une définition donnée à un autre endroit. Disons que vous voulez chercher *cast in one's lot with*. Vous pouvez chercher sous *cast* et sous *lot:* mais l'entrée de référen-

ce vous référera à *throw* dans la locution *throw in one's lot with*. C'est que *cast* est un mot beaucoup plus rare aujourd'hui et ainsi, la forme habituelle et plus fréquente de cet idiotisme commence par le verbe *throw*.

Une entrée d'index vous renverra à toutes les autres entrés contenant le mot de l'index. Par exemple, le mot *chin* est suivi des locutions dont il fait partie, e.g., *keep one's chin up, stick one's chin (or neck) out, take it on the chin, up to the chin*.

## ETIQUETTES INDIQUANT LA PARTIE DU DISCOURS

Les idiotismes lexémiques (tels que présentés plus haut) sont porteurs d'une étiquette de partie du discours. Parfois, comme dans le cas de plusieurs locutions adverbiales, une double étiquette doit leur être attachée, parce que la locution en question a deux emplois grammaticaux, e.g., *in commission* peut être soit adverbe soit adjectif. Plusieurs locutions prépositionnelles sont des adverbes dans leur sens littéral, mais sont des adjectifs dans leur sens idiomatique.

*V.* veut dire verbe: il a été attaché aux locutions contenant un verbe et un adverbe: un verbe et une préposition: ou un verbe, une préposition et un adverbe. *V. Phr.* veut dire "verbal phrase" (prédicat): sont inclus sous cette étiquette les verbes qui ont un objet, les verbes qui ont un sujet et les verbes attachés à une locution prépositionelle.

## ETIQUETTES DÉCRIVANT L'USAGE DES IDIOTISMES

Il est important pour vous, dont l'anglais n'est pas la langue maternelle de réfléchir à l'emploi que vous faites d'un certain idiotisme dans un certain contexte. L'étiquette *informal* «langue familière» indique que la forme s'emploie en conversation mais devrait être évitée en composition. *Formal* «langue recherchée» indique le contraire: c'est une forme que les gens n'emploient pas d'habitude en conversation mais qu'ils écriront volontiers dans une dissertation et dont ils se serviront lorsqu'ils donnent une conférence à l'université. *Literary* «langue littéraire» vous éveille au fait que les gens savent en général que la forme est une citation; vous auriez l'air bizarre si vous employiez ces expressions trop souvent. *Vulgar* «vulgaire» indique que vous devriez éviter cette forme complètement. *Substandard* «inférieure au niveau moyen» veut dire qu'une forme n'est employée que par ceux qui sont moins instruits; *nonstandard* «qui n'est pas standard» signifie qu'une locution semble être une gaucherie d'expression. *Regional labels* «régionalisme» sont ce qui nous révèlent l'origine géographique d'une forme et l'emploie qu'on en fait dans ce milieu, e.g., *chiefly British* «strictement anglais d'Angleterre» veut dire que les Américains n'emploient cette expression que rarement, *Southern* «du sud» signifie qu'une forme est beaucoup plus fréquente au sud qu'au nord des Etats-Unis.

Les formes qui sont récentes, ayant fait leur entrée dans la langue pendant ces six ou sept dernières années, apparaissent dans un appendice faisant suite au texte principal du dictionnaire.

*Adam Makkai/Jean-Luc Garneau*

# Vorwort

## WAS IST EIN IDIOM?

Wenn wir jedes Wort in einem Text verstehen, und den Sinn des Ganzen doch nicht begreifen, dann müssen wir davon ausgehen, daß uns die Idiomatismen verwirren. Nehmen wir zum Beispiel an, daß jemand das Folgende liest, oder hört:

*Sam is a real cool cat. He never blows his stack and hardly ever flies off the handle. What's more, he knows how to get away with things . . . Well, of course, he is getting on, too. His hair is pepper and salt, but he knows how to make up for lost time by taking it easy. He gets up early, works out, and turns in early. He takes care of the hot dog stand like a breeze until he gets time off. Sam's got it made; this is it for him.*

Die Bemerkung, daß wir es hier nicht mit einem gehobenen literarischen Stil zu tun haben, erübrigt sich; die meisten Amerikaner werden jedoch die in der vorliegenden Textpassage vorkommenden Ausdrücke oft gebrauchen, besonders wenn sie im vertrauten Kreis miteinander reden. Ein Fremder oder ein erst kürzlich in dieses Land Eingewanderter wird zwar schon früher gelernt haben, daß *cool* 'kühl', *cat* 'Katze', *blow* 'blasen, wehen', *stack* 'Haufen, Stapel', *fly* 'fliegen', *handle* 'Griff, Stiel, Öhr', etc. bedeuten, es folgt daraus aber bei weitem nicht, daß die obige amerikanisch-englische Gabrauchssprache auch verstanden wird, da eine leicht zu handhabenbe Wörterbuchinformation allein nicht genügen kann, den Sinn der vorliegenden Formen zu enthüllen. Wie aus diesen Beobachtungen hervorgeht, ist ein Idiom nichts anderes, als eine Gruppe von Wörtern, die einzeln und ursprünglich eine andere Bedeutung haben, einen neuen Sinn zu verleihen. Die 'Übersetzung' dieses vertraulich-slangartigen Textes in eine troken-formalere und verhältnismäßig idiomentfrei englische Fassung könne so lauten:

*Sam is really a calm person. He never loses control of himself and hardly ever becomes too angry. Furthermore, he knows how to manage his business financially by using a few tricks . . . Needless to say, he, too, is getting older. His hair is beginning to turn gray, but he knows how to compensate for wasted time by relaxing. He rises early, exercises, and goes to bed early. He manages his frankfurter stand without visible effort, until it is someone else's turn to work there. Sam is successful; he has reached his life's goal.*

*Sam ist wirklich ein ruhiger Mensch Er verliert niemals die Beherrschung, und wird fast nie allzu ärgerlich. Außerdem weiß er darüber Bescheid, wie er seine finanziellen Geschäfte mittels einiger Kniffe zu führen hat... Selbstverständlich ist auch er nicht mehr der Jüngste. Seine Haare werden langsam grau, aber er weiß, daß man die verlorengegangene Zeit durch Gemütsruhe ersetzen kann. Er steht früh auf, turnt, und geht früh zu Bett. Er versieht die Arbeit in seinem Heißwurst-Verkaufsstand ohne sichtliche Anstrengung, bis ihn dort jemand ablöst. Sam ist erfolgreich, er hat sein Lebensziel erreicht.*

Wenn wir nun die Struktur der phraseologischen Einheiten des Slangtextes zu erklären versuchten, so wäre das Ergebnis unserer Arbeit ein kleines idiomatisches Wörterbuch, das wie folgt aussehen würde:

| | |
|---|---|
| *to be a (real) cool cat* | 'eine wirkliche ruhiger Mensch sein' |
| *to blow one's stack* | 'die Beherrschung verlieren, plötzlich in Wut geraten' |
| *to fly off the handle* | 'sich erzürnen, ärgerlich werden' |
| *what's more* | 'außerdem, darüberhinaus' |

| | |
|---|---|
| *to get away with something* | 'eine gesetzwirdrige oder knifflige Handlung vornehmen und mit heiler Haut davonkommen' |
| *of course* | 'selbstverständlich, natürlich' |
| *to be getting on* | 'älter werden', 'altern' |
| *pepper and salt* | 'mit grauen Strähnen vermischte dunkle Haarfarbe' |
| *to make up for something* | 'gutmachen, kompensieren' |
| *lost time* | 'durch sinnlose Betätigung verschwendete Zeit' |
| *to take it easy* | 'sich keine Sorgen machen', 'sich nicht aus der Ruehe bringen lassen' |
| *to get up* | 'aufstehen' |
| *to work out* | 'turnen' |
| *to turn in* | 'abends zu Bett gehen' |
| *to take care of something* | 'sich für etwas Sorge tragen', 'sich um etwas kümmern' |
| *like a breeze* | 'ohne Anstrengung, leicht' |
| *time off* | 'Freizeit' |
| *to have got it made* | 'erfolgreich sein, es geschafft haben' |
| *this is it* | 'das ist es, in einer Lage sein, in der man sein Zeit erreicht hat' |

Viele Idiome der vorliegenden kleinen Wortauslese sind in diesem Wörterbuch zu finden. Bemerkenswert ist gerade jener Umstand, daß die meinsten dieser Idiome leicht mit den herkömmlichen, allgemein üblichen Satzteilen zu identifizieren sind. Manche sind offensichtlich verbaler Natur, z.B. *get away with, get up, work out, turn in,* usw. Ebenso häufig sind die Idiome von substantivischem Charakter, beispielsweise *hot dog* (nicht 'heisser Hund', sondern 'heißes Würstchen mit Senf und/oder anderen Beilagen zwischen zwei länglichen Brötchen'), *White House* 'das Weiße Haus, Residenz des Präsidenten der Ver-einigten Staaten', usw. Viele haben eine prädikative Funktion, wie *pepper and salt* 'ergrauende, dunkle Haare', andere wiederum sind adverbialer Natur, wie in unserem Beispiel: *like a breeze* ('ohne Anstrengung, leicht'/oder wie in der Redewendung *hammer and tongs* (nicht 'hammer und Kneifzange' sondern 'heftig, gewaltsam').

Die Idiome, die in einem bestimmten Zusammenhang mit den bekannten Bestandteilen eines Satzes stehen, werden LEXEMISCHE IDIOME 'lexemic idioms' genannt.

Die andere, sehr wichtige Gruppe von Idiomen besteht aus längeren formelhaften Redewendungen. Oft machen solche Idiome einen ganzen kleinen Satz aus, wie unsere Beispiele *to fly off the handle* 'sich erzürnen. ärgerlich werden' und *to blow one's stack* 'die Beherrschung verlieren'. Davon gibt es im Amerikanischen Englisch eine große Anzahl. Hier sind einige der bekanntesten: *to kick the bucket* 'sterben', *to be up the creek* 'in der Klemme sitzen', usw. Diese Idiome heißen 'tournures', auf gut Deutsch Redewendungen, laut linguistischer Definition, phraseologische Einheiten.

Ihre Form ist festgeleft, und lediglich eine geringe Anzahl solcher Idiome kann umgewandelt oder anders gesagt werden, ohne ihren ursprünglichen Sinn zu verlieren. Manche von ihnen sind völlig unveränderbare Redewendungen.

Die nächste wichtige Klasse von Idiomen bilden die bekannten Sprüche und Sprichwörter.

Warum ist die englische Sprache und besonders ihre amerikanische Variante dermaßen reich an Idiomen? Höchst wahrscheinlich liegt es daran, daß in einer schnell sich entwickelnden großindustriellen Gesellschaft Tag für Tag neue Begriffe und sprachliche Konzepte entstehen und immer mehr neue Benennungen und Ausdrücke zur Kommunikation benötigt werden. Die menschliche Natur mit unserer angeborenen Bequemlichkeit ist aber so beschaffen, daß wir anstatt aus dem phonetischen Bestand der Sprache brandneue Wörter zu schöpfen, lieber die schon vorhandenen Wörter gebrauchen, indem wir sie in einer neuen sinntragenden Form zusammenstellen. Dies scheint jedoch auf alle Sprachen zuzutreffen.

# TIPS FÜR DEN GEBRAUCH DIESES WÖRTERBUCHS

Dieses Wörterbuch der Idiome wurde für jene Studenten, Berufstätige und Einwanderer zusammengestellt, die Englisch schon gelernt haben, aber die Sprache fließender und natürlicher sprechen wollen. Es enthält die oben angeführten Arten von Redewendungen: Lexemische, phraseologische, und spruchartige Idiome, deren spezifischer Sinn nicht mit der Einzelbedeutung der darin vorkommenden Wörter identifiziert werden kann. Der Leser wird die Bedeutung mancher Idiome von vorherein kennen, die meisten aber werden für ihn wahrscheinlich neu sein. Der Gebrauch diese Nachschlagewerkes wird beträchtlich erleichtert, wenn wir nach allgemein verbreiteten Ausdrücken suchen, wie z.B. *boyfriend, girlfriend, outer space, piggy bank, get even, give up, going to, keep on, keep your mouth shut.*

Ein Wörterbuch ist, wie jedes andere Werkzeug: Man muß sich damit vertraut machen, bevor es einem nützen kann. Es ist also ratsam, die folgende Anleitung aufmerksam durchzulesen und zu .üben, wie und wo man die gesuchten Idiome im Buch findet. Bald wird es mit automatischer Leichtigkeit gehen. Sollten wir einen idiomatischen Ausdruck hören, der in diesem Wörterbuch nicht enthalten ist, dann wird die Übung zur Fähigkeit beitragen, den Sinn eines Idioms selbst zu entschlüsseln. Es ist empfehelenswert ein kleines Wörterbuch der Idiome für den Eigengebrauch anzulegen. Der Verleger zeigt sich dankbar für alle Bemerkungen und Vorschläge der Leser.

Wenn irgendetwas in einem Fachtext, Roman oder Zeitungsartikel unverständlich ist, kann man vorerst im allgemeinen Schul- oder im erläuternden Wörterbuch nachschlagen; fehlt dort das Gesuchte, dann verspricht dieses Wörterbuch mehr Erfolg.

Wie findet man heraus, ob dieses Werk beim Verstehen eines schwierigen englischen Satzes Hilfestellung leistet? Manchmal sind auch unbekannte Ausdrücke mittels der Struktur der Wortzusammensetzungen einfach zu lösen, wie *puppy love, fun house, dog-eat-dog, mixed-up.* Ist der Ausdruck aber doch nicht zu enträtseln, so ist es am besten, ein wichtiges Wort des schwierigsten Teiles nachzuschlagen. Steht das gesuchte Wort am Anfang des Idioms, so wird der ganze Satz(teil) samt Erklärung bei diesem Wort zu finden sein. Der Ausdruck *bats in the belfry* (nicht 'Fledermäuse im Kirchturm' sondern 'er ist nicht richtig im Oberstübchen', 'er ist meschugge', 'übergeschnappt') steht unter dem Buchstaben 'B' beim Wort *bats.* Ist das gewählte Wort nicht das erste im Satz, dann finden wir eine ganze Liste von Idiomen, die dieses Wort enthalten. Zum Beispiel das Wort *toe* 'Zehe' ist in den folgenden Ausdrücken zu finden: *Curl one's hair or curl one's toes, on one's toes, step on the toes (of somebody).* Es kann natürlich vorkommen, daß man einen Satz nicht deshalb mißversteht (oder gar nicht versteht), weil Idiome darin vorkommen, sondern nur deswegen, weil uns auch die Ursprüngliche Bedeutung der Wörter unbekannt ist. Es versteht sich von selbst, daß in diesem Fall ein allgemeines Wörterbuch benützt werden soll. Natürlich gibt es mehr Idiome als in diesem Band erhalten sind; dieses Buch enthält nur die meistgebrauchten Idiome des Amerikanischen English. Das Britische Englisch und das in Australien gesprochene Englisch weisen sicherlich manche idiomatische Wendungen auf, die nicht zum Bestandteil der nordamerikanischen Sprache geworden sind. Ein Wörterbuch, das alle Idiome der englischen Sprache enthielte, wäre ein unterdialektisches Wörterbuch der englischen Idiome. Ein solches Buch gibt es vorläufig nicht, wir wollen aber hoffen, daß die Zusammenstellung dieses erwünschten Werkes lediglich eine Zeitfrage ist.

## ARTEN VON EINTRAGUNGEN

In diesem Wörterbuch finden wir vier Arten von Eintragungen: Haupteintragungen, Ableitungseintragungen, Referenzeintragungen und Index-Eintragungen. Eine Haupteintragung enthält die volle Erklärung des Idioms. Eine Ableitungseintragung ist ein Ausdruck, der von einem anderen Idiom herrührt, der aber von seinem Ursprung getrennt wäre, wenn er seine einreihung laut Alphabet erhielte.

Diese abgeleiteten Idiome finden sich im vorliegenden Wörterbuch im Anschluß an die Haupteintragung, so wie der Ausdruck *fence sitter* unter der Haupteintragung *sit on the fence,* also bei 'S' und nicht by 'F' vorkommt. Die Erläuterung, wie dieser Ausdruck zu gebrauchen ist, wird auch in der Haupteintragung gegeben, aber es wurden überall dort Sondererklärungen beigefügt, wo das Verstehen des abgeleiteten Idioms aufgrund der ursprünglichen Redewendung schwierig gewesen wäre. Wenn ein gegebenes Idiom als unterschiedlicher Satzteil gebraucht wird, erscheint jeder Satzteil in diesem Band als Sondereintragung. Eine anderswo hinweisende Eintragung dient dazu, eine Erklärung zu finden, die an einer anderen Stelle im Wörterbuch enthalten ist. Die Index-Eintragung führt zu allen Ausdrücken, die das gesuchte Stichwort enthalten.

## SATZTEILBEZEICHNUNGEN

Da (wie schon erörtert worden ist) die lexemischen Idiome mit Satzteilen identifizierbar sind, wurden sie mit Satzteilbezeichnungen versehen. Es kommt oft vor, daß ein englisches Idiom eine syntaktische Doppelrolle innehat. Das ist eine bekannte Schwierigkeit dieser Sprache. Im Falle eines einfachen Wortes sieht das so aus: *man* kann ein Hauptwort sein, wie in diesem Satz: *he is a good man* 'er ist ein guter Mensch', es kann aber ebenso als Zeitwort dienen: *John will man the post tonight* 'heute nacht wird John den Posten besetzen/übernehmen'. Diese syntaktische Pluralität besteht auch bei mehrteiligen Idiomen. Der Ausdruck *in commission* 'in Betrieb sein' kann sowohl prädikativ als auch adverbial sein. Viele präpositionalen Wortgruppen sind adverbialer Art in ihrem engsten Sinn, aber adjektivisch in ihrer unvorhersehbaren idiomatischen Bedeutung.

Das Zeichen *v* steht für 'verb' d.h. 'Zeitwort', und wurde solchen Wortgruppen zugeteilt, die ein Zeitwort und ein Bestimmungswort, oder ein Zeitwort und ein Verhältniswort, oder alle drei enthalten.

Die Abkürzung *v. phr.* steht für *verbal phrase,* d.h. für solche längeren Ausdrücke, die verbalen Charakter im Satz haben; diese beinhalten Zeitwörter mit einem Objekt, Zeitwörter mit erweitertem Subjekt und Zeitwörter mit präpositionalen Wortverbindungen.

## GEBRAUCHSHINWEISE

Derjenige, der Englisch nicht als seine Muttersprache spricht, muß besonders darauf achten, ob der Gebrauch gewisser Idiome in einer Bestimmten Umgebung passend ist oder nicht. Die Bezeichnung *slang* weist darauf hin, daß das Idiom nur im engen Freundeskreis angewandt werden soll. *Informal* 'ungebunden' macht darauf aufmerksam, daß diese Form im Gespräch volkommen einwandfrei, aber in schriftlicher Fassung zu vermeiden ist. *Formal* bezeichnet das Gegenteil; solche Ausdrücke hören wir im gesprochenen Englisch selten, wärend sie ziemlich häufig in der Schriftsprache und in Vorlesungen vorkommen. *Literary* ist ein Hinweis darauf, daß wir mit einem literarischen Zitat zu tun haben, und diejenigen, die das gebrauchen, wissen zumeist Bescheid (obwohl nicht ausnahmslos), aber ein Ausländer soll mit Zitaten vorsichtig umgehen. *Vulgar* bezeichnet, daß der Ausdruck zu vermeiden ist. Natürlich kann es nicht schaden, wenn mach auch diese Art von Idiomen kennt und versteht, da der von einem Menschen gern gebrauchte Wortschatz nicht wenig zu seiner Beurteilung beiträgt. Regionale Bezeichnungen sind einschränkender Natur, und geben die geographische Herkunft und Verbreitung einer Ausdrucksform an. *Chiefly British* bedeutet 'in England üblich', aber in Nordamerika selten zu hören. *Southern* bedeutet daß das Idiom in den Südstaaten viel beliebter ist, als im nördlichen Teil der USA.

*Adam Makkai/Doris Jutta Glatzl*

# הקדמה

## מה הוא ניב?

אם אתה מבין כל מלה בטקסט ועדיין אין
לך מושג מה פרוש הדבר, כל הסיכויים
שמדובר בניב. למשל נניח שקראת (או
שמעת) את הקטע הבא:

*Sam is a real cool cat. He never
blows his stack and hardly ever flies off
the handle. What's more, he knows how to
get away with things . . . Well, of course,
he is getting on, too. His hair is pepper
and salt, but he knows how to make up for
lost time by taking it easy. He gets up
early, works out, and turns in early. He
takes care of the hot dog stand like a
breeze until he gets time off. Sam's got it
made; this is it for him.*

כמובן אין זה סגנון ספרותי גבוה, אבל
רוב האמריקאים, ביחוד כאשר הם משוחחים
בינם לבין עצמם, משתמשים בביטויים
כאלה. אם אתה זר בארה"ב ולמדת את
המלים *cool* 'יקרירי', *cat* 'חתולי', *blow* 'לנשוף',
*stack* 'ערמהי', *fly* 'לעוףי', *handle* 'ידיתי',
וכולי, עדיין לא תוכל להבין את הדוגמה
מאנגלית אמריקאית מדוברת שמופיעה
למעלה, מכיוון שהמידע המילוני הזה לבדו לא
יתן את המובן של הביטויים האלה. ניב - כפי
שמתברר מההערות הללו - הוא יחום מובן
חדש לצרוף מלים שכבר יש להן מובן משלהן.
בהמשך נמצא תרגום של אותו הטקסט
משפת הדיבור העממית האמריקאית
היומיומית לשפה יותר פורמלית שיחסית
כמעט אין בה מונחים אידיומטיים.

*Sam is really a calm person. He never
loses control of himself and hardly ever
becomes too angry. Furthermore, he
knows how to manage his business financially by using a few tricks . . . Needless to
say, he, too, is getting older. His hair is
beginning to turn gray, but he knows how
to compensate for wasted time by relaxing.*

*He rises early, exercises and goes to
bed early. He manages his frankfurter
stand without visible effort, until it is*

*someone else's turn to work there. Sam is
successful; he has reached his life's goal.*

רצית להסביר איך מסודרות היחידות בקטע
הזה, כי אז היה עליך לכתוב מילון ניבים קטן.
כגון זה:

| | |
|---|---|
| *to be a (real) cool cat* | להיות אדם רגוע ושלו |
| *to blow one's stack* | לאבד שליטה עצמית |
| *to fly off the handle* | |
| *what's more* | חוץ מזה |
| *to get away with something* | לעשות מעשה רע ולא להענש או להנזק ממנו |
| *of course* | כמובן |
| *to be getting on* | להזדקן |
| *pepper and salt* | שיער שיבה מעורב בשיער שחור |
| *to make up for something* | לפצות על משהו |
| *lost time* | זמן מבוזבז |
| *to take it easy* | לנוח להרגע לא לדאוג |
| *to get up* | לקום מהמטה בבוקר |
| *to work out* | להתעמל לעשות גימנסטיקה |
| *to turn in* | ללכת לישון בלילה |
| *like a breeze* | בלי מאמץ בקלות |
| *time off* | תקופת חופש מהעבודה |
| *to have got it made* | להצליח להיות מוצלח |
| *this is it* | להיות במצב שאין טוב ממנו כשיש די ממשהו להרגיש סיפוק מהמצב הנוכחי |

**ביטויים רבם ברשימה הזאת נמצאם**
במלון הגיל. הדבר המעניין בקשר לרובם הוא
שאפשר ליחס להם חלקי דבור. כלומר, כמה
מהביטויים האלה משמשים כפעלים, כמו
למשל *get away with, get up, turn in*. ואילו

XXIX

אחרים, שווים במספר, משמשים כשמות
עצם. למשל hot dog ו- cool cat הם שמות.
רבים מהביטויים הם תארים, למשל בדוגמה
pepper and salt, שפרושה שיער שיבה
מעורבב עם שיער שחור. רבים הם תארי
פעלים כמו בדוגמאות like a breeze יבלי
מאמץ, בקלות,' hammer and tongs,'
באלימות', she ran after him hammer
and tongs המתואמים עם חלקי הדיבור
נקראים ניבים לקסמיים.

הקבוצה השניה החשובה ביותר
מורכבת מביטויים ארוכים מאלה, רבים
מכילים משפט שלם או קטע ממשפט, כמו
fly off the handle לאבד שליטה עצמית,
blow one's stack לכעוס. יש ביטויים רבים
מהסוג הזה באנגלית אמריקאית. הנפוצים
ביותר הם to kick the bucket למות, to be up
the creek להיות בצרה או במצב מסוכן,
caught between the devil and the deep
blue sea חייב לבחור בין שתי ברירות שאף
אחת מהן אינה נעימה, to seize the bull by
the horns להתמודד ביושר עם בעיה קשה.
ביטויים כאלה נקראים בצרפתית tournures
שפרוש הדבר צירוף לשוני דמיוני או ביתר
פשטות ניבים מורכבים. משותף לכל אלה
שאין להם יחס ישיר לחלקי הדיבור, וכדי
להגדיר אותם דרושה פרפרזה ולא רק מלה
אחת.

צורת הניב קבועה מראש ורק מעטים
מהם יכולים להרשות שינויים קטנים בלי
להרום את פרושם המורכב. רבים מהם
לגמרי קפואים מלה במלה ולא יכולים להופיע
בצירוף אחר. נחשוב למשל על kick the.
bucket במשפט פסיבי, מקבלים צורה בלתי
רצויה כמו the bucket has been kicked by,
the cowboy שאין פרושה שהאדם הזה מת.
במקום זאת פרוש הדבר שבעט בדלי. ניבים
מהסוג הזה ידועים כמבנים לגמרי קפואים.
עלינו לשים לב, בכל זאת, שאפשר להטות
אפילו ניב מסוג זה בעבר ועתיד. כלומר,
אפשר להגיד the cowboy kicked the bucket,
וגם he the cowboy will kick the bucket,
has kicked the bucket וכך הלאה. דוברי

אנגלית אינם תמיד מסכימים בינם
לבין עצמם, וכן גם מומחי הדקדוק, אם
מותר להשתמש באידיום הזה בצורת
gerund) gerund הוא שם עצם בני מפועל עם
ing-. למשל singing שׂ-sing, eating שׂ-eat,
his kicking the וכולי ספק גדול אם המשפט
bucket surprised us all היה מתקבל בעיני
דוברי אנגלית, ולכן מוטב להמנע ממנו.

הקבוצה הבאה, מבחינת הגודל, היא
זאת של ביטויים שהם מליצות ואמרות
ופתגמים. ביניהם מונים אנו את don't count,
שפרוש your chickens before they're hatched
הדבר אל תחגוג את תוצאות המשימה לפני
שהן ידועות, כי יתכן שתכשל, ואז תראה
מגוהץ; don't wash your dirty linen in public
(אל תתלונן בקשר לבעיות משפחתיות לפני
זרים כי זה לא עסקם) וכולי. רבים מאלה
נובעים ממקור ספרותי או באים אלינו
מדוברי האנגלית הראשונים בצפון אמריקה.

שאי אפשר לנבא את מובן הביטוי
מהמללים אשר בו (או לפחות את הפרוש
המדויק) הוא לא הקריטריון היחיד
לאידיומטיות. ביטויים קבועים או יחידות
המרכבות ממלים רבות יכולים להיות
אידיומטיים אף כי פרושם ברור מראש.
הדבר שאידיומטי בהם הוא הצורה שהם
בנויים. למשל? How about a drink? (אWhat do
you say, Joe? (במקום להגיד שלום כשנפגשים)
just to be on the safe side, just in case; as a
matter of fact; ורבים אחרים.

מקרה אחר שנחשב לאידיומטי הוא
כאשר משתמשים במלה יחידה בצורה
מפתיעה שמובנה שונה בהחלט מן הפירוש
הרגיל. למשל lemon כדי לתאר שעונים
פגומים מכוניות או מכונות שאינן פועלות,
לתאר פגישה מאכזבת בין בחור ובחורה
שיוצאים ביחד או בחינה קשה; my math)
exam was a dog, my car is a lemon).

מדוע האנגלית וביחוד זאת הנפוצה
באמריקה כל כך אידיומטית? הסיבה
הסבירה ביותר היא שכאשר אנחנו מפתחים
מושגים חדשים יש לנו צורך בביטויים
חדשים כדי להביע אותם, אבל במקום לגזור

מלה חדשה משורשים או להמציא שורש
חדש מצלילי השפה, דוברי האנגלית מצרפים
מילים קיימות כדי להביע מובן מורכב חדש.
זה נכון במידה מסוימת בקשר לכל השפות.
בעצם, אין שום שפה בעולם שאין בה ניבים.
למשל, נסתכל על הביטוי הסיני שפירושו
מהר: XX (מה שננג), שבאופן מלולי אפשר
היה לתרגם כעל כעל סוס'. למה שמשמעו
המהירות יהיה קשור לרכיבה על גבו של
סוס? התשובה ברורה בימים עברו, לפני
הרכבת, המכונית, והאוירון, הדרך המהירה
ביותר להגיע ממקום למקום היתה לרכב על
סוס. לכן, להגיד XX (מה שננג), בסינית היה
כאילו אמרנו אנו: מהר! לדהור כעל סוס!
ביטוי כזה לא היה קשה לנו להבין. אבל כדי
להבין אותו, דובר השפה צריך לדעת שזה
ניב, והזר היה צריך ללמוד אותו.

בכל זאת כשלומדים ניב חדש, בקלות
אפשר לנחש שזה לא נכון. נתבונן בביטוי האנגלי
*Oh, well. the die is cast!* מה היית מנחש
שפירוש הדבר - בהנחה שאינך יודע? אולי
היית מסיק שמוותרים על משהו בגלל
ה *Oh, well* - בעצם, פרוש יהביטוי בחרתי
בדבר שאי אפשר לחזור ממנו ועלי לחיות עם
התוצאות'. עכשיו נוכל לשחזר איך נוצר
הניב הזה. את הקוביה שזורקים במשחקי
מזל אסור לזרוק מחדש כדי לקבל מספר
אחר. לעשות כך מנוגד לחוקי המשחק. בין
אם הגרלת אחד, שלוש או שש, עליך לשאת
בתוצאות הזריקה, כלומר לזכות או להפסיד.
(רבים מכם בוודאי יודעים שקיסר השתמש
בביטוי הזה כאשר חצה את הרוביקון, מעשה
שהוביל למלחמה). ובכן איך תשתמש בניב
אם רק למדת אותו? קודם כל, חכה עד
שתשמע אותו מפי דובר אנגלית בשיחה
טבעית. אל תנסה להשתמש בביטוי הזה עד
אשר תהיה לך שליטה בדקדוק אנגלי יסודי.
אחרי שתשמע את הביטוי לפחות פעמיים
ותבין את פרושו, תוכל לנסות להשתמש בו.

נגיד שיש לך שתי הצעות עבודה, אחת
מובטחת, אבל עם משכורת נמוכה, ובשניה
תרוויח יותר כסף, אבל עוד לא הובטחה לך.
מכיוון שאתה חושש שמא תשאר מחוסר

עבודה, אתה מקבל את ההצעה הראשונה,
ואחרי כן מתברר שההצעה השניה אושרה.
כמובן אתה מרגיש קצת מאוכזב. תוכל
במקרה כזה להגיד: *Oh, well, the die is cast...*
אם תנסה זאת עם דובר אנגלית אמריקאי
והוא יסתכל עליך בהבנה ולא ישאל למה
אתה מתכוון, כי אז הצלחת למצוא שמוש
מתאים לניב החדש שבפיך. אפשר להפיק
הרבה נחת מהצלחה שכזו. אמריקאים
מנומסים יותר אל זרים מרוב האומות, אבל
בכל זאת הם מבחינים בין אנגלית שוטפת
לזאת שאינה. אם אדם תמיד מדבר בשפה
גבוהה ומליצית ואף פעם אינו משתמש בניב
במקום הנכון, הוא עלול לקבל שם של דובר
זר בעל סגנון יבש וחסר דמיון, או יראה
רציני ורשמי מדי. השמוש בניבים, על פי כן,
הוא חשוב למדי. עשוי הוא לעורר הרגשה
של הבנה הדדית.            ככל שאתה שולט
באנגלית אידיומטית        ככה יכבדוך
האמריקאים וירגישו אתך בנוח, ויחשבו
לעצמם: הנה אדם נחמד ונעים - ראו כמה יפה
הוא מתבטא.

עכשיו נעבור על כמה נימוקים מעשיים
בקשר לשימוש במילון הניבים האמריקאים.

## איך להשתמש במילון הזה

המילון הזה ניתן לשימוש על ידי זרים,
תלמידים, פועלים, מהגרים - וכן כל מי שרוצה
לשפר את האנגלית שבפיו ולדבר שפה
שוטפת ואידיומטית. יש כאן ביטויים מהסוג
שהזכרנו מקודם: ניבים לקסמיים, צרופי
לשון דמיוניים, ניבים משליים או ספרותיים.
כאשר משפט או חלק ממשפט הוא בעל מובן
מיוחד שאי אפשר להבין מהמלים אשר בו, כי
אז נדע שמדובר בניב יתכן שאתה כבר מכיר
כמה מהביטויים הללו או שתוכל לנחש את
פרושם. חפש בספר את הניבים המנונים
מטה. כל הסיכויים שאתה כבר מכירם היטב.
תרגיל זה יעזור לך להבין כיצד משתמשים
בספר הזה. למשל:

*boyfriend, girl friend, outer
space, get even, give up, going
to, keep on, keep your mouth*

*shut, lead somebody by the nose, look after, show off, throw away, all over, in love, mixed up. out of this world, piggy bank, throw away, I'll say, both X and Y.*

מילון הוא כמו כל מכשיר אחר עליך להתרגל אליו וללמוד איך להשתמש בו לפני שהוא יועיל לך. עיין בהוראות בתשומת לב עיין וחזור כדי שתתחיל חיפוש הניבים יהיה לך קל וטבעי. אם תשמע ביטוי מורכב או ניב שאינו במילון הזה, אחרי שתתרגל לניבים שבמילון, תתפתח אצלך חוש לביטויים כאלה ותוכל למצוא את הפירוש ולרשום אותו לעצמך שמור רשימת ניבים פרטית משלך ליד המילון הרגיל. אם תקרא מאמר טכני, או רומן או קטע מעיתון שיש בו ביטוי לא מובן, חפש במילון הרגיל שלך. אם לא ימצא שם, נסה כאן.

איך לברר אם המילון הזה יכול להיות לך לעזר בפענוח משפט קשה? לפעמים קל לראות איזו פסוקית היא הניב; כמו ב-*puppy love, mixed up, dog-eat-dog, fun house* אם לא ברור היכן הניב מתחיל או נגמר, בחר במלה חשובה מהחלק הקשה ביותר במשפט וחפש אותה. אם היא המלה הראשונה בניב, כי אז תמצא את כל הפסוקית, ואחריה הסבר. למשל, הביטוי *bats in the belfry* מופיע תחת אחרי המלה *bats*. אם המלה שבה בחרת אינה הראשונה בניב, תמצא רשימה של ניבים שהמלה מופיעה בהם. למשל, המלה תמצא בהגדרות של *curl one's hair OR curl one's toes, step on the toes (of somebody).* כמובן, לפעמים תמצא שאינך מבין משפט ואין זה בגלל הניבים שבו. במקרה כזה, מוטב להשתמש במילון רגיל. נוסף לזה, יש לציין שקיימים ניבים אנגליים רבים שאינם מופיעים במילון זה. כאן רשומים רק הניבים הנפוצים ביותר באנגלית אמריקאית. באנגלית בריטית למשל או באנגלית המדוברת באוסטרליה, יש ניבים רבים שאינם מקובלים באנגלית אמריקאית.

# הערכים לסוגיהם

במילון זה יש ארבעה מיני ערכים: ערך ראשי, ערך כלול, ארך הפניה וערך מפתח. ערך כלול נגזר מניב אחר, אבל היה יכול לקבל הגדרה משל עצמו. ערך כלול מופיע תחת ערך ראשי ונשען של הגדרתו. (למשל *fence-sitter* תחת *sit on the fence*). כל ערך כלול כולל דוגמה ופרפרזה. הסבר נוסף מצורף כאשר קשה להבין את הניב הנגזר מהמקור שממנו נגזר. כאשר ניב ניתן לשימוש ביותר מחלק דיבור אחד (כמו שם וגם פועל), רשום כאן ערך נפרד לכל שימוש.

ערך הפניה מפנה את הקורא להסבר הנמצא תחת ערך אחר. נניח שאתה רוצה למצוא *cast in one's lot with*, תוכל לחפש תחת *cast*, וגם תחת *lot*, אבל ערך הפניה יפנה אותך אל *throw*, מפני ש-*cast* היא מילה הרבה יותר נדירה ולכן הצורה הנפוצה יותר של הניב הזה מתחילה בפועל *throw*.

ערך מפתח מוביל את הקורא לכל הערכים האחרים שבהם מופיעה מלת המפתח. על כן אחרי המלה *chin* מופיעות כל הפסוקיות שבהן היא נמצאת, למשל:

*keep one's chin up, stick one's chin (or neck) out, take it on the chin, up to the chin in.*

# חלקי הדיבור

הניבים שממלאים תפקיד דקדוקי מסוים מצוינים כאן כשייכים לאחד מחלקי הדיבור. לפעמים ניב ממלא יותר מתפקיד אחד, (למשל אלה שמתחילים במלת שימוש), ואז הם מקבלים ציון כפול. הניב *in commission* הוא גם תואר וגם תואר הפועל. רבות מפסוקיות השימוש הן תארי פועל בפירושן המלולי, אבל תארים במובן הבלתי צפוי בתור ניבים. פעלים מצוינים ב-*v-(verb):* ניב שבו יש פועל ותואר הפועל, פועל ומלת שימוש או פועל, מלת שימוש ותואר הפועל נחשבים ל-*v-* פסוקית פועל מסומנת כ-*v. phr.-(verbal phrase):* סימון זה כולל

פעלים עם מושא או נושא ופעלים יחד עם פסוקית שימוש.

## ציון המשלב

עליך לשים לב אם רצוי להשתמש בניב מסוים בתנאים חברתיים כל-שהם. ציון המשלב *slang* מזהיר שבניב הזה מוטב להשתמש רק בין חברים טובים. לעומת זאת *informal* מציין שמותר להשתמש בניב זה בשיחה יומיומית אבל עלינו להמנע ממנו בכתב. ואילו *formal* מביעה בדיוק את ההפך: זה דבר שאנשים לרוב אינם אומרים, אבל נוהגים הם לכתוב כך בחיבורים ולהשמיע את הביטוי בנאומים או בהרצאות באוניברסיטה. אם מצוין הניב כ-*literary* סימן שיודעים כולם שזאת ציטטה; לא רצוי להשתמש בביטויים כאלה לעיתים תכופות מדי. ציון המשלב *vulgar* מזהיר אותנו כלל לא להשתמש בביטוי. צריך להמנע ממנו. אבל טוב להכיר ביטויים כאלה כששומעים אותם כי אז נוכל לשפוט את הדובר על פי המלים שבפיו. ניב מסומן כ-*substandard* משמש דוברים פחות משכילים. ואילו *nonstandard* נחשב לבלתי שוטף אם ביטוי מסווג כ-*archaic* (נדיר בספר זה) פרוש הדבר שהוא מוגבל לאנגלית תנ"כית או מזמן שקספיר. *dialect* פירושו שהביטוי הזה מוגבל למקורו הגאוגרפי; למשל, *chiefly British* פירושו שאמריקאים כמעט שלא משתמשים בו; *Southern* מציין שהביטוי נפוץ הרבה יותר בדרום ארה"ב מאשר בצפון.

אדם מקאי/תרגום: איה כ"ץ
*Adam Makkai/Aya Katz*

# Premessa

## CHE COS'E' UN'ESPRESSIONE IDIOMATICA?

Se non si capisce ciascuna parola in un certo testo e non si riesce ad interpretare tale testo, il motivo sicuro per questo è la presenza nel testo di espressioni idiomatiche sconosciute. Per esempio, supponiamo che si è presentati con il seguente testo:

*Sam is a real cool cat. He never blows his stack and hardly ever flies off the handle. What's more, he knows how to get away with things . . . Well, of course, he is getting on, too. His hair is pepper and salt, but he knows how to make up for lost time by taking it easy. He gets up early, works out, and turns in early. He takes care of the hot dog stand like a breeze until he gets time off. Sam's got it made; this is it for him.*

Va senza dire che non si tratta di un testo di grande qualità letteraria, ma la maggior parte degli americani, specialmente quando conversano tra di loro, utilizzano espressioni proprio come quelle contenute in questo testo. Se non si conosce la cultura americana, pur conoscendo vocaboli come *cool* "fresco," *cat* "gatto," *blow* "soffiare," *stack* "mucchio," *fly* "volare," *handle* "maniglia, manico," e così via, non si sarà in grado di capire il testo riportato sopra, per il motivo che le definizioni di un vocabolario regolare non forniranno i significati idiomatici delle parole. Ma sono proprio questi significati che si dorvanno conoscere per interpretare il testo nella sua globalità. L'uso idiomatico di una parola sta, ovviamente, nell'assegnare un nuovo significato alla stessa parola. Ecco, perciò, una "traduzione" letterale del testo idiomatico riportato sopra. Questa riflette uno stile più formale e privo relativamente di idiomaticità:

*Sam is really a calm person. He never loses control of himself and hardly ever becomes too angry. Further-*

*more, he knows how to manage his business financially by using a few tricks . . . Needless to say, he, too, is getting older. His hair is beginning to turn gray, but he knows how to compensate for wasted time by relaxing. He rises early, exercises, and goes to bed early. He manages his frankfurter stand without visible effort, until it is someone else's turn to work there. Sam is successful; he has reached his life's goal.*

Ora, se si dovesse spiegare come sono organizzate le unità in questo testo, si avrebbe bisogno di un dizionarietto di espressioni idiomatiche che avrebbe la seguente forma:

| | |
|---|---|
| *to be a (real) cool cat* | essere una persona molto calma |
| *to blow one's stack* | perdere l'auto-controllo, arrabbiarsi |
| *to fly off the handle* | arrabbiarsi fortemente |
| *what's more* | per di più |
| *to get away with something* | cavarsela |
| *of course* | certo, naturalmente |
| *to be getting on* | invecchiarsi |
| *pepper and salt* | capelli che stanno diventando grigi |
| *to make up for something* | riprendere, riacquistare, rifare |
| *lost time* | tempo perduto |
| *to take it easy* | stare calmo, non preoccuparsi |
| *to get up* | alzarsi dal letto |
| *to work out* | fare esercizio, fare ginnastica |
| *to turn in* | andare a dormire la sera |
| *to take care of something* | pensarci |
| *like a breeze* | con facilità, facilmente, senza alcuno sforzo |
| *time off* | tempo libero |
| *to have got it made* | essere arrivato, avere successo |
| *this is it* | avercela fatta |

Gran parte delle espressioni in questo elenco sono ritrovabili nel presente dizionario. E' interesante notare che esse sono classificabili secondo le cosiddette "parti del discorso": e cioè, dal punto di vista grammatical alcune fungono da verbi *(get away with, get up, work out, turn in, etc.)*, alcune da nomi *(hot dog, White House* "Casa Bianca,"*)* altre da aggettivi *(pepper and salt)*, altre ancora da avverbi *(like the breeze, hammer and tongs* "in modo violento,"*)* e così via. Le espressioni che si possono correlare alle parti del discorso sono lessemi idiomatici.

L' altro tip di espressione idiomatica di una certa frequenza nel discorso comune è costituito da frasi intere come *to fly off the handle* "perdere l'auto-controllo" e *to blow one's stack* "arrabbiarsi fortenmente." Ce ne sono veramente tante in inglese di frasi di questo tipo, alcune delle quali sono assai famose: *to kick the bucket* "morire," *to be up the creek* "essere in pericolo," *to be caught between the devil and the deep blue sea* "essere tra l'incudine ed il martello," *to seize the bull by the horns* "risolvere un problema concretamente," e così via. In francese, espressioni di questo tipo si chiamano *tournures*, cioè, "giri di parole," ma si possono anche denominare semplicemente delle *frasi idiomatiche*. La loro caratteristica saliente è il fatto che non sono assegnabili facilmente ad una parte del discorso, e, per di più, che ne sono esplicabili ne termini di una parafrasi.

La loro forma è fissa e non può essere alterata senza modificare il significato. Sono delle "formule rigide" che non si possono parafrasare, né facilmente spiegare. L'espressione *to kick the bucket,* per esempio, non può essere modificata in nessuna maniera: la forma passiva *the bucket has been kicked by the cowboy* non significa più che "il cowboy è morto," ma invece che "il cowboy ha dato un calcio al secchio." Espressioni di questo tipo sono forme completamente fisse, anche se possono essere modificate in quanto al loro tempo verbale: *the cowboy kicked the bucket, the cowboy will kick the bucket, he has kicked the bucket,* ecc. le quali significano irspettivamente che il cowboy "morì," "morirà," e "è morto," Solo il caso del gerundio (forma verbale terminante in *-ing*) presenta un'ambiguità interpretativa, per cui è meglio evitare frasi tipo *His kicking the bucket surprised us all.*

Un altro tipo assai consistente di espressioni idiomatiche è costituito dai detti e dai proverbi, e cioè, da espressioni come *don't count your chickens before they're hatched* ("una rondine non fa primavera,") *don't wash your dirty linen in public* ("non far conoscere agli altri i propri problemi domestici,") ecc. Molte di queste espressioni hanno una lunga ed illustre tradizione letteraria, essendo state tramandate al continente americano dai primi parlanti d'inglese.

Perché è così "idiomatico" l'inglese, specialmente nella sua versione americana? La risposta più probabile a questo quesito è il bisogno di creare nuovi significati semplicemente ricombinando le parole già esistenti nella lingua, ed evitando perciò d'inventare nuove parole in base alle risorse fonetiche della lingua. Questa forma di creatività si manifesta in tutte le lingue del mondo. Non esiste una lingua che non abbia espressioni idiomatiche. In cinese, per esempio, l'espressione *mǎ shāng* "velocemente," significa letteralmente "groppa di cavallo." In che modo è associabile il concetto di "velocemente" con una "groppa di cavallo?" La risposta risulta ovvia se si considera che prima dell'avvento del treno, dell'automobile, e dell'aeroplano, il modo più veloce per giungere a destino era a cavallo. Quindi, l'espressione cinese *mǎ shāng* corrisponde all'inglese *hurry up! We must go on horse back* ("Andiamo velocemente"). Tali forme, quindi, non sono affatto incomprensibili, ma uno studente straniero della lingua le dovrà imparare correttamente, altrimenti rischia di essere incompreso. Si consideri, per esempio, l'espressione *Oh well, the die is cast!* Cosa significa? Ovviamente, contiene un elemento di sorpresa, visto la presenza dell'interiezione *Oh well*. Essa significa: "Ho sbagliato, e dovrò accettarne le conseguenze!" Da un punto di vista etimologico tale espressione deriva probabilmente dal fatto che nei giochi d'azzardo una volta che è stato buttato giù un dado sul tavolo, non importerà se dimostra il numero uno, tre, o sei; il fatto sta che bisognerà accettarne le conseguenze, per cui si potrà vincere o perdere. Alcuni pensano, invece, che tale frase fu usata da Cesare quando attraversò il Rubicone, azione dalla quale conseguì una guerra.

Come sarà possibile usare un'espressione come questa, appena determinato il suo significato? Anzitutto, sarà necessario ascoltare come viene usata nei suoi contesti naturali da parlanti nativi; non è consigliabile usarla senza conoscere prima la grammatica dell'inglese. In seguito a diverse osservazioni circa il suo uso coretto, si sarà più in grado di usarla per conto proprio. Ecco uno scenario plausibile in proposito: Poniamo che un individuo riceva due offerte di impiego, uno delle quali ha prospettive di stipendio più alto; e poniamo l'individuo accetti quella meno lucrosa per qualche motivo; allora l'espressione *Oh well, the die is cast,* è del tutto applicabile alla situazione in questione. Un parlante nativo che sentirà tale espressione in riferimento a questo scenario la capirà perfettamente, e la troverà del tutto adatta. Anche se gli americani tendono ad essere assai tolleranti rispetto agli stranieri, sanno giudicare correttamente il livello di competenza linguistica raggiunto da un qualsiasi straniero. Chi usa uno stile troppo formale e letterale è spesso giudicato come troppo serio e uggioso. *Perciò, l'abilità di padroneggiare le espressioni idiomatiche è importantissima, poiché consente di avvicinarsi all'interlocutore.* Più espressioni idiomatiche si conoscono, più probabile è un tale avvicinamento.

## COME USARE QUESTO DIZIONARIO

Chi non consoce la lingua inglese come un nativo, non importa a quale ambito sociale appartenga, può facilmente usare questo dizionario allo scopo di rendere la propria conoscenza della lingua più idiomatica. Esso contiene i tipi d'espressione menzionati sopra: *frasi idiomatiche, forme fisse,* ecc. Le espressioni idiomatiche si riconoscono subito quando il significato non è determinaible in base al significato delle singole parole che le compongono. Alcune di queste saranno già familiari al lettore, il quale potrà ricercarle facilmente nel presente libro: *boyfriend, girlfriend, outer space, piggy bank, get even, give up, going to, keep on, keep your mouth shut,* *lead someone by the nose, look after, show off, throw away, all over, in love, mixed up, out of this world, throw away, I'll say, both X and Y.*

Questo dizionario è uno strumento che si deve conoscere prima di usare. Quindi, sarà necessario leggere le sue didascalie con attenzione e fare qualche "prova iniziale," ricercando in esso diverse espressioni idiomatiche. In tal modo sarà molto più facile familiarizzarsi con questo strumento, utilizzandolo assieme ad un vocabolario normale quando si leggono testi tecnici, romanzi, o anche articoli di giornale. Chi desidera veramente imparare a parlare idiomaticamente dovrà notare per iscritto qualsiasi espressioni che vuole veramente imparare, appena l'avrà ritrovata nel dizionario.

Questo dizionario sarà anche utile per l'interpretazione di intere frasi. Se la frase contiene un'espressione come *puppy love fun house, dog-eat-dog, mixed-up,* si potrà semplicemente ricercarla in modo alfabetico; diversamente, sarà necessario determinare qual è parola chiave in una data espressione e poi ricercarla in modo alfabetico. Se è la prima parola dell'espressione, allora è proprio questa che si dovrà ricercare alfabeticamente: per esempio, l'espressione *bats in the belfry* appare alfabeticamente in rapporto alla parola *bats.* Se invece non è la prima parola, bisognerà seguire un'altra modalità di ricerca: per esempio, la parola *toe* in una data espressione sarà ritrovata come una voce in *curl one's hair, curl one's toes, on one's toes, step on the toes (of somebody).* Ovviamente, nel caso di espressioni non-idiomatiche, si dovrà consultare un vocabolario regolare. E' da notare che non è stato possibile includere in questo dizionario tutte le espressioni idiomatiche dell'inglese parlato in America. Inoltre, nell'inglese parlato in Gran Bretagna in Australia esistono frasi idiomatiche che non fanno parte del repertorio espressivo dell'inglese parlato sul continente nordamericano.

## TIPO DI VOCI RACCOLTE IN QUESTO DIZIONARIO

Ci sono quattro tipi di voce raccolti in questo dizionario: *voci principali, voci* continuate o unite, *voci di richiamo*, e *voci indice*. Nel caso di *voci principali* si tratta di un'espressione spiegata nella sua totalità. Nel caso di una *voce continuata* si tratta di un'espressione derivata da un'altra che altrimenti sarebbe separata da essa se fosse messa in ordine alfabetico (per es., *fence-sitter* viene collocata dopo *sit on the fence* e poi illustrata o spiegata secondo la necessità); un'espressione che appartiene a più di una parte del discorso viene spiegata separatamente. Le voci di richiamo permettono di ricercare frasi come *cast in one's lot with* sia in base a *cast* che a *lot*. In questo caso il lettore troverà la voce nel contesto di *throw in one's lot with*: per il motivo che *cast* è una parola di scarsa frequenza, mentre *throw* è di frequenza elevata. Infine, la voce indice permette di ritrovare tutte le altre voci che la contengono: per es., la parola *chin* è seguita dalle espressioni di cui è una componente, e cioè, *keep one's chin up, stick one's chin (or neck) out, take it on the chin, up to the chin.*

## VOCI CLASSIFICATE SECONDO LE PARTI DEL · DISCORSO

Le espressioni che corrispondono a specifiche parti del discorso saranno classificate in modo correlativo. Per esempio, le espressioni preposizionali sono assegnate a due categorie grammaticali: e.g., *in com-* *mission* può essere usata sia come frase aggettivale che come avverbiale. E' da notare che molte di queste espressioni sono avverbiali quando vengono usate con un significato letterale, ma aggettivali quando sono usate in modo idiomatico. La sigla *v.* rappresenta un verbo; e cioè essa indica le espressioni contenenti un verbo e un avverbio, un verbo e una preposizione, oppure un verbo, una preposizione e un avverbio. La sigla *v. phr.* indica qualsiasi frase verbale (verbo più complemento, verbo più frase preposizionale, ecc.).

## VOCI CON USI RESTRITTIVI

E' ovviamente importante saper usare una qualsiasi espressione in modo appropriato; perciò l'etichetta *slang* indica che è da usare solo con amici che si conoscono intimamente; *uso informale* indica che è da usare sollo nelle conversazioni informali, e *uso formale* nei testi, orali o scritti, che esigono un livello più formale di discorso; *uso letterario* indica che si tratta di una citazione, e che, quindi, è da usare di rado; *volgare* indica che è da evitare, anche se viene usata da qualche nativo; *substandard* indica un uso incolto, e *nonstandard* un uso grossalano; *arcaico* indica un uso ormai sorpassato; *regionale* indica un uso ristretto ad un'area geografica (*generalmente britannico* indica uno scarso uso in America, e *meridionale* un uso particolarmente caratteristico nel sud degli Stati Uniti).

*Adam Makkai/Marcel Danesi*

# 序文

## イディオムとは何か

あるテキストに分からない単語は一つもないのに、全体で一体どういう意味なのか理解できないとしたら、その原因は恐らくイディオムにあるだろう。たとえば次の文章を読んだ(または聞いた)としよう。

*Sam is a real cool cat. He never blows his stack and hardly ever flies off the handle. What's more, he knows how to get away with things . . . Well, of course, he is getting on, too. His hair is pepper and salt, but he knows how to make up for lost time by taking it easy. He gets up early, works out, and turns in early. He takes care of the hot dog stand like a breeze until he gets time off. Sam's got it made; this is it for him.*

　言うまでもなく、これはすぐれた文学的文体ではないが、大概のアメリカ人は、特に彼ら同士で話す時には、この種の表現を使うだろう。さて、もしあなたがアメリカにいる外国人で、*cool*「涼しい、冷静な」、*cat*「ねこ」、*blow*「吹く」、*stack*「堆積」、*fly*「飛ぶ」、*handle*「取手」等々の単語を学んでいたとしても、上に挙げた会話体のアメリカ英語は分からないだろう。辞書の与えるこういった基礎的な知識だけではここで使われたいろいろな形の意味は与えられないからである。イディオムとは―今言ったことから分かるように―すでにそれぞれ自身の意味を持っている一群の語に新しい意味を付与することである。下に示すのは、この高度にイディオマティックな口語アメリカ英語のテキストを、もっと形式張っていて、比較的イディオムを用いない英語に翻訳したものである。

*Sam is really a calm person. He never loses control of himself and hardly ever becomes too angry. Furthermore, he knows how to manage his business financially by using a few tricks . . . Needless to say, he, too, is getting older. His hair is beginning to turn gray, but he knows how to compensate for wasted time by relaxing. He rises early, exercises, and goes to bed early. He manages his frankfurter stand without visible effort, until it is someone else's turn to work there. Sam is successful; he has reached his life's goal.*

さて、もしこのテキストで意味の単位が如何に構成されているかを説明するとしたら、イディオム小辞典を作らねばならないだろう。それは次のようになるだろう。

| | |
|---|---|
| to be a (real) cool cat | 本当に落ち着いた人だ |
| to blow one's stack | 自制を失う、かっとなる |
| to fly off the handle | 激怒する |
| what's more | さらに、その上 |
| to get away with something | (罰せられたりせずに)ある事をうまくやり遂げる |
| of course | もちろん |
| to be getting on | 年をとる |
| pepper and salt | (頭髪が)ごま塩 |
| to make up for something | ある事の埋め合わせをする |
| lost time | むだにした時間 |
| to take it easy | 気楽にやる、のんきにやる |
| to get up | 起床する |
| to work out | 体操をする |
| to turn in | 就寝する |
| to take care of something | ある事の面倒を見る |
| like a breeze | たやすく |
| time off | 休み時間 |
| to have got it made | 成功する |
| this is it | これで終わりだ |

　この小さな見本のリストに挙げたイディオムの多くはこの辞書に見出される。興味深いことに、これらのイディオムの大多数は我々が親しんでいるいずれかの品詞に容易に当てはめることができる。たとえば *get away with, get out, turn in* のようなイディオムは明らかに動詞的である。同様に多数のイディオムは名詞的である。たとえば *hot dog*「ホット・ドッグ」や *White House*「ホワイト・ハウス」は名詞である。上の文にある「ごま塩」の意味の *pepper and salt* のような形容詞的なものも多い。*like the breeze*「たやすく」、*hammer and tongs*「激しく」(たとえば *She ran after him hammer and tongs.*「彼女は猛烈に彼の後を追った」)など多くは副詞的である。このように我々が親しんでいる品詞と関連しているイディオムを「語彙

的イディオム」(lexemic idiom) と呼ぶことができる。

　もう一つの大変重要なイディオムのグループはもっと形が大きい。上例の to fly off the handle「自制を失う」や to blow one's stack「激怒する」のように、しばしば一つの節 (clause) 全体の長さに近い。このようなイディオムはアメリカ英語には非常に多い。最も有名なものを幾つか挙げれば、to kick the bucket「死ぬ」、to be up the creek「苦境にある」、to be caught between the devil and deep blue sea「二つのいやなことのどちらかを選ばねばならない、進退きわまる」、to seize the bull by the horns「敢然と難局に当たる」などである。この種のイディオムは「言い回し」(フランス語から来た tournure) または「句イディオム」(phraseological idiom) と呼ばれている。それらに共通しているのは、それらがある文法的品詞とすぐには関連せずに、2語以上のパラフレーズを必要とすることである。

　これらのイディオムの形は固定していて、ごく少数のものを除けば、別の言い方や書き方をすると、イディオムの意味が破壊されてしまう。多くのものは完全に固定していて、それ以外の形で現われることはあり得ない。たとえば kick the bucket というイディオムを考えて頂きたい。これを受動態にすれば、たとえば The bucket has been kicked by the cowboy のようになるが、これはイディオムとしては受け入れられず、もはや「カウボーイは死んだ」ではなく、「カウボーイが足でバケツをけった」という意味になる。しかしながら、注意して頂きたいが、このイディオムでも時制によって変化させることはできるのである。たとえば The cowboy kicked the bucket, The cowboy will kick the bucket, He has kicked the bucket などと言ってもよい。たとえば、His kicking the bucket surprised us all..のようにこのイディオムを動名詞 (sing から singing、eat から eating のように動詞に -ing をつけて派生した名詞を動名詞と言う) の形で使ってよいかどうかについては、文法家も一般の話し手も意見が一致しない。この形は避けるのが一番よい。

　次に大きなイディオムのクラスは十分確立した言い習わしや諺である。これには Don't count your chickens before they're hatched.「失敗するかもともともないかねないから仕事の結果も分からないうちから祝ったりする、捕らぬたぬきの皮算用」とか Don't wash your dirty linen in public.「家庭の問題について関係ない他人にぐちをこぼすな、内輪の恥をさらけ出すな」といった有名なタイプが含まれる。これらの多くはよく知られた文学的な出所から出ていたり、北米大陸で最も早く英語を話した人々から我々に伝えられたものである。

　なぜ英語、それも特にアメリカ英語にはこんなにイディオムが多いのだろうか。我々が新しい概念を発達させるにつれてそのために新しい表現を必要とするが、我々の言語の音から全く新しい語を造り出す代わりに、我々はすでに存在する二つ以上の語を使って、それらを合わせて新しい意味を持たせる、というのが一番有力な理由であろう。しかし、これはこれまでに知られているすべての言語について言えることである。事実、イディオムを持たない言語はない。たとえば「速く」という意味の中国語の表現を考えてみよう。それは mǎ shāng (馬上) で、文字通りに訳せば 'horse back' という意味である。どうして「速い」という概念が馬の背と結び付けられるのだろうか。一寸考えれば答えは明らかになる。昔、まだ汽車も自動車もない頃、ある場所から他の場所へ行く一番速い方法は馬に、つまり馬の背に乗ることだった。そこで中国語の mǎ shāng は英語ならば Hurry up! We must go 'on horse back'. つまり Hurry up! We must go quickly. と言うようなものである。このような形は英語でも決して理解できないことはないだろうが、話し手はそれがイディオムだと悟らねばならないだろうし、外国人はそれを学ばねばならないだろう。しかしながら、イディオムを学ぶ時に、人は不正確な推測をすることがある。英語のイディオム Oh well, the die is cast! を考えて頂きたい。あなたはこれがどんな意味だと思うだろうか—あなたがそれを知らなかったとして。Oh well という部分があるので、恐らくこの話し手は何かに仕方なく従っているのだとあなたは推測するだろう。この表現の意味は「取り返しのつかない決定をしてしまってそれに従わねばならない」ということである。今このイディオムの生成過程を再建してみることができる。賭博で投げられたさいは2度投げることはできない。それは規則違反である。1が出ようと、3が出ようと、6が出ようと、投げた結果に甘んじなければならない、つまり、場合に応じて勝つか負けるかしなければならない。(この句はシーザーがルビコン川を渡った時に使って、その結果戦争になったということを知っている人もいるだろう。)

それでは、たった今このイディオムを覚えて、あなたはそれを正確に使えるだろうか。まず第一に、英語を母国語とする人が自然な文脈の中で使うのを聞くまで待たなければならない。英文法の基礎をマスターするまでは、自分でイディオムを使う実験をしてはならない。そのイディオムが使われるのを2回以上聞いてその意味が十分に分かったら、自分で使ってみてもよい。一方は確実だが給料は低く、他方は給料は多いが反りである二つの仕事の話があったと想像してみなさい。臆病と完全な失職の恐れのために低い給料の仕事を承諾した丁度その時に、もっとよい話が舞い込んで、あなたは当然気をくじかれる。その時、*Oh well, the die is cast...*と言えるのである。これを英語を母国語とする人に使ってみて、相手が同情の色を見せ、そして *What do you mean?* と言わなければ、あなたは覚えたてのイディオムを適切な文脈に使うことに初めて成功したわけになる。これは貴重な体験になる。生粋のアメリカ人はふつう他の国の人々よりも外国人に対して丁寧な反応を示すが、彼らはあなたがどの位流暢に話すかはっきり言うことができる。もしいつも堅苦しく大げさな表現を使って、適切な場所にイディオムを使わなければ、その人は無味乾燥で想像力のない話し手か、あまりにまじめで形式張ろうとしている話し手だという評判を得るかもしれない。<u>したがって、イディオムの使用は極めて大切である。それは聞き手との連帯感を呼び起こすことができるのである。</u>あなたが正しい文脈でイディオムをたくさん使えば使うほど、生粋のアメリカ人はあなたに対してくつろいだ気持になり、それだけ一層「これはよい親しみのある人だ―実にうまく自分の考えを話すことができる」と心の中で思うだろう。

次に『現代熟語辞典』の使い方に関する幾つかの実際的な問題を見ることにしよう。

## 本辞典の使い方

この辞典は英語を母国語としない人、学生、労働者、移住者―要するに英語をもっと流暢にもっとイディオマティックに使いたいと思っている人が使うと効果があるだろう。本辞典には上に挙げた型の句、すなわち特別の意味を持った語彙的イディオム (lexemic idiom)、句イディオム (phrase idiom)、諺的イディオム (provervial idiom)が載せてある。あなたがある句を構成している個々の語を辞書で

調べて分かっても、その句が持つ特別な意味を正しく理解できない時に、その句はイディオムである。イディオムの幾つかをあなたはすでに知っているかもしれないし、あるいはその意味を想像できるかもしれない。すでによく知っているかもしれないが、次のイディオムのどれでも本辞典で引いてみると、この辞典の使い方を理解するのに役立つだろう。：*boyfriend, girlfriend, outer space, piggy bank, get even, give up, going to, keep on, keep your mouth shut, lead somebody by the nose, look after, show off, throw away, all over, in love, mixed-up, out of this world, I'll say, both X and Y.*

辞書も他の道具と同じである。それがあなたのためによく働いてくれるためには、あなたがそれに慣れ親しんで、使い方を学ばねばならない。使用法指示を何度も注意深く読んで、イディオムを調べる練習をしなさい。そのように、イディオムを捜して見つければ、それはあなたの第二の天性になるだろう。本辞典をしばらく使った後で、ここに載っていないイディオマティックな表現を耳にしたら、その意味を突き止めてそれを自分で書き留める力がついているだろう。あなた自身のイディオムのリストを家のふつうの辞書のすぐそばに置きなさい。専門書や小説や新聞記事を読んで分からない表現があったら、まずふつうの学校用辞書を調べて、そこに見つからなかったら、この辞典を使いなさい。

この辞典が難文の理解を助けるかどうか、どうしたら分かるだろうか。*puppy love, fun house, dog-eat-dog, mixed up* などのように句がどれだかすぐに分かることもあるだろう。もし分からなければ、一番難しい部分から重要な1語を取り出して、それを捜しなさい。もしそれがイディオムの最初の語ならば、句全体が見つかり、その後に説明がある。たとえば *bats in the belfry* という表現は本辞典ではbの *bats* の所に挙げてある。取り出した語がイディオムの最初の語でない場合は、その語を含むリストを見い出すだろう。たとえば、*toe* という語は *curl one's hair / curl one's toe, on one's toe, step on the toes (of somebody)* の項に見い出される。もちろん、ある文が分からない理由がイディオムのためでないこともあるだろうが、その場合には、ふつうの辞書が役に立つだろう。また、イディオムの数は本辞典に載っているよりも多い。ここに載せたのはアメリカ英語で最もよく使われるものだけである。たとえばイギリス英語や

オーストラリアで話される英語には確かにアメリカ英語にはないイディオマティックな表現が沢山ある。

## 項目の型

本辞典には4種類の項目がある。独立項目、追い込み項目、相互参照項目、索引項目である。独立項目はイディオムの完全な説明を含んでいる。追い込み項目は他のイディオムから派生しているがそのアルファベットの位置に置かれると基本的なイディオムから離れてしまう句である。これらの派生イディオムは独立項目の終わりに追い込んで(たとえば *fence-sitter* は *sit on the fence* の項にある) 説明とパラフレーズをつけた。主要項目の説明から派生項目を理解することが難しいと思われる場合にはさらに説明をつけた。イディオムが二つ以上の品詞に用いられる場合は、それぞれの用法を別見出しにした。

相互参照項目はその定義が別の場所にあることを示す。たとえば *cast in one's lot with* を調べたいと思ったとしよう。あなたは *cast* と *lot* の項を見ることができるが、相互参照項目によって *throw in one's lot with* という句を参照するように指示される。これは *cast* が今日ではずっとまれな語なので、このイディオムのふつうの、もっと頻度の高い形は *throw* という動詞で始まるからである。

索引項目は索引語を含む他のすべての項目を指示する。たとえば *chin* という語の後に、*keep one's chin up, stick one's chin (or neck) out, take it on the chin, up to the chin* など *chin* を含む句が挙げてある。

## 品詞表示

はっきりした文法形式類と関連するイディオムには品詞表示がつけられている。たとえば、〔動〕は、「動詞」及び「動詞句」を表し、「動詞＋副詞」、「動詞＋前置詞」、「動詞＋前置詞＋副詞」(以上、原著では*v.*と表示)、「動詞＋目的語」、「動詞＋主格補語」、「動詞＋前置詞句」(以上、原著では *v. phr.* と表示)を含む。品詞表示にはその他、〔名〕〔代〕〔形〕〔副〕〔前〕〔接〕〔感〕がある。また、多くの前置詞句の場合のように、ある句が二つの文法的用法を持っているために、二つの表示をつけなければならないこともあった。たとえば *in commission* は副詞的か形容詞的かである。そのような時は〔副、形〕と表示した。前置詞句の多くは文字通りの意味では副詞的であるが、予言できないイディオマティックな意味では形容詞的である。

## 用法指示

あるイディオムをある環境で使うことが適切かどうかに特に注意を払わねばならない。*sl. (slang* 「俗語」) はあるイディオムがお互いにごく親しい友人の間でだけ使われていることを示す。*inf. (informal* 「口語的」) はある形が会話では用いられるが、改まった作文では避けるべきことを示す。*form. (formal* 「形式張った」) はその反対で、通常話す時には使わず、エッセイで書いたり、講演や大学の講義で用いる形である。*lit. (literary* 「文学的」) は、人々がその形が引用であることを知っているということに注意を喚起するのであって、こういう形をあまり使うのは不適当である。(卑語) (*(vulgar* 「卑俗な」) はその形を全く避けるべきことを示す。使用する言葉によって人を判断することができるのだから、その形を卑俗だと分かることはもちろん重要である。(非標準語) は、*substandard* 「標準語以下の」―主に教育の低い人々が使う形を示す―、及び *nonstandard* 「非標準語の」―ある句がぎこちないと感じられるという意味である―を示す。(古風) (*archaic* 「古風な」、本書ではまれにしか用いていない) はある形が現代英語ではもはや用いられないことを意味する。*regional labels*「地域表示」はある形の地理的起源と使用を示す。たとえば (英国語法) (*Chiefly British* 「主に英国」) はアメリカ人はめったに使わないという意味であり、(南部方言) (*Southern* 「南部」) はある形が米国北部よりも南部でずっとよく行われていることを意味する。

*Adam Makkai/Richard C. Goris*

XLI

# Предисловие

## ЧТО ТАКОЕ ИДИОМА?

Если в незнакомом тексте Вы понимаете каждое слово, но не можете понять смысла, Ваши затруднения, вероятно, вызваны идиоматическими выражениями. Предположим, Вы прочитали или услышали следующий текст:

*Sam is a real cool cat. He never blows his stack and hardly ever flies off the handle. What's more, he knows how to get away with things . . . Well, of course, he is getting on, too. His hair is pepper and salt, but he knows how to make up for lost time by taking it easy. He gets up early, works out, and turns in early. He takes care of the hot dog stand like a breeze until he gets time off. Sam's got it made; this is it for him.*

Очевидно, что этот стиль нельзя назвать строго литературным, но, тем не менее, американцы в разговоре друг с другом часто употребляют такие выражения. Если Вы иностранец и знаете слова *cool* (прохладно), *cat* (кошка), *blow* (дуть), *stack* (куча), *fly* (лететь), *handle* (ручка) и т.д., Вы не поймете данный образец разговорного американского английского языка, потому что те переводы слов, которые находятся в обычных английских словарях, не дадут Вам точного значения приведенных выше выражений. Из этого следует, что идиома — это новое, неожиданное значение группы слов, каждое из которых обладает своим собственным значением. Ниже Вы найдете перевод этого разговорного и нелитературного текста на более формальный вариант американского диалекта:

*Sam is really a calm person. He never loses control of himself and hardly ever becomes too angry. Furthermore, he knows how to manage his business financially by using a few tricks . . . Needless to say, he, too, is getting older. His hair is beginning to turn gray, but he knows how to compensate for wasted time by relaxing. He rises early, exercises, and goes to bed early. He manages his frankfurter stand without visible effort, until it is someone else's turn to work there. Sam is successful; he has reached his life's goal.*

*Сэм очень тихий человек. Он никогда не теряет контроль над собой и редко сердится. Кроме того, он знает, как вести свое дело с финансовой точки зрения, употребляя некоторые хитрости . . . Безусловно, он тоже стареет. Его волосы седеют, но он умеет восстанавливать потраченные силы отдыхом. Он рано встает, делает гимнастику и рано ложится. Со своей работой в колбасном магазине он справляется без особого труда, успевая все сделать до того, как его сменят. Сэм вполне счастлив, — он достиг цели своей жизни.*

Идиоматические выражения, употребленные в этом тексте, можно организовать в следующий небольшой словарь:

| | |
|---|---|
| to be a (real) cool cat | «быть очень спокойным человеком» |
| to blow one's stack | «потерять контроль над собой, рассердиться» |
| to fly off the handle | «прийти в ярость» |
| what's more | «помимо этого, кроме того» |
| to get away with something | «смошенничать, оставшись безнаказанным» |
| of course | «конечно» |
| to be getting on | «постареть» |
| pepper and salt | «седеющие черные или темные волосы» |

| | |
|---|---|
| to make up for something | «восполнить что-то» |
| lost time | «потерянное время» |
| to take it easy | «не обращать внимания» |
| to get up | «встать утром» |
| to work out | «делать гимнастику» |
| to turn in | «лечь спать» |
| to take care of something | «отвечать за что-то» |
| like a breeze | «легко, элегантно, без усилий» |
| time off | «время отдыха» |
| to have got it made | «быть счастливым, довольным, удачливым» |
| this is it | «вот и все, что нужно» |

Некоторые идиомы из этого небольшого списка можно найти в нашем словаре. Большая часть идиом принадлежит обыкновенным грамматическим классам или частям речи. Так, например, некоторые идиомы по своей природе—типичные глаголы: *get away with, get up, work out, turn in* и т.д. Не меньшее число идиоматических выражений—имена. Так, *hot dog* (сосиска в хлебе), *The White House* (Белый Дом—официальная резиденция американского президента)—имена существительные. Некоторые из идиом—имена прилагательные; так, в нашем примере *pepper and salt* (седеющие черные или темные волосы) обозначает цвет волос. Многие из этих выражений, как, например, *like a breeze* (легко), *hammer and tongs* (*violently,* насильственно)—наречия. Идиоматические выражения, относящиеся к одному из обыкновенных грамматических классов, называются *лексемными идиомами (lexemic idioms).*

Вторая основная группа идиом состоит из фраз, таких как наши примеры *to fly off the handle* (потерять контроль над собой) и *to blow one's stack* (прийти в ярость). В американском варианте английского языка подобные выражения встречаются очень часто. Некоторые из наиболее известных следующие: *to kick the bucket (die,* умереть, сыграть

в ящик, отбросить копыта), *to be up the creek (in danger,* быть в опасности), *to seize the bull by the horns (face a problem squarely,* разрешать проблему или задачу, стоящую перед нами, взять быка за рога) и т.д. Идиомы этой группы называются *оборотами* речи, по-английски *tournures* (из французского языка). Они не принадлежат одному какому-либо грамматическому классу (*части речи*), и переводить их нужно не словом, а группой слов.

Форма подобных идиоматических выражений устоялась; многие из них совсем «застыли» и не могут функционировать в другой форме. Рассмотрим, например, идиому *to kick the bucket (die,* умереть). Употребив эту форму в пассивном залоге, мы отказываемся от идиоматического смысла, получив выражение *the bucket has been kicked by the cowboy* (ковбой ударил ведро ногой). Впрочем, даже это выражение может изменяться по времени, так как мы можем сказать *the cowboy kicked the bucket, the cowboy will kick the bucket, the cowboy has kicked the bucket* и т.д. Проблема, можно ли употреблять это идиоматическое выражение в герундивной форме (*герундив,* gerundive—слово, производное от глагола с помощью суффикса *-ing,* например, *singing* от *sing, eating* от *eat* и т.д.), не решена окончательно учеными-лингвистами и носителями языка. Правильная эта форма или нет, мы не рекомендуем употреблять выражения типа *his kicking the bucket surprised us all.*

Следующий большой класс идиом состоит из поговорок, таких как *don't count your chickens before they're hatched (do not celebrate the outcome of an undertaking prematurely—you may fail and will look ridiculous);* буквально: «не считайте кур, пока они не вылупились из яиц»; русский вариант поговорки звучит: «цыплят по осени считают». Большое число поговорок пришло в американский вариант английского языка из литературных источников или же от первых английских иммигрантов в Америку.

Своим рождением идиомы обязаны тому, что мы чаще используем уже существующие слова для выражения новых идей, чем создаем новые слова с помощью фонем языка. Фактически нет языков, в которых не было бы идиом. Возьмем, например, слова *ма шанг*, китайское выражение, которое значит «быстро». Переведенное дословно, оно означает «лошадиная спина». Связь понятий *лошадиной спины* и *быстроты* очевидна: раньше, до появления поезда, автомобиля и самолета, быстрее всего было путешествовать верхом на лошади. Китайское выражение *ма шанг* было бы аналогом русской фразы: «Торопитесь, нам надо ехать *на лошадиной спине*!» Такая форма была бы вполне понятной носителю русского языка, но иностранец должен был бы понять, что это идиома. Даже если иностранец никогда не слышал выражения *ма шанг* (лошадиная спина), он может догадаться, что это значит; однако, во многих случаях подобные догадки ошибочны.

Например, возьмем английскую идиому *the die is cast* (жребий брошен). Вряд ли, не зная ее точного выражения, Вы догадаетесь, что это выражение значит: «Я решил, и больше не могу изменить свое решение». Зная точное значение, Вы можете догадаться, как возникло это идиоматическое выражение: кость, брошенная во время игры в кости, по правилам может быть брошена только один раз, независимо от результата. Многие знают, что эту фразу произнес Юлий Цезарь, когда перешел Рубикон, что явилось началом войны.

Как научиться употреблять идиоматическое выражение правильно? Прежде всего, подождите, пока Вы не услышите идиому от человека, для которого американский английский—родной язык. Если Вы неоднократно слышали идиому и вполне поняли ее значение, Вы сами можете начать употреблять это выражение. Предположим, молодая девушка очень хочет выйти замуж. Она может выбирать между двумя возможными женихами, назовем их Павел и Николай. Павел немолод, некрасив и небогат, но он уже сделал предложение и готов жениться хоть завтра. Николай красив и богат, но он пока не собирается жениться и неизвестно, женится ли когда-нибудь. После некоторого раз-

мышления девушка решает принять предложение Павла, боясь остаться старой девой. Если вскоре после свадьбы Николай признается ей, что мечтает быть ее мужем, нашей героине останется только сказать *"Oh, well, the die is cast..."* («Что делать, жребий брошен»). Если, оказавшись в подобной ситуации, Вы произносите эту фразу, беседуя с американцем, и он смотрит на Вас с сочувствием и не переспрашивает: «Что Вы имеете в виду?»—считайте, что Вы достигли первого успеха, употребив новую идиому в правильном контексте. Американцы относятся к иностранцам более лояльно, чем другие нации, но они, конечно, оценят, сколь бегло Вы говорите по-английски. Использование идиом поможет Вам установить контакт со слушателем и избежать репутации «слишком серьезного» человека. Чем больше идиом Вы употребляете в правильном контексте, тем лучше о Вас будут думать Ваши собеседники.

## КАК ПОЛЬЗОВАТЬСЯ ЭТИМ СЛОВАРЕМ?

Словарь был составлен для людей, говорящих по-английски, но не родившихся в Америке. Словарь содержит *лексемные идиомы, фразеологические единицы* и *поговорки*, имеющие особенное значение. Возможно, некоторые из идиоматических выражений Вам уже знакомы, и Вы понимаете, что они означают. Найдите в словаре перевод одной из следующих идиом, значение которой Вы уже знаете,—это поможет Вам понять, как пользоваться этой книгой: *boyfriend, girlfriend, piggy bank, get even, give up, going to, keep on, keep your mouth shut, lead somebody by the nose, look after, show off, throw away, all over, in love, mixed-up, out of this world, I'll say.*

Чтобы научиться пользоваться словарем, несколько раз внимательно изучите предписания и попрактикуйтесь в нахождении значения идиоматических выражений. Если Вы услышите идиому, которой нет в книге, то, имея некоторый опыт работы с нашим словарем, Вы сможете найти ее значение и выписать его для себя. Заведите Ваш собственный список идиом и храните его вместе с Вашим обычным словарем. Пошлите нам Ваши наблюдения и замечания.

Как узнать, поможет ли Вам «Словарь идиом» понять трудную фразу? Иногда догадаться, о чем идет речь, не сложно, как в выражениях *puppy love, fun house, dog-eat-dog, mixed-up.* Если же Вы не можете перевести выражение, выберите основное слово из самой трудной части и найдите его в словаре. Если это первое слово идиомы, Вы найдете всю фразу и перевод к ней. Таким образом, выражение *bats in the belfry* напечатано в этом словаре под буквой *b*, слово *bats.* Если слово, которое Вы выбрали, не первое слово идиомы, Вы найдете список идиом, которые содержат это слово. Например, слово *toe* (палец ноги) Вы найдете в статьях *curl one's hair or curl one's toes, on one's toes, step on the toes (of somebody).* Конечно, Вы можете столкнуться с тем, что не понимаете некоторые фразы, потому что Вам незнакомы обыкновенные слова, а не из-за обилия идиоматических выражений. В этом случае Вам поможет обычный словарь. Обратите внимание, что в этом словаре приведены наиболее употребительные выражения только американского английского языка, без учета идиоматики, например, британского или австралийского диалектов. Словарь, содержащий идиомы всех диалектов английского языка, был бы *международным словарем английских идиоматических выражений.* В настоящее время такой книги нет, но надеемся, что в будущем она будет написана.

## ТИПЫ СЛОВАРНЫХ СТАТЕЙ

Этот словарь содержит четыре типа статей: *Главные статьи, продолжающиеся статьи, статьи-ссылки и указательные статьи. Главная статья* включает полное объяснение идиомы. *Продолжающаяся статья* — фраза, происходящая от другой идиомы, но которая была бы самостоятельной единицей, если бы она была напечатана в своем собственном алфавитном месте. Эти производные идиомы приводятся в конце главной статьи, например, *fence sitter* «человек, сидящий на заборе» в конце статьи *sit on the fence* «сидеть на заборе». В тех случаях, когда понять производную форму, опираясь на основное объяснение, затруднительно, приводятся дополнительные объяснения. Если идиома может употребляться в форме различных частей речи, приводится отдельная статья на каждый случай.

Ссылки показывают, что объяснение можно найти в другом месте. Предположим, Вы хотите посмотреть выражение *cast in one's lot with* (решить стать соучастниками или партнерами). Вы можете посмотреть на слово *cast* (бросать) или на слово *lot* (судьба); ссылка направит Вас к слову *throw* в фразе *throw in one's lot with.* Причиной этого является тот факт, что слово *cast* (бросать)—употребляется в сегодняшнем английском языке гораздо режеъ чем слово *throw.* Следовательно, более распространенная форма этой идиомы начинается глаголом *throw.*

Указательная статья ведет нас ко всем другим статьям, содержащим искомое слово. Таким образом, слово *chin* (подбородок) сопровождается фразами, в которых Вы найдете слово *chin,* таких как *keep one's chin up, stick one's chin (OR neck) out, take out, take it on the chin, up to the chin.*

## УКАЗАТЕЛИ ЧАСТЕЙ РЕЧИ

*Лексемные идиомы,* которые мы обсуждали раньше, сопровождены указателем части речи. В некоторых случаях, таких, как, скажем, в случае предложных фраз, употреблен двойной указатель, потому что данная фраза имеет два грамматических употребления. Буква *v* значит *verb* (глагол); она напечатана в фразах, содержащих глагол и наречие, или глагол и предлог, или все три, то есть глагол, предлог и наречие. Сокращение *v. phr.* означает *"verbal phrase"* как, например, *look up, look in* и т.д., то есть сочетание глагола с существительным: глагол с дополнением, глагол с подлежащим и глагол с предложной фразой.

## ОГРАНИЧИТЕЛЬНЫЕ УКАЗАТЕЛИ

Иностранцу, для которого американский английский—неродной язык, следует обратить особое внимание на то, в какой ситуации какую идиому можно употреблять. В этом читателю словаря помогут ограничительные указатели. Так, указатель *slang* (слэнг) показывает, что идиома употребляется только в фамильярном разговоре очень близкими друзьями. Указатель *informal* (неформальный) показывает, что выражение может употребляться в разговоре, но не должно встречаться в формальных сочинениях. Указатель *formal* (формальный) имеет противоположное значение; он указывает, что форма употребляется только в научных работах или при чтении лекции в университете. Указатель *literary* (литературный) напоминает, что интересующая Вас идиома—широко известная цитата; ее не стоит употреблять слишком часто. Указатель *vulgar* (вульгарный, грубый) показывает, что Вам не следует употреблять эту форму. Однако, иметь представление о подобных формах необходимо, чтобы иметь возможность судить о людях по языку, который они употребляют. Указатель *substandard* (не соответствующий языковой норме) показывает, что форма употребляется малообразованными людьми; *nonstandard* (нестандартный) значит, что фраза неуклюжая. Указатель *archaic* (архаический) редко употребляется в этой книге; он означает, что форма очень редка в современном английском языке. Географические указатели показывают, где идиома образовалась и где употребляется. *Chiefly British* (главным образом британское) значит, что американцы редко употребляют эту форму; *southern* (южный) значит, что идиома употребляется чаще на юге США, чем на севере. Молодые формы, которые образовались не более шести или семи лет назад, находятся в приложении к главному словарю.

*Adam Makkai/Maya Aleksandrovna Glinberg*

# Prefacio

## ¿QUÉ ES UN MODISMO?

Si usted entiende todas las palabras de un texto y aún no comprende su significado, es posible que tenga dificultad con los modismos. Por ejemplo, suponga que usted lee (u oye) lo siguiente:

*Sam is a real cool cat. He never blows his stack and hardly ever flies off the handle. What's more, he knows how to get away with things . . . Well, of course, he is getting on, too. His hair is pepper and salt, but he knows how to make up for lost time by taking it easy. He gets up early, works out, and turns in early. He takes care of the hot dog stand like a breeze until he gets time off. Sam's got it made; this is it for him.*

No es necesario mencionar que tal párrafo carece de estilo literario, pero la mayoría de los estadounidenses, especialmente en conversación, usan expresiones de este tipo. Si usted es un extranjero en E.U.A. y ha aprendido las palabras *cool* (frío a tibio), *cat* (gato, animal común doméstico), *blow* (expirar aire con fuerza), *stack* (pila de cosas u objetos amontonados), *fly* (impulsarse por el aire), *handle* (parte de un objeto designada a tomarse con la mano), todavía no comprenderá el párrafo recién visto porque esta información básica de diccionario no es suficiente para darle el significado a la combinación de palabras usadas. Un modismo—como puede verse—es la asignación de un nuevo significado a un grupo de palabras que ya tienen su propio significado. Observe en el siguiente párrafo cómo ese texto lleno de modismos típicos del inglés estadounidense común se traduce a una versión más formal y relativamente exenta de modismos:

*Sam is really a calm person. He never loses control of himself and hardly ever becomes too angry. Furthermore, he knows how to manage his business financially by using a few tricks . . . Needless to say, he, too, is getting older. His hair is beginning to turn gray, but he knows how to compensate for wasted time by relaxing. He rises early, exercises, and goes to bed early. He manages his frankfurter stand without visible effort, until it is someone else's turn to work there. Sam is successful; he has reached his life's goal.*

Si uno fuera a explicar cómo están organizadas las palabras en este texto, crearía un pequeño diccionario de modismos que tendría la siguiente forma:

| | |
|---|---|
| *to be a (real) cool cat* | ser realmente calmo, ser sumamente tranquilo |
| *to blow one's stack* | perder el control, enojarse |
| *to fly off the handle* | enfurecerse |
| *what's more* | además, de paso, adicionalmente |
| *to get away with something* | cometer un acto ilegítimo o tramposo sin repercusiones o daño |
| *of course* | naturalmente |
| *to be getting on* | envejecer |
| *pepper and salt* | cabello negro u oscuro, tornándose canoso |
| *to make up for something* | recuperar algo |
| *lost time* | tiempo perdido, tiempo desperdiciado |
| *to take it easy* | descansar, despreocuparse |
| *to get up* | levantarse |
| *to work out* | hacer ejercicio, hacer gimnasia |
| *to turn in* | acostarse |
| *to take care of something* | ocuparse de algo, encargarse de algo, cuidar algo |
| *like a breeze* | sin esfuerzo, elegantemente, fácilmente |
| *time off* | período de inactividad en el empleo o en el sitio de empleo |

| *to have got it made* | tener buen éxito, haber cumplido |
| *this is it* | estar en una posición o en un sitio, o tener posesión de un objeto, tras lo cual más no es necesario |

Muchos de los modismos en esta pequeña lista de ejemplos pueden ser hallados en este mismo diccionario. Lo interesante de la mayoría de estos modismos es que pueden ser identificados fácilmente con las partes de la oración. De esta manera algunos modismos son claramente de naturaleza verbal, tales como *get away with, get up work out, turn in*, etc. Una gran cantidad son de naturaleza nominal, como *hot dog* y *cool cat*, es decir, son sustantivos. Muchos son adjetivos, como en el ejemplo *pepper and salt* (cabello tornándose canoso), indicativo del color del cabello. Otros son adverbiales, como los ejemplos *like the breeze* (fácilmente, sin esfuerzo) y *hammer and tongs* (violentamente).

Estos modismos que correlacionan con las familiares partes de la oración se pueden llamar modismos lexémicos.

El otro grupo importante de modismos es más grande. Frecuentemente son del tamaño de una oración completa, como son nuestros ejemplos *to fly off the handle* (enfurecerse) y *to blow one's stack* (perder el control). El inglés norteamericano se caracteriza por tener muchos de este grupo. Algunos de los más famosos son *to kick the bucket* (morirse), *to be up the creek* (estar en un aprieto o en una situación peligrosa), *to be caught between the devil and the deep blue sea* (tener que optar entre dos alternativas igualmente desagradables), *to seize the bull by the horns* ("tomar el toro por los astas", es decir, enfrentarse con un problema y tratarlo con equidad), y otros. Los modismos de este tipo se llaman *tournures* (del francés), "giros de frase", o simplemente modismos *fraseológicos*. Lo que tienen en común es que no se correlacionan fácilmente con una parte de la oración determinada y requieren una paráfrasis mayor que una mera palabra.

Su forma es fija y solamente un número limitado de estos modismos puede ser dicho o escrito de cualquier otra forma sin destruir su significado. Muchos de ellos son completamente rígidos y no pueden tener ninguna otra forma. Considere el modismo *kick the bucket*, por ejemplo. Si se pone en voz pasiva, se obtiene una forma tan inaceptable como *the bucket has been kicked by the cowboy*, la cual ya no indica que murió el vaquero, sino que éste pateó el balde. Modismos de este tipo son considerados *formas completamente congeladas*. Fíjese, sin embargo, que hasta este modismo puede ser conjugado: por ejemplo, es correcto decir *the cowboy kicked the bucket* o *the cowboy will kick the bucket*.

El próximo grupo de modismos importante es el de los refranes y proverbios. Estos incluyen ejemplos tan conocidos como *don't count your chickens before they're hatched* (no celebre el resultado de una empresa prematura pues, de fracasar ésta, sufrirá el ridículo); *don't wash your dirty linen in public* ("la ropa sucia se lava en casa") y otros. Muchos de éstos tuvieron origen en fuentes literarias muy conocidas o vienen a nosotros de los primitivos colonos norteamericanos, para quienes dichos, refranes y proverbios eran parte de su cultura oral.

¿Por qué es el inglés, y especialmente el inglés estadounidense, tan sobrecargado de modismos? Mientras desarrollamos nuevos conceptos, necesitamos nuevas expresiones para ellos, pero en vez de crear una nueva palabra de los sonidos de la lengua, preferimos usar palabras existentes y las combinamos para obtener un nuevo sentido. Esto, sin embargo, parece ocurrir en todas las lenguas. Considere la expresión china *mǎ shāng* para "rápidamente". Traducida al pie de la letra, *mǎ shāng* significa "lomo de caballo" y uno se pregunta por qué el concepto de "rapidez" está asociado con el lomo del caballo. Reflexionemos un momento. En tiempos pasados, antes de que se inventaran el tren, el automóvil y el avión, la manera más rápida de llegar de un lugar a otro era montado a caballo, es decir, a lomo de caballo. Por esto, *mǎ shāng* equivale a "¡vamos a galopar!" y, por extensión, "¡apurémonos!" En español, "vamos a galopar" sería fácilmente comprendido por todos y todos sabrían que se trata de un modismo, mientras que el extranjero tendría que aprenderlo como tal.

No obstante, hay ocasiones en que la persona puede adivinar incorrectamente. Considere el modismo inglés *Oh well, the die is cast!* Si desconoce su significado, ¿qué le sugiere esta frase? Tal vez por la expresión *Oh well* puede suponer que el que lo dijo está consintiendo a algo. Sin embargo, este modismo significa "Tomé una decisión y ahora tengo que vivir con ella". Al tratar de reconstruir este modismo aparece la imagen del dado tirado. Recordamos, entonces, que, según las reglas del juego de dados, la tirada puede ser una sola sean cuales sean las consecuencias. La frase fue usada por César cuando cruzó el Rubicón, un evento, que desencadenó la guerra.

¿Cómo, entonces, acabando de aprenderlo, va usted a usar este modismo correctamente? Antes que nada, asegúrese de conocer los rudimentos básicos de la gramática inglesa. Luego, escuche como lo emplea la persona cuyo idioma materno es el inglés. Después de haber escuchado más de una vez el uso del modismo y comprender completamente su significado, podrá usarlo usted mismo. Imagínese tener dos ofertas de trabajo, una segura, pero de menos salario, y otra que pague más, pero sólo tentativa. Nervioso y atemorizado de terminar sin empleo alguno, acepta· la de menor sueldo, pocas horas antes de recibir una oferta definitiva por el trabajo mejor pagado. La frustración lo lleva entonces a exclamar, *Oh well, the die is cast . . .* Y si un norteamericano lo oye, asiente con comprensión y no le pregunta—¿qué dijo?—ha logrado usted su primer éxito en el uso correcto de un modismo recientemente aprendido. Los estadounidenses suelen tratar a los extranjeros con más cortesía que los de otras naciones, pero prefieren a los que se les asemejan. Si una persona siempre usa expresiones versadas y afectadas y jamás usa un modismo en el momento apropiado, puede obtener la reputación de ser un orador pedante y sin imaginación, o uno demasiado serio y formal. El uso de modismos es, por consiguiente, de suma importancia pues puede establecer lazos de solidaridad con el oyente. Mientras más modismos use dentro del contexto apropiado, más cómodos se sentirán los estadounidenses con usted y más se dirán "¡qué simpática y amable es esta persona y qué bien se expresa!"

Veremos ahora algunas consideraciones prácticas con relación al presente libro.

## COMO USAR ESTE DICCIONARIO

Recapitulemos. Cuando una frase tiene un significado especial que nadie puede descifrar correctamente aun cuando las palabras individuales que la componen son comprendidas fácilmente, se trata de un modismo. Este diccionario se destina a personas de habla no inglesa...estudiantes, obreros, profesionales, todos los que deseen perfeccionar su inglés y mejorar su posición social. Contiene frases con significado especial de los tipos anteriormente mencionados, es decir, modismos lexémicos, modismos fraseológicos y proverbios. Sugerimos buscar en el libro algunos modismos que Ud. indudablemente ya conoce como práctica para el uso adecuado de este libro: *boyfriend, girlfriend, outer space, piggy bank, get even, give up, going to, keep on, keep your mouth shut, lead somebody by the nose, look after, show off, throw away, all over, in love, mixed-up, out of this world, throw away, I'll say.*

Un diccionario es como cualquier otra herramienta: Debe familiarizarse con él y aprender a usarlo antes de obtener buenos resultados. Repase las instrucciones y practique buscando modismos determinados. Semejante práctica le familiarizará hasta tal punto con los modismos que le permitirá deducir el significado de muchos modismos desconocidos que escucha por primera vez. Mantenga su propia lista de modismos en casa, al lado de su diccionario corriente. Al leer un texto técnico, o una novela o un artículo de periódico y no comprender una expresión, búsquela primero en su diccionario corriente y, si no lo encuentra, recurra al volumen que ahora lee.

¿Cómo puede saber usted si este diccionario puede ayudarle a entender una oración difícil? Algunas veces el modismo es de fácil interpretación, como en el caso de *puppy love, fun house, dog-eat-dog, mixed-up.* En los demás casos, seleccione una palabra clave de la parte más difícil de la oración y búsquela. Si es la primera palabra del modismo, encontrará la frase completa, seguida por una explicación. Así, la expresión *bats in the belfry* se encuentra en este diccionario bajo la *b* en la palabra *bats.* Si la palabra que usted escogió no es la primera, encontrará una lista de modismos que contienen esa palabra. Por ejemplo, la palabra *toe* se encontrará bajo expresiones como *curl one's hair* o *curl one's toes, on one's toes, step on the toes (of somebody)*. Podría ocurrir, por supuesto, que la razón de no comprender una oración sea ajena a todo modismo: en ese caso, recurra a su diccionario corriente. También, por supuesto, hay muchos más modismos de los que se encuentran en este libro: le damos aquí los más frecuentemente usados en los Estados Unidos. El inglés británico, por ejemplo, o el inglés hablado en Australia posee muchos modismos que no forman parte del inglés estadounidense. Un diccionario que contenga todos los modismos de la lengua inglesa mundial no existe en el presente, aunque tarde o temprano saldrá a luz.

## TIPOS DE ARTICULOS

Este diccionario contiene cuatro clases de artículos: artículos principales, artículos continuados, artículos de referencias cruzadas, y artículos alfabéticos. Un artículo principal incluye una explicación completa del modismo. Un artículo continuado es una frase derivada de otro modismo pero que estaría separada de éste si hubiese sido anotada en orden alfabético. Estos modismos derivados han sido añadidos al final del artículo principal (por ejemplo, *fence-sitter* en *on the fence*) y van acompañados de una segunda explicación cuando el derivado de la explicación principal es difícil de comprender.

Un artículo de referencia cruzada le guía a una definición en otro sitio. Suponga que desea encontrar *cast in one's lot with*. Puede buscar bajo *cast* y bajo *lot*, pero el artículo de referencia cruzada lo encauzará al término *throw* en la frase *throw in one's lot with*. La razón para esto es que *cast* es una palabra mucho menos usada en la actualidad, siendo *throw* la versión más corriente y frecuente de este modismo.

Un artículo alfabético lo dirige a todos los otros artículos que contienen la palabra en orden alfabético. Así, la palabra *chin* es seguida por las frases donde se encuentra, por ejemplo, *keep one's chin up, stick one's chin out, take it on the chin, up to the chin*.

## CLASIFICACIONES SEGUN LAS PARTES DE LA ORACION

Los modismos lexémicos antes vistos van acompañados por indicadores de la parte de la oración a la cual están vinculados. Algunas veces, como con muchas frases preposicionales, una segunda clasificación ha sido necesaria porque la frase obtenida tiene dos usos gramaticales: por ejemplo, *in commission* puede ser adverbial o adjetival.

*v* indica verbo y fue designada a frases que contienen un verbo y un adverbio, verbo y preposición o verbo, preposición y adverbio.

*v. phr.* indica "frase verbal" e incluye a verbos con un objeto, verbos con un complemento de sujeto y verbos con frases preposicionales.

## CLASIFICACIONES RESTRICTIVAS

Le aconsejamos determinar en cada ocasión si es apropiado o no usar determinado modismo. La clasificación *slang* indica que el modismo es usado solamente entre íntimos amigos. *Informal* señala que la expresión es usada en conversación, pero que debiera evitarse en una composición formal. *Formal* indica lo contrario: ésta es una forma que la gente generalmente no emplea al hablar, sino que utiliza por escrito en un ensayo o durante un discurso universitario. *Literary* le advierte que el modismo es una cita conocida y que sería poco apropiado usarla muy seguido. *Vulgar* es señal de evitar este modismo por completo, aunque reconociendo que su conocimiento puede serle importante para juzgar al usuario. *Substandard* indica que el modismo es empleado principalmente por gente poco educada. *Nonstandard* significa que la frase resultante de este modismo es torpe y debiera evitarse. *Archaic* (raramente usada en este libro) significa que el modismo pertenece al inglés bíblico o antiguo. Algunos modismos se identifican según su origen geográfico; por ejemplo, *Chiefly British* significa que los estadounidenses raramente lo usan; *Southern* significa que el modismo es mucho más corriente en el sur de los Estados Unidos que en el norte.

*Adam Makkai/Verónica Cortés*

L

# Preface to the Fourth Edition

The fourth edition of *A Dictionary of American Idioms* published by Barron's Educational Series in 2004 follows three previous, highly successful editions, the first of which appeared in 1975. Thus, we have 29 years of continuous experience with ongoing changes in the living vocabulary of American English, which gives this updated version of the English language such widespread appeal.

There can be little doubt that English has become the world language. In the nineteenth century, while Britain was the world's major colonial power, it was British English that held sway wherever English was taught. In the twentieth century, after two World Wars, America emerged as the planet's leading industrial power. After the collapse of communism in the early '90s, the United States was left as the world's only superpower, for better or for worse. (Think of the space program and the computer industry in this regard, and you will readily agree that this is indeed the case.)

The United States has always been a country of immigrants. This trend continues unabated. Whatever anyone thinks of American politics at home or abroad at any given time, the fact remains that the number of Americans "escaping" abroad are infinitesimally small in comparison to the hundreds of thousands of people who come to America in search of a brighter future for themselves and for their children. It is for learners of American English, both the beginners and the advanced, that a book such as this can be particularly useful. Native speakers also will find it both intellectually challenging and entertaining to check their internalized vocabulary against what they find on these pages.

Idioms sometimes have more than one form. Take as an example: *speak of the devil,* versus *talk of the devil.* Both occur and, therefore, both are correct. We have in this updated fourth edition given many such variants. Each idiom is defined and a sample sentence in which it can be used is provided.

Some 1,600 entries have been added to the new edition, making this book one of the most comprehensive dictionaries of American idioms currently available.

Readers often wonder where and how an idiom originated. This is a dictionary less concerned with the history of a given idiom than with its current use. We have added "Biblical" and "Shakespearean" when it seemed warranted, but numerous idioms such as *kick the bucket,* for instance, have several competing explanations, so that we could write a separate study about the origin of idioms. The present editor has consistently tried to answer readers' questions in the hope that, in the future, an expanded version also will include historical narratives.

We hope that you will find the fourth revised and expanded edition to be both educationally useful and entertaining. We look forward to your comments and queries.

Adam Makkai, Ph.D.
Professor of English and Linguistics
University of Illinois at Chicago (UIC)
e-mail: *admakkai@uic.edu*

**a bad penny always turns up (again)** An unwanted or unsavory character is likely to show up when least expected.—A proverb. ♦*"Who's coming?" Father asked. "It's Uncle Joe, the drunkard," I answered. "Oh, that's the case of a bad penny always turning up again," Father said with a sigh.*

**abide by** *v.* To accept and obey; be willing to follow. ♦*A basketball player may know he did not foul, but he must abide by the referee's decision.* ♦*The members agree to abide by the rules of the club.*

**a bit** *n., informal* A small amount; some. ♦*There's no sugar in the sugar bowl, but you may find a bit in the bag.* ♦*If the ball had hit the window a bit harder, it would have broken it.*—Often used like an adverb. ♦*This sweater scratches a bit.*—Also used like an adjective before *less, more.* ♦*Janet thought she could lose weight by eating a bit less.* ♦*"Have some more cake?" "Thanks. A bit more won't hurt me."*—Often used adverbially after verbs in negative, interrogative, and conditional sentences, sometimes in the form *one bit.* ♦*"Won't your father be angry?" "No, he won't care a bit."*

**abound in** *v. phr.* To have plenty of something. ♦*Our university abounds in talented undergraduates.*

**about-face** *n.* A sudden change of course or a decision opposite to what was decided earlier. ♦*Her decision to become an actress instead of a dentist was an about-face from her original plans.*

**about time** *n. phr.* Finally, but later than it should have been; at last. ♦*Mother said, "It's about time you got up, Mary."* ♦*The basketball team won last night. About time.*

**about to 1.** Close to; ready to.—Used with an infinitive. ♦*We were about to leave when the snow began.* ♦*I haven't gone yet, but I'm about to.* Compare GOING TO, ON THE POINT OF. **2.** *informal* Having a wish or plan to.—Used with an infinitive in negative sentences. ♦*"Will she come with us?" asked Bill. "She's not about to," answered Mary.*

**above all** *adv. phr.* Of first or highest importance; most especially. ♦*Children need many things, but above all they need love.* Syn. FIRST AND LAST.

**above suspicion** *adj. phr.* Too good to be suspected; not likely to do wrong. ♦*The umpire in the game must be above suspicion of supporting one side over the other.*

**a breath of fresh air** *n. phr.* Something new, pleasant, or invigorating. ♦*Sue's arrival at our law firm was a breath of fresh air.*

**abscond from** *v. phr.* To go away suddenly and furtively, usually having been part of some shady business. ♦*Joe absconded from our shop when we discovered that the books had been tampered with.*

**abscond with** *v. phr.* To steal or embezzle something. ♦*Al absconded with the uncounted extra cash after we closed for the evening.*

**absence makes the heart grow fonder** When we don't see someone or something for a long while, we rejoice all the more when we meet again.—A proverb. ♦*"How long will you be gone?" Sue asked, when her husband joined the marines. "Just six months," Joe answered. "It will be over soon; besides, absence makes the heart grow fonder!"*

**absent-minded** *adj.* Lost in thought; forgetful; unable to concentrate on the task at hand. ♦*"What's the matter with Joe? Why is he so absent-minded?" Pete asked. "I think it's because he is about to get married," I answered, "and he's thinking about the wedding plans."*

**absent without leave (AWOL)** *adj.* Absent without permission; used mostly in the military. ♦*Jack left Fort Sheridan without asking his commanding officer, and was punished for going AWOL.*

**absolve from** *v. phr.* To forgive; to allow not to repay a debt. ♦*Joe is very religious; he goes to confession every Saturday. He hopes he will be absolved from his sins that way.* ♦*"How much do I owe you?" Pete asked. "Nothing," I replied, "you are absolved from your debt."*

**absorb in** *v. phr.* Pay total attention to something. ♦ *"Why isn't Sue coming to dinner?" mother asked. "She is completely absorbed in studying for her exam tomorrow," Joe explained.*

**abstain from** *v. phr.* To not participate in the consumption of something; said of alcoholic beverages, cigarettes, sex, and drugs. ♦ *"Won't you have a glass of sherry and a cigar?" Joe asked the priest. "No thanks," he replied. "I abstain from those things."*

**abut against** *v. phr.* Reach up to; as far as; touch, said of streets, lots, buildings, and the like. ♦ *Our old cornfield abuts against the Fox River.* ♦ *Our campus abuts against the Eisenhower Expressway.*

**Acapulco gold** *n., slang* Marijuana of an exceptionally high quality. ♦ *Jack doesn't just smoke pot; he smokes Acapulco gold.*

**accede to** *v. phr.* to inherit the position of someone of importance. ♦ *When England's King George the Sixth died, his daughter, Elizabeth, acceded to the throne.*

**ace up one's sleeve** *or* **have something up one's sleeve** *n., or v. phr.* To have a hidden asset or trick unknown by the opposition, like someone who cheats at cards and has winning cards hidden in his shirtsleeve. ♦ *We all hope that the government has something up its sleeve in the war against terrorism.*

**ache for** *or* **be itching to** *v. phr.* To long for something or someone powerfully. ♦ *"I am aching for a piece of chocolate cake," the pregnant woman said.*

**acid test** *n. phr.* A powerful way of determining if something is genuine or false, going back to the days when gold was differentiated from brass by dipping an object into hydrochloric acid. ♦ *The acid test of a good marriage is fidelity and truthfulness.*

**according to** *prep.* **1.** So as to match or agree with; so as to be alike in. ♦ *Many words are pronounced according to the spelling but some are not.* ♦ *The boys were placed in three groups according to height.* **2.** On the word or authority of. ♦ *According to the Bible, Adam was the first man.*

**according to one's own lights** *adv. phr.* In accordance with one's conscience or inclinations. ♦ *Citizens should vote according to their own lights.*

**account for** *v. phr.* **1.** To rationally or scientifically explain the reason for something. ♦ *The view that the earth revolves around its axis and circles the sun in a year accounts much better for the changing of the seasons than the old geocentric view.* **2.** To render accurate inventory of cash, personnel, objects, etc. ♦ *Joe was fired because he failed to account for the missing $50,000.* ♦ *A good platoon commander accounts for every enlisted man under his command.*

**ace in the hole** *n. phr.* **1.** An ace given to a player face down so that other players in a card game cannot see it. ♦ *When the cowboy bet all his money in the poker game he did not know that the gambler had an ace in the hole and would win it from him.* **2.** *informal* Someone or something important that is kept as a surprise until the right time so as to bring victory or success. ♦ *The lawyer's ace in the hole was a secret witness who saw the accident.* Compare CARD UP ONE'S SLEEVE.

**Achilles' heel** *n. phr., literary* A physical or psychological weakness named after the Greek hero Achilles who was invulnerable except for a spot on his heel. ♦ *John's Achilles' heel is his lack of talent with numbers and math.*

**acid head** *n., slang* A regular user of LSD on whom the hallucinogenic drug has left a visible effect. ♦ *The reason John acts so funny is that he is a regular acid head.*

**acid rock** *n., slang* A characteristic kind of rock in which loudness and beat predominate over melody; especially such music as influenced by drug experiences. ♦ *John is a regular acid rock freak.*

**acoustic perfume** *n., slang* Sound for covering up unwanted noise, such as music over loudspeakers in a noisy construction area. ♦ *Let's get out of here—this acoustic perfume is too much for my ears.*

**acquaint with** *v. phr.* To make something or somebody known to someone; to introduce someone or something to another person. ♦ *"Let me acquaint you with who's who at work," John said to the new employee.*

**acquire a taste for** *v. phr.* To become fond of something; get to like something. *♦Jack acquired a taste for ripe cheeses when he went to France.*

**across the board** *adv. phr.* **1.** So that equal amounts of money are bet on the same horse to win a race, to place second, or third. *♦I bet $6 on the white horse across the board.*—Often used with hyphens as an adjective. *♦I made an across-the-board bet on the white horse.* **2.** *informal* Including everyone or all, so that all are included. *♦The president wanted taxes lowered across the board.*—Often used with hyphens as an adjective. *♦The workers at the store got an across-the-board pay raise.*

**across the tracks** See THE TRACKS.

**act as** *v. phr.* To function in the capacity of something to assure a desired result. *♦Did you know that if you have a bad sunburn and no lotion to relieve it, sour cream can act as a good replacement?*

**actions speak louder than words** What you do shows your character better and is more important than what you say.—A proverb. *♦John promised to help me, but he didn't. Actions speak louder than words.*

**act of faith** *n. phr.* An act or a deed that shows unquestioning belief in someone or something. *♦It was a real act of faith on Mary's part to entrust her jewelry to her younger sister's care.*

**act of God** *n.* An occurrence (usually some sort of catastrophe) for which the people affected are not responsible; said of earthquakes, floods, etc. *♦Hurricane Andrew destroyed many houses in Florida, but some types of insurance did not compensate the victims, claiming that the hurricane was an act of God.*

**act one's age** *or* **be one's age** *v. phr.* To do the things that people expect someone of your age to do, not act as if you were much younger than you are. *♦Mr. O'Brien was playing tag with the children at the party. Then Mrs. O'Brien said, "Henry! Act your age!" and he stopped.*

**act out** *v.* **1.** To show an idea, story, or happening by your looks, talk, and movements. *♦He tried to act out a story that he had read.* **2.** To put into action. *♦All his life he tried to act out his beliefs.*

**act up** *v., informal* **1.** To behave badly; act rudely or impolitely. *♦The dog acted up as the postman came to the door.* **2.** To work or run poorly (as a machine); skip; miss. *♦The car acted up because the spark plugs were dirty.*

**add fuel to the flame** *v. phr.* To make a bad matter worse by adding to its cause; spread trouble, increase anger or other strong feelings by talk or action. *♦Bob was angry with Ted and Ted added fuel to the flame by laughing at him.*

**addicted to** *adj. phr.* So used to something that doing without it becomes unbearably painful. *♦People addicted to smoking have a hard time giving up cigarettes.*

**add in** *v. phr.* **1.** To increase the contents of a mixture prepared as food. *♦This soup tastes quite nice, but you had better add in some sour cream and some salt.* **2.** To calculate a previously neglected sum as part of a previous calculation as in balancing one's checking account. *♦I think we had better add in all the gas mileage and the motels on the way before turning in the bill to the boss for our field trip.*

**add insult to injury** *v. phr.* **1.** To hurt someone's feelings after doing him harm. *♦He added insult to injury when he called the man a rat after he had already beaten him up.* **2.** To make bad trouble worse. *♦We started on a picnic, and first it rained, then to add insult to injury, the car broke down.*

**add up** *v.* **1.** To come to the correct amount. *♦The numbers wouldn't add up.* **2.** *informal* To make sense; be understandable. *♦His story didn't add up.*

**add up to** *v.* **1.** To make a total of; amount to. *♦The bill added up to $12.95.* **2.** *informal* To mean; result in. *♦The rain, the mosquitoes, and the heat added up to a spoiled vacation.*

**ad lib** *v. phr.* To improvise; interpolate during speech. *♦When the actress forgot her lines during the second act, she had to ad lib in order to keep the show going.*

**adhere to** *v. phr.* To stick to something; to observe the laws and regulations of an organization. *♦Both the dictators Hitler and Stalin demanded of their* *followers that they adhere to Nazi and communist ideology strictly.*

**advance on** *or* **upon** *v. phr.* To get nearer to; to gain in distance during pursuit of criminals or the army of the enemy. ♦ *The American troops were soon advancing on the Germans after they landed at the beaches of Normandy toward the end of World War II.*

**a few** *n. or adj.* A small number (of people or things); some. ♦ *The dry weather killed most of Mother's flowers, but a few were left.* A few is different in meaning from *few,* which emphasizes the negative; *a few* means 'some,' *few* means 'not many.' ♦ *We thought no one would come to lunch, but a few came.* Sometimes *a few* is used with *only,* and then it is negative. ♦ *We thought many people would come to lunch, but only a few came.*—Sometimes used like an adverb. ♦ *Three students have no seats; we need a few more chairs.*

**affix to** *v. phr.* To add in writing; glue to; stamp onto a piece of paper. ♦ *"Would you please affix your signature to the document?" the banker asked, as we were closing the car loan.*

**afoul of** *prep.* **1.** In collision with. ♦ *The boat ran afoul of a buoy.* **2.** In or into trouble with. ♦ *The thief ran afoul of the night watchman.* ♦ *Speeders can expect to fall afoul of the law sometimes.*

**afraid of one's shadow** *adj. phr., informal* Scared of small or imaginary things; very easily frightened; jumpy; nervous. ♦ *Mrs. Smith won't stay alone in her house at night; she is afraid of her own shadow.*

**a friend in need is a friend indeed** A genuine friend on whom one can always depend.—A proverb; often shortened to "a friend in need...." ♦ *When John's house burned down, his neighbor Jim helped him and his family with shelter, food, and clothing. Jim said, "John, a friend in need is a friend indeed—this describes you."*

**after all** *adv. phr.* **1.** As a change in plans; anyway.—Used with emphasis on *after.* ♦ *Bob thought he couldn't go to the party because he had too much homework, but he went after all.* **2.** For a good reason that you should remember.—Used with emphasis on *all.* ♦ *Why shouldn't Betsy eat the cake? After all, she baked it.*

**after a while** *informal or* **in a while** *adv. phr.* Later, at some time in the future; after a time that is not short and not long. ♦ *"Dad, will you help me make this model plane?" "After a while, Jimmy, when I finish reading the newspaper."*

**after hours** *adv. or adj. phr.* Not during the regular, correct, or usual time; going on or open after the usual hours. ♦ *The store was cleaned and swept out after hours.*

**after one's own heart** *adj. phr., informal* Well liked because of agreeing with your own feelings, interests, and ideas; to your liking—agreeable. Used after *man* or some similar word. ♦ *He likes baseball and good food; he is a man after my own heart.*

**after the dust clears/when the dust settles** *adv. phr.* When a troubling, confusing, or disastrous event is finally over. ♦ *John invited Tim for dinner, but since Tim's father had just died, he replied, "Thanks. I'd like to come after the dust settles."*

**against all odds** *adv. phr.* In spite of chances to the contrary; in defiance of the chances of winning. ♦ *The U.S. marines refused to surrender to the Germans during the Battle of the Bulge, against all odds.*

**against it** See UP AGAINST IT.

**against the clock** *or* **against time** *adv. phr.* **1.** As a test of speed or time; in order to beat a speed record or time limit. ♦ *John ran around the track against time, because there was no one else to race against.* **2.** As fast as possible; so as to do or finish something before a certain time. ♦ *It was a race against the clock whether the doctor would get to the accident soon enough to save the injured man.* **3.** So as to cause delay by using up time. ♦ *The outlaw talked against time with the sheriff, hoping that his gang would come and rescue him.*

**against the grain** *adv. phr.* **1.** Across rather than with the direction of the fibers (as of wood or meat). ♦ *He sandpapered the wood against the grain.* **2.** So as to annoy or trouble, or to cause anger or dislike.—Usually follows *go.* ♦ *His coarse and rude ways went against the grain with me.*

**Agent Orange** *n.* A herbicide used as a defoliant during the Vietnam War, considered by some to cause birth defects and cancer, hence, by extension, an instance of 'technological progress pollution.' ♦ *If things continue as they have, we'll all be eating some Agent Orange with our meals.*

**agitate for** *or* **agitate against** *v. phr.* To animatedly and excitedly persuade others to act in a certain way. ♦ *The peace demonstrators were agitating for an immediate withdrawal of U.S. troops from Iraq.*

**agree with** *v.* To have a good effect on, suit. ♦ *The meat loaf did not agree with him.* ♦ *The warm, sunny climate agreed with him, and he soon grew strong and healthy.*

**ahead of** *prep.* **1.** In a position of advantage or power over. ♦ *He studies all the time, because he wants to stay ahead of his classmates.* **2.** In front of; before. ♦ *The troop leader walked a few feet ahead of the boys.* **3.** Earlier than; previous to, before. ♦ *Betty finished her test ahead of the others.*

**ahead of the game** *adv. or adj. phr., informal* **1.** In a position of advantage; winning (as in a game or contest); ahead (as by making money or profit); making it easier to win or succeed. ♦ *The time you spend studying when you are in school will put you ahead of the game in college.* **2.** Early; too soon; beforehand. ♦ *When Ralph came to school an hour early, the janitor said, "You're ahead of the game."*

**ahead of time** *adv. phr.* Before the expected time; early. ♦ *The new building was finished ahead of time.* Contrast BEHIND TIME.

**a hell of a** *or* **one hell of a** *adj., or adv. phr. informal* Extraordinary; very. ♦ *He made a hell of a shot during the basketball game.* ♦ *Max said seven months was a hell of a time to have to wait for a simple visa.*

**aim high** *v. phr.* (given as advice) To set your goals high; to be ambitious. ♦ *If you want to achieve a comfortable position by the time you're fifty, you must aim high!*

**ain't that the limit?** *v. phr.* When someone does something disgusting, illegal, or outrageous, people often make the remark that worse behavior can hardly be expected. ♦ *Not only did they rob the house, they smeared mud on the walls and poured the garbage on the floor. Ain't that the limit?*

**airbus** *n.* A trade name, also used informally for a wide-bodied airplane used chiefly as a domestic passenger carrier. ♦ *Airbuses don't fly overseas, but mainly from coast to coast.*

**air one's dirty linen in public** *or* **wash one's dirty linen in public** *v. phr.* To talk about your private quarrels or disgraces where others can hear; make public something embarrassing that should be kept secret. ♦ *No one knew that the boys' mother was a drug addict, because the family did not wash its dirty linen in public.*

**airquake** *n.* An explosive noise of undetermined origin usually heard in coastal communities and appearing to come from some higher point in elevation. ♦ *What was that awful noise just now?—I guess it must have been an airquake.*

**air shuttle** *n., informal* Air service for regular commuters operating between major cities at not too far a distance, e.g., between Boston and New York City; such flights operate without reservation on a frequent schedule. ♦ *My dad takes the air shuttle from Boston to New York once a week.*

**airy nothings** *n. phr.* Trivial or superficial remarks; meaningless compliments. ♦ *John's popularity is based on the fact that he is a master at whispering airy nothings.*

**a la** *prep.* In the same way as; like. ♦ *Billy played ball like a champion today, a la the professional ball players.* ♦ *Joe wanted to shoot an apple off my head a la William Tell.* [From French *à la*, in the manner of.]

**albatross around one's neck** *n. phr., literary* Guilt, the haunting past, an unforgettable problem. ♦ *Even though it was an accident, John's father's death has been an albatross around John's neck.*

**a little** *n. or adj.* A small amount (of); some.—Usually *a little* is different in meaning from *little*, which emphasizes the negative; *a little* means 'some'; but *little* means 'not much.' We say ♦ *"We thought that the paper was all gone, but a little was left."* But we say, ♦ *"We* thought we still had a bag of flour, but little was left." Also, we say, ♦ "Bob was sick yesterday, but he is a little better today." But we say, ♦ "Bob was sick yesterday, and he is little better today." Sometimes a little is used with only, and then it is negative. ♦ We thought we had a whole bag of flour, but only a little was left. ♦ We have used most of the sugar; but a little is left. Often used as an adverb. ♦ Usually the teacher just watched the dancing class, but sometimes she danced a little to show them how. Sometimes used with very for emphasis. ♦ The sick girl could not eat anything, but she could drink a very little tea.

**a little bird told me** To have learned something from a mysterious, unknown, or secret source. ♦ "Who told you that Dean Smith was resigning?" Peter asked. "A little bird told me," Jim answered.

**a little knowledge is a dangerous thing** literary A person who knows a little about something may think he knows it all and make bad mistakes.—A proverb. ♦ John has read a book on driving a car and now he thinks he can drive. A little knowledge is a dangerous thing.

**alive and kicking** adj. phr. Very active; vigorous; full of energy. ♦ Grandpa was taken to the hospital with pneumonia, but he was discharged yesterday and is alive and kicking.

**alive with** prep., informal Crowded with; filled with. ♦ The lake was alive with fish. ♦ The stores were alive with people the Saturday before Christmas.

**all along** or (informal) **right along** adv. phr. All the time; during the whole time. ♦ I knew all along that we would win. ♦ I knew right along that Jane would come.

**all at once** adv. phr. 1. At the same time; together. ♦ The teacher told the children to talk one at a time; if they all talked at one time, she could not understand them. ♦ Bill can play the piano, sing, and lead his orchestra all at once. 2. or **all of a sudden** Without warning; abruptly; suddenly; unexpectedly. ♦ All at once we heard a shot and the soldier fell to the ground.

**all better** adj. phr. Fully recovered; all well again; no longer painful.—

Usually used to or by children. ♦ "All better now," he kept repeating to the little girl.

**all but** adv. phr. Very nearly; almost. ♦ Crows all but destroyed a farmer's field of corn.

**all chiefs and no Indians** n. phr. All bosses and no workers; a situation at work where everyone wants to give orders and no one wishes to work.—A proverb. ♦ The problem with this company is that it's all chiefs and no Indians.

**all ears** adj. phr., informal Very eager to hear; very attentive.—Used in the predicate. ♦ Go ahead with your story; we are all ears.

**alley cat** n., slang 1. A stray cat. 2. A person (usually a female) of rather easygoing, or actually loose, sexual morals; a promiscuous person. ♦ You'll have no problem dating her; she's a regular alley cat.

**all eyes** adj. phr., informal Wide-eyed with surprise or curiosity; watching very closely.—Used in the predicate. ♦ At the circus the children were all eyes.

**all fired up** adj. phr. A state of feeling upset; feeling rowdy. ♦ Mark got all fired up when Mary rejected his invitation.

**all gone** adj. phr. Used up; exhausted (said of supplies); done with; over with. ♦ We used to travel a lot, but, alas, those days are all gone.

**all hours** n. phr., informal Late or irregular times. ♦ The boy's mother said he must stop coming home for meals at all hours.

**all in** adj. phr., informal Very tired; exhausted. ♦ The players were all in after their first afternoon of practice.

**all in a day's work** or **all in the day's work** adj. phr., informal Unpleasant or bad but to be expected; not harder than usual; not unusual. ♦ When the car had a flat tire, Father said that it was all in a day's work.

**all in all**[1] n. phr., literary The person or thing that you love most. ♦ She was all in all to him. ♦ Music was his all in all.

**all in all**[2] or **in all** adv. phr. When everything is thought about; in summary; altogether. ♦ All in all, it was a pleasant day's cruise. ♦ All in all, the pilot of an airplane must have many abilities and years of experience before he can be appointed. ♦*Counting the balls on the green, we have six golf balls in all.*

**all in good time** *adv. phr.* Some time soon, when the time is ripe for an event to take place. ♦*"I want to get married, Dad," Mike said. "All in good time, Son," answered his father.*

**all in one piece** *adv. phr.* Safely; without damage or harm. ♦*John's father was terribly concerned when his son was sent to war as a pilot, but he came home all in one piece.*

**all kinds of** *adj. phr., informal* Plenty of. ♦*People say that Mr. Fox has all kinds of money.*

**all manner of** *adj. phr., formal* Many different kinds of; all sorts of. ♦*In a five-and-ten-cent store you can buy all manner of things.*

**all of a sudden** See ALL AT ONCE 2.

**all out** *adv. phr., informal* With all your strength, power, or determination; to the best of your ability; without holding back.—Usually used in the phrase go all out. ♦*We went all out to win the game.*

**all-out effort** *n.* A great and thorough effort at solving a given problem. ♦*The President is making an all-out effort to convince Congress to pass the pending bill on health care.*

**all-out war** *n.* Total war including civilian casualties as opposed to a war that is limited only to armies. ♦*Hitler was waging an all-out war when he invaded Poland.*

**all over** *adv. phr.* **1.** In every part; everywhere. ♦*He has a fever and aches all over.* ♦*I have looked all over for my glasses.* **2.** *informal* In every way; completely. ♦*She is her mother all over.* **3.** *informal* Coming into very close physical contact, as during a violent fight; wrestling. ♦*Before I noticed what happened, he was all over me.*

**allow for** *v.* To provide for; leave room for; give a chance to; permit. ♦*She cut the skirt four inches longer to allow for a wide hem.* ♦*Democracy allows for many differences of opinion.*

**all right**[1] *adv. phr.* **1.** Well enough. *The new machine is running all right.* **2.** *informal* I am willing; yes. ♦*"Shall we watch television?" "All right."* **3.** *informal* Beyond question, certainly.—

Used for emphasis and placed after the word it modifies. ♦*It's time to leave, all right, but the bus hasn't come.*

**all right**[2] *adj. phr.* **1.** Good enough; correct; suitable. ♦*His work is always all right.* **2.** In good health or spirits; well. ♦*"How are you?" "I'm all right."* **3.** *slang* Good. ♦*He's an all right guy.*

**all right for you** *interj.* I'm finished with you! That ends it between you and me!—Used by children. ♦*All right for you! I'm not playing with you any more!*

**all roads lead to Rome** *literary* The same end or goal may be reached by many different ways.—A proverb. ♦*"I don't care how you get the answer," said the teacher, "All roads lead to Rome."*

**all set** *adj. phr.* Ready to start. ♦*"Is the plane ready for takeoff?" the bank president asked. "Yes, Sir," the pilot answered. "We're all set."*

**all shook up** *also* **shook up** *adj., slang* In a state of great emotional upheaval; disturbed; agitated. ♦*What are you so shook up about?*

**all's for the best** A stoical statement indicating acceptance of the inevitable.—A proverb. ♦*"Everyone will have to die some day," Joe said as they were leaving the hospital. "All's for the best," his wife consoled him. "Poor mother is in her nineties."*

**all smiles** *adj. phr.* Very happy; completely satisfied. ♦*Mary was all smiles when she got word that she was selected for the Miss America contest.* ♦*Why is Sam all smiles? Did he just receive a promotion?*

**all systems go** *Originally from space English, now general colloquial usage.* Everything is complete and ready for action; it is now all right to proceed. ♦*After they wrote out the invitations, it was all systems go for the wedding.*

**all that** *adj. phr.* Very good looking. ♦*Sarah thinks that Peter is all that.*

**all that glitters is not gold** *or* **not all that glitters is gold** Objects, people, or situations that appear attractive may turn out to be fake or downright harmful.—A proverb. ♦*"Joe's fancy new computer keeps quitting on him. He should have stuck with his old one. Goes to show that all that glitters is not gold.*

**all the¹** *adj. phr., dial.* The only. ♦*A hut was all the home he ever had.*

**all the²** *adv. phr.* Than otherwise; even.— Used to emphasize comparative adjectives, adverbs, and nouns. ♦*Opening the windows made it all the hotter.*

**all the better** See ALL THE 2.

**all there** *or* **all here** *adj. phr., informal* Understanding well; thinking clearly; not crazy.—Usually used in negative sentences. ♦*Joe acted queerly and talked wildly, so we thought he was not all there.*

**all the same¹** *or* **all one** *n. phr.* Something that makes no difference; a choice that you don't care about. ♦*If it's all the same to you, I would like to be waited on first.* ♦*You can get there by car or by bus—it's all one.*

**all the same²** *or* **just the same** *adv. phr., informal* As if the opposite were so; nevertheless; anyway; anyhow; still. ♦*Everyone opposed it, but Sally and Bob got married all the same.* ♦*Mary is deaf, but she takes tap dancing lessons just the same.*

**all the thing** *or* **all the rage, the in thing** *n. phr.* The fashionable or popular thing to do, the fashionable or most popular artist or form of art at a given time. ♦*After "The Graduate" Dustin Hoffman was all the rage in the movies.* ♦*It was all the thing in the late sixties to smoke pot and demonstrate against the war in Vietnam.*

**all the time** *adv. phr.* **1.** *or* **all the while** During the whole period; through the whole time. ♦*Mary went to college in her home town and lived at home all the while.* ♦*Most of us were surprised to hear that Mary and Tom had been engaged all year, but Sue said she knew it all the time.* **2.** Without stopping; continuously ♦*Most traffic lights work all the time.* **3.** Very often; many times. ♦*Ruth talks about her trip to Europe all the time, and her friends are tired of it.*

**all the traffic will bear** *or* **that's all the traffic will bear** *n. phr.* The situation, whether financial, commercial, or other, precludes anything more.—A proverb. ♦*"Should we increase our productivity before year's end?" Ted asked the director. "I think we've got all the traffic will bear," the director replied.*

**all the way** *or* **the whole way** *adv. phr.* **1.** From start to finish during the whole distance or time. ♦*Jack climbed all the way to the top of the tree.* ♦*Joe has played the whole way in the football game and it's almost over.* **2.** In complete agreement; with complete willingness to satisfy.—Often used in the phrase *go all the way with.* ♦*I go all the way with what George says about Bill.* ♦*Mary said she was willing to kiss Bill, but that did not mean she was willing to go all the way with him.*

**all the worse** See ALL THE 2.

**all things considered** *adv. phr.* Everything being taken into account; having weighed the pros and cons of an argument. ♦*All things considered, the best defense against terror attacks is a good offense.*

**all things to all men** *adv. phr.* To make oneself indispensable to everyone. ♦*I hope he won't wear himself out; my brother John is so eager to help others, he is in a real sense all things to all men.*

**all thumbs** *adj., informal* Awkward, especially with your hands; clumsy. ♦*Harry tried to fix the chair but he was all thumbs.*

**all told** *adv. phr., informal* Counting or including everything. ♦*Including candy sale profits we have collected $300 all told.*

**all up** *adj. phr., informal* Near to certain death or defeat without any more chance or hope. ♦*With their ammunition gone the patrol knew that it was all up with them.*

**all very well** *adj.* All right; very good and correct; very true.—Usually followed by a *but* clause. ♦*It's all very well for you to complain but can you do any better?*

**all walks of life** *n. phr.* All socioeconomic groups; all professions and lines of work. ♦*A good teacher has to be able to communicate with students from all walks of life.* ♦*A clever politician doesn't alienate people from any walk of life.*

**all wet** *adj., slang* Entirely confused or wrong; mistaken. ♦*When the Wright brothers said they could build a flying machine, people thought they were all wet.*

**all work and no play makes Jack a dull boy** Too much hard work without time out for play or enjoyment is not good for anyone.—A proverb. ♦ *Bill's mother told him to stop studying and to go out and play, because all work and no play makes Jack a dull boy.*

**all year round** *adv. phr.* Always; all the time; throughout all seasons of the year. ♦ *In California the sun shines all year round.*

**almighty dollar** *n. phr.* The power of wealth. ♦ *Too many people have no place for art or meditation in their lives, since all they do is chase the almighty dollar.*

**along for the ride** *adv. phr., informal* Being in a group for the fun or the credit without doing any of the work. ♦ *He wants no members in his political party who are just along for the ride.*

**along in years** *or* **on in years** *adj. phr.* Elderly; growing old. ♦ *As Grandfather got on in years, he became quiet and thoughtful.*

**alongside of** *prep.* **1.** At or along the side of. ♦ *We walked alongside of the river.* **2.** Together with. ♦ *I played alongside of Tom on the same team.* **3.** *informal* Compared with or to; measured next to. ♦ *His money doesn't look like much alongside of a millionaire's.*

**a lot** *n., informal* A large number or amount; very many or very much; lots. ♦ *I learned a lot in Mr. Smith's class.* ♦ *A lot of our friends are going to the beach this summer.*—Often used like an adverb. ♦ *Ella is a jolly girl; she laughs a lot.*—Also used as an adjective with *more, less,* and *fewer.* ♦ *There was a good crowd at the game today, but a lot more will come next week.*—Often used with *whole* for emphasis. ♦ *Jerry is a whole lot taller than he was a year ago.*

**a lot riding on** *or* **lot riding on** *or* **lots riding on** *phrasal idiom* A great deal depending on something. ♦ *If you want to gain admission to graduate school, there's a lot riding on your Graduate Record Examination as well as on your undergraduate grades.*

**alpha and omega** *n. phr.* The beginning and the end of something. ♦ *For investors, the alpha and omega of human society is the Stock Exchange; for a priest or minister, it is God and the church.*

**alpha wave** *n.* A brain wave, 8–12 cycles per second, associated with a state of relaxation and meditation and, hence, free of anxieties. ♦ *Try to produce some alpha waves; you will instantly feel a lot better.*

**always look on the bright side** *v. phr.* Advice given to a pessimist indicating that everything "bad" may have something "good" in it as well.—A proverb. ♦ *"OK, so you're in the hospital. But at least you don't have to drive 30 miles to work and back! Always look on the bright side!"* Mary said to her husband.

**a man is known by the company he keeps** An adage reminding people that they are often judged by the nature of their friends.—A proverb. ♦ *John's looks and health deteriorated when he joined up with a pot-smoking hippie band. It's true that a man is known by the company he keeps.*

**ambulance chaser** *n.* An attorney who specializes in representing victims of traffic accidents. By extension, a lawyer of inferior rank or talent. ♦ *Don't hire Jones; he's just another ambulance chaser.*

**American plan** *n.* A system of hotel management in which meals are included with the room, as opposed to the European plan that does not include meals. ♦ *American tourists in Europe sometimes expect that their meals will be included, because they are used to the American plan.*

**amount to** *v.* Signify; add up to. ♦ *John's total income didn't amount to more than a few hundred dollars.*

**a must** *n.* **1.** An inevitability; a necessity. *Visas in many foreign countries are a must.* **2.** An extremely interesting or memorable event, such as a free concert given by an international celebrity. ♦ *Alfred Brendel's Beethoven master classes are open to the public and are not to be missed; they're a must.*

**an apple a day keeps the doctor away** A saying often heard emphasizing the virtues of simple living and a healthy diet.—A proverb. ♦ *So you have poor digestion? Take more fruit. Don't you remember the old saying, "An apple a day keeps the doctor away?"*

**and all** *informal* And whatever goes with it; and all that means. ♦ *We don't go out* much nowadays, with the new baby and all. ♦ *Jack's employer provided the tools and all.*

**and how!** *interj. informal* Yes, that is certainly right!—Used for emphatic agreement. ♦ *"Did you see the game?" "And how!"* ♦ *"Isn't Mary pretty?" "And how she is!"*

**and so forth** *or* **and so on** And more of the same kind; and further amounts or things like the ones already mentioned. ♦ *The costumes were red, pink, blue, purple, yellow, and so forth.* Compare WHAT HAVE YOU.

**and sundry** *n. phr.* All, both collectively and individually. ♦ *All and sundry showed up at the new governor's inaugural ball.*

**and the like** *n. phr.* Things of a similar nature. ♦ *I like McDonald's, Wendy's, Kentucky Fried Chicken, and the like.* ♦ *When I go out to the beach I take towels, a mat, suntan lotion, and the like.*

**and then some** And a lot more; and more too. ♦ *It would cost all the money he had and then some.*

**and what not** See WHAT NOT.

**an elephant never forgets** Often heard as a remark about people with an exceptionally sharp, long-range memory.—A proverb. ♦ *"How come you recognized me after twenty years?" John asked his friend. "I am like an elephant, you know," came the answer, "and an elephant never forgets."*

**angel dust** *n., slang* Phencyclidine, an addictive hallucinatory narcotic drug extremely dangerous to the users' health, also called PCP. ♦ *Mike has gone from grass to angel dust; he will end up in the morgue.*

**another day, another dollar** Often said by people at the end of a day of hard work. They have not made a fortune, but are getting by on a daily basis.—A proverb. ♦ *"Well, it's Friday again," said Joe. "Yeah, another day, another dollar," his tired partner replied.*

**answer for** *v.* **1.** To take responsibility for; assume charge or supervision of. ♦ *The secret service has to answer for the safety of the president and his family.* **2.** To say you are sure that (someone) has good character or ability; guarantee; sponsor. ♦ *When people*

thought Ray had stolen the money, the principal said, "Ray is no thief. I'll answer for him." **3.** Take the blame or punishment for. ♦ *When Mother found out who ate the cake, Tom had to answer for his mischief.*

**answer one's calling** *v. phr.* To fulfill one's destiny in terms of work or profession by doing what one has a talent for. ♦ *Don answered his calling when he became a chiropractor. Susy answered her calling when she became a violinist.*

**answer the call of nature** *or* **obey the call of nature** *v. phr., slang* To go to the bathroom to relieve oneself by urinating or defecating. ♦ *Ted was hiking in the mountains when suddenly he had to answer the call of nature, but since there was no bathroom in the woods, he excused himself and disappeared behind the bushes.*

**answer to** *v.* To be named; go by a certain name or designation; be accountable. ♦ *When you walk my dog, please remember that he answers to the name "Caesar."* ♦ *As head of the company she does not have to answer to anyone.*

**ante up** *v., informal* To produce the required amount of money in order to close a transaction; to pay what one owes. ♦ *"I guess I'd better ante up if I want to stay an active member of the Association," Max said.*

**ants in one's pants** *n. phr., slang* Nervous overactivity; restlessness. ♦ *You have ants in your pants today. Is something wrong?*

**a number** *n.* A rather large number; numbers.—Used when there are more than several and fewer than many. ♦ *We knew the Smiths rather well; we had visited them a number of times.*— Used like an adjective before *less, more.* ♦ *We have not set up enough folding chairs; we need a number more.*

**any number** *n., informal* A large number; many. ♦ *There are any number of reasons for eating good food.*

**any old how / any old way** *adv. phr., informal* Doing something in a casual, haphazard, or careless way. ♦ *"John," the teacher said, "you can't just do your homework any old way; you must pay attention to my instructions!"*

**any port in a storm** Any help is welcome in an emergency.—A proverb. ♦ *The* *motel we stopped in was nothing to brag about, but we were so exhausted that it was a clear case of any port in a storm.*

**anything but** *adv. phr.* Quite the opposite of; far from being. ♦ *I don't mean he's lazy—anything but!* ♦ *The boys knew they had broken the rules, and they were anything but happy when they were called to the office.*

**anything goes!** You can do as you please; anything is permissible.—A proverb. ♦ *Wars may be planned, but how they play out is really unpredictable. In the heat of battle, anything goes!"*

**anything like** *or* **anywhere near** *adv.* Nearly.—Used in negative, interrogative, and conditional sentences, often in the negative forms *nothing like* or *nowhere near.* ♦ *It's not anything like as hot today as it was yesterday.* ♦ *Do you think that gold ring is worth anywhere near a hundred dollars?* ♦ *Today's game was nowhere near as exciting as yesterday's game.* ♦ *Studying that lesson should take nothing like two hours.*

**anywhere near** See ANYTHING LIKE *or* ANYWHERE NEAR.

**any which way** See EVERY WHICH WAY.

**apart** See JOKING ASIDE *or* JOKING APART, POLES APART, TELL APART.

**apart from** *or* **aside from** *prep. phr.* Beside or besides; in addition to. ♦ *Aside from being fun and good exercise, swimming is a very useful skill.*

**appear on the scene** *v. phr.* To make an impact in a given circle of friends, acquaintances, and colleagues. ♦ *American film history changed for good when Meryl Streep and Al Pacino appeared on the scene.*

**apple of discord** *n. phr.* The reason for a prolonged quarrel (from the story of Venus and Paris in Homer's *Iliad*). ♦ *The unfair distribution of wealth will always remain the apple of discord in society.*

**apple of one's eye** *n. phr.* Something or someone that is adored; a cherished person or object. ♦ *Charles is the apple of his mother's eye.*

**apple-pie order** *n. phr., informal* Exact orderly arrangement, neatness; tidy arrangement. ♦ *Like a good secretary, she kept the boss's desk in apple-pie order.*

**apply oneself to something** *v. phr.* To make oneself work hard at something;

to undertake a task in earnest. ♦ *If you want to get an A in English grammar, you must apply yourself to it.*

**apron strings** *n. phr.* The nearly complete influence of another person. ♦ *Suzie is so immature, I am afraid she will never free herself from her mother's apron strings.*

**apropos of** *prep., formal* In connection with; on the subject of, about; concerning. ♦ *Apropos of higher tuition, Mr. Black told the boy about the educational loans that banks are offering.* ♦ *Mr. White went to see Mr. Richards apropos of buying a car.*

**arch over** *v. phr.* To cover; to make a curved roof over a space. ♦ *The corridor between the gym and the assembly hall was arched over to keep the students out of the snow and rain.*

**argue down** *v. phr.* To defeat an opponent in a debating contest. ♦ *Central High's students were rather well prepared, but Jefferson High's debating team succeeded in arguing them down.*

**Argus-eyed** *adj. phr.* Extraordinarily observant, watchful, sharp-sighted (from an ancient Greek legend about Argus, who had a hundred eyes) ♦ *The Argus-eyed chief of detectives solved the puzzling crime in two short days.*

**are you kidding?** *v. phr.* Ironically derisive exclamation meaning "Surely you are not serious" or "What you say must be a joke." ♦ *You say you will move to Fiji to teach American football… . Are you kidding?*

**arm and a leg** *n., slang* An exorbitantly high price that must be paid for something that isn't really worth it. ♦ *It's true that to get a decent apartment these days in New York you have to pay an arm and a leg.*

**armed to the teeth** *adj. phr.* Having all needed weapons; fully armed. ♦ *The paratroopers were armed to the teeth.*

**arm in arm** *adv. phr.* With your arm under or around another person's arm, especially in close comradeship or friendship. ♦ *Sally and Joan were laughing and joking together as they walked arm in arm down the street.* ♦ *When they arrived at the party, the partners walked arm in arm to meet the hosts.* Compare HAND IN HAND.

**around Robin Hood's barn** *adv. phr.* In a roundabout, tricky, indirect sort of way. ◆ *They weren't at all straight with me; they were leading me around Robin Hood's barn.*

**around the clock** *also* **the clock around** *adv. phr.* For 24 hours a day continuously all day and all night. ◆ *The factory operated around the clock until the order was filled.* ◆ *He studied around the clock for his history exam.*—**round-the-clock** *adj.* ◆ *That filling station has round-the-clock service.*

**around the corner** *adv. phr.* Soon to come or happen; close by; near at hand. ◆ *The fortune teller told Jane that there was an adventure for her just around the corner.*

**arrive at** *v. phr.* To reach a decision; to come to a conclusion. ◆ *After a prolonged discussion the president's advisers arrived at the decision to bring the war to the terrorists.*

**as a last resort** *adv. phr* In lieu of better things; lacking better solutions. ◆ *"We'll sleep in our sleeping bags as a last resort," John said, "since all the motels are full."*

**as a matter of fact** *adv. phr.* Actually; really; in addition to what has been said; in reference to what was said.—Often used as an interjection. ◆ *It's not true that I cannot swim; as a matter of fact, I used to work as a lifeguard in Hawaii.*

**as a matter of form** *adv. phr.* Routinely; without extra importance; merely as a formality. ◆ *You are asked to put your signature here merely as a matter of form.*

**as an aside** *adv. phr.* Said as a remark in a low tone of voice; used in theaters where the actor turns toward the audience as if to 'think out loud.' ◆ *During the concert Tim said to his wife as an aside, "The conductor has no idea how to conduct Beethoven."*

**as a rule** *adv. phr.* Generally; customarily. ◆ *As a rule, the boss arrives at the office about 10 A.M.*

**as best as one can** *adv. phr.* As well as you can; by whatever means are available; in the best way you can. ◆ *The car broke down in the middle of the night, and he had to get home as best as he could.* ◆ *George's foot hurt, but he played the game as best as he could.*

**as far as** *or* **so far as** *adv. phr.* **1.** To the degree or amount that; according to what, how much, or how far. ◆ *John did a good job as far as he went, but he did not finish it.* ◆ *So far as the weather is concerned, I do not think it matters.* ◆ *As far as he was concerned, things were going well.* **2.** To the extent that; within the limit that. ◆ *He has no brothers so far as I know.*

**as far as that goes** *or* **as far as that is concerned** *or* **so far as that is concerned** *also* **so far as that goes** *adv. phr.* While we are talking about it; also; actually. ◆ *You don't have to worry about the girls. Mary can take care of herself, and as far as that goes, Susan is pretty independent, too.* ◆ *I didn't enjoy the movie, and so far as that is concerned, I never like horror movies.*

**as follows** A list of things that come next; what is listed next.—Followed by a colon. ◆ *My grocery list is as follows: bread, butter, meat, eggs, sugar.*

**as for** *prep.* **1.** In regard to; speaking of; concerning. ◆ *We have plenty of bread, and as for butter, we have more than enough.* **2.** Speaking for. ◆ *Most people like the summer but as for me, I like winter much better.*

**as good as** *adv. phr.* Nearly the same as; almost. ◆ *She claimed that he as good as promised to marry her.* ◆ *He as good as called me a liar.* ◆ *We'll get to school on time, we're as good as there now.* ◆ *The man who had been shot was as good as dead.*

**as good as one gets** See GIVE AS GOOD AS ONE GETS.

**as good as one's promise** See AS GOOD AS ONE'S WORD.

**as good as one's word** *or* **good as one's word** *adj. phr.* Trustworthy; sure to keep your promise. ◆ *The coach said he would give the players a day off if they won, and he was as good as his word.* ◆ *We knew she was always good as her word, so we trusted her.*

**as hard as nails** *adj. phr.* Very unfeeling; cruel, and unsympathetic. ◆ *Uncle Joe is as hard as nails; although he is a millionaire, he doesn't help his less fortunate relatives.*

**aside from** See APART FROM.

**aside of** *prep.*, *dialect* Beside; by the side of. ♦ *Mary sits aside of her sister on the bus.*

**as if** *or* **as though** *conj.* **1.** As (he, she, it) would if; in the same way one would if seeming to show. ♦ *The baby laughed as if he understood what Mother said.* ♦ *The book looked as though it had been out in the rain.* **2.** That. ♦ *It seems as if you are the first one here.*

**as is** *adv.* Without changes or improvements; with no guarantee or promise of good condition.—Used after the word it modifies. ♦ *They agree to buy the house as is.* ♦ *He bought an old car as is.*

**as it were** *adv. phr.* As it might be said to be; as if it really were; seemingly.— Used with a statement that might seem silly or unreasonable, to show that it is just a way of saying it. ♦ *In many ways children live, as it were, in a different world from adults.*

**ask for** *v.*, *informal* To make (something bad) likely to happen to you; bring (something bad) upon yourself. ♦ *Charles drives fast on worn-out tires; he is asking for trouble.* ♦ *The workman lost his job, but he asked for it by coming to work drunk several times.*

**ask for one's hand** *v. phr.* To ask permission to marry someone. ♦ *"Sir," John said timidly to Mary's father, "I came to ask for your daughter's hand."*

**ask for the moon** *or* **cry for the moon** *v. phr.* To want something that you cannot reach or have; try for the impossible. ♦ *John asked his mother for a hundred dollars today. He's always asking for the moon.*

**ask out** *v. phr.* To invite someone on a date. ♦ *"I met a terrific girl," Joe said. "Well, then, you must ask her out soon!" Peter replied.*

**ask yourself!** *v. phr.* Be sensible, be reasonable, and you'll find the right answer. ♦ *"Should I marry someone thirty years older?" Joe asked Peter. "Come on, man, ask yourself!" Peter answered with a laugh.*

**asleep at the switch** *adj. phr.* **1.** Asleep when it is one's duty to move a railroad switch for cars to go on the right track. ♦ *The new man was asleep at the switch and the two trains crashed.* **2.** *informal* Failing to act promptly as expected; not alert to an opportunity. ♦ *When the* ducks flew over, the hunter was asleep at the switch and missed his shot.

**as likely as not** *adv. phr.* Probably. ♦ *As likely as not, he will disappear forever.*

**as long as** *or* **so long as** *conj.* **1.** Since; because; considering that. ♦ *As long as you are going to town anyway, you can do something for me.* **2.** Provided that; if. ♦ *You may use the room as you like, so long as you clean it up afterward.*

**as luck would have it** *adv. clause* As it happened; by chance; luckily or unluckily. ♦ *As luck would have it, no one was in the building when the explosion occurred.* ♦ *As luck would have it, there was rain on the day of the picnic.*

**as much** *n.* The same; exactly that. ♦ *Don't thank me, I would do as much for anyone.* ♦ *Did you lose your way? I thought as much when you were late in coming.*

**as much as** *adv. phr.* **1.** *or* **much as** Even though; although. ♦ *As much as I hate to do it, I must stay home and study tonight.* **2.** *or* **so much as** Just the same as; almost; practically; really. ♦ *By running away he as much as admitted that he had taken the money.* ♦ *You as much as promised you would help us.*

**as of** *prep.* At or until (a certain time). ♦ *I know that as of last week he was still unmarried.* ♦ *As of now we don't know much about Mars.*

**as one man** *adv. phr.* Unanimously; together; involving all. ♦ *The audience arose as one man to applaud the great pianist.*

**aspire to** *v.phr.* To want something, to aim to achieve a certain goal. ♦ *Many a U.S. senator aspires to the presidency, but very few ever make it.*

**as regards** *prep.* Regarding; concerning; about. ♦ *You needn't worry as regards the cost of the operation.* ♦ *He was always secretive as regards his family.*

**as soon as** *conj.* Just after; when; immediately after. ♦ *As soon as the temperature falls to 70, the furnace is turned on.* ♦ *As soon as you finish your job let me know.* ♦ *He will see you as soon as he can.*

**as the crow flies** *adv. clause* By the most direct way; along a straight line between two places. ♦ *It is seven miles to the next town as the crow flies, but it is ten miles by the road, which goes around the mountain.*

**as the story goes** *adv. phr.* As the story is told; as one has heard through rumor. ♦ *As the story goes, Jonathan disappeared when he heard the police were after him.*

**as though** See AS IF.

**a stitch in time saves nine** It is better to prepare something while it is still not entirely broken, since later it would take much more of an effort.—A proverb. ♦ *We had better fix the old car before we leave; you know how they say "a stitch in time saves nine."*

**as to** *prep.* **1.** In connection with; about; regarding. ♦ *There is no doubt as to his honesty.* ♦ *As to your final grade, that depends on your final examination.* Syn. WITH RESPECT TO. **2.** According to; following; going by. ♦ *They sorted the eggs as to size and color.*

**as usual** *adv. phr.* In the usual way; as you usually do or as it usually does. ♦ *As usual, Tommy forgot to make his bed before he went out to play.* ♦ *Only a week after the fire in the store, it was doing business as usual.*

**as well** *adv. phr.* **1.** In addition; also, too; besides. ♦ *The book tells about Mark Twain's writings and about his life as well.* ♦ *Tom is captain of the football team and is on the baseball team as well.* **2.** Without loss and possibly with gain. ♦ *After the dog ran away, Father thought he might as well sell the dog house.* ♦ *Since he can't win the race, he may as well quit.* ♦ *It's just as well you didn't come yesterday, because we were away.*

**as well as** *conj.* In addition to; and also; besides. ♦ *Hiking is good exercise as well as fun.* ♦ *He was my friend as well as my doctor.* ♦ *The book tells about the author's life as well as about his writings.*

**as ye sow, so shall ye reap** *or* **as you make your bed, so you must lie in it** One's actions bear definite consequences and one has to face them.—A proverb. ♦ *When the leader of a murderous gang was shot himself, the local minister said: "As ye sow, so shall ye reap."*

**as yet** *adv. phr.* Up to the present time; so far; yet. ♦ *We know little as yet about the moon's surface.* ♦ *She has not come as yet.*

**as you make your bed, so you must lie in it** See AS YE SOW, SO SHALL YE REAP.

**as you please 1.** As you like, whatever you like or prefer; as you choose. ♦ *You may do as you please.* **2.** *informal* Very.—Used after an adjective or adverb often preceded by *as.* ♦ *She was dressed for the dance and she looked as pretty as you please.*

**at a blow** *or* **at a stroke** *or* **at one stroke** *adv. phr.* Immediately; suddenly; with one quick or forceful action. ♦ *The pirates captured the ship and captured a ton of gold at a blow.* ♦ *A thousand men lost their jobs at a stroke when the factory closed.*

**at all** *adv. phr.* At any time or place, for any reason, or in any degree or manner.—Used for emphasis with certain kinds of words or sentences. **1.** Negative ♦ *It's not at all likely he will come.* **2.** Limited ♦ *I can hardly hear you at all.* **3.** Interrogative ♦ *Can it be done at all?* **4.** Conditional ♦ *She will walk with a limp, if she walks at all.*

**at all costs** *adv. phr.* At any expense of time, effort, or money. Regardless of the results. ♦ *Mr. Jackson intended to save his son's eyesight at all costs.*

**at all hours** *adv. phr.* Any time; all the time; at almost any time. ♦ *The baby cried so much that we were up at all hours trying to calm her down.*

**at a loss** *adj. phr.* In a state of uncertainty; without any idea; puzzled. ♦ *A good salesman is never at a loss for words.* ♦ *When Don missed the last bus, he was at a loss to know what to do.*

**at anchor** *adj. phr.* Held by an anchor from floating away; anchored. ♦ *The ship rode at anchor in the harbor.*

**at any rate** *adv. phr.* In any case; anyhow. ♦ *It isn't much of a car, but at any rate it was not expensive.*

**at a premium** *adv. phr.* At a high price due to special circumstances. ♦ *When his father died, Fred flew to Europe at a premium because he had no chance to buy a less expensive ticket.*

**at a set time** *prep. phr.* At a particular, pre-specified time. ♦ *Do we have to eat in this hotel at a set time, or may we come down whenever we want?*

**at a time** *adv. phr.* At once; at one time; in one group or unit; together. ♦ *He checked them off one at a time as they came in.* ♦ *He ran up the steps two at a time.*

**at bay** *adv. or adj. phr.* In a place where you can no longer run away; unable to go back farther; forced to stand and fight, or face an enemy; cornered. ♦ *The police chased the thief to a roof, where they held him at bay until more policemen came to help.*

**at best** *or* **at the best** *adv. phr.* **1.** Under the best conditions; as the best possibility. ♦ *A coal miner's job is dirty and dangerous at best.* ♦ *We can't get to New York before ten o'clock at best.* **2.** In the most favorable way of looking at something; even saying the best about the thing. ♦ *The treasurer had at best been careless with the club's money, but most people thought he had been dishonest.*

**at call** *adj. or adv. phr.* **1.** Ready or nearby for use, help, or service; on request. ♦ *Auto insurance agents all over the country are at the insured person's call, wherever he may travel.* **2.** At the word of command; at an order or signal. ♦ *The dog was trained to come at call.*

**at close range** *adv. phr.* Close by; in proximity. ♦ *The police officer fired at the fleeing murder suspect at close range.*

**at cross purposes** *adv. phr.* With opposing meanings or aims; with opposing effect or result; with aims which hinder or get in each other's way. ♦ *Tom's parents acted at cross purposes in advising him; his father wanted him to become a doctor, but his mother wanted him to become a minister.*

**at daggers drawn** *adv. phr.* In a state ready to kill; in great anger; anticipating fighting and hostility. ♦ *When they were discussing divorce, Mike and Sue went at it all day at daggers drawn.*

**at death's door** *adj. or adv. phr.* Very near death; dying. ♦ *He seemed to be at death's door from his illness.*

**at each other's throats** *prep. phr.* Always arguing and quarreling. ♦ *Joan and Harry have been at each other's throats so long that they have forgotten how much they used to love one another.*

**at ease** *or* **at one's ease** *adj. or adv. phr.* **1.** In comfort; without pain or bother. ♦ *You can't feel at ease with a toothache.* **2.** *or* **at one's ease** Comfortable in one's mind; relaxed, not troubled.—Often used in the phrase *put at ease* or *put at one's ease.* ♦ *We put Mary at her ease during the thunderstorm by reading her stories.* **3.** Standing with your right foot in place and without talking in military ranks. ♦ *The sergeant gave his men the command "At ease!"*

**at every turn** *adv. phr.* Every time; all the time; continually without exception. ♦ *Because of his drinking, the man was refused a job at every turn.*

**at face value** *prep. phr.* What one can actually hear, read, or see; literally. ♦ *John is so honest that you can take his words at face value.* ♦ *This store's advertisements are honest; take them at face value.*

**at fault** *adj. phr.* Responsible for an error or failure; to blame. ♦ *The driver who didn't stop at the red light was at fault in the accident.*

**at first** *adv. phr.* In the beginning; at the start. ♦ *The driver didn't see the danger a first.* ♦ *At first the job looked good to Bob, but later it became tiresome.*

**at first blush** *adv. phr.* When first seen; without careful study. ♦ *At first blush the offer looked good, but when we studied it, we found things we could not accept.*

**at first glance** *or* **at first sight** *adv. or adj. phr.* After a first quick look. ♦ *At first sight, his guess was that the whole trouble between the two men resulted from personalities that did not agree.* ♦ *Tom met Mary at a party, and it was love at first sight.*

**at great length** *prep. phr.* **1.** In great detail. ♦ *Jim told us the story of his life at great length.* **2.** For a long time. ♦ *The boring speaker rambled on at great length.*

**at half mast** *prep. phr.* Halfway up or down; referring primarily to flagposts, but may be used jokingly. ♦ *When a president of the United States dies, all flags are flown at half mast.*

**at hand** *also* **at close hand** *or* **near at hand** *adv. phr.* **1.** Easy to reach; nearby. ♦ *When he writes, he always keeps a dictionary at hand.* **2.** *formal* Coming soon; almost here. ♦ *Examinations are past and Commencement Day is at hand.*

**at heart** *adv. phr.* **1.** In spite of appearances; at bottom; in reality. ♦ *His manners are rough but he is a kind man at* *heart.* **2.** As a serious interest or concern; as an important aim or goal. ♦ *He has the welfare of the poor at heart.*

**at home** *adv. or adj. phr.* **1.** In the place where you live or come from. ♦ *I went to his house, but he was not at home.* **2.** Knowing what to do or say; familiar; comfortable. ♦ *Charles and John enjoy working together because they feel at home with each other.*

**at issue** *adj. phr.* **1.** In dispute; to be settled by debate, by vote, by battle, or by some other contest. ♦ *His good name was at issue in the trial.* ♦ *The independence of the United States from England was at issue in the Revolutionary War.* **2.** Not in agreement; in conflict; opposing. ♦ *His work as a doctor was at issue with other doctors' practice.*

**at it** *adj. phr.* Busily doing something; active. ♦ *His rule for success was to keep always at it.* ♦ *The couple who owned the little cleaning shop were at it early and late.*

**at large** *adv. or adj. phr.* **1.** Not kept within walls, fences, or boundaries; free. ♦ *The killer remained at large for weeks.* Compare AT LIBERTY. ♦ *Cattle and sheep roamed at large on the big ranch.* **2.** In a broad, general way; at length; fully. ♦ *The superintendent talked at large for an hour about his hopes for a new school building.* **3.** As a group rather than as individuals; as a whole; taken together. ♦ *The junior class at large was not interested in a senior yearbook.* **4.** As a representative of a whole political unit or area rather than one of its parts; from a city rather than one of its wards, or a state rather than one of its districts. ♦ *He was elected congressman at large.*

**at last** *also* **at long last** *adv. phr.* After a long time; finally. ♦ *The war had been long and hard, but now there was peace at last.* ♦ *The boy saved his money until at last he had enough for a bicycle.*

**at least** *adv. phr.* **1.** *or* **at the least** At the smallest guess; no fewer than; no less than. ♦ *You should brush your teeth at least twice a day.* ♦ *At least three students are failing in mathematics.* **2.** Whatever else you may say; anyhow; anyway. ♦ *She broke her arm, but at least it wasn't the arm she writes with.* ♦ *He's not coming—at least that's what he said.*

**at leisure** *adj. or adv. phr.* **1.** Not at work; not busy; with free time; at rest. ♦ *Come and visit us some evening when you're at leisure.* **2.** *or* **at one's leisure** When and how you wish at your convenience; without hurry. ♦ *You may read the book at your leisure.*

**at length** *adv. phr.* **1.** In detail; fully. ♦ *You must study the subject at length to understand it.* ♦ *The teacher explained the new lesson at length to the students.* **2.** In the end; at last; finally. ♦ *The movie became more and more exciting, until at length people were sitting on the edge of their chairs.*

**at liberty** *adv. or adj. phr.* Free to go somewhere or do something; not shut in or stopped. ♦ *The police promised to set the man at liberty if he told the names of the other robbers.*

**at loggerheads** *adj. or adv. phr.* In a quarrel; in a fight; opposing each other. ♦ *The two senators had long been at loggerheads on foreign aid.* ♦ *Because of their barking dog, the Morrises lived at loggerheads with their neighbors.*

**at long last** See AT LAST.

**at loose ends** *adj. phr.* Without a regular job or settled habits; uncertain what to do next; having nothing to do for a while; undecided; unsettled; restless. ♦ *Feeling at loose ends, I went for a long walk.* ♦ *He had finished college but hadn't found a job yet, so he was at loose ends.*

**at most** *or* **at the most** *adv. phr.* By the largest or most generous guess; at the upper limit; by the maximum account; not more than; at best; at worst. ♦ *It was a minor offense at most.* ♦ *He had been gone 15 minutes at the most.*

**at odds** *adj. phr.* In conflict or disagreement; opposed. ♦ *The boy and girl were married a week after they met and soon found themselves at odds about religion.*

**at once** *adv. phr.* Without delay; right now or right then; immediately. ♦ *Put a burning match next to a piece of paper and it will begin burning at once.*

**at one** *adj. phr.* **1.** In union or harmony; in agreement or sympathy. Not usually used informally. ♦ *He felt at one with all the poets who have sung of love.* **2.** Of the same opinion, in agreement. ♦ *Husband and wife were at one on everything but money.*

**at one's beck and call** *or* **at the beck and call of** *adj. phr.* Ready and willing to do whatever someone asks; ready to serve at a moment's notice. ♦ *A good parent isn't necessarily always at the child's beck and call.*

**at one's best** *prep. phr.* In best form; displaying one's best qualities. ♦ *Tim is at his best when he has had a long swim before a ballgame.*

**at one's door** *or* **at one's doorstep** *adv. phr.* Very close; very near where you live or work. ♦ *Johnny is very lucky because there's a swimming pool right at his doorstep.*

**at one's earliest convenience** *adv. phr* At the first moment when one is able to do something; used as a term of politeness. ♦ *Please answer at your earliest convenience.*

**at one's elbow** *adv. phr.* Close beside you; nearby. ♦ *The president rode in an open car with his wife at his elbow.*

**at one's feet** *adv. phr.* Under your influence or power. ♦ *She had a dozen men at her feet.* ♦ *Her voice kept audiences at her feet for years.*

**at one's fingertips** *adv. phr.* **1.** Within easy reach; quickly touched; nearby. ♦ *Seated in the cockpit, the pilot of a plane has many controls at his fingertips.* **2.** Readily usable as knowledge or skill; familiar. ♦ *He had several languages at his fingertips.*

**at one's heels** *adv. phr.* Close behind; as a constant follower or companion. ♦ *The boy got tired of having his little brother at his heels all day.*

**at one's leisure** See AT LEISURE 2.

**at one's service** *adv. phr.* **1.** Ready to serve or help you; prepared to obey your wish or command; subject to your orders. ♦ *He placed himself completely at the president's service.* ♦ *"Now I am at your service," the dentist told the next patient.* **2.** Available for your use; at your disposal. ♦ *He put a car and chauffeur at the visitor's service.*

**at one's wit's end** *or* **at wit's end** *adj. phr.* Having no ideas as to how to meet a difficulty or solve a problem; feeling puzzled after having used up all of your ideas or resources; not knowing what to do; puzzled. ♦ *The designer was at his wit's end: he had tried out wings of many different kinds but none would fly.*

**at one time** *adv. phr.* **1.** In the same moment; together. ♦ *Let's start the dance again all at one time.* **2.** At a certain time in the past; years ago. ♦ *At one time most school teachers were men, but today there are more women than men.*

**at pains** *adj. phr.* Making a special effort. ♦ *At pains to make a good impression, she was prompt for her appointment.*

**at present** *adv. phr.* At this time; now. ♦ *It took a long time to get started, but at present the road is half finished.* ♦ *At present the house is empty, but next week a family will move in.*

**at random** *adv. phr.* With no order, plan, or purpose; in a mixed-up, or thoughtless way. ♦ *His clothes were scattered about the room at random.*

**at sea¹** *adv. or adj. phr.* **1.** On an ocean voyage; on a journey by ship. ♦ *They had first met at sea.* **2.** Out on the ocean; away from land. ♦ *By the second day the ship was well out at sea.* ♦ *Charles had visited a ship in dock, but he had never been on a ship at sea.*

**at sea²** *adj. phr.* Not knowing what to do; bewildered; confused; lost. ♦ *The job was new to him, and for a few days he was at sea.*

**at sight** *or* **on sight** *adv. phr.* The first time the person or thing is seen; as soon as the person or thing is seen. ♦ *First graders learn to read many words on sight.* ♦ *Mary had seen many pictures of Grandfather, so she knew him on sight.*

**at ——— stage of the game** *adv. phr.* At (some) time during an activity; at (some) point. ♦ *At that stage of the game, our team was doing so poorly that we were ready to give up.* ♦ *It's hard to know what will happen at this stage of the game.*

**at stake** *adj. phr.* Depending, like a bet, on the outcome of something uncertain; in a position to be lost or gained. ♦ *The team played hard because the championship of the state was at stake.*

**at swords' points** *adj. phr.* Ready to start fighting; very much opposed to each other; hostile; quarreling. ♦ *The mayor and the reporter were always at swords' points.*

**at that** *adv. phr., informal* **1.** As it is; at that point; without more talk or waiting. ♦ *Ted was not quite satisfied with his haircut but let it go at that.* **2.** In addition; also. ♦ *Bill's seat mate on the plane was a girl and a pretty one at that.*

**at the drop of a hat** *adv. phr., informal* **1.** Without waiting; immediately; promptly. ♦ *If you need a baby-sitter quickly, call Mary, because she can come at the drop of a hat.* **2.** Whenever you have a chance; with very little cause or urging. ♦ *He was quarrelsome and ready to fight at the drop of a hat.*

**at the eleventh hour** *prep. phr.* At the last possible time. ♦ *Aunt Mathilda got married at the eleventh hour; after all, she was already 49 years old.*

**at the end of one's rope** See END OF ONE'S ROPE.

**at the end of the day** *adv. phr.* After all previous arrangements have been completed; finally; at last. ♦ *At the end of the day, the hostile foreign government will have to realize that it is better to cooperate with the U.N.*

**at the mercy of** *or* **at one's mercy** *adj. phr.* In the power of; subject to the will and wishes of; without defense against. ♦ *The small grocer was at the mercy of people he owed money to.*

**at the outset** *adv. phr.* At the start; at the beginning. ♦ *"You'll live in the cheaper barracks at the outset; later you can move into the better cabins," the camp director said to the new boys.*

**at the outside** *adv. phr.* Maximally; at the utmost. ♦ *This old house can cost no more than $40,000 at the outside.*

**at the point of** *prep.* Very near to; almost at or in. ♦ *When Mary broke her favorite bracelet, she was at the point of tears.* ♦ *The boy hurt in the accident lay at the point of death for a week, then he got well.*

**at the psychological moment** *v. phr.* At the critical moment; in the nick of time. ♦ *The ping-pong game stood at 21:21 when, at the psychological moment, the American team won with two slams, ending the game at 23:21.*

**at the ready** *adj. phr.* Ready for use. ♦ *The sailor stood at the bow, harpoon at the ready, as the boat neared the whale.*

**at the same time** *adv. phr.* **1.** In the same moment; together. ♦ *The two runners reached the finish line at the same time.*

**2.** In spite of the fact; even though; however; but; nevertheless. ♦ *John did pass the test; at the same time, he didn't know the subject very well.*

**at the seams** See BURST AT THE SEAMS.

**at the table** *or* **at table** *adv. phr.* At a meal; at the dinner table. ♦ *The telephone call came while they were all at table.*

**at the tip of one's tongue** *or* **on the tip of one's tongue** *adv. phr. informal* **1.** Almost spoken; at the point of being said. ♦ *It was at the tip of my tongue to tell him, when the phone rang.* **2.** Almost remembered; at the point where one can almost say it but cannot because it is forgotten. ♦ *I have his name on the tip of my tongue.*

**at the top of one's voice** *or* **at the top of one's lungs** *adv. phr.* As loud as one can; with the greatest possible sound; very loudly. ♦ *He was singing at the top of his voice.* ♦ *He shouted at the top of his lungs.*

**at this juncture** *adv. phr.* Now; at this critical point; at this conjuncture of affairs. ♦ *At this juncture it is wiser to retire than to fight a bankrupt company.*

**at this rate** *or* **at that rate** *adv. phr.* At a speed like this or that; with progress like this or that. ♦ *"Three 100's in the last four tests! At this rate you'll soon be teaching the subject," Tom said to Mary.*

**at times** *adv. phr.* Not often; not regularly; not every day; not every week; occasionally; sometimes. ♦ *At times Tom's mother lets him hold the baby.* ♦ *You can certainly be exasperating, at times!* ♦ *We have pie for dinner at times.*

**attribute to** *v. phr.* To believe something to have been said or written by someone. ♦ *The saying "An Iron Curtain has descended across Europe" is attributed to Winston Churchill.*

**at will** *adv. phr.* As you like; as you please or choose freely. ♦ *With an air conditioner you can enjoy comfortable temperatures at will.*

**at wits end** See AT ONE'S WIT'S END.

**at work** *adj. phr.* Busy at a job; doing work. ♦ *The teacher was soon hard at work correcting that day's test.* ♦ *Jim is at work on his car.*

**at worst** *or* **at the worst** *adv. phr.* **1.** Under the worst conditions; as the worst possibility. ♦ *When Don was caught cheating on the examination he thought that at worst he would get a scolding.* **2.** In the least favorable view; to say the worst about a thing. ♦ *The treasurer had certainly not stolen any of the club's money; at worst, he had forgotten to write down some of the things he had spent money for.*

**Aunt Tom** *n., slang, originally from Black English* A successful professional or business woman who, due to her success in a masculine profession, doesn't care about the women's liberation movement or the passing of the Equal Rights Amendment to the U.S. Constitution. ♦ *Hermione is a regular Aunt Tom; she'll never vote for the ERA.*

**average out** *v. phr.* To reach a certain average after proper calculation. ♦ *"My monthly salary averages out to no more than $1,500," the young teaching assistant sadly remarked.*

**avoid like the plague** *or* **shun as one would the plague** See GIVE WIDE BERTH TO.

**awake to** *v. phr.* To begin to understand something; become alert and watchful of something. ♦ *America had to awake to the dangers posed by domestic terrorism.*

**awkward age** *n.* Adolescence; awkwardness during adolescence. ♦ *Sue used to be an "ugly duckling" when she was at the awkward age, but today she is a glamorous fashion model.*

**AWOL** See ABSENT WITHOUT LEAVE.

**ax to grind** *n. phr., informal* Something to gain for yourself: a selfish reason. ♦ *In praising movies for classroom use he has an ax to grind; he sells motion picture equipment.*

**babe in the woods** *n. phr.* A person who is inexperienced or innocent in certain things. ♦ *He is a good driver, but as a mechanic he is just a babe in the woods.*

**baby** See WAR BABY.

**baby boom** *n.* A sudden increase in the birth rate. ♦ *The universities were filled to capacity due to the baby boom that followed World War II.*

**baby grand** *n.* A small grand piano no longer than three feet, maximally four feet. ♦ *This apartment can't take a regular grand piano, so we'll have to buy a baby grand.*

**baby kisser** *n., slang* A person campaigning for votes in his quest for elected political office; such persons often kiss little children in public. ♦ *Nixon was a baby kisser when he ran for vice president with Eisenhower.*

**back and forth** *adv.* Backwards and forwards. ♦ *The tiger is pacing back and forth in his cage.* Compare TO AND FRO.

**back away** *v.* To act to avoid or lessen one's involvement in something; draw or turn back; retreat. ♦ *The townspeople backed away from the building plan when they found out how much it would cost.*

**back door** *n., slang, citizen's band radio jargon* Rear of vehicle. ♦ *I am watching your back door.*

**back down** *or* **back off** *v., informal* To give up a claim; not follow up a threat. ♦ *Bill said he could beat Ted, but when Ted put up his fists Bill backed down.* ♦ *Harry claimed Joe had taken his book, but backed down when the teacher talked with him.*

**back in circulation** *adv. phr.* **1.** Socially active once again (said about people); back on the dating circuit after a divorce or a romantic breakup. ♦ *Now that Sally is divorced from Jim she is back in circulation.* **2.** Once again available to the public (said about types of paper money, rare coins, or other commercially available goods). ♦ *In the USA the two-dollar bill was back in circulation for a short time only in the 1950s and 1960s.*

**back in the saddle** *adv. phr.* Back in the daily routine. ♦ *After his prolonged illness and stay in the hospital, Joe is back in the saddle.*

**back number** *n.* Something out of fashion, or out of date. ♦ *Among today's young people a waltz like "The Blue Danube" is a back number.*

**backfire** *v.* To misfire; to have a reverse effect from what was intended. ♦ *Mimi's gossip about the Head of the Department backfired when people began to mistrust her.*

**backhanded compliment** *n. phr.* A remark that sounds like a compliment but is said sarcastically. ♦ *"Not bad for a girl" the coach said, offering a backhanded compliment.*

**back of** *or* **in back of** *prep.* **1.** In or at the rear of; to the back of; behind. ♦ *The garage is back of the house.* ♦ *Our car was in back of theirs at the traffic light.* **2.** *informal* Being a cause or reason for; causing. ♦ *Hard work was back of his success.* **3.** *informal* In support or encouragement of; helping. ♦ *Get in back of your team by cheering them at the game.*

**back one up on something** *v. phr.* To corroborate; to bear witness to the truth of what one has said. ♦ *"I was nowhere near the scene of the crime," Joe said. "You must back me up on that!"*

**back out** *v. phr.* **1.** To move backwards out of a place or enclosure. ♦ *Bob slowly backed his car out of the garage.* **2.** To withdraw from an activity one has promised to carry out. ♦ *Jim tried to back out of the engagement with Jane, but she insisted that they get married.*

**backseat driver** *n., informal* A bossy person in a car who always tells the driver what to do. ♦ *The man who drove the car became angry with the backseat driver.*

**back street** *n.* A street not near the main streets or from which it is hard to get to a main street. ♦ *We got lost in the back streets going through the city and it took us a half hour to find our way again.*

**back talk** *n.* A sassy, impudent reply. ♦ *Such back talk will get you nowhere, young man!*

**back the wrong horse** *v. phr.* To support a loser. ♦ *In voting for George Bush, voters in 1992 were backing the wrong horse.*

**back-to-back** *adv.* **1.** Immediately following. ♦ *The health clinic had back-to-back appointments for the new students during the first week of school.* **2.** Very close to, as if touching. ♦ *Sardines are always packed in the can back-to-back.*

**back to square one** *or* **back to the basics** *or* **back to the drawing board** *adv. phr.* To start at the beginning again in an attempt to correct whatever mistakes were made initially. ♦ *After the first American rockets misfired, NASA decided to go back to square one.*

**back to the salt mines** *informal* Back to the job; back to work; back to work that is as hard or as unpleasant as working in a salt mine would be.—An overworked phrase, used humorously. ♦ *The lunch hour is over, boys. Back to the salt mines!*

**back to the wall** *or* **back against the wall** *adv. phr.* In a trap, with no way to escape; in bad trouble. ♦ *The soldiers had their backs to the wall.* ♦ *He was in debt and could not get any help; his back was against the wall.* ♦ *The team had their backs to the wall in the second half.*

**back up** *v.* **1.** To move backwards. ♦ *The train was backing up.* **2.** To help or be ready to help; stay behind to help; agree with and speak in support of. ♦ *Jim has joined the Boy Scouts and his father is backing him up.* **3.** To move behind (another fielder) in order to catch the ball if he misses it. ♦ *The shortstop backed up the second baseman on the throw.*

**back-up** *adj.* Supplementary; auxiliary; kept in need for safety. ♦ *When at war, it is essential to keep the lines open for back-up troops and supplies.* ♦ *When the policeman saw what happened, he called in for back-up support.*

**backward and forward** *or* **backwards and forwards** *adv. phr.* To the full extent; in all details; thoroughly; completely. ♦ *He understood automobile engines backwards and forwards.*

**bad actor** *n., informal* A person or animal that is always fighting, quarreling, or doing bad things. ♦ *The boy was a bad actor and nobody liked him.*

**bad blood** *n., informal* Anger or misgivings due to bad relations in the past between individuals or groups. ♦ *There's a lot of bad blood between Max and Jack; I bet they'll never talk to each other again.* Compare BAD SHIT.

**bad egg** *n., slang* A ne'er-do-well; good-for nothing; a habitual offender. ♦ *The judge sent the bad egg to prison at last.*

**bad mouth (someone)** *v., slang* To say uncomplimentary or libelous things about someone; deliberately to damage another's reputation. ♦ *It's not nice to bad mouth people.*

**bad news** *n., slang* An event, thing, or person which is disagreeable, or an unpleasant surprise. ♦ *What's the new professor like?—He's all bad news to me.*

**bad paper** *n., slang* **1.** A check for which there are no funds in the bank. **2.** Counterfeit paper money. ♦ *Why are you so mad?—I was paid with some bad paper.*

**bad seed** *n. phr.* A person who never does anything well; a person who veers from the straight and narrow and acts like a criminal. ♦ *Jim is a bad seed; he doesn't belong in our family.*

**bad shit** *n., vulgar, avoidable* An unpleasant event or situation, such as a long-lasting and unsettled quarrel or recurring acts of vengeance preventing two people or two groups from reaching any kind of reconciliation. ♦ *There is so much bad shit between the two gangs that I bet there will be more killings this year.*

**bad trip** *n., slang, also used colloquially* A disturbing or frightening experience, such as terrifying hallucinations, while under the influence of drugs; hence, by colloquial extension any bad experience in general. ♦ *Why's John's face so distorted?—He had a bad trip.* ♦ *How was your math exam?—Don't mention it; it was a bad trip.*

**bag and baggage** *adv., informal* With all your clothes and other personal belongings, especially movable possessions; completely. ♦ *If they don't pay their hotel bill they will be put out bag and baggage.*

**bail out¹** *v.* **1.** To secure release from prison until trial by leaving or promising money or property for a while.

♦*When college students got into trouble with the police, the college president would always bail them out.* **2.** *informal* To free from trouble by giving or lending money.* ♦*He started a small business, which prospered after his father had to bail him out a couple of times.*

**bail out**[2] *v.* To jump from an airplane and drop with a parachute. ♦*When the second engine failed, the pilot told everyone to bail out.*

**bail out**[3] *v.* To dip water from a filling or leaking boat; throw water out of a boat to prevent its sinking. ♦*Both men were kept busy bailing out the rowboat after it began to leak.*

**baker's dozen** *n., informal* Thirteen. ♦*"How many of the jelly doughnuts, Sir?" the salesclerk asked. "Oh, make it a baker's dozen."*

**balance** See HANG IN THE BALANCE, OFF BALANCE.

**balk at** *or* **baulk at** *or* **jib at** *v. phr.* To be unwilling to face or agree to something. ♦*The Iraqis kept balking at every sensible proposal made to them by the U.N.*

**ball game** *n., slang, also informal* The entire matter at hand; the whole situation; the entire contest. ♦*You said we can get a second mortgage for the house? Wow! That's a whole new ball game.*

**ball of fire** *n., informal* A person with great energy and ability; a person who can do something very well. ♦*He did poorly in school but as a salesman he is a ball of fire.* ♦*The new shortstop is a good fielder but certainly no ball of fire in batting.*

**ball up** *v., slang* To make a mess of; confuse. ♦*Don't ball me up.* ♦*Hal balled up the business with his errors.*—Often used in the passive. ♦*He was so balled up that he did not know if he was coming or going.*

**baloney** *n., informal* Nonsense, unbelievable, trite, or trivial. ♦*John brags that he's won the $10 million lottery, and I think it's just a lot of baloney.* ♦*"Will you marry Joe?" mother asked. "Baloney," Susie answered with a disgusted look.*

**banana oil** *n., slang* Flattery that is an obvious exaggeration; statements that are obviously made with an ulterior motive. ♦*Cut out the banana oil; flattery will get you nowhere!*

**band together** *v. phr.* To join a group to exert united force. ♦*The inhabitants of the ecologically threatened area banded together to stop the company from building new smokestacks.*

**bandy around** *v. phr.* To talk disrespectfully about something or someone or without caring whether what is said is true or false; to chatter away about something in a facetious, nonserious manner. ♦*Several ridiculous ideas were bandied about on how to rescue the company, but the only ones that made sense came from the stockholders.*

**bang up** *adj., informal* Very successful; very good; splendid; excellent. ♦*The football coach has done a bang-up job this season.* ♦*John did a bang-up job painting the house.*

**bank on** *v., informal* To depend on; put one's trust in; rely on. ♦*He knew he could bank on public indignation to change things, if he could once prove the dirty work.* ♦*The students were banking on the team to do its best in the championship game.*

**baptism of fire** *n. phr.* The experience of the first real battle with live ammunition and a real chance to die. ♦*Many a nineteen-year-old had his baptism of fire during the Gulf War.*

**bargain for** *or* **bargain on** *v.* To be ready for; expect. ♦*When John started a fight with the smaller boy he got more than he bargained for.* ♦*The final cost of building the house was much more than they had bargained on.*

**bargain hunter** *n. phr.* A person who likes to shop in inexpensive stores, such as factory outlets and garage sales, and always looks for the lowest possible price. ♦*Having lived in the bargaining environment of the Far East, my wife and I have become regular bargain hunters.*

**barge in** *v. phr., informal* To appear uninvited at someone's house or apartment, or to interrupt a conversation. ♦*I'm sorry for barging in like that, Sir, but my car died on me and there is no pay phone anywhere.*

**bark up the wrong tree** *v. phr., informal* To choose the wrong person to deal with or the wrong course of action; mistake an aim. ♦*If he thinks he can fool me, he is barking up the wrong* tree. ♦ *He is barking up the wrong tree when he blames his troubles on bad luck.* ♦ *The police were looking for a tall thin man, but were barking up the wrong tree; the thief was short and fat.*

**bark worse than one's bite** *informal* Sound or speech more frightening or worse than your actions. ♦ *The small dog barks savagely, but his bark is worse than his bite.* ♦ *The boss sometimes talks roughly to the men, but they know that his bark is worse than his bite.* ♦ *She was always scolding her children, but they knew her bark was worse than her bite.*

**barn burner** *n. phr. (sports terminology)* A very close game with an uncertain outcome to the end. ♦ *The Bulls beat the Pistons 110 to 109 in a barn burner.*

**base on balls** *n.* First base given to a baseball batter who is pitched four balls outside of the strike zone. ♦ *He was a good judge of pitchers and often received bases on balls.*

**basket case** *n., slang, also informal* **1.** A person who has had both arms and both legs cut off as a result of war or other misfortune. **2.** A helpless person who is unable to take care of himself, as if carted around in a basket by others. ♦ *Stop drinking, or else you'll wind up a basket case!*

**bat an eye** *or* **bat an eyelash** *v. phr., informal* To show surprise, fear, or interest; show your feelings.—Used in negative sentences. ♦ *Bill told his story without batting an eyelash, although not a word of it was true.* Compare STRAIGHT FACE.

**bat around** See BANDY AROUND.

**bats in one's belfry** *or* **bats in the belfry** *n. phr., slang* Wild ideas in his mind; disordered senses; great mental confusion. ♦ *When he talked about going to the moon he was thought to have bats in his belfry.*

**batting average** *n. phr.* Degree of accomplishment (originally used as a baseball term). ♦ *Dr. Grace has a great batting average with her heart transplant operations.*

**battle of nerves** *n. phr.* A contest of wills during which the parties do not fight physically but try to wear each other out. ♦ *It has been a regular battle of nerves to get the new program accepted at the local state university.*

**bawl out** *v., informal* To reprove in a loud or rough voice; rebuke sharply; scold. ♦ *The teacher bawled us out for not handing in our homework.*

**be about to** *or* **be just about to do something** *v. phr.* Be at the verge of starting a certain act of doing something. ♦ *Mr. Brown was about to play tennis when it started to rain.*

**beach bunny** *n., slang* An attractive girl seen on beaches—mostly to show off her figure; one who doesn't get into the water and swim. ♦ *What kind of a girl is Susie?—She's a beach bunny; she always comes to the Queen's Surf on Waikiki but I've never seen her swim.*

**be a drag** *v. phr.* Be boring; soporiphic, somniferous ♦ *My math teacher is the biggest drag I've ever met.* ♦ *People who overexplain obvious things can be a drag.*

**be a fly on the wall** *v. phr.* To eavesdrop on a secret conversation. ♦ *How I wish I could be a fly on the wall to hear what my fiance's parents are saying about me!* See EAVESDROP.

**be after someone or something** *v. phr.* To hound or pursue someone or something; to chase or keep after a person or a goal. ♦ *John is after Mary in a real big way.* ♦ *Ted is after his boss' job.*

**be a full house** *or* **have a full house** *v. phr.* To be so crowded that there is not enough space for anyone else. ♦ *Because there was a full house there was only standing room left at the concert.*

**be a good hand at** *v. phr.* To be talented, gifted, or skilled in some activity. ♦ *Florian is a good hand at both gardening and building.*

**be all at sea** *v. phr.* To find oneself at a loss; to have lost one's way; to be unable to find where one has to go, or what the truth is in a given matter. ♦ *When it comes to Chinese grammar, Steven is all at sea.*

**be all for someone or something** *or* **be for some or something** *v. phr.* To support, to be in favor of. ♦ *How can one be for that piece of legislation, when one knows that it will benefit only the privileged?* ♦ *The urban masses are all for the Reverend Jessie Jackson.*

**be an item** *v. phr.* To be a couple; belong to one another. ♦ *No one is surprised to* *see them together anymore; it is generally recognized that they are an item.*

**be a poor hand at** *v. phr.* To be inept, untalented, or clumsy in some activity. ♦ *Archibald is a poor hand at tennis so no one wants to play with him.* Contrast BE A GOOD HAND AT.

**bear a grudge** *v. phr.* To persist in bearing ill feeling toward someone after a quarrel or period of hostility. ♦ *Come on, John, be a good sport and don't bear a grudge because I beat you at golf.* Contrast BURY THE HATCHET.

**bear a hand** See LEND A HAND.

**bear down** *v.* **1.** To press or push harder; work hard at; give full strength and attention. ♦ *The sergeant bears down on lazy soldiers.* **2.** To move toward in an impressive or threatening way.— Often used with *on.* ♦ *While he was crossing the street a big truck bore down on him.* ♦ *The little ship tried to escape when the big pirate ship bore down.*

**bear down on** *or* **upon** *v. phr.* To draw constantly nearer with great speed and force. ♦ *The police cars were bearing down on the bank robbers' get-away car.*

**beard the lion in his den** *or* **beard somebody in his den** *v. phr.* Face the enemy in his own surroundings where he can be the most dangerous. ♦ *When the marines entered Baghdad to topple the despot's government, they were bearding the lion in his den.*

**bear fruit** *v. phr.* To yield results. ♦ *We hope that the company's new investment policy will bear fruit.*

**bear in mind** See IN MIND.

**bear in the air** *or* **bear in the sky** *n. phr., slang, citizen's band jargon* A police helicopter flying overhead watching for speeders. ♦ *Slow down, good buddy, there's a bear in the air.*

**bear one's cross** See CARRY ONE'S CROSS.

**bear out** *v.* To show to be right; prove; support. ♦ *Modern findings do not bear out the old belief that the earth is flat.* ♦ *Seward's faith in his purchase of Alaska was borne out, even though it was once called "Seward's Folly."*

**bear the brunt** *v. phr.* To shoulder or manage the hardest part of an undertaking, such as work, negotiations, or battle. ♦ *The marines bore the brunt of many a battle during the Gulf War.*

**bear trap** *n., slang, citizen's band radio jargon* A police radar unit designed to catch speeders. ♦ *Watch the bear trap at exit 101.*

**bear up** *v.* **1.** To hold up; carry; support; encourage. ♦ *The old bridge can hardly bear up its own weight any more.* **2.** To keep up one's courage or strength; last.—Often used with *under.* ♦ *This boat will bear up under hurricane winds.* ♦ *She bore up well at the funeral.*

**bear watching** *v. phr.* **1.** To be worth watching or paying attention to; have a promising future. ♦ *That young ball player will bear watching.* **2.** To be dangerous or untrustworthy. ♦ *Those tires look badly worn; they will bear watching.*

**bear with** *v., formal* To have patience with; not get angry with. ♦ *Your little sister is sick. Try to bear with her when she cries.* ♦ *It is hard to bear with criticism.*

**be a steal** *v. phr.* To cost very little; to be inexpensive. ♦ *"You mean to say that you paid only $8,000 for that fantastic new sports car? That's a steal!" Joe cried with envy.*

**beat about the bush** *or* **beat around the bush** *v. phr., slang* To talk about things without giving a clear answer; avoid the question or the point. ♦ *He beat about the bush for a half hour without coming to the point.*

**beat a retreat** *v. phr.* **1.** To give a signal, esp. by beating a drum, to go back. ♦ *The Redcoats' drums were beating a retreat.* **2.** To run away. ♦ *The cat beat a hasty retreat when he saw the dog coming.*

**beat around the bush** See BEAT ABOUT THE BUSH.

**beat down** *v.* **1.** To crush or break the spirit of; win over; conquer. ♦ *All their defenses were beaten down by the tanks.* **2.** *informal a.* To try to get reduced; force down by discussing. ♦ *Can we beat down the price?* **b.** To persuade or force (someone) to accept a lower price or easier payments. ♦ *He tried to beat us down, so we did not sell the house.* **3.** To shine brightly or hotly. ♦ *At noon the sun beat down on our heads as we walked home.*

**beaten path** *or* **track** *n. phr.* The usual route or way of operating that has been conventionally established. ♦ *If we* *always follow the beaten path, we'll never have the courage to try something new.*

**beat into one's head** *v. phr., informal* To teach by telling again and again; repeat often; drill, also, to be cross and punish often. ♦ *Tom is lazy and stubborn and his lessons have to be beaten into his head.*

**beat it** *v., slang* To go away in a hurry; get out quickly. ♦ *When he heard the crash he beat it as fast as he could.*—Often used as a command. ♦ *The big boy said, "Beat it, kid. We don't want you with us."*

**beat one to it** *v. phr.* To arrive or get ahead of another person. ♦ *I was about to call you, John, but you have beat me to it! Thanks for calling me.*

**beat one's brains out** or **beat one's brains** *v. phr., slang* To try very hard to understand or think out something difficult; tire yourself out by thinking. ♦ *It was too hard for him and he beat his brains out trying to get the answer.*

**beat one's gums** *v. phr., slang* To engage in idle talk, or meaningless chatter; generally to talk too much. ♦ *"Stop beating your gums, Jack," Joe cried. "I am falling asleep."*

**beat one's head against a wall** *v. phr.* To struggle uselessly against something that can't be beaten or helped; not succeed after trying very hard. ♦ *Trying to make him change his mind is just beating your head against a wall.*

**be at pains** *v. phr.* To be extremely desirous to do something; to take the trouble to do something. ♦ *The captain was at pains to see that everybody got safely into the lifeboats.*

**beat the bushes** also **beat the brush** *v. phr., informal* To try very hard to find or get something. ♦ *The mayor was beating the bushes for funds to build the playground.*

**beat the drum** *v. phr.* To attract attention in order to advertise something or to promote someone, such as a political candidate. ♦ *Mrs. Smith has been beating the drum in her town in order to get her husband elected mayor.*

**beat the —— out of** or **lick the —— out of** or **whale the —— out of** *v. phr., informal* To beat hard; give a bad beating to.—Used with several words after *the*, as *crap, daylights, living daylights,*

*tar.* ♦ *The big kid told Charlie that he would beat the daylights out of him if Charlie came in his yard again.*

**beat the pants off** *v. phr.* **1.** To prevail over someone in a race or competition. ♦ *Jim beat the pants off George in the swimming race.* **2.** To give someone a severe physical beating. ♦ *Jack beat the pants off the two young men who were trying to hold him up in Central Park.*

**beat the rap** *v. phr.* To escape the legal penalty one ought to receive. ♦ *In spite of the strong evidence against him, the prisoner beat the rap and went free.*

**beat the shit out of** *v. phr., vulgar, avoidable* See KNOCK THE LIVING DAYLIGHTS OUT OF.

**beat time** *v. phr.* To follow the rhythm of a piece of music by moving one's fingers or feet. ♦ *Jack was beating time with his foot during the concert, which annoyed his neighbor.*

**beat to** *v., informal* To do something before someone else does it. ♦ *We were planning to send a rocket into space but the Russians beat us to it.*

**beat to the punch** or **beat to the draw** *v. phr., slang* To do something before another person has a chance to do it. ♦ *John was going to apply for the job, but Ted beat him to the draw.* ♦ *Lois bought the dress before Mary could beat her to the punch.*

**beat up** *v., informal* To give a hard beating to; hit hard and much; thrash; whip. ♦ *When the new boy first came, he had to beat up several neighborhood bullies before they would leave him alone.*—Also used with *on*. ♦ *The tough boy said to Bill, "If you come around here again, I'll beat up on you."*

**beauty sleep** *n.* A nap or rest taken to improve the appearance. ♦ *She took her beauty sleep before the party.* ♦ *Many famous beauties take a beauty sleep every day.*

**beaver** *n., slang, vulgar, avoidable, citizen's band radio jargon* A female, especially one driving along the highway and operating a CB radio. ♦ *I didn't know there was a beaver aboard that eighteen wheeler.*

**be blown away** *v. phr.* Be extremely pleased and enchanted by someone or something. ♦ *"I was blown away with* your presentation," a commentator said, when Jim finished his paper.

**be cast away** *v. phr.* To be shipwrecked. ♦ *The Swiss Family Robinson were cast away just like Robinson Crusoe.*

**because of** *prep.* On account of; by reason of; as a result of. ♦ *The train arrived late because of the snowstorm.*

**become of** *v. phr.* To happen to; befall. ♦ *What will become of the children, now that both parents are in jail?*

**bed down** *v. phr.* To prepare a temporary place to go to sleep. ♦ *The mountain climbers bedded down in a different hut each night during their excursion.*

**bed of nails** *n. phr.* A difficult or unhappy situation or set of circumstances. ♦ *"There are days when my job is a regular bed of nails," Jim groaned.* Contrast BED OF ROSES.

**bed of roses** *or* **bowl of cherries** *n. phr.* A pleasant easy place, job, or position; an easy life. ♦ *A coal miner's job is not a bed of roses.* ♦ *After nine months of school, summer camp seemed a bowl of cherries.*

**bed of thorns** *n. phr.* A thoroughly unhappy time or difficult situation. ♦ *I'm sorry I changed jobs; my new one turned out to be a bed of thorns.*

**beef about** *v. phr.* To complain about something. ♦ *Stop beefing about your job, Jack. You could have done a lot worse!*

**beef up** *v., informal* To make stronger by adding men or equipment; make more powerful; reinforce. ♦ *The general beefed up his army with more big guns and tanks.*

**bee in one's bonnet** *n. phr., informal* A fixed idea that seems fanciful, odd, or crazy. ♦ *Grandmother has some bee in her bonnet about going to the dance.*

**be even-Steven** *v. phr.* To be in a position of owing no favors or debt to someone. ♦ *Yesterday you paid for my lunch, so today I paid for yours; now we're even-Steven.*

**be far out** *v. phr.* To be so unusual as to defy credibility or likeability. ♦ *My history teacher is so far out that I have difficulty understanding what she's saying.*

**before long** *adv. phr.* In a short time; without much delay; in a little while, soon. ♦ *Class will be over before long.* ♦ *We were tired of waiting and hoped the bus would come before long.*

**before one can say Jack Robinson** *adv. cl., informal* Very quickly; suddenly.— An overused phrase. ♦ *Before I could say Jack Robinson, the boy was gone.* Compare IN A FLASH, RIGHT AWAY.

**before you know it** *adv. phr.* Sooner than one would expect. ♦ *Don't despair; we'll be finished with this work before you know it!*

**be from** *v. phr.* To hail from a certain place; be the native of a certain country or locality. ♦ *"Where are you from?" the teacher asked the new student. "I am from Shanghai, China," she answered.*

**beg** See BEGGING.

**be game** *v. phr.* To be cooperative, willing, sporting. ♦ *When I asked Charlie to climb Mount McKinley with us, he said he was game if we were.*

**begin with** *adv. phr.* As a preliminary statement; in the first place. ♦ *To begin with, you are far too young to get married.*

**beg off** *v.* To ask to be excused. ♦ *I accepted an invitation to a luncheon, but a headache made me beg off.*

**be good!** *v. phr.* A frequent substitute for "Good-bye" or "au revoir." ♦ *When John left Jim's house he said, "Be good!" while they were shaking hands.*

**beg the question** *v. phr., literary* To accept as true something that is still being argued about, before it is proved true; avoid or not answer a question or problem. ♦ *Laura told Tom that he must believe her argument because she was right. Father laughed and told Laura she was begging the question.*

**be hard on** *v. phr.* To be strict or critical with another; be severe. ♦ *"Don't be so hard on Jimmy," Tom said. "He is bound to rebel as he gets older."*

**behind bars** *adv. phr.* In jail; in prison. ♦ *He was a pickpocket and had spent many years behind bars.* ♦ *That boy is always in trouble and will end up behind bars.*

**behind one's back** *adv. phr.* When one is absent; without one's knowledge or consent; in a dishonest way; secretly; sneakily. ♦ *Say it to his face, not behind his back.* ♦ *It is not right to criticize a person behind his back.*

**behind the eight-ball** *adj. phr., slang* In a difficult position; in trouble. ♦ *Bill* *can't dance and has no car, so he is behind the eight-ball with the girls.*

**behind the scenes** *adv. phr.* Out of sight; unknown to most people; privately. ♦ *Much of the committee's work was done behind the scenes.* ♦ *John was president of the club, but behind the scenes Lee told him what to do.*

**behind the times** *adj. phr.* Using things not in style; still following old ways; old-fashioned. ♦ *The science books of 30 years ago are behind the times now.*

**behind time** *adv. or adj. phr.* **1a.** Behind the correct time; slow. ♦ *That clock is behind time.* **1b.** Behind schedule; late. ♦ *The train is running behind time today.* **2.** Not keeping up; not at the proper time; overdue. ♦ *Your lessons are good, but why are you behind time?* ♦ *We are behind time in paying the rent.*

**be iffy** *v. phr.* To be questionable, or uncertain as to the desired outcome. ♦ *It's iffy whether there will be any pay raises this year, because the state is deeply in the red.*

**be-in** *n., slang, hippie culture* A gathering or social occasion with or without a discernible purpose, often held in a public place like a park or under a large circus tent. ♦ *The youngsters really enjoyed the great springtime jazz be-in at the park.*

**be in a stew** *v. phr.* To be worried, harassed, upset. ♦ *Al has been in a stew ever since he got word that his sister was going to marry his worst enemy.*

**be in bed with** *v. phr.* To be in alliance with an individual or a group of people; to work for the same cause. ♦ *Allegedly Saddam Hussein was in bed with the Al Qaeda terrorists.* ♦ *In some cities the police are in bed with the gangs.*

**be in good hands** *v. phr.* To be well cared for; trustworthily treated, or guarded. ♦ *"We are sure our daughter Suzanne is in good hands with the nuns in Lausanne, Switzerland," said the girl's father.*

**be in labor** *v. phr.* To be in parturition; experience the contractions of childbirth. ♦ *Jane had been in labor for eight hours before her twin daughters were finally born.*

**be in someone else's shoes** *v. phr.* To be in someone else's situation. ♦ *Fred has had so much trouble recently that we ought to be grateful we're not in his shoes.*

**be into something** *v. phr., informal* To have taken something up partly as a hobby, partly as a serious interest of sorts (basically resulting from the new consciousness and self-realization movement that originated in the late Sixties). ♦ *Did you know that Syd is seriously into transcendental meditation?* ♦ *Jack found out that his teenage son is into pot smoking and gave him a serious scolding.*

**be itching to** *v. phr.* To have a very strong desire to do something. ♦ *Jack is itching to travel abroad.*

**be it so** See SO BE IT.

**belabor the point** *v. phr.* To overexplain something to the point of obviousness, resulting in ridicule. ♦ *"Lest I belabor the point," the teacher said, "I must repeat the importance of teaching good grammar in class."*

**believe it or not,** *or* **you may not believe it** Often heard when one announces that something unusual will be communicated.—A proverb. ♦ *Believe it or not, I have won the Lottery! You may not believe it, but I got nominated for the Pulitzer Prize!*

**believe one's ears** *v. phr.* **1.** To believe what one hears; trust one's hearing.— Used with a negative or limiter, or in an interrogative or conditional sentence. ♦ *He thought he heard a horn blowing in the distance, but he could not believe his ears.* **2.** To be made sure of (something). ♦ *Is he really coming? I can hardly believe my ears.*

**believe one's eyes** *v. phr.* **1.** To believe what one sees; trust one's eyesight.— Used with a negative or limiter or in an interrogative or conditional sentence. ♦ *Is that a plane? Can I believe my eyes?* **2.** To be made sure of seeing something. ♦ *She saw him there but she could hardly believe her eyes.*

**bellyache** *v.* To constantly complain. ♦ *Jim is always bellyaching about the amount of work he is required to do.*

**belly up** *adj., informal* Dead, bankrupt, or financially ruined. ♦ *Tom and Dick struggled on for months with their tiny computer shop, but last year they went belly up.*

**belly up** *v., informal* To go bankrupt, become afunctional; to die. ♦ *Uncompetitive small businesses must eventually all belly up.*

**be looking up** *v .phr.* To be promising or improving. ♦ *Now that I got the new job, my life is looking up again.*

**below par** *adj.* or *adv.* Below standard. ♦ *Bob was fired because his work has been below par for several months now.* Contrast UP TO PAR *or* UP TO SNUFF.

**below the belt** *adv. phr.* **1.** In the stomach; lower than is legal in boxing. ♦ *He struck the other boy below the belt.* **2.** *informal* In an unfair or cowardly way; against the rules of sportsmanship or justice; unsportingly; wrongly. ♦ *Pete told the students to vote against Harry because he was bound to a wheelchair and would therefore make a poor congressman, but they thought Pete was hitting below the belt.*

**belt out** *v., slang* To sing with rough rhythm and strength; shout out. ♦ *She belted out ballads and hillbilly songs one after another all evening.* ♦ *Young people enjoy belting out songs.*

**be my guest!** *v. phr.* Said to someone wishing to borrow something not too valuable or worth returning it; also said to someone who wants one to do him or her a small favor such as giving him or her a seat on a bus, etc. ♦ *"Can I borrow that red tie?" Joe asked his roommate Tim. "But of course! Be my guest!" Tim answered.*

**bench warmer** See WARM THE BENCH.

**bend one's ear** *v. phr.* To talk for a long time without any pause or interruption. ♦ *"Let's go home, it is getting late," Joe said, but his host kept bending his ear for two more painful hours.*

**bend over backward** *or* **lean over backward** *v. phr., informal* To try so hard to avoid a mistake that you make the opposite mistake instead; do the opposite of something that you know you should not do; do too much to avoid doing the wrong thing; also, make a great effort; try very hard. ♦ *Mary was afraid the girls at her new school would be stuck up, but they leaned over backward to make her feel at home.*

**beneath contempt** *adj. phr.* Something so bad or so reprehensible that it doesn't even seem worthy of one's looking down on it; usually said in exaggeration. ♦ *Joe's conduct at the governor's inaugural ball was beneath contempt.*

**beneath one** *adj. phr.* Below one's ideals or dignity. ♦ *Bob felt it would have been beneath him to work for such low wages.*

**benefit of the doubt** *v. phr.* If someone is accused of a crime or a misdemeanor but is not proven guilty, one is entitled to a presumption of innocence in a court of law. In private life when we are not sure whether to believe someone or not, we may wish to extend them the presumption of innocence, i.e., the "benefit of the doubt." ♦ *It's better to give people the benefit of the doubt than to go around accusing innocent friends.*

**bent on** *or* **bent upon** Very decided, determined, or set. ♦ *The sailors were bent on having a good time.* ♦ *The policeman saw some boys near the school after dark and thought they were bent on mischief.* ♦ *The bus was late, and the driver was bent upon reaching the school on time.*

**bent out of shape** *adj. phr.* **1.** To be distorted from one's or an object's original, proper form. ♦ *The plane was so full of luggage that my suitcase was bent all out of shape.* **2.** angry. ♦ *My boss treated me so unfairly that after the meeting I was bent out of shape.*

**be news to** *v. phr.* To receive a surprising piece of unexpected or new information. ♦ *It is news to me that my spinster sister Matilda eloped to Hawaii with Algernon Doolittle.*

**be nuts about** *v. phr.* To be enthusiastic or very keen about someone or something; be greatly infatuated with someone. ♦ *Hermione is nuts about modern music.* ♦ *"I am nuts about you, Helen," Jim said. "Please let's get married!"*

**be off** *v. phr.* **1.** *v.* To be in error; miscalculate. ♦ *The estimator was off by at least 35% on the value of the house.* **2.** *v.* To leave. ♦ *Jack ate his supper in a hurry and was off without saying goodbye.* **3.** *adj.* Cancelled; terminated. ♦ *The weather was so bad that we were told that the trip was off.* **4.** *adj.* Crazy. ♦ *I'm sure Aunt Mathilda is a bit off; no one in her right mind would say such things.* **5.** *adj.* Free from work; having vacation time. ♦ *Although we were off for the rest of the day, we couldn't go to the beach because it started to rain.*

**be on** *v. phr.* **1.** To be in operation; be in the process of being presented. ♦ *The news is on now on Channel 2; it will be off in five minutes.* **2.** To be in the process of happening; to take place. ♦ *We cannot travel now to certain parts of Africa, as there is a civil war on there right now.* **3.** To be on duty. ♦ *"Is the night guard on Saturday and Sunday?" the new tenant asked the landlady. "No, he's off on weekends," she answered.*

**be oneself** *v.* To act naturally; act normally without trying unduly to impress others. ♦ *Just try being yourself; I promise people will like you more.*

**be on one** *v. phr.* To be the task of a given member of a company to pick up the bill in a restaurant, etc. ♦ *"By the way, this lunch was on me," said Uncle Joe to everyone's delight.*

**be on the outs with** *v. phr.* To not be on speaking terms with someone; be in disagreement with someone. ♦ *Jane and Tom have been on the outs with one another since Tom started to date another woman.*

**be on the verge of** *v. phr.* To be about to do something; be very close to. ♦ *We were on the verge of going bankrupt when, unexpectedly, my wife won the lottery and our business was saved.*

**be on to** *v. phr.* To understand the motives of someone; not be deceived. ♦ *Jack keeps telling us how wealthy his family is, but we are on to him.*

**be onto a good thing** *v. phr.* To understand and avail oneself of a fortunate circumstance. ♦ *Jim's secret as a writer is that he always knows when he is on to a good thing.*

**be out** *v. phr.* **1.** To not be at home or at one's place of work. ♦ *I tried to call but they told me that Al was out.* **2.** To be unacceptable; not be considered; impossible. ♦ *I suggested that we hire more salespeople but the boss replied that such a move was positively out.* **3.** To be poorer by; suffer a loss of. ♦ *Unless more people came to the church picnic, we realized we would be out $500. at least.* **4.** To be in circulation, in print, published. ♦ *Jane said that her new novel won't be out for at*

least another month. **5.** A baseball term indicating that a player has been declared either unfit to continue or punished by withdrawing him. ♦ *The spectators thought that John was safe at third base, but the umpire said he was out.* **6.** To be on duty in public, usually out of doors, e.g. policeman or mailman, etc. ♦ *Why are there so many police officers out today?* **7.** To be made known. ♦ *The government wanted to keep secret the story about the girlfriend of the president but it is out now.* **8.** To be unconscious. ♦ *When Jim was hit by the car behind him, he was out for about two minutes.*

**be out of it** *v. phr.* **1.** To not be aware of what is happening around one. ♦ *Joe has been studying so hard for his finals that he didn't get any sleep for several days; the poor guy is totally out of it.* **2.** To be thoroughly exhausted. ♦ *Dad has been working so hard finishing the basement that he is out of it for the rest of the evening.*

**be out to** *v. phr.* To intend to do; to plan to commit. ♦ *The police felt that the gang may be out to rob another store.*

**be over** *v. phr.* To be ended; be finished. ♦ *The show was over by 11 P.M.* ♦ *The war will soon be over.*

**be peanuts** *v. phr.* To be of very little value due to the great abundance and commonality of the item in question. ♦ *"How much did you pay for that used computer?" "Fifty bucks." "Hey, that's really peanuts."*

**be seeing you!** *v. phr.* (short for nice to be seeing you, instead of good-bye) Farewell! ♦ *"Be seeing you," Joe said before he hung up the telephone.*

**be set on** *or* **upon** *v. phr.* To be determined about something. ♦ *Tom is set upon leaving his Chicago job for Tokyo, Japan, although he speaks only English.*

**beside oneself** *adj. phr.* Very much excited; somewhat crazy. ♦ *She was beside herself with fear.* ♦ *He was beside himself, he was so angry.* ♦ *When his wife heard of his death, she was beside herself.*

**beside the point** *or* **beside the question** *adj. or adv. phr.* Off the subject; about something different. ♦ *What you meant to do is beside the point; the fact is you didn't do it.*

**best man** *n.* The groom's aid (usually his best friend or a relative) at a wedding. ♦ *When Agnes and I got married, my brother Gordon was my best man.*

**best-seller** *n.* An item (primarily said of books) that outsells other items of a similar sort. ♦ *Catherine Neville's novel* The Eight *has been a national best-seller for months.* ♦ *Among imported European cars, the Volkswagen is a best-seller.*

**be that as it may** *adv. phr.* Nevertheless. ♦ *"Be that as it may," said Mr. Smith before concluding his speech, "I am still opposed to the idea of appeasing a tyrannical regime."*

**be the making of** *v. phr.* To account for the success of someone or something. ♦ *The strict discipline that we had to undergo in graduate school was the making of many a successful professor.* ♦ *The relatively low cost and high gas mileage are the making of Chevrolet's Geo Metro cars.*

**bet one's boots** *or* **bet one's bottom dollar** *or* **bet one's shirt** *v. phr., informal* **1.** To bet all you have. ♦ *This horse will win. I would bet my bottom dollar on it.* ♦ *Jim said he would bet his boots that he would pass the examination.* **2.** *or* **bet one's life.** To feel very sure; have no doubt. ♦ *Was I scared when I saw the bull running at me? You bet your life I was!*

**bet on it** *v. phr.* A guarantee given by someone during a conversation indicating that the listener feels certain about what was asserted. *"Will we see you at Nancy's wedding?" father asked. "You can bet on it," Nancy's brother replied.*

**bet on the wrong horse** *v. phr., informal* To base your plans on a wrong guess about the result of something; misread the future; misjudge a coming event. ♦ *To count on the small family farm as an important thing in the American future now looks like betting on the wrong horse.*

**better half** *n., informal* One's marriage partner (mostly said by men about their wives.) ♦ *"This is my better half, Mary," said Joe.*

**better late than never** It is better to come or do something late than never.—A proverb. ♦ *The firemen didn't arrive at the house until it was half burned, but it was better late than never.*

**better off** *adj. phr.* Richer, wealthier. ♦ *My neighbors the Smiths are a lot better off than we are.*

**better off without** *adj. phr.* In a more advantageous position in the absence of some desired possession. ♦ *John is really better off without a car than with one. He is blind in one eye and kept getting into all sorts of traffic accidents.*

**better safe than sorry** Often heard when people are making seemingly unnecessary preparations, such as getting gas masks for a feared chemical attack by terrorists.—A proverb. ♦ *"Better safe than sorry," Tim said, and kept on practicing putting on his gas mask.*

**better than** *prep. phr.* More than; greater than; at a greater rate than. ♦ *The car was doing better than eighty miles an hour.* ♦ *It is better than three miles to the station.*

**between a rock and a hard place** See BETWEEN THE DEVIL AND THE DEEP BLUE SEA.

**between life and death** *adv. phr.* In danger of dying or being killed; with life or death possible. ♦ *He held on to the mountainside between life and death while his friends went to get help.*

**between the devil and the deep blue sea** *or literary* **between two fires** *or* **between a rock and a hard place** *adv. phr.* Between two dangers or difficulties, not knowing what to do. ♦ *The pirates had to fight and be killed or give up and be hanged; they were between the devil and the deep blue sea.* ♦ *The boy was between a rock and a hard place; he had to go home and be whipped or stay in town all night and be picked up by the police.* ♦ *When the man's wife and her mother got together, he was between two fires.*

**between two shakes of a lamb's tail** See BEFORE ONE CAN SAY JACK ROBINSON.

**be up to no good** *v. phr., informal* To be plotting and conniving to commit some illegal act or crime. ♦ *"Let's hurry!" Susan said to her husband. "It's dark here and those hoodlums obviously are up to no good."*

**be up to something** *v. phr., informal* **1.** To feel strong enough or knowledgeable enough to accomplish a certain task. ♦ *Are you up to climbing all the way to the 37th floor?* ♦ *Are we up to meeting* the delegation from Moscow and speaking Russian to them? **2.** Tendency to do something mischievous. ♦ *I'm afraid Jack is up to one of his old tricks again.*

**beware of Greeks bearing gifts** Often said about people who make one a gift with false pretenses.—A proverb. ♦ *The new boss at the firm promised everyone a brand new set of office furniture, but we cannot trust the man. He will surely want us to work longer hours. Well, beware of Greeks bearing gifts, as the saying goes.*

**be with one** *v. phr.* To give attention to a person after a period of waiting. ♦ *"I'll be with you in a moment, sir," the salesman at the store said, while answering the phone.*

**be wound up** *v. phr.* To be tense, nervous. ♦ *The young surgeon was all wound up before his first major operation.*

**be wound up in** *v. phr.* To be heavily absorbed in some activity that demands full attention. ♦ *"Why is John so absent-minded these days?" Jerry asked. "He is all wound up in his research project," his wife replied.*

**beyond a shadow of doubt** *adv. phr.* Undoubtedly, certainly, for sure. ♦ *A jury of twelve people must come to a conclusion beyond a shadow of doubt that the accused was guilty or innocent.*

**beyond belief** *adj. phr.* Incredible. ♦ *It is almost beyond belief that suicide pilots were able to destroy the World Trade Center.*

**beyond measure** *adj. or adv. phr., formal* So much that it can not be measured or figured without any limits. ♦ *With her parents reunited and present at her graduation, she had happiness beyond measure.*

**beyond one's depth** *adj. or adv. phr.* **1.** Over your head in water; in water too deep to touch bottom. ♦ *Jack wasn't a good swimmer and nearly drowned when he drifted out beyond his depth.* **2.** In or into something too difficult for you; beyond your understanding or ability. ♦ *Bill decided that his big brother's geometry book was beyond his depth.* ♦ *Sam's father started to explain the atom bomb to Sam but he soon got beyond his depth.*

**beyond one's means** *adj. phr.* Too expensive, not affordable. ♦ *Unfortunately, a* new Mercedes Benz is beyond my means right now.

**beyond question**[1] *adj. phr.* Not in doubt certain; sure.—Used in the predicate. ♦ *People always believe anything that Mark says; his honesty is beyond question.* Contrast IN QUESTION.

**beyond question**[2] *or* **without question** *adv. phr.* Without doubt or argument; surely; unquestionably. ♦ *Beyond question, it was the coldest day of the winter.* ♦ *John's drawing is without question the best in the class.*

**beyond reasonable doubt** *adv. phr. formal and legal* Virtually certain; essentially convincing. ♦ *The judge instructed the jurors to come up with a verdict of guilty only if they were convinced beyond a reasonable doubt that Algernon was the perpetrator.*

**beyond the pale** *adv. or adj. phr.* In disgrace; with no chance of being accepted or respected by others; not approved by the members of a group. ♦ *After the outlaw killed a man he was beyond the pale and not even his old friends would talk to him.* ♦ *Tom's swearing is beyond the pale; no one invites him to dinner anymore.*

**beyond a shadow of a doubt** *adv. phr., formal and legal* Absolutely certain, totally convincing. ♦ *Fred burglarized Mrs. Brown's apartment, beyond a shadow of a doubt.*

**bide one's time** *v. phr.* To await an opportunity; wait patiently until your chance comes. ♦ *Refused work as an actor, Tom turned to other work and bided his time.*

**bid fair** *v., literary* To seem likely; promise. ♦ *He bids fair to be a popular author.* ♦ *The day bids fair to be warm.*

**big as life** *or* **large as life** *adj. phr.* **1.** *or* **life-size** The same size as the living person or thing. ♦ *The statue of Jefferson was big as life.* ♦ *The characters on the screen were life-size.* **2.** *or* **big as life and twice as natural** *informal* In person; real and living. ♦ *I had not seen him for years, but there he was, big as life and twice as natural.*

**big cheese** *or* **big gun** *or* **big shot** *or* **big wheel** *or* **big wig** *n., slang* An important person; a leader; a high official; a person of high rank. ♦ *Bill had been a* *big shot in high school.* ♦*John wanted to be the big cheese in his club.*

**big daddy** *n., slang, informal* The most important, largest thing, person or animal in a congregation of similar persons, animals, or objects. ♦*The whale is the big daddy of everything that swims in the ocean.* ♦*The H-bomb is the big daddy of all modern weapons.* ♦*Al Capone was the big daddy of organized crime in Chicago during Prohibition.*

**big deal** *interj., slang, informal* (loud stress on the word *deal*) Trifles; an unimportant, unimpressive thing or matter. ♦*So you became college president—big deal!*

**big frog in a small pond** *n. phr., informal* An important person in a small place or position; someone who is respected and honored in a small company, school, or city; a leader in a small group. ♦*As company president, he had been a big frog in a small pond, but he was not so important as a new congressman in Washington.*

**big hand** *n.* Loud and enthusiastic applause. ♦*When Pavarotti finished singing the aria from* Rigoletto, *he got a very big hand.*

**big head** *n., informal* Too high an opinion of your own ability or importance; conceit. ♦*When Jack was elected captain of the team, it gave him a big head.*

**big house** *n.* A large jail or prison. ♦*The rapist will spend many years in the big house.*

**big lie, the** *n., informal* A major, deliberate misrepresentation of some important issue made on the assumption that a bold, gross lie is psychologically more believable than a timid, minor one. ♦*We all heard the big lie during the Watergate months.* ♦*The pretense of democracy by a totalitarian regime is part of the big lie about its government.*

**big mouth** *or* **big-mouthed** See LOUD MOUTH, LOUD-MOUTHED.

**big shot** *or* **big wig** *n.* An important or influential person. ♦*Elmer is a big shot in the State Assembly.*

**big stink** *n., slang* A major scandal; a big upheaval. ♦*I'll raise a big stink if they fire me.*

**big taste** *n. phr.* A yearning for a drug fix. ♦*I saw you taking a blast from dope yesterday. Your big taste is only going to get worse unless you seek treatment.*

**big time** *n., informal* **1.** A very enjoyable time at a party or other pleasurable gathering. ♦*I certainly had a big time at the club last night.* **2.** The top group; the leading class; the best or most important company. ♦*After his graduation from college, he soon made the big time in baseball.* ♦*Many young actors go to Hollywood, but few of them reach the big time.*

**big-time** *adj.* Belonging to the top group; of the leading class; important. ♦*Jean won a talent contest in her home town, and only a year later she began dancing on big-time television.* Often used in the phrase *big-time* operator. ♦*Just because Bill has a new football uniform he thinks he is a big-time operator.*

**big top** *n.* The main tent under which a circus gives its show; the circus and circus life. ♦*The book tells of life with Barnum and Bailey under the big top.*

**big wheel** *n., informal* An influential or important person who has the power to do things and has connections in high places. ♦*Uncle Ferdinand is a big wheel in Washington; maybe he can help you with your problem.*

**big yawn** *n.* A very boring person, story or event. ♦*I love my grandma very much, but the stories she tells are a big yawn.*

**bird has flown** *slang* The prisoner has escaped; the captive has got away. ♦*When the sheriff returned to the jail, he discovered that the bird had flown.*

**bird in the hand is worth two in the bush (a)** Something we have, or can easily get, is more valuable than something we want that we may not be able to get; we shouldn't risk losing something sure by trying to get something that is not sure.—A proverb. ♦*Johnny has a job as a paperboy, but he wants a job in a gas station. His father says that a bird in the hand is worth two in the bush.*

**bird of a different feather** *n. phr.* A person who is free thinking and independent. ♦*Syd won't go along with recent trends in grammar; he created his own. He is a bird of a different feather.*

**bird of ill omen** *n. phr.* A person that augurs ill, always predicting the worst possibility. ♦ *"Stop being such an old bird of ill omen! You always say that life will be ruined on Earth because of an asteroid impact."*

**birds of a feather flock together** People who are alike often become friends or are together; if you are often with certain people, you may be their friends or like them.—A proverb. ♦ *Don't be friends with bad boys. People think that birds of a feather flock together.*

**birds and the bees (the)** *n. phr., informal* The facts we should know about our birth. ♦ *At various ages, in response to questions, a child can be told about the birds and the bees.*

**bird watcher** *n.* A person whose hobby is to study birds close-up in their outdoor home. ♦ *A bird watcher looks for the first robin to appear in the spring.*

**birthday suit** *n.* The skin with no clothes on; complete nakedness. ♦ *The little boys were swimming in their birthday suits.*

**bite an elbow** *v. phr.* To miss or lose a chance. ♦ *John really bit an elbow when he refused to take Sue to the prom.*

**bite off more than one can chew** *v. phr., informal* To try to do more than you can; be too confident of your ability. ♦ *He started to repair his car himself, but realized that he had bitten off more than he could chew.*

**bite one's head off** *v. phr.* To answer someone in great anger; answer furiously. ♦ *I'm sorry to tell you that I lost my job, but that's no reason to bite my head off!*

**bite one's lips** *v. phr.* To force oneself to remain silent and not to reveal one's feelings. ♦ *I had to bite my lips when I heard my boss give the wrong orders.*

**bite the dust** *v. phr., informal* **1.** To be killed in battle. ♦ *Captain Jones discharged his gun and another guerrilla bit the dust.* **2.** To fall in defeat; go down before enemies; be overthrown; lose. ♦ *Our team bit the dust today.*

**bite the hand that feeds one** *v. phr.* To turn against or hurt a helper or supporter; repay kindness with wrong. ♦ *He bit the hand that fed him when he complained against his employer.*

**bitter pill** *n.* Something hard to accept; disappointment. ♦ *Jack was not invited to the party and it was a bitter pill for him.*

**black and blue** *adj.* Badly bruised. ♦ *Poor Jim was black and blue after he fell off the apple tree.*

**black and white** *n. phr.* **1.** Print or writing; words on paper, not spoken; exact written or printed form. ♦ *He insisted on having the agreement down in black and white.* **2.** The different shades of black and white of a simple picture, rather than other colors. ♦ *He showed us snapshots in black and white.*

**black-and-white** *adj.* Divided into only two sides that are either right or wrong or good or bad, with nothing in between; thinking or judging everything as either good or bad. ♦ *The old man's religion shows his black-and-white thinking; everything is either completely good or completely bad.*

**black day** *n.* A day of great unhappiness; a disaster. ♦ *It was a black day when our business venture collapsed.*

**black eye** *n.* **1.** A dark area around one's eye due to a hard blow during a fight, such as boxing. ♦ *Mike Tyson sported a black eye after the big fight.* **2.** Discredit. ♦ *Bob's illegal actions will give a black eye to the popular movement he started.*

**blackout** *n.* (stress on *black*) **1.** The darkening of a city during an air raid by pulling down all curtains and putting out all street lights. ♦ *The city of London went through numerous blackouts during World War II.* **2.** A cessation of news by the mass media. ♦ *There was a total news blackout about the kidnapping of the prime minister.*

**black out** *v.* **1.** To darken by putting out or dimming lights. ♦ *In some plays the stage is blacked out for a short time and the actors speak in darkness.* ♦ *In wartime, cities are blacked out to protect against bombing from planes.* **2.** To prevent or silence information or communication; refuse to give out truthful news. ♦ *In wartime, governments often black out all news or give out false news.* ♦ *Dictators usually black out all criticism of the government.* **3.** *informal* To lose consciousness; faint. ♦ *It had been a hard and tiring day, and she suddenly blacked out.*

**black sheep** *n.* A person in a family or a community considered unsatisfactory or disgraceful. ♦*My brother Ted is a high school dropout who joined a circus; he is the black sheep in our family.*

**blank amazement** *n. phr.* Utterly prostrating amazement; total surprise. ♦*Everyone had a look of blank amazement, when in the middle of Mother's birthday party, the door opened and a cowboy on horseback rode into the dining room.*

**blank check** *n.* **1.** A bank check written to a person who can then write in how much money he wants. ♦*John's father sent him a blank check to pay his school bills.* **2.** *informal* Permission to another person to do anything he decides to do. ♦*The teacher gave the pupils a blank check to plan the picnic.*

**blank despair** *n. phr.* Helpless despair. ♦*Poor Mary was in blank despair when John announced his decision to get a divorce.*

**blast off** *v.* **1.** To begin a rocket flight. ♦*The astronaut will blast off into orbit at six o'clock.* **2.** *Also* **blast away** *informal* To scold or protest violently. ♦*The coach blasted off at the team for poor playing.*

**blaze a trail** *v. phr.* **1.** To cut marks in trees in order to guide other people along a path or trail, especially through a wilderness. ♦*Daniel Boone blazed a trail for other hunters to follow in Kentucky.* **2.** To lead the way; make a discovery; start something new. ♦*Henry Ford blazed a trail in manufacturing automobiles.*

**bleeding-heart liberal** *n. phr.* A reasonably well-situated member of the bourgeoisie, who for sentimental reasons of left-leaning political views, always espouses the liberal cause, whether sensibly or not. ♦*Many bleeding-heart liberals, who once thought that marijuana should be legalized, change their minds when their own children become addicted to drugs.*

**blessing in disguise** *n. phr.* Some unexpected good that came about as the result of something bad or undesirable. ♦*"It was a blessing in disguise that I forgot my car keys and had to go back for them," Joe said. "If I hadn't, I would not have noticed that I left the burner on in the kitchen, and I could have had a fire."*

**bless one's heart** *v. phr.* To thank someone; consider one the cause of something good that has happened. ♦*Aunt Jane, bless her heart, left me half a million dollars!*

**bless one's lucky star** *or* **bless one's stars** *v. phr.* To be grateful for one's good luck. (Also given as advice.) ♦*"I must bless my lucky star for having married such a wonderful woman as you," Joe said to Mary.*

**blind alley** *n.* **1.** A narrow street that has only one entrance and no exit. ♦*The blind alley ended in a brick wall.* **2.** A way of acting that leads to no good results. ♦*John did not take the job because it was a blind alley.*

**blind as a bat/beetle/mole/owl** *adj. phr.* Anyone who is blind or has difficulty in seeing; a person with very thick glasses. ♦*Without my glasses I am blind as a bat.*

**blind date** *n.* An engagement or date arranged by friends for people who have not previously known one another. ♦*A blind date can be a huge success, or a big disappointment.*

**blind leading the blind** One or more people who do not know or understand something trying to explain it to others who do not know or understand. ♦*Jimmy is trying to show Bill how to skate. The blind are leading the blind.*

**blind spot** *n.* **1.** A place on the road that a driver cannot see in the rearview mirror. ♦*I couldn't see that truck behind me, Officer, because it was in my blind spot.* **2.** A matter or topic a person refuses to discuss or accept. ♦*My uncle Ted has a real blind spot about religion.*

**blip out** *or* **bleep out** *v. phr., informal* To delete electronically a word on television or on radio either because it mentions the name of an established firm in a commercial or because it is a censored word not allowed for television audiences, resulting in a sound resembling the word "bleep." ♦*What was the old product they compared Spic-n-Span to?—I don't know; they've bleeped it out.*

**blockhead** *n., informal* An unusually dense, or stupid person whose head is therefore exaggeratedly compared to a solid block of wood. ♦*Joe is such a blockhead that he flunked every course as a freshman.*

**blood and iron** *n. phr.* Military power as opposed to diplomacy. ♦*There are situations when all diplomacy fails and one must reluctantly resort to blood and iron.*

**blood and thunder** *n. phr.* The violence and bloodshed of stories that present fast action rather than understanding of character. ♦*Crime movies and westerns usually have lots of blood and thunder.*—Often used like an adjective. ♦*John likes to watch blood-and-thunder stories on television.*

**blood is thicker than water** Persons of the same family are closer to one another than to others; relatives are favored or chosen over outsiders. ♦*Mr. Jones hires his relatives to work in his store. Blood is thicker than water.*

**blood runs cold** *also* **blood freezes** *or* **blood turns to ice** You are chilled or shivering from great fright or horror; you are terrified or horrified.— Usually used with a possessive. ♦*The horror movie made the children's blood run cold.* ♦*Mary's blood froze when she had to walk through the cemetery at night.* ♦*Oscar's blood turned to ice when he saw the shadow pass by outside the window.*

**blot on the landscape** *n. phr.* Something that spoils the scenery, disfigures the landscape. ♦*All that uncollected garbage the city is unable to dispose of is quite a blot on the landscape.*

**blot out** *v. phr.* **1.** To obstruct; cover; obscure. ♦*The high-rise building in front of our apartment house blots out the view of the ocean.* **2.** To wipe out of one's memory. ♦*Jane can't remember the details when she was attacked in the streets; she blotted it out of her memory.*

**blow a fuse** *or* **blow a gasket** *or* **blow one's top** *or* **blow one's stack** *v. phr., slang* To become extremely angry; express rage in hot words. ♦*When Mr. McCarthy's son got married against his wishes, he blew a fuse.* ♦*When the umpire called Joe out at first, Joe blew his top and was sent to the showers.*

**blow hot and cold** *v. phr.* To change your ways or likes often; be fickle or changeable. ♦*Tom blows hot and cold*

about coming out for the baseball team; he cannot decide. ♦*Mary blew hot and cold about going to college; every day she changed her mind.*

**blow in** *v., slang* To arrive unexpectedly or in a carefree way. ♦*The house was already full of guests when Bill blew in.*

**blow into** *v., slang* To arrive at (a place) unexpectedly or in a carefree way. ♦*Bill blows into college at the last minute after every vacation.* ♦*Why Tom, when did you blow into town?*

**blow it** *v. phr.* To make a major blunder; to commit an error. ♦*That English test was so easy I can't understand how I could have blown it.*

**blown to smithereens** *adj. phr.* Utterly shattered by an explosion; blown to tiny fragments. ♦*During the Blitz in World War II, Hitler's V2 rockets blew many buildings in London to smithereens.*

**blow one's brains out** *v. phr.* **1.** To shoot yourself in the head. ♦*Mr. Jones lost all his wealth, so he blew his brains out.* **2.** *slang* To work very hard; overwork yourself. ♦*The boys blew their brains out to get the stage ready for the play.* ♦*Mary is not one to blow her brains out.*

**blow one's cool** *v. phr., slang, informal* To lose your composure or self-control. ♦*Whatever you say to the judge in court, make sure that you don't blow your cool.*

**blow one's lines** *or* **fluff one's lines** *v. phr., informal* To forget the words you are supposed to speak while acting in a play. ♦*The noise backstage scared Mary and she blew her lines.*

**blow one's mind** *v. phr., slang, informal; originally from the drug culture* **1.** To become wildly enthusiastic over something as if understanding it for the first time in an entirely new light. ♦*Read Lyall Watson's book* Supernature, *it will simply blow your mind!* **2.** To lose one's ability to function, as if due to an overdose of drugs. ♦*Joe is entirely incoherent—he seems to have blown his mind.*

**blow one's own horn** *or* **toot one's own horn** *v. phr., slang* To praise yourself; call attention to your own skill, intelligence, or successes; boast. ♦*A person who does things well does not have to* *toot his own horn; his abilities will be noticed by others.*

**blow one's top** *v. phr.* To become very excited, angry, hysterical, or furious. ♦*"No need to blow your top, Al," his wife said, "just because you lost a few dollars."*

**blow out** *v. phr.* **1.** To cease to function; fail; explode (said of tires and fuses). ♦*The accident occurred when Jim's tire blew out on the highway.* ♦*The new dishwasher blew out the fuses in the whole house.* **2.** To extinguish. ♦*Jane blew out her birthday cake candles before offering pieces to the guests.*

**blowout** *n.* **1.** An explosion of a tire or a fuse. ♦*Jim's van veered sharply to the right after his car had a blowout.* **2.** A big party. ♦*After graduation from college, my son and his friends staged a huge blowout.*

**blow over** *v.* To come to an end; pass away with little or no bad effects. ♦*The sky was black, as if a bad storm were coming, but it blew over and the sun came out.* ♦*He was much criticized for the divorce, but it all blew over after a few years.*

**blow taps** *v. phr.* To sound the final bugle call of the evening in a camp or military base. ♦*After taps is blown the boy scouts go to their bunks to sleep.*

**blow the gaff** *v. phr.* To open one's mouth to reveal a secret. ♦*When Al cheated on his wife, his younger brother blew the gaff on him.*

**blow the lid off** *v. phr., informal* Suddenly to reveal the truth about a matter that has been kept as a secret either by private persons or by some governmental agency. ♦*The clever journalists blew the lid off the Watergate cover-up.*

**blow the whistle on** *v. phr., slang* **1.** To inform against; betray. ♦*The police caught one of the bank robbers, and he blew the whistle on two more.* **2.** To act against, stop, or tell people the secrets of (crime or lawlessness). ♦*The mayor blew the whistle on gambling.* ♦*The police blew the whistle on hot rodding.*

**blow up** *v.* **1a.** To break or destroy or to be destroyed by explosion. ♦*He blew up the plane by means of a concealed bomb.* **1b.** *informal* To explode with anger or strong feeling; lose control of

yourself. ♦*When Father bent the nail for the third time, he blew up.* **1c.** To stop playing well in a game or contest, usually because you are in danger of losing or are tired; *especially*: To lose skill or control in pitching baseball. ♦*The champion blew up and lost the tennis match.* **2.** *informal* To be ruined as if by explosion; be ended suddenly. ♦*The whole scheme for a big party suddenly blew up.* **3a.** To pump full of air; inflate. ♦*He blew his tires up at a filling station.* **3b.** To make (something) seem bigger or important. ♦*It was a small thing to happen but the newspapers had blown it up until it seemed important.* **4.** To bring on bad weather; also, to come on as bad weather. ♦*The wind had blown up a storm.* **5.** To copy in bigger form; enlarge. ♦*He blew up the snapshot to a larger size.*

**blow up in one's face** *v. phr., informal* To fail completely and with unexpected force. ♦*The thief's plan to rob the bank blew up in his face when a policeman stopped him.*

**blue blood** *n. phr.* Aristocratic blood, hence aristocratic rank or condition. ♦*"Why is Algernon always so proud and self-assured?" Michael asked. "Because he has blue blood," Vanessa, Algernon's sister, replied.*

**blue collar worker** *n. phr.* A manual laborer who is probably a labor union member. ♦*Because Jack's father is a blue collar worker, Jack was so anxious to become an intellectual.*

**blue in the face** *adj. phr., informal* Very angry or upset; excited and very emotional. ♦*Tom argued with Bill until he was blue in the face.*

**blue Monday** *n.* A Monday when you have to work after a happy weekend. ♦*It was blue Monday and John nodded sleepily over his books.*

**blue-pencil** *v.* To edit. ♦*The editor blue-penciled John's manuscript.*

**blurt out** *v. phr.* To suddenly say something even if one was not planning to do so, or if it was not expected of them. ♦*"My brother Bob is in jail," Tony blurted out, before anybody could stop him.*

**body blow** *n., informal* A great disappointment; a bitter failure. ♦*When he* *failed to get on the team it came as a body blow to him.*

**bog down** *v. phr.* To be immobilized in mud, snow, etc.; slow down. ♦*Our research got bogged down for a lack of appropriate funding.* ♦*Don't get bogged down in too much detail when you write an action story.*

**bog down, to get bogged down** *v. phr., mostly intransitive or passive* **1.** To stop progressing; to slow to a halt. ♦*Work on the new building bogged down, because the contractor didn't deliver the needed concrete blocks.* **2.** To become entangled with a variety of obstacles making your efforts unproductive or unsatisfying. ♦*The novelist wrote little last summer because she got bogged down in housework.*

**boggle the mind** *v. phr., informal* To stop the rational thinking process by virtue of being too fantastic or incredible. ♦*It boggles the mind that John should have been inside a flying saucer!*

**boil down** *v.* **1.** To boil away some of the water from; make less by boiling. ♦*She boiled down the maple sap to a thick syrup.* **2.** To reduce the length of; cut down; shorten. ♦*The reporter boiled the story down to half the original length.* **3.** To reduce itself to; come down to; be briefly or basically. ♦*The whole discussion boils down to the question of whether the government should fix prices.*

**boil over** *v. phr.* **1.** To rise due to boiling and overflow down the sides of a pan or a pot. ♦*"Watch out!" Jane cried. "The milk is boiling over on the stove!"* **2.** To become enraged to the point of being unable to contain oneself. ♦*John took a lot of abuse from his boss, but after 25 minutes he suddenly boiled over and told him what he thought of him.*

**boiling point** *n.* **1.** The temperature at which a liquid boils. ♦*The boiling point of water is 212° Fahrenheit.* **2.** The time when you become very angry. ♦*He has a low boiling point.* ♦*After being teased for a long time, John reached the boiling point.* ♦*When John made the same mistake for the fourth time, his teacher reached the boiling point.*

**bolt from the blue** *n. phr.* Something sudden and unexpected; an event that you did not see coming; a great and usually unpleasant surprise; shock. ♦*His decision to resign was a bolt from the blue.*

**bonehead** *n., slang* An unusually dense or stupid person. ♦*John is such a bonehead—small wonder he flunks all of his courses.*

**bone of contention** *n. phr.* Something to fight over; a reason for quarrels; the subject of a fight. ♦*The use of the car was a bone of contention between Joe and his wife.*

**bone to pick** *or* **crow to pick** *n. phr., informal* A reason for dispute; something to complain of or argue about.— Often used jokingly. ♦*"I have a bone to pick with you," he said.* ♦*There was always a crow to pick about which one would shave first in the morning.* Compare BONE OF CONTENTION.

**bone up** *v., informal* To fill with information; try to learn a lot about something in a short time; study quickly. ♦*Carl was boning up for an examination.* ♦*Jim had to make a class report the next day on juvenile delinquency, and he was in the library boning up on how the courts handle it.*

**boob tube** *n. phr. slang* A television set. ♦*Why is Bobby getting so heavy? Because he's sitting all day in front of the boob tube.*

**boot hill** *n.* A cemetery in the old Wild West where cowboys and cops and robbers used to be buried with their boots on. Hence, jokingly, any cemetery. ♦*Good old Joe, the cowboy, is resting comfortably in the nearby boot hill.*

**border on** *v. phr.* To be adjacent to; come close to; adjoin. ♦*Our village borders on the Mississippi River.* ♦*John's actions border on irresponsibility.*

**bore to death** See TO DEATH.

**bore to tears** *v. phr.* To fill with tired dislike; tire by dullness or the same old thing bore. ♦*The party was dull and Roger showed plainly that he was bored to tears.* ♦*Mary loved cooking, but sewing bores her to tears.*

**born out of wedlock** *adj. phr.* Born to parents who are not married to each other; without legal parents. ♦*Sometimes when a married couple can't have children, they adopt a child* *who was born out of wedlock.* ♦ *Today we no longer make fun of children born out of wedlock.*

**born with a silver spoon in one's mouth** *adj. phr.* Born to wealth and comfort; provided from birth with everything wanted; born rich. ♦ *The stranger's conduct was that of a man who had been born with a silver spoon in his mouth.*

**born with two left feet** *n. phr.* An extremely awkward or clumsy person. ♦ *Poor Jerry drops everything he touches; he must have been born with two left feet.*

**born under a lucky star** *adj. phr.* Extraordinarily lucky and successful. ♦ *Joe Smith grew up in an orphanage and never knew his parents, yet at the age of twenty-six he was a self-made billionaire working in the insurance business. Surely, he must have been born under a lucky star.*

**born yesterday** *adj. phr.* Inexperienced and easily fooled; not alert to trickery; easily deceived or cheated. ♦ *I won't give you the money till I see the bicycle you want to sell me. Do you think I was born yesterday?*

**borrowed plumes** *n. phr.* Borrowed fame or reputation; the state of glorying in the fame of another person. ♦ *Joe's brother won the Nobel Prize in medicine, so ever since then Joe has been parading around in borrowed plumes.*

**borrow trouble** *v. phr.* To worry for nothing about trouble that may not come; make trouble for yourself needlessly. ♦ *Don't borrow trouble by worrying about next year. It's too far away.* ♦ *You are borrowing trouble if you try to tell John what to do.*

**bosom friend** *n. phr.* A very close friend; an old buddy with whom one has a confidential relationship. ♦ *Sue and Jane have been bosom friends since their college days.*

**boss one around** *v. phr.* To keep giving someone orders; to act overbearingly toward someone. ♦ *"If you keep bossing me around, darling," Tom said to Jane, "the days of our relationship are surely numbered."*

**botch up** *v. phr.* To ruin, spoil, or mess something up. ♦ *"I botched up my chemistry exam," Tim said, with a resigned sigh.*

**bother the life out of one** *or* **bother heck out of one** *or* **bother the hell out of one** *v. phr.* To irritate someone in a major way. ♦ *The new boss at work has been bothering hell out of everyone with his unreasonable demands.*

**bottle blond** *n., slang* A person who is obviously not a natural blond but whose hair is artificially colored. ♦ *I doubt that Leonora's hair color is natural; she strikes me as a bottle blond.*

**bottleneck** *n.* A heavy traffic congestion. ♦ *In Chicago the worst bottleneck is found where the Kennedy and the Eden's expressways separate on the way to the airport.*

**bottle up** *v.* **1.** To hide or hold back; control. ♦ *There was no understanding person to talk to, so Fred bottled up his unhappy feeling.* **2.** To hold in a place from which there is no escape; trap. ♦ *Our warships bottled up the enemy fleet in the harbor.*

**bottom dollar** *n., v. phr., informal* One's last penny, one's last dollar. ♦ *He was down to his bottom dollar when he suddenly got the job offer.*

**bottom drop out** *or* **bottom fall out** *v. phr. informal* **1.** To fall below an earlier lowest price. ♦ *The bottom dropped out of the price of peaches.* **2.** To lose all cheerful qualities; become very unhappy, cheerless, or unpleasant. ♦ *The bottom dropped out of the day for John when he saw his report card.*

**bottomless pit** *n. phr.* Someone who eats an unusually large amount of food. ♦ *My teenager son eats as though he has a bottomless pit.*

**bottom line** *n., informal* (stress on *line*) **1.** The last word on a controversial issue; a final decision. ♦ *"Give me the bottom line on the proposed merger," said John.* **2.** The naked truth without embellishments. ♦ *Look, the bottom line is that poor Max is an alcoholic.* **3.** The final dollar amount; for example, the lowest price two parties reach in bargaining about a sale. ♦ *"Five-hundred," said the used car dealer, "is the bottom line. Take it or leave it."*

**bottom line** *v., informal* (stress on *bottom*) To finish; to bring to a conclusion. ♦ *Okay, you guys, let's bottom line this project and break for coffee.*

**bottom out** *v. phr.* To reach the lowest point (said chiefly of economic cycles). ♦ *According to the leading economic indicators the recession will bottom out within the next two months.*

**bounce a check** *v. phr.* To write a check for something that is not covered by sufficient deposits in the bank. ♦ *Better make sure there is enough money in the bank, otherwise you may bounce a check, for which the bank charges a penalty!*

**bounce off the walls** *v. phr.* To be nervous enough to be comparable to a tennis ball that keeps bouncing off hard surfaces. ♦ *A day before my final exams I was nervous enough to bounce off the walls.*

**bound for** *adj. phr.* On the way to; going to. ♦ *I am bound for the country club.* ♦ *The ship is bound for Liverpool.*

**bound up with** *v. phr.* To be connected; be involved with. ♦ *Tuition at our university is bound up with the state budget.*

**bowl over** *v., informal* **1.** To knock down as if with a bowled ball. ♦ *The taxi hit him a glancing blow and bowled him over.* **2.** To astonish with success or shock with misfortune; upset; stun. ♦ *He was bowled over by his wife's sudden death.* ♦ *The young actress bowled over everybody in her first movie.*

**bow out** *v., informal* **1.** To give up taking part; excuse yourself from doing any more; quit. ♦ *Mr. Black often quarreled with his partners, so finally he bowed out of the company.* ♦ *While the movie was being filmed, the star got sick and had to bow out.* **2.** To stop working after a long service; retire. ♦ *He bowed out as train engineer after forty years of railroading.*

**box office** *n., informal* **1.** The place at movies and theaters where tickets may be purchased just before the performance instead of having ordered them through the telephone or having bought them at a ticket agency. ♦ *No need to reserve the seats; we can pick them up at the box office.* **2.** *adj.* A best selling movie, musical, or drama (where the tickets are all always sold out and people line up in front of the box office). ♦ *Denzel Washington's last movie was a box office smash.*

**boyfriend** *n., informal* **1.** A male friend or companion. ♦ *"John and his boyfriends have gone to the ball game," said his mother.* **2.** A girl's steady date, a woman's favorite man friend; a male lover or sweetheart. ♦ *Jane's new boyfriend is a senior in high school.*

**boys will be boys** Boys are only children and must sometimes get into mischief or trouble or behave too roughly. ♦ *Boys will be boys and make a lot of noise, so John's mother told him and his friends to play in the park instead of the back yard.*

**brain bucket** *n., slang* A motorcycle helmet. ♦ *If you want to share a ride with me, you've got to wear a brain bucket.*

**brain drain** *n., informal* **1.** The loss of the leading intellectuals and researchers of a country due to excessive emigration to other countries where conditions are better. ♦ *Britain suffered a considerable brain drain to the United States after World War II.* **2.** An activity requiring great mental concentration resulting in fatigue and exhaustion ♦ *That math exam I took was a regular brain drain.*

**brainstorm** *v.* (stress on *brain*) To have a discussion among fellow researchers or co-workers on a project in order to find the best solution to a given problem. ♦ *Dr. Watson and his research assistants are brainstorming in the conference room.*

**brainstorm** *n.* A sudden insight; a stroke of comprehension. ♦ *Listen to me, I've just had a major brainstorm, and I think I found the solution to our problem.*

**brain trust** *n.* A group of specially trained, highly intelligent experts in a given field. ♦ *Albert Einstein gathered a brain trust around himself at the Princeton Institute of Advanced Studies.*

**brainwash** *v. phr.* To change someone's way of thinking mostly about politics or religion, by constantly bombarding them with the desired information under duress, until the victim "believes" what he or she is being told. ♦ *Both the Nazis and the Communists used to brainwash the population with their ideology.*

**brainwashing** *n.* The act of submitting someone to unrelenting propaganda. ♦ *The Iraqi regime is guilty of brain-*

*washing the population into a personality cult for Saddam Hussein.*

**branch off** *v.* To go from something big or important to something smaller or less important; turn aside. ♦*At the bridge a little road branches off from the highway and follows the river.* ♦*Martin was trying to study his lesson, but his mind kept branching off onto what girl he should ask to go with him to the dance.*

**branch out** *v.* To add new interests or activities; begin doing other things also. ♦*First Jane collected stamps; then she branched out and collected coins, too.* ♦*John started a television repair shop; when he did well, he branched out and began selling television sets too.*

**brand-new** *also* **bran-new** *adj.* As new or fresh as when just made and sold by the manufacturer; showing no use or wear. ♦*He had taken a brand-new car from the dealer's floor and wrecked it.*

**brass hat** *n., slang* **1.** A high officer in the army, navy, or air force. ♦*The brass hats in Washington often discuss important secrets.* **2.** Any person who has a high position in business, politics, or other work. ♦*Mr. Woods, the rich oil man, is a political brass hat.*

**brave it out** *v. phr.* To endure something difficult or dangerous through to the end; keep on through trouble or danger. ♦*It was a dangerous ocean crossing in wartime, but captain and crew braved it out.*

**brazen it out** *v. phr.* To pretend you did nothing wrong; be suspected, accused, or scolded without admitting you did wrong; act as if not guilty. ♦*The teacher found a stolen pen that the girl had in her desk, but the girl brazened it out; she said someone else must have put it there.*

**bread and butter** *n. phr.* The usual needs of life; food, shelter, and clothing. ♦*Ed earned his bread and butter as a bookkeeper, but added a little jam by working with a dance band on weekends.*

**bread-and-butter letter** *n.* A written acknowledgment of hospitality received. ♦*Jane wrote the Browns a bread-and-butter letter when she returned home from her visit to them.*

**breadbasket** *n., slang* The stomach. ♦*John is stuffing his breadbasket again.*

**break a leg** *or* **fall through the trapdoor** *v. phr,* A wish or command. Good luck to you! Used mainly by actors and other performers, but also said to people setting out on a journey. ♦*"Fall through the trapdoor, Romeo," the director said to the new actor.* ♦*"Break a leg, Johnny!" his sister Sue said to Johnny as he was leaving for Europe by plane.*

**break away** *or* **break loose** *v. phr.* To liberate oneself from someone or something. ♦*Jane tried to break loose from her attacker, but he was too strong.*

**break camp** *v. phr.* To take down and pack tents and camping things; take your things from a camping place. ♦*The scouts broke camp at dawn.*

**break down** *v.* (stress on *down*) **1.** To smash or hit (something) so that it falls; cause to fall by force. ♦*The firemen broke down the door.* **2.** To reduce or destroy the strength or effect of; weaken; win over. ♦*By helpful kindness the teacher broke down the new boy's shyness.* **3.** To separate into elements or parts; decay. ♦*Water is readily broken down into hydrogen and oxygen.* **4.** To become unusable because of breakage or other failure; lose power to work or go. ♦*The car broke down after half an hour's driving.* ♦*His health broke down.*

**break even** *v. phr., informal* (stress on *even*) To end a series of gains and losses having the same amount you started with; have expenses equal to profits; have equal gain and loss. ♦*If you gamble you are lucky when you break even.*

**break-even** *n.* The point of equilibrium in a business venture when one has made as much money as one had invested, but not more—that would be "profit." ♦*"We've reached the break-even point at long last!" Max exclaimed with joy.*

**break ground** *v. phr.* To begin a construction project by digging for the foundation; especially, to turn the formal first spadeful of dirt. ♦*City officials and industrial leaders were there as the company broke ground for its new building.*

**break in** *v.* (stress on *in*) **1a.** To break from outside. ♦*The firemen broke in the door of the burning house.* **1b.** To enter by force or unlawfully. ♦*Thieves broke in while the family was away.* **2.** To enter suddenly or interrupt. ♦ *A stranger broke in on the meeting without knocking.* ♦ *The secretary broke in to say that a telegram had arrived.* **3.** To make a start in a line of work or with a company or association; begin a new job. ♦ *He broke in as a baseball player with a minor league.* **4.** To teach the skills of a new job or activity to. ♦ *An assistant foreman broke in the new man as a machine operator.* **5.** To lessen the stiffness or newness of by use. ♦ *Breaking in a new car requires careful driving at moderate speeds.*

**break-in** *n.* (stress on *break*) A robbery; a burglary. ♦ *We lost our jewelry during a break-in.*

**break into** *v.* **1.** To force an entrance into; make a rough or unlawful entrance into. ♦ *Thieves broke into the store at night.* **2.** *informal* To succeed in beginning (a career, business, or a social life) ♦ *He broke into television as an actor.* **3.** To interrupt. ♦ *He broke into the discussion with a shout of warning.* **4.** To begin suddenly. ♦ *He broke into a sweat.* ♦ *She broke into tears.*

**break it up!** *v. phr. command* Disperse; stop the gathering (or fight), and keep moving away from the scene. ♦ *"Come on you guys! Break it up!" the coach shouted, when the two basketball teams started a brawl in mid-court.*

**break new ground** *v. phr.* **1.** To start a new activity previously neglected by others; do pioneering work. ♦ *Albert Einstein broke new ground with his theory of relativity.* **2.** To begin something never done before. ♦ *The school broke new ground with reading lessons that taught students to guess the meaning of new words.*

**break off** *v.* **1.** To stop suddenly. ♦ *The speaker was interrupted so often that he broke off and sat down.* ♦ *When Bob came in, Jean broke off her talk with Linda and talked to Bob.* **2.** *informal* To end a friendship or love. ♦ *I hear that Tom and Alice have broken off.*

**break one's balls** *v. phr., slang, vulgar, avoidable* To do something with maximum effort; to do something very difficult or taxing ♦ *I've been breaking my balls to buy you this new color TV set and you aren't the least bit appreciative!*

**break one's heart** *v. phr.* To discourage greatly; make very sad or hopeless.

♦ *His son's disgrace broke his heart.* ♦ *When Mr. White lost everything he had worked so hard for, it broke his heart.*

**break one's neck** *v. phr., slang* To do all you possibly can; try your hardest.—Usually used with a limiting adverb or negative. ♦ *John nearly broke his neck trying not to be late to school.*

**break one's word** *v. phr.* To renege on a promise. ♦ *When Jake broke his word that he would marry Sarah, she became very depressed.*

**break out** *v.* **1.** To begin showing a rash or other skin disorder.—Often used with *with.* ♦ *He broke out with scarlet fever.* **2.** To speak or act suddenly and violently. ♦ *He broke out laughing.* ♦ *She broke out, "That is not so!"* **3.** To begin and become noticeable. ♦ *Fire broke out after the earthquake.* ♦ *War broke out in 1812.* **4.** *informal* To bring out; open and show. ♦ *When Mr. Carson's first son was born, he broke out the cigars he had been saving.*

**break out in laughter** *v. phr.* To burst out in sudden uncontrollable laughter. ♦ *Every time Joe tells a joke I break out in laughter.*

**break out in tears** *or* **break out into tears** *v. phr.* To suddenly start crying without being able to stop. ♦ *When Sue heard that her husband was killed in action, she broke out in tears.*

**break the ice** *v. phr., informal* **1.** To conquer the first difficulties in starting a conversation, getting a party going, or making an acquaintance. ♦ *To break the ice Ted spoke of his interest in mountain climbing, and they soon had a conversation going.* **2.** To be the first person or team to score in a game. ♦ *The Wolves broke the ice with a touchdown.*

**break the news** *v. phr.* To reveal new information, sometimes in the midst of a regularly scheduled broadcast, or by personal visit or telephone call. ♦ *The army has the sad job of breaking the news to family members when one of theirs has been killed in action or is mission in action.*

**break the record** *v. phr.* To set or to establish a new mark or record. ♦ *Algernon broke the record in both the pentathlon and the decathlon and took* home two gold medals from the Olympics.

**break through** v. (stress on *through*) To be successful after overcoming a difficulty or bar to success. ♦ *Dr. Salk failed many times but he finally broke through to find a successful polio vaccine.*

**breakthrough** n. (stress on *break*) A point of sudden success after a long process of experimentation, trial, and error. ♦ *The U.S. Space Program experienced a major breakthrough when Armstrong and Aldrin landed on the moon in June of 1969.*

**break up** v. phr. (stress on *up*) To end a romantic relationship, a marriage, or a business partnership. ♦ *Tom and Jane broke up because Tom played so much golf that he had no time for her.*

**break up** v. (stress on *up*) **1.** To break into pieces. ♦ *The workmen broke up the pavement to dig up the pipes under it.* ♦ *River ice breaks up in the spring.* **2.** *informal* To lose or destroy spirit or self-control.—Usually used in the passive. ♦ *Mrs. Lawrence was all broken up after her daughter's death, and did not go out of the house for two months.* **3.** To come or to put to an end, especially by separation; separate. ♦ *Some men kept interrupting the speakers, and finally broke up the meeting.* ♦ *The party broke up at midnight.*—Often used in the informal phrase *break it up.* ♦ *The boys were fighting, and a passing policeman ordered them to break it up.* **4.** *informal* To stop being friends. ♦ *Mary and June were good friends and did everything together, but then they had a quarrel and broke up.*

**break-up** n. (stress on *break*) The end of a relationship, personal or commercial. ♦ *The break-up finally occurred when Smith and Brown decided to sue each other for embezzlement.*

**break with** v. To separate yourself from; end membership in; stop friendly association with ♦ *He broke with the Democratic party on the question of civil rights.*

**breathe down one's neck** v. phr., *informal* To follow closely; threaten from behind; watch every action. ♦ *Too many creditors were breathing down his neck.* ♦ *The carpenter didn't like to work for Mr. Jones, who was always breathing down his neck.*

**breathe easily** or **breathe freely** v. To have relief from difficulty or worry; relax; feel that trouble is gone; stop worrying. ♦ *Now that the big bills were paid, he breathed more easily.* ♦ *His mother didn't breathe easily until he got home that night.*

**breathe one's last** v. phr. To die. ♦ *The wounded soldier fell back on the ground and breathed his last.*

**breathing room** n. phr. Freedom from coercive, marital, or managerial control. ♦ *"You've got to give me some breathing room!" Sue cried, "or I'll file for divorce right now!"*

**breeze in** v. phr., *slang, informal* To walk into a place casually (like a soft blowing wind). ♦ *Betsie breezed in and sat down at the bar.*

**bright and early** adj. phr. Prompt and alert; on time and ready; cheerful and on time or before time. ♦ *He came down bright and early to breakfast.* ♦ *She arrived bright and early for the appointment.*

**bright-eyed and bushy-tailed** adj. phr. Lively, eager, healthy, like a young puppy dog. ♦ *"Good morning Bobby," father said, "you sure look bright-eyed and bushy-tailed this fine day! Any special plans?"*

**bring about** v. To cause; produce; lead to. ♦ *The war had brought about great changes in living.* ♦ *Drink brought about his downfall.*

**bring an end to** v. phr. To stop something. ♦ *We must bring an end to the tribal warfare and the rule of the landlords in Afghanistan.*

**bring around** or **bring round** v. **1.** *informal* To restore to health or consciousness cure. ♦ *He was quite ill, but good nursing brought him around.* **2.** To cause a change in thinking; persuade; convince; make willing. ♦ *After a good deal of discussion he brought her round to his way of thinking.*

**bringdown** n., *slang, informal* (stress on *bring*) **1.** (from *bring down*, past *brought down*). A critical or cutting remark said sarcastically in order to deflate a braggard's ego. ♦ *John always utters the right bringdown when he encounters a braggard.* **2.** A person who depresses and saddens others by being a chronic complainer. ♦ *John is a regular bringdown.*

**bring down** *v. phr., slang, informal* (stress on *down*) **1.** To deflate (someone's ego). ♦*John brought Ted down very cleverly with his remarks.* **2.** To depress (someone). ♦*The funeral brought me down completely.*

**bring down the house** *v. phr., informal* To start an audience laughing or clapping enthusiastically. ♦*The president made a fine speech which brought down the house.*

**bring grits to one's mill** *or* **it is all grits to one's (the) mill** *v.* To obtain profit-yielding work, work that brings in monetary reward.—A proverb. ♦*"Every bump on a rear fender brings grits to my mill," said the manager of the body shop.*

**bring home** *v.* To show clearly; emphasize; make (someone) realize; demonstrate. ♦*The accident caused a death in his family, and it brought home to him the evil of drinking while driving.*

**bring home the bacon** *v. phr., informal* **1.** To support your family; earn the family living. ♦*He was a steady fellow, who always brought home the bacon.* **2.** To win a game or prize. ♦*The football team brought home the bacon.*

**bring in** *v.* To tune one's radio so that a station can be heard. ♦*"Can you bring in the BBC on that portable machine of yours?"*

**bring into focus** *v. phr.* To make something clearly known, understood. ♦*September 11, 2001 brought into focus the importance of preparedness against domestic terrorism.*

**bring into line** *v. phr.* To make someone conform to the accepted standard. ♦*Sam had to be brought into line when he refused to take his muddy shoes off the cocktail table.*

**bring into play** *v. phr.* To cause something to have an effect or influence or force. ♦*Who knows, what details may be brought into play when the talks about a postwar Iraq begin.*

**bring into the open** *v. phr.* To cause something to be publicly known, no longer kept as a secret ♦*The Iraqis must bring into the open their caches of weapons of mass destruction, if they are to be trusted by the United Nations.*

**bring off** *v.* To do (something difficult); perform successfully (an act of skill); accomplish (something requiring unusual ability). ♦*He tried several times to break the high jump record, and finally he brought it off.*

**bring on** *v.* To result in; cause; produce. ♦*The murder of Archduke Franz Ferdinand in the summer of 1914 brought on the First World War.* ♦*Spinal meningitis brought on John's deafness when he was six years old.* ♦*Reading in a poor light may bring on a headache.*

**bring one down a peg or two** *v. phr.* To deflate an overinflated ego, to put someone in his or her place. ♦*Stanley has too high an opinion of himself; clearly he has to be brought down a peg or two.*

**bring one down to earth** *or* **bring one down to earth with a bang** *or* **bring one down to earth with a bump** *v. phr.* To make someone face the unpleasant truth and reality; to make someone give up living in the clouds. ♦*The cruel dictator believed that he and his cohorts were invincible, so the civilized world had to bring him down to earth with a bump.*

**bring one in on the ground floor** *v. phr.* To offer someone employment at a low rank or at the beginning phases of a company in the hope that such an employee will keep growing with the institution. ♦*When the University of Illinois at Chicago opened its gates in 1965, many a new assistant professor was hoping that being brought in on the ground floor would eventually put him or her in an advantageous position.*

**bring one into the world** *v. phr.* To give birth to a child. ♦*Many couples believe that it is a bad idea to bring someone into the world during wartime or uncertain economic conditions.*

**bring one to his feet** *v. phr.* To be so effective as a performer or speechmaker that the audience rises to its feet and applauds enthusiastically. ♦*Luciano Pavarotti's performance in Il Trovatore, when he sang the high C note, brought the entire Lyric Opera to its feet.*

**bring out** *v.* **1.** To cause to appear; make clear. ♦*His report brought out the foolishness of the plan.* ♦*Brushing will bring out the beauty* of your hair. **2.** To help (an ability or skill) grow or develop. ♦ *The teacher's coaching brought out a wonderful singing voice of great power and warmth.* **3.** To offer to the public by producing, publishing, or selling. ♦ *He brought out a new play.* ♦ *The company brought out a line of light personal airplanes.*

**bring suit against** *v. phr.* To sue someone in a court of law. ♦ *Fred brought suit against Tom for fraud and embezzlement.*

**bring to** *v.* (stress on *to*) **1.** To restore to consciousness; wake from sleep, anesthesia, hypnosis, or fainting. ♦ *Smelling salts will often bring a fainting person to.* **2.** To bring a ship or boat to a stop. ♦ *Reaching the pier, he brought the boat smartly to.*

**bring to a close** *v. phr.* To terminate; cause to end. ♦ *The meeting was brought to an abrupt close when the speaker collapsed with a heart attack.*

**bring to a dead end** *v. phr.* To prevent the further advance of an object or a project. ♦ *The investigation of the missing girl was suddenly brought to a dead end when the accused criminal committed suicide in jail before the trial.*

**bring to a head** *v. phr.* To cause some activity to reach the point of culmination. ♦ *Time is running out, gentlemen, so let us bring this discussion to a head.*

**bring to attention** *v. phr.* To cause soldiers to stand upright and stiffly. ♦ *The sergeant brought the company to attention when the lieutenant arrived.*

**bring to bay** *v. phr.* To chase or force into a place where escape is impossible without a fight; trap; corner. ♦ *The police brought the robber to bay on the roof and he gave up.* ♦ *The fox was brought to bay in a hollow tree and the dogs stood around it barking.*

**bring to light** *v. phr.* To discover (something hidden); find out about; expose. ♦ *Many things left by the ancient Egyptians in tombs have been brought to light by scientists and explorers.*

**bring to mind** *v. phr.* To remember somebody or something. ♦ *No matter how hard I tried, I couldn't bring to mind the year my father was born.*

**bring to one's knees** *v. phr.* To seriously weaken the power or impair the func-

tion of. ♦ *The fuel shortage brought the automobile industry to its knees.*

**bring to pass** *v. phr., informal* To make (something) happen; succeed in causing. ♦ *The change in the law was slow in coming, and it took a disaster to bring it to pass.*

**bring to rest** *v. phr.* To cause something, such as an engine, to stop. ♦ *The farmer managed to bring his tractor to rest in the field after a brief struggle.*

**bring to terms** *v. phr.* To make (someone) agree or do; make surrender. ♦ *The war won't end until we bring the enemy to terms.*

**bring to the (a) boil** *v. phr.* **1.** To heat a liquid until it begins to boil. ♦ *Water is normally brought to the boil at 100°C (212°F) but at higher altitudes water is brought to the boil at lower temperatures.* **2.** To cause something such as a previously dormant problem to reach a state of crisis or urgency. ♦ *The attack on the Twin Towers of the World Trade Center brought to a boil the constant danger of domestic terrorism.*

**bring up** *v.* **1.** To take care of (a child); raise, train, educate. ♦ *He gave much attention and thought to bringing up his children.* ♦ *Joe was born in Texas but brought up in Oklahoma.* **2.** *informal* To stop; halt.—Usually used with *short.* ♦ *He brought the car up short when the light changed to red.* ♦ *Bill started to complain, I brought him up short.* **3.** To begin a discussion of; speak of; mention. ♦ *At the class meeting Bob brought up the idea of a picnic.*

**bring up the rear** *v. phr.* **1.** To come last in a march, parade, or procession; end a line. ♦ *The governor and his staff brought up the rear of the parade.* **2.** *informal* To do least well; do the most poorly of a group; be last. ♦ *In the race, John brought up the rear.* ♦ *In the basketball tournament, our team brought up the rear.*

**bring** *or* **wheel in** *or* **out** *or* **up the big guns** *v. phr.* To make use of a concealed plan in order to defeat an opponent in an argument or in a game, debate, or competition. ♦ *The new computer software company decided to bring out the big guns to get ahead of the competition.*

**bring up to date** *v. phr.* To make something current, or to share contemporary information with someone. ♦ *This poor old provincial radio station has to be brought up to date with some new equipment.* ♦ *"Let me bring you up to date on the state of our college's ruinous finances," the Dean said to the new applicant.*

**bring up to standard** *v. phr.* To make an outmoded piece of equipment or the working conditions of employees conform with the current state of the art, considered the standard at the time. ♦ *Chicago's antiquated subway system must soon be brought up to standard.*

**broke to the wide, wide world** *adj. phr.* Penniless; having no money at all. ♦ *"I couldn't get a penny out of John for his membership dues; the poor guy seems to be broke to the wide, wide world."*

**broken record** *n. phr.* Someone who keeps repeating the same stories over and over again, like an old-fashioned gramophone record that is stuck in a given groove. ♦ *Poor Grandpa is getting senile; he keeps repeating his wartime stories again and again and is beginning to sound like a broken record.*

**Bronx cheer** *n. phr., slang* A loud sound made with tongue and lips to show opposition or scorn. ♦ *When he began to show anti-union feelings, he was greeted with Bronx cheers all around.*

**browbeat into** *v. phr.* To coerce someone to do or say something by brute force or blackmail. ♦ *In the democratic West the police are not expected to browbeat the accused to admit to any wrongdoing.*

**brown-bagger** *n., slang, informal* A person who does not go to the cafeteria or to a restaurant for lunch at work, but who brings his homemade lunch to work in order to save money. ♦ *John became a brown-bagger not because he can't afford the restaurant, but because he is too busy to go there.*

**brown-nose** *v., slang, avoidable, though gaining in acceptance* To curry favor in a subservient way, as by obviously exaggerated flattery. ♦ *Max brown-noses his teachers, that's why he gets all A's in his courses.*

**brown paper bag** *n., slang, citizen's band radio jargon* An unmarked police car.
♦ *The beaver got a Christmas card because she didn't notice the brown paper bag at her back door.*

**brush aside** *v. phr.* To ignore; give no reply. ♦ *Brushing aside the editor's comments, the young novelist proceeded with his story, which was subsequently rejected by the publisher.*

**brush back** *v.* To throw a baseball pitch close to. ♦ *The pitcher threw a high inside pitch to brush the batter back.*

**brush off** *or* **give the brush off** *v. phr.* **1.** To refuse to hear or believe; quickly and impatiently; not take seriously or think important. ♦ *John brushed off Bill's warning that he might fall from the tree.* **2.** *informal* To be unfriendly to; not talk or pay attention to (someone); get rid of. ♦ *Mary brushed off Bill at the dance.*

**brush up** *or* **brush up on** *v.* To refresh one's memory of or skill at by practice or review; improve; make perfect. ♦ *She spent the summer brushing up on her American History as she was to teach that in the fall.* ♦ *He brushed up his target shooting.*

**bubble gum music** *n., slang* The kind of rock'n'roll that appeals to young teenagers. ♦ *When will you learn to appreciate Mozart instead of that bubble gum music?*

**bubble over with** *v. phr.* To show extraordinary enthusiasm for somebody or something; considered a sign of naïvety. ♦ *Tim was bubbling over with joy when Sue accepted his invitation to the prom.*

**bubble trouble** *n., slang, citizen's band radio jargon* Tire trouble, flat tire. ♦ *The eighteen wheeler ahead of me seems to have bubble trouble.*

**bucket of bolts** *n., slang* A very old and shaky car that barely goes. ♦ *When are you going to get rid of that old bucket of bolts?*

**buckle down** *or* **knuckle down** *v.* To give complete attention (to an effort or job); attend. ♦ *They chatted idly for a few moments then each buckled down to work.* ♦ *Jim was fooling instead of studying; so his father told him to buckle down.*

**buckle under** *v. phr.* To admit one's defeat; to allow one's resistance to crumble; to yield. ♦ *The cruel dictator's* *forces will inevitably buckle under the democratic coalition forces' assault.*

**buck passer, buck-passing** See PASS THE BUCK.

**buffeting of fate** *or* **the buffets of fate** *n. phr.* Those unforeseeable and incalculable forces of both nature and society that cause one to change one's life, such as get a divorce, emigrating, etc. ♦*The buffeting of fate made many early Americans go west.*

**bug-eyed** *adj., slang* Wide-eyed with surprise. ♦*He stood there bug-eyed when told that he had won the award.*

**bug out** *v. phr.* To get out of a place in a great hurry; to escape. ♦*"Come on! Lets bug out!" Sergeant O'Leary cried, when the enemy started to shoot at the foxhole where the marines hid.*

**buggy-whip** *n., slang* An unusually long, thin radio antenna on a car that bends back like a whip when the car moves fast. ♦*He's very impressed with himself ever since he got a buggy whip.*

**bughouse¹** *n., slang* An insane asylum. ♦*They took Joe to the bughouse.*

**bughouse²** *adj., slang* Crazy, insane. ♦*Joe's gone bughouse.*

**bug in one's ear** *n. phr., informal* A hint; secret information given to someone to make him act; idea. ♦*I saw Mary at the jeweler's admiring the diamond pin; I'll put a bug in Henry's ear.*

**build a fire under** *v. phr.* To urge or force (a slow or unwilling person) to action; get (someone) moving; arouse. ♦*The health department built a fire under the restaurant owner and got him to clean the place up by threatening to cancel his license.*

**build castles in the air** *or* **build castles in Spain** *v. phr.* To make impossible or imaginary plans, dream about future successes that are unlikely. ♦*He liked to build castles in the air, but never succeeded in anything.* ♦*To build castles in Spain is natural for young people and they may work hard enough to get part of their wishes.*

**build on sand** *v. phr.* To lay a weak or insufficient foundation for a building, a business, or a relationship. ♦*"I don't want to build my business on sand,"* John said, *"so please, Dad, give me that loan I requested."*

**build up** *v.* **1.** To make out of separate pieces or layers; construct from parts. ♦*Johnny built up a fort out of large balls of snow.* **2.** To cover over or fill up with buildings. ♦*A driver should slow down when he comes to an area that is built up.* **3a.** To increase slowly or by small amounts; grow. ♦*John built up a bank account by saving regularly.* **3b.** To make stronger or better or more effective. ♦*Fred exercised to build up his muscles.* **3c.** *informal* To advertise quickly and publicize so as to make famous. ♦*The press agent built up the young actress.*

**build up to** *v. phr.* To be in the process of reaching a culmination point. ♦*The clouds were building up to a violent storm.* ♦*Their heated words were building up to a premature divorce.*

**bulk up** *v. phr.* To get larger and firmer muscles by lifting weights. ♦*Peter bulked up considerably after having pumped some iron at Bally's health club for a year.*

**bullet lane** *n., slang, citizen's band radio jargon* The passing lane. ♦*Move over into the bullet lane, this eighteen wheeler is moving too slow.*

**bull in a china shop** *n. phr.* A rough or clumsy person who says or does something to anger others or upset plans; a tactless person. ♦*We were talking politely and carefully with the teacher about a class party, but John came in like a bull in a china shop and his rough talk made the teacher say no.*

**bull session** *n., slang* A long informal talk about something by a group of persons. ♦*After the game the boys in the dormitory had a bull session until the lights went out.*

**bullshit** *n., vulgar, but gaining in acceptance by some* Exaggerated or insincere talk meant to impress others. ♦*"Joe, this is a lot of bullshit!"*

**bullshit** *v., vulgar to informal, gaining in social acceptance by some* To exaggerate or talk insincerely in an effort to make yourself seem impressive. ♦*"Stop bullshitting me, Joe, I can't believe a word of what you're saying."*

**bullshit artist** *n., slang, vulgar, but gaining in social acceptance* A person who habitually makes exaggerated or insincerely flattering speeches designed to impress others. ♦*Joe is a regular bull-*

shit artist, small wonder he keeps getting promoted ahead of everyone else.

**bully for you!** adj. phr., exclamation Good for you! Congratulations! You have done very well! ♦ *"Bully for you, Alvin!" the class cried out as one man, when we learned that Alvin had won the Illinois state lottery.*

**bum around** v. phr., slang To aimlessly wander in no definite direction, like a vagabond. ♦ *Jim had been bumming around in the desert for three days and nights before he was able to remember how he got there in the first place.*

**bumper to bumper** adj. phr. Heavily congested with hardly any progress made or room to maneuver. ♦ *The traffic on all major highways around Chicago was bumper to bumper; naturally we were two hours late.*

**bump into** v., informal To meet without expecting to; happen to meet; come upon by accident. ♦ *Ed was surprised to bump into John at the football game.*

**bump off** v., slang To kill in a violent way; murder in gangster fashion. ♦ *Hoodlums in a speeding car bumped him off with Tommy guns.*

**bump on a log** n. phr. A boring or uninteresting, dull person. ♦ *Small wonder the girls don't like poor Joe; he is such a bump on a log.*

**bum's rush** n. phr., slang **1.** Throwing or pushing someone out from where he is not wanted. ♦ *When John tried to go to the party where he was not invited, Bill and Fred gave him the bum's rush.* **2.** To hurry or rush (someone). ♦ *The salesman tried to give me the bum's rush.*

**bum steer** n. Wrong or misleading directions given naively or on purpose. ♦ *Man, you sure gave me a bum steer when you told me to go north on the highway; you should have sent me south!*

**bundle of laughs** n. phr. A very amusing person, thing, or event. ♦ *Uncle Lester tells so many jokes that he is a bundle of laughs.*

**bundle of nerves** adj. phr. Extremely nervous, jumpy, fidgety, restless. ♦ *Is your son Bobby always such a bundle of nerves? You should have him seen by a doctor for hyperactivity.*

**burden of proof** v. phr. The imperative necessity for the prosecution to convince the jury that the accused is indeed guilty. ♦ *In a court of law the burden of proof rests always with the prosecution.*

**burden of (the) years** v. phr. The physical debilities of old age; aches and pains, etc. ♦ *Poor Grandpa is showing the burden of years; he is able to do less and less around the house.*

**burn a hole in one's pocket** v. phr. To make you want to buy something; be likely to be quickly spent. ♦ *Money burns a hole in Linda's pocket.*

**burn down** v. phr. To burn to the ground; be totally gutted by fire. ♦ *The old frame house burned down before the firefighters could get to it.*

**burning question** v. phr. A subject that is responsible for generating a lot of excitement and discussion by the public at large. ♦ *The burning question for the United States often is whether or not to follow what the U.N. wishes, or to go its own way.*

**burn one's bridges** also **burn one's boats** v. phr. To make a decision that you cannot change; remove or destroy all the ways you can get back out of a place you have got into on purpose; leave yourself no way to escape a position. ♦ *When Dorothy became a nun, she burned her bridges behind her.*

**burn one's fingers** v. phr., informal To get in trouble doing something and fear to do it again; learn caution through an unpleasant experience. ♦ *Some people can't be told; they have to burn their fingers to learn.*

**burn out** v. phr. (stress on *out*) **1.** To destroy by fire or by overheating. ♦ *Mr. Jones burned out the clutch on his car.* **2.** To destroy someone's house or business by fire so that they have to move out. ♦ *Three racists burned out the black family's home.* **3a.** To go out of order; cease to function because of long use or overheating. ♦ *The light bulb in the bathroom burned out, and Father put in a new one.* ♦ *The electric motor was too powerful, and it burned out a fuse.* **3b.** To break, tire, or wear out by using up all the power, energy, or strength of. ♦ *Bill burned himself out in the first part of the race and could not finish.* ♦ *The farmer burned out his field by planting the same crop every year for many years.*

**burn-out** *n.* (stress on *burn*) A point of physical or emotional exhaustion. ♦ *There are so many refugees all over the world that charitable organizations as well as individuals are suffering from donor burn-out.*

**burn rubber** *v. phr., slang* 1. To start up a car or a motorcycle from dead stop so fast that the tires leave a mark on the road. ♦ *The neighborhood drag racers burned a lot of rubber—look at the marks on the road!* 2. To leave in a hurry. ♦ *I guess I am going to have to burn rubber.*

**burnt child dreads the fire** *or* **once bitten, twice shy** A person who has suffered from doing something has learned to avoid doing it again.—A proverb. ♦ *Once Mary had got lost when her mother took her downtown. But a burnt child dreads the fire, so now Mary stays close to her mother when they are downtown.*

**burn the candle at both ends** *v. phr.* To work or play too hard without enough rest; get too tired. ♦ *He worked hard every day as a lawyer and went to parties and dances every night; he was burning the candle at both ends.*

**burn the midnight oil** *v. phr.* To study late at night. ♦ *Exam time was near, and more and more pupils were burning the midnight oil.*

**burn to a crisp** *v. phr.* To burn black; burn past saving or using especially as food. ♦ *While getting breakfast, Mother was called to the telephone, and when she got back, the bacon had been burned to a crisp.*

**burn up** *v.* 1. To burn completely; destroy or be destroyed by fire. ♦ *Mr. Scott was burning up old letters.* ♦ *The house burned up before the firemen got there.* 2. *informal* To irritate, anger, annoy. ♦ *The boy's laziness and rudeness burned up his teacher.*

**burn up the road** *v. phr., informal* To drive a car very fast. ♦ *Speed demons burning up the road often cause accidents.*

**burst at the seams** *v. phr., informal* To be too full or too crowded. ♦ *John ate so much he was bursting at the seams.*

**burst into** *v. phr.* 1. To enter suddenly. ♦ *Stuart burst into the room, screaming angrily.* 2. To break out. ♦ *The crowd burst out cheering when the astronauts paraded along Fifth Avenue.*

**burst into flames** *v. phr.* To begin to burn suddenly. ♦ *The children threw away some burning matches and the barn burst into flames.*

**burst into tears** *v. phr.* To suddenly start crying. ♦ *Mary burst into tears when she heard that her brother was killed in a car accident.*

**burst one's bubble** *v. phr.* To disappoint someone. ♦ *I hate to burst your bubble, but you didn't get the job you applied for.*

**burst out** *v. phr.* 1. To escape. ♦ *Very few inmates ever managed to burst out from Alcatraz in the Bay of San Francisco.* 2. To speak suddenly. ♦ *You will make a lot of enemies if you always burst out so suddenly and don't think before opening your mouth.*

**burst with joy or pride** *v. phr.* To be so full of the feeling of joy or pride that one cannot refrain from showing one's exuberant feelings. ♦ *Armstrong and Aldrin burst with pride when they stepped out on the moon in July 1969.*

**bury the hatchet** *v. phr., informal* To settle or end a war; make peace. ♦ *The two men had been enemies a long time, but after the flood they buried the hatchet.*

**bust out** *v. phr.* To escape, as from jail. ♦ *The prisoners made a careful plan how to bust out of the maximum security prison, but after only half a day at large they were recaptured by the police.*

**bust up** *v. phr., slang* To terminate a partnership, a relationship, a friendship, or a marriage. ♦ *If Jack keeps drinking the way he does, it will bust up his marriage to Sue.*

**busybody** *n. phr.* A person who often unnecessarily interferes with the business of others under the pretext of trying to offer his help; a nosey person. ♦ *"Stop being such a busybody," Joe warned the new employee. "This is not the way to succeed at this kind of work."*

**busy work** *n.* Work that is done not to do or finish anything important, but just to keep busy. ♦ *When the teacher finished all she had to say it was still a half hour before school was over. So she gave the class a test for busy work.*

**but good** *adv. phr., informal* Very much so; thoroughly completely; forcefully.—Used for emphasis. ♦*Tom fell and broke his leg. That taught him but good not to fool around in high trees.*

**butterfingers** *n. phr.* Someone who is clumsy and easily drops things. ♦*"You had better do some hand-muscle exercises," Joe's doctor said, "or you'll remain a butterfingers, which can be embarrassing."*

**butterflies in one's stomach** *n. phr.* A queer feeling in the stomach caused by nervous fear or uncertainty; a feeling of fear or anxiety in the stomach. ♦*When Bob walked into the factory office to ask for a job, he had butterflies in his stomach.*

**butter up** *v., informal* To try to get the favor or friendship of (a person) by flattery or pleasantness. ♦*He began to butter up the boss in hope of being given a better job.*

**butter wouldn't melt in one's mouth** *informal* You act very polite and friendly but do not really care, you are very nice to people but are not sincere. ♦*The new secretary was rude to the other workers, but when she talked to the boss, butter wouldn't melt in her mouth.*

**butt in** *v., slang* To join in with what other people are doing without asking or being asked; interfere in other people's business; meddle. ♦*Mary was explaining to Jane how to knit a sweater when Barbara butted in.* Often used with *on.* ♦*John butted in on Bill and Tom's fight, and got hurt.*

**button down** *v., slang* (stress on *down*) To state precisely, to ascertain, to pin down, to peg down. ♦*First let's get the facts buttoned down, then we can plan ahead.*

**button-down** *adj. phr., slang* (stress on *button*) Well-groomed, conservatively dressed. ♦*Joe is a typical button-down type.*

**buttonhole** *v.* To approach a person in order to speak with him or her in private. ♦*After waiting for several hours, Sam managed to buttonhole his boss just as she was about to leave the building.*

**button one's lip** *also* **zip one's lip** *v. phr., slang* To stop talking; keep a secret; shut your mouth; be quiet. ♦*The man was getting loud and insulting and the cop told him to button his lip.* ♦*John wanted to talk, but Dan told him to keep his lip buttoned.*

**butt out** See MIND ONE'S OWN BUSINESS.

**buy for a song** *v. phr.* To buy something very cheaply. ♦*Since the building on the corner was old and neglected, I was able to buy it for a song.*

**buy off** *v.* To turn from duty or purpose by a gift. ♦*When the police threatened to stop the gambling business, the owner bought them off.*

**buy out** *v.* **1.** To buy the ownership or a share of; purchase the stock of. ♦*He bought out several small stockholders.* **2.** To buy all the goods of; purchase the merchandise of. ♦*Mr. Harper bought out a nearby hardware store.*

**buy up** *v. phr.* To purchase the entire stock of something. ♦*The company is trying to buy up all the available shares.*

**buzz off** *v. phr.* (given as a command). To disappear, to get lost. ♦*"Buzz off, kid!" the class bully yelled, when Johnny tried to say something.*

**buzz on** *v. phr.* To complain about or chide someone for some minor mishap. ♦*There was no reason for Mom to buzz on like that; all I did was spill some coffee on the table.*

**buzz word** *n.* A word that sounds big and important in a sentence but, on closer inspection, means little except the speaker's indication to belong to a certain group. ♦*The politician's speech was nothing but a lot of misleading statements and phony promises hidden in a bunch of buzz words.*

**by** *or* **in my book** *adv. phr.* In my opinion; as far as I am concerned; in my judgment. ♦*By my book, Mr. Murgatroyd is not a very good department head.*

**by all means** *also* **by all manner of means** *adv. phr.* Certainly, without fail. ♦*He felt that he should by all means warn Jones.*

**by all odds** *adv. phr.* Without question; certainly. ♦*He was by all odds the strongest candidate.*

**by a long shot** *adv. phr., informal* By a big difference; by far.—Used to add emphasis. ♦*Bert was the best swimmer in the race, by a long shot.* ♦*Our team didn't win—not by a long shot.*

**by and by** *adv.* After a while; at some time in the future; later. ♦ *Roger said he would do his homework by and by.* ♦ *The mother knew her baby would be a man by and by and do a man's work.*

**by and large** *adv. phr.* As it most often happens; more often than not; usually; mostly. ♦ *There were bad days, but it was a pleasant summer, by and large.* ♦ *By and large, women can bear pain better than men.*

**by chance** *adv. phr.* Without any cause or reason; by accident; accidentally. ♦ *Tom met Bill by chance.* ♦ *The apple fell by chance on Bobby's head.*

**by choice** *adv. phr.* As a result of choosing because of wanting to; freely. ♦ *John helped his father by choice.*

**by dint of** *prep.* By the exertion of; by the use of; through. ♦ *His success in college was largely by dint of hard study.*

**by ear** *adv. phr.* **1.** By sound, without ever reading the printed music of the piece being played. ♦ *The church choir sang the hymns by ear.* **2.** Waiting to see what will happen. ♦ *I don't want to plan now; let's just play it by ear.*

**by far** *adv. phr.* By a large difference; much. ♦ *His work was better by far than that of any other printer in the city.* ♦ *The old road is prettier, but it is by far the longer way.*

**by fits and starts** *or* **jerks** *adv. phr.* With many stops and starts, a little now and a little more later; not all the time; irregularly. ♦ *You will never get anywhere if you study just by fits and starts.*

**by heart** *adv. phr.* By exact memorizing; so well that you remember it; by memory. ♦ *The pupils learned many poems by heart.*

**by hook or by crook** *adv. phr.* By honest or dishonest ways in any way necessary. ♦ *The wolf tried to get the little pigs by hook or by crook.*

**by inches** *adv. phr.* By small or slow degrees; little by little; gradually. ♦ *The river was rising by inches.* ♦ *He was dying by inches.*

**by leaps and bounds** *adv. phr.* With long steps; very rapidly. ♦ *The school enrollment was going up by leaps and bounds.*

**by means of** *prep.* By the use of; with the help of. ♦ *By means of monthly pay-*ments, people can buy more than in the past.

**by mistake** *adv. phr.* As the result of a mistake; through error. ♦ *He picked up the wrong hat by mistake.*

**by no means** *or* **not by any means** *also* **by no manner of means** *or* **not by any manner of means** *adv. phr.* Not even a little; certainly not. ♦ *He is by no means bright.* ♦ *"May I stay home from school?" "By no means."* ♦ *Dick worked on his project Saturday, but he is not finished yet, by any means.*

**B.Y.O.** *(Abbreviation) informal* Bring Your Own. Said of a kind of party where the host or hostess does not provide the drinks or food but people bring their own.

**B.Y.O.B.** *(Abbreviation) informal* Bring Your Own Bottle. Frequently written on invitations for the kind of party where people bring their own liquor.

**by oneself** *adv. phr.* **1.** Without any others around; separate from others; alone. ♦ *The house stood by itself on a hill.* ♦ *Tom liked to go walking by himself.* **2.** Without the help of anyone else; by your own work only. ♦ *John built a flying model airplane by himself.*

**by the book** *adv. phr.* Without taking any liberties with a stated procedure; following the rules and regulations to the letter. ♦ *A good police officer does it by the book when he arrests a suspected criminal.*

**by the dozen** *or* **by the hundred** *or* **by the thousand** *adv. phr.* Very many at one time; in great numbers. ♦ *Tommy ate cookies by the dozen.* Often used in the plural, meaning even larger numbers. ♦ *The ants arrived at the picnic by the hundreds.* ♦ *The enemy attacked the fort by the thousands.*

**by the piece** *adv. phr.* Counted one piece at a time, separately for each single piece. ♦ *John bought boxes full of bags of potato chips and sold them by the piece.*

**by the same token** *adv. phr.* A propos of which; this reminds me of another thing; actually this is similar to what was talked about before. ♦ *By the same token, let me mention that not only is the entire state budget shot, but the university won't be getting any money either.*

**by the seat of one's pants** See FLY BY THE SEAT OF ONE'S PANTS.

**by the skin of one's teeth** *adv. phr.* By a narrow margin; with no room to spare; barely. ♦ *The drowning man struggled, and I got him to land by the skin of my teeth.* ♦ *She passed English by the skin of her teeth.*

**by the sweat of one's brow** *adv. phr.* By hard work; by tiring effort; laboriously. ♦ *Even with modern labor-saving machinery, the farmer makes his living by the sweat of his brow.*

**by the way** *also* **by the bye** *adv. phr.* Just as some added fact or news; as something else that I think of.—Used to introduce something related to the general subject, or brought to mind by it. ♦ *We shall expect you; by the way, dinner will be at eight.* ♦ *I was reading when the earthquake occurred, and, by the way, it was* The Last Days of Pompeii *that I was reading.*

**by turns** *adv. phr.* First one and then another in a regular way; one substituting for or following another according to a repeated plan. ♦ *On the drive to Chicago, the three men took the wheel by turns.*

**by virtue of** *also* **in virtue of** *prep.* On the strength of; because of; by reason of. ♦ *By virtue of his high rank and position, the president takes social leadership over almost everyone else.*

**by way of** *prep.* **1.** For the sake or purpose of; as. ♦ *By way of example, he described his own experience.* **2.** Through; by a route including; via. ♦ *He went from New York to San Francisco by way of Chicago.*

**by word of mouth** *adv. phr.* From person to person by the spoken word; orally. ♦ *The news got around by word of mouth.* ♦ *The message reached him quietly by word of mouth.*

**caged in** or **caged up** *adj. phr.* Caught, squeezed in; deprived of one's freedom of physical or intellectual motion. ♦*"Why is Jerry so restless?" Elvira asked. "I think he feels caged up by his new job."* ♦*Parents of young children often feel entirely caged in.*

**cake walk** See PIECE OF CAKE, IT'S A CINCH, WALK IN THE PARK.

**calculated risk** *n.* An action that may fail but is judged more likely to succeed. ♦*The sending of troops to the rebellious island was a calculated risk.*

**call a halt** *v. phr.* To give a command to stop. ♦*The scouts were tired during the hike, and the scoutmaster called a halt.* ♦*When the children's play, got too noisy, their mother called a halt.*

**call a spade a spade** *v. phr.* To call a person or thing a name that is true but not polite; speak bluntly; use the plainest language. ♦*A boy took some money from Dick's desk and said he borrowed it, but I told him he stole it; I believe in calling a spade a spade.*

**call back** *v. phr.* To return a phone call. ♦*"I can't speak now, but can I call you back in an hour?"*

**call down** also **dress down** *v., informal* To scold. ♦*Jim was called down by his teacher for being late to class.* ♦*Mother called Bob down for walking into the kitchen with muddy boots.*

**call even a snowflake a spade** See POT CALLS THE KETTLE BLACK.

**call for** *v.* **1.** To come or go to get (someone or something). ♦*John called for Mary to take her to the dance.* **2.** To need; require. ♦*The cake recipe calls for two cups of flour.* ♦*Success in school calls for much hard study.*

**call girl** *n., slang* A prostitute catering to wealthy clientele, especially one who is contacted by telephone for an appointment. ♦*Rush Street is full of call girls.*

**calling down** also **dressing down** *n. phr., informal* A scolding; reprimand. ♦*The judge gave the boy a calling down for speeding.*

**call in question** or **call into question** or **call in doubt** *v. phr.* To say (something) may be a mistake; express doubt about; question. ♦*Bill called in ques-*

tion Ed's remark that basketball is safer than football.

**call it a day** *v. phr.* To declare that a given day's work has been accomplished and go home; to quit for the day. ♦*"Let's call it a day," the boss said, "and go out for a drink."*

**call it a night** *v. phr.* To declare that an evening party or other activity conducted late in the day is finished. ♦*I am so tired that I am going to call it a night and go to bed.*

**call it quits** *v. phr., informal* **1.** To decide to stop what you are doing; quit. ♦*When Tom had painted half the garage, he called it quits.* **2.** To agree that each side in a fight is satisfied; stop fighting because a wrong has been paid back; say things are even. ♦*Pete called Tom a bad name, and they fought till Tom gave Pete a bloody nose; then they called it quits.* **3.** To cultivate a habit no longer. ♦*"Yes, I called it quits with cigarettes three years ago."*

**call names** *v. phr.* To use ugly or unkind words when speaking to someone or when talking about someone.—Usually used by or to children. ♦*Bill got so mad he started calling Frank names.*

**call off** *v.* To stop (something planned); quit; cancel. ♦*The baseball game was called off because of rain.*

**call of the wild** *n. phr.* The appeal of nature in the raw; the city worker's desire to escape into nature. ♦*My neighbor has got the call of the wild; he packed up his tent and set out on a trip to discover Alaska.*

**call on** or **call upon** *v.* **1.** To make a call upon; visit. ♦*Mr. Brown called on an old friend while he was in the city.* **2.** To ask for help. ♦*He called on a friend to give him money for the busfare to his home.*

**call one's bluff** *v. phr., informal* To ask someone to prove what he says he can or will do. (Originally from the card game of poker.) ♦*Tom said he could jump twenty feet and so Dick called his bluff and said "Let's see you do it!"*

**call one's shot** *v. phr.* **1.** To tell before firing where a bullet will hit. ♦*An expert rifleman can call his shot regu-*

*larly.* ♦*The wind was strong and John couldn't call his shots.* **2.** *or* **call the turn** To tell in advance the result of something before you do it. ♦*Mary won three games in a row, just as she said she would. She called her turns well.*

**call on the carpet** *v. phr., informal* To call (a person) before an authority (as a boss or teacher) for a scolding or reprimand. ♦*The worker was called on the carpet by the boss for sleeping on the job.*

**call the roll** *v. phr.* To read out the names on a certain list, usually in alphabetical order. ♦*The sergeant called the roll of the newly enlisted volunteers in the army.*

**call the shots** *v. phr., informal* To give orders; be in charge; direct; control. ♦*Bob is a first-rate leader who knows how to call the shots.*

**call the tune** *v. phr., informal* To be in control; give orders or directions; command. ♦*Bill was president of the club but Jim was secretary and called the tune.*

**call to account** *v. phr.* **1.** To ask (someone) to explain why he did something wrong (as breaking a rule). ♦*The principal called Jim to account after Jim left school early without permission.* **2.** To scold (as for wrong conduct); reprimand. ♦*The father called his son to account for disobeying him.*

**call to arms** *v. phr.* To summon into the army. ♦*During World War II millions of Americans were called to arms to fight for their country.*

**call to mind** *v. phr.* To remember; cause to remember. ♦*Your story calls to mind a similar event that happened to us a few years back.*

**call to order** *v. phr.* **1.** To open (a meeting) formally. ♦*The chairman called the committee to order.* ♦*The president pounded with his gavel to call the convention to order.* **2.** To warn not to break the rules of a meeting. ♦*The judge called the people in the court room to order when they talked too loud.*

**call out** *v. phr.* **1.** To shout; speak loudly. ♦*My name was called out several times, but I was unable to hear it.* **2.** To summon someone. ♦*If the rioting con-*tinues, the governor will have to call out the National Guard.*

**call up** *v.* (stress on *up*) **1.** To make someone think of; bring to mind; remind. ♦*The picture of the Capitol called up memories of our class trip.* **2.** To tell to come (as before a court). ♦*The district attorney called up three witnesses.* **3.** To bring together for a purpose; bring into action. ♦*Jim called up all his strength, pushed past the players blocking him, and ran for a touchdown.* ♦*The army called up its reserves when war seemed near.* **4.** To call on the telephone. ♦*She called up a friend just for a chat.*

**call-up** *n. phr.* (stress on *call*) An occasional invitee from another or a junior group to play in another sports club. ♦*"Who is that player?" "He's a call-up from the minor league."*

**call upon** (stress on *call*) See CALL ON.

**calm before the storm** *or* **lull before the storm** *n. phr.* The ominous quiet before an excess of noise or the tenuous peace before war. ♦*"Why is everything so quiet?" Jenny asked. "We can't become too happy about it," her husband George answered. "It's only the calm before the storm."*

**calm down** *v. phr.* To become quiet; relax. ♦*"Calm down, Mr. Smith," the doctor said with a reassuring smile. "You are going to live a long time."*

**camp follower** *n.* **1.** A man or woman who goes with an army, not to fight but to sell something. ♦*Nowadays camp followers are not allowed as they were long ago.* **2.** A person who goes with a famous or powerful person or group in hope of profit. ♦*A man who runs for president has many camp followers.*

**camp out** *v.* To live, cook, and sleep out of doors (as in a tent). ♦*We camped out near the river for a week.*

**cancel out** *v.* To destroy the effect of; balance or make useless. ♦*The boy got an "A" in history to cancel out the "C" he got in arithmetic.* ♦*Tom's hot temper cancels out his skill as a player.*

**cancer stick** *n., slang* A cigarette. ♦*Throw away that cancer stick! Smoking is bad for you!*

**canned heat** *n.* Chemicals in a can which burn with a hot, smokeless flame. ♦*Some people use canned heat to keep* *food warm.* ♦*The mountain climbers used canned heat for cooking.*

**canned laughter** *n.*, *informal* The sounds of laughter heard on certain television programs that were obviously not recorded in front of a live audience and are played for the benefit of the audience from a stereo track to underscore the funny points. ♦*"How can there be an audience in this show when it is taking place in the jungle?—Why, it's canned laughter you're hearing."*

**canned music** *n.* Recorded music, as opposed to music played live. ♦*"Let us go to a real concert, honey," Mike said. "I am tired of all this canned music we've been listening to."*

**can of worms** *n.*, *slang*, *informal* **1.** A complex problem, or complicated situation. ♦*Let's not get into big city politics—that's a different can of worms.* **2.** A very restless, jittery person. ♦*Joe can't sit still for a minute—he is a can of worms.*

**can't have it both ways** See HAVE ONE'S CAKE AND EAT IT TOO.

**can't help but** *(informal)* ALSO *(formal)* **cannot but** *v. phr.* To be forced to; can only; must. ♦*When the streets are full of melting snow, you can't help but get your shoes wet.*

**can't make an omelette without breaking (some) eggs** To achieve a certain goal one must sometimes incur damage, experience difficulties, or make sacrifices.—A proverb. ♦*When we drove across the country, we put a lot of mileage on our car and had a flat tire, but it was a pleasant trip. "Well, you can't make an omelette without breaking some eggs," my wife said with a smile.*

**can't make bricks without straw** Often heard when one sees someone trying to produce something without the proper ingredients, no matter how insignificant they may seem.—A proverb. ♦*That fancy new printer of yours won't work without toner. Go and get some—you can't make bricks without straw, you know!*

**can't see the wood for the trees** *or* **can't see the woods for the trees** *or* **can't see the forest for the trees** *v. phr.* To be unable to judge or understand the whole because of attention to the parts; criticize small things and not see

the value or the aim of the future achievement. ♦*Teachers sometimes notice language errors and do not see the good ideas in a composition; they cannot see the woods for the trees.*

**can you beat it?** *phrasal idiom* Are you able to exceed what has been accomplished; can you do better than what you saw? ♦*Stanley was hired as college president in the South—can you beat it?*

**cap the climax** *v. phr.* To exceed what is already a high point of achievement. ♦*Sam's piano recital was great, but Bill's performance capped the climax.*

**cards stacked against one** See STACK THE CARDS.

**card up one's sleeve** *n. phr.*, *informal* Another help, plan, or argument kept back and produced if needed; another way to do something. ♦*John knew his mother would lend him money if necessary, but he kept that card up his sleeve.* ♦*Bill always has a card up his sleeve, so when his first plan failed he tried another.* Compare ACE IN THE HOLE 2.

**care about** *v. phr.* **1.** To be fond of; to like something. ♦*I care a great deal about my family.* **2.** To mind something; to be worried. ♦*Parents usually care about their children when they leave home for the first time.* **3.** To be interested in. ♦*John cares much about classical music.*

**care for** *v. phr.* Have regard for someone or something. ♦*Albert is the kind of selfish person who cares only for himself.*

**carp at** *v. phr.* To complain about in an unpleasant, irritating manner. ♦*When will you stop carping about how bad things are at your job?*

**car pool** *n.* A group of people who take turns driving each other to work or on some other regular trip. ♦*It was John's father's week to drive his own car in the car pool.*

**car pool lane** *n. phr.* A special lane on busy four-lane highways reserved for cars that have at least two people riding in them. ♦*"You can go faster by getting over into the car pool lane," Jean said to her husband. "After all, we have the two children with us!"*

**carriage trade** *n.*, *literary* Rich or upper class people. ♦*The hotel is so expensive that only the carriage trade stays there.*

♦*The carriage trade buys its clothes at the best stores.*

**carrot and stick** *n. phr.* The promise of reward and threat of punishment, both at the same time. ♦*John's father used the carrot and stick when he talked about his low grades.*

**carry a torch** *or* **carry the torch** *v. phr.* **1.** To show great and unchanging loyalty to a cause or a person. ♦*Although the others gave up fighting for their rights, John continued to carry the torch.* **2.** *informal* To be in love, usually without success or return. ♦*He is carrying a torch for Anna, even though she is in love with someone else.*

**carry a tune** *v. phr.* To sing the right notes without catching any false ones. ♦*Al is a wonderful fellow, but he sure can't carry a tune and his singing is a pain to listen to.*

**carry away** *v.* To cause very strong feeling; excite or delight to the loss of cool judgment. ♦*The music carried her away.* ♦*He let his anger carry him away.*—Often used in the passive. ♦*She was carried away by the man's charm.*

**carry coals to Newcastle** *v. phr.* To do something unnecessary; bring or furnish something of which there is plenty. ♦*The man who waters his grass after a good rain is carrying coals to Newcastle.* [Newcastle is an English city near many coal mines, and coal is sent out from there to other places.]

**carrying charge** *n.* An extra cost added to the price of something bought on weekly or monthly payments. ♦*The price of the bicycle was $50. Jim bought it for $5.00 a month for ten months plus a carrying charge of $1 a month.*

**carry off** *v.* **1.** To cause death of; kill. ♦*Years ago smallpox carried off hundreds of Indians of the Sioux tribe.* Compare WIPE OUT. **2.** To succeed in winning. ♦*Jim carried off two gold medals in the track meet.* **3.** To succeed somewhat unexpectedly. ♦*The spy planned to deceive the enemy soldiers and carried it off very well.*

**carry off the palm** *or* **bear off the palm** *v. phr., literary* To gain the victory; win. ♦*John carried off the palm in the tennis championship match.* ♦*Our army bore off the palm in the battle.* [From the fact that long ago a palm leaf was given to the winner in a game as a sign of victory.]

**carry on** *v.* **1.** To work at; be busy with; manage. ♦*Bill and his father carried on a hardware business.* ♦*Mr. Jones and Mr. Smith carried on a long correspondence with each other.* **2.** To keep doing as before; continue. ♦*After his father died, Bill carried on with the business.* **3a.** *informal* To behave in a noisy, foolish, and troublesome manner. ♦*The boys carried on in the swimming pool until the lifeguard ordered them out.* **3b.** *informal* To make too great a show of feeling, such as anger, grief, and pain. ♦*John carried on for ten minutes after he hit his thumb with the hammer.* **4.** *informal* To act in an immoral or scandalous way; act disgracefully. ♦*The neighbors said that he was carrying on with an underage girl.*

**carry one's cross** *or* *(literary)* **bear one's cross** *v. phr.* To live with pain or trouble; keep on even though you suffer or have trouble. ♦*Weak ankles are a cross Joe carries while the other boys play basketball.*

**carry out** *v.* To put into action; follow; execute. ♦*The generals were determined to carry out their plans to defeat the enemy.*

**carry over** *v.* **1.** To save for another time. ♦*What you learn in school should carry over into adult life.* **2.** To transfer (as a figure) from one column, page, or book to another. ♦*When he added up the figures, he carried over the total into the next year's account book.* **3.** To continue in another place. ♦*The story was carried over to the next page.*

**carry the ball** *v. phr., informal* To take the most important or difficult part in an action or business. ♦*When the going is rough, Fred can always be depended on to carry the ball.*

**carry the banner** *v. phr.* To support a cause or an ideal with obvious advocacy. ♦*Our college is carrying the banner for saving the humpback whale, which is on the list of endangered species.*

**carry the day** *v. phr., informal* To win completely; to succeed in getting one's aim accomplished. ♦*The defense attorney's summary before the jury helped him carry the day.*

**carry through** v. **1a.** To put into action. ♦ *Mr. Green was not able to carry through his plans for a hike because he broke his leg.* **1b.** To do something you have planned; put a plan into action. ♦ *Jean makes good plans but she cannot carry through with any of them.* **2.** To keep (someone) from failing or stopping; bring through; help. ♦ *When the tire blew out, the rules Jim had learned in driving class carried him through safely.*

**carry weight** n. To be influential; have significance and/or clout; impress. ♦ *A letter of recommendation from a full professor carries more weight than a letter from an assistant professor.*

**cart before the horse (to put)** n. phr., informal Things in wrong order; something backwards or mixed up.—An overused expression. Usually used with put but sometimes with get or have. ♦ *To get married first and then get a job is getting the cart before the horse.*

**carte blanche** n. phr. The freedom to act any way one wishes, or to spend as much as one wants to. ♦ *Jerry is such a spoiled brat because his parents gave him carte blanche even before he was out of high school.*

**cart off** or **cart away** v., informal To take away, often with force or with rough handling or behavior. ♦ *The police carted the rioters off to jail.*

**carved** or **chiseled** or **inscribed in granite** / **written in stone** adj. phr. Holy; unchangeable; noble and of ancient origin. ♦ *You should wear shoes when you come to class, although this is not carved in granite.* ♦ *The Constitution of the United States is so hard to change that one thinks of it as written in stone.*

**carve up** v. phr. To divide according to military occupation zones, especially after a major war. ♦ *The map of Europe was badly carved up both after World War I and after World War II.*

**case in point** n. phr. An example that proves something or helps to make something clearer. ♦ *An American can rise from the humblest beginnings to become president. Abraham Lincoln is a case in point.*

**case the joint** v. phr., slang **1.** To study the layout of a place one wishes to bur-glarize. ♦ *The hooded criminals carefully cased the joint before robbing the neighborhood bank.* **2.** To familiarize oneself with a potential workplace or vacation spot as a matter of preliminary planning. ♦ *"Hello Fred," he said. "Are you working here now?" "No, not yet," Fred answered. "I am merely casing the joint."*

**cash-and-carry**[1] adj. Selling things for cash money only and letting the customer carry them home, not having the store deliver them; also sold in this way. ♦ *This is a cash-and-carry store only.* ♦ *You can save money at a cash-and-carry sale.*

**cash-and-carry**[2] adv. With no credit, no time payments, and no deliveries. ♦ *Some stores sell cash-and-carry only.* ♦ *It is cheaper to buy cash-and-carry.*

**cash crop** n. A crop grown to be sold. ♦ *Cotton is a cash crop in the South.* ♦ *They raise potatoes to eat, but tobacco is their cash crop.*

**cash in** v. **1.** To exchange (as poker chips or bonds) for the value in money. ♦ *When the card game ended, the players cashed in their chips and went home.* **2.** or **cash in one's chips** slang To die. ♦ *When the outlaw cashed in his chips, he was buried with his boots on.*

**cash in on** v., informal To see (a chance) and profit by it; take advantage of (an opportunity or happening). ♦ *Mr. Brown cashed in on people's great interest in camping and sold three hundred tents.*

**cash on the barrelhead** n. phr., informal Money paid at once; money paid when something is bought. ♦ *Father paid cash on the barrelhead for a new car.* ♦ *Some lawyers want cash on the barrelhead.*

**cast** or **shed** or **throw light upon** v. phr. To explain; illuminate; clarify. ♦ *The letters that were found suddenly cast a new light on the circumstances of Tom's disappearance.* ♦ *Einstein's General Theory of Relativity threw light upon the enigma of our universe.*

**cast about** also **cast around** v., literary **1.** To look everywhere; search. ♦ *The committee was casting about for an experienced teacher to take the retiring principal's place.* **2.** To search your mind; try to remember something; try to think of something. ♦ *The teacher cast around for an easy way to explain the lesson.*

**cast down** *adj.* Discouraged; sad; unhappy.—Used less often than the reverse form, *downcast.* ♦ *Mary was cast down at the news of her uncle's death.*

**cast in one's lot with** *formal* See THROW IN ONE'S LOT WITH.

**cast off** *v.* **1a.** *or* **cast loose** To unfasten; untie; let loose (as a rope holding a boat). ♦ *The captain of the boat cast off the line and we were soon out in open water.* **1b.** To untie a rope holding a boat or something suggesting a boat. ♦ *We cast off and set sail at 6 A.M.* **2.** To knit the last row of stitches. ♦ *When she had knitted the twentieth row of stitches she cast off.* **3.** To say that you do not know (someone) any more; not accept as a relative or friend. ♦ *Mr. Jones cast off his daughter when she married against his wishes.*

**cast oneself on someone's mercy** *v. phr.* To declare that someone, especially an accused person in a court of law, is dependent on someone else's pity, e.g., that of the judge and the jury. ♦ *Having run out of all possible defense strategies, the accused decided to throw himself on the mercy of the court.*

**cast out** *v., formal* To force (someone) to go out or away; banish; expel. ♦ *After the scandal, he was cast out of the best society.*

**cast pearls before swine** *or* **cast one's pearls before swine** *n. phr., literary* To waste good acts or valuable things on someone who won't understand or be thankful for them, just as pigs won't appreciate pearls.—Often used in negative sentences. ♦ *I won't waste good advice on John any more because he never listens to it. I won't cast pearls before swine.*

**cast the first stone** *v. phr., biblical* To be the first to blame someone, lead accusers against a wrongdoer. ♦ *Jesus said that a person who was without sin could cast the first stone.*

**catch-as-catch-can¹** *adv. phr.* In a free manner; in any way possible; in the best way you can. ♦ *On moving day everything is packed and we eat meals catch-as-catch-can.*

**catch-as-catch-can²** *adj. phr.* Using any means or method; unplanned; free. ♦ *Politics is rather a catch-as-catch-can business.*

**catch at** *v.* **1.** To try to catch suddenly; grab for. ♦ *The boy on the merry-go-round caught at the brass ring, but did not get it.* **2.** To seize quickly; accept mentally or physically. ♦ *The hungry man caught at the sandwich and began to eat.*

**catch cold** *v. phr.* **1.** *or* **take cold** To get a common cold-weather sickness that causes a running nose, sneezing, and sometimes sore throat and fever or other symptoms. ♦ *Don't get your feet wet or you'll catch cold.* **2.** *informal* To catch unprepared or not ready for a question or unexpected happening. ♦ *I had not studied my lesson carefully, and the teacher's question caught me cold.*

**catch (someone) dead** *v. phr., informal* To see or hear (someone) in an embarrassing act or place at any time. Used in the negative usually in the passive. ♦ *John wouldn't be caught dead in the necktie he got for Christmas.*

**catch fire** *v. phr.* **1.** To begin to burn. ♦ *When he dropped a match in the leaves, they caught fire.* **2.** To become excited. ♦ *The audience caught fire at the speaker's words and began to cheer.*

**catch flak** *or* **take flak** *v. phr.* To draw fire from an air defense gun as it shoots at enemy bombers, hence to be in for criticism by others. ♦ *The American B-52 bombers took a lot of flak over Germany during World War II.* ♦ *Joe's father has just come home late and he's catching flak again from his disgruntled wife.*

**catch hold of** *v. phr.* To grasp a person or a thing. ♦ *"I've been trying to catch hold of you all week," John said, "but you were out of town."* ♦ *The mountain climber successfully caught hold of his friend's hand and thereby saved his life.*

**catch it** *or* **get it** *v. phr., informal* To be scolded or punished.—Usually used of children. ♦ *John knew he would catch it when he came home late for supper.* ♦ *Wow, Johnny! When your mother sees those torn pants, you're going to get it.*

**catch it in the neck** *or* **get it in the neck** *v. phr., slang* To be blamed or punished. ♦ *Tom got it in the neck because he forgot to close the windows when it rained.* ♦ *Students get it in the neck when they lose library books.*

**catch off balance** *v. phr.* To confront someone with physical force or with a statement or question he or she is not prepared to answer or deal with; to exploit the disadvantage of another. ♦ *Your question has caught me off balance; please give me some time to think about your problem.*

**catch off guard** *v. phr.* To challenge or confront a person at a time of lack of preparedness or sufficient care. ♦ *The suspect was caught off guard by the detective and confessed where he had hidden the stolen car.*

**catch on** *v., informal* **1.** To understand; learn about.—Often used with *to.* ♦ *You'll catch on to the job after you've been here awhile.* ♦ *Don't play any tricks on Joe. When he catches on, he will beat you.* **2.** To become popular; be done or used by many people. ♦ *The song caught on and was sung and played everywhere.* **3.** To be hired; get a job. ♦ *The ball player caught on with a big league team last year.*

**catch one's breath** *v. phr.* **1.** To breathe in suddenly with fear or surprise. ♦ *The beauty of the scene made him catch his breath.* **2a.** To rest and get back your normal breathing, as after running. ♦ *After running to the bus stop, we sat down to catch our breath.* **2b.** To relax for a moment after any work. ♦ *After the day's work we sat down over coffee to catch our breath.*

**catch one's death of** *or* **take one's death of** *v. phr., informal* To become very ill with (a cold, pneumonia, flu). ♦ *Johnny fell in the icy water and almost took his death of cold.* Sometimes used in the short form "catch your death." ♦ *"Johnny! Come right in here and put your coat and hat on. You'll catch your death!"*

**catch one's drift** *v. phr.* To understand what one's interlocutor is trying to imply, or is hinting at; to be able to figure out where a conversation is headed. ♦ *"If I am catching your drift right," Mary said sadly, "you're not really interested in marriage."*

**catch one's eye** *v. phr.* To attract your attention. ♦ *I caught his eye as he* moved through the crowd, and waved at him to come over. ♦ *The dress in the window caught her eye when she passed the store.*

**catch red-handed** *v. phr.* To apprehend a person during the act of committing an illicit or criminal act. ♦ *Al was caught red-handed at the local store when he was trying to walk out with a new camera he had not paid for.*

**catch sight of** *v. phr.* To see suddenly or unexpectedly. ♦ *Allan caught sight of a kingbird in a maple tree.*

**catch some rays** *v. phr., slang, informal* To get tanned while sunbathing. ♦ *Tomorrow I'll go to the beach and try to catch some rays.*

**catch some Z's** *v. phr., slang, informal* To take a nap, to go to sleep. (Because of the *z* sound resembling snoring.) ♦ *I want to hit the sack and catch some Z's.*

**catch the flu** *or* **catch a cold** *v. phr.* To contract influenza or some other communicable disease of short duration. ♦ *"Why is Joe not at work again?" the office manager asked. "He's caught the flu again," Joe's brother Tom replied.*

**catch-22** *n., informal* From Joseph Heller's novel *Catch-22,* set in World War II. **1.** A regulation or situation that is self-contradictory or that conflicts with another regulation. In Heller's book it referred to the regulation that flight crews must report for duty unless excused for reasons of insanity, but that any one claiming such an excuse must, by definition, be sane. ♦ *Government rules require workers to expose any wrongdoing in their office, but the Catch-22 prevents them from doing so, because they are not allowed to disclose any information about their work.* **2.** A paradoxical situation. ♦ *The Catch-22 of job-hunting was that the factory wanted to hire only workers who had experience making computers but the only way to get the experience was by working at the computer factory.*

**catch up** *v.* **1.** To take or pick up suddenly; grab (something). ♦ *She caught up the book from the table and ran out of the room.* **2.** To capture or trap (someone) in a situation; concern or interest very much.—Usually used in the passive with *in.* ♦ *We were so caught up in the movie we forgot what time it* *was.* **3.** To go fast enough or do enough so as not to be behind; overtake; come even.—Often used with *to* or *with.* ♦ *Johnny ran hard and tried to catch up to his friends.* ♦ *Mary missed two weeks of school; she must work hard to catch up with her class.* Compare UP TO. **4.** To find out about or get proof to punish or arrest.—Usually used with *with.* ♦ *A man told the police where the robbers were hiding, so the police finally caught up with them.* **5.** To result in something bad; bring punishment.—Usually used with *with.* ♦ *The boy's fighting caught up with him and he was expelled from school.* ♦ **6.** To finish; not lose or be behind.—Used with *on* and often in the phrase *get caught up on.* ♦ *Frank stayed up late to get caught up on his homework.*

**catch up with** *v. phr.* To come level with someone being pursued; to reach the same level of income, education, etc., as someone emulated. ♦ *John is afraid that he will never be able to catch up with his older brother, who was nominated for the Nobel Prize in medicine.*

**catch with one's pants down** *v. phr., slang* To surprise someone in an embarrassing position or guilty act. ♦ *They thought they could succeed in the robbery, but they got caught with their pants down.*

**catch you later** Good-bye, see you around, etc. ♦ *"I must run now," Jerry said, "but I'll catch you later and we can talk some more."*

**cater to** *v. phr.* To provide what is needed to fulfill a demand; e.g., food at a party, flattering words to a haughty superior, etc. ♦ *The television industry caters to all sorts of taste in home entertainment.* ♦ *If you don't stop catering to the boss' vanity, everybody will start to hate you in the office.*

**cat got one's tongue** *v. phr.* You are not able or willing to talk because of shyness. Usually used about children or as a question to children. ♦ *The little girl had a poem to recite, but the cat got her tongue.*

**cat has nine lives** *v. phr.* A cat can move so fast and jump so well that he seems to escape being killed many times. ♦ *We thought our cat would be killed when he fell from the roof of the house. He was not, but he used up one of his nine lives.*

**cathouse** *n., slang* A house of ill repute, a house of prostitution. ♦ *Massage parlors are frequently cathouses in disguise.*

**cat's meow** or **cat's pajamas** *n., slang* Something very wonderful, special, or good. ♦ *John's new bike is really the cat's meow.* ♦ *Mary's party is going to be the cat's pajamas.*

**catnap** *n. phr.* A short period of rest during which one falls asleep, even if only lightly. ♦ *I like to take a catnap in the afternoon.*

**caught short** *adj. phr., informal* Not having enough of something when you need it. ♦ *Mrs. Ford was caught short when the newspaper boy came for his money a day early.* ♦ *The man was caught short of clothes when he had to go on a trip.*

**cause a stir** *v. phr.* To cause a considerably greater reaction than was anticipated. ♦ *The well-known dramatic actress caused quite a stir when she accepted* Playboy *magazine's offer to pose in the nude as Playmate of the Month.*

**cause eyebrows to raise** *v. phr.* To do something that causes consternation; to shock others. ♦ *When Algernon entered Orchestra Hall barefoot and wearing a woman's wig, he caused eyebrows to raise.*

**cavalry are coming** or **cavalry are here** or **marines have landed** or **send in the cavalry** Help is on its way; the rescuers are approaching.—A proverb. ♦ *Jane was struggling with the new furniture when Jerry arrived from work. "The cavalry are coming!" Jane cried out with a laugh.*

**cave in** *v.* **1.** To fall or collapse inward. ♦ *The mine caved in and crushed three miners.* ♦ *Don't climb on that old roof. It might cave in.* **2.** *informal* To weaken and be forced to give up. ♦ *The children begged their father to take them to the circus until he caved in.* ♦ *After the atomic bomb, Japan caved in and the war ceased.*

**cease fire** *v.* To give a military command ordering soldiers to stop shooting. ♦ *"Cease fire!" the captain cried, and the shooting stopped.*

**cease-fire** *n.* A period of negotiated nonaggression, when the warring parties involved promise not to attack.

♦ *Unfortunately, the cease-fire in Bosnia was broken many times by all parties concerned.*

**century** See TURN OF THE CENTURY.

**C.E.O.** *n.* Abbreviation of "Chief Executive Officer." The head of a company, factory, firm, etc. ♦ *We are very proud of the fact that our C.E.O. is a young woman.*

**chain gang** *n.* A group of convicts or slaves in the old South who were chained together. ♦ *Chain gangs are no longer an acceptable way of punishment, according to modern criminologists.*

**chain letter** *n.* A letter which each person receiving it is asked to copy and send to several others. ♦ *Most chain letters die out quickly.*

**chain-smoke** *v.* To smoke cigarettes or cigars one after another without stopping. ♦ *Mr. Jones is very nervous. He chain-smokes cigars.* **chain smoker** *n.* ♦ *Mr. Jones is a chain smoker.* **chain-smoking** *adj. or n.* ♦ *Chain smoking is very dangerous to health.*

**chain stores** *n.* A series of stores in different locations, joined together under one ownership and general management. ♦ *The goods in chain stores tend to be more uniform than in independent ones.*

**chained to the oars** *adj. phr.* The condition of being forced to do strenuous and unwelcome labor against one's wishes for an extended period of time. ♦ *Teachers in large public schools frequently complain that they feel as if they had been chained to the oars.*

**chalk it up to experience** *v. phr.* To record in memory a failure so as to avoid repeating the same mistake in the future. ♦ *When the Jones' new business venture selling computers from door to door had failed, Mr. Jones said "OK, let's chalk this one up to experience and start doing something else."*

**chalk up** *v., informal* **1.** To write down as part of a score; record. ♦ *The scorekeeper chalked up one more point for the home team.* **2.** To make (a score or part of a score); score. ♦ *The team chalked up another victory.* ♦ *Bob chalked up a home run and two base hits in the game.* ♦ *Mary chalked up good grades this term.*

**champ at the bit** *v. phr.* To be eager to begin; be tired of being held back; want to start. ♦ *The horses were champing at the bit, anxious to start racing.*

**chance it** *v. phr.* To be willing to risk an action whose outcome is uncertain. ♦ *"Should we take the boat out in such stormy weather?" Jim asked. "We can chance it," Tony replied. "We have enough experience."*

**chance of a snowball in hell** *or* **chance of a fart in a windstorm** *slang; the second version is vulgar, hence avoidable* To have practically no chance at all of accomplishing what one has set out to do.—A proverb. ♦ *If we continue to move as slowly as we do, we'll have the chance of a snowball in hell to arrive at the Olympics in time.*

**chance on** *also* **chance upon** *v.* To happen to find or meet; find or meet by accident. ♦ *On our vacation we chanced upon an interesting antique store.* ♦ *Mary dropped her ring in the yard, and Mother chanced on it as she was raking.*

**chances are** *v. phr.* To be likely; to be probable; to have a good chance that something is decidable as to its being true or false. ♦ *Chances are it won't rain anymore today because the sky cleared up entirely.*

**change color** *v. phr.* **1.** To become pale. ♦ *The sight was so horrible that Mary changed color from fear.* ♦ *Bill lost so much blood from the cut that he changed color.* **2.** To become pink or red in the face; become flushed; blush. ♦ *Mary changed color when the teacher praised her drawing.*

**change hands** *v. phr.* To change or transfer ownership. ♦ *Ever since our apartment building changed hands, things are working a lot better.*

**change horses in the middle of a stream** *or* **change horses in midstream** *v. phr.* To make new plans or choose a new leader in the middle of an important activity. ♦ *When a new president is to be elected during a war, the people may decide not to change horses in the middle of a stream.*

**change off** *v., informal* To take turns doing something; alternate. ♦ *John and Bill changed off at riding the bicycle.*

**change of heart** *n. phr.* A change in the way one feels or thinks about a given task, idea or problem to be solved. ◆ *Joan had a change of heart and suddenly broke off her engagement to Tim.*

**change of life** *n. phr.* The menopause (primarily in women). ◆ *Women usually undergo a change of life in their forties or fifties.*

**change of pace** *n. phr.* A quick change in what you are doing. ◆ *John studied for three hours and then read a comic book for a change of pace.*

**change one's mind** *v. phr.* To alter one's opinion or judgment on a given issue. ◆ *I used to hate Chicago, but as the years passed I gradually changed my mind and now I actually love living here.*

**change one's tune** *v. phr., informal* To make a change in your story, statement, or claim; change your way of acting. ◆ *The man said he was innocent, but when they found the stolen money in his pocket he changed his tune.*

**chapter and verse** *adv. phr.* Entirely, authoritatively, and exhaustively. ◆ *When the police were interrogating Jeff about the serial murders in town, he gave them every last detail, chapter and verse.*

**charge account** *n.* An agreement with a store through which you can buy things and pay for them later. ◆ *Mother bought a new dress on her charge account.*

**charge off** *v.* To consider or record as a loss, especially in an account book. ◆ *The store owner charged off all of the last season's stock of suits.*

**charge something to something** *v.* **1.** To place the blame on; make responsible for. ◆ *John failed to win a prize, but he charged it to his lack of experience.* **2.** To buy something on the credit of. ◆ *Mrs. Smith bought a new pocketbook and charged it to her husband.*

**charge up** *v. phr.* **1.** To submit to a flow of electricity in order to make functional. ◆ *I mustn't forget to charge up my razor before we go on our trip.* **2.** To use up all the available credit one has on one's credit card(s). ◆ *"Let's charge dinner on the Master Card," Jane said. "Unfortunately I can't," Jim replied. "All of my credit cards are completely charged up."*

**charge with** *v. phr.* To accuse someone in a court of law. ◆ *The criminal was charged with aggravated kidnapping across a state line.*

**charmed life** *n.* A life often saved from danger; a life full of lucky escapes. ◆ *He was in two airplane accidents, but he had a charmed life.*

**chart out** *v. phr.* To set or establish a plan for some activity. ◆ *The mountain climbers charted out their activities for each day for their trip to Mount Everest.*

**chase after** See RUN AFTER.

**chasing the rainbow** *v. phr.* To pursue unrealistic dreams and expectations. ◆ *It would be better for my spinster aunt to marry the mailman and settle down than to be chasing the rainbow like some romantic schoolgirl.*

**cheapskate** *n., informal* A selfish or stingy person; a person who will not spend much.—An insulting term. ◆ *None of the girls like to go out on a date with him because he is a cheapskate.*

**cheap shot** *n. phr.* An unbecomingly unfair and unsporting statement made against someone. ◆ *The radio commentator said that the senator's portrayal of his opponent as a criminal was nothing but a cheap shot; in fact, his police record showed no more than one arrest when he protested against the war in Vietnam as a young student.*

**cheat on someone** *or* **something** *v. phr.* **1.** To be unfaithful to one's husband, wife, or "significant other." ◆ *"Do you think Albert cheats on Vanessa?" "Well, in fact, she cheats on him as well."* **2.** To use crib notes during a final examination, a cause for dismissal from most colleges and universities. ◆ *Oliver was thrown out of West Point Military Academy because he cheated on his final math exam.*

**check in** *v.* **1a.** To sign your name (as at a hotel or convention). ◆ *The last guests to reach the hotel checked in at 12 o'clock.* **1b.** *informal* To arrive. ◆ *The friends we had invited did not check in until Saturday.* **2.** To receive (something) back and make a record of it. ◆ *The coach checked in the football uniforms at the end of the school year.* ◆ *The students put their books on the* *library desk, and the librarian checked them in.*

**check into** *v. phr.* **1.** To register in a hotel, motel, or hospital. ♦ *The doctor recommended that I should check into the nearest hospital.* **2.** To investigate. ♦ *The FBI decided to check into the background of a number of suspicious characters in our neighborhood.*

**check off** *v.* To put a mark beside (the name of a person or thing on a list) to show that it has been counted. ♦ *The teacher checked off each pupil as he got on the bus.*

**check on someone/thing** *or* **check up on someone/thing** *v.* To try to find out the truth or rightness of; make sure of; examine; inspect; investigate. ♦ *We checked on Dan's age by getting his birth record.*

**check out** *v.* **1a.** To pay your hotel bill and leave. ♦ *The last guests checked out of their rooms in the morning.* **1b.** *informal* To go away; leave. ♦ *I hoped our guest would stay but he had to check out before Monday.* **2a.** To make a list or record of. ♦ *They checked out all the goods in the store.* **2b.** To give or lend (something) and make a record of it. ♦ *The boss checked out the tools to the workmen as they came to work.* **2c.** To get (something) after a record has been made of it. ♦ *I checked out a book from the library.* **3.** *informal* To test (something, like a part of a motor). ♦ *The mechanic checked out the car battery.* ♦ *"He checked out from the motel at nine," said the detective, "then he checked out the air in the car tires and his list of local clients."* **4.** *slang* To die. ♦ *He seemed too young to check out.*

**check up** *v.* (stress on *up*) To find out or try to find out the truth or correctness of something; make sure of something; investigate. ♦ *Mrs. Brown thought she had heard a burglar in the house, so Mr. Brown checked up, but found nobody.* ♦ *Bill thought he had a date with Janie, but phoned her to check up.*

**checkup** *n.* (stress on *check*) A periodic examination by a physician or of some equipment by a mechanic. ♦ *I am overdue for my annual physical checkup.* ♦ *I need to take my car in for a checkup.*

**check with** *v. phr.* **1.** To consult. ♦ *I want to check with my lawyer before I sign*

*the papers.* **2.** To agree with. ♦ *Does my reconciliation of our account check with the bank statement?*

**cheer on** *v. phr.* To vociferously encourage a person or a team during a sports event. ♦ *The spectators at the stadium cheered on their home team.*

**cheer up** *v.* **1.** To feel happy; stop being sad or discouraged; become hopeful, joyous, or glad. ♦ *Jones was sad at losing the business, but he cheered up at the sight of his daughter.* ♦ *Cheer up! The worst is over.* **2.** To make cheerful or happy. ♦ *The support of the students cheered up the losing team and they played harder and won.* ♦ *We went to the hospital to cheer up a sick friend.* ♦ *Flowers cheer up a room.*

**cheesebox** *n., slang* A small, suburban house built by a land developer available at low cost and resembling the other houses around it. ♦ *They moved to a suburb, but their house is just a cheesebox.*

**cheesecake** *n., slang, informal* A showing of the legs of an attractive woman or a display of her breasts as in certain magazines known as cheesecake magazines. ♦ *Photographer to model: "Give us some cheesecake in that pose!"*

**cherished belief** *or* **cherished beliefs** *n. phr.* A set of beliefs or opinions to which one is likely to cling stubbornly without giving revision a chance. ♦ *It is a cherished belief among many racists that other races are inferior to their own.*

**cherry farm** *n., slang* A correctional institution of minimal security where the inmates, mostly first offenders, work as farmhands. ♦ *Joe got a light sentence and was sent to a cherry farm for six months.*

**chew out** *v., slang* To scold roughly. ♦ *The boy's father chewed him out for staying up late.* ♦ *The coach chews out lazy players.*

**chew the cud** *v. phr.* **1.** Said of animals, such as cows, to ruminate. ♦ *After grazing for several hours the cow lies down and chews the cud.* **2.** Said of people, to mentally go over what was heard or read, as if ruminating. ♦ *John was sitting in his rocking chair and chewing the cud over the lecture he heard earlier that day.*

**chew the fat** *or* **chew the rag** *v. phr., slang* To talk together in an idle, friendly fashion; chat. ♦ *We used to meet after work, and chew the fat over coffee and doughnuts.* ♦ *The old man would chew the rag for hours with anyone who would join him.*

**chew the scenery** *v. phr., slang* To act overemotionally in a situation where it is inappropriate; to engage in histrionics. ♦ *I don't know if Joe was sincere about our house, but he sure chewed up the scenery!*

**chicken-brained** *adj.* Stupid; narrow-minded; unimaginative. ♦ *I can't understand how a bright woman like Helen can date such a chicken-brained guy as Oliver.*

**chicken feed** *n., slang* A very small sum of money. ♦ *John and Bill worked very hard, but they were only paid chicken feed.* ♦ *Mr. Jones is so rich he thinks a thousand dollars is chicken feed.*

**chicken-hearted** *adj.* Cowardly; excessively timid. ♦ *"Come on, let's get on that roller coaster," she cried. "Don't be so chicken-hearted."*

**chicken-livered** *adj., slang, colloquial* Easily scared; cowardly. ♦ *Joe sure is a chicken-livered guy.*

**chicken out** *v. phr., informal* To stop doing something because of fear; to decide not to do something after all even though previously having decided to try it. ♦ *I used to ride a motorcycle on the highway, but I've chickened out.*

**chickens come home to roost** *informal* Words or acts come back to cause trouble for a person; something bad you said or did receives punishment; you get the punishment that you deserve. ♦ *Fred's chickens finally came home to roost today. He was late so often that the teacher made him go to the principal.*—Often used in a short form. ♦ *Mary's selfishness will come home to roost some day.*

**chicken switch** *n., slang, Space English* **1.** The emergency eject button used by test pilots in fast and high flying aircraft by means of which they can parachute to safety if the engine fails; later adopted by astronauts in space capsules. ♦ *Don't pull the chicken switch, unless absolutely necessary.* **2.** The

panic button; a panicky reaction to an unforeseen situation, such as unreasonable or hysterical telephone calls to friends for help. ♦ *Joe pulled the chicken switch on his neighbor when the grease started burning in the kitchen.*

**children and fools speak the truth** Children and fools say things without thinking; they say what they think or know when grown-ups might not think it was polite or wise to do so.—A proverb. ♦ *"Uncle Willie is too fat," said little Agnes. "Children and fools speak the truth," said her father.*

**children should be seen and not heard** A command issued by adults to children ordering them to be quiet and not to interrupt.—A proverb. ♦ *Your children should not argue so loudly. Haven't you taught them that children should be seen and not heard?*

**child's play** *adj.* Easy; requiring no effort. ♦ *Mary's work as a volunteer social worker is so agreeable to her that she thinks of it as child's play.*

**chilled to the marrow** *or* **frozen to the marrow** *adj. phr.* Extremely cold; chilled both inside and outside. ♦ *The mountain climbers were chilled to the marrow during their climb of Mount Everest.*

**chill out** *v. phr., slang* To relax. ♦ *After the boisterous party at her girlfriend's house, Kathy was just chilling out at home.*

**chime in** *v.* **1.** *informal* To join in. ♦ *The whole group chimed in on the chorus.* ♦ *When the argument got hot, John chimed in.* **2.** To agree; go well together.—Usually used with *with*. ♦ *Dick was happy, and the holiday music chimed in with his feelings.*

**China syndrome** *n., informal* From the title of the movie with Jane Fonda and Jack Lemmon. The possibility that an industrial nuclear reactor might explode, literally affecting the other side of the planet (as if by eating a hole through the earth all the way to China.) ♦ *Antinuclear demonstrators are greatly worried about the China syndrome.*

**chip in** *or* **kick in** *v., informal* To give together with others, contribute. ♦ *The pupils chipped in a dime apiece for the teacher's Christmas present.* ♦ *All the neighbors kicked in to help after the fire.*

**chip off the old block** *n. phr.* A person whose character traits closely resemble those of his parents. ♦ *I hear that Tom plays the violin in the orchestra his father conducts; he sure is a chip off the old block.*

**chip on one's shoulder** *n. phr., informal* A quarrelsome nature; readiness to be angered. ♦ *He went through life with a chip on his shoulder.* ♦ *Jim often gets into fights because he goes around with a chip on his shoulder.*

**chips are down** *phrasal idiom* Said when a situation has reached its most critical or worst point. ♦ *When the enemy opened fire, the chips were really down.*

**chisel** *or* **muscle in on** *v. phr.* To illegitimately and forcefully intrude into someone's traditional sales or professional arena of operation. ♦ *Tim has a good sales territory, but he is always afraid that someone might chisel in on it.* ♦ *Las Vegas casino owners are concerned that the Mafia might muscle in on their territory.*

**choke off** *v.* To put a sudden end to; stop abruptly or forcefully. ♦ *The war choked off diamond shipments from overseas.*

**choke up** *v.* **1a.** To come near losing calmness or self-control from strong feeling; be upset by your feelings. ♦ *When one speaker after another praised John, he choked up and couldn't thank them.* **1b.** *informal* To be unable to do well because of excitement or nervousness. ♦ *Bill was a good batter, but in the championship game he choked up and did poorly.* **2.** To fill up; become clogged or blocked; become hard to pass through. ♦ *The channel had choked up with sand so that boats couldn't use it.*

**chomp at the bit** See CHAMP AT THE BIT.

**choose up sides** *v. phr.* To form two teams with two captains taking turns choosing players. ♦ *The boys chose up sides for a game of softball.* ♦ *Tom and Joe were the captains. They chose up sides.*

**chosen people** *or* **the C.P.** *n. phr.* The Jewish people. ♦ *In the days of the Old Testament the Jews were considered to be the Chosen People.*

**chow line** *n., slang* A line of people waiting for food. ♦ *The chow line was already long when John got to the dining hall.* ♦ *The soldiers picked up trays and got into the chow line.*

**Christmas card** *n., slang, citizen's band radio jargon* A speeding ticket. ♦ *Smokey just gave a Christmas card to the eighteen wheeler we passed.*

**Christmas club** *n.* A plan for putting money in the bank to be saved for Christmas shopping. ♦ *John deposits $10 each week in the Christmas club.*

**chuck out** *v. phr.* To discard; to throw something out that is of no more use. ♦ *If you have too many used old clothes and not even the Salvation Army can take them, just chuck them out.*

**chum around with** *v. phr.* **1.** To be close friends with someone. ♦ *They have been chumming around with one another for quite some time.* **2.** To travel around with someone. ♦ *Jack is planning to chum around with Tim in Europe this summer.*

**circumstances alter cases** *formal* The way things are, or happen, may change the way you are expected to act. ♦ *John's father told him never to touch his gun, but one day when Father was away, John used it to shoot a poisonous snake that came into the yard. Circumstances alter cases.*

**claim check** *n.* A ticket needed to get back something. ♦ *The man at the parking lot gave Mrs. Collins a claim check.*

**clamp down** *v., informal* To put on strict controls; enforce rules or laws. ♦ *After the explosion, police clamped down and let no more visitors inside the monument.* ♦ *The school clamped down on smoking.*

**clam up** *v., slang* To refuse to say anything more; stop talking. ♦ *The suspect clammed up, and the police could get no more information out of him.*

**class action suit** *n. phr.* A lawsuit brought by several individuals suffering from the same problem against an employer, an institution, or an industry, etc. ♦ *Numerous American victims of secondhand smoke joined in successful class action suits against some major cigarette manufacturing companies.*

**clay pigeon** *n., slang, informal* **1.** A popular target at practice shooting made of clay and roughly resembling a pigeon; an easy target that doesn't move. ♦ *All he can shoot is a clay pigeon.* **2.** A person who, like a clay pigeon in target practice, is immobilized or is in a sensitive position and is therefore easily criticized or otherwise victimized. ♦ *Poor Joe is a clay pigeon.* **3.** A task easily accomplished like shooting an immobile clay pigeon. ♦ *The math exam was a clay pigeon.*

**clean bill of health** *n. phr.* **1.** A certificate that a person or animal has no infectious disease. ♦ *The government doctor gave Jones a clean bill of health when he entered the country.* **2.** *informal* A report that a person is free of guilt or fault. ♦ *The stranger was suspected in the bank robbery, but the police gave him a clean bill of health.*

**clean break** *n. phr.* A complete separation. ♦ *Tom made a clean break with his former girlfriends before marrying Pamela.*

**clean hands** *n. phr., slang* Freedom from guilt or dishonesty; innocence. ♦ *John grew up in a bad neighborhood, but he grew up with clean hands.* ♦ *There was much proof against Bill, but he swore he had clean hands.*

**clean out** *v.* **1.** *slang* To take everything from; empty; strip. ♦ *George's friends cleaned him out when they were playing cards last night.* ♦ *The sudden demand for paper plates soon cleaned out the stores.* **2.** *informal* To get rid of; remove; dismiss. ♦ *The new mayor promised to clean the crooks out of the city government.*

**cleanse the Augean stables** *or* **clean the Augean stables** *v. phr. from Greek mythology* To get rid of corruption or immoral behavior. ♦ *There was so much corruption in City Hall that the governor decided to cleanse the Augean stables.*

**clean slate** *n. phr.* A record of nothing but good conduct, without any errors or bad deeds; past acts that are all good without any bad ones. ♦ *Johnny was sent to the principal for whispering. He had a clean slate so the principal did not punish him.*

**clean sweep** *n. phr.* A complete victory. ♦ *Our candidate for the United States Senate made a clean sweep over his opponent.*

**clean up** *v. phr.* **1.** To wash and make oneself presentable. ♦ *After quitting for the day in the garage, Tim decided to clean up and put on a clean shirt.* **2.** To finish; terminate. ♦ *The secretary promised her boss to clean up all the unfinished work before leaving on her Florida vacation.* **3.** *informal* To make a large profit. ♦ *The clever investors cleaned up on the stock market last week.*

**clean-up** *n.* **1.** An act of removing all the dirt from a given set of objects. ♦ *What this filthy room needs is an honest clean-up.* **2.** The elimination of pockets of resistance during warfare or a police raid. ♦ *The FBI conducted a clean-up against the drug pushers in our district.*

**clear and present danger** *n. phr.* A state of affairs that equals a major emergency, compelling the government and other agencies to take immediate action to avert the danger inherent in the situation. ♦ *Domestic terrorism after 9/11/01 presents a case of clear and present danger.*

**clear-cut** *adj.* Definite; well defined. ♦ *The president's new policy of aggressive action is a clear-cut departure from his old methods of unilateral appeasement.*

**clear-eyed** *adj.* Understanding problems or events clearly; being able to tell very well the results of a way of acting. ♦ *Tom is very clear-eyed. He knows he doesn't have much chance of winning the race, but he will try his best.* ♦ *He is a clear-eyed and independent commentator on the news.*

**clear off** *v. phr.* To clear the table of cutlery, plates, foods, etc. ♦ *While the guests were chatting away, the hostess and her daughter cleared off the family dining table.*

**clear one's name** *v. phr.* To prove someone is innocent of a crime or misdeed of which he has been accused. ♦ *The falsely accused rapist has been trying in vain to clear his name.*

**clear out** *v.* **1.** To take everything out of; empty. ♦ *When Bill was moved to another class he cleared out his desk.* **2.** *informal* To leave suddenly; go away; depart. ♦ *The cop told the boys to clear out.* ♦ *Bob cleared out without paying his room rent.* ♦ *Clear out of here! You're bothering me.* Compare BEAT IT.

**clear the air** *v. phr.* To remove angry feelings, misunderstanding, or confusion. ♦ *The president's statement that he would run for office again cleared the air of rumors and guessing.* ♦ *When Bill was angry at Bob, Bob made a joke, and it cleared the air between them.*

**clear the decks** *v. phr.* To put everything in readiness for a major activity; to eliminate unessentials. ♦ *The governor urged the State Assembly to clear the decks of all but the most pressing issues to vote on.*

**clear up** *v.* **1.** To make plain or clear; explain; solve. ♦ *The teacher cleared up the harder parts of the story.* ♦ *Maybe we can clear up your problem.* **2.** To become clear. ♦ *The weather cleared up after the storm.* **3.** To cure. ♦ *The pills cleared up his stomach trouble.* **4.** To put back into a normal, proper, or healthy state. ♦ *The doctor can give you something to clear up your skin.* ♦ *Susan cleared up the room.* **5.** To become cured. ♦ *This skin trouble will clear up in a day or two.*

**cliff dweller** *n., slang, informal* A city person who lives on a very high floor in an apartment building. ♦ *Joe and Nancy have become cliff dwellers—they moved up to the 30th floor.*

**cliff-hanger** *n., informal* A sports event or a movie in which the outcome is uncertain to the very end, keeping the spectators in great suspense and excitement. ♦ *Did you see* The Fugitive? *It's a regular cliff-hanger.*

**climb the corporate ladder** See CORPO-RATE LADDER.

**climb the wall** *v. phr., slang. informal* **1.** To react to a challenging situation with too great an emotional response, frustration, tension, and anxiety. ♦ *By the time I got the letter that I was hired, I was ready to climb the wall.* **2.** To be so disinterested or bored as to be most anxious to get away at any cost. ♦ *If the chairman doesn't stop talking, I'll climb the wall.*

**clinging vine** *n.* A very dependent woman; a woman who needs much love and encouragement from a man. ♦ *Mary is a clinging vine; she cannot do anything without her husband.*

**clip joint** *n. slang* A low-class night club or other business where people are cheated. ♦ *The man got drunk and lost all his money in a clip joint.*

**clip one's wings** *v. phr.* To limit or hold you back, bring you under control; prevent your success. ♦ *When the new president tried to become dictator, the generals soon clipped his wings.*

**cloak-and-dagger** *adj.* Of or about spies and secret agents. ♦ *It was a cloak-and-dagger story about some spies who tried to steal atomic secrets.*

**clock in** *or* **punch in** *v. phr.* To mechanically register the time at which one starts to work, e.g., by using a clock that stamps the time on one's attendance card. ♦ *What time should we clock in? Do I have to punch in every time I come to work?*

**clock out** *v. phr.* To register on a stamping machine united with a clock the time that one leaves work. ♦ *Yesterday I clocked out at 6 P.M.*

**clock watcher** *n. phr., informal* A worker who always quits at once when it is time; a man who is in a hurry to leave his job. ♦ *When Ted got his first job, his father told him to work hard and not be a clock watcher.*

**close at hand** *adj. phr.* Handy; close by; within one's range. ♦ *I always keep my pencils and erasers close at hand when I work on a draft proposal.*

**close call** *or* **shave** *n. phr.* A narrow escape. ♦ *That sure was a close call when that truck came near us from the right!* ♦ *When Tim fell off his bicycle in front of a bus, it was a very close shave.*

**closed book** *n.* A secret; something not known or understood. ♦ *The man's early life is a closed book.* ♦ *For Mary, science is a closed book.* ♦ *The history of the town is a closed book.*

**closed-door** *adj.* Away from the public; in private or in secret; limited to a few. ♦ *The officers of the club held a closed-door meeting.* ♦ *The committee decided on a closed-door rule for the investigation.* Compare IN PRIVATE.

**close down** *or* **shut down** *v.* To stop all working, as in a factory; stop work entirely; *also:* to stop operations in. ♦ *The factory closed down for Christmas.* ♦ *The company shut down the condom plant for Easter.*

**closed shop** *n. phr.* **1.** A plant or factory that employs only union workers. ♦ *Our firm has been fighting the closed shop policy for many years now.* **2.** A profession or line of work dominated by followers of a certain mode of thinking and behaving that does not tolerate differing views or ideas. ♦ *Certain groups of psychologists, historians, and linguists often behave with a closed-shop mentality.*

**close finish** *n. phr.* An exciting race or contest during which it is difficult to tell who will be the winner. ♦ *The presidential election of 2000 between Republican George W. Bush and Democrat Al Gore was a very close finish.*

**close in** *v.* To come in nearer from all sides. ♦ *We wanted the boat to reach shore before the fog closed in.*—Often used with *on.* ♦ *The troops were closing in on the enemy.*

**close its doors** *v. phr.* **1.** To keep someone or something from entering or joining; become closed. ♦ *The club has closed its doors to new members.* **2.** To fail as a business; go bankrupt. ♦ *The fire was so damaging that the store had to close its doors.* ♦ *Business was so poor that we had to close our doors after six months.*

**close-knit** *adj.* Closely joined together by ties of love, friendship, or common interest; close. ♦ *The Joneses are a close-knit family.* ♦ *The three boys are always together. They form a very close-knit group.*

**close one's eyes** *or* **shut one's eyes** *v. phr.* To refuse to see or think about. ♦ *The park is beautiful if you shut your eyes to the litter.* ♦ *The ice was very thin, but the boys shut their eyes to the danger and went skating.* Compare OPEN ONE'S EYES.

**close on the heels** *adv. phr.* Only a little way behind the leader in a chase or competition. ♦ *The silver medal winner at the Olympics was close on the heels of the gold medalist, who won the race.*

**close out** *v.* To sell the whole of; end (a business or a business operation) by selling all the goods; *also,* to sell your stock and stop doing business. ♦ *The store closed out its stock of garden supplies.* ♦ *Mr. Jones closed out his grocery.*

**close quarters** *n. phr.* Limited, cramped space. ♦ *With seven boy scouts in a tent, they were living in very close quarters.*

**close ranks** *v. phr.* **1.** To come close together in a line especially for fighting. ♦ *The soldiers closed ranks and kept the enemy away from the bridge.* **2.** To stop quarreling and work together; unite and fight together. ♦ *The Democrats and Republicans closed ranks to win the war.* ♦ *The leader asked the people to close ranks and plan a new school.*

**close the books** *v. phr.* To stop taking orders; end a bookkeeping period. ♦ *The tickets were all sold, so the manager said to close the books.* ♦ *The department store closes its books on the 25th of each month.*

**close the door** *or* **bar the door** *or* **shut the door** *v. phr.* To prevent any more action or talk about a subject. ♦ *The president's veto closed the door to any new attempt to pass the bill.* ♦ *Joan was much hurt by what Mary said, and she closed the door on Mary's attempt to apologize.*

**close to home** *adv.* Too near to someone's personal feelings, wishes, or interests. ♦ *When John made fun of Bob's way of walking, he struck close to home.*

**close-up** *n.* A photograph, motion picture, or video camera shot taken at very close range. ♦ *Directors of movies frequently show close-ups of the main characters.*

**close up shop** *v. phr.* **1.** To shut a store at the end of a day's business, *also,* to end a business. ♦ *The grocer closes up shop at 5 o'clock.* ♦ *After 15 years in business at the same spot, the garage closed up shop.* **2.** *informal* To stop some activity; finish what you are doing. ♦ *After camping out for two weeks, the scouts took down their tents and closed up shop.* ♦ *The committee finished its business and closed up shop.*

**cloud over** *v. phr.* To have a sad or depressed expression come over one's face. ♦ *Jim's face clouded over when he heard the bad news about his dismissal from the firm.*

**cloud up** *v. phr.* To become less transparent, i.e., more opaque. ♦ *A light fog clouded up the yacht's windows.*

**cloven hoof** *n. phr.* A manifestation of evil; the sign of the devil. ♦ *Sooner or later the devil reveals his presence by showing his cloven hoof.*

**cluck and grunt** *n., slang, avoid it in restaurants* The familiar restaurant dish of ham and eggs; since ham is made of pork (and pigs grunt) and eggs come from hens (which cluck). ♦ *"I am sorry I can't fix you an elaborate meal, but I can give you a quick cluck and grunt."*

**clue in** *v. phr.* To give someone a tip, a hint, or the necessary information as to what is going on. ♦ *Would you please clue me in on what the salaries will be like at the factory next year?*

**clutch at a straw** *or* **clutch at straws** *v. phr.* To hang on even to the weakest or flimsiest of handles, physical or mental, in an attempt to salvage a hopeless situation. ♦ *When the police made it quite clear that they knew about everything, the accused felon began to clutch at straws to save himself.*

**coast along** *v. phr.* **1.** Of cars, boats, and planes: To proceed without having to adjust the flow of fuel, as when one sets one's car at a certain speed by using the cruise control. ♦ *We were comfortably coasting along at 60 m.p.h.* **2.** Of people: To advance without any special effort. ♦ *John is no longer trying to achieve anything new in life; he is just coasting along.* **3.** Of businesses, establishments, etc.: To advance without effort. ♦ *Work at the shop is just coasting along these days.*

**coast is clear** No enemy or danger is in sight; there is no one to see you. ♦ *When the teacher had disappeared around the corner, John said, "Come on, the coast is clear."* ♦ *The men knew when the night watchman would pass. When he had gone, and the coast was clear, they robbed the safe.*

**cock-and-bull story** *n. phr.* An exaggerated or unbelievable story. ♦ *"Stop feeding me such cock-and-bull stories,"* the detective said to the suspect.

**cockeyed** *adj.* Drunk; intoxicated. ♦ *Frank has been drinking all day and, when we met, he was so cockeyed he forgot his own address.*

**cocksure** *adj.* Overconfident; very sure. ♦ *Paul was cocksure that it wasn't going to snow, but it snowed so much that we had to dig our way out of the house.*

**C.O.D.** *n. phr.* Abbreviation of "cash on delivery." ♦ *If you want to receive a piece of merchandise by mail and pay when you receive it, you place a C.O.D. order.*

**coffee break** *n.* A short recess or time out from work in which to rest and drink coffee. ♦ *The girls in the office take a coffee break in the middle of the morning and the afternoon.*

**coffee fix** *n. phr.* The view that coffee, since it contains caffeine, is a drug that is able to wake one up or sharpen one's attention. ♦ *One afternoon, when it was time to sit down and take my final exam, I first decided to give myself a coffee fix.*

**coffin nail** *n., slang* A cigarette. ♦ *"I stopped smoking," Algernon said. "In fact, I haven't had a coffin nail in well over a year."*

**coin money** *or* **mint money** *v. phr., informal* To make a lot of money quickly; profit heavily; gain big profit. ♦ *Fred coined money with many cigarette vending machines and juke boxes.*

**cold cash** *or* **hard cash** *n.* Money that is paid at the time of purchase; real money; silver and bills. ♦ *Mr. Jones bought a new car and paid cold cash for it.* ♦ *Some stores sell things only for cold cash.*

**cold comfort** *n.* Something that makes a person in trouble feel very little better or even worse. ♦ *Mary spent her vacation sick in bed and Jane's letter about her trip was cold comfort.*

**cold feet** *n. phr., informal* A loss of courage or nerve; a failure or loss of confidence in yourself. ♦ *Ralph was going to ask Mary to dance with him but he got cold feet and didn't.*

**cold fish** *n., informal* A queer person; a person who is unfriendly or does not mix with others. ♦ *No one knows the new doctor, he is a cold fish.* ♦ *Nobody invites Eric to parties because he is a cold fish.*

**cold light of reason** *n. phr.* An issue or a matter viewed entirely soberly, and without emotion. ♦ *By the cold light of reason, we must admit that our son John, no matter how much we love him, deserves to spend a year in jail for having sold drugs in the streets.*

**cold-shoulder** *v., informal* To act towards a person; with dislike or scorn; be unfriendly to. ♦ *It is impolite and unkind to cold-shoulder people.*

**cold shoulder** *n., informal* Unfriendly treatment of a person, a showing of dislike for a person or of looking down on a person.—Used in the clichés *give the cold shoulder* or *turn a cold shoulder to* or *get the cold shoulder.* ♦ *When Bob asked Mary for a date she gave him the cold shoulder.*

**cold snap** *n.* A short time of quick change from warm weather to cold. ♦ *The cold snap killed everything in the garden.*

**cold spell** *n. phr.* A period of extraordinarily cold weather. ♦ *"You men had better dress warm in this cold spell!" the staff sergeant said to his enlisted men shivering inside the tent.*

**cold turkey** *adv., slang, informal* **1.** Abruptly and without medical aid to withdraw from the use of an addictive drug or from a serious drinking problem. ♦ *Joe is a very brave guy; he kicked the habit cold turkey.* **2.** *n.* An instance of withdrawal from drugs, alcohol, or cigarette smoking. ♦ *Joe did a cold turkey.*

**cold war** *n.* A struggle that is carried on by other means and not by actual fighting; a war without shooting or bombing. ♦ *After World War II, a cold war began between Russia and the United States.*

**collect dust** *v. phr.* To sit in storage and remain unused. ♦ *"What happened to your twenty-speed racing bike?" John asked. "It's just sitting in our old garage, collecting dust."*

**collector's item** *n.* Something rare or valuable enough to collect or save. ♦ *Jimmy's mother found an old wooden doll in the attic that turned out to be a collector's item.*

**College Boards** *n.* A set of examinations given to test a student's readiness and ability for college. ♦ *College Boards test both what a student has learned and his ability to learn.*

**color guard** *n.* A military guard of honor for the flag of a country; *also:* a guard of honor to carry and protect a flag or banner (as of a club). ♦ *There were four marines in the color guard in the parade.*

**color scheme** *n.* A plan for colors used together as decoration. ♦ *The color scheme for the dance was blue and silver.* ♦ *Mary decided on a pink and white color scheme for her room.*

**come about** *v.* **1.** To take place; happen; occur. ♦ *Sometimes it is hard to tell how a quarrel comes about.* ♦ *When John woke up he was in the hospital, but he didn't know how that had come about.* **2.** *nautical use* To change direction; to turn around. ♦ *When you want to bring the sailing boat home, you first have to come about.*

**come a cropper 1.** To fall off your horse. ♦ *John's horse stumbled, and John came a cropper.* **2.** To fail. ♦ *Mr. Brown did not have enough money to put into his business and it soon came a cropper.*

**come across** *v.* **1.** *or* **run across** To find or meet by chance. ♦ *He came across a dollar bill in the suit he was sending to the cleaner.* ♦ *The other day I ran across a book that you might like.* ♦ *I came across George at a party last week; it was the first time I had seen him in months.* **2.** To give or do what is asked. ♦ *The robber told the woman to come across with her purse.* ♦ *For hours the police questioned the man suspected of kidnapping the child, and finally he came across with the story.*

**come again** *v., informal* Please repeat; please say that again.—Usually used as a command. ♦ *"Harry has just come into a fortune," my wife said. "Come again?" I asked her, not believing it.* ♦ *"Come again," said the hard-of-hearing man.*

**come alive** *or* **come to life** *v.* **1.** *informal* To become alert or attentive; wake up and look alive; become active. ♦ *When Mr. Simmons mentioned money, the boys came alive.* ♦ *Bob pushed the starter button, and the engine came alive with a roar.* **2.** To look real; take on a bright, natural look. ♦ *Under skillful lighting, the scene came alive.* ♦ *The president came alive in the picture as the artist worked.*

**come along** *v.* To make progress; improve; succeed. ♦ *He was coming along well after the operation.* ♦ *Rose is coming right along on the piano.*

**come a long way** *v. phr.* To show much improvement; make great progress. ♦ *The school has come a long way since its beginnings.* ♦ *Little Jane has come a long way since she broke her leg.*

**come and get it!** *v. phr. informal, slang* An invitation to come to the dinner table or to the kitchen counter and

start eating. ♦ *"Come and get it!"*
*Mother shouted from the kitchen, and*
*we all ran in to eat as if we had been*
*starving for weeks.*

**come apart at the seams** *v. phr., slang,*
*informal* To become upset to the point
where one loses self-control and composure as if having suffered a sudden
nervous breakdown. ♦ *After his*
*divorce Joe seemed to be coming apart*
*at the seams.*

**come around** See COME ROUND.

**come at** *v.* **1.** To approach; come to or
against; advance toward. ♦ *The young*
*boxer came at the champion cautiously.*
**2.** To understand (a word or idea) or
master (a skill); succeed with. ♦ *The*
*sense of an unfamiliar word is hard to*
*come at.*

**come back** *v., informal* (stress on *back*) **1.**
To reply; answer. ♦ *The lawyer came*
*back sharply in defense of his client.*
♦ *No matter how the audience heckled*
*him, the comedian always had an*
*answer to come back with.* **2.** To get a
former place or position back; to reach
again a place which you have lost.
♦ *After a year off to have her baby, the*
*singer came back to even greater fame.*
♦ *It is hard for a retired prize fighter to*
*come back and beat a younger man.*

**comeback** *n., v. phr., slang, citizen's band*
*radio jargon* (stress on *come*) A return
call. ♦ *Thanks for your comeback.*

**come back to earth** *or* **come down to**
**earth** *v. phr.* To return to the real
world; stop imagining or dreaming;
think and behave as usual. ♦ *Bill was*
*sitting and daydreaming so his mother*
*told him to come down to earth and to*
*do his homework.*

**come back to haunt** *v. phr.* Often heard
when a problem returns from
someone's past. ♦ *The condemned*
*rapist's past came back to haunt him,*
*when the police mistakenly arrested*
*him because he resembled another*
*wanted fugitive.*

**come between** *v.* To part; divide; separate. ♦ *John's mother-in-law came to*
*live in his home, and as time passed she*
*came between him and his wife.* ♦ *Bill's*
*hot rod came between him and his*
*studies, and his grades went down.*

**come by** *v.* To get; obtain; acquire. ♦ *A*
*good job like that is hard to come by.*

♦ *Money easily come by is often easily*
*spent.* ♦ *How did she come by that*
*money?*

**come clean** *v. phr., slang* To tell all; tell
the whole story; confess. ♦ *The boy*
*suspected of stealing the watch came*
*clean after long questioning.*

**come close to** *v. phr.* To be on the verge
of something happening. ♦ *Your idea*
*comes close to a perfect solution. The*
*acrobat came close to falling down*
*from the parallel bars.* ♦ *Your qualifica-*
*tions come close to what we were*
*looking for at our firm.*

**comedown** *n.* (stress on *come*)
Disappointment; embarrassment;
failure. ♦ *It was quite a comedown for*
*Al when the girl he took for granted*
*refused his marriage proposal.*

**come down** *v.* (stress on *down*) **1.** To
reduce itself; amount to no more
than.—Followed by *to.* ♦ *The quarrel*
*finally came down to a question of*
*which boy would do the dishes.* **2.** To
be handed down or passed along,
descend from parent to child; pass
from older generation to younger
ones. ♦ *Mary's necklace had come*
*down to her from her grandmother.*

**come down hard on** *v., informal* **1.** To
scold or punish strongly. ♦ *The prin-*
*cipal came down hard on the boys for*
*breaking the window.* **2.** To oppose
strongly. ♦ *The minister in his sermon*
*came down hard on drinking.*

**come down off one's high horse** *v. phr.*
To become less arrogant; to assume a
more modest disposition. ♦ *The*
*boastful candidate for Congress*
*quickly came down off his high horse*
*when he was soundly beaten by his*
*opponent.*

**come down on like a ton of bricks** *v.*
*phr., slang* To direct one's full anger at
somebody. ♦ *When the janitor was late*
*for work, the manager came down on*
*him like a ton of bricks.*

**come down to earth** See COME BACK TO
EARTH.

**come down with** *v., informal* To become
sick with; catch. ♦ *We all came down*
*with the mumps.* ♦ *After being out in*
*the rain, George came down with a*
*cold.*

**come forward** *v. phr* To offer oneself, as
to help ♦ *The chairperson of the cul-*

*tural festival asked people to come forward and volunteer their time and money.*

**come from** *v. phr.* **1.** To hail from a certain place; to be native of a certain country and locality. ♦ *Is it true that you come from Hawaii?* **2.** To inquire about or to state one's background, which is responsible for one's opinion and decision regarding a certain affair. ♦ *Let me tell you where I am coming from on the question of war.*

**come from far and wide** *v. phr.* To originate or hail from many different places. ♦ *The students at this university come from far and wide and speak many languages.*

**come full circle** *v. phr., informal* **1.** To become totally opposed to one's own earlier conviction on a given subject. ♦ *Today's conservative businessperson has come full circle from former radical student days.* **2.** To change and develop, only to end up where one started. ♦ *From modern permissiveness, ideas about child raising have come full circle to the views of our grandparents.*

**come hell or high water** *adv. phr., informal* No matter what happens; whatever may come. ♦ *Grandfather said he would go to the fair, come hell or high water.*

**come home to roost** See CHICKENS COME HOME TO ROOST.

**come in** *v.* **1.** To finish in a sports contest or other competition. ♦ *He came in second in the hundred-yard dash.* **2.** To become the fashion; begin to be used. ♦ *Swimming trunks for men came in after World War I; before that men used full swim suits.*

**come in for** *v.* **1.** To receive. ♦ *He came in for a small fortune when his uncle died.* ♦ *His conduct came in for much criticism.* **2.** To receive blame or praise. ♦ *The mayor of New York City, Rudolph Giuliani, came in for a lot of praise in the wake of 9/11/01.*

**come in handy** *v. phr., informal* To prove useful. ♦ *The French he learned in high school came in handy when Tom was in the army in France.*

**come into** *v.* To receive, especially after another's death; get possession of. ♦ *He came into a lot of money when his father died.*

**come into a person's life** *v. phr.* To attain the status of "significant other" in a person's life. ♦ *"Matilda came into my life as my nurse when I was almost dying in the hospital. Now we're married and have four children," John said gratefully.*

**come into focus** *v. phr.* To become clearly understood in every detail. ♦ *The role of our urban commuter campus is coming more and more into focus now that private universities charge such high tuition rates.*

**come into force** *v. phr.* To attain enforceable legal status. ♦ *The law passed by Congress won't came into force until the president signs the bill into law.*

**come into one's own** *v. phr.* To receive the wealth or respect that you should have. ♦ *John's grandfather died and left him a million dollars; when John is 21, he will come into his own.*

**come into play** *v. phr.* To begin having a noticeable effect. ♦ *It is difficult to predict what forces might come into play after the terrorists have been eliminated.*

**come of** *v.* **1.** To result from. ♦ *After all the energy we spent on that advertising campaign, absolutely nothing came of it.* **2.** To become of; happen to. ♦ *"Whatever became of your son, Peter?"*

**come of age** See OF AGE.

**come off** *v.* **1.** To take place; happen. ♦ *The picnic came off at last, after being twice postponed.* **2.** *informal* To do well; succeed. ♦ *The attempt to bring the quarreling couple together again came off, to people's astonishment.*

**come off as** *v. phr.* To give the impression of possessing certain qualities. ♦ *Wilbur is often disliked because he has a tendency to come off as a vulgar person.*

**come off it** *also* **get off it** *v. phr., slang* Stop pretending; bragging, or kidding; stop being silly.—Used as a command. ♦ *"So I said to the duchess..." Jimmy began. "Oh, come off it," the other boys sneered.* ♦ *Fritz said he had a car of his own. "Oh, come off it," said John. "You can't even drive."*

**come off** *or* **through with flying colors** *v. phr.* To succeed; triumph. ♦ *John came off with flying colors in his final exams at college.*

**come on** *v.* **1.** To begin; appear. ♦ *Rain came on toward morning.* ♦ *He felt a cold coming on.* **2.** To grow or do well; thrive. ♦ *The wheat was coming on.* ♦ *His business came on splendidly.* **3.** or **come upon.** To meet accidentally; encounter; find. ♦ *He came on an old friend that day when he visited his club.* ♦ *He came upon an interesting idea in reading about the French Revolution.* **4.** *informal* Let's get started; let's get going; don't delay; don't wait.—Used as a command. ♦ *"Come on, or we'll be late," said Joe, but Lou still waited.* **5.** *informal* Please do it!—Used in begging someone to do something. ♦ *Sing us just one song, Jane, come on!*

**come-on** *n., slang* An attractive offer made to a naive person under false pretenses in order to gain monetary or other advantage. ♦ *Joe uses a highly successful come-on when he sells vacant lots on Grand Bahama Island.*

**come one's way** *v. phr.* To be experienced by someone; happen to you. ♦ *Tom said that if the chance to become a sailor ever came his way, he would take it.*

**come on strong** *v. phr., slang* To overwhelm a weaker person with excessively strong language, personality, or mannerisms; to insist extremely strongly and claim something with unusual vigor. ♦ *Joe came on very strong last night about the War in Indochina; most of us felt embarrassed.*

**come on to** *v. phr.* To make sexual advances. ♦ *"I think my boss is coming on to me; what should I do?" Mary complained to her husband.*

**come on the scene** *v. phr.* To make a major splash in society; to become noted. ♦ *When Elvis Presley first came on the scene with his new style of singing, many older people were shocked and amazed.*

**come out** *v.* **1.** *Of a girl:* To be formally introduced to polite society at about age eighteen, usually at a party; begin to go to big parties. ♦ *In society, girls come out when they reach the age of about eighteen, and usually it is at a big party in their honor; after that they are looked on as adults.* **2.** To be published. *The book came out two weeks ago.* **3.** To become publicly known. ♦ *The truth finally came out at his trial.* **4.** To end; result; finish. ♦ *How did the story come out?* ♦ *The game came out as we had hoped.* ♦ *The snapshots came out well.* **5.** To announce support or opposition; declare yourself (for or against a person or thing). ♦ *The party leaders came out for an acceptable candidate.* ♦ *Many Congressmen came out against the bill.* **6.** See GO OUT FOR.—**coming-out** *adj.* Introducing a girl to polite society. ♦ *Mary's parents gave her a coming-out party when she was 17.*

**come out ahead** *v. phr.* To emerge as a winner either monetarily or otherwise. ♦ *John decided to live dangerously and went to Las Vegas to gamble with only $100. He had $200 when he got home. His wife remarked, "You lucky dog; you always come out ahead, don't you?"*

**come out for** *v. phr.* To support; declare oneself in favor of another, especially during a political election. ♦ *Candidates for the presidency of the United States are anxious for the major newspapers to come out for them.*

**come out in the open** *v. phr.* **1.** To reveal one's true identity or intentions. ♦ *Fred finally came out in the open and admitted that he was gay.* **2.** To declare one's position openly. ♦ *The conservative Democratic candidate came out in the open and declared that he would join the Republican party.*

**come out of the closet** *v. phr.* To expose something about oneself that was previously kept as a secret. Used mostly in connection with homosexuals. ♦ *I heard that Al is coming out of the closet, after living with Joe for more than twenty years!*

**come out with** *v. phr.* **1.** To make a public announcement of; make known. ♦ *He came out with a clear declaration of his principles.* **2.** To say. ♦ *He comes out with the funniest remarks you can imagine.*

**come over** *v.* **1.** To take control of; cause sudden strong feeling in; happen to. ♦ *A sudden fit of anger came over him.* ♦ *A great tenderness came over her.* ♦ *What has come over him?* **2.** To visit someone. ♦ *Why don't you come over some time? We would love to have you pay us a visit.*

**come round** *or* **come around** *v.* **1.** To happen or appear again and again in regular order. ♦ *And so Saturday night came around again.* ♦ *I will tell him when he comes round again.* **2.** *informal* To get back health or knowledge of things; get well from sickness or a faint. ♦ *Jim has come around after having had stomach ulcers.* **3.** To change direction. ♦ *The wind has come round to the south.* **4.** *informal* To change your opinion or purpose to agree with another's. ♦ *Tom came round when Dick told him the whole story.*

**comes to the same thing** *or* **comes to the same thing at the end** *v. phr.* To amount to the identical sum of money, situation, etc. ♦ *It comes to the same thing at the end whether I write out the check or my wife does; our assets are shared in any event.*

**come through** *v., informal* To be equal to a demand; meet trouble or a sudden need with success; satisfy a need. ♦ *John needed money for college and his father came through.*

**come through for** *v. phr.* To come to the aid of someone as promised or as expected. ♦ *I knew my brother Jack would come through for me; he loaned me the money to survive when I lost my job.*

**come to** *v.* (stress on *to*) **1.** To wake up after losing consciousness; get the use of your senses back again after fainting or being knocked out. ♦ *The boxer who was knocked out did not come to for five minutes.* ♦ *The doctor gave her a pill and after she took it she didn't come to for two days.* **2.** (stress on *come*) To get enough familiarity or understanding to; learn to; grow to.—Used with an infinitive. ♦ *John was selfish at first, but he came to realize that other people counted, too.* **3.** To result in or change to; reach the point of; arrive at. ♦ *Mr. Smith lived to see his invention come to success.* **4.** To have something to do with; be in the field of; be about.—Usually used in the phrase *when it comes to.* ♦ *Joe is not good in sports, but when it comes to arithmetic he's the best in the class.*

**come to a dead end** *v. phr.* To reach a point from which one cannot proceed further, either because of a physical obstacle or because of some forbidding circumstance. ♦ *The factory expansion project came to a dead end because of a lack of funds.*

**come to a head** *v. phr.* To reach a point where immediate and urgent decision is unavoidable. ♦ *Discussions have come to a head regarding the enlargement of the European Union. Seven new nations are now scheduled to join.*

**come to blows** *v. phr.* To begin to fight. ♦ *The two countries came to blows because one wanted to be independent from the other.*

**come together** See FALL IN *or* IN TO PLACE.

**come to grief** *v. phr.* To have a bad accident or disappointment; meet trouble or ruin; end badly; wreck; fail. ♦ *Bill came to grief learning to drive a car.*

**come to grips with** *v. phr.* **1.** To get hold of (another wrestler) in close fighting. ♦ *After circling around for a minute, the two wrestlers came to grips with each other.* **2.** To struggle seriously with (an idea or problem). ♦ *Mr. Blake's teaching helps students come to grips with the important ideas in the history lesson.* ♦ *Harry cannot be a leader, because he never quite comes to grips with a problem.*

**come to life** See COME ALIVE.

**come to light** *v. phr.* To be discovered; become known; appear. ♦ *New facts about ancient Egypt have recently come to light.*

**come to mind** *v. phr.* To occur to someone. ♦ *A new idea for the advertising campaign came to mind as I was reading your book.*

**come to nothing** *also formal* **come to naught** *v. phr.* To end in failure; fail; be in vain. ♦ *The dog's attempts to climb the tree after the cat came to nothing.*

**come to one's senses** *v. phr.* **1.** Become conscious again; wake up. ♦ *The boxer was knocked out and did not come to his senses for several minutes.* **2.** To think clearly; behave as usual or as you should; act sensibly. ♦ *Don't act so foolishly. Come to your senses!*

**come to pass** *v. phr., literary* To happen; occur. ♦ *Strange things come to pass in troubled times.*

**come to rest** *v. phr.* To stop. ♦ *The runaway truck finally came to rest in a* *muddy cornfield although all of its brakes were gone.*

**come to terms** *v. phr.* To reach an agreement. ♦ *Management and the labor union came to terms about a new arrangement and a strike was prevented.*

**come to the ears of someone** *v. phr.* To hear as gossip, story, or rumor. ♦ *It came to my ears that poor Jack started drinking again.*

**come to the point** *or* **get to the point** *v. phr.* To talk about the important thing; reach the important facts of the matter; reach the central question or fact. ♦ *A good newspaper story must come right to the point and save the details for later.*

**come to think of it** *v. phr., informal* As I think again; indeed; really. ♦ *Come to think of it, I should write my daughter today.*

**come to this** *v. phr.* To reach a certain condition, usually a negative or bad one. ♦ *So it really came to this, that we are getting divorced after twenty years together?*

**come true** *v.* To really happen; change from a dream or a plan into a fact. ♦ *It was a dream come true when he met the president.*

**come unglued** *or* **come unstrung** *v. phr.* To lose one's composure; to become very upset. ♦ *I'm going to come unglued if you keep controlling my work all the time.*

**come up** *v.* **1.** To become a subject for discussion or decision to talk about or decide about. ♦ *The question of wage increases came up at the board meeting.* ♦ *Mayor Jones comes up for reelection this fall.* **2.** To be equal; match in value.—Used with *to.* ♦ *The new model car comes up to last year's.* **3.** To approach; come close. ♦ *We saw a big black bear coming up on us from the woods.* ♦ *Christmas is coming up soon.* **4.** To provide; supply; furnish.—Used with *with.* ♦ *The teacher asked a difficult question, but finally Ted came up with a good answer.*

**come up for air** *v. phr.* To stop doing what one is doing and take a break. ♦ *"I've got to stop and come up for some air, you guys," Tim said. "This is hard work."*

**come up in the world** *or* **rise in the world** *v. phr.* To gain success, wealth, or importance in life; rise to a position of greater wealth or importance. ♦ *He had come up in the world since he peddled his wife's baked goods from a pushcart.*

**come up short** *v. phr.* To have less than the correct amount to be paid for something; to be found wanting in matters other than monetary. ♦ *I went to the grocery store where the bill came to $73, but I only had $40, so I came up short by $33.* ♦ *Every time Tim wants to join the basketball team, he is rejected because he is so small; poor guy keeps coming up short.*

**come up smelling like a rose** *v. phr.* To escape from a difficult situation or misdeed unscathed or without punishment. ♦ *It is predicted that Congressman Brown, in spite of the current investigation into his financial affairs, will come up smelling like a rose at the end.*

**come up to** *v. phr.* To equal. ♦ *The meals cooked in most restaurants do not come up to those prepared at home.*

**come up with** *v. phr.* **1.** To offer. ♦ *We can always depend on John Smith to come up with a good solution for any problem we might have.* **2.** To produce on demand. ♦ *I won't be able to buy this car, because I cannot come up with the down payment you require.* **3.** To find. ♦ *How on earth did you come up with such a brilliant idea?*

**come what may** *adv. phr.* Even if troubles come; no matter what happens; in spite of opposition or mischance. ♦ *Charles has decided to get a college education, come what may.*

**comfortable as an old shoe** *adj. phr., informal* Pleasant and relaxed; not stiff, strict or too polite; easy to talk and work with. ♦ *The stranger was as comfortable as an old shoe, and we soon were talking like old friends.*

**coming out party** *n. phr.* A debutante party in which a young girl is formally introduced to society. ♦ *Coming out parties used to be more popular in the early twentieth century than nowadays, primarily because they cost a lot of money.*

**comings and goings** *n. pl., informal* **1.** Times of arriving and going away; movements. ♦ *I can't keep up with the* children's comings and goings. **2.** Activities; doings; business. ♦ *Mary knows all the comings and goings in the neighborhood.*

**command module** *n., Space English* **1.** One of the three main sections of the basic Apollo spacecraft. It weighs six tons and is cone shaped. It contains crew compartments and from it the astronauts can operate the lunar module (LM), the docking systems, etc. **2.** *Informal transferred sense.* The cockpit, the chief place where a person does his most important work. ♦ *My desk is my command module.*

**common ground** *n.* Shared beliefs, interests, or ways of understanding; ways in which people are alike. ♦ *Bob and Frank don't like each other because they have no common ground.*

**common lot** *n. phr.* The inevitable circumstances of life. ♦ *We're all born without teeth, hair, and illusions, and we shall all die without teeth, hair, and illusions. This is our common lot.*

**common touch** *n.* The ability to be a friend of the people; friendly manner with everyone. ♦ *Voters like a candidate who has the common touch.*

**company man** *n., informal* A worker who always agrees with management rather than labor.—Usually used to express dislike or disapproval. ♦ *Joe was a company man and refused to take a part in the strike.* Compare YES-MAN.

**compare notes** *v. phr., informal* To exchange thoughts or ideas about something; discuss together. ♦ *Mother and Mrs. Barker like to compare notes about cooking.*

**condemn to** *v. phr.* To force someone into an undesirable and unfortunate condition or position. ♦ *John's inability to hold down a job condemns his entire family to a life of poverty.* ♦ *Alan's polio condemned him to a life on crutches and later to a wheelchair.*

**congregate housing** *n., informal* A form of housing for elderly persons in which dining facilities and services are shared in multiple dwelling units. ♦ *Jerry put Grandma in a place where they have congregate housing.*

**conjure up** **1.** To bring to mind. ♦ *Your remark about sandy beaches conjures*

up memories of Hawaii and the Bahamas. **2.** To cause to appear as if by magic. ♦ *Peter's mother conjured up a fabulous meal, although everybody thought that her refrigerator was empty and it was after store-closing hours.*

**conk out** *v. phr., slang, informal* To fall asleep suddenly with great fatigue or after having drunk too much. ♦ *We conked out right after the guests had left.*

**conspiracy of silence** *n. phr.* An organized way to treat someone as a nonperson; a concerted avoidance of mentioning someone or their work. ♦ *When Oscar Wilde got out of the Jail of Redding, London society greeted him with a conspiracy of silence.*

**consumer goods** *or* **consumer items** *n.* Food and manufactured things that people buy for their own use. ♦ *In time of war, the supply of consumer goods is greatly reduced.*

**control room** *n.* A room containing the panels and switches used to control something (like a TV broadcast). ♦ *While a television program is on the air, engineers are at their places in the control room.*

**control tower** *n.* A tower with large windows and a good view of an airport so that the traffic of airplanes can be seen and controlled, usually by radio. ♦ *We could see the lights at the control tower as our plane landed during the night.*

**convenience store** *n. phr.* A small store attached to a gas station or standing by itself, e.g., a 7-Eleven (meaning that it is open 11 hrs, 7 days a week) where soft drinks, cigarettes, and sandwich makings, along with candy, are available. ♦ *"Is there a convenience store near by?" the out-of-town driver asked.*

**conversation piece** *n.* Something that interests people and makes them talk about it; something that looks unusual, comical, or strange. ♦ *Uncle Fred has a glass monkey on top of his piano that he keeps for a conversation piece.*

**cook one's goose** *v. phr., slang* To ruin someone hopelessly; destroy one's future expectations or good name. ♦ *The dishonest official knew his goose was cooked when the newspapers printed the story about him.*

**cook up** *v., informal* To plan and put together; make up; invent. ♦ *The boys cooked up an excuse to explain their absence from school.*

**cook up a mess** or **cook up a fine mess** *v. phr.* To create chaos and disorder around oneself by socially unacceptable behavior. ♦ *Joe sure cooked up a fine mess when he started to invite his female students to his home without telling his wife about it.*

**cool as a cucumber** *adj. phr., informal* Very calm and brave; not nervous, worried, or anxious; not excited; composed. ♦ *Bill is a good football quarterback, always cool as a cucumber.*

**cool, calm, and collected** *adj. phr.* Describing a desired quality in people, especially ones in a leadership position, whereby the person is alert, yet not excited and ready to act. ♦ *Peter Murphy would make a fine commanding officer. I don't know anyone else quite so cool, calm, and collected as he is.*

**cool customer** *n.* Someone who is calm and in total control of himself; someone showing little emotion. ♦ *Jim never gets too excited about anything; he is a cool customer.*

**cool down** or **cool off** *v.* To lose or cause to lose the heat of any deep feeling (as love, enthusiasm, or anger); make or become calm, cooled or indifferent; lose interest. ♦ *A heated argument can be settled better if both sides cool down first.* ♦ *The neighbor's explanation about his illness cooled the argument down.*

**cool it** *v. phr. most often used as a command* To calm down; simmer down; relax, take it easy! ♦ *When Mr. Smith got home he heard a lot of noise from his son's room where six high school students were rehearsing for a play. "Nice to have you all here," he said, "but please cool it, won't you? I have a headache."*

**cool one down** *v. phr.* To make someone become less excited or upset. ♦ *"My sister has been shouting all day long, because she broke up with her boy friend. What can I do to cool her down?" Tom asked his mother. "Take her to see a good movie," the mother answered. "Maybe that will do the trick."*

**cool one's heels** *v. phr., slang* To be kept waiting by another's pride or rudeness; be forced to wait by someone in power or authority; wait. ♦ *I was left to cool my heels outside while the others went into the office.*

**coop up** *v. phr.* To hedge in; confine; enclose in a small place. ♦ *How can poor Jane work in that small office, cooped up all day long?*

**cop a feel** *v. phr., vulgar, avoidable* To attempt to arouse sexually by manual contact, usually by surprise. ♦ *John talks big for a 16 year old, but all he's ever done is cop a feel in a dark movie theater.*

**cop a plea** *v. phr., slang, colloquial* To plead guilty during a trial in the hope of getting a lighter sentence as a result. ♦ *The murderer of Dr. Martin Luther King, Jr., copped a plea of guilty, and got away with a life sentence instead of the death penalty.*

**cop out** *v. phr., slang, informal* (stress on *out*) To avoid committing oneself in a situation where doing so would result in difficulties. ♦ *Nixon copped out on the American people with Watergate.*

**cop-out** *n. phr., slang, informal* (stress on *cop*) An irresponsible excuse made to avoid something one has to do, a flimsy pretext. ♦ *Come on, Jim, that's a cheap cop-out, and I don't believe a word of it!*

**copy cat** *n.* Someone who copies another person's work or manner.—Usually used by children or when speaking to children. ♦ *He called me a copy cat just because my new shoes look like his.*

**corn ball** *n., slang, informal* **1.** A superficially sentimental movie or musical in which the word *love* is mentioned too often; a theatrical performance that is trivially sentimental. ♦ *That movie last night was a corn ball.* **2.** A person who behaves in a superficially sentimental manner or likes performances portraying such behavior. ♦ *Suzie can't stand Joe; she thinks he's a corn ball.*

**corn belt** *n.* The Midwest; the agricultural section of the United States where much corn is grown. ♦ *Kansas is one of the states that lies within the corn belt.*

**corporate ladder** *n. phr.* The series of advancements in pay, promotions in rank, and other perks that one has to go through in order to arrive at the top in large business settings. ♦ *Joe was made by Mother Nature to be a top executive; why, he climbs the corporate ladder like a pro.*

**cost a bomb** *or* **an arm and a leg** *v. phr.* To be extremely expensive. ♦ *My new house has cost us an arm and a leg and we're almost broke.*

**cotton** See ON TOP OF THE WORLD *also* SITTING ON HIGH COTTON.

**cotton picking, cotton-pickin'** *adj., slang, colloquial* Worthless, crude, common, messy. ♦ *Keep your cotton picking hands off my flowers!* ♦ *You've got to clean up your room, son, this is a cotton-pickin' mess!*

**couch case** *n., slang, informal* A person judged emotionally so disturbed that people think he ought to see a psychiatrist (who, habitually, make their patients lie down on a couch). ♦ *Joe's divorce messed him up so badly that he became a couch case.*

**couch doctor** *n., slang, colloquial* A psychoanalyst who puts his patients on a couch following the practice established by Sigmund Freud. ♦ *I didn't know your husband was a couch doctor, I thought he was a gynecologist!*

**couch potato** *n.* A person who is addicted to watching television all day. ♦ *Poor Ted has become such a couch potato that we can't persuade him to do anything.*

**cough up** *v., slang* **1.** To give (money) unwillingly; pay with an effort. ♦ *Her husband coughed up the money for the party with a good deal of grumbling.* **2.** To tell what was secret; make known. ♦ *He coughed up the whole story for the police.*

**could do with** *v. phr., informal* To wish to have something. ♦ *After a hot day's work out in the open, we could do with a nice hot shower and something cold to drink.*

**could go for** See COULD DO WITH.

**couldn't care less** *v. phr., informal* To be indifferent; not care at all. ♦ *The students couldn't care less about the band; they talked all through the concert.* Also heard increasingly as *could care less* (nonstandard in this form.)

**countdown** *n., Space English, informal* **1.** A step-by-step process which leads to the launching of a rocket. ♦ *Countdown starts at 23:00 hours tomorrow night and continues for 24 hours.* **2.** Process of counting inversely during the acts leading to a launch; liftoff occurs at zero. **3.** The time immediately preceding an important undertaking, borrowed from Space English. ♦ *We're leaving for Hawaii tomorrow afternoon; this is countdown time for us.*

**count heads** *or* **count noses** *v. phr., informal* To count the number of people in a group. ♦ *On the class picnic, we counted heads before we left.* ♦ *The usher was told to look out into the audience and count noses.*

**count in** *v. phr.* To consider someone or something as part of a group of people or a set of objects. ♦ *If you are buying tickets to the Lyric Opera for tomorrow evening's performance, please count us in.*

**count off** *v.* **1.** To count aloud from one end of a line of men to the other, each man counting in turn. ♦ *The soldiers counted off from right to left.* **2.** To place into a separate group or groups by counting. ♦ *The coach counted off three boys to carry in the equipment.* ♦ *Tom counted off enough newspapers for his route.*

**count on** *v.* To depend on; rely on; trust. ♦ *The team was counting on Joe to win the race.* ♦ *I'll do it; you know you can count on me.*

**count one's chickens before they're hatched** *v. phr., informal* To depend on getting a profit or gain before you have it; make plans that suppose something will happen; be too sure that something will happen. Usually used in negative sentences. ♦ *Maybe some of your customers won't pay, and then where will you be? Don't count your chickens before they're hatched.*

**count one's lucky stars** See LUCKY STAR.

**count out** *v.* **1.** To leave (someone) out of a plan; not expect (someone) to share in an activity; exclude. ♦ *"Will this party cost anything? If it does, count me out, because I'm broke."* **2.** To count out loud to ten to show that (a boxer who has been knocked down in a fight) is beaten or knocked out if he does not get up before ten is counted. ♦ *The champion was counted out in the third round.* **3a.** To add up; count again to be sure of the amount. ♦ *Mary counted out the number of pennies she had.* **3b.** To count out loud (especially the beats in a measure of music). ♦ *The music teacher counted out the beats "one-two-three-four," so the class would sing in time.*

**count to ten** *v. phr., informal* To count from one to ten so you will have time to calm down or get control of yourself; put off action when angry or excited so as not to do anything wrong. ♦ *Father always told us to count to ten before doing anything when we got angry.*

**county mounty** *n., slang, citizen's band radio jargon* Sheriff's deputy. ♦ *The county mounties are parked under the bridge.*

**cover a lot of ground** *v. phr.* To process a great deal of information and various facts. ♦ *Professor Brown's thorough lecture on asteroids covered a lot of ground today.*

**covered-dish supper** *or* **potluck supper** A meal to which each guest brings a share of the food. ♦ *Dolly made a chicken casserole for the covered-dish supper.*

**cover for** *v. phr.* **1.** To provide an excuse. ♦ *My cousin Ernie called in an excited voice, and told me to cover for him by saying that he spent the night at my place, if his wife inquires about his whereabouts.* **2.** To substitute for someone at work. ♦ *When faculty have to take a trip abroad, colleagues often cover for one another.*

**cover girl** *n.* A pretty girl or woman whose picture is put on the cover of a magazine. ♦ *Ann is not a cover girl, but she is pretty enough to be.*

**cover ground** *or* **cover the ground** *v. phr.* **1.** To go a distance; travel. ♦ *Mr. Rogers likes to travel in planes, because they cover ground so quickly.* **2.** *informal* To move over an area at a speed that is pleasing; move quickly over a lot of ground. ♦ *Jack's new car really covers ground!* **3.** To give or receive the important facts and details about a subject. ♦ *The class spent two days studying the Revolutionary War, because they couldn't cover that much ground in one day.*

**cover one's tracks** *or* **cover up one's tracks** *v. phr.* **1.** To hide and not leave anything, especially foot marks, to show where you have been, so that no one can follow you. ♦ *The deer covered his tracks by running in a stream.* **2.** *informal* To hide or not say where you have been or what you have done; not tell why you do something or what you plan to do. ♦ *The boys covered their tracks when they went swimming by saying that they were going for a walk.*

**cover the waterfront** *v. phr.* To talk or write all about something; talk about something all possible ways. ♦ *The principal pretty well covered the waterfront on student behavior.*

**cover up** *v., informal* (stress on *up*) **1.** To hide something wrong or bad from attention. ♦ *The spy covered up his picture-taking by pretending to be just a tourist.* **2.** *In boxing:* To guard your head and body with your gloves, arms, and shoulders. ♦ *Jimmy's father told him to cover up and protect his chin when he boxed.* **3.** To protect someone else from blame or punishment; protect someone with a lie or alibi.— Often used with *for.* ♦ *The burglar's friend covered up for him by saying that he was at his home when the robbery occurred.*

**cover-up** *n.* (stress on *cover*) A plan or excuse to escape blame or punishment; lie, alibi. ♦ *When the men robbed the bank, their cover-up was to dress like policemen.*

**cowboy** *n., slang, informal* A person who drives his car carelessly and at too great a speed in order to show off his courage. ♦ *Joe's going to be arrested some day—he is a cowboy on the highway.*

**cow college** *n., slang* **1.** An agricultural college; a school where farming is studied. ♦ *A new, bigger kind of apple is being grown at the cow college.* **2.** A new or rural college not thought to be as good as older or city colleges. ♦ *John wanted to go to a big college in New York City, not to a cow college.*

**cow's tail** *n., dialect* A person who is behind others. ♦ *John was the cow's tail at the exam.*

**cozy up** *v., slang* To try to be close or friendly; try to be liked.—Usually used with *to*. ♦ *John is cozying up to Henry so he can join the club.*

**crack a book** *v. phr., slang* To open a book in order to study.—Usually used with a negative. ♦ *Many students think they can pass without cracking a book.*

**crack a bottle** *v. phr.* To open a new bottle of alcoholic beverage. ♦ *On birthdays it is customary to crack a bottle and offer one's best wishes.*

**crack a joke** *v. phr., informal* To make a joke; tell a joke. ♦ *The men sat around the stove, smoking and cracking jokes.*

**crack a smile** *v. phr., informal* To let a smile show on one's face; permit a smile to appear. ♦ *Bob told the whole silly story without even cracking a smile.*

**crack down** *v. phr., informal* To enforce laws or rules strictly; require full obedience to a rule. ♦ *After a speeding driver hit a child, the police cracked down.*—Often used with *on*. ♦ *Police suddenly cracked down on the selling of liquors to minors.*

**crack of dawn** *n. phr.* The time in the morning when the sun's rays first appear. ♦ *The rooster crows at the crack of dawn and wakes up everybody on the farm.*

**cracked up** *adj. phr., informal* Favorably described or presented; praised.—Usually used in the expression *not what it's cracked up to be*. ♦ *The independent writer's life isn't always everything it's cracked up to be.*

**crack open** *v. phr.* **1.** To destroy someone's argument. ♦ *A clever attorney usually succeeds in cracking open his client's case.* **2.** To solve a mystery. ♦ *The local police cracked open the case of several complex kidnappings.*

**crack under the strain** *v. phr.* To suffer a nervous breakdown. ♦ *Jane cracked under the strain of worrying about her son, who just joined the army when war started.*

**crackpot** *n., attrib. adj., informal* **1.** *n.* An eccentric person with ideas that don't make sense to most other people. ♦ *Don't believe what Uncle Noam tells you—he is a crackpot.* **2.** *attrib. adj.* Eccentric or lunatic. ♦ *That's a crackpot idea.*

**crack the whip** *v. phr., informal* To get obedience or cooperation by threats of punishment. ♦ *If the children won't*

behave when I reason with them, I have to crack the whip.

**crack up** *v.* **1.** To wreck or be wrecked; smash up. ♦ *The airplane cracked up in landing.* **2.** *informal* To become mentally ill under physical or mental overwork or worry. ♦ *It seemed to be family problems that made him crack up.* **3.** burst into laughter *or* cause to burst into laughter. ♦ *That comedian cracks me up.*

**cramp one's style** *v. phr., informal* To limit your natural freedom; prevent your usual behavior; limit your actions or talk. ♦ *It cramped his style a good deal when he lost his money.* ♦ *Army rules cramped George's style.*

**crank call** *n. phr.* An anonymous phone call made by the caller as a threat or as a tasteless joke. ♦ *I won't pick up the receiver for the next couple of days, because I've been getting lots of crank calls, and I want to make the caller think that I have left town.*

**crank out** *or* **whip out** *v. phr.* To manufacture things quickly in large numbers. ♦ *During World War II, American industry cranked out boat after boat and plane after plane.*

**crash dive** *n.* A sudden dive made by a submarine to escape an enemy; a dive made to get deep under water as quickly as possible. ♦ *The captain of the submarine told his crew to prepare for a crash dive when he saw the enemy battleship approaching.*

**crash-dive** *v.* **1.** To dive deep underwater in a submarine as quickly as possible. ♦ *We shall crash-dive if we see enemy planes coming.* **2.** To dive into (something) in an airplane. ♦ *When the plane's motor was hit by the guns of the enemy battleship, the pilot aimed the plane at the ship and crash-dived into it.*

**crashing bore** *n. phr., slang* An extremely boring person. ♦ *Our math teacher is the most crashing bore we have ever experienced; he puts us to sleep!*

**crash the gate** *v. phr., slang* To enter without a ticket or without paying; attend without an invitation or permission. ♦ *Three boys tried to crash the gate at our party but we didn't let them in.*

**crash with** *v. phr.* To sleep temporarily in the home of a close friend, usually without paying for it and with little if any comfort, such as on a couch, under the dining table, in a sleeping bag, etc. ♦ *"We'd love to come to the convention, but we have no money, even for a cheap motel," John said. "No problem," Mike replied, "you can crash with us."*

**crawl out of the woodwork** *v. phr.* To suddenly appear as from nowhere; said of unsavory characters such as thieves, burglars, pimps, etc. ♦ *"When did you crawl out of the woodwork?" Sergeant O'Malley asked the petty criminal at the beginning of the interrogation.*

**crazy** *or* **mad** *or* **nuts about** *adj. phr., informal* Excessively fond of; infatuated with. ♦ *Jack is totally nuts about Liz, but she is not too crazy about him.*

**cream of the crop** *n. phr.* The best of a group; the top choice. ♦ *The students had drawn many good pictures and the teacher chose the cream of the crop to hang up when the parents came to visit.*

**creature comforts of home** *n. phr.* The conveniences of modern life, such as running hot water, air conditioning, a built-in dishwasher, etc. ♦ *Helen gave up the dilapidated country cottage she inherited from her parents, and moved into a modern city condominium in order to enjoy all the creature comforts of modern living.*

**creature of habit** *n. phr.* A person who does things out of habit rather than by thought. ♦ *Our boss is a creature of habit, so let us not confuse him with too many new ideas.*

**credibility gap** *n., hackneyed phrase, politics* An apparent discrepancy between what the government says and what one can observe for oneself. ♦ *There was a tremendous credibility gap in the USA during the Watergate years.*

**creep up on** *v.* **1.** To crawl towards; move along near the ground; steal cautiously towards so as not to be seen or noticed. ♦ *The mouse did not see the snake creeping up on it over the rocks.* **2.** *or* **sneak up on** To come little by little; arrive slowly and unnoticed. ♦ *The woman's hair was turning gray as age crept up on her.*

**crew cut** *or* **crew haircut** *n.* A boy's or man's hair style, cut so that the hair stands up in short, stiff bristle. ♦ *Many boys like to get crew cuts during the summer to keep cooler.*

**crocodile tears** *n.* Pretended grief; a show of sorrow that is not really felt. ♦ *When his rich uncle died, leaving him his money, John shed crocodile tears.*

**crop up** *v.* To come without warning; appear or happen unexpectedly. ♦ *Problems cropped up almost every day when Mr. Reed was building his TV station.*

**cross a bridge before one comes to it** *v. phr.* To worry about future events or trouble before they happen—Usually used in negative sentences, often as a proverb. ♦ *"Can I be a soldier when I grow up, Mother?" asked Johnny. "Don't cross that bridge until you come to it," said his mother.*

**cross-check**[1] *v.* To test the truth of by examining in different ways or by seeing different reports about. ♦ *If you see something in a book that may not be true, be sure to crosscheck it in other books.*

**cross-check**[2] *n.* The testing of the truth of by checking one report against another or others. ♦ *A cross-check with other books will show us if this story is true.*

**cross fire** *n.* **1.** Firing in a fight or battle from two or more places at once so that the lines of fire cross. ♦ *The soldiers on the bridge were caught in the cross fire coming from both sides of the bridge.* **2.** Fast or angry talking back and forth between two or more people; *also,* a dispute; a quarrel. ♦ *There was a cross fire of excited questions and answers between the parents and the children who had been lost in the woods.*

**cross one's fingers** *v. phr.* **1a.** To cross two fingers of one hand for good luck. ♦ *Mary crossed her fingers during the race so that Tom would win.* **1b.** *or* **keep one's fingers crossed** *informal* To wish for good luck. ♦ *Keep your fingers crossed while I take the test.* **2.** To cross two fingers of one hand to excuse an untruth that you are telling. ♦ *Johnny crossed his fingers when he told his mother the lie.*

**cross one's heart** *or* **cross one's heart and hope to die** *v. phr., informal* To say that what you have said is surely true; promise seriously that it is true.— Often used by children in the longer form. Children often make a sign of a cross over the heart as they say it, for emphasis. ♦ *"Cross my heart, I didn't steal your bicycle," Harry told Tom.* ♦ *"I didn't tell the teacher what you said. Cross my heart and hope to die," Mary said to Lucy.*

**cross one's mind** *or* **pass through one's mind** *v. phr.* To be a sudden or passing thought; be thought of by someone; come to your mind; occur to you. ♦ *When Jane did not come home by midnight, many terrible fears passed through her mother's mind.*

**cross one's path** *v. phr.* To meet or encounter someone; to come upon someone more by accident than by plan. ♦ *Surprisingly, I crossed John's path in Central Park one afternoon.*

**cross street** *n.* A street that crosses a main street and runs on both sides of it. ♦ *Elm Street is a cross street on Main Street and there is a traffic light there.*

**cross swords** *v. phr., literary* To have an argument with; fight.—Often used with *with*. ♦ *Don't argue with the teacher; you're not old enough to cross swords with her.*

**cross the wire** *v. phr.* To finish a race. ♦ *The Russian crossed the wire just behind the American.*

**crow before one is out of the woods** *v. phr.* To be glad or brag before you are safe from danger or trouble.—Usually used in negative sentences, often as a proverb, "Don't crow before you are out of the woods." ♦ *John thought his team would win because the game was almost over, but he didn't want to crow before they were out of the woods.*

**crowd in on** *or* **crowd in upon** *v. phr.* To fill the memory of someone by hearing something or looking at something. ♦ *Happy nostalgia for my days in Hawaii crowded in on me as I was rearranging my old photo album.*

**crown jewels** *n. pl.* The crown, staff, and jewels used for the crowning of a king or queen; the crown and jewels representing royal power and authority. ♦ *The crown jewels are handed down from one king to the next when the new king is crowned.*

**crumbs from the rich man's table** *n. phr.* the *Gospel of Luke* Insignificant, minor gifts received from a wealthy person. ♦ *A week at the Smiths' seaside villa, after saving their daughter's life impressed John as crumbs from the rich man's table.*

**crux of the matter** *n. phr.* The basic issue at hand; the core essence that one must face. ♦ *The crux of the matter is that he is incompetent and we will have to fire him.*

**cry** *or* **scream bloody murder** *v. phr.* To bitterly and loudly complain against an indignity. ♦ *Pete cried bloody murder when he found out that he didn't get the promotion he was hoping for.*

**cry buckets** *v. phr.* To shed an excessive amount of tears. ♦ *Grandma is crying buckets over the loss of our cat.*

**cry for** *or* **cry out for** *v., informal* To need badly; be lacking in. ♦ *It has not rained for two weeks and the garden is crying for it.* ♦ *The school is crying out for good teachers.*

**cry on one's shoulder** *v. phr.* To find a willing listener to whom one can complain all one wants for psychological comfort. ♦ *"I am sorry to be crying on your shoulders, Dad," Tim said, "but I lost my job and my wife left me. I have no one else to talk to."*

**cry out** *v.* **1.** To call out loudly; shout; scream. ♦ *The woman in the water cried out "Help!"* **2.** To complain loudly; protest strongly.—Used with *against*. ♦ *Many people are crying out against the new rule.*

**cry over spilled milk** *or* **cry over spilt milk** *v. phr., informal* To cry or complain about something that has already happened; be unhappy about something that cannot be helped. ♦ *You have lost the game but don't cry over spilt milk.*

**crystal ball** *n.* **1.** A ball, usually made of quartz crystal (glass) that is used by fortune-tellers. ♦ *The fortune-teller at the fair looked into her crystal ball and told me that I would take a long trip next year.* **2.** Any means of predicting the future. ♦ *My crystal ball tells me you'll be rich.*

**crystal gazing** *n.* The attempt to predict future events. ♦ *The magician's specialty was crystal gazing.*

**cry wolf** *v. phr.* To give a false alarm; warn of a danger that you know is not there. ♦ *The general said that the candidate was just crying wolf when he said* that the army was too weak to fight for the country.

**cub scout** *n.* A member of the Cub Scouts, the junior branch of the Boy Scouts for boys 8–10 years of age. ♦*Jimmie is only seven, too young to be a Cub Scout.*

**cue in** *v. phr., informal* To add new information to that which is already known. ♦*Let's not forget to cue in Joe on what has been happening.*

**culture vulture** *n., slang, informal* A person who is an avid cultural sightseer, one who seeks out cultural opportunities ostentatiously, such as going to the opera or seeing every museum in a town visited, and brags about it. ♦*My Aunt Mathilda is a regular culture vulture; she spends every summer in a different European capital going to museums and operas.*

**cup of tea** *also* **dish of tea** *n. phr., informal* **1.** Something you enjoy or do well at; a special interest, or favorite occupation. Used with a possessive. ♦*You could always get him to go for a walk: hiking was just his cup of tea.* **2.** Something to think about; thing; matter. ♦*That's another cup of tea.*

**curb service** *n.* Waiting on customers while they sit in their cars. ♦*Families with small children often look for hamburger stands that offer curb service.*

**curdles one's milk** *or* **curdles one's blood** *adj. phr.* Horrible; unspeakable, repugnant. ♦*What the Taliban did to their women in Afghanistan curdles one's blood.*

**curiosity killed the cat** *informal* Getting too nosy may lead a person into trouble.—A proverb. ♦*"Curiosity killed the cat," Fred's father said, when he found Fred hunting around in closets just before Christmas.*

**curl one's hair** *v. phr., slang* To shock; frighten; horrify; amaze. ♦*Wait till you read what it says about you—this'll curl your hair.*

**curl up** *v.* **1.** To become curly or wavy. ♦*Bacon curls up when it is cooked.* **2.** To roll oneself into a ball. ♦*Tim curled up in bed and was asleep in five minutes.*

**curry favor** *v.* To flatter or serve someone to get his help or friendship. ♦*Jim tried to curry favor with the new*

girl by telling her she was the prettiest girl in the class.

**Custer's last stand** *n. phr., from American history* A form of desperate resistance ending in one's extermination, as happened to the famous American officer named Custer while fighting the Indians. ♦*"We're all about to lose our jobs here," said Mr. Smith, the foreman, "but we figured we might as well stage a Custer's last stand before we go home."*

**cut a class** *v. phr.* To be truant; to deliberately miss a class and do something else instead. ♦*"If you keep cutting classes the way you do, you will almost surely flunk this course," John's professor said to him.*

**cut a deal** *or* **hammer out** *v. phr.* To reach an agreement after long and arduous negotiations. ♦*It took the airline employees four weeks to hammer out an agreement with the management.* ♦*I know you're just as anxious to get down to business as I am, so let us cut a deal here and now.*

**cut a figure** *v. phr.* To make a favorable impression; carry off an activity with dignity and grace. ♦*With his handsome face and sporty figure, Harry cuts quite a figure with all the ladies.*

**cut across** *v.* **1.** To cross or go through instead of going around; go a short way. ♦*John didn't want to walk to the corner and turn, so he cut across the yard to the next street.* **2.** To go beyond to include; stretch over to act on; affect. ♦*The love for reading cuts across all classes of people, rich and poor.*

**cut-and-dried** *adj. phr.* Decided or expected beforehand; following the same old line; doing the usual thing. ♦*The decision of the judge was cut-and-dried.*

**cut and run** *v., informal* To abandon an unfavorable situation. ♦*When the price of coffee dropped sharply many investors wanted to cut and run.*

**cut a swathe** *v. phr.* **1a.** To mow a path through a field. ♦*The farmer cut a swathe through the high grass with his scythe.* **1b.** To cut down as if by mowing. ♦*The machine gun cut a swathe in the lines of enemy soldiers.* **2.** *informal* To attract notice; make an impression; seem important. ♦*John* *tries to show off and cut a big swathe with the girls.*

**cut back** *v.* **1.** To change direction suddenly while going at full speed. ♦*The halfback started to his left, cut back to his right, and ran for a touchdown.* **2.** To use fewer or use less. ♦*The school employed forty teachers until a lower budget forced it to cut back.*

**cut back** *v. phr.* (stress on *back*) To diminish; lessen; decrease (said of budgets). ♦*The state had to cut back on the university budget.*

**cutback** *n.* (stress on *cut*) An act of decreasing monetary sources. ♦*The cutback in military spending has caused many bases to be closed.*

**cut both ways** *or* **cut two ways** *v. phr.* To have two effects; cause injury to both sides. ♦*People who gossip find it cuts both ways.*

**cut corners** *v. phr.* **1.** To take a short way; not go to each corner. ♦*He cut corners going home in a hurry.* **2.** To save cost or effort; manage in a thrifty way; be saving. ♦*John's father asked him to cut corners all he could in college.* **3.** To do less than a very good job; do only what you must do on a job. ♦*He had cut corners in building his house, and it didn't stand up well.*

**cut down** *v.* To lessen; reduce; limit. ♦*Tom had to cut down expenses.* ♦*The doctor told Mr. Jones to cut down on smoking.*

**cut down to size** *v. phr., informal* To prove that someone is not as good as he thinks. ♦*The big boy told John he could beat him, but John was a good boxer and soon cut him down to size.*

**cut ice** *v. phr., informal* To make a difference; make an impression; be accepted as important.—Usually used in negative, interrogative, or conditional sentences. ♦*When Frank had found a movie he liked, what others said cut no ice with him.*

**cut in** *v.* **1.** To force your way into a place between others in a line of cars, people, etc.; push in. ♦*After passing several cars, Fred cut in too soon and nearly caused an accident.*—Often used with *on.* ♦*A car passed Jean and cut in on her too close; she had to brake quickly or she would have hit it.* **2.** To stop a talk or program for a time; interrupt. ♦*While we were watching the late show, an announcer cut in to tell who won the election.* **3.** *informal* To tap a dancer on the shoulder and claim the partner. ♦*Mary was a good dancer and a boy could seldom finish a dance with her; someone always cut in.*—Often used with *on.* ♦*At the leap year dance, Jane cut in on Sally because she wanted to dance with Sally's handsome date.* **4.** To connect to an electrical circuit or to a machine. ♦*Harry threw the switch and cut in the motor.* **5.** *informal* To take in; include. ♦*When John's friends got a big contract, they cut John in.*

**cut into** *v.* **1.** To make less; reduce. ♦*The union made the company pay higher wages, which cut into the profits.* ♦*At first Smith led in votes, but more votes came in and cut into his lead.* **2.** To get into by cutting in. ♦*While Bill was passing another car, a truck came around a curve heading for him, and Bill cut back into line quickly.*

**cut it out** *v. phr., slang* See LET ALONE.

**cut loose** *v.* **1.** To free from ties or connections; cut the fastenings of. ♦*The thief hastily cut the boat loose from its anchor.* **2.** *informal* To break away from control; get away and be free. ♦*The boy left home and cut loose from his parents' control.* **3.** *informal* To behave freely or wildly. ♦*The men had come to the convention to have a good time, and they really cut loose.*

**cut off** *v.* **1.** To separate or block. ♦*The flood cut the townspeople off from the rest of the world.* ♦*The woods cut off the view.* **2.** To interrupt or stop. ♦*The television show was cut off by a special news report.* ♦*We were told to pay the bill or the water would be cut off.* **3.** To end the life of; cause the death of. ♦*Disease cut Smith off in the best part of life.* **4.** To give nothing to at death; leave out of a will. ♦*Jane married a man her father hated, and her father cut her off.* **5.** To stop from operating; turn a switch to stop. ♦*The ship cut off its engines as it neared the dock.*

**cut off one's nose to spite one's face** *v. phr.* To suffer from an action intended originally to harm another person. ♦*In walking out and leaving his employer in the lurch, John really cut off his nose to* *spite his face, since no business wanted to hire him afterwards.*

**cut-offs** *n., colloquial* (stress on *cut*) Pants cut to the length of shorts and usually left unhemmed so as to look old and worn, e.g., considered cool and elegant. ♦*Jack always wears cut-offs during the summer.*

**cut one's losses** *v. phr.* To stop spending time, money, or energy on unprofitable projects and concentrate on what goes well. ♦*"Just cut your losses, Jim," his father suggested, "and get on with the rest of your life."*

**cut one's throat** *v. phr., informal* To spoil one's chances; ruin a person. ♦*He cut his own throat by his carelessness.*

**cut out**[1] *v., slang* **1.** To stop; quit. ♦*All right, now—let's cut out the talking.* ♦*He was teasing the dog and Joe told him to cut it out.* **2.** To displace in favor. ♦*John cut out two or three other men in trying for a better job.*

**cut out**[2] *adj.* **1.** Made ready; given for action; facing. ♦*Mary agreed to stay with her teacher's children all day; she did not know what was cut out for her.*—Often used in the phrase *have one's work cut out for one.* ♦*If Mr. Perkins wants to become a senator, he has his work cut out for him.* **2.** Suited to; fitted for. ♦*Warren seemed to be cut out for the law.*

**cut out the dead wood** *v. phr.* To remove useless parts, personnel, or methods. ♦*Our business will probably start to show a quarterly profit, if we can just get rid of some dead wood.* ♦

**cut rate**[1] *n.* A lower price; a price less than usual. ♦*Toys are on sale at the store for cut rates.*

**cut-rate**[2] *adj.* Sold for a price lower than usual; selling cheap things. ♦*If you buy cut-rate things, be sure they are good quality first.*

**cut short** *v.* To stop or interrupt suddenly; end suddenly or too soon. ♦*Rain cut short the ball game.* ♦*An auto accident cut short the man's life.*

**cut some slack** *v. phr., from sportfishing* Give someone more freedom or more room to maneuver. ♦*"Cut me some slack, you guys!" John emphatically urged his colleagues. "I am suffocating under such close supervision."*

**cut teeth** *v. phr.* To have teeth grow out through the gums. ♦*The baby was cross because he was cutting teeth.*

**cut the cord** *v. phr., informal, with reference to the umbilical cord at birth* To separate from a source of security. ♦*"Well, Johnny finally did it. He left home and took an apartment in the city. He finally cut the cord."*

**cut the ground from under** *v. phr. informal* To make (someone) fail; upset the plans of; spoil the argument for (a person) in advance. ♦*Paul wanted to be captain but we cut the ground from under him by saying that Henry was the best player on the team.* ♦*Several workers applied for the retiring foreman's job, but the owner cut the ground from under them by hiring a foreman from another company.*

**cut the mustard** *v. phr., slang* To do well enough in what needs to be done; to succeed. ♦*His older brothers and sisters helped Max through high school, but he couldn't cut the mustard in college.*

**cut-throat** *adj.* Severe; intense; unrelenting. ♦*There is cut-throat competition among the various software companies today.*

**cut to pieces** *v. phr.* **1.** To divide into small parts with something sharp; cut badly or completely. ♦*Baby has cut the newspaper to pieces with scissors.* **2.** To destroy or defeat completely. ♦*When Dick showed his book report to his big sister for correction, she cut it to pieces.*

**cut to the bone** *v. phr.* To make (something) the least or smallest possible amount; reduce severely; leave out everything extra or unnecessary from. ♦*Father cut Jane's allowance to the bone for disobeying him.* ♦*When father lost his job, our living expenses had to be cut to the bone.*

**cut to the quick** *v. phr.* To hurt someone's feelings deeply. ♦*The children's teasing cut Mary to the quick.*

**cut up** *v.* **1.** *informal* To hurt the feelings of; wound.—Usually used in the passive. ♦*John was badly cut up when Susie gave him back his ring.* **2.** *slang* To act funny or rough; clown. ♦*Joe would always cut up if there were any girls watching.*

**cut your coat according to your cloth** Often heard as advice given when one tries to live beyond one's means. To spend no more than what you can afford.—A proverb. ♦*When John came home for the fifth time the same semester asking for extra money, his father said, "You should really have enough. Cut your coat according to your cloth."*

**cybercrime** *n. phr.* A new kind of crime that came in with the general availability of the personal computer; such as breaking into a bank or stealing someone's identity together with their credit card numbers, etc. ♦*"My brother Sam, whom I used to envy for his knowledge of computers, is doing fifteen years in jail for committing a major cybercrime."*

**daily dozen** *n.*, *informal* Gymnastic exercises; *especially*, several different exercises done daily. ◆*The boys did their daily dozen early each morning.*

**damned if one does, damned if one doesn't** *adj. phr.* No matter what one does, someone is likely to criticize one. ◆*No matter what decisions I make, there are always some people who will approve them and those who won't. It is a classical case of "damned if I do, damned if I don't."*

**damn with faint praise** *v. phr.* To express one's dislike or scorn for a piece of writing, music, scholarship, or art, by not saying anything directly against it, but praising it in such general terms that amount to condemnation. ◆*When it comes to Milton scholarship, Stanley Fish is a master of damning the work of his colleagues with faint praise.*

**dance around** *v. phr.* To avoid coming to grips with something. ◆*The divorcing couple danced around the issue of child custody for several months before they were able to come an amicable arrangement.*

**dance to another tune** *v. phr.* To talk or act differently, usually better because things have changed; be more polite or obedient because you are forced to do it. ◆*Johnny refused to do his homework but punishment made him dance to another tune.*

**dare say** *v. phr.* To think probable; suppose; believe.—Used in first person. ◆*There is no more ice cream on the table, but I dare say we can find some in the kitchen.*

**dare one to do something** *v. phr.* To challenge someone to do something. ◆*"I dare you to jump off that rock into the sea," Fred said to Jack.*

**Dark Continent** *n. phr.*, *old-fashioned, avoidable* The continent of Africa. ◆*In the nineteenth century British and other European explorers used to refer to Africa as the "Dark Continent."*

**dark horse** *n.*, *informal* A political candidate little known to the general voting public; a candidate who was not expected to run. ◆*Every once in a while a dark horse candidate gets elected president.*

**dark of the moon** *n. phr.*, *literary* A time when the moon is not shining or cannot be seen. ◆*It was the dark of the moon when the scouts reached camp and they had to use flashlights to find their tents.*

**dash light** *n.* A light on the front inside of a car or vehicle. ◆*Henry stopped the car and turned on the dash lights to read the road map.*

**dash off** *v.* To make, do, or finish quickly; especially, to draw, paint, or write hurriedly. ◆*John can dash off several letters while Mary writes only one.* ◆*Charles had forgotten to write his English report and dashed it off just before class.*

**date back** *v. phr.* To go back to a given period in the past. ◆*My ancestors date back to the sixteenth century.*

**dawdle away** *v. phr.* To waste time, etc. ◆*Jane dawdled the whole day away trying to polish the tarnished old silverware she inherited from her grandmother.*

**dawn on** *v.* To become clear to. ◆*It dawned on Fred that he would fail the course if he did not study harder.*

**day and night** *or* **night and day** *adv.* **1.** For days without stopping; continually. ◆*Some filling stations on great highways are open day and night 365 days a year.* **2.** Every day and every evening. ◆*The girl knitted day and night to finish the sweater before her mother's birthday.*

**day by day** *adv.* Gradually. ◆*The patient got better day by day.*

**daydream** *v.* To spend time in reverie; be absentminded during the day. ◆*John spends so much time daydreaming that he never gets anything done.*

**day in and day out** *or* **day in, day out** *adv. phr.* Regularly; consistently; all the time; always. ◆*He plays good tennis day in and day out.*—Also used with several other time words in place of *day: week, month, year.* ◆*Every summer, year in, year out, the ice cream man comes back to the park.*

**day in court** *n. phr.* A chance to be heard; an impartial hearing; a chance to explain what one has done. ◆*The* *letters from the faculty members to the dean gave Professor Smith his day in court.*

**daylight saving time** *also* **daylight saving** *or* **daylight time** *or* **fast time** *n.* A way of keeping time in summer that is one or two hours ahead of standard time.—Abbreviation DST. ♦ *Father said that next week it will get dark later because we will change to daylight saving time.* ♦ *We go off daylight saving in the fall.*

**daylight robbery** See HIGHWAY ROBBERY.

**day of grace** *n. phr.* An extension period after the due date of some contract or bond. ♦ *The premium is due on the first of each month, but they allow ten days of grace.*

**day of reckoning** *n. phr.* **1.** A time when one will be made to account for misdeeds. ♦ *When the criminal was caught and brought to trial his victims said, "finally, the day of reckoning has come."* **2.** A time when one's will and judgment are severely tested. ♦ *"You always wanted to run the department," the dean said to Professor Smith. "Now here is your chance; this is your day of reckoning."*

**day off** *n.* A day on which one doesn't have to work, not necessarily the weekend. ♦ *Monday is his day off in the restaurant, because he prefers to work on Saturdays and Sundays.*

**day-to-day** *adj.* Daily; common; everyday. ♦ *For best results, students' homework should be checked on a day-to-day basis.*

**days are numbered** (Someone or something) does not have long to live or stay. ♦ *When a man becomes ninety years old, his days are numbered.*

**dead ahead** *adv., informal* Exactly in front; before. ♦ *Jim was driving in a fog, and suddenly he saw another car dead ahead of him.*

**dead and buried** *adj. phr.* Gone forever. ♦ *Slavery is dead and buried in twentieth-century America.*

**dead and done with** *adj. phr.* Obsolete; irrelevant; no longer considered important. ♦ *"What about the Smith family estate?" the new bank employee asked. "That's been dead and done with for quite some time," the vice president answered.*

**dead and gone** *adj. phr.* Said of persons who have vanished without a trace. ♦ *"What ever happened to the Millers?" the young journalist inquired. "I am trying to write about famous people in your town." "All dead and gone," the sheriff answered. "You're wasting your time."*

**dead as a doornail** *adj. phr.* Completely dead without the slightest hope of resuscitation. ♦ *This battery is dead as a doornail; no wonder your car won't start.*

**deadbeat** *n., slang* **1.** A person who never pays his debts and who has a way of getting things free that others have to pay for. ♦ *You'll never collect from Joe—he's a deadbeat.* **2.** **dead beat** *adj. phr.* Totally exhausted. ♦ *I feel dead beat all day after yawning through three boring meetings.*

**dead but he won't lie down** *or* **dead man who won't lie down** *n. phr.* Someone whose prime time has been over for quite a while, but who nevertheless, ignorantly, keeps speaking up and making irrelevant remarks as a sign of his stupidity. ♦ *That old gentleman next door, who still believes that the sun is circling the earth, is a dead man who won't lie down.*

**dead center** *n.* The exact middle. ♦ *The treasure was buried in the dead center of the island.* Often used like an adverb. ♦ *The arrow hit the circle dead center.*

**dead duck** *n., slang* A person or thing in a hopeless situation or condition; one to whom something bad is sure to happen. ♦ *When the pianist broke her arm, she was a dead duck.*

**dead end** *n. phr.* A hopeless situation, from which one is unable to advance. ♦ *That job in Podunk, Missouri, where he works as a short-order cook, is a dead end for my poor cousin Joe.*

**dead-end** *v. phr.* To end in an obstacle, to be blocked off. ♦ *MacLaren Lane in Lake Bluff dead-ends in a meadow full of weeds.*

**deadhead** *n., slang* An excessively dull or boring person. ♦ *You'll never get John to tell a joke—he's a deadhead.*

**dead letter** *n. phr.* An undeliverable letter that ends up in a special office holding such letters. ♦ *There is a dead letter office in most major cities.*

**deadline** *n.* A final date by which a project, such as a term paper, is due. ♦*The deadline for the papers on Shakespeare is November 10.*

**dead loss** *n. phr.* A total waste; a complete loss. ♦*Our investment in Jack's company turned out to be a dead loss.*

**dead on one's feet** *adv. phr., informal* Very tired but still standing or walking; too tired to do more; exhausted. ♦*After the soldiers march all night, they are dead on their feet.*

**deadpan** *adj., adv., slang* With an expressionless or emotionless face; without betraying any hint of emotion. ♦*She received the news of her husband's death deadpan.*

**dead pedal** *n., slang, citizen's band radio jargon* A slow moving vehicle. ♦*Better pass that eighteen wheeler, Jack; it's a dead pedal.*

**dead ringer** *n. phr.* A person who strongly resembles someone else. ♦*Charlie is a dead ringer for his uncle.*

**dead set against** *adj. phr.* Totally opposed to someone or something. ♦*Jack is dead set against the idea of marriage, which upsets Mary.*

**dead tired** *adj. phr., informal* Very tired; exhausted; worn out. ♦*She was dead tired at the end of the day's work.*

**dead to the world** *adj. phr., informal* **1.** Fast asleep. ♦*Tim went to bed very late and was still dead to the world at 10 o'clock this morning.* **2.** As if dead; unconscious. ♦*Tom was hit on the head by a baseball and was dead to the world for two hours.*

**dead-end** *n.* A street closed at one end; a situation that leads nowhere. ♦*Jim drove into a dead-end street and had to back out.* ♦*Mary was in a dead-end job.*

**dead-end** *v.* To not continue normally but end in a closure (said of streets). ♦*Our street dead-ends on the lake.*

**deal in** *v. phr.* To sell; do business in a certain commodity. ♦*Herb's firm deals in sporting goods.*

**deal with** *v. phr.* **1.** To conduct negotiations or business dealings with. ♦*John refuses to deal with the firm of Brown and Miller.* **2.** To handle a problem. ♦*Ted is a very strong person and dealt with the fact that his wife had left him much better than anyone else I know.*

**Dear John letter** *n. phr.*—A note or a letter informing one that a romantic relationship or a marriage is over. ♦*Jane left a "Dear John letter" on the table and went home to live with her parents.*

**dear me** *interj.* Used to show surprise, fear, or some other strong feeling. ♦*Dear me! My purse is lost, what shall I do now?*

**death knell** *n. formal* **1.** The ringing of a bell at a death or funeral. ♦*The people mourned at the death knell of their friend.* **2.** *literary* Something which shows a future failure. ♦*His sudden deafness was the death knell of his hope to become president.*

**decked out** *adj. phr., informal* Dressed in fancy clothes; specially decorated for some festive occasion. ♦*The school band was decked out in bright red uniforms with brass buttons.* ♦*Main Street was decked with flags for the Fourth of July.*

**deep-six** *v., slang* To throw away; dispose of. ♦*As the police boat came near, the drug smugglers deep-sixed their cargo.*

**deep water** *n.* Serious trouble or difficulty. ♦*When Dad tried to take Mom's place for a day, he found himself in deep water.*

**defer to** *v. phr.* Show respect toward someone, or to yield to someone else's wishes. ♦*On the question of war or appeasement, we had better defer to the president and his close associates.*

**deliver the goods** *v. phr.* **1.** To carry things and give them to the person who wants them. ♦*Lee delivered the goods to the right house.* **2.** *slang* To succeed in doing well what is expected. ♦*This personal computer surely delivers the goods.*

**delta wave** *n., informal, semi-technical* A brain wave 1–3 cycles per second, associated with very deep sleep. ♦*Good night, honey, I'm off to produce some delta waves.*

**Dennis the Menace** *n. phr.* After the notorious comic strip character of a young boy who always creates trouble for the grownups. Any hyperactive little boy who needs calming down. ♦*"Your son, Joey, is becoming a regular 'Dennis the Menace'," Jane said to Elvira.*

**devil incarnate** *n. phr.* A person who is totally devoid of a human conscience, who can commit any heinous crime without the least regret. ◆ *Adolf Hitler and Joseph Stalin were perfect examples of what one calls "the devil incarnate."*

**devil-may-care** *adj.* Not caring what happens; unworried. ◆ *Johnny has a devil-may-care feeling about his school work.*

**devil-may-care attitude** *n. phr.* An attitude of no concern for financial or other loss. ◆ *"Easy come, easy go," John said in a devil-may-care attitude when he lost all of his money during a poker game.*

**devil of it** *or* **heck of it** *n. phr.* **1.** The worst or most unlucky thing about a trouble or accident; the part that is most regrettable. ◆ *When I had a flat tire, the devil of it was that my spare tire was flat too.* **2.** Fun from doing mischief.—Used after *for.* ◆ *The boys carried away Miss White's front gate just for the devil of it.*

**devil to pay** *n. phr.* Great trouble.—Used after *the.* ◆ *There'll be the devil to pay when the teacher finds out who broke the window.*

**diamond cuts diamond** Just as the hardest stone, a diamond, can be cut only with another diamond, it takes an extraordinary person to have an effect on another of similar qualities.—A proverb. ◆ *The physicist Niels Bohr alone was able to exert major influence on Albert Einstein's thinking, but that's understandable—diamond cuts diamond.*

**diamond in the rough** *n. phr.* A very smart person without a formal education who may have untutored manners. ◆ *Jack never went to school but he is extremely talented; he is a veritable diamond in the rough.*

**die away** *or* **die down** *v.* To come slowly to an end; grow slowly less or weaker. ◆ *The wind died down.* ◆ *His mother's anger died away.*

**die for** *v. phr.* Almost irresistibly, very strongly. To wish or yearn for something. ◆ *"I am dying for a glass of cold water," the man lost in the desert said.*

**die in one's boots** *or* **die with one's boots on** *v. phr., informal* To be killed or hanged rather than die in bed. ◆ *The*

badmen of the Old West usually died in their boots.

**die is cast** *v. phr., literary* To make an irrevocable decision. ◆ *Everything was ready for the invasion of Europe, the die had been cast, and there was no turning back now.*

**die hard** *v. phr* (stress on *hard*) To be slow to cease; slow to go out of fashion. ◆ *Old beliefs and superstitions die hard.* ◆ *Racism and segregation in the South of the United States died hard.*

**diehard** *adj. phr.* (Stress on *die*) **1.** (of objects, tools, instruments, etc.) Possessing the ability to withstand extended use and depletion of energy. ◆ *If you want your flashlight to work for several weeks, you had better get some diehard batteries.* **2.** (of people) A staunch adherer to a religion, a political view, or some set of values. ◆ *Nick is a diehard Roman Catholic and a registered Republican voter besides, but his younger brother Pete is a diehard agnostic and a libertarian.*

**die in harness** *v. phr.* To die while one is at work. ◆ *The 90-year-old novelist was sitting at his desk typing when he died of a sudden heart attack. He was a most dedicated worker, who died in harness.*

**die in the last ditch** *v. phr.* To die while fighting to the very last minute as if defending a besieged castle or the like. ◆ *The evil dictator was hoping that his special guard would die in the last ditch for him, but most of them defected.*

**die off** *v.* To die one at a time. ◆ *The flowers are dying off because there has been no rain.*

**die on the vine** *or* **wither on the vine** *v. phr.* To fail or collapse in the planning stages. ◆ *The program for rebuilding the city died on the vine.*

**die out** *v.* To die or disappear slowly until all gone. ◆ *This kind of bird is dying out.*

**different strokes for different folks** Everyone has different interests and tastes and should therefore be treated accordingly.—A proverb. ◆ *A crying baby needs to be changed and a pacifier put in his mouth, but a complaining teenager needs some intelligent advice. After all it is "different strokes for different folks."*

**dig down** *v., slang* To spend your own money. ◆ *"So you broke Mrs. Brown's* window?" Tom's father said. "You'll have to dig down and pay for it."

**dig in** *v., informal* **1.** To dig ditches for protection against an enemy attack. ♦*The soldiers dug in and waited for the enemy to come.* **2a.** To go seriously to work; work hard. ♦*John dug in and finished his homework very quickly.* **2b.** To begin eating. ♦*Mother set the food on the table and told the children to dig in.*

**dig one's heels in** *or* **dig one's toes in** *v. phr.* To offer strong resistance; to refuse changing one's mind under the influence of another. ♦*The dean tried to persuade Professor Doolittle to retire, but he dug his heels in and refused to listen to reason.*

**dig out** *v.* **1.** To find by searching; bring out (something) that was put away. ♦*The newspaper printed an old story dug out of their records.* **2.** *informal* To escape.—Usually used with *of.* Often used in the phrase *dig oneself out of a hole.* ♦*The pitcher dug himself out of a hole by striking the batter out.*

**dig up** *v., informal* To find or get (something) with some effort. ♦*Sue dug up some useful material for her English composition.* ♦*Jim asked each boy to dig up twenty-five cents to pay for the hot dogs and soda.*

**dime a dozen** *adj. phr., informal* Easy to get and so of little value; being an everyday thing because there are many of them; common. ♦*Mr. Jones gives A's to only one or two students, but in Mr. Smith's class, A's are a dime a dozen.*

**dim out** *v. phr.* To become gradually darker either by deliberately fading the lights or because of a partial power failure known as a "brownout." ♦*The lights dimmed out in the theater as the new act began.* ♦*All over Los Angeles the lights dimmed out for an hour during California's electric power shortage.*

**dine out** *v. phr.* To not eat at home but to go to a restaurant. ♦*"Let's dine out tonight, honey," she said to her husband. "I am tired of cooking dinner every night."*

**dine out on** *v. phr.* To gain social advantage and success and often a free meal on account of some past accomplishment that is no longer followed by new deeds of merit. ♦*The former revolu-*

tionary student leader, now fat and complacent, keeps dining out on stories of the revolution.*

**dip into** *v. phr.* **1.** To scan or sample lightly and briefly (said of printed materials). ♦*I didn't get a chance to read all of* War and Peace, *but I dipped into it here and there.* **2.** To take money out of a savings account or a piggy bank. ♦*I am sorry to have to say that I had to dip into the piggy bank; I took out $6.75.*

**dirt cheap** *adj.* Extremely inexpensive. ♦*The apartment we are renting is dirt cheap compared to other apartments of similar size in this neighborhood.*

**dirty look** *n., informal* A look that shows dislike. ♦*Miss Parker sent Joe to the principal's office for giving her a dirty look.*

**dirty old man** *n. phr.* An older man who shows an unhealthy interest in young girls. ♦*"Stay away from Uncle Algernon, Sally," her mother warned. "He is a dirty old man."*

**dirty one's hands** *or* **soil one's hands** *v. phr.* To lower or hurt one's character or good name; do a bad or shameful thing. ♦*The teacher warned the children not to dirty their hands by cheating in the examination.* ♦*I would not soil my hands by going with bad people and doing bad things.*

**dirty story** *n. phr.* An improper or obscene story. ♦*Uncle Bill is much too fond of telling dirty stories in order to embarrass his friends.*

**dirty trick** *n. phr.* A treacherous action; an unfair act. ♦*That was a dirty trick John played on Mary when he ran away with her younger sister.*

**disappear** *or* **evaporate** *or* **vanish into thin air** *v. phr.* To disappear quickly, without leaving a trace. ♦*Money seems to disappear into thin air these days.*

**discretion is the better part of valor** *literary* When you are in danger or trouble, good sense helps more than foolish risks; it is better to be careful than to be foolishly brave.—A proverb. ♦*When you are facing a man with a knife, discretion is the better part of valor.*

**dish out** *v.* **1.** To serve (food) from a large bowl or plate. ♦*Ann's mother asked her to dish out the beans.* **2.** *informal* To give in large quantities. ♦*That teacher* *dished out so much homework that her pupils complained to their parents.* **3.** *slang* To scold; treat or criticize roughly. ◆*Jim likes to dish it out, but he hates to take it.*

**dish the dirt** *v. phr., slang* To gossip, to spread rumors about others. ◆*Stop dishing the dirt, Sally, it's really quite unbecoming!*

**disk jockey** *n.* An employee at a radio station or in a dance club who puts on the records that will be broadcast. ◆*Jack is working as a disk jockey at the local FM station.*

**dispose of** *v.* **1.** To throw away; give away, or sell; get rid of. ◆*John's father wants to dispose of their old house and buy a new one.* ◆*The burglars had difficulty in disposing of the stolen jewelry.* **2.** To finish with; settle; complete. ◆*The boys were hungry, and quickly disposed of their dinner.* ◆*The committee soon disposed of all its business.* **3.** To destroy or defeat. ◆*The champion disposed of the other fighter by knocking him out in the second round.* ◆*Our planes disposed of two enemy planes.*

**dive into** *v. phr.* **1.** To conduct a rapid search inside a container, such as a suitcase, etc. ◆*Jane nervously dived into her suitcase in search of her lost wedding ring.* ◆*Joe dived his hands into both pockets trying to find his car keys.* **2.** To eagerly start eating. ◆*Hardly had Mother put the food on the table, when I eagerly dived into it, just like a kid.* **3.** To eagerly and keenly join some ongoing activity. ◆*Al dived into the political discussion without knowing much about the subject.* **4.** To enter a place suddenly and often in secret. ◆*The police were following the robber, when he suddenly dived into an abandoned railway car and disappeared from sight.*

**divvy up** *v. phr., slang* To share. ◆*The four bank robbers decided to divvy up the two million dollars they stole in cash, so each one got $250,000.*

**do a double take** *v. phr., informal* To look again in surprise; suddenly understand what is seen or said. ◆*John did a double take when he saw Bill in girls' clothes.*

**do a good turn to one** *v. phr.* To render service or benefit to a person; to prac-

tice charity. ◆*The new country doctor decided to treat poor people free, thereby doing them a good turn.*

**do a job on** *v. phr., slang* To damage badly; do harm to; make ugly or useless. ◆*Jane cut her hair and really did a job on herself.*

**do a stretch** *v. phr.* To spend time in jail serving one's sentence. ◆*Jake has disappeared from view for a while; he is doing a stretch for dope smuggling.*

**do away with** *v.* **1.** To put an end to; stop. ◆*The teachers want to do away with cheating in their school.* ◆*The city has decided to do away with overhead wires.* **2.** To kill; murder. ◆*The robbers did away with their victims.*

**do business** *v. phr.* To be in a commercial relationship with an individual or a firm. ◆*"Always glad to do business with you, gentlemen," John said. "You are always punctual, precise, and honest."*

**do by someone** *or* **something** *v.* To deal with; treat.—Used with a qualifying adverb between *do* and *by.* ◆*Andy's employer always does very well by him.*

**do credit** *or* **do credit to** *also (informal)* **do proud** To add to or improve the reputation, good name, honor, or esteem of; show (you) deserve praise. ◆*Mary's painting would do credit to a real artist.*

**doctor up** *v. phr.* To meddle with; adulterate. ◆*You don't have to doctor up this basic salad with a lot of extras as I am trying to lose weight.*

**do duty for** *v. phr.* To substitute for; act in place of. ◆*The bench often does duty for a table.*

**doesn't add up to a can of beans** *v. phr.* To be of little or no value. (Said of plans, ideas, etc.) ◆*"That's a fairly interesting concept you got there, Mike, but the competition is bound to say that it doesn't add up to a can of beans."*

**doesn't grow on trees** Said of goods and services that are hard to obtain; chiefly about money.—A proverb. ◆*"You have to work hard in America, my friend," John said to the naïve immigrant. "After all, money doesn't grows on trees."*

**do for** *v., informal* To cause the death or ruin of; cause to fail.—Used usually in the passive form *done for.* ◆*The poor* *fellow is done for and will die before morning.* ◆ *If Jim fails that test, he is done for.*

**do for a living** *v. phr.* Pursue as an occupation. ◆ *"What do you do for a living?" Mary asked John. "I am a dentist," John replied.*

**dog days** *n. phr.* The hottest days of the year in the Northern Hemisphere (July and August). ◆ *"The dog days are upon us," John said. "It's time to go swimming in the lake."*

**dog-eared** *adj. phr.* Worn, used a lot; especially about pages in books that have been turned in to mark where the reader has stopped. ◆ *"Why is this old edition of Shakespeare all dog-eared?" the new English teacher asked. "Because the school has no money to buy a new one," the librarian answered. "All our books here are dog-eared."*

**dog-eat-dog**[1] *n.* A way of living in which every person tries to get what he wants for himself no matter how badly or cruelly he must treat others to get it; readiness to do anything to get what you want. ◆ *In some early frontier towns it was dog-eat-dog.*

**dog-eat-dog**[2] *adj.* Ready or willing to fight and hurt others to get what you want. ◆ *During the California gold rush, men had a dog-eat-dog life.*

**doggy bag** *n. phr.* A small styrofoam, plastic, or paper container in which food left on one's plate in a restaurant may be taken home instead of being thrown away. The food is mostly for oneself and not for a "dog." ◆ *"Waiter, may I have a doggy bag, please?" "But of course, Sir," the waiter replied. "Every restaurant has them these days."*

**dog in the manger** *n. phr.* A person who is unwilling to let another use what he himself has no use for. ◆ *Although Valerie lives alone in that big house, she is like a dog in the manger when it comes to letting someone sharing it with her.*

**dog one's steps** *v. phr.* To follow someone closely. ◆ *All the time he was in Havana, Castro's police were dogging his steps.*

**dog's life** *n. phr.* A life of misery, poverty, and unhappiness. ◆ *Diogenes, the Greek philosopher, lived a dog's life inside an empty barrel.*

**dog tag** *n. phr.* A small metal plate on a chain worn around the neck by those in the United States armed forces, giving the person's name, rank, and serial number. ◆ *If our soldiers didn't have dog tags, it would be hard to identify them in case of a battle casualty.*

**do in** *v., slang* **1.** To ruin; destroy. ◆ *Mr. Smith's business was done in by a fire that burned down his store.* **2a.** To kill; murder. ◆ *The poor man was done in by two gangsters who ran away after the crime.* **2b.** To make tired; exhaust. ◆ *The boys were done in after their long hike.* **3.** To cheat; swindle. ◆ *Mr. Jones was done in by two men who claimed to be collecting money for orphans and widows.*

**do justice to** *v. phr.* **1.** To do (something) as well as you should; do properly. ◆ *The newspaper man did not do justice to the story.* **2.** To eat or drink with enthusiasm or enjoyment. ◆ *The boy did justice to the meal.*

**dole out** *v. phr.* To measure out sparingly. ◆ *Since the water ration was running low in the desert, the camp commandant doled out small cups of water to each soldier.*

**doll up** *v., slang* **1.** To dress in fine or fancy clothes. ◆ *The girls dolled up for the big school dance of the year.* ◆ *The girls were all dolled up for the Christmas party.* **2.** To make more pretty or attractive. ◆ *The classrooms were all dolled up with Christmas decorations.*

**done deal** *n. phr.* A business or political deal or agreement, which was completed some time ago, without making officially public. ◆ *"Who will be the next head of our department?" Professor Fisher asked. "Why, Patrick McInerney, of course, didn't you know?" "It was never announced." "You're right, it was not, but it is a done deal."*

**done for** *adj. phr.* Finished; dead. ◆ *When the police burst in on the crooks, they knew they were done for.*

**done with** *adj. phr.* Finished; completed. ◆ *As soon as you're done with your work, give us a call.*

**don't get smart** *v. phr.* A phrase idiom issued as a warning, meaning that if the addressee answers back, he or she may get into trouble. ◆ *"Don't you get* *smart with me, Johnny! I know what's good for you,"* father thundered angrily. *"Go and do your homework."*

**don't give me that** See TELL IT TO THE MARINES.

**don't give up the ship** *phrasal idiom* Advice given to someone who is about to stop doing a difficult task, comparable to a sea captain trying to save a sinking boat. ◆ *"Your business is having some difficulties right now, John,"* his brother Mike said, *"but I suggest that you don't give up the ship just yet. Better times lie ahead."*

**don't I know it?** *v. phr.* This idiom expresses that the speaker knows something rather well; the question form enhances this fact ruefully or sarcastically. ◆ *"So my wife is sleeping with another guy… Man, don't I know it?"*

**don't mind me** *v. phr., informal, ironic* Often heard as an excuse when someone bumps into someone else in a narrow corridor, in the library stacks, on a bus or a streetcar, etc. Excuse me. ◆ *"Don't mind me, Miss,"* the clumsy man said, *while trampling on the librarian's foot.*

**don't shoot the messenger** Said when one hears some bad news brought by some innocent person. One has a tendency to get angry or irritated at the message bearer who had nothing to do with the message's contents.—A proverb. ◆ *"Sir, I just saw your wife walk into a motel room with your colleague, but please don't shoot the messenger."*

**don't shut the stable door after the horse has gone** *proverbial idiom* It is useless to take precautionary measures to prevent something unpleasant from happening after the event took place.—A proverb. ◆ *"Why give our daughter, Jenny, birth control pills now that she's gotten pregnant by her boyfriend? No use shutting the stable door after the horse has gone."*

**don't sweat it** *v. phr., slang* See TAKE IT EASY.

**don't take any wooden nickels** *v. phr.* Protect yourself; take care of yourself; don't let anybody cheat you by giving you something worthless.—A proverb. ◆ *"The part of that country you're going to, John,"* Peter said, *"is full of*

*hoodlums and tricksters. Be careful, and don't take any wooden nickels."*

**don't tell me—let me guess** *v. phr.* A humorous, anticipatory saying used when one knows what's coming. ◆ *"Don't tell me—let me guess—you got fired again,"* Mary said to her husband, *when he came home sadly, carrying all of his papers.*

**do one a good turn** *v. phr.* To perform an act of kindness, friendship, or help to another person, unselfishly, without expectation of reward. ◆ *"I'll be happy to help you any time you need it,"* John said. *"After all you have done me so many good turns."*

**do one dirt** *v. phr.* **1.** To besmirch one's reputation by spreading false gossip about the person. ◆ *Poor Mr. Wong was done dirt by the other restaurant owners in the city who spread the false rumor that he was using dog meat in his dishes.* **2.** To cheat someone in a seemingly honest business transaction. ◆ *I am afraid to do business with those guys, because they may do me dirt.*

**do one good** *v. phr.* To benefit. ◆ *The fresh air will do you good after having been inside the house all day.*

**do one good** *or* **do one's heart good** *v. phr.* To give satisfaction; please; gratify. ◆ *It does my heart good to see those children play.*

**do one's best** *v. phr.* To perform at one's optimum capacity; spare no effort in fulfilling one's duties. ◆ *"I've really done my best teaching you people,"* the tired professor said on the last day of classes. *"I hope you got something out of this course."*

**do one's bit** *or* **part** *v. phr.* To shoulder one's share of responsibility in a communal undertaking; shirk one's obligation. ◆ *"Let me go home and rest, fellows,"* John said. *"I think I've done my bit for this project."*

**do one's thing** *or* **do one's own thing** *v. phr., informal* **1.** To do what one does well and actually enjoys doing. ◆ *Two thousand fans paid $15 each to hear the rock group do their thing.* **2.** To follow one's bent; for example, to be engaged in left-wing politics, some sort of meditation, or use of drugs (particularly in the sixties). ◆ *The hippies were doing their own thing when the cops came* and busted them. **3.** To be engaged in an unusual activity that strikes others as odd. ♦ *Leave Jim alone, he's just doing his own thing when he's standing on his head.*

**do one's worst** *v. phr.* To do one's utmost by resorting to every foul means possible. ♦ *Hitler did his worst to drive out the Allied invasion from Europe, but he failed.*

**do-or-die** *adj.* Strongly decided, very eager and determined. ♦ *With a real do-or-die spirit the team scored two touchdowns in the last five minutes of the game.* ♦ *The other army was larger but our men showed a do-or-die determination and won the battle.*

**do over** *v. phr.* **1.** To renovate; redecorate. ♦ *The new owners are going to do over the entire building in the fall.* **2.** To repeat. ♦ *Please do that math problem over until you get it right.*

**dope out** *v., slang* To think of something that explains. ♦ *The detectives tried to dope out why the man was murdered.*

**dope up** *v. phr.* **1.** To feed drugs to a person or an animal. ♦ *The favorite race horse was disqualified, because they found out that it had been doped up.* **2.** To take a lot of vitamins and some anticold medicine to get over a fever faster. ♦ *Agnes beat the cold by doping herself up with aspirin, vitamin C, and an antihistamine.*

**do someone out of something** *v., informal* To cause to lose by trickery or cheating. ♦ *The clerk in the store did me out of $2.00 by overcharging me.*

**dose of one's own medicine** *or* **taste of one's own medicine** *n. phr.* Being treated in the same way you treat others; something bad done to you as you have done bad to other people. ♦ *Jim was always playing tricks on other boys. Finally they decided to give him a dose of his own medicine.*

**do tell** *interj., informal* An inelegant expression used to show that you are a little surprised by what you hear. ♦ *"You say George is going to get married after all these years? Do tell!" said Mrs. Green.*

**dote on** *or* **dote upon** *v. phr.* To entertain or to display too much affection for a child or a grown-up. ♦ *The Browns dote on their grandchildren so much*

that we're afraid the kids will be spoiled.

**do the honors** *v. phr.* To act as host or hostess (as in introducing guests, carving, or paying other attentions to guests.) ♦ *The president of the club will do the honors at the banquet.*

**do the trick** *v. phr., informal* To bring success in doing something; have a desired result. ♦ *Jim was not passing in English, but he studied harder and that did the trick.* ♦ *The car wheels slipped on the ice, so Tom put sand under them, which did the trick.*

**do things by halves** *v. phr.* To do things in a careless and incomplete way. ♦ *When he reads a book he always does it by halves; he seldom finishes it.*

**do to death** *v. phr.* To overdo; do something so often that it becomes extremely boring or tiresome. ♦ *The typical car chase scene in motion pictures has been done to death.*

**dot the i's and cross the t's** *v. phr.* To be careful, thorough, and pay close attention to detail. ♦ *"The best way to get an A on the final exam," the teacher said, "is for every one to dot the i's and cross the t's."*

**double back** *v.* **1.** To turn back on one's way or course. ♦ *The escaped prisoner doubled back on his tracks.* **2.** To fold over; usually in the middle. ♦ *The teacher told Johnny to double back the sheet of paper and tear it in half.*

**double check** *n.* A careful second check to be sure that something is right; a careful look for errors. ♦ *The policeman made a double check on the doors in the shopping area.*

**double-check** *v.* **1.** To do a double check on; look at again very carefully. ♦ *When the last typing of his book was finished, the author double-checked it.* **2.** To make a double check; look carefully at something. ♦ *The proofreader double-checks against errors.*

**double-cross** *v.* To promise one thing and deliver another; to deceive. ♦ *The lawyer double-crossed the inventor by manufacturing the gadget instead of fulfilling his promise to arrange a patent for his client.*

**double date** *n., informal* A date on which two couples go together. ♦ *John and*

*Nancy went with Mary and Bill on a double date.*

**double-date** *v., informal* To go on a double date; date with another couple. ♦*John and Nancy and Mary and Bill double-date.*

**double duty** *n.* Two uses or jobs; two purposes or duties. ♦*Our new washer does double duty; it washes the clothes and also dries them.*

**double for** *v. phr.* To act as a replacement for someone either out of friendship, or as a mutual arrangement. ♦*Dr. Abrahamian often doubles for Dr. Frank in the operating room; conversely, Dr. Frank also doubles for Dr. Abrahamian.*

**double-header** *n.* Two games or contests played one right after the other, between the same two teams or two different pairs of teams. ♦*The Yankees and the Dodgers played a double-header Sunday afternoon.*

**double nickel** *adv., slang, citizen's band radio jargon* The nationally enforced speed limit on some highways—55 MPH. ♦*We'd better go double nickel on this stretch, partner; there's a bear in the air.*

**double-park** *v.* To park a car beside another car which is at the curb. ♦*If you double-park, you block other cars from passing.*

**double-talk** *n.* **1.** Something said that is worded, either on purpose or by accident, so that it may be understood in two or more different ways. ♦*The politician avoided the question with double-talk.* **2.** Something said that does not make sense; mixed up talk or writing; nonsense. ♦*The man's explanation of the new tax bill was just a lot of double-talk.*

**double up** *v.* **1.** To bend far over forward. ♦*Jim was hit by the baseball and doubled up with pain.* **2.** To share a room, bed, or home with another. ♦*When relatives came for a visit, Ann had to double up with her sister.*

**do up** *v.* **1a.** To clean and prepare for use or wear; launder. ♦*Ann asked her mother to do up her dress.* **1b.** To put in order; straighten up; clean. ♦*At camp the girls have to do up their own cabins.* **2.** To tie up or wrap. ♦*Joan asked the clerk to do up her purchases.* **3a.** To set

and fasten (hair) in place. ♦*Grace helped her sister to do up her hair.* **3b.** *informal* To dress or clothe. ♦*Suzie was done up in her fine new skirt and blouse.*

**do well by** *v. phr.* To benefit; help; treat exceptionally well. ♦*In his will Grandpa did well by all of his grandchildren and left each of them one million dollars.*

**do what comes naturally** *v. phr., informal* To engage in an activity that doesn't have to be taught, since it is a universal instinct, such as sex. ♦*"Did your daughter finish high school?" John asked. "I'm afraid she hasn't. She doesn't do much of anything, except what comes naturally."*

**do with** *v.* **1.** To find enough for one's needs; manage.—Usually follows *can.* ♦*Some children can do with very little spending money.* **2.** To make use of; find useful or helpful.—Follows *can* or *could.* ♦*After a hard day's work, a man can do with a good, hot meal.*

**do without** *or* **go without** *v.* **1.** To live or work without (something you want); manage without. ♦*We had to go without hot food because the stove was broken.* **2.** To live or work without something you want; manage. ♦*If George cannot earn money for a bicycle, he will have to do without.*

**down and out** *adj. phr.* Without money; without a job or home; broke. ♦*Poor Sam lost his job after his wife had left him; he is really down and out.*

**down-and-outer** *n. phr.* A person who has lost everything and is penniless. ♦*Joe goes from shelter to shelter asking for food and a place to sleep; he's become a regular down-and-outer.*

**down in the dumps** *or* **down in the mouth** *adj. phr., informal* Sad or discouraged; gloomy; dejected. ♦*The boys were certainly down in the dumps when they heard that their team had lost.*

**download** *v. phr.* To get some program or information off the Internet and save it either on a floppy disk, the hard disk, or in temporary memory. ♦*"Where did you get that fancy program? Did it cost a lot?" Mary asked. "No, not at all," Sam answered. "I downloaded it free."*

**down on** *adj. phr., informal* Having a grudge against; angry at. ♦*John is* *down on his teacher because she gave him a low grade.*

**down one's alley** *or* **up one's alley** *adj. phr., slang* Suited to your tastes and abilities; what you like or like to do. ♦ *Computers are right down Jim's alley.*

**down on one's luck** *adj., informal* Having bad luck; having much trouble; not successful in life. ♦ *Harry asked me to lend him ten dollars, because he was down on his luck.*

**down payment** *n.* A retainer paid to a prospective seller. ♦ *How much of a down payment do you require for this new car?*

**down the drain** *adj. or adv. phr., informal* Wasted; lost. ♦ *It is money down the drain if you spend it all on candy.* ♦ *Our plans to go swimming went down the drain when it rained.*

**down the garden path** *or* **down the primrose path** *adv. phr.* In a misleading way. ♦ *Professor Bloch created a phony argument to see if anyone would catch on; he was leading the class down the primrose path.*

**down the hatch!** *v. phr., informal* Let us drink! ♦ *When we celebrated Mom's birthday, we all raised our glasses and cried in unison, "Down the hatch!"*

**down the line** *adv. phr., informal* **1.** Down the road or street; straight ahead. ♦ *The church is down the line a few blocks.* **2.** All the way; completely; thoroughly. ♦ *Bob always follows the teacher's directions right down the line.*

**downtime** *n. phr.* Intermittent period during which a computer installation does not work, either because of power failure or some internal problem specific to the given system. ♦ *"We can't complete your transaction without our computers, Sir; we're having a downtime. Please come back in half an hour."*

**down-to-earth** *adj.* Showing good sense; practical. ♦ *The committee's first plan for the party was too fancy, but the second was more down-to-earth.*

**down to the last detail** *adv. phr.* In complete detail from the beginning to the end, no matter how small. ♦ *The new employee recounted his past employment history down to the last detail.*

**down to the wire** *adj., slang* **1.** Running out of time, nearing a deadline. ♦ *Bob is down to the wire on his project* **2.**

Being financially almost broke, being very low on cash or other funds. ♦ *We can't afford going to a restaurant tonight—we're really down to the wire!*

**down under** *adv. phr.* In the Southern Hemisphere, e.g., Australia, South America, New Zealand, or South Africa. ♦ *"Down under, where I come from, we're having summer when you have winter, and vice versa."*

**down with a disease** *adj. phr.* Ill or sick. ♦ *Aunt Liz is down with the flu this week; she has to stay in bed.*

**do you know where I'm coming from?** *v. phr.* Do you understand what I'm saying? ♦ *I think life is way too expensive in cities like New York, Chicago, and Los Angeles. Do you know where I'm coming from?*

**do you mind?** *v. phr.* Mind your own business! Stop bothering me! ♦ *"Do you mind?" Jennifer cried crossly, when Alfred rudely interrupted her narrative during dinner.*

**do you see what I see?** *v. phr.* Used to express astonishment at an unexpected sight. ♦ *"Do you see what I see?" Sue cried out in amazement, when three little gray men emerged from a flying saucer in their backyard.*

**do yourself a favor** *v. phr.* Advice given to people, who apparently don't know how to take care of themselves or what would benefit them. ♦ *"Do yourself a favor, Johnny," his big brother Tim said. "Start eating less and exercise more."*

**doze off** *v. phr.* To unintentionally fall asleep due to fatigue or boredom. ♦ *It is considered impolite to doze off during a university lecture.*

**drag in** *v.* To insist on bringing (another subject) into a discussion; begin talking about (something different.) ♦ *No matter what we talk about, Jim drags in politics.*

**drag into the mire** *v. phr.* **1.** To besmirch one. ♦ *The unscrupulous competition tried to drag the honest Mr. Brown into the mire.* **2.** To drag someone down to one's own level. ♦ *"If you keep going out with that gang," his father warned Bob, "they will drag you into the mire, right where they are."*

**drag on** *or* **drag out** *v.* **1.** To pass very slowly. ♦ *The cold winter months* dragged on until we thought spring would never come. **2.** To prolong; make longer. ♦ *The meeting would have been over quickly if the members had not dragged out the argument about dues.*

**drag on the market** *n. phr.* An article for which the demand has fallen off, thus causing an oversupply. ♦ *Your type of word processor went out of style and is now a drag on the market.*

**drag oneself up by one's boot straps** See PULL ONESELF UP BY THE BOOT STRAPS.

**drag one's feet** *or* **drag one's heels** *v. phr.* To act slowly or reluctantly. ♦ *The city employees said the mayor had promised to raise their pay, but was now dragging his feet.*

**drag out** See DRAG ON.

**drag race** *n., slang* An automobile race in which the drivers try to cover a certain distance (usually one quarter mile) in the shortest possible time. ♦ *Drag races are often held on airport landing strips.*

**drag strip** *n., slang* A place where drag races are held. ♦ *Before the race Paul loaded his racer onto the trailer to take it out of town to the drag strip for the race.*

**draw a blank** *v. phr., informal* **1.** To obtain nothing in return for an effort made or to get a negative result. ♦ *I looked up all the Joneses in the telephone book but I drew a blank every time I asked for Archibald Jones.* **2.** To fail to remember something. ♦ *I am trying to think of the name but I keep drawing a blank.* **3.** To be consistently unsuccessful at doing something. ♦ *I keep trying to pass that math exam but each time I try it I draw a blank.*

**draw a conclusion** *v. phr.* To make an inference. ♦ *After he failed to keep an appointment with me for the third time, I drew the conclusion that he was an unreliable person.*

**draw a line** *or* **draw the line** *v. phr.* **1.** To think of as different. ♦ *The law in this country draws a line between murder and manslaughter.* ♦ *Can you draw the line between a lie and a fib?* **2.** To set a limit to what will be done; say something cannot be done. ♦ *We would like to invite everybody to our party, but we have to draw a line somewhere.*—Often used with *at.* ♦ *Mrs. Jones draws the*

line at permitting the children to play in their father's den. ♦ *People fighting for their freedom often do not draw the line at murder.*

**draw a long breath** *or* **take a long breath** *v. phr.* To breathe deeply when getting ready to speak or act. ♦ *Father asked who broke the window. Jim drew a long breath and admitted that he had done it.*

**draw a parallel** *v. phr.* To make a comparison. ♦ *It is easy to draw a parallel between the characters of Saint Francis of Assisi and Great Saint Theresa of Aquila, but this doesn't mean that all saints are alike.*

**draw and quarter** *v. phr. literary* **1.** To execute someone in the barbaric medieval fashion of having him torn into four pieces by four horses tearing his body in four different directions. ♦ *The captured foreign marauders were drawn and quartered by the angry citizens of ancient Frankfurt.* **2.** To punish someone very severely. ♦ *"If you miss another homework assignment, John," the teacher said, "I'll have you drawn and quartered."*

**draw back** *v.* To move back; back away; step backward; withdraw; move away from. ♦ *When the man spotted the rattlesnake, he drew back and aimed his shotgun.* ♦ *The children drew back from the dog when it barked at them.*

**drawback** *n.* Disadvantage; obstacle; hindrance. ♦ *The biggest drawback of Bill's plan is the cost involved.*

**draw blood** *v. phr., informal* To make someone feel hurt or angry. ♦ *If you want to draw blood, ask Jim about his last money-making scheme.* ♦ *Her sarcastic comments drew blood.*

**draw fire** *v. phr.* **1.** To attract or provoke shooting; be a target. ♦ *The general's white horse drew the enemy's fire.* **2.** To bring criticism or argument; make people say bad things about you. ♦ *Having the newest car in your group is sure to draw fire.*

**drawing card** *n.* The most important figure in a multi-person event; the top entertainer during a show; the best professor or researcher at a university, etc. ♦ *The biggest drawing card at many a university is the resident Nobel Laureate.*

**draw interest** *v. phr.* To earn interest on invested capital. ♦ *My savings account draws 4.5% interest.*

**draw lots** *v. phr.* To select at random from a series in order to determine precedents or apportionment. ♦ *The refugees to be evacuated drew lots on who would get a place on the first airplane out of the besieged city.*

**draw near** *v. phr.* To approach; come near. ♦ *The time is drawing near when classes will end and vacation will begin.*

**draw off** *v. phr.* To drain away; deflect. ♦ *A light flanking attack was made in order to draw off the enemy's fire.*

**draw on** *v. phr.* **1.** To arrive; approach. ♦ *As midnight drew on, the New Year's Eve party grew louder and louder.* **2.** To secure funds from a bank or person. ♦ *Jack kept drawing on his bank account so much that several of his checks bounced.*

**draw one's attention to** *v. phr.* To make someone notice something. ♦ *"Let me draw your attention to the motion picture versions of Tolstoy's* War and Peace, *and Hemingway's* The Old Man and the Sea, *if you don't have the time to read them in book form."*

**draw out** *v. phr.* **1.** To take out; remove. ♦ *The hunter drew out his gun and shot the snake.* **2.** To make (a person) talk or tell something. ♦ *Jimmy was bashful but Mrs. Wilson drew him out by asking him about baseball.* **3.** To make come out; bring out. ♦ *The bell of the ice-cream truck drew the children out of the houses.* **4.** To make longer or too long; stretch. ♦ *The Smiths drew out their vacation at the beach an extra week.*

**draw to a close** *v. phr.* To finish; terminate; come to an end. ♦ *The meeting drew to a close around midnight.*

**draw up** *v.* **1.** To write (something) in its correct form; put in writing. ♦ *The rich man had his lawyers draw up his will so that each of his children would receive part of his money when he died.* **2.** To plan or prepare; begin to write out. ♦ *The two countries drew up a peace treaty after the war ended.* **3.** To hold yourself straight or stiffly, especially because you are proud or angry. ♦ *When we said that Mary was getting fat, she drew herself up angrily and walked out of the room.* **4.** To stop or

come to a stop. ♦ *A big black car drew up in front of the house.*

**dream of** *v.* To think about seriously; think about with the idea of really doing; consider seriously.—Usually used with a negative. ♦ *I wouldn't dream of wearing shorts to church.*

**dream up** *v. phr.* To conduct, to invent something to fill a need. ♦ *"How are we going to explain to Mom and Dad where we spent last weekend?" Jenny asked her boyfriend excitedly. "Don't worry, honey," Jack answered, "I'm sure we can dream up some acceptable explanation."*

**drenched to the skin** *adj. phr.* Thoroughly soaked through in a heavy downpour of rain, through all of one's clothes. ♦ *The farmhand came in from the field and asked for a dry towel, saying, "Sorry to bother you, ma'am, but I'm drenched to the skin."*

**dressing down** *n., informal* A scolding. ♦ *The sergeant gave the soldier a good dressing down because his shoes were not shined.*

**dress up** *v.* **1a.** To put on best or special clothes. ♦ *Billy hated being dressed up and took off his best suit as soon as he got home from church.* **1b.** To put on a costume for fun or clothes for a part in a play. ♦ *Mary was dressed up to play Cinderella in her school play.* **2.** To make (something) look different; make (something) seem better or more important. ♦ *A fresh coat of paint will dress up the old bicycle very much.*

**dribs and drabs** *n. phr.* Portions; small bits. ♦ *John paid Oliver back what he owed him in dribs and drabs.*

**drift apart** *v. phr.* To gradually become estranged from one another; said of married couples or formerly close friends. ♦ *"I don't understand what happened to Mary and John. They were as close as you can be." "Well, after she finished college and started to work as a nurse, they just drifted apart. She is now married to a doctor."*

**drift off** *v. phr.* **1.** To fall asleep. ♦ *He kept nodding and drifting off to sleep while the lecturer was speaking.* **2.** To depart; leave gradually. ♦ *One by one, the sailboats drifted off over the horizon.*

**drink down** *v. phr.* To drink in one gulp; swallow entirely. ♦ *Steve was so thirsty* *that he drank down six glasses of orange juice in rapid succession.*

**drink in** *v. phr.* To absorb with great interest. ♦ *The tourists stood on the beach drinking in the wonderful Hawaiian sunset.*

**drink like a fish** *v. phr.* To drink (alcoholic beverages) in great quantities; to be addicted to alcohol. ♦ *John is a nice guy but, unfortunately, he drinks like a fish.*

**drink up** *v. phr.* To finish drinking; empty one's glass. ♦ *"Drink up that cough syrup," the nurse said, "and never mind the taste."*

**drive a bargain** *or* **drive a hard bargain** *v. phr.* **1.** To buy or sell at a good price; succeed in a trade or deal. ♦ *Jack drove a hard bargain with the real estate agent when we bought his new house.* **2.** To make an agreement that is better for you than for the other person; make an agreement to your advantage. ♦ *The French drove a hard bargain in demanding that Germany pay fully for World War I damages.*

**drive at** *v.* To try or want to say; mean.— Used in the present participle. ♦ *Jack had been talking for half an hour before anyone realized what he was driving at.*

**drive home** *v. phr.* To argue convincingly; make a strong point. ♦ *The doctor's convincing arguments and explanation of his X-ray pictures drove home the point to Max that he needed surgery.*

**drive-in** *adj./n.* A kind of movie theater, fast food restaurant, or church, where the customers, spectators, or worshippers do not leave their automobiles but are served the food inside their cars, can watch a motion picture from inside their cars, or can participate in a religious service in their cars. ♦ *Let's not waste time on the road; let's just eat at the next drive-in restaurant.* ♦ *There is a drive-in theater not far from where we live.*

**drive off** **1.** *v. phr.* To stave off an attacker. ♦ *The army drove off the attackers with much effort and many casualties.* **2.** To make go away; to get rid of something. ♦ *These pills will help you to drive off your headaches.*

**drive one ape, bananas, crazy, mad** *or* **nuts** *v. phr., informal* To irritate, frus-

trate, or tickle someone's fancy so badly that they think they are going insane. ♦ *"Stop teasing me, Mary," John said. "You are driving me nuts."* ♦ *"You are driving me bananas with all your crazy riddles," Steve said.*

**drive one up the wall** See DRIVE ONE APE, BANANAS, CRAZY, MAD, *or* NUTS.

**drive to the wall** *v. phr.* To defeat someone completely; to ruin someone. ♦ *Poor Uncle Jack was driven to the wall by his angry creditors when his business failed.*

**drive someone bananas** *or* **drive someone nuts** *or* **drive someone ape** *v. phr., slang informal* To excite someone to the point that he or she goes out of his or her mind; to drive someone crazy. ♦ *You're driving me bananas/nuts with that kind of talk!*

**drool over** *v. phr.* To show too much love to the point of being disgusting. ♦ *"Stop drooling over your puppy dog; you'll become the laughingstock of the whole neighborhood."*

**drop a bomb** See DROP A BRICK, PUT ONE'S FOOT IN IT, PUT ONE'S FOOT IN ONE'S MOUTH.

**drop a bombshell** *v. phr.* To announce some sensationally good or shockingly bad news. ♦ *Freddy dropped a bombshell when he told his astonished parents that he had just married a widow with seven children.*

**drop a brick** See PUT ONE'S FOOT IN IT.

**drop a line** *v. phr.* To write someone a short letter or note. ♦ *Please drop me a line when you get to Paris; I'd like to know that you've arrived safely.*

**drop back** *v.* To move or step backwards; retreat. ♦ *The soldiers dropped back before the enemy's attack.* ♦ *The quarterback dropped back to pass the football.*

**drop behind** *v. phr.* To fail to remain level on a par with an individual or a group of people. ♦ *When Joe started to smoke pot, his schoolwork dropped behind that of his classmates.*

**drop by** *or* **stop by** *v.* **1.** or **drop around** To make a short or unplanned visit; go on a call or errand; stop at someone's home. ♦ *Drop by any time you're in town.* ♦ *My sister dropped around last night.* ♦ *Don't forget to stop by at the gas station.* Syn. DROP IN. **2.** or **drop into** To stop (somewhere) for a short visit or a short time. ♦ *We dropped by the club to see if Bill was there, but he wasn't.* ♦ *I dropped into the drugstore for some toothpaste and a magazine.*

**drop dead** *v., slang* To go away or be quiet; stop bothering someone.— Usually used as a command. ♦ *"Drop dead!" Bill told his little sister when she kept begging to help him build his model airplane.*

**drop from the face of the earth** *n. phr.* To suddenly disappear without letting one's friends and relatives know where one has gone. ♦ *"Have you dropped from the face of the earth?" Joe asked his kid brother Jeff, when after not seeing him for a year they accidentally met in Hawaii.*

**drop in** *v.* To make a short or unplanned visit; pay a call.—Often used with *on.* ♦ *We were just sitting down to dinner when Uncle Willie dropped in on us.*

**drop in the bucket** *n. phr.* A relatively small amount; a small part of the whole. ♦ *Our university needs several million dollars for its building renovation project; $50,000 is a mere drop in the bucket.*

**drop names** *v. phr.* To impress people by mentioning famous names. ♦ *He likes to pretend he's important by dropping a lot of names.*

**drop off** *v.* **1.** To take (someone or something) part of the way you are going. ♦ *Joe asked Mrs. Jones to drop him off at the library on her way downtown.* **2.** To go to sleep. ♦ *Jimmy was thinking of his birthday party as he dropped off to sleep.* **3.** To die. ♦ *The patient dropped off in his sleep.* **4.** *or* **fall off** To become less. ♦ *Business picked up in the stores during December, but dropped off again after Christmas.*

**drop off to sleep** *v. phr.* To unexpectedly and suddenly fall asleep lightly and for a short time, as in a doctor's waiting room, during watching a boring motion picture, etc. ♦ *The old lady in Dr. Gordon's waiting room dropped off to sleep; Phyllis woke her up when it was time for her to go in to see him.*

**dropout** *n.* (stress on *drop*) Someone who did not finish school, high school and college primarily. ♦ *Tim is having a hard time getting a better job as he was a high-school dropout.*

**drop out** *v.* (stress on *out*) To stop attending; quit; stop; leave. ♦ *Teenagers who drop out of high school have trouble finding jobs.*

**drop the ball** *v. phr.* To drop out of rhythm and make a mistake during the course of an activity; to falter; to miss an important opportunity. ♦ *I wish that Sam hadn't dropped the ball on his admission to college; now he'll have to remain only a high school graduate.*

**drown one's sorrows** *or* **drown one's troubles** *v. phr., informal* To drink liquor to try to forget something unhappy. ♦ *When his wife was killed in an auto accident, Mr. Green tried to drown his sorrows in whiskey.*

**drown out** *v.* To make so much noise that it is impossible to hear (some other sound). ♦ *The actor's words were drowned out by applause.*

**drum out of** *v. phr.* To make someone in the army, a club, a fraternity, etc. leave in shame as punishment for some offense. ♦ *The young lieutenant, who tried to seduce the general's wife, got drummed out of the army.*

**drum up** *v.* **1.** To get by trying or asking again and again; attract or encourage by continued effort. ♦ *The car dealer tried to drum up business by advertising low prices.* **2.** To invent. ♦ *I will drum up an excuse for coming to see you next week.*

**dry out** *v. phr.* To cure an alcoholic. ♦ *A longtime alcoholic, Uncle Steve is now in the hospital getting dried out.*

**dry up** *v.* **1.** To become dry. ♦ *The reservoir dried up during the four-month drought.* **2.** To disappear or vanish as if by evaporating. ♦ *The Senator's influence dried up when he was voted out of office.*

**duck out** *v. phr.* To avoid; escape from something by skillful maneuvering. ♦ *Somehow or other Jack always manages to duck out of any hard work.*

**duck soup** *n., slang* **1.** A task easily accomplished or one that does not require much effort. ♦ *That history test was duck soup.* **2.** A person who offers no resistance; a pushover. ♦ *How's the new history teacher?—He's duck soup.*

**due east** *or* **due west** *or* **due north** *or* **due south** *adv. phr.* Directly east, west, north, or south to the degree and minute, without the slightest deviation. ♦ *"How do we get to Cape Good Hope, captain?" the smaller boat telegraphed the ocean cruiser. "We lost our sea maps." "Sail due east for twenty miles and you'll run right into it," the captain answered via Morse code.*

**due to** *prep.* Because of; owing to; by reason of. ♦ *His injury was due to his careless use of the shotgun.*

**dullville** *n. phr., slang* A boring, dull, or uninteresting event. ♦ *"Our grammar class is always a dullville," the students complained. "Just rules after rules, never a living example."*

**dumb as a box of rocks** *adj. phr.* Extremely stupid. ♦ *Oliver is handsome and strong enough to be Mr. Universe; unfortunately, however, he is also as dumb as a box of rocks.*

**dumb down** *v. phr.* To leave out details; to put it in laymen's terms ♦ *"I was exploring the biological basis of metabolic respiration and found that lipids provide the most energy potential, followed by proteins and carbohydrates, especially polysaccharides." "Dumb it down for me; I'm not a biology major." "OK, I said that eating fats gives you the most energy after proteins, followed by carbohydrates."*

**dumb bunny** *n., slang, informal* Any person who is gullible and stupid. ♦ *Jack is a regular dumb bunny.*

**dumbwaiter** *n.* A small elevator for carrying food, dishes, etc., from one floor to another in hotels, restaurants, or large homes. ♦ *The banquet was delayed because the dumbwaiter broke down and the food had to be carried upstairs by hand.*

**dump on one** *v. phr.* To take advantage of someone; to deceive. ♦ *I have been dumped on so often that I no longer trust people.*

**dump something on one** *v. phr.* To make another do one's work in one's place, most often without any compensation

and without asking the victim's consent. ♦ *Stanley is a nasty and selfish boss; he dumps all the work on the unsuspecting, overworked, and reluctant employees in the office.*

**dust off** *v., informal* **1.** To get ready to use again. ♦ *Four years after he graduated from school, Tom decided to dust off his algebra book.* **2.** To throw a baseball pitch close to. ♦ *The pitcher dusted off the other team's best hitter.*

**Dutch courage** *n. phr.* Courage artificially induced by strong drink. ♦ *Those guys over there look like a really tough bunch, but I bet you it's nothing but Dutch courage. I saw them come out of the bar a moment ago.*

**dutch treat** *n., informal* A meal in a restaurant or an outing at the movies, concert, or theater where each party pays his or her own way. ♦ *"I am willing to accept your invitation," Mary said, "but it will have to be Dutch treat."*

**duty bound** *adj. phr.* Forced to act by what you believe is right. ♦ *John felt duty bound to report that he had broken the window.*

**duty calls** *n. phr.* One must attend to one's obligations. ♦ *"I'd love to stay and play more poker," Henry said, "but duty calls and I must get back to the office."*

**dwell on** *or* **dwell upon** *v.* To stay on a subject; not leave something or want to leave; not stop talking or writing about. ♦ *Joe dwelt on his mistake long after the test was over.* ♦ *Our eyes dwelled on the beautiful sunset.* ♦ *The principal dwelled on traffic safety in his talk.*

**dyed-in-the-wool** *adj. phr.* Thoroughly committed; inveterate; unchanging. ♦ *Max is a dyed-in-the-wool Conservative Republican.*

**dying to** *adj. phr.* Having a great desire to; being extremely eager to. ♦ *Seymour is dying to date Mathilda, but she keeps refusing him.*

**each and every** *adj. phr.* Every.—Used for emphasis. ♦ *The captain wants each and every man to be here at eight o'clock.*

**eager beaver** *n. phr., slang* A person who is always eager to work or do anything extra, perhaps to win the favor of his leader or boss. ♦ *Jack likes his teacher and works hard for her, but his classmates call him an eager beaver.*

**eagle eye** *n.* Sharp vision like that of an eagle; the ability to notice even the tiniest details. ♦ *The new boss keeps an eagle eye on all aspects of our operation.*

**eager for the fray** *or* **ready for the fray** *adj. phr.* Anxious to fight or struggle, or to participate in a competitive game. ♦ *The college basketball team was eager for the fray.*

**early bird** *n* An early riser from bed. ♦ *Jane and Tom are real early birds; they get up at 6 A.M. every morning.*

**early bird catches the worm** *or* **early bird gets the worm** A person who gets up early in the morning has the best chance of succeeding; if you arrive early or are quicker, you get ahead of others.—A proverb. ♦ *When Billy's father woke him up for school he said, "The early bird catches the worm."*

**earn a living** *or* **make a living** *v. phr.* To earn enough money to cover all basic necessities such as food, shelter, clothing, and transportation; to be gainfully employed. ♦ *"There has to be an easier way to make a living than collecting garbage in Chicago," Joe said. "Go back to school, then," his father suggested, "then you can earn a living as a computer programmer, clerk, whatever you care to study!"*

**earn one's keep** *v. phr.* To merit one's salary or keep by performing the labor or chores that are expected of one. ♦ *John earned his keep at the music conservatory by cleaning all the musical instruments every day.*

**ears burn** *informal* To feel embarrassment or shame at hearing others talk about you. ♦ *Joan overheard the girls criticizing her and it made her ears burn.*

**ear to the ground** *n. phr., informal* Attention directed to the way things are going, or seem likely to go, or to the way people feel and think. ♦ *Reporters keep an ear to the ground so as to know as soon as possible what will happen.*

**ease off** *or* **ease up** *v.* To make or become less nervous; relax; work easier. ♦ *When the boss realized that John had been overworking, he eased off his load.*

**easier said than done** *adj. phr.* This idiom is often heard when one braggingly suggests that he or she can accomplish something difficult, meaning that talking is much less than acting.—A proverb. ♦ *"I've decided to swim across Lake Michigan on Christmas day," Johnny said. "That's easier said than done, son," his father replied.*

**easygoing** *adj.* Amiable in manner; relaxed; not excited. ♦ *Because Al has an easygoing personality, everybody loves him.*

**easy come, easy go** *truncated sent. informal* Something you get quickly and easily may be lost or spent just as easily. ♦ *Grandfather thought Billy should have to work for the money Father gave him, saying "Easy come, easy go."*

**easy does it** *informal* Let's do it carefully, without sudden movements and without forcing too hard or too fast; let's try just hard enough but not too hard. ♦ *"Easy does it," said the boss as they moved the piano through the narrow doorway.*

**easy mark** *n.* A foolishly generous person; one from whom it is easy to get money. ♦ *Bill is known to all the neighborhood beggars as an easy mark.*

**easy money** *n. informal* Money gained without hard work; money that requires little or no effort. ♦ *The movie rights to a successful play mean easy money to the writer of the play.*

**eat at** *v. phr.* To irritate; to bother; to gradually bring to ruin. ♦ *"What's eating at you anyway?" Joe asked his brother. "I guess I am upset because I had a fight with my boss at work."*

**eat away** *v.* 1. To rot, rust, or destroy. ♦ *Rust was eating away the pipe.*

♦*Cancer ate away the healthy flesh.*
**2.** To gradually consume. ♦*The ocean waves were gradually eating the volcanic rocks until they turned into black sand.*

**eat away at** *v. phr.* To psychologically gnaw at; to worry someone. ♦*Fear of the comprehensive examination was eating away at Sam.*

**eat crow** *v. phr.* To admit you are mistaken or defeated; take back a mistaken statement. ♦*John had boasted that he would play on the first team; but when the coach did not choose him, he had to eat crow.*

**eat dirt** *v. phr., informal* To act humble; accept another's insult or bad treatment. ♦*Mr. Johnson was so afraid of losing his job that he would eat dirt whenever the boss got mean.*

**eat (live) high on the hog** *or* **eat (live) high off the hog** *v. phr.* To eat or live well or elegantly. ♦*For the first few days after the check arrived, they ate high on the hog.*

**eat humble pie** *v. phr.* To be humbled; to accept insult or shame; admit your error and apologize. ♦*Tom told a lie about George, and when he was found out, he had to eat humble pie.*

**eat in** *v. phr.* To eat at home instead of going to a restaurant. ♦*It would be nice not to have to cook a meal at home, but we are broke, so we'll just eat in.*

**eating one** *v. phr.* To cause someone to be angry or ill-humored. ♦*We can't figure out what's eating Burt, but he hasn't spoken one pleasant word all day.*

**eat like a bird** *v. phr.* To eat very little; have little appetite. ♦*Mrs. Benson is on a diet and she eats like a bird.*

**eat like a horse** *v. phr.* To eat a lot; eat hungrily. ♦*The harvesters worked into the evening, and then came in and ate like horses.*

**eat one out of house and home** *v. phr.* **1.** To eat so much as to cause economic hardship. ♦*Our teenaged sons are so hungry all the time that they may soon eat us out of house and home.* **2.** To overstay one's welcome. ♦*We love Bob and Jane very much, but after two weeks we started to feel that they were eating us out of house and home.*

**eat one's cake and have it too** *v. phr.* To use or spend something and still keep it; have both when you must choose one of two things. Often used in negative sentences. ♦*Mary wants to buy a beautiful dress she saw at the store, but she also wants to save her birthday money for camp. She wants to eat her cake and have it too.*

**eat one's fill** *v. phr.* To eat as much as one's stomach can hold; until one is completely satisfied, feeling no more hunger. ♦*We were so poor in Eastern Europe during World War II that nobody ever had a chance to eat his fill.*

**eat one's heart out** *v. phr.* To grieve long and hopelessly; to become thin and weak from sorrow. ♦*For months after her husband's death, Joanne simply ate her heart out.*

**eat one's words** *also* **swallow one's words** *v. phr.* To take back something you have said; admit something is not true. ♦*John had called Harry a coward, but the boys made him eat his words after Harry bravely fought a big bully.*

**eat out** *v.* **1.** To eat in a restaurant; eat away from home. ♦*Fred ate out often even when he wasn't out of town.* **2.** To rust, rot, or be destroyed in time. ♦*Rust had eaten out the gun barrel.*

**eat out of one's hand** *v. phr., informal* To trust someone fully; believe or obey someone without question. ♦*Helen is so pretty and popular that all the boys eat out of her hand.*

**eat up** *v.* **1.** To eat all of. ♦*After hiking all afternoon, they quickly ate up all of the dinner.* **2.** To use all of. ♦*Idle talk had eaten up the hour before they knew it.* **3.** *slang* To accept eagerly; welcome. ♦*Jim told Martha that she was as smart as she was beautiful and Martha ate it up.*

**eavesdrop** *or* **be a fly on the wall** *v. phr.* To overhear surreptitiously and furtively what others are saying to each other in confidence. ♦*If you want to find out what those thieves are up to, you will have to eavesdrop on their conversations.* ♦*I'd love to be a fly on the wall when the Nobel Committee is deliberating on who to give next year's Peace Prize to.*

**edge away** *v. phr.* To withdraw or retreat gradually. ♦*Frightened by the growling tiger guarding its catch, the hunter carefully edged away.*

**edge in** *v.* To move slowly; get in quietly, especially with some difficulty, by force or without a big enough opening. ♦ *People had crowded around the senator, but Don succeeded in edging in.* ♦ *Harry edged the book in on the shelf.*

**edge in (on)** *v. phr.* **1.** To gradually approach an individual or a group with the intent of taking over or wielding power. ♦ *Jack was edging in on the firm of Smith and Brown and after half a year actually became its vice president.* **2.** To approach for capture (said of a group). ♦ *The hunters were edging in on the wounded leopard.*

**edge out** *v.* To defeat in competition or rivalry; take the place of; force out. ♦ *Harry edged out Tom for a place in Mary's affections.*

**egg on** *v.* To urge on; excite; lead to action. ♦ *Joe's wife egged him on to spend money to show off.*

**egg on one's face** *n. phr.* Embarrassment; humiliation caused by a claim made, which subsequently turns out to be false. ♦ *Tim announced with great relish that he got the directorship of the firm. He sure had a lot of egg on his face the next day, when it turned out that he was not even considered for the post.*

**ego trip** *n. phr.* An action that gives the person involved a sensation of being far more important than he or she actually is; a "delusion of grandeur." ♦ *With all that talk about how many women he had during his lifetime, Ted is on one hell of an ego trip.*

**either a feast or a famine** See FEAST OR A FAMINE.

**either hide or hair** See HIDE OR HAIR.

**eke out** *v.* **1.** To fill out or add a little to; increase a little. ♦ *Mr. Jones eked out a country teacher's small salary by hunting and trapping in the winter.* **2.** To get (little) by hard work; to earn with difficulty. ♦ *Fred eked out a bare living by farming on a rocky hillside.*

**elbow grease** *n.* Exertion; effort; energy. ♦ *"You'll have to use a little more elbow grease to get these windows clean," Mother said to Ed.*

**elbow one's way into** *or* **out of** *v. phr.* To force entry into a place by using one's elbows. ♦ *The bus was so crowded that, in order to get off in time, we had to elbow our way to the exit door.*

**elbow room** *n.* Adequate space to move around or to work in. ♦ *He doesn't require a huge office, but we must at least give him elbow room.*

**eleventh hour** *adj. phr.* Pertaining to the last minutes; the last opportunity to accomplish a task. ♦ *The editors made several eleventh hour changes in the headlines of the morning paper.*

**Emerald Isle** *n. phr.* The popular name of Ireland. ♦ *"Have you ever been to the Emerald Isle?" Kelly asked Patrick. "Unfortunately not," Patrick answered, "but my grandparents live in Dublin, so we're planning to visit them next summer and also to see some of Ireland."*

**Empire State** *n. phr.* The nickname of the state of New York. ♦ *"How did you guess I was from New York? Is it my accent?" Ginny asked. "No," Peter answered, "I just took a peek at your Empire State license plate."*

**end in itself** *n. phr.* Something wanted for its own sake; a purpose, aim, or goal we want for itself alone and not as a way to something else. ♦ *The miser never spent his gold because for him it was an end in itself.*

**end of one's rope** *or* **end of one's tether** *n. phr., informal* The end of your trying or imagining; the last of your ability, or ideas of how to do more. ♦ *Frank was out of work and broke, and he was at the end of his rope.* ♦ *The doctor saw that Mother had reached the end of her tether, and told us to send her away for a holiday.*

**end of the world** *n. phr.* A tragic event. ♦ *"It's not the end of the world, John, that Suzie doesn't want to marry you right now. Ask her again in a few months."*

**end run** *n.* A football play in which a back tries to run around one end of the opponent's line. ♦ *Smith's end run scored the winning touchdown.*

**ends of the earth** *n. phr.* **1.** Some of the most distant locations on planet earth. ♦ *I have traveled for twenty years with the U.S. Navy; I have been literally to the ends of the earth.* **2.** Unlimited effort exerted to gain someone's love. ♦ *"For you, my love, I'd go to the ends of the earth, if you will only have me."*

**end up** *v.* **1.** To come to an end; be ended or finished; stop. ♦ *How does the story* *end up?* **2.** To finally reach or arrive; land. ♦*I hope you don't end up in jail.* **3.** *informal* To die, be killed. ♦*The gangster ended up in the electric chair.* **4.** *or* **finish up**. To put an end to; finish; stop. ♦*The politician finally ended up his speech.*

**end zone** *n.* Either of the marked areas behind the goal line. ♦*He caught a pass in the end zone for a touchdown.*

**engage in small talk** *v. phr.* To converse with a stranger or casual acquaintance about matters of no great importance in order to make the time go faster. ♦*The patients in the doctor's waiting room engaged in small talk complaining about the hot weather.*

**English as (she) is spoken** *n. phr.* A humorous way to refer to the English language as it is spoken by foreigners or by illiterate natives. ♦*The familiar phrases "Long time no see" and "No can do" are examples of English as she is spoken.*

**enlarge on** *or* **enlarge upon** *or* **expand on** *or* **expand upon** *v.* To talk or write more about; say or explain more completely or at greater length. ♦*The teacher enlarged on the uses of atomic power.*

**en masse** *adv. phr.* As a group; in one big mass or group.—Used after the word it modifies. ♦*The school turned out en masse to cheer the returning astronaut.*

**enough is enough** That's enough, let's not have any more; that will do, let's cut it short; that's the limit, let's stop there. ♦*"I don't mind good clean fun, but enough is enough," the principal said.*

**enter into** *v. phr.* To begin something. ♦*The parties entered into negotiations in earnest about the salary raises.* ♦*John entered into chemotherapy against a milder form of cancer.*

**entertain hopes** *or* **entertain high hopes** *v. phr.* To feel very optimistic that a planned activity will succeed as anticipated. ♦*Joe entertained high hopes of being able to marry his boss' daughter, who was the heiress to a huge fortune.*

**equal to** *adj. phr.* Able to meet, do, or control; able to do something about. ♦*The situation took quick thinking, but John was equal to it.* ♦*When a guest upset the coffee pot, Mrs. Smith's tact and quickness of mind were equal to the occasion.*

**equal to the occasion** *adj. phr.* Capable of handling the situation. ♦*Although he had never before assisted in childbirth, the taxi driver proved equal to the occasion and helped deliver the baby in his cab.*

**errand of mercy** *n. phr.* A trip taken with the intention of bringing good news to someone in need; to bring food or medicine, or the like, without expectation of payment or recompense. ♦*Sister Prudence got on her bicycle to run a series of errands of mercy in her neighborhood, where many elderly handicapped people lived.*

**escape unscathed** *v. phr.* To get away from a dangerous situation or captivity without any bodily harm to oneself. ♦*The captive American marines took a vote to try to leave the enemy prisoner of war camp, and managed to escape unscathed.*

**even a worm will turn** *v. phr.* When pushed into a corner, even a generally cautious or cowardly person will fight back. ♦*John may look like a weak pushover, but don't press him too hard, because even a worm will turn.*

**even Homer sometimes nods** Even a great poet or novelist may produce boring or less successful passages.—A proverb. ♦*I've been reading Tolstoy's* War and Peace *but I must confess that I sometimes felt like falling asleep. I guess it's because even Homer sometimes nods.*

**even so** *adv.* Although that is true; nevertheless; still. ♦*The fire was out, but even so, the smell of smoke was strong.*

**even Steven** *adj. phr.* Free of indebtedness toward one another. ♦*"You have paid me back my $100," John said, "so now we're even Steven."*

**ever and anon** *adv. phr.* Every now and then; intermittently. ♦*"Do you still write poetry?" Tim asked. "Yeah, sort of ever and anon," the old poet answered.*

**ever so much** *adv.* Very much; truly. ♦*I am ever so much in your debt for your kind assistance when I needed it most.*

**everybody and his dog** *v. phr.* Absolutely everyone; the whole community. ♦*"Don't shout so loud, for heaven's sake!" Valerie complained in a bitter voice. "Do you want everybody and his dog to hear that we're having a fight?"*

**every cock crows on his own dunghill** People have a tendency to brag aloud about their bravery or their accomplishments on their own turf.—A proverb. ♦ *"It's a bit disgusting how this dictator keeps saying how he is invincible and in the right,"* Peter said. *"Sure,"* Tim replied, *"every cock crows on his own dunghill."*

**every cloud has a silver lining** Every trouble has something hopeful that you can see in it, like the bright edge around a dark cloud.—A proverb. ♦ *The doctor told Tommy to cheer up when he had measles. "Every cloud has a silver lining," he said.*

**every dog has his day** Everyone will have his chance or turn; everyone is lucky or popular at some time.—A proverb. ♦ *Jack will be able to go to boxing matches like his brother when he grows up. Every dog has his day.*

**every inch** *adv. phr.* To the last part, in every way; completely. ♦ *He was every inch a man.* ♦ *Henry looked every inch a soldier.*

**every Jack has his Jill** For every man there is a suitable woman partner somewhere in the world; one just has to keep looking for her.—A proverb. ♦ *"I'll never find a suitable woman to marry,"* Peter complained to his father. *"Never fear, son,"* the father replied, *"every Jack has his Jill somewhere."*

**every last man** *also* **every man jack** *n. phr.* Every single man; each man without exception. ♦ *I want every last man to be here on time tomorrow morning.* ♦ *Every man jack of you must do his duty.*

**every man has his price** A set phrase stating that every human being can be bought if the price is high enough.—A proverb. ♦ *"Although common wisdom has it that every man has his price, I for one will never betray my country,"* the young American soldier said proudly. *"We'll see,"* Ivan Ivanovich Smerdyakov, the ruthless Soviet agent replied.

**every now and then** *or* **every now and again** *or* **every so often** *or* **every once in a while** *adv. phr.* At fairly regular intervals; fairly often; repeatedly. ♦ *John comes to visit me every now and then.* ♦ *It was hot work, but every so*

often Susan would bring us something cold to drink.

**every other** *adj. phr.* Every second; every alternate. ♦ *The milkman comes every other day.*

**every single** *or* **every last** *adj. phr.* Every.—Used for emphasis. ♦ *When she got home she found every last tomato in the box was rotten.*

**every so often** See EVERY NOW AND THEN.

**every time one turns around** *adv. phr.,* *informal* Very often. ♦ *Mr. Winston must be rich. He buys a new suit every time he turns around.*

**every Tom, Dick, and Harry** See TOM, DICK, AND HARRY

**every which way** *also* **any which way** In all directions. ♦ *Bricks and boards were scattered in confusion on the ground every which way, just as they had fallen after the tornado.*

**except for** *or formal* **but for** *prep.* **1.** With the exception of; if (a certain person or thing) were left out; omitting. ♦ *Except for John, the whole class passed the test.* **2.** Without. ♦ *I'd have been lost but for you.*

**exception proves the rule** Something unusual that does not follow a rule tests that rule to see if it is true; if there are too many exceptions, the rule is no good.—A proverb. ♦ *Frank is very short but is a good basketball player. He is the exception that proves the rule.*

**excuse oneself** *v. phr.* **1.** To think of reasons for not being to blame; think yourself not at fault. ♦ *John excused himself for his low grades on the ground that the teacher didn't like him.* **2.** To ask to be excused after doing something impolite. ♦ *John excused himself for his tardiness, saying his watch was wrong.* **3.** To ask permission to leave a group or place. ♦ *The committee meeting lasted so long that Mr. Wilkins excused himself to keep an appointment.*

**exert oneself** *v. phr.* To make an effort; try hard; work hard. ♦ *Susan exerted herself all year to earn good marks.* ♦ *Jerry exerted himself to please the new girl.*

**expand on** *or* **expand upon** See ENLARGE ON *or* ENLARGE UPON.

**explain away** *v.* To explain (something) so that it does not seem true or important. ♦ *John explained away his unfin-*

*ished homework by showing the teacher his broken arm in a cast.*

**explain oneself** *v. phr.* **1.** To make your meaning plainer; make your first statement clear. ♦ *When we didn't understand Fritz, he went on to explain himself.* **2.** To give a good reason for something you did or failed to do which seems wrong. ♦ *When Jack brought Mary home at three o'clock in the morning, her father asked him to explain himself.*

**explode a bombshell** *v. phr., informal* To say something startling; suggest or show something astonishing or shocking. ♦ *The police exploded a bombshell when they arrested the kindly old banker for stealing money from the bank.*

**express oneself** *v. phr.* To say what you think or feel; put your thoughts or feelings into words by speaking or writing. ♦ *The boy expressed himself well in debate.*

**extend one's sympathy to** *v. phr.* To offer one's condolences on the occasion of a death or similarly tragic event. ♦ *All of Tom's colleagues extended their sympathy to him when his wife and daughter were killed in a car accident.*

**eye-catcher** *n.* Something that strongly attracts the eye. ♦ *That new girl in our class is a real eye-catcher.*

**eye-filling** *adj., literary* Attractive to the eye; beautiful; especially grand; splendid; majestic. ♦ *The mountains in the distance were an eye-filling sight.*

**eye-opener** See OPEN ONE'S EYES.

**eye out** Careful watch or attention; guard.—Used after *keep, have* or *with.* ♦ *Keep an eye out. We're close to Joe's house.* Usually used with *for.* ♦ *Mary has her eye out for bargains.*

**eyes are bigger than one's stomach** *informal* You want more food than you can eat. ♦ *Annie took a second big helping of pudding, but her eyes were bigger than her stomach.*

**eye shadow** *n. phr.* A cream used to darken the eyelids in order to make the eyes more noticeable. ♦ *Jane's mother told her that girls in the ninth grade shouldn't be using eye shadow.*

**eyes in the back of one's head** *n. phr., informal* Ability to know what happens when your back is turned. ♦ *Mother must have eyes in the back of her head, because she always knows when I do something wrong.*

**eyes open 1.** Careful watch or attention; readiness to see—Usually used with *for.* ♦ *Keep your eyes open for a boy in a red cap and sweater.* **2.** Full knowledge; especially of consequences; understanding of what will or might result.—Used with *have* or *with.* ♦ *Automobile racing is dangerous. Bob went into it with his eyes open.*

**eyes pop out** *informal* (You) are very much surprised.—Used with a possessive noun or pronoun. ♦ *When Joan found a new computer under the Christmas tree, her eyes popped out.*

**eye to 1.** Attention to.—Usually used with *have* or *with.* ♦ *Have an eye to spelling in these test papers.* **2.** Plan for, purpose of.—Usually used with *have* or *with.* ♦ *Save your money now with an eye to the future.*

**face down** v. phr. To get the upper hand over someone by behaving forcefully; disconcert someone by the displaying of great self-assurance. ◆ *The night guard faced down the burglar by staring him squarely in the face.*

**face lift** n. phr. **1.** A surgical procedure designed to make one's face look younger. ◆ *Aunt Jane, who is in her seventies, had an expensive face lift and now she looks as if she were 40.* **2.** A renovation, a refurbishing. ◆ *Our house needs a major face lift to make it fit in with the rest of the neighborhood.*

**face the music** v. phr., informal To go through trouble or danger, especially because of something you did; accept your punishment. ◆ *The official who had been taking bribes was exposed by a newspaper, and had to face the music.*

**face-to-face**[1] adv. phr. **1.** With your face looking toward the face of another person; each facing the other. ◆ *Turning a corner, he found himself face-to-face with a policeman.* **2.** In the presence of another or others. ◆ *She was thrilled to meet the President face-to-face.* **3.** To the point where you must do something.—Used with *with*. ◆ *The solution of the first problem brought him face-to-face with a second problem.*

**face-to-face**[2] adj. Being in the presence of a person; being right with someone. ◆ *The British prime minister came to Washington for a face-to-face meeting with the president.*

**face up to** v. phr. **1.** To bravely confront a person or a challenge; admit. ◆ *Jack doesn't want to face up to the fact that Helen doesn't love him anymore.* **2.** To confess something to someone; confess to having done something. ◆ *Jim had to face up to having stolen a sweater from the department store.*

**face value** n. **1.** The worth or price printed on a stamp, bond, note, piece of paper money, etc. ◆ *The savings bond had a face value of $25.* **2.** The seeming worth or truth of something. ◆ *She took his stories at face value and did not know he was joking.*

**faced with** adj. phr. Confronted with. ◆ *We were all faced with the many wars that broke out in the wake of the collapse of communism.*

**facts of life** n. phr. **1.** The truth which we should know about sex, marriage, and births. ◆ *His father told him the facts of life when he was old enough.* **2.** The truths one learns about people and their good and bad habits of life, work or play. ◆ *As a cub reporter he would learn the facts of life in the newspaper world.*

**fact of the matter is** See AS A MATTER OF FACT.

**fade away** v. phr. To gradually disappear with the passage of time. ◆ *Fred's parents died in a traffic accident and he suffered their loss terribly, but eventually the pain started to fade away.*

**fail to do** v. phr. To neglect to do something that is expected of one. ◆ *Tom waited for Jane for nearly an hour, but she failed to show up.*

**fair and square** adv. phr., informal Without cheating; honestly. ◆ *He won the game fair and square.*

**fair enough** adj. phr. Plausible, acceptable. ◆ *"How about our offer for your house?" the realtor asked. "That's fair enough" Mr. Brown replied.*

**fair-haired boy** n., informal A person that gets special favors; favorite; pet. ◆ *If he wins the election by a large majority, he will become his party's fair-haired boy.*

**fair play** n. Equal and right action (to another person); justice. ◆ *The visiting team did not get fair play in the game.*

**fair sex** n., informal Women in general; the female sex. ◆ *"Better not use four-letter words in front of a member of the fair sex," Joe said.*

**fair shake** n., informal Honest treatment. ◆ *Joe has always given me a fair shake.*

**fair-weather enemy** n. phr. A country that is another country's competitor, short of war. ◆ *The Soviet Union was America's fair-weather enemy during the Cold War.*

**fair-weather friend** n. phr. A person who is a friend only while one is very successful. ◆ *John didn't realize how many fair-weather friends he had until his* *firm had to declare bankruptcy and people turned their backs on him.*

**fairy godmother** *n.* **1.** A fairy believed to help and take care of a baby as it grows up. **2.** A person who helps and does much for another. ♦ *The rich man played fairy godmother to the boys and had a baseball field made for them.*

**fairy tale** *or* **story** *n.* An inaccurate, even false account of something; a result of wishful thinking. ♦ *Jeff said he was going to be promoted soon, but we all suspect that it is only one of his customary fairy tales.*

**fall all over** *v. phr., informal* To show too much love or thanks toward (someone). ♦ *She must love him. Every time you see them, she's falling all over him.*

**fall apart** *v. phr.* To lose control over one's composure; to suffer a nervous breakdown. ♦ *Suzie almost fell apart when her husband left her for a younger woman.*

**fall asleep at the switch** *v. phr.* To fail to perform an expected task; be remiss in one's duty. ♦ *The dean promised our department $250,000 but the foundation never sent the money because someone in the dean's office fell asleep at the switch.*

**fall away** *v. phr.* To decline; diminish. ♦ *I was shocked to see how haggard Alan looked; he seems to be falling away to a shadow.*

**fall back** *v.* To move back; go back.— Usually used with a group as subject. ♦ *The army fell back before their stubborn enemies.* ♦ *The crowd around the hurt boy fell back when someone shouted "Give him air!"*

**fall back on** *or* **fall back upon** *v.* **1.** To retreat to. ♦ *The enemy made a strong attack, and the soldiers fell back on the fort.* **2.** To go for help to; turn to in time of need. ♦ *When the big bills for Mother's hospital care came, Joe was glad he had money in the bank to fall back on.*

**fall behind** *v.* To go slower than others and be far behind them. ♦ *Frank's lessons were too hard for him, and he soon fell behind the rest of the class.*

**fall between two stools** *v. phr.* To fail to achieve one's desired goal due to hesitation between two available alternatives. ♦ *You had better make up your*

*mind which job to accept; if you hesitate too long you may find yourself fallen between two stools.*

**fall by the wayside** *also* **drop by the wayside** *v. phr.* To give up or fail before the finish. ♦ *George, Harry, and John entered college to become teachers, but Harry and John fell by the wayside, and only George graduated.*

**fall down on the job** *v. phr., informal* To fail to work well. ♦ *The boss was disappointed when his workers fell down on the job.*

**fall due** *or* **come** *or* **become due** *v. phr.* To reach the time when a bill or invoice is to be paid. ♦ *Our car payment falls due on the first of every month.*

**fall flat** *v., informal* To be a failure; fail. ♦ *His joke fell flat because no one understood it.*

**fall for** *v., slang* **1.** To begin to like very much. ♦ *Dick fell for baseball when he was a little boy.* **2.** To begin to love (a boy or a girl.) ♦ *Helen was a very pretty girl and people were not surprised that Bill fell for her.* **3.** To believe (something told to fool you.) ♦ *Nell did not fall for Joe's story about being a jet pilot.*

**fall from grace** *v. phr.* To go back to a bad way of behaving; do something bad again. ♦ *The boy fell from grace when he lied.*

**fall guy** *n. slang* The "patsy" in an illegal transaction; a sucker; a dupe; the person who takes the punishment others deserve. ♦ *When the Savings and Loan Bank failed, due to embezzlement, the vice president had to be the fall guy, saving the necks of the owners.*

**fall head over heals in love** See HEAD OVER HEALS.

**fall in** *v.* **1.** To go and stand properly in a row like soldiers. ♦ *The captain told his men to fall in.* **2.** To collapse. ♦ *The explosion caused the walls of the house to fall in.*

**fall in for** *v.* To receive; get. ♦ *The team manager fell in for most of the blame when his team lost the playoffs.*

**fall into the clutches of** *v. phr.* To fall victim of someone. ♦ *If you keep cultivating such dangerous company, you may fall into the clutches of criminals.*

**falling-out** *n.* Argument; disagreement; quarrel. ♦ *The boys had a falling-out when each said that the other had broken the rules.*

**fall in line** *or* **fall into line** See IN LINE, INTO LINE.

**fall in love** See IN LOVE.

**fall in** *or* **into place** *or* **fall together** *v. phr.* **1.** To suddenly make sense; find the natural or proper place for the missing pieces of a puzzle. ♦ *When the detectives realized that a second man was seen at the place of the murder, the pieces of the puzzle began to fall into place.* **2.** To result in the best possible arrangement or situation. ♦ *Peter was glad that everything fell together at the job interview, just as he had expected.* ♦ *All the arrangements for our trip around the world have finally fallen into place, so we are finally able to leave.*

**fall in with** *v., informal* **1.** To meet by accident. ♦ *Mary fell in with some of her friends downtown.* **2.** To agree to help with; support. ♦ *I fell in with Jack's plan to play a trick on his father.* **3.** To become associated with a group detrimental to the newcomer. ♦ *John fell in with a wild bunch; small wonder he flunked all of his courses.*

**fall into the habit of** *v. phr.* To develop the custom of doing something. ♦ *Jack has fallen into the bad habit of playing poker for large sums of money every night.*

**fall off the wagon** *v. phr., slang alcoholism and drug culture* To return to the consumption of an addictive, such as alcohol or drugs, after a period of abstinence. ♦ *Poor Joe has fallen off the wagon again—he is completely incoherent today.*

**fall on** *or* **fall upon** *v.* **1.** To go and fight with; attack. ♦ *The robbers fell on him from behind trees.* **2.** *formal* To meet (troubles). ♦ *The famous poet fell upon unhappy days.*

**fall on deaf ears** See TURN A DEAF EAR TO.

**fall on stony ground** *v. phr., Biblical* To be placed in an inhospitable environment where the chances of survival are nil. ♦ *All the good advice John's father gave his son fell on stony ground, as the boy never listened to reasonable advice and became a drug addict.*

**fallout** *n.* **1.** Result of nuclear explosion; harmful radioactive particles. *Some experts consider fallout as dangerous as the bomb itself.* **2.** Undesirable aftereffects in general. ♦ *As a fallout of Watergate, many people lost their faith in the government.*

**fall out** *v.* **1.** To happen. ♦ *As it fell out, the Harpers were able to sell their old car.* **2.** To quarrel; fight; fuss; disagree. ♦ *The thieves fell out over the division of the loot.* **3.** To leave a military formation. ♦ *You men are dismissed. Fall out!* **4.** To leave a building to go and line up. ♦ *The soldiers fell out of the barracks for inspection.*

**fall over backwards** *or* **fall over oneself** *v. phr.* To do everything you can to please someone; try very hard to satisfy someone. ♦ *The hotel manager fell over backwards to give the movie star everything she wanted.*

**fall short** *v.* To fail to reach (some aim); not succeed. ♦ *His jump fell three inches short of the world record.*

**fall through** *v., informal* To fail; be ruined; not happen or be done. ♦ *Jim's plans to go to college fell through at the last moment.*

**fall through the trap door** See BREAK A LEG.

**fall to** *v.* (stress on *to*) **1.** To begin to work. ♦ *The boys fell to and quickly cut the grass.* **2.** To begin to fight. ♦ *They took out their swords and fell to.* **3.** To begin to eat. ♦ *The hungry boys fell to before everyone sat down.* **4.** Begin; start. ♦ *The old friends met and fell to talking about their school days.*

**fall to pieces** *v. phr.* To disintegrate; collapse. ♦ *After the death of Alexander the Great, his empire started to fall to pieces.*

**familiarity breeds contempt** When someone becomes accustomed to something or someone, one's earlier respect degenerates into disregard.— A proverb. ♦ *Newly hired faculty from other universities always get higher salaries, while the faithful who do not move around get underpaid. This is because familiarity breeds contempt.*

**family tree** *n.* Ancestry. ♦ *My family tree can be traced back to the sixteenth century.*

**famous last words** *n. phr.* Issued as a warning after an optimistic statement indicating that the person with the optimistic outlook could easily be wrong. ♦*"Such a terrible thing as the exploding of a skyscraper with a hijacked airplane could never happen in America!" Joe said. "Famous last words!" Peter answered.*

**fancy doing something**—An expression of surprise. ♦*Fancy meeting you here in such an unexpected place!*

**fancy pants** *n., slang* A man or boy who wears clothes that are too nice or acts like a woman or girl; sissy. ♦*The first time they saw him in his new band uniform, they yelled "Hey, fancy pants, what are you doing in your sister's slacks?"*

**fan out** *v. phr.* To spread in several directions. ♦*The main road fans out at the edge of the forest in four different directions.*

**fan the breeze** *v. phr.* To swing and miss the ball in baseball. ♦*The batter tried to hit a home run, but he fanned the breeze.*

**fan the flames** See ADD FUEL TO THE FLAME.

**far afield** *adj. phr.* Remote; far from the original starting point. ♦*When we started to discuss theology, Jack was obviously getting far afield from the subject at hand.*

**far and away** *adv. phr.* Very much. ♦*The fish was far and away the biggest ever caught on the lake.*

**far and near** *n. phr.* Far places and near places; everywhere. ♦*People came from far and near to hear him speak.*

**far and wide** *adv. phr.* Everywhere, in all directions. ♦*The wind blew the papers far and wide.*

**far be it from me to** *adv. phr.* A sometimes falsely modest disclaimer stating that the person doesn't really mean what he or she is about to say, when in fact he or she actually means it. ♦*"Far be it from me to criticize the government's decision to go to war, but wouldn't it have been better to wait for United Nations consensus in the matter?"*

**farfetched** *adj.* Exaggerated; fantastic. ♦*Sally told us some farfetched story about having been kidnapped by little green men in a flying saucer.*

**far cry** *n.* Something very different. ♦*His last statement was a far cry from his first story.* ♦*The first automobile could run, but it was a far cry from a modern car.*

**far from accurate** *adj. phr.* Quite inaccurate. ♦*I am afraid that your estimate concerning the purchase of the new equipment for our factory is far from accurate.*

**far from it** *adv. phr.* Not even approximately; not really at all. ♦*"Do you think she spent $100 on that dress?" Jane asked. "Far from it," Sue replied. "It must have cost at least $300."*

**far gone** *adj. phr.* In a critical or extreme state. ♦*He was so far gone by the time the doctor arrived, that nothing could be done to save his life.*

**farm out** *v.* **1.** To have another person do (something) for you; send away to be done. ♦*Our teacher had too many test papers to read, so she farmed out half of them to a friend.* **2.** To send away to be taken care of. ♦*While Mother was sick, the children were farmed out to relatives.* **3.** To send a player to a league where the quality of play is lower. ♦*The player was farmed out to Rochester to gain experience.*

**far-out** *adj.* **1.** Very far away; distant. ♦*Scientists are planning rocket trips to the moon and far-out planets.* **2.** *informal* Very different from others; queer; odd, unusual. ♦*He enjoyed being with beatniks and other far-out people.* ♦*Susan did not like some of the paintings at the art show because they were too far-out for her.*

**fast and furious** *adj. or adv. phr.* Very fast; with much speed and energy. ♦*When I last saw her she was driving fast and furious down the street.*

**fast buck** or **quick buck** *slang* Money earned quickly and easily, and sometimes dishonestly. ♦*You can make a fast buck at the golf course by fishing balls out of the water trap.* ♦*He isn't interested in a career; he's just looking for a quick buck.*

**fast talker** *n., slang, informal* A con artist or a swindler, one who is particularly apt to get away with illegitimate transactions because of the clever way he talks. ♦*I wouldn't trust Uncle Joe if I were you,—he is a fast talker.*

**fasten on** *v. phr.* To attach; tie something to make it secure. ♦ *"Fasten on your life jackets when you get into the life boats," the captain said.*

**fat chance** *n. phr., slang* Little or no possibility; almost no chance. ♦ *Jane is pretty and popular; you will have a fat chance of getting a date with her.*

**fat city** *n., slang* A state of contentment due to wealth and position. ♦ *Bully for the Smiths; they have arrived in Fat City.*

**fate worse than death** *n. phr.* Extraordinarily severe punishment, inhumane treatment, unbearable ordeal. ♦ *To be tortured by the terrorist dictator's thugs is a fate worse than death.*

**fat is in the fire** Something has happened that will cause trouble or make a bad situation worse. ♦ *He found out you took it? Well, the fat's in the fire now.*

**fat of the land** *n. phr.* The best and richest food, clothes, everything. ♦ *When I'm rich I'll retire and live off the fat of the land.*

**faultfinding** *n.* Recrimination; nagging; criticism. ♦ *All of this constant fault-finding will only to lead to trouble between you and your wife.*

**favorite son** *n.* A man supported by his home state for president. ♦ *At a national convention, states often vote for their favorite sons first; then they change and vote for another man.*

**fear and trembling** *or* **fear and trepidation** *n. phr.* Great fear. ♦ *He came in fear and trembling to tell his father he had a bad report card .*

**feast one's eyes on** *v. phr.* To look at and enjoy very much. ♦ *He feasted his eyes on the beautiful painting.*

**feast or a famine** *n. phr.* Plenty or very little; big success or bad failure. ♦ *He is very careless with his money, it is always a feast or a famine with him.*

**feather in one's cap** *n. phr.* Something to be proud of; an honor. ♦ *It was a feather in his cap to win first prize.*

**feather one's nest** *v. phr., informal* **1.** To use for yourself money and power, especially from a public office or job in which you are trusted to help other people. ♦ *The man feathered his nest in politics by getting money from contrac-*

tors who built roads. **2.** To make your home pleasant and comfortable; furnish and decorate your house. ♦ *Furniture stores welcome young couples who want to feather their nests.*

**fed up** *(informal)* ALSO *(slang)* **fed to the gills** *or* **fed to the teeth** *adj. phr.* Having had too much of something; at the end of your patience; disgusted; bored; tired. ♦ *People get fed up with anyone who brags all the time.* ♦ *John quit football because he was fed to the gills with practice.*

**feed a cold and starve a fever** When one has a cold one ought to eat a great deal, but when one has a fever, as when one has the flu, one ought to eat as little as possible.—A proverb. *"Why are you bringing me a six-course meal in bed, Grandma?" Jimmy asked all sniffling and coughing. "Well, you know what they say," Grandma answered. "Feed a cold and starve a fever!"*

**feed one a line** *v. phr.* To deceive one, to tell one a lie. ♦ *Mr. Smith promised Sam a job but Sam soon discovered that he was being fed a line when Mr. Smith gave the job to someone else.*

**feel a different person** *v. phr.* To feel recovered and well again after some illness or draining ordeal. ♦ *After she finally managed to get rid of her alcoholic husband, Irene felt like a different person.*

**feel a draft** *v. phr., slang* To have the sensation that one is not welcome in a place; that one has gotten a cold reception. ♦ *Let's go, Suzie, I feel a draft.*

**feel at home** *v. phr.* To feel comfortable, relaxed, at ease. ♦ *"When you're at our place for a weekend," my sister-in-law said, "you must feel at home and tell me what you like to eat."*

**feel blue** *or* **have the blues** *v. phr.* To feel sad, lonely, or depressed due to lovesickness or some other unfortunate circumstance. ♦ *John's wife left town with another guy; that's why he is feeling so blue.* ♦ *Mike has the blues because his mother just passed away.*

**feel down** *v. phr.* To feel tired, miserable, exhausted, sad, or depressed. *John doesn't eat right; that's why he feels down so often.* ♦ *"You're feeling down just now, because Suzie left you," the* *psychologist said, "but you're young, and life is long. Pretty soon you will find someone else."*

**feel for someone** *v. phr., informal* To be able to sympathize with someone's problems. ♦*I can really feel for you, John, for losing your job.*

**feel free to do** *v. phr.* To take the liberty to engage in an activity. ♦*Please feel free to take off your jackets; this is an informal party.*

**feel in one's bones** *or* **know in one's bones** *v. phr.* To have an idea or feeling but not know why. ♦*I feel in my bones that tomorrow will be a sunny day.* ♦*I know in my bones that God will protect us.*

**feel like** *v., informal* To want to do or have. ♦*I just don't feel like pancakes this morning.*

**feel like a million** *or* **feel like a million dollars** *v. phr., informal* To be in the best of health and spirits. ♦*I feel like a million this morning.* ♦*He had a headache yesterday but feels like a million dollars today.*

**feel like a new man** *v. phr.* To feel healthy, vigorous, and well again after a major physical illness or emotional upheaval. ♦*Ted felt like a new man after his successful heart bypass operation.*

**feel low** *v. phr.* To be depressed; be in low spirits. ♦*I don't know what's the matter with Mary, but she says she has been feeling very low all afternoon.*

**feel one's age** *v. phr.* To be conscious of one's advancing years and to give signs of one's waning powers and energy. ♦*"I started to feel my age," Grandpa said. "I'm ninety, you know, and it's getting harder and harder to stay up all night dancing with the girls than when I was only eighty."*

**feel one's way** *v. phr.* To proceed cautiously by trial and error; probe. ♦*I won't ask her to marry me directly; I will feel my way first.*

**feel or look small** *v. phr.* To have the impression that one is insignificant, foolish, or humiliated. ♦*"I feel small next to Hemingway," the young student of creative writing said.*

**feel out** *v.* To talk or act carefully with someone and find what he thinks or can do. ♦*John felt out his father about letting him have the car that evening.* ♦*At first the boxers felt each other out.*

**feel out of it** *v. phr.* To sense that one is not in one's normal condition; to feel strange. ♦*I don't know what's the matter with me today. I just feel completely out of it. Maybe it's because I didn't sleep at all last night.*

**feel out of place** *v. phr.* To experience the sensation of not belonging in a certain place or company. ♦*Dave felt out of place among all those chess players as he knows nothing about chess.*

**feel ten feet tall** *v. phr.* To feel self-confident, happy, optimistic, full of energy. ♦*Winning the Nobel Prize for medicine, made Dr. McDermott feel ten feet tall.*

**feel the pinch** *v. phr.* To be short of money; experience monetary difficulties. ♦*If we are going to have a recession, everybody will feel the pinch.*

**feel up** *v. phr., vulgar, avoid* To arouse sexually by manual contact. ♦*You mean to tell me that you've been going out for six months and he hasn't ever tried to feel you up?*

**feel up to something** *v. phr., informal* To feel adequately knowledgeable, strong, or equipped to handle a given task. ♦*Do you feel up to jogging a mile a day with me?*

**feet of clay** *n. phr.* A hidden fault or weakness in a person which is discovered or shown. ♦*The famous general showed he had feet of clay when he began to drink liquor.*

**feet on the ground** *n. phr.* An understanding of what can be done; sensible ideas. Used with a possessive. ♦*John has his feet on the ground; he knows he cannot learn everything at once.*

**fellow traveler** *n.* A sympathizer with a political movement who does not officially belong to the political party in question. ♦*Many Germans after World War II were innocently accused of being fellow travelers of Nazism.* ♦*During the McCarthy era, many Americans were accused of being Communist fellow travelers.*

**fence in** *or* **hedge in** *or* **hem in** *v.* To keep (someone) from doing what he or she would like to do. Usually used in the passive. ♦*Mary felt fenced in because her father would not let her drive a car or have dates with boys.* ♦*John didn't like his job because he* had to do the same kind of work all the time. He felt that he was hemmed in.

**fence-sitter** *n.* A person unable to pick between two sides; a person who does not want to choose. ♦ *Dad says he is a fence-sitter because he doesn't know which man he wants for president.*

**fence-sitting** *n. or adj.* Choosing neither side. ♦ *You have been fence-sitting for too long. It is time you made up your mind.*

**fence with** *or* **spar with** *v.* To talk with (someone) as if you were fighting like a swordsman or boxer; to give skillful answers or arguments against (someone). ♦ *The governor was an expert at fencing with reporters at press conferences.*

**fender bender** *n. phr.* A minor traffic accident during which the damaged vehicle remains drivable and no one is seriously injured. ♦ *Three days ago a young man hit my car from behind, but nothing serious happened. It was just a fender bender and his insurance will take care of the damage.*

**ferret out** *literary or* **smell out** *or* **sniff out** *v.* To hunt or drive from hiding; to bring out into the open; search for and find. ♦ *John ferreted out the answer to the question in the library.* ♦ *Jane smelled out the boys' secret hiding place in the woods.*

**few and far between** *adj. phr.* Not many; few and scattered; not often met or found; rare.—Used in the predicate. ♦ *People who will work as hard as Thomas A. Edison are few and far between.*

**fiddle around** See FOOL AROUND 3.

**fiddle while Rome burns** *v. phr.* To amuse oneself with some trivial activities while a major crisis, disaster, or war is in progress. ♦ *As Hitler's Third Reich fell apart toward the end of World War II, the Nazi German movie industry churned out one ridiculous and sentimental love story after another; they were obviously fiddling while Rome burned.*

**fiddle with** *v. phr.* To carelessly play with something. ♦ *If Jimmy continues to fiddle with our computer, he is liable to ruin it.*

**fifth column** *n. phr.* A group or organization within a country that works to bring about the country's downfall, usually through acts of espionage and sabotage. ♦ *The Communist Party in the United States was considered by Senator McCarthy to be the Soviet Union's fifth column.*

**fifth wheel** *n. phr.* An unwanted, extra person, who feels awkward and uncomfortable in the company of those he or she is with. ♦ *My spinster Aunt Helen often spent Christmas and New Year's Eve with us, but she frequently complained that she felt like a fifth wheel.*

**fifty-fifty**[1] *adv., informal* Equally; evenly. ♦ *When Dick and Sam bought an old car, they divided the cost fifty-fifty.*

**fifty-fifty**[2] *adj., informal* **1.** Divided or shared equally. ♦ *It will be a fifty-fifty arrangement; half the money for me and half for you.* **2.** Half for and half against; half good and half bad. ♦ *There is only a fifty-fifty chance that we will win the game.*

**fight fire with fire** *v. phr. slightly formal, of Biblical origin* To fight back in the same way one was attacked; make a defense similar to the attack. ♦ *The candidate was determined to fight fire with fire in the debate.*

**fight it out** See SLUG IT OUT.

**fighting chance** *n. phr.* A chance that necessitates struggle and courage; a slim chance. ♦ *The doctor told the family that Jack had a fighting chance to recover.*

**fight off** *v. phr.* **1.** To struggle against someone so as to free oneself; push an attacker back. ♦ *Suzy fought off her two attackers in Central Park with a couple of karate chops.* **2.** To strive to overcome something negative. ♦ *After twelve hours at the computer terminal, Jane had to fight off her overwhelming desire to go to sleep.*

**fight tooth and nail** See TOOTH AND NAIL.

**figure in** *v.* **1.** *informal* To add to a total; remember to put down in figures. ♦ *We figured in the travel expenses but forgot the cost of meals.* **2.** To have a part in; be partly responsible for. ♦ *Mary's good grades figured in her choice as class president.*

**figure on** *v.* **1.** To expect and think about while making plans. ♦ *We did not figure on having so many people at the picnic.*

2. To depend on; be sure about. ♦ *You can figure on him to be on time.*

**figure out** *v.* **1.** To find an answer by thinking about (some problem or difficulty); solve. ♦ *Tom couldn't figure out the last problem on the arithmetic test.* ♦ *Sam couldn't figure out how to print a program until the teacher showed him how.* **2.** To learn how to explain; understand. ♦ *Laurence is an odd boy; I can't figure him out.*

**figure up** *v. phr.* To calculate; add up. ♦ *If you can figure up how many phone calls I've made from your home, I will pay you right away.*

**filled to capacity** *adj. phr.* Completely full. ♦ *All hotels in town during the summer Olympic games were filled to capacity so many people decided to sleep out in the open.*

**fill in** *v.* **1.** To write words needed in blanks; put in; fill. ♦ *You should fill in all the blanks on an application for a job.* **2.** *informal* To tell what you should know. ♦ *The teacher filled in Mary about class work done while she was sick.* **3.** To take another's place; substitute. ♦ *The teacher was sick and Miss Jones filled in for her.*

**fill (in) the gap** *v. phr.* To supply a missing piece of information; provide a clue during the course of solving a mystery. ♦ *Sherlock Holmes said, "These fingerprints are bound to fill the gap in our investigation."*

**fill one in (on)** *v. phr.* To inform; to bring up to date. ♦ *The president depends on his advisors to fill him in on every new development both domestically and abroad.*

**fill one's shoes** *v. phr.* To take the place of another and do as well; to substitute satisfactorily for. ♦ *When Jack got hurt, the coach had nobody to fill his shoes.*

**fill out** *v.* **1.** To put in what is missing; complete; finish; *especially,* to complete (a printed application blank or other form) by writing the missing facts in the blank spaces; to write down facts which are asked for in (a report or application.) ♦ *After Tom passed his driving test he filled out an application for his driver's license.* **2.** To become heavier and fatter; gain weight. ♦ *The girl was pale and thin after her sickness, but in a few months she filled out.*

**fill the bill** *v. phr., informal* To be just what is needed; be good enough for something; be just right. ♦ *The boss was worried about hiring a deaf boy, but after he tried Tom out for a few weeks, he said that Tom filled the bill.*

**fill up** *or* **fill it up** *or* **fill her up** *v. phr.* To fill entirely. (Said by the driver of a car to a gas station attendant). ♦ *When the attendant asked Andrew how much gas he wanted in the tank, Andrew replied, "Fill her up."*

**filthy rich** *adj. phr.* Extremely rich but without cultural refinement; nouveau riche. ♦ *"The Murgatroyds are filthy rich," Ted complained. "They are rolling in money but they never learned how to behave properly at a dinner table."*

**finders keepers** *or* **finders keepers, losers weepers** *informal* Those who find lost things can keep them.—Used usually by children to claim the right to keep something they have found. ♦ *I don't have to give it back; it's finders keepers.* ♦ *Finders keepers, losers weepers! It's my knife now!*

**find fault** *v. phr.* To find something wrong; complain; criticize. ♦ *She tries to please him, but he always finds fault.*

**find it in one's heart** *v. phr.* To be able or willing because of your nature. ♦ *Can you find it in your heart to forgive me?*

**find oneself** *v. phr.* To find out what one is fitted for and succeed in that. ♦ *Mary tried several lines of work, but at last found herself as a teacher.* ♦ *Sometimes young people move around a long time from job to job before they find themselves.*

**find** *or* **get one's bearings** *v. phr.* To know where one is or where one is headed. ♦ *"Without a compass," the sergeant warned the enlisted men, "you will never find your bearings in the desert."*

**find out** *v.* **1.** To learn or discover (something you did not know before.) ♦ *I don't know how this car works, but I'll soon find out.* ♦ *He watched the birds to find out where they go.* **2.** To get facts; to get facts about. ♦ *He wrote to find out about a job in Alaska.* **3.** To discover (someone) doing wrong; catch. ♦ *The boy knew that if he cheated on the test the teacher would find him out.*

**find out the hard way** See HARD WAY.

**fine feathers do not make fine birds** *literary* A person who wears fine clothes may not be as good as he looks.—A proverb. ♦ *Mary is pretty and she wears pretty clothes, but she is very mean. Fine feathers do not make fine birds.*

**fine line** *n. phr.* A subtle distinction between two different things that resemble each other. ♦ *There is a fine line separating genius from insanity.*

**fine-tooth comb** *n. phr.* Great care; careful attention so as not to miss anything. ♦ *The police searched the scene of the crime with a fine-tooth comb for clues.*

**finger in the pie** *n. phr., informal* Something to do with what happens; part interest or responsibility. ♦ *When the girls got up a Christmas party, I felt sure Alice had a finger in the pie.* ♦ *The Jones Company was chosen to build the new hospital and we knew Mr. Smith had a finger in the pie.*

**finishing touch** *n. phr.* The last thing that needs to be added to make something complete. ♦ *The finishing touch on John's education was his receiving the degree of Ph.D. with distinction.*

**fire away** *v. phr.* To keep asking whatever questions someone wants. ♦ *During his press interview the president, who was in an unusually good mood, kept encouraging the journalists to fire away.*

**firebug** *n.* An arsonist; one who willfully sets fire to property. ♦ *The police caught the firebug just as he was about to set another barn ablaze in the country.*

**fire's gone out** *phrasal idiom* Said when a relationship that was passionate at the beginning has cooled down and is held together by habit and inertia. ♦ *"Why are Jean and Tom behaving so formally and coldly toward one another?" Peter asked. "I guess the fire's gone out between them," Sue answered.*

**fire up** *v. phr.* To make someone excited or eager to do something. ♦ *John is all fired up about going to China for a year; I'm afraid he may be cooled off by some of the living conditions over there.*

**firing squad** *n.* A group of soldiers chosen to shoot a prisoner to death or to fire shots over a grave as a tribute.

♦ *A dictator often sends his enemies before a firing squad.*

**firm footing** *n. phr.* An established position or place on which one can stand during construction; a solid position in one's job. ♦ *"Give me a chair to stand on while I am putting up these heavy books," Joe said. "I need some firm footing."* ♦ *John's excellent education gave him a firm footing in the profession.*

**firsthand** *adj.* Fresh; genuine; from the original source. ♦ *John says he got the information firsthand from the president himself.*

**first and foremost** *adv. phr.* As the most important thing; first. ♦ *First and foremost they needed food.* ♦ *First and foremost, we must keep America free.*

**first class** *n.* **1.** The first rank; the highest class; the best group. ♦ *The pianist was quite good but he was not in the first class.* **2.** The most expensive or comfortable class of travel; the best or one of the best groups in which to travel, especially by ship, train, or airplane. ♦ *Most people can't afford the first class when they take a long journey by ship.* **3.** The way of sending all mail that includes letters and post cards, anything written by hand or typewriter, and anything sealed so that it cannot be inspected, and that is the most expensive class of mail but receives the best treatment. ♦ *The usual way to send a letter is by first class.*

**first-class**[1] *adj.* **1.** Of the highest class or best kind; excellent; first-rate. ♦ *It was a first-class TV program.* **2.** Of the best or most expensive class of travelling. ♦ *Mr. Jones bought a first-class plane ticket to Chicago.* **3.** Belonging to the class of mail for sending letters, post cards, and handwritten or typewritten mail that is sealed. ♦ *It is expensive to send a heavy letter by first-class mail.*

**first-class**[2] *adv.* With the best material; in the best or most expensive way. ♦ *When Mr. Van Smith goes anywhere he always travels first-class.* ♦ *"How did you send the package?" "First-class."*

**first come, first served** *truncated sent. informal* If you arrive first, you will be served first; people will be waited on in the order they come; the person who comes first will have his turn first.

♦ *Get in line for your ice cream, boys. First come, first served.* ♦ *The rule in the restaurant is first come, first served.* ♦ *There are only a few seats left so it's first come, first served.*

**first cousin** *n.* The child of your aunt or uncle. ♦ *Tom's only first cousin was Ralph, the son of his Uncle John.*

**first of all** *adv. phr.* Chiefly; primarily; as the first thing. ♦ *After we get to Chicago, we will, first of all, try to find a reliable used car.*

**first off** *adv. phr., informal* Before anything else; first. ♦ *First off, I want you to mow the lawn.*

**first-rate** *adj. phr.* Excellent, outstanding, superior. ♦ *John received a first-rate education at Princeton University.*

**first-run** *adj. phr.* Shown for the first time; new. ♦ *The local theater showed only first-run movies.*

**first thing off the bat** *adv. phr.* Immediately; at once. ♦ *He called home from Paris first thing off the bat as he stepped off the plane.*

**first things first** Other things must wait until the most important and necessary things are done. ♦ *Study your lessons before you go out to play. First things first.*

**fish for** *v., informal* To try to get or to find out (something), by hinting or by a roundabout way to try to lead someone else to give or tell you what you want by hinting. ♦ *Near examination time, some of the students fish for information.*

**fish for a compliment** *v. phr.* To try to make someone pay a compliment. ♦ *When Jim showed me his new car, I could tell that he was fishing for a compliment.*

**fish in muddy** *or* **troubled waters** *v. phr.* To take advantage of a troubled or confusing situation; seek personal advantage. ♦ *With the police disorganized after the collapse of communism in Europe, many criminals started to fish in troubled waters.*

**fish or cut bait** *v. phr., informal* **1.** Decide what you want to do and stop wasting time; either act now or give someone else a chance or turn. ♦ *Jack couldn't decide whether to go to college or get a job, so his father told him to fish or cut bait.* **2.** either

try hard and do your best, or quit. ♦ *Frank missed football practice so often that the coach told him to fish or cut bait.*

**fish out of water** *n. phr.* A person who is out of his proper place in life; someone who does not fit in. ♦ *She was the only girl at the party not in a formal dress and she felt like a fish out of water.*

**fish story** *n. phr.* An unlikely or improbable tale. ♦ *Hunters and fishermen often exaggerate their successes by telling fish stories.*

**fit as a fiddle** *adj. phr.* In very good health. ♦ *The man was almost 90 years old but fit as a fiddle.*

**fit for** *v. phr.* To be suited for; be prepared for. ♦ *"What kind of job is Ted fit for?" the social worker asked.*

**fit for a king** *adj. phr.* Very elegant, luxurious, beautiful, expensive. ♦ *The new condominium Joe and Mary bought is fit for a king.*

**fit in with** *v. phr.* To fall into agreement or accord with. ♦ *His plans to take a vacation in early July fit in perfectly with the university schedule.*

**fit like a glove** *v. phr.* To fit perfectly. ♦ *Her new dress fits her like a glove.*

**fit out** *or* **fit up** *v.* To give things needed; furnish. ♦ *The soldiers were fitted out with guns and clothing.* ♦ *The government fitted out warships and got sailors for them.*

**fit to be tied**[1] *adj. phr., informal* Very angry or upset. ♦ *She was fit to be tied when she saw the broken glass.*

**fit to be tied**[2] *adv. phr., substandard* Very hard.—Used for emphasis. ♦ *Uncle Willie was laughing fit to be tied at the surprised look on Mother's face.*

**fit to hold a candle to** *adj. phr., always in the negative* Much inferior to; worth less; cannot be compared with someone or something. ♦ *"I am not fit to hold a candle to Professor Teller when it comes to nuclear physics," Joe said.*

**five o'clock shadow** *n. phr.* A very short growth of beard on a man's face who did shave in the morning but whose beard is so strong that it is again visible in the afternoon. ♦ *"You have a five o'clock shadow, honey," Irene said, "and we're going to the opera. Why don't you shave again quickly?"*

**fix one up with** *v. phr.* To make arrangements for two people to meet or date;

usually said in a matchmaking context. ♦ *"I don't have anyone to take to the opera this weekend,"* Jack complained to Jerry. *"Let me fix you up with my sister, Jane,"* Jerry answered. *"She feels lonely, too."*

**fix someone's wagon** *or* **fix someone's little red wagon** *v. phr., informal* **1.** (Said to a child as a threat) To administer a spanking. ♦ *Stop that right away or I'll fix your (little red) wagon!* **2.** (Said of an adult) To thwart or frustrate another, to engineer his failure. ♦ *If he sues me for slander, I will counter-sue him for malicious prosecution. That will fix his wagon!*

**fix someone up with** *v. phr., informal* To help another get a date with a woman or man by arranging a meeting for the two. ♦ *Say Joe, can you possibly fix me up with someone this weekend? I am so terribly lonesome!*

**fix up** *v. phr.* **1.** To repair. ♦ *The school is having the old gym fixed up.* **2.** To arrange. ♦ *I think I can fix it up with the company so that John gets the transfer he desires.* **3.** To arrange a date that might lead to a romance or even to marriage. ♦ *Mary is a great matchmaker; she fixed up Ron and Betty at her recent party.*

**fizzle out** *v., informal* **1.** To stop burning; die out. ♦ *The fuse fizzled out before exploding the firecracker.* **2.** To fail after a good start; end in failure. ♦ *The party fizzled out when everyone went home early.*

**flag down** *v., informal* To stop by waving a signal flag or as if waving a signal flag. ♦ *A policeman flagged down the car with his flashlight.*

**flakeball** *or* **flake** *n., slang, drug culture* A disjointed, or "flaky" person, who is forgetful and incoherent, as if under the influence of narcotics.

**flare up** *v.* (stress on *up*) **1.** To burn brightly for a short time especially after having died down. ♦ *The fire flared up again and then died.* **2.** To become suddenly angry. ♦ *The mayor flared up at the reporter's remark.* **3.** To begin again suddenly, especially for a short time after a quiet time. ♦ *Mr. Gray's arthritis flared up sometimes.*

**flare-up** *n.* (stress on *flare*) The reoccurrence of an infection or an armed conflict. ♦ *He had a flare-up of his arthritis.*

*There was a bad flare-up of hostilities in some countries.*

**flash card** *n.* A card with numbers or words on it that is used in teaching a class. ♦ *The teacher used flash cards to drill the class in addition.*

**flash in the pan** *n. phr., slang* A person or thing that starts out well but does not continue. ♦ *The new opera star was a flash in the pan.*

**flash through one's mind** *v. phr.* To suddenly occur to someone; to suddenly think of something or remember something. ♦ *I was already sitting in the bus several stops away from home, when it flashed through my mind that I probably hadn't turned off the stove in my kitchen.*

**flat as a pancake** *adj. phr.* Very level; very flat; having no mountains or hills. ♦ *A great part of the American Midwest is as flat as a pancake.*

**flatfoot** *n., slang, derogatory* A policeman. ♦ *"What does Joe do for a living?—He's a flatfoot."*

**flat-footed** *adj., informal* **1.** Straightforward; forthright; direct; outright. ♦ *The governor issued a flat-footed denial of the accusation.* **2.** Not ready; not prepared;—usually used with *catch*. ♦ *The teacher's question caught Tim flat-footed.*

**flat-out** *adv. phr., informal* **1.** Without hiding anything; plainly; openly. ♦ *The student told his teacher flat-out that he was not listening to her.* **2.** At top speed; as fast as possible. ♦ *He saw two men running flat-out from the wild rhinoceros.*

**flea in one's ear** *n. phr., informal* An idea or answer that is not welcome; an annoying or surprisingly sharp reply or hint. ♦ *I'll put a flea in his ear if he bothers me once more.*

**flea market** *n. phr.* A place where antiques, second-hand things, and cheap articles are sold, and especially one in the open air. ♦ *There are many outdoor flea markets in Europe.*

**flesh and blood** *n.* **1.** A close relative (as a father, daughter, brother); close relatives. Used in the phrase *one's own flesh and blood.* ♦ *Such an answer from her—and she's my own flesh and blood, too!* **2.** The appearance of being real or alive. ♦ *The author doesn't give his* *characters any flesh and blood.* **3.** The human body. ♦ *Before child labor laws, small children often worked 50 or 60 hours a week in factories. It was more than flesh and blood could bear.*

**flesh out** *v., informal* **1.** To add to; make fuller, bigger, or longer. ♦ *The author fleshed out his story by adding more about his war experiences.* **2.** *also* **flesh up** To become heavier, put on weight, or flesh. ♦ *He lost weight after his illness but is beginning to flesh out again.* See FILL OUT.

**flight of fancy** *n. phr.* An imaginative excursion; a poetical or rhetorical extravaganza. ♦ *Many a piece of literature may start out first as a flight of fancy.*

**fling enough dirt and some will stick** If someone accuses a person often and repeatedly, people will believe the accusation or at least parts of it, whether it is true or false.—A proverb. ♦ *It is an unfortunate habit of some politicians during campaigns to say bad things about their opponents, because some of it will be believed—fling enough dirt and some will stick.*

**flip-flop**[1] *v., informal* To alternate the positions of; exchange the places of; switch. ♦ *The football coach had one play in which he flip-flopped his left halfback and fullback.*

**flip-flop**[2] *n., informal* A complete change; a switch from one thing to an entirely different one. ♦ *John wanted to be a carpenter like his father, but when he saw the print shop he did a flip-flop and now he's learning printing.*

**flip-flop**[3] *adj. phr., informal* Involving or using a change from one of two places, positions, or alternatives to the other. ♦ *The machine was controlled by a flip-flop switch.*

**flip off** *v. phr.* To make a vulgar gesture with one's hand. ♦ *Ted has a terrible habit; each time he feels the least bit frustrated, he flips off.*

**flip one's lid** *also* **flip one's wig** *slang* **1.** To lose one's temper. ♦ *When that pushy salesman came back Mom really flipped her lid.* **2.** To lose your mind; become insane. ♦ *When he offered me three times the pay I was getting, I thought he had flipped his lid.* **3.** To become unreasonably enthusiastic.

♦ *She flipped her lid over a hat she saw in the store window.*

**flip out** *v. phr., slang, informal* To go insane, to go out of one's mind. ♦ *It is impossible to talk to Joe today—he must have flipped out.*

**float** *or* **fly like a butterfly, sting like a bee** *phrasal idiom* Your appearance could look small but you are stronger than you look. ♦ *Mickey's appearance is rather deceptive—he floats like a butterfly, but stings like a bee.*

**floor one** *v. phr.* To shock or surprise someone. ♦ *When my daughter called from Reno, Nevada, and announced that she had gotten married an hour ago, I was completely floored.*

**floorwalker** *n.* A section manager in a department store. ♦ *To exchange this pair of shoes, you must first get the floorwalker's approval.*

**floppy disk** *n. phr.* A 3.5-inch-wide diskette used to store information in connection with personal computers, whether IBM compatible, or McIntosh. ♦ *The floppy disk is the twenty-first century's electronic paper.*

**flotsam and jetsam** *n. phr.* **1.** Ruinous remains floating in the sea after a shipwreck. ♦ *The fishermen on shore saw a lot of flotsam and jetsam being moved by the waves.* **2.** Human wreckage. ♦ *On the embankment we saw the flotsam and jetsam of exhausted immigrants standing in line for admission to America.*

**flower child** *n., slang, informal* **1.** A young person who believes in nonviolence and carries flowers around to symbolize his peace-loving nature. ♦ *Flower children are supposed to be nonviolent, but they sure make a lot of noise when they demonstrate!* **2.** Any person who cannot cope with reality. ♦ *"Face facts, Suzie, stop being such a flower child!"*

**flower power** *n., slang* The supposed power of love and nonviolence as intended to be used by members of the anti-culture to change American society. ♦ *The young people were marching for flower power.*

**flowers of speech** *n. phr.* Rhetorical devices of speech; figures of speech and other stylistic embellishments. ♦ *Mr. Chisolm would be a much more* *effective speaker if he didn't use so many tired, old, and trite flowers of speech.*

**fluff stuff** *n.*, *slang, citizen's band radio jargon* Snow. ♦*We can expect some fluff stuff this afternoon.*

**flunk out** *v. phr.* To have to withdraw from school or college because of too many failing grades. ♦*Fred flunked out of college during his junior year.*

**flush it** *v. phr., slang* **1.** To fail (something). ♦*I really flushed it in my math course.* **2.** *interj., used imperatively* Expression registering refusal to believe something considered stupid or false. ♦*"You expect me to buy that story? Flush it!"*

**fly at one's throat** *v. phr.* To attack you suddenly with great anger. ♦*When Tom called Dick a bad name, Dick flew at his throat.*

**fly ball** *n.* A baseball hit high into the air. ♦*He hit an easy fly ball to center field.*

**fly blind** *v. phr.* **1.** To fly an airplane by instruments alone. ♦*In the heavy fog he had to fly blind.* **2.** *informal* To do something without understanding what you are doing. ♦*I'm glad the car runs now; I was flying blind when I fixed it.*

**fly-by-night**[1] *adj.* Set up to make a lot of money in a hurry, then disappear so people can't find you to complain about poor work, etc.; not trustworthy; not reliable. ♦*Mrs. Blank bought her vacuum cleaner from a new company; when she tried to have it fixed, she found it was a fly-by-night business.*

**fly-by-night**[2] *n., informal* **1.** A company that sells many cheap things for a big profit and then disappears. ♦*A dependable company honors its guarantees, but a fly-by-night only wants your money.* **2.** A person who does not pay his bills, but sneaks away (as at night.) ♦*Hotels are bothered by fly-by-nights.*

**fly by the seat of one's pants** *v. phr., slang* To fly an airplane by feel and instinct rather than with the help of the instruments. ♦*Many pilots in World War I had to fly by the seat of their pants.*

**flying high** *adj., slang* Very happy; joyful. ♦*Jack was flying high after his team won the game.*

**flying tackle** *n., informal* A tackle made by jumping through the air at the person to be tackled. ♦*The policeman stopped the burglar with a flying tackle.*

**fly in the face of** *or* **fly in the teeth of** *v. phr.* To ignore; go against; show disrespect or disregard for. ♦*You can't fly in the face of good business rules and expect to be successful.*

**fly in the ointment** *n. phr., informal* An unpleasant part of a pleasant thing; something small that spoils your fun. ♦*We had a lot of fun at the beach; the only fly in the ointment was George's cutting his foot on a piece of glass.*

**fly off on a tangent** *v. phr.* To suddenly stop doing what one was engaged in and to shift to something else. ♦*John will never amount to anything in his work; he constantly flies off on a tangent and so never completes anything.*

**fly off the handle** *v. phr., informal* To become very angry. ♦*John flew off the handle whenever Mary made a mistake.* ♦*The children's noise made the man next door fly off the handle.*

**fly the coop** *v. phr., slang* To leave suddenly and secretly; run away. ♦*The robbers flew the coop before the police arrived.*

**flying visit** *n. phr.* A visit of very short duration. ♦*Tom came to New York for only a flying visit.* ♦*We had hardly eaten lunch when he had to leave.*

**fly into a rage** *or* **temper** *v. phr.* To become very angry. ♦*Each time we mention the name of her ex-husband, Sue flies into a rage.*

**foam at the mouth** *v. phr., slang* To be very angry, like a mad dog. ♦*By the time Uncle Henry had the third flat tire he was really foaming at the mouth.*

**fob off** *v., informal* **1.** To get something false accepted as good or real. ♦*The peddler fobbed off pieces of glass as diamonds.* **2.** To put aside; not really answer but get rid of. ♦*Her little brother asked where she was going, but she fobbed him off with an excuse.*

**foggy bottom** *n., slang* An area in downtown Washington, D.C. where many offices of the Department of State are located; hence figuratively, the U.S. Department of State. ♦*The press secretary gave us a lot of foggy bottom double-talk about the hostage crisis in the Near East.*

**foil one's plot** *v. phr.* To frustrate one's plans; to uncover what the enemy is up to and to take effective counter measures. ♦ *The marines found out what the terrorists were up to through excellent intelligence, so they managed to foil their plot.*

**fold up** *v., informal* To collapse; fail. ♦ *The team folded up in the last part of the season.* ♦ *The new restaurant folded up in less than a year.*

**follow in one's footsteps** *also* **follow in one's tracks** *v. phr.* To follow someone's example; follow someone exactly. ♦ *He followed in his father's footsteps and became a doctor.*

**follow one's heart** *v. phr.* To do what one wishes to do rather than to follow the voice of reason. ♦ *Instead of accepting a lucrative job in his father's business, Jim followed his heart and became a missionary in the jungle.*

**follow one's nose** *v. phr., informal* **1.** To go straight ahead; continue in the same direction. ♦ *Just follow your nose and you'll get there.* **2.** To go any way you happen to think of. ♦ *Oh, I don't know just where I want to go. I'll just follow my nose and see what happens.*

**follow out** *v. phr., informal* **1.** To do fully; finish (what you are told to do.) ♦ *The boy followed out the instructions and made a fine model plane.* **2.** To keep working at (something) until it is finished; give (something) your attention until it comes to an end or conclusion. ♦ *The student followed out all the index references in the encyclopedia until he found what he wanted to know.*

**follow suit** *v. phr.* **1.** To play a card of the same color and kind that another player has put down. ♦ *When diamonds were led, I had to follow suit.* **2.** To do as someone else has done; follow someone's example. ♦ *When the others went swimming, I followed suit.*

**follow through** *v. phr.* To finish an action that you have started. ♦ *Bob drew plans for a table for his mother, but he did not follow through by making it.*

**follow up** *v. phr., informal* **1.** To chase or follow closely and without giving up. ♦ *The hunters followed up the wounded buffalo until it fell dead.* **2.** Make (one action) more successful by doing something more. ♦ *After Mary sent a letter to*

apply for a job; she followed it up by going to talk to the personnel manager. **3a.** To hunt for (more news about something that has already been in the newspapers, radio, or TV news); find more about. ♦ *The day after news of the fire at Brown's store, the newspaper sent a reporter to follow up Mr. Brown's future plans.* **3b.** To print or broadcast (more news about some happening that has been in the news before). ♦ *The fire story was printed Monday, and Tuesday's paper followed it up by saying that Mr. Brown planned to build a bigger and better store at the same place.*

**follow-up** *n.* Additional work or research by means of which an earlier undertaking's chances of success are increased. ♦ *I hope you'll be willing to do a bit of follow-up.*

**fond of** Having a liking for; attracted to by strong liking. ♦ *Alan is fond of candy.* ♦ *Uncle Bill was the children's favorite, and he was fond of them too.*

**food for thought** *n. phr.* Something to think about or worth thinking about; something that makes you think. ♦ *The teacher told John that she wanted to talk to his father, and that gave John food for thought.* ♦ *There is much food for thought in this book.*

**fool and his money are soon parted** A foolish person soon wastes his money.—A proverb. ♦ *Jimmy spends all his pennies for candy. A fool and his money are soon parted.*

**fool around** *or* **mess around** *or* **play around** *or* **monkey around** *v., informal* **1.** To spend time playing, fooling, or joking instead of being serious or working; waste time. ♦ *If you go to college, you must work, not fool around.* **2.** To treat or handle carelessly. ♦ *Bob cut himself by fooling around with a sharp knife.* ♦ *Suzie says she wishes John would quit playing around with the girls and get married.* **3.** *or* **fiddle around** To work or do something in an irregular or unplanned way; tinker. ♦ *Jimmy likes to monkey around with automobile engines.*

**fool away** *or* **fritter away** *v., informal* To waste foolishly. ♦ *Paul failed history because he fooled away his time instead of studying.* ♦ *The man won a lot of* *money, but he soon frittered it away and was poor again.*

**foolproof** *adj.* So constructed that not even a fool can spoil it; easy. ♦ *This entrance examination is so easy that it is actually foolproof.*

**fools rush in where angels fear to tread** Often heard when unwise people rashly and thoughtlessly tackle situations when even the most circumspect take their time assessing the odds, and think twice about how to proceed.—A proverb. ♦ *It's no good to choose war as one's first option; diplomacy should be tried first—only fools rush in where angels fear to tread.*

**foot in the door** *n. phr., informal* The first step toward getting or doing something; a start toward success; opening. ♦ *Don't let Jane get her foot in the door by joining the club or soon she'll want to be president.*

**footloose and fancy-free** *adj. phr.* Free and free to do what one wants (said of unmarried men). ♦ *Ron is a merry bachelor and seems to enjoy greatly being footloose and fancy-free.*

**foot the bill** *v. phr.* To cover the expenses of; pay for something. ♦ *The bride's father footed two-thirds of the bill for his daughter's wedding.* Compare PICK UP THE TAB.

**for all 1.** In spite of; even with, despite.— Used for contrast. ♦ *For all his city ways, he is a country boy at heart.* **2.** *also* **for aught** To the extent that.— Used like a negative with *care* and *know.* ♦ *For all I care, you can throw it away.* ♦ *For all he knows, we might be in Boston.*

**for all I know** *adv. phr.* To the extent that I am familiar with the situation or the circumstances. ♦ *For all I know, Suzie may have left town.*

**for all one cares** *adv. phr.* In the opinion of one who is not involved or who does not care what happens. ♦ *For all Jane cares, poor Tom might as well drop dead.*

**for all one is worth** With all of your strength; as hard as you can. ♦ *Roger ran for all he was worth to catch the bus.*

**for all one knows** *adv. phr.* According to the information one has; probably. ♦ *For all we know, Ron and Beth might have eloped and been married in a French chateau.*

**for all that** *adv. phr.* In spite of what has been said, alleged, or rumored. ♦ *Well, for all that, we think that she is still the most deserving candidate for Congress.*

**for all the world** *adv. phr.* **1.** Under no circumstances. ♦ *Betty said she wouldn't marry Jake for all the world.* **2.** Precisely; exactly. ♦ *It began for all the world like a successful baseball season for the UIC Flames, when suddenly they lost to the Blue Demons.*

**for as much as** *conj., formal* Because; since. ♦ *For as much as the senator is eighty years old, we feel he should not run for reelection.*

**for a song** *adv. phr., informal* At a low price; for a bargain price; cheaply. ♦ *They bought the house for a song and sold it a few years later at a good profit.*

**for a while** *adv. phr.* For a short period of time. ♦ *For a while I used to think that I'd become a musician, but soon enough I changed my mind and went into medicine.*

**for better or worse** *or* **for better or for worse** *adv. phr.* **1.** With good or bad effect, depending on how one looks at the matter. ♦ *The historian did justice, for better or worse, to the careers of several famous men.* **2.** Under any eventuality; forever; always. ♦ *Alex and Masha decided to leave Moscow and come to Chicago, for better or for worse.* **3.** *(Marriage vows)* Forever, for as long as one may live. ♦ *With this ring I thee wed, for richer or poorer, in sickness and in health, for better or worse, til death do us part.*

**forbidden fruit** *n. phr.* **1.** Something stolen. ♦ *"What's all that fancy stuff you're carrying in your pockets?" Jim asked. "We knocked off a small jeweler yesterday evening and this is my forbidden fruit," Fred answered.* **2.** Illicit pleasure. ♦ *Sleeping with another man's wife is forbidden fruit.*

**force one's hand** *v. phr.* To make you do something or tell what you will do sooner than planned. ♦ *Ben did not want to tell where he was going, but his friend forced his hand.*

**force to be reckoned with** *n. phr.* A formidable organization, power, or individual person. ♦ *The new boss' wife doesn't say very much, but she sure is a force to be reckoned with.*

**for crying out loud** *informal* Used as an exclamation to show that you feel surprised or cross. ♦ *For crying out loud, look who's here!*

**for days on end** *adv. phr.* For a long time; for many days. ♦ *The American tourists tried to get used to Scottish pronunciation for days on end, but still couldn't understand what the Scots were saying.*

**for dear life** *adv. phr.* As though afraid of losing your life. ♦ *When the horse began to run, she held on for dear life.*

**foregone conclusion** *n. phr.* A conclusion or result taken for granted. ♦ *When Doolittle assumed the deanship of our college, it was a foregone conclusion that all new department heads would be his old friends.*

**forget it** See NO WAY.

**forgive and forget** *v. phr.* To finally decide to no longer think of one's past mistake or offense and to bear no grudge against the person. ♦ *Jack and Helen have been divorced for ten years, so they decided to forgive and forget all past grievances for their children's sake.*

**forever and a day** *adv. phr., informal* For a seemingly endless time; forever; always. Used for emphasis. ♦ *We waited forever and a day to find out who won the contest.*

**for example** *or* **for instance** *adv. phr.* As an example; as proof; to give an example or illustration. ♦ *Not only rich men become president. For example, Lincoln was born poor.* ♦ *There are jobs more dangerous than truck driving; for instance, training lions.*

**for fear** Because of fear. ♦ *He left an hour early for fear of missing his train.*

**for fear of** *adv. phr.* Because of being afraid of something; on account of being scared. ♦ *Dave refuses to go to Europe for fear of an airplane crash and for fear of a shipwreck.*

**for free** *adj. phr. substandard* Without having to pay; free. ♦ *Hey you guys, look at this balloon! They're for free down at the new store.*

**for fun** *prep. phr.* As amusement, not seriously, as a joke. ♦ *Let's try to play Beethoven's* Emperor *Concerto together, you on one piano, and I on another one.*

**forget oneself** *v. phr.* To do something one should have remembered not to do; do something below one's usual conduct although one knows better; let one's self-control slip. ♦ *He forgot himself only once at dinner—when he belched.*

**forgive and forget** *v.* To have no bad feelings about what happened in the past. ♦ *After the argument the boys decided to forgive and forget.*

**for good** *also* **for good and all** Permanently, forever, for always. ♦ *He hoped that the repairs would stop the leak for good.* ♦ *When John graduated from school, he decided that he was done with study for good and all.*

**for good measure** *adv. phr.* As something more added to what is expected or needed; as an extra. ♦ *He sold me the car at a cheap price and included the radio for good measure.*

**for Heaven's sake!** *adv. phr.* Please. ♦ *"Help me, for Heaven's sake!" the injured man cried.*

**for hours on end** *adv. phr.* For many hours; for a very long time. ♦ *We have been trying to get this computer going for hours on end, but we need serious professional help.*

**for instance** See FOR EXAMPLE.

**for keeps** *adv. phr.* **1.** For the winner to keep. ♦ *They played marbles for keeps.* **2.** *informal* For always; forever. ♦ *He left town for keeps.* **3.** Seriously, not just for fun. ♦ *This is not a joke, it's for keeps.*

**fork over** *or* **fork out** *also* **fork up** *v.* To pay; pay out. ♦ *He had to fork over fifty dollars to have the car repaired.* Compare HAND OVER.

**fork over a lot of money** *v. phr.* To pay an excessive amount of money often unwillingly. ♦ *"According to my divorce decree," Alan complained, "I have to fork over a lot of money to my ex-wife every month."*

**for laughs** *adv. phr.* For pleasure; for fun; as a joke. ♦ *The college boys climbed up into the girls' dorms and stole some of their dresses just for laughs, but they were punished all the same.*

**forlorn hope** *n. phr.* **1.** Something done in utter desperation. ♦ *John phoned Mary the day before she was to marry Ted in the forlorn hope that she would change her mind and marry him instead.* **2.** An undertaking that is extremely unlikely to succeed. ♦ *Trying to dig for gold in Illinois is a forlorn hope.*

**for love or money** *adv. phr.* For anything; for any price. Used in negative sentences. ♦ *I wouldn't give him my dog for love or money.*

**for nothing** *adv. phr.* In vain. ♦ *The job they advertised in Leeds, England, was canceled before my plane arrived, so both the trip and the perfunctory interview were for nothing.*

**for old times' sake** *adv. phr.* In memory of bygone times; for friendship's sake. ♦ *"When the divorced couple got old, they had dinner together every once in a while, for old times' sake.*

**for one** As the first of several possible examples; as one example. ♦ *Many people do not like certain foods. I for one do not like cabbage.*—Also used with similar words instead of *one.* ♦ *Several materials can be used to make the box: plywood, for one; masonite, for another; sheet metal, for a third.*

**for one's part** *also* **on one's part** *adv. phr.* As far as you are concerned; the way you feel or think. ♦ *I don't know about you, but for my part I don't want to go to that place.*

**for one thing** *adv. phr.* As one thing of several; as one in a list of things. ♦ *The teacher said, "You get a low mark, for one thing, because you did not do your homework."*

**for openers** *or* **for starters** *adv. phr.* To begin with; first of all. ♦ *"Why aren't we hiring new people? I'll tell you why. For openers, we have no money." "You can skip the rest," the applicant said.* ♦ *"Why does everyone flatter Dr. Doolittler constantly?" the new assistant professor asked. "For starters he is the new dean," a seasoned older colleague answered. "You want to hear more?"*

**for real**[1] *adj. phr., informal* Not practice or play; earnest, real, serious. ♦ *The war games were over now. This battle was for real.*

**for real**[2] *adv. phr., substandard* Not for practice; really; seriously. ♦ *Let's do our work for real.*

**for one's sake** *adv. phr., informal* Used with different possessive nouns to show surprise, crossness, or impatience. ♦ *For heaven's sake, where did you come from?* ♦ *For Pete's sake, look who's here!* ♦ *Well, for pity's sake, I wish you'd told me sooner.* ♦ *Oh, for gosh sake, let me do it.*

**for short** *adv. phr.* So as to make shorter; as an abbreviation or nickname. ♦ *The National Broadcasting Company is called NBC for short.*

**for sure** *or* **for certain** *adv. phr.* **1.** Without doubt; certainly; surely. ♦ *He couldn't tell for sure from a distance whether it was George or Tom.* ♦ *He didn't know for certain which bus to take.* ♦ *I know for certain that he has a car.* **2.** *slang* Certain. ♦ *"That car is smashed so badly it's no good any more." "That's for sure!"*

**for that matter** *adv. phr.* With regard to that; about that. ♦ *I don't know, and for that matter, I don't care.* ♦ *Alice didn't come, and for that matter, she didn't even telephone.*

**for the asking** *adv. phr.* By asking; by asking for it; on request. ♦ *John said I could borrow his bike any time. It was mine for the asking.*

**for the best** *adj. or adv. phr.* good or best; not bad as thought; lucky; well, happily. ♦ *Maybe it's for the best that your team lost; now you know how the other boys felt.*

**for the better** *adj. or adv. phr.* With a better result; for something that is better. ♦ *The doctor felt that moving Father to a dry climate would be for the better.*

**for the birds** *adj. phr., slang* Not interesting; dull; silly; foolish; stupid. ♦ *I think history is for the birds.* ♦ *I saw that movie. It's for the birds.*

**for the devil** *or* **heck** *or* **the hell of it** *adv. phr.* For no specific reason; just for sport and fun. ♦ *We poured salt into Uncle Tom's coffee, just for the heck of it.*

**for the life of one** *adv., informal* No matter how hard you try.—Used for emphasis with negative statements. ♦ *I can't for the life of me remember his name.*

**for the most part** *adv. phr.* In general; mostly; most of the time; commonly; generally. ♦ *European countries are, for the most part, tired of war.*

**for the sake of** *or* **for one's sake** *adv. phr.* On behalf of; for the benefit of. ♦ *For the sake of truth and freedom, Dr. Sakharov, the Soviet dissident, was willing to be banished from Moscow.*

**for the time being** *also literary* **for the nonce** *adv. phr.* For now; for a while; temporarily. ♦ *Sue hasn't found an apartment yet; she's staying with her aunt for the time being.*

**for the worse** *adj. phr. or adv. phr.* For something that is worse or not as good, with a worse result. ♦ *He bought a new car but it turned out to be for the worse.* ♦ *The sick man's condition changed for the worse.*

**for to** *prep. phr., dialect* So that you can; to. ♦ *Simple Simon went a-fishing for to catch a whale.*

**forty winks** *n. phr., informal* A short period of sleep; a nap. ♦ *When the truck driver felt sleepy, he stopped by the side of the road to catch forty winks.*

**for what it is worth** *adv. phr.* Often said when one wants to sound modest or start a statement with the disclaimer that they aren't entirely sure about the value of what they are about to communicate. Also said ironically. ♦ *In my humble opinion, for what it's worth, you ought to close the factory, since we're losing incredible sums of money.*

**foul one's own nest** *v. phr.* To denigrate one's own country or family. ♦ *Peter sure fouled his own nest when in a drunken stupor he blurted out that the family fortune started during Prohibition when his grandfather used to work for Al Capone.*

**foul play** *n.* Treachery; a criminal act (such as murder). ♦ *After they discovered the dead body, the police suspected foul play.* ♦ *"She must have met with foul play," the chief inspector said when they couldn't find the 12-year-old girl who had disappeared.*

**foul up** *v., informal* (stress on *up*) **1.** To make dirty. ♦ *The birds fouled up his newly washed car.* **2.** To tangle up. ♦ *He tried to throw a lasso but he got the rope all fouled up.* **3.** To ruin or spoil by stupid mistakes; botch. ♦ *He fouled the whole play up by forgetting his part.* **4.** To make a mistake; to blunder. ♦ *Blue suit and brown socks! He had fouled up again.* **5.** To go wrong. ♦ *Why do some people foul up and become criminals?*

**foul-up** *n.* (stress on *foul*) **1.** *informal* A confused situation; confusion; mistake. ♦ *The luncheon was handled with only one or two foul-ups.* **2.** *informal* A breakdown. ♦ *There was a foul-up in his car's steering mechanism.* **3.** *slang* A person who fouls up or mixes things. ♦ *He had gotten a reputation as a foul-up.*

**foundation garment** *n.* A close-fitting garment designed for women to wear underneath their clothes to make them look slim; a piece of woman's underwear. ♦ *Jane wears a foundation garment under her evening dress.*

**four corners** *n.* All parts of a place. ♦ *People came from the four corners of the world to see him.* ♦ *He has been to the four corners of the country.*

**four-eyes** *n., slang* A person who wears glasses.—A rude expression. ♦ *Hey, four-eyes, come over here.*

**four-leaf clover** *n.* A small green plant with four leaves which many people think means good luck because clover plants usually have three leaves. ♦ *John has a four-leaf clover in his pocket. He thinks he will have good luck now .*

**four-letter words** *n. phr.* Crude or crass language, pertaining to sex or excretion, which happens to consist of four letters; swearing. ♦ *It is bad manners to use four-letter words in front of ladies.* ♦ *Not all words that have four letters in them are "four-letter-words"; e.g.* love *and* nice, *which are l,o,v,e and n,i,c,e.*

**fourth world** *n., informal* The poor nations of the world, as distinguished from the oil-rich nations of the third world. ♦ *Sri Lanka will never join OPEC, since it is a fourth world nation.*

**fraidy-cat** *or* **fraid-cat** *or* **scaredy-cat** *or* **scared cat** *n., informal* A shy person; someone who is easily frightened.— Usually used by or to children. ♦ *Tom was a fraidy-cat and wouldn't go in the water.*

**frame of mind** *n. phr.* One's mental outlook; the state of one's psychological condition. ♦ *There is no use trying to talk to him while he is in such a negative frame of mind.*

**fraught with danger** *or* **fraught with peril** *adj. phr.* Attended with much risk or danger; likely to produce peril and harm. ♦ *All wars, no matter how just, are always fraught with danger.* ♦ *High-mountain climbing is always fraught with peril.*

**freak** *n., slang* **1.** A good, or well-liked person, the opposite of a square, someone with long hair and who is likely (or known) to be a marijuana smoker or a drug user. Also said of homosexuals. ◆ *Is Joe a square, establishment type?—Oh no, he's a regular freak.* **2.** ——— **freak** An enthusiast, a person who does or cultivates something in excess. ◆ *Ellen is a film-freak.*

**freak-out**[1] *n., slang* An act of losing control; a situation that is bizarre or unusual. ◆ *The party last night was a regular freak-out.*

**freak out**[2] *v. phr., slang* To lose control over one's conscious self due to the influence of hallucinogenic drugs. ◆ *Joe freaked out last night.*

**free agent** *n.* A professional player who does not have a contract with a team. ◆ *The Giants signed two free agents who had been released by the Cardinals.*

**free and easy** *adj.* Not strict; relaxed or careless. ◆ *They were free and easy with their money and it was soon gone.*

**free ball** *n.* A ball in football that is in play, that is not in the possession of anyone, that is not a legally thrown forward pass, and that belongs to the first team which can grab it. ◆ *A Notre Dame player fell on a free ball and recovered it for his team.*

**free enterprise** *n. phr.* A system in which private business is controlled by as few government rules as possible. ◆ *The United States is proud of its free enterprise.*

**free hand** *n.* Great freedom. ◆ *The teacher had a free hand in her classroom.*

**freeload** *v.* To have oneself supported in terms of food and housing at someone else's expense. ◆ *When are you guys going to stop freeloading and do some work?*

**free rein** *n.* Freedom to do what you want. ◆ *Father is strict with the children, but Mother gives them free rein.*

**free throw** *n.* A shot at the basket in basketball without interference from opponents. ◆ *Mike scored the winning point on a free throw.*

**free-for-all** *n.* **1.** Unlimited, free access to something everybody wants. ◆ *The Smith's party was a lavish free-for-all; everybody could eat and drink as much as they wanted.* **2.** A barroom, tavern, or street fight in which everybody participates. ◆ *The celebration after the soccer game victory turned into an uncontrollable free-for-all.*

**fret and fume** *v. phr.* To worry with the connotation of anger; vexing oneself with made-up accusations regarding the causes of one's troubles. ◆ *Poor John frets and fumes all the time about his unhappy fate, although nobody really tries to hurt him.*

**freeze out** *v., informal* To force out or keep from a share or part in something by unfriendly or dishonest treatment. ◆ *The other boys froze John out of the club.*

**freeze over** *v.* To become covered with ice. ◆ *The children wanted the lake to freeze over so they could ice-skate.*

**french fried potato** *or* **french fry** *n.* A narrow strip of potato fried in deep fat.—Usually used in the plural. ◆ *Sue ordered a hamburger and french fries.*

**French leave** *n.* The act of slipping away from a place secretly and without saying good-bye to anyone. ◆ *"It's getting late," Rob whispered to Janet. "Let's take French leave and get out of here."*

**fresh from** *adj.* Recently returned from; experienced in. ◆ *Tom was fresh from two years in Paris and was very condescending in matters pertaining to cuisine and wines.*

**friction tape** *n.* Black cloth tape with one sticky side used around electric wires. ◆ *The boy fixed his cracked baseball bat with some friction tape.*

**friend in need** *n. phr.* A dependable friend, who is likely to come to one's aid even if one is unable to offer anything in return. ◆ *As the old saying says, "A friend in need is a friend indeed."*

**friendly fire** *n. phr., military* An accident during a battle when one is shot not by the enemy but by one's own comrades in arms in error due to faulty reconnaissance. ◆ *Both during the first and the second Gulf Wars, several American and British soldiers were killed by friendly fire.*

**frightened to death** See TO DEATH.

**from A to Z** *or* **from alpha to omega** *adv. phr.* From beginning to end, taken from the Latin and the Greek alphabet's first and last letters, respectively. ♦ *Arabic students in certain schools memorize the entire Koran from A to Z.* ♦ *Some Christian theologians know the entire New Testament from alpha to omega.*

**from hand to hand** *adv. phr.* From one person to another and another. ♦ *The box of candy was passed from hand to hand.*

**from head to heels** *or* **from top to toe** *adv. phr.* In one's entirety, without skipping any detail; wholly; entirely. ♦ *The movie director looked at all the girls who wanted a part in the new film from head to heels.* ♦ *The tired athlete was aching from top to toe.*

**from Missouri** *adj. phr., slang* Doubtful; suspicious. ♦ *Don't try to fool me. I'm from Missouri.*

**from pillar to post** *adv. phr.* From one place to another many times. ♦ *Sarah's father changed jobs several times a year, and the family was moved from pillar to post.*

**from rags to riches** *adv. phr.* Suddenly making a fortune; becoming rich overnight. ♦ *The Smiths went from rags to riches when they unexpectedly won the lottery.*

**from scratch** *adv. phr., informal* With no help from anything done before; from the beginning; from nothing. ♦ *Dick built a radio from scratch.*

**from the bottom of one's heart** *or* **with all one's heart** *adv. phr.* With great feeling; sincerely. ♦ *The people welcomed the returning soldiers from the bottom of their hearts.*

**from the cradle to the grave** *adv. phr.* During all one's life, from birth to death. ♦ *John was a thoroughly decent human being from the cradle to the grave.*

**from the ground up** *adv. phr.* From the beginning; entirely; completely. ♦ *After the fire they had to rebuild their cabin from the ground up.*

**from the heart** *adv.* Sincerely; honestly. ♦ *John always speaks from the heart.*

**from the sublime to the ridiculous** *adv. phr.* Covering an entire range of things or ideas from the extremely lofty and elevated to the negligible and trivial. ♦ *The couple's prenuptial negotiations covered absolutely every detail of their future life together from the sublime to the ridiculous.*

**from the word "go"** *adv. phr.* From start to finish; completely. ♦ *He may look French but he is a New Yorker from the word "go."*

**from time immemorial** *or* **time out of mind** *adv. phr.* Starting in very remote, ancient prehistorical times. ♦ *The island of Crete in the Mediterranean was probably inhabited from time immemorial, although historians are not sure by what people.* ♦ *Some Greek myths have started in prehistorical ages, time out of mind.*

**from time to time** *adv. phr.* Not often; not regularly; sometimes; occasionally; at one time and then again at another time. ♦ *Even though the Smiths have moved, we still see them from time to time.* ♦ *Mother tries new recipes from time to time, but the children never like them.*

**from way back** *adv. phr.* From a previous time; from a long time ago. ♦ *They have known one another from way back when they went to the same elementary school.*

**front and center** *adv., slang* Used as a command to a person to go to someone who wants him. ♦ *Front and center, Smith. The boss wants to see you.*

**front court** *n.* The half of a basketball court that is a basketball team's offensive zone. ♦ *The guard brought the ball up to the front court.*

**front office** *n., informal* The group of persons who manage a business; the officers. ♦ *The front office decides how much the workers are paid.*

**frown upon** *v. phr.* To look with disfavor upon somebody or something. ♦ *Everybody in her family frowns upon her attachment to him.*

**frozen to the marrow** See CHILLED TO THE MARROW.

**fuck around** *v. phr., vulgar, avoidable* 1. To be promiscuous. ♦ *John fucks around with the secretaries.* 2. To play at something without purpose, to mess around. ♦ *He doesn't accomplish anything, because he fucks around so much.*

**fuck off** *v. phr., vulgar, avoidable* 1. Go away! ♦ *Can't you see you're bothering me? Fuck off!* 2. To be lazy. ♦ *John said*

*"I don't feel like working, so I'll fuck off today."*

**fuck up** *v. phr., vulgar, avoidable* To make a mess of something or oneself. ♦ *Because he was totally unprepared, he fucked up his exam.* ♦ *He is so fucked up he doesn't know whether he is coming or going.*

**fuck-up** *n. vulgar, avoidable* A mess; a badly botched situation. ♦ *What a fuck-up the dissolution of the USSR created!*

**fuddy-duddy** *n.* A person whose ideas and habits are old-fashioned. ♦ *His students think Professor Jones is an old fuddy-duddy.*

**full blast** *adv.* At full capacity. ♦ *With all the research money at their disposal, the new computer firm was going ahead full blast.*

**full-bodied** *adj.* Mature; of maximum quality. ♦ *The wines from that region in California have a rich, full-bodied flavor.*

**full-fledged** *adj.* Having everything that is needed to be something; complete. ♦ *A girl needs three years of training to be a full-fledged nurse.*

**full of oneself** *adj. phr., informal* Interested only in yourself. ♦ *Joe would be a nice boy if he would stop being so full of himself.*

**full of the moon** *n. phr., literary* The moon when it is seen as a full circle; the time of a full moon. ♦ *The robbers waited for a dark night when the full of the moon was past.*

**full tilt** *adv.* At full speed; at high speed. ♦ *He ran full tilt into the door and broke his arm.*

**fun and games** *n., slang, informal* **1.** A party or other entertaining event. **2.** Something trivially easy. **3.** Petting, or sexual intercourse. **4.** (Ironically) An extraordinary difficult task. ♦ *How was your math exam? (With a dismayed expression):—Yeah, it was all fun and games, man.*

**fun house** *n.* A place where people see many funny things and have tricks played on them to make them laugh or have a good time. ♦ *The boys and girls had a good time looking at themselves in mirrors in the fun house.*

**funny bone** *n.* **1.** The place at the back of the elbow that hurts like electricity when accidentally hit. ♦ *He hit his funny bone on the arm of the chair.* **2.** *or informal* **crazy bone** Sense of humor; understanding jokes. ♦ *Her way of telling the story tickled his funny bone.*

**fuss and feathers** *n., informal* Unnecessary bother and excitement. ♦ *She is full of fuss and feathers this morning.*

**gain ground** v. phr. **1.** To go forward; move ahead. ◆ *The soldiers fought hard and began to gain ground.* **2.** To become stronger; make progress; improve. ◆ *Under Lincoln, the Republican Party gained ground.*

**gain steam** v. phr. To increase in momentum. ◆ *People's interest in protecting the environment has gained steam in recent years.*

**gallows' humor** n. phr. Bitter joke(s) that make fun of a very serious matter, e.g. death, imprisonment, etc. ◆ *When the criminal was led to the electric chair on Monday morning, he said, "Nice way to start the week, eh?"*

**gamble on that** or **may gamble on that** v. phr. Said about something that is very certain as assurance. ◆ *"Is the sun going to shine in Hawaii?" John, who has never been there, asked Leilani. "You may gamble on that," she answered with a smile.*

**game at which two can play** n. phr. A plan, trick, or way of acting that both sides may use. ◆ *Rough football is a game two can play.* ◆ *Politics is a game at which two can play.*

**game is up** or slang **jig is up** The secret or plan won't work; we are caught or discovered. ◆ *The jig's up; the principal knows the boys have been smoking in the basement.*

**gang up on** or **gang up against** v. phr., informal To jointly attack someone, either physically or verbally; take sides in a group against an individual. ◆ *The class bully was stronger than all the other boys, so they had to gang up on him to put him in his place.*

**garage sale** or **yard sale** n. phr. A sale organized in order to get rid of unwanted, older things. ◆ *Our neighbors are having a garage sale and put up posters all over the neighborhood on trees and lampposts.*

**garbage down** v. phr., slang To eat eagerly and at great speed without much regard for manners or social convention. ◆ *The children garbaged down their food.*

**garbage in—garbage out** n. phr. A computer doesn't put out anything that was not programmed into it by a human being, whether meaningful or meaningless material. ◆ *"I don't trust the data coming out of my personal computer," Uncle Norman said. "Not to worry," his wife Christine answered, "it's garbage in—garbage out. We'll make sure that what goes in is accurate to begin with."*

**garden apartment** n. An apartment with a garden near it. ◆ *The couple live in a garden apartment.*

**garden state** n. phr. The nickname of the state of New Jersey. ◆ *I can tell that the car ahead of us is from New Jersey; it says "Garden State" on the license plate.*

**gas guzzler** n. phr. A larger automobile, such as an SUV, or one of older vintage that consumes much more gasoline than a smaller, newer model. ◆ *John spends a lot of money on gasoline, because he drives a gas guzzler.*

**gas up** v., informal **1.** To fill the gasoline tank. ◆ *The mechanics gassed up the planes for their long trip.* **2.** To fill the tank with gasoline. ◆ *The big truck stopped at the filling station and gassed up.*

**gather in** v. informal To catch. ◆ *The end gathered in the pass and went over for a touchdown.*

**gee whiz** interj., informal Used as an exclamation to show surprise or other strong feeling. Rare in written English. ◆ *Gee whiz! I am late again.*

**generation gap** n., informal, hackneyed phrase The difference in social values, philosophies, and manners between children and their parents, teachers and relatives which causes a lack of understanding between them and frequently leads to violent confrontations. ◆ *My daughter is twenty and I am forty, but we have no generation gap in our family.*

**generous to a fault** adj. phr. Excessively generous. ◆ *Generous to a fault, my Aunt Elizabeth gave away all her rare books to her old college.*

**germane to the matter** or **germane to the subject** adj. phr. Pertinent or relevant to a given subject. ◆ *What you say* *sounds interesting, but it isn't strictly germane to the subject.*

**get a black eye** *v. phr.* **1.** To receive a dark ring around the eye after being hit by someone's fist or an object. ♦*In the fistfight Tom got a black eye from Pete.* ♦*Sue got a black eye when she ran into a tree.* **2.** To have one's character denigrated. ♦*Our firm received a black eye because of all the consumer complaints that were lodged against our product.*

**get a break** *v. phr.* To receive a stroke of luck. ♦*Bill got a break when he won the lottery.*

**get a checkup** *v. phr.* Undergo a medical examination. ♦*It is a good idea to get a periodic checkup, especially after one has been in the hospital.*

**get accustomed to** *or* **grow accustomed to** *v. phr.* To become thoroughly familiar with something to the point of missing it when it goes away. ♦*Immigrants to the United States sooner or later all get accustomed to talking about dimes, nickels, and pennies, as they also get accustomed to inches, miles, pounds, and measuring temperature in Fahrenheit.*

**get across** *v.* **1.** To explain clearly, make (something) clear; to make clear the meaning of. ♦*Mr. Brown is a good coach because he can get across the plays.* **2.** To become clear. ♦*The teacher tried to explain the problem, but the explanation did not get across to the class.*

**get a feel for** *or* **get the hang of** *v. phr.* To gain an understanding of how something works, to become more skilled at handling something. ♦*I was trying to learn how to play chess, but I can't seem to get a feel for it.* ♦*John practiced surfing long enough, until he got the hang of it.*

**get a fix** *or* **give a fix** *v. phr., slang, drug culture* To provide (someone) with an injection of narcotics. ♦*The neighborhood pusher gave Joe a fix.* Contrast GET A FIX ON.

**get a fix on** *v. phr., informal* Receive a reading of a distant object by electronic means, as by radar or sonar. ♦*Can you get a fix on the submarine?* Contrast GET A FIX.

**get after** *v., informal* **1.** To try or try again to make someone do what he is supposed to do. ♦*Ann's mother gets after her to hang up her clothes.* **2.** To scold or make an attack on. ♦*The police are getting after the crooks in the city.*

**get a grip on** *v. phr.* To take firm control of something. ♦*If Tim wants to keep his job, he had better get a grip on himself and start working harder.* Contrast LOSE ONE'S GRIP.

**get ahead** *v.* **1.** *informal* To become successful. ♦*The person with a good education finds it easier to get ahead.* **2.** To be able to save money; get out of debt. ♦*After Father pays all the doctor bills, maybe we can get a little money ahead and buy a car.*

**get a head start on** *v. phr.* To receive preliminary help or instruction in a particular subject so that the recipient is in a favorable position compared to his or her peers. ♦*At our school, children get a head start on their reading ability thanks to a special program.*

**get (a) hold of oneself** *v. phr.* To gain composure over oneself, to stop being upset or excited. ♦*"Get hold of yourself, son!" John's father told him. "Stop yelling at your little sister, just because she put on your jacket."*

**get a leg up on one** *v. phr.* To gain an advantage over someone else. ♦*I practiced my Ping-Pong game for several weeks until at last I got a leg up on my best friend Jim, who is actually a champion.*

**get a life** *v. phr., slang* To decide to look out for oneself, to come out from one's shell, to stop being under the thumb of another. ♦*"All my life I was doing things for my husband, who treated me very shabbily. Too bad that he is dead, but at long last I'll try to get a life," the recently widowed Mrs. Goodman said.*

**get a load of** *v. phr., slang* **1.** To take a good look at; see (something unusual or interesting.)—Often used to show surprise or admiration. ♦*Get a load of Dick's new car!* **2.** To listen to carefully or with interest, especially exciting news.—Often used as a command: **1.** *Get a load of this: Alice got married yesterday!*

**get along** *also* **get on** *v.* **1.** To go or move away; move on. ♦*The policeman told the boys on the street corner to get along.* **2.** To go forward; make progress; advance. ♦ *John is getting along well in school. He is learning more every day.* **3.** To advance; become old or late. ♦ *It is getting along towards sundown.* ♦ *Grandmother is 68 and getting along.* **4.** To get or make what you need; manage. ♦ *It isn't easy to get along in the jungle.* ♦ *We can get along on $100 a week.* **5.** To live or work together in a friendly way; agree, cooperate; not fight or argue. ♦ *We don't get along with the Jones family.* ♦ *Jim and Jane get along fine together.* ♦ *Don't be hard to get along with.*

**get a kick out of** *v. phr.* To be greatly thrilled; derive pleasure from. ♦ *Tom and Marty get a kick out of playing four hands on the piano.*

**get a line on** *v. phr.* To receive special, sometimes even confidential information about something. ♦ *Before Bill accepted his new position, he got a line on how the business was being run.*

**get along** *or* **on in years** *v. phr.* To age; grow old. ♦ *My father is getting along in years; he will be ninety on his next birthday.*

**get a move on** *informal or slang* **get a wiggle on** *v. phr.* To hurry up; get going.—Often used as a command. ♦ *Get a move on, or you will be late.*

**get an eyeful** *or* **take an eyeful** *v. phr.* To have a long, careful look at something. ♦ *"Sergeant, come and take an eyeful of this terrible sight here," the policeman said, pointing at the dead body of the murder victim.* ♦ *"Take an eyeful of these wonderful paintings!" the museum director said to the special guests before opening the show.*

**get a raise** *v. phr.* To receive an increment in salary. ♦ *Because of his good work, Ted got a raise after May 1.*

**get a rise out of** *v. phr., slang* **1.** To have some fun with (a person) by making (him) angry; tease. ♦ *The boys get a rise out of Joe by teasing him about his girl friend.* **2.** *vulgar, avoid* To be sexually aroused (said of males) ♦ *Jim always gets a rise out of watching adult movies.*

**get an earful** *v. phr., informal* To hear more (of usually unwelcome news) than one expects or wishes to hear. ♦ *I asked how Tim and his wife were getting along, and I certainly got an earful.*

**get around** *v.* **1a.** To go to different places; move about. ♦ *Mary's father really gets around; Monday he was in Washington; Wednesday he was in Chicago; and today he is in New York.* **1b.** *or* **get about** To become widely known especially by being talked about. ♦ *Bad news gets around quickly.* **2a.** *informal* To get by a trick or flattery what you want from (someone). ♦ *Mary knows how to get around her father.* **2b.** *informal* To find a way of not obeying or doing; escape from. ♦ *Some people try to get around the tax laws.*

**get around to** *v.* To do (something) after putting it off; find time for. ♦ *Mr. Lee hopes to get around to washing his car next Saturday.*

**get at** *v.* **1.** To reach an understanding of; find out the meaning. ♦ *This book is very hard to get at.* **2.** To do harm to. ♦ *The cat is on the chair trying to get at the canary.* **3.** To have a chance to do; attend to. ♦ *I hope I have time to get at my homework tonight.* **4.** To mean; aim at; hint at. ♦ *What the teacher was getting at in this lesson was that it is important to speak correctly.*

**getaway car** *n. phr.* A vehicle parked near the scene of a crime in which the criminals escape. ♦ *The police intercepted the getaway car at a major crossroads.*

**get away** *v.* **1.** To get loose or get free; become free from being held or controlled; succeed in leaving; escape. ♦ *As Jim was trying the bat, it got away from him and hit Tom.* ♦ *The bank robbers used a stolen car to get away.* **2.** To begin; start. ♦ *We got away early in the morning on the first day of our vacation.*

**get away with** *v., informal* To do (something bad or wrong) without being caught or punished. ♦ *Some students get away without doing their homework.*

**get away with murder** *v. phr., informal* To do something very bad without being caught or punished. ♦ *John is scolded if he is late with his homework, but Robert gets away with murder.*

**get a word in** *or* **get a word in edgewise** *also* **get a word in edgeways** *v. phr.* To find a chance to say something when others are talking. ♦ *Mary talked so* much that Jack couldn't get a word in edgewise.

**get back at** v., informal To do something bad to (someone who has done something bad to you) hurt in return. ♦ The elephant waited many years to get back at the man who fed him red pepper.

**get back on one's feet** v. phr. To once again become financially solvent; regain one's former status and income, or health. ♦ Max got back on his feet soon after his open heart surgery. ♦ Tom's business was ruined due to the inflation, but he got back on his feet again.

**get back to one** v. phr. To recontact someone, especially by phone. ♦ "I'm sorry, I must hang up now, but I'll get back to you in an hour or so," John said to Fred on his cell phone.

**get back together** v. phr. To reconcile, to become friendly again after a disagreement, separation, or divorce. ♦ John and Mary got back together again after six years of being divorced.

**get behind** v. 1. To go too slowly; be late; do something too slowly. ♦ The post office got behind in delivering Christmas mail. 2. informal To support; help. ♦ A club is much better if members get behind their leaders. ♦ We got behind Mary to be class president. 3. informal To explain; find out the reason for. ♦ The police are questioning many people to try and get behind the bank robbery.

**get busy** v. phr. To accelerate the pace in one's activities. ♦ We've got to get busy if we want to make the deadline.

**get by** v., informal 1. To be able to go past; pass. ♦ The cars moved to the curb so that the fire engine could get by. 2. To satisfy the need or demand. ♦ Mary can get by with her old coat this winter. 3. Not to be caught and scolded or punished. ♦ The boy got by without answering the teacher's question because a visitor came in.

**get cracking** v. phr., slang, informal To hurry up, to start moving fast. (Used mostly as an imperative). ♦ Come on, you guys, let's get cracking! (Let's hurry up!)

**get credit for** v. phr. To be given points of merit, recognition, or praise for labor or intellectual contribution. ♦ Our firm got a lot of credit for developing parts of the space shuttle.

**get one down** v. phr., informal 1. To make (someone) unhappy; cause low spirits; cause discouragement. ♦ Low grades are getting Helen down. 2. To swallow; digest. ♦ The medicine was so bitter I couldn't get it down. 3. To depress a person's spirit. ♦ Working at such an awful job got Mike down.

**get down cold** v. phr. To memorize perfectly. ♦ Terry got the text of his speech down cold.

**get down off your high horse** See OFF ONE'S HIGH HORSE.

**get down to** v., informal To get started on, being on. ♦ Let's get down to work.

**get down to brass tacks** also **get down to cases** v. phr., informal To begin the most important work or business; get started on the most important things to talk about or know. ♦ A busy doctor wants his patients to get down to brass tacks.

**get down to business** or **work** v. phr. To start being serious; begin to face a problem to be solved, or a task to be accomplished. ♦ Gentlemen, I'm afraid the party is over and we must get down to business.

**get down to the nitty gritty** See GET DOWN TO BRASS TACKS.

**get dressed** v. phr. To put on all of one's usual clothing. ♦ One has to get dressed before leaving home for work.

**get even** v., informal 1. To owe nothing. ♦ Mr. Johnson has a lot of debts, but in a few years he will get even. 2. To do something bad to pay someone back for something bad; get revenge; hurt back. Jack is waiting to get even with Bill for tearing up his notebook.

**get going** v., informal 1. To excite; stir up and make angry. ♦ Talking about her freckles gets Mary going. 2. or chiefly British **get cracking** To begin to move; get started. ♦ The teacher told Walter to get going on his history lesson. ♦ The foreman told the workmen to get cracking.

**get gray hair** or **get gray** v. phr., informal To become old or gray from worrying; become very anxious or worried. Often used with over. ♦ "If John doesn't join the team, I won't get gray hair over it," the coach said.

**get his** *or* **hers** *v. phr.* To receive one's proper reward or punishment. ♦*Tim will get his when his wife finds out that he's been seeing other women.*

**get hitched** *v. phr.* To get married. ♦*After a long period of dating, Fred and Mary finally got hitched.*

**get hold of** *v.* **1.** To get possession of. ♦*Little children sometimes get hold of sharp knives and cut themselves.* **2.** To find a person so you can speak with him. ♦*Mr. Thompson spent several hours trying to get hold of his lawyer.*

**get in** *v. phr.* **1.** To be admitted. ♦*Andy wants to go to medical school but his grades aren't good enough for him to get in.* **2.** To arrive. ♦*What time does the plane from New York get in?* **3.** To enter. ♦*"Get in the car, and let's go,"* Tom said in a hurry.* **4.** To put in stock; receive. ♦*The store just got in a new shipment of shoes from China.*

**get in on** *v. phr.* To be permitted to participate; become privy to; be included. ♦*This is your chance to get in on a wonderful deal with the new company if you're willing to make an investment.*

**get in on the ground floor** *v. phr.* To be one of the first members or employees to participate in the growth of a firm, educational institution, etc. ♦*Mr. Smith who joined the new college as an instructor, got in on the ground floor, and wound up as its president after twenty years.*

**get in on the** *or* **one's act** *v. phr.* To do something because others are engaged in the same act; join others. ♦*John's business is succeeding so well that both of his brothers want to get in on the act.*

**get in one's hair** See IN ONE'S HAIR.

**get in one's way** See IN ONE'S WAY.

**get in the way** *v. phr.* To block the progress of someone or something, either physically or otherwise, e.g., socially, emotionally, etc. ♦*The huge truck got in the way of John's car, so he had to sit and wait until it moved away.* ♦*My poor health got in the way of my work.*

**get into** See BE INTO SOMETHING.

**get in(to)** *v. phr.* To enter. ♦*I can't get into my apartment, as I lost my keys.*

**get into line** *v. phr.* To cooperate; conform. ♦*The maverick members of the party were advised to get into line unless they wanted to be expelled.*

**get into the spirit** *v. phr.* To become greatly interested or enthusiastic about something. ♦*The religious holidays are times of the year when people usually get into the spirit of charity and family togetherness.*

**get it** *v. phr.* To understand. ♦*The professor certainly knows a great deal, but he talks so fast that half of the class just doesn't get what he's talking about.* ♦*"Did you get what I said?" "Yes I got it; message received loud and clear."*

**get it backwards** *v. phr.* To misunderstand, to arrive at the wrong interpretation of something. ♦*"No you silly, Joan didn't leave her husband, Peter left her. You got it backwards."*

**get in with** *v. phr.* To join up with; begin to associate with; be accepted by. ♦*He got in with the wrong gang of boys and wound up in jail.* ♦*She got in with her father's firm and made a successful career of it.*

**get in wrong** *v. phr.* To incur the anger or dislike of someone; come into disfavor. ♦*Although he means well, Fred is always getting in wrong with someone at the office.*

**get it** *v.* To understand; comprehend; grasp. ♦*"I can't get it," John said. "Why do you spend so much on clothes."*

**get it all together** *v. phr.* **1.** To be in full possession and control of one's mental faculties; have a clear purpose well pursued. ♦*You've sure got it all together, haven't you?* **2.** Retaining one's self-composure under pressure. ♦*A few minutes after the burglars left he got it all together and called the police.* **3.** To be well built, stacked (said of girls and women.) ♦*Sue's sure got it all together, hasn't she?*

**get (it** *or* **something) in** *or* **into one's head** *v. phr.* To become possessed of an idea; develop a fixed idea. ♦*Jack got it into his head to become a marine and nothing we could say would make him change his mind.*

**get lost** *v. phr., slang* Go away!—Used as a command. ♦*Get lost! I want to study.* ♦*John told Bert to get lost.*

**get mixed up** See MIXED UP.

**get more than one bargained for** *phrasal idiom* To get more in a pejorative sense than what one expected to get.

♦ *After the childless couple used fertility pills to have a child, they had quadruplets, which was a lot more than they bargained for.*

**get off** v. 1. To come down from or out of. ♦ *The ladder fell, and Tom couldn't get off the roof.* ♦ *The bus stopped, the door opened, and Father got off.* 2. To take off. ♦ *Joe's mother told him to get his wet clothes off.* 3. To get away; leave. ♦ *Mr. Johnson goes fishing whenever he can get off from work.* ♦ *William got off early in the morning.* 4. To go free. ♦ *Mr. Andrews got off with a $5 fine when he was caught passing a stop sign.* 5. To make (something) go. ♦ *John got a letter off to his grandmother.* 6. To tell. ♦ *The governor got off several jokes at the beginning of his speech.* 7. To write a quick letter or note to someone. ♦ *I got off a Christmas card just in time to my relatives.* 8. *sexual taboo, avoidable* To ejaculate. ♦ *If you think administrative work makes me get off, you are sadly mistaken.*

**get off cheap** v. phr. 1. To receive a lesser punishment than one deserves. ♦ *Ted could have been sentenced to fifteen years in prison; he got off cheap by receiving a reduced sentence of five years.* 2. To pay less than the normal price. ♦ *If you had your car repaired for only $75, you got off cheap.*

**get off easy** v. phr., informal To have only a little trouble; escape something worse. ♦ *John got off easy because it was the first time he had taken his father's car without permission.*

**get off on a tangent** See FLY OFF ON A TANGENT.

**get off one's back** v. phr., slang, colloquial To stop criticizing or nagging someone. ♦ *"Get off my back! Can't you see how busy I am?"*

**get off one's case** or **back** or **tail** v. phr. To stop bothering and constantly checking up on someone; quit hounding one. ♦ *"Get off my case!" he cried angrily. "You're worse than the cops."*

**get off one's tail** v. phr., slang To get busy, to start working. ♦ *OK you guys! Get off your tails and get cracking!*

**get off on the wrong foot** v. phr. To make a bad start; begin with a mistake. ♦ *Peggy got off on the wrong foot with her new teacher; she chewed gum in class and the teacher didn't like it.*

**get off the ground** v. phr., informal To make a successful beginning; get a good start; go ahead; make progress. ♦ *Our plans for a party didn't get off the ground because no one could come.*

**get off to a flying** or **running start** v. phr. To have a promising or successful beginning. ♦ *Ron got off to a flying start in business school when he got nothing but A's.*

**get on** or **get onto** v., informal 1. To speak to (someone) roughly about something he did wrong; blame; scold. ♦ *Mrs. Thompson got on the girls for not keeping their rooms clean.* ♦ *The fans got on the new shortstop after he made several errors.* 2. To grow older. ♦ *Work seems harder these days; I'm getting on, you know.*

**get one's act together** v. phr. To control one's performance at work or in one's personal affairs more efficiently than before. ♦ *Democracy would prevail much more easily in many parts of the world if the intelligentsia in the countries concerned could only get their act together.*

**get one's back up** v. phr., informal To become or make angry or stubborn. ♦ *Fred got his back up when I said he was wrong.*

**get one's brains fried** v. phr., slang also used colloquially 1. To sit in the sun and sunbathe for an excessive length of time. ♦ *Newcomers to Hawaii should be warned not to sit in the sun too long—they'll get their brains fried.* 2. To get high on drugs. ♦ *He can't make a coherent sentence anymore—he's got his brains fried.*

**get on one's case** v. phr. To keep checking up on someone; to put pressure on someone; to keep bothering someone. ♦ *Peter's parents are always getting on his case to find a nice girl to marry and start a family of his own.*

**get one's dander up** or **get one's Irish up** v. phr. To become or make angry. ♦ *The boy got his dander up because he couldn't go to the store.* ♦ *The children get the teacher's dander up when they make a lot of noise.*

**get one's ducks in a row** v. phr., informal To get everything ready. ♦ *The scoutmaster told the boys to get their ducks in a row before they went to camp.*

**get one's feet on the ground** See FEET ON THE GROUND.

**get one's feet wet** *v. phr., informal* To begin; do something for the first time.

**get one's foot in the door** See FOOT IN THE DOOR.

**get one's gears turning** *v. phr.* To start thinking in a novel and creative way in order to achieve a certain goal, such as solving a knotty problem. ♦ *You need to get your gears turning if you want to win the competition on building the new metropolitan airport.*

**get one's goat** *v. phr., informal* To make a person disgusted or angry. ♦ *The boy's laziness all summer got his father's goat.* ♦ *The slow service at the cafe got Mr. Robinson's goat.*

**get one's hands on** See LAY ONE'S HANDS ON.

**get one's number** *or* **have one's number** *v. phr., informal* To find out or know what kind of person somebody is. ♦ *The girls got their new roommate's number the first week of school.*

**get one's rear in gear** *v. phr., slang* To hurry up, to get going. ♦ *I'm gonna have to get my rear in gear.*

**get one's second wind** See SECOND WIND.

**get one's signals crossed** *or* **get one's wires crossed** *v. phr.* To communicate with someone so as to result in misunderstanding, either because of the language used, or bad telephone connection, etc. ♦ *I thought we were going to meet for lunch on Wednesday, but when my friend didn't show up I called him, and he swore he thought it was going to be on Thursday. Apparently we got our signals crossed.*

**get one's teeth into** *or* **sink one's teeth into** *v. phr., informal* To have something real or solid to think about; go to work on seriously; struggle with. ♦ *Frank chose a subject for his report that he could sink his teeth into.*

**get on one's good side** *v. phr.* To gain the favor of someone; flatter or please another. ♦ *A clever lobbyist knows how to get on the good side of both the House of Representatives and the Senate.*

**get on one's nerves** *v. phr.* To make you nervous. *John's noisy eating habits get on your nerves.* ♦ *Children get on their parents' nerves by asking so many questions.*

**get one** *or* **something off one's mind** *v. phr.* To make a deliberate effort to forget some strange or unhappy event or person in one's life; an effort not to dwell on some past misery. ♦ *Many sensitive viewers have a hard time getting the image of wounded children off their minds.* ♦ *John was trying very hard to get his former girlfriend, Mary, off his mind.*

**get one's way** *v. phr.* To see to it that matters turn out according to one's own wishes. ♦ *It is a bad sign in a marriage if one party always gets his or her way.* ♦ *In a group of people it is usually the most strong-willed person who gets his or her way.*

**get one's wires crossed** See GET ONE'S SIGNALS CROSSED.

**get one wrong** *v. phr.* To misinterpret; misunderstand another. ♦ *Don't get me wrong; I didn't mean to criticize you.*

**get on the stick** *v. phr., slang, informal* To get moving; to stop being idle and to start working vigorously. ♦ *All right, man, let's get on the stick!* Compare ON THE BALL, GET OFF ONE'S TAIL.

**get on to one** *v. phr.* To figure someone out; understand what someone else is up to. ♦ *The FBI is on to Jim's secret trading with the enemy.*

**get** *or* **have one's say** See DAY IN COURT.

**get out** *v. phr.* **1.** leave or depart. ♦ *"Get out of here!" the teacher shouted angrily to the misbehaving student.* ♦ *"Driver, I want to get out by the opera."* **2.** To publish; produce. ♦ *Our press is getting out two new books on ecology.* **3.** To escape; leak out. ♦ *We must not let the news about this secret invention get out.*

**get out and around** *v. phr.* To leave home to participate in some social activity. ♦ *John gets out and around so much that he is in danger of becoming a social butterfly.*

**get out of** *v. phr.* **1.** To be excused from; avoid. ♦ *He got out of jury duty because of his illness.* **2.** To gain from; extract from. ♦ *Tom complained that he didn't get anything out of the course on grammar.*

**get out of the way** See OUT OF THE WAY.

**get out of hand** See OUT OF HAND, OUT OF CONTROL.

**get over** v. **1.** To finish. ♦ *Tom worked fast to get his lesson over.* **2.** To pass over. ♦ *It was hard to get over the muddy road.* **3.** To get well from; recover from. ♦ *The man returned to work after he got over his illness.* **4.** To accept or forget (a sorrow or suprise.) ♦ *It is hard to get over the death of a member of your family.*

**get popped** v. phr. slang To get shot. ♦ *If you walk around in this particular neighborhood at night, you might get popped.*

**get rattled** v. phr. To become confused, overexcited, or nervous. ♦ *The thief got so rattled when he saw the police following him that he drove his car into a ditch.*

**get real** v. phr., informal To come to grips with reality; to face facts as they really are. ♦ *"Stop daydreaming, my dear,"* Mike said to his sister. *"You'll never win the lottery and your husband isn't coming back. Get real—you need a job!"*

**get rid of** See RID OF.

**get set** v. phr. To get ready to start. ♦ *The runners got set.* ♦ *The seniors are getting set for the commencement.*

**get smart with one** v. phr. To start sassing someone; to answer back impudently; to act like a know-it-all. ♦ *When Johnny started to argue with his father about absolutely everything as if he knew more than his dad, Mr. Smith admonished his son: "Don't you get smart with me, young man, or I'll cut your weekly allowance."*

**get someone going** v. phr. To have someone believe a story that isn't true; to tease someone. ♦ *You really got me going there for a while when you said that you won some money on the lottery and that you'll take me to Paris.*

**get something out of one's system** v. phr. **1.** To eliminate some food item or drug from one's body. ♦ *John will feel much better once he gets the addictive sleeping pills out of his system.* **2.** To free oneself of yearning for something in order to liberate oneself from an unwanted preoccupation. ♦ *Ted bought a new cabin cruiser that he'd been wanting for a long time, and he says he is glad that he's finally got it out of his system.*

**get something over with** See OVER WITH 1.

**get something straight** v. phr. To clearly comprehend an issue. ♦ *"Let me get this straight,"* Burt said. *"You want $85,000 for this miserable shack?"*

**get stoned** v. phr., slang To become very drunk or high on some drug. ♦ *Poor Fred was so stoned that Tom had to carry him up the stairs.*

**get stuck** v. phr. **1.** To be victimized; be cheated. ♦ *The Smiths sure got stuck when they bought that secondhand car; it broke down just two days after they got it.* **2.** To become entrapped or embroiled in a physical, emotional, or social obstacle so as to be unable to free oneself. ♦ *Tom and Jane are stuck in a bad marriage.*

**get (all) the breaks** v. phr. To be fortunate; have luck. ♦ *That fellow gets all the breaks! He's been working here only six months, and he's already been promoted to vice president!*

**get the ax** v. phr., slang **1.** To be fired from a job. ♦ *Poor Joe got the ax at the office yesterday.* **2.** To be dismissed from school for improper conduct, such as cheating. *Joe got caught cheating on his final exam and he got the ax.* **3.** To have a quarrel with one's sweetheart or steady ending in a termination of the relationship. ♦ *Joe got the ax from Betsie—they won't see each other again.*

**get the ball rolling** or **set the ball rolling** or **start the ball rolling** informal To start an activity or action; make a beginning; begin. ♦ *George started the ball rolling at the party by telling a new joke.*

**get the better of** or **get the best of** v. phr. **1.** To win over, beat; defeat. ♦ *Our team got the best of the visitors in the last quarter.* ♦ *George got the better of Robert in a game of checkers.* **2.** or **have the best of** or **have the better of** To win or be ahead in (something); gain most from (something.) *Bill traded an old bicycle tire for a horn; he got the best of that deal.*

**get the bounce** or **get the gate** v. phr., slang **1.** or **get the air** To lose one's sweetheart; not be kept for a friend or lover. ♦ *Joe is sad because he just got the gate from his girl.* ♦ *Shirley was afraid she might get the air from her* boyfriend if she went out with other boys while he was away. **2.** or **get the sack** also **get the hook** To be fired; lose a job. ♦ *Uncle Willie can't keep a job; he got the sack today for sleeping on the job.* ♦ *You're likely to get the bounce if you are absent from work too much.*

**get the brush-off** v. phr., slang **1.** To be paid no attention; not be listened to or thought important. ♦ *My idea for a party got the brush-off from the other students.* **2.** To be treated in an unkind or unfriendly way; be ignored. ♦ *Frank and Jane had an argument, so the next time he telephoned her, he got the brush-off.*

**get the drift** or **get my drift** or **get someone's drift** v. phr. To begin to understand what someone else means without being completely specific. ♦ *"I think I am beginning to get the drift," John said, when his boss explained the ruinous state of the economy. "No raises next year, right?" "I'm afraid so," his boss answered.*

**get the eye** v. phr., informal **1.** To be looked at, especially with interest and liking. ♦ *The pretty girl got the eye as she walked past the boys on the street corner.* **2.** To be looked at or stared at, especially in a cold, unfriendly way. ♦ *When Mary asked if she could take home the fur coat and pay later, she got the eye from the clerk.*

**get the feel of** v. phr. To become used to or learn about, especially by feeling or handling; get used to the experience or feeling of; get skill in. ♦ *You'll get the feel of the job after you've been there a few weeks.*

**get the go-ahead** or **the green light** v. phr. To receive the permission or signal to start or to proceed. ♦ *We had to wait until we got the go-ahead on our research project.*

**get the goods on** or **have the goods on** v. phr. slang To find out true and, often, bad information about; discover what is wrong with; be able to prove the guilt of. ♦ *The police had the goods on the burglar before he came to trial.*

**get the hang of** See GET A FEEL FOR.

**get the jitters** v. phr. To become very nervous or excited. ♦ *I always get the jitters when I sit in an airplane that's about to take off.*

**get the jump on** or **have the jump on** v. phr., slang To get ahead of; start before (others); have an advantage over. ♦ *Our team got the jump on their rivals in the first minutes of play, and held the lead to win.*

**get the lead out of one's pants** v. phr., slang To get busy; work faster. ♦ *The coach told the players to get the lead out of their pants.*

**get the lowdown on** v. phr. To receive the full inside information on a person or thing. ♦ *We need to get the lowdown on Peter before we can decide whether or not to hire him.*

**get the message** or **get the word** v. phr., slang To understand clearly what is meant. ♦ *The principal talked to the students about being on time, and most of them got the message.*

**get the sack** v. phr., slang **1.** To be fired or dismissed from work. ♦ *John got the sack at the factory last week.* **2.** To be told by one's lover that the relationship is over. ♦ *Joanna gave Sam the sack.*

**get the show on the road** v. phr., informal To start a program; get work started. ♦ *It was several years before the rocket scientists got the show on the road.*

**get the worst of** also **have the worst of** v. phr. To lose; be defeated or beaten in; suffer most. ♦ *Joe got the worst of the argument with Molly.* Often used in the phrase *the worst of it.* If you start a fight with Jim, you may get the worst of it. ♦ *The driver of the car got the worst of it in the accident.*

**get through** v. phr. **1.** To finish. ♦ *Barry got through his homework by late evening.* **2.** To pass a course or an examination. ♦ *I got through every one of my courses except mathematics.*

**get through one's head** v. phr. **1.** To understand or believe. ♦ *Jack couldn't get it through his head that his father wouldn't let him go to camp if his grades didn't improve.* **2.** To make someone understand or believe. ♦ *I'll get it through his head if it takes all night.*

**get through to** v. To be understood by; make (someone) understand. ♦ *When the rich boy's father lost his money, it took a long time for the idea to get* *through to him that he'd have to work and support himself.*

**get to** *v. phr., informal* **1.** To begin by chance; begin to.—Used with a verbal noun or an infinitive. ♦*I got to know Mary at the party.* ♦*I was just getting to know John when he moved away.* **2.** To have a chance to; be able to. *The Taylors wanted to go to the beach Saturday, but it rained and they didn't get to.* ♦*Did you get to see the king?*

**get to first base** *or* **reach first base** *v. phr.* To make a good start; really begin; succeed. ♦*Joe had a long paper to write for history class, but when the teacher asked for it, Joe hadn't got to first base yet.* ♦*Suppose Sam falls in love with Betty. Can he even get to first base with her?* ♦*If you don't dress neatly, you won't get to first base when you look for a job.*

**get together** *v.* To come to an agreement; agree. ♦*Mother says I should finish my arithmetic lesson, and Father says I should mow the lawn. Why don't you two get together?*

**get-together** *n.* A party; a gathering. ♦*I hate to break up this nice get-together but we must leave.*

**get to the bottom of** *v. phr.* To find out the real cause of. ♦*The doctor made several tests to get to the bottom of the man's headaches.*

**get to the heart of** *v. phr.* To find the most important facts about or the central meaning of; understand the most important thing about. ♦*You can often get to the heart of people's unhappiness by letting them talk.*

**get to the point** See COME TO THE POINT.

**get underway** *v. phr.* To set out on a journey; start going. ♦*We are delighted that our new Ph.D. program finally got underway.*

**get under one's skin** *v. phr.* To bother; upset. ♦*Children who talk too much in class get under the teacher's skin.*

**get up** *v.* **1.** To get out of bed. ♦*John's mother told him that it was time to get up.* **2.** To stand up; get to your feet. ♦*A man should get up when a woman comes into the room.* **3.** To prepare; get ready. ♦*Mary got up a picnic for her visitor.* ♦*The students got up a special number of the newspaper to celebrate the school's 50th birthday.* **4.** To dress

up. *One of the girls got herself up as a witch for the Halloween party.* **5.** To go ahead. ♦*The wagon driver shouted, "Get up!" to his horses.*

**get up** *or* **rise with the chickens** *v. phr.* To rise very early in the morning. ♦*All the farmers in this village get up with the chickens.*

**get-up** *n.* (stress on *get*) Fancy dress or costume. ♦*Some get-up you're wearing!*

**get-up-and-go** *also* **get-up-and-get** *n. phr., informal* Energetic enthusiasm; ambitious determination; pep; drive; push. ♦*Joe has a lot of get-up-and-go and is working his way through school.*

**get up on the wrong side of the bed** *v. phr., informal* To awake with a bad temper. ♦*Henry got up on the wrong side of the bed and wouldn't eat breakfast.*

**get up the nerve** *v. phr.* To build up your courage until you are brave enough; become brave enough. ♦*Jack got up the nerve to ask Ruth to dance with him.*

**get what's coming to one** *or slang* **get one's** *v. phr.* To receive the good or bad that you deserve; get what is due to you; get your share. ♦*At the end of the movie the villain got what was coming to him and was put in jail.*

**get wind of** *v. phr.* To get news of; hear rumors about; find out about. ♦*The police got wind of the plans to rob the bank.*

**get wise** *v. phr., slang* To learn about something kept secret from you; become alert. ♦*One girl pretended to be sick on gym days when she had athletics, until the teacher got wise and made her go anyway.*

**get with it** *v. phr., slang* To pay attention; be alive or alert; get busy. The students get with it just before examinations. ♦*The coach told the team to get with it.*

**get wrong** *v. phr.* To misunderstand something. ♦*"You got it all wrong!" the boss said to Mr. Brown. "We aren't closing down the plant; we are just downsizing it a bit."*

**ghost of a** Least trace of; slightest resemblance to; smallest bit even of; a very little. Usually used with *chance* or *idea* in negative sentences, or with *smile*. ♦*There wasn't a ghost of a chance that Jack would win.* ♦*We didn't have the ghost of an idea where to look for John.*

**ghost-writer** *n.* A writer whose identity remains a secret and who writes for another who receives all the credit. ♦ *It is rumored that John Smith's best-selling novel was written by a ghost-writer.*

**gift of gab** *or* **gift of the gab** *n. phr., informal* Skill in talking; ability to make interesting talk that makes people believe you. ♦ *Many men get elected because of their gift of gab.*

**gild the lily** *also* **paint the lily** *v. phr.* To add unnecessarily to something already beautiful or good enough. ♦ *To talk about a beautiful sunset is to gild the lily.*

**gild the pill** *or* **sugarcoat the pill** *v. phr.* To make something more acceptable; to soften something harsh; to tone down something unpleasant. ♦ *When the boss had to dismiss two hundred workers from his small factory, he decided to sugarcoat the pill by giving them six months of extra severance pay.*

**gilt-edged** *adj.* Of the highest quality. ♦ *Government saving bonds are considered by many to be a gilt-edged investment.*

**gin mill** *n., slang* A bar where liquor is sold. ♦ *Rush Street in Chicago is full of gin mills.*

**G.I.** *or* **"government issue"** *n.* An American soldier. ♦ *After the war many GI's were able to get a free education.*

**gird one's loins** *v. phr., literary* To prepare for action; get ready for a struggle or hard work. ♦ *David girded up his loins and went out to meet the giant Goliath.* ♦ *Seniors must gird their loins for the battles of life.*

**girlfriend** *n., informal* **1.** A female friend or companion. ♦ *Jane is spending the night at her girlfriend's house.* **2.** A boy's steady girl; the girl or woman partner in a love affair; girl; sweetheart. ♦ *John is taking his girlfriend to the dance.*

**give a bad mark** *v. phr.* To think less of a person; to condemn one for something the person had done. ♦ *You didn't show up for dinner last night; we had been waiting for you for three hours. I am going to give you a bad mark for that! Please phone next time if you can't make it.*

**give a dog a bad name** *v. phr.* Ruining a person's reputation by spreading false rumors about him. ♦ *The main business of some tabloids is to give a dog a bad name.*

**give a dog a bad name and hang him** *v. phr.* Ruining a person's reputation and then condemning him, making the false accusation irreversible. ♦ *Once enough bad rumors were circulated about the actor, nobody wanted to employ him. It was a case of giving a dog a bad name and hanging him, too.*

**give a hand** See LEND A HAND.

**give a hard time** *v. phr., informal* **1.** To give trouble by what you do or say; complain. ♦ *Jane gave her mother a hard time on the bus by fighting with her sister and screaming.* **2.** To get in the way by teasing or playing; kid. ♦ *Don't give me a hard time, boys. I'm trying to study.*

**give a lift** *or* **give a ride** *v. phr.* To invite someone into one's car and take them where they want to go. ♦ *Can I give you a lift to the train station?* ♦ *While my car was being repaired, my neighbor gave me a ride to work.*

**give-and-take** *n. phr.* **1.** A sharing; giving and receiving back and forth between people; a giving up by people on different sides of part of what each one wants so that they can agree. ♦ *There has to be give-and-take between two countries before they can be friends.* **2.** Friendly talking or argument back and forth. Friendly sharing of ideas which may not agree; also: an exchange of teasing remarks. ♦ *After the meeting there was a lot of give-and-take about plans for the dance.*

**give an ear to** *or* **lend an ear to** *v. phr., literary* To listen to. ♦ *The king lent an ear to the complaints of his people.*

**give a pain** *v. phr., slang* To make (you) disgusted; annoy. ♦ *John's bad manners give his teacher a pain.*

**give as good as one gets** *v. phr.* To be able to give back blow for blow; defend yourself well in a fight or argument. *The Americans gave as good as they got in the war with the English.*

**give away** *v.* **1.** To give as a present. ♦ *Mrs. Jones has several kittens to give away.* **2.** To hand over (a bride) to her husband at the wedding. ♦ *Mr. Jackson* *gave away his daughter.* **3.** To let (a secret) become known; tell the secret of. ♦ *The little boy gave away his hiding place when he coughed.*

**giveaway** *or* **dead giveaway** *n.* (stress on *give*) **1.** An open secret. ♦ *By mid-afternoon, it was a dead giveaway who the new boss would be.* **2.** A forced or sacrifice sale at which items are sold for much less than their market value. ♦ *The Simpson's garage sale was actually a big giveaway.* **3.** A gift; something one doesn't have to pay for. ♦ *The tickets to the concert were a giveaway.*

**give a wide berth** *v. phr.* To keep away from; keep a safe distance from. ♦ *Mary gave the barking dog a wide berth.* ♦ *Jack gave a wide berth to the fallen electric wires.*

**give birth to** *v. phr.* **1.** To bear live offspring. ♦ *The mother gave birth to twin baby girls.* **2.** To bring about; create; occasion. ♦ *Beethoven gave birth to a new kind of symphony.*

**give chase** *v. phr.* To chase or run after someone or something. ♦ *The policeman gave chase to the man who robbed the bank.*

**give color to** *or* **lend color to** *v. phr.* To make (something) seem true or likely. ♦ *The way the man ate lent color to his story of near starvation.*

**give credence to** *v. phr.* **1.** To be willing to believe that something is true. ♦ *Larry gave credence to the rumor that Fred used to be a convict.*

**give fits** *v. phr. informal* To upset; bother very much. ♦ *Paul's higher grades give John fits.*

**give forth** *v. phr.* To emit; produce. ♦ *When the gong was struck it gave forth a rich, resounding sound.*

**give free rein to** See GIVE REIN TO.

**give gray hair** *v. phr., informal* To make (someone) anxious, confused, or worried. ♦ *The traffic problem is enough to give a policeman gray hairs.*

**give ground** *v. phr.* To go backward under attack; move back; retreat. ♦ *After fighting for a while the troops slowly began to give ground.*

**give in** *v.* To stop fighting or arguing and do as the other person wants; give someone his own way; stop opposing someone. ♦ *After Billy proved that he*

*could ride a bicycle safely, his father gave in to him and bought him one.*

**give it a rest** *v. phr.* To stop trying to achieve something that is doomed to failure. ♦ *"Look, John you'll never be a concert pianist. You're making noise, that's all. Sober up and give it a break!"*

**give it one's all** *v. phr.* To exert maximum effort in order to achieve a certain goal. ♦ *It's too bad John didn't succeed in business; he certainly tried to give it his all.*

**give it one's best shot** See GIVE IT ONE'S ALL.

**give it some thought** *v. phr.* To wait and see; consider something after some time has elapsed. ♦ *"Will you buy my car?" Fred asked. "Let me give it some thought," Jim answered.*

**give it to** *v. phr., informal* **1.** To give punishment to; beat. ♦ *The crowd yelled for the wrestler to give it to his opponent.* **2.** To scold. ♦ *Jerry's mother gave it to him for coming home late.*

**give it to one straight** *v. phr.* To be direct; be frank. ♦ *I asked the doctor to give it to me straight how long I have to live.*

**give me some skin** *or* **slip me five** *v. phr., slang* To shake hands; to strike one's palm in friendship and agreement. ♦ *"Give me some skin, brother!" the gang leader said to the new member. "I'll give you five anytime, man," the new boy answered with a broad grin.*

**give me a break!** *or* **come off it!** *or* **come on!** *or* **spare me!** *or* **don't give me that!** *v. phr., exclamation.* I don't believe what you said. ♦ *"Give me a break! That's absurd!" "Come off it, man, you're saying crazy things!" "You can't remember where you spent the night? Spare me, please! That's total nonsense!"* ♦ *"You're going to run for president? Don't give me that! You'll never get to first base!"*

**give no quarter** *v. phr.* To be ruthless and show no mercy. ♦ *The enemy soldiers gave no quarter and shot all the prisoners.*

**give notice** *v. phr.* To inform an employer, an employee, a landlord, or a tenant of the termination of a contractual agreement of service or tenancy. ♦ *Max gave notice at the bank where he was working.*

**given to** *adj. phr.* Having a tendency to; addicted to. ♦ *Phil is given to telling* fantastic tales about his chateau in France.

**give off** *v.* To send out; let out; put forth. ♦*Rotten eggs give off a bad smell.*

**give one a break** *v. phr.* Give one a chance to do something, or to forgive one for having made a mistake. ♦*Although Sam did poorly on his entrance exam, the school gave him a break and admitted him anyway. "I am sorry, boss!" John said. "It will never happen again. Please give me a break and don't fire me!"*

**give one a call** See GIVE ONE A RING.

**give one a (good) going-over** See GO OVER 1.

**give one a lift** *v. phr.* **1.** To give someone a ride. ♦*Jack gave me a lift in his new car.* **2.** To comfort someone. ♦*Talking to my doctor yesterday gave me a lift.*

**give one an inch, and he will take a mile** If you give some people a little or yield anything, they will want more and more; some people are never satisfied. ♦*If you give him an inch, he'll take a mile.*

**give one a piece of one's mind** *v. phr., informal* To scold angrily; say what you really think to (someone). ♦*The sergeant gave the soldier a piece of his mind for not cleaning his boots.*

**give one a ring** *also informal* **give a buzz** To call on the telephone. ♦*Alice will give her friend a buzz tonight.*

**give one enough rope and he will hang himself** *informal* Give a bad person enough time and freedom to do as he pleases, and he may make a bad mistake or get into trouble and be caught.—A proverb. ♦*Johnny is always stealing and hasn't been caught. But give him enough rope and he'll hang himself.*

**give one pause** *v. phr.* To astonish someone; cause one to stop and think. ♦*"Your remark gives me pause," Tom said, when Jane called him an incurable gambler.*

**give oneself airs** *v. phr.* To act proud; act vain. ♦*John gave himself airs when he won first prize.*

**give oneself away** *v. phr.* To show guilt; show you have done wrong. ♦*The thief gave himself away by spending so much money.*

**give oneself up** *v.* To stop hiding or running away; surrender. ♦*The thief gave himself up to the police.*

**give oneself up to** *v. phr.* Not to hold yourself back from; let yourself enjoy. ♦*Uncle Willie gave himself up to a life of wandering.*

**give one some of his or her own medicine** *v. phr.* To treat someone the way he or she treats others (used in the negative). ♦*The gangster beat up an innocent old man, so when he resisted arrest, a policeman gave him a little of his own medicine.*

**give one's due** *v. phr.* To be fair to (a person), give credit that (a person) deserves. ♦*We should give a good worker his due.*

**give one's right arm for** *v. phr.* To give something of great value; sacrifice. ♦*During our long hike in the desert, I would have given my right arm for an ice cold drink.*

**give one's word** *v. phr.* To seriously promise. ♦*"You gave me your word you would marry me," Mary bitterly complained, "but you broke your word."*

**give one the crazies** *v. phr., slang* To produce an unwarrantedly extreme reaction to something. ♦*As soon as I call my boyfriend, my mom starts to give me the crazies.*

**give one the eye** *v. phr., slang* **1.** To look at, especially with interest and liking. ♦*A pretty girl went by and all the boys gave her the eye.* **2.** To look or stare at, especially in a cold or unfriendly way. ♦*Mrs. Jones didn't like Mary and didn't speak. She just gave her the eye when they met on the street.*

**give one the runaround** *v. phr.* To give someone numerous excuses and delays instead of attending to the matter at hand; to give someone meaningless busywork. ♦*The bureaucracy at that firm is so bad that one cannot accomplish anything; they're constantly giving me the runaround.*

**give or take** *v. phr.* To add or subtract. Used with a round number or date to show how approximate it is. ♦*The house was built in 1900, give or take five years.*

**give out** *v.* **1.** To make known; let it be known; publish. ♦*Mary gave out that she and Bob were going to be married.* **2.** To let escape; give. ♦*The cowboy gave out a yell.* **3.** to give to people; distribute. ♦*The barber gives out free lollipops to all the children.* **4.** To fail; collapse. *Tom's legs gave out and he couldn't run any farther.* ♦*The chair gave out under the fat man.* **5.** To be finished or gone. ♦*When the food at the party gave out, they bought more.* ♦*The teacher's patience gave out.*

**give pause** *v. phr.* To cause you to stop and think; make you doubt or worry. ♦*The bad weather gave John pause about driving to New York City.*

**give rein to** *or* **give free rein to** *v. phr.* To remove all restrictions or limitations from someone or something. ♦*When she wrote her first mystery novel, the talented novelist gave rein to her imagination.*

**give rise to** *v. phr.* To be the reason for; cause. *A branch floating in the water gave rise to Columbus' hopes that land was near.*

**give someone his rights** *or* **read someone his rights** *v. phr., informal* **1.** The act of advising arrested criminals that they have the right to remain silent and that everything they say can be held against them in a court of law; that they have the right to the presence of an attorney during questioning and that if they can't afford one and request it, an attorney will be appointed for them by the state. ♦*The cops gave Smith his rights immediately after the arrest.* **2.** To sever a relationship by telling someone that he or she can go and see a divorce lawyer or the like. ♦*Sue gave Mike his rights before she slammed the door in his face.*

**give the ax** *v. phr., colloquial* **1.** Abruptly to finish a relationship. ♦*She gave me the ax last night.* **2.** To fire an employee in a curt manner. ♦*His boss gave John the ax last Friday.*

**give the benefit of the doubt** *v. phr.* To believe (a person) is innocent rather than guilty when you are not sure. ♦*George's grade was higher than usual and he might have cheated, but his teacher gave him the benefit of the doubt.*

**give the bounce** *or* **give the gate** *v. phr., slang* **1.** *or* **give the air** To stop being a friend or lover to (a person); separate from. ♦*Mary gave John the bounce after she saw him dating another girl.*

♦*Bill and Jane had an argument and Bill is giving her the gate.* **2.** *or* **give the sack** *also* **give the hook** To fire from a job; dismiss. ♦*The ball team gave Joe the gate because he never came to practice.*

**give the creeps** See THE CREEPS.

**give the devil his due** *v. phr.* To be fair, even to someone who is bad; tell the truth about a person even though you don't like him. ♦*I don't like Mr. Jones, but to give the devil his due, I must admit that he is a good teacher.*

**give the finger** *v. phr.* To make a vulgar gesture with the hand. ♦*Jim never learned how to behave in good company; when he dislikes someone or something he still just gives the finger, as he did when he was a teenager.*

**give the glad eye** *v. phr., slang* To give (someone) a welcoming look as if saying "come over here, I want to talk to you." ♦*I was surprised when Joe gave me the glad eye.*

**give the go-ahead** *or* **give the green light** *v. phr.* To give one's consent or proceed with a certain activity; to issue the command to go forward. ♦*When John at age sixteen successfully got his first driver's license, his father gave him the green light to drive the family car.* ♦*The platoon commander gave the troops the long awaited go-ahead.*

**give the go-by** *v. phr.* To pay no attention to a person; avoid. ♦*John fell in love with Mary, but she gave him the go-by.*

**give the hook** See GIVE THE BOUNCE 2.

**give the pink slip** See LAY OFF 2.

**give the sack** See GIVE THE BOUNCE 2.

**give the shirt off one's back** *v. phr., informal* To give away something or everything that you own. ♦*He'd give you the shirt off his back.*

**give the show away** *v. phr.* To reveal a plan or information that is supposed to be secret. ♦*You have read further in the book than I have, but please don't tell me where the treasure was buried; otherwise you'd be giving the show away.*

**give the slip** *v.* To escape from (someone); run away from unexpectedly; sneak away from. ♦*Some boys were waiting outside the school to beat up Jack, but he gave them the slip.*

**give the willies** *v. phr.* To cause someone to be uncomfortable, fearful, or nervous. ♦*Sue hates to camp out in a tent; the buzzing of the mosquitoes gives her the willies.*

**give thought to** *v. phr.* To consider; think about. ♦*Have you given any thought to the question of how to sell Grandpa's old house?*

**give to understand** *v. phr.* To make a person understand by telling him very plainly or boldly. ♦*Frank was given to understand in a short note from the boss that he was fired.*

**give up** *v.* **1.** To stop trying to keep; surrender; yield. ♦*The dog had the ball in his mouth and wouldn't give it up.* **2.** To stop doing or having; abandon; quit. ♦*The doctor told Mr. Harris to give up smoking.* ♦*Jane hated to give up her friends when she moved away.* **3.** To stop hoping for, waiting for, or trying to do. ♦*Johnny was given up by the doctors after the accident, but he lived just the same.* **4.** To stop trying; quit; surrender. ♦*The war will be over when one of the countries gives up.*

**give (one) up for** *v. phr.* To abandon hope for someone or something. ♦*After Larry had not returned to base camp for three nights, his fellow mountain climbers gave him up for dead.*

**give up the ghost** *v. phr.* To die; stop going. ♦*After a long illness, the old woman gave up the ghost.*

**give up the ship** *v. phr.* To stop fighting and surrender; stop trying or hoping to do something.* ♦*"Don't give up the ship, John," said his father when John failed a test.*

**give voice** *v. phr., formal* To tell what you feel or think; especially when you are angry or want to object.—Used with *to.* ♦*Willie gave voice to his pain when the dog bit him by crying loudly.*

**give way** *v.* **1.** To go back; retreat. ♦*The enemy army is giving way before the cannon fire.* **2.** To make room, get out of the way. ♦*The children gave way and let their mother through the door.* **3.** To lose control of yourself; lose your courage or hope; yield. ♦*Mrs. Jones didn't give way during the flood, but she was very frightened.* **4.** To collapse; fail. ♦*The river was so high that the dam gave way.* ♦*Mary's legs gave way and she fainted.* **5.** To let yourself be persuaded; give permission. ♦*Billy*

kept asking his mother if he could go to the movies and she finally gave way.

**give way to** *v. phr.* **1a.** To make room for; allow to go or pass; yield to. ♦*John gave way to the old lady and let her pass.* **1b.** To allow to decide. ♦*Mrs. Rogers gave way to her husband in buying the car.* **1c.** To lose control of (your feelings), not hold back. ♦*Timmy gave way to his feelings when his dog died.* **2. or give place to.** To be replaced by. ♦*When she saw the clowns, the little girl's tears gave way to laughter.*

**give wide berth to** *v. phr.* To avoid coming into contact with a physical object, a place, or certain people and certain kinds of activity. ♦*After the newspapers published an article about numerous attacks in Hyde Park, people started to give wide berth to the place.*

**glad hand** *n., informal* A friendly handshake; a warm greeting. ♦*The politician went down the street on election day giving everyone the glad hand.*

**glad rags** *n., slang* Clothes worn to parties or on special occasions; best clothes. ♦*Mrs. Owens put on her glad rags for the party.*

**glance off** *v. phr.* To ricochet. ♦*The bullet glanced off the wall and wounded an innocent bystander.*

**glass ceiling** *n. phr.* A level of maximum success in corporations or large businesses, beyond which certain groups of people, such as women or minorities, can rise only seldom and with great difficulty. ♦*"They're pretending to be nice to me," Mary complained, "but they'll never make me CEO of the company. It's impossible to break the glass ceiling in this industry."*

**globe-trotter** *n.* One who has traveled far and wide. ♦*Tim and Nancy are regular globe-trotters; there are few countries they haven't been to.*

**gloss over** *v.* To try to make what is wrong or bad seem right or not important; try to make a thing look easy; pretend about; hide. ♦*John glossed over his mistake by saying that everybody did the same thing.*

**glutton for punishment** *n. phr.* A greedy person; someone who wants too much of something, such as food or drink, which will make him sick. ♦*Fred eats* *so much red meat that he is a regular glutton for punishment.*

**gnaw at one** See EAT AWAY AT.

**go about** *v.* **1.** To be busy with; keep busy at or working on; start working on; do. ♦*Just go about your business and don't keep looking out of the window.* **2.** To move from one place or person to another. ♦*Some people go about telling untrue stories.*

**go about one's business** *v. phr.* To mind one's own affairs. ♦*Fred kept bothering me with his questions all day, so I finally told him to go about his business and leave me alone.*

**go after** *v.* To try to get. ♦*"First find out what job you want and then go after it,"* said Jim's father.

**go against the grain** See AGAINST THE GRAIN 2.

**go ahead** *v.* To begin to do something; not wait. ♦*"May I ask you a question?" "Go ahead."*

**go astray** *v. phr.* To become lost. ♦*The letter has obviously gone astray; otherwise it would have been delivered a long time ago.*

**goal line** *n.* A line that marks the goal in a game (as football.) ♦*The fullback went over the goal line from five yards out.*

**go all out** See GIVE IT ONE'S ALL.

**go along** *v.* **1.** To move along; continue. ♦*Uncle Bill made up the story as he went along.* **2.** To go together or as company; go for fun.—Often used with *with.* ♦*Mary went along with us to Jane's house.* **3.** To agree; cooperate.—Often used with *with.* ♦*"Jane is a nice girl." "I'll go along with that,"* said Bill. ♦*Just because the other boys do something bad, you don't have to go along with it.*

**go ape** *v. phr., slang* To become highly excited or behave in a crazy way. ♦*Amy went ape over the hotel and beautiful beaches.*

**go around** *v.* **1a.** To go from one place or person to another. *Mr. Smith is going around looking for work.* ♦*Don't go around telling lies like that.* ♦*Chicken pox is going around the neighborhood.* ♦*A rumor is going around school that we will get the afternoon off.* **1b.** To go together; keep company.—Usually used with *with.* ♦*Bill goes around with* boys older than he is because he is big for his age. **2.** To be enough to give to everyone; be enough for all. ♦*There are not enough desks to go around in the classroom.*

**go around in circles** See IN A CIRCLE.

**goat** *v.* **1.** To start to fight with; attack. ♦*The dog and the cat are going at each other again.* **2.** To make a beginning on; approach; tackle. ♦*How are you going to go at the job of fixing the roof?*

**go at it hammer and tongs** *v. phr., informal* **1.** To attack or fight with great strength or energy; have a bad argument. ♦*Bill slapped George's face and now they're going at it hammer and tongs in back of the house.* **2.** To start or do something with much strength, energy, or enthusiasm. ♦*The farmer had to chop down a tree and he went at it hammer and tongs.*

**go away** *v. phr.* **1.** To leave home for a weekend; to take a vacation; to travel. ♦*"What you need," Dr. Gordon said, "is to go away for a couple of weeks and have a rest."* **2.** Stop bothering someone. ♦*How many times did I tell you to go away and leave me alone?* **3.** To cease; to stop. ♦*My headache finally went away after I took two migraine pills.*

**go-back** *n. phr.* (stress on *go*) Merchandise left at the checkout counter in a supermarket because the customer didn't have enough money to pay for it. ♦*"This is a go-back!" the cashier cried. "Take it back to the shelf!"*

**go back on one's word** *v. phr.* To renege; break a promise. ♦*Patrick went back on his word when he refused to marry Karen in spite of his earlier promise.*

**gobble up** *v. phr.* **1.** To completely devour. ♦*The boys were famished after the steep mountain climb, and gobbled up all the leftovers in the refrigerator.* **2.** To uncritically accept. ♦*The naïve villagers gobbled up all the false news the tyrannical state-run television fed them.*

**go bail for** *v. phr.* To advance the necessary money as security in order to release an accused person until trial. ♦*The arrested driver had no trouble finding someone to go bail for him.*

**go broke** *v. phr., slang* To lose all one's money; especially by taking a chance;

owe more than you can pay. ♦*The inventor went broke because nobody would buy his machine.*

**go-between** *n.* An intermediary. ♦*They expect Mr. Smith to act as a go-between in the dispute between management and labor.*

**go bust** *v. phr., slang* To become bankrupt. ♦*Our company lost a lot of money and went bust.*

**go by** *v.* **1.** To go or move past; pass. ♦*Bob had to go by the post office on his way to school, so he mailed the letter.* **2.** To follow; copy; obey. ♦*Mother goes by a pattern when she makes a dress.* ♦*If you ride a bicycle, you must go by the rules of the road.* **3.** To be known by; be called. ♦*Many actors do not go by their real names.* **4.** To pass; be over; end. ♦*Time goes by quickly on vacation.* **5.** To stop for a short visit; go to someone's house for a short while. ♦*"Have you seen Bill lately?" "Yes, I went by his house last week."*

**go by the board** *also* **pass by the board** *v. phr.* To go away or disappear forever; be forgotten or not used. ♦*Tom had several chances to go to college, but he let them go by the board.*

**go by the name of** *v. phr.* To be called. ♦*Adolf Schicklegruber went by the name of Adolf Hitler.*

**God forbid** *interj.* May God prevent (something from happening); I hope that will not happen or is not true. ♦*Someone told the worried mother that her son might have drowned. She said, "God forbid!"*

**God knows** *or* **goodness knows** *or* **heaven knows** *informal* **1.** Maybe God knows but I don't know and no one else knows.—Often used with *only.* ♦*Do you know where Susan is? God only knows!* **2.** Surely; certainly. ♦*Goodness knows, the poor man needs the money.* ♦*Heaven only knows, I have tried hard enough.*

**go down** *v. phr.* **1.** To deteriorate in quality. ♦*This hotel, which used to be one of the best, has gone down during the past few years.* **2.** To become lower in price. ♦*It is said that the price of milk is expected to go down soon.* **3.** To sink. ♦*The Titanic went down with a lot of people aboard.*

**go down in history** *or* **go down in the records** *v. phr.* To be remembered or recorded for always. ♦*The lives of great men go down in history.* ♦*The boy's straight A's for four years of college went down in the records.* ♦*The president said that the day the war ended would go down in history.*

**go down into the clinker** *v. phr.* To go to ruin; to perish. ♦*"The war isn't over yet," the general warned. "If the troops don't act with utmost caution, they may go down into the clinker."*

**go down the drain** *v. phr.* To be lost or wasted forever. ♦*If he doesn't pass the bar examination tomorrow, his best efforts to become a lawyer will go down the drain.*

**go Dutch** *v. phr., informal* To go out for fun together but have each person pay for himself. ♦*Sometimes boys and girls go Dutch on dates.* ♦*The girl knew her boyfriend had little money, so she offered to go Dutch.*

**go fly a kite** *v. phr., slang* To go away; leave. Usually used as a command, to show that you do not accept someone's ideas. ♦*Harry was tired of John's advice and told him to go fly a kite.*

**go for** *v. phr., informal* **1.** To try to get; aim for; try for. ♦*Our team is going for the championship in the game tonight.* **2.** To favor; support; like. *Susie really goes for ice cream.* ♦*Bob goes for Jane in a big way.* **3.** To attack; begin to fight or argue with. ♦*The mugger jumped out of the bush and went for Jack.*

**go for a ride** *or* **go for a spin** *v. phr.* To drive a car for pleasure usually for a short time. ♦*"Would you like to take the new Buick out for a spin before you make a decision?" the salesman asked the customer. "OK," the customer agreed, "let's go for a ride."*

**go for broke** *v. phr., slang* To risk everything on one big effort; use all your energy and skill; try as hard as possible. ♦*The racing car driver decided to go for broke in the biggest race of the year.*

**go from bad to worse** *adv. phr.* To change from a bad position or condition to a worse one; become worse. ♦*Jack's conduct in school has gone from bad to worse.*

**go from strength to strength** *v. phr.* To move forward, increasing one's fame, power, or fortune in a series of successful achievements. ♦ *Our basketball team has gone from strength to strength.*

**go-getter** *n.* A person who works hard to become successful; an active, ambitious person who usually gets what he wants. ♦ *The governor of the state has always been a go-getter.*

**go-go** *adj., slang, informal* **1.** vigorous youthful, unusually active. ♦ *Joe is a go-go kind of guy.* **2.** Of a discotheque or the music or dances performed there. **3a.** unrestrained **3b.** very up-to-date, hip. ♦ *Mary wore handsome go-go boots to the discotheque last night.*

**go halfway** *or* **go halfway to meet one** *or* **meet one halfway** *v. phr.* To give up part of what you want or to do your share in reaching an agreement with someone. ♦ *Our neighbors are willing to go halfway to meet us and pay their share for a fence between our houses.*

**go halves** *v. phr., informal* To share half or equally become partners. ♦ *The girl bought a box of candy and went halves with her roommate.*

**go haywire** *v. phr., informal* Mixed-up, out of order, not in regular working condition. ♦ *My computer has gone all haywire; I have to call the repair man.*

**go hog wild** *v. phr., slang* To become extremely agitated and go out of control. ♦ *After the soccer game was won, the fans went hog wild.*

**go in a circle** *or* **go in circles** See IN A CIRCLE.

**go in for** *v. phr., informal* To try to do; take part in; take pleasure in. ♦ *Most girls do not go in for rough games.* ♦ *Mrs. Henry goes in for simple meals.*

**going for one** *adj. phr.* Working to help; in one's favor. ♦ *The young woman surely will get the job; she has everything going for her.*

**going on** *adv. phr.* Almost; nearly. ♦ *Joe is going on six years old.* ♦ *It is going on six o'clock.*

**going through changes** *v. phr., slang, informal* To be in trouble, to have difficulties, to be trapped in unfavorable circumstances. ♦ *"What's the matter with Joe?"—"He's going through changes."*

**going to** Can be expected to; planning to.—Used after *is* (or *was*, etc.), with an infinitive, in the same way *will* is used, to show future. ♦ *Some day that big tree is going to rot and fall.* Sometimes used without the infinitive. ♦ *That worn rope hasn't broken yet, but it's going to.* ♦ *Put some more wood on the fire. "I'm going to."*

**go in one ear and out the other** *v. phr., informal* To be not really listened to or understood; be paid no attention. ♦ *The teacher's directions to the boy went in one ear and out the other.*

**go into** *v.* **1a.** To go or fit inside of; able to be put in. ♦ *The table is too big to go into the closet.* **1b.** To be able to be divided into; be divisible into. ♦ *Two goes into four two times.* **2.** To enter a state or condition of; pass into. *John went into a fit of temper when he didn't get his own way.* **3.** To be busy in or take part in; enter as a job or profession. ♦ *The mayor went into politics as a very young man.* **4.** To start to talk about; bring up the subject of; examine. ♦ *We'll talk about the dead mouse after dinner, Billy. Let's not go into it now.*

**go into a nose dive** See GO INTO A TAIL SPIN.

**go into a tailspin** *or* **go into a nose dive** *v. phr., informal* To fall or go down badly; collapse; give up trying. ♦ *The team went into a tailspin after their captain was hurt, and they were badly beaten.* **2.** *informal* To become very anxious, confused, or mentally sick; give up hope. ♦ *The man went into a tailspin after his wife died and he never got over it.*

**go into orbit** *v. phr., slang* **1.** To become very happy or successful. ♦ *Our team has gone into orbit.* **2.** To lose one's temper or control completely; become very angry. ♦ *John was afraid his father would go into orbit when he found out about the car accident.*

**go it** *v. phr., informal* **1.** To go fast; run hard; not to spare yourself.—Often used as a command. ♦ *The coach yelled to the runner to go it.* ♦ *At the party the girls cheered for their partners to go it.* ♦ *The boys called, "Go it!" to the dog chasing the cat.* **2.** To live; continue to do or work. ♦ *John wants to leave home and go it alone.*

**go jump in the lake** *v. phr., informal* To go away and quit being a bother.

♦*George was tired of Tom's advice and told him to go jump in the lake.*

**golden mean** *or* **golden medium** *or* **happy medium** *n. phr.* The happy middle ground between two equally bad extremes. ♦*One ought not to overeat or to starve oneself to death; the smart way to take care of one's health is to choose a golden mean diet and eat a little of everything with moderation.*

**goldfish bowl** *n., slang, informal* **1.** A situation in which it is not possible to keep things secret for any length of time. ♦*Washington Society is a goldfish bowl.* **2.** An apartment or place that provides no privacy for its occupant, e.g., an office that has too many windows. ♦*Joe's office is a goldfish bowl, that's why I didn't let him kiss me there.*

**golf widow** *n., informal* A woman whose husband is often away from home playing golf. ♦*Mrs. Thompson didn't like being a golf widow.*

**go legit** *v. phr.* To start practicing a legitimate business after having been operating outside of the law. ♦*"The old days are over," the crime boss said to his friends. "We are going legit as of right now."*

**go like clockwork** *or* **go off like clockwork** *v. phr., informal* To run smoothly and regularly like the workings of a clock; go smoothly and without difficulty; go on time or as planned. ♦*The car's motor went like clockwork after Bob fixed it.*

**go native** *v. phr.* To behave like a native (said of European Americans in tropical countries). ♦*Mainlanders often go native in Hawaii.*

**gone with the wind** *adj. phr.* Gone forever; past; vanished. ♦*All the deer that used to live here are gone with the wind.* ♦*Joe knew that his chance to get an "A" was gone with the wind when he saw how hard the test was.*

**good and———** *adv., informal* Very; completely. ♦*John's father was good and mad when John came home late.* ♦*Susan wouldn't come out till she was good and ready.*

**good buddy** *n., slang, citizen's band radio jargon* Salutation used by truckers and automobile drivers who have CB radios. ♦*What's the Smokey situation, good buddy?*

**good cheer** *n. phr.* Happiness; optimistic disposition. ♦*Everyone likes John because he is a person of good cheer.*

**good clean fun** *n. phr.* Harmless amusement; recreational activity not involving alcohol, drugs, etc. ♦*The boys had some good, clean fun climbing the Sierra Nevada.*

**good deal** *or* **great deal** *n., informal* A large amount; much.—Used with *a.* ♦*Mrs. Walker's long illness cost her a good deal.* ♦*George spends a great deal of his time watching television.* ♦*George is a good deal like his father; they both love to eat.*

**good egg** *slang or informal* **good scout** *n. phr.* A friendly, kind or good-natured person, a nice fellow. ♦*Tommy is such a good egg that everybody wants to be his friend.*

**good faith** *n.* **1.** Belief in another person's honesty; trust. ♦*Uncle Dick let me have the keys to his candy store to show his good faith.*—Often used in the phrase *in good faith.* ♦*The teacher accepted Bob's excuse for being late in good faith.* **2.** Honesty of purpose; trustworthiness. ♦*John agreed to buy Ted's bicycle for $20, and he paid him $5 right away to show his good faith.*

**good for** *or* **hurrah for** *adj. phr.* Used with a name or pronoun to praise someone. ♦*Good for George! He won the 100-yard dash.* ♦*You got 100 on the test? Hurrah for you.*

**good-for-nothing** *adj. phr.* Worthless. ♦*While Janice works hard each day, her good-for-nothing husband hangs around in the bars.*

**good grief!** *interj., informal* Wow! Indication of surprise, good or bad. ♦*"Good grief," Joe cried out loud. "Is this all you will pay me for my hard work?"* ♦*What a figure Melanie has, good grief! I wonder if she would be willing to go out with me.*

**good head on one's shoulders** *n. phr.* Good sense; good judgment. ♦*Jack has a good head on his shoulders; he never drives too fast.*

**good many** *or* **great many** *n. or adj.* A large number (of); very many. Used with *a.* ♦*We found some fall flowers, but the frost had already killed a good many.* ♦*A great many of the houses were knocked down by the earthquake.*

**goodness gracious** *interj., slightly archaic* Exclamation of surprise and a certain degree of disapproval. ♦*"Can my boyfriend stay overnight, Dad?"* Melanie asked. "Goodness gracious, most certainly not!" her father replied. "What would the neighbors think?"*

**good question** *n. phr.* A question difficult to answer because of a lack of information or because the answer is classified. ♦*"How much longer will this war last?" the journalist asked the general. "That's a good question," the general replied. "We just don't know."*

**good riddance** *n.* A loss that you are glad about. Often used as an exclamation, and in the sentence *good riddance to bad rubbish.* To show that you are glad that something or somebody has been taken or sent away. ♦*The boys thought it was good riddance when the troublemaker was sent home.* ♦*"I'm going and won't come back," said John. "Good riddance to bad rubbish!" said Mary.*

**Good Samaritan** *n. phr., Biblical* A person who helps another in distress unselfishly, even if they are not friends or related in any way. ♦*"Be a Good Samaritan and help me out!" John asked his boss. "All right, but just this once," the boss answered.*

**good show!** *adj. phr.* Excellent; terrific; wonderful. ♦*"Good show, boys!" the coach cried, when our team won the game.*

**go off** *v.* **1.** To leave; to depart. ♦*Helen's mother told her not to go off without telling her.* **2a.** To be fired; explode. ♦*The firecracker went off and scared Jack's dog.* **2b.** To begin to ring or buzz. ♦*The alarm clock went off at six o'clock and woke Father.* **3.** To happen. ♦*The party went off without any trouble.* ♦*The parade went off without rain.*

**go off half-cocked** *also* **go off at half cock** *v. phr., informal* To act or speak before getting ready; to do something too soon. ♦*Bill often goes off half cocked.* ♦*Mr. Jones was thinking about quitting his job, but his wife told him not to go off at half cock.*

**go off like clockwork** See GO LIKE CLOCKWORK.

**go off on a tangent** See FLY OFF ON A TANGENT.

**go off the deep end** *or* **go overboard** *v. phr., informal* To act excitedly and without careful thinking. ♦*John has gone off the deep end about owning a motorcycle.* ♦*Some girls go overboard for handsome movie and television actors.*

**goof off** *v., slang* To loaf or be lazy; not want to work or be serious; fool around. ♦*Tom didn't get promoted because he goofed off all the time and never did his homework.*

**go off in a huff** *v. phr.* To depart in anger. ♦*Marian went off in a huff just because Jeff failed to open the door for her.*

**goof up** See GOOF OFF.

**go on** *v.* **1a.** To continue; not stop. ♦*After he was hit by the ball, Billy quit pitching and went home, but the game went on.* **1b.** To continue after a pause; begin with the next thing. ♦*"Go on! I'm listening," said Mother.* ♦*The teacher pointed to the map, and went on, "But the land that Columbus came to was not India."* **1c.** To pass. ♦*The years went on, and Betty's classmates became gray-haired men and women.* **2.** To happen. ♦*Mr. Scott heard the noise and went to see what was going on in the hall.* **3.** To talk for too long, often angrily. ♦*We thought Jane would never finish going on about the amount of homework she had.* **4.** To fit on; be able to be worn. ♦*My little brother's coat wouldn't go on me. It was too small.* **5.** Stop trying to fool me; I don't believe you.—Used as a command, sometimes with *with*. ♦*When Father told Mother she was the prettiest girl in the world, Mother just said, "Oh, go on, Charles."*

**go on a diet** *v. phr.* To start eating food containing fewer calories and less cholesterol in order to lose weight and control one's blood pressure, etc. ♦*Doctor Gordon recommended that I should go on a diet and exercise more.*

**go on record** *v. phr.* To make an official statement as opposed to an informal one; say something officially that may be quoted with the person's name added for reference. ♦*I want to go on record that I oppose the merger with the firm of Catwallender and Swartvik.*

**go on strike** *v. phr.* To start a demonstration usually organized by one's labor union in order to exact higher wages or better treatment from one's employers. ♦ *The flight attendants' union went on general strike, so the country's second-biggest airline was out of commission for two weeks.*

**go one's way** *v. phr.* **1.** To start again or continue to where you are going. ♦ *The milkman left the milk and went his way.* **2.** To go or act the way you want to or usually do. ♦ *Joe just wants to go his way and mind his own business.*

**goose bumps** *or* **goose pimples** *n. plural, informal* Small bumps that come on a person's skin when he gets cold or afraid. ♦ *Nancy gets goose bumps when she sees a snake.* ♦ *Ann, put on your sweater; you're so cold you have goose pimples on your arms.*

**go out** *v. phr.* **1.** To pass out of date or style. ♦ *Short skirts are gradually going out.* **2.** To stop giving off light or burning. ♦ *Put more wood on the fire or it will go out.* **3.** To leave. ♦ *When I called Sue, her mother said that she had just gone out.*

**go out of business** *v. phr.* To cease functioning as a commercial enterprise. ♦ *The windows of the store are all boarded up because they went out of business.*

**go out of one's way** *v. phr.* To make an extra effort; do more than usual. ♦ *Jane went out of her way to be nice to the new girl.*

**go out the window** *v. phr., informal* To go out of effect; be abandoned. ♦ *During the war, the school dress code went out the window.*

**go out with one** *v. phr.* To date someone. ♦ *"May I ask your daughter for a date, sir?" Fred asked politely. "She is too young to go out with anyone," the father replied. "Why don't you come back next year?"*

**go over** *v.* **1.** To examine; think about or look at carefully. ♦ *The teacher went over the list and picked John's name.* ♦ *The police went over the gun for fingerprints.* **2.** To repeat; do again. *Don't make me go all over it again.* ♦ *We painted the house once, then we went over it again.* ♦ **3.** To read again; study. ♦ *After you finish the test, go over it again to look for mistakes.* ♦ *They went over their lessons together at night.* **4.** To cross; go to stop or visit; travel. ♦ *We*

*went over to the other side of the street.* ♦ *I'm going over to Mary's house.* ♦ *We went over to the next town to the game.* **5.** To change what you believe. ♦ *Joe is a Democrat, but he says that he is going over to the Republicans in the next election.* ♦ *Many of the natives on the island went over to Christianity after the missionaries came.* **6.** To be liked; succeed.—Often used in the informal phrase *go over big.* ♦ *Bill's joke went over big with the other boys and girls.* ♦ *Your idea went over well with the boss.*

**go over like a lead balloon** *v. phr., informal* To fail to generate a positive response or enthusiasm; to meet with boredom or disapproval. ♦ *The president's suggested budget cuts went over like a lead balloon.*

**go over one's head** *v. phr.* **1.** To be too difficult to understand. ♦ *Penny complains that what her math teacher says simply goes over her head.* **2.** To do something without the permission of one's superior. ♦ *Fred went over his boss's head when he signed the contract on his own.*

**go over with a fine-tooth comb** See FINE-TOOTH COMB.

**go postal** *v. phr.* To lose control over oneself and become angry enough to start shooting at innocent bystanders (as was done by a disgruntled employee in a post office in Chicago). ♦ *"Oh, I'm so glad I found you, Professor. Here is my term paper. I was stuck in traffic and I thought I was gonna go postal," Ms. Murphy said, handing in her paper at the very last possible moment.*

**Gordian knot** *n. phr. Greek antiquity, from Alexander the Great.* A very tough and apparently insolvable problem, which, given the right decisive action, can nevertheless be solved. ♦ *"I am not going to try to figure out who embezzled the money at this firm," the director said. "I will solve the Gordian knot by firing everybody in one fell swoop and hiring a whole new office staff."*

**go right over one's head** See BEYOND ONE.

**go somebody one better** *v. phr., informal* To do something better than (someone else); do more or better than; beat.

*John made a good dive into the water, but Bob went him one better by diving in backwards.*

**go stag** *v. phr.* **1.** To go to a dance or party without a companion of the opposite sex. *♦When Sally turned him down, Tom decided to go stag to the college prom.* **2.** To participate in a party for men only. *♦Mrs. Smith's husband frequently goes stag, leaving her at home.*

**go steady** *v. phr.* To go on dates with the same person all the time; date just one person. *♦Jean went steady with Bob for a year; then they had a quarrel and stopped dating each other.*

**go straight** *v. phr., slang* To become an honest person; lead an honest life. *♦After the man got out of prison, he went straight.*

**got a thing going** *v. phr., slang, informal* To be engaged in a pleasurable or profitable activity with someone else as a partner either in romance or in mutually profitable business. *♦"You two seem to have got a thing going, haven't you?"* *♦"You've got a good thing going with your travel bureau, why quit now?"*

**go the whole hog** *or* **go whole hog** *v. phr., informal* To do something completely or thoroughly; to give all your strength or attention to something. *♦The family went whole hog at the fair, and spent a lot of money.*

**go through** *v.* **1.** To examine or think about carefully; search. *♦I went through the papers looking for Jane's letter.* *♦Mother went through the drawer looking for the sweater.* **2.** To experience; suffer; live through. *♦Frank went through many dangers during the war.* **3.** To do what you are supposed to do; do what you promised. *♦I went through my part of the bargain, but you didn't go through your part.* **4.** To go or continue to the end of; do or use all of. *♦Jack went through the magazine quickly.* *♦We went through all our money at the circus.* **5.** To be allowed; pass; be agreed on. *♦I hope the new law we want goes through Congress.*

**go through fire and water** *v. phr.* To undergo great dangers and risk. *♦Our troops had go through fire and water to liberate Europe during World War II.*

**go through hell and high water** *v. phr., informal* To go through danger, or trouble. *♦John is ready to go through hell and high water to help his friends.*

**go through the motions** *v. phr.* To pretend to do something by moving or acting as if you were really doing it; do something without really trying hard or caring. *♦The team was so far behind in the game that they just went through the motions of playing at the end.*

**go through with** *v. phr.* To finish; do as planned or agreed; not stop or fail to do. *♦The boys don't think Bob will go through with his plans to spend the summer at a camp.*

**go through (something) with a fine-tooth comb** *v. phr.* To examine something in great detail and minutely. *♦I went through my study with a fine-tooth comb, yet I was unable to find the lost files.* *♦The firm's accountant went through all the books with a fine-tooth comb and in the end found the missing amount of money.*

**go to** *v.* To be ready to do; start doing something. *♦When Jack went to write down the telephone number, he had forgotten it.*

**go to any length** *v. phr.* To do everything you can. *♦Bill will go to any length to keep Dick from getting a date with Mary.*

**go to bat for** *v. phr., informal* To help out in trouble or need; give aid to. *♦Mary went to bat for the new club program.*

**go to bed with the chickens** *v. phr., informal* To go to bed early at night. *♦On the farm John worked hard and went to bed with the chickens.* *♦Mr. Barnes goes to bed with the chickens because he has to get up at 5 A.M.*

**go to bed with someone** *v. phr.* To have sexual relations with someone. *♦"John is very nice, I agree. Have you gone to bed with him yet?" Sue's sister asked.*

**go together** *v.* **1.** To go with the same boy or girl all the time; date just one person. Herbert and Thelma go together. **2.** To be suitable or agreeable with each other; match. *♦Roast turkey and cranberries go together.* *♦Ice cream and cake go together.*

**go to great lengths** See GO TO ANY LENGTH.

**go to hell** See GO TO THE DEVIL.

**go to it!** *v. phr.* An expression of encouragement meaning go ahead; proceed.

♦*"Go to it!" my father cried enthusiastically, when I told him I had decided to become a doctor.*

**go to one's account** *v. phr.* To die. ♦*The terrorists will go to their account sooner or later.*

**go to one's head** *v. phr.* **1.** To make one dizzy. ♦*Beer and wine go to a person's head.* **2.** To make someone too proud; make a person think he is too important. ♦*The girl's fame as a movie actress went to her head.*

**go to pieces** *v. phr.* To become very nervous or sick from nervousness; become wild. ♦*The man went to pieces when the judge said he would have to go to prison for life.*

**go to pot** *v. phr., informal* To be ruined; become bad; be destroyed. ♦*The motel business went to pot when the new highway was built.*

**go to seed** *or* **run to seed** *v. phr.* **1.** To grow seeds. ♦*Onions go to seed in hot weather.* **2.** To lose skill or strength; stop being good or useful. ♦*Mr. Allen was a good carpenter until he became rich and went to seed.*

**go to show** *or* **go to prove** *v. phr., informal* To seem to prove; act or serve to show (a fact); demonstrate.—Often used after *it.* ♦*The hard winter at Valley Forge goes to show that our soldiers suffered a great deal to win the Revolution.*

**go to the chair** *v. phr.* To be executed in the electric chair. ♦*After many stays of execution, the criminal finally had to go to the chair.*

**go to the devil** *v. phr., informal* **1.** To go away, mind your own business.—Used as a command; considered rude. ♦*George told Bob to go to the devil.* ♦*"Go to the devil!" said Jack, when his sister tried to tell him what to do.*

**go to the dogs** *v. phr., informal* To go to ruin; to be ruined or destroyed. ♦*The man went to the dogs after he started drinking.*

**go to the other extreme** *v. phr.* To swing to the opposite side in an opinion and especially in the course of one's behavior, like a pendulum. ♦*John was a dedicated pacifist before the war, but when the Allies emerged victorious, he suddenly went to the other extreme, advocating future preemptive wars.*

**go to the trouble** *or* **take the trouble** *v. phr.* To make trouble or extra work for yourself; bother. ♦*John told Mr. Brown not to go to the trouble of driving him home.*

**go to town** *v. phr., slang* **1.** To do something quickly or with great force or energy; work fast or hard. ♦*The boys went to town on the old garage, and had it torn down before Father came home from work.* **2.** *or* **go places.** To do a good job; succeed. ♦*Our team is going to town this year, we have won all five games that we played.* ♦*Dan was a good student and a good athlete; we expect him to go places in business.*

**go to waste** *v. phr.* To be wasted or lost; not used. ♦*Joe's work on the model automobile went to waste when he dropped it.*

**go to wrack and ruin** *v. phr.* To fall apart and be ruined; to become useless. ♦*The car will soon go to wrack and ruin standing out in all kinds of weather.*

**go under** *v.* **1.** To be sunk. ♦*The ship hit an iceberg and went under.* **2.** To fail; be defeated. ♦*The filling station went under because there were too many others on the street.*

**go under the hammer** *v. phr.* To be auctioned off. ♦*Our old family paintings went under the hammer when my father lost his job.*

**go up** *v.* **1.** To go or move higher; rise. ♦*Many people came to watch the weather balloon go up.* ♦*The path goes up the hill.* **2.** To be able to become heard; become loud or louder. ♦*A shout went up from the crowd at the game.* **3.** Grow in height while being built; to be built. ♦*The new church is going up on the corner.* **4.** To increase. ♦*Prices of fruit and vegetables have gone up.*

**go up in smoke** *or* **go up in flames** *v. phr.* To burn; be destroyed by fire. **1.** ♦*The house went up in flames.* ♦*The barn full of hay went up in smoke.* **2.** Disappear; fail; not come true. ♦*Jane's hopes of going to college went up in smoke when her father lost his job.*

**go up in the air** *v. phr.* To become angry; lose one's temper. ♦*Herb is so irritable these days that he goes up in the air for no reason at all.*

**go with** *v.* **1.** To match; to look good with. ♦*A yellow blouse goes with her blonde hair.* **2.** To go out in the company of. *Tom goes with the girl who lives across the street.*

**go without saying** *v. phr.* To be too plain to need talking about; not be necessary to say or mention. ♦*It goes without saying that children should not be given knives to play with.*

**go wrong** *v. phr.* **1.** To fail; go out of order. ♦*Something went wrong with our car and we stalled on the road.* **2.** To sink into an immoral or criminal existence. ♦*In a large city many young people go wrong every year.*

**grab a bite to eat** *v.phr.* To have a quick and informal meal in a fast-food place or inexpensive restaurant. ♦*Let's not spend a lot of money and just grab a bite to eat during shopping.*

**grab bag** *n.* **1.** A bag from which surprise packages are chosen; a bag in which there are many unknown things. ♦*The children brought packages to be sold from the grab bag at the school carnival.* **2.** A group of many different things from which to choose; a variety. ♦*The TV program was a grab bag for young and old alike.*

**grab the bull by the horns** *or* **seize the bull by the horns** See TAKE THE BULL BY THE HORNS.

**grace period** *or* **period of grace** *n.* The time or extra time allowed in which to do something. ♦*The teacher gave the class a week's period of grace to finish workbooks.*

**grandstand** *v., slang, informal* To show off, to perform histrionics needlessly. ♦*Stop grandstanding and get down to honest work!*

**grandstander** *n., slang, informal* A showoff, a person who likes to engage in histrionics. ♦*Many people think that Evel Knievel is a grandstander.*

**graphic description** *or* **graphic descriptions** *n. phr.* Extremely detailed, often brutal scenes of the dead, etc. ♦*"What follows are some graphic descriptions of the battle," the television announcer said. "Sensitive viewers and children may not wish to see these."*

**grasp at straws** *or* **clutch at straws** *v. phr.* To depend on something that is useless or unable to help in a time of trouble or danger; try something with little hope of succeeding. ♦*The robber clutched at straws to make excuses. He said he wasn't in the country when the robbery happened.*

**grass is always greener on the other side of the fence** *or* **grass is always greener on the other side of the hill** We are often not satisfied and want to be somewhere else; a place that is far away or different seems better than where we are. ♦*John is always changing his job because the grass always looks greener to him on the other side of the fence.*

**grass roots** *n. phr* Of or by common people. ♦*The cause of nature conservation was taken up by grass roots organizations.*

**graveyard shift** *n. phr.* The work period lasting from sundown to sunup, when one has to work in the dark or by artificial light. ♦*"Why are you always so sleepy in class?" Professor Brown asked Sam. "Because I have to work the graveyard shift beside going to school," Sam answered.*

**gravy train** *n., slang, informal* The kind of job that brings in a much higher income than the services rendered would warrant. ♦*Jack's job at the Athletic Club as Social Director is a regular gravy train.*

**grease-ball** *n., slang, derogatory, avoidable* An immigrant from a southern country, such as Mexico, Italy, or Spain; a person with oily looking black hair. ♦*Mr. White is a racist; he calls Mr. Lopez from Tijuana a grease-ball because he has dark hair.*

**grease monkey** *n., slang, derogatory, avoidable* **1.** A person who greases or works on machinery; a mechanic or worker in a garage or gasoline station. ♦*The grease monkey was all dirty when he came out from under the car.* **2.** Airplane mechanic. ♦*Jack was a grease monkey in the Air Force.*

**grease one's palm** *or* **grease the palm** *slang* **1.** To pay a person for something done or given, especially dishonestly; bribe. ♦*Some politicians will help you if you grease their palms.* **2.** To give a tip; pay for a special favor or extra help. ♦*We had to grease the palm of the waiter to get a table in the crowded restaurant.*

**grease the wheels** *v. phr., informal* To do something or act to make something go smoothly or happen in the way that is wanted. ♦ *Mr. Davis asked a friend to grease the wheels so he could borrow money from the bank.*

**greasy spoon** *n., informal* Any small, inexpensive restaurant patronized by workers or people in a hurry; a place not noted for its excellence of cuisine or its decor. ♦ *I won't have time to eat lunch at the club today; I'll just grab a sandwich at the local greasy spoon.*

**great guns** *adv. phr., informal* **1.** Very fast or very hard.—Usually used in the phrases *blow great guns, go great guns.* ♦ *The men were going great guns to finish the job.* **2.** Very well; successfully. ♦ *Smith's new store opened last week and it's going great guns.*

**great minds think alike** When two people happen to think of the same idea, they jokingly quote this saying.—A proverb. ♦ *"I am tired of cooking tonight," Suzie said. "Let's go to a restaurant." "Just what I was going to suggest," Tom replied. "Goes to show that great minds think alike."*

**great oaks from little acorns grow** As great oak trees grow from tiny acorns, so many great people or things grew from a small and unimportant beginning, so be patient.—A proverb. ♦ *Many great men were once poor, unimportant boys. Great oaks from little acorns grow.*

**Greek to** *adj. phr.* Strange; alien; incomprehensible. ♦ *I can't figure out what language those people in the elevator are speaking, but whatever it is, it's all Greek to me.*

**green around the gills** *or* **pale around the gills** *adj. phr., slang* Pale-faced from fear or sickness; sickly; nauseated. ♦ *Bill's father took him for a ride in his boat while the waves were rough, and when he came back he was green around the gills.* ♦ *The car almost hit Mary crossing the street, and she was pale around the gills because it came so close.*

**green-eyed monster** *n. phr.* Jealousy; envy. ♦ *When John's brother got the new bicycle, the green-eyed monster made John fight with him.*

**green power** *n., slang, informal* The social prestige or power money can buy one. ♦ *In American political elections the candidates that win are usually the ones who have green power backing them.*

**green thumb** *n., informal* A talent for gardening; ability to make things grow. ♦ *Mr. Wilson's neighbors say his flowers grow because he has a green thumb.*

**green with envy** *adj. phr.* Very jealous; full of envy. ♦ *The other boys were green with envy when Joe bought a second-hand car.*

**grin and bear it** *v. phr., informal* To be as cheerful as possible in pain or trouble; do something without complaining. ♦ *If you must have a tooth drilled, all you can do is grin and bear it.*

**grind to a halt** *v. phr., informal* To slow down and stop like a machine does when turned off. ♦ *The old car ground to a halt in front of the house.*

**grin from ear to ear** *v. phr.* To smile very broadly; to be very happy about something. ♦ *"What are you grinning from ear to ear about?" Peter asked. "You won't believe it, but I won the lottery," John replied.*

**gross out** *v., slang* To commit a vulgar act; to repel someone by saying a disgusting or vulgar thing. ♦ *You are going to gross out people if you continue talking like that.*

**gross-out session** *n., slang, avoidable* A verbal contest between teen-agers in which the object of the game is to see who can be more disgusting or vulgar than anybody else. ♦ *When Jim got home he found his two teen-age sons engaged in a gross-out session; he bawled them out and cut their weekly allowance.*

**ground floor** *n.* **1.** First floor of a house or building. ♦ *Mrs. Turner has an apartment on the ground floor.* **2.** *informal* The first or best chance, especially in a business. ♦ *That man got rich because he got in on the ground floor of the television business.*

**ground rule** *n.* A rule, usually not written, of what to do or how to act in case certain things happen.—Usually used in the plural. ♦ *When you go to a new school, you don't know the ground rules of how you are supposed to behave.*

**ground zero** *n.* **1.** A place of total devastation. ♦ *Hiroshima and Nagasaki were ground zero after the atomic bomb was dropped on them in August 1945.*

**2.** After September 11, 2001: The place in New York City where the World Trade Center stood that was brought down by suicide terrorists. ♦ *Many tourists come to see ground zero, the place where the World Trade Center once stood.* **3.** A very messy and disorganized place. ♦ *"Why must you turn your room into a total ground zero?" Father asked indignantly.*

**growing pains** *n.* **1.** Pains in children's legs supposed to be caused by changes in their bodies and feelings as they grow. ♦ *The little girl's legs hurt, and her mother told her she had growing pains.* **2.** *informal* Troubles when something new is beginning or growing. ♦ *The factory has growing pains.*

**grow on** *or* **grow upon** *v.* **1.** To become stronger in; increase as a habit of. ♦ *The habit of eating before going to bed grew upon John.* **2.** To become more interesting to or liked by. ♦ *The more Jack saw Mary, the more she grew on him.*

**grow out of** *v. phr.* **1.** To outgrow; become too mature for. ♦ *As a child he had a habit of scratching his chin all the time, but he grew out of it.* **2.** To result from; arise. ♦ *Tom's illness grew out of his tendency to overwork and neglect his health.*

**grow up** *v.* To increase in size or height; become taller or older; reach full height. **1.** ♦ *Johnny is growing up; his shoes are too small for him.* ♦ *I grew up on a farm.* ♦ *The city has grown up since I was young.* **2.** To become adult in mind or judgment; become old enough to think or decide in important matters. ♦ *Tom wants to be a coach when he grows up.*

**gulp down** *v. phr.* To eat or drink in a great hurry. ♦ *It is considered unhealthy to gulp one's food down too fast.* ♦ *Gulping down ice water in the hot weather may give one a sore throat.*

**gum up** *v., slang* To cause not to work or ruin; spoil; make something go wrong. ♦ *Jimmy has gummed up the typewriter.*

**gun for** *v., informal* **1.** To hunt for with a gun; look hard for a chance to harm or defeat. ♦ *The cowboy is gunning for the man who stole his horse.* **2.** To try very hard to get. ♦ *The man is gunning for first prize in the golf tournament.*

**gung-ho** *adj., colloquial* Enthusiastic, full of eagerness in an uncritical or unsophisticated manner. ♦ *Suzie is all gung-ho on equal rights for women, but fails to see the consequences.*

**guns or butter** *or* **guns and butter** *or* **guns before butter** *n. phr.* The choice between a country's ability to wage war and feed the population properly, or the desire to do both, or the statement that one is rich and powerful enough to do both. ♦ *Countries that don't care for affluence and wish to fight may opt for guns before butter. Wealthy countries that are able to keep society affluent and wage war simultaneously, may speak of the economy's strength to have both guns and butter. Some may simply ask, "Is it going to be guns or butter?"*

**gut feeling** *n. phr.* An instinctive reaction. ♦ *I have a gut feeling that they will never get married in spite of all they say.*

**gut reaction** *n. phr.* A mental or physical response that springs from one's depths. ♦ *My gut reaction was to get out of here as fast as possible.*

**gut talk** *n. phr.* Sincere, honest talk. ♦ *We admire people who speak gut talk and tell exactly what they think and feel.*

**had better** *informal* Should; must. ◆ *I had better leave now, or I'll be late.*

**hail from** *v., informal* To have your home in; come from; be from; *especially,* to have been born and raised in. ◆ *Mrs. Gardner hails from Mississippi.*

**haircut place** *n., slang, citizen's band radio jargon* Bridge or overpass with tight clearance. ◆ *Are we going to make it in that haircut place?*

**hairdo** *n.* Style or manner of arranging, combing, or wearing one's hair. ◆ *"How do you like my new hairdo?" Jane asked, as she left the beauty parlor.*

**hair stand on end** *informal* The hair of your head rises stiffly upwards as a sign or result of great fright or horror. ◆ *When he heard the strange cry, his hair stood on end.* ◆ *The sight of the dead man made his hair stand on end.*

**hale and hearty** *adj. phr.* In very good health; well and strong. ◆ *Grandfather will be 80 years old tomorrow, but he is hale and hearty.* ◆ *That little boy looks hale and hearty, as if he is never sick.*

**half a chance** *or* **a half chance** *n.* An opportunity; a reasonable chance. ◆ *Just give yourself half a chance and you will quickly get used to your new job.*

**half a loaf is better than none** *or* **half a loaf is better than no bread** Part of what we want or need is better than nothing.—A proverb. ◆ *Albert wanted two dollars for shoveling snow from the sidewalk but the lady would only give him a dollar, so he said that half a loaf is better than none.*

**half a mind** *also* **half a notion** *n. phr., informal* A wish or plan that you have not yet decided to act on; a thought of possibly doing something.—Used after *have* or *with* and before *to* and an infinitive. ◆ *I have half a mind to stop studying and go to the movies.* ◆ *Jerry went home with half a mind to telephone Betty.*

**half-and-half¹** *adj.* As much one thing as the other. ◆ *We asked the coach if more boys than girls were interested in debating, and he said it was about half-and-half.* ◆ *The show last night was neither very good nor very poor—just half-and-half.*

**half-and-half²** *n.* A mixture of milk and cream in equal parts, used with cereal or coffee. ◆ *John uses half-and-half with his cereal, but his wife, who is dieting, uses milk.*

**half an eye** *n. phr.* A slight glance; a quick look. ◆ *While Mary was cooking she kept half an eye on the baby to see that he didn't get into mischief.*

**half-baked** *adj., informal* Not thought out or studied thoroughly; not worth considering or accepting. ◆ *We cannot afford to put the government in the hands of people with half-baked plans.*

**half-hearted** *adj.* Lacking enthusiasm or interest. ◆ *Phil made several half-hearted attempts to learn word processing, but we could see that he didn't really like it.*

**half-holiday** *n.* A day on which you get out of school or work in the afternoon. ◆ *The principal said that Tuesday would be a half-holiday.*

**half the battle** *n. phr.* A large part of the work. ◆ *When you write an essay for class, making the outline is half the battle.* ◆ *To see your faults and decide to change is half the battle of self-improvement.*

**half-time** *n.* A rest period in the middle of certain games. ◆ *I saw Henry at the football game and I went over and talked to him at half-time.*

**ham actor** *n. phr., slang* An untalented actor; someone who tries so hard to act that his performance becomes foolishly exaggerated. ◆ *Fred is a ham actor who, instead of memorizing his lines, keeps moving around in a ridiculous way.*

**ham it up** *v. phr., slang* To do more than look natural in acting a part; pretend too much; exaggerate. ◆ *When Tom told the teacher he was too sick to do homework, he really hammed it up.* ◆ *The old-fashioned movies are funny to us because the players hammed it up.*

**hammer and tongs** *adv. phr.* Violently. ◆ *Mr. and Mrs. Smith have been at it all day, hammer and tongs.*

**hammer at** *or* **hammer away at** *v.* **1.** To work steadily at; keep at. ◆ *That lesson is not easy, but hammer away at it and you will get it right.* **2.** To talk about again and again; emphasize. ♦ *The speaker hammered at his opponent's ideas.*

**hammer out** *v.* **1.** To write or produce by hard work. ♦ *The President sat at his desk till midnight hammering out his speech for the next day.* **2.** To remove, change, or work out by discussion and debate; debate and agree on (something). ♦ *Mrs. Brown and Mrs. Green have hammered out their difference of opinion.*

**hand down** *v.* To arrange to give or leave after death. ♦ *In old times, property was usually handed down to the oldest son at his father's death.*

**hand in glove** *or* **hand and glove** *adj. or adv. phr.* Very close or friendly; working together; in very close agreement or cooperation. ♦ *The Navy and the Coast Guard work hand and glove, especially in war time.* ♦ *Judges and others in high office sometimes are hand in glove with gangsters to cheat and steal.*

**hand in hand** *adv. phr.* **1.** Holding hands. ♦ *Bob and Mary walked along hand in hand in the park.* Compare ARM IN ARM. **2.** Accompanying each other; together; closely connected.—Used with *go.* ♦ *Ignorance and poverty often go hand in hand.*

**hand it to** *v. phr., informal* To admit the excellence of; give credit or praise to. ♦ *You have to hand it to Jim; he is very careful and hard-working in all he does.*

**handle to one's name** *n. phr., slang* A special title used before your name. ♦ *Jim's father has a handle to his name. He is Major Watson.* ♦ *Bob came back from the University with a handle to his name and was called Dr. Jones.*

**handle with gloves** *or* **handle with kid gloves** *v. phr., informal* **1.** To treat very gently and carefully. ♦ *An atomic bomb is handled with kid gloves.* **2.** To treat with great tact and diplomacy. ♦ *Aunt Jane is so irritable that we have to treat her with kid gloves.*

**hand-me-down** *n., informal* Something given away after another person has no more use for it; especially, used clothing. ♦ *Alice had four older sisters, so all her clothes were hand-me-downs.*

**hand on** *v.* To pass along to the next person who should have it. ♦ *Everyone*

in class should read this, so when you have finished, please hand it on. ♦ *In the early days, news was handed on from one person to another.*

**hand on the torch** *v. phr.* To give the power to the next person in office, or to the younger generation. ♦ *Before the director announced his retirement officially, he called John to his office and said, "Time to hand on the torch, John. You are my chosen successor."*

**handout** *n.* (stress on *hand*) **1.** A free gift of food, clothes, etc. ♦ *The homeless people were standing in a long line for various handouts.* **2.** A typed and photocopied sheet or sheets of paper outlining the main points made by a speaker. ♦ *Please look at page three of the handout.*

**hand out** *v., informal* (stress on *out*) To give (things of the same kind) to several people. ♦ *The teacher handed out the examination papers.* ♦ *Handing out free advice to all your friends will not make them like you.*

**hand over** *v.* To give control or possession of; give (something) to another person. ♦ *When Mr. Jones gets old, he will hand over his business to his son.*

**hand over fist** *adv. phr., informal* Fast and in large amounts. ♦ *Fred may get a pony for Christmas because his father is making money hand over fist.* ♦ *Business is so bad that the store on the corner is losing money hand over fist.*

**hand over hand** *adv. phr.* By taking hold with one hand over the other alternately. ♦ *The only way to climb a rope is hand over hand.*

**hand-pick** *v., informal* To choose very carefully. ♦ *The political bosses hand-picked a man for mayor who would agree with them.*

**hands-down** *adj., informal* **1.** Easy. ♦ *The Rangers won a hands-down victory in the tournament.* **2.** Unopposed; first; clear. ♦ *Johnny was the hands-down favorite for president of the class.*

**hands down** *adv., informal* **1.** Without working hard; easily. ♦ *The Rangers won the game hands down.* **2.** Without question or doubt; without any opposition; plainly. ♦ *John was hands down the best writer in the class.*

**hands off** *informal* Keep your hands off or do not interfere; leave that alone.—

Used as a command. ♦ *I was going to touch the machine, but the man cried, "Hands off!" and I let it alone.*

**hands-off** *adj., informal* Leaving alone, not interfering; inactive. ♦ *The United States told the European governments to follow a hands-off policy toward Latin America.*

**handsome is as handsome does** *informal* A person must act well and generously so that he will be truly worth respecting.—A proverb. ♦ *Everyone thinks that Bob is a very handsome boy, but he is very mean too. Handsome is as handsome does.*

**hands up** *informal* Hold up your hands! Put your hands up high and keep them there!— Used as a command. ♦ *The sheriff pointed his gun at the outlaws and called out, "Hands up!"*

**hand something to someone on a silver platter** *v. phr.* To give a person a reward that has not been earned. ♦ *The lazy student expected his diploma to be handed to him on a silver platter.*

**hand to hand** *adv. phr.* Close together, near enough to hit each other. ♦ *The two soldiers fought hand to hand until one fell badly wounded.* ♦ *In modern naval warfare, men seldom fight hand to hand.*

**hand-to-hand** *adj.* Close to each other; near enough to hit each other. ♦ *The result of the battle was decided in hand-to-hand combat.*

**hand-to-mouth** *adj.* Not providing for the future; living from day to day; not saving for later. ♦ *Many native tribes lead a hand-to-mouth existence, content to have food for one day at a time.*

**handwriting on the wall** *n. phr.* A sign that something bad will happen. ♦ *John's employer had less and less work for him; John could read the handwriting on the wall and looked for another job.*

**hang around** *v., informal* **1.** To pass time or stay near without any real purpose or aim; loaf near or in. ♦ *The principal warned the students not to hang around the corner drugstore after school.* **2.** To spend time or associate. ♦ *Jim hangs around with some boys who live in his neighborhood.*

**hang by a thread** *or* **hang by a hair** *v. phr.* To depend on a very small thing;

be in doubt. ♦ *For three days Tom was so sick that his life hung by a thread.*

**hang in effigy** *or* **burn in effigy** *v. phr.* To hang or burn a figure, usually a stuffed dummy, representing a person who is disliked or scorned. ♦ *When the high school team lost the championship game, the coach was hung in effigy by the townspeople.* ♦ *During World War II, Hitler was sometimes burned in effigy in the United States.*

**hang in the balance** *v. phr.* To have two equally possible results; to be in doubt; be uncertain. ♦ *She was very sick and her life hung in the balance for several days.*

**hang in (there)** *v. phr., slang, informal* To persevere; not to give up; to stick to a project and not lose faith or courage. ♦ *Hang in there old buddy; the worst is yet to come.*

**hang on** *v.* **1.** To hold on to something, usually tightly. ♦ *Jack almost fell off the cliff, but managed to hang on until help came.* **2a.** To continue doing something; persist. ♦ *The grocer was losing money every day, but he hung on, hoping that business would improve.* **2b.** To hold a lead in a race or other contest while one's opponents try to rally. ♦ *The favorite horse opened an early lead and hung on to win as two other horses almost passed him in the final stretch.* **3.** To continue to give trouble or cause suffering. ♦ *Lou's cold hung on from January to April.* **4.** To continue listening on the telephone. ♦ *Jerry asked John, who had called him on the phone, to hang on while he ran for a pencil and a sheet of paper.*

**hang one on** *v. phr., slang* **1.** To give a heavy blow to; hit hard. ♦ *The champion hung one on his challenger in the second round and knocked him out of the ring.* **2.** To get very drunk. ♦ *After Smith lost his job, he went to a bar and hung one on.*

**hang one's head** *v. phr.* To bend your head forward in shame. ♦ *Johnny hung his head when the teacher asked him if he broke the window.*

**hang on the words of** *also* **hang on the lips of** *v. phr.* To listen very attentively to. ♦ *Ann hangs on every word of her history teacher and takes very careful notes.*

**hang onto** v. To hold tightly; keep firmly. ♦ *The child hung onto its mother's apron, and would not let go.* ♦ *John did not like his job, but decided to hang onto it until he found a better one.*

**hang onto your hat** or **hold onto your hat** or **hold your hat** v. phr., informal **1.** Watch out; be prepared.—Used as a command, usually to warn of an unexpected action. ♦ *"Hold onto your hat," said Jim as he stepped on the gas and the car shot forward.* **2.** Get ready for a surprise.—Used as a command, usually to warn of unexpected news. ♦ *"Hold onto your hat," said Mary. "Jim asked me to marry him."*

**hang out** v. **1.** slang To spend your time idly or lounging about. ♦ *The teacher complained that Joe was hanging out in poolrooms instead of doing his homework.* **2.** slang To live; reside. ♦ *Two policemen stopped the stranger and asked him where he hung out.* **3.** To reach out farther than the part below. ♦ *The branches of the trees hung out over the road.* ♦ *The upper floor of that house hangs out above the first.*

**hang out one's shingle** v. phr., informal To give public notice of the opening of an office, especially a doctor's or lawyer's office, by putting up a small signboard. ♦ *The young doctor hung out his shingle and soon had a large practice.*

**hangover** n. (stress on *hang*) A bad feeling of nausea and/or headache the day after one has had too much to drink. ♦ *Boy, did I have a hangover after that party yesterday!*

**hang over** v. (stress on *over*) **1.** To be going to happen to; threaten. ♦ *Great trouble hangs over the little town because its only factory has closed down.* **2.** To remain to be finished or settled. ♦ *The committee took up the business that hung over from its last meeting.*

**hang over one's head** v. phr. To be a danger or threat to you. ♦ *Death hangs over a bullfighter's head every time he performs.*

**hang ten** v., slang **1.** To be an outstanding performer on a surfboard or on a skateboard (referring to the user's ten toes). ♦ *I bet I am going to be able to hang ten if you let me practice on your*

skateboard. **2.** To be a survivor despite great odds. ♦ *Don't worry about Jack, he can hang ten anywhere!*

**hang together** v. **1.** To stay united; help and defend one another. ♦ *The club members always hung together when one of them was in trouble.* **2.** informal To form a satisfactory whole; fit together. ♦ *Jack's story of why he was absent from school seems to hang together.*

**hang up** v. (stress on *up*) **1.** To place on a hook, peg, or hanger. ♦ *When the children come to school, they hang up their coats in the cloakroom.* **2a.** To place a telephone receiver back on its hook and break the connection. ♦ *Carol's mother told her she had talked long enough on the phone and made her hang up.* **2b.** To put a phone receiver back on its hook while the other person is still talking.—Used with *on.* ♦ *I said something that made Joe angry, and he hung up on me.*

**hang-up** n., informal (stress on *hang*) **1.** A delay in some process. ♦ *The mail has been late for several days; there must be some hang-up with the trucks somewhere.* **2.** A neurotic reaction to some life situation probably stemming from a traumatic shock which has gone unconscious. ♦ *Doctor Simpson believes that Suzie's frigidity is due to some hang-up about men.*

**happen on** or **happen upon** v. literary To meet or find accidentally or by chance. ♦ *The Girl Scouts happened on a charming little brook not far from the camp.*

**happy as the day is long** adj. phr. Cheerful and happy. ♦ *Carl is happy as the day is long because school is over for the summer.*

**happy camper** v. phr. A person who is satisfied or happy about a given situation, someone who doesn't complain. ♦ *John is generally a happy camper, especially when pursuing the outdoor sports.* ♦ *Hermione was not a happy camper when Suzanne got the promotion she had hoped for.*

**happy-go-lucky** See FOOTLOOSE AND FANCY-FREE.

**happy hour** n., informal A time in bars or restaurants when cocktails are served at a reduced rate, usually one hour before they start serving dinner.

♦*Happy hour is between 6 and 7 P.M. at Celestial Gardens.*

**happy hunting ground** *n. phr.* **1.** The place where, in American Indian belief, a person goes after death; heaven. ♦*The Indians believed that at death they went to the happy hunting ground.* **2.** *informal* A place or area where you can find a rich variety of what you want, and plenty of it. ♦*The forest is a happy hunting ground for scouts who are interested in plants and flowers.*

**happy medium** See GOLDEN MEAN *or* GOLDEN MEDIUM.

**hard-and-fast** *adj.* Not to be broken or changed; fixed; strict. ♦*The teacher said that there was a hard-and-fast rule against smoking in the school.*

**hard as nails** *adj. phr., informal* **1.** Not flabby or soft; physically very fit; tough and strong. ♦*After a summer of work in the country, Jack was as hard as nails, without a pound of extra weight.* **2.** Not gentle or mild; rough; stern. ♦*John works for a boss who is as hard as nails and scolds John roughly whenever he does something wrong.*

**hard-boiled** *adj.* Unrefined; tough; merciless. ♦*"Because you were two minutes late," my hard-boiled boss cried, "I will deduct fifteen minutes worth from your salary!"*

**hard disk** *n. phr.* The central memory in personal computers of all brands, sometimes called the "Winchester." Originally they came 40 to 100 megabytes; but nowadays 64 gigabytes are not uncommon. ♦*"Sam, please get me a new hard drive! I need at least 30 gigabytes to store all my data."*

**hard facts** *n. phr.* Circumstances established beyond any doubt. ♦*"You can't argue with hard facts," the judge said.*

**hard feeling** *n.* Angry or bitter feeling; enmity.—Usually used in the plural. ♦*Jim asked Andy to shake hands with him, just to show that there were no hard feelings.*

**hard-fisted** *adj.* **1.** Able to do hard physical labor; strong. ♦*Jack's uncle was a hard-fisted truck driver with muscles of steel.* **2.** Not gentle or easy-going; tough; stern. ♦*The new teacher was a hard-fisted woman who would allow no nonsense.* **3.** Stingy or mean; not generous with money. ♦*The hard-*

*fisted banker refused to lend Mr. Jones more money for his business.*

**hard going** *adj. phr.* Fraught with difficulty. ♦*Dave finds his studies of math hard going.*

**hardheaded** *adj.* Stubborn; shrewd; practical. ♦*Don is a hardheaded businessman who made lots of money, even during the recession.*

**hardhearted** *adj.* Unsympathetic; merciless. ♦*Jack is so hardhearted that even his own children expect nothing from him.*

**hard-hitting** *adj.* Working hard to get things done; strong and active; stubbornly eager. ♦*The boys put on a hard-hitting drive to raise money for uniforms for the football team.*

**hard line** *n. phr.* Tough political policy. ♦*Although modern economists were trying to persuade him to open up to the West, Castro has always taken the hard line approach.*

**hardly any** *or* **scarcely any** Almost no or almost none; very few. ♦*Hardly any of the students did well on the test, so the teacher explained the lesson again.* ♦*Charles and his friends each had three cookies, and when they went out, hardly any cookies were left.*

**hardly ever** *or* **scarcely ever** *adv. phr.* Very rarely; almost never; seldom. ♦*It hardly ever snows in Florida.* ♦*Johnny hardly ever reads a book.*

**hard-nosed** *adj., slang* Tough or rugged; very strict; not weak or soft; stubborn, especially in a fight or contest. ♦*Joe's father was a hard-nosed army officer who had seen service in two wars.*

**hard nut to crack** *also* **tough nut to crack** *n. phr., informal* Something difficult to understand or to do. ♦*Tom's algebra lesson was a hard nut to crack.*

**hard of hearing** *adj.* Partially deaf. ♦*Some people who are hard of hearing wear hearing aids.*

**hard-on** *n. vulgar, avoidable.* An erection of the male sexual organ.

**hard pill to swallow** *n. phr.* News or information that is hard or painful to accept. ♦*The announcement that the state is bankrupt and that threre won't be any salary raises for the next two years was a very hard pill to swallow.*

**hard put** *or* **hard put to it** *adj.* In a difficult position; faced with difficulty;

barely able. ♦ *John was hard put to find a good excuse for his lateness in coming to school.*

**hard sell** *n., informal* A kind of salesmanship characterized by great vigor, aggressive persuasion, and great eagerness on the part of the person selling something; opposed to 'soft sell'. ♦ *Your hard sell turns off a lot of people; try the soft sell for a change, won't you?*

**hard-top** *n.* **1.** A car that has a metal roof; a car that is not a convertible. ♦ *Every spring Mr. Jones sells his hardtop and buys a convertible.* **2.** or **hardtop convertible** A car with windows that can be completely lowered with no partitions left standing, and with a top that may or may not be lowered. ♦ *Mr. Brown's new car is a hardtop convertible.*

**hard up** *adj., informal* Without enough money or some other needed thing. ♦ *Dick was hard up and asked Lou to lend him a dollar.*

**hard way** *n.* The harder or more punishing of two or more ways to solve a problem, do something, or learn something.—Used with *the.* ♦ *The challenger found out the hard way that the champion's left hand had to be avoided.*

**harebrained** *adj.* Thoughtless; foolish. ♦ *Most of the harebrained things Ed does may be attributable to his youth and lack of experience.*

**hark back** *v. literary* **1.** To recall or turn back to an earlier time or happening. ♦ *Judy is always harking back to the good times she had in college.* **2.** To go back to something as a beginning or origin. ♦ *The slit in the back of a man's coat harks back to the days when men rode horseback.*

**harp away at** or **on** *v.* To mention again and again. ♦ *In his campaign speeches, Jones harps on his rival's wealth and powerful friends.*

**harum-scarum**[1] *adv., informal* In a careless, disorderly or reckless way. ♦ *Jim does his homework harum-scarum, and that is why his schoolwork is so poor.*

**harum-scarum**[2] *adj., informal* Careless, wild, or disorderly in one's acts or performance; reckless. ♦ *Jack is such a harum-scarum boy that you can never depend on him to do anything right.*

**hash out** *v., informal* To talk all about and try to agree on; discuss thoroughly. ♦ *The teacher asked Susan and Jane to sit down together and hash out their differences.*

**hat in hand** *adv. phr., informal* In a humble and respectful manner. ♦ *They went hat in hand to the old woman to ask for her secret recipe.*

**hatchet job** *n. phr., slang* **1.** The act of saying or writing terrible things about someone or something, usually on behalf of one's boss or organization. ♦ *When Phil makes speeches against the competition exaggerating their weaknesses, he is doing the hatchet job on behalf of our president.* **2.** A ruthless, wholesale job of editing a script whereby entire paragraphs or pages are omitted. ♦ *Don, my editor, did a hatchet job on my new novel.*

**hatchet man** *n., colloquial* **1.** A politician or newspaper columnist whose job is to write and say unfavorable things about the opposition. ♦ *Bill Lerner is the hatchet man for the mayor's party; he smears all the other candidates regularly.* **2.** An executive officer in a firm whose job it is to fire superfluous personnel, cut back on the budget, etc., in short, to do the necessary but unpleasant things. ♦ *The firm hired Cranhart to be hatchet man; his title is that of executive vice president.*

**hate one's guts** *v. phr., slang* To feel a very strong dislike for someone. ♦ *Dick said that he hated Fred's guts because Fred had been very mean to him.*

**hats off to** or **one's hat is off to** *truncated phr. informal* Used to recognize and praise a job well-done. ♦ *Hats off to anyone who runs the twenty-six mile race.* ♦ *My hat is off to the chef who created this delicious meal.*

**haul down one's colors** or **strike one's colors** *v. phr* **1.** To pull down a flag, showing you are beaten and want to stop fighting. ♦ *After a long battle, the pirate captain hauled down his colors.* **2.** To admit you are beaten; say you want to quit. ♦ *After losing two sets of tennis, Tom hauled down his color.*

**haul in** or **haul up** or **pull in** *v. slang* To bring before someone in charge for punishment or questioning; arrest.

♦*John was hauled in to court for speeding.*
**haul over the coals** *or* **rake over the coals** *v. phr.* To criticize sharply; rebuke; scold. ♦ *The sergeant raked the soldier over the coals for being late for roll call.*
**have** *or* **get** *or* **develop a crush on** *v. phr.* To be infatuated with someone. ♦ *Walter has a terrible crush on his English teacher, but she is a lot older and doesn't take it seriously.*
**have a ball** *v. phr., slang* Enjoy yourself very much; have a wonderful time. ♦ *Mary and Tim have a ball exploring the town.*
**have a beef against one** *or* **hold a beef against one** *phrasal idiom* To have a complaint against one. ♦ *John behaves very embarrassed around the director; I guess he must have a beef against him.* ♦ *Why hold a beef against me? I didn't cause your troubles!*
**have a big head** *v. phr.* To be conceited; be excessively proud; think too highly of oneself. ♦ *Albert is a nice enough guy, but alas, he has a big head.*
**have a blast** *v. phr.* To have a big celebration, a joyous party; to have a great time. ♦ *When Professor Doolittle retired, he invited the entire department to his country house and we all had a blast.*
**have a bone to pick** See BONE TO PICK.
**have a corner on** *v. phr.* To have a monopoly on some product or trade secret. ♦ *We cannot compete with the big telephone companies, because they have a corner on the market.*
**have a field day** *v. phr.* To enjoy great success or unlimited opportunity. ♦ *The visiting basketball team was so weak that our school had a field day scoring one point after another.*
**have a fit** *or* **have fits** *or* **throw a fit** *v. phr.* **1.** To have a sudden illness with stiffness or jerking of the body. ♦ *Our dog had a fit yesterday.* **2.** *informal* To become angry or upset. ♦ *Father will throw a fit when he sees the dent in the car.* ♦ *Howard will have a fit when he learns that he lost the election.*
**have a ghost of a chance** *v. phr.* To have hardly any chance at all. ♦ *Will the Kurds every have their own independent state? Under the present circumstances they have a ghost of a chance at best.*

**have a go at** *v. phr., informal* To try, especially after others have tried. ♦ *She had a go at pottery, but did not do very well.*
**have a good head on one's shoulders** *v. phr.* To be smart; intelligent; well educated. ♦ *Rob is not the handsomest guy in the world but the girls appreciate him because he has a good head on his shoulders.*
**have a (good) head for** *v. phr.* To have a special talent in a certain area. ♦ *Joan has quite a good head for business administration.*
**have a (good) mind to** *v. phr.* To consider doing; intend to with a high degree of probability. ♦ *I have a good mind to tell my boss that he doesn't know how to run our enterprise.*
**have a good one** *v. phr., greeting on departure* This idiom is used when one says good-bye to someone wishing them a pleasant day or upcoming time without naming the time itself. ♦ *"Have a good one," the storekeeper said to Mr. Schwartz before July Fourth. "You, too!" Mr. Schwartz answered.*
**have a hand in** *v. phr.* To have a part in or influence over; to be partly responsible for. ♦ *Ben had a hand in getting ready the Senior play.*
**have a heart** *v. phr., informal* To stop being mean; be kind, generous, or sympathetic. ♦ *Have a heart, Bob, and lend me two dollars.*
**have a heart-to-heart talk** *v. phr.* To confide in someone with great intimacy. ♦ *Jill and her mother had a heart-to-heart talk before she decided to move in with Andrew.*
**have a knack for** *v. phr.* To have an innate talent for something. ♦ *We can't understand how our son became a piano virtuoso, since nobody plays any instrument in the family. We guess he just has a knack for music and the piano in particular.*
**have all one's buttons** *or* **have all one's marbles** *v. phr., slang* To have all your understanding; be reasonable.— Usually used in the negative or conditionally. ♦ *Mike acts sometimes as if he didn't have all his buttons.* ♦ *He would not go to town barefooted if he had all his marbles.*
**have a long face** *or* **have on a long face** *v. phr.* To be and look sad. ♦ *David had*

a long face when he heard that he would not get the promotion he had hoped for.

**have a long fuse** *v. phr.* To be a patient person, not to lose one's cool even under constant irritation. ♦ *If you want to be a grade school teacher, you had better have a long fuse.*

**have a mind of one's own** *v. phr.* To be independent in one's thinking and judgment. ♦ *Tom has always had a mind of his own so there is no use trying to convince him how to vote.*

**have an affair with** *v. phr.* To have a sexual relationship with someone, either before marriage or outside of one's marriage. ♦ *Tom and Jane had a long and complex affair but they never got married.*

**have an ear for** *v. phr.* To have a keen perception; have a taste or a talent for; be sensitive to something. ♦ *I have no ear whatsoever for foreign languages or music.*

**have an edge on** *v. phr., informal* **1.** To have an advantage over someone or something else in the course of an evaluative comparison. ♦ *I can't beat you at tennis, but I have an edge on you in ping-pong.* **2.** To be mildly intoxicated; to have had a few drinks. ♦ *Joe sure had an edge on when I saw him last night.*

**have an eye for** *v. phr.* To be able to judge correctly of; have good taste in. ♦ *She has an eye for color and style in clothes.*

**have an eye on** *or* **have one's eye on** *v. phr., informal* **1.** To look at or think about (something wanted); have a wish for; have as an aim. ♦ *John has his eye on a scholarship so he can go to college.*

**have a nose for** *v. phr.* To have a natural talent to find out secrets, etc. ♦ *Small wonder Mr. Murphy became chief of police in Chicago; he has a nose for investigative work.*

**have a peg to hang on** *v. phr.* To have someone to blame for something. ♦ *The boss made a bad mistake at work, so he blamed poor Jack. Lucky for him that he had a peg to hang his own mistake on.*

**have a say in** *or* **a voice in** *v. phr.* To have the right to express one's opinion or cast a vote in a pending matter. ♦ *Our*

boss is friendly and democratic; he always encourages us to have a say in what we will do next.

**have a screw loose** *v. phr., slang* To act in a strange way; to be foolish. ♦ *Now I know he has a screw loose—he stole a police car this time.*

**have a short fuse** *v. phr.* To be impatient; have a hard time taking abuse and irritation. ♦ *Jack has a very short fuse; it's better not to mess with him.*

**have a shot at** *v. phr.* To have a chance at succeeding by trying to do something. ♦ *"Do you think we have a shot at winning the lottery?" Jim asked. "It's very hard to win the lottery. It's a long shot in any event," Peter replied.*

**have a snowball's chance in hell** *v. phr.* To be condemned to failure; enjoy a zero chance of success. ♦ *Pessimists used to think that we had a snowball's chance in hell to put a man on the moon; yet we did it in July, 1969.*

**have a soft spot in one's heart for** *v. phr.* To be sympathetically inclined towards; entertain a predilection for. ♦ *Ron always had a soft spot in his heart for intellectual women wearing miniskirts.*

**have a sweet tooth** *v. phr.* To be excessively fond of dessert items, such as ice cream, pies, etc. ♦ *Jill has a sweet tooth; she always orders cake after a meal in a restaurant.*

**have a time** *v. phr., informal* **1.** To have trouble; have a hard time. ♦ *Poor Susan had a time trying to get the children to go to bed.* **2.** To have a good time; to have fun.—Used with a reflexive pronoun. ♦ *Mary had herself a time dancing at the party.*

**have a way with** *v. phr.* To be able to lead, persuade, or influence. ♦ *Ted will be a good veterinarian, because he has a way with animals.*

**have a way with words** *v. phr.* To be talented at speech; be able to influence others by expressing oneself succinctly and persuasively. ♦ *The reason why John was elected to Congress at such a young age is that he really has a way with words.*

**have a word with** *v. phr.* **1.** To talk, discuss, or speak briefly with. ♦ *Robert, I need to have a word with you about tomorrow's exam.* **2.** To engage in a sincere discussion with the purpose of persuading the other person or let him or her know of one's dissatisfaction. ♦ *Our boss has been making funny decisions lately; I think we ought to have a word with him.*

**have been around** *v. phr., informal* Have been to many places and done many things; know people; have experience and be able to take care of yourself. ♦ *It's not easy to fool him; he's been around.*

**have come to stay** *v. phr.* To be generally accepted, be permanent. ♦ *Smaller sized compact cars made in Japan have come to stay.*

**have dibs on** *or* **put dibs on** *v. phr., slang* To demand a share of something or to be in line for the use of an object usable by more than one person. ♦ *Don't throw your magazine away! I put (my) dibs on it, remember?*

**have done with** *v.* To stop doing or using something. ♦ *When you have done with that paintbrush, Barbara, I would like to use it.*

**have eyes only for** *v. phr.* To see or want nothing else but; give all your attention to; be interested only in. ♦ *All the girls liked Fred, but he had eyes only for Helen.*

**have got it up there** *v. phr.* To be intellectually superior; to be smart. ♦ *John's success is easy to explain; he's really got it up there.*

**have got to** *v. phr.* Must; be in great need to do something; be obliged to. ♦ *I am sorry but we have got to leave, otherwise, we'll miss the last train.*

**have had it** *v. phr., slang* To have experienced or suffered all you can; to have come to the end of your patience or life. ♦ *"I've had it," said Lou, "I'm resigning from the job of chairman right now."*

**have had one's moments** *v. phr.* An expression describing someone's positive or negative behavior in the past. ♦ *John is generally a kind person, but his daughter says that he, too, had his moments.* ♦ *Mr. White is generally very stingy with his money, but when he saw real need he, too, had his moments of generosity.*

**have** *or* **hold the whip over** *v. phr.* To control; dominate. ♦ *Eugene has always held the whip over his younger brothers and sisters.*

**have in mind** *v. phr.* To plan; intend; select. ♦ *We don't know whom our boss has in mind for the new position.*

**have in the palm of one's hand** *v. phr.* To completely control; have a project finished, all wrapped up. ♦ *Our boss felt that if he could calm his critics he would soon have the entire factory in the palm of his hand.*

**have it** *v. phr.* **1.** To hear or get news; understand. ♦ *I have it on the best authority that we will be paid for our work next week.* **2.** To do something in a certain way. ♦ *Bobby must have it his way and play the game by his rules.* **3.** To claim; say. ♦ *Rumor has it that the school burned down.* **4.** To allow it— Usually used with *will* or *would* in negative sentences. ♦ *Mary wanted to give the party at her house, but her mother wouldn't have it.* **5.** To win. ♦ *When the senators vote, the ayes will have it.* **6.** To get or find the answer; think of how to do something. ♦ *"I have it!" said John to Mary. "We can buy Mother a nice comb for her birthday."* **7.** *informal* To have an (easy, good, rough, soft) time; have (certain kinds of) things happen to you; be treated in a (certain) way by luck or life. ♦ *Everyone liked Joe and he had it good until he got sick.*

**have it both ways** *v. phr.* Two incompatible approaches to the same problem cannot happen at the same time. ♦ *John wants to keep both his wife and his mistress; he doesn't understand that he must choose—you can't have it both ways.*

**have it coming** *v. phr.* To deserve the good or bad things that happen to you. ♦ *I feel sorry about Jack's failing that course, but he had it coming to him.* ♦ *Everybody said that Eve had it coming when she won the scholarship.*

**have it in for** *v. phr., informal* To wish or mean to harm; have a bitter feeling against. ♦ *After John beat Ted in a fight, Ted always had it in for John.*

**have it made** *v. phr., slang* To be sure of success; have everything you need. ♦ *With her fine grades Alice has it made and can enter any college in the country.*

**have it out** *v. phr.* To settle a difference by a free discussion or by a fight. ♦ *The former friends finally decided to have it* *out in a free argument and they became friends again.*

**have it over** *or* **have it all over** *v. phr.* To be better than; be superior to. ♦ *A jeep has it over a regular car on rough mountain trails.*

**have lots (everything) going for one** *v. phr.* To have abilities or qualities that help in achieving one's goal; assets working in one's favor. ♦ *The young woman will surely get the job; she has everything going for her.*

**have no business** *v. phr.* To have no right or reason. ♦ *Jack had no business saying those nasty things about Dick.*

**have none of** *v. phr.* To refuse to approve or allow. ♦ *The boss said she would have none of Mike's arguing.*

**have nothing on** *or* **not have anything on** *v. phr.* Not to be any better than; to have no advantage over. ♦ *Although the Smiths have a Rolls Royce, they have nothing on the Jones' who have a Cadillac and a Jaguar.* **2.** To have no information or proof that someone broke the law. ♦ *Mr. James was not worried when he was arrested because he was sure they had nothing on him.*

**have nothing to do with** *v. phr.* To not be involved with; not care about. ♦ *Our firm has nothing to do with oil from the Near East; we are interested in solar energy.*

**have off** *v. phr.* To not have to work, such as on weekends or on holidays. ♦ *"May I speak to John?" a customer at the store asked. "I am afraid you can't, he has his day off."*

**have on** *v.* **1.** To be dressed in; wear. ♦ *Mary had on her new dress.* **2.** To have (something) planned; have an appointment; plan to do. ♦ *I'm sorry I can't attend your party, but I have a meeting on for that night.*

**have one's ass in a sling** *v. phr., slang, vulgar, avoid!* To be in an uncomfortable predicament; to be in the doghouse; to be at a disadvantage. ♦ *Al sure had his ass in a sling when the boss found out about his juggling the account.*

**have one's cake and eat it too** *v. phr.* To enjoy two opposite advantages. ♦ *You can either spend your money going to Europe or save it for a down payment on a house, but you can't do both. That*

*would be having your cake and eating it, too.*

**have one's ear** *v. phr.* To have access to someone in power; receive audiences rather frequently. ♦ *The national security advisor has the president's ear.*

**have one's ears on** *v. phr., slang, citizen's band radio jargon* To have one's CB radio in receiving condition. ♦ *Good buddy in the eighteen wheeler southbound, got your ears on?*

**have oneself** *v. phr., nonstandard* To enjoy—Sometimes used in very informal speech to provide emphasis. ♦ *After working hard all day, John had himself a good night's sleep.*

**have one's fill** *v. phr.* To be satisfied; be surfeited; be overindulged. ♦ *Howard says he's had his fill of expensive golf tournaments in Europe.*

**have one's fling** *v. phr.* To have one or more romantic and/or sexual experiences, usually before marriage. ♦ *Jack has had his fling and now seems to be ready to get married and settle down.*

**have one's hand in the till** See ROB THE TILL.

**have one's hands full** *v. phr.* To have as much work as you can do; be very busy. ♦ *The plumber said that he had his hands full and could not take another job for two weeks.*

**have one's head in the sand** See HIDE ONE'S HEAD IN THE SAND.

**have one's head screwed on backwards** *v. phr.* To lack common sense; behave in strange and irrational ways. ♦ *Henry seems to have his head screwed on backwards; he thinks the best time to get a suntan is when it is raining and to sleep with his shoes on.*

**have one's hide** *v. phr., informal* To punish severely. ♦ *John's mother said she would have his hide if he was late to school again.*

**have one's way** *v. phr.* To make one's will prevail over that of others. ♦ *Jim is a very strong-willed person; he wants to have his way all the time.*

**have one's wits about one** *v. phr.* To be alert; remain calm; not panic. ♦ *Sam was the only one who kept his wits about him when the floodwaters of the Mississippi broke into our yard.*

**have one's work cut out** See CUT OUT 1.

**have (someone) over** *v. phr.* To invite

someone; to treat someone to a meal, a snack, or some conversation at one's home. ♦ *Our new neighbors really seem like nice people; shouldn't we have them over to our place?*

**have qualms about** *v. phr.* To feel uneasy about; hesitate about something. ♦ *Mike had no qualms in telling Sue that he was no longer in love with her.*

**have rocks in one's head** *v. phr., informal* To be stupid; not have good judgment. ♦ *When Mr. James quit his good job with the coal company to begin teaching school, some people thought he had rocks in his head.*

**have second thoughts about** See SECOND THOUGHT(S).

**have seen better days** See SEE BETTER DAYS.

**have (someone) by the balls** *v. phr., slang, vulgar, avoidable* To have someone at a disadvantage or in one's power. ♦ *The kidnappers had the company by the balls for six long weeks.*

**have (something) down pat** *v. phr.* To know the details of something entirely, in every detail. ♦ *"Can we trust Jim with making that deal with our Japanese partners?" the company director asked. "I am sure we can," Jim's supervisor answered. "He has all the details down pat."*

**have (something) going for one** *v. phr., slang, informal* To have ability, talent; good looks, and/or influence in important places helping one to be successful. ♦ *Well now, Pat Jones, that's another story—she's got something going for her.*

**have something on** *v. phr., informal* To have information or proof that someone did something wrong. ♦ *Although Miss Brown is not a good worker, her boss does not fire her because she has something on him.*

**have something on the ball** *v. phr., slang, colloquial* To be smart, clever; to be skilled and have the necessary know-how. ♦ *You can trust Syd; he's got a lot on the ball* OR *he's got something on the ball.*

**have the blues** See FEEL BLUE.

**have the constitution of an ox** *v. phr.* To be able to work extremely hard and to have the stamina to overcome misfortune. ♦ *Stan, who has lost both of his*

parents within one year and is constantly working late, seems to be indestructible, as if he had the constitution of an ox.

**have the courage of one's convictions** *v. phr.* To be brave enough to act according to your beliefs. ♦ *Steve showed that he had the courage of his convictions by refusing to help another student cheat in the exam.*

**have the guts to do something** *v. phr., informal* To be brave enough to do something difficult or dangerous. ♦ *Jack wants to marry Jill, but he doesn't have the guts to pop the question.*

**have the last laugh** *or* **get the last laugh** *v. phr.* To make someone seem foolish for having laughed at you. ♦ *Other schools laughed at us when our little team entered the state championship, but we had the last laugh when we won it.*

**have the lead** *v. phr.* To occupy the most prominent part in something. ♦ *Maria has the lead in our school play.*

**have the makings of** *v. phr.* To possess the basic ingredients; have the basic qualities to do something. ♦ *Tom is still young but he seems to have the makings of an excellent pianist.*

**have the right-of-way** *v. phr.* To have priority in proceeding in traffic on a public highway while other vehicles must yield and wait. ♦ *"Go ahead," he said. "We have the right-of-way at this intersection."*

**have time on one's hands** *v. phr.* To have the leisure to do something; to be free to do something. ♦ *Let Aunt Mary do some baby-sitting for us next month; she has recently retired, her children are gone, and she has time on her hands.*

**have time to kill** *v. phr.* To be free to spend one's time idly, playing, or pursuing one's favorite hobby or sport. ♦ *Come on and let's play some ping-pong. I've got some time to kill and you, too, can use a bit of relaxation.*

**have to do with** *v. phr.* **1.** To be about; be on the subject of or connected with. ♦ *The book has to do with airplanes.* **2.** To know or be a friend of; work or have business with.—Usually used in negative sentence. ♦ *Tom said he didn't want to have anything to do with the new boy.*

**have two strikes against one** *or* **have two strikes on one** *v. phr.*, *informal* To have things working against you; be hindered in several ways; be in a difficult situation; be unlikely to succeed. ◆ *Children from the poorest parts of a city often have two strikes against them before they enter school.*

**have what it takes** *v. phr.* To be suited to do something; to possess the ability, skill, and qualifications to carry out a certain task. ◆ *"Can we make John vice president of the firm?" the director asked. "He certainly has what it takes," John's supervisor replied.*

**have words with** *v. phr.* To quarrel with someone; to argue; to have a heated verbal contest. ◆ *"Why is Mom so upset?" Suzie asked. "She and Dad had words again," Suzie's brother replied.*

**head above water** *n. phr.* out of difficulty; clear of trouble. ◆ *Business at the store is bad. They can't keep their heads above water.*

**head and shoulders** *adv. phr.* **1.** By the measure of the head and shoulders. ◆ *The basketball player is head and shoulders taller than the other boys.* **2.** By far; by a great deal; very much. ◆ *She is head and shoulders above the rest of the class in singing.*

**head back** *v. phr.* To start to return to the place where one came from. ◆ *"It's raining; I think we'd better head back and try to reach the other side of the mountain tomorrow," the leader of the excursion advised his companions.*

**head for** *v. phr.* To go in the direction of. ◆ *We left early in the morning and headed for Niagara Falls.*

**head for the hills** *v. phr.*, *informal* To get far away in a hurry; run away and hide.—Often used imperatively. ◆ *Head for the hills. The bandits are coming.*

**head-hunting** *n.*, *slang*, *informal* **1.** The custom of seeking out, decapitating, and preserving the heads of enemies as trophies **2.** A search for qualified individuals to fill certain positions. ◆ *The president sent a committee to the colleges and universities to do some head-hunting; we hope he finds some young talent.* **3.** A systematic destruction of opponents, especially in politics. ◆ *Billings was hired by the party to do some head-hunting among members of the opposition.*

**head in the clouds** See IN THE CLOUDS.

**head in the sand** See HIDE ONE'S HEAD IN THE SAND.

**head off** *v.* **1.** To get in front of and stop, turn back, or turn aside. ◆ *The sheriff said to head the cattle thieves off at the pass.* **2.** To block; stop; prevent. ◆ *He will get into trouble if someone doesn't head him off.*

**head off for the four winds** *v. phr.* To go in all directions of the compass. ◆ *The U.S. Marines and Infantry had to head off for the four winds in Iraq to liberate the country.*

**head-on** *adj.* or *adv. phr.* **1.** With the head or front pointing at; with the front facing; front end to front end. ◆ *Our car skidded into a head-on crash with the truck.* ◆ *In the fog the boat ran head-on into a log.* **2.** In a way that is exactly opposite; against or opposed to in argument. ◆ *If you think a rule should be changed, a head-on attack against it is best.*

**head out** *v.* **1.** To go or point away. ◆ *The ship left port and headed out to sea. The car was parked beside the house. It was headed out towards the street.* **2.** *informal* Leave; start out. ◆ *I have a long way to go before dark. I'm going to head out.*

**head over heels** *also* **heels over head 1a.** In a somersault; upside down; head first. ◆ *It was so dark Bob fell head over heels into a big hole in the ground.* **1b.** In great confusion or disorder; hastily. ◆ *The children all tried to come in the door at once, head over heels.* **2.** *informal* Completely; deeply. ◆ *He was head over heels in debt.* ◆ *She was head over heels in love.*

**head shrinker** *n.*, *slang*, *informal* A psychoanalyst, also called a *shrink*. ◆ *Forrester is falling apart; his family physician sent him to a head shrinker (to a shrink).*

**head start** *n.* **1.** A beginning before someone; lead or advantage at the beginning. ◆ *The other racers knew they couldn't catch Don if he got too big a head start.* **2.** A good beginning. ◆ *The teacher gave the class a head start on the exercise by telling them the answers to the first two problems.*

**heads or tails** *n. phr.* The two sides of a coin, especially when the coin is tossed in the air in order to decide which of two alternatives are to be followed. ♦ *Tom tossed a quarter in the air and said, "Tails, I win; heads you win."*

**head up** *v., informal* **1.** To be at the head or front of. ♦ *The elephants headed up the whole parade.* **2.** To be the leader or boss of. ♦ *Mr. Jones will head up the new business.*

**heap coals of fire on one's head** *v. phr., literary* To be kind or helpful to someone who has done wrong to you, so that he is ashamed. ♦ *Alice heaped coals of fire on Mary's head by inviting her to a party after Mary had gossiped about her.*

**hear a pin drop** *v. phr.* Absolute silence. ♦ *It's so quiet in the room you could hear a pin drop.*

**hear from one** *v. phr.* To receive news. ♦ *Have you heard from your son recently?*

**heart bleeds for one** *v. phr.* To show exaggerated sympathy for some one, said ironically. ♦ *"I won the lottery and now I am worried about what to do with all that money," John said. "My heart really bleeds for you," his brother answered with a sneer.*

**heartbreaker** *n.* One with numerous admirers of the opposite sex; one with whom others fall in love readily. ♦ *Tom, who has four girls in love with him at college, has developed the reputation of being a heartbreaker.*

**heart and soul**[1] *n.* Eager love; strong feeling; great enthusiasm. Often used with a singular verb. ♦ *When Mr. Pitt plays the piano, his heart and soul is in it.*

**heart and soul**[2] *adv.* Wholly and eagerly; with all one's interest and strength; completely. ♦ *Will you try to make our city a better place? Then we are with you heart and soul.*

**heart goes out** *to formal* You feel very sorry for; you feel pity or sympathy for.—Used with a possessive. ♦ *Our hearts went out to the young mother whose child had died.*

**heart in one's mouth** *or* **heart in one's boots** A feeling of great fear or nervousness. ♦ *When the bear came out of the woods towards us, our hearts were in our mouths.*

**heart is in the right place** *or* **have one's heart in the right place.** To be kindhearted, sympathetic or well-meaning; have good intentions. ♦ *Tom looks very rough but his heart is in the right place.*

**heart miss a beat** See HEART SKIP A BEAT.

**heart of gold** *n. phr.* A kind, generous, or forgiving nature. ♦ *John has a heart of gold. I never saw him angry at anyone.* ♦ *Mrs. Brown is a rich woman with a heart of gold.*

**heart of stone** *n. phr.* A nature without pity. ♦ *Mr. Smith has a heart of stone. He whipped his horse until it fell down.*

**heart of the matter** *n. phr.* The essence of something. ♦ *The heart of the matter is that if you want to succeed in life you must work harder than the average person.*

**heart set** See SET ONE'S HEART ON.

**heart sink** To lose hope, courage, or eagerness; be very disappointed. ♦ *The soldiers' hearts sank when they saw that they were surrounded by Iraqis.*

**heart skip a beat** *or* **heart miss a beat 1.** The heart leaves out or seems to leave out a beat; the heart beats hard or leaps from excitement or strong feeling. ♦ *When Paul saw the bear standing in front of him, his heart skipped a beat.* **2.** To be startled or excited from surprise, joy, or fright. ♦ *When Linda was told that she had won, her heart missed a beat.*

**heart stand still** *v. phr.* To be very frightened or worried. ♦ *Everybody's heart stood still when the President announced that war was declared.*

**heart-stopper** *n. phr.* Something such as bad news that causes great surprise or even shock. ♦ *It was a heart-stopper for the Smith family when they got word that their son was killed in action.*

**heart-to-heart** *adj.* Speaking freely and seriously about something private. ♦ *The father decided to have a heart-to-heart talk with his son about smoking.*

**hearty of the party** *or* **life and soul of the party** *v. phr.* The liveliest, most attractive person at a gathering of friends, the one to whom most people pay attention. ♦ *No matter how hard she was trying, Helen could not compete with Vanessa, who once more turned out to be the hearty of the party.* ♦ *John is always the life and soul of the party.*

**heated argument** *n. phr.* A loud, often violent quarrel; a shouting match. ♦ *"What's all that noise?" my guests asked. "Nothing special," I answered. "My youthful neighbors are having one of their heated arguments."*

**heated retort** *n. phr.* Angry reply; furious rebuttal; passionate reply. ♦ *When his boss scolded him for a poor quarter in earnings, John made a heated retort and blamed the company's situation on the boss.*

**heat wave** *n. phr.* A period of very hot weather. ♦ *The Midwest was experiencing an unusually severe heat wave.* Contrast COLD SPELL.

**heave in sight** *v. phr.* To seem to rise above the horizon at sea and come into sight; come into view; become visible.— Usually used of ships. ♦ *A ship hove in sight many miles away on the horizon.*

**heaven knows** *or* **heaven only knows** See GOD KNOWS.

**heavenly days!** *interj., informal* Exclamation of amazement and disbelief with negative coloring. ♦ *Heavenly days! Look what happened! The dog did it again on the Persian carpet!*

**heave to** *v.* To bring a ship to a stop; bring a sailing ship to a standstill by setting the sails in a certain way. ♦ *"Heave to!" the captain shouted to his crew.* ♦ *We fired a warning shot across the front of the pirate ship to make her heave to.*

**heavy-duty** *adj.* Made for long or hard use; very strong. ♦ *The lumberman used heavy-duty trucks for hauling logs down the mountains.*

**heavy-footed** *adj.* **1.** Slow and clumsy in walking or movement; awkward in using your feet. ♦ *The fat man tried to dance, but he was too heavy-footed.* **2.** Awkward in choice and order of words; not smooth and graceful; clumsy. ♦ *In Mary's compositions, the words seem to dance, but John's compositions are always heavy-footed.* **3.** *or* **lead-footed** *informal* Likely to drive an automobile fast. ♦ *Jerry is a bad driver because he is too heavy-footed.*

**heavy-handed** *adj.* **1.** Not skillful or graceful; clumsy. ♦ *George is heavy-handed and seldom catches the ball.* **2.** Likely to hit or punish hard; harsh or cruel in making (someone) obey.

♦ *Years ago many fathers were heavy-handed bosses in their homes.*

**heavy heart** *n. phr.* A feeling of being weighed down with sorrow; unhappiness. ♦ *They had very heavy hearts as they went to the funeral.*

**heck of it** See DEVIL OF IT.

**hedge about** *or* **hedge in** **1.** To surround with a hedge or barrier; protect or separate by closing in. ♦ *The little garden is hedged in to keep the chickens out.* **2.** To keep from getting out or moving freely; keep from acting freely; block in. ♦ *The boys are hedged in today. They can only play in the backyard.*

**heels over head** See HEAD OVER HEELS.

**he laughs best who laughs last** A person should go ahead with what he is doing and not worry when others laugh at him. When he succeeds he will enjoy laughing at them for being wrong more than they enjoyed laughing at him.—A proverb. ♦ *Everyone laughed at Mary when she was learning to ski. She kept falling down. Now she is the state champion. He laughs best who laughs last.*

**hell and high water** *n. phr.* Troubles or difficulties of any kind. ♦ *After John's father died he went through hell and high water, but he managed to keep the family together.*

**hell-on-wheels** *n., slang* A short-tempered, nagging, or crabby person especially one who makes another unhappy by constantly criticizing him even when he has done nothing wrong. ♦ *Finnegan complains that his wife is hell on wheels; he is considering getting a divorce.*

**help oneself** *v. phr.* To take what you want; take rather than ask or wait to be given. ♦ *Help yourself to another piece of pie.*

**help out** *v.* **1.** To be helpful or useful; help sometimes or somewhat. ♦ *Mr. Smith helps out with the milking on the farm.* ♦ *Tom helps out in the store after school.* **2.** To help (someone) especially in a time of need; aid; assist. ♦ *Jane is helping out Mother by minding the baby.*

**helter-skelter** *adv.* **1.** At a fast speed, but in confusion. ♦ *When the bell rang, the pupils ran helter-skelter out of the door.* **2.** In a confusing group; in disorder.

♦ *The movers piled the furniture helter-skelter in the living room of the new house.*

**he-man** *n., informal* A man who is very strong, brave, and healthy. ♦ *Larry was a real he-man when he returned from service with the Marines.*

**hem and haw** *v. phr.* **1.** To pause or hesitate while speaking, often with little throat noises. ♦ *The man was a poor lecturer because he hemmed and hawed too much.* **2.** To avoid giving a clear answer; be evasive in speech. ♦ *The principal asked Bob why he was late to school, and Bob only hemmed and hawed.*

**hen party** *n. phr., informal* A party to which only women or girls are invited. ♦ *The sorority gave a hen party for its members.*

**here and now**[1] *adv. phr.* At this very time and place; right now; immediately. ♦ *I want my dime back, and I want it here and now.*

**here and now**[2] *n.* The present time and place; today. ♦ *"I want my steak here and now!"*

**here and there** *adv. phr.* **1.** In one place and then in another. ♦ *Here and there in the yard little yellow flowers had sprung up.* **2.** In various directions. ♦ *We went here and there looking for berries.*

**here goes** *interj., informal* I am ready to begin; I am now ready and willing to take the chance; I am hoping for the best.—Said especially before beginning something that takes skill, luck, or courage. ♦ *"Here goes!" said Charley, as he jumped off the high diving board.*

**here goes nothing** *interj., informal* I am ready to begin, but this will be a waste of time; this will not be anything great; this will probably fail.—Used especially before beginning something that takes skill, luck or courage. ♦ *"Here goes nothing," said Bill at the beginning of the race.*

**here to-day and gone to-morrow** See FOOTLOOSE AND FANCY-FREE.

**here we are** *or* **here we are again** See THERE YOU GO.

**hide one's face** *or* **hide one's head** *v. phr.* **1.** To lower your head or turn your face away because of shame or embarrassment. ♦ *The teacher found out that Tom had cheated, and Tom hid his*

head. **2.** To feel embarrassed or ashamed. ♦ *We will beat the other team so badly that they will hide their heads in shame.*

**hide one's head in the sand** *or* **bury one's head in the sand** *or* **have one's head in the sand** To keep from seeing, knowing, or understanding something dangerous or unpleasant; to refuse to see or face something. ♦ *If there is a war, you cannot just bury your head in the sand.*

**hide one's light under a bushel** *v. phr.* To be very shy and modest and not show your abilities or talents; be too modest in letting others see what you can do. ♦ *All year long Tom hid his light under a bushel and the teacher was surprised to see how much he knew when she read his exam paper.*

**hide or hair** *or* **hide nor hair** *n. phr., informal* A sign or trace of someone that is gone or lost; any sign at all of something missing. Usually used in negative or interrogative sentence. ♦ *Tommy left the house this morning and I haven't seen hide or hair of him since.* ♦ *A button fell off my coat and I could find neither hide nor hair of it.*

**hide out** *v. phr.* To go into hiding, as in the case of a criminal on the run. ♦ *He tried to hide out but the police tracked him down.*

**hideout** *n.* A place where one hides. ♦ *The wanted criminal used several hideouts but he was captured in the end.*

**high and dry** *adv. or adj. phr.* **1.** Up above the water; beyond the reach of splashing or waves. ♦ *Mary was afraid she had left her towel where the tide would reach it, but she found it high and dry.* **2.** Without anyone to help; alone and with no help. ♦ *When the time came to put up the decorations, Mary was left high and dry.*

**high and low** *adv.* Everywhere. ♦ *The police were searching for the criminal high and low, but they couldn't find him.*

**high-and-mighty** *adj., informal* Feeling more important or superior to someone else; too proud of yourself. ♦ *Mary become high-and-mighty when she won the prize, and Joan would not go around with her any more.*

**high as a kite** *adj.* **1.** As excited and happy as one can possibly be. ♦ *When*

*Eric won the lottery he was high as a kite.* **2.** Intoxicated or under the influence of some drug. ♦*Jeff has been drinking again and he is high as a kite.*

**highbrow** *adj.* Very well educated or even over-educated; belonging to the educated middle class; sophisticated. ♦*Certain novels are not for everyone and are considered as highbrow entertainment.*

**high camp** *n., slang, show business* **1.** Kitsch, or pretentious material in bad taste that is still liked by higher class audiences. ♦*The* Potsdam Quartet *is a play full of high camp.* **2.** An exaggerated movie or theater scene that loses believability. ♦*Scarecrow and Mrs. King and Sledge Hammer are so full of high camp that no sensible people watch them anymore.* **middle camp** and **low camp** refer to theatrical kitsch preferred by middle class and low class audiences, respectively.

**high-class** *adj.* Of the best quality; very good; superior.—Avoided by many careful speakers. ♦*When Mr. Brown got a raise in pay, Mrs. Brown started to look for a high-class apartment.*

**higher education** *n.* Schooling after graduation from high school, especially in a college or university. ♦*Tom plans to get his higher education at the state university.*

**higher-up** *n., informal* One of the people who has one of the more important positions in an organization; an important official. ♦*The teacher's problem was discussed by the higher-ups.*

**high fashion** or **high style** *n. phr.* The new style in women's dress set each season by designers in Paris or other fashion centers and accepted by fashionable women. ♦*The high styles designed in Paris are often quickly copied by makers of cheap clothing.*

**high gear** *n. phr., informal* Top speed; full activity. ♦*Production got into high gear after the vacation.*

**high-handed** *adj.* Depending on force rather than right; bossy; dictatorial. ♦*Mr. Smith was a high-handed tyrant in his office.*

**high hopes** *n. phr.* Great expectations. ♦*John had high hopes of being named vice president of the company, but he lost out to a colleague.*

**high on** *adj. phr.* **1.** Intoxicated on some drug or alcoholic drink. ♦*Rob was severely scolded by the dean for always being high on marijuana.* **2.** Enthusiastic about something. ♦*Jeff is high on Beethoven and Brahms.*

**high place** *n. phr.* A position of responsibility, honor, and power. ♦*Jones had reached a high place in the government at Washington.*

**high-powered** *adj. phr.* Extremely energetic and influential. ♦ *Mr. Horner is a high-powered attorney; small wonder he charges so much.*

**high seas** *n. phr.* The open ocean, not the waters near the coast. ♦*It was a big powerful liner built to sail on the high seas.* ♦ *The ships of every country have the right to sail on the high seas.*

**high season** *n. phr.* The time of year when the largest number of passengers are travelling; the time when airfare costs more. ♦ *We had to pay $100 more for our tickets because it was the high season.*

**high-sounding** *adj.* Sounding important; said for showing off; too fancy. ♦ *The politician's speech was full of high-sounding words.*

**high-strung** *adj.* Nervous; sensitive; tense. ♦*Gary has been rather high-strung lately because of too much work at the office.*

**high time** *adj. phr., used predicatively* (stress on *time*) Dire, necessary, and sufficient circumstances prompting action. ♦*It is high time we sold the old house; it will fall apart within a year.*

**highway robbery** *n. phr.* **1.** A hold-up of or theft from a person committed on an open road or street usually by an armed man. ♦ *Highway robbery was common in England in Shakespeare's day.* **2.** An extremely high price or charge; a profiteer's excessive charge. ♦ *To someone from a small town, the prices of meals and theater tickets in New York often seem to be highway robbery.*

**hinge on** or **hinge upon** *v.* To depend on as decisive: be decided by. ♦*In a dictatorship, everything hinges on one man.* ♦ *A tobacco grower's income for the year may hinge on what the weather is like in a few summer weeks.*

**hip to** *adj. phr., slang* Knowledgeable about something. ♦ *Ted prides* *himself on being hip to the latest trends in popular music.*

**hired man** *n. phr.* A man employed to do jobs every day about a house or farm. ♦ *The hired man was sick, and a lot of the daily chores were not done.*

**hire out** *v., informal* **1.** To accept a job; take employment. ♦ *Frank hired out as a saxophonist with a dance band.* **2.** To rent (as owner). ♦ *John used to hire out his tractor sometimes when he didn't need it himself.*

**hit-and-run** *adj.* **1.** Of or about an accident after which a motorist drives away without giving his name and offering help. ♦ *Judges are stern with hit-and-run drivers.* **2.** Striking suddenly and leaving quickly. ♦ *The bandits often made hit-and-run attacks on wagon trains.*

**hit a nerve** *v. phr.* To affect someone strongly and negatively. ♦ *When John called his sister a hooker, the remark hit a nerve so strongly that she gave him a slap in the face.*

**hit a snag** *or* **run into trouble** *v. phr.* To encounter unexpected difficulties or problems. ♦ *Sam was repairing my broken computer when he suddenly hit a snag, and said that we needed a new hard disk.* ♦ *The construction engineer ran into trouble suddenly when he found that the beams were too weak to hold up the walls.*

**hit between the eyes** *v. phr., informal* To make a strong impression on; surprise greatly. ♦ *To learn that his parents had endured poverty for his sake hit John between the eyes.*

**hit bottom** *or* **touch bottom** *v. phr., informal* **1.** To be at the very lowest. ♦ *In August there was a big supply of corn and the price hit bottom.* **2.** To live through the worst; not to be able to go any lower. ♦ *When they lost all their money they thought they had touched bottom and things would have to get better.*

**hitch one's wagon to a star** *v. phr.* To aim high; follow a great ambition or purpose. ♦ *John hitched his wagon to a star and decided to try to become President.*

**hither and thither** *or* **hither and yon** *adv. phr., literary* In one direction and then in another. ♦ *Bob wandered hither and thither looking for a playmate.*

**hit home** *v. phr.* To go directly to the mark; strike a vulnerable spot. ♦ *His remark hit home when he referred to those who do not contribute sufficiently to the college fund drive.*

**hit it off** *v. phr., informal* To enjoy one another's company; be happy and comfortable in each other's presence. ♦ *Tom and Fred hit it off well with each other.* ♦ *Mary and Jane hit it off from the first.*

**hit on** *or* **hit upon** *v.* To happen to meet, find, or reach; to choose or think by chance. ♦ *There seemed to be several explanations of the crime, but the detectives hit on the right one the first time.*

**hit on all cylinders** *v. phr.* **1.** To run smoothly or at full power without any missing or skipping.—Said of a motor. ♦ *The mechanic tuned the car engine until it was hitting on all cylinders.* **2.** *informal* To think or work well; to use all your ability. ♦ *The football team was hitting on all cylinders and scored a big victory.*

**hit one in the pocket** *or* **hit one in the wallet** *v. phr.* To hurt one economically. ♦ *The expenditure of the war against terrorism has hit all of us in the pocket.*

**hit one's stride** *v. phr.* **1.** To walk or run at your best speed; reach your top speed or game. ♦ *The horse began to hit his stride and moved ahead of the other horses in the race.* **2.** To do your best work; do the best job you are able to. ♦ *Mary didn't begin to hit her stride in school until the fifth grade.*

**hit on one** *v. phr.* To flirt with someone. ♦ *"Why are you hitting on me?" Suzie asked, "when your pretty wife is standing just a few feet away from us?"*

**hit-or-miss** *also* **hit-and-miss** *adj.* Unplanned; uncontrolled; aimless; careless. ♦ *John did a lot of hit-or-miss reading, some of it about taxes.* ♦ *Mary packed her bag in hurried, hit-or-miss fashion.*

**hit or miss** *also* **hit and miss** *adv.* In an unplanned or uncontrolled way; aimlessly; carelessly. ♦ *George didn't know which house on the street was Jane's, so he began ringing doorbells hit or miss.*

**hit parade** *n.* **1.** A list of songs or tunes arranged in order of popularity. ♦ *Tom was overjoyed when his new song was* named on the hit parade on the local radio station. **2.** slang A list of favorites in order of popularity. ♦ *Jack is no longer number one on Elsie's hit parade.*

**hit the books** *v. phr., informal* To study your school assignments, prepare for classes. ♦ *Jack broke away from his friends, saying, "I've got to hit the books."*

**hit the bull's-eye** *v. phr., informal* To go to the important part of the matter; reach the main question. ♦ *John hit the bull's-eye when he said the big question was one of simple honesty.*

**hit the ceiling** *or* **hit the roof** *v. phr., slang* To become violently angry; go into a rage. ♦ *When Elaine came home at three in the morning, her father hit the ceiling.*

**hit the deck** *v. phr.* To get up from bed, to start working. (From sailor's language as in *"All hands on the deck!"*) ♦ *OK boys, it's time to hit the deck!*

**hit the dirt** *v. phr., slang military* To take cover under gunfire by falling on the ground. ♦ *We hit the dirt the moment we heard the machine gun fire.*

**hit the fan** *v. phr., informal* To become a big public problem or controversy. ♦ *The whole mess hit the fan when the judge was arrested for drunken driving for the second time.*

**hit the hay** *or* **hit the sack** *v. phr., slang* To go to bed. ♦ *Louis was so tired that he hit the sack soon after supper.*

**hit the high spots** *v. phr.* To consider, mention, or see only the more important parts of something such as a book, war, or school course. ♦ *The first course in general science hits only the high spots of the physical sciences.*

**hit the jackpot** *v. phr., slang* To be very lucky or successful. ♦ *Mr. Brown invented a new gadget which hit the jackpot.*

**hit the nail on the head** *v. phr.* To get something exactly right; speak or act in the most fitting or effective way. ♦ *The mayor's talk on race relations hit the nail on the head.*

**hit the road** *v. phr., slang* **1.** To become a wanderer; to live an idle life; become a tramp or hobo. ♦ *When Jack's wife left him, he felt a desire to travel, so he hit the road.* **2.** To leave, especially in a car. ♦ *It is getting late, so I guess we will hit*

the road for home. ♦ *He packed his car and hit the road for California.*

**hit the roof** See HIT THE CEILING.

**hit the sack** See HIT THE HAY.

**hit the sauce** *v. phr., slang* To drink alcoholic beverages—especially heavily and habitually. ♦ *When Sue left him, Joe began to hit the sauce.*

**hit the spot** *v. phr., informal* To refresh fully or satisfy you; bring back your spirits or strength—used especially of food or drink. ♦ *A cup of tea always hits the spot when you are tired.*

**hitting skins** *n. phr., slang* Sex. *"What is Jim the best at?" the prospective employer asked. "Not much that I know of," Tracy answered, "except for hitting skins."*

**hit town** *v. phr.* To arrive in town. ♦ *Give me a phone call as soon as you hit town.*

**hive of industry** *n. phr.* An extremely busy place for work. ♦ *Kaiser Industries, Ltd. became a veritable hive of industry during World War II, when it started to build landing craft for the allied forces.*

**hoe one's own row** *v. phr.* To make your way in life by your own efforts; get along without help. ♦ *David's father died when he was little, and he has always had to hoe his own row.*

**hog-tie** *v., informal* **1.** To tie (an animal) so it is unable to move or escape. ♦ *The Cowboy caught a calf and hog-tied it.* **2.** To make someone unable to act freely; limit. ♦ *The welfare worker wanted to help at once, but rules and regulations hog-tied her, so she could only report the case.*

**hoist with one's own petard** *adj. phr.* Caught in your own trap or trick. ♦ *Jack carried office gossip to the boss until he was hoisted by his own petard.*

**hold a candle to** *also* **hold a stick to** *v. phr.* To be fit to be compared with; be in the same class with. ♦ *Henry thought that no modern physicist could hold a candle to Einstein.*

**hold a grudge against** See NURSE A GRUDGE.

**hold all the trumps** *v. phr.* To have the best chance of winning; have all the advantages; have full control. ♦ *Fred has $200 and I have no money, so he holds all the trumps and can buy whatever he wants with it.*

**hold back** *v.* **1.** To stay back or away; show unwillingness. ♦ *John held back from social activity because he felt embarrassed with people.* **2.** To keep someone in place; prevent from acting. ♦ *The police held back the crowd.*

**hold court** *v. phr.* **1.** To hold a formal meeting of a royal court or a court of law. ♦ *Judge Stephens allowed no foolishness when he held court.* **2.** *informal* To act like a king or queen among subjects. ♦ *Even at sixteen, Judy was holding court for numbers of charmed boys.*

**hold down** *v.* **1.** To keep in obedience; keep control of; continue authority or rule over. ♦ *Kings used to know very well how to hold down the people.* **2.** *informal* To work satisfactorily at. ♦ *John had held down a tough job for a long time.*

**hold everything** See HOLD IT.

**hold forth** *v.* **1.** To offer; propose. ♦ *As a candidate, Jones held forth the promise of a bright future.* **2.** To speak in public; preach.—Usually used with little respect. ♦ *Senator Smith was holding forth on free trade.*

**hold good** *v.* **1.** To continue to be good; last. ♦ *The coupon on the cereal box offered a free toy, but the offer held good only till the end of the year.* **2.** To continue; endure; last. ♦ *The agreement between the schools held good for three years.*

**hold no brief for** *v. phr.* To argue in support of; defend.—Usually used with a negative. ♦ *I hold no brief for John, but I do not think he was responsible for the accident.* ♦ *The lawyer said he held no brief for thievery, but he considered the man should be given another chance.*

**hold in** *or* **hold inside** *v. phr.* To not let others know what one thinks or feels; to dissemble. ♦ *You'll never figure Samantha out; she holds everything inside.*

**hold in suspense** *v. phr.* To not let one know what's happening, or what the outcome of a story might be. ♦ *A good mystery writer, such as Agatha Christie, always holds the audience in suspense.*

**hold no brief for one** *v. phr.* To be far from advocating something; to be far from be a supporter of someone or something. ♦ *It is common knowledge the competing candidates for presi-*

*dency of the United States hold no brief for one another.*

**hold it** *or* **hold everything** *v. phr., informal* To stop something one is doing or getting ready to do.—Usually used as a command. ♦ *The pilot was starting to take off, when the control tower ordered "Hold it!"*

**hold off** *v.* **1a.** To refuse to let (someone) become friendly. ♦ *The president's high rank and chilly manner held people off.* **1b.** To be rather shy or unfriendly. ♦ *Perkins was a scholarly man who held off from people.* **2.** To keep away by fighting; oppose by force. ♦ *The kidnapper locked himself in the house and held off the police for an hour.* **3.** To wait before (doing something); postpone; delay. ♦ *Jack held off paying for the television set until the dealer fixed it.*

**hold on** *v.* **1.** To keep holding tightly; continue to hold strongly. ♦ *As Ted was pulling on the rope, it began to slip and Earl cried, "Hold on, Ted!"* **2.** To wait and not hang up a telephone; keep a phone for later use. ♦ *Mr. Jones asked me to hold on while he spoke to his secretary.* **3.** To keep on with a business or job in spite of difficulties. ♦ *It was hard to keep the store going during the depression, but Max held on and at last met with success.* **4.** *informal* To wait a minute; stop.—Usually used as a command. ♦ *"Hold on!" John's father said, "I want the car tonight."*

**hold one's breath** *v. phr.* **1.** To stop breathing for a moment when you are excited or nervous. ♦ *The race was so close that everyone was holding his breath at the finish.* **2.** To endure great nervousness, anxiety, or excitement. ♦ *John held his breath for days before he got word that the college he chose had accepted him.*

**hold one's end up** *or* **hold up one's end** *or* **keep one's end up** *or* **keep up one's end** *v. phr., informal* To do your share of work; do your part. ♦ *Mary washed the dishes so fast that Ann, who was drying them, couldn't keep her end up.* ♦ *Bob said he would lend me his bicycle if I repaired the flat tire, but he didn't keep up his end of the bargain.*

**hold one's fire** *or* **hold fire** *v. phr.* To keep back arguments or facts; keep from telling something. ♦ *Tom could* *have hurt Fred by telling what he knew, but he held his fire.*

**hold one's hand** *v. phr.* To comfort one. ♦ *"Thanks for holding my hand during my obligatory retirement," Professor Miller said to his junior colleague. "Your hand-holding helped me through a difficult period in my life."*

**hold one's head high** *v. phr.* To be proud. ♦ *After several unsuccessful attempts at passing the special examination for foreign medical graduates, Steve passed his exam on the fourth try, and can now hold his head high.*

**hold one's head up** *v. phr.* To show self-respect; not be ashamed; be proud. ♦ *When Mr. Murray had paid off his debts, he felt that he could hold his head up again.*

**hold one's horses** *v. phr., informal* To stop; wait; be patient. ♦ *"Hold your horses!" Mr. Jones said to David when David wanted to call the police.*

**hold one's own** *v. phr.* To keep your position; avoid losing ground; keep your advantage, wealth, or condition without loss. ♦ *Mr. Smith could not build up his business, but he held his own.* ♦ *The team held its own after the first quarter.* ♦ *Mary had a hard time after the operation, but soon she was holding her own.*

**hold one's peace** *v. phr., formal* To be silent and not speak against something; be still; keep quiet. ♦ *I did not agree with the teacher, but held my peace as he was rather angry.*

**hold one's temper** *or* **keep one's temper** *v. phr.* To make yourself be quiet and peaceful; not become angry. ♦ *Dave can't keep his temper when he drives in heavy traffic.*

**hold one's tongue** *v. phr.* To be silent; keep still; not talk. ♦ *The teacher told Fred to hold his tongue*

**hold on to** *v. phr.* **1a.** *or* **hold to** To continue to hold or keep; hold tightly. ♦ *The old man held on to his job stubbornly and would not retire.* **1b.** To stay in control of. ♦ *Ann was so frightened that she had to hold onto her husband in order to not scream.* **2.** To continue to sing or sound. ♦ *The singer held on to the last note of the song for a long time.*

**hold on to your hat** See HANG ON TO YOUR HAT.

**holdout** *n.* A rebel who refuses to go with the majority. ♦ *Sam was a lone holdout in town; he refused to sell his old lakefront cottage to make place for a skyscraper.*

**hold out** *v. phr.* **1.** To put forward; reach out; extend; offer. ♦ *Mr. Ryan held out his hand in welcome.* **2.** To keep resisting; not yield; refuse to give up. ♦ *The city held out for six months under siege.* Compare HANG ON, HOLD ON. **3.** To refuse to agree or settle until one's wishes have been agreed to. ♦ *The strikers held out for a raise of five cents an hour.* **4.** *slang* To keep something from; refuse information or belongings to which someone has a right. ♦ *Mr. Porter's partner held out on him when the big payment came in.*

**hold out hope** *v. phr.* To give encouragement to people in difficulty. ♦ *The U.S. central command held out hope for our prisoners of war.*

**holdover** *n.* **1.** A successful movie or theater production that plays longer than originally planned. ♦ *Because of its great popularity,* Star Wars *was a holdover in most movie theaters.* **2.** A reservation not used at the time intended, but used later. ♦ *They kept my seat at the opera as a holdover because I am a patron.*

**hold over** *v.* **1.** To remain or keep in office past the end of the term. ♦ *The new President held the members of the Cabinet over for some time before appointing new members.* **2.** To extend the engagement of; keep longer. ♦ *The theater held over the feature film for another two weeks.* **3.** To delay action on; to postpone; to defer. ♦ *The directors held over their decision until they could get more information.*

**hold still** *v. phr.* To remain motionless. ♦ *"Hold still," the dentist said. "This won't hurt you at all."*

**hold the bag** *v. phr.* To be made liable for or victimized. ♦ *We went out to dinner together but when it was time to pay I was left holding the bag.*

**hold the fort** *v. phr.* **1.** To defend a fort successfully; fight off attackers. ♦ *The little group held the fort for days until help came.* **2.** *informal* To keep a position against opposing forces. ♦ *Friends* of civil liberties held the fort during a long debate. **3.** *informal* **to keep service or operations going** ♦ *Mother and Father went out and told the children to hold the fort.*

**hold the line** *v. phr.* To keep a situation or trouble from getting worse; hold steady; prevent a setback or loss. ♦ *The company held the line on employment.*

**hold the stage** *v. phr.* **1.** To continue to be produced and to attract audiences. ♦ *"Peter Pan" holds the stage year after year at its annual Christmas showing in London.* **2.** To be active in a group; attract attention. ♦ *We had only an hour to discuss the question and Mr. Jones held the stage for most of it.*

**hold true** *or* **hold good** *v. phr.* To remain true. ♦ *It has always held true that man cannot live without laws.* ♦ *Bob is a good boy and that holds true of Jim.*

**holdup** *n.* (stress on *hold*) **1.** Robbery. ♦ *John fell victim to a highway holdup.* **2.** A delay, as on a crowded highway. ♦ *Boy we're late! What's causing this holdup?*

**hold up** *v.* (stress on *up*) **1.** To raise; lift. ♦ *John held up his hand.* **2.** To support; bear; carry. ♦ *The chair was too weak to hold up Mrs. Smith.* **3.** To show; call attention to; exhibit. ♦ *The teacher held up excellent models of composition for her class to imitate.* **4.** To check; stop; delay. ♦ *The wreck held up traffic on the railroad's main line tracks.* **5.** *informal* To rob at gunpoint. ♦ *Masked men held up the bank.* **6.** To keep one's courage or spirits up; remain calm; keep control of oneself. ♦ *The grieving mother held up for her children's sake.* **7.** To remain good; not get worse. ♦ *Sales held up well.* ♦ *Our team's luck held up and they won the game.* ♦ *The weather held up and the game was played.* **8.** To prove true. ♦ *The police were doubtful at first, but Tony's story held up.* **9.** To delay action; defer; postpone. ♦ *The President held up on the news until he was sure of it.*

**hold up one's end** See HOLD ONE'S END UP.

**hold water** *v. phr.* **1.** To keep water without leaking. ♦ *That pail still holds water.* **2.** *informal* To prove true; stand testing; bear examination.—Usually used in negative, interrogative, or con-

ditional sentences. ♦ *Ernest told the police a story that wouldn't hold water.*

**hold your hat** See HANG ON TO YOUR HAT.

**hole in one** *n. phr.* A shot in golf that is hit from the tee and goes right into the cup. ♦ *Many golfers play for years and never get a hole in one.*

**hole-in-the-wall** *n. phr.* A small place to live, stay in, or work in; a small, hidden, or inferior place. ♦ *The jewelry store occupied a tiny hole-in-the-wall.* ♦ *When Mr. and Mrs. Green were first married, they lived in a little hole-in-the-wall in a cheap apartment building.* **2.** *slang,* citizen's band radio jargon. A tunnel. ♦ *Let's get through this hole in the wall, then we'll change seats.*

**hole out** *v.* To finish play in golf by hitting the ball into the cup. ♦ *The other players waited for Palmer to hole out before they putted .*

**hole up** *also* **hole in** *v., slang* To take refuge or shelter; put up; lodge. ♦ *The thief holed up at an abandoned farm.*

**holier-than-thou** *adj.* Acting as if you are better than others in goodness, character, or reverence for God; acting as if morally better than other people. ♦ *Most people find holier-than-thou actions in others hard to accept.*

**holistic health** *n., informal, semi-technical* The maintenance of health and the avoidance of disease through such psychogenic practices and procedures as biofeedback, meditation, alternative methods of childbirth, and avoidance of drugs. ♦ *The Murgatroyds are regular holistic health freaks—why, they won't even take aspirin when they have a headache.*

**hollow out** *v.* To cut or dig out or to cut or dig a hole in; make a cut or cave in; excavate. ♦ *The soldier hollowed out a foxhole in the ground to lie in.*

**holy cow** *or* **holy mackerel** *or* **holy Moses** *interj., informal*—Used to express strong feeling (as astonishment, pleasure, or anger); used in speech or when writing conversation. ♦ *"Holy cow! They can't do that!" Mary said when she saw the boys hurting a much smaller boy.*

**holy terror** *n., informal* A very disobedient or unruly child; brat. ♦ *All the children are afraid of Johnny because he's a holy terror.*

**home brew** *n. phr.* A beer or other malt liquor made at home, not in a brewery. ♦ *Home brew reached its greatest popularity in America during national prohibition.*

**home is where the heart is** *from Latin.* It matters less where one is physically than whether one feels a sense of belonging.—A proverb. *Many military families get moved around the United States and even abroad, so they are used to the idea that "home is where the heart is."*

**home on** *or* **home in on** *v.* To move toward a certain place by following a signal or marker. ♦ *The airplane homed in on the radio beacon.* ♦ *The ship homed on the lights of New York harbor.*

**home plate** *n.* The base in baseball where the batter stands and that a runner must touch to score. ♦ *The runner slid across home plate ahead of the tag to score a run.*

**home run** *n.* A hit in baseball that allows the batter to run around all the bases and score a run. ♦ *Frank hit a home run over the left field wall in the second inning.*

**honest broker** *n. phr.* A person hired or appointed to act as an agent in a legal, business, or political situation where impartial advice is needed in order to settle a dispute. ♦ *Michael has been asked to act as an honest broker to settle the argument between the employees and the management.*

**honest penny** *v. phr.* To make honest money at some work to earn an honest living. ♦ *John may not be a wealthy man, but he was never in jail and with his hard work he certainly earns an honest penny.*

**honest to goodness** *or* **honest to God** *adj. phr., informal* Really; truly; honestly.—Used to emphasize something said. ♦ *"Honest to goodness, Jane, I think you are the messiest girl in the world," said Mother.*

**honest-to-goodness** *or* **honest-to-God** *adj. phr., informal* Real; genuine.—Used for emphasis. ♦ *She served him honest-to-goodness deep dish apple pie.*

**honeymoon is over** The first happy period of friendship and cooperation between two persons or groups is over.

♦ *A few months after a new President is elected, the honeymoon is over and Congress and the President begin to criticize each other.*

**honky-tonk** *n.* A cheap nightclub or dance hall. ♦ *There were a number of honky-tonks near the army camp.*

**hooked on** *adj.* **1.** Addicted to a substance such as cigarettes, coffee, tea, drugs, or alcohol. ♦ *Fred is hooked on grass, but Tim is only hooked on tea.* **2.** Enthusiastic or very supportive of something. ♦ *I am hooked on the local symphony.*

**hook, line and sinker** *adv. phr., informal* Without question or doubt; completely. ♦ *Johnny was so easily fooled that he fell for Joe's story, hook, line and sinker.*

**hookup** *n.* (stress on *hook*) A connection, electrical or otherwise, between two instruments or two individuals. ♦ *Edwin and Hermione are a perfect couple; they have got the right hookup.*

**hook up** *v. phr.* (stress on *up*) To connect or fit together. ♦ *The company sent a man to hook up the telephone.* ♦ *They could not use the gas stove because it had not been hooked up.*

**hook up with one** *v. phr.* To start living with a member of the opposite sex without the benefit of marriage. ♦ *"I didn't know your daughter got married," Tom's colleague said. "No, she isn't married at all; she just hooked up with a friend from college. That's modern kids for you!"*

**hope against hope** *v. phr.* To try to hope when things look black; hold to hope in bad trouble. ♦ *The mother continued to hope against hope although the plane was hours late.* ♦ *Jane hoped against hope that Joe would call her.*

**hope for the best** *v. phr.* To be optimistic about the outcome of a situation. ♦ *Try not to get pessimistic and always hope for the best no matter what trouble you are in.*

**hop in** *or* **hop into** *v. phr.* To enter a vehicle, mostly a private car. ♦ *When Sam needed to get to the hospital in a hurry and was waiting for the bus in the rain, his friend Ted said, as he drove by: "Hop in, old man; let me give you a lift."*

**hop to it** *v. phr., slang* To get started; start a job; get going. ♦ *"There's a lot to* do today, so let's hop to it," the boss said.

**hopped up** *adj., slang* **1.** Doped with a narcotic drug. ♦*Police found Jones hiding in an opium den, among other men all hopped up with the drug.* **2.** Full of eagerness; excited. ♦*Fred was all hopped up about going over the ocean.*

**horizontal mambo** *n. phr., slang* Sex. ♦*"What's going on in the next room? What's all that panting and wheezing I hear?" Sue's father asked his college-age son as he entered the house. "I guess its just some horizontal mambo between Sis and her boyfriend," the son replied.*

**horn in** *v., slang* To come in without invitation or welcome; interfere. Often used with *on*. ♦*Jack would often horn in on conversations discussing things he knew nothing about.*

**horns of a dilemma** *n. phr.* Two choices possible in a situation in which neither is wanted. Usually used after *on*. ♦*Joe found himself on the horns of a dilemma; if he went to work, he'd miss seeing Mary; if he stayed out, he'd be too broke to take her anywhere.*

**horselaugh** *n. phr.* A loud, sarcastic, and derisive laugh. ♦*When the speaker praised politics as one of the oldest and noblest professions, his audience of college students gave him a horselaugh.*

**horse around** *v., slang* To join in rough teasing; play around. ♦*They were a bunch of sailors on shore leave, horsing around where there were girls and drinks.*

**horse of a different color** *or* **horse of another color** *n. phr., informal* Something altogether separate and different. ♦*Anyone can be broke, but to steal is a horse of a different color.*

**horse opera** *n. phr.* A Western movie in which cowboys and horses play a major part. ♦*John Wayne played in many horse operas.*

**horseplay** *n.* Rough, practical joking. ♦*The newlyweds couldn't get a wink of sleep all night because there was a lot of yelling and screaming outside of their window—the usual horseplay.*

**horse sense** *n., informal* A good understanding about what to do in life; good judgment; wisdom in making decisions. ♦*Some people are well educated and read many books, but still do not have much horse sense.*

**horse trade** *n.* **1.** The sale of a horse or the exchange of two horses. ♦*It was a horse trade in which the owner of the worse animal gave a rifle to make the trade equal.* **2.** *informal* A business agreement or bargain arrived at after hard and skillful discussion. ♦*Party leaders went around for months making horse trades to get support for their candidate.* ♦

**hot air** *n., informal* Nonsense, exaggerated talk, wasted words characterized by emotion rather than intellectual content. ♦*That was just a lot of hot air what Joe said.*

**hot and bothered** *adj., informal* Excited and worried, displeased, or puzzled.— *Fritz got all hot and bothered when he failed in the test.* ♦*Leona was all hot and bothered when her escort was late in coming for her.*

**hot and heavy** *adv. phr., informal* Strongly; vigorously; emphatically. ♦*Fred got it hot and heavy when his wife found out how much he had lost at cards.*

**hot dog** *n. phr., informal* A frankfurter or wiener in a roll. ♦*The boys stopped on the way home for hot dogs and coffee.*

**hot dog!** *interj., informal* Hurrah!—A cry used to show pleasure or enthusiasm. ♦*"Hot dog!" Frank exclaimed when he unwrapped a birthday gift of a small record player.*

**hot flashes** *n. phr.* A time in women's life during or after menopause they experience sudden sensations of intense heat. ♦*"Why are you so unhappy?" Jean's husband asked with concern. "I am having one of my lousy hot flashes," she replied in a grumpy mood.*

**hot-headed** *adj. phr.* Someone easily irritated; one who loses his or her temper at even the least provocation. ♦*Tom is a generally very patient and nice fellow, but he can be awfully hot-headed sometimes.*

**hotly contested** *adj. phr.* Contentious; hard-fought; keenly competitive. *The Democratic and the Republican nominees for the vacant Senate seat fought a hotly contested campaign.*

**hot number** *n., slang* A person or thing noticed as newer, better, or more popular than others. ♦*John invented a new* can opener that was a hot number in the stores.

**hot off the press** *adj. phr.* Just appeared in print. ♦ *This is the latest edition of the Chicago Tribune; it's hot off the press.*

**hot one** *n., slang, informal* Something out of the ordinary; something exceptional, such as a joke, a person whether in terms of looks or intelligence. ♦ *Joe's joke sure was a hot one.* ♦ *Sue is a hot one, isn't she?*

**hot potato** *n., informal* A question that causes strong argument and is difficult to settle. ♦ *Many school boards found segregation a hot potato in the 1960s.*

**hot rod** *n., informal* An older automobile changed so that it can gain speed quickly and go very fast. ♦ *Hot rods are used by young people especially in drag racing.*

**hot seat** *n., slang* **1.** The electric chair used to cause death by electrocution in legal executions. ♦ *Many a man has controlled a murderous rage when he thought of the hot seat.* **2.** *informal* A position in which you can easily get into trouble. ♦ *A judge in a beauty contest is on the hot seat. If he chooses one girl, the other girls will be angry with him.*

**hot stuff** *n., slang, citizen's band radio jargon* Coffee. ♦ *Let's stop and get some hot stuff.*

**hot under the collar** *adj. phr., informal* Angry. ♦ *Mary gets hot under the collar if you joke about women drivers.*

**hot water** *n. informal* Trouble.—Used with *in, into, out, of.* ♦ *John's thoughtless remark about religion got John into a lot of hot water.*

**housebroken** *adj.* Trained to go outside to relieve themselves (said of domestic pets, primarily dogs). ♦ *All young puppies must eventually be housebroken.*

**house detective** *n.* A detective employed by a hotel, store, or other business to watch for any trouble. ♦ *The one-armed man sweeping the bank floor was really the house detective.*

**household name** *n. phr.* The name of a person who is recognized by almost everyone, due to frequent appearances on television or being seen in newspapers and in public. ♦ *Hardly anyone knew Elvis Presley before he became a household name after being discharged from the U.S. Army.*

**household word** *n. phr.* A well-known company or brand name. IBM, KLEENEX, MACINTOSH, *and* XEROX *have all become household words in every English-speaking country.*

**housekeeper** *n. phr.* A hired woman who works in the household of a family as cleaning woman, cook, etc. ♦ *Many women, who could not find other employment, used to work as housekeepers, especially in the old days.*

**house of cards** *n. phr.* Something badly put together and easily knocked down; a poorly founded plan, hope, or action. ♦ *John's business fell apart like a house of cards..*

**house of ill fame** *or* **of ill repute** *n. phr.* A bordello; a brothel. ♦ *At the edge of town there is a house of ill repute run by a Madame who used to be a singer in a bar.*

**hover over** *v. phr.* **1.** To remain close or above. ♦ *The rescue helicopter was carefully hovering above the stranded rock climbers.* **2.** To watch over; supervise. ♦ *"Mother!" Phillip cried, "if you don't stop hovering over me, I'll go bananas!"*

**how about** *or* **what about** *interrog.—* Used to ask for a decision, action, opinion, or explanation. **1.** Will you have something or agree on something? ♦ *How about another piece of pie?* ♦ *What about a game of tennis?* **2.** Will you lend or give me? ♦ *How about five dollars until Friday?* **3.** What is to be done about? ♦ *What about the windows? Shall we close them before we go?* **4.** How do you feel about? What do you think about? What is to be thought or said? ♦ *What about women in politics?*

**how about that** *or* **what about that** *informal* An expression of surprise, congratulation, or praise. ♦ *When Jack heard of his brother's promotion, he exclaimed, "How about that!"*

**how can you?** *or* **how could you ?** *adv. phr.* Elliptical for "How can you behave this way?" or "How could you be so foolish?" said in indignant surprise. ♦ *When Joe found out that his brother Sam had left his wonderful doctor wife for an unmarried bartender with five children, he exclaimed in horror, "How could you?"*

**how come** *informal also nonstandard* **how's come** *interrog.* How does it happen that? Why? ♦*How come you are late?* ♦*You're wearing your best clothes today. How come?*

**how does it play?** *adv. phr.* What is the reaction? How do the people evaluate what is happening? ♦*"What I need to know is," the public relations director of the famous daily newspaper asked, "how our attempt at liberating Iraq is playing in the Arab streets, now that Baghdad has fallen."*

**how does that grab you?** *adv. phr., slang* What do you reply to that? What do you think of that? ♦*The income tax cut will have to be less than the president promised before the second Gulf War. Now let me ask you, how does that grab you?*

**how do you do** *formal greeting* How are you?—Usually as a reply to an introduction; it is in the form of a question but no answer is expected. ♦*"Mary, I want you to meet my friend Fred. Fred, this is my wife, Mary." "How do you do, Mary?" "How do you do, Fred?"*

**how goes it?** *v. phr. interrog.* How are you and your affairs in general progressing? ♦*Jim asked Bill, "how goes it with the new wife and the new apartment?"*

**how has life been treating you?** or **how's the world treating you?** *adv. phr.* How are you faring? How are you doing? ♦*"How has life been treating you?" Ted asked his old friend John. "Fine, thanks," John replied, "and how's the world treating you?"*

**howling success** *n., informal* A great success; something that is much praised; something that causes wide enthusiasm. ♦*The party was a howling success.*

**howl with the wolves** *v. phr.* To agree with those who are in power. ♦*John gets around at the university because he howls with the wolves.*

**how so** *interrog.* How is that so? Why is it so? How? Why? ♦*I said the party was a failure and she asked. "How so?"* ♦*He said his brother was not a good dancer and I asked him, "How so?"*

**how's that** *informal* What did you say? Will you please repeat that? ♦*"I've just been up in a balloon for a day and a half." "How's that?"* ♦*"The courthouse is on fire." "How's that again?"*

**how's tricks?** *adv. phr., informal* A friendly greeting meaning "How are you?, how are things going?" etc. ♦*"How's tricks?" John greeted his old roommate from college. "Have you made your first million yet?"*

**how the wind blows** See WAY THE WIND BLOWS.

**hue and cry** *n.* **1.** An alarm and chase after a supposed wrongdoer; a pursuit usually by shouting men. ♦*"Stop, thief," cried John as he ran. Others joined him, and soon there was a hue and cry.* **2.** An excited mass protest, alarm, or outcry of any kind. ♦*The explosion was so terrible that people at a distance raised a great hue and cry about an earthquake.*

**hug the road** *v. phr.* To stay firmly on the road; ride smoothly without swinging. ♦*A heavy car with a low center of gravity will hug the road.* ♦*At high speeds a car will not hug the road well.*

**huh-uh** or **hum-um** or **uh-uh** *adv., informal* No.—Used only in speech or to record dialogue. ♦*Did Mary come? Huh-uh.* ♦*Is it raining out? Uh-uh.*

**hunky-dory** *adj.* OK; satisfactory; fine. ♦*The landlord asked about our new apartment and we told him that so far everything was hunky-dory.*

**hunt and peck** *n. phr., informal* Picking out typewriter keys by sight, usually with one or two fingers; not memorizing the keys. ♦*Many newspaper reporters do their typing by hunt and peck.*—Often used, with hyphens, as an adjective. ♦*Mr. Barr taught himself to type, and he uses the hunt-and-peck system.*

**hunt down** *v.* **1.** To pursue and capture; look hard for an animal or person until found and caught. ♦*The police hunted down the escaped prisoner.* **2.** To search for (something) until one finds it. ♦*Professor Jones hunted down the written manuscript in the Library of Congress.*

**hunt for bargains** *v. phr.* To seek inexpensive things, frequent sales. ♦*After living in Hong Kong for four years, we learned how to hunt for bargains, even back in Chicago.*

**hunt up** v. To find or locate by search. ♦*When John was in Chicago, he hunted up some old friends.* ♦*The first thing Fred had to do was to hunt up a hotel room.*

**hurry on with** or **make haste with** v. phr. To make rapid progress in an undertaking. ♦*Sue promised to hurry on with the report and send it out today.*

**hurry up** v. phr. To rush (an emphatic form of hurry). ♦*Hurry up or we'll miss our plane.*

**hurt someone's feelings** v. phr. To offend one's pride or self-image. ♦*Don't talk to Helen like that; you're bound to hurt her feelings.*

**hush-hush** adj., informal Kept secret or hidden; kept from public knowledge; hushed up; concealed. ♦*The company had a new automobile engine that it was developing, but kept it a hush-hush project until they knew it was successful.*

**hush up** v. **1.** To keep news of (something) from getting out; prevent people from knowing about. ♦*It isn't always easy to hush up a scandal.* **2.** informal To be or make quiet; stop talking, crying, or making some other noise.—Often used as a command. ♦*"Hush up," Mother said, when we began to repeat ugly gossip.*

**I been there before** or **I've been there before** v. phr. I know what it's like; I know all about that; I've had similar experiences. ♦ *"It's terrible to be laid off on such short notice," John complained. "I know," Tom answered, "I've been there before."*

**I beg to differ** or **excuse me!** v. phr. I disagree with what you said. ♦ *"All people who use marijuana are criminals," the old lady opined. "I beg to differ with you on that," John said. "Some people get a doctor's prescription for it to reduce their pain caused by cancer."*

**I bet!** or **I'll bet!** v. phr. offered as reinforcement of what was heard; meaning "I believe you, I am sure you did, or will do something." ♦ *"I know when the weather will turn," the retired sea captain said. "After all, I have sailed around the world a few dozen times." "I bet," the admiring listener responded.*

**I can't wait** or **I can hardly wait!** v. phr. Eagerly anticipating something. ♦ *"You will be flown to Stockholm, Sweden, at our expense to be able to accompany your husband, who has won the Nobel Prize for Literature," the voice on the other end of the phone announced. "I can hardly wait!" Mrs. Kertész, the Nobel Laureate's wife replied.*

**icebreaker** n. phr. A joke or a funny anecdote used at the beginning of a formal presentation or question-and-answer session after a lecture, which puts the participants at ease, allowing a flow of free conversation. ♦ *"I always welcome an icebreaker in a formal situation," Sir Randolph Quirk, the president of the British Academy said after a heavily attended and televised conference in Singapore.*

**I couldn't agree with you more** v. phr. meaning: "How right you are!" ♦ *"We need a little more love between human beings on planet Earth," the Reverend Blomerly said. "I couldn't agree with you more," his parishioner answered.*

**I couldn't care less** v. phr. It really doesn't matter to me; I am entirely indifferent in the matter. ♦ *"The Milky Way Galaxy will definitely collide with the Andromeda Galaxy in a billion year's time," the*

lecturer in astronomy said, trying to impress Miss Curtis. *"is interesting that," the pretty young girl answered, "but I really couldn't care less. My problems are more immediate."*

**I declare** interj., dialect Well; oh my; truly.—Used for emphasis. ♦ *I declare, it has been a very warm day!* ♦ *Mother said, "I declare, John, you have grown a foot."*

**idiot box** n. A television set. ♦ *Phil has been staring at the idiot box all afternoon.*

**I don't care if I do!** or **I don't mind if I do!** v. phr., informal Yes, please! ♦ *"Would you care to have another drink?" the host asked Suzanne. "I don't care if I do," she answered flirtatiously.* ♦ *"Have some more cake, Steve!" his aunt encouraged the rare visitor. "I don't mind if I do," Steve said, holding out his plate.*

**if anything** adv. phr. More likely; instead; rather. ♦ *The weather forecast is not for cooler weather; if anything, it is expected to be warmer.*

**if I say so myself** v. phr. A phrase pointing out that the speaker believes strongly in what he or she said, and is adding him- or herself as the authority to back up the statement. ♦ *"Your daughter, Sam," Joe said, "is beautiful enough to run for the Miss America contest, if I say so myself."*

**if it ain't broke, don't fix it** informal If something is in good working order, there is no need to start changing it, as such interference may lead to ruining the thing.—A proverb. ♦ *Too many new ideas are floating around in various experimental sciences, and so we're tempted to change everything around us. Yet there is wisdom in the old saying "If it ain't broke, don't fix it!"*

**if it's not one thing it's another** If a certain thing doesn't go wrong, another most probably will. ♦ *When John lost his keys and his wallet, and his car wouldn't start, he exclaimed in despair, "If it's not one thing it's another."*

**if need be** adv. phr. If the need arises. ♦ *If need be, I can come early tomorrow and work overtime.*

**if only** I wish. ♦*If only it would stop raining!* ♦*If only Mother could be here.*

**if the hill will not come to Muhammad, Muhammad will go to the hill** If one person will not go to the other, then the other must go to him.—A proverb. ♦*Grandfather won't come to visit us, so we must go and visit him. If the hill won't come to Muhammad, then Muhammad will go to the hill.*

**if the shoe fits, wear it** If what is said describes you, you are meant.—A proverb. ♦*I won't say who, but some children are always late. If the shoe fits, wear it.*

**if worst comes to worst** If the worst thing happens that be imagined; if the worst possible thing happens; if troubles grow worse. ♦*If worst comes to worst and Mr. Jones loses the house, he will send his family to his mother's farm.*

**if you can't lick them, join them** If you cannot defeat an opponent or get him to change his attitude, plans, or ways of doing things, the best thing to do is to change your ideas, plans, etc. ♦*"The small car manufacturers are winning over the big car makers," the president of an American car factory said. "If we want to stay in business, we must do as they do. In other words, if you can't lick them, join them."*

**if you don't like it, you can lump it** *informal* If you don't like what I have proposed, you may just quit the entire discussion and go away.—A proverb. ♦*Before Grandmother died she called in her two grandsons and told them,: "I will leave you each an equal amount of $25,000." "Is that all?" the boys replied indignantly. "I can give it all to the church, you know!" the grandmother answered, and added, "If you don't like it, you can lump it!"*

**I give up!** *v. phr., informal* When confronted with a puzzle to solve or a difficult game to win, such as chess, the party that cannot come up with the right answer or wants to concede defeat uses this phrase. ♦*"Who invented the electric locomotive?" the teacher asked. "Was it Bell, Morse, or Kandó?" The boy waited a while, and then said, "I don't know, sir; I give up!."*

**I got your number** *v. phr.* I figured out what you're up to. ♦*"You've sneaking around my back all day, you little scoundrel!" Father said. " I got your number—you are trying to put up a homemade rocket launcher in the backyard!"*

**I have to hand it to you!** *v. phr., informal* Compliment; congratulations, I recognize that you are very good at it indeed. ♦*"Now that is quite a model airplane you built," Father said proudly. "I have to hand it to you; you've got talent."*

**I hear you** *v. phr.* I am in sympathy with what you are saying. ♦*"I am being treated very shabbily at my place of employment," Joe complained to his brother. "I hear you, man," his brother answered. "Why don't you quit?"*

**I'll be damned!** *or* **I'll be darned!** *or* **I'll be...!** I am greatly surprised; I can hardly believe what you said; I cannot understand why something is happening or has happened.—A proverb. ♦*"I'll be damned if I understand what my daughter sees in that idiot Jim!" Sylvia's father exclaimed.*

**I'll bet you my bottom dollar** *interj., informal* An exaggerated assertion of assurance. ♦*I'll bet you my bottom dollar that the Cubs will win this year.*

**I'll bet you the hole of a doughnut** *v. phr., said as a joke* I am willing to bet you, but nothing worthwhile, as a hole in a doughnut is empty air. ♦*"I'll bet you the hole of a doughnut, that we'll have another frost even as late as May," the meteorologist said with an impish smirk.*

**I'll eat my hat** *v. phr., informal* Often heard when someone wants to express great surprise or disbelief, meaning that what I heard is so outlandish, strange, unbelievable that my reaction to it will be equally out of the ordinary. ♦*I'll eat my hat if that idiot Jim makes the honor roll.* ♦*If you find a single misquote in my article, I'll eat my hat.*

**I'll leave it to you** *or* **leave it to someone** *phr. v.* To let someone else make an important decision; to allow another person to be in control. ♦*"When should we leave?" John asked his wife. "I'll leave it to you, dear," she replied.* ♦*The head of the department decided to leave the scheduling of classes to his administrative assistant.*

**I'll say** *or* **I tell you** *interj., informal* I agree with this completely.—Used for emphasis. ♦ *Did the children all enjoy Aunt Sally's pecan pie? I'll say!* ♦ *I'll say this is a good movie!*

**I'll tell you what** *or* **tell you what** *informal* Here is an idea. ♦ *The hamburger stand is closed, but I'll tell you what, let's go to my house and cook some hot dogs.*

**ill at ease** *adj. phr.* Not feeling at ease or comfortable; anxious; worried; unhappy. ♦ *When Joe first went to dancing school, he was ill at ease, not knowing how to act.*

**ill-favored** *adj.* Ugly; unprepossessing. ♦ *Oddly enough, the father had less trouble in marrying off his ill-favored daughter than her prettier sister.*

**ill-gotten gains** *n. phr.* Goods or money obtained in an illegal or immoral fashion. ♦ *The jailed criminal had plenty of time to think about his ill-gotten gains.*

**I'm from Missouri** I am skeptical; I don't believe what you said unless you show me.—A proverb. ♦ *"I won two air tickets and a week in a hotel in Hawaii," John said. "I hope you're coming." "You know me, John," Mary replied, "I'm from Missouri. I'll believe you when you show them to me."*

**impose on** *v.* To try to get more from (a person who is helping you) than he or she intended to give. ♦ *Don't you think you are imposing on your neighbor when you use his telephone for half an hour?*

**improve on** *or* **improve upon** *v.* To make or get one that is better than (another). ♦ *Dick made good marks the first year, but he thought he could improve on them.*

**I'm telling you** *informal* It is important to listen to what I am saying. ♦ *Marian is a smart girl but I'm telling you, she doesn't always do what she promises.*

**I'm with you on that** *or* **I'm with you, pal** The speaker registers agreement informally and enthusiastically. ♦ *"All twentieth-century dictatorships have failed," the political science major said to his roommate, Tom. "I'm with you on that," Tom replied.*

**in a bad frame of mind** *adv. phr.* In an unhappy mood. ♦ *Make sure the boss is not in a bad frame of mind when you ask him for a raise.*

**in a bad way** *adv. phr., informal* In trouble or likely to have trouble. ♦ *If you have only those two girls to help you, you are in a bad way.* ♦ *Mrs. Jones has cancer and is in a bad way.*

**in a big way** *adv. phr., informal* As fully as possible; with much ceremony. ♦ *Our family celebrates birthdays in a big way.*

**in a bind** *or* **in a box** *adv. phr., informal* Likely to have trouble whether you do one thing or another. ♦ *Sam is in a bind because if he carries home his aunt's groceries, his teacher will be angry because he is late, and if he doesn't, his aunt will complain.*

**in absentia** *adv. phr., formal* When the person is absent.—Used in graduation exercises when presenting diplomas to an absent student or during a court case. ♦ *On Commencement Day, Joe was sick in bed and the college gave him his bachelor's degree in absentia.*

**in accordance with** *adv. phr.* In consonance with something; conforming to something. ♦ *Employees at this firm are expected to always behave in accordance with the rules.*

**in a certain condition** *or* **in an interesting condition** *adj. phr.* Pregnant. ♦ *"Your daughter Mary looks rather pale these days," Tom's brother remarked. "Didn't you know?" Tom replied. "She is in a certain condition."*

**in a circle** *or* **in circles** *adv. phr.* Without any progress; without getting anywhere; uselessly. ♦ *The committee debated for two hours, just talking in circles.*

**in addition** *adv. phr.* As something extra; besides. ♦ *He has two cars and in addition a motorboat.*

**in advance** *or* **in advance of** *adv. phr.* **1.** In front; ahead (of the others); first. ♦ *In the parade, the band will march in advance of the football team.* ♦ *The soldiers rode out of the fort with the scouts in advance.* **2.** Before doing or getting something. ♦ *The motel man told Mr. Williams he would have to pay in advance.*

**in a family way** *or* **in the family way** *adj. phr., informal* Going to have a baby. ♦ *Sue and Liz are happy because their mother is in the family way.*

**in a fix** *adv. phr.* In trouble. ♦*Last night Jack wrecked his car and now he is in a fix.*

**in a flash** *also* **in a trice** *adv. phr.* Very suddenly. ♦*We were watching the bird eat the crumbs; then I sneezed, and he was gone in a flash.*

**in a flutter** *adv. phr., informal* In a state of nervous excitement. ♦*Whenever Norm and Cathy are near one another, both are in a flutter; they must be in love.*

**in a fog** *or* **in a haze** *adv. phr.* Mentally confused; not sure what is happening. ♦*I was so upset that for two days I went around in a haze, not even answering when people spoke to me.*

**in a good frame of mind** *adv. phr.* In a happy mood. ♦*After a relaxing holiday in the Bahamas, the boss was in a very good frame of mind.*

**in a hole** *or* **in a spot** *adj. phr., informal* In an embarrassing or difficult position; in some trouble. ♦*When the restaurant cook left at the beginning of the busy season, it put the restaurant owner in a hole.*

**in a huff** *adv. phr., informal* Angrily. ♦*Ellen went off in a huff because she didn't get elected class president.*

**in a hurry** *or* **in a rush** *adv. phr.* Quickly, rapidly. ♦*If you want to find the bank open, we must get there in a hurry.* ♦*I am sorry about the many typos in my manuscript, but I had to finish it in a great rush.*

**in a jam** *adv. phr., informal* In a predicament; in a situation fraught with difficulty. ♦*If you continue to disregard the university instructions on how to take a test, you'll wind up in a jam with the head of the department.*

**in a jiffy** *adv. phr., informal* Immediately; right away; in a moment. ♦*Wait for me; I'll be back in a jiffy.*

**in all** *adv. phr.* **1.** All being counted; altogether. ♦*You have four apples and I have three bananas, making seven pieces of fruit in all.* ♦*In all we did very well.*

**in and out** *adv. phr.* **1.** Coming in and going out often. ♦*He was very busy Saturday and was in and out all day.*

**in a nutshell** *adv. phr., informal* In a few words; briefly; without telling all about it. ♦*We are in a hurry, so I'll give you the story in a nutshell.*

**in any case** *also* **in any event** *or* **at all events** *adv. phr.* **1.** No matter what happens; surely; without fail; certainly; anyhow; anyway. ♦*It may rain tomorrow, but we are going home in any case.* **2.** Regardless of anything else; whatever else may be true; anyhow; anyway. ♦*I don't know if it is a white house or a brown house. At all events, it is a big house on Main Street.*

**in a pickle** *adv. phr., informal* In a quandary; in a difficult situation. ♦*I was certainly in a pickle when my front tire blew out.*

**in a pig's eye** *adv., slang, informal* Hardly; unlikely; not so. ♦*Would I marry him? In a pig's eye.*

**in a pinch** *adv. phr., informal* In an emergency. ♦*Dave is a good friend who will always help out in a pinch.*

**in arms** *adv. phr.* Having guns and being ready to fight; armed. ♦*When our country is at war, we have many men in arms.*

**in arrears** *adv. phr.* Late or behind in payment of money or in finishing something.—Usually used of a legal debt or formal obligation. ♦*Poor Mr. Brown! He is in arrears on his rent.*

**in a rush** See IN A HURRY.

**in a rut** *adv. phr.* Stuck in an unchanging, boring job, marriage, or other situation in life. ♦*"Why is Mary so sad?" her brother Joe asked. "She feels that she is in a rut," Mary's husband replied.*

**in a sense** *adv. phr.* In some ways but not in all; somewhat. ♦*In a sense, arithmetic is a language.*

**inasmuch as** *conj. also* **for as much as** *formal* Because; for the reason that; since. ♦*Inasmuch as the waves are high, I shall not go out in the boat.*

**in at the kill** *adj. phr., informal* Watching or taking part, usually with pleasure, at the end of a struggle; present at the finish. ♦*Frank and John have been quarreling for a long time and tonight they are having a fight. Bill says he wants to be in at the kill, because he is Frank's friend.*

**in a way** *adv. phr.* **1.** *also informal* **in a kind of way** *or informal* **in a sort of way** To a certain extent; a little; somewhat. ♦*I like Jane in a way, but she is very proud.* **2.** In one thing. ♦*In a way, this book is easier; it is much shorter.*

**in a while, crocodile** *or* **see you later, alligator!** *adv. phr.* A joking way to say later, not now. ♦*When John's six-year-old son kept nagging about lunch in the zoo, John said, "In a while, crocodile!"* ♦*When the boy's friend left after little Johnny's birthday, Johnny's father said to the boy, "See you later, alligator!"*

**in a world of one's own** *or* **in a world by oneself 1.** In the place where you belong; in your own personal surroundings; apart from other people. ♦*They are in a little world of their own in their house on the mountain.* **2a.** In deep thought or concentration. ♦*Mary is in a world of her own when she is playing the piano.* **2b.** *slang* Not caring about or connected with other people in thoughts or actions.—Usually used sarcastically. ♦*That boy is in a world all by himself. He never knows what is happening around him.*

**in a zone** *adv., slang, informal* In a daze; in a daydream; in a state of being unable to concentrate. ♦*Professor Smith puts everyone in a zone.*

**in bad form** *adv. phr.* Violating social custom or accepted behavior. ♦*When Bob went to the opera in blue jeans and without a tie, his father-in-law told him that it was in bad form.*

**in behalf of** *or* **on behalf of** *prep., formal* **1.** In place of; as a representative of; for. ♦*John accepted the championship award on behalf of the team.* **2.** As a help to; for the good of. ♦*The minister worked hard all his life in behalf of the poor.*

**in black and white** See BLACK AND WHITE.

**in brief** *or* **in short** *or* **in a word** *adv. phr.* Briefly; to give the meaning of what has been said or written in a word or in a few words; in summary. ♦*The children could play as long as they liked, they had no work to do, and nobody scolded them; in short, they were happy.* ♦*The speaker didn't know his subject, nor did he speak well; in brief, he was disappointing.* ♦*John is smart, polite, and well-behaved. In a word, he is admirable.*

**in case** *adv. phr., informal* **1.** In order to be prepared; as a precaution; if there is need.—Usually used in the phrase *just in case.* ♦*The bus is usually on time,* but start early, just in case. **2. in case** *or* **in the event** *conj.* If it happens that; if it should happen that; if; lest. ♦*Tom took his skates in case they found a place to skate.* ♦*In the event that our team wins, there will be a big celebration.* ♦*What shall we do in case it snows?*

**in case of** *also* **in the event of** *prep.* In order to meet the possibility of; lest there is; if there is; if there should be. ♦*Take your umbrellas in case of rain.* ♦*The wall was built along the river in case of floods.*

**inch (one's way) along** *v. phr.* To proceed slowly and with difficulty. ♦*When the electricity failed, it took John half an hour to inch his way along the corridors of the office building.*

**in character** *adv. or adj. phr.* **1.** In agreement with a person's character or personality; in the way that a person usually behaves or is supposed to behave; as usual; characteristic; typical; suitable. ♦*John was very rude at the party, and that was not in character because he is usually very polite.* **2.** Suitable for the part or the kind of part being acted; natural to the way a character in a book or play is supposed to act. ♦*It would not have been in character for Robin Hood to steal from a poor man.*

**in charge** *adv. or adj. phr.* **1.** In authority or control; in a position to care for or supervise; responsible. ♦*If you have any questions, ask the boss. He's in charge.* **2.** Under care or supervision. ♦*During your visit to the library, you will be in the librarian's charge.*

**in charge of** *prep.* **1.** Responsible for; having supervision or care of. ♦*Marian is in charge of selling tickets.* **2.** *or* **in the charge of** Under the care or supervision of. ♦*Mother puts the baby in the charge of the baby-sitter while she is out.*

**in check** *adv. phr.* In a position where movement or action is not allowed or stopped; under control; kept quiet or back. ♦*The soldiers tried to keep the attacking Iraqis in check until help came.* ♦*Mary couldn't hold her feelings in check any longer and began to cry.*

**in circulation** *or* **into circulation** *adj. phr., informal* Going around and doing things as usual; joining what others are doing. ♦*John broke his leg and was out* *of school for several weeks, but now he is back in circulation again.*

**inclined to** *adj. phr.* Having a tendency to; positively disposed toward. ◆*I am inclined to fall asleep after a heavy meal.*

**in clover** *or* **in the clover** *adv. or adj. phr., informal* In rich comfort; rich or successful; having a pleasant or easy life. ◆*They live in clover because their father is rich.* ◆*When we finish the hard part we'll be in the clover.*

**in cold blood** *adv. phr.* Without feeling or pity; in a purposely cruel way; coolly and deliberately. ◆*The bank robbers planned to shoot in cold blood anyone who got in their way.*

**in command** *adv. phr.* In control of; in charge. ◆*Helen is in command of the situation.*

**in commission** *or* **into commission** *adv. or adj. phr.* **1.** On duty or ready to be put on duty by a naval or military service; in active service. ◆*The old battleship has been in commission for twenty years.* **2.** In proper condition; in use or ready for use; working; running. ◆*The wheel of my bicycle was broken, but it is back in commission now.*

**in common** *adv. phr.* Shared together or equally; in use or ownership by all. ◆*Mr. and Mrs. Smith own the store in common.*

**in consequence** *adv. phr.* As a result; therefore; so. ◆*Jennie got up late, and in consequence she missed the bus.*

**in consequence of** *prep., formal* As a result of. ◆*In consequence of the deep snow, school will not open today.* ◆*In consequence of his promise to pay for the broken window, Bill was not punished.*

**in consideration of** *adv. phr.* **1.** After thinking about and weighing; because of. ◆*In consideration of the boy's young age, the judge did not put him in jail.* **2.** In exchange for; because of; in payment for. ◆*In consideration of the extra work Joe had done, his boss gave him an extra week's pay.*

**in days** *or* **weeks** *or* **years to come** *adv. phr.* In the future. ◆*In the years to come I will be thinking of my father's advice about life.*

**in deep** *adj. phr.* Seriously mixed up in something, especially trouble. ◆*George*

*began borrowing small sums of money to bet on horses, and before he knew it he was in deep.*

**in defiance of** *prep.* Acting against; in disobedience to. ◆*The girl chewed gum in defiance of the teacher's rule.*

**in demand** *adj. phr.* Needed; wanted. ◆*Men to shovel snow were in demand after the snow storm.*

**Indian giver** *n. phr.* A person who gives one something, but later asks for it back.—An ethnic slur; avoid! ◆*John gave me a beautiful fountain pen, but a week later, like an Indian giver, he wanted it back.*

**Indian summer** *n. phr.* A dry and warm period of time late in the fall, usually in October. ◆*After the cold and foggy weather, we had a brief Indian summer, during which the temperature was up in the high seventies.*

**in dire straits** *adv. phr.* In a difficult, terrible situation. ◆*"I am badly in need of an interest-free loan of $5,000, John!" the old roommate from college called to say. "What's the matter? Have you tried your bank?" "I am in such dire straights that they won't give it to me," came the reply.* ◆*The mountain climbers were in dire straights because they had been lost for days without food and water.*

**in dispute** *adj. phr.* Disagreed about; being argued. ◆*The penalty ordered by the referee was in dispute by one of the teams.*

**in doubt** *adv. phr.* In the dark; having some question or uncertainty. ◆*When in doubt about any of the words you're using, consult a good dictionary.*

**in due course** *or* **in due season** *or* **in due time** See IN GOOD TIME 2.

**in due season** *or* **in due time** See IN GOOD TIME.

**industrial park** *n.* A complex of industrial buildings and/or businesses usually located far from the center of a city in a setting especially landscaped to make such buildings look better. ◆*The nearest supermarket that sells car tires is at the industrial park twenty miles from downtown.*

**in earnest** *adv. or adj. phr.* Seriously; in a determined way. ◆*Bill did his homework in earnest.*—Often used like a predicate adjective. Sometimes used with *dead*, for emphasis. ◆*Betty's* *friends thought she was joking when she said she wanted to be a doctor, but she was in dead earnest.*

**in effect** *adv. or adj. phr.* **1.** The same in meaning or result. ♦*The teacher gave the same assignment, in effect, that she gave yesterday.* **2.** Necessary to obey; being enforced. ♦*The coach says that players must be in bed by midnight, and that rule is in effect tonight.*

**in error** *adv. phr.* Wrong; mistaken. ♦*You were in error when you assumed that he would wait for us.*

**in evidence** *adj. phr.* Easily seen; noticeable. ♦*The tulips were blooming; spring was in evidence.*

**I never liked it, anyway** *v. phr.* Similar to "sour grapes," this saying is heard when one loses or breaks something in order to comfort oneself jokingly.—A proverb. ♦*"I lost my new digital camera!" John sighed. "Oh, it doesn't matter," he added. "I didn't like it, anyway!"*

**in fact** *also* **in point of fact** *adv. phr.* Really truthfully.—Often used for emphasis. ♦*It was a very hot day; in fact, it was 100 degrees.*

**in favor of** *prep.* On the side of; in agreement with. ♦*Everyone in the class voted in favor of the party.* ♦*Most girls are in favor of wearing lipstick.*

**in fear of** *adj. phr.* Fearful of; afraid of. ♦*They live so close to the border that they are constantly in fear of an enemy attack.*

**in for** *prep., informal* Unable to avoid; sure to get. ♦*On Christmas morning we are in for some surprises.*

**in for a penny, in for a dollar** *or* **pound** Once you got into a deal on a low level, you're in all the way, which may be costly.—A proverb. ♦*When Mr. Smith decided to invest in Mr. Brown's company, everything went well at the beginning. When things started to go badly, Mr. Smith wanted to get out of the business. At this point Mr. Brown reminded his partner: "In for a penny, in for a pound."*

**in force** *adj. phr.* **1.** To be obeyed. ♦*New times for eating meals are now in force.* **2.** In a large group. ♦*People went to see the parade in force.*

**in front of** *prep.* Ahead of; before. ♦*A big oak tree stood in front of the building.*

**in full swing** *adj. phr.* Actively going on; in full action. ♦*All of the children were planting seeds; the gardening project was in full swing.*

**in general**[1] *adv. phr.* Usually; very often. ♦*The weather in Florida is warm in general.*

**in general**[2] *adj. phr.* Most; with few exceptions. ♦*Boys in general like active sports more than girls do.*

**in glass houses** See PEOPLE WHO LIVE IN GLASS HOUSES SHOULD NOT THROW STONES.

**in good** *adj. phr., informal* Well liked; accepted.—Used with *with.* ♦*The boy washed the blackboards so that he would get in good with his teacher.* ♦*Although Tom was younger, he was in good with the older boys.*

**in good faith** See GOOD FAITH.

**in good time** *or* **in good season** *adv. phr.* **1.** A little early; sooner than necessary. ♦*The school bus arrived in good time.* ♦*We reached the station in good season to catch the 9:15 bus for New York.* **2.** *or* **in due course** *or* **in due season** *or* **in due time** In the usual amount of time; at the right time; in the end. ♦*Spring and summer will arrive in due course.*

**in great measure** *adv. phr.* To a great extent; largely. ♦*The Japanese attack on Hawaii was in great measure a contributing factor to President Roosevelt's decision to enter World War II.*

**in hand** *adv. or adj. phr.* **1.** Under control. ♦*The baby-sitter kept the children well in hand.* **2.** In your possession; with you.—Often used in the phrase *cash in hand.* ♦*Tom figured that his cash in hand with his weekly pay would be enough to buy a car.* **3.** Being worked on; with you to do. ♦*We should finish the work we have in hand before we begin something new.*

**in harm's way** *or* **into harm's way** *adv. phr.* In danger of getting wounded or killed either in a war or in the police force. ♦*America worries about sending U.S. troops into harm's way.* ♦*Many reporters during the war lived in harm's way.*

**in honor of** *prep.* As an honor to; for showing respect or thanks to. ♦*We celebrate Mother's Day in honor of our mothers.*

**in hot water** See HOT WATER.

**in** *or* **into orbit** *adj. phr.* Thrilled; exuberantly happy; in very high spirits. ◆*When Carol won the lottery she went right into orbit.*

**in** *or* **into the clear** *adj. phr.* Free; cleared of all responsibility and guilt. ◆*Because of the new evidence found, Sam is still in the clear, but Harry is still behind bars.*

**in** *or* **into the doldrums** *adj. phr.* Inactive; sluggish; depressed. ◆*The news of our factory's going out of business put all of us in the doldrums.*

**in** *or* **into the limelight** *adv. phr.* In the center of attention. ◆*Some people will do almost anything to be able to step into the limelight.*

**in keeping** *adj. phr.* Going well together; agreeing; similar. ◆*Having an assembly on Friday morning was in keeping with the school program.*

**in kind** *adv. phr.* In a similar way; with the same kind of thing. ◆*Lois returned Mary's insult in kind.*

**in league with** *or informal* **in cahoots with** *prep.* In secret agreement or partnership with (someone); working together secretly with, especially for harm. ◆*People once believed that some women were witches in league with the devil.*

**in light of** *also* **in the light of** *adj. phr.* **1.** As a result of new information; by means of new ideas. ◆*The teacher changed John's grade in the light of the extra work in the workbook.* **2.** Because of. ◆*In light of the muddy field, the football team wore their old uniforms.*

**in line** *adj. phr.* **1.** In a position in a series or after someone else. ◆*John is in line for the presidency of the club next year.* **2.** Obeying or agreeing with what is right or usual; doing or being what people expect or accept; within ordinary or proper limits. ◆*The coach kept the excited team in line.*

**in line with** *prep.* In agreement with. ◆*In line with the custom of the school, the students had a holiday between Christmas and New Year's Day.*

**in love** *adj. phr.* Liking very much; loving. ◆*Tom and Ellen are in love.* ◆*Mary is in love with her new wristwatch.*

**in luck** *adj. phr.* Being lucky; having good luck; finding something good by chance. ◆*Mary dropped her glasses but they did not break. She was in luck.*

**in memory of** *prep.* As something that makes people remember (a person or thing); as a reminder of; as a memorial to. ◆*Many special ceremonies are in memory of famous people.*

**in mind** *adv. phr.* **1.** In the center of your thought; in your close attention. ◆*You have to be home by 11 o'clock. Keep that in mind, Bob.* ◆*Bear in mind the rules of safety when you swim.*

**in mint condition** *adj. phr.* Excellent; as good as new. ◆*Grandma seldom uses her car; it is already ten years old, but it is still in mint condition.*

**in name** *adj. or adv. phr.* Having a title, but not really doing what someone with the title is expected to do. ◆*The old man is a doctor in name only. He does not have patients now.*

**in need of** *adj. phr.* Destitute; lacking something. ◆*The young girl is so ill that she is seriously in need of medical attention.*

**inner city** *n., colloquial* Densely populated neighborhoods in large metropolitan areas inhabited by low income families usually of minority backgrounds, such as Mexicans, Puerto Ricans, or African Americans; characterized by slums and government-owned high rises. ◆*Joe comes from the inner city—he may need help with his tuition.*

**in no time** *or* **in nothing flat** *adv. phr., informal* In a very little time; soon; quickly. ◆*When the entire class worked together they finished the project in no time.* ◆*The bus filled with students in nothing flat.*

**in no uncertain terms** See IN SO MANY WORDS 2.

**in on** *prep.* **1.** Joining together for. ◆*The children collected money from their classmates and went in on a present for their teacher.* **2.** Told about; having knowledge of. ◆*Bob was in on the secret.*

**in one ear and out the other** See GO IN ONE EAR AND OUT THE OTHER.

**in one fell swoop** *or* **at one fell swoop** *adv. phr.* **1.** *literary* In one attack or accident; in one bad blow. ◆*The millionaire lost his money and his friends at one fell swoop.* **2.** At one time; at the same time. ◆ *Three cars drove into the driveway, and Mrs. Crane's dinner guests all arrived at one fell swoop.*

**in one's behalf** *or* **on one's behalf** *adv. phr., informal* **1.** For someone else; in your place. ◆ *My husband could not be here tonight, but I want to thank you on his behalf.* **2.** For the good of another person or group; as a help to someone. ◆ *My teacher went to the factory and spoke in my behalf when I was looking for a job.*

**in one's blood** *or* **into one's blood** *adv. phr.* Agreeing perfectly with one's sympathies, feelings, and desires. ◆ *Living in a warm section of the country gets in your blood.*

**in one's cups** *adj. phr., literary* Drunk. ◆ *The man was in his cups and talking very loudly.*

**in one's element** *adv. phr.* **1.** In one's natural surroundings. ◆ *The deep-sea fish is in his element in deep ocean water.* **2.** Where you can do your best. ◆ *John is in his element working on the farm.*

**in one's face** *adv. phr.* **1.** Against your face. ◆ *The trick cigar blew up in the clown's face.* ◆ *A cold wind was in our faces as we walked to school.* **2.** In front of you. ◆ *I told the boys that they were wrong, but they laughed in my face.*

**in one's favor** *adv. or adj. phr.* In a way that is good for you. ◆ *Bob made good grades in high school, and that was in his favor when he looked for a job.*

**in one's footsteps** See FOLLOW IN ONE'S FOOTSTEPS.

**in one's glory** *adj. phr.* Pleased and contented with yourself. ◆ *When John won the race, he was in his glory.*

**in one's good graces** *or* **in one's good books** *adv. phr.* Approved of by you; liked by someone. ◆ *Bill is back in the good graces of his girlfriend because he stopped drinking.*

**in one's hair** *adj. phr., informal* Bothering you again and again; always annoying. ◆ *John got in Father's hair when he was trying to read the paper by running and shouting.*

**in one's heart of hearts** *adv. phr.* Deep down where it really matters; in one's innermost feelings. ◆ *In my heart of hearts, I think you're the nicest person in the whole world.*

**in one's mind's eye** *adv. phr.* In the memory; in the imagination. ◆ *In his mind's eye he saw again the house he had lived in when he was a child.*

**in one's right mind** *adj. phr.* Accountable; sane and sober. ◆ *If you were in your right mind, you wouldn't be saying such stupid things to our boss.*

**in one's shell** *or* **into one's shell** *adv. or adj. phr., informal* In or into bashfulness; into silence; not sociable; unfriendly. ◆ *The teacher tried to get Rose to talk to her, but she stayed in her shell.*

**in one's shoes** *also* **in one's boots** *adv. phr.* In or into one's place or position. ◆ *How would you like to be in a lion tamer's boots?*

**in one's tracks** *adv. phr., informal* **1.** Just where one is at the moment; abruptly; immediately. ◆ *Mary stopped dead in her tracks, turned around, and ran back home.*

**in one's way** *adv. or adj. phr.* **1.** Within reach; likely to be met; before you. ◆ *The chance to work for a printer was put in my way.* **2.** *or* **in the way** In your path as a hindrance; placed so as to block the way. ◆ *A tree had fallen across the street and was in Jim's way as he drove.*

**in on the ground floor** *adv. phr.* At the start of a new enterprise or new business, giving employees a chance to grow with the place. ◆ *"Should we accept appointments at this university, which has been functioning for only one year?" John asked a colleague. "I think it would be a good idea, because we would be getting in on the ground floor, and in ten or fifteen years we will be the senior faculty."*

**in order** *adv. or adj. phr.* **1.** In arrangement; in the proper way of following one another. ◆ *Line up and walk to the door in order.* ◆ *Name all the presidents in order.* **2.** In proper condition. ◆ *The car was in good working order when I bought it.* **3.** Following the rules; proper; suitable. ◆ *Is it in order to ask the speaker questions at the meeting?* ◆ *At the end of a program, applause for the performers is in order.*

**in order to** *or* **so as to** *conj.* For the purpose of; to.—Used with an infinitive. ◆ *In order to follow the buffalo, the hunters often had to move their camps.* ◆ *We picked apples so as to make a pie.*

in part *adv. phr.* To some extent; partly; not wholly.—Often used with *large* or *small.* ♦ *We planted the garden in part with flowers. But in large part we planted vegetables.* ♦ *Tom was only in small part responsible.*

in particular *adv. phr.* In a way apart from others; more than others; particularly; especially. ♦ *The speaker talked about sports in general and about football in particular.*

in passing *adv. phr.* While talking about that subject; as extra information; also. ♦ *The writer of the story says he grew up in New York and mentions in passing that his parents came from Italy.*

in person *also* in the flesh *adv. phr.* Yourself; personally. ♦ *The governor cannot march in the parade in person today, but his wife will march.*

in place¹ *adv. phr.* **1a.** In the right or usual place or position. ♦ *Nothing is in place after the earthquake. Even trees and houses are turned over.* ♦ **1b.** In one place. ♦ *Our first exercise in gym class was running in place.* **2.** In proper order. ♦ *Stay in place in line, children.*

in place² *adj. phr.* In the right place or at the right time; suitable; timely. ♦ *A dog is not in place in a church.*

in place of See INSTEAD OF.

in plain English *adv. phr.* Plainly; simply; in clear language. ♦ *Stop beating around the bush and saying that John "prevaricates"; in plain English he is a liar.*

in poor shape *adv. phr.* In a bad condition. ♦ *Most of the streets of Chicago are in poor shape due to the heavy snow and frost during the winters.*

in practice¹ *also* into practice *adv. phr.* In actual doing. ♦ *The idea sounds good but will it work in practice?*

in practice² *adj. phr.* In proper condition to do something well through practice. ♦ *A pianist gets his fingers in practice by playing scales.*

in print *adj. phr.* Obtainable in printed form from a printer or publisher; printed. ♦ *The author has finished writing his book but it is not yet in print.* ♦ *It is a very old book and no longer in print.*

in private *adj. or adv. phr.* Not openly or in public; apart from others; confidentially; secretly. ♦ *The teacher told Susan that she wanted to talk to her in private after class.*

in progress *adj. phr.* Going ahead; being made or done; happening. ♦ *Plans are in progress to build a new school next year.*

in public *adv. phr.* **1.** In a place open to the people; in such a way that the public may see, hear, or know; not secretly; openly. ♦ *The mayor has told his friends that he is sick but will not admit it in public.*

in question *adj. phr.* **1.** In doubt; in dispute; being argued about or examined. ♦ *I know Bill would be a good captain for the team. That is not in question. But does he want to be captain?* **2.** Under discussion; being talked or thought about. ♦ *The girls in question are not in school today.*

in quotes See INVERTED COMMAS.

in reason *adv. phr., formal* Following the rules of reasoning; sensibly; reasonably. ♦ *One cannot in reason doubt that freedom is better than slavery.*

in reference to *or* with reference to *or* in regard to *or* with regard to *prep.* In connection with; from the standpoint of; concerning; regarding; about. ♦ *I am writing with reference to your last letter.* ♦ *I spoke to him with regard to his low marks.* ♦ *In regard to the test tomorrow, it is postponed.*

in relation to *or* with relation to *prep.* In connection with; in dealing with; as concerns; in comparison to; respecting; about. ♦ *With relation to his job, skill is very important.* ♦ *In relation to Texas, Rhode Island is quite a small state.*

in respect to *or* with respect to In connection with; related to; about; on. ♦ *The teacher told stories about Washington and Lincoln in respect to the importance of being honest.*

in return *adv. phr.* In order to give back something; as payment; in recognition or exchange.—Often used with *for.* ♦ *How much did John give you in return for your bicycle?* ♦ *I hit him in return for the time he hit me.*

in reverse *adj. or adv. phr.* In a backward direction; backward. ♦ *John hit the tree behind him when he put the car in reverse without looking first.*

in round figures *adv. phr.* As an estimated number; as a rounded-off figure containing no decimals or fractions. ♦*Skip the cents and just tell me in round figures how much this car repair will cost.*

**ins and outs** *n. phr.* The special ways of going somewhere or doing something; the different parts. ♦*Jerry's father is a good life insurance salesman; he knows all the ins and outs of the business.*

**in search of** *or literary* **in quest of** *prep.* Seeking or looking for; in pursuit of. ♦*Many men went West in search of gold.*

**in season** *adv. or adj. phr.* **1.** *literary* At the proper or best time. ♦*Fred's father told him that he was not old enough yet but that he would learn to drive in season.* **2a.** At the right or lawful time for hunting or catching. ♦*Deer will be in season next week.* ♦*In spring we'll go fishing when trout are in season.* **2b.** At the right time or condition for using, eating, or marketing; in a ripe or eatable condition. ♦*Christmas trees will be sold at the store in season.*

**in secret** *adv. phr.* In a private or secret way; in a hidden place. ♦*The miser buried his gold in secret and no one knows where it is.*

**in shape** *or* **in condition** *adj. phr.* In good condition; able to perform well. ♦*Mary was putting her French in shape for the test.*

**in short** See IN BRIEF.

**in short order** *adv. phr.* Without delay; quickly. ♦*Johnny got ready in short order after his father said that he could come to the ball game if he was ready in time.*

**in short supply** *adj. phr.* Not enough; in too small a quantity or amount; in less than the amount or number needed. ♦*We have five people and only four beds, so the beds are in short supply.*

**inside and out** See INS AND OUTS, INSIDE OUT 2.

**inside dope** *n. phr.* Secret information about the inner workings of a business, an organization, or some place of employment. ♦*"How does one get ahead at the Chicago Tool and Die Company?" Peter asked his friend Tom, who had been working there for several years. "I'll give you the inside dope," Tom replied. "Rule number one: never disagree with the boss; he is very vain."*

**inside of** *prep.* In; within; on or in an inside part of; not beyond; before the end of. ♦*There is a broom inside of the closet.* ♦*There is a label on the inside of the box.* ♦*Hand your papers in to me inside of three days.*

**inside out** *adv.* **1.** So that the inside is turned outside. ♦*Mother turns the stockings inside out when she washes them.* **2.** *or* **inside and out** *also* **in and out** In every part; throughout; completely. ♦*We searched the house inside and out for the kitten.*

**inside track** *n. phr.* **1.** The inside, shortest distance around a curved racetrack; the place that is closest to the inside fence. ♦*A big white horse had the inside track at the start of the race.* **2.** *informal* An advantage due to special connections or information. ♦*I would probably get that job if I could get the inside track.*

**insofar as** *conj.* To the extent that; to the point that; as much as. ♦*You will learn your lessons only insofar as you are willing to keep studying them.*

**in so many words** *adv. phr.* **1.** In those exact words. ♦*He hinted that he thought we were foolish but did not say so in so many words.* **2.** *or* **in no uncertain terms** In an outspoken way; plainly; directly. ♦*I told him in so many words that he was crazy.* ♦*Bob was very late for their date, and Mary told Bob in no uncertain terms what she thought of him.*

**in spite of** *prep. phr.* Against the influence or effect of; in opposition to; defying the effect of; despite. ♦*In spite of the bad storm John delivered his papers on time.*

**instead of** *or* **in place of** *also formal* **in lieu of** *prep.* In the place of; in substitution for; in preference to; rather than. ♦*I wore mittens instead of gloves.* ♦*The grown-ups had coffee but the children wanted milk in place of coffee.* ♦*The magician appeared on the program in lieu of a singer.*

**in step** *adv. or adj. phr.* **1.** With the left or right foot stepping at the same time as another's or to the beat of music; in matching strides with another person or persons. ♦*The long line of soldiers marched all in step: Left, right! Left, right!* **2.** In agreement; abreast.—Often followed by *with*. ♦ *Mary wanted to stay in step with her friends and have a car too.*

**in stitches** *adj. phr., informal* Laughing so hard that the sides ache; in a fit of laughing hard. ♦ *The comedian was so funny that he had everyone who was watching him in stitches.*

**in stock** *adj. phr.* Having something ready to sell or use; in present possession or supply; to be sold. ♦ *The store had no more red shoes in stock, so Mary chose brown ones instead.*

**in store** *adj. or adv. phr.* 1. Saved up in case of need; ready for use or for some purpose. ♦ *The squirrel has plenty of nuts in store for the winter.* 2. Ready to happen; waiting.—Often used in the phrase *hold* or *have in store.* ♦ *What does the future hold in store for the boy who ran away?* ♦ *There is a surprise in store for Helen when she gets home.*

**in substance** *adv. phr.* In important facts; in the main or basic parts; basically; really. ♦ *In substance the weather report said that it will be a nice day tomorrow.*

**in terms of** *prep.* 1. In the matter of; on the subject of; especially about; about. ♦ *He spoke about books in terms of their publication.* ♦ *What have you done in terms of fixing the house?* 2. As to the amount or number of. ♦ *We swam a great distance. In terms of miles, it was three.*

**in that** *conj.* For the reason that; because. ♦ *I like the city, but I like the country better in that I have more friends there.*

**in the air** *adv. phr.* 1. In everyone's thoughts. ♦ *Christmas was in the air for weeks before.* ♦ *The war filled people's thoughts every day; it was in the air.* 2. Meeting the bodily senses; surrounding you so as to be smelled or felt. ♦ *Spring is in the air.*

**in the bag** *adj. phr., informal* Sure to be won or gotten; certain. ♦ *We thought we had the game in the bag.*

**in the balance** See HANG IN THE BALANCE.

**in the ballpark** *adv. phr.* In roughly the amount mentioned. ♦ *"Will the new employee cost us $75,000 a year?" Tom asked the director. "You're in the ballpark," the director replied.*

**in the black** *adv. or adj. phr., informal* In a successful or profitable way; so as to make money. ♦ *A business must stay in the black to keep on.*

**in the can** *adj., slang, movie jargon* Ready; finished; completed; about to be duplicated and distributed to exhibitors. ♦ *No sneak previews until it's all in the can!*

**in the cards** *also* **on the cards** *adj. phr., informal* To be expected; likely to happen; foreseeable; predictable. ♦ *It was in the cards for the son to succeed his father as head of the business.*

**in the clear** *adj. phr.* 1. Free of anything that makes moving or seeing difficult; with nothing to limit action. ♦ *The plane climbed above the clouds and was flying in the clear.* ♦ *Jack passed the ball to Tim, who was in the clear and ran for a touchdown.* 2. *informal* Free of blame or suspicion; not thought to be guilty. ♦ *Steve was the last to leave the locker room, and the boys suspected him of stealing Tom's watch, but the coach found the watch and put Steve in the clear.* 3. Free of debt; not owing money to anyone. ♦ *Bob borrowed a thousand dollars from his father to start his business, but at the end of the first year he was in the clear.*

**in the clouds** *adj. phr.* Far from real life; in dreams; in fancy; in thought. ♦ *When Alice agreed to marry Jim, Jim went home in the clouds.*—Often used with *head, mind, thoughts.* ♦ *Mary is looking out the window, not at the chalkboard; her head is in the clouds again.*

**in the cold light of day** *adv. phr.* After sleeping on it; after giving it more thought; using common sense and looking at the matter unemotionally and realistically. ♦ *Last night my ideas seemed terrific, but in the cold light of day I realize that they won't work.*

**in the dark** *adj. phr.* 1. In ignorance; without information. ♦ *John was in the dark about the job he was being sent to.*

**in the dead of night** *adv. phr.* In total darkness. ♦ *The inmates tried to escape from the maximum security prison in the dead of night.*

**in the doghouse** *adj. phr., slang* In disgrace or disfavor. ♦ *Our neighbor got in the doghouse with his wife by coming home drunk.*

**in the door** See FOOT IN THE DOOR.

**in the driver's seat** *adv. phr.* In control; having the power to make decisions. ♦ *Stan is in the driver's seat now that he has been made our supervisor at the factory.*

**in the event of** See IN CASE OF.

**in the extreme** *adv. phr.* Extraordinarily. ♦ *"Why does Mary allow John to do anything he wants?" Suzie asked. "Because she loves him in the extreme," Mary's brother replied.*

**in the face of** *adv. phr.* **1.** When met or in the presence of; threatened by. ♦ *He was brave in the face of danger.* **2.** Although opposed by; without being stopped by. ♦ *Talking continued even in the face of the teacher's command to stop.*

**in the first place** *adv. phr.* **1.** Before now; in the beginning; first. ♦ *Carl patched his old football but it soon leaked again. He should have bought a new one in the first place.*

**in the flesh** See IN PERSON.

**in the forefront** *adv. phr.* Way out; leading. ♦ *The University of Chicago is in the forefront of medical research.*

**in the groove** *adj. phr., slang* Doing something very well; near perfection; at your best. ♦ *The band was right in the groove that night.* ♦ *It was an exciting football game; every player was really in the groove.*

**in the heat of the moment** *adv. phr.* In great anger; not thinking. ♦ *In the heat of the moment, John killed his wife when he found her in bed with their neighbor. He pleaded temporary insanity and got away with two years in jail.*

**in the hole** *adv. or adj. phr., informal* **1a.** Having a score lower than zero in a game, especially a card game; to a score below zero. ♦ *John went three points in the hole on the first hand of the card game.* **1b.** Behind an opponent; in difficulty in a sport or game. ♦ *We had their pitcher in the hole with the bases full and no one out.* **2.** In debt; behind financially. ♦ *John went in the hole with his hot dog stand.*

**in the know** *adj. phr., informal* Knowing about things that most people do not know about; knowing secrets or understanding a special subject. ♦ *In a print shop, Mr. Harvey is in the know, but in a kitchen he can't even cook an egg.*

**in the lap of luxury** *adv. phr.* Well supplied with luxuries; having most things that money can buy. ♦ *Mike grew up in the lap of luxury.*

**in the lap of the gods** *also* **on the knees of the gods** *adv. phr., literary* Beyond human control; not to be decided by anyone. ♦ *Frank had worked hard as a candidate, and as election day came he felt that the result was in the lap of the gods.* ♦ *The armies were evenly matched and the result of the battle seemed to be on the knees of the gods.*

**in the least** *adv. phr.* Even a little; in any degree or amount.—Used in negative, interrogative, and conditional sentences. ♦ *Mike was not upset in the least by the storm.* ♦ *It is no trouble to help you. Not in the least.*

**in the line of duty** *adj. phr.* Done or happening as part of a job. ♦ *The policeman was shot in the line of duty.*

**in the line of fire** *adv. phr.* In a dangerous position between two opposing parties. ♦ *John is right in the line of fire between the company's director and the vice president, who couldn't agree on John's proposal about the budget.*

**in the long run** *adv. phr.* In the end; in the final result. ♦ *John knew that he could make a success of the little weekly paper in the long run.*

**in the long term** See IN THE LONG RUN.

**in the loop** *adj. phr.* Knowledgeable about; involved in something. ♦ *John felt a great deal of responsibility, because he was in the loop on all essential decisions at the new bank.*

**in the lurch** See LEAVE IN THE LURCH.

**in the market for** *adj. phr.* Wishing to buy; ready to buy. ♦ *Mr. Jones is in the market for a new car.*

**in the middle** *adv. or adj. phr.* In between two sides of an argument; caught between two dangers. ♦ *Mary found herself in the middle of the quarrel between Joyce and Ethel.*

**in the middle of nowhere** *adv. phr.* In a deserted, faraway place. ♦ *When my car stopped on the highway in the middle of nowhere, it took forever to get help.*

**in the mood (for)** *adj. phr.* **1.** Interested in doing something. ♦ *Sorry, I'm just not in the mood for a heavy dinner* *tonight.* **2.** Feeling sexy. ♦ *I am sorry, darling, I am just not in the mood tonight.*

**in the nick of time** *adv. phr.* Just at the right time; barely soon enough; almost too late. ♦ *The doctor arrived in the nick of time to save the child from choking to death.*

**in the open** *adj. phr.* Publicly known; common knowledge. ♦ *Ever since he worked up the courage to come out of the closet, Professor Chisolm's former secret he is gay is now out in the open.*

**in the picture** *adj. phr.* Understanding what goes on; part of the whole; included in matters. ♦ *Would you please clue me in on what's happening at the firm? I am a new employee and I am not yet in the picture.*

**in the pink** *or* **in the pink of condition** *adj. phr., informal* In excellent health; strong and well; in fine shape. ♦ *Mr. Merrick had aged well; he was one of those old men who always seem in the pink of condition.* ♦ *After a practice and a rubdown, Joe felt in the pink.*

**in the prime of life** *adv. phr.* At the peak of one's creative abilities; during the most productive years. ♦ *Poor John lost his job due to restructuring when he was in the prime of his life.*

**in the public eye** *adj. phr.* Widely known; often seen in public activity; much in the news. ♦ *The senator's activity kept him in the public eye.*

**in the raw** *adj. or adv. phr.* **1.** In the simplest or most natural way; with no frills. ♦ *Henry enjoyed going into the woods and living life in the raw.* **2.** *informal* Without any clothing; naked. ♦ *In the summer the boys slept in the raw.*

**in real time** *adv. phr.* As something happens; immediately; synchronously on several continents. ♦ *American television stations have been broadcasting the news from Iraq in real time.*

**in the red** *adv. or adj. phr., informal* In an unprofitable way; so as to lose money. ♦ *A large number of American radio stations operate in the red.*

**in the right** *adj. phr.* With moral or legal right or truth on your side; in agreement with justice, truth, or fact; correct. ♦ *In many disputes, it is hard to say who is in the right.*

**in the running** *adj. or adv. phr.* Having a chance to win; not to be counted out; among those who might win. ♦ *At the beginning of the last lap of the race, only two horses were still in the running.* ♦ *A month before Joyce married Hal, three of Joyce's boyfriends seemed to be still in the running.*

**in the saddle** *adv. or adj. phr.* In command; in control; in a position to order or boss others. ♦ *Getting appointed chief of police put Stevens in the saddle.*

**in the same boat** *adv. or adj. phr.* In the same trouble; in the same fix; in the same bad situation. ♦ *When the town's one factory closed and hundreds of people lost their jobs, all the storekeepers were in the same boat.*

**in the same breath** *adv. phr.* **1.** At the same time; without waiting. ♦ *John would complain about hard times, and in the same breath boast of his prizewinning horses.* **2.** In the same class; in as high a group—Usually used in the negative with *mention, speak,* or *talk.* ♦ *Mary is a good swimmer, but she should not be mentioned in the same breath with Joan.*

**in the sand** *See* HIDE ONE'S HEAD IN THE SAND.

**in the short run** *adv. phr.* In the immediate future. ♦ *We are leasing a car in the short run; later we might buy one.*

**in the soup** *adj. phr., slang* In serious trouble; in confusion; in disorder. ♦ *When his wife overdrew their bank account without telling him, Mr. Phillips suddenly found himself really in the soup.*

**in the spotlight** *adv. phr.* In the center of attention, with everybody watching what one is doing. ♦ *It must be difficult for the President to be in the spotlight wherever he goes.*

**in the twinkling of an eye** *See* BEFORE ONE CAN SAY JACK ROBINSON.

**in the wake of** *prep., literary* As a result of; right after; following. ♦ *Many troubles follow in the wake of war.*

**in the way** *See* IN ONE'S WAY.

**in the wind** *adj. phr.* Seeming probable; being planned; soon to happen. ♦ *Changes in top management of the company had been in the wind for weeks.*

**in the works** *adv. or adj. phr.* In preparation; being planned or worked on; in progress. ♦*John was told that the paving of his street was in the works.*

**in the world** *or* **on earth** *adv. phr., informal* Of all possible things; ever.— Usually used for emphasis after words that ask questions, as *who, why, what,* etc. ♦*Where in the world did you find that necktie?* ♦*The boys wondered how on earth the mouse got out of the cage.*

**in the wrong** *adj. phr.* With moral or legal right or truth against you; against justice, truth, or fact; wrong. ♦*In attacking a smaller boy, Jack was plainly in the wrong.*

**in time** *adv. or adj. phr.* **1.** Soon enough. ♦*We got to Washington in time for the cherry blossoms.* ♦*We got to the station just in time to catch the bus.* **2.** In the end; after a while; finally. ♦*Fred and Jim did not like each other at first, but in time they became friends.* **3.** In the right rhythm; in step. ♦*The marchers kept in time with the band.*

**into a nose dive** See GO INTO A TAIL SPIN *or* GO INTO A NOSE DIVE.

**into a tail spin** See GO INTO A TAIL SPIN.

**into effect** *adv. phr.* Into use or operation. ♦*The new rule was put into effect at once.* ♦*The judge ordered the old suspended penalty into effect.*

**into line** *adv. phr.* **1.** Into agreement. ♦*The department's spending was brought into line with the budget.* **2.** Under control. ♦*The players who had broken training rules fell into line when the coach warned them that they would be put off the team.*

**into practice** See IN PRACTICE.

**into question** *adv. phr.* Into doubt or argument.—Usually used with *call, bring* or *come.* ♦*This soldier's courage has never been called into question.*

**into thin air** *adv. phr.* Without anything left; completely. ♦*When Bob returned to the room, he was surprised to find that his books had vanished into thin air.*

**in toto** *adv. phr.* As a whole; in its entirety; totally; altogether. ♦*The store refused the advertising agency's suggestion in toto.*

**in touch** *adj. phr.* Talking or writing to each other; giving and getting news. ♦*John kept in touch with his school friends during the summer.* ♦*The man claimed to be in touch with people on another planet.*

**in tow** *adj. phr.* **1.** Being pulled. ♦*The tugboat had the large ocean liner in tow as they came into the harbor.* **2.** Being taken from place to place; along with someone. ♦*Janet took the new girl in tow and showed her where to go.*

**in trust** *adv. or adj. phr.* In safe care for another. ♦*The money was held by the bank in trust for the widow.* ♦*At his death Mr. Brown left a large sum in trust for his son until he was twenty-five.*

**in tune** *adv. or adj. phr.* **1.** At the proper musical pitch; high or low enough in sound. ♦*The piano is in tune.* **2.** Going well together; in agreement; matching; agreeable.—Often used with *with.* ♦*In his new job, John felt in tune with his surroundings and his associates.*

**in turn** *adv. phr.* According to a settled order; each following another. ♦*Each man in turn got up and spoke.*

**in two** *adv. phr.* Into two parts or pieces; into two divisions. ♦*John and Mary pulled on the wishbone until it came in two.*

**in two shakes of a lamb's tail** *adv., informal* Quickly; in no time at all. ♦*I'll be back in two shakes of a lamb's tail.*

**in vain** *adv. phr.* **1.** Without effect; without getting the desired result; without success. ♦*The drowning man called in vain for help.*

**in view** *adv. or adj. phr.* **1.** In sight; visible. ♦*We came around a bend and there was the ocean in view.* **2.** As a purpose, hope, or expectation. ♦*John had his son's education in view when he began to save money.*

**in view of** *prep.* After thinking about; because of. ♦*Schools were closed for the day in view of the heavy snowstorm.* ♦*In view of rising labor costs, many companies have turned to automation.*

**in with** *prep.* In friendship, favor, or closeness with; in the trust or liking of. ♦*It took the new family some time to get in with their neighbors.*

**I.O.U.** *adj. phr.* I owe you, abbreviated; a promissory note. ♦*I had to borrow some money from John and, in order to remind both of us, I wrote him an I.O.U. note for $250.*

**iron horse** *n., informal* A railroad locomotive; the engine of a railroad train. ♦ *In its first days, the iron horse frightened many people as it roared across country scattering sparks.*

**iron in the fire** *n. phr.* Something you are doing; one of the projects with which a person is busy; job. ♦ *John had a number of irons in the fire, and he managed to keep all of them hot.*—Usually used in the phrase *too many irons in the fire.* ♦ *"Ed has a dozen things going all the time, but none of them seem to work out." "No wonder. He has too many irons in the fire."*

**iron out** *v., informal* To discuss and reach an agreement about (a difference); find a solution for (a problem); remove (a difficulty). ♦ *The House and Senate ironed out the differences between their two different tax bills.*

**is** *or* **are** *or* **was** *or* **will be history** *adj. phr.* Dead; defeated; finished; done with; often used as a threat. ♦ *Move one finger buddy, and you are history! Why worry about Mao Zedong? He is history.* ♦ *Don't worry too much about the terrorists; in a few years they will be history.*

**is it cricket** *or* **would it be cricket?** *v. phr.* Be allowed; be fair game; permissible; socially acceptable. Used both as question and as a statement. ♦ *It's not cricket to inquire about one's grade before the rest of the class is told.* ♦ *Would it be cricket to take a peek if I made the list of the finalists for the scholarship?*

**is that so** *informal* **1.** Oh, indeed? That's interesting.—Used in simple acceptance or reply. ♦ *"The Republicans have pulled a trick at city hall." "Is that so?"* **2.** Surely not?—Used in disbelief or sarcasm. ♦ *"The moon is made of green cheese." "Is that so?"* ♦ *"I'm going to take your girlfriend to the dance," said Bob. "Oh, is that so!" said Dick. "Try it and you'll be sorry."*

**it all depends** *adv. phr.* To be relative, please clarify your meaning. ♦ *"Do you consider yourself a rich man?" John asked. " It all depends on what you mean," Peter replied.*

**it can't happen here** *v. phr.* Heard from people who are astonished at some really bad news. ♦ *When the terrorists exploded the U.S. Embassy in Kenya, the old lady from New York remarked, "It can't happen here."*

**itching palm** *n., slang* A wish for money; greed. ♦ *The bellboys in that hotel seem always to have itching palms.*

**itchy feet** *adj. phr.* Anxious to travel; bitten by wanderlust. ♦ *My brother John is constantly traveling somewhere, it seems he can never stop. He's got itchy feet, for sure.*

**it figures** *informal sentence* It checks out; it makes sense; it adds up. ♦ *It figures that Bob got the highest raise at our firm; he is the most productive salesman.*

**it happens all the time** *v. phr.* Said of something that happens as a common occurrence; is nothing out of the ordinary.—A proverb. ♦ *"A guy ran into my car the other day at a red light." "Oh, that's nothing," said the policeman. "In a big city like Chicago, it happens all the time."*

**it is an ill wind that blows nobody good** No matter how bad a happening is, someone can usually gain something from it.—A proverb. ♦ *When Fred got hurt in the game John got a chance to play. It's an ill wind that blows nobody good.*

**it never rains but it pours** One good thing or bad thing is often followed by others of the same kind.—A proverb. ♦ *John got sick, then his brothers and sisters all got sick. It never rains but it pours.*

**it's a cinch** *informal sentence* It is very easy. ♦ *"What about the final exam?" Fred asked. "It was a cinch," Sam answered.*

**it's a deal** *informal sentence* Consider it done; OK; it is agreed. ♦ *"How much for this used car?" Bill asked. "Two thousand," the man answered. "I'll give $1,500," Bill said. "It's a deal!" the owner answered as they sealed the transaction.*

**it's a different ball game** Different rules apply.—A proverb. ♦ *Being in college is one thing, but to be working for a Ph.D. in graduate school is a different ball game.*

**it's a gas** *or* **it's a gasser** *or* **it's a gig** *or* **it's a giggle** *adj. phr., slang* A highly amusing, laughable thing. ♦ *Every joke John tells is a real gasser.* ♦ *Professor*

*Doolittle's lecture often turns into a giggle.*

**it's a go** *or* **it's all go** *adj. phrase, informal* Agreed; it's OK; we can proceed. ♦*"Are we going to Europe this summer, or not?" John's family wanted to know. "I have good news," John replied. "It's a go!"*

**it's a lemon** *adj. phr. informal* The thing is badly made; it won't work. ♦*"I sure bought myself a lemon," John said. "This car will never work." ♦ "What's wrong with your watch? You're always late." "It is a lemon, I must admit," John said.*

**it's all good clean fun** *adj. phr., informal* A saying often heard when one makes fun of others at their expense, or when committing some other mischief. ♦*When the Harvard undergraduate fraternity conducted a panty raid on the girls' dormitory, they were caught by the campus police. "Can't you think of something better to do?" the officer asked. "But sir, it's all good clean fun!" the leader of the boys answered.*

**it's all right by me** *adj. phrase, a proverb* OK, I agree. ♦*"Shall we go to the movies tonight?" Ted asked his wife. "It's all right by me," his wife Sue replied.*

**it's a shame** *or* **it's a real shame** *adj. phr.* It is too bad; it is unfortunate. ♦*It's a real shame that Grandmother's first operation didn't succeed, and she must go back for more surgery.*

**it's a small world!** *phr.* How nice to see you; I am surprised to run into you here.—A proverb. ♦*When John and Jerry saw each other for the first time in ten years after graduation from high school, both exclaimed simultaneously, "It's a small world!"*

**it's as simple as that** *adj. phr.* Not a big problem, do not worry about it, this is a trivial matter. ♦*"Would you help me change this tire?" John asked the gas station attendant, "I don't know how to do it." When the man finished the job he said, "It's as simple as that!"*

**it's been** ——— , **it's been real** *informal* Shortened form for "it has been real nice (being with you)"—used colloquially between very close friends.

**it's boloney** *(or* **bologna** *or* **baloney)— no matter how thin you slice it** *adj.*

*phr.* It is sheer nonsense, no matter how hard you try to prove the opposite. ♦*The members of the UFO cult believed that if they commit suicide, the UFO will gather up their souls and take them to another solar system. One should be tolerant toward different religious beliefs, but this one is boloney, no matter how thin you slice it.*

**it's high time** *informal sentence* It is overdue. ♦*It is high time for John Browning to be promoted to full professor; he has written a great deal but his books went unnoticed.*

**it shouldn't happen to a dog!** *v. phr., a proverb* To be too disagreeable and unjust to be wished even on a dog. ♦*Poor John was mugged, robbed, beaten, and thrown unconscious in a ditch by the gang. He was lucky to survive the attack. This is the kind of thing that shouldn't happen to a dog!*

**it's not my bag** *phrasal idiom, slang* It's not my thing, not my affair, not in my karma. ♦*"Come on, brother, let's rob that store; it will be a cakewalk," the guy in tattered clothes said to John. "Sorry," John replied. "That sort of thing is not my bag."*

**it's your funeral** *n. phrase, a proverb* The consequences will be your concern, not mine.—A proverb. ♦*"You had better play it by the book when you see the new director," John said to Ted. "Why should I care?" Ted replied, somewhat irritated. "Look," John said, "do as you wish! After all, it's your funeral."*

**it takes one to know one** One recognizes talent more easily if one has talent oneself.—A proverb. ♦*"You really are a first-class poet!" the Nobel Laureate for Literature said to an outstanding colleague. "Thanks, it takes one to know one."*

**it takes two to tango** Co-operation is always necessary in order to accomplish something, whether good or bad.—A proverb. ♦*If you won't help me restore the business to normal, we'll never get anyplace. You should know that it takes two to tango. ♦ "Who starts all those quarrels next door?" Suzie asked her girlfriend Mable. "I think it's the husband," Mable replied, "but the wife must also be involved. After all it takes two to tango."*

**it won't wash** *or* **that won't wash** *v. phr.* It will never be believed; it will never pass the test of truth.—A proverb. ◆*Your story about meeting the little green men from the flying saucer just won't wash.*

**Ivy League** *n.* A small group of the older and more famous eastern U.S. colleges and universities. ◆*Several Ivy League teams play each other regularly each year.* ◆*Harvard, Yale, and Princeton were the original Ivy League.*

**I wasn't born yesterday** *v. phr.* I am not naïve or credulous enough to believe what you said.—A proverb. ◆*So you want me to believe that you're the sister of Princess Anastasia Romanoff? Come on, I wasn't born yesterday.*

**I wouldn't know** *v. phr., informal* I couldn't say; I am not sure; I don't know. Also said in order to avoid a direct answer. *"How much does your brother make these days?"* Joe pumped Ted for information. *Ted, who knew perfectly well how much his brother made, didn't want to answer, so he said "I wouldn't know."*

**I, you, one (really) dig it!** *v. phr., informal* To really be wildly enthusiastic about something; also asked as a question. ◆*I really dig the Country Western songs those girls are singing.* ◆*John digs his newly found hippie life.* ◆*Do you dig drugs?*

**jack of all trades** n., informal (Often followed by the words "master of none.") A person who is knowledgeable in many areas. Can be used as praise, or as a derogatory remark depending on the context and the intonation. ♦ "How come Joe did such a sloppy job?" Mary asked. "He's a jack of all trades," Sally answered.

**jack-rabbit start** n., informal A very sudden start from a still position; a very fast start from a stop. ♦ Bob made a jack-rabbit start when the traffic light turned green.

**jack up** v. 1. To lift with a jack. ♦ The man jacked up his car to fit a flat tire. 2. informal To make (a price) higher; raise. ♦ Just before Christmas, some stores jack up their prices.

**jailbait** n., slang A girl below the legal age of consent for sex; one who tempts you to intimacy which is punishable by imprisonment. ♦ Stay away from Arabella, she is a jailbait.

**jailbird** n., informal A convict; someone who is in jail or has been recently released from prison. ♦ Because Harry was a jailbird, it was understandably hard for him to find a job after being imprisoned.

**jar on** v. phr. To irritate. ♦ The constant construction noise was beginning to jar on the nerves of the members of the meeting.

**jawbreaker** n. 1. A large piece of hard candy or bubblegum. ♦ Billy asked his mother for a quarter to buy some jawbreakers and a chocolate bar. 2. informal A word or name that is hard to pronounce. ♦ His name, Nissequogue, is a real jawbreaker.

**jaw drop** or **jaw drop a mile** informal Mouth fall wide open with surprise.— Used with a possessive. ♦ Tom's jaw dropped a mile when he won the prize.

**jaws tight** adj., slang, informal Angry; uptight; tense. ♦ Why are you getting your jaws so tight?

**jazz up** v., slang To brighten up; add more noise, movement, or color; make more lively or exciting. ♦ The party was very dull until Pete jazzed it up with his drums.

**jerry-built** adj. 1. Built poorly or carelessly of cheap materials; easily broken. ♦ That jerry-built cabin will blow apart in a strong wind. 2. Done without careful preparation or thought; planned too quickly. ♦ When the regular television program didn't come on, a jerry-built program was substituted at the last minute.

**Jesus boots** or **Jesus shoes** n., slang Men's sandals, particularly as worn by hippies and very casually dressed people. ♦ I dig your Jesus boots, man, they look cool.

**jet set,** or **jet-setter** n. phr. A trendy affluent person who travels a lot, especially by airplane, and dresses like a Hollywood star. ♦ Tom is so rich he is a member of the jet set. Both Tom and his brother Jerry are jet-setters.

**John Hancock** or **John Henry** n., informal Your signature; your name in writing. ♦ The man said, "Put your John Hancock on this paper." ♦ Joe felt proud when he put his John Henry on his very first driver's license.

**Johnny-come-lately** n. Someone new in a place or group; newcomer; also: a new person who takes an active part in group affairs before the group has accepted him; upstart. ♦ Everybody was amazed when a Johnny-come-lately beat the old favorite in the race.

**Johnny-on-the-spot** adj. phr. At the right place when needed; present and ready to help; very prompt; on time. ♦ A good waterboy is always Johnny-on-the-spot.

**join forces** or **join hands** v. phr. To get together for the same aim; group together for a purpose; unite. ♦ The students and the graduates joined forces to raise money when the gym burned down.

**join the army and see the world—the next world** Poking fun at the recruiting slogan "join the army and see the world"; this saying implies that you may die.—A proverb. ♦ "Join the army and see the world!" Sergeant O'Toole said to the class of graduating seniors. "You mean the next world?" Tim O'Brien, the class' smart aleck asked sarcastically.

**joking aside** *or* **joking apart** *v. phr., informal* No fooling; without exaggerating; seriously. ♦*Joking apart, there must have been over a hundred people in the room.*

**jot down** *v. phr.* To quickly commit to writing; make a quick note of something. ♦ *Let me jot down your address so that I can send you a postcard from Europe.*

**jug-eared** *adj.* With ears that stick out like the handles of a jug. ♦ *Tommy was a red-headed, freckle-faced, jug-eared boy.*

**juice dealer** *n., slang* An underworld money lender who charges exorbitant fees to his clientele and frequently collects payment by physical force. ♦*No matter how broke you are, never go to a juice dealer.*

**jump all over** See JUMP ON.

**jump at** *v.* To take or accept quickly and gladly. ♦*Johnny jumped at the invitation to go swimming with his brother.*

**jump bail** *or* **skip bail** *v. phr., informal* To run away and fail to come to trial, and so to give up a certain amount of money already given to a court of law to hold with the promise that you would come. ♦ *The robber paid $2000 bail so he wouldn't be put in jail before his trial, but he jumped bail and escaped to Mexico.*

**jump ball** *n.* The starting of play in basketball by tossing the ball into the air between two opposing players, each of whom jumps and tries to hit the ball to a member of his own team. ♦ *Two players held onto the ball at the same time and the referee called a jump ball.*

**jump down one's throat** *v. phr.* To suddenly become very angry at someone; scold severely or angrily. ♦ *The teacher jumped down Billy's throat when Billy admitted he did not do his homework.*

**jumping-off place** *n. phr.* **1.** A place so far away that it seems to be the end of the world. ♦ *Columbus' sailors were afraid they would arrive at the jumping-off place if they sailed farther west.* **2.** The starting place of a long, hard trip or of something difficult or dangerous. ♦ *The jumping-off place for the explorer's trip through the jungle was a little village.*

**jump on** *or* **jump all over** *or* **land on** *or* **land all over** *v. phr., informal* To scold; criticize; blame. ♦ *Tom's boss jumped all over Tom because he made a careless mistake.* ♦*Janice landed on Robert for dressing carelessly for their date.* ♦*"I don't know why Bill is always jumping on me; I just don't understand him," said Bob.*

**jump on the bandwagon** *or* **get on the bandwagon** *v. phr., informal* To join a popular cause or movement. ♦*At the last possible moment, the senator jumped on the winning candidate's bandwagon.*

**jump out of one's skin** *v. phr., informal* To be badly frightened; be very much surprised. ♦*The lightning struck so close to Bill that he almost jumped out of his skin.*

**jump pass** *n.* A pass (as in football or basketball) made by a player while jumping. ♦ *The Bruins scored when the quarterback tossed a jump pass to the left end.*

**jump-start** *v. phr.* To restart an enterprise or business with vigorous action. ♦ *The president of the United States decided to jump-start the economy with a tax cut stimulus package.*

**jump the gun** *also* **beat the gun** *v. phr.* **1.** To start before the starter's gun in a race. ♦ *The runners were called back because one of them jumped the gun.* **2.** *informal* To start before you should; start before anyone else. ♦ *The new students were not supposed to come before noon, but one boy jumped the gun and came to school at eight in the morning.*

**jump the track** *v. phr.* **1.** To go off rails; go or run the wrong way. ♦ *The train jumped the track and there was a terrible accident.* **2.** *informal* To change from one thought or idea to another without plan or reason; change the thought or idea you are talking about to something different. ♦*Bob didn't finish his algebra homework because his mind kept jumping the track to think about the new girl in class.*

**jump through a hoop** *v. phr., informal* To do whatever you are told to do; obey any order. ♦*Bob would jump through a hoop for Mary.*

**jump to a conclusion** *v. phr.* To decide too quickly or without thinking or finding the facts. ♦*Jerry saw his dog limping on a bloody leg and jumped to the conclusion that it had been shot.*

**junked up** *adj. or v. phr., slang, drug culture* To be under the influence of drugs, especially heroine. ♦ *You can't talk to Billy, he's all junked up.*

**junk food** *n. phr.* The name given to hamburgers, hot dogs, french fries, and the like available at fast-food restaurants. ♦ *"Eat a regular home-cooked meal,"* Dr. Gordon suggested. *"Stay away from junk food."*

**junk mail** *n. phr.* Unwanted and unsolicited mail stuffed into one's mailbox both at home and at work, usually advertisements of one sort or another. ♦ *"Did you check the mailbox, honey?"* Ted asked his wife. *"Yes, but it's only junk mail,"* she answered.

**just about** *adv., informal* Nearly; almost; practically. ♦ *Just about everyone in town came to hear the mayor speak.*

**just for the fun of it** *or* **just for the hell of it** *adv. phr.* Merely as a matter of amusement. ♦ *"I'll bring a goat to class,"* Bob said to his classmates, *"just for the fun of it; I want to see what kind of a face Professor Brown will make."*

**just for the record** *adv. phr.* Let me make my position clear; let's get things straight. ♦ *"Just for the record Sam,"* Ted said, *"you still owe me $100 from last time. I hope you understand that I can't give you further loans until you repay me."*

**just in case** *adv. phr.* For an emergency; in order to be protected. ♦ *"Here are my house keys, Sue,"* Tom said. *"I'll be back in two weeks, but you should have them, just in case...."*

**just in time** See IN TIME.

**just now** *adv. phr.* **1.** Just at this moment; at this time. ♦ *Mr. Johnson isn't here just now. Will you phone back later?* **2.** *informal* A very short time ago; only a moment ago; only a little while ago. ♦ *"Where could that boy have gone so quickly? He was here just now!"*

**just so**[1] *adj.* Exact; exactly right. ♦ *Mrs. Robinson likes to keep her house just so, and she makes the children take off their shoes when they come in the house.*

**just so**[2] *conj.* Provided; if. ♦ *Take as much food as you want, just so you don't waste any food.*

**just so**[3] *adv. phr.* With great care; very carefully. ♦ *In order to raise healthy African violets you must treat them just so.*

**just the other way** *or* **the other way around** *adv. phr.* Just the opposite. ♦ *One would have thought that Goliath would defeat David, but it was the other way around.*

**just the same** See ALL THE SAME.

**just what the doctor ordered** *n. phr., informal* Exactly what is needed or wanted. ♦ *"Ah! Just what the doctor ordered!"* exclaimed Joe when Mary brought him a cold soda.

**kangaroo court** *n.* A self-appointed group that decides what to do to someone who is supposed to have done wrong. ◆ *The Chicago mob held a kangaroo court and shot the gangster who competed with Al Capone.*

**keel over** *v.* **1.** To turn upside down; tip over; overturn.—Usually refers to a boat. ◆ *The strong wind made the sailboat keel over and the passengers fell into the water.* **2.** *informal* To fall over in a faint; faint. ◆ *When the principal told the girl her father died, she keeled right over.*

**keen about** *or* **on** *adj. phr.* Very enthusiastic about someone or something. ◆ *It is well known that Queen Elizabeth is keen on horses.*

**keep abreast (of) someone** *or* **something** *v. phr.* To be informed of the latest developments. ◆ *It is difficult to keep abreast of all the various wars that are being waged on planet Earth.*

**keep a civil tongue in one's head** *v. phr.* To be polite in speaking. ◆ *He was very angry with his boss, but he kept a civil tongue in his head.*

**keep a close check on** See KEEP TAB(S) ON.

**keep after** *v.,* *informal* To speak to (someone) about something again and again; remind over and over again. ◆ *Sue's mother had to keep after her to clean her bedroom.*

**keep an eye on** *or* **keep one's eye on** *or* **have one's eye on** *v. phr.* **1.** To watch carefully; not stop paying attention to. ◆ *A good driver keeps his eye on the road.* ◆ *The teacher had her eye on me because she thought I was cheating.* **2.** To watch and do what is needed for; mind. ◆ *Mother told Jane to keep an eye on the baby while she was in the store.*

**keep an eye open** *or* **keep an eye out for** See KEEP AN EYE ON.

**keep a stiff upper lip** *v. phr.* To be brave; face trouble bravely. ◆ *John was very much worried about his sick daughter, but he kept a stiff upper lip.*

**keep a straight face** See STRAIGHT FACE, DEADPAN.

**keep at** *v.* To continue to do; go on with. ◆ *Mary kept at her homework until she finished it.*

**keep away** *v. phr.* To remain at a distance from. ◆ *Her mother advised Diane to keep away from men offering a ride.*

**keep back** *v. phr.* To refrain or be restrained from entering; remain back. ◆ *The police had a hard time keeping back the crowd when the astronauts came to town after walking on the moon.*

**keep body and soul together** *v. phr.* To keep alive; survive. ◆ *John was unemployed most of the year and hardly made enough money to keep body and soul together.*

**keep books** *v. phr.* To keep records of money gained and spent; do the work of a bookkeeper. ◆ *Miss Jones keeps the company's books.*

**keep company** *v. phr.* **1.** To stay or go along with (someone) so that he will not be lonely to visit with (someone). ◆ *John kept Andy company while his parents went to the movies.* **2.** To go places together as a couple; date just one person. ◆ *Who is Bill keeping company with now?*

**keep cool** *v. phr.* Remain calm; remain unexcited. ◆ *The main thing to remember in an emergency situation is to not lose one's head and keep cool.*

**keep down** *v.* Keep from progressing or growing; keep within limits; control. ◆ *You can't keep a good man down.*

**keep from** *v.,* *informal* To hold yourself back from; stop or prevent yourself from (doing something). ◆ *Jill can't keep from talking about her trip.*—Usually used with *can* in the negative. ◆ *You can't keep from liking Jim.*

**keep good time** See KEEP TIME.

**keep house**[1] *v. phr.* To do the necessary things in a household; do the cooking and cleaning. ◆ *Since their mother died, Mary and her brother keep house for their father.*

**keep house**[2] *also* **play house** *v. phr.,* *informal* To live together without being married. ◆ *Bob and Nancy keep house these days.*

**keep in mind** See IN MIND.

**keep in touch with** *v. phr.* To remain in communication with; maintain contact with. ◆ *Don't forget to keep in touch,* *either by letter or phone, when you're in Europe!*

**keep late hours** *v. phr.* To go to bed late; habitually stay up (and work) late. ◆ *"If you always keep such late hours, your health might suffer," Tom's doctor said.*

**keep off** *v. phr.* To refrain from entering; stay away from. ◆ *"Keep off the grass," the sign in the park indicated.*

**keep on** *v.* **1.** To go ahead; not stop; continue. ◆ *Columbus kept on until he saw land.*—Often used before a present participle. ◆ *Relentlessly, the boy kept on asking about outer space.* **2.** To allow to continue working for you. ◆ *The new owner kept Fred on as gardener.*

**keep one at a distance** *or* **keep one at arm's length** *v. phr.* To avoid (someone's) company; not become too friendly toward. ◆ *Betty likes Bill and is trying to be friendly, but he keeps her at arm's length.*

**keep (one) posted** *v. phr.* To receive current information; inform oneself. ◆ *My associates phoned me every day and kept me posted on new developments in our business.*

**keep one's balance** *v. phr.* To stay even-tempered; not become overexcited. ◆ *Mike has the best personality to run our office; he always keeps his balance.*

**keep one's chin up** *v. phr.* To be brave; be determined; face trouble with courage. ◆ *He didn't think that he would ever get out of the jungle alive, but he kept his chin up.*

**keep one's cool** *or* **keep one's head** *v. phr.* To stay in control of one's composure; stay calm. ◆ *"Keep your cool, John, when you face the director," Ted advised. "He has a tendency to get on people's nerves." Fred succeeded in keeping his head when the building burst into flames.*

**keep one's distance** *v. phr.* To be cool toward someone; avoid being friendly. ◆ *Mary did not like her co-worker, Betty, and kept her distance from her.*

**keep one's end up** See HOLD ONE'S END UP.

**keep one's eye on** See KEEP AN EYE ON.

**keep one's eye on the ball** *v. phr., informal* To be watchful and ready; be wide-awake and ready to win or succeed; be smart. ◆ *Tom is just starting on*

the job but if he keeps his eye on the ball, he will be promoted.

**keep one's eyes open** See EYES OPEN.

**keep one's eyes peeled** *or* **keep one's eyes skinned** *v. phr., informal* To watch carefully; be always looking. ◆ *The bird-watcher kept his eyes peeled for bluebirds.*

**keep one's feet on the ground** See FEET ON THE GROUND.

**keep one's fingers crossed** See CROSS ONE'S FINGERS 1b.

**keep one's hand in** *v. phr.* To keep in practice; continue to take part. ◆ *After he retired from teaching, Mr. Brown kept his hand in by giving a lecture once in a while.*

**keep one's head** *also* **keep one's wits about one** *v. phr.* To stay calm when there is trouble or danger. ◆ *When Tim heard the fire alarm he kept his head and looked for the nearest exit.*

**keep one's head above water** *v. phr.* To remain solvent; manage to stay out of debt. ◆ *Herb's income declined so drastically that he now has difficulty keeping his head above water.*

**keep one's mouth shut** *v. phr., informal* To be or stay silent.—Rude when used as a command. ◆ *When the crooks were captured by the police, their leader warned them to keep their mouths shut.*

**keep one's nose clean** *v. phr., slang* To stay out of trouble; do only what you should do. ◆ *The policeman warned the boys to keep their noses clean unless they wanted to go to jail.*

**keep one's nose to the grindstone** *or* **have one's nose to the grindstone** *or* **hold one's nose to the grindstone** *v. phr., informal* To work hard all the time; keep busy with boring or tiresome work. ◆ *Sarah keeps her nose to the grindstone and saves as much as possible to start her own business.*

**keep one's own counsel** *v. phr., formal* To keep your ideas and plans to yourself. ◆ *John listened to what everyone had to say in the discussion, but he kept his own counsel.*

**keep one's shirt on** *v. phr., slang* To calm down; keep from losing your temper or getting impatient or excited. ◆ *John said to Bob, "Keep your shirt on."*

**keep one's wits about one** See KEEP ONE'S HEAD.

**keep one's word** *v. phr.* To do what one has promised; fulfill one's promise. ♦ *Paul kept his word and paid me the $250 that he owed me right on time.*

**keep on truckin'** *v. phr.* Advice given to one about to despair, saying that one has to keep working, doing what one's job demands, or to encourage a vigorous or self-assertive action. ♦ *"OK, gang, this is going to be a great show. I know the practice is tiring, but let's keep on truckin.'"*

**keep open house** *v. phr.* To offer hospitality and entertain those who come at any given time on a certain day or afternoon. ♦ *Beth and Charlie have a cottage by the lake where they keep open house on Saturday afternoons during the summer.*

**keep out (of)** *v. phr.* **1.** To stay out; remain out of. ♦ *The sign on the fence said, "Danger! Keep out!"* **2.** To stave off; not allow in. ♦ *The border patrol near El Paso, Texas, is trying to keep illegal immigrants out of the United States.*

**keep pace** *v. phr.* To go as fast; go at the same rate; not get behind. ♦ *When Bill was moved to a more advanced class, he had to work hard to keep pace.*

**keep plugging along** *v. phr., informal* To continue to work diligently and with great effort, often against hardship. ♦ *Bob was not particularly talented but he kept plugging along year after year, and eventually became vice president.*

**keep (something) bottled up** See BOTTLE UP.

**keep step with** *v. phr.* To maintain the same degree of progress as someone else. ♦ *The United States has no choice but to keep step with potential enemies in terms of modern defense systems.*

**keep tab on** *or* **keep tabs on** *v. phr., informal* **1.** To keep a record of. ♦ *The government tries to keep tabs on all the animals in the park.* **2.** To keep a watch on; check. ♦ *The house mother kept tabs on the girls to be sure they were clean and neat.*

**keep the ball rolling** *v. phr., informal* To keep up an activity or action; not allow something that is happening to slow or stop. ♦ *Clyde kept the ball rolling at the party by telling funny jokes.*

**keep the change!** *v. phr.* Don't give me any money back. Said to taxi drivers, waiters, etc, when one wants to give them a tip. ♦ *"Keep the change!" Ted said, after handing a $20 bill to the cab driver, who wanted to return $3.50 to him.*

**keep the faith** *v. phr.* To not abandon hope; stay committed to the cause of democracy and racial equality. ♦ *"Keep the faith, Baby," my neighbor said as he raised his fingers to show the "V" for victory sign.*

**keep the home fires burning** *v. phr.* To keep things going as usual while someone is away; wait at home to welcome someone back. ♦ *While John was in the army, Mary kept the home fires burning.*

**keep the wolf (wolves) from the door** *v. phr.* To avoid hunger, poverty, and/or creditors. ♦ *"I don't like my job," Mike complained, "but I must do something to keep the wolves from the door."*

**keep things humming** *v. phr.* To cause thing to perform smoothly and efficiently. ♦ *Until Mr. Long joined our computer center, we had all sorts of problems, but he has corrected them and really keeps things humming.*

**keep time** *v. phr.* **1.** To show the right time. ♦ *My watch has not kept good time since I dropped it.* **2.** To keep the beat; keep the same rhythm; keep in step. ♦ *Many people are surprised at how well deaf people keep time with the music when they dance.*

**keep to oneself** See TO ONESELF 2.

**keep track** *v. phr.* To know about changes; stay informed or up-to-date; keep a count or record. ♦ *What day of the week is it? I can't keep track.*

**keep under one's hat** *v. phr., informal* To keep secret; not tell. Often used as a command. ♦ *Keep it under your hat.*

**keep up** *v.* **1a.** To go on; not stop; continue. ♦ *The rain kept up for two days and the roads were flooded.* **1b.** To go on with (something); continue steadily; never stop. ♦ *Mrs. Smith told John to keep up the good work.* **2a.** To go at the same rate as others. ♦ *John had to work hard to keep up.* **2b.** To keep (something) at the same level or rate or in good condition. ♦ *Grandfather was too poor to keep up his house.* **3.** To keep informed.— Usually used with *on* or *with.* ♦ *Mary is* *interested in politics and always keeps up with the news.*

**keep up appearances** *v. phr.* To maintain an outward show of prosperity in spite of financial problems. ♦ *Mr. Smith's widow had a hard time keeping up appearances after her husband's death.*

**keep up on** *v. phr.* To keep cultivating a habit in order not to forget it. ♦ *Ted tries to keep up on his saxophone playing whenever he has the time.*

**keep up one's end** See HOLD ONE'S END UP.

**keep up with** See KEEP STEP WITH, KEEP ABREAST OF.

**keep up with the Joneses** *v. phr.* To follow the latest fashion; try to be equal with your neighbors. ♦ *Mrs. Smith kept buying every new thing that was advertised. Finally Mr. Smith told her to stop trying to keep up with the Joneses and to start thinking for herself.*

**keep watch** *v. phr.* To be vigilant; be alert; guard. ♦ *The police have asked the neighborhood to keep watch against an escaped convict.*

**keep your fingers crossed** See CROSS ONE'S FINGERS.

**kettle of fish** *v. phr., informal* Something to be considered; how things are; a happening; business. ♦ *He had two flat tires and no spare on a country road at night, which was certainly a pretty kettle of fish.*

**keyed up** *adj., informal* Excited; nervous; anxious to do something. ♦ *Mary was all keyed up about the exam.*

**kick against the pricks** *v. phr., literary* To fight against rules or authority in a way that just hurts yourself. ♦ *Johnny kicked against the pricks in his foster home until he learned that he could trust his new family.*

**kick around** *v., informal* **1.** To act roughly or badly to; treat badly; bully. ♦ *John likes to kick around the little boys.* **2.** To lie around or in a place; be treated carelessly; be neglected. ♦ *The letter kicked around on my desk for days.* **3.** *slang* To talk easily or carelessly back and forth about; examine in a careless or easygoing way. ♦ *Bob and I kicked around the idea of going swimming, but it was hot and we were too lazy.*

**kick back** *v., slang, informal* (stress on *back*) To pay money illegally for favor-

able contract arrangements. ♦ *I will do it if you kick back a few hundred for my firm.*

**kickback** *n., slang, informal* (stress on *kick*) Money paid illegally for favorable treatment. ♦ *He was arrested for making kickback payments.*

**kick down** *v. phr., slang* To shift an automobile, jeep, or truck into lower gear by hand-shifting. ♦ *Joe kicked the jeep down from third to second, and we slowed down.*

**kick in** *v.* to start. ♦ *The payments on the new car won't kick in until February!*

**kick in the pants** *or* **kick in the teeth** *n. phr., informal* Unexpected scorn or insult when praise was expected; rejection. ♦ *Mary worked hard to clean up John's room, but all she got for her trouble was a kick in the teeth.*

**kick it** *v. phr., slang* To end a bad or unwanted habit such as drinking, smoking, or drug addiction. ♦ *Farnsworth finally kicked it; he's in good shape.*

**kickoff** *n.* (stress on *kick*) The start of something, like a new venture, a business, a sports event, or a concert season. ♦ *Beethoven's Ninth will be the kickoff for this summer season at Ravinia.*

**kick off** *v. phr.* (stress on *off*) **1.** *informal* To begin; launch; start. ♦ *The candidate kicked off his campaign with a speech on television.* **2.** *slang* To die. ♦ *Mr. Jones was almost ninety years old when he kicked off.*

**kick oneself** *v. phr., informal* To be sorry or ashamed; regret. ♦ *Mary could have kicked herself for letting the secret out before it was announced officially.*

**kick out** *or* **boot out** *v., informal* To make (someone) go or leave; get rid of; dismiss. ♦ *The boys made so much noise at the movie that the manager kicked them out.* ♦ *The chief of police was booted out of office because he was a crook.*

**kick over** *v.* **1.** *Of a motor:* To begin to work. ♦ *He had not used his car for two months and when he tried to start it, the motor would not kick over.* **2.** *slang* To pay; contribute. ♦ *The gang forced all the storekeepers on the block to kick over $500 a week.* **3.** *slang* To die. ♦ *Mrs. O'Leary's cow kicked over this morning.*

**kick the bucket** *v. phr., slang* To die. ♦ *Old Mr. Jones kicked the bucket just two days before his ninety-fourth birthday.*

**kick up** *v., informal* To show signs of not working right. ♦ *John had had too much to eat and his stomach started to kick up.*

**kick up a fuss** *or* **kick up a row** *or* **raise a row** *also* **kick up a dust** *v. phr., informal* To make trouble; make a disturbance. ♦ *When the teacher gave the class five more hours of homework, the class kicked up a fuss.* ♦ *When the teacher left the room, two boys kicked up a row.*

**kick up one's heels** *v. phr., informal* To have a merry time; celebrate. ♦ *When exams were over the students went to town to kick up their heels.*

**kiddie car** *n., slang, citizen's band radio jargon* A school bus. ♦ *Watch out for that kiddie car coming up behind you!*

**kill off** *v.* To kill or end completely; destroy. ♦ *The factory dumped poisonous wastes into the river and killed off the fish.*

**kill or cure** *phrasal idiom* Drastic treatment or action that will either ruin one or set things right. Said mostly of certain kinds of medicine or food. ♦ *This new wonder drug will either kill me or cure me.* ♦ *This Indian soup is so hot that it will kill or cure whoever tastes it.*

**kill the goose that laid the golden egg** To spoil something that is good or something that you have, by being greedy.—A proverb. ♦ *Communist China decided to keep Capitalism alive in Hong Kong. They don't want to kill the goose that laid the golden egg.*

**kill time** *v. phr.* To cause the time to pass more rapidly; waste time. ♦ *The plane trip to Hong Kong was long and tiring, but we managed to kill time by watching several movies.*

**kill two birds with one stone** *v. phr.* To succeed in doing two things by only one action; get two results from one effort. ♦ *Mother stopped at the supermarket to buy bread and then went to get Jane at dancing class; she killed two birds with one stone.*

**kind of** *or* **sort of** *adv. phr., informal* Almost but not quite; rather. ♦ *A guinea pig looks kind of like a rabbit,* but it has short ears. ♦ *The teacher sort of frowned but then smiled.*

**kindred spirits** *n. phr.* People who resemble each other in numerous ways, including their ways of thinking and feeling. ♦ *They are kindred spirits; they both like to go on long walks in the forest.*

**king's ransom** *n. phr.* **1.** An excessively large sum of money extorted by kidnappers to let someone go free. ♦ *The Smith family had to pay a king's ransom for the freedom of their seven-year-old son.* **2.** An exorbitant fee one is forced to pay. ♦ *The realtors exacted a king's ransom for that choice lot on the corner.*

**kiss off** *v. phr., slang* Go away, leave me alone! ♦ *"Kiss off, Buster," the bartender said, when the neighborhood drunk, who didn't have any money, asked for another glass of whiskey.*

**kiss of death** *n. phr.* A curse, a very bad thing. ♦ *Having unsafe sex with a stranger can often be the kiss of death.*

**kiss someone** *or* **something goodbye** *v. phr.* To lose or give up someone or something forever. ♦ *"If you won't marry Jane," Peter said to Tom, "you might as well kiss her goodbye."* ♦ *People who bet on a losing horse at the races might as well kiss their money goodbye.*

**kitty corner** *adv. phr.* Diagonally, or turning, so as to make a large object fit through a narrow doorway. ♦ *The movers cleverly moved the larger pieces of furniture kitty corner from one room to the next.*

**kith and kin** *or* **kith or kin** *n. phr.* A relative, even if not a very close one. ♦ *"Why won't you help poor John, when he is in such trouble?" Mary asked her husband. "He just pretends to be close," Ted answered, "but he is no kith or kin of ours."*

**knee-deep** *or* **neck-deep** *adv. or adj. phr.* **1.** Very much; deeply; having a big part in. ♦ *Johnny was knee-deep in trouble.* **2.** Very busy; working hard at. ♦ *We were neck-deep in homework before the exams.*

**kneeling bus** *n., informal* A bus equipped with a hydraulic device to enable it to drop almost to curb level for greater ease of boarding and leaving vehicle, as a convenience for elderly or handicapped passengers. *The man on crutches was pleased to see the kneeling bus.*

**knight in shining armor** *n. phr.* The ideal boyfriend, lover, or future husband, who may take a young woman away to a better life. *"So Jim got you pregnant, and then he left you, is that right?" Mary asked her sister Joan. "Yes," Joan replied, "but I used to think of him as my knight in shining armor before he revealed his true face."*

**knock about** *or* **knock around** *v.* To travel without a plan; go where you please. *After he graduated from college, Joe knocked about for a year seeing the country before he went to work in his father's business.*

**knock cold** *v. phr., informal* To render unconscious. *The blow on the chin knocked Harry cold.*

**knock down** *v. phr.* To reduce; lower. *The realtors said that if we decided to buy the house, they would knock the price down by 10%.*

**knock (one or something) down with a feather** *v. phr.* To push a person or institution that doesn't need energetic destroying, one that would crumble at the least push. *That regime overseas talks loudly, but is really only a paper tiger. I believe that we could knock it down with a feather.*

**knocked out** *adj., slang* Intoxicated; drugged; out of one's mind. *Jim sounds so incoherent, he must be knocked out.*

**knock for a loop** *or* **throw for a loop** *v. phr., slang* To surprise very much. *The news of their marriage threw me for a loop.*

**knock it off** *v. phr., slang, informal* **1.** To stop talking about something considered not appropriate or nonsensical by the listener.—Used frequently as an imperative. *Come on, Joe, knock it off, you're not making any sense at all!* **2.** To cease doing something; to quit.—Heavily favored in the imperative. *Come on boys, knock it off, you're breaking the furniture in my room!*

**knock off** *v. phr., slang* **1.** To burglarize someone. *They knocked off the Manning residence.* **2.** To murder someone. *The gangsters knocked off Herman.*

**knock off one's feet** *v. phr.* To surprise (someone) so much that he does not know what to do. *When Charlie was given the prize, it knocked him off his feet for a few minutes.*

**knock one up** *v. phr. vulgar, avoidable* To get a woman pregnant. *Did you hear that poor Suzie got knocked up by her careless boyfriend when they were vacationing together in the mountains?*

**knock one's block off** *v. phr., slang* To hit someone very hard; beat someone up. *Stay out of my yard or I'll knock your block off.*

**knock oneself out** *v. phr., informal* To work very hard; make a great effort. *Mrs. Ross knocked herself out planning her daughter's wedding.*

**knock on wood** *v. phr.* To knock on something made of wood to keep from having bad luck.—Many people believe that you will have bad luck if you talk about good luck or brag about something, unless you knock on wood; often used in a joking way. *Charles said, "I haven't been sick all winter." Grandfather said, "You'd better knock on wood when you say that."*

**knockout** *n., slang* (stress on *knock*) **1.** Strikingly beautiful woman. *Sue is a regular knockout.* **2.** A straight punch in boxing that causes one's opponent to fall and lose consciousness. *The champion won the fight with a straight knockout.*

**knock out** *v. phr.* (stress on *out*) To make helpless, unworkable, or unusable. *The soldier knocked out two enemy tanks with his bazooka.*

**knock over** *v. phr.* To overturn; upset. *I accidentally knocked over the Chinese lamp that fell on the floor and broke.*

**knock the bottom out of something** *v. phr.* To render invalid or ineffective. *Vigorous new research knocked the bottom out of various older theories about the structure of the universe.*

**knock the living daylights out of** *v. phr., slang, informal* To render (someone) unconscious (said in exaggeration). *The news almost knocked the living daylights out of me.*

**knotty problem** *n. phr.* A very complicated and difficult problem to solve. *Doing one's income tax properly can present a knotty problem.*

**know a thing or two about** *v. phr.* To be experienced in; have a fairly considerable knowledge of. ♦ *Tom has dealt with many foreign traders; he knows a thing or two about stocks and bonds.*

**know chalk from cheese** To be very stupid; to be unable to distinguish valuable things from rubbish.—A proverb. ♦ *Poor Jerry will never amount to much; the poor guy doesn't even know chalk from cheese.*

**know-how** *n., slang* Expertise; ability to devise and construct. ♦ *The United States had the know-how to beat the Soviet Union to the moon in 1969.*

**know if one is coming or going** *or* **know whether one is coming or going** *v. phr.* To feel able to think clearly; know what to do.—Usually used in the negative or with limiters. ♦ *My cousin is so much in love that she scarcely knows whether she's coming or going.*

**know-it-all** *n.* A person who acts as if he knows all about everything; someone who thinks no one can tell him anything new. ♦ *After George was elected class president, he wouldn't take suggestions from anyone; he became a know-it-all.*

**know one in high places** *v. phr.* To be connected with people in power. ♦ *Ted's grandfather was the mayor of Chicago so he knows people in high places.*

**know one's own mind** *v. phr.* To not hesitate or vacillate; be definite in one's ideas or plans. ♦ *It is impossible to do business with Fred, because he doesn't know his own mind.*

**know one's place** *v. phr.* To be deferential to one's elders or superiors. ♦ *Ken is a talented teaching assistant, but he has a tendency to tell the head of the department how to run things. Somebody ought to teach him to know his place.*

**know one's way around** *or* **know one's way about** *v. phr.* **1.** To understand how things happen in the world; be experienced in the ways of the world. ♦ *The sailor had been in the wildest ports in the world. He knew his way around.*

**know (something) inside out** *v. phr.* To be extremely well conversant with something; be an expert in; have thorough knowledge of. ♦ *Tom knows the stock market inside out.*

**know (something) like the back of one's hand** *phrasal idiom* To know something thoroughly, inside out. ♦ *John is a man-about-town; he knows London like the back of his hand.*

**know shit from shinola** *vulgar, avoidable* To be ignorant enough to confuse things of unequal value.—A proverb. ♦ *Algernon talks big, but he doesn't know shit from shinola about money matters.*

**know the ropes** See THE ROPES.

**know the score** See THE SCORE.

**know what's what** See KNOW SOMETHING INSIDE OUT.

**know where one stands** *v. phr.* To be aware of one's monetary or social position. ♦ *"Excuse me, sir!" Ted said to the company director, "I hate to bother you, but I'd really like to know where I stand. Will I get a pay raise next year?"*

**know which side one's bread is buttered on** *v. phr.* To know who can help you and try to please him; know what is for your own gain. ♦ *Dick was always polite to the boss; he knew which side his bread was buttered on.*

**know which way to turn** See NOT KNOW WHICH WAY TO TURN.

**knuckle under** *v. phr.* To do something because you are forced to do it. ♦ *Bobby refused to knuckle under to the bully.*

**labor of love** n. phr. Something done for personal pleasure and not pay or profit. ◆ *Building the model railroad was a labor of love for the retired engineer.*

**labor under** v. phr. To be the victim of; suffer from. ◆ *Ken is obviously laboring under the delusion that Jennifer will marry him out of love.*

**ladies' room** n. phr. A public toilet and restroom for women. ◆ *Can you please tell me where the ladies' room is?*

**lady friend** n. **1.** A woman friend. ◆ *His aunt stays with a lady friend in Florida during the winter.* **2.** A woman who is the lover of a man. ◆ *The lawyer took his lady friend to dinner.*

**lady-killer** n., informal **1.** Any man who has strong sex appeal toward women. ◆ *Joe is a regular lady-killer.* **2.** A man who relentlessly pursues amorous conquests, is successful at it, and then abandons his heartbroken victims. ◆ *The legendary Don Juan of Spain is the most famous lady-killer of recorded history.*

**lady of the house** n. phr. Female owner, or wife of the owner, of the house; the hostess. ◆ *"Dinner is served," the lady of the house announced to her guests.*

**lady's man** n. A man or boy who likes to be with women or girls very much and is popular with them. ◆ *Charlie is quite a lady's man now.*

**laid out** adj. Arranged. ◆ *Her house is very conveniently laid out.*

**laid up** adj. Sick; confined to bed. ◆ *I was laid up for a couple of weeks with an ear infection.*

**lame duck** n., informal An elected public official who has been either defeated in a new election or whose term cannot be renewed, but who has a short period of time left in office during which he can still perform certain duties, though with somewhat diminished powers. ◆ *In the last year of their second terms, American presidents are lame ducks.*

**landing ship** n. A ship built to land troops and army equipment on a beach for an invasion. ◆ *The landing ship came near the beach, doors in the bow opened, and marines ran out.*

**land of Lincoln** n. phr. The state of Illinois's nickname. ◆ *I could tell you're from Illinois, because it says "Land of Lincoln" on your license plate.*

**land of nod** n. phr. Sleep. ◆ *The little girl went off to the land of nod.*

**land on one's feet** also **land on both feet** v. phr., informal To get yourself out of trouble without damage or injury and sometimes with a gain; be successful no matter what happens. ◆ *No matter what trouble he gets into, Julius always seems to land on his feet.*

**landslide** n. An overwhelming victory during a political election. ◆ *Ronald Reagan won the election of 1980 in a landslide.*

**lap up** v. **1.** To eat or drink with the tip of the tongue. ◆ *The kitten laps up its milk.* **2.** informal To take in eagerly. ◆ *She flatters him all the time and he just laps it up.*

**lardhead** n., slang A stupid or slow-witted person. ◆ *You'll never convince Algernon; he's a lardhead.*

**large as life** See BIG AS LIFE.

**large order** n. phr. Difficult job; a difficult task to fulfill. ◆ *It is a large order to educate three children in college at the same time.*

**lash out** v. **1.** To kick. ◆ *The horse lashed out at the man behind him.* **2.** To try suddenly to hit. ◆ *The woman lashed out at the crowd with her umbrella.* **3.** To attack with words. ◆ *The senator lashed out at the administration.*

**last but not least** adv. phr. In the last place but not the least important. ◆ *Billy will bring sandwiches, Alice will bring cake, Susan will bring cookies, John will bring potato chips, and last but not least, Sally will bring the lemonade.*

**last ditch** n. The last place that can be defended; the last resort. ◆ *They will fight reform to the last ditch.*

**last-ditch** adj. Made or done as a last chance to keep from losing or failing. ◆ *He threw away his cigarettes in a last-ditch effort to stop smoking.*

**last-ditch effort** See LAST DITCH.

**last lap** n. phr. The final stage. ◆ *Although the trip had been very interesting, we were glad that we were on the last lap of our tiring journey.*

**last laugh** See HAVE THE LAST LAUGH.

**last leg** *n. phr.* **1.** Final stages of physical weakness before dying. ♦ *The poor old man was on his last leg in the nursing home.* **2.** The final stage of a journey. ♦ *The last leg of our round-the-world trip was Paris to Chicago.*

**last of the Mohicans** *n. phr.* The last individual belonging to a certain group, such as a tribe, generation, or practitioners of a rare or dying art. ♦ *Woodcuts are a vanishing art; George Buday, who lived in England and made them, was one of the last of the Mohicans.*

**last out** *v.* **1.** To be enough until the end of. ♦ *There is enough food in the house to last out the snowstorm.* **2.** To continue to the end of; continue to live after; live or go through. ♦ *The old man is dying; he won't last out the night.*

**last straw** *or* **straw that breaks the camel's back** *n. phr.* A small trouble which follows other troubles and makes one lose patience and be unable to bear them. ♦ *Bill had a bad day in school yesterday. He lost his knife on the way home, then he fell down, and when he broke a shoe lace, that was the last straw and he began to swear.*

**last word** *n.* **1.** The last remark in an argument. ♦ *I never win an argument with her. She always has the last word.* **2.** The final say in deciding something. ♦ *The superintendent has the last word in ordering new desks.* **3.** *informal* The most modern thing. ♦ *Mr. Green's Jaguar is the last word in cars.*

**latch on** *or* **latch onto** *v., informal* **1.** To get hold of; grasp or grab; catch. ♦ *He looked for something to latch onto and keep from falling.* **2.** *slang* To get into your possession. ♦ *The banker latched onto a thousand shares of stock.* **3.** *slang* To understand. ♦ *The teacher explained the idea of jet engines until the students latched onto it.* **4.** *informal* To keep; to hold. ♦ *The poor woman latched onto the little money she had left.*

**laugh all the way to the bank** *v. phr.* To have made a substantial amount of money either by lucky investment or by some fraudulent deal and rejoice over one's gains. ♦ *If you had done what I suggested, you, too, could be laughing all the way to the bank.*

**laughing matter** *n.* A funny happening; a silly situation.—Usually used with

no. ♦ *John's failing the test is no laughing matter!*

**laugh in one's beard** See LAUGH UP ONE'S SLEEVE.

**laugh in one's sleeve** See LAUGH UP ONE'S SLEEVE.

**laugh off** *v.* To dismiss with a laugh as not important or not serious; not take seriously. ♦ *He had a bad fall while ice skating but he laughed it off.*

**laugh one out of** *v. phr.* To cause another to forget his/her worries and sorrows by joking. ♦ *Jack was worried about getting airsick, but his son and daughter laughed him out of it.*

**laugh one out of court** *v. phr.* To render a person or project ridiculous by laughter and scorn. ♦ *Proponents of solar energy were originally laughed out of court, but with the world's oil crisis on the increase, they will soon be heard again.*

**laugh one's head off** *v. phr., informal* To laugh very hard; be unable to stop laughing. ♦ *Paul's stories are so wildly funny that I laugh my head off whenever he starts telling one of them.*

**laugh up one's sleeve** *or* **laugh in one's sleeve** *or* **laugh in one's beard** To be amused but not show it; hide your laughter. ♦ *He was laughing up his sleeve when Joe answered the phone because he knew the call would be a joke.*

**launch window** *n., Space English; informal* **1.** A period of time when the line-up of planets, Sun, and Moon are such as to make favorable conditions for a specific space launch. ♦ *The mission was canceled until the next launch window which will be exactly six weeks from today.* **2.** A favorable time for starting some kind of ambitious adventure. ♦ *My next launch window for a European trip isn't until school is over in June.*

**laundry list** *n. phr.* A list of things to buy or to do. ♦ *The government has a whole laundry list of things to accomplish before U.S. troops can be withdrawn from Iraq.*

**law-abiding** *adj.* Obeying or following the law. ♦ *Michael had been a law-abiding citizen all his life.*

**law and order** *n. phr.* A state of affairs where crime and criminals are kept in check by a strong and well-organized police force, a conservative set of political values. ♦ *The Republican candidate for president was a strong law and order advocate.*

**law of averages** *n. phr.* The idea that you can't win all the time or lose all the time. ♦ *The Celtics have won 10 games in a row but the law of averages will catch up with them soon.*

**law unto oneself** *n. phr., literary* A person who does only what he wishes; a person who ignores or breaks the law when he doesn't like it. ♦ *Everybody in Germany feared Hitler because he was a law unto himself.*

**lay a finger on** *v. phr.* To touch or bother, even a little.—Used in negative, interrogative, and conditional sentences. ♦ *Don't you dare lay a finger on the vase!* ♦ *If you so much as lay a finger on my boy, I'll call the police.*

**lay an egg** *v. phr., slang* To fail to win the interest or favor of an audience. ♦ *His joke laid an egg.* ♦ *Sometimes he is a successful speaker, but sometimes he lays an egg.*

**lay aside** *v. phr.* **1.** To put off until another time; interrupt an activity. ♦ *The president laid aside politics to turn to foreign affairs.* **2.** To save. ♦ *They tried to lay aside a little money each week for their vacation.*

**lay at one's door** *v. phr., literary* To blame (something) on a person. ♦ *The failure of the plan was laid at his door.*

**lay away** *v.* **1.** To save. ♦ *She laid a little of her pay away each week.* **2.** To bury (a person).—Used to avoid the word *bury,* which some people think is unpleasant. ♦ *He was laid away in his favorite spot on the hill.*

**lay-away plan** *n.* A plan for buying something that you can't pay cash for; a plan in which you pay some money down and pay a little more when you can, and the store holds the article until you have paid the full price. ♦ *She could not afford to pay for the coat all at once, so she used the lay-away plan.*

**lay bare** *v. phr.* To expose; reveal; divulge. ♦ *During his testimony the witness laid bare the whole story of his involvement with the accused.*

**lay by** *v.* To save, especially a little at a time. ♦ *The farmer laid by some of his best corn to use the next year for seed.*

**lay down** *v.* **1.** To let (something) be taken; give up or surrender (something). ♦ *The general told the troops to lay down their arms.* ♦ *He was willing to lay down his life for his country.* **2.** To ask people to follow; tell someone to obey; make (a rule or principle). ♦ *The committee laid down rules about the size of tennis courts.*

**lay down one's arms** *v. phr.* To cease fighting; surrender. ♦ *The Civil War ended when the Confederate army finally laid down its arms.*

**lay down one's cards** See LAY ONE'S CARDS ON THE TABLE.

**lay down one's life** *v. phr.* To sacrifice one's life for a cause or person; suffer martyrdom. ♦ *The early Christians often laid down their lives for their faith.*

**lay down the law** *v. phr.* **1.** To give strict orders. ♦ *The teacher lays down the law about homework every afternoon.* **2.** To speak severely or seriously about a wrongdoing; scold. ♦ *The principal called in the students and laid down the law to them about skipping classes.*

**lay eyes on** *or* **set eyes on** *v. phr.* To see. ♦ *I didn't know the man; in fact, I had never set eyes on him.*

**lay hands on** *v. phr.* **1.** To get hold of; find; catch. ♦ *If the police can lay hands on him, they will put him in jail.* **2.** To do violence to; harm; hurt. ♦ *They were afraid that if they left him alone in his disturbed condition he would lay hands on himself.*

**lay hold of** *v. phr.* **1.** To take hold of; grasp; grab. ♦ *He laid hold of the rope and pulled the boat ashore.* **2.** To get possession of. ♦ *He sold every car he could lay hold of.* **3.** *Chiefly British* To understand. ♦ *Some ideas in this science book are hard to lay hold of.*

**lay in** *v.* To store up a supply of; to get and keep for future use. ♦ *Before school starts, the principal will lay in plenty of paper for the students' written work.*

**lay into** *or* **light into** *v., informal* **1.** To attack physically; go at vigorously. ♦ *The two fighters laid into each other as soon as the bell rang.* ♦ *John loves Italian food and he really laid into the spaghetti.* **2.** *slang* To attack with words. ♦ *The senator laid into the opponents of his bill.*

**lay it on** *or* **lay it on thick** *also* **put it on thick** *or* **spread it on thick** *or* **lay it on with a trowel** *v. phr., informal* To persuade someone by using very much flattery; flatter. ♦ *Bob wanted to go to the movies. He laid it on thick to his mother.*

**lay it on the line** See LAY ON THE LINE 2.

**layoff** *n.* (stress on *lay*) A systematic or periodical dismissal of employees from a factory or a firm. ♦ *Due to the poor economy, the car manufacturer announced a major layoff starting next month.*

**lay off** *v. phr.* (stress on *off*) **1.** To mark out the boundaries or limits. ♦ *He laid off a baseball diamond on the vacant lot.* **2.** To put out of work. ♦ *The company lost the contract for making the shoes and laid off half its workers.* **3.** *slang* To stop bothering; leave alone.—Usually used in the imperative. ♦ *Lay off me, will you?* **4.** *slang* To stop using or taking. ♦ *His doctor told him to lay off cigarettes.*

**lay of the land** *also* **how the land lies** *n. phr.* **1.** The natural features of a piece of land, such as hills and valleys. ♦ *The style of house the contractor builds depends partly on the lay of the land.* **2.** The way something is arranged; the important facts about something; how things are. ♦ *The banker wanted to check the lay of the land before buying the stock.*

**lay on** *v.* **1.** To spread on or over a surface; apply. ♦ *He told us that we should lay on a second coat of paint for better protection against the weather.*

**lay one's cards on the table** *or* **lay down one's cards** *or* **put one's cards on the table** *v. phr., informal* To let someone know your position and interest openly; deal honestly; act without trickery or secrets. ♦ *In talking about buying the property, Peterson laid his cards on the table about his plans for it.*

**lay oneself open to** *v. phr.* To make oneself vulnerable to; expose oneself. ♦ *If you don't perform your job properly, you will lay yourself open to criticism.*

**lay one's hands on** *or* **get one's hands on** *v. phr.* **1.** To seize in order to punish or treat roughly. ♦ *If I ever lay my hands on that boy he'll be sorry.* **2.** To get possession of. ♦ *He was unable to lay his hands on a camel for the school play.* **3.** *or* **lay one's hand on** *or* **put one's hand on** To find; locate. ♦ *He keeps a file of letters so he can lay his hands on one whenever he needs it.*

**lay on the line** *or* **put on the line** *v. phr., informal* **1.** To pay or offer to pay. ♦ *The bank is putting $5,000 on the line as a reward to anyone who catches the robber.* **2.** To say plainly so that there can be no doubt; tell truthfully. ♦ *I'm going to lay it on the line for you, Paul. You must work harder if you want to pass.* **3.** To take a chance of losing; risk. ♦ *Frank decided to lay his job on the line and tell the boss that he thought he was wrong.*

**lay out** *v. phr.* **1.** To prepare (a dead body) for burial. ♦ *The corpse was laid out by the undertaker.* **2.** *slang* To knock down flat; to hit unconscious. ♦ *A stiff blow to the jaw laid the boxer out in the second round.* **3.** To plan. ♦ *Come here, Fred, I have a job laid out for you.* **4.** To mark or show where work is to be done. ♦ *The foreman laid out the job for the new machinist.* **5.** To plan the building or arrangement of; design. ♦ *The architect laid out the interior of the building.* **6.** *slang* To spend; pay. ♦ *How much did you have to lay out for your new car?*

**layout** *n.* General situation; arrangement; plan. ♦ *The layout of their apartment overlooking Lake Michigan was strikingly unusual.*

**layover** *n.* A stopover, usually at an airport or in a hotel due to interrupted air travel. ♦ *There were several layovers at O'Hare last month due to bad weather.*

**lay over** *v.* **1.** To put off until later; delay; postpone. ♦ *We voted to lay the question over to our next meeting for decision.* **2.** To arrive in one place and wait some time before continuing the journey. ♦ *We had to lay over in St. Louis for two hours waiting for a plane to Seattle.*

**lay rubber** *or* **lay a patch** *v. phr., slang* To take off in a car or a motorcycle so fast that the tires (made of rubber) leave a mark on the pavement. ♦ *Look at those crazy drag racers; they laid rubber in front of my house.*

**lay the blame at one's door** *v. phr.* To say that another person or group is responsible for one's own failure. ♦ *The angry coach laid the blame at the* door of the players when our college lost the basketball game.

**lay to rest** v. phr., informal **1.** To put a dead person into a grave or tomb; bury. ♦ President Kennedy was laid to rest in Arlington National Cemetery. **2.** To get rid of; put away permanently; stop. ♦ The rumor that the principal had accepted another job was laid to rest when he said it wasn't true.

**lay up** v. **1.** To collect a supply of; save for future use; store. ♦ Bees lay up honey for the winter. **2.** To keep in the house or in bed because of sickness or injury; disable. ♦ Jack was laid up with a twisted knee and couldn't play in the final game. **3.** To take out of active service; put in a boat dock or a garage. ♦ Bill had to lay up his boat when school started.

**lay waste** v. phr., literary To cause wide and great damage to; destroy and leave in ruins; wreck. ♦ Enemy soldiers laid waste the land.

**lead a dog's life** v. phr., informal To live a hard life, work hard, and be treated unkindly. ♦ Some poorer college students led a dog's life.

**lead a merry chase** v. phr. To delay or escape capture by (someone) skillfully; make (a pursuer) work hard. ♦ Valerie is leading her boyfriend a merry chase.

**lead by the nose** v. phr., informal To have full control of; make or persuade (someone) to do anything whatever. ♦ Don't let anyone lead you by the nose; use your own judgment and do the right thing.

**leading light** n. phr. A prominent person in a community, company, or group. ♦ Alan is the leading light of our discussion group on music.

**lead off** v. To begin; start; open. ♦ Richard led off the chess game with a knight. ♦ We always let Henry lead off. ♦ Mr. Jones led off with the jack of diamonds.

**lead on** v. phr. To encourage you to believe something untrue or mistaken. ♦ We were led on to think that Jeanne and Jim were engaged to be married.

**lead one a merry dance** v. phr. To cause someone unusual discomfort or expense; tire someone by causing one to overdo. ♦ With her personal extravagances Carol led her husband a merry dance.

**lead the way** v. phr. To go before and show how to go somewhere; guide. ♦ The boys need someone to lead the way on their hike. ♦ That school led the way in finding methods to teach reading.

**lead to** v. phr. To result in. ♦ Such a heavy arms race can only lead to war.

**leaf through** v. phr. To scan or glance through a book or other reading matter. ♦ I only had time to leaf through the program before the concert started.

**leak out** v. phr. To become known; escape. ♦ The famous beauty queen tried to keep her marriage a secret, but news of it soon leaked out.

**leak to** v. phr. To purposely let a secret be known, as if conveying it in the strictest confidence. ♦ The movie star's secret divorce was leaked to the tabloids by her housekeeper.

**lean on** v. phr., slang, informal To pressure (someone) by blackmailing, threats, physical violence, or the withholding of some favor in order to make the person comply with a wish or request. ♦ I would gladly do what you ask if you only stopped leaning on me so hard!

**lean-to** n. **1.** A shed for tools, such as spades, hoes, etc., attached to the wall of a house. ♦ Jo looked for the garden hose in the lean-to. **2.** A small cabin in the country. ♦ They spend their weekends in their modest lean-to in Wisconsin.

**leap year** n. Every fourth year during which the month of February contains 29 rather than 28 days. ♦ During a leap year one must wait a day longer for one's February paycheck.

**learn by heart** See BY HEART.

**learn by rote** v. phr. To blindly memorize what was taught without thinking about it. ♦ If you learn a subject by rote, it will be difficult to say anything original about it.

**learn one's way around** See KNOW ONE'S WAY AROUND.

**learn the hard way** See HARD WAY.

**learn the ropes** See THE ROPES.

**leatherneck** n., slang, informal A member of the United States Marine Corps. ♦ I didn't know your son Joe became a leatherneck.

**leave a bad taste in one's mouth** *v. phr.* To feel a bad impression; make you feel disgusted. ♦ *His rudeness to the teacher left a bad taste in my mouth.*

**leave alone** See LET ALONE.

**leave a door open** *v. phr.* To not do something that cannot be undone. ♦ *"I know you dislike the boss at your place of work, but don't resign in anger; leave a door open!" John advised his younger brother.*

**leave at the altar** *v. phr.* **1.** To decide not to marry someone in the last minute; jilt. ♦ *Ed left poor Susan at the altar.* **2.** To overlook and skip for promotion; not fulfill deserved expectation. ♦ *Once again I didn't get my promotion and was left at the altar.*

**leave behind** *v. phr.* **1.** Abandon. ♦ *Refugees on the run must sometimes leave old and sick people behind.* **2.** To forget; go away without. ♦ *We had reached our car when we noticed that we had left our keys behind.*

**leave flat** *v. phr., informal* To quit or leave suddenly without warning when wanted or needed; desert; forsake; abandon. ♦ *My car ran out of gas and left me flat, ten miles from town.*

**leave hanging** *or* **leave hanging in the air** *v. phr.* To leave undecided or unsettled. ♦ *Because the committee could not decide on a time and place, the matter of the spring dance was left hanging.*

**leave high and dry** See HIGH AND DRY.

**leave holding the bag** *or* **leave holding the sack** *v. phr., informal* **1.** To cause (someone) not to have something needed; leave without anything. ♦ *In the rush for seats, Joe was left holding the bag.* **2.** To force (someone) to take the whole responsibility or blame for something that others should share. ♦ *After the party, the other girls on the clean-up committee went away with their dates, and left Mary holding the bag.*

**leave in the lurch** *v. phr.* To desert or leave alone in trouble; refuse to help or support. ♦ *Bill quit his job, leaving his boss in the lurch.*

**leave it at that** *v. phr.* To avoid further and more acrimonious disagreement; not argue or discuss any further. ♦ *Our opinion on health care is obviously different, so let's just leave it at that.*

**leave much to be desired** *v. phr.* To be highly flawed, bad, unsatisfactory. ♦ *"How is you health these days?" Dr. Gordon asked, when one of her patients returned from an extended stay abroad. "I am afraid," the patient answered, "it leaves much to be desired."*

**leave it to one** *v. phr.* To delegate; give someone authority or responsibility to carry out a certain job. ♦ *Leave it to Ted to make the office Christmas party a resounding success; he is a terrific organizer.*

**leave no stone unturned** *v. phr.* To try in every way; miss no chance; do everything possible.—Usually used in the negative. ♦ *The police will leave no stone unturned in their search for the bank robbers.*

**leave off** *v.* To come or put to an end; stop. ♦ *Marion put a marker in her book so that she would know where she left off.*

**leave one cold** *v. phr.* To be of no interest to one at all. ♦ *I tried to take Fred to the Symphony Center, but unfortunately, classical music leaves him entirely cold. All he is interested in is Country and Western music.*

**leave one's mark** *v. phr.* To leave an impression upon; influence someone. ♦ *Tolstoy never won the Nobel Prize, but he left his mark on world literature.*

**leave open** *v. phr.* To remain temporarily unsettled; subject to further discussion. ♦ *Brad said that the question of health insurance would be left open until some future date.*

**leave out** *v. phr.* To skip; omit. ♦ *The printer accidentally left out two paragraphs from Alan's novel.*

**leave out in the cold** See OUT IN THE COLD.

**leave out of account** *v. phr.* To fail to consider; forget about. ♦ *The picnic planners left out of account that it might rain.* Contrast TAKE INTO ACCOUNT.

**leave over** *v. phr.* (stress on *over*) To leave unfinished. ♦ *They gave us such huge portions of food in our favorite Chinese restaurant that we had to leave lots over and take it home in a doggy bag.*

**leave something up to someone** *v. phr.* To hand over the right to decide a certain matter to someone else. ♦ *I leave it* up to you, sir, what you want to do about next year's budget.

**leave to one's own devices** v. phr. To not worry about how someone will succeed, but to allow a person to take care of himself or herself and his or her own affairs. ◆*John is a big boy now; no need to always rush to his aid. We can leave him to his own devices.*

**leave well enough alone** See LET WELL ENOUGH ALONE.

**leave word with** v. phr. To leave a message. ◆*Hank left word with his secretary where he could be reached by phone while he was away from his office.*

**left-handed** adj., informal **1.** Using the left hand habitually. **2.** Crooked; phoney. ◆*Morris is such a left-handed guy.* **3.** Clumsy; untoward; awkward. ◆*Grab that hammer and stop acting so left-handed.*

**left-handed compliment** An ambiguous compliment which is interpretable as an offense. ◆*I didn't know you could look so pretty! Is that a wig you're wearing?*

**leftovers** n. phr. (stress on left) Food that remains uneaten from a meal. ◆*May we take home some of these delicious leftovers?*

**left-wing** adj. That which is or belongs to a group of people in politics that favors radical change in the direction of socialism or communism. ◆*The left-wing faction called for an immediate strike.*

**legal age** or **lawful age** The age at which a person is allowed to do a certain thing or is held responsible for an action. ◆*In most states the legal age for voting is 21.*

**leg man** n., informal **1.** An errand boy; one who performs messenger services, or the like. ◆*Joe hired a leg man for the office.* **2.** Slang, semi-vulgar, avoid! A man who is particularly attracted to good looking female legs and pays less attention to other parts of the female anatomy. ◆*Herb is a leg man.*

**leg to stand on** n. phr. A firm foundation of facts; facts to support your claim.— Used in the negative. ◆*Jerry's answering speech left his opponent without a leg to stand on.*

**leg work** n., informal The physical end of a project, such as the typing of research

reports; the physical investigating of a criminal affair; the carrying of books to and from libraries; etc. ◆*Joe, my research assistant, does a lot of leg work for me.*

**lemon law** n. phr. A law in effect in some states that allows customers to return a faulty product for a full refund, after they have proven that they tried to fix the item more than once. ◆*"Dad, our car is a lemon," Mark and Sylvia bitterly complained. "I think Wisconsin has a lemon law," Sylvia's father answered. "See if they will give you a refund."*

**lend a hand** or **give a hand** also **bear a hand** v. phr. To give help; make yourself useful; help. ◆*Dick saw a woman with a flat tire and offered to give her a hand with it.*

**lend an ear to** See GIVE AN EAR TO.

**lend color to** See GIVE COLOR TO.

**lend credence to** v. phr. To believe. ◆*We cannot lend credence to enemy propaganda.*

**lend itself to** v. phr. To give a chance for or be useful for; to be possible or right for. ◆*This poem lends itself to our program very well.*

**lend oneself to** v. phr. To give help or approval to; encourage; assist. ◆*Alice wouldn't lend herself to the plot to steal the teacher's chalk.*

**less than** adv. Not; little. ◆*We were busy and less than delighted to have company that day.* ◆*The boys were less than happy about having a party.*

**less than no time** n. phr., informal Very quickly. ◆*We can be ready to go in less than no time.* ◆*It took Sally less than no time to get dinner ready.*

**let alone** conj. phr. **1.** Even less; certainly not.—Used after a negative clause. ◆*I can't add two and two, let alone do fractions.* **2.** **let alone** or **leave alone** v. To stay away from; keep hands off; avoid. ◆*When Joel gets mad, just let him alone.*

**let be** v. To pay no attention to; disregard; forget. ◆*Let her be; she has a headache.*

**let bygones be bygones** v. phr. To let the past be forgotten. ◆*We should let bygones be bygones and try to get along with each other.*

**letdown** n. A disappointment; a heartbreak. ◆*It was a major letdown for John when Mary refused to marry him.*

**let down** v. phr. **1.** To allow to descend; lower. ♦ *Harry let the chain saw down on a rope and then climbed down himself.* **2.** To relax; stop trying so hard; take it easy. ♦ *The horse let down near the end of the race and lost.* **3.** To fail to do as well as (someone) expected; disappoint. ♦ *The team felt they had let the coach down.*

**let down easy** v. phr. To refuse or say no to (someone) in a pleasant manner; to tell bad news about a refusal or disappointment in a kindly way. ♦ *The boss tried to let Jim down easy when he had to tell him he was too young for the job.*

**let down one's hair** See LET ONE'S HAIR DOWN.

**let drop** v. phr. **1.** To cease to talk about; set aside; forget. ♦ *This is such an unpleasant subject that I suggest we let it drop for a few days.* **2.** To disclose; hint. ♦ *He unexpectedly let drop that he was resigning and joining another firm.*

**let go** v. **1a.** To stop holding something; loosen your hold; release. ♦ *The boy grabbed Jack's coat and would not let go.*—Often used with *of.* ♦ *When the child let go of her mother's hand, she fell down.* **1b.** To weaken and break under pressure. ♦ *The old water pipe suddenly let go and water poured out of it.* **2.** To pay no attention to; neglect. ♦ *Robert let his teeth go when he was young and now he has to go to the dentist often.* **3.** To allow something to pass; do nothing about. ♦ *The children teased Frank, but he smiled and let it go.* **4.** To discharge from a job; fire. ♦ *Mr. Wilson got into a quarrel with his boss and was let go.* **5.** To make (something) go out quickly; shoot; fire. ♦ *Robin Hood let go an arrow at the deer.* **6.** or **let oneself go** informal To be free in one's actions or talk; relax. ♦ *The cowboys worked hard all week, but on Saturday night they went to town and let themselves go.*

**let go of** v. phr. To release one's grasp. ♦ *As soon as Sally let go of the leash, her dog ran away.*

**let grass grow under one's feet** v. phr. To be idle; be lazy; waste time.—Used in negative, conditional, and interrogative sentences. ♦ *The new boy joined the football team, made the honor roll, and found a girlfriend during the first month of school. He certainly did not let any grass grow under his feet.*

**let it all hang out** v. phr., slang, informal Not to disguise anything; to let the truth be known. ♦ *Sue can't deceive anyone; she just lets it all hang out.*

**let it lay** v. phr., used imperatively, slang Forget it; leave it alone; do not be concerned or involved. ♦ *Don't get involved with Max again—just let it lay.*

**let it rip** v. phr., used imperatively, slang Don't be concerned; pay no attention to what happens. ♦ *Why get involved? Forget about it and let it rip.* **2.** (Imperatively) Do become involved and make the most of it; get in there and really try to win. ♦ *Come on man, give it all you've got and let it rip!*

**let it spread** v. phr., slang Said to people who are worried that they would gain too much weight. ♦ *"How about some more cake?" the hostess asked John. "I am afraid, I can't." John answered. "Let it spread," the hostess said. "You aren't that overweight."*

**let know** v. phr. To inform. ♦ *Please let us know the time of your arrival.*

**let loose** v. **1a.** or **set loose** or **turn loose** To set free; loosen or give up your hold on. ♦ *The farmer opened the gate and let the bull loose in the pasture.* **1b.** or **turn loose** To give freedom (to someone) to do something; to allow (someone) to do what he wants. ♦ *The children were turned loose in the toy store to pick the toys they wanted.* **1c.** To stop holding something; loosen your hold. ♦ *Jim caught Ruth's arm and would not let loose.* **2a.** informal To let or make (something) move fast or hard; release. ♦ *The fielder let loose a long throw to home plate after catching the ball.* **2b.** informal To release something held. ♦ *Those dark clouds are going to let loose any minute.* **3.** informal To speak or act freely; disregard ordinary limits. ♦ *The boss told Jim that some day she was going to let loose and tell him what she thought of him.*

**let loose the dogs of war** or **unleash the dogs of war** or **let slip the dogs of war** To start and wage war.—A proverb. ♦ *When diplomacy fails, nations may have to unleash the dogs of war.*

**let me see** or **let us see** informal **1.** Let us find out by trying or performing an

action. ♦ *Let me see if you can jump over the fence.* **2.** Give me time to think or remember. ♦ *I can't come today. Let me see. How about Friday?*
**let off** *v.* **1.** To discharge (a gun); explode; fire. ♦ *Willie accidentally let off his father's shotgun and made a hole in the wall.* **2.** To permit to go or escape; excuse from a penalty, a duty, or a promise. ♦ *Two boys were caught smoking in school but the principal let them off with a warning.* **3.** *or informal* **let off the hook** To miss a chance to defeat or score against, especially in sports or games. ♦ *The boxer let his opponent off the hook many times.*
**let off steam** *or* **blow off steam** *v. phr.* **1.** To let or make steam escape; send out steam. ♦ *The janitor let off some steam because the pressure was too high.* **2.** *informal* To get rid of physical energy or strong feeling through activity; talk or be very active physically after forced quiet. ♦ *After the long ride on the bus, the children let off steam with a race to the lake.*
**let on** *v. informal* **1.** To tell or admit what you know.—Used in the negative. ♦ *Frank lost $50 but he didn't let on to his mother.* **2.** To try to make people believe; pretend. ♦ *The old man likes to let on that he is rich.*
**let one have it** *v. phr.* **1a.** *slang* To hit hard. ♦ *He drew back his fist and let the man have it.* **1b.** *slang* To use a weapon on; to shoot or knife. ♦ *The guard pulled his gun and let the robber have it in the leg.* **1c.** *slang* To attack with words; scold; criticize. ♦ *Mary kept talking in class until the teacher became angry and let her have it.* **2.** *informal* To tell about it.—Used in the imperative phrase, *let's have it.* ♦ *Now, Jack, let's have it from the beginning.*
**let one in on** *v. phr.* To reveal a secret to; permit someone to share in. ♦ *If I let you in on something big we're planning, will you promise not to mention it to anyone?*
**let one's hair down** *or* **let down one's hair** *v. phr., informal* Act freely and naturally; be informal; relax. ♦ *Kings and queens can seldom let their hair down.*
**let out** *v.* **1a.** To allow to go out or escape. ♦ *The guard let the prisoners out of jail*

to work in the garden. ♦ *Mother won't let us out when it rains.* **1b.** *informal* To make (a sound) come out of the mouth; utter. ♦ *A bee stung Charles. He let out a yell and ran home.* ♦ *Father told Betty to sit still and not let out a peep during church.* **2.** To allow to be known; tell. ♦ *I'll never tell you another secret if you let this one out.* **3.** To make larger (as clothing) or looser; allow to slip out (as a rope). ♦ *Father hooked a big fish on his line. He had to let the line out so the fish wouldn't break it.* **4.** *informal* To allow to move at higher speed. ♦ *The rider let out his horse to try to beat the horse ahead of him.* **5.** *informal* To dismiss or be dismissed. ♦ *The coach let us out from practice at 3 o'clock.* ♦ *I'll meet you after school lets out.*
**let pass** *v. phr.* To disregard; overlook. ♦ *Herb may have overheard what was said about him, but he decided to let it pass.*
**let ride** *v. phr., informal* To allow to go on without change; accept (a situation or action) for the present. ♦ *The committee could not decide what to do about Bob's idea, so they let the matter ride for a month or so.*
**let's don't** *also* **don't let's** *nonstandard* Let's not; let us not; I suggest that we don't. ♦ *"Let's go out and play," said Fred. "Let's don't until the rain stops," said Mary.* ♦ *Don't let's go now. Let's go tomorrow instead.*
**let's roll** *v. phr.* Let's start the competition, the battle, the fight. ♦ *"Let roll!" said the leader of the hijacked plane heading for the White House, after which the passengers disarmed the hijackers, with the plane finally crashing in Pennsylvania.*
**let sleeping dogs lie** Do not make (someone) angry and cause trouble or danger; do not make trouble if you do not have to.—A proverb. ♦ *Don't tell Father that you broke the window. Let sleeping dogs lie.*
**let slip** *v. phr.* To unintentionally reveal. ♦ *Ellen let it slip that she had been a witness to the accident.*
**letter-perfect** *adj. phr.* Memorized perfectly; perfect to the last letter. ♦ *The actor was letter-perfect in his role.*
**let the cat out of the bag** *v. phr., informal* To tell about something that is

supposed to be a secret. ♦ *We wanted to surprise Mary with a birthday gift, but Allen let the cat out of the bag by asking her what she would like.—* Sometimes used in another form. ♦ *Well, the cat is out of the bag—everybody knows about their marriage.*

**let the chips fall where they may** *v. phr.* To pay no attention to the displeasure caused others by your actions. ♦ *The senator decided to vote against the bill and let the chips fall where they may.*

**let the grass grow under one's feet** *v. phr., informal* To waste time; be slow or idle. ♦ *Grandpa spends so much time sitting and thinking that Grandma accuses him of letting the grass grow under his feet.*

**let up** *v., informal* **1.** To become less, weaker, or quiet; become slower or stop. ♦ *It's raining as hard as ever. It's not letting up at all.* **2.** To do less or go slower or stop; relax; stop working or working hard. ♦ *Let up for a minute. You can't work hard all day.* ♦ *Jim ran all the way home without letting up once.* **3.** To become easier, kinder, or less strict.—Usually used with *on.* ♦ *Let up on Jane. She is sick.*

**let well enough alone** *or* **leave well enough alone** *v. phr.* To be satisfied with what is good enough; not try to improve something because often that might cause more trouble. ♦ *Ethel made a lot of changes in her test paper after she finished. She should have let well enough alone, because she made several new mistakes.*

**level best** *adj. phr.* One's utmost; one's very best. ♦ *Eric refused to stay in school although his parents did their level best to make him finish.*

**levelheaded** *adj. phr.* Having good common sense; practical; reasonable. ♦ *What our office needs is a good, levelheaded manager.*

**level off** *or* **level out** *v.* **1.** To make flat or level. ♦ *The steamroller leveled out the gravel roadbed and then the concrete was poured.* **2.** To move on an even level. ♦ *The airplane leveled out at 30,000 feet.* ♦ *After going up for six months, the cost of living leveled off in September.*

**level playing field** *n. phr.* Equal opportunity; fair chance for both competitors in a game or employment. ♦ *In a democracy people should be afforded a level playing field in all walks of life.*

**level with** *v. phr.* To tell someone the truth; not engage in lies and subterfuge. ♦ *"You can level with me," his father said. "Did you break that window?"*

**lick into shape** *v. phr.* To make perfect; drill; train. ♦ *The sergeant licked the new volunteer army into shape in three months.*

**lick one's boots** *v. phr.* To flatter or act like a slave; do anything to please another. ♦ *A wise prime minister would not want his friends and officials to lick his boots.*

**lick one's chops** *v. phr., informal* To think about something pleasant; enjoy the thought of something. ♦ *John is licking his chops about the steak dinner tonight.*

**lie around** *v. phr.* To be unused; inert. ♦ *This old typewriter has been lying around ever since Grandpa died.*

**lie down on the job** *v. phr., informal* To purposely fail to do your job; neglect a task; loaf. ♦ *Bill isn't trying to learn his lessons. He is lying down on the job.*

**lie in state** *v. phr.* Of a dead person: To lie in a place of honor, usually in an open coffin, and be seen by the public before burial. ♦ *When the president died, thousands of people saw his body lying in state.*

**lie in wait** *v. phr.* To watch from hiding in order to attack or surprise someone; to ambush. ♦ *The driver of the stagecoach knew that the thieves were lying in wait somewhere along the road.*

**lie low** *or nonstandard* **lay low** *v., informal* **1.** To stay quietly out of sight; try not to attract attention; hide. ♦ *After holding up the bank, the robbers lay low for a while.* **2.** To keep secret one's thoughts or plans. ♦ *I think he wants to be elected president, but he is lying low and not saying anything.*

**lie through one's teeth** *v. phr.* To lie uninhibitedly and unashamedly. ♦ *Everyone in the courtroom could sense that the accused was lying through his teeth.*

**lie to** *v.* Of a ship: To stay in one place facing against the wind; stop. ♦ *Our ship will lie to outside the harbor until daylight.*

**life and soul of the party** See HEARTY OF THE PARTY.

**life begins at forty** A quasi-proverbial idiom praising the virtue of having reached middle age.—A proverb. ♦ *"Never mind that you turned thirty-five, Suzie," her husband said. "Life begins at forty!"*

**life of Riley** *n. phr., informal* A soft easy life; pleasant or rich way of living. ♦ *He's living the life of Riley. He doesn't have to work anymore.*

**life of the party** *n. phr.* A person who makes things enjoyable or interesting for a group of people. ♦ *Bill is the life of the party at school. He is always making us laugh.*

**lift a finger** *or* **lift a hand** *also* **raise a hand** *v. phr.* **1.** To do something; do your share; to help.—Usually used in the negative. ♦ *We all worked hard except Joe. He wouldn't lift a finger.*

**lift one's spirits** *v. phr.* To make someone feel better. ♦ *Listening to some nice classical music usually lifts one's spirits.*

**light at the end of the tunnel** *n. phr.* The first sign of hope after a long period of difficulties. ♦ *Ted was near bankruptcy, but after some successful business transactions there was finally light at the end of the tunnel.*

**lighten up** *v. phr.* To put oneself in a better mood, or do it to others. ♦ *"Lighten up, Sam," the doctor suggested. "You worry too much."* ♦ *Joe tried to lighten up the party with a few innocent jokes.*

**light-fingered** *adj.* Given to stealing; having a tendency to be dishonest or a kleptomaniac. ♦ *I always suspected that Freddie might be lightfingered and my suspicions were confirmed when he was arrested for shoplifting.*

**light housekeeping** *n., slang* An arrangement in which an unmarried couple live together. ♦ *Are Joe and Sue married?—Oh, no,—it's just a case of light housekeeping.*

**light on** *also* **light upon** *v.* To pick out by sight from among others; see; notice. ♦ *Her eyes lighted upon the row of boxes, and she asked what was in them.*

**light out** *v., slang* **1.** To run as fast as you can. ♦ *The boy lit out for home with the bully chasing him.* **2.** To go away in a

hurry; leave suddenly.—Often used with *for.* ♦ *Jack won't be in town long. He wants to light out as soon as he has enough money saved.*

**light up** *v.* Suddenly to look pleased and happy. ♦ *Martha's face lit up when she saw her old friend.*

**like a fish out of water** See FISH OUT OF WATER.

**like a hole in the head** *adv. phr.* Not at all; scarcely; grudgingly; in an unwelcome manner. ♦ *Joan needs her mother-in-law to stay with her for a week like a hole in the head.*

**like anything** *adv. phr.* To an extreme degree. ♦ *He swore like anything when he found out that he hadn't been promoted.*

**like clockwork** See GO LIKE CLOCKWORK *or* GO OFF LIKE CLOCKWORK.

**like father, like son** A son is usually like his father in the way he acts.—A proverb. ♦ *Mr. Jones and Tommy are both quiet and shy. Like father, like son.*

**like hell** *adv., slang, vulgar, avoid!* **1.** With great vigor. ♦ *As soon as they saw the cops, they ran like hell.* **2.** *interj.* Not so; untrue; indicates the speaker's lack of belief in what he heard. ♦ *Like hell you're gonna bring me my dough!*

**like hell I will** *or* **across my dead body** *or* **not across my dead body** See ACROSS MY DEAD BODY.

**like it or lump it** See TAKE IT OR LEAVE IT.

**like looking for a needle in a haystack** See NEEDLE IN A HAYSTACK.

**like mad** *or* **like crazy** *adv., slang, informal* With great enthusiasm and vigor; very fast. ♦ *We had to drive like mad (like crazy) to get there on time.*

**little rabbits have big ears** See LITTLE PITCHERS HAVE BIG EARS.

**like two peas in a pod** *adj. phr.* Closely similar; almost exactly alike. ♦ *The twin sisters Eve and Agnes are like two peas in a pod.*

**like water** *adv. phr.* As something easily poured out or wasted; freely.—Usually used in the phrase *spend money like water.* ♦ *During the World Wars, the United States spent money like water.*

**like water off a duck's back** *adv. phr., informal* Without changing your feelings or opinion; without effect.

♦ *Advice and correction roll off him like water off a duck's back.*

**line of fire** *n. phr.* The path that something fired or thrown takes. ♦ *When the bandit and the police began to shoot, John was almost in their line of fire.*

**line of least resistance** *or* **path of least resistance** *n. phr.* The easiest way; the way that takes least effort. ♦ *Some parents take the path of least resistance with their children and let them do as they please.*

**line one's pockets** *also* **line one's purse** *v. phr., informal* To get a lot of money unfairly; get rich by being dishonest. ♦ *The policeman lined his pockets by taking bribes.*

**lineup** *n.* (stress on *line*) **1.** An alignment of objects in a straight line. ♦ *A lineup of Venus and the moon can be a very beautiful sight in the night sky.* **2.** An arrangement of suspects through a one-way mirror so that the victim or the witness of a crime can identify the wanted person. ♦ *She picked out her attacker from a police lineup.*

**line up** *v. phr.* (stress on *up*) **1.** To take places in a line or formation; stand side by side or one behind another; form a line or pattern. ♦ *The boys lined up and took turns diving off the springboard.* **2.** To put in line. ♦ *John lined up the pool balls.* **3.** To adjust correctly. ♦ *The garage man lined up the car's wheels.* **4a.** *informal* To make ready for action; complete a plan or agreement for; arrange. ♦ *The superintendent lined up all the new teachers he needed before he went on vacation.* **4b.** *informal* To become ready for action; come together in preparation or agreement. ♦ *Larry wanted to go to the seashore for the family vacation, but the rest of the family lined up against him.*

**lion's share** *n. phr.* A disproportionate share; the largest part. ♦ *The manager always gets the lion's share of the company's profits.*

**lips are sealed** *See* MUM IS THE WORD.

**lip service** *n.* Support shown by words only and not by actions; a show of loyalty that is not proven in action.— Usually used with *pay.* ♦ *By holding elections, communism pays lip service to democracy, but it offers only one candidate per office.*

**liquid assets** *n. phr.* Those belongings that can be easily converted into cash. ♦ *Herb asked for a loan and the bank manager told him to bring in proof of all his liquid assets.*

**liquor up** *v. phr., slang* To drink an excessive amount of liquor before engaging in some activity as if comparing oneself to a car that needs to be filled before a journey. ♦ *Joe always liquors up before he takes Sue for a dance.*

**listen in** *v.* **1.** To listen to a radio broadcast. ♦ *We found them listening in to the president's speech.* **2.** To listen to the talk of others, often to talk that is not intended for your ears; eavesdrop. ♦ *When Mary talked to her boyfriend on the telephone, her little brother listened in.*

**listen to reason** *v. phr.* To listen to and think about advice that you are given. ♦ *It will save you a lot of trouble if you will just listen to reason.*

**listen who's talking** *or* **look who's talking** *v. phr., informal* Said to one mockingly who under the circumstances had better keep quiet. ♦ *"Divorce is a bad thing," said the famous actress, who had just married for the seventh time, when her daughter got a divorce. "Look who's talking," her daughter said.*

**litterbug** *n., slang, informal* A person who leaves garbage in a public place, such as a park or beach or a street; one who litters. ♦ *Don't be a litterbug; keep the city clean!*

**little does one think** *v. phr.* To not realize; not expect; be hardly aware of. ♦ *Little did Ed think that very soon he would be the father of twin daughters.*

**little frog in a big pond** *or* **small frog in a big pond** *n. phr.* An unimportant person in a large group or organization. ♦ *In a large company, even a fairly successful man is likely to feel like a little frog in a big pond.*

**little pitchers have big ears** Little children often overhear things they are not supposed to hear, or things adults do not expect they would notice.—A proverb. ♦ *Be especially careful not to swear in front of little children. Little pitchers have big ears.*

**little strokes fell great oaks** *a proverb* Lots of minor acts in a sequence can accomplish great tasks. ♦ *The men got discouraged when building the tower seemed impossible. The architect comforted them by saying: "Little strokes fell great oaks."*

**lit up like a Christmas tree** *adj. phr., informal* To be drunk. ♦ *On New Year's Eve Ned was lit up like a Christmas tree.*

**live and learn** You learn more new things the longer you live; you learn by experience.—A proverb. ♦ *"Live and learn," said Mother. "I never knew that the Indians once had a camp where our house is."*

**live and let live** *v. phr.,* To live in the way you prefer and let others live as they wish without being bothered by you. ♦ *Father scolds Mother because she wears her hair in curlers and Mother scolds Father because he smokes a smelly pipe. Grandfather says it's her hair and his pipe; live and let live.*

**live down** *v.* To remove (blame, distrust or unfriendly laughter) by good conduct; cause (a mistake or fault) to be forgiven or forgotten by not repeating it. ♦ *John's business failure hurt him for a long time, but in the end he lived it down.*

**live from hand to mouth** *v. phr.* To live on little money and spend it as fast as it comes in; live without saving for the future; have just enough. ♦ *Mr. Johnson got very little pay, and the family lived from hand to mouth when he had no job.*

**live high off the hog** *or* **eat high on the hog** See EAT (LIVE) HIGH ON THE HOG *or* EAT (LIVE) HIGH OFF THE HOG.

**live in** *or* **room in** *v., informal* To live in the school you attend or the place where you work. ♦ *Jack decided to live in during his freshman year at college.* ♦ *Many women advertise for mother's helpers to room in with families and help take care of children.*

**live in a fool's paradise** *v. phr.* To deceive oneself; tell oneself unreal stories. ♦ *His information is based on a lot of misunderstanding—the poor guy is living in a fool's paradise.*

**live in an ivory tower** *v. phr.* To be blind to real life; live an unrealistically sheltered existence. ♦ *Professor Nebelmacher has no idea of the cost of living; he lives in an ivory tower.*

**live in the fast lane** *v. phr., informal* To live a full and very active life pursuing wealth and success. ♦ *They have been living in the fast lane ever since they arrived in New York City.*

**live it up** *v. phr., informal* To pursue pleasure; enjoy games or night life very much; have fun at places of entertainment. ♦ *Joe had had a hard winter in lonesome places; now he was in town living it up.*

**liven up** *v. phr.* To make oneself or others more lively or active. ♦ *Graduate student applicants livened up when they found out that there were scholarships available at the university.* ♦ *We will need a few clever musicians to liven up this dreary party with some dancing.*

**live off someone** *v. phr.* To be supported by someone. ♦ *Although Eric is already 40 years old, he has no job and continues to live off his elderly parents.*

**live on borrowed time** *v. phr.* To live or last longer than was expected. ♦ *Ever since his operation, Harvey felt he was living on borrowed time.*

**live out** *v.* **1.** To finish (a period of time); spend. ♦ *After retiring, John and his wife lived out their lives in Florida.* **2.** To last through; endure to the end of. ♦ *We lived out the winter on short ration.*

**live out of a suitcase** *v. phr.* To have no permanent residence or a permanent place to hang one's clothes. ♦ *When Jennifer accepted her new job, she had no idea that she would have to live out of a suitcase for six months.*

**live up to** *v.* To act according to; come up to; agree with; follow. ♦ *So far as he could, John had always tried to live up to the example he saw in Lincoln.*

**live wire** *n. phr.* **1.** An electrically charged wire, usually uninsulated. ♦ *The electrician was severely burned by the live wire.* **2.** An alert or energetic person. ♦ *To sell the new merchandise, our company needs several salespeople who are live wires.*

**live within one's means** See CUT YOUR COAT ACCORDING TO YOUR CLOTH.

**living end** *adj., slang* Great; fantastic; the ultimate. ♦ *That show we saw last night was the living end.*

**loaded for bear** *adj. phr., slang* Ready for action; prepared and eager. ♦ *Frank* liked the new merchandise and as he set out on his rounds as a salesman, he felt really loaded for bear. ♦ The football team arrived Friday noon, loaded for bear.

**load up (on)** v. phr. To buy more than one needs for a future time when there might be a shortage. ♦ Florida residents often load up on fresh drinking water and canned goods when there is a hurricane watch.

**loan shark** n. phr. A money lender who charges excessive interest. ♦ Why go to a loan shark when you can borrow from the bank at the legal rate?

**local yokel** n., slang, citizen's band radio jargon City police officer, as opposed to state police or highway patrol. ♦ There's a local yokel westbound on the move.

**lock on** v. phr. To find a mobile target, such as a tank or a boat, by radar, sonar, or radio signal. ♦ The U.S. Army's success in battle is largely due to its ability to lock on even distant targets.

**lock, stock, and barrel** n. phr. Everything; completely. ♦ The robbers emptied the whole house—lock, stock, and barrel.

**lock the barn door after the horse is stolen** To be careful or try to make something safe when it is too late.—A proverb. ♦ After Mary failed the examination, she said she would study hard after that. She wanted to lock the barn door after the horse was stolen.

**lock up** v. phr., slang To be assured of success. ♦ How did your math test go?—I locked it up, I think.

**lodge a complaint** v. phr. To make a complaint; complain. ♦ If our neighbors don't stop this constant noise, I will have to lodge a complaint with the management.

**log in** v. phr. To register at work at the beginning. ♦ All employees at this firm are required to log in at the start of their work day.

**log off** v. phr. To finish using the e-mail or the Internet on one's computer. ♦ Every evening I finish my work at the computer and I log off.

**log on** v. phr. To start work on the Internet or one's e-mail on a computer. ♦ I log on twice a day to see if I have e-mail.

**log out** v. phr. To register at the end of one's work day. ♦ All employees are required to log out at the end of the work day, just as they logged in when they started.

**Lone Star State** n. phr. Texas. ♦ The Lone Star State is one of the largest in the United States, next to only California in size.

**lone wolf** n. A man who likes to work or live alone. ♦ Jones is a good pitcher, but he is a lone wolf.

**long and short of it** n. phr. The essence; the whole story in a nutshell. ♦ The long and short of it is that he is lazy and doesn't really want to find a job.

**long ball** n. A baseball hit far enough to be a home run. ♦ The White Sox need a player who can hit the long ball.

**long face** n. A sad look; disappointed look. ♦ He told the story with a long face.

**long for** v. phr. To desire greatly; miss someone or something badly. ♦ All I am longing for is a little peace and quiet after a hard day's work. ♦ John was longing for Suzie even after they had been divorced for three years.

**longhair**[1] 1. n., slang A male hippie. ♦ Who's that longhair?—It's Joe. 2. An intellectual who prefers classical music to jazz or acid rock. ♦ Catwallender is a regular longhair; he never listens to modern jazz.

**longhair**[2] adj., slang Pertaining to classical art forms, primarily in dancing and music. ♦ Cut out that longhair Mozart Symphony and put on a decent pop record!

**long haul** or **long pull** n., informal 1. A long distance or trip. ♦ It is a long haul to drive across the country. 2. A long length of time during which work continues or something is done; a long time of trying. ♦ A boy crippled by polio may learn to walk again, but it may be a long haul.—Used in the phrase over the long haul. ♦ Over the long haul, an expensive pair of shoes may save you money.

**long shot** n. 1. A bet or other risk taken though not likely to succeed. ♦ The horse was a long shot, but it came in and paid well.

**long time no see** informal, greeting I haven't seen you for quite a long while—a joking imitation of Pidgin English. ♦ *"Long time no see," said Mr. Wong, the furniture shop owner, when we visited him in Hong Kong after several years.*

**long-winded** *adj.* Tedious; overlong; given to too much talking. ♦ *Everyone was bored by the old man's long-winded stories.*

**look after** *also* **see after** *v.* To watch over; attend to. ♦ *John's mother told him to look after his younger brother.* ♦ *When he went to Europe, Mr. Jenkins left his son to see after the business.*

**look a gift horse in the mouth** To complain if a gift is not perfect.—A proverb. Used with a negative. ♦ *John gave Joe a baseball but Joe complained that the ball was old. His father told him not to look a gift horse in the mouth.*

**look alive** *v.* Act lively; be quick; wake up and work; be busy; hurry.—Often used as a command. ♦ *"Look alive there," the boss called.*

**look around** *v. phr.* To reconnoiter the scenery for goods and services or a romantic partner. ♦ *"Look around in California for a nice girlfriend," Aunt Agnes encouraged her nephew, Steve. "Don't be a lone wolf." ♦ We decided to take our time and look around for the best buy before purchasing a house.*

**look at** *v.* To have a way of thinking or feeling toward; think about something in a certain way. ♦ *Is he a hero or a villain? That depends on how you look at it.*

**look at the world through rose-colored glasses** *or* **see with rose-colored glasses** *v. phr.* To see everything as good and pleasant; not see anything hard or bad. ♦ *If you see everything through rose-colored glasses, you will often be disappointed.*

**look back** *v.* To review the past; think of what has happened. ♦ *Murphy looked back on his early struggles as having made him feel especially alive.*

**look bleak** *v.* To indicate misfortune; appear threatening or ruinous. ♦ *As prices dropped lower and lower, things looked bleak for Henry's company.*

**look daggers** *v. phr.* To show anger with a look; express hate or enmity by a look or stare; look fiercely. ♦ *Mary did*

not dare talk back to her father, but she looked daggers.

**look down on** *also* **look down upon** *v.* To think of (a person or thing) as less good or important; feel that (someone) is not as good as you are, or that (something) is not worth having or doing; consider inferior. ♦ *Mary looked down on her classmates because she was better dressed than they were.*

**look down one's nose at** *v. phr., informal* To think of as worthless; feel scorn for. ♦ *The banker's wife has beautiful china cups, and she looked down her nose at the plastic cups that Mrs. Brown used.*

**look facts in the face** *v. phr.* To be practical and realistic. ♦ *"You will never be a mountain climber, Joe," his doctor said. "After all, you have lost a leg in the war. Look facts in the face and be glad that you can walk with an artificial leg."*

**look for** *v.* **1.** To think likely; expect. ♦ *We look for John to arrive any day now.* **2.** To try to find; search for; hunt. ♦ *Fred spent all day looking for a job.* **3.** To do things that cause (your own trouble); make (trouble) for yourself; provoke. ♦ *Joe often gets into fights because he is always looking for trouble.*

**look for a needle in a haystack** See NEEDLE IN A HAY STACK.

**look forward to** *v.* **1.** To expect. ♦ *At breakfast, John looked forward to a difficult day.* **2.** To expect with hope or pleasure. ♦ *Frank was looking forward to that evening's date.*

**look high and low for** *v. phr.* To look everywhere; search all over. ♦ *Everyone has been looking high and low for the lost key but no one could find it.*

**look in on** *v.* To go to see; make a short visit with; make a call on. ♦ *The doctor looked in on Mary each day while she was in the hospital.*

**look in the eye** *or* **look in the face** *v. phr.* To meet with a steady look; to face bravely or without shame. ♦ *We often believe a person who looks us in the eye, but it does not prove he is truthful.*

**look into** *v.* To find out the facts about; examine; study; inspect. ♦ *Mr. Jones said he was looking into the possibility of buying a house.*

**look like a million bucks** See LOOK LIKE A MILLION DOLLARS.

**look like a million dollars** *v. phr., informal* To look well and prosperous; appear healthy and happy and lucky; look pretty and attractive. ♦ *John came back from Florida driving a fine new car, tanned and glowing with health. He looked like a million dollars.*

**look like the cat that ate the canary** *or* **look like the cat that swallowed the canary** *v. phr.* To seem very self-satisfied; look as if you had just had a great success. ♦ *When she won the prize, she went home looking like the cat that swallowed the canary.*

**look on** *or* **look upon** *v.* **1.** To regard; consider; think of. ♦ *The stuff had always been looked on as a worthless factory waste.* **2.** To be an observer; watch without taking part. ♦ *Fred had never been able to do more than look on at athletic sports.*

**look one's age** *v. phr.* To appear in accordance with one's real age. ♦ *Grandpa looks his age, but then he just had his nineth-fifth birthday last week.* ♦ *Agnes sure doesn't look her age. She is fifty-nine, but she doesn't look a day older than thirty-five.*

**look oneself** *v. phr.* To appear self-possessed and well; look or seem in full possession of your abilities and in good health; to appear all right or normal. ♦ *Mary had had a long illness, but now she looked quite herself again.*

**look out** *or* **watch out** *v.* **1.** To take care; be careful; be on guard.—Usually used as a command or warning. ♦ *"Look out!" John called, as the car came toward me.* ♦ *"Look out for the train," the sign at the railroad crossing warns.* **2.** To be alert or watchful; keep watching. ♦ *A collector of antique cars asked Frank to look out for a 1906 gas head lamp.* **3.** *informal* To watch or keep (a person or thing) and do what is needed; provide protection and care. —Used with *for.* ♦ *Lillian looked out for her sister's children one afternoon a week.*

**look out for** *v. phr.* To watch out for; be on the alert. ♦ *There were signs along the highway warning drivers to look out for deer crossing.*

**look over** *v.* To look at and try to learn something about; look at every part or piece of or at every one of; examine; inspect; study. ♦ *We looked over several kinds of new cars before deciding.*

**look over one's shoulder** *v. phr.* To constantly supervise one in an obtrusive and irritating way. ♦ *It drives me crazy when my mom keeps looking over my shoulder while I'm doing my homework.*

**look to** *v.* **1.** To attend to; get ready for; take care of. ♦ *The president assigned a man to look to our needs.* **2.** To go for help to; depend on. ♦ *The child looks to his mother to cure his hurts.*

**look up** *v.* **1.** *informal* To improve in future chances; promise more success. ♦ *The first year was tough, but business looked up after that.* **2.** To search for; hunt for information about; find. ♦ *It is a good habit to look up new words in a dictionary.* **3.** To seek and find. ♦ *While he was in Chicago, Henry looked up a friend of college days.*

**look up to** *v.* To think of (someone) as a good example to copy; honor; respect. ♦ *Young children look up to older ones, so older children should be good examples.*

**look who's talking** See LISTEN WHO'S TALKING.

**loose cannon** *n. phr.* A person who has lost control over himself or herself and is behaving wildly and unpredictably. ♦ *Sheriff Madigan had to be asked to quit his job. After his wife's death he started drinking heavily, and has generally become a loose cannon.*

**loose ends** *n.* **1.** Parts or things that should be finished or put together. ♦ *Mary's composition had many loose ends.*

**loose lips sink ships** *from World War II.* Revealing too much information will eliminate opportunities and may put American troops in harm's way; revealing closely guarded production or manufacturing secrets will give the competition an edge.—A proverb. ♦ *"You're talking too much about your work," the director warned Joe. "Don't you know that loose lips sink ships?"*

**loosen up** *v. phr.* To become relaxed, more informal. ♦ *"Come on, Ted," Bonnie said to her husband. "Loosen up a bit. You've been working too hard lately. Why don't we go to see a good movie or to the concert?"*

**lord it over** *v. phr.* To act as the superior and master of; dominate; be bossy over; control. ♦ *The office manager lorded it over the clerks and typists.*

**lose face** *v.* To be embarrassed or shamed by an error or failure; lose dignity, influence or reputation; lose self-respect or the confidence of others. ♦ *Many Japanese soldiers were killed in World War II because they believed that to give up or retreat would make them lose face.*

**lose ground 1.** To go backward; retreat. ♦ *The soldiers began to lose ground when their leader was killed.* **2.** To become weaker; get worse; not improve. ♦ *The sick man began to lose ground when his cough grew worse.*

**lose heart** *v. phr.* To feel discouraged because of failure; to lose hope of success. ♦ *The team had won no games and it lost heart.*

**lose one's cool** See BLOW ONE'S COOL.

**lose oneself** *v. phr.* **1.** To go wrong; miss your way; become unable to find the right direction. ♦ *Fred lost himself in the confusion of downtown Boston streets.* **2.** To conceal yourself; hide. ♦ *The pickpocket lost himself in the crowd and escaped the police.* **3.** To become deeply interested and forget yourself; become absorbed. ♦ *Sometimes Harry would lose himself in a book for an afternoon at a time.*

**lose one's grip** *v. phr.* To fail in control or command; lose your strength, force, or ability to lead. ♦ *Mr. Jones began to lose his grip: he no longer wanted the hard jobs, and he left decisions to others.*

**lose one's head (over)** *v. phr.* **1.** To panic. ♦ *"Let's not lose our heads," the captain cried. "We have good lifeboats on this vessel."* **2.** To become deeply infatuated with someone. ♦ *Don't lose your head over Jane; she is already married.*

**lose one's heart** *v. phr.* To fall in love; begin to love. ♦ *She lost her heart to the soldier with the broad shoulders and the deep voice.*

**lose one's marbles** *v. phr.* To go mad; become crazed. ♦ *Stan must have lost his marbles; he is hopelessly pursuing a happily married woman.*

**lose one's shirt** *v. phr., slang* To lose all or most of your money. ♦ *Mr. Matthews lost his shirt betting on the horses.*

**lose one's temper** *v. phr.* To lose control over one's anger; to get angry. ♦ *He lost his temper when he broke the key in the lock.*

**lose one's tongue** *v. phr., informal* To be so embarrassed or surprised that you cannot talk. ♦ *The man would always lose his tongue when he was introduced to new people.*

**lose one's touch** *v. phr.* To forget how to do something well, effortlessly, and smoothly. ♦ *John used to be able to sight-read any piece of classical music you put in front of him. Nowadays he fumbles, like a beginner. We can't figure out what made him lose his touch.*

**lose out** *v.* To fail to win; miss first place in a contest; lose to a rival. ♦ *John lost out in the rivalry for Mary's hand in marriage.*

**lose sight of** *v. phr.* **1.** Not to be able to see any longer. ♦ *I watched the plane go higher and higher until I lost sight of it.* **2.** To forget; overlook. ♦ *No matter how rich and famous he became, he never lost sight of the fact that he had been born in the slums.*

**lose sleep over** *v. phr.* To worry about something. ♦ *"The tests have turned out to be negative, you're doing just fine. Just go home and don't lose any sleep over your health," the doctor said to Joe.*

**lose the thread of one's discourse** *or* **lose one's train of thought** *v. phr.* To forget what one was going to say next; forget where one was in telling a story. ♦ *"Help me; where was I?" Joe asked his friends. "I am afraid I lost my train of thought."* ♦ *Older people sometimes lose the thread of their discourse.*

**lose touch** *v. phr., informal* To fail to keep in contact or communication.— Usually used with *with.* ♦ *After she moved to another town, she lost touch with her childhood friends.*

**lose track** *v. phr.* To forget about something; not stay informed; fail to keep a count or record. ♦ *What's the score now? I've lost track.*—Used with *of.* ♦ *John lost track of the money he spent at the circus.*

**lost cause** *n. phr.* A movement that has failed and has no chance to be revived. ♦ *Communism in Eastern Europe has become a lost cause.*

**lost to view** *adj. phr.* Gone from one's sight; off the radar screen; vanished. ♦*At first the marines could see the enemy soldiers in the field, but after a sudden cloudburst, they were lost to view.* ♦*The submarine commander was able to observe the enemy destroyer for a while, but the vessel went off the radar screen and became lost to view.*

**lost upon** *adj.* Wasted. ♦*Tim's generosity is completely lost upon Sue; he can't expect any gratitude from her.*

**loud mouth** *or* **big mouth** *n., slang* A noisy, boastful, or foolish talker. ♦*Fritz is a loud mouth who cannot be trusted with secrets.*

**loud-mouthed** *or* **big-mouthed** *adj., slang* Talking noisily, boastfully, or foolishly. ♦*Fred was a loud-mouthed fellow, whose talk no one listened to.*

**lounge lizard** *n. phr.* A well-dressed male fortune hunter who sits around in bars and other public places, and attends many social events to try to pick up wealthy women through smart conversation. ♦*Harry has the reputation of being a lounge lizard; he is looking for a rich wife.*

**louse up** *v., slang* To throw into confusion; make a mess of; spoil; ruin. ♦*The rain loused up the picnic.*

**love affair** *n.* A friendship between lovers; a romance or courtship. ♦*The love affair of Bob and Jane went on for months.*

**love-in** *n., slang, informal* A festival or occasion to celebrate life, human sensuality, the beauty of nature, human sexuality, and universal love; affairs so conceived by some frequently deteriorate into obscenity and drug using sessions in parody of their stated purpose. ♦*The hippies gathered for a big love-in in the Haight-Ashbury district of San Francisco.*

**lovers' lane** *n.* A hidden road or walk where lovers walk or park in the evening. ♦*A parked car in a lonely lovers' lane often is a chance for holdup men.*

**lowbrow** *n.* A person of limited culture; a nonintellectual. ♦*Some people claim that only lowbrows read the comics.*

**lowdown** *n., slang, informal* The inside facts of a matter; the total truth. ♦*Nixon never gave the American people the lowdown on Watergate.*

**lower the boom** *v. phr., informal* To punish strictly; check or stop fully. ♦*The police lowered the boom on open gambling.*

**low-key** *adj.* Relaxed and easygoing. ♦*Surprisingly, dinner with the governor was a low-key affair.*

**luck of the Devil** *or* **the Devil's own luck** *n. phr.* Incredible, fantastic luck. ♦*John keeps winning lots of money in Las Vegas, and hardly ever loses. He appears to have the luck of the Devil.*

**luck out** *v. phr., slang, informal* **1.** Suddenly to get lucky when in fact the odds are against one's succeeding. ♦*I was sure I was going to miss the train as I was three minutes late, but I lucked out; the train was five minutes late.* **2.** To be extraordinarily fortunate. ♦*Catwallender really lucked out at Las Vegas last month; he came home with $10,000 in cash.* **3.** (By sarcastic opposition) to be extremely unfortunate; to be killed. ♦*Those poor marines sure lucked out in Saigon, didn't they?*

**lucky star** *n.* A certain star or planet which, by itself or with others, is seriously or jokingly thought to bring a person good luck and success in life. ♦*Ted was unhurt in the car accident, for which he thanked his lucky stars.*

**lump in one's throat** *n. phr.* A feeling (as of grief or pride) so strong that you almost sob. ♦*The bride's mother had a lump in her throat.*

**lump sum** *n.* The complete amount; a total agreed upon and to be paid at one time. ♦*The case was settled out of court with the plaintiff receiving a lump sum of half a million dollars for damages.*

**lunar module (L.M.)** *or* **Lem** *n., Space English* That portion of the rocket assemblage on a flight to the Moon in which the astronauts descend to the Moon's surface. ♦*Building the L.M. was one of the most expensive parts of the American space program.*

**lust for** *v. phr.* To physically yearn for; hanker after; want something very strongly. ♦*Ed has been lusting after Meg for a very long time.*

**mad about** *adj. phr.* **1.** Angry about. ♦*What is Harriet so mad about?* **2.** Enthusiastic about. ♦*Dan is mad about pop music.*

**mad as a hatter** *or* **mad as a March hare** *adj. phr.* Not able to think right; crazy. ♦*Anyone who thinks the moon is made of green cheese is mad as a hatter.*

**mad as a hornet** *or* **mad as a wet hen** *adj. phr., informal* In a fighting mood; very angry. ♦*When my father sees the dent in his fender, he'll be mad as a hornet.* ♦*Mrs. Harris was mad as a wet hen when the rabbits ate her tulips.*

**made of money** *adj. phr.* Very rich; wealthy. ♦*Mr. Jones buys his children everything they want. He must be made of money.*

**made-to-measure** *or* **tailor-made** *adj.* Made to fit a special set of measurements or needs. ♦*John has a new made-to-measure suit.*

**made to order** *adj. phr.* **1.** Made specially in the way the buyer wants instead of all the same in large amounts; made especially for the buyer. ♦*Mr. Black's clothes were all made to order.* **2.** Just right. ♦*The weather was made to order for the hike.*

**magic carpet** *n.* **1.** A rug said to be able to transport a person through the air to any place he wishes. ♦*The caliph of Baghdad flew on his magic carpet to Arabia.* **2.** Any form of transportation that is comfortable and easy enough to seem magical. ♦*Mr. Smith's new car drove so smoothly it seemed like a magic carpet.*

**maiden speech** *n. phr.* One's first public speech, usually before some legislative body. ♦*It was the new congressman's maiden speech and everyone was listening very keenly.*

**maiden voyage** *n. phr.* The first voyage of a boat. ♦*The* Titanic *sank on her maiden voyage to America from England.*

**mail order** *n. phr.* A purchase made by mail. ♦*If you don't have a chance to go to a store, you can sometimes make a purchase by mail order.*

**main drag** *n., colloquial* **1.** The most important street or thoroughfare in a town. ♦*Lincoln Avenue is the main drag of our town.* **2.** The street where the dope pushers and the prostitutes are. ♦*Wells Street is the main drag of Chicago, actionwise.*

**main squeeze** *n., slang* **1.** The top ranking person in an organization or in a neighborhood; an important person, such as one's boss. ♦*Mr. Bronchard is the main squeeze in this office.* **2.** The top person in charge of an illegal operation, such as drug sales, etc. ♦*Before we can clean up this part of town, we must arrest the main squeeze.* **3.** One's principal romantic or sexual partner. ♦*The singer's main squeeze is a member of the band.*

**majority leader** *n.* The leader of the political party with the most votes in a legislative house. ♦*The majority leader of the House of Representatives tried to get the members of his party to support the bill.*

**make a beeline for** *v. phr.* To go in a straight line toward. ♦*When the bell rang Ted made a beeline for the door of the classroom.*

**make** *or* **build a better mousetrap and the world will beat a path to your door** Often heard when one invents an improved version of a commonly used item, comparable in its simplicity to a mousetrap.—*A proverb.* ♦*Volkswagen improved the little car called "the bug." Goes to show that if you build a better mousetrap, the world will beat a path to your door.*

**make a big deal about** *v. phr., informal* To exaggerate an insignificant event. ♦*Jeff said, "I'm sorry I banged into you in the dark. Don't make a big deal out of it."*

**make a blunder** *v. phr.* To make a bad mistake; spoil something by carelessness. ♦*The chancellor of our university was forced to resign because administrators at our medical school made a blunder with experimental subjects.*

**make a clean breast of** *v. phr.* To admit (your guilt); tell all about (your wrong doing); confess everything. ♦*Arthur worried because he cheated on the test, and finally he went to the teacher and made a clean breast of it.*

**make a clean sweep of** *v. phr.* **1.** Achieve a complete victory. ♦*In 1980 the Reagan Republicans made a clean sweep of the western states.* **2.** To eliminate thoroughly and completely. ♦*The new attorney general is expected to make a clean sweep of all the old administrative personnel.*

**make a comeback** *v. phr.* To reappear on the social, sports, artistic, or professional scene after a period of inactivity, absence, or illness. ♦*The legendary Michael Jordan made a comeback when he came out of retirement and started playing basketball again.*

**make a day of it** *v. phr., informal* To do something all day. ♦*When they go to the beach they take a picnic lunch and make a day of it.*

**make a dent in** *v. phr., informal* To make less by a very small amount; reduce slightly.—Usually used in the negative or with such qualifying words as *hardly* or *barely.* ♦*Mary studied all afternoon and only made a dent in her homework.*

**make a difference** *or* **make the difference** *v. phr.* To change the nature of something or a situation; be important; matter. ♦*John's good score on the test made the difference between his passing or failing the course.*

**make a face** *v. phr., informal* To twist your face; make an ugly expression on your face (as by sticking out your tongue). ♦*The boy made a face at his teacher when she turned her back.*

**make a fast buck** See FAST BUCK.

**make a federal case out of** See MAKE A BIG DEAL ABOUT, MAKE A MOUNTAIN OUT OF A MOLEHILL.

**make a fool of** *or (informal)* **make a monkey of** *v. phr.* To make (someone) look foolish. ♦*The boy made a fool of himself.*

**make after** *v. phr.* To chase something; run after something. ♦*The mouse escaped from the kitchen corner and the cat made after it.*

**make a fuss over** *v. phr.* **1.** To quarrel about something or someone. ♦*I want you kids to stop fussing about who gets the drumstick.* **2.** To be excessively concerned about someone or something; worry. ♦*Let's not fuss over such an insignificant problem!* **3.** To show exaggerated care or preoccupation about a person or an animal. ♦*Aunt Hermione is constantly fussing over her old lapdog.*

**make a go of** *v. phr.* To turn into a success. ♦*He is both energetic and highly skilled at trading; he is sure to make a go of any business that holds his interest.*

**make a hit** *v. phr., informal* To be successful; be well-liked; get along well. ♦*Mary's new red dress made a hit at the party.*

**make a killing** *v. phr.* To earn or suddenly win a very large sum of money. ♦*Herb bought a lot of soybean stock when the price was low and sold it when the price went up. Small wonder he made a huge killing.*

**make a living** *v. phr.* To earn one's livelihood. ♦*It is easier to make a living in the United States than in many other countries.*

**make allowances** *v. phr.* To judge results by the circumstances. ♦*When a small boy is helping you, you must make allowances for his age.*

**make a long story short** *v. phr.* To summarize a lengthy narrative. ♦*"So, to make a long story short," he said, "I made a killing on the stock market."*

**make a match** *v. phr.* To bring a man and woman together for the purpose of an engagement or marriage. ♦*Sheila's aunt is anxious to make a match between her and an attractive, wealthy man.*

**make a mess of** See SCREW UP.

**make a motion** *v. phr.* To propose in some committee meeting or legislative group that a certain action be taken. ♦*The secretary made a motion that the minutes of the last meeting be accepted.*

**make a mountain out of a molehill** To think a small problem is a big one; try to make something unimportant seem important. ♦*You're not hurt badly, Johnny. Stop trying to make a mountain out of a molehill with crying.*

**make a move** *v. phr.* **1.** To budge; change places. ♦*"If you make a move," the masked gangster said, "I'll start shooting."* **2.** To go home after dinner or a party. ♦*"I guess it's time to make a move," Roy said at the end of the party.*

**make a name for oneself** *v. phr.* To become recognized in a field of endeavor; become a celebrity. ♦*Bill has made a name for himself both as a pianist and as a composer.*

**make an end of** *v. phr.* To make (something) end; put a stop to; stop. ♦*To make an end of rumors that the house was haunted, a reporter spent the night there.*

**make an example of** *v. phr.* To punish (someone) publicly to show what happens when someone does wrong. ♦*The Pilgrims made an example of a thief by putting him in the stocks.*

**make an exhibition of oneself** *v. phr.* To behave foolishly or embarrassingly in public. ♦*Stop drinking so much and making an exhibition of yourself.*

**make an issue** *v. phr.* To complain about something; protest against a certain way of treatment; to animatedly discuss and bring something into question. ♦*The mailman always mixes up the letters, putting them into the wrong boxes, but he is such a nice helpful person that we won't make an issue over this.*

**make a night of it** *v. phr., informal* To spend the whole night at an activity. ♦*The boys and girls at the dance made a night of it.*

**make a nuisance of oneself** *v. phr.* To constantly bother others. ♦*The screaming kids made a nuisance of themselves around the swimming pool.*

**make a pass at** *v. phr., slang, informal* Make advances toward a member of the opposite sex (usually man to a woman) with the goal of seducing the person. ♦*We've been dating for four weeks but Joe has never even made a pass at me.*

**make a pig of oneself** *v. phr., informal* To overindulge; eat too much. ♦*Mary said, "This dessert is so delicious that I am going to make a pig of myself and have some more."*

**make a play for** *v. phr., slang* To try to get the interest or liking of; flirt with; attract. ♦*Bob made a play for the pretty new girl.*

**make a plug for** *or* **put in a plug for** To ask for a favor; recommend; promote a cause or a friend. ♦*"Let me put in a plug for publishing this article by one of my colleagues," Professor Fish asked the editor of the Journal of American Speech.*

**make a point** *v. phr.* To try hard; make a special effort.—Used with *of* and a verbal noun. ♦*He made a point of remembering to get his glasses fixed.*

**make a practice of** *v. phr.* To make a habit of; do regularly. ♦*Make a practice of being on time for work.*

**make a quick buck** See FAST BUCK.

**make a racket** *v. phr.* To cause a lot of noisy disturbance. ♦*I wish the kids playing in the street wouldn't make such a racket while I'm trying to take a nap.*

**make a scene** *v. phr.* To act hysterically; attract unfavorable attention. ♦*I didn't want Kate to make a scene in front of all of those people, so I gave her the money she wanted.*

**make a splash** *v. phr.* To cause a sensation. ♦*The brilliant young pianist, barely 14 years old, made quite a splash on the concert circuit.*

**make a stab at** *v. phr.* To try doing something at random without sufficient preparation. ♦*The singer was not familiar with the aria but she decided to make a stab at it anyhow.*

**make a stand** *v. phr.* **1.** To take a firm position on an issue. ♦*He keeps talking about politics but he never makes a stand for what he believes in.* **2.** To take up a defensive position against the enemy. ♦*The retreating troops decided to make a stand by the river.*

**make a touch** *v. phr.* To borrow money; try to borrow money. ♦*He is known to make a touch whenever he is hard up for cash.*

**make a virtue of necessity** *v. phr.* Make the best of things as they are; do cheerfully what you do. ♦*After Mr. Wilson lost all his money, he made a virtue of necessity and found a new and interesting life as a teacher.*

**make away with** *v., informal* Take; carry away; cause to disappear. ♦*Two masked men held up the clerk and made away with the payroll.*

**make-believe** *n.* False; untrue; created by illusion. ♦*The creatures of* Star Wars *are all make-believe.*

**make believe** *v.* To act as if something is true while one knows it is not; pretend. ♦*Let's make believe we have a million dollars.*

**make book** *v. phr.* To serve as a bookmaker taking bets on the horse races.

♦ *The police were out to prosecute anybody who made book illegally.*

**make bricks without straw** *v. phr.* To make something without the wherewithal; do something the hard way; do a job under hard conditions. ♦*John could not go to a library, and writing the report was a job of making bricks without straw.*

**make certain** *v. phr.* Ascertain; assure; insure. ♦*I need delivery confirmation on that priority mail. I want to make certain that my friend got my manuscript.*

**make clear** *or* **make it perfectly clear** *v. phr.* To clarify; explain; assert forcefully. ♦*"Let me make clear what I think," the director said. "People absent without a doctor's certificate will get their pay reduced.* ♦*I want to make it perfectly clear that cheating on final exams will result in disciplinary action.*

**make conversation** *v. phr.* To talk with someone just so that there will be talk. ♦*John made conversation with the stranger so that he would not feel left out.*

**make do** *v. phr.* To use a poor substitute when one does not have the right thing. ♦*Many families manage to make do on very little income.*

**make ends meet** *v. phr.* To have enough money to pay one's bills; earn what it costs to live. ♦*Both husband and wife had to work to make ends meet.*

**make eyes at** *v. phr., informal* To look at a girl or boy in a way that tries to attract him to you; flirt. ♦*The other girls disliked her way of making eyes at their boyfriends instead of finding one of her own.*

**make faces at** *v. phr.* To grimace; scowl. ♦*"Stop making faces at each other, you children," my aunt said, "and start eating."*

**make for** *v.* To go toward; start in the direction of. ♦*The children took their ice skates and made for the frozen pond.*

**make free with** *v.* **1.** To take or use (things) without asking. ♦*Bob makes free with his roommate's clothes.* **2.** To act toward (someone) in a rude or impolite way. ♦*The girls don't like Ted because he makes free with them.*

**make friends** *v. phr.* To become friends; form a friendship. ♦*You can make friends with an elephant by giving him peanuts.*

**make fun of** *or* **poke fun at** *v. phr., informal* To joke about; laugh at; tease; mock. ♦*Men like to make fun of the trimmings on women's hats.* ♦*James poked fun at the new pupil because her speech was not like the other pupils.*

**make good** *v. phr.* **1.** To do what one promised to do; make something come true. ♦*Joe made good his boast to swim across the lake.* **2.** To compensate; pay for loss or damage. ♦*The policeman told the boy's parents that the boy must make good the money he had stolen or go to jail.* **3.** To do good work at one's job; succeed. ♦*Kate wanted to be a nurse. She studied and worked hard in school. Then she got a job in the hospital and made good as a nurse.*

**make good time** *v. phr.* To make unimpeded progress on a journey; arrive at one's destination sooner than estimated. ♦*There was not much traffic on the expressway so we made good time on our way to the airport.*

**make haste** *v. phr.* To move fast; hurry. ♦*Mary saw that she had hurt Jane's feelings, and made haste to say she was sorry.*

**make hay while the sun shines** *v. phr.* To do something at the right time; not wait too long. ♦*Dick had a free hour so he made hay while the sun shone and got his lesson for the next day.*

**make head or tail of** *v. phr., informal* To see the why of; finding a meaning in; understand.—Used in negative, conditional, and interrogative sentences. ♦*Can you make head or tail of the letter?*

**make headway** *v. phr.* To move forward; make progress. ♦*The university is making headway with its campus reorganization project.*

**make it hot** *v. phr., informal* To bring punishment; cause trouble. ♦*Dick threatened to make it hot for anyone who tied knots in his pajama legs again.*

**make it snappy** *v. phr., informal* To move quickly; be fast; hurry.—Usually used as a command. ♦*"Make it snappy," Mother said, "or we'll be late for the movie."*

**make it to the big time** *v. phr., informal* To succeed in becoming famous and rich, a part of the elite. ♦ *Kim Novak used to work as a supermarket checkout girl before she was discovered by a Hollywood director; after that she made it to the big time in Alfred Hitchcock's films.*

**make it with** *v. phr., slang, informal* **1.** To be accepted by a group. ♦ *Joe finally made it with the in crowd in Hollywood.* **2.** *vulgar* To have sex with (someone). ♦ *I wonder if Joe has made it with Sue.*

**make light of** *v. phr.* To treat an important matter as if it were trivial. ♦ *One ought to know which problems to make light of and which ones to handle seriously.*

**make little of** *v. phr.* To make (something) seem unimportant; belittle. ♦ *Tom made little of his saving the drowning boy.*

**make love** *v. phr.* **1.** To be warm, loving, and tender toward someone of the opposite sex; try to get him or her to love you too. ♦ *There was moonlight on the roses and he made love to her in the porch swing.* **2.** To have sexual relations with (someone). ♦ *It is rumored that Alfred makes love to every girl he hires as a secretary.*

**make merry** *v. phr., literary* To have fun, laugh, and be happy. ♦ *In Aesop's fable the grasshopper made merry while the ant worked and saved up food.*

**make mincemeat (out) of** *v. phr.* To destroy completely. ♦ *The defense attorney made mincemeat of the prosecution's argument.*

**make neither head nor tail of** *v. phr.* To be unable to figure something out. ♦ *This puzzle is so complicated that I can make neither head nor tail of it.*

**make no bones** *v. phr., informal* **1.** To have no doubts; not to worry about right or wrong; not to be against.— Used with *about.* ♦ *The boss made no bones about hiring extra help for the holidays.* **2.** To make no secret; not keep from talking; admit.—Used with *about* or *of the fact.* ♦ *John thinks being poor is no disgrace and he makes no bones of the fact.*

**make no mistake** *v. phr,. always in the negative* To be certain; understand me well; don't think wrong thoughts. ♦ *"We suffered great losses and a ter-*

*rible shock on 9/11/01, but make no mistake—no terrorist shall ever intimidate us Americans," the mayor of New York said.*

**make of** *v. phr.* To interpret; understand. ♦ *What do you make of his sudden decision to go to Africa?*

**make off** *v.* To go away; run away; leave. ♦ *A thief stopped John on a dark street and made off with his wallet.*

**make one feel at home** *v. phr.* To be hospitable; welcome; make someone feel at ease. ♦ *They are very popular hosts because they always manage to make their guests feel at home.*

**make one out to be** *v. phr.* To accuse someone of being something. ♦ *Don't make me out to be such a grouch; I am really quite happy-go-lucky.*

**make one's bed and lie in it** To be responsible for what you have done and so to have to accept the bad results. ♦ *Billy smoked one of his father's cigars and now he is sick. He made his bed, now let him lie in it.*

**make one's blood boil** or **make the blood boil** *v. phr., informal* To make someone very angry. ♦ *When someone calls me a liar it makes my blood boil.*

**make one's day** *v. phr.* To cause one to feel to have been successful; to please someone. (Often used in the imperative as an exclamation; used as a threat.) ♦ *"Go ahead and try to shoot me!" the sheriff cried at the outlaws reaching for his own gun. "Make my day!"*

**make oneself at home** *v. phr.* To feel comfortable; act as if you were in your own home. ♦ *If you get to my house before I do, help yourself to a drink and make yourself at home.*

**make oneself scarce** *v. phr., slang* To leave quickly; go away. ♦ *The boys made themselves scarce when they saw the principal coming to stop their noise.*

**make one's head spin** *v. phr.* To be bewildered; be confused. ♦ *It makes my head spin to think about the amount of work I still have to do.*

**make one's mark** *v. phr.* To become known to many people; do well the work you started to do; make a reputation. ♦ *Shakespeare made his mark as a playwright.*

**make one's mouth water** *v. phr.* **1.** To look or smell very good; make you want very much to eat or drink something you see or smell. ♦*The pies in the store window made Dan's mouth water.* **2.** To be attractive; make you want to have something very much. ♦*Judy loves Swiss chocolates, and the ones in the store window made her mouth water.*

**make one's pile** *v. phr.* To make one's fortune. ♦*The rich man made his pile in the stock market.*

**make one's skin crawl** *v. phr.* To disgust someone; horrify and upset someone with revulsion. ♦*The sight of the enormous scorpion climbing up her bed, made Suzie's skin crawl.* ♦*The discovery of a dead body in the closet made everyone's skin crawl.*

**make one's way** *v. phr.* **1.** To go forward with difficulty; find a path for yourself. ♦*They made their way through the crowd.* **2.** To do many hard things to earn a living; make a life work for yourself. ♦*He was anxious to finish school and make his own way in the world.*

**make one tick** *v. phr.* To cause to operate; to motivate. ♦*He is so secretive that we are unable to figure out what makes him tick.*

**make or break** *v. phr.* To bring complete success or failure, victory or defeat. ♦*Playing the role of Hamlet will make or break the young actor.*

**make out** *v.* **1.** To write the facts asked for (as in an application blank or a report form); fill out. ♦*The teacher made out the report cards and gave them to the students to take home.* **2.** To see, hear, or understand by trying hard. ♦*It was dark, and we could not make out who was coming along the road.* **3.** *informal* To make someone believe; show; prove. ♦*Charles and Bob had a fight, and Charles tried to make out that Bob started it.* **4.** *informal* Do well enough; succeed. ♦*John's father wanted John to do well in school and asked the teacher how John was making out.* **5.** To kiss or pet. ♦*What are Jack and Jill up to?—They're making out on the back porch.*

**make out a check** *v. phr.* To write one a check. ♦*"How can I pay you?" Mrs. Smith asked the clerk in the store. "Just make out a check to Cash," the clerk replied.*

**make over** *v.* **1.** To change by law something from one owner to another owner; change the name on the title (lawful paper) from one owner to another. ♦*Mr. Brown made over the title to the car to Mr. Jones.* **2.** To make something look different; change the style of. ♦*He asked the tailor to make over his pants.*

**make room for someone or something** *v. phr.* To accommodate a person physically; create space for someone; allow into one's life or sphere of activities. ♦*"So you're pregnant again?" Barry asked his wife, Donna Jo. "We already have four children," she answered. "We can always make room for a fifth one.*

**make rounds** *v. phr.* To travel the same route, making several stops along the way. ♦*The doctor makes the rounds of the hospital rooms.*

**make sense** *v. phr.* **1.** To be something you can understand or explain; not be difficult or strange. ♦*The explanation in the school book made no sense because the words were hard.* **2.** To seem right to do; sound reasonable or practical. ♦*Does it make sense to let little children play with matches?*

**make sit up** *v. phr.* To shock to attention; surprise; create keen interest. ♦*Her sudden appearance at the party and her amazingly low-cut dress made us all sit up.*

**make small talk** See SMALL TALK.

**make (something) fly** *v. phr.* To make something work; render something viable or functional. ♦*Bob has terrific ideas about how to improve sales, but he can't make them fly.*

**make something of** *v. phr.* **1.** To make (something) seem important. ♦*When girls see another girl with a boy, they often try to make something of it.* **2.** To start a fight over; use as an excuse to start a quarrel. ♦*Ann didn't like what Mary said about her. She tried to make something of what Mary said.*

**make sport of** See MAKE FUN OF.

**make sure** *v. phr.* To see about something yourself; look at to be sure. ♦*Father makes sure that all the lights are off before he goes to bed.*

**makes you think, doesn't it** *adj. phr.* Something that makes one wonder or reconsider a proposal; reevaluate a situation. ♦ *"Susie is really nice, and I like her a lot,"* Bob said, *"but she smokes three packs of cigarettes a day. Makes you think, doesn't it?"*

**make the best of** *v. phr.* To do something you do not like to do and not complain; accept with good humor. ♦ *The girl did not like to wash dishes but she made the best of it.*

**make the feathers fly** *v. phr., informal* 1. To enjoy working; be strong and work hard. ♦ *When Mrs. Hale did her spring cleaning she made the feathers fly.*

**make the grade** *v. phr., informal* 1. To make good; succeed. ♦ *It takes hard study to make the grade in school.* 2. To meet a standard; qualify. ♦ *That whole shipment of cattle made the grade as prime beef.*

**make the most of** *v. phr.* To do the most you can with; get the most from; use to the greatest advantage. ♦ *She planned the weekend in town to make the most of it.*

**make the punishment fit the crime** Punishment should not be too severe or too light; it should be measured and proportional to the transgression committed.—A proverb. ♦ *In the Middle Ages if someone stole a chicken, his or her hand was cut off as punishment. It's probably worth two weeks in jail, but no more. The judges back then didn't know how to make the punishment fit the crime.*

**make the scene** *v. phr., slang* To be present; to arrive at a certain place or event. ♦ *I am too tired to make the scene; let's go home.*

**make the supreme sacrifice** *v. phr.* To die. ♦ *The American military honors those who make the supreme sacrifice for their country.*

**make time** *v. phr., slang* 1. To be successful in arriving at a designated place in short or good time. ♦ *We're supposed to be there at 6 P.M., and it's only 5:30—we're making good time.* 2. To be successful in making sexual advances to someone. ♦ *Joe sure is making time with Sue, isn't he?*

**make tracks** *v. phr., informal* To go fast; get a speedy start; hurry. ♦ *Man, it's time we made tracks!*

**makeup** *n.* (stress on *make*) 1. Cosmetics. ♦ *All the actors and actresses put on a lot*

of makeup. 2. *Attributive auxiliary* in lieu of, or belated. ♦ *The professor gave a makeup to the sick students.*

**make up** *v.* (stress on *up*) 1. To make by putting things or parts together. ♦ *A car is made up of many different parts.* 2. To invent; think and say something that is new or not true. ♦ *Jean makes up stories to amuse her little brother.* 3a. To do or provide (something lacking or needed); do or supply (something not done, lost, or missed); get back; regain; give back; repay. ♦ *I have to make up the test I missed last week.* 3b. To do what is lacking or needed; do or give what should be done or given; get or give back what has been lost, missed, or not done; get or give instead; pay back.—Used with *for.* ♦ *We made up for lost time by taking an airplane instead of a train.* 4. To put on lipstick and face paint powder. ♦ *Clowns always make up before a circus show.* ♦ *Tom watched his sister make up her face for her date.* 5. To become friends again after a quarrel. ♦ *Mary and Joan quarreled, but made up after a while.* 6. To try to make friends with someone; to win favor.—Followed by *to.* ♦ *The new boy made up to the teacher by sharpening her pencils.*

**make up one's mind** *v. phr.* To choose what to do; decide. ♦ *They made up their minds to sell the house.*

**make waves** *v. phr., informal* Make one's influence felt; create a disturbance, a sensation. ♦ *Joe Catwallender is the wrong man for the job; he is always trying to make waves.*

**make way** *v. phr.* To move from in front so someone can go through; stand aside. ♦ *When older men retire they make way for younger men to take their places.*

**malfunction** *n. phr., slang* A problem. ♦ *Stop complaining. What's your malfunction?*

**mama's boy** *n. phr., informal* A boy who depends too much on his mother; a sissy. ♦ *The other boys called Tommy a mama's boy because he wouldn't come out to play unless his mother stayed near him.*

**man *or* the man** *n., slang* 1. The police; a policeman. ♦ *I am gonna turn you in to* *the man.* **2.** The boss; the leader; the most important figure in an organization or outfit. ◆*The man will decide.*

**man-about-town** *n. phr.* A sophisticate; an idler; a member of café society; one who knows where the best plays and concerts are given. ◆*Ask Mark where to go when you're in New York City; he's a real man-about-town.*

**man in the moon** *n. phr.* An imaginary or nonexistent person (often used to indicate a person of ignorance). ◆*Stop asking me such difficult questions about nuclear physics; I know as much about it as the man in the moon.*

**man in the street** *n. phr.* The man who is just like most other men; the average man; the ordinary man. ◆*The newspaper took a poll of the man in the street.*

**man of few words** *n. phr.* A man who doesn't talk very much; a man who says only what is needed. ◆*The principal is a man of few words, but the pupils know what he wants.*

**man of his word** *n. phr.* A man who keeps his promises and does the things he agrees to do; a man who can be trusted. ◆*My uncle is a man of his word.*

**man of letters** *n. phr.* A writer; an author; a scholar. ◆*Chekhov was not only a practicing physician but also a first-rate man of letters.*

**man of means** *n. phr.* A rich person. ◆*He became a man of means by successfully playing the stock market.*

**man of straw** *or* **straw man** *n. phr.* A phony issue; an imaginary adversary; an allegation, made about a set of opponents or opposing theories, created to destroy it more easily in a self-serving, one-sided argument. ◆*It is bad scholarship to set up a man of straw to prove one's point.*

**man-of-war** *n. phr.* **1.** A stinging jellyfish in the Gulf of Mexico. ◆*"No swimming today," the sign said, "as we have a man-of-war alert."* **2.** A large battleship displaying its national flag or insignia. ◆*The shipwreck victims were picked up by an American man-of-war.* **3.** The albatross bird. ◆*After several days at sea we noticed some men-of-war majestically sailing through the skies.*

**man-to-man** *adj.* Honest and full in the telling; not hiding anything embar-rassing. ◆*Tom and his father had a man-to-man talk about his smoking pot.*

**many a** *adj.* Many (persons or things)—Used with a singular noun. ◆*Many a boy learns to swim before he can read.*

**many moons ago** *adv. phr.* A long, long time ago. ◆*Many moons ago, when I was young, I was able to dance all night.*

**map out** *v. phr.* To arrange; lay out; plan. ◆*The candidate will meet with his campaign manager tomorrow to map out his campaign strategy.*

**mare's nest** *n. phr.* Something that doesn't exist; a discovery that proves to be worthless. ◆*He claims that he has discovered a gasoline substitute but we suspect it will turn out to be a mare's nest.*

**markdown** *n.* (stress on *mark*) A reduction in price. ◆*Joan asked, "Do you like my new sandals? They were markdowns at Marshall Field's."*

**mark down** *v. phr.* (stress on *down*) **1.** To lower the price. ◆*The department store marked down their prices on women's sandals.* **2.** To give a poor grade to a student. ◆*Peter was marked down for his numerous spelling errors.* **3.** To make a written note of something. ◆*Here is my phone number; mark it down.*

**marked man** *n. phr.* A man whose behavior has made him the object of suspicion; a man whose life may be in danger. ◆*When Dave dared to criticize the dictator openly, he became a marked man.*

**mark my words** See READ MY LIPS.

**mark off** *v. phr.* Mark with lines; lay out in sections. ◆*The field will be marked off in accordance with the special track events that will take place tomorrow.*

**mark one's words** *v. phr.* To pay close attention to what one says; an emphatic expression indicating prophecy. ◆*"It will certainly rain tomorrow," he said. "Mark my words."*

**mark time** *v. phr.* **1.** To move the feet up and down as in marching, but not going forward. ◆*The officer made the soldiers mark time as a punishment.* **2.** To be idle; waiting for something to happen. ◆*The teacher marked time until all the children were ready for the test.* **3.** To seem to be working or doing something, but really not doing it. ♦ *It was so hot that the workmen just marked time.*

**marry in haste, repent at leisure** If one accepts a deal, job, or position too fast, one may come to regret it later.—A proverb. ♦ *"I am really unhappy with this overseas assignment," John complained to his brother Ted. "Well, I told you to wait and look around some more, remember?" Ted answered. "Marry in haste, repent at leisure, as the saying goes."*

**marry money** *v. phr.* To marry a rich person. ♦ *Ellen married money when she became Hal's wife.*

**masking tape** *n.* A paper tape that is stuck around the edges of a surface being painted to keep the paint off the surface next to it. ♦ *The painters put masking tape around the window frames to keep the paint off the glass.*

**master copy** *n.* **1.** A perfect text to which all copies are made to conform; a corrected version used as a standard by printers. ♦ *The master copy must be right, because if it isn't, the mistakes in it will be repeated all through the edition.* **2.** A stencil from which other copies are made. ♦ *Mr. Brown told his secretary to save the master copy so that they could run off more copies whenever they needed them.* .

**master key** *n. phr.* A key that opens a set of different locks. ♦ *The building janitor has a master key to all of the apartments in this building.*

**mastermind** *v.* To create; direct; invent the central plan for several individuals to follow. ♦ *Lenin masterminded the Bolshevik Revolution in Russia.*

**mastermind** *n.* A person who supplies the intelligence for a project and/or undertakes its management. ♦ *Winston Churchill was the mastermind in the war against Hitler.*

**master of ceremonies** *or* **M.C.** *or* **emcee** *n.* The person in charge of introducing the various participants in a show or entertainment. ♦ *Bob Hope was the M.C. of many memorable shows.*

**matter of course** *n. phr.* Something always done; the usual way; habit; rule. ♦ *Bank officers ask questions as a matter of course when someone wants to borrow money.*

**matter of fact** *n. phr.* Something that is really true; something that can be proved. ♦ *The town records showed that it was a matter of fact that the two boys were brothers.* Used for emphasis in the phrase *as a matter of fact.* ♦ *I didn't go yesterday, and as a matter of fact, I didn't go all week.*

**matter-of-fact** *adj.* **1.** Simply telling or showing the truth; not explaining or telling more. ♦ *The newspaper gave a matter-of-fact account of the murder trial.* **2.** Showing little feeling or excitement or trouble; seeming not to care much. ♦ *He was a very matter-of-fact person.*

**matter of opinion** *n. phr.* Something that may or may not be true; something that people do not all agree on. ♦ *Whether or not he was a good general is a matter of opinion.*

**matter of record** *n. phr.* A fact or event that is kept officially as a legal record. ♦ *A birth certificate or a marriage license is a matter of record.*

**M.C.** *or* **emcee** *v.* To act as master of ceremonies at a show. ♦ *The famous actor emceed the entire television show.*

**mean as a junkyard dog** *adj. phr.* Exceedingly nasty. ♦ *It's OK if you disagree with me, but why do you have to be mean as a junkyard dog?*

**mean beans** *or* **amount to a hill of beans** *adj. phr., slang* To amount to nothing or extremely little. ♦ *Ted boasts a lot about his new invention, but frankly, the whole thing means beans.* ♦ *Uncle Noam's new ideas don't amount to a hill of beans.*

**mean business** *v. phr., informal* To decide strongly to do what you plan to do; really mean it; be serious. ♦ *The boss said he would fire us if we didn't work harder and he means business.*

**means to an end** *n. phr.* An action leading to some end or purpose. ♦ *Money for him was just a means to an end; actually he wanted power.*

**mean well** *v. phr.* To have good intentions. ♦ *Fred generally means well, but he has a tendency to be tactless.*

**measure off** *v. phr.* To mark by measuring. ♦ *She measured off three yards with which to make the new dress.*

**measure up** *v.* To be equal; be of fully high quality; come up. ♦ *Lois' school work didn't measure up to her ability.*

**meatball** *n., slang* A dull, boring, slow-witted, or uninteresting person. ♦ *You'll never get an interesting story out of that meatball—stop inviting him.*

**meet halfway** See GO HALFWAY.

**meet one's death** *v. phr.* To die. ♦ *Algernon met his death in a car accident.*

**meet one's eye** *v. phr.* To be in plain view or come into plain view; appear clearly or obviously. ♦ *On a first reading the plan looked good, but there was more to it than met the eye.*

**meet one's match** *v. phr.* To encounter someone as good as oneself. ♦ *The champion finally met his match and lost the game.*

**meet one's Waterloo** *v. phr.* To be defeated; lose an important contest. ♦ *After seven straight victories the team met its Waterloo.*

**meet up with** *v. phr.* To meet by accident; come upon without planning or expecting to. ♦ *The family would have arrived on time, but they met up with a flat tire.*

**meet with** *v.* **1.** To meet (someone), usually by accident. ♦ *In the woods he met with two strangers.* **2.** To meet together, usually by plan; join; have a meeting with. ♦ *The two scouts met with the officers to talk about plans for the march.* **3.** To experience (as unhappiness); suffer (as bad luck); have (as an accident or mishap). ♦ *The farmer met with misfortune; his crops were destroyed by a storm.*

**meet with an untimely end** *v. phr.* To die prematurely. ♦ *Many young soldiers, barely out of high school, meet with an untimely end.*

**melting pot** *n. phr.* A country where different nationalities mingle and mix with the result that, in the second generation, most people speak the main language of the country and behave like the majority. ♦ *It is no longer considered entirely true that the United States is a melting pot; many immigrants speak a second language.*

**melt in one's mouth** *v. phr.* **1.** To be so tender as to seem to need no chewing. ♦ *The chicken was so tender that it melted in your mouth.* **2.** To taste very good; be delicious. ♦ *Mother's apple pie really melts in your mouth.*

**mend one's fences** *v. phr., informal* To do something to make people like or follow you again; strengthen your friendships or influence. ♦ *John saw that his friends did not like him, so he decided to mend his fences.*

**mend one's ways** *v. phr.* To reform; change one's behavior from negative to positive. ♦ *He had better mend his ways or he'll wind up in jail.*

**mental telepathy** *n. phr.* The passing of one person's thoughts to another without any discoverable talking or carrying of signals between them. ♦ *Most or all men who practice mental telepathy on stage have really trained themselves to detect tiny clues from the audience.*

**mercy killing** *n. phr.* The act of killing a terminally ill patient or animal in order to avoid further suffering. ♦ *Mercy killing of humans is illegal in most countries, yet many doctors practice it secretly.*

**mess around** *v. phr.* **1.** To engage in idle or purposeless activity. ♦ *Come on, you guys,—start doing some work, don't just mess around all day!* **2.** *vulgar* To be promiscuous; to indulge in sex with little discrimination as to who the partner is. ♦ *Allen needs straightening out; he's been messing around with the whole female population of his class.*

**mess up** *v. phr., slang, informal* **1.** To cause trouble; to spoil something. ♦ *What did you have to mess up my accounts for?* **2.** To cause someone emotional trauma. ♦ *Sue will never get married; she got messed up when she was a teenager.* **3.** To beat up someone physically. ♦ *When Joe came in after the fight with the boys, he was all messed up.*

**method in (to) one's madness** *n. phr.* A plan or organization of ideas hard to perceive at first, but that becomes noticeable after longer and closer examination. ♦ *We thought he was crazy to threaten to resign from the university but, when he was offered a tenured full professorship, we realized that there had been method in his madness.*

**mickey mouse**[1] *adj., slang* Inferior; second rate; chicken; easy; gimmicky. ♦ *Watch out for Perkins; he's full of mickey mouse ideas.*

**mickey mouse²** *n.* *(derogatory)* A stupid person; a policeman; a white man (as used by blacks).

**middle ground** *n.* A place halfway between the two sides of an argument; a compromise. ♦ *The committee found a middle ground between the two proposals.*

**middleman** *n.* A person or small business standing in an intermediary position between two parties. ♦ *A retail merchant is the middleman between the factory and the consumer.*

**middle of the road** *n. phr.* A way of thinking which does not favor one idea or thing too much; being halfway between two different ideas. ♦ *The teacher did not support the boys or the girls in the debate, but stayed in the middle of the road.*

**middle-of-the-road** *adj.* Favoring action halfway between two opposite movements or ideas; with ideas halfway between two opposite sides; seeing good on both sides. ♦ *The men who wrote the Constitution followed a middle-of-the-road plan on whether greater power belonged to the United States government or to the separate states.*

**might as well** *adv. phr.* For no particular reason; as an alternative. ♦ *Since the weather is too hot outside, we might as well turn on the air conditioner and eat inside.*

**mile markers** *n., slang, citizen's band radio jargon* Small signs along interstate highways usually bearing a number. ♦ *The Smokey is located at 131 mile marker.*

**miles away** *adj. phr.* Inattentive; not concentrating. ♦ *When Betty said, "We have theater tickets for tonight," Ken didn't react as his mind was miles away.*

**mill around** *v. phr.* To move impatiently in no particular direction. ♦ *The crowd milled around, waiting for the arrival of the president.*

**mills of God** *or* **God's mills** *n. phr.* Eventual vindication after a long time; rehabilitation in due course or delayed punishment that eventually catches up with the perpetrator. ♦ *The innocent man who was mistakenly imprisoned for many years, took comfort in the thought that the mills of God grind slow but sure.*

**millstone around one's neck** *n. phr.* An intolerable burden. ♦ *Max said that his old car was a millstone around his neck.*

**mince words** *v. phr.* To choose words carefully for the sake of politeness or deception. ♦ *I like people who speak frankly and truthfully without mincing words.*

**mind boggles** *v. phr.* *or* **mind-boggling** *adj. phr.* A comment made on any marked absurdity or incredibly news or statement. ♦ *The mind boggles when one hears of the suicide of the UFO cult followers, who believed that after committing suicide their souls would be picked up by a UFO.* ♦ *It is mind-boggling to think of what the Nazis did to innocent people in the concentration camps.*

**mind like a steel trap** *n. phr.* A very quick and understanding mind, which is quick to catch an idea. ♦ *A successful lawyer must have a mind like a steel trap.*

**mind one's own business** *v. phr.* To not interfere in the affairs of others. ♦ *He finally got tired of her criticism and told her to mind her own business.*

**mind one's p's and q's** *v. phr.* To be very careful what you do or say; not make mistakes. ♦ *When the principal of the school visited the class the students all minded their p's and q's.*

**mind over matter** *n. phr.* The power of the mind over physical matters, such as illness, fear, etc.—A proverb. ♦ *Advocates of alternative medicine discourage the taking of too many drugs and point out that since most illnesses are psychosomatic, one might as well use "mind over matter" to cure oneself.*

**mind you** *v. phr., informal* I want you to notice and understand. ♦ *Mind you, I am not blaming him.*

**mine of information** *n. phr.* A person, a book, etc., that is a valuable source of information. ♦ *A dictionary can be a mine of information.*

**minority leader** *n. phr.* The leader of the political party that has fewer votes in a legislative house. ♦ *The minority leader of the Senate supported the bill.*

**minutes of the meeting** *n. phr.* The notes taken by the recording secretary of an official body or an association recording of what was said and transacted during the given session. ♦ *"Shall we accept the minutes of our last meeting as read by the secretary?" the chairman asked.*

**misfire** *v.* To fail to appeal; fall flat. ♦ *The standup comic's jokes misfired with the audience.*

**miss a trick** *v. phr.* To fail to see, hear, or notice something of even the slightest importance. ♦ *He never misses a trick when it comes to the stock market.*

**miss by a mile** *v. phr., informal* **1.** To shoot at something and be far from hitting it; not hit near. ♦ *Jack's first shot missed the target by a mile.* **2.** To be very wrong; be far from right. ♦ *Lee tried to guess on the examination, but his answers missed by a mile.* **3.** To fail badly; not succeed at all. ♦ *John Brown wanted to be governor but in the election he missed by a mile.*

**missing link** *n.* **1.** Something needed to complete a group; a missing part of a chain of things. ♦ *The detective hunted for the fact that was the missing link in the case.* **2.** An unknown extinct animal that was supposed to be a connection between man and lower animals. ♦ *The missing link would be half man and half ape.*

**miss out** *v., informal* To fail; lose or not take a good chance; miss something good. ♦ *You missed out by not coming with us; we had a great time.*

**miss the boat** *also* **miss the bus** *v. phr., informal* To fail through slowness; to put something off until too late; do the wrong thing and lose the chance. ♦ *Ted could have married Lena but he put off asking her and missed the boat.*

**miss the point** *v. phr.* To be unable to comprehend the essence of what was meant. ♦ *The student didn't get a passing grade on the exam because, although he wrote three pages, he actually missed the point.*

**misty-eyed** *or* **dewy-eyed** *adj. phr.* **1.** Having eyes damp with tears; emotional. ♦ *The teacher was misty-eyed when the school gave her a retirement gift.* **2.** Of the kind who cries easily; sentimental. ♦ *The movie appealed to dewy-eyed girls.*

**mixed bag** *n. phr.* A varied set of people, ideas, objects, or circumstances, including both the good and the bad.

♦ *There was a mixed bag of people at the press conference.*

**mixed blessing** *n.* Something good that has bad features. ♦ *John's new car was a mixed blessing. The other students were always asking John to drive it.*

**mixed up** *adj. phr.* **1.** *informal* Confused in mind; puzzled. ♦ *Bob was all mixed up after the accident.* **2.** Disordered; disarranged; not neat. ♦ *The papers on his desk were mixed up.* **3.** *informal* Joined or connected (with someone or something bad). ♦ *Harry was mixed up in a fight after the game.*

**mix up** *v.* To confuse; make a mistake about. ♦ *Jimmy doesn't know colors yet; he mixes up purple with blue.* ♦ *Even the twins' mother mixes them up.*

**mom-and-dad operation** *or* **mom-and-pop operation** *n. phr.* A very small business, sometimes run out of one's home, that has no employees and is done by a husband-and-wife team. ♦ *Jack and Suzie became small desktop publishers doing everything themselves; it has been a typical mom-and-dad operation ever since.*

**money is no object** *informal sentence* The price of something is irrelevant. ♦ *Please show me your most beautiful mink coat; money is no object.*

**money makes the world go 'round** Most things in the world depend on finances.—A proverb. ♦ *John has outstanding plans, but he will never succeed in implanting them, because he lacks the capital. We had to remind him that "money makes the world go 'round."*

**money talks** *v. phr.* People tend to believe and admire those who are rich; while a poor person may speak the truth, he or she is seldom listened to. ♦ *There are two solutions to the problem of how to improve automobiles, solar energy, and more oil. Unfortunately the oil concerns are bound to win out, because "money talks."*

**money to burn** *n. phr., informal* Very much money, more than is needed. ♦ *Dick's uncle died and left him money to burn.*

**monkey around** See FUCK AROUND, HORSE AROUND, MESS AROUND.

**monkey business** *n., slang, informal*
**1.** Any unethical, illegitimate, or objectionable activity that is furtive or deceitful, e.g., undercover sexual advances, cheating, misuse of public funds, etc. ♦ *There is a lot of monkey business going on in that firm; you'd better watch out who you deal with!*
**2.** Comical or silly actions; goofing off. ♦ *Come on boys, let's cut out the monkey business and get down to work!*

**monkey love** *n. phr.* An exaggerated show of affection often covering up true and meaningful fondness and caring, which may include occasional punishment. ♦ *The Chisolms are guilty of showering their children with monkey love. It would be far better for the two teenagers to be told occasionally that they are out of line.*

**monkey on one's back** *n. phr., informal* An unsolved or nagging problem. ♦ *"My math course is a real monkey on my back," Jack complained.*

**monkey wrench** See THROW A MONKEY WRENCH.

**moonshine** *n.* Illegally distilled alcoholic beverage made at home, mostly on a farm. ♦ *Grandpa is at it again in the barn, making moonshine out of plums.*

**moot point** *n. phr.* A point not worth discussing because of its hypothetical nature. ♦ *To discuss what would have happened to Europe if Hitler had won World War II is a moot point.*

**mop the floor with** *or* **mop up the floor with** *or* **wipe the floor with** *or* **wipe up the floor with** *v. phr., slang* To defeat very clearly or quickly; to beat badly. ♦ *Our team wiped the floor with the visiting team.*

**mop up** *v. phr.* To disperse or liquidate isolated groups or detachments of opposing forces. ♦ *Our forces won the basic battle but there still remain pockets of resistance they must mop up.*

**more Catholic than the pope** See OUT-HEROD HEROD.

**more often than not** *adv. phr.* More than half the time; fifty-one or more times out of a hundred; not quite usually, but fairly regularly. ♦ *Nancy comes over on Saturday more often than not.*

**more or less** *adv. phr.* **1.** Somewhat; rather; mostly; fairly. ♦ *Earl made some mistakes on the test, but his answers* were more or less right. **2.** About; nearly; not exactly, but almost. ♦ *It is a mile, more or less, from his home to the school.*

**more power to you** *adj. phr., a proverb* Expressing encouragement and congratulations when someone accomplishes something difficult. ♦ *When the double amputee started to participate in a walking marathon, people exclaimed, "More power to you!"*

**more than** *adv.* Over what you might expect; very. ♦ *They were more than glad to help.* ♦ *He was more than upset by the accident.*

**more than meets the eye** *adj. phr.* More than is physically apparent; more than one is deducible or can be surmised. ♦ *"There is more to this apparent accident," Detective Sergeant Jones said, "than meets the eye. I suspect foul play."*

**more than pleased** *adj. phr.* Very grateful; very pleased; delighted. ♦ *I am more than pleased that both of my daughters found such wonderful husbands.*

**more the merrier** *n. phr.* The more people who join in the fun, the better it will be.—Used in welcoming more people to join others in some pleasant activity. ♦ *Come with us on the boat ride; the more the merrier.*

**morning after** *n., slang* The effects of drinking liquor or staying up late as felt the next morning; a hangover. ♦ *One of the troubles of drinking too much liquor is the morning after.* ♦ *Jack woke up with a big headache and knew it was the morning after.*

**mouse click** *or* **mouse clicks away** *adj. phr.* Easy to gain access to; just as easy as to make a click with one's "mouse" at a home personal computer. ♦ *You can find anything you need in our store; we are just a mouse click away.*

**mouth-watering** *adj.* Smelling or looking very good to eat. ♦ *It was a mouth-watering meal.*

**move a muscle** *v. phr.* To move even a very little.—Used in negative sentences and questions and with *if.* ♦ *The deer stood without moving a muscle until the hunter was gone.* ♦ *The robber said he would shoot the bank worker if he moved a muscle.*

**move heaven and earth** *v. phr.* To try every way; do everything you can. ♦*Joe moved heaven and earth to be sent to Washington.*

**move in on** *v. phr., slang, colloquial* To take over something that belongs to another. ♦*He moved in on my girlfriend and now we're not talking to each other.*

**move in the wrong circles** *v. phr.* To fall in with the wrong crowd and under their negative influence, either because they are doing bad things or because they are in political favor with the present government. ♦*Mike's son became a dope addict because in high school he moved in the wrong circles.*

**move over** *v. phr.* **1.** Shift one's position from right to left, forward or backward. ♦*We had to move the dinner table over to be able to put down the new suitcases temporarily.* **2.** To yield one's place in the arts, music, dancing, etc., because of new younger talent. ♦*"Move over, Elvis!" "Michael Jackson is coming!"*

**moving spirit** *n. phr.* The main figure behind a business or an activity; the one who inspires the others. ♦*Mr. Smith is the moving spirit behind our expansion plans.*

**much less** *conj.* And also not; and even less able or likely to.—Used after a negative clause. ♦*I never even spoke to the man, much less insulted him.*

**much of a muchness** *or* **too much of a muchness** *n. phr.* Similarity; much of the same substance, value, or significance. ♦*"Won't you have some more cake?" my aunt Meggie asked. "Thanks, I can't. I'm full." "Anything wrong with it?" she kept on prodding. "No, it just too much of a muchness; I mean, too much cream."*

**mud in your eye** *n. phr., informal* A cheering exclamation when people drink, much like "cheers!" ♦*Each time John raised his glass he said, "Well, here's mud in your eye!"*

**mug shot** *n. phr.* A police photograph showing the arrested person's full face and profile. ♦*"Go over these mug shots," Sergeant O'Malley said, "and tell me if you find the person who held up the liquor store!"*

**mull over** *v. phr.* To consider; think over. ♦*He mulled over the offer for some time, but finally rejected it.*

**mum is the word** You must keep the secret; keep silent; don't tell anyone.— Often used as an interjection. ♦*We are planning a surprise party for John and mum is the word.*

**muscle in on** *v. phr.* To intrude; penetrate; force oneself into another's business or territory. ♦*The eastern Mafia muscled in on the western Mafia's turf and a shooting war was started.*

**musical chairs** *n. phr.* (Originally the name of a children's game.) The transfer of a number of officers in an organization into different jobs, especially each other's jobs. ♦*The boss regularly played musical chairs with department heads to keep them fresh on the job.*

**music to one's ears** *n. phr.* Something one likes to hear. ♦*When the manager phoned to say I got the job, it was music to my ears.*

**my God** *or* **my goodness** *interj.* Used to express surprise, shock, or dismay. ♦*My God! What happened to the car?*

**my home is my castle** *chiefly British* One's home is impregnable, a place of safety, privacy and security.—A proverb. ♦*"Where will you spend your retirement years, sir?" The student asked the famous scientist. "At home, of course," the professor answered, "I won't be bothered by journalists on this island. My home is my castle, as they say."*

**my lips are sealed** *informal sentence* A promise that one will not give away a secret. ♦*"You can tell me what happened," Helen said. "My lips are sealed."*

**nail down** v. phr., informal To make certain; make sure; settle. ◆Joe had a hard time selling his car, but he finally nailed the sale down when he got his friend Sam to give him $300.

**nail one's colors to the mast** literary To let everyone know what you think is right and refuse to change. ◆During the election campaign the candidate nailed his colors to the mast on the question of civil rights.

**naked truth** n. phr. The pure, unadulterated truth. ◆"Are you, or are you not a Republican?" John asked his college roommate, Ted. "The naked truth is, old friend," that I am a typical 'swing voter'—sometimes I vote for a Democrat, and sometimes for a Republican."

**name calling** See CALL NAMES.

**named after** adj. phr. Given the same name as someone. ◆Archibald was named after his father.

**name day** n. The day of the saint for whom a person is named. ◆Lawrence's name day is August 10, the feast of St. Lawrence.

**namedropper** n. phr. A person who is always mentioning well-known names. ◆Since her move to Hollywood she has become a regular namedropper.

**name is mud** informal (You) are in trouble; a person is blamed or no longer liked.—Used in the possessive. ◆If you tell your mother I spilled ink on her rug my name will be mud.

**name of the game** n., informal The crux of the matter; that which actually occurs under the disguise of something else. ◆Getting medium income families to support the rest of society—that's the name of the game!

**narrow down** v. phr. To limit within very strict margins. ◆Of the numerous applicants, the list has been narrowed down to just a few.

**narrow escape** n. phr. An escape by a very small margin; a near miss. ◆If the truck that hit his car had been coming faster, it would have killed him; it was certainly a narrow escape that he only had a broken arm!

**narrow-minded** adj. phr. Limited in outlook; resistant to new ideas; bigoted.

◆Jack is generally very open about everything, but when it comes to politics, he is terribly narrow-minded.

**nasty-nice** adj. Unkind in a polite way; disagreeable while pretending to be gracious. ◆The bus driver has a nasty-nice way of showing his dislike.

**natives are restless** The locals are in a rebellious mood; taken from colonial days when certain African tribes rebelled against the British; used in other contexts.—A proverb. ◆"What's happening on campus?" Professor Brown asked. "Why is everyone talking so excitedly?" "The natives are restless," a colleague answered, "because they forced the chancellor to resign over the budget."

**natural-born** adj. **1.** Being a (citizen) because you were born in the country. ◆Mr. and Mrs. Schmidt came to the United States from Germany and are naturalized citizens but their children are natural-born citizens. **2.** Born with great ability to become (something); having great ability (as in a sport or art) almost from the start. ◆Mozart was a natural-born musician. He could play the piano well when he was only six years old.

**near at hand** See AT HAND.

**neck and neck** adj. or adv., informal Equal or nearly equal in a race or contest; abreast; tied. ◆At the end of the race the two horses were neck and neck.

**neck of the woods** n. phr., informal Part of the country; place; neighborhood; vicinity. ◆We visited Illinois and Iowa last summer; in that neck of the woods the corn really grows tall.

**needle in a haystack** n. phr., informal Something that will be very hard to find. ◆"I lost my class ring somewhere in the front yard," said June. Jim answered, "Too bad. That will be like finding a needle in a haystack."

**neither fish nor fowl** also **neither fish, flesh, nor fowl** Something or someone that does not belong to a definite group or known class; a strange person or thing; someone or something odd or hard to understand. ◆The man is neither fish nor fowl; he votes Democrat or Republican according to which will do him the most good.

**neither here nor there** *adj. phr.* Not important to the thing being discussed; off the subject; not mattering. ♦ *The boys all like the coach but that's neither here nor there; the question is, "Does he know how to teach football?"*

**neither rhyme nor reason** *n. phr.* No emotional or intellectual substance. ♦ *As far as I am concerned, his proposal makes no sense; it has neither rhyme nor reason.*

**nervous breakdown** *n.* A mild or severe attack of mental illness; a collapse of a person's ability to make decisions and solve problems because of overwork, great mental strain, or the like. ♦ *When the mother saw her baby run over, she suffered a nervous breakdown.*

**Nervous Nellie** *n., informal* A timid person who lacks determination and courage. ♦ *I say we will never win if we don't stop being Nervous Nellies!*

**nest egg** *n.* Savings set aside to be used in the future. ♦ *Herb says he doesn't have to worry about his old age because he has a nest egg in the bank.*

**never a dull moment** Something out of the ordinary is happening all the time, good or bad.—A proverb. ♦ *When the Mississippi flooded their house, the Smiths remarked with a wry sense of humor, "Never a dull moment…"*

**never mind** *v. phr.* Don't trouble about it; don't worry about it; forget it; skip it.—Usually used in speaking or when writing dialogue. ♦ *"What did you say?" "Oh, never mind." ♦ "What about money?" "Never mind that. I'll take care of it."*

**never say die** *v. phr.* Don't quit; don't be discouraged. ♦ *"Never say die!" John said, as he got on his feet and tried to ice skate again.*

**new blood** *n.* Something or someone that gives new life or vigor, fresh energy or power. ♦ *New blood was brought into the company through appointment of younger men to important positions.*

**new broom sweeps clean** A new person makes many changes.—A proverb. ♦ *The new superintendent has changed many of the school rules. A new broom sweeps clean.*

**new deal** *n., informal* **1.** A complete change; a fresh start. ♦ *People had been on the job too long; a new deal*

was needed to get things out of the old bad habits. **2.** Another chance. ♦ *The boy asked for a new deal after he had been punished for fighting in school.*

**newfangled** *adj.* Newly invented or contrived; excessively complex. ♦ *Dorothy felt that many newfangled gadgets in Kate's all-electric kitchen weren't really necessary.*

**new flame** *n. phr.* A new girlfriend or boyfriend. ♦ *John is very excited; he has a new flame.*

**new lease on life** *n. phr.* A new chance to live; an improved manner of living. ♦ *After his illness and his retirement, living in Hawaii was a new lease on life.*

**new man** *n.* A person who has become very much better. ♦ *Diet and exercise made a new man of him.*

**new money** *n. phr.* People who have become rich recently. ♦ *Since Bob's father invented a new computer component, Bob and his family are new money.*

**newshawk** *n.* A newspaper reporter. ♦ *There are always a lot of newshawks following the president.*

**new wine in old bottles** *Biblical* New ideas presented in an old, familiar form.—A proverb. ♦ *John writes wonderfully interesting new poetry in sonnet form. A successful case of "new wine in old bottles."*

**next door** *adv. or adj.* **1.** In or to the next house or apartment. ♦ *He lived next door to me.* **2.** Very close.—Used with *to.* ♦ *The sick man was next door to death.*

**next to**[1] *adv.* Almost; nearly. ♦ *It was next to unthinkable that the boy would steal.*

**next to**[2] *prep.* Just after; second to. ♦ *Next to his family, baseball was his greatest love.*

**next to nothing** *n. phr.* Very little; almost nothing. ♦ *They gave me next to nothing for my old car when I traded it in for a new one.*

**nibble at** *or* **nibble away at** Compare EAT AT.

**nice going** *n. phr.* Wonderful progress that deserves congratulations, offered as praise. ♦ *"Nice going, Johnny!" the boy's father said, when he heard his eleven-year-old son play a Bach solo sonata on the violin.*

**night and day** See DAY AND NIGHT.

**nightcap** *n.* A good-night drink; a drink taken just before bedtime. ♦ *Would you like to come up to my place for a nightcap?*

**night letter** *n.* A telegram sent at night at a cheaper rate and delivered in the morning. ♦ *I waited until after six o'clock in the evening before sending the telegram home because I can say more for the same price in a night letter.*

**night life** *n. phr.* Entertainment at night. ♦ *People in the city are able to find more night life than those who live in the country.*

**night on the town** *n. phr.* An evening of drinks, dinner, and entertainment. ♦ *"We haven't been doing anything for so long," Mary complained to her husband. "Let's go and have a night on the town!"*

**night owl** *n. phr.* One who sleeps during the day and stays up or works during the night. ♦ *Tom hardly ever sleeps at night; he prefers to work by lamp light and has become a regular night owl.*

**nine days' wonder** *n. phr.* An unusual occurrence that first causes surprise or consternation, but that will be soon forgotten. ♦ *Many a Hollywood scandal involving divorces and marriages is nothing but a nine days' wonder.*

**nine-to-five job** *n. phr.* A typical office job that starts at 9 A.M. and ends at 5 P.M. with a one-hour lunch break at 12 noon or 1 P.M. ♦ *We professors are not too well paid but I could never get used to a nine-to-five job.*

**nip and tuck** *adj. or adv., informal* Evenly matched; hard fought to the finish. ♦ *The game was nip and tuck until the last minute.*

**nip in the bud** *v. phr.* To check at the outset; prevent at the start; block or destroy in the beginning. ♦ *The police nipped the plot in the bud.*

**nitpick** *v. phr.* To argue about something small or relatively insignificant in an annoying manner. ♦ *Stop nitpicking at every little detail! Our work is finished and is quite good on the whole.*

**nitty-gritty** *n. phr.* The minute details of an agreement or contract. ♦ *All right, then, now that we have agreed on the broad outlines of the deal, let's get down to the nitty-gritty!*

**no account**[1] *adj.* Of no importance. ♦ *The lowly clerk's opinion is of no account in this matter.*

**no account**[2] *n. phr.* A person of low social station. ♦ *Fred was first considered a no account but he soon proved himself to be a person of great ability.*

**nobody home** *slang* **1.** Your attention is somewhere else, not on what is being said or done here; you are absent-minded. ♦ *The teacher asked him a question three times but he still looked out the window. She gave up, saying, "Nobody home."* **2.** You are feeble-minded or insane. ♦ *He pointed to the woman, tapped his head, and said, "Nobody home."*

**nobody's fool** *n. phr.* A smart person; a person who knows what he is doing; a person who can take care of himself. ♦ *In the classroom and on the football field, Henry was nobody's fool.*

**no-brainer** *n. phr.* Something easy to do or solve that requires little or no thinking. ♦ *How do we decide the salary raises for next year? I tell you how; it's a no-brainer—nobody gets any, because the state cut our budget.*

**no comment** *adj. phr.* I have no answer to give; I refuse to discuss the issue. Often said by political figures during press interviews. ♦ *"Will you run for president of the United States next year, Senator?" "No comment," the senator answered, and quickly got into his car.*

**nodding acquaintance** *n.* Less than casual acquaintance. ♦ *I have never spoken to the chancellor; we have only a nodding acquaintance.*

**no deal** *or* **no dice** *or* **no go** *or* **no sale** *slang* Not agreed to; refused or useless; without success or result; no; certainly not.—Used in the predicate or to refuse something. ♦ *Billy wanted to let Bob join the team, but I said that it was no deal because Bob was too young.* ♦ *"Let me have a dollar." "No dice!" answered Joe.* ♦ *I tried to get Mary on the telephone but it was no go.* ♦ *"Let's go to the beach tomorrow." "No sale, I have my music lesson tomorrow."*

**no doubt** *adv.* **1.** Without doubt; doubtless; surely; certainly. ♦ *No doubt Susan was the smartest girl in her class.* **2.** Probably. ♦ *John will no doubt telephone us if he comes to town.*

**no end** *adv., informal* **1.** Very much; exceedingly. ♦*Jim was no end upset because he couldn't go swimming.* **2.** Almost without stopping; continually. ♦*The baby cried no end.*

**no end to** *or informal* **no end of** So many, or so much of, as to seem almost endless; very many or very much. ♦*There was no end to the letters pouring into the post office.*

**no expense spared** *adj. phr.* Money has been spent freely. ♦*The Smiths completely refurbished their new home and even had a heated swimming pool put in, no expense spared.*

**no foolin'** *or* **no fooling** *v. phr.* A humorous way of affirming something, saying "Yes indeed." ♦*"Do you actually want to buy my old horse?" the old farmer asked the recently retired university professor, who moved down to Texas. "No foolin', my man," the professor answered. "I've been riding ever since I was a kid."*

**no frills** *n. phr.* A firm or product that offers no extras; a generic product that carries no expensive label. ♦*We went on a no frills trip to Europe with few luxuries.*

**no good** *adj. phr.* Not satisfactory; not adequate; not approved. ♦*He was no good at arithmetic.* ♦*He tried appealing to the man's pride, but it did no good.*

**no great shakes** *adj., informal* Mediocre; unimportant. ♦*Joe Wilson is no great shakes.*

**no hard feelings** *n. phr.* A lack of resentment or anger; a state of peace and forgiveness. ♦*"No hard feelings," he said. "You should feel free to make constructive criticism any time."*

**no ifs, ands, or buts about it** *adj. phr.* Absolutely certain; without a doubt. ♦*"I am afraid your condition calls for immediate surgery," the doctor said. "Are you sure, Doctor," the patient inquired. "No ifs, ands, or buts about it!" the physician replied.*

**no harm in looking** *v. phr., informal* The excuse of husbands whose eyes wander. ♦*"Why are you staring at that salesgirl?" Mary nervously asked her husband. "No harm in looking," he replied. "You must admit she has a striking figure."*

**no kidding** *n. phr.* Without jokes or teasing; honestly spoken. ♦*"You actu-*

*ally won the lottery?" Dick asked. "No kidding," Joe replied. "I really did."*

**no longer** *adv.* Not any more; not at the present time. ♦*He could no longer be trusted and they had to let him go.*

**no love lost** *n. phr.* Bad feeling; ill will. ♦*Bob and Dick both wanted to be elected captain of the team, and there was no love lost between them.*

**no matter** **1.** Not anything important. ♦*I wanted to see him before he left but it's no matter.* **2.** It makes no difference; regardless of. ♦*She was going to be a singer no matter what difficulties she met.*

**no matter what** *adv. phr.* Under any circumstances. ♦*We will go to Europe this summer, no matter what.* ♦*Charles had decided to go to the footb*

**none of ones' business** *n. phr., informal* Something that doesn't concern someone; something one should not interfere with or inquire about. ♦*"How old are you actually?" the inexperienced young journalist asked the famous actress. "None of your business, young man!" she replied indignantly.*

**none too** *adv.* Not very; not at all. ♦*The doctor arrived none too soon as Lucy's fever was alarmingly high.*

**nonstarter** *n.* An idea, plan, or project that doesn't work or is obviously no good. ♦*His plan to start a new private school is a nonstarter because he is unable to organize anything.*

**no percentage** *n. phr.* No advantage; no profit. ♦*There is no percentage in complaining about the zero raise policy of our university next year; there isn't anything anyone can do about it.*

**no picnic** *n. phr.* Something arduous; something that requires great effort to accomplish. ♦*It is no picnic to climb Mount Everest.*

**no sale** See NO DEAL.

**nose about** *or* **nose around** *v. phr., informal* To look for something kept private or secret; poke about; explore; inquire; pry. ♦*In Grandmother's attic, Sally spent a while nosing about in the old family pictures.*

**nose down** *v., of an aircraft* To head down; bring down the nose of. ♦*The big airliner began to nose down for a landing.*

nose in[1] *or* nose into[1] *informal* Prying or pestering interest in; unwelcome interest in; impolite curiosity. ♦ *He always had his nose in other people's business.*

nose in[2] *or* nose into[2] *v.* To move in close; move slowly in with the front first. ♦ *The ship nosed into the pier.* ♦ *The car nosed into the curb.*

nose in a book *n. phr.* Busy interest in reading.—Used with a possessive. ♦ *Mother can't get Mary to help do the housework; she always has her nose in a book.*

nose is out of joint See PUT ONE'S NOSE OUT OF JOINT.

nose out *v., informal* **1.** To learn by effort (something private or secret); uncover. ♦ *The principal nosed out the truth about the stolen examination.* **2.** To defeat by a nose length; come in a little ahead of in a race or contest. ♦ *The horse we liked nosed out the second horse in a very close finish.*

nose out of *informal* Curious attention; bothering.—Usually used with a possessive and usually used with *keep.* ♦ *When Billy asked his sister where she was going she told him to keep his nose out of her business.*

nose over *v.* To turn over on the nose so as to land upside down. ♦ *The airplane made a faulty landing approach and nosed over.*

nose up *v.* To head up; incline the forward end upwards; move up. ♦ *The airplane nosed up through the cloud bank.*

no-show *n., informal* A person who makes a reservation, e.g., at a hotel or at an airline, and then neither claims nor cancels it. ♦ *The airlines were messed up because of a great number of no-show passengers.*

no sooner —— than As soon as; at once when; immediately when. ♦ *No sooner did he signal to turn than the other car turned in front of him.*

no spring chicken *n. phr.* A person who is no longer young. ♦ *Even though she is no spring chicken anymore, men still turn their heads to look at her.*

no sweat[1] *adj., slang, informal* Easily accomplished, uncomplicated. ♦ *That job was no sweat.*

no sweat[2] *adv.* Easily. ♦ *We did it no sweat.*

not a leg to stand on *n. phr., informal* No good proof or excuse; no good evidence or defense to offer. ♦ *The man with a gun and $300 in his pocket was accused of robbing an oil station. He did not have a leg to stand on.*

not all there *adj. phr.* Not completely alert mentally; absentminded; not together. ♦ *Bill is a wonderful guy but he is just not all there.*

not bad *or* not so bad *or* not half bad *adj., informal* Pretty good; all right; good enough. ♦ *The party last night was not bad.* ♦ *It was not so bad, as inexpensive vacations go.* ♦ *The show was not half bad.*

not breathe a word *v. phr.* To keep a confidence well; to not reveal a secret. ♦ *"I won the lottery!" Jack whispered in his wife's ear. "Don't you breathe a word!" "OK, honey; mum is the word."*

not by a long shot See BY A LONG SHOT.

not by any means See BY NO MEANS.

notch See TIGHTEN ONE'S BELT.

not cricket *adj. phr.* Not "comme il faut"; not proper; not to be done in polite society. ♦ *It's not cricket to look into your playing partner's hand of cards when playing for money.*

not feel oneself (today) *v. phr.* To be unhinged; to not feel good physically or emotionally. ♦ *The weather must be affecting me—I haven't been feeling myself all day.*

not for all the coffee in Brazil *or* not for all the tea in China *or* not for anything in the world *or* not for love or money See NOT FOR THE WORLD.

not for the world *or* not for worlds *adv. phr.* Not at any price; not for anything. ♦ *I wouldn't hurt his feelings for the world.* ♦ *Not for worlds would he let his children go hungry.*

not give a damn *or* darn *or* not to give a hoot *v. phr., always negative* To not care about something; be scornfully unconcerned; said in disdain and derision. ♦ *"Myron is in jail again for shoplifting," Myron's brother said to Bob. "Sorry," Bob replied, "but I tried to help him for years without success. At this point I don't give a damn what happens to him."*

not give a thought *v. phr.* To disregard something as important, given as advice. ♦ *"I still owe you $5 from last year," Bob said to his wealthy lawyer* brother. *"Don't give it a thought,"* the brother answered.

**not have a prayer** *v. phr.* To have no chance at all ♦*John keeps hoping to win the U.S. Open golf tournament, but in reality he doesn't have a prayer.*

**not have the heart to** *v. phr.* To not be insensitive or cruel. ♦*My boss did not have the heart to lay off two pregnant women when they most needed their jobs.*

**nothing doing** *adv. phr., informal* I will not do it; certainly not; no indeed; no. ♦*"Will you lend me a dollar?" "Nothing doing!"*

**nothing if not** *adv. phr.* Without doubt; certainly. ♦*With its bright furnishings, flowers, and sunny windows, the new hospital dayroom is nothing if not cheerful.*

**nothing of the kind** *adv. phr.* On the contrary. ♦*"Did you quit your job?"* he asked. *"No, I did nothing of the kind,"* she answered.

**nothing short of** *adv. phr.* Absolutely; thoroughly; completely. ♦*Olivier's performance in* Hamlet *was nothing short of magnificent.*

**nothing to boast about** *or* **nothing to write home about** *or* **nothing to wire home about** *adj. phr.* Nothing interesting or significant; nothing to brag about. ♦*This is the fifth time in a year that I hit a lamppost with my car. My driving is nothing to write home about, I guess.*

**nothing to it** *adj. phr.* Presenting no serious challenge; easily accomplished. ♦*Once you learn how to tread water, swimming is really easy; there is nothing to it.*

**nothing to sneeze at** See SNEEZE AT.

**not if I can help it** *adv. phr.* I will not do something if it can be avoided. ♦*"Will you go and work in sub-zero weather in northern Alaska?" John's brother asked. "Not if I can help it," came the reply.*

**not in the least** *adv. phr.* Not at all. ♦*She was not in the least interested in listening to a long lecture on ethics.*

**not know which way to turn** *v. phr.* To be puzzled about getting out of a difficulty; not know what to do to get out of trouble. ♦*When Jane missed the last bus home, she didn't know which way to turn.*

**not one iota** *(n. phr)* from the Bible referring to the Greek letter *"i."* Not at all; not in the least. ♦*Not an iota must be changed or omitted in that valuable, ancient manuscript while you try deciphering it.*

**not on your life** *adv. phr., informal* Certainly not; not ever; not for any reason.—Used for emphasis. ♦*I wouldn't drive a car with brakes like that—not on your life.*

**not over until the fat lady sings** *or* **it's not over until it's over** *adv. phr., from old-fashioned country circus performances, or sports, said in jest* Ongoing activities do not come to an end until the proper conclusion. ♦*During the lengthy court trial jurors were getting restless and many wanted to leave, until the foreman said, "It's not over until the fat lady sings."*

**not so hot** *or* **not too hot** *adj. phr.* Ineffective; not very good. ♦*His plans to rebuild the house in a hurry obviously weren't so hot.*

**not the only fish in the sea** *n. phr.* One of many; not the only one of the kind; not the only one available. ♦*He said he could find other girls—she was not the only fish in the sea.*

**not the only pebble on the beach** *n. phr.* Not the only person to be considered; one of many. ♦*George was acting pretty self-important and we finally had to tell him that he wasn't the only pebble on the beach.*

**not the smartest tool in the shed** *adj. phr., informal* Not the most intelligent person in a given setting. ♦*Poor Jerry has been suffering from a bad inferiority complex all his life; he has been told too often that he is not the smartest tool in the shed.*

**not the thing** *n. phr.* Not the accepted form of action; something socially improper. ♦*It is simply not the thing to wear blue jeans to the opera.*

**not to amount to a hill of beans** See MEANS BEANS.

**not to get to first base** *v. phr.* To fail to make initial progress; have no success at all. ♦*I tried various ways to make Mary interested in me as a potential husband, but I couldn't even get to first base.*

**not to give one the time of day** *v. phr., slang, informal* To dislike someone strongly enough so as to totally ignore him. ♦ *Sue wouldn't give Helen the time of day.*

**not to give quarter** *v. phr.* **1.** To be utterly unwilling to show mercy; not to allow a weaker or defeated party the chance to save themselves through escape. ♦ *The occupying foreign army gave no quarter—they took no prisoners, shot everyone, and made escape impossible.* **2.** To argue so forcefully during a negotiation or in a court of law as to make any counter-argument or counter-proposal impossible. ♦ *The District Attorney hammered away at the witnesses and gave no quarter to the attorney for the defense.*

**not to know one from Adam** *v. phr.* To not know a person; be unable to recognize someone. ♦ *I have no idea who that guy is that Jane just walked in with; I don't know him from Adam.*

**not to know the first thing about** *v. phr.* To be totally ignorant about a certain issue. ♦ *Al assured us that he didn't know the first thing about Mary's whereabouts.*

**not to know what to make of** *v. phr.* To be unable to decipher; be unable to identify; not know how to decide what something really is. ♦ *I got a mysterious letter asking me to meet Santa Claus at 6 P.M. at the supermarket. Is this a joke? I don't know what to make of it.*

**not to know whether one is coming or going** *v. phr.* To be completely confused. ♦ *He was so perplexed he didn't know whether he was coming or going.*

**not to lift a finger** *v. phr.* To not help in the slightest degree. ♦ *"My husband won't lift a finger to help me," she complained, "although we have 12 people coming for dinner."*

**not to mention** *or* **not to speak of** *or* **to say nothing of** Without ever needing to speak of; in addition to; besides.—Used to add something to what you have said or explained. ♦ *They have three fine sons, not to speak of their two lovely daughters.*

**not to miss a beat** *v. phr. negative only* To do without hesitation; go on undisturbed. ♦ *John is the most clever and most poised engineer we ever had at this auto plant; he simply never misses a beat.* ♦ *Ervin is a terrific pianist with a phenomenal memory; he just never misses a beat.*

**not to say 'boo!' to a goose** *v. phr.* To be too shy to say anything. ♦ *Poor Jerry is so self-conscious and shy that he doesn't say "boo" to a goose.*

**not to see the forest for the trees** *v. phr. negative only* To be unable to see the total picture in a situation because of being lost in the details. ♦ *Ernie is a great toolmaker, but sometimes he needs reminding what the whole project is about; otherwise he doesn't see the forest for the trees.*

**not to touch (something) with a ten-foot pole** *v. phr.* To consider something completely undesirable or uninteresting. ♦ *Some people won't touch spinach with a ten-foot pole.*

**not to worry** *phrasal idiom, offered as advice, always negative* Relax, troubles will go away, don't get upset. ♦ *"How will I ever learn how to drive?" Phil said worriedly, "I am afraid of highways." "Not to worry," the instructor answered. "It's just a question of time. You will soon get used to it and overcome your fears."*

**not worth a dime** See NOT WORTH A TINKER'S DAMN.

**not worth a hill of beans** See NOT WORTH A TINKER'S DAMN.

**not worth a tinker's damn** *or* **not worth a tinker's dam** *adj. phr., informal* Not worth anything; valueless. ♦ *I am not familiar with the subject so my opinion would not be worth a tinker's dam.*

**not worth the paper it's written on** *adj. phr.* Entirely worthless, mostly because of the falsehoods contained in a document. ♦ *This entire accusation of Mr. Brown is a total fabrication; it isn't worth the paper it is written on.* ♦ *I don't know how Ollie ever got a Ph.D. His diploma isn't worth the paper it is written on.*

**no two ways about it** *n. phr.* No other choice; no alternative. ♦ *The boss said there were no two ways about it; we would all have to work late to finish the job.*

**no use** *n.* **1.** No purpose; no object; no gain. ♦ *There's no use in crying about your broken bicycle.* **2.** Bad opinion; no respect; no liking.—Used after have. ♦ *He had no use for dogs after a dog bit him.*

**no use crying over spilled milk** *or* **no use crying over spilt milk** See CRY OVER SPILLED MILK.

**now and then** *or* **now and again** *adv. phr.* Not often; not regularly; occasionally; sometimes. ♦ *Now and then he goes to a ball game.*

**now ———— now** *coord. adv.* Sometimes... sometimes; by turns; at one time... then at another.—Often used with adjectives that are very different or opposite, especially to show change. ♦ *The weather changed every day; it was now hot, now cool.*

**no way** *adv.* Not at all; never; under no circumstances. ♦ *Do you think I will do the house chores alone? No way!*

**no wonder** *also* **small wonder** *adj.* Not surprising; to be expected. ♦ *It is no wonder that the children love to visit the farm.*

**now or never** *adv. phr.* This is the right time to do something; at other times the opportunity to carry out such an activity will not be there. ♦ *Mary was thirty-nine when she got pregnant for the first time after fifteen years of marriage. "Should I have this child?" she asked her doctor. "It's now or never," the doctor answered.*

**now that** *conj.* Since; because; now. ♦ *Now that dinner is ready, wash your hands.*

**now you're talking** *adv. phr.* This is the right attitude, now you are on the right track, this is the way to make sense. ♦ *"OK, I will try to overcome my fears and learn how to be a good driver," Phil said to his driving instructor, who replied, "Now you're talking!"*

**nuke a tater** *v. phr.* **1.** To bake a potato in a microwave oven. ♦ *"We have no time for standard baked potatoes in the oven," she said. "We'll just have to nuke a tater."*

**null and void** *adj.* Not worth anything; no longer valid. ♦ *Both the seller and the buyer agreed to forget about their previous contract and to consider it null and void.*

**number among** *v. phr.* Consider as one of; consider to be a part of. ♦ *I number Al among my best friends.*

**number one**[1] *or* **Number One**[1] *n. phr., informal* Yourself; your own interests; your private or selfish advantage. Usually used in the phrase *look out for number one.* ♦ *He was well known for his habit of always looking out for number one.*

**number one**[2] *adj. phr.* **1.** Of first rank or importance; foremost; principal. ♦ *Tiger Woods is easily America's number one golfer.* **2.** Of first grade; of top quality; best. ♦ *That is number one western steer beef.*

**nurse a drink** *v. phr., informal* To hold a drink in one's hand at a party, pretending to be drinking it or taking extremely small sips only. ♦ *John's been nursing that drink all evening.*

**nurse a grudge** *v. phr.* To keep a feeling of envy or dislike toward some person; remember something bad that a person said or did to you, and dislike the person because of that. ♦ *Mary nursed a grudge against her teacher because she thought she deserved a better grade in English.*

**nurture a snake in one's bosom** *or* **nourish a snake in one's bosom** To be good and friendly to a false friend who will never repay one's friendship, but will betray his or her benefactor.—A proverb. ♦ *When we supported Dale Edwards for promotion at the university, we had no idea that we were nurturing a snake in our bosom. He subsequently opposed every sensible proposal.*

**nut case** *n. phr.* A very silly, crazy, or foolish person. ♦ *I am going to be a nut case if I don't go on a vacation pretty soon.*

**nuts and bolts of** *n. phr.* The basic facts or important details of something. ♦ *"Ted will be an excellent trader," his millionaire grandfather said, "once he learns the nuts and bolts of the profession."*

**nutty as a fruitcake** *adj. phr., slang* Very crazy; entirely mad. ♦ *He looked all right, as we watched him approach, but when he began to talk, we saw that he was as nutty as a fruitcake.*

**occupy oneself** *v. phr.* To make oneself busy with. ♦ *Having retired from business, he now occupies himself with his stamp collection.*

**occur to someone** *v. phr.* To think of something. ♦ *"Did it ever occur to you that you might be better off looking for a job elsewhere?" Peter asked. "No," John replied, "but it did occur to me to ask for a raise."*

**oddball** *n., slang, informal* An eccentric person; one who doesn't act like everyone else. ♦ *John is an oddball—he never invites anyone.*

**odd jobs** *n. phr.* Work that is not steady or regular in nature; small, isolated tasks. ♦ *Dan does odd jobs for his neighbors, barely making enough to eat.*

**odds and ends** *n. phr.* Miscellaneous items; remnants. ♦ *After the great annual clearance sale there were only a few odds and ends left in the store.*

**odds are** *phrasal idiom* Chances are; the likelihood is; what will probably happen is x or y. ♦ *Odds are it will rain tonight.* ♦ *Odds are the price of gasoline will go down after the war in Iraq has come to an end.*

**odds are against** *v. phr.* The likelihood of success is not probable; the chances of success are poor. ♦ *The odds are against her getting here before Monday.*

**odds-on** *adj., informal* Almost certain; almost sure; probable. ♦ *Ed is the odds-on choice for class president, because he has good sense and good humor.*

**of age** *adj. phr.* **1a.** Old enough to be allowed to do or manage something. ♦ *Mary will be of driving age on her next birthday.* **1b.** Old enough to vote; having the privileges of adulthood. ♦ *The age at which one is considered of age to vote, or of age to buy alcoholic drinks, or of age to be prosecuted as an adult, varies within the United States.* **2.** Fully developed; mature. ♦ *Education for the foreign born came of age when bilingual education was accepted as a necessary part of the public school system.*

**of course** *adv. phr.* **1.** As you would expect; naturally. ♦ *Bob hit Herman, and Herman hit him back, of course.* **2.** Without a doubt; certainly; surely. ♦ *Of course you know that girl; she's in your class.*

**of every stripe and color** *adj. phr.* All kinds; from everywhere; different both physically and otherwise. ♦ *"What kind of people did you see at the meeting?" Ted asked. "There were people there of every stripe and color, from several dozen countries on all known continents," John replied.*

**off-again, on-again** *or* **on-again, off-again** *adj. phr., informal* Not settled; changeable; uncertain. ♦ *John and Susan had an off-again, on-again romance.*

**off and on** *also* **on and off** *adv.* Not regularly; occasionally; sometimes. ♦ *It rained off and on all day.*—Sometimes used with hyphens like an adjective. ♦ *A worn-out cord may make a hearing aid work in an off-and-on way.*

**off balance** *adj. phr.* **1.** Not in balance; not able to stand up straight and not fall; not able to keep from turning over or falling; unsteady. ♦ *Never stand up in a canoe; it will get off balance and turn over.* **2.** Not prepared; not ready; unable to meet something unexpected. ♦ *The teacher's surprise test caught the class off balance, and nearly everyone got a poor mark.*

**off base** *adj. phr., informal* Not agreeing with fact; wrong. ♦ *The idea that touching a toad causes warts is off base.*

**offbeat** *adj., informal* Nonconventional; different from the usual; odd. ♦ *Linguistics used to be an offbeat field, but nowadays every self-respecting university has a linguistics department.*

**off center** *adv. phr.* Not exactly in the middle. ♦ *Mary hung the picture off center, because it was more interesting that way.*

**off-center** *adj., informal* Different from the usual pattern; not quite like most others; odd. ♦ *Roger's sense of humor was a bit off-center.*

**off-color** *or* **off-colored** *adj.* **1.** Not of the proper hue or shade; not matching a standard color sample. ♦ *The librarian complained that the painter had used an off-color green on the walls.* **2.** *informal* Not of the proper kind for polite society; in bad taste; dirty. ♦ *When Joe told his off-color story, no one was pleased.*

**off day** *n. phr.* A period when one is not functioning at his or her best; a period of weakness. ♦ *The champion was obviously having an off day; otherwise she would have been able to defeat her opponent.*

**off duty** *adj.* Not supposed to be at work; having free time; not working. ♦ *Sailors like to go sight-seeing, when they are off duty in a foreign port.*

**off (one/he/she/it) goes!** *v. phr.* Said of a person, a vehicle, or a memorable thing who/which has started leaving or moving, both as a statement of fact (declarative assertion) or as a command (imperative). ♦ *When the boat hit the water in the formal launching ceremony, they cried out simultaneously, "Off she goes!"*

**off guard** *adj.* In a careless attitude; not alert to coming danger; not watching. ♦ *Tim's question caught Jean off guard, and she told him the secret before she knew it.*

**offhand** *adj.* **1.** Informal; casual; careless. ♦ *Dick found Bob's offhand manner inappropriate for business.* **2.** In an improvised fashion. ♦ *Offhand, I would guess that at least five thousand people attended the festival.*

**off-key** *adj., informal* **1.** Not proper; queer. ♦ *When George told jokes at the funeral, everyone thought his action was off-key.* **2.** In a false key. ♦ *John always sings off-key.*

**off limits** See OUT OF BOUNDS.

**off one's back** *adj. phr.* **1.** *informal* Stopped from bothering one; removed as an annoyance or pest. ♦ *"Having a kid brother always following me is a nuisance," Mary told her mother. "Can't you get him off my back?"*

**off one's chest** *adj. phr., informal* Told to someone and so not bothering you anymore; not making you feel worried or upset, because you have talked about it. ♦ *After Dave told the principal that he had cheated on the test, he was glad because it was off his chest.*

**off one's hands** *adv. phr.* No longer in your care or possession. ♦ *Ginny was glad to have the sick dog taken off her hands by the doctor.*

**off one's high horse** *adj. phr., informal* **1.** Not acting proud and scornful; humble and agreeable. ♦ *The girls were so kind to Nancy after her mother died that she came down off her high horse and made friends with them.*

**off one's rocker** *or* **off one's trolley** *adj. phr., informal* Not thinking correctly; crazy; silly; foolish. ♦ *Tom is off his rocker if he thinks he can run faster than Bob can.* ♦ *If you think you can learn to figure skate in one lesson, you're off your trolley.*

**offshoot** *n.* A derivative; a side product. ♦ *The discovery of nuclear reactors was an offshoot of research in quantum physics.*

**off the air** *adj. phr.* Not broadcasting; observing radio silence. ♦ *The talk show is off the air on Wednesdays and Fridays.*

**off the beam** *adv. or adj. phr.* **1.** *(Of an airplane)* Not in the radio beam that marks the path to follow between airports; flying in the wrong direction. ♦ *A radio signal tells the pilot of an airplane when his plane is off the beam.* **2.** *slang* Wrong; mistaken. ♦ *Maud was off the beam when she said that the girls didn't like her.*

**off the beaten track** *adv. phr.* Not well known or often used; not gone to or seen by many people; unusual. ♦ *We are looking for a vacation spot that is off the beaten track.*

**off the cuff** *adv. phr., informal* Without preparing ahead of time what you will say; without preparation. ♦ *Some presidents like to speak off the cuff to newspaper reporters but others prefer to think questions over and write their answers.*

**off-the-cuff** *adj., informal* Not prepared ahead of time.—Used of a speech or remarks. ♦ *Jack was made master of ceremonies because he was a good off-the-cuff speaker.*

**off the hook** *adv. phr.* Out of trouble; out of an awkward or embarrassing situation. ♦ *Thelma found she had made two dates for the same night; she asked Sally to get her off the hook by going out with one of the boys.*

**off the mark** *adv. phr.* Having missed the target; gone astray. ♦ *Your comments to the boss were way off the mark; I am* afraid he will start watching you very closely from now on.

**off the phone** *adj. phr.* Finished; through; having stopped talking. ♦ *"Please let me know when you're off the phone," John said to his wife. "I have to make some important calls." ♦ "Get off the phone, you chattering teenager!" John yelled at his sixteen-year-old daughter, who kept talking on the phone for hours.*

**off the record**[1] *adv. phr.* Confidentially. ♦ *"Off the record," the boss said, "you will get a good raise for next year, but you'll have to wait for the official letter."*

**off the record**[2] *adj. phr.* Not to be published or told; secret; confidential. ♦ *The president told the reporters his remarks were strictly off the record.*—Sometimes used with hyphens, before the noun. ♦ *The governor was angry when a newspaper printed his off-the-record comments.*

**off the table** *adv. phr.* Not included in the agenda; not to be discussed; not a part of scheduled debate. ♦ *Salary raises at our university are off the table for the next two years due to the state's financial difficulties.*

**off the top of one's head** *adv. or adj. phr., informal* Without thinking hard; quickly. ♦ *Vin answered the teacher's question off the top of his head.*

**off the wagon** *adj. phr., slang* No longer refusing to drink whiskey or other alcoholic beverages; drinking liquor again, after stopping for a while. ♦ *When a heavy drinker quits he must really quit. One little drink of whiskey is enough to drive him off the wagon.*

**off the wall** *adj. phr.* Strange; out of the ordinary; stupid. ♦ *He has been making off-the-wall remarks all day; something must be the matter with him.*

**of late** *adv. phr., formal* In the recent past; not long ago; a short time ago; lately; recently. ♦ *There have been too many high school dropouts of late.*

**of necessity** *adv. phr.* Because there is no other way; because it must be; necessarily. ♦ *Being a professional actor of necessity means working nights and Sundays.*

**of old** *adj. phr.* Of ancient times; of long ago. ♦ *Knights of old had to wear armor in battle.*

**of one's life** *adj. phr.* The best or worst; greatest.—Usually describing a time or effort. ♦ *His race for the presidency was the political fight of his life.*

**of one's own accord** *or* **of one's own free will** *adv. phr.* Without suggestion or help from anyone else; without being told; voluntarily. ♦ *On her mother's birthday, Betsy did the dishes of her own accord. ♦ John hates baths I can't believe he would take one of his own free will.*

**of service** *adj. phr.* Valuable as a source of aid; helpful; useful. ♦ *A good jack-knife is often of service to a camper.*

**of sorts** *or* **of a sort** *adj. phr.* Not especially good; not very good; of common quality. ♦ *Joel was a magician of sorts, and popular at parties.*

**of the same mind** *adv. phr.* In agreement; in consonance. ♦ *It is a good thing when father and son are of the same mind regarding business and politics.*

**oil and water** *n. phr.* Two very different things that will not mix. ♦ *Mimi and Helen are sisters, but they really are as different as oil and water. ♦ You can't make a Jew worship in a mosque, and you can't make a Muslim worship in a synagogue. They may resemble one another outwardly, but inside they are oil and water.*

**old as the hills** *adj. phr.* Very old; ancient. ♦ *"Why didn't you laugh?" she asked. "Because that joke is as old as the hills," he answered.*

**old bag** *n. phr., slang, avoidable* Old, ragged woman. ♦ *"Who's that poor old bag over there?" John asked. "For your information," Ted answered, "that poor old bag is my mother." "Oh, I am so sorry," John said. "I hope I didn't offend you."*

**old boy network** *n. phr.* A system whereby men who went to the same school help each other to get good jobs, regardless of their ability or training. ♦ *Peter got his lucrative job thanks to the old boy network rather than because of his qualifications.*

**old college try** *n. phr.* An attempt to win a favor from another by mentioning the fact that one had gone to the same college or university as the party from whom the favor is requested. ♦ *Since he needed a job, he decided to use the* *old college try when he contacted Jerry, but it didn't work.*

**old country** *n. phr.* Primarily Europe, but also any country other than the United States where one originally came from. ♦ *Al's wife was born in Chicago but Al himself is from the old country, Ireland.*

**old flame** *n. phr.* An erstwhile lover. ♦ *Did you know that Meg was one of Howard's old flames?*

**old guard** *n. phr.* People whose ideas may be out of date, but who have been in power for a long time. ♦ *There will not be any change in policy at the company, as long as the old guard still works here.*

**old hand** *n. phr.* An experienced and highly skilled expert at some particular job. ♦ *Uncle Joe is an old hand at repairing car engines.*

**old hat** *adj., informal* Old-fashioned; not new or different. ♦ *By now, putting satellites in orbit is old hat to space scientists.*

**old head on young shoulders** *adj. phr.* Said of someone much wiser than the number of his or her years would warrant.—A proverb. ♦ *"Your son is a very precocious person; watch out for him," John said to Ted. "What do you mean?" Ted asked. "He has an old head on young shoulders," Ted went on. "It is obvious from all the remarks he makes."*

**old maid** *n. phr.* A spinster; a woman who has never married. ♦ *Because my old maid aunt is a terrific cook as well as a good-looking woman, nobody understands why she never married.*

**old stamping ground** See HAPPY HUNTING GROUND.

**old story** *n.* An everyday occurrence; something that often happens. ♦ *Jane's temper tantrums were an old story.*

**old-timer** *n.* An old person who remembers bygone days, matters, and personalities. ♦ *There was an old-timer at the party who told us interesting details about World War II.*

**old world** *n. phr.* Europe, the continent; a continental manner. ♦ *Tom had an old world manner that thoroughly charmed all the ladies.*

**olive branch** *n. phr.* An overture; a symbol of peace. ♦ *Tired of the constant fighting, the majority government extended an olive branch to the militant minority.*

**on account** *adv. phr.* As part payment of a debt; to lessen the amount owed. ♦ *John paid $10 down and $5 on account each month for his bicycle.*

**on account of** *prep.* As a result of; because of. ♦ *The picnic was held in the gym on account of the rain.*

**on a diet** *adv. phr.* In a weight-losing program characterized by eating low-calorie food. ♦ *John is on a diet; he's already lost twenty pounds.*

**on a dime** *adv. phr., informal* In a very small space. ♦ *Bob can turn that car on a dime.*

**on-again, off-again** See OFF-AGAIN, ON-AGAIN.

**on all fours** *adv. phr.* **1.** On all four legs; on hands and knees. ♦ *Fido sat up to "beg" but dropped down on all fours to eat the dog biscuit Sam gave him.* **2.** *informal* On a level of equality; of the same value. ♦ *Wigs may be widely used, but they are still not on all fours with beautiful natural hair.*

**on an average** *or* **on the average** *adv. phr.* In most cases; usually. ♦ *On the average, Mr. Blank trades in his car for a new one every three years.*

**on and off** See OFF AND ON.

**on an even keel** *adv. phr., informal* In a well-ordered way or condition; orderly. ♦ *When the football rally became a riot, the principal stepped to the platform and got things back on an even keel.*

**on a pedestal** *adv. phr.* Lovingly honored and cared for. ♦ *Bill is always waiting on his fiancee and bringing her flowers and candy. He has certainly put her on a pedestal.*

**on approval** *adv. phr.* With the understanding that the thing may be refused. ♦ *Mr. Grey bought his camera on approval.* ♦ *The company offered to send a package of stamps on approval.*

**on a roll** *adv. phr.* Having a good time; doing well; progressing very well. ♦ *The poet had a great time with his new volume; he produced poem after poem. He was on a roll, as never before.*

**on a shoestring** *adv. phr.* With little money to spend; on a very low budget. ♦ *The couple was seeing Europe on a shoestring.*

**on behalf of** See IN BEHALF OF.

**on board**[1] *prep.* On (a ship). ♦ *Joan was not on board the ship when it sailed.*

**on board**[2] *adv. or adj. phr.* On a ship. ♦ *A ship was leaving the harbor, and we saw the people on board waving.*

**on borrowed time** See LIVE ON BORROWED TIME.

**on call** *adj. phr.* **1.** Having to be paid on demand. ♦ *Jim didn't have the money ready even though he knew the bill was on call.* **2.** Ready and available. ♦ *This is Dr. Kent's day to be on call at the hospital.*

**once and for all** *adv. phr.* **1.** One time and never again; without any doubt; surely; certainly; definitely. ♦ *For once and for all, I will not go swimming with you.* **2.** Permanently. ♦ *The general decided that two bombs would destroy the enemy and end the war once and for all.*

**once in a blue moon** *adv. phr.* Very rarely; very seldom; almost never. ♦ *Coin collecting is interesting, but you find a valuable coin only once in a blue moon.*

**once in a while** *adv. phr.* Not often; not regularly; sometimes; occasionally. ♦ *We go for a picnic in the park once in a while.*

**once-over** *n., slang* **1.** A quick look; a swift examination of someone or something.—Usually used with *give* or *get.* ♦ *The new boy got the once-over from the rest of the class when he came in.* **2.** *or* **once-over-lightly** A quick or careless job, especially of cleaning or straightening; work done hastily for now. ♦ *Ann gave her room a quick once-over-lightly with the broom and dust cloth.*

**once upon a time** *adv. phr.* Sometime before now, long ago. Used at the beginning of fairy stories. ♦ *Once upon a time there lived a king who had an ugly daughter.*

**on cloud nine** *adj. phr., slang* Too happy to think of anything else; very happy. ♦ *Ada has been on cloud nine since the magazine printed the story she wrote.*

**on condition that** *conj.* Providing that; if. ♦ *I will lend you the money on condition that you pay it back in one month.*

**on credit** *adv. pr.* Without having to pay in cash or with a check; on a charge by signature or by credit card to be paid later. ♦ *We bought our new car on credit because we had no cash to pay*

for it in full. ♦ *Most people buy their first home on credit.*

**on deck** *adv. or adj. phr.* **1.** On a floor of a ship open to the outdoors. ♦ *The passengers were playing shuffleboard on deck.* ♦ *The sailors kept busy cleaning and painting on deck.* **2.** *informal* Ready to do something; present. ♦ *The scout leader told the boys to be on deck at 8:00 Saturday morning for the hike.*

**on deposit** *adv. phr.* In a bank. ♦ *I have almost $500 on deposit in my account.*

**on duty** *adj. phr.* Doing one's job; supervising. ♦ *Two soldiers are on duty guarding the gates.*

**one and the same** *adj. phr.* The same; identical. ♦ *Erle Stanley Gardner and A. A. Fair are one and the same person.*

**one-armed bandit** *n., slang* A slot machine, like those used in Las Vegas and other gambling places. ♦ *Joe was playing the one-armed bandit all day— and he lost everything he had.*

**on easy street** *adj. phr., informal* Having enough money to live very comfortably; rather rich. ♦ *After years of hard work, the Grants found themselves on easy street.*

**one damn thing after another** *or* **ODTAA** (pronounced owed-tay) *n. phr.* If there is one problem, there will be more. ♦ *First I lost my wallet, then a kid broke the window, and, lastly, my car refused to start. It was just one damn thing after another!*

**on edge** *adj. phr.* Excited or nervous; impatient. ♦ *The magician kept the children on edge all through his show.*

**one eye on** *informal* Watching or minding (a person or thing) while doing something else; part of your attention on.—Used after *have, keep,* or *with.* ♦ *Jane had one eye on the baby as she ironed.*

**one foot in the grave** *n. phr.* Near to death. ♦ *The dog is fourteen years old, blind, and feeble. He has one foot in the grave.*

**one for the books** *n. phr., informal* Very unusual; a remarkable something. ♦ *The newspaper reporter turned in a story that was one for the books.*

**one for the road** *n. phr.* A last drink before one leaves a party. ♦ *"How about one for the road?" John asked his guests before they left his house.*

**one-horse** *adj. phr.* Insignificant; modest; provincial. ◆*Arnold's business is a one-horse operation; he never had a single employee.*

**one man's meat is another man's poison** What is good for one person is not necessarily good for another.—A proverb. ◆*Even though Jeff likes to swim in ice cold water, his brother Tim hates it. This is understandable, however, because one's man's meat is another man's poison.*

**on end** *adj. phr.* Seemingly endless.—Used with plural nouns of time. ◆*Judy spent hours on end writing and re-writing her essay.*

**one-night stand** *n. phr.* **1.** A single performance given by a traveling company while on a tour. ◆*After they went bankrupt in the big cities, the traveling jazz quartet played one-night stands in the country.* **2.** A brief affair or sexual encounter. ◆*"With AIDS all around us," said Jane, "nobody is having one-night stands anymore."*

**one of these days** *or* **some of these days** *adv. phr.* Someday; sometime soon. ◆*One of these days Herbert will be famous.*

**one of us** *n. phr.* A friend; someone who thinks and reacts to things as we do; not an outsider. ◆*"Is Mike reliable?" Fred asked anxiously. "Oh yes, absolutely. You can say anything to him, really...He is one of us, you know," Ted assured him.*

**one on the city** *n., slang* A glass of water (which is provided free of charge, as a free gift from the city). ◆*What will you have?—Oh, just give me one on the city.*

**one's money's worth** *n. phr.* A fair return on one's money spent or invested. ◆*I wouldn't say that the trip was a great bargain, but I feel that we got our money's worth.*

**one's own master** *n. phr.* A person whose livelihood does not depend on others; a free person; a self-employed individual, who is not under the influence of others. ◆*"It is not surprising that George speaks so openly and sincerely; he doesn't owe allegiance to anyone, he is self-employed and doing remarkably well; in short his is his own master."*

**one's own worst enemy** *n. phr.* A person who has a tendency to hurt himself either by being physically clumsy, or by saying the wrong things at the wrong time to the wrong people, or by making the wrong choices in every walk of life. ◆*Albert ought to understand that nobody is against him; it's just that he is his own worst enemy.*

**one swallow doesn't make a summer** One manifestation of an expected larger event does not necessarily mean that the event itself is happening just yet.—A proverb. ◆*When the first customer entered their new cosmetics shop, June said to her partner, Liz, who believed that they were going to be rich instantly, "Hold it, Liz. One swallow doesn't make a summer."*

**one's pride and joy** *n. phr.* Something or someone that one is extremely proud of. ◆*John's daughter, who is a violin virtuoso, is his pride and joy.*

**one that got away** *n. phr.* Someone that one has almost married, but didn't. Said meaning both "good riddance" and "that was unfortunate." ◆*"Who is that lovely lady at the other table?" John asked his friend Ted. "Oh, that's my former fiancée, Joan, who fell in love with another guy a months before we were going to get married. She is the one that got away."*

**one-two** *n.* **1.** A succession of two punches, the first a short left, followed by a hard right punch, usually in the jaw. ◆*Ali gave Frazier the one-two.* **2.** Any quick or decisive action which takes the opposition by surprise, thereby ensuring victory. ◆*He gave us the old one-two and won the game.*

**one up** *adj. phr.* Having an advantage; being one step ahead. ◆*John graduated from high school; he is one up on Bob, who dropped out.*

**one-upmanship** *v., informal* Always keeping ahead of others; trying to keep an advantage. ◆*No matter what I do, I find that Jim has already done it better. He's an expert at one-upmanship.*

**on faith** *adv. phr.* Without question or proof. ◆*He looked so honest that we accepted his story on faith.*

**on file** *adv. phr.* Placed in a written or electronic file; on record. ◆*We are sorry we cannot hire you right now but we will keep your application on file.*

**on foot** *adv. or adj. phr.* **1.** By walking. ♦*Sally's bicycle broke and she had to return home on foot.* **2.** Being planned. ♦*The reporter said that a civil rights demonstration was on foot.* ♦*Plans have been set on foot for a party for Miss Jackson, because she is retiring.*

**on guard** *adj. phr.* Watchful; watching. ♦*The police warned people to be on guard for pickpockets during the Christmas rush.*

**on hand** *adv. phr.* **1a.** Nearby; within reach. ♦*Always have your dictionary on hand when you study.* **1b.** Here. ♦*Soon school will end and vacation will be on hand.* **2.** Present. ♦*Mr. Blake's secretary is always on hand when he appears in public.* **3.** In your possession; ready. ♦*The Girl Scouts have plenty of cookies on hand.*

**on hold** *adv. phr.* **1.** Left waiting while making a telephone call. ♦*"Sorry sir," the secretary said, "I'll have to put you on hold for a minute."* **2.** Waiting; temporarily halted. ♦*"Put your marriage plans on hold, son, and wait until after graduation," his father said seriously.*

**on ice** *adv. or adj. phr., slang* **1.** The same as won; sure to be won. ♦*The score was 20–10 in the last inning, and our team had the game on ice.* **2.** Away for safekeeping or later use; aside. ♦*The senator was voted out of office. He is on ice until the next election.*

**on leave** *adv. phr.* Having vacation; to not be on active duty. ♦*"Can I speak to Dr. Smith?" the patient asked. "Try again in two days," the nurse replied. "He is still on leave."*

**only too glad** *or* **only too happy** *or* **only too pleased** *adj. phr.* Eager to comply or please; very willing to do something. ♦*"Would you watch the kids while we're gone?" Joan asked her neighbor Mary, who had no children of her own. "I'd be only too glad to do so," Mary eagerly replied.*

**on occasion** *adv. phr.* Sometimes; occasionally. ♦*We go to New York on occasion.*

**on one hand** *adv. phr.* Looking at a thing in one of two possible ways; from one point of view.—Usually used with *on the other hand.* ♦*John wants to be a printer or a teacher; on one hand, printing pays better; on the other hand, teaching is more fun.*

**on one's account** *adv. phr.* For your good; because you want to help or please someone. ♦*I hope you didn't bring tea to the picnic just on my account.*

**on one's back** *adj. phr., informal* Making insistent demands of you; being an annoyance or bother. ♦*My wife has been on my back for weeks to fix the front door screen.*

**on one's bad side** *or* **on the bad side of one** *adj. phr., informal* Not liked by someone; not friendly with a person. ♦*Sally's boyfriend got on Father's bad side by keeping Sally out too late after the dance.*

**on one's chest** *adj. phr., informal* Hidden in your thoughts or feelings and bothering you; making you feel worried or upset; that is something you want to talk to someone about. ♦*"Well, Dave," said the coach, "You look sad—what's on your chest?"*

**on one's coattails** *adv. phr.* Because of another's merits, success, or popularity. ♦*Bob and Jim are best friends. When Jim was invited to join a fraternity, Bob rode in on his coattails.*

**on one's feet** *adv. phr.* **1.** Standing or walking; not sitting or lying down; up. ♦*Before the teacher finished asking the question, George was on his feet ready to answer it.* **2.** Recovering; getting better from sickness or trouble. ♦*Jack is back on his feet after a long illness.*

**on one's good behavior** *adv. phr.* Behaving right to make a good impression. ♦*The minister is coming to dinner, and Mother wants us to be on our good behavior.*

**on one's good side** *or* **on the good side of one** *adj. phr., informal* Friendly with someone; liked by a person. ♦*Successful workers stay on the good side of their bosses.*

**on one's hands** *adv. or adj. phr.* In your care or responsibility; that you must do something about. ♦*Mrs. Blake left her five children with me while she shopped. I could not get anything done with the children on my hands.*

**on one's head** *or* **upon one's head** *adv. phr.* On one's self. ♦*When the school board fired the superintendent of schools, they brought the anger of the parents upon their heads.*

**on one's high horse** *adj. phr., informal* **1.** Acting as if you are better than others; being very proud and scornful. ♦ *Martha was chairman of the picnic committee, and at the picnic she was on her high horse, telling everyone what to do.* **2.** Refusing to be friendly because you are angry; in a bad temper. ♦ *Joe was on his high horse because he felt Mary wasn't giving him enough attention.*

**on one's honor** *adj. phr.* Bound by one's honesty; trusted. ♦ *The students were not supervised during the examination. They were on their honor not to cheat.*

**on one's knees** *adj. phr.* **1.** Pleading; begging very hard. ♦ *The boys were on their knees for hours before their parents agreed to their camping plans.* **2.** In a very weak condition; near failure. ♦ *When the graduates of the school heard that it was on its knees they gave money generously so that it would not close.*

**on one's last legs** *adj. phr.* Failing; near the end. ♦ *The blacksmith's business is on its last legs.*

**on one's mind** *adv. phr.* In one's thoughts. ♦ *What's on your mind?*

**on one's nerves** See GET ON ONE'S NERVES.

**on one's own** *adj. phr.* With no help from others. ♦ *Being on your own may be a frightening experience.*

**on one's own account** *or informal* **on one's own hook** *adv. phr.* **1.** For yourself; as a free agent; independently. ♦ *After they had picked out the class gift, members of the committee did some shopping on their own account.*

**on one's own feet** See STAND ON ONE'S OWN FEET.

**on one's own time** *adv. phr.* During one's free time; not during working or school hours. ♦ *If you want to play football, you'll have to do it on your own time.*

**on one's part** *or* **on the part of one** *adj. phr.* **1.** Of or by you; of someone's. ♦ *When Miss Brown said I was a good student, that was pure kindness on her part.*

**on one's shoulders** *adv. or adj. phr.* In your care; as your responsibility. ♦ *The success of the program rests on your shoulders.*

**on one's toes** *adj. phr., informal* Alert; ready to act. ♦ *The successful ball player is always on his toes.*

**on one's uppers** *adj. phr., informal* Very poor. ♦ *Mr. White had been out of work for several months and was on his uppers.*

**on pain of** *also* **under pain of** *prep., formal* At the risk of; under penalty of. ♦ *The workers went on strike on pain of losing their jobs.*

**on paper** *adv. or adj. phr.* Judging by appearances only and not by past performance; in theory; theoretically. ♦ *On paper, the American colonies should have lost the Revolutionary War.*

**on pins and needles** *adj. phr., informal* Worried; nervous. ♦ *Many famous actors are on pins and needles before the curtain opens for a play.*

**on purpose** *adv. phr.* For a reason; because you want to; not accidentally. ♦ *Jane did not forget her coat; she left it in the locker on purpose.*

**on record** *adj. phr.* **1.** An official or recorded statement or fact; said for everyone to know. ♦ *The two candidates went on television to put their ideas on record.* **2.** Known to have said or done a certain thing.—Usually used with *as.* ♦ *The mayor went on record as opposing a tax raise.*

**on sale** *adj. phr.* Selling for a special low price. ♦ *Tomato soup that is usually sold for ninety cents a can is now on sale for seventy cents.*

**on schedule**[1] *adv. phr.* As planned or expected; at the right time. ♦ *The school bus arrived at school on schedule.*

**on schedule**[2] *adj. phr.* Punctual; as planned. ♦ *The new airline claims to have more on schedule arrivals than the competition.*

**on second thought** See SECOND THOUGHT.

**on speaking terms** *adv. phr.* To be familiar with someone so as to actually speak with that person instead of just waving or nodding; cordial. ♦ *John and Tim have been on speaking terms for many years, but otherwise they are not very close.* ♦ *Mary and Ted are no longer on speaking terms; they were divorced ten years ago.*

**on strike** *adv. phr.* To not be working as a matter of protest against low wages or other unacceptable employment conditions. ♦ *"Why are those people walking around in front of the store carrying signs?" the foreign visitor asked Ted. "Because they are on strike," he explained.*

**on tenterhooks** *adv. phr.* To be in a state of painful suspense; to feel anxious and impatient to receive some news, good or bad. ♦ *When Rose's father was near death, her husband told me, "We are on tenterhooks waiting for the phone call every day." ♦ The young poet was on tenterhooks until his new manuscript was accepted by Princeton University Press.*

**on the air** *adj. or adv. phr.* Broadcasting or being broadcast on radio or TV. ♦ *His show is on the air at six o'clock.*

**on the alert** *adj. phr.* Alert; watchful; careful. ♦ *Campers must be on the alert for poison ivy and poison oak.*

**on the average** See ON AN AVERAGE.

**on the ball** *adj. phr., informal* **1.** Paying attention and doing things well.— Used after *is* or *get.* ♦ *The coach told Jim he must get on the ball or he cannot stay on the team.* **2.** That is a skill or ability; making you good at things.— Used after *have.* ♦ *John will succeed in life; he has a lot on the ball.*

**on the bandwagon** *adj. phr., informal* In or into the newest popular group or activity; in or into something you join just because many others are joining it.—Often used after *climb, get,* or *jump.* ♦ *When all George's friends decided to vote for Bill, George climbed on the bandwagon too.*

**on the beam** *adv. or adj. phr.* **1.** (Of an airplane) In the radio beam that marks the path to follow between airports; flying in the right direction. ♦ *A radio signal tells the pilot of an airplane when he is flying on the beam.* **2.** *slang* Doing well; just right; good or correct. ♦ *Kenneth's answer was right on the beam.*

**on the bench 1.** Sitting in a law court as a judge. ♦ *Judge Wyzanski is on the bench this morning.* **2.** Sitting among the substitute players. ♦ *The coach had to keep his star player on the bench with a sprained ankle.*

**on the blink** *adj. phr.* Faulty; malfunctioning; inoperative. ♦ *I need to call a competent repairman because my computer is on the blink again.*

**on the block** *adj. phr.* To be sold; for sale. ♦ *The vacant house was on the block.*

**on the brain** *adj. phr., slang* Filling your thoughts; too much thought about; almost always in mind. ♦ *Mary Ann has boys on the brain.*

**on the brink of** *adv. phr.* Facing a new event that's about to happen. ♦ *"I am on the brink of a new discovery," our physics professor proudly announced.*

**on the button** *adv., adj., slang* At the right place; at the heart of the matter. ♦ *John's remark was right on the button.*

**on the cheap** *adv. phr.* Inexpensively; on a tight budget. ♦ *She buys most of her clothes on the cheap in secondhand stores.*

**on the contrary** *adv. phr.* Exactly the opposite; rather; instead. ♦ *"You don't like football, do you?" "On the contrary, I like it very much."*

**on the dole** *adv. phr.* Drawing unemployment benefits. ♦ *When Jim lost his job he got on the dole and is still on it.*

**on the dot** *also* **on the button** *adv. phr., informal* Exactly on time; not early and not late. ♦ *Susan arrived at the party at 2:00 P.M. on the dot.*

**on the double!** *adv. phr.* Hurry up! ♦ *"Let's go! On the double!" the pilot cried, as he started up the engine of the small plane.*

**on the eve of** *prep.* Just before (an event). ♦ *On the eve of the election, the president proposed a plan to cut taxes.*

**on the face of it** *adv. phr.* Apparently; as it seems. ♦ *His statement that he is a millionaire is, on the face of it, false.*

**on the fast track** *adv. phr.* In a position where one rises through the ranks of an organization faster than one would normally. ♦ *John got three early promotions one after another; he sure seems to be on the fast track!*

**on the fence** *adj. or adv. phr.* Not able, or not wanting to choose; in doubt; undecided.—Often used with *sit.* ♦ *Mrs. Jones has decided to vote for the Democrats, but Mr. Jones is still on the fence.*

**on the fly[1]** *adv. phr.* **1.** While in the air; in flight. ♦ *The bird caught a bug on the fly.* **2.** *informal* Between other activities; while busy with many things. ♦ *The president was so busy that he had to dictate letters on the fly.*

**on the fly[2]** *adj. phr., informal* Busy; going somewhere in a hurry; going about doing things. ♦ *Getting the house ready for the visitors kept Mother on the fly all day.*

**on the go** *adj. phr., informal* Active and busy. ♦ *Successful businessmen are on the go most of the time.*

**on the heels of** *prep.* Just after; following (something, especially an event).— Often used with *hard* for emphasis. ♦ *Hard on the heels of the women's liberation parade, homosexuals declared a "gay pride week."*

**on the hour** *adv. phr.* Each time the hour has zero minutes and zero seconds. ♦ *The uptown bus goes past the school on the hour.*

**on the house** *adj. phr., informal* Paid for by the owner. ♦ *At the opening of the new hotel, the champagne was on the house.*

**on the job** *adj. phr., informal* Working hard; not wasting time. ♦ *Joe was on the job all of the time that he was at work.*

**on the lam** *adj. or adv. phr., slang* Running away, especially from the law; in flight. ♦ *The bank robber was on the lam for ten months before the police caught him.*

**on the level** *adj. phr., informal* Honest and fair; telling the whole truth. ♦ *Our teacher respects the students who are on the level with her.*

**on the line** See LAY ON THE LINE *or* PUT ON THE LINE.

**on the lookout** *adj. phr.* Watching closely. ♦ *Forest rangers are always on the lookout for forest fires.*

**on the loose** *adj. phr., informal* Free to go; not shut in or stopped by anything. ♦ *The zookeeper forgot to close the gate to the monkey cage and the monkeys were on the loose.*

**on the make** *adj., slang* **1.** Promiscuous or aggressive in one's sexual advances. ♦ *I can't stand Murray; he's always on the make.* **2.** Pushing to get ahead in one's career; doing anything to succeed. ♦ *The new department head is a young man on the make, who expects to be company president in ten years.*

**on the market** *adj. phr.* For sale. ♦ *In the summer many fresh vegetables are on the market.*

**on the mend** *adj. phr.* Healing; becoming better. ♦ *John's broken leg is on the mend.*

**on the money** *adv. phr.* Exactly right; exactly accurate. ♦ *Algernon won the lottery; the numbers he picked were right on the money.*

**on the move** *adj. or adv. phr.* **1.** Moving around from place to place; in motion. ♦ *It was a very cold day, and the teacher watching the playground kept on the move to stay warm.* **2.** Moving forward; going somewhere. ♦ *The candidate promised that if people would make him president, he would get the country on the move.*

**on the nose** *adv. phr., informal* Just right; exactly. ♦ *The airplane pilot found the small landing field on the nose.*

**on the other hand** *adv. phr.* Looking at the other side; from another point of view.—Used to introduce an opposite or different fact or idea. ♦ *Jim wanted to go to the movies; his wife, on the other hand, wanted to stay home and read.*

**on the outs** *adj. phr., informal* Not friendly; having a quarrel. ♦ *Mary and Sue were on the outs.*

**on the phone** *adv. phr.* Using the telephone; speaking to someone by telephone. ♦ *Please don't disturb me when I am on the phone.*

**on the point of** *prep.* Ready to begin; very near to.—Usually used with a verbal noun. ♦ *The baby was on the point of crying when her mother finally came home.*

**on the Q.T.** *adv. phr., informal* Secretly; without anyone's knowing. ♦ *The teachers got the principal a present strictly on the Q.T.*

**on the right track** *adv. phr.* Going in the right direction; proceeding correctly. ♦ *The detectives were on the right track in trying to find the kidnapped girl.* ♦ *John quit literature for chemistry, which suits his talents much better. He is now finally on the right track.*

**on the road** *adv. or adj. phr.* **1.** Traveling; moving from one place to another. ♦ *When we go on vacation, we take a lunch to eat while on the road.* **2.** Changing; going from one condition to another. ♦ *Mary was very sick for several weeks, but now she is on the road to recovery.*

**on the rocks** *adj. phr.* **1.** *informal* Wrecked or ruined. ♦ *Mr. Jones' business and marriage were both on the rocks.* **2.** With ice only. ♦ *At the restaurant, Sally ordered orange juice on the rocks.*

**on the ropes** *adv. or adj. phr.* **1.** Against the ropes of a boxing ring and almost not able to stand up. ♦ *The fighter was on the ropes and could hardly lift his gloves.* **2.** Almost defeated; helpless; near failure. ♦ *The new supermarket took most of the business from Mr. Thomas's grocery, and the little store was soon on the ropes.*

**on the run** *adv. or adj. phr.* **1.** In a hurry; hurrying. ♦ *Jane called "Help!" and Tom came on the run.* **2.** Going away from a fight; in retreat; retreating. ♦ *The enemy soldiers were on the run.*

**on the safe side** *adv. phr.* Provided for against a possible emergency; well prepared. ♦ *"Please double-check these proofs, Mr. Brown," the printer said, "just to be on the safe side."*

**on the same page with** *adv. phr.* In agreement with someone; subscribing to the same values. ♦ *It will be interesting to see if the European Union and the United States can be on the same page as far as the war against terrorism is concerned.*

**on the same wavelength** *adv. phr.* To think exactly the same way as someone else; agree with someone concerning an important issue. ♦ *The president and the national security advisor are on the same wavelength when it comes to national defense.* ♦ *Will the Palestinians and the Israelis ever be on the same page as far as statehood is concerned?*

**on the same page** See ON THE SAME WAVELENGTH.

**on the shelf** *adv. or adj. phr., informal* Laid aside; not useful anymore. ♦ *When a girl grows up, she puts childish habits on the shelf.*

**on the side** *adv. phr., informal* **1.** In addition to a main thing, amount or quan-

tity; extra. ♦ *He ordered a hamburger with onions and French fries on the side.* **2.** *or* on the ——— side Tending toward; rather. ♦ *Grandmother thought Jane's new skirt was on the short side.*

**on the sly** *adv. phr.* So that other people won't know; secretly. ♦ *The boys smoked on the sly.*

**on the spot** *adv. or adj. phr.* **1.** *or* upon the spot At that exact time and at the same time or place; without waiting or leaving. ♦ *The news of important events is often broadcast on the spot over television.* **2.** *informal also* in a spot In trouble, difficulty, or embarrassment. ♦ *Mr. Jones is on the spot because he cannot pay back the money he borrowed.* **3.** *slang* In danger of murder; named or listed for death. ♦ *After he talked to the police, the gangsters put him on the spot.*

**on the spur of the moment** *adv. phr.* On a sudden wish or decision; suddenly; without thought or preparation. ♦ *John had not planned to take the trip; he just left on the spur of the moment.*

**on the stage** *adv. or adj. phr.* In or into the work of being an actor or actress. ♦ *John's brother is on the stage.*

**on the strength of** *prep.* With faith or trust in; depending upon; with the support of. ♦ *Bill started a restaurant on the strength of his experience as a cook in the army.*

**on the string** *or* **on a string** *adv. phr., informal* Under your influence or control; obedient to every wish. ♦ *The baby had his mother on a string.*

**on the table** *adv. phr.* To be part of the agenda; be included in what is to be discussed and decided. ♦ *"Is Palestinian statehood on the table?" the representative from the Arab League asked. "Not yet, but it will soon be on the table," the secretary of the United Nations answered.*

**on the take** *adv. phr.* Bribable; corrupt. ♦ *Officer O'Keefe was put on three months' probation because it was alleged that he was on the take.*

**on the tip of one's tongue** *adv. phr.* About to say something, such as a name, a telephone number, etc., but unable to remember it for the moment. ♦ *"His name is on the tip of my tongue," Tom said. "It will come to me in a minute."*

**on the town** *adv. or adj. phr., informal* In or into a town to celebrate; having a good time or enjoying the amusements in a town. ♦*When the sailors got off their ship they went out on the town.*

**on the track of** *or* **on the trail of** *adv. or adj. phr.* Hunting or looking for; trying to find; following. ♦*The hunter is on the track of a deer.* ♦*The lawyer is on the trail of new proof in the case.*

**on the up and up** *adj. phr., informal* Honest; trustworthy; sincere. ♦*We felt that he was honest and could be trusted. This information is on the up and up.*

**on the wagon** *adv. phr.* Participating in an alcohol addiction program; not touching any alcoholic beverage. ♦*Jim's doctor and his family finally managed to convince him that he was an alcoholic and should go on the wagon.*

**on the wane and on the wax** *adv. phr.* Decreasing and increasing.—Said of the moon. ♦*The moon is regularly on the wane and on the wax at regular intervals lasting half a month.*

**on the warpath** *adj. phr., informal* **1.** Very angry. ♦*When Mother saw the mess in the kitchen she went on the warpath.* **2.** Making an attack; fighting. ♦*The government is on the warpath against narcotics.*

**on the watch** *adj. phr.* Alert; watchful. ♦*The customs inspector was on the watch for diamond smugglers.*

**on the way** *or* **on one's way** *adv. or adj. phr.* Coming; going toward a place or goal; started. ♦*Help was on the way.* ♦*The train left and Bill was on his way to New York.*

**on the whole** *adv. phr.* **1.** In the most important things; in most ways. ♦*On the whole, Billy did very well in school this year.* **2.** In most cases; usually. ♦*On the whole, men are stronger than women.*

**on the wing** *adv. or adj. phr.* **1.** In the air; while flying. ♦*The duck flew away, but John shot it on the wing.* **2.** *informal* In constant motion; always very busy. ♦*Susan was on the wing doing things to get ready for her trip.* ♦ **3.** *informal* Moving from one place to another; traveling; going somewhere. ♦*Mary's husband is a traveling salesman and he's always on the wing.*

**on the wrong track** *adv. phr.* Lost; pursuing the wrong lead. ♦*Professor MacAlister confessed that his chemical experiments were on the wrong track.*

**on time** *adv. or adj. phr.* **1.** At the time arranged; not late; promptly. ♦*The train left on time.* ♦*Mary is always on time for an appointment.* **2.** On the installment plan; on credit, paying a little at a time. ♦*John bought a car on time.*

**on top** *adv. or adj. phr., informal* In the lead; with success; with victory. ♦*The horse that everyone had expected would be on top actually came in third.*

**on top of** *prep.* **1.** On the top of; standing or lying on; on. ♦*When the player on the other team dropped the ball, Bill fell on top of it.* **2.** *informal* Very close to. **3.** *informal* In addition to; along with. ♦*Mary worked at the store all day and on top of that she had to baby-sit with her brother.* **4.** *informal* Managing very well; in control of. ♦*Although his new job was very complicated, John was on top of it within a few weeks.* **5.** Knowing all about; not falling behind in information about; up-to-date on. ♦*Mary stays on top of the news by reading newspapers and magazines.*

**on top of the world** *or* **sitting on top of the world** *also* **(Southern) sitting on high cotton** *adj. phr., informal* Feeling pleased and happy; feeling successful. ♦*John was on top of the world when he found out that he got into college.* ♦*The girls were sitting on high cotton because their basketball team had won the trophy.*

**on trial** *adv. or adj. phr.* **1.** For testing or trying out for a time before making a decision. ♦*I was lucky that I had bought the machine on trial because I didn't like it and was able to return it.* **2.** In a court being tried for a crime before a judge or jury. ♦*John White was on trial for murder.*

**open a can of worms** See CAN OF WORMS, PANDORA'S BOX

**open and aboveboard** *adj. phr.* Honest. ♦*Jacob felt that the firm he was doing business with wasn't entirely open and aboveboard.*

**open and shut** See CUT AND DRIED.

**open-door policy** *n. phr.* A policy that states that newcomers are welcome to join the company, firm, or country in question. ♦ *During the nineteenth century the United States had an open-door policy regarding immigration.*

**open doors** *v. phr.* To give others a chance to better their position in life; get ahead. ♦ *The summer camp financed by the city is opening doors for aspiring young musicians and singers, who want to try out at the local symphony center.*

**open fire** *v. phr.* To begin shooting. ♦ *The big warship turned its guns toward the enemy ship and opened fire.*

**openhanded** *adj.* Generous; liberal. ♦ *Although not wealthy himself, Bob was always very openhanded with those who needed help.*

**open heart** *n.* **1.** No hiding of your feelings; frankness; freedom. ♦ *She spoke with an open heart of her warm feelings for her pupils.* **2.** Kindness; generosity. ♦ *She contributed to the fund with an open heart.*

**open its doors** *v. phr.* **1.** To allow someone or something to enter or join; become open. ♦ *That college was started for women only, but a few years ago it opened its doors to men.* **2.** To begin doing business; open. ♦ *Proffitts Department Store is having a birthday sale; it first opened its doors fifty years ago this month.*

**open letter** *n. phr.* A public message in the form of a letter addressed to a particular person or to a group. ♦ *There was an open letter to the president of the United States in today's morning paper.*

**open market** *n. phr.* Goods or securities available for purchase by all. ♦ *The stocks of certain companies are on the open market.*

**open marriage** *n. phr.* An arrangement by mutual agreement between husband and wife whereby they are both allowed to have extramarital affairs. ♦ *Chances are the open marriage arrangement they had didn't work out too well so they are getting a divorce.*

**open-minded** *adj.* Having no dogmatic or biased views on matters of theory, religion, politics, etc. ♦ *Fred is easy to talk to about anything; he is a highly intelligent and open-minded person.*

**open one's eyes** *or* **open up one's eyes** *v. phr.* To make a person see or under-

stand the truth; make a person realize; tell a person what is really happening or what really exists. ♦ *John's eyes were opened up to the world of nature when he visited his grandfather's farm.*—**eye opener** *n.* Something that makes you understand the truth. ♦ *Pam's first visit to school was a real eye-opener.*

**open one's heart** *v. phr.* **1.** To talk about your feelings honestly; confide in someone. ♦ *John felt much better after he opened his heart to Betty.* **2.** To be sympathetic to; give love or help generously. ♦ *Mrs. Smith opened her heart to the poor little boy.*

**open onto** *v. phr.* To have a view of. ♦ *Our apartment in Chicago has a set of windows that open onto Lake Michigan.*

**open question** *n. phr.* A debatable issue. ♦ *Whether assisted suicide is legal and moral or not is still an open question, recent publicity on the matter notwithstanding.*

**open secret** *n. phr.* Something that is supposed to be a secret but that everyone knows. ♦ *It is an open secret that Mary and John are engaged.*

**open sesame** *n. phr., literary* Immediate means of entrance, or unobstructed access to something. ♦ *Tom mistakenly believed that his wealth would be an open sesame to the world of creative arts.*

**open shop** *n. phr.* A factory or firm that employs both union and non-union labor. ♦ *The firm refuses to adopt an open shop policy.*

**open the door** *v. phr.* To allow more action or discussion; give a chance. ♦ *Learning to read and write opens the door to a better job and better living conditions.*

**open the floodgates** *v. phr.* To let loose an outburst of human activity or emotion. ♦ *It would open the floodgates of anger and discontent if the university raised tuition too soon.*

**open up** *v.* **1.** To show for the first time; make clear; reveal. ♦ *The story of Helen Keller's life opened up a whole new world to Mary.* **2.** To make available; present an opportunity; offer. ♦ *The building of the railroad opened up new lands to the pioneers.* **3.** *informal* To go faster. ♦ *When they got out on the* *highway John opened up and drove at 65 miles per hour.* **4.** *informal* To begin to shoot. ♦ *When they got close to the enemy lines, they opened up with all they had.* **5.** *informal* To begin to talk frankly. ♦ *After John learned to trust Mr. Jones, he opened up and told him how he felt.* **6.** To spread out. ♦ *After a while the road opened up and they traveled more quickly.* **7.** To become available. ♦ *When she got her college diploma, many new jobs opened up.*

**opposite number** *n. phr.* A person occupying the same position as somone in a different group, organization, or country. ♦ *The opposite number of the President of the United States in Germany is the Chancellor of the Federal Republic.*

**opposite sex** *n. phr.* The sex different from the one being discussed or mentioned. ♦ *Fred came out and said he was gay, having never had any interest in the opposite sex.*

**optional origin** *n.* Stipulation in international commodities contract whereby the seller may ship from either his foreign or his domestic resources. ♦ *Be sure to enter that in the books as an optional origin order.*

**order about** *or* **around** *v. phr.* To dictate arrogantly to someone; domineer. ♦ *Dan orders his younger colleagues around in a most unpleasant way.*

**or other** *adv.*—Used to emphasize indefinite words or phrases beginning with *some* (as *someone, something, somewhere, somehow, sometime*). ♦ *I'll think of something or other for the program.* ♦ *Someone or other will take the letters to the post office.*

**or so** *adv.* About; or a little more. ♦ *Mr. Brown will be back in a day or so.* ♦ *The book cost $5 or so.*

**or words to that effect** *n. phr.* An expression used when one cannot quote something exactly, but gives a paraphrase of what was said, meaning "that is the rough meaning of what I am quoting." ♦ *Ted complained that his boss was a common thief, or words to that effect.*

**other fish to fry** *n. phr., informal* Other things to do; other plans. ♦ *They wanted John to be the secretary, but he had other fish to fry.*

**other half** *n. phr.* One's husband or wife. ♦ *"Where is your other half?" Suzanne asked Mary. "He is still at work," Mary replied.*

**out and about** See UP AND ABOUT.

**out-and-out** *adj.* Extreme; complete; thorough. ♦ *The candidate was an out-and-out conservative.*

**out at the elbows** *adj. phr.* Poorly or shabbily dressed. ♦ *Roy walks around out at the elbows, but it's not because he is penniless, but more in imitation of a certain style.*

**out back** *adv. phr.* In one's backyard. ♦ *On the Fourth of July they were out back making preparations for their holiday barbecue.*

**outback** *n.* **1.** The remote and uncultivated wilderness areas of Australia or New Zealand, with very few inhabitants. ♦ *Mike and Barbara roughed it in the Australian outback for nearly two years.* **2.** Any remote, sparsely populated region. ♦ *Tom's old ranch in Texas is next to an arid outback.*

**out cold** *adv. or adj., informal* Unconscious; in a faint. ♦ *The ball hit Dick in the head and knocked him out cold for ten minutes.*

**outer space** *n.* What is outside of the earth's air. ♦ *An astronaut cannot live without oxygen when he goes into outer space.*

**out for** *prep.* Joining, or planning to join; taking part in; competing for a place in. ♦ *John is out for the basketball team.* ♦ *Mary is going out for the school newspaper.*

**out from under** *adj. phr., informal* Free from something that worries you; seeing the end; finished.—Usually used with *be* or *get.* ♦ *John had so many debts, he couldn't get out from under.*

**out-Herod Herod** *or* **more Catholic than the pope** *v. phr.* To exaggeratedly do or overdo something, usually done by neophytes in a religious or political context. ♦ *Former Nazis, who joined the Communist Party to protect themselves in Eastern Europe after World War II, were often guilty of persecuting noncommunists, thus out-Heroding Herod.* ♦ *Recent converts to Roman Catholicism often try to be more Catholic than the Pope.*

**out in force** *adv. phr.* Present in very large numbers; en masse. ♦ *On the Fourth of July the police cars are out in force in the Chicago area.*

**out in left field** *adj. phr., informal* Far from the right answer; wrong; astray. ♦ *Johnny tried to answer the teacher's question but he was way out in left field.* **2.** Speaking or acting very queerly; crazy. ♦ *The girl next door was always queer, but after her father died, she was really out in left field and had to go to a hospital.*

**out in the cold** *adj. phr., informal* Alone; not included. ♦ *All the other children were chosen for parts in the play, but John was left out in the cold.*

**out in the open** See COME OUT IN THE OPEN.

**out like a light** *adj. phr., informal* **1.** Fast asleep; to sleep very quickly. ♦ *As soon as the lights were turned off, Johnny was out like a light.* **2.** In a faint; unconscious. ♦ *Johnny was hit by a ball and went out like a light.*

**out loud** *adv. phr.* In an ordinary speaking voice and not whispering or talking quietly; so everybody can hear; aloud. ♦ *The teacher read the final grades out loud.*

**out of** *prep.* **1a.** From the inside to the outside of. ♦ *John took the apple out of the bag.* **1b.** In a place away from. ♦ *No, you can't see Mr. Jones; he is out of the office today.* **2.** From a particular condition or situation; not in; from; in a way changed from being in. ♦ *The drugstore is going out of business.* **3.** Beyond the range of. ♦ *The plane is out of sight now.* **4.** From (a source). ♦ *Mother asked Billy who started the fight, but she couldn't get anything out of him.* **5.** Because of; as a result of. ♦ *Mary scolded Joan out of jealousy.* **6.** Without; not having. ♦ *The store is out of coffee.* **7.** From (a material). ♦ *The house is built out of stone.* . **8.** From among. ♦ *The man picked Joe out of the crowd.*

**out of a clear sky** *or* **out of a clear blue sky** See OUT OF THE BLUE.

**out of action** *adv. phr.* Useless; crippled; damaged so as to be quiescent. ♦ *American bombers put Nazi heavy industry out of action during World War II.*

**out of all proportion** *adv. phr.* Disproportionate; lopsided. ♦ *The news cov-*

erage of the sensational celebrity double murder has grown out of all proportion, obscuring the international news.

**out of bounds** *adv. or adj. phr.* **1.** Outside of the boundary lines in a game; not on or inside the playing field. ♦ *Bill thought he had scored a touchdown, but he had stepped out of bounds before he reached the goal line.* **2.** Outside of a circumscribed area for a certain kind of work, such as construction or military site. ♦ *The captain's cabin is out of bounds to the passengers on the ship.* **3.** Outside of safe or proper limits; not doing what is proper; breaking the rules of good behavior. ♦ *John was out of bounds when he called Tom a liar in the meeting.*

**out of breath** *adj. or adv. phr.* Not breathing easily or regularly; gasping; panting. ♦ *The fat man was out of breath after climbing the stairs.*

**out of character** *adv. or adj. phr.* **1.** Not in agreement with a person's character or personality; not in the way that a person usually behaves or is expected to behave; not usual; unsuitable; uncharacteristic. ♦ *Mary is a nice girl. Her fit of temper was out of character.* **2.** Not in character; unsuitable for a part or character. ♦ *It isn't always out of character for a young actor to play an old man, if he is a good actor.*

**out of circulation** *adj. phr., informal* Not out in the company of friends, other people, and groups; not active; not joining in what others are doing. ♦ *John has a job after school and is out of circulation with his friends.*

**out of commission** *adj. phr.* **1.** Retired from active military service; no longer on active duty. ♦ *When the war was over, many warships were placed out of commission.* 1. **2.** Not in use or not working; so that it cannot work or be used. ♦ *The strike put the airline out of commission for a week.*

**out of date** *adj. phr.* Old fashioned; superseded; no longer valid; too old to be used. ♦ *Father's suit is out of date; he needs a new one.*

**out of earshot** *adv. phr.* Too far to be heard by the naked ear. ♦ *Make sure you are out of earshot before you tell me anything in confidence.* ♦ *If you are out of earshot, use your cell phone.*

**out of fashion** *adj. phr.* Having passed from vogue; out of the current mode. ♦ *The miniskirt is now out of fashion in most quarters, but it may very well come back some day.*

**out of gas** *adv. phr.* **1.** Out of fuel (said of automobiles). ♦ *Be sure you don't run out of gas when you go on a long distance trip by car.* **2.** Rundown; depleted of energy; in poor physical condition. ♦ *Mary said she had to take a break from her job as she was running totally out of gas.*

**out of hand** *adv. phr.* **1.** Out of control. ♦ *Bobby's birthday party got out of hand and the children were naughty.* **2.** Suddenly, quickly without examination of possible truth or merit; without any consideration.—Often used after *dismiss* or *reject.* ♦ *The senator rejected out of hand the critics' call for his resignation.*

**out of harm's way** *adv. phr.* No longer in danger. ♦ *Our liberated prisoners of war were out of harm's way at last when they were liberated by the marines.*

**out of here** *adv. phr.* Soon to be gone; about to leave in a rush. ♦ *"Just give me my change, and I am out of here," John said impatiently to the slow salesman.*

**out of keeping** *adj. phr.* Not going well together; not agreeing; not proper. ♦ *Loud talk was out of keeping in the library.*

**out of kilter** *adj. phr., informal* **1.** Not balanced right; not in a straight line or lined up right. ♦ *The wheels of my bicycle were out of kilter after it hit the tree.* **2.** Needing repair; not working right. ♦ *My watch runs too slowly; it must be out of kilter.*

**out of line** *adj. phr.* Not obeying or agreeing with what is right or usual; doing or being what people do not expect or accept; outside ordinary or proper limits; not usual, right, or proper. ♦ *Mrs. Green thought the repair man's charge was out of line.*

**out of line with** *prep.* Not in agreement with. ♦ *The price of the bicycle was out of line with what Bill could afford.*

**out of luck** *adj. phr.* Being unlucky; having bad luck; having something bad happen to you. ♦ *All of the girls had dates so Ben was out of luck.*

**out of nowhere** *adv. phr.* Without having been seen before; suddenly and unexpectedly. ♦ *Mr. Jones was driving too fast on the express highway when a police patrol car appeared out of nowhere and stopped him.*

**out of one's blood** *adv. phr.* Separate from one's feelings, interests, or desires. ♦ *When Tom moved to the city, he couldn't get the country out of his blood.*

**out of one's depth** or **out of one's ground** *adv. phr.* In a situation in which one feels unprepared or not ready to react intelligently. ♦ *When it comes to rocket science, I feel out of my depth.*

**out of one's element** *adv. phr.* Outside of your natural surroundings; where you do not belong or fit in. ♦ *Wild animals are out of their element in cages.*

**out of one's hair** *adj. phr., informal* Rid of as a nuisance; relieved of as an annoyance. ♦ *Harry got the boys out of his hair so he could study.*

**out of one's head** or **out of one's mind** or **out of one's senses** also **off one's head** *adj. phr., informal* Acting in a crazy way; especially, wildly crazy. ♦ *The patient was feverish and out of his head and had to be watched.*

**out of one's pocket** *adv. phr.* Having sustained a financial loss; poorer by a said amount. ♦ *The show was so bad that, besides having a lousy time, I was also $35 out of my pocket.*

**out of one's senses** See OUT OF ONE'S HEAD.

**out of one's shell** *adv. phr., informal* Out of one's bashfulness or silence; into friendly conversation—Usually used after *come.* ♦ *The other girls tried to draw Ella out of her shell, but without success.*

**out of (one's) reach** *adv. phr.* Unreachable; unattainable; unobtainable. ♦ *Sam wanted to be a United States senator but he came to realize that such a dream was out of his reach.*

**out of order** *adv. or adj. phr.* **1.** In the wrong order; not coming after one another in the right way. ♦ *Peter wrote the words of the sentence out of order.* **2.** In poor condition; not working properly. ♦ *Our television set is out of order.* **3.** Against the rules; not suitable. ♦ *The judge told the people in the courtroom that they were out of order because they were so noisy.*

**out of place** *adj. phr.* In the wrong place or at the wrong time; not suitable; improper. ♦ *Joan was the only girl who wore a formal at the party, and she felt out of place.*

**out-of-pocket expenses** *n. phr.* Expenses one has to pay for oneself, not the company that sends one on a given assignment, such as tips for waiters, cab drivers, etc. ♦ *Luckily, my out-of-pocket expenses didn't amount to more than $15.*

**out of practice** *adj. phr.* Not in proper condition; unable to do something well because of lack of practice. ♦ *The basketball team got out of practice during the Christmas holidays.*

**out of print** *adj. phr.* No longer obtainable from the publisher because the printed copies have been sold out; no longer printed. ♦ *The book is out of print. An edition of one thousand copies was sold and no more copies were printed.*

**out of range** *adv. phr.* Unreachable socially, financially, or intellectually. ♦ *"I'd like to date the college beauty queen, but she is out of range for me,"* John sighed sadly. ♦ *"I'd like to buy a new Mercedes Benz,"* Ted said, *"but it is out of range for us right now."* ♦ *"Medical school is out of range for me now,"* Mike said, after he took a look at the tuition costs.

**out of season** *adv. phr.* **1.** Not at the right or lawful time for hunting or catching. ♦ *The boys were caught fishing out of season.* **2.** Not at the usual time for growing and selling. ♦ *The corn we get out of season is different from the kind we grow here.*

**out of shape** *or* **out of condition** *adj. phr.* **1.** Not in good condition; not able to perform well. ♦ *Jack's pitching arm got out of condition during the winter, when he wasn't using it.* **2.** Not look the same; changed. ♦ *Someone sat on father's new hat and mashed it. It is now out of shape.*

**out of sight** *adv. phr.* **1.** Not within one's field of vision. ♦ *The sailboat disappeared out of sight over the horizon.* **2.** Extremely expensive. ♦ *The builder's*

estimate was so high that it was out of sight. **3.** Unbelievable; fantastic; incredible (both in the positive and the negative sense; an exaggeration.) ♦ *Roxanne is such a stunning beauty, it's simply out of sight.* **4.** Unreachable; unrealizable; belonging to the world of fiction and fantasy. ♦ *Max's dreams about winning the Senatorial election are really out of sight; he admits it himself.*

**out of sight, out of mind** If one doesn't see something for an extended period of time, one tends to forget about it.— A proverb. ♦ *After Caroline moved out of town, Ray soon found other women to date. As the saying goes, "out of sight, out of mind."*

**out of sorts** *adj. phr.* In an angry or unhappy mood; in a bad temper; grouchy. ♦ *Bob was out of sorts because he didn't get a bicycle for his birthday.*

**out of step** *adv. or adj. phr.* **1.** Not in step; not matching strides or keeping pace with another or others. ♦ *George always marches out of step with the music.* **2.** Out of harmony; not keeping up.—Often followed by *with.* ♦ *Just because you don't smoke, it doesn't mean you are out of step with other boys and girls your age.*

**out of stock** *adj. phr.* Having none for sale or use; no longer in supply; sold out. ♦ *When Father tried to get tires for an old car, the man in the store said that size was out of stock and were not sold anymore.*

**out of the blue** *or* **out of a clear sky** *or* **out of a clear blue sky** *adv. phr., informal* Without any warning; by surprise; unexpectedly. ♦ *The cowboy thought he was alone but suddenly out of a clear sky there were bandits all around him.*

**out of the corner of one's eye** *adv. phr.* Without looking at a person or thing directly or openly; secretly; without being noticed. ♦ *The cat looked at the mouse out of the corner of his eye.*

**out of the frying pan into the fire** Out of one trouble into worse trouble; from something bad to something worse.— A proverb. ♦ *The policeman was out of the frying pan into the fire. After he escaped from the gang, he was captured by terrorists.*

**out of the game** *adv. phr.* Losing; out of competition; to have no more chance to participate or win. ♦ *"Will John ever become captain of the football team?"* Ted asked. *"No,* Peter answered. *"With his broken legs and arms after his car accident he is out of the game."*

**out of the hole** *adv. or adj. phr., informal* **1a.** With a score better than zero in a game; especially a card game, to a score above zero. ♦ *It took us a long time to get out of the hole in the card game.* **1b.** Even with an opponent after being behind; out of trouble in a sport or game. ♦ *The team played very hard, but could not get out of the hole.* **2.** Out of debt; ahead financially. ♦ *It was a small business, but it was wisely managed, and it kept out of the hole.*

**out of the loop** Contrast IN THE LOOP.

**out of the ordinary** *adj. phr.* Outside or beyond common experience; unusual; wonderful; extraordinary. ♦ *This juggler was out of the ordinary because he could juggle with his feet as well as his hands.*

**out of the picture** *adv. phr.* No longer a possibility or in the running; rejected. ♦ *Mark assured Carol that his ex-wife was completely out of the picture.*

**out of the question** *adj. phr.* Not worth considering; unthinkable; impossible. ♦ *It sometimes snows as late as June in the mountains, but the summer campers thought that snow was out of the question.*

**out of the red** *adv. phr.* Having reached solvency; no longer in debt. ♦ *Under the new management, our company finally got out of the red.*

**out of the running** *adj. or adv. phr.* Having no chance to win; not among the real contenders; not among those to be considered. ♦ *John had been out of the running since his first date with Mary, but he didn't realize it.*

**out of the swim** *adj. phr.* Not doing what others are doing; not active in business or social affairs. ♦ *Mary had to stay home and take care of Mother while she was sick, and soon felt out of the swim.*

**out of the way** *adv. phr.* **1.** Not where people usually go; difficult to reach. ♦ *When Tom comes to visit her, Aunt Sally puts her lamps and vases out of the way.*—Often used with hyphens before a noun. ♦ *Gold was found in an out-of-the-way village in the mountains, and soon a good road and airfield were built.* **2.** Not what is usual or proper; strange. ♦ *To leave before the guest of honor would be out of the way.* ♦ *I'm sorry if I said something out of the way.* **3.** *or* **out of one's way** Not able to stop or bother you. ♦ *Tom wished the visitors were out of the way so that he could have the cake for himself.*

**out of the woods** See CROW BEFORE ONE IS OUT OF THE WOODS.

**out of thin air** *adv. phr.* Out of nothing or from nowhere. ♦ *The teacher scolded Dick because his story was made out of thin air.*

**out of this world** *adj. phr., slang* Wonderfully good or satisfying; terrific; super. ♦ *The dress in the store window was out of this world!*

**out of touch** *adj. phr.* Not writing or talking with each other; not getting news anymore. ♦ *On his island Robinson Crusoe was out of touch with world news.*

**out of town** *adv. phr.* Having left one's usual residence or place of work on a longer trip. ♦ *"Mr. Smith is out of town until Monday," the secretary said. "May I take a message?"*

**out of tune** *adv. or adj. phr.* **1.** Out of proper musical pitch; too low or high in sound. ♦ *The band sounded terrible, because the instruments were out of tune.* **2.** Not in agreement; in disagreement; not going well together.—Often used with *with.* ♦ *What Jack said was out of tune with how he looked; he said he was happy, but he looked unhappy.*

**out of turn** *adv. phr.* **1.** Not in regular order; at the wrong time. ♦ *By taking a day off out of turn, Bob got the schedule mixed up.* **2.** Too hastily or wrongly; at the wrong time or place; so as to annoy others. ♦ *Dick loses friends by speaking out of turn.*

**out of wedlock** See BORN OUT OF WEDLOCK.

**out of whack** *adj. phr., slang* **1.** Needing repair; not working right. ♦ *Ben was glad the lawn mower got out of whack, because he didn't have to mow the lawn.* **2.** Not going together well; not in agreement. ♦ *The things Mr. Black* *does are out of whack with what he says.*

**out of work** *adv. phr.* Having no income-producing job; unemployed. ♦*When too many people are out of work, it is a sign that the economy is in a recession.*

**out on a limb** *adv. phr.* With your beliefs and opinions openly stated; in a dangerous position that can't be changed. ♦*The president went out on a limb and supported a foreign aid bill that many people were against.*

**out on bail** *adv. phr.* Released from prison because a security deposit known as "bail" has been put up by an individual or a bail bond broker. ♦*The murder suspect was out on a one million dollar bail awaiting trial.*

**out on parole** *adv. phr.* Released from prison but still under the supervision of the police. ♦*Although Henry is out on parole he must watch his step very carefully. If he commits another burglary he may have to go to jail for a very long time.*

**out on the town** *adv. phr.* Going from one bar or restaurant to the next in order to celebrate an event. ♦*They all went out on the town to celebrate Tom's promotion to vice president.*

**outside of** *prep.* **1.** Not in; outside. ♦*I would not want to meet a lion outside of a zoo.* **2.** Except for; not including. ♦*Outside of Johnny, all the boys on the basketball team are over six feet tall.*

**outtakes** *n. phr.* The scenes not included in the final product when editing films. ♦*If you want to see the actress in the nude, you will have to look at the outtakes.*

**out to lunch** *adj., slang, informal* **1.** Gone for the midday meal. **2.** Inattentive; daydreaming; inefficient; stupid. ♦*Neil Bender is just out to lunch today; he's in a fog.*

**overall** *adj.* All inclusive; comprehensive. ♦*What our department needs is an overall revamping of our undergraduate curriculum.*

**over a barrel** *also* **over the barrel** *adv. phr., informal* In the power of your enemies; not able to do anything about what happens to you; in a helpless condition; trapped. ♦*Bill had Tom over a barrel because Tom owed him money.*

**over age** *adj. phr.* Too old; not young enough; above the legal age. ♦*Grandfather wanted to fight in World War II, but he could not because he was over age.*

**over and above** *adv. phr.* Besides; more than; in excess of something. ♦*The new department head was given a large summer research allowance over and above his already huge salary.*

**over and done with** *adj. phr.* Finished; completed; forgotten. ♦*Norm and Meg's affair has been over and done with for a long time.*

**over and over (again)** See TIME AND AGAIN.

**overhead** *n.* Expenses incurred in the upkeep of one's plant and premises, employees' salaries, etc., which are not due to the cost of individual items or products. ♦*"Our overhead is killing us!" the used car lot owner complained. "We have to move to a cheaper place."*

**over my dead body** *or* **not over my dead body** *or* **like hell I will** *adv. phr.* Under no circumstances; by no means. ♦*"Did you hear they want to appoint Mort Doolittle as dean of the college?" Joe asked. "Over my dead body they will!" I replied.*

**overnight** *adj.* Rapidly. ♦*When Tom won the lottery he became a rich man overnight.*

**over one's head** *adv. or adj. phr.* **1.** Not understandable; beyond your ability to understand; too hard or strange for you to understand. ♦*The lesson today was hard; it went over my head.* **2.** To a more important person in charge; to a higher official. ♦*When Mary's supervisor said no, Mary went over her head to the person in charge of the whole department.*

**overstay one's welcome** *v. phr.* To remain longer at a party or one's house than desired by the host, thereby making an unpleasant nuisance of oneself. ♦*"At the risk of overstaying my welcome, may I use your guestroom for a few more days?" John asked his old college roommate. "But of course!" Ted answered. "You will never overstay your welcome with us!"*

**over the hill** *adj., informal* Past one's prime; unable to function as one used to; senile. ♦ *Poor Mr. Jones is sure not like he used to be; well, he's over the hill.*

**over the hump** *adj. phr., informal* Past the most difficult part; past the crisis; out of danger. ♦ *Mary was failing math, but she is over the hump now.*

**over the long haul** See IN THE LONG RUN. Contrast OVER THE SHORT HAUL.

**over the short haul** See IN THE SHORT RUN. Contrast OVER THE LONG HAUL.

**over the top** *adv. phr.* **1.** Out of the trenches and against the enemy. ♦ *The plan was to spend the night in the trenches and go over the top at dawn.* **2.** Over the goal. ♦ *Our goal was to collect a half million dollars for the new school building, but we went over the top.*

**over with¹** *prep.* At the end of; finished with; through with. ♦ *They were over with the meeting by ten o'clock.*

**over with²** *adj., informal* At an end; finished. ♦ *After the hard test, Jerry said, "I'm glad that's over with!"*

**owe it to** *v. phr.* To be in someone's debt. ♦ *I owe it to my doctor that I am no longer in need of a costly operation.*

**owing to** *adv. phr.* Because; on account of. ♦ *Owing to my aunt's generosity, I inherited the old family house.* ♦ *Owing to unexpectedly cold weather, I came down with the flu.*

**own up** *v., informal* To take the blame; admit your guilt; confess. ♦ *When Mother saw that someone had broken the vase, Billy owned up to it.*

**pack a punch** *or* **pack a wallop** *v. phr.,* *slang* **1.** To be able to give a powerful blow; have a dangerous fist. ◆*He packed a mean punch.* **2.** To have a violent effect; be powerful. ◆*It was vodka, and it packed quite a wallop.*

**pack off** *v., informal* To send away; dismiss abruptly. ◆*When an Englishman got in trouble long ago, his family would pack him off to Australia or some other distant land.*

**pack rat** *n., informal* A person who cannot part with old, useless objects; an avid collector of useless things; a junk hoarder. ◆*"Why are there so many things in this room?" John asked. "It is my brother's room, and he is a pack rat; he is unable to throw stuff away."*

**packed (in) like sardines** *adj. phr.* So tightly crowded that there is hardly room to turn. ◆*The trains are so full during rush hour that we must go to work packed in like sardines.*

**pack of lies** *n. phr.* An unbelievable story; unprovable allegations. ◆*What Al told us about his new girlfriend was nothing but a pack of lies.*

**pack one's bag** *v. phr.* To leave a place out of anger, annoyance, or disagreement. ◆*"This place is beginning to irritate me," she said to her friend. "I want to pack my bags and get out of here."*

**pack up** *v. phr.* To pack one's suitcase for traveling; prepare a package. ◆*Without saying a single word, the unhappy husband packed up and left.*

**paddle one's own canoe** *v. phr., informal* To work without help; earn your own living; support yourself. ◆*After his father died, John had to paddle his own canoe.*

**paddy wagon** *n., informal* A police van used for transporting prisoners to jail or the police station. ◆*The police threw the demonstrators into the paddy wagon.*

**pad the bill** *v. phr.* To add false expenses to a bill; make a bill larger than it really was. ◆*The salesman padded the bill for his traveling expenses by exaggerating his food expenses.*

**pain in the ass** *or* **pain in the neck** *n., slang, vulgar with ass* An obnoxious or bothersome person or event. ◆*Phoebe Hochrichter is a regular pain in the neck/ass.*

**paint a gloomy picture** *v. phr.* To describe something in a gloomy, pessimistic way. ◆*We are sad because the weather forecast has painted a gloomy picture for all of next week when we go on vacation.*

**paint a picture** *v. phr.* To describe a situation in a certain way, positively or negatively. ◆*John is an eternal optimist; he always paints a rosy picture about the future of the American economy.* ◆*Ted is an eternal pessimist; he always paints a dark picture of the future.*

**paint oneself into a corner** *v. phr.* To get oneself into a bad situation that is difficult or impossible to get out of. ◆*By promising to both lower taxes and raise the defense budget, the president has painted himself into a corner.*

**paint the town red** *or* **paint the town** *v. phr., slang* To go out to drink and have a good time; celebrate wildly; carouse. ◆*It was the sailors' first night ashore; they painted the town red.*

**pair off** *v.* **1.** To make a pair of; put two together; associate; match. ◆*Mrs. Smith paired off her guests by age and tastes.* **2.** To belong to a pair; become one of a pair. ◆*Jane paired off with Alice in a tennis doubles match.* **3.** To divide or join into pairs. ◆*Later in the day the picnic crowd paired off for walks and boat rides.*

**pair up** *v.* **1.** To make a pair of; match. ◆*When she finished the mending, she paired up the socks.* **2.** To form a pair; to be or become one of a pair.

**palm off** *v., informal* **1.** To sell or give (something) by pretending it is something more valuable; to sell or give by trickery. ◆*He palmed off his own painting as a Rembrandt.* **2.** To deceive (someone) by a trick or lie. ◆*He palmed his creditors off with a great show of prosperity.* **3.** To introduce someone as a person he isn't; present in a false pretense. ◆*He palmed the girl off as a real Broadway actress.*

**Pandora's box** *n. phr., literary* A thing or problem that, if activated, will give rise to many unmanageable problems. ♦ *If they insist on having that inquiry, they will open up a Pandora's box.*

**pan gravy** *n.* Gravy made with meat drippings with seasoning and often a little water. ♦ *His wife liked cream gravy, but he preferred pan gravy.*

**pan out** *v., informal* To have a result, especially a good result; result favorably; succeed. ♦ *Edison's efforts to invent an electric light bulb did not pan out until he used tungsten wires.*

**pant for** *v. phr.* To desire something very deeply. ♦ *He is panting for his girlfriend, who went out of town to see her family.*

**paper trail** *n. phr.* Records that establish a traceable chronology of past transactions and events. ♦ *If you want to be a responsible accountant, always leave an appropriate paper trail.* ♦ *The embezzler was easily caught by the police because he left a paper trail of all of his illegitimate business deals.*

**parade rest** *n.* A position in which soldiers stand still, with feet apart and hands behind their backs. ♦ *The marines were at parade rest in front of the officials' platform.*

**parallel bars** *n.* Two horizontal bars the same distance apart, that are a few feet above the floor of a gymnasium. ♦ *The boys exercised on the parallel bars in the gym.*

**parcel out** *v.* To give out in parts or shares; divide. ♦ *He parceled out the remaining food to the workers.*

**pardon my French** *v. phr.* To apologize for having uttered a vulgarity. ♦ *"What the bloody hell is this asshole doing here?" John said, and added blushingly, "Pardon my French, but I really dislike this guy."*

**par for the course** *n. phr., informal* Just what was expected; nothing unusual; a typical happening.—Usually refers to things going wrong. ♦ *When John came late again, Mary said, "That's par for the course."*

**pare down** *v. phr.* To limit; economize; reduce. ♦ *With a smaller income per month, the family had to pare down their household expenses.*

**parliamentary law** *n.* The rules for legislative or other meetings. ♦ *The club followed parliamentary law at the business meeting.*

**parrot-fashion** *adv.* Like a parrot; by rote memorization and without any understanding. ♦ *The candidate delivered a speech that was prepared for him and he read it parrot-fashion.*

**partake of** *v., formal* **1.** To take some of; receive a share of; eat. ♦ *He partook of ordinary country fare as he traveled.* **2.** To have the same qualities as; show the characteristics of. ♦ *Her way of cooking partook of both Italian and American habits.*

**part and parcel** *n. phr.* A necessary or important part; something necessary to a larger thing.—Usually followed by of. ♦ *Freedom of speech is part and parcel of the liberty of a free man.*

**part company** *v. phr.* **1.** To part with someone; leave each other; separate. ♦ *George parted company with the others at his front door.* **2.** To be different from someone in opinion or action; follow your own way; disagree; differ. ♦ *The mayor parted company with the newspapers on raising taxes.*

**partial to** *v. phr.* Having a weakness for; favorable toward. ♦ *He seems to be partial to blondes while his brother is partial to redheads.*

**parting of the ways** *n. phr.* A time or place where a choice must be made; a deciding point. ♦ *He had come to a parting of the ways: he had to choose the high school courses that would prepare him for college, or the courses that would prepare him for business.*

**parting shot** *n. phr.* A clever or witty remark that one makes on leaving a group of people with whom one had a disagreement. ♦ *"We don't want your business," Suzie said, "because you don't have any money." "OK," Ted replied with a grin, "but just for your information, I won $25,000,000 on the lottery yesterday." He sounded his parting shot, and showed her the certified check.* ♦ *"I feel sorry for you that you bought that uninhabited, worthless island full of soft wood and birds," said the seller, after the signing of the contract. "Well, how about three million pairs of chopsticks a year?" the buyer sounded his parting shot.*

**part of the action** *or* **piece of the action** *or* **piece of the pie** *n. phr.* Participation in some desirable activity, said when one wants to be included in a situation from which one expects to benefit. ♦ *"Give me a piece of the action, Dad!" Peter yelled at his father, when he opened a new branch of the highly profitable family business.*

**part of the furniture** *n. phr.* In a job or position for so long that one is taken entirely for granted, like a part of the physical surroundings. ♦ *He has been working in the same office for so many years now that people consider him to be a part of the furniture.*

**part with** *v.* **1.** To separate from; leave. ♦ *He parted with us at the end of the trip.* **2.** To let go. *They were sorry to part with the old house.* ♦ *He had to part with his secretary when she got married.*

**party animal** See SOCIAL BUTTERFLY.

**party line** *n. phr.* Ideas, policies, and goals set forth by the leadership of a group or organization. ♦ *Dan seldom has an original idea but he keeps faithfully repeating his company's party line.*

**party pooper** *n. phr.* A humorless person, who habitually manages to spoil the fun of others at a gathering of friends. ♦ *"Come on, John! Have a drink and cheer up! Why are you such a party pooper?" Ted tried to cheer his friend up. "I am no party pooper, you idiot!" John replied, "Haven't you heard that I'm having surgery tomorrow?"*

**party to** *adj. phr.* Concerned with; participating in. ♦ *The prosecution has been trying to show that the defendant was party to a fraud.*

**pass around** *v. phr.* To circulate from one to another; distribute something among a group of people. ♦ *Why doesn't he pass around the appetizers to the guests?*

**pass away** *v.* **1.** To slip by; go by; pass. ♦ *Forty years had passed away since they had met.* **2.** To cease to exist; end; disappear; vanish ♦ *When automobiles became popular, the use of the horse and buggy passed away.* **3.** To have your life stop; die. ♦ *He passed away at eighty.*

**passed ball** *n.* A pitched baseball missed by the catcher when he should have been able to catch it. ♦ *The batter sin-*

*gled and went to second on a passed ball.*

**pass for** *v. phr.* To be taken for; be considered as. ♦ *Charles speaks Arabic so fluently that he could easily pass for an Arab.*

**pass muster** *v. phr., informal* To pass a test or check-up; be good enough. ♦ *His work was done carefully, so it always passed muster.*

**pass off** *v.* **1.** To sell or give (something) by false claims; offer (something fake) as genuine. ♦ *The dishonest builder passed off a poorly built house by pretending it was well constructed.* **2.** To claim to be someone you are not; pretend to be someone else. ♦ *He passed himself off as a doctor until someone checked his record.* **3.** To go away gradually; disappear. ♦ *Tom's morning headache had passed off by that night.* **4.** To reach an end; run its course from beginning to end. ♦ *The party passed off well.*

**pass on** *v.* **1.** To give an opinion about; judge; settle. ♦ *The college passed on his application and found him acceptable.* ♦ *The committee recommended three people for the job and the president passed on them.* **2.** To give away (something that has been outgrown.) ♦ *As he grew up, he passed on his clothes to his younger brother.* **3.** To die. ♦ *Mary was very sorry to hear that her first grade teacher had passed on.*

**pass out** *v., informal* **1.** To lose consciousness; faint. ♦ *She went back to work while she was still sick, and finally she just passed out.* **2.** *or slang* **pass out cold** To drop into a drunken stupor; become unconscious from drink. ♦ *After three drinks, the man passed out.*

**pass over** *or* **pass by** *v.* To give no attention to; not notice; ignore. ♦ *In choosing men to be given a salary raise, the foreman passed Mr. Hart by.*

**pass the buck** *v. phr., informal* To make another person decide something or accept a responsibility or give orders instead of doing it yourself; shift or escape responsibility or blame; put the duty or blame on someone else. ♦ *If you break a window, do not pass the buck; admit that you did it.*—**buckpasser** *n. phr.* A person who passes the buck. ♦ *Mr. Jones was a buck-passer even at home, and tried to make his wife make all the decisions.*—**buck-passing** *n. or adj.* ♦ *Buck-passing clerks in stores make customers angry.*

**pass the hat** *v. phr.* To solicit money; take up collections for a cause. ♦ *The businessmen's club frequently passes the hat for contributions toward scholarships.*

**pass the time of day** *v. phr.* To exchange greetings; stop for a chat. ♦ *They met at the corner and paused to pass the time of day.*

**pass up** *v.* To let (something) go by; refuse. ♦ *Mary passed up the dessert because she was on a diet.*

**pass upon** *v. phr.* To express an opinion about; judge. ♦ *George said he wanted his wife to pass up the new house before he decided to buy it.*

**pass with flying colors** See WITH FLYING COLORS.

**past master** *n. phr.* An expert. ♦ *Alan wins so often because he is a past master at chess.*

**past one's peak** *adj. phr.* No longer as strong, efficient, or able as one once was, usually because of advanced age and decreased ability. ♦ *He used to be a terrific athlete but we're afraid he is past his peak.*

**pat-a-cake** *n.* A clapping game that keeps time to a nursery rhyme. ♦ *Mother played pat-a-cake with the baby.*

**patch up** *v.* **1.** To mend a hole or break; repair; fix. ♦ *The lovers patched up their quarrel.* **2.** To put together in a hurried or shaky way. ♦ *They patched up a hasty peace.*

**pat oneself on the back** *v. phr.* To be proud of oneself; give oneself credit for having achieved something; praise oneself. ♦ *When Eleanor won the lottery after trying in vain for many years, she patted herself on the back.* ♦ *You deserve to pat yourself on the back for saving that child's life by getting him out of the burning house.*

**pat on the back**[1] *v. phr.* **1.** To clap lightly on the back in support, encouragement, or praise. ♦ *The coach patted the player on the back and said a few encouraging words.* **2.** To make your support or encouragement for (someone) felt;

praise. ♦ *After he won the game, everyone patted him on the back for days.*

**pat on the back**[2] *n. phr.* **1.** An encouraging tap of the hand on someone's back; a show of sympathy or support. ♦ *I gave her a pat on the back and told her she had done fine work.* **2.** A word or gesture of praise or other encouragement; applause. ♦ *Pats on the back weren't enough; he wanted hard cash.*

**pave the way** *v. phr.* To make preparation; make easy. ♦ *Aviation paved the way for space travel.*

**pay a call** *v. phr.* To visit someone. ♦ *"Come and pay us a call some time, when you're in town," Sue said to Henry.*

**pay as one goes** *v. phr.* To pay cash; to pay at once; to avoid charging anything bought; to avoid debt entirely by paying cash.—Usually used with *you.* ♦ *It is best to pay as you go; then you will not have to worry about paying debts later.*

**pay attention** *v. phr.* To listen to someone; hear and understand someone alertly. ♦ *"Pay attention, children!" the teacher cried. "Here is your homework for next week!"*

**pay a visit** *v. phr.* To visit someone, usually by previous arrangement. ♦ *"It's your turn to pay me a visit," John said, "I've been to your place several times."*

**pay court to** *v. phr.* To woo; to shower with attention. ♦ *He had been paying court to her for three long years before he worked up the courage to ask her to marry him.*

**pay dirt** *n., slang* **1.** The dirt in which much gold is found. ♦ *The man searched for gold many years before he found pay dirt.* **2.** *informal* A valuable discovery.—Often used in the phrase *strike pay dirt.* ♦ *When Bill joined the team, the coach struck pay dirt.*

**pay down** *v. phr.* **1.** To give as a deposit on some purchase, the rest of which is to be paid in periodic installments. ♦ *"How much can you pay down on the house, sir?" the realtor asked.* **2.** To decrease a debt with periodical payments. ♦ *I'd like to pay down the charges on my credit cards.*

**pay for** *v.* To have trouble because of (something you did wrong or did not do); be punished or suffer because of.

♦ *Mary was very mean to John because she wanted to make him pay for all the years in which he had ignored her.*

**pay in advance** See IN ADVANCE.

**pay lip service to** See LIP SERVICE.

**payoff** *n.* (stress on *pay*) Culmination point; climax. ♦*After many months of patient labor on your book, the payoff comes when you see the first printed copy.*

**pay off** *v. phr.* (stress on *off*) **1.** To pay the wages of. ♦ *The men were paid off just before quitting time, the last day before the holiday.* **2.** To pay and discharge from a job. ♦*When the building was completed he paid off the laborers.* **3.** To hurt (someone) who has done wrong to you; get revenge on. ♦*When Bob tripped Dick, Dick paid Bob off by punching him in the nose.* **4.** *informal* To bring a return; make profit. ♦*At first Mr. Harrison lost money on his investments, but finally one paid off.* **5.** *informal* To prove successful, rewarding, or worthwhile. ♦*John studied hard before the examination, and it paid off. He made an A.*

**pay one a left-handed compliment** See LEFT-HANDED COMPLIMENT.

**pay one back in his own coin** *v. phr.* To retaliate. ♦*Jim refused to help Bob when he needed it most, so Bob decided to pay him back in his own coin and told him to go and look for help elsewhere.*

**pay one's respect to** *v. phr.* To discharge one's social obligations by visiting someone or by calling them on the phone. ♦ *The newly arrived people paid their respects to their various neighbors during their first couple of weeks in town.*

**pay one's way** *v. phr.* **1.** To pay in cash or labor for your expenses. ♦*He paid his way by acting as a guide.* **2.** To be profitable; earn as much as you cost someone; be valuable to an employer; to yield a return above expenses. ♦*The bigger truck paid its way from the start.*

**pay out** See PAY OFF.

**pay the piper** *or* **pay the fiddler** *v. phr.* To suffer the results of being foolish; pay or suffer because of your foolish acts or wasting money. ♦*Bob had spent all his money and got into debt, so now he must pay the piper.*

**pay through the nose** *v. phr., informal* To pay at a very high rate; pay too much. ♦ *There was a shortage of cars; if you found one for sale, you had to pay through the nose.*

**pay up** *v.* To pay in full; pay the amount of; pay what is owed. ♦*The monthly installments on the car were paid up.*

**pecking order** *n.* The way people are ranked in relation to each other (for honor, privilege, or power); status classification; hierarchy. ♦*After the president was in office several months, his staff developed a pecking order.*

**peel off** *v.* To dive away from a group of airplanes in a flight formation; bring one plane down from a group. ♦*As the group neared the home base, pilot after pilot peeled off for a landing.*

**peeping Tom** *n.* A man or boy who likes sly peeping. ♦*He was picked up by the police as a peeping Tom.*

**peg away** *v.* To work methodically, industriously, or steadily. ♦ *Thomson pegged away for years at a shoe repair business.*

**peg to hang something on** *n. phr.* A pretext or an excuse; an opportunity; or a theme. ♦*Economic depression provides many pegs to hang various theories on.* ♦ *The lack of experience of the new employees turned out to be a convenient peg for the director to hang his problems on.*

**penalty box** *n.* A place where penalized hockey players are required to go to wait until the penalty is over. ♦*Two players got into a fight and were sent to the penalty box for two minutes.*

**penny for one's thoughts** Please tell me what you are thinking about; what's your daydream. ♦*"A penny for your thoughts!" he exclaimed.*

**penny pincher, penny pinching** See PINCH PENNIES.

**penny wise and pound foolish** Wise or careful in small things but not careful enough in important things.—A proverb. ♦ *Mr. Smith's fence is rotting and falling down because he wouldn't spend money to paint it. He is penny wise and pound foolish.*

**pen pal** *n.* A friend who is known to someone through an exchange of letters. ♦*John's pen pal writes him letters about school in Alaska.*

**people who live in glass houses should not throw stones** Do not complain about other people if you are as bad as they are.—A proverb. ◆ *Mary says that Betty is promiscuous, but Mary is a call girl. People who live in glass houses should not throw stones.*

**pep talk** *n., informal* A speech that makes people feel good so they will try harder and not give up. ◆ *The football coach gave the team a pep talk.*

**perish the thought** *v. phr.* Let us not even think of it; may it never come true.—Used as an exclamation. ◆ *If John fails the college entrance exam— perish the thought—he will go back to high school for one more year.*

**perk up** *v.* To get or give back pep, vigor, health, or spirit; become or make more lively; liven up. ◆ *He perked up quickly after his illness.*

**pester the life out of someone** *v. phr.* To irk; irritate; annoy a person. ◆ *Helen pesters the life out of her poor husband by constantly demanding money for new clothes and jewelry.*

**pet name** *n. phr.* A special or abbreviated name indicating affection. ◆ *He never calls his wife her real name, "Elizabeth," but only such pet names as "honey," "honey bunch," "sweetheart," and "sugar."*

**peter out** *v., informal* To fail or die down gradually; grow less; become exhausted. ◆ *The mine once had a rich vein of silver, but it petered out.*

**pet peeve** *n. phr.* Something that particularly annoys someone. ◆ *The grunting noise Jim makes with his stuffed-up nose is a pet peeve of most people who know him.*

**photo finish** *n. phr.* A close finish in a race of people or animals, where the camera must decide the actual result, sometimes by millimeters. ◆ *The black horse was declared the winner in a photo finish.*

**pick a fight** See PICK A QUARREL.

**pick a hole in** *or* **pick holes in** *v. phr., informal* To find a mistake in or things wrong with; criticize; blame. ◆ *Mary is always picking holes in what the other girls do.*

**pick and choose** *v.* To select with much care; choose in a fussy way; take a long time before choosing. ◆ *He was never one to pick and choose.*

**pick apart** *or* **pick to pieces** *v. phr.* To criticize harshly; find things wrong with; find fault with. ◆ *They picked the play to pieces.*

**pick a pocket** *v. phr.* To steal by removing from the pocket of another. ◆ *While on the train, somebody picked his pocket and took the last dollar he had.*

**pick a/the lock** *v. phr.* To burglarize; open illegally; open a lock without the regular key. ◆ *The robber got into the house by picking the lock.*

**pick a quarrel** *v. phr.* To seek the opportunity for a fight or a quarrel. ◆ *When Charlie has too much to drink, he has a tendency to pick a quarrel with whomever happens to be around.*

**pick at** *v.* **1.** To reach or grasp for repeatedly. ◆ *The baby kept picking at the coverlet.* **2.** To eat without appetite; choose a small piece every little while to eat. ◆ *He picked at his food.* **3.** To annoy or bother continually; find fault with. ◆ *They showed their displeasure by continually picking at her.*

**pick holes in** *v. phr.* To criticize or find fault with something, such as a speech, a statement, a theory, etc. ◆ *It is easier to pick holes in someone else's argument than to make a good one yourself.*

**pick-me-up** *n. phr.* Something you take when you feel tired or weak. ◆ *Mary always carried a bar of chocolate in her pocketbook for a pick-me-up.*

**pickpocket** *n.* A thief; a petty criminal who steals things and money out of people's pockets on a bus, train, etc. ◆ *In some big cities many poor children become pickpockets out of poverty.*

**pick off** *v.* **1.** To pull off; remove with the fingers. ◆ *He picked off the burs that had stuck to his overcoat.* **2.** To shoot, one at a time; knock down one by one. ◆ *The sniper picked off the slower soldiers as they came out into the road.*

**pick of the bunch** *or* **pick of the crop** See CREAM OF THE CROP.

**pick on** *v.* **1.** *informal* To make a habit of annoying or bothering (someone); do or say bad things to (someone). ◆ *Other boys picked on him until he decided to fight them.* **2.** To single out; choose; select. ◆ *He visited a lot of colleges, and finally picked on Stanford.*

**pick on somebody your own size** A person should not fight with someone much weaker.—A proverb. ♦ *When the fifteen-year-old Johnny started to beat up on his seven-year-old brother, their father said, "Pick on somebody your own size, Johnny, or I will box your ears, and then you'll know what it feels like."*

**pick one's teeth** *v. phr.* To clean one's teeth with a toothpick. ♦ *It is considered poor manners to pick one's teeth in public.*

**pick one's way** *v. phr.* To go ahead carefully in difficult or unfamiliar places; advance with care. ♦ *He picked his way across the rough and rocky hillside.*

**pick out** *v.* **1.** To choose. ♦ *It took Mary a long time to pick out a dress at the store.* **2.** To see among others; recognize; tell from others. ♦ *We could pick out different places in the city from the airplane.* **3.** To find by examining or trying; tell the meaning. ♦ *The box was so dirty we couldn't pick out the directions on the label.*

**pick over** *v.* To select the best of; look at and take what is good from; choose from. ♦ *She picked the apples over and threw out the bad ones.*

**pick the brains of** *v. phr.* To get ideas or information about a particular subject by asking an expert. ♦ *If you have time, I'd like to pick your brains about home computers.*

**pickup** *n.*, (stress on *pick*) **1.** A rugged, small truck. ♦ *When he got into the lumber business, Max traded in his comfortable two-door sedan for a pickup.* **2.** Scheduled meeting in order to transfer merchandise or stolen goods. ♦ *The dope pushers usually make their pickup on Rush Street.* **3.** A person who is easy to persuade to go home with the suitor. ♦ *Sue is said to be an easy pickup.*

**pick up** *v.* (stress on *up*) **1.** To take up; lift. ♦ *During the morning Mrs. Carter picked up sticks in the yard.* **2.** *informal* To pay for someone else. ♦ *After lunch, in the restaurant, Uncle Bob picked up the check.* **3.** To take on or away; receive; get. ♦ *At the next corner the bus stopped and picked up three people.* **4.** To get from different places at different times; a little at a time; col-

lect. ♦ *He had picked up rare coins in seaports all over the world.* **5.** To get without trying; get accidentally. ♦ *He picked up knowledge of radio just by staying around the radio station.* **6a.** To gather together; collect. ♦ *When the carpenter finished making the cabinet, he began picking up his tools.* **6b.** To make neat and tidy; tidy up; put in order. ♦ *Pick up your room before Mother sees it.* **6c.** To gather things together; tidy a place up. ♦ *It's almost dinner time, children. Time to pick up and get ready.* **7.** To catch the sound of. ♦ *He picked up Chicago on the radio.* **8.** To get acquainted with (someone) without an introduction; make friends with (a person of the other sex). ♦ *Mother told Mary not to walk home by herself from the party because some stranger might try to pick her up.* **9.** *informal* To take to the police station or jail; arrest. ♦ *Police picked the man up for burglary.* **10.** To recognize the trail of a hunted person or animal; find. ♦ *State police picked up the bandit's trail.* **11.** To make (someone) feel better; refresh. ♦ *A little food will pick you up.* **12a.** To increase (the speed); make (the speed) faster. ♦ *The teacher told her singing class to pick up the tempo.* **12b.** To become faster; become livelier. ♦ *The speed of the train began to pick up.* **13.** To start again after interruption; go on with. ♦ *The class picked up the story where they had left it before the holiday.* **14.** *informal* To become better; recover; gain. ♦ *He picked up gradually after a long illness.*

**pick up the tab** *v. phr.* To pay the bill in a restaurant; be the one who underwrites financially what others are doing. ♦ *"I am always the one who picks up the tab," Charlie complained bitterly. "Others get away with being freeloaders."*

**pick up the pieces** *or* **pick up the thread** *v. phr.* To continue living life normally, after some tragedy that put a major roadblock in one's way. ♦ *After her husband's untimely death, it took Jane a year to pick up the pieces.* ♦ *John developed a writer's block, and it took him several weeks to pick up the thread and continue writing his novel.*

**pick up the threads** *v. phr.* To resume an occupation or a piece of work after a longer break. ♦*After his trip to Europe Ed will pick up the threads as if there had been no interruption.*

**picture of health** *n. phr.* A strikingly healthy, good-looking person. ♦*I can't believe that John has just come home from the hospital—he is the very picture of health.*

**Pidgin English** *n. phr.* A jargon that consists of some mispronounced English words and some foreign words used by Orientals in talking with Westerners. ♦*You can conduct a lot of business in Pidgin English in the Far East.*

**piece of cake** *adj., slang* Easy. ♦*The final exam was a piece of cake.*

**piece of the pie** See PART OF THE ACTION.

**piecework** *n.* Work paid for in accordance with the quantity produced. ♦*Al prefers working on a piecework basis to being on a regular salary because he feels he makes more that way.*

**pie in the sky** *n. phr., informal* An unrealistic wish or hope. ♦*Our trip to Hawaii is still only a pie in the sky.*

**pigeonhole** *v.* 1. To set aside; defer consideration of. ♦*The plan was pigeonholed until the next committee meeting.* 2. To typecast; give a stereotypical characterization to someone. ♦*It was unfair of the committee to pigeonhole him as a left-wing troublemaker.*

**pigeonhole** *n.* 1. Small compartment for internal mail in an office or a department. ♦*"You can just put your late exam into my pigeonhole," said Professor Brown to the concerned student.* 2. One of the small compartments in a desk or cabinet. ♦*He keeps his cufflinks in a pigeonhole in his desk.*

**piggy-back** *adj. or adv.* Sitting or being carried on the shoulders. ♦*When Mary sprained her ankle, John carried her piggy-back to the doctor.*

**piggy bank** *n.* A small bank, sometimes in the shape of a pig, for saving coins. ♦*John's father gave him a piggy bank.*

**pigheaded** *adj.* Stubborn; unwilling to compromise. ♦*"Stop being so pigheaded!" she cried. "I, too, can be right sometimes!"*

**pig in a poke** *n. phr.* An unseen bargain; something accepted or bought without looking at it carefully. ♦*Buying land by mail is buying a pig in a poke: sometimes the land turns out to be under water.*

**pig out** *v. phr.* 1. To eat a tremendous amount of food. ♦*"I always pig out on my birthday," she confessed.* 2. To peruse; have great fun with; indulge in for a longer period of time. ♦*"Go to bed and pig out on a good mystery story," the doctor recommended.*

**pile up** *v. phr.* (stress on *up*) 1. To grow into a big heap. ♦*He didn't go into his office for three days and his work kept piling up.* 2. To run aground. ♦*Boats often pile up on the rocks in the shallow water.* 3. To crash. ♦*One car made a sudden stop and the two cars behind it piled up.*

**pile-up** *n.* (stress on *pile*) 1. A heap; a deposit of one object on top of another. ♦*There is a huge pile-up of junked cars in this vacant lot.* 2. A large number of objects in the same place, said of traffic. ♦*I was late because of the traffic pile-up on the highway.*

**pillar of society** *n. phr.* A leading figure who contributes to the support and the well-being of his/her society; a person of irreproachable character. ♦*Mrs. Brown, the director of our classical symphony fund, is a true pillar of society.*

**pinch and scrape** *v. phr.* To save as much money as possible by spending as little as possible. ♦*They are trying to buy their first house so they are pinching and scraping every penny they can.*

**pinch-hit** *v.* 1. *informal* To act for a while, or in an emergency, for another person; take someone's place for a while. ♦*I asked him to pinch-hit for me while I was away.* ♦*When our teacher was sick, Mrs. Harris was called as a pinch-hitter.*—**pinch-hitting** *adj. or n.* ♦*Pinch-hitting for another teacher is a hard job.*

**pinch pennies** *v. phr., informal* Not spend a penny more than necessary; be very saving or thrifty. ♦*When Tom and Mary were saving money to buy a house, they had to pinch pennies.*—**penny-pincher** *n., informal* A stingy or selfish person; miser. ♦*He spent so little money that he began to get the name of a penny-pincher.*—**penny-**

**pinching** adj. or n., informal ♦Bob saved enough money by penny-pinching to buy a bicycle.

**pin curl** n. A curl made with a hair clip or bobby pin. ♦Mary washed her hair and put it up in pin curls.

**pin down** v. **1a.** To keep (someone) from moving; make stay in a place or position; trap. ♦Mr. Jones' leg was pinned down under the car after the accident. **1b.** To keep (someone) from changing what (he) says or means; make (someone) admit the truth; make (someone) agree to something. ♦Mary didn't like the book but I couldn't pin her down to say what she didn't like about it. **2.** To tell clearly and exactly; explain so that there is no doubt. ♦The police tried to pin down the blame for the fire in the school.

**pine away** v. phr. To waste away with grief. ♦After George was sent abroad, his wife pined away for him so much that she became ill.

**pin money** n. phr. Extra money used for incidentals. ♦She has a regular full-time job but she earns extra pin money by doing a lot of baby-sitting.

**pin one's ears back** v. phr., slang **1.** To beat; defeat. ♦After winning three games in a row, our team had our ears pinned back by the visitors. **2.** To scold. ♦Mrs. Smith pinned Mary's ears back for not doing her homework.

**pin one's faith on** v. phr. To depend upon; trust. ♦We pinned our faith on our home basketball team to win the state finals, and they did!

**pint-size** adj., informal Very small. ♦The new pint-size, portable TV sets have a very clear picture.

**pinup girl** v. phr. An attractive girl whose picture is pinned or tacked to the wall by an admirer. ♦Some Hollywood actresses are understandably very popular pinup girls among male soldiers.

**pious fraud** n. phr. A deception practiced in order to promote a cause that is considered to be beneficial to the public. ♦The Catholic priests committed an act of pious fraud when they made the statue of the Virgin Mary shed some red tears in order to stop the gang violence in their neighborhood.

**pipe down** v. **1.** To call (sailors) away from work with a whistle. ♦He piped the men down after boat drill. **2.** slang To stop talking; shut up; be quiet. ♦"Oh, pipe down," he called.

**pipe dream** n., informal An unrealizable, financially unsound, wishful way of thinking; an unrealistic plan. ♦Joe went through the motions of pretending that he wanted to buy that $250,000 house, but his wife candidly told the real estate lady that it was just a pipe dream.

**pipe up** v., informal To speak up; to be heard. ♦Everyone was afraid to talk to the police, but a small child piped up.

**pip-squeak** n., informal A small, unimportant person. ♦If the club is really democratic, then every little pip-squeak has the right to say what he thinks.

**piss into the wind** v. phr. vulgar, avoidable To cause problems for oneself by going against powerful prevailing trends. ♦John wants to reform the company, but I am afraid he is merely pissing into the wind, because the boss managed to persuade all employees not to change the daily routine.

**piss off** v., slang, vulgar, avoid! To bother; annoy; irritate. ♦You really piss me off when you talk like that.—**pissed off** adj. ♦Why act so pissed off just because I made a pass at you?

**pit against** v. To match against; oppose to; put in opposition to; place in competition or rivalry with. ♦The game pits two of the best pro football teams in the East against each other.

**pit-a-pat** adv. With a series of quick pats. ♦When John asked Mary to marry him, her heart went pit-a-pat.

**pitch a curve** or **a curve ball** v. phr. To catch someone unawares; confront someone with an unexpected event or act. ♦My professor pitched me a curve ball when he unexpectedly confronted me with a complicated mathematical equation that was way over my head.

**pitch dark** adj. Totally, completely dark. ♦A starless and moonless night in the country can be pitch dark.

**pitch in** v., informal **1.** To begin something with much energy; start work eagerly. ♦Pitch in and we will finish the job as soon as possible. **2.** To give help or money for something; contribute. ♦Everyone must pitch in and work together.

**pitch into** *v., informal* **1.** To attack with blows or words. ♦ *He pitched into me with his fists.* **2.** To get to work at; work hard at. ♦ *She pitched into the work and had the house cleaned up by noon.*

**plain Jane** *n. phr.* A common or simple looking young woman or girl. ♦ *When we were in school, Ann was a plain Jane, but she blossomed out and even won the title of Miss Indiana.*

**plain** *or* **smooth sailing** *n. phr.* An uncomplicated, unhampered, or easy course. ♦ *For a graduate of such a famous university as he was, that assignment was plain sailing.*

**plain white wrapper** *n., slang, citizen's band radio jargon* Unmarked police car. ♦ *There's a plain white wrapper at your rear door!*

**plan on** *v.* **1.** To have the plan of; have in mind.—Used with a verbal noun. ♦ *I plan on going to the movies after I finish my homework.* ♦ *Mary was planning on seeing John at the baseball game.* **2.** To think you will do or have; be sure about; expect. ♦ *I'm hoping to go away for the weekend, but I'm not planning on it.*

**platonic love** *n. phr.* Great affection toward another person without sex. ♦ *They are platonic lovers; they do everything together except make love.*

**play along (with)** *v.* Cooperate; make no trouble. ♦ *The honest jockey refused to play along with the bookmaker's illegal plan.*

**play a part in** *v. phr.* To be instrumental in; have a role in; be concerned with. ♦ *Some First Ladies play a greater part in political life than others.*

**play a role in** See PLAY A PART IN.

**play around** See FOOL AROUND.

**play a waiting game** *v. phr.* To withhold action until one's chances for success improve. ♦ *Ray would like to be vice president of the company so he is playing a waiting game in the hope that the president will soon recognize his abilities.*

**play ball** *v. phr. informal* To join in an effort with others; cooperate. ♦ *To get along during Prohibition, many men felt that they had to play ball with gangsters.*

**play by ear** *v. phr.* **1.** To play a musical instrument by remembering the tune, not by reading music. ♦ *Mary does not know how to read music. She plays the piano by ear.* **2.** *informal* To decide what to do as you go along; to fit the situation.—Used with *it.* ♦ *It was her first job and she didn't know what to expect, so she had to play it by ear.*

**play cat and mouse with** *v. phr.* To tease or fool (someone) by pretending to let him go free and then catching him again. ♦ *The policeman decided to play cat and mouse when he saw the woman steal the dress in the store.*

**play down** *v.* To give less emphasis to; make (something) seem less important; divert attention from; draw notice away from. ♦ *A salesman's job is to emphasize the good points of his merchandise; he must play down any faults it has.*

**played out** *adj. phr.* Tired out; worn out; finished; exhausted. ♦ *It had been a hard day, and by night he was played out.*

**play fair** *v. phr.* To do what is right to others; act in a fair and truthful way. ♦ *The boys like the principal because he always plays fair.*

**play fast and loose** *v. phr.* To do as you please without caring what will happen to other people; act so carelessly or unfairly that people cannot depend on you; be very unreliable. ♦ *He played fast and loose with the company's good name.*

**play favorites** *v. phr.* To treat certain people preferentially; be kinder to some people than to others. ♦ *A good teacher must never play favorites with her students.*

**play footsie** *v. phr., slang, informal* **1.** Touch the feet of a member of the opposite sex under the table as an act of flirtation. ♦ *Have you at least played footsie with her?* **2.** To engage in any sort of flirtation or collaboration, especially in a political situation. ♦ *The mayor was suspected of playing footsie with the Syndicate.*

**play for keeps** *v. phr.* To take an action of finality and irreversibility. ♦ *"Are you serious about me?" she asked. "Yes," he replied. "I want to marry you. I play for keeps."*

**play hard to get** *v. phr.* To act as if one weren't interested; be fickle; be coy.

♦ *"Professor Brown is playing very hard to get," our dean said, "but I know he will accept our offer and come to teach here."*

**play havoc with** *or* **raise havoc with** *v. phr.* To cause destruction; ruin; injure badly. ♦ *The storm played havoc with the apple orchard.*

**play hooky** *v. phr., informal* To stay out of school to play. ♦ *Carl is failing in school because he has played hooky so many times during the year.*

**play into one's hands** *v. phr.* To be or do something that another person can use against you; help an opponent against yourself. ♦ *Mary and Bobby wanted the last piece of cake, but Bobby played into Mary's hands by trying to grab it.*

**play it close to the vest** *v. phr.* To handle matters secretly and confidentially; not reveal one's intentions. ♦ *The dean is playing it so close to the vest that nobody has any idea who will be the next head of the department.*

**play off** *v.* **1.** To match opposing persons, forces, or interests so that they balance each other. ♦ *Britain tried to play off European nations against each other so that she would have a balance of power.* **2.** To finish the playing of (an interrupted contest.) ♦ *The visitors came back the next Saturday to play off the game stopped by rain.* **3.** To settle (a tie score) between contestants by more play. ♦ *When each player had won two matches, the championship was decided by playing off the tie.*

**play on** *or* **play upon** *v.* **1.** To cause an effect on; influence. ♦ *A heavy dose of television drama played on his feelings.* **2.** To work upon for a planned effect; excite to a desired action by cunning plans; manage. ♦ *The makeup salesman played on the woman's wish to look beautiful.*

**play one for** *v., informal* To treat (someone) as; act toward (someone) as; handle (someone) as; handle as. ♦ *He played the man for a sucker.*

**play one's cards right** *or* **play one's cards well** *v. phr., informal* To use abilities and opportunities so as to be successful; act cleverly; make the best use of your place or skills. ♦ *People liked Harold, and he played his cards well— and soon he began to get ahead rapidly.*

**play ostrich** *v. phr.* To refuse to face painful facts or unpleasant truths. ♦ *She plays ostrich when it comes to her husband's drinking problem.*

**play politics** *v. phr.* To make secret agreements for your own gain; handle different groups for your own advantage. ♦ *Mary always gets what she wants by playing office politics.*

**play safe** *or* **play it safe** *v. phr., informal* To be very careful; accept small gains or none to avoid loss; avoid danger for the sake of safety. ♦ *Tom didn't know what the other driver would do, so he played it safe and stopped his own car.*

**play second fiddle** *v. phr., informal* To act a smaller part; follow another's lead; be less noticed. ♦ *His wife had the stronger mind and he played second fiddle to her.*

**play the field** *v. phr., informal* To date many different people; not always have dates with the same person. ♦ *Al had a steady girlfriend, but John was playing the field.*

**play the game** *v. phr., informal* To obey the rules; do right; act fairly. ♦ *"That's not playing the game," we told him when he wanted to desert his wife.*

**play the market** *v. phr.* To try to make money on the stock market by buying and selling stocks. ♦ *Sometimes Mr. Smith makes a lot of money when he plays the market, and sometimes he loses.*

**play (the) Monday morning quarterback** *v. phr.* To practice hindsight; be wise after an event has happened. ♦ *"You shouldn't have invested all your money in that uncertain, new company," Jack said. "Small wonder you lost a fortune." "That is unfair!" Tom replied. "You are playing the Monday morning quarterback."*

**play to the gallery** *v. phr.* To try to get the approval of the audience. ♦ *Whenever John recites in class he seems to be playing to the gallery.*

**play tricks on** *v. phr.* To make another the victim of some trick or joke. ♦ *Al got angry when his classmates played a trick on him by hiding his clothes while he was swimming.*

**play up** *v.* To call attention to; talk more about; emphasize. ♦ *The coach played up the possibilities, and kept our minds off our weaknesses.*

**play up to** *v. phr., slang* **1.** To try to gain the favor of, especially for selfish reasons; act to win the approval of; try to please. ♦ *He played up to the boss.* **2.** To use (something) to gain an end; to attend to (a weakness). ♦ *He played up to the old lady's vanity to get her support.*

**play with fire** *v. phr.* To put oneself in danger; to take risks. ♦ *Leaving your door unlocked in New York City is playing with fire.*

**plot thickens** *v. phr.* Becoming more intense, more complex, more difficult to see though. ♦ *When three different people all confessed to the same murder, the detective exclaimed, "Well! The plot thickens!"*

**plough the sands** *or* **plow the sands** *v. phr.* To do something futile or useless. ♦ *If you try to persuade the gang to become saints, you're plowing the sands.*

**plough** *or* **plow through** *v. phr.* Pass through laboriously. ♦ *Sam had to plough through hundreds of pages of American history to get ready for his test.*

**plow into** *v.* **1.** To attack vigorously. ♦ *He plowed into his work and finished it in a few hours.* **2.** To crash into with force. ♦ *A truck plowed into my car and smashed the fender.*

**pluck up** *v.* **1.** To have (courage) by your own effort; make yourself have (courage). ♦ *He plucked up courage when he saw a glimmer of hope.* **2.** To become happier; feel better; cheer up. ♦ *He plucked up when his wife recovered.*

**plug in** *v. phr.* To connect (an electrical appliance) to a power wire by putting its plug into a receptacle or hole. ♦ *The integrated circuit has multiplied the number of small radios that need not be plugged in.*

**plug into** *v.* To connect (an electrical appliance) to a power wire by inserting its plug into a receptacle or hole. ♦ *He thought he had left the lamp plugged into the wall, and so was puzzled when it wouldn't light that night.*

**plume oneself** *v. phr., literary* To be proud of yourself; boast. ♦ *He plumed himself on having the belle of the ball as his date.*

**plunk down** *v., informal* **1.** To drop down; fall. ♦ *After walking a mile we plunked down on a bench to rest.* **2.** To drop something noisily or firmly. ♦ *He plunked the heavy suitcase down at the station.* **3.** To pay out, primarily an excessive amount ♦ *I had to plunk down $55 for a concert ticket.*

**pocket money** See SPENDING MONEY.

**pockets of resistance** *n. phr.* Isolated areas where the fighting continues after the main battle is over. ♦ *Even after the marines had taken over the entire country, there still remained a few isolated pockets of resistance.*

**point-blank** *adv.* Straightforwardly; bluntly; directly. ♦ *Sue refused point-blank to discuss marriage with Sam.*

**point of view** *n.* Attitude; opinion. ♦ *From the American point of view, Fidel Castro is a bad neighbor to have.*

**point out** *v.* **1.** To show by pointing with the finger; point to; make clear the location of. ♦ *The guide pointed out the principal sights of the city.* **2.** To bring to notice; call to attention; explain. ♦ *The policeman pointed out that the law forbids public sale of firecrackers.*

**point up** *v.* To show clearly; emphasize. ♦ *The increase in crime points up the need for greater police protection.*

**poison-pen** *adj.* Containing threats or false accusations; written in spite or to get revenge, and usually unsigned. ♦ *Mrs. Smith received a poison-pen letter telling her that her husband was untrue.*

**poke around** *or* **poke about** *v.* **1.** To search about; look into and under things. ♦ *The detective poked around in the missing man's office.* **2.** To move slowly or aimlessly; do little things. ♦ *He didn't feel well, and poked around the house.*

**poles apart** *adj.* Completely different. ♦ *The two brothers were poles apart in personality.*

**polish off** *v., informal* **1.** To defeat easily. ♦ *The Dodgers polished off the Yankees in four straight games in the 1963 World Series.* **2.** To finish completely; finish doing quickly, often in order to do something else. ♦ *The boys were hungry and polished off a big steak.* ♦ *Mary polished off her homework early so that she could watch TV.*

**polish the apple** *v. phr., slang* To try to make someone like you; to try to win favor by flattery. *♦Susan is the teacher's pet because she always polishes the apple.*—**apple-polisher** *n., slang* A person who is nice to the one in charge in order to be liked or treated better; a person who does favors for a superior. *♦Joe is an apple-polisher. He will do anything for the boss.*—**apple-polishing** *n., slang* Trying to win someone's good-will by small acts currying favor; the behavior of an apple-polisher. *♦When John brought his teacher flowers, everyone thought he was apple-polishing.*

**pool one's resources** *v. phr.* To utilize and share one's resources into a commonly accessibly repository. *♦"Let us pool our resources," the three local shoe manufacturers said, before they put their respective signatures on the merger that made them into one big company.*

**pooped out** *adj., slang* Worn out; exhausted. *♦The heat made them feel pooped out.*

**poor as a church mouse** *adj. phr., informal* Penniless; broke; extremely poor. *♦The newly arrived boat people were poor as church mice.*

**poor-mouth** *v.* To be constantly complaining about one's poverty; keep saying how one cannot afford the better things in life. *♦Uncle Jack indulges in an awful lot of poor-mouthing, but we know that he has three million dollars stashed away in a secret savings account.*

**pop in** *v. phr.* To suddenly appear without announcement. *♦"Just pop into my office any time you're on campus," Professor Brown said.*

**pop into one's head** *v. phr.* To suddenly remember or to think of something. *♦It suddenly popped into my head that April 20th is my daughter's birthday, so I stopped at a pay phone and gave her a call.*

**pop one's cork** See BLOW A FUSE, FLY OFF THE HANDLE, LOSE ONE'S MARBLES, LOSE ONE'S TEMPER.

**pop the question** *v. phr., slang* To ask someone to marry you. *♦After the dance he popped the question.*

**pop up** *v.* **1.** *or* **bob up** To appear suddenly or unexpectedly; show up; come out. *♦After no one had heard from him for years, John popped up in town again.*

**port of call** *n. phr.* **1.** Any of the ports that a ship visits after the start of a voyage and before the end; a port where passengers or cargo may be taken on or put off; an in-between port. *♦Savannah is a port of call for many Atlantic coasting vessels.* **2.** A place you visit regularly or often; a stop included on your usual way of going. *♦It was an obscure little restaurant which I had made something of a port of call.*

**port of entry** *n. phr.* **1.** A port where things brought into the country to sell may pass through customs. *♦Other ports of entry have been taking business from New York.* **2.** A port where a citizen of another country may legally enter a country; a port having passport and immigration facilities. *♦Airports have joined seaports as ports of entry for the visiting foreigner.*

**potboiler** *n.* A book, play, or film written for the primary purpose of earning money for the author. *♦"Reading a cheap potboiler helps me go to sleep," the professor wryly remarked.*

**pot calling the kettle black** *informal* The person who is criticizing someone else is as guilty as the person he or she accuses; the charge is as true of the person who makes it as of the one he or she makes it against. *♦Bill said John was cheating at a game but John replied that the pot was calling the kettle black.*

**potluck** See TAKE POTLUCK.

**potluck supper** See COVERED-DISH SUPPER.

**potshot** *n.* A direct shot at an easy, stationary target from behind a protected position or camouflage; criticism. *♦Modern journalists like to take potshots at the president of the United States.*

**pound away at** *v. phr.* **1.** To attack; criticize. *♦In his campaign speeches the candidate kept pounding away at the administration's foreign policy.* **2.** To work industriously. *♦Mike was pounding away at the foundation of his new house with shovels and pickaxes.*

**pound out** *v. phr.* **1.** To play a piece of music very loudly on a percussion instrument. ♦ *The boy was pounding out the tune "Mary had a little lamb" on the marimba.* **2.** To flatten something with a hammer. ♦ *The bodyshop uses special hammers to pound out the indentations in the bodies of cars.* **3.** To produce a piece of writing on a typewriter in haste and without much care. ♦ *She hurriedly pounded out a letter of recommendation for the foreign graduate student.*

**pound the pavement** *v. phr., informal* To walk up and down the streets; tramp about. ♦ *John pounded the pavement looking for a job.*

**pour money down the drain** *v. phr.* To spend one's money unwisely; to waste one's funds. ♦ *"Stop supporting Harry's drug habit," Ralph said. "You're just pouring money down the drain."*

**pour oil on troubled waters** *v. phr.* To quiet a quarrel; say something to lessen anger and bring peace. ♦ *The troops were nearing a bitter quarrel until the leader poured oil on the troubled waters.*

**pour out** *v.* **1.** To tell everything about; talk all about. ♦ *Mary poured out her troubles to her pal.* **2.** To come out in great quantity; stream out. ♦ *The people poured out of the building when they heard the fire alarm.*

**powder room** *n.* The ladies' rest room. ♦ *When they got to the restaurant, Mary went to the powder room to wash up.*

**power behind the throne** *n. phr.* The person with the real power backing up the more visible partner (usually said about the wives of public figures). ♦ *It is rumored that the First Lady is the power behind the throne in the White House.*

**praise to high heaven** *or* **praise to the skies** *v. phr.* To shower someone with extreme, exaggerated praise. ♦ *The theater critic, who was in love with the mediocre actress, decided to gain her favors by praising her to high heaven.*

**pray to the toilet** *v. phr,. slang* To vomit from having consumed too much alcohol. ♦ *"What's that ugly noise coming from the bathroom?" John's father asked. "He is praying to the toilet, as usual," John's younger brother replied.*

**preach to the saved** *or* **preach to the choir** *v. phr.* To be engaged in persuading a group of people about something they already believe in. ♦ *"You are preaching to the saved!" John exclaimed, when Jerry was trying to convince him to give up smoking. "I quit a long time ago, cold turkey!"*

**presence of mind** *n. phr.* Effective and quick decision-making ability in times of crisis. ♦ *When Jimmy fell into the river, his father had the presence of mind to dive in after him and save him from drowning.*

**press box** *n.* The place or room high in a sports stadium that is for newspaper men and radio and television announcers. ♦ *In baseball the official scorer sits in the press box.*

**press conference** *n. phr.* A meeting with news reporters. ♦ *The reporters questioned the president about foreign affairs at the press conference.*

**press one's luck** *or* **push one's luck** *v. phr.* To depend too much on luck; expect to continue to be lucky. ♦ *If you're lucky at first, don't press your luck.*

**press the flesh** *v., slang* To shake hands with total strangers by the hundreds, keeping an artificial smile all the way, in order to raise one's popularity during political elections. ♦ *Incumbent Governor Maxwell was pressing the flesh all day long at six different hotels.*

**pressure group** *n. phr.* An organization whose goal it is to create changes by lobbying for the benefit of its own members. ♦ *Certain unscrupulous pressure groups stop at nothing to achieve their selfish aims.*

**pretty penny** *n. phr.* A large amount of money. ♦ *Their new house is so big and modern that we're sure it must have cost them a pretty penny.*

**prevail upon** *or* **prevail on** *v.* To bring to an act or belief; cause a change in; persuade. ♦ *He prevailed upon me to believe in his innocence.*

**prey on** *or* **prey upon** *v.* **1.** To habitually kill and eat; catch for food. ♦ *Cats prey on mice.* **2.** To capture or take in spoils of war or robbery. ♦ *Pirates preyed on American ships in the years just after the Revolutionary War.* **3.** To cheat; rob. ♦ *Gangsters preyed on businesses of many kinds while the sale of liquor was prohibited.* **4.** To have a tiring and weakening effect on; weaken. ♦ *Ill health had preyed on him for years.*

**prey on one's mind** *v. phr.* To afflict; worry. ♦ He couldn't sleep because his many debts were preying on his mind.

**price on one's head** *n. phr.* Reward offered to anyone who catches a thief or a murderer. ♦ *The hotel manager learned that the quiet man taken from his room by the police was a murderer with a price on his head.*

**prick up one's ears** *v. phr., informal* To come to interested attention; begin to listen closely; try to hear. ♦ *The woman pricked up her ears when she heard them talking about her.*

**pride must take a pinch** One must endure the minor pains and hardships one encounters while being made pretty.—A proverb. ♦ *"Mother,"* Sue cried, *"stop pulling my hair!" "Just a moment, young lady,"* the mother answered, while combing her hair. *"Don't you know that pride must take a pinch?"*

**pride oneself on** *v. phr.* To be proud of; take satisfaction in; be much pleased by. ♦ *She prided herself on her beauty.*

**prime of life** *n. phr.* The healthiest and most vigorously active time of one's life. ♦ *"I am getting old,"* John complained, *"I just had my fortieth birthday." "Come on, Dad,"* his son replied, *"you're just coming into the prime of your life!"*

**private eye** *n., colloquial* A private investigator; a detective. ♦ *Buddy Ebsen played a private eye on "Barnaby Jones."*

**promises, promises!** *n. phr.* used as a teasing exclamation Often heard when one makes a semithreatening statement that the addressee wishes to belittle, it also indicates disbelief. ♦ *"I shall marry you, you beautiful woman!" the old millionaire said to the young bar dancer. "Promises, promises!" she answered with a flirtatious smile.*

**promise the moon** *v. phr.* To promise something impossible. ♦ *I can't promise you the moon, but I'll do the best job I can.*

**proof of the pudding is in the eating** Only through actual experience can the value of something be tested.—A proverb. ♦ *He was intrigued by the ads about the new high mileage sports cars.*

*"Drive one, sir," the salesman said. "The proof of the pudding is in the eating."*

**pros and cons** *n. phr.* The relative advantages and disadvantages of a matter at hand. ♦ *I want to move to Hawaii, when I retire. Can you tell me what are the pros and cons of living there?*

**psyched up** *adj., informal* Mentally alert; ready to do something. ♦ *The students were all psyched up for their final exams.*

**psychological moment** *n. phr.* The critical time during a game or some other activity; the nick of time. ♦ *The two ping-pong table players were battling each other tooth and nail, when the foreign visitor missed the psychological moment and failed to return the opponent's backhand slam.*

**psych out** *v. phr., slang, informal* **1.** To find out the real motives of (someone). ♦ *Sue sure has got Joe psyched out.* **2.** To go berserk; to lose one's nerve. ♦ *Joe says he doesn't ride his motorcycle on the highway anymore because he's psyched out.*

**public-address system** *n.* A set of devices for making a speaker's voice louder so that he can be heard by more people. ♦ *The public-address system broke down during the senator's speech.*

**public enemy** *n. phr.* A famous criminal. ♦ *Al Capone of Chicago used to be Public Enemy Number One during Prohibition.*

**public speaker** *n.* A person who speaks to the public. ♦ *A public speaker must appeal to all kinds of people.*

**puffed up** *adj.* Elated; proud; conceited. ♦ *Just because Bob inherited some money from his father is no reason for him to act so puffed up.*

**pull a fast one** *v. phr.* To gain the advantage over one's opponent unfairly; deceive; trick. ♦ *When Smith was told by his boss that he might be fired, he called the company president, his father-in-law, and pulled a fast one by having his boss demoted.*

**pull an all-nighter** *v. phr.* To stay up and work through the night without a break. ♦ *"Why are you so tired?" John asked his friend. "I had to pull an all-nighter, as we were shorthanded at work," Ted answered.*

**pull date** n., informal The date stamped on baked goods, dairy products, or other perishable foods indicating the last day on which they may be sold before they must be removed from the shelves in a retail store. ♦ *This pie is way past the pull date—small wonder it's rotten.*

**pull down** v. To earn. ♦ *Mr. Blake pulls down $500 a week.* ♦ *John pulled down an A in algebra by studying hard.*

**pull for** v. phr. To encourage someone; show support for a person or a team. ♦ *"Who are you pulling for? Harvard or Yale?" Tom asked during the annual football contest between the old rivals. "Yale, of course," Alan answered. "That was my undergraduate alma mater."*

**pull in** See HAUL IN.

**pull in** or **pull into** v. phr. To park one's car by leaving the road. ♦ *Let's pull into the driveway before it starts raining.* ♦ *We left the highway and pulled into a diner parking lot for a cup of coffee.*

**pull in one's horns** or **draw in one's horns** v. phr., informal 1. To reduce your boasts; calm down from a quarrel; back down on a promise. ♦ *He said he could beat any man there single-handed, but he pulled in his horns when Jack came forward.* 2. To cut back from one's usual way of living; reduce spending or activities; save. ♦ *After the business failed, Father had to pull in his horns.*

**pull off** v., informal To succeed in (something thought difficult or impossible); do. ♦ *The bandits pulled off a daring bank robbery.*

**pull one's chain** See PULL ONE'S LEG.

**pull one's chestnuts out of the fire** To do someone else a great favor which they don't really deserve, doing oneself a disfavor in the process. ♦ *Small countries often have to pull the chestnuts out of the fire for their more powerful neighbors.*

**pull oneself together** v. phr. To become calm after being excited or disturbed; recover self-command; control yourself. ♦ *It had been a disturbing moment, but he was able to pull himself together.*

**pull oneself up by the bootstraps** or **pull oneself up by one's own bootstraps** adv. phr. To succeed without help; succeed by your own efforts. ♦ *He had to pull himself up by the bootstraps.*

**pull one's hair out over** or **tear one's hair out over** v. phr. To stay upset because of a frustrating event or situation. ♦ *Mary was pulling her hair out over her husband's drinking, until she realized that the only solution was to send him to a doctor.* ♦ *Don't tear your hair out over the new boss. He is here to stay; it can't be helped.*

**pull one's leg** v. phr., informal To get someone to accept a ridiculous story as true; fool someone with a humorous account of something; trick. ♦ *For a moment, I actually believed that his wife had royal blood. Then I realized he was pulling my leg.*

**pull one's punches** v. phr., informal 1. Not to hit as hard as you can. ♦ *Jimmy pulled his punches and let Paul win the boxing match.* 2. To hide unpleasant facts or make them seem good.—Usually used in the negative. ♦ *The mayor spoke bluntly; he didn't pull any punches.*

**pull one's weight** v. phr. To do your full share of work; do your part. ♦ *When Mother was sick in the hospital, Father said each child must pull his own weight.*

**pullout** n. (stress on *pull*) An evacuation. ♦ *The pullout of the American military proceeded on schedule.*

**pull out** v. phr. (stress on *out*) 1. To withdraw; leave unceremoniously. ♦ *The defeated army hastily pulled out of the occupied territories.* 2. To leave (said about trains). ♦ *The train pulled out of Grand Central Station just as the foreign students got there.* 3. To remove by order; evacuate. ♦ *Napoleon pulled his beaten troops out of Russia.*

**pull out of a hat** v. phr., informal To get as if by magic; invent; imagine. ♦ *Let's see you pull an excuse out of your hat.*

**pull over** v. To drive to the side of the road and stop. ♦ *The policeman told the speeder to pull over.*

**pull rank** v. phr., slang, informal To assert one's superior position or authority on a person of lower rank as in exacting a privilege or a favor. ♦ *How come you always get the night duty? The boss pulled rank on me.*

**pull something on one** *v. phr.* To perpetrate something prejudicial; deceive. ♦ *Larry pulled a very dirty trick on Ann when, after going with her for three years, he suddenly married another girl.*

**pull strings** *or* **pull wires** *v. phr., informal* To secretly use influence and power, especially with people in charge or in important jobs to do or get something; make use of friends to gain your wishes. ♦ *If you want to see the governor, Mr. Root can pull strings for you.* ♦ *Jack pulled wires and got us a room at the crowded hotel.*

**pull the chestnuts out of the fire** *v. phr.* To perform a difficult, dangerous, or illicit work on behalf of someone else. ♦ *The new boss is using his colleagues to pull the chestnuts out of the fire for him.*

**pull the plug on** *v. phr., slang* To expose (someone's) secret activities. ♦ *The citizens' committee pulled the plug on the mayor, and he lost his election.*

**pull the rug out from under** *v. phr., informal* To withdraw support unexpectedly from; to spoil the plans of. ♦ *Bill thought he would be elected, but his friends pulled the rug out from under him and voted for John.*

**pull the wool over one's eyes** *v. phr., informal* To fool someone into thinking well of you; deceive. ♦ *The businessman had pulled the wool over his partner's eyes about their financial position.*

**pull through** *v.* **1.** To help through; bring safely through a difficulty or sudden trouble; save. ♦ *A generous loan showed the bank's faith in Father and pulled him through the business trouble.* **2.** To recover from an illness or misfortune; conquer a disaster; escape death or failure. ♦ *By a near-miracle, he pulled through after the smashup.*

**pull together** *v.* To join your efforts with those of others; work on a task together; cooperate. ♦ *Many men must pull together if a large business is to succeed.*

**pull up** *v.* **1.** To check the forward motion of; halt; stop. ♦ *He pulled up his horse at the gate.* **2.** To tell (someone) to stop doing something; say (someone) is doing wrong and must stop; scold. ♦ *Jim talked rudely to Mother, and*

*Father pulled him up.* **3.** To stop moving forward; halt. ♦ *The car slowed down and pulled up at the curb.* **4.** To come even with; move up beside. ♦ *The other boat pulled up alongside us.*

**pull up one's socks** *v. phr.* To try to do better, either in terms of one's behavior or at a task one is performing. ♦ *I'll have to pull up my socks if I am going to finish my work today.*

**pull up short** *v. phr.* To suddenly stop. ♦ *He pulled up short in his red car at the corner when he saw a pregnant lady crossing.*

**pull up stakes** *v. phr., informal* To leave the place where you have been living. ♦ *We are going to pull up stakes and move to California.*

**pump iron** *v. phr.* To exercise in a gym by weight lifting or moving other metallic heavy-weight gym equipment. ♦ *Ever since Bob decided to become an athlete, he has been pumping iron in the gymnasium.*

**pump up** *or* **fire up** *v. phr.* To fill with enthusiasm; excite. ♦ *The coach had to pump up the team at halftime by giving an intimidating speech.*

**punch-drunk** *adj.* **1.** Dazed or become dulled in the mind from being hit in the head. ♦ *He was a punch-drunk boxer who made his living shining shoes.* **2.** In a foggy state of mind; groggy. ♦ *Mary was so thrilled at winning the contest she acted punch-drunk.*

**puppy love** *also* **calf love** *n., informal* The first love of very young people. ♦ *When John and Mary began going around together in junior high school, their parents said it was just puppy love.*

**pure and simple** *adj.* Simply stated; basic.—Follows the noun it modifies and is used for emphasis. ♦ *The problem, pure and simple, is finding a baby-sitter.*

**purse strings** *n.* Care or control of money. ♦ *Dad holds the purse strings in our family.*

**push around** *v., informal* To be bossy with; bully. ♦ *Don't try to push me around!*

**push comes to shove** *v. phr.* Often heard when a bad situation, which is difficult to tolerate, suddenly comes to a head and steady, slow pressure is replaced by a sudden explosion of events.—A proverb. ◆ *I am afraid that when push comes to shove during the present economic slump, many of us will be fired.*

**push the envelope** *v. phr.* To strain a delicate situation to the utmost; engage in exaggerated demands. ◆ *If you want to succeed with these difficult peace negotiations, you had better stop pushing the envelope.* ◆ *"You're pushing the envelope!" John warned his colleague. "The boss will not listen to you if you won't stop."*

**push off** or **shove off** *v.* 1. To push a boat away from the shore. ◆ *Before Tom could reach the boat, Jake had shoved off.* 2. *slang* To start; leave. ◆ *We were ready to push off at ten o'clock, but had to wait for Jill.* ◆ *Jim was planning to stay at the beach all day, but when the crowds arrived he shoved off.*

**push on** *v. phr.* To press forward; proceed forward laboriously. ◆ *The exhausted mountain climbers pushed on, despite the rough weather, as the peak was already in sight.*

**pushover** *n.* (stress on *push*) 1. Something easy to accomplish or overcome. ◆ *For Howard steering a boat is a pushover as he was raised on a tropical island.* 2. A person easily seduced. ◆ *It is rumored that she is a pushover when she has a bit to drink.*

**push over** *v. phr.* (stress on *over*) To upset; overthrow. ◆ *She is standing on her feet very solidly; a little criticism from you certainly won't push her over.*

**push the panic button** *v. phr., slang* To become very much frightened; nervous or excited, especially at a time of danger or worry. ◆ *John thought he saw a ghost and pushed the panic button.*

**push-up** *n.* An exercise to build strong arms and shoulders, in which you lie on your stomach and push your body up on your hands and toes. ◆ *At the age of seventy, Grandpa still does twenty push-ups every day.*

**push up daisies** *v. phr., slang* To be dead and buried. ◆ *I'll be around when you're pushing up daisies.*

**put about** *v. phr.*—Nautical usage. To turn in the opposite direction; turn around. ◆ *When we saw the storm clouds thickening in the sky, we put about quickly and raced ashore.*

**put a bee in one's bonnet** See BEE IN ONE'S BONNET.

**put a bug in one's ear** or **put a flea in one's ear** See BUG IN ONE'S EAR.

**put across** *v.* 1. To explain clearly; make yourself understood; communicate. ◆ *He knew how to put his ideas across.* 2. *informal* To get (something) done successfully; bring to success; make real. ◆ *He put across a big sales campaign.*

**put a damper on** *v. phr.* To take away one's hopes of success; put an obstacle in one's way. ◆ *Peter put a damper on my chances of getting a better position.* ◆ *Never put a damper on a young student's enthusiasm.*

**put a good face on** *v. phr.* To assume or maintain a brave attitude toward something bad in order to make it look better and act bravely. ◆ *When Claire learned that she had breast cancer, she tried to put a good face on it by comforting her family, saying that 95% of breast cancer cases are cured if caught in time.*

**put a lid on it** *v. phr.* To keep quiet about something. ◆ *When we found out that the company treasurer embezzled six million dollars, the director became afraid and tried to put a lid on it.* Compare COVER UP, COVER ONE'S TRACKS.

**put all one's eggs in one basket** *v. phr.* To place all your efforts, interests, or hopes in a single person or thing. ◆ *To buy stock in a single company is to put all your eggs in one basket.*

**put a new face on** *v. phr.* To alter the aspect of something; change. ◆ *Mr. Merryman's announcement of his candidacy for governor puts an entirely new face on the political scene in our state.*

**put an end to** or **put a stop to** *v. phr.* 1. To make (something) end; stop; end. ◆ *The farmer built an electric fence around his field to put an end to trespassing.* 2. To destroy or kill. ◆ *The new highway took most of the traffic from the old road and put an end to Mr. Hanson's motel business.*

**put aside** *v. phr.* 1. To save; put something aside for a special purpose. ◆ *Peter puts $100 aside every week.* 2. To let go of; put away. ◆ *The teacher* to the students, *"Put your books aside and start writing your tests!"*

**put a spoke in one's wheel** See THROW A MONKEY WRENCH.

**put away** *v.* **1.** To put in the right place or out of sight. *♦She put away the towels.* **2.** To lay aside; stop thinking about. *♦He put his worries away for the weekend.* **3.** *informal* To eat or drink. *♦He put away a big supper and three cups of coffee.* **4.** *informal* To put in a mental hospital. *♦He had to put his wife away when she became mentally ill.* **5.** To put to death for a reason; kill. *♦He had his dog put away when it became too old and unhappy.*

**put back the clock** *or* **turn back the clock** *v. phr.* To go back in time; relive the past. *♦If I could put back the clock, I'd give more thought to preparing for a career. ♦Richard wishes that he had lived in frontier days, but he can't turn back the clock.*

**put by** *v.* To save for the future; lay aside. *♦He had put by a good sum during a working lifetime.*

**putdown** *n.* (stress on *put*) An insult. *♦It was a nasty putdown when John called his sister a fat cow.*

**put down** *v. phr.* (stress on *down*) **1.** To stop by force; crush. *♦In 24 hours the general had entirely put down the rebellion.* **2.** To put a stop to; check. *♦She had patiently put down unkind talk by living a good life.* **3.** To write a record of; write down. *♦He put down the story while it was fresh in his mind.* **4.** To write a name in a list as agreeing to do something. *♦The banker put himself down for $1000.* **5.** To decide the kind or class of; characterize. *♦He put the man down as a bum.* **6.** To name as a cause; attribute. *♦He put the odd weather down to nuclear explosions.* **7.** To dig; drill; sink. *He put down a new well.*

**put down roots** See SETTLE DOWN **1.**

**put forth** *v. phr.* To produce; issue; send out. *♦The chairman of the board put forth an innovative proposal that was circulated by mail.*

**put heads together** *v. phr.* To cooperate with someone else in order to find the solution to a given problem. *♦"Come on, let's put our heads together and find a way out of the firm's financial chaos," the director suggested to his colleagues.*

**put ideas into one's head** *v. phr.* To persuade someone to do something negative; put one up to something. *♦Bill would never have poured glue into his father's shoes if the neighbor's son hadn't been putting ideas into his head.*

**put in** *v.* **1.** To add to what has been said; say (something) in addition to what others say. *♦My father put in a word for me and I got the job.* **2.** To buy and keep in a store to sell. *♦He put in a full stock of drugs.* **3.** To spend (time). *♦He put in many years as a printer.* **4.** To plant. *♦He put in a row of radishes.* **5.** To stop at a port on a journey by water. *♦After the fire, the ship put in for repairs.* **6.** To apply; ask.—Used with *for.* *♦When a better job was open, he put in for it.*

**put in a word for** *v. phr.* To speak in favor of someone; recommend someone. *♦"Don't worry about your job application," Sam said to Tim. "I'll put in a word for you with the selection committee."*

**put in an appearance** *also* **make an appearance** *v. phr.* To be present, esp. for a short time; visit; appear. *♦The president put in an appearance at several dances the evening after he was sworn in.*

**put in one's place** *v. phr., informal* To criticize someone for impolite boldness; remind someone of low rank or position; reduce someone's unsuitable pride; deflate. *♦She was a teacher who could put a troublemaker in his place with just a glance.*

**put in the way of** *or* **put in one's way** *v. phr.* To set before (someone); give to (someone); show the way to; help toward. *♦The librarian put me in the way of a lot of new material on the subject of my report.*

**put off** *v.* **1.** *informal* To cause confusion in; embarrass; displease. *♦I was rather put off by the shamelessness of his proposal.* **2.** To wait and have (something) at a later time; postpone. *♦They put off the picnic because of the rain.* **3.** To make (someone) wait; turn aside. *♦When he asked her to name a day for their wedding, she put him off.* **4.** To draw away the attention; turn aside; distract. *♦Little Jeannie began to tell the guests some family secrets, but

*Father was able to put her off.* **5.** To move out to sea; leave shore. ♦ *They put off in small boats to meet the coming ship.*

**put on** *v. phr.* **1.** To dress in. ♦ *The boy took off his clothes and put on his pajamas.* **2a.** To pretend; assume; show. ♦ *The child was putting on airs.* **2b.** To exaggerate; make too much of. ♦ *That's rather putting it on.* **3.** To begin to have more (body weight); gain (weight). ♦ *Mary was thin from sickness, and the doctor said she must put on ten pounds.* **4a.** To plan and prepare; produce; arrange; give; stage. ♦ *The senior class put on a dance.* ♦ *The actor put on a fine performance.* **4b.** To make (an effort). ♦ *The runner put on an extra burst of speed and won the race.* **5.** To choose to send; employ on a job. ♦ *The school put on extra men to get the new building ready.*

**put-on** *n.* An act of teasing; the playing of a practical joke on someone. ♦ *Eric didn't realize that it was a put-on when his friends phoned him that he won the lottery.*

**put on airs** *v. phr.* To show conceit; act in a superior or condescending manner. ♦ *The fact that her parents own a villa in Capri is no reason for Amanda to keep putting on airs.*

**put on an act** *v. phr.* **1.** To perform a play. ♦ *The seventh grade put on a lovely act for Christmas for the parents.* **2.** To pretend. ♦ *"If you always put on an act," her father said, "people will never know who you really are."*

**put one in** *v. phr., slang* To be allowed to sleep at someone's house. ♦ *"Put me in," Mary asked Jane, when she was beaten up by her husband.*

**put one in one's place** See CUT DOWN TO SIZE.

**put one in the picture** *v. phr.* To inform someone of all the facts about a given situation. ♦ *Once you're back from your overseas trip, we'll put you in the picture about recent developments at home.*

**put one on a pedestal** *v. phr.* To exaggeratedly worship or admire a person. ♦ *Daniel puts Elaine on a pedestal and caters to her every whim.*

**put one through one's paces** *v. phr.* To train and discipline someone; test one's abilities. ♦ *The new recruits were certainly put through their paces by the drill sergeant.*

**put one wise** *v. phr.* To bring one up-to-date; inform someone; explain. ♦ *Our old friend David put us wise as to where the best used cars could be found in Chicago.*

**put one's back to it** *v. phr.* To make a real effort; to try. ♦ *You can finish the job by noon if you put your back to it.*

**put one's best foot forward** *v. phr., informal* To try to make a good impression; try to make a good appearance; do one's best. ♦ *During courtship, it is natural to put your best foot forward.*

**put oneself in another's place** or **put oneself in another's shoes** *v. phr.* To understand another person's feeling imaginatively; try to know his feelings and reasons with understanding; enter into his trouble. ♦ *If you will put yourself in the customer's place you may realize why the thing isn't selling.*

**put one's finger on** also **lay one's finger on** *v. phr.* To find exactly. ♦ *We called in an electrician hoping he could put his a finger on the cause of the short circuit.*

**put one's foot down** *v. phr., informal* To take a decided stand; be stubborn in decision. ♦ *When it came to smoking pot at parties, our parents put their foot down.*

**put one's foot in it** or **put one's foot in one's mouth** *v. phr., informal* To speak carelessly and rudely; hurt another's feelings without intending to; make a rude mistake. ♦ *He put his foot in it with his remark about self-made men because Jones was one of them.*

**put one's hand to** or **set one's hand to** or **turn one's hand to** *v. phr.* To start working at; try to do. ♦ *Hal does a good job at everything that he turns his hand to.*

**put one's hand to the plow** or **set one's hand to the plow** *v. phr.* To start doing something of importance; give yourself to a big job. ♦ *We felt that he had put his hand to the plow, and we didn't like it when he quit.*

**put one's life on the line** *v. phr.* To risk one's own life in the line of duty. ♦ *Firefighters and police officers frequently put their lives on the line while trying to save others.*

**put one's money where one's mouth is** *v. phr.* To follow through with a stated intention.—A proverb. ♦ *The governor has been promising to clean up corruption in the motor vehicle department, but nothing has ever been done. Isn't it time to put his money where his mouth is?*

**put one's name on the line** *v. phr.* To risk one's reputation by standing up for a cause. ♦ *Ted put his name on the line when he decided to stand up for gay liberation at the university.*

**put one's nose out of joint** *v. phr., informal* **1.** To make you jealous; leave you out of favor. ♦ *When Jane accepted Tom's invitation it put Jack's nose out of joint.* **2.** To ruin your plans; cause you disappointment. ♦ *Joe's mother put his nose out of joint by not letting him go to the movie.*

**put one's house in order** *or* **set one's house in order** *v. phr.* To arrange your affairs in good order. ♦ *When Mr. Black died, his lawyer helped the widow put her house in order.*

**put one's shoulder to the wheel** *v. phr.* To make a great effort yourself or with others; try hard; cooperate. ♦ *The company was failing in business until a new manager put his shoulder to the wheel.*

**put on one's thinking cap** *v. phr.* To think hard and long about some problem or question. ♦ *Miss Stone told her pupils to put on their thinking caps before answering the question.*

**put on the back burner** See ON ICE.

**put on the dog** *v. phr.* To behave ostentatiously in terms of dress and manner. ♦ *"Stop putting on the dog with me,"* Sue cried at Roy. *"I knew the real you from way back!"*

**put on the map** *v. phr.* To make (a place) well known. ♦ *The first successful climb of Mount Matterhorn put Zermatt, Switzerland, on the map.*

**put on weight** *v. phr.* To become fat, heavier, or obese. ♦ *Jack put on an awful lot of weight since he stopped exercising and started watching television all day.*

**put out** *v.* **1.** To make a flame or light stop burning; extinguish; turn off. ♦ *Please put the light out when you leave the room.* ♦ *The firemen put out the blaze.* **2.** To prepare for the public; produce; make. ♦ *For years he had put out a weekly newspaper.* ♦ *It is a small restaurant, which puts out an excellent dinner.* **3.** To invest or loan money. ♦ *He put out all his spare money at 4 percent or better.* **4.** To make angry; irritate; annoy. ♦ *It puts the teacher out to be lied to.* **5.** *informal* To cause inconvenience to; bother. ♦ *He put himself out to make things pleasant for us.* **6.** To retire from play in baseball. ♦ *The runner was put out at first base.* **7.** To go from shore; leave. ♦ *A Coast Guard boat put out through the waves.* **8.** *vulgar, avoidable* Said of women easy and ready to engage in sexual intercourse. ♦ *It is rumored that Hermione gets her promotions as fast as she does because she puts out.*

**put out of the way** *v. phr.* To kill. ♦ *The old dog was very sick, and Father had the animal doctor put him out of the way.*

**put over** *v.* **1.** To wait to a later time; postpone. ♦ *They put over the meeting to the following Tuesday.* **2.** *informal* To make a success of; complete. ♦ *He put over a complex and difficult business deal.* **3.** *informal* To practice deception; trick; fool.—Used with *on.* ♦ *George thought he was putting something over on the teacher when he said he was absent the day before because his mother was sick.*

**put someone on** *v.* To play a joke on someone by saying or doing things that are only pretense; kid. ♦ *When the voice on the phone told Mrs. Jones she had won a $10,000 prize, she thought someone was putting her on.*

**put (something) on the table** *or* **have (something) on the table** *v. phr.* To make something a subject of discussion or negotiation. ♦ *It is high time to put the question of a separate Palestinian state on the table.* ♦ *We cannot discuss the legalization of marijuana, because the subject is not on the table.*

**put that in your pipe and smoke it** *v. phr., informal* To understand something told you; accept something as fact or reality; not try to change it.—Usually used as a command, normally only in speech, and often considered rude. ♦ *I am not going to do what you ask of me and you can put that in your pipe and smoke it.*

**put the bite on** *v. phr., slang* To ask (for money, favors, etc.) ♦ *John put the bite on his friend for several tickets to the dance.*

**put the blame on** *v. phr.* To cause someone to become the scapegoat for a crime or some unpleasant event. ♦ *Mary put the blame on her mother-in-law for ruining her marriage by saying bad things about her to her husband.* ♦ *Don't put the blame on others before you search your own soul.*

**put the cart before the horse** See CART BEFORE THE HORSE.

**put their heads together** *or* **lay their heads together** *v. phr., informal* To plan or consider things together; discuss something as a group; talk it over. ♦ *They put.laid their heads together and decided on a gift.*

**put the screws on** *v. phr.* To pressure someone to confess, to pay up a debt; do what is wanted. ♦ *The police detectives really put the screws on the suspect, in order to make him tell the truth.* ♦ *The loan shark put the screws on the small business owners to make them repay their debts with all the interest.*

**put the word out** *v. phr.* To disseminate information about an important matter, good or bad. ♦ *The neighborhood watch group put out the word that a convicted rapist, who was recently released, had moved into their vicinity.* ♦ *I want you to put out the word that John's book of poetry is so good that he might just win the Pulitzer Prize.*

**put through** *v. phr.* **1.** To carry out; arrange. ♦ *If Jim can put through one more financial transaction like this one, we will be rich.* **2.** To connect. (said of telephone calls) ♦ *The telephone operator had to put me through to Zambia as there is no direct dialing there yet.*

**put through the mill** See PUT THROUGH ONE'S PACES.

**put through one's paces** *v. phr., informal* To test the different abilities and skills of a person or a thing; call for a show of what one can do. ♦ *He put his new car through its paces.*

**put to it** *adj. phr.* Hard pressed; having trouble; in difficulty; puzzled. ♦ *When he lost his job, he was rather put to it for a while to provide for his family.*

**put to sea** *v. phr.* To start a voyage. ♦ *The captain said the ship would put to sea at six in the morning.* ♦ *In the days of sailing ships, putting to sea depended on the tides.*

**put to shame** *v. phr.* **1.** To disgrace. ♦ *The cleanliness of European cities puts our cities to shame.* **2.** To do much better than surpass. ♦ *Einstein put other physicists to shame when he proved his theory of relativity correct.*

**put to sleep** *v. phr.* **1.** To cause to fall asleep. ♦ *Mother used to put us to sleep by telling us a good-night story and giving us a kiss.* **2.** To kill with an injection (said of animals). ♦ *Dr. Murphy, the veterinarian, put our sick, old dog to sleep.*

**put to the sword** *v. phr., literary* To kill (people) in war, especially with a sword. ♦ *The Romans put their enemies to the sword.*

**put to use** *v. phr.* To use. ♦ *Henry decided to put his dictionary to use.*

**put two and two together** *v. phr.* To make decisions based on available proofs; reason from the known facts; conclude; decide. ♦ *He had put two and two together and decided where they had probably gone.*

**put up** *v.* **1a.** To make and pack (especially a lunch or medicine); get ready; prepare. ♦ *Every morning Mother puts up lunches for the three children.* **1b.** To put food into jars or cans to save; can. ♦ *Mother is putting up peaches in jars.* **1c.** To store away for later use. ♦ *The farmer put up three tons of hay for the winter.* **2.** To put in place; put (something) where it belongs. ♦ *After he unpacked the car, John put it up.* **3.** To suggest that (someone) be chosen a member, officer, or official. ♦ *The club decided to take in another member, and Bill put up Charles.*—Often used with *for.* ♦ *The Republicans put Mr. Williams up for mayor.* **4.** To put (hair) a special way; arrange. ♦ *Aunt May puts up her hair in curlers every night.* **5.** To place on sale; offer for sale. ♦ *She put the house up for sale.* **6a.** To provide lodging for; furnish a room to. ♦ *The visitor was put up in the home of Mr. Wilson.* **6b.** To rent or get shelter; take lodging; stay in a place to sleep. ♦ *The traveler put up at a motel.* ♦ *We* *put up with friends on our trip to Canada.* **7.** To make; engage in. *He put up a good fight against his sickness.* **8.** To furnish (money) or something needed; pay for. ◆ *He put up the money to build a hotel.*

**put-up** *adj.* Artificially arranged; plotted; phony; illegal. ◆ *The FBI was sure that the bank robbers worked together with an insider and that the whole affair was a put-up job.*

**put up a (brave, good,** etc.**) fight** *v. phr.* To resist. ◆ *He put up a good fight but he was bound to lose in the end to the older, more experienced chess player.*

**put up a (brave** or **good) front** *v. phr.* To act courageously, even though one is actually afraid. ◆ *When Joe was taken in for his open heart surgery, he put up a brave front, although his hands were shaking.*

**put up or shut up** *v. phr. informal* **1.** To bet your money on what you say or stop saying it.—Often used as a command; often considered rude. ◆ *The man from out of town kept saying their team would beat ours and finally John told him "Put up or shut up."* **2.** To prove something or stop saying it.—Often used as a com-mand; often considered rude. ◆ *George told Al that he could run faster than the school champion and Al told George to put up or shut up.*

**put upon** *v.* To use (someone) unfairly; expect too much from.—Used in the passive or in the past participle. ◆ *Martha was put upon by the bigger girls.*

**put up to** *v. phr., informal* To talk to and make do; persuade to; get to do. ◆ *Older boys put us up to painting the statue red.*

**put up with** *v.* To accept patiently; bear. ◆ *We had to put up with Jim's poor table manners because he refused to change.*

**put wise** *v., slang* To tell (someone) facts that will give him an advantage over others or make him alert to opportunity or danger. ◆ *The new boy did not know that Jim was playing a trick on him, so I put him wise.*

**put words into one's mouth** *v. phr.* To say without proof that another person has certain feelings or opinions; claim a stand or an idea is another's without asking; speak for another without right. ◆ *When he said "John here is in favor of the idea." I told him not to put words in my mouth.*

**quality time** *n. phr.* A good leisure time spent with friends in conversation as during a major holiday; a serious time spent with one's children or other family members. ◆*"Come over after dinner, and let's have some quality time together,"* Bob said to his friends. ◆*Parents ought to spend some quality time with their children every day and not just send them to bed in a hurry.*

**queer fish** *n.* A strange or unusual person who does odd things. ◆*Uncle Algernon dresses in heavy furs in the summer and short-sleeved shirts in the winter. No wonder everyone considers him a queer fish.*

**quick fix** *or* **stopgap** *n. phr.* A simple short-term solution to a problem. ◆*Putting duct tape on a broken car bumper is just a quick fix that won't last very long.* ◆*To hire a substitute lecturer to teach English grammar instead of hiring a permanent faculty member is just a stopgap solution.*

**quick on the trigger** *or* **trigger happy** *adj. phr.* Ready to shoot without warning; fast with a gun. ◆*He's a dangerous criminal quick on the trigger.* **2.** *informal* Fast at answering questions or solving problems. ◆*In class discussions John is always quick on the trigger.*

**quick on the uptake** *adj. phr.* Smart; intelligent. ◆*Eleanor is very witty and quick on the uptake.*

**quick study** *n. phr.* One who acquires new skills and habits in record time. ◆*Sue is new at her job but people have confidence in her because she is a quick study.*

**quite a bit** *also formal* **not a little** *n. or adj. phr.* Rather a large amount; rather much; more than a little. ◆*Six inches of snow fell today, and quite a bit more is coming tonight.*—Sometimes used like an adverb. ◆*Harry was sick quite a bit last winter.*

**quite a few** *or* **quite a number** *also formal* **not a few** *n. or adj. phr.* Rather a large number; more than a few. ◆*Quite a few went to the game.* ◆*The basket had quite a few rotten apples in it.*—The phrase *quite a number* is used like an adjective only before *less, more.* ◆*Few people saw the play on the first night but quite a number came on the second night.*—Sometimes used like an adverb. ◆*We still have quite a few more miles to go before we reach New York.*

**quite the thing** *n. phr.* The socially proper thing to do. ◆*In polite society it is quite the thing to send a written thank you note to one's host or hostess after a dinner party.*

**rabbit food** n. phr., slang Vegetables; healthy food. ◆Sally looks a lot better and lost a lot of weight ever since she stopped eating junk food and heavy meats and became a rabbit food fan.

**race against time** v. phr. To be in a great hurry to finish a given project by a specified deadline. ◆The workers were racing against time to finish the campus modernization project.

**race to stand still** v. phr. To be so far behind in one's work that one must exert an effort similar to that needed to win a race in order simply not to fall even further behind. ◆"Could you review this book for us, Professor Brown?" the editor asked. "Unfortunately, no," the professor answered. "I'm so behind in my work that I am racing to stand still."

**rack and ruin** n. phr. Complete decay; condition of decline. ◆The entire house had been so neglected that it had gone to rack and ruin.

**rack one's brain** v. phr. To try your best to think; make a great mental effort; especially: to try to remember something you have known. ◆Bob racked his brain trying to remember where he left the book.

**radio ham** n. phr. Someone whose hobby is the operating of shortwave radio. ◆The code letters C.Q. are used by radio hams to invite other radio hams to join in the conversation.

**rag doll** n. A doll made of cloth and filled with soft stuffing. ◆My baby brother won't go to bed without his rag doll.

**rag trade** n. phr. The clothing industry. ◆My brother is working in the rag trade, manufacturing dresses.

**railroad** v. To force through; push through by force. ◆The bill was railroaded through the state legislature due to the influence of some very wealthy sponsors.

**rain cats and dogs** or **rain buckets** or **rain pitchforks** v. phr., informal To rain very hard; come down in torrents. ◆In the middle of the picnic it started to rain cats and dogs, and everybody got soaked. ◆Terry looked out of the window and said, "It's raining pitchforks, so we can't go out to play right now."

**raincheck** n. 1. A special free ticket to another game or show that will be given in place of one canceled because of rain. ◆When the drizzle turned into a heavy rain the manager announced that the baseball game would be replayed the next day. He told the crowd that they would be given rainchecks for tomorrow's game as they went out through the gates. 2. informal A promise to repeat an invitation at a later time. ◆Bob said, "I'm sorry you can't come to dinner this evening, Dave. I'll give you a raincheck."

**rained out** adj. Stopped by rain. ◆The ball game was rained out in the seventh inning.

**rain on** v. phr., slang To bring misfortune to (someone); to complain to (someone) about one's bad luck. ◆Don't rain on me.

**rain or shine** adv. phr. 1. If the weather is stormy or if it is fair. ◆The parade will start promptly, rain or shine. 2. No matter; if your luck is good or bad. ◆Sam knows he can depend on his family, rain or shine.

**rainproof** adj. Resistant to rain; something that will not soak in water; referring to a material that repels water. ◆"I don't need an umbrella," she said, "as my coat is rainproof."

**rainy day** n. A time of need; especially: a time when you really need money. ◆Squirrels gather acorns for a rainy day. ◆Each week Mrs. Carlson saved a little money for a rainy day.

**raise a row** v. phr. To cause a disturbance, a fuss, or a scene. ◆He raised quite a row when he noticed that someone had scratched his brand new car.

**raise a stink** v. phr. To cause a disturbance; complain; protest strongly. ◆Quite a stink was raised in the office when the boss discovered that several employees had left early.

**raise Cain** v. phr., slang To be noisy; cause trouble. ◆When John couldn't go on the basketball trip with the team he raised Cain.

**raise eyebrows** v. phr. To shock people; cause surprise or disapproval. ◆The news that the princess was engaged to a commoner raised eyebrows all over the kingdom.

**raise funds** *or* **money** *v. phr.* To solicit donations for a charity or a specific project. ♦ *Our church is trying to raise the funds for a new organ.*

**raise hackles** *or* **raise one's hackles** *v. phr.* To make (someone) upset or annoyed; arouse hostility. ♦ *Attempts to add new ingredients to the beer raised hackles among all the old brew masters.*

**raise one's sights** *v. phr.* To aim high; be ambitious. ♦ *Teenage boys sometimes think too much of themselves and have a tendency to raise their sights too high.*

**raise one's voice** *v. phr.* To speak loudly, as if in anger or in protest. ♦ *"I'm sorry, Sir," Peter said. "I didn't mean to raise my voice."*

**raise red flags** *n. phr.* Signal that danger is approaching. ♦ *The World Health Organization has been raising red flags all over the world about the new disease known as Severe Acute Respiratory Syndrome, or SARS.*

**raise the devil** *or* **raise heck** *or* **raise hob** *or* **raise ned** *v. phr., informal* To make trouble; start a fight or an argument. ♦ *Mr. Black raised heck when he saw the dented fender. He blamed the other driver.* ♦ *Some teenage boys raised the devil in town on Halloween night and damaged a lot of property.*

**raise the roof** *v. phr., informal* **1.** To make a lot of noise; be happy and noisy. ♦ *The gang raised the roof with their singing.* **2.** To scold loudly. ♦ *Mother raised the roof when she saw the dog's muddy footprints on her new bedspread.*

**rake in** *v. phr.* To realize great profits; take in money. ♦ *Because of the heavy snowfall, ski lodge operators in the Rocky Mountains have been raking in the dough this winter season.*

**rake off** *v. phr.* To illegally expropriate part of a sum paid. ♦ *The secretary-treasurer of the association has been caught raking off some of the membership dues.*

**rake over the coals** See HAUL OVER THE COALS.

**rake up** *v. phr.* To expose; gather; bring to light. ♦ *Let's forget about the past; there's no need to rake up all those old memories.*

**ramble on about** *v. phr.* To chatter on idly and without a purpose. ♦ *When Ted has too much to drink, he always rambles on about the good old days.*

**ram down one's throat** See SHOVE DOWN ONE'S THROAT.

**rank and file** *n. phr.* Ordinary people; the regular membership of an organization; the enlisted privates in the Army. ♦ *The secretary of the association sends letters annually to the rank and file.*

**rant and rave** *v. phr.* To quarrel almost violently with someone without any intention of stopping. *"♦ Stop ranting and raving," Sally begged her husband, who blamed his wife for his misfortune.*

**rap one's knuckles** *v. phr.* To scold or punish. ♦ *The principal rapped our knuckles for cheating on the test.* ♦ *Why rap my knuckles? It wasn't my fault.*

**rat on** See BLOW THE WHISTLE, RAT OUT.

**rat out** *or* **rat out on** *v. phr., slang* To desert; to leave at a critical time. ♦ *Joe ratted out on Sue when she was seven months pregnant.*

**rat race** *n., slang* A very confusing, crowded, or disorderly rush; a confusing scramble, struggle, or way of living that does not seem to have a purpose. ♦ *This job is a rat race. The faster you work, the faster the boss wants you to work.*

**rate with someone** *v. phr.* To be esteemed highly by another. ♦ *The professor really rates with both the graduate students and the undergraduates.*

**rattle off** *or* **reel off** *v.* To say quickly without having to stop to think; recite easily and rapidly. ♦ *When Roger was seven he could rattle off the names of all the states in alphabetical order.* ♦ *Joan memorized the "Gettysburg Address" so well that she could reel it off.*

**rattle one's saber** *v. phr.* To threaten another government or country without subsequent acts of war. ♦ *It is considered an act of demagoguery on the part of politicians to rattle their sabers.*

**rave about** *v. phr.* To talk very enthusiastically about someone or something. ♦ *Hank praised the new TV show very highly but we didn't think it was anything to rave about.*

**raw deal** *n. phr.* Unfair treatment; inequity. ♦ *Barry got a raw deal when* *he was sent to teach the class on advanced nuclear physics; he's an inexperienced graduate student.*

**raze to the ground** *v. phr.* To flatten; completely destroy. ♦*The conquering Red Army razed many German cities to the ground.* ♦*Three Turkish towns were razed to the ground by the violent earthquake.*

**razzle-dazzle** *n., slang* Fancy display; showing off. ♦*He is such a good player that he doesn't have to add razzle-dazzle to his game.*

**reach for the sky** *v. phr., slang* **1.** To put your hands high above your head or be shot.—Usually used as a command. ♦*A holdup man walked into a gas station last night and told the attendant "Reach for the sky!"* **2.** To set one's aims high. ♦*"Why medical technician?" asked her father. "Reach for the sky! Become a physician!"*

**read between the lines** *v. phr.* To understand all of a writer's meaning by guessing at what he has left unsaid. ♦*A clever foreign correspondent can often avoid censorship by careful wording, leaving his audience to read between the lines.*

**read into** *v. phr.* To attribute extra meaning to; deduce from; consider to be implicit in. ♦*Just because Fred's letters sounded so friendly Mary was wrong to read anything serious into them.*

**read my lips** *or* **mark my words** *v. phr.* Often heard when one wants to make the point that what was said is to be taken very seriously; a promise that what was said will be kept. ♦*"There will be no tax increase; read my lips!" former President George Herbert Walker Bush said, but unfortunately soon afterward there was a tax increase.* ♦*"Mark my words," the surgeon general said. "If you don't stop smoking, you could develop lung cancer!"*

**read off** *v. phr.* To read in a speaking voice from a list. ♦*The secretary read off the names of those present in alphabetical order.*

**read one like a book** *v. phr., informal* To understand someone completely; know what he will think or do at any time. ♦*John's girlfriend could read him like a book.*

**read one one's rights** *v. phr.* To give to an arrested person the legally required statement regarding the rights of such a person. ♦*"Read him his rights," Sergeant," the captain said, "and book him for breaking and entering."*

**read one's mind** *v. phr.* To know what someone else is thinking. ♦*I have known John so long that I can read his mind.*—**mind reader** *n.* ♦*That's exactly what I was going to say. You must be a mind reader!*

**read the riot act** *v. phr.* To give someone a strong warning or scolding. ♦*Three boys were late to class and the teacher read the riot act to them.*

**read over** *v. phr.* To read hurriedly in a rather superficial manner. ♦*The professor said he had no time to read my essay thoroughly but that he had read it over and would comment later in detail.*

**read up on** *v. phr.* To study carefully in preparation for an examination or other special purpose. ♦*Since Mr. and Mrs. Lee are going to take their American citizenship exams soon, they must read up on the Constitution and the three branches of government.*

**ready-made** *adj.* Mass-produced; machine made. ♦*I buy all my dresses ready-made because I can't afford to have them made to order.*

**ready money** *n. phr.* Cash on hand. ♦*Frank refuses to buy things on credit, but, if he had the ready money, he would buy that lovely old house.*

**real sport** *n. phr.* A person who willingly cooperates or gladly does someone a favor. ♦*I love John for many reasons, but most of all, because he is a real sport: he always carries Mr. Brown, who is in a wheelchair, upstairs.*

**rear end** *n.* **1.** The back part (usually of a vehicle) ♦*The rear end of our car was smashed when we stopped suddenly and the car behind us hit us.*—Often used like an adjective, with a hyphen. ♦*A head-on crash is more likely to kill the passengers than a rear-end crash.* **2.** Rump; backside. ♦*Bobby's mother was so annoyed with his teasing that she swatted his rear end.*

**rear its head** *v. phr.* To appear; emerge. ♦*After decades of certainty that tuberculosis had been eradicated globally, it* *suddenly reared its ugly head right here in the United States.*

**reckon with** *v.* To consider as one of the things which may change a situation; consider (something) that will make a difference in the results. ♦ *The coach said the opposing pitcher had a fast ball to be reckoned with.*

**reckon without** *v.* To fail to consider as one of the things which might change a situation; not think about. ♦ *The committee for the class picnic party made careful plans for a beach party but they reckoned without a sudden change in the weather.*

**redcap** *n.* A porter at an airport or at a railroad station. ♦ *Mr. Smith works as a redcap at Chicago's O'Hare Airport.*

**red cent** *n. phr.* The one-cent coin; a copper coin; very little money. ♦ *Poor Oscar is so broke he doesn't have a red cent to his name.*

**red eye** *adj. phr.* Bloodshot eyes that are strained from too much reading. ♦ *Poor Tim has a red eye; he must have been studying too late again.*

**red eye** *n. phr., informal* A night flight. ♦ *The company refused to pay for him to take a more expensive daytime flight, so he had to come in on the red eye.*

**red-faced** *adj. phr.* Visibly embarrassed. ♦ *"What on earth are you so red-faced about?" Sally asked her husband, Ted. "I managed to get myself fired from my job by badmouthing the boss while he was listening to our meeting, on closed circuit TV." Ted answered all embarassed.*

**red flag to a bull** *or* **red rag to a bull,** *or* **red rug to a bull** *n. phr.* An extraordinarily powerful irritant that provokes violent reaction. ♦ *Anti-Semitism is a red flag to a bull for all Jewish people.*

**red-handed** *adj.* In the very act; while committing a crime or evil action. ♦ *The criminal was caught red-handed while holding up the neighborhood bank at gunpoint.*

**red herring** *n. phr.* A false scent laid down in order to deceive; a phony or misleading story designed to cause confusion. ♦ *That story about the president having an affair was a red herring created by the opposition in order to discredit him.*

**red-letter day** *n. phr.* A holiday; memorable day (usually printed in red on calendars). ♦ *The Fourth of July is a red-letter day.*

**red-light district** *n. phr.* A district of brothels or where prostitutes hang out. ♦ *Most unwisely, the young sailor decided to spend his leave on shore by haunting the red-light districts of the port of call.*

**red tape** *n. phr.* Unnecessary bureaucratic routine; needless but official delays. ♦ *If you want to get anything accomplished in a hurry, you have to find someone in power who can cut through all that red tape.*

**refine on** *or* **refine upon** *v.* **1.** To make better; improve. ♦ *Mary was asked to refine on her first outline to make it clearer and more exact.* **2.** To be better than; surpass. ♦ *Modern medical techniques refine on those of the past.*

**regain one's feet** *v. phr.* To get back up again after falling down. ♦ *Tom fell while he skied down the hill but he regained his feet quickly.*

**regular guy** *or* **regular fellow** *n., informal* A friendly person who is easy to get along with; a good sport. ♦ *You'll like Tom. He's a regular guy.*

**relative to 1.** On the subject of; about. ♦ *Relative to school athletics, the principal said the students should not allow athletics to interfere with homework.* **2.** In comparison with; in proportion to. ♦ *Relative to the size of an ant, a blade of grass is as tall as a tree.*

**remains to be seen** *adj. phr.* Said when someone remains skeptical about a statement or promise made; I want proof of what was said. ♦ *"John will surely have a brilliant career as a concert pianist," his mother proudly announced. "That remains to be seen," John's father replied, "I don't think he practices enough."*

**remember the Alamo** *or* **remember Pearl Harbor** This is often heard when one wants to issue a warning in jest, meaning, "Don't forget history; we can climb out of any misery."—A proverb. ♦ *When John got fired from his job by the new boss, his old college roommate, a teacher of history, comforted him by saying, "Don't give up, John! Remember the Alamo!"*

**repeat oneself** *v. phr.* To say the same thing over again, often in the same words; repeat ideas because you forget what you said or because you want to stress their importance. ♦*Grandfather is forgetful and often repeats himself when he tells a story.*

**resign oneself** *v. phr.* To stop arguing; accept something which cannot be changed. ♦*When Jane's father explained that he could not afford to buy her a new bicycle, she finally resigned herself to riding the old one.*

**rest assured** *v. phr.* To be convinced; persuaded; certain and unworried. ♦*"Please rest assured," he said seriously, "that I will keep all of my promises."*

**rest on one's laurels** *v. phr.* To be satisfied with the success you have already won; stop trying to win new honors. ♦*Getting an A in chemistry almost caused Mike to rest on his laurels.*

**rest on one's oars** *v. phr.* To stop trying; stop working for a while; rest. ♦*The man who wants to become a millionaire can never rest on his oars.*

**rest room** *n.* A room or series of rooms in a public building which has things for personal comfort and grooming, such as toilets, washbowls, mirrors, and often chairs or couches. ♦*Sally went to the rest room to powder her nose.*

**return the compliment** *v. phr.* To say or do the same to someone that he has said or done to you; pay someone back. ♦*Mary said, "I love your new hairdo" and Suzy returned the compliment with "What a pretty dress you're wearing, Mary."* ♦*John punched Jerry in the nose, and Jerry returned the compliment.*

**return to the fold** *v. phr.* To regain membership in a given church denomination or political party, after having strayed from one's fellow believers or comrades. ♦*After several years spent as an atheist, John returned to the fold of the Catholic Church.*

**rev up** *v. phr., informal, slang* **1.** To press down sharply several times on the accelerator of an idling car in order to get maximum acceleration. ♦*The race driver revved up his car by pumping his accelerator.* **2.** To get oneself ready in order to accomplish a demanding or difficult task. ♦*The boys were getting all revved up for the football game.*

**rhyme or reason** *n. phr.* A good plan or reason; a reasonable purpose or explanation.—Used in negative, interrogative, or conditional sentences. ♦*Don could see no rhyme or reason to the plot of the play.*

**ride herd on** *v. phr.* **1.** To patrol on horseback around a herd of animals to see that none of them wanders away. ♦*Two cowboys rode herd on the cattle being driven to market.* **2.** *informal* To watch closely and control; take care of. ♦*A special legislative assistant rides herd on the bills the president is anxious to have congress pass.*

**ride on one's coattails** *v. phr.* To succeed in a certain endeavor by attaching oneself to the greater weight of another person or corporate body. ♦*"We will never get our Ph.D. program approved on our own," said the head of the modern dance department, "but we might succeed if we stay in the Division of Fine Arts, riding on their coattails, as it were."*

**ride out** *v.* To survive safely; endure. ♦*The captain ordered all sails lowered so the ship could ride out the storm.*

**ride roughshod over** *v. phr.* To do as you wish without considering the wishes of (another person); treat with scorn or lack of courtesy; show no sympathy for. ♦*The city officials rode roughshod over the people who did not want their homes torn down for a new school.*

**ride shotgun** *v. phr.* To ride next to the driver in a car, in the seat for the front passenger. ♦*I really dislike riding shotgun; in case of an accident it is considered the "death seat."*

**rideshare** *v. phr.* To share a car with a fellow commuter to save on gasoline and toll prices. ♦*The Smiths and the Kowalskis decided to rideshare, since both families were living and working in the same place.*

**ride the brake** *or* **ride the clutch** *v. phr., informal* To keep your foot on the pedal. ♦*Riding the brake is a bad habit for a driver to form.*

**ride the gravy train** *v. phr.* To live a life of plenty and luxury. ♦*Those who have a wealthy executive or heir to a fortune for a spouse can ride the gravy train without doing any work.*

**ride up** *or* **crawl up** *v.* To slip gradually upward on the body. ♦ *Shorts that ride up can be very uncomfortable.*

**riding for a fall** *adj. phr.* Behaving in an overconfident way that is likely to lead to trouble; being too sure of yourself; doing something dangerous. ♦ *The student who does not study for exams is riding for a fall.*

**riding high** *adj.* Attracting attention; enjoying great popularity. ♦ *After scoring the winning touchdown, John is riding high with his classmates.*

**rid of** Free of; away from; without the care or trouble. ♦ *I wish you'd get rid of that cat!*

**right along** *adv. phr., informal* **1a.** On your way satisfactorily or without trouble. ♦ *They fixed the engine and the train ran right along.* **1b.** On your way without delay. ♦ *Don't wait for me. Go right along.*

**right and left** *adv. phr.* In or from every direction; all around; on all sides. ♦ *When the talk ended, questions were thrown at the speaker right and left.*

**right around the corner** See AROUND THE CORNER.

**right away** *or informal* **right off** *also informal* **right off the bat** *adv. phr.* Immediately; as the next thing in order; without delay. ♦ *Phil's mother told him to do his homework right away so that he could enjoy the weekend.* ♦ *Jill knew the answer right off.* ♦ *The teacher said he could not think of the title of the book right off the bat.*

**right down** *or* **up one's alley** *adv. phr.* In accordance with one's specialty or predilection. ♦ *This kind of preclassical music is right up Bill's alley; after all, he wrote his Ph.D. on Bach.*

**right-hand man** *v. phr.* A valued and indispensable assistant. ♦ *The chancellor of the university never goes anywhere without the vice chancellor, his right-hand man, whose judgment he greatly trusts.*

**right on** *adj., interj., slang, informal* **1.** Exclamation of animated approval "Yes," "That's correct," "You're telling the truth," "we believe you," etc. ♦ *Orator: And we shall see the promised land! Crowd: Right on!* **2.** Correct; to the point; accurate. ♦ *The reverend's remark was right on!*

**right out** *or* **straight out** *adv.* Plainly; in a way that hides nothing; without waiting or keeping back anything. ♦ *When Ann entered the beauty contest her little brother told her straight out that she was crazy.*

**right-wing** *adj.* Being or belonging to a political group which opposes any important change in the way the country is run. ♦ *Some countries with right-wing governments have dictators.*

**rig out** *v. phr.* To overdecorate; doll up; dress up. ♦ *Ann arrived all rigged out in her newest Parisian summer outfit.*

**ring a bell** *v. phr.* To make you remember something; sound familiar. ♦ *When Ann told Jim the name of the new teacher it rang a bell, and Jim said, "I went to school with John Smith."*

**ring in** *v. phr., informal* **1.** To bring in (someone or something) from the outside dishonestly or without telling; often: hire and introduce under a false name. ♦ *Bob offered to ring him in on the party by pretending he was a cousin from out of town.* **2.** To ring a special clock that records the time you work. ♦ *We have to ring in at the shop before eight o'clock in the morning.*

**ring in the New Year** *v. phr.* To clink with glasses filled with champagne and wish one another a happy New Year at midnight on December 31. ♦ *We rang in the New Year and wished one another peaceful and worry-free times.*

**ringleader** *n. phr.* The chief of an unsavory group; a higher-up. ♦ *The FBI finally caught up with the ringleader of the dope smugglers from South America.*

**ring out** *v.* To ring a special clock that records the time you leave work. ♦ *Charles can't leave early in his new job; he has to ring out.*

**ring true** *v. phr.* To have a tone of genuineness; sound convincing. ♦ *I believed his sob story about how he lost his fortune, because somehow it all rang true.*

**ring up** *v.* **1.** To add and record on a cash register. ♦ *The supermarket clerk rang up Mrs. Smith's purchases and told her she owed $33.* ♦ *Business was bad Tuesday; we didn't ring up a sale all morning.* **2.** *informal* To telephone. ♦ *Sally rang up Sue and told her the news.*

**rip into** *or* **tear into** *v., informal* **1.** To start a fight with; attack. ♦ *The puppy is tearing into the big dog.* **2.** To quarrel with; scold. ♦ *Mrs. Brown ripped into her daughter for coming home late.*

**rip off** *v., slang* (stress on *off*) Steal. ♦ *The hippies ripped off the grocery store.*

**rip-off** *n., slang* (stress on *rip*) An act of stealing or burglary. ♦ *Those food prices are so high, it's almost a rip-off.*

**rise and shine** *v. phr.* Said by parents to their sleeping children, who have to get up and go to school.—A proverb. ♦ *"Rise and shine!" Mother's voice rang out, as the boys pulled the covers over their heads, refusing to get up.*

**rise as one man** *v. phr.* To stand up spontaneously and simultaneously, as if the crowd were one person, both in a theater or in real life in politics. ♦ *The audience rose as one man after Maestro Georg Solti put down his baton, having conducted Beethoven's Ninth Symphony.* ♦ *The Hungarian nation rose as one man in 1956 against Soviet oppression.*

**rise from the ashes** *v. phr.* To rise from ruin; start anew. ♦ *A year after flunking out of medical school, Don rose from the ashes and passed his qualifying exams for the M.D. with honors.*

**rise to** *v.* To succeed in doing what is expected by trying especially hard in or on; show that you are able to do or say what is needed or proper in or on. ♦ *Jane was surprised when the principal handed her the prize, but she rose to the occasion with a speech of thanks.*

**rise up** *v. phr.* To stage a rebellion; revolt. ♦ *The people finally rose up and communism came to an end in Eastern Europe.*

**rise with the lark** *or* **rise with the birds** *v. phr.* To get up early in the morning. ♦ *Farmers usually rise with the lark.*

**risk life and limb** *v. phr.* To live dangerously. ♦ *John has been risking life and limb ever since he became a race car driver.*

**risk one's neck** *v. phr.* To put oneself in a potentially dangerous situation. ♦ *"I refuse to risk my neck for my new boss," John said.*

**road gang** *n.* A group of men who work at road construction. ♦ *Football players often work with road gangs during summer vacations.*

**road hog** *n ., informal* A car driver who takes more than his share of the road. ♦ *A road hog forced John's car into the ditch.*

**road show** *n.* A theatrical play that is performed for a few days in one town and then moves to other towns. ♦ *Many actors get their start in road shows.*

**road sign** *n.* A sign on which there is information about a road or places; a sign with directions to drivers. ♦ *The road sign said Westwood was four miles away.*

**road test** *n.* **1.** A test to see if you can drive a car. ♦ *Jim took the road test and got his driver's license last week.* **2.** A test to see if a car works all right on the road. ♦ *Most new cars are given road tests before they are put on the market.* ♦ *After he repaired the car, the mechanic gave it a road test.*

**road to perdition** *or* **road to ruin** *n. phr.* A lifestyle that will lead to illness, jail, and even death. ♦ *Many young gang members are unaware of the fact that they have chosen the road to perdition.* ♦ *Doing drugs means having chosen the road to ruin.*

**roasting ear** *n.* An ear of corn young and tender enough to be cooked and eaten; *also* corn cooked on the cob. ♦ *At the Fourth of July picnic we had fried chicken and roasting ears.*

**rob one blind** *v. phr.* To take everything away from someone in a holdup or by dishonest court action. ♦ *When John was divorced from Melanie, she robbed him blind.*

**rob Peter to pay Paul** *v. phr.* To change one duty or need for another; take from one person or thing to pay another. ♦ *Trying to study a lesson for one class during another class is like robbing Peter to pay Paul.*

**rob the cradle** *v. phr., informal* To have dates with or marry a person much younger than yourself. ♦ *When the old woman married a young man, everyone said she was robbing the cradle.*

**rock-bottom** *n.* The lowest possible point. ♦ *The nation's morale hit rock bottom in the hours following the pres-*

*ident's assassination.*—Often used like an adjective, with a hyphen. ♦ *The rock-bottom price of this radio is $25.*

**rock hound** *n., slang* A person who studies and collects rocks for a hobby. ♦ *Many young rock hounds grow up to be geologists.*

**rock one's word** *v. phr.* To make a major impression in a given circle of friends or professional colleagues. ♦ *Noam Chomsky's work has rocked the world of linguistics.*

**rock 'n' roll** *or* **rock and roll** *n.* A style of popular music with heavily accented rhythm. ♦ *Rock 'n' roll appeals mostly to youngsters nine to sixteen years old.*

**rock the boat** *v. phr., informal* To make trouble and risk losing or upsetting something; cause a disturbance that may spoil a plan. ♦ *Politicians don't like to rock the boat around election time.*

**roll around** *v., informal* To return at a regular or usual time; come back. ♦ *When winter rolls around, out come the skis and skates.*

**roll back out to sea** *v. phr., nautical and meteorological* This idiom is used when coastal fog recedes from the land. ♦ *The Coast Guard issued a warning to all small boats not to set out until the fog rolls back out to sea.*

**roll in** *v. phr., nautical and meteorological* Said when a thunderstorm or the fog is coming toward the coast from the sea. ♦ *The small boats were not allowed to set out to sea because a thunderstorm was rolling in.* ♦ *Small aircraft were not allowed to take off, because the fog was rolling in.*

**roller coaster ride** *n. phr.* Extreme emotional upheaval, due to ups and down's in one's life. ♦ *Poor Mary has been on an emotional roller coaster ride. First her husband died; then she met a wonderful new man, who also died. She doesn't know what to do next.*

**rolling stone gathers no moss** A person who changes jobs or where he lives often will not be able to save money or things of his own.—A proverb. ♦ *Uncle Willie was a rolling stone that gathered no moss. He worked in different jobs all over the country.*

**roll out the red carpet** *v. phr.* 1. To welcome an important guest by putting a red carpet down for him to walk on. ♦ *They rolled out the red carpet for the Queen when she arrived in Australia.* 2. To greet a person with great respect and honor; give a hearty welcome. ♦ *Margaret's family rolled out the red carpet for her teacher when she came to dinner.*

**roll up one's sleeves** To get ready for a hard job; prepare to work hard or seriously. ♦ *When Paul took his science examination, he saw how little he knew about science. He rolled up his sleeves and went to work.*

**Roman collar** *n.* The high, plain, white collar worn by priests and clergymen. ♦ *The man with the Roman collar is the new Episcopalian preacher.*

**Rome wasn't built in a day** Great things are not accomplished overnight; great deeds take a long time.—A proverb. ♦ *It takes a long time to write a successful novel, but don't worry: Rome wasn't built in a day, as the saying goes.*

**room and board** *n. phr.* A room for rent with meals included. ♦ *A room alone in that country costs only $10 a day, but room and board together run $22 a day.*

**room clerk** *or* **desk clerk** *n.* A person who is responsible for assigning rooms and providing service to guests in hotels, motels, inns, etc. ♦ *At first-class hotels, room clerks are trained to be at the service of every guest.*

**room service** *n.* Service provided to hotel guests in their rooms. *Also:* The hotel workers who give this service. ♦ *We called for room service when we wanted ice.*

**room with** *v. phr.* 1. To live in a furnished room with someone as a roommate without having an affair. ♦ *I roomed with him in college for four years.* 2. To live together as husband and wife without the benefit of marriage. ♦ *Dan and Sue have been rooming together for quite a while.*

**root and branch** *adv. phr.* Thoroughly, entirely, so as to prevent the destroyed item from coming back to life. ♦ *Terrorism must be destroyed root and branch, if we want to live in safety.*

**root-bound** *adj.* 1. Having a limited amount of space for root growth. ♦ *After seven or eight years day lilies become root-bound and will not bloom* *well unless they are divided.* **2.** Liking the familiar place where you live and not wanting to go away from it; having a sentimental attachment to one place. ♦ *Mr. Jones has lived in Connecticut all his life. He is too root-bound to consider moving to another state.*

**root for** *v. phr.* To cheer for; applaud; support. ♦ *During the Olympics one usually roots for the team of one's own country.*

**root of all evil** *n. phr.* The desire to enrich oneself financially Money and greed, i.e., the desire to enrich oneself financially. ♦ *The love of money is the root of all evil.* ♦ *Chasing the almighty dollar is the root of all evil.*

**rope in** *v., informal* **1.** To use a trick to make (someone) do something; deceive; fool. ♦ *The company ropes in high school students to sell magazine subscriptions by telling them big stories of how much money they can earn.* **2.** To get (someone to join or help); persuade to do something. ♦ *Martha roped in Charles to help her decorate the gym for the party.*

**rope into** *v., informal* **1.** To trick into; persuade dishonestly. ♦ *Jerry let the big boys rope him into stealing some apples.* **2.** To get (someone) to join in; persuade to work at. ♦ *It was Sue's job to bathe the dog but she roped Sam into helping her.*

**rope off** *v. phr.* To divide into sections by use of a rope. ♦ *The police roped off the section of the street where the president was expected to jog.*

**rose-colored glasses** See LOOK AT THE WORLD THROUGH ROSE-COLORED GLASSES.

**rotten egg** *n., informal* A person whose character or way of acting is not good. ♦ *His friends have all learned that Stanley is a rotten egg.*

**rotten to the core** *adj. phr.* **1.** Thoroughly decayed or spoiled. ♦ *This apple is inedible; it is brown and soft and rotten to the core.* **2.** In total moral collapse. ♦ *The Communist government of Cuba is rotten to the core.*

**rough-and-ready** *adj.* **1.** Not finished in detail; not perfected; rough but ready for use now. ♦ *We asked Mr. Brown how long it would take to drive to Chicago and his rough-and-ready answer was*

*two days.* **2.** Not having nice manners but full of energy and ability. ♦ *Jim is a rough-and-ready character; he'd rather fight than talk things over.*

**rough-and-tumble 1.** *n.* Very rough, hard fighting or arguing that does not follow any rules. ♦ *Many people don't like the rough-and-tumble of politics.* **2.** *adj.* Fighting or arguing in a very rough and reckless way; struggling hard; not following rules or laws. ♦ *It took strong men to stay alive in the rough-and-tumble life of the western frontier.*

**roughhouse** *n.* Riotous play or commotion. ♦ *I told the boys they can play in the attic if there is no roughhouse.*

**roughhouse** *v.* To play very wildly; be running around as young boys usually do. ♦ *"Stop roughhousing this minute,"* Grandma cried. *"Your father will be home soon."*

**rough idea** *n. phr.* A fairly accurate, but not final approximation of the status of a situation. ♦ *Can you give me a rough idea about next year's salaries?*

**rough it** *v. phr.* To live like primitive people; live with little of the comfort and equipment of civilization. ♦ *Scouts like to rough it in the woods on weekend hikes.*

**roughneck** *n.* A low, coarse fellow. ♦ *The only boys in the neighborhood are a bunch of roughnecks, and Mrs. Smith is unhappy about the fact that her son is rapidly becoming one of them.*

**rough up** *v.* To attack or hurt physically; treat roughly; beat. ♦ *Three boys were sent home for a week because they roughed up a player on the visiting team.*

**roughly speaking** *adv. phr.* Approximately; in general terms. ♦ *Roughly speaking, about 250 people attended the annual convention of the Dictionary Society of America.*

**round-eyed** *or* **wide-eyed** *also* **large-eyed** *adj.* Very much surprised; astonished; awed. ♦ *The people were round-eyed when they learned what the computer could do.* ♦ *The children were wide-eyed at the sight of the Christmas tree and didn't make a sound.*

**round off** *v.* **1.** To make round or curved. ♦ *John decided to round off the corners of the table he was making so that no one would be hurt by bumping them.*

2. To change to the nearest whole number. ♦ *The teacher said to round off the averages.* 3. To end in a satisfactory way; put a finishing touch on; finish nicely. ♦ *We rounded off the dinner with mixed nuts.*

**round out** v. phr. To complete; make whole. ♦ *He needs only one or two more rare compact discs to round out his collection of Vivaldi.*

**round robin** n. phr. A contest or games in which each player or team plays every other player or team in turn.— Often used like an adjective. ♦ *The tournament will be a round robin for all the high school teams in the city.*

**round the clock** See AROUND THE CLOCK.

**round trip** n. A return trip; passage to a place and back. ♦ *The ticket agent explained that a ticket for a round trip to Hawaii at certain times of the year may cost less than a one-way ticket during the high season.*

**roundup** n. (stress on *round*) A muster; an inspection; a gathering together. ♦ *The police roundup of all suspected drug dealers took place early in the morning.*

**round up** v. (stress on *up*) 1. To bring together (cattle or horses). ♦ *Cowboys round up their cattle in the springtime to brand the new calves.* 2. *informal* To collect; gather. ♦ *Dave rounded up many names for his petition.*

**rubdown** n. A massage. ♦ *The chiropractor gave his patient a powerful rubdown.*

**rub down** v., phr. 1. To dry the body of (an animal or person) by rubbing. ♦ *Stablemen rub down a horse after a race.* 2. To rub and press with the fingers on the body of (a person) to loosen muscles or prevent stiffness; massage. ♦ *Trainers rub down an athlete after hard exercise.*

**rub elbows** also **rub shoulders** v. phr. To be in the same place (with others); meet and mix. ♦ *On a visit to the United Nations Building in New York, you may rub elbows with people from far-away lands.*

**rub it in** v. phr., *slang* To remind a person again and again of an error or short-coming; tease; nag. ♦ *I know my black eye looks funny. You don't need to rub it in.*

**rub off** v. To pass to someone near as if by touching. ♦ *Jimmy is very lucky; I wish some of his luck would rub off on me.*

**rub one's nose in something** v. phr. To put someone to shame by reminding them of some past mistake. ♦ *"I am sorry that I made a mistake in last year's accounting," John said to the director. "I have corrected that since, and it will never happen again. Why must you keep rubbing my nose in it?"*

**rub out** v. *slang* To destroy completely; kill; eliminate. ♦ *The gangsters told the storekeeper that if he did not pay them to protect him, someone would rub him out.*

**rub salt into one's wounds** v. phr., *informal* To deliberately add pain when one feels shame, regret, or defeat. ♦ *Must you rub salt into my wounds by telling me how much fun I missed by not going to the party?*

**rub the wrong way** v. phr., *informal* To make (someone) a little angry; do something not liked by (someone); annoy; bother. ♦ *John's bragging rubbed the other boys the wrong way.*

**rub up against** v. phr. To come into contact with. ♦ *In that business one naturally has to rub up against all kinds of people.*

**ruffle feathers** or **ruffle one's feathers** v. phr. Insult or disturb slightly; offend. ♦ *The author ruffled some feathers by his portrait of his hometown.*

**rule of thumb** n. phr. A simple and practical method that has proven successful or useful in the past. ♦ *It is a very good rule of thumb to look up all unfamiliar words in a good dictionary.*

**rule out** v. 1. To say that (something) must not be done; not allow; *also:* decide against. ♦ *The principal ruled out dances on school nights.* 2. To show that (someone or something) is not a possibility; make it unnecessary to think about; remove (a chance). ♦ *The doctor took X rays to rule out the chance of broken bones.* 3. To make impossible; prevent. *Father's illness seems to rule out college for Jean.*

**rule the roost** v. phr., *informal* To be leader or boss; be in charge. ♦ *Jim is very bossy; he always wants to rule the roost.*

**rumor has it** adv. phr. According to gossip; as people say. ♦ *Rumor has it* *that Jane and Mike are not getting married after all.*

**run a fever** See RUN A TEMPERATURE.

**run after** *or* **chase after** *v.* **1.** To try to find; look for; hunt. ◆*The Dramatic Club has to run all over town after things for setting the stage when it puts on a play.* **2.** *informal* To seek the company of; chase. ◆*Some boys spend a lot of time and money running after girls.*

**run along** *v.* To go away; leave. ◆*Joan said she had errands to do and must run along.*

**run amok** *or* **run amuck** *v. phr.* To act wildly and strangely. ◆*The entire company has been running amok after the unexpected resignation of our director.*

**run a risk** *or* **take a risk** *v. phr.* To be open to danger or loss; put yourself in danger; be unprotected. ◆*I was afraid to run the risk of betting on the game.*

**run around in circles** *v. phr.* To waste time in repetitive movements; be confused. ◆*There was such a crowd in the lobby that I ran around in circles trying to find my group.*

**run around** *or* **chase around** *v., informal* To go to different places for company and pleasure; be friends. ◆*Tim hasn't been to a dance all year; with school work and his job, he hasn't time to run around.*

**run around like a chicken with its head cut off** See RUN AROUND IN CIRCLES.

**run a temperature** *v. phr.* To have a body temperature that is above normal;· have a fever. ◆*We took the baby to the doctor because he was running a temperature.*

**run a tight ship** *v. phr.* To run an organization with a firm hand, with strict rules and regulations. ◆*Our dean of the college runs a very tight ship; he tolerates no mistakes.*

**run away** *or* **run off** *v.* To leave and not plan to come back; go without permission; escape. ◆*Many times Tommy said he would run away from home, but he never did.*

**run away with** *v.* **1.** To take hold of; seize. ◆*The boys thought they saw a ghost in the old house last night; they let their imagination run away with them.* **2.** To be much better or more noticeable than others in; win easily. ◆*Our team ran away with the game in the last half.*

**run circles around** *also* **run rings around** *v. phr.* To show that you can do a task much better than; do better than (someone) very easily. ◆*Frank ran rings around the other boys on the basketball team.*

**run down** *v.* (stress on *down*) **1.** To crash against and knock down or sink. ◆*Jack rode his bicycle too fast and almost ran down his little brother.* **2a.** To chase until exhausted or caught. ◆*The dogs ran down the wounded deer.* **2b.** To find by hard and thorough search; *also:* trace to its cause or beginning. ◆*The policeman ran down proof that the burglar had robbed the store.* **3.** *informal* To say bad things about; criticize. ◆*Suzy ran down the club because the girls wouldn't let her join.* **4.** To stop working; not run or go. ◆*The battery in Father's car ran down this morning.* **5.** To get into poor condition; look bad. ◆*A neighborhood runs down when the people don't take care of their houses.*

**run-down** *adj.* (stress on *run*) In poor health or condition; weak or needing much work. ◆*Grandma caught a cold because she was very run-down from loss of sleep.*

**run dry** *v. phr.* To dry up; lose the water content. ◆*After many years of use, our well ran dry.*

**run errands** *v. phr.* To carry messages or perform similar minor tasks. ◆*Peter runs errands for our entire neighborhood to make some extra money.*

**run for it** *or* **make a run for it** *v. phr.* To dash for safety; make a speedy escape. ◆*The bridge the soldiers were on started to fall down and they had to run for it.*

**run for one's money** *n. phr.* **1.** A good fight; a hard struggle.—Usually used with *give* or *get.* ◆*Our team didn't win the game, but they gave the other team a run for their money.* **2.** Satisfaction; interest; excitement.—Usually used with *give* or *get.* ◆*People like to watch the champion fight because they get a good run for their money from him.*

**run for the office of** *v. phr.* To enter a political race as a candidate of the Democratic or the Republican Party, or as an independent. ◆*John decided to run for the office of county treasurer.* ◆*We have no idea who will run for the* *office of president of the United States in the year 2012.*

**run in** *v. phr.* (stress on *in*) **1.** *informal* To take to jail; arrest. ♦ *The policeman ran the man in for peddling without a license.* **2.** To make a brief visit. ♦ *The neighbor boy ran in for a minute to see Bob's newest model rocket.* Syn. DROP IN. Compare STOP OFF.

**run-in** *n.* (stress on *run*) **1.** A traffic accident. ♦ *My car was wrecked when I had a run-in with a small truck.* **2.** A violent quarrel. ♦ *John had a nasty run-in with his boss and was fired.*

**run in the blood** *or* **run in the family** *v. phr.* To be a common family characteristic; be learned or inherited from your family. ♦ *Red hair runs in the family.*

**run into** *v.* **1.** To mix with; join with. ♦ *If the paint brush is too wet, the red paint will run into the white on the house.* ♦ *This small brook runs into a big river in the valley below.* **2.** To add up to; reach; total. ♦ *Car repairs can run into a lot of money.* ♦ *A good dictionary may run into several editions.* **3a.** Bump; crash into; hit. ♦ *Joe lost control of his bike and ran into a tree.* **3b.** To meet by chance. ♦ *I ran into Joe yesterday on Main Street.* **3c.** Be affected by; get into. ♦ *I ran into trouble on the last problem on the test.*

**run into a brick wall** *or* **run into a stone wall** See STONE WALL.

**run into the ground** *v. phr., informal* **1.** To do or use (something) more than is wanted or needed. ♦ *It's all right to borrow my hammer once in a while, but don't run it into the ground.* **2.** To win over or defeat (someone) completely. ♦ *We lost the game today, but tomorrow we'll run them into the ground.*

**run its course** *v. phr.* To fulfill a normal development; terminate a normal period. ♦ *Your flu will run its course; in a few days you'll be back on your feet.*

**run late** *v. phr.* To be tardy, or habitually be late, often because of poor planning of one's day. ♦ *If Ted keeps running late at the firm, he may get into serious trouble with the director.*

**run low on** *v. phr.* To face a shortage of something essential. ♦ *"We are running low on drinking water and bathroom tissue," Jean said to her husband. "I am running low on gas," he replied, "so*

*let's get going and take care of all of our needs at once."*

**run off** *v., phr.* (stress on *off*) **1.** To produce with a printing press or duplicating machine. ♦ *The print shop ran off a thousand copies of the newspaper.* **2.** To drive away. ♦ *The boys saw a dog digging in mother's flower bed, and they ran him off.*

**run-off** *n.* (stress on *run*) A second election held to determine the winner when the results of the first one were inconclusive. ♦ *The senatorial race was so close that the candidates will have to hold a run-off.*

**run off at the mouth** *v. phr.* To talk too much; be unable to stop talking. ♦ *"Shut up, John," our father cried. "You are always running off at the mouth.*

**run of luck** *n. phr.* A period of good luck. ♦ *I had a run of luck last Saturday when I went fishing and caught seven big trout within one hour.*

**run-of-the-mill** *adj.* Of a common kind; ordinary; usual. ♦ *It was just a run-of-the-mill movie.*

**runner-up** *n.* The person who finishes second in a race or contest; the one next after the winner. ♦ *Sylvia was runner-up in the Miss Illinois contest.*

**running start** *n. phr.* Good progress at the beginning. ♦ *Contributions of $5000 before the drive began gave the charity fund a running start.*

**run one's head against a stone wall** *or* **bang one's head against a wall** *or* **hit one's head against a wall** *or* **run one's head against a wall** *v. phr.* To willfully ignore the facts and tempt fate by trying to do the impossible. ♦ *Ted is the most stubborn person I know; instead of coming to grips with reality, he is constantly running his head against a stone wall by proposing impossible schemes at his workplace.*

**run out** *v.* **1a.** To come to an end; be used up. ♦ *We'd better do our Christmas shopping; time is running out.* **1b.** To use all of the supply; be troubled by not having enough. ♦ *The car ran out of gas three miles from town.* **2.** *informal* To force to leave; expel. ♦ *Federal agents ran the spies out of the country.*

**run out on** *v. phr.* To leave someone in the lurch; abandon another. ♦ *When Ted ran out on Delores, she got so* *angry that she sued him for divorce.*

**run over** *v.* **1.** To be too full and flow over the edge; spill over. ♦*Billy forgot he had left the water on, and the tub ran over.* **2.** To try or go over (something) quickly; practice briefly. ♦*During the lunch hour, Mary ran over her history facts so she would remember them for the test.* **3.** To drive on top of; ride over. ♦*At night cars often run over small animals that are blinded by the headlights.*

**run ragged** *v. phr.* To tire out; make nervous by too much worry or work. ♦*Trying to keep up with too many clubs, sports, and activities in addition to his homework ran Tom ragged.*

**run riot** *v. phr.* **1.** To act freely or wildly; not control yourself. ♦*John let his imagination run riot, thinking he was hunting lions in Africa.* **2.** To be or grow in great numbers or large amounts. ♦*Daisies ran riot in the meadow.*

**run scared** *v. phr.* To expect defeat, as in a political campaign. ♦*The one-vote defeat caused him to run scared in every race thereafter.*

**run short** *v. phr.* **1.** To not have enough. ♦*We are running short of sugar.* **2.** To be not enough in quantity. ♦*We are out of potatoes and the flour is running short.*

**runs in the blood** *v. phr.* Said when someone acts like his or her parents or other close relatives; when one's behavior seems to be hereditary.—A proverb. ♦*John writes remarkable short stories, just like his father and grandfather. Literary talent for the Smiths apparently runs in the blood.*

**run that by me again!** *v. phr., informal command* Repeat what you just said, as I couldn't understand you. ♦*"Run that by me again," Ted cried. "This telephone connection is very bad."*

**run the gauntlet** *v. phr.* **1.** To be made to run between two lines of people facing each other and be hit by them with clubs or other weapons. ♦*Joe had to run the gauntlet as part of his initiation into the club.* **2.** To face a hard test; bear a painful experience. ♦*Ginny had to run the gauntlet of her mother's questions about how the ink spot got on the dining room rug.*

**run the show** *v. phr.* To direct the given activity; be in charge of what is being done. ♦*When the Cabinet meets in the White House, it is the president of the United States, who runs the show.*

**run through** *v.* **1.** To make a hole through, especially with a sword; pierce. ♦*The pirate was a good swordsman, but the hero finally ran him through.* **2.** To spend recklessly; use up wastefully. ♦*The rich man's son quickly ran through his money.* **3.** To read or practice from beginning to end without stopping. ♦*The visiting singer ran through his numbers with the orchestra just before the program.*

**run to** *v. phr.* To approximate; reach. ♦*It has been estimated that the casualties will run to over 300,000 killed by cholera and starvation in the crowded refugee camps.*

**run true to form** *v. phr.* To follow a usual way; act as expected; agree with how a person usually acts. ♦*Tim's actions ran true to form. He bothered his mother until she gave him his way.*

**run up** *v. phr.* **1.** To add to the amount of; increase. ♦*Karl ran up a big bill at the bookstore.* **2.** To pull (something) upward on a rope; put (something) up quickly. ♦*The pirates ran up the black flag.*

**run up against** See UP AGAINST.

**run wild** *v. phr.* To be or go out of control. ♦*The students ran wild during spring vacation.*

**run with the hare and hunt (ride) with the hounds** *v. phr.* To appear to support both parties in a conflict; to conduct things in ambiguous ways. ♦*Critics accused the king of running with the hare and hunting with the hounds.*

**running commentary** *n. phr.* A continual series of remarks. ♦*My chiropractor gives me a running commentary on the health care debate while he is giving me a rubdown.*

**rush hour** *n. phr.* The time roughly from 7 to 9 A.M., and 3 to 6 P.M. in major American cities, when cars can only go slowly; the busiest commuting time. ♦*It's a bad idea to try driving during rush hour, when everyone is trying to get to work or home from work.*

**rush off** *v. phr.* To depart in great haste. ♦*I have no time to eat breakfast this morning; there is a special meeting so I must rush off to work.*

**Russian roulette** *n.* A game of chance in which one bullet is placed in a revolver, the cartridge cylinder is spun, and the player aims the gun at his own head and pulls the trigger. ♦ *Only a fool would risk playing Russian roulette.*

**rust away** *v. phr.* To disappear gradually through the process of rust or corrosion. ♦ *If you refuse to paint those metal bars on the window, they will soon rust away.*

**rustproof** *adj.* Free from rusting or corrosion; permeated with anti-rust chemical agents. ♦ *My new watch is rustproof and waterproof and I can wear it while swimming or taking a shower.*

**saber rattling** or **sword rattling** n. A show of military strength usually to frighten; a threat of military force. ♦ *The dictator marched his troops and tanks along the border of our country and did some saber rattling.*

**sack in/out** v., slang To go to sleep for a prolonged period (as in from night to morning). ♦ *Where are you guys going to sack in/sack out?*

**sack rat** n. phr., slang A person who sleeps too much. ♦ *My roommate John in a regular sack rat; it takes a major effort to wake him up for breakfast.*

**sacred cow** n. A person or thing that is never criticized, laughed at, or insulted even if it deserves such treatment. ♦ *Motherhood is a sacred cow to most politicians.*

**saddled with** adj. phr. Burdened with; handicapped. ♦ *The business was so saddled with debt that the new owner had a hard time making a go of it for a couple of years.*

**safe and sound** adj. phr. Not harmed; not hurt; safe and not damaged. ♦ *The children returned from their trip safe and sound.*

**safety glass** n. Two panes of glass with a sheet of plastic between them so that the glass will not break into pieces. ♦ *Safety glass is used in cars because it does not break into pieces.*

**safety in numbers** n. phr. Protection against trouble by being in a group. ♦ *Peter said, "Stay in a group; there is safety in numbers."*

**safety island** or **safety zone** n. A raised area in a highway or road to be used only by people walking. ♦ *John was half-way across the street when the light changed. He stayed on the safety island until it changed again.*

**safe haven** n. phr. A place where someone who is pursued by the enemy or by the police can hide. ♦ *Our troops found safe haven in a liberated part of the enemy's capital city.* ♦ *The criminals found temporary safe haven in an abandoned factory, where they were eventually found and arrested by the police.*

**sail into** v., informal **1.** To attack with great strength; begin hitting hard.

♦ *George grabbed a stick and sailed into the dog.* **2.** To scold or criticize very hard. ♦ *The coach really sailed into Bob for dropping the pass.*

**sail (right) through** v. phr. To conclude easily and rapidly; finish something. ♦ *The bright young man sailed through the bar exam in record time.*

**sailor collar** n. A large square collar like those worn by sailors. ♦ *Mary's blouse has a sailor collar.*

**sailor's yarn** n. phr. An improbable or exaggerated story. ♦ *John is a great conversationalist, but we think that most of his stories are sailor's yarns.*

**sail the seven seas** v. phr. To be traveling all over the world, mostly by boat. ♦ *"What does Ted do, now that he is retired as a wealthy man?" Peter asked. "He is enjoying life and sailing the seven seas," Ted's son replied.*

**sail under false colors** v. phr. To pretend to be what you are not; masquerade. ♦ *They found out that Smith was an escaped convict who had been sailing under false colors as a lawyer.*

**salad days** n. phr., informal The period of one's youth; a period of inexperience. ♦ *He was silly and immature during his salad days in high school.*

**sales check** or **sales slip** n. A paper which the clerk gives the person who bought something; a paper that shows what you bought in a store and how much you paid for it. ♦ *Mary brought the sales check when she returned the dress so she could get her money back.*

**sales talk** n. A speech made to point out all the good reasons why the sale would help someone who might buy the product. ♦ *The coach gave a sales talk on exercise in the school assembly.*

**salt away** v., informal To save (money) for the future. ♦ *Every week Joe salts away half of his pay.*

**same diff** or **same difference** n. phr. No difference at all; exactly the same thing. ♦ *"Do you prefer working in the New York office, or in the Chicago office?" Ted asked John. "Same difference," John answered with a shrug of the shoulder.*

**same here** *informal* And it is the same with me; and the same for me.—Used only in speech. ♦ *Mary ordered an ice cream soda, and Jill said, "Same here."*

**sandman is coming** *or* **dustman is coming** *v. phr.* Said by parents when sleepy children start to rub their eyes, and it is time for them to be put to bed.—A proverb. ♦ *"The sandman is coming, right?" his mother said to Tommy. "Time to go to bed!"*

**sand trap** *n.* A low place on a golf course that is filled with sand to stop the ball. ♦ *The golfer lost four strokes trying to get the ball out of the sand trap.*

**sandwich board** *n.* Two advertising signs worn by a man, one on his chest and the other on his back. ♦ *The man walking along Main Street wore a sandwich board saying "Eat at Joe's."*

**salt of the earth** *n. phr., informal* One who helps to make society good and wholesome; a basically good or valuable person. ♦ *Everyone here considers Syd and Susan the salt of the earth because they are so generous.*

**saved by the bell** *v. phr.* Said when one is saved by a lucky accident or unexpected intervention, as when the bell rings, putting an end to a session.—A proverb. ♦ *The reporter began to ask embarrassing questions, when his cell phone rang, forcing him to stop. "Saved by the bell!" I exclaimed, and left the room.*

**save face** *v. phr.* To save your good reputation, popularity, or dignity when something has happened or may happen to hurt you; hide something that may cause you shame. ♦ *The colonel who lost the battle saved face by showing his orders from the general.*

**save for a rainy day** See RAINY DAY.

**save one's breath** *v. phr., informal* To keep silent because talking will not help; not talk because it will do no good. ♦ *Save your breath; the boss will never give you the day off.*

**save one's neck** *or* **save one's skin** *v. phr., slang* To save from danger or trouble. ♦ *Betty saved Tim's neck by typing his report for him; without her help he could not have finished on time.*

**save the day** *v. phr.* To bring about victory or success, especially when defeat is likely. ♦ *The forest fire was nearly out of control when suddenly it rained heavily and saved the day.*

**save up** *v. phr.* To put away for future use; keep as savings; save. ♦ *John was saving up for a new bicycle.*

**saving grace** *n. phr.* A single good attribute; a redeeming quality. ♦ *Felicity is not very attractive but her intelligence and wit are her saving grace.*

**savings account** *n.* An account in a bank, where people put money to save it, and the bank uses the money and pays interest every year. ♦ *If you leave your money in your savings account for six months or a year, the bank will pay interest on it.*

**sawed-off** *adj., informal* Shorter than usual; small of its kind. ♦ *The riot police carried sawed-off shotguns.* ♦ *Jimmy was a sawed-off, skinny runt.*

**say a mouthful 1.** *v. phr., slang* To say something of great importance or meaning; say more by a sentence than the words usually mean.—Usually in past tense. ♦ *Tom said a mouthful when he guessed that company was coming to visit. A dozen people came.* **2.** *v. phr., informal* To vent one's honest opinion, even in anger. ♦ *He sure said a mouthful when he told his boss what was wrong with our business.*

**say it with flowers** *or* **say it with diamonds** *v. phr.* If you want to please your mother, wife, or girlfriend, don't talk too much, but rather give her a present.—A proverb. ♦ *"Mother's Day is coming," John said to his wife. "What shall I get for your and my mother?" "It doesn't really matter, as long as you say it with flowers," she replied. "As for me, you might as well say it with diamonds!"*

**say one's peace** *or* **speak one's piece** *v. phr.* To say openly what you think; say, especially in public, what you usually say or are expected to say. ♦ *Every politician got up and said his piece about how good the mayor was and then sat down.*

**say the least (of it)** *adv. phr.* To put it in an understated way, temperately or mildly. ♦ *Mr. Rockefeller doesn't have to worry where his next meal is coming from, to say the least.*

**say when** *v. phr., informal* Said while pouring one a drink, meaning "Tell me when you think have enough." ♦ *"Say when," John said to Ted at the party. "When!" Ted replied, but only when the glass was practically full of whiskey.*

**says who** *or* **says you** *v. phr., slang* I don't believe or accept that.—An expression of rebuff often used to make fun of someone or oppose him. ♦ *"I am the strongest boy on the block." "Says you."* ♦ *"You can't take Mary to the party—she's my girl." "Says who?"*

**say-so** *n.* Approval; permission; word. ♦ *Father got angry because I took his new car out without his say-so.*

**say the word** *v. phr., informal* To say or show that you want something or agree to something; show a wish, willingness, or readiness; give a sign; say yes; say so. ♦ *Just say the word and I will lend you the money.*

**say uncle** *also* **cry uncle** *v. phr., informal* To say that you surrender; admit that you have lost; admit a defeat; give up. ♦ *The bully twisted Jerry's arm and said, "Cry uncle."*

**scale** See TO SCALE.

**scale down** *v.* To make smaller or less; decrease. ♦ *Tom built a scaled down model of the plane.*

**scandal sheet** *n.* A newspaper that prints much shocking news and scandal. ♦ *The scandal sheet carried big headlines about the murder.*

**scaredy-cat** *or* **scared-cat** See FRAIDY-CAT.

**scare away** *or* **off** *v. phr.* To cause to flee; frighten away. ♦ *Jake is a confirmed bachelor; the best way to scare him off is to start talking about marriage.*

**scare out of one's wits** *or* **scare stiff** *or* **scare the daylights out of** *v. phr., informal* To frighten very much. ♦ *The owl's hooting scared him out of his wits.* ♦ *The child was scared stiff in the dentist's chair.* ♦ *Pete's ghost story scared the daylights out of the smaller boys.*

**scare up** *or* **scrape up** *v., informal* To find, collect, or get together with some effort when needed. ♦ *The boy scared up enough money to go to college.* ♦ *He managed to scrape up the money for his speeding fine.*

**school of hard knocks** *n. phr.* Life outside of school or college; life out in the world; the ordinary experience of learning from work and troubles. ♦ *He never went to high school; he was educated in the school of hard knocks.*

**scot-free** *adj. phr.* Without punishment; completely free. ♦ *In spite of his obvious* guilt, the jury acquitted him and he got off scot-free.

**scotch broth** *n.* A thick barley soup with vegetables and mutton or beef. ♦ *Mother cooked a hearty scotch broth for dinner.*

**scout around** *v. phr.* To search for; look around. ♦ *When we first came to town, we had to scout around for a suitable apartment.*

**scrape the bottom of the barrel** *v. phr., informal* To use or take whatever is left after the most or the best has been taken; accept the leftovers. ♦ *The garage owner had to scrape the bottom of the barrel to find a qualified mechanic to work for him.*

**scrape together** *v. phr.* To quickly assemble, usually from scanty ingredients. ♦ *We were so hungry we had to scrape together some lunch from all kinds of frozen leftovers.*

**scrape up** See SCARE UP.

**scratch around for** *v. phr.* To search randomly for something. ♦ *If you scratch around for a more reliable used car, maybe you'll feel more confident on the road.*

**scratch one's back** *v. phr., informal* To do something kind and helpful for someone or to flatter him in the hope that he will do something for you. Usually used in the expression *"You scratch my back and I'll scratch yours."* ♦ *Mary asked Jean to introduce her to her brother. Jean said, "You scratch my back and I'll scratch yours."*

**scratch the surface** *v. phr.* To learn or understand very little about something.—Usually used with a limiting adverb (as *only, hardly*). ♦ *We thought we understood Africa but when we made a trip there we found we had only scratched the surface.*

**scream bloody murder** *v. phr., informal* To yell or protest as strongly as one can. ♦ *When the thief grabbed her purse, the woman screamed bloody murder.*

**scream one's head off** *or* **yell one's head off** See SCREAM BLOODY MURDER.

**screen test** *n.* A short movie made to see if an actor or actress is good enough or the right one to play a part. ♦ *Ellen acted well on the stage, but she failed her screen test.*

**screw around** *v. phr., vulgar, avoidable* To hang around idly without accomplishing anything, to loaf about, to beat or hack around. ♦ *You guys are no longer welcome here; all you do is screw around all day.*

**screw up** *v. phr., slang, semi-vulgar, best avoided* (stress on *up*) **1.** To make a mess of, to make an error which causes confusion. ♦ *The treasurer screwed up the accounts of the Society so badly that he had to be fired.* **2.** To cause someone to be neurotic or maladjusted. ♦ *Her divorce screwed her up so badly that she had to go to a shrink.*

**screw-up** *n.* (stress on *screw*) A mistake; an error; a confusing mess. ♦ *"What a screw-up!" the manager cried, when he realized that the bills were sent to the wrong customers.*

**screw up one's courage** *or* **pluck up one's courage** *v. phr.* To force yourself to be brave. ♦ *The small boy screwed up his courage and went upstairs in the dark.*

**scrounge around** *v. phr., slang* **1.** To search for an object aimlessly without having one clearly in mind. ♦ *I don't know what's the matter with him, he is just scrounging around all day long.* **2.** To look around for a way to get a free drink or a free meal. ♦ *Sue and her husband are so broke they never eat properly; they just scrounge around from one place to the next until someone offers them something.*

**scuttlebutt** *n. phr, old naval expression* Gossip. ♦ *"Did you hear the latest?" Ted asked his friend, Jim. "No, what's up?" "Well, they appointed Harvey Smith vice president of the company." "Are you sure?" "Not, not entirely; it may be just scuttlebutt."*

**sea legs** *n. phr.* **1.** Adjustment to being in a boat that is rocking on the sea. ♦ *This is my first transatlantic trip so give me a day to get my sea legs before you make me dance.* **2.** Adjustment to a new job or situation. ♦ *"I have just been transferred here and I haven't found my sea legs yet," the new colleague joked.*

**search me** *informal* I don't know; how should I know?—May be considered rude. ♦ *When I asked her what time it was, she said, "Search me, I have no watch."*

**search one's heart** *or* **search one's soul** *v. phr., formal* To study your reasons and acts; try to discover if you have been fair and honest. ♦ *The teacher searched his heart trying to decide if he had been unfair in failing Tom.*—**heart-searching** *or* **soul-searching** *n. or adj.* ♦ *The minister preached a soul-searching sermon about the thoughtless ways people hurt each other.*

**search out** *v.* To search for and discover; find or learn by hunting. ♦ *The police were trying to search out the real murderer.*

**search with a fine-tooth comb** See FINE-TOOTH COMB.

**seasonable weather** *n. phr.* Weather as one expects at the given season. ♦ *We are having seasonable weather this spring in Chicago, which is unfortunately not always the case.*

**seat belt** *n.* A strong strap used to protect a person in a moving car or other vehicle by holding him in his seat. ♦ *Passengers in automobiles should wear seat belts for safety.*

**second best** *n.* Something that is lower than or not quite as good as the best. ♦ *There were ten boys in the race. Jack won and Fred was a close second best.*

**second best** *adv.* Second; in second place. ♦ *The team came off second best in the game.*

**second-best** *adj.* Next to best; second in rank. ♦ *Mary wore her second-best dress.*

**second childhood** *n. phr.* Senility; dotage. ♦ *"Grandpa is in his second childhood; we must make allowances for him at the dinner table," my mother said, as Grandpa dropped food all over the place.*

**second class** *n.* **1.** The second best or highest group; the class next after the first. ♦ *Joe was good enough in arithmetic to be put in the second class but was not good enough for the first.* **2.** The place or quarters, especially on a ship, train, or airplane which people travel who pay the next to the highest fare. ♦ *Aunt May bought a ticket to travel in the second class on the boat trip.* **3.** A class of mail that includes magazines and newspapers published at least four times a year.

**second-class**[1] *adj.* **1.** Belonging in the class that is next to the highest or next best. ♦ *The periodical came as second-class mail.* **2.** Not so good as others; second-rate. ♦ *They were never given full democratic rights but were always treated as second-class citizens.*

**second-class**[2] *adv.* By second class. ♦ *We went second-class on the train to New York.*

**second cousin** *n.* A child of your father's or mother's first cousin. ♦ *Mary and Jane are second cousins.*

**second-guess** *v. phr.* **1.** To criticize another's decision with advantage of hindsight. ♦ *The losing team's coach is always second-guessed.* **2.** To guess what someone else intends or would think or do. ♦ *Television planners try to second-guess the public.*

**secondhand** *adj.* Used; not new; pre-owned. ♦ *Sometimes a secondhand car is just as reliable as a brand new one.*

**second nature** *n.* Something done without any special effort, as if by natural instinct. ♦ *Cutting tall trees has become second nature to the experienced lumberjack.*

**second-rate** *adj.* Of mediocre or inferior quality. ♦ *The movie received a bad review; it was second-rate at best.*

**second-run** *adj.* Of a movie: Shown in many movie theaters before, and allowed to be shown later in other movie theaters. ♦ *Tickets to second-run movies cost much less.*

**second sight** *n. phr.* Intuition; prescience; clairvoyance. ♦ *Some police departments employ psychics to find missing persons or objects as they are said to have second sight.*

**second thought** *n.* A change of ideas or opinions resulting from more thought or study. ♦ *Your second thoughts are very often wiser than your first ideas.*

**second to none** *adj. phr.* Excellent; first rate; peerless. ♦ *Our new State University campus is second to none. There is no need to pay all that high tuition at a private college.*

**second wind** *also* **second breath** *n.* **1.** The easier breathing that follows difficult breathing when one makes a severe physical effort, as in running or swimming. ♦ *We climbed with labored breathing for half an hour, but then got our second wind and went up more easily.* **2.** *informal* The refreshed feeling you get after first becoming tired while doing something and then becoming used to it. ♦ *Tom became very tired of working at his algebra, but after a while he got his second wind and began to enjoy it.*

**section gang** *or* **section crew** *n.* A group of railroad workers who watch and repair a number of miles of track. ♦ *The section crew was called out to fix the broken bridge.*

**section hand** *n.* A worker who repairs railway track; one of the men in a section gang. ♦ *The section hands moved off the track while the train went by.*

**security blanket** *n., slang, colloquial* An idea, person, or object that one holds on to for psychological reassurance or comfort as infants usually hang on to the edge of a pillow, a towel, or a blanket. ♦ *Sue has gone to Aunt Mathilda for a chat; she is her security blanket.*

**see a lot of** *v. phr.* To go out regularly with someone; have an affair with someone. ♦ *They have been seeing a lot of each other lately.*

**see a man about a dog** *or* **see a man about a horse** *v. phr.* To go to the bathroom.—A proverb. ♦ *"Excuse me, but I have to go see a man about a dog," Peter said. "Go ahead. It's the second room on the left," his host replied.*

**see about** *v.* **1.** To find out about; attend to. ♦ *If you are too busy, I'll see about the train tickets.* **2.** *informal* To consider; study. ♦ *I cannot take time now but I'll see about your plan when I have time.*

**see better days** *v. phr.* **1.** To enjoy a better or happier life. ♦ *Mr. Smith is poor now, but he will see better days.* **2.** To become old, damaged, or useless. Used in the perfect tense. ♦ *Our car wasn't old, but it had seen better days.*

**see beyond one's nose** *or* **see beyond the end of one's nose** *v. phr.* To make wise judgments about questions of importance to yourself and others; act with farseeing understanding. Used in negative, conditional, and interrogative sentences. ♦ *He couldn't save money or make plans for the future; he just never saw beyond the end of his nose.*

**see daylight** v. phr., informal To know that an end or success is near. ♦ We thought we would never finish building the house, but now we can see daylight.

**see eye to eye** v. phr. To agree fully; hold exactly the same opinion. ♦ Though we did not usually agree, we saw eye to eye in the matter of reducing taxes.

**see fit** or **think fit** v. phr. To decide that an action is necessary, wise, or advisable; choose. ♦ Jim asked "Dad, what time should I come home after the dance?" His father answered, "You may do as you see fit."

**see how the cat jumps** or **see which way the cat jumps** v. phr. To see which way or how things will proceed; how matters will turn out.—A proverb. ♦ "What will happen when the new boss takes over?" Mike asked, worried. "We'll just have to see how the cat jumps." Peter tried to calm him down.

**see how the land lies** v. phr., informal To reconnoiter; investigate. ♦ Before going there in person to ask for a job, you had better see how the land lies and who does what.

**seeing is believing** Seeing something is good proof. ♦ Bill told Joe he had passed his test, but Joe said, "Seeing is believing."

**see into** v. To know or understand the real nature or meaning of. ♦ Suddenly the teacher saw into Linda's strange actions.

**see off** v. To go to say or wave goodbye to. ♦ When Marsha flew to Paris, Flo saw her off at the airport.

**see one home** v. phr. To walk a person home. ♦ "Let me see you home, dear," Nick said to Jenny at the end of the party.

**see one's way clear** v. phr. To know no reason for not doing something; feel that you are free. ♦ John finally saw his way clear to help his friends.

**see out** v. 1. To go with to an outer door. ♦ A polite man sees his company out after a party. 2. To stay with and finish; not quit. ♦ Pete's assignment was hard but he saw it out to the end.

**see reason** v. phr. To think or act sensibly, especially after realizing what the facts are on a certain matter and accepting advice about it. ♦ He finally saw reason and reshaped his sales strategy by lowering the prices.

**see red** v. phr., informal To become very angry. ♦ Whenever anyone teased John about his weight, he saw red.

**see service** v. phr. 1. To be used over a considerable period of time. ♦ This old camera of mine has already seen six years of service. 2. To serve in a military sense. ♦ Colonel Hutchins has seen service in World War II, Korea, Vietnam, and the Persian Gulf.

**see someone's point** v. phr. To agree with someone. ♦ "No matter how just, war is always costly," John said. "I see your point," Tom replied, nodding.

**see stars** v. phr., informal To imagine you are seeing stars as a result of being hit on the head. ♦ When Ted was hit on the head by the ball, he saw stars.

**see the color of one's money** v. phr., informal To know that you have money to spend. ♦ Before I show you the diamond, let me see the color of your money.

**see the last of** v. phr. To say good-bye to someone or something; get rid of something. ♦ We were glad to see the last of the winter.

**see the light** v. phr., informal To understand or agree, often suddenly; accept another's explanation or decision. ♦ Mary thought it was fun to date older boys but when they started drinking, she saw the light.

**see the light at the end of the tunnel** v. phr., informal To anticipate the happy resolution of a prolonged period of problems. ♦ We've been paying on our house mortgage for many years, but at long last we can see the light at the end of the tunnel.

**see the light of day** v. phr. To be born or begun. ♦ The children visited the old house where their great-grandfather first saw the light of day.

**see things** v. phr., informal To imagine sights which are not real; think you see what is not there. ♦ She woke her husband to tell him she had seen a face at the window, but he told her she was seeing things.

**see through** v. 1. To understand the real meaning of or reason for; realize the falseness of. ♦ The teacher saw through the boy's story of having to help at home. 2. To do (something) until finished; stay with until the end. ♦ Once

*Charles started a job, he saw it through till it was finished.* **3.** To help and encourage (a person) through trouble or difficulty. ♦ *Mrs. Miller saw Jane through her sickness.* **4.** To be enough for; last. ♦ *This money will see us through the week.*

**see to** *also* **look to** *v.* To attend to; take care of; do whatever needs to be done about. ♦ *While Donna bought the theatre tickets, I saw to the parking of the car.*

**see to it** *v. phr.* To take care; take the responsibility; make sure. Used with a noun clause. ♦ *We saw to it that the child was fed and bathed.*

**seed money** *n. phr.* A small grant or donation for others to be able to start a new venture. ♦ *All you need is some seed money and you can set up your own desk-top publishing firm.*

**seize on** *v.* To make use of (a happening or idea.) ♦ *Bob seized on the rain as an excuse for missing school.*

**seize on** *or* **upon** *v. phr.* To latch onto. ♦ *Whenever Herb is in a romantic mood, Irene seizes on it and starts talking about marriage, which is not what Herb had in mind.*

**seize the bull by the horns** See TAKE THE BULL BY THE HORNS.

**seize the opportunity** *v. phr.* To exploit a chance. ♦ *His wealthy uncle offered to send him to Harvard and he wisely seized the opportunity.*

**self-conscious** *adj.* Embarrassed; shy. ♦ *Edith has a freckled face and sometimes she is very self-conscious about it.*

**self-made** *adj.* Having achieved wealth, fame, and success on one's own without outside help. ♦ *John D. Rockefeller is one of the most famous self-made men in America.*

**self-possessed** *adj.* Confident; sure of one self. ♦ *Before he made his first million, he used to be shy, but afterwards he became very self-possessed.*

**self-seeking** *adj.* Given to egotism and self-aggrandizement. ♦ *Al is the most self-seeking person I've ever met, he is not fun to be around.*

**sell down the river** *v. phr.* To give harmful information about someone or something to one's enemies; betray. ♦ *The traitor sold his country down the river to the enemy army.*

**sell like hotcakes** *v. phr.* To be a best-seller, an extremely popular item.—A proverb. ♦ *John Grisham's mystery novels sell like hotcakes.* ♦ *After September 11, 2001, American flags sold like hotcakes.*

**sell off** *v. phr.* To liquidate one's holdings of certain set items. ♦ *The retired professor had to sell off his rare butterfly collection to meet his health expenses.*

**sell one a bill of goods** *v. phr.* To persuade another to acquire something useless; defraud. ♦ *We were sure sold a bill of goods when Alfred persuaded us to buy his expensive custom-built car.*

**sell one on** *v. phr.* To persuade someone to do something. ♦ *We were able to sell our wealthy uncle on the idea of having a joint family vacation in Hawaii.*

**sellout** *n.* (stress on *sell*) **1.** A betrayal or act of treason. ♦ *The spy's behavior during the Cold War was a classical sellout.*

**sell out** *v.* (stress on *out*) **1a.** To sell all of a certain thing which a store has in stock. ♦ *In the store's January white sale the sheets and pillowcases were sold out in two days.* **1b.** To sell all the stock and close the store; go out of business. ♦ *The local hardware store sold out last month and was replaced by a cafe.* **2.** *informal* To be unfaithful to your country for money or other reward; be disloyal; sell a secret; accept a bribe. ♦ *In the Revolutionary War, Benedict Arnold sold out to the British.*

**sell short** *v.* To think (a person or thing) less good or valuable than is true; underestimate. ♦ *Don't sell the team short; the players are better than you think.*

**sell snow to the Eskimos** *v. phr.* To sell something to people who already have a large quantity of the same or similar goods. ♦ *My Alaskan friend said, "One of the hottest businesses in Alaska is refrigeration. You could say that I, as a refrigerator expert, am selling snow to the Eskimos."*

**send C.O.D.** See C.O.D.

**send a message** *v. phr.* **1.** To give off a signal, such as a scent or a call, notifying members of the opposite sex that the female of the species is in heat and is ready to mate. ♦ *The smell of the rutting does sent a strong message to the*

*bucks throughout the entire forest.*
**2.** To make a geopolitical move or statement, which will be interpreted by the targeted foreign power or others about the originator's unspoken but clearly implied intentions and possibilities. ♦ *The United States sent a powerful message not only to the Middle East but the entire world by toppling the regime of Iraqi dictator Saddam Hussein in just one month.*

**send off** *v. phr.* (stress on *off*) To say good-bye to someone ceremoniously. ♦ *They sent us off to the Mainland from our first visit to Hawaii with an elaborate champagne party at the pier.*

**send-off** *n. phr.* (stress on *send*) A demonstration of affection or respect at someone's departure, as a retirement ceremony. ♦ *When our colleague retired after 35 years of teaching, we all got together at the Faculty Club and gave him a terrific send-off.*

**send one packing** *v. phr.* To fire someone summarily. ♦ *When the boss caught Smith stealing from the cash register, he sent him packing.*

**send to the minors** *v. phr.* To dismiss someone; tell them off; terminate a relationship. ♦ *"What did you do to your girlfriend?" Ernie asked Bert, when Bert started dating Jane. "I sent her to the minors," Bert answered with a sneer.*

**send up** *v. phr., colloquial* To sentence (someone) to prison. ♦ *Did you know that Milton Shaeffer was sent up for fifteen years?*

**send word** *v. phr.* To send notification to; advise. ♦ *When his father fell seriously ill, we sent word to Mike to come home as quickly as possible.*

**senior citizen** *n.* An older person, often one who has retired from active work or employment. *Mrs. North, the history teacher, is a senior citizen.*

**separate the grain from the chaff** See SEPARATE THE MEN FROM THE BOYS.

**separate the men from the boys** *v. phr., informal* To show who has strength, courage and loyalty and find who do not. ♦ *The mile run separates the men from the boys.*

**separate the sheep from the goats** See SEPARATE THE MEN FROM THE BOYS.

**serve a sentence** *v. phr.* To be in jail. ♦ *Charlie served four years of an eight-*

*year sentence, after which he was paroled and released.*

**serve notice** *v. phr.* **1.** To notify one's employer in a formal or legal manner that one is quitting the former's employment. ♦ *She gave notice to her boss that she was quitting because of marriage.* **2.** To notify an employee or a tenant that one no longer needs their services or wishes to have them as tenants. ♦ *The new landlady gave notice to several families in our building because they were late in paying their rent.*

**serve one right** *v. phr.* To be what (someone) really deserves as a punishment; be a fair exchange for what (someone) has done or said or failed to do or say. ♦ *He failed his exam; it served him right because he had not studied.*

**serve up** *v.* To prepare and serve (as a food). ♦ *Father caught a trout and Mother served it up at dinner.*

**set ablaze** *v. phr.* To cause to burn by lighting with a match or other incendiary device. ♦ *The criminals poured gasoline on the house and set it ablaze with a small lighter.*

**set about** *v.* To begin; start. ♦ *Benjamin Franklin set about learning the printer's trade at an early age.*

**set aside** *v.* **1.** To separate from the others in a group or collection. ♦ *She set aside the things in the old trunk which she wanted to keep.* **2.** To select or choose from others for some purpose. ♦ *The governor set aside a day for thanksgiving.* **3.** To pay no attention to (something); leave out. ♦ *The complaint was set aside of no importance.* **4.** *formal* To refuse to accept; annul; cancel as worthless or wrong. ♦ *The Supreme Court set aside the decision of the lower courts.*

**setback** *n.* (stress on *set*) A disadvantage; a delay. ♦ *We suffered a major setback when my wife lost her job.*

**set back** *v.* (stress on *back*) **1.** To cause to put off or get behind schedule; slow up; check. ♦ *The cold weather set back the planting by two weeks.* **2.** *informal* To cause to pay out or to lose (a sum of money); cost. ♦ *His new car set him back over $3000.*

**set back on one's heels** *or* **knock back on one's heels** *v. phr., informal* To give an unpleasant surprise; upset suddenly; stop or turn back (someone's) progress. ◆ *Jean was doing very well in school until sickness knocked her back on her heels.*

**set down** *v.* **1.** To write; record. ◆ *He set down all his important thoughts in his dairy.* **2.** To stop a bus or other vehicle and let (someone) get off. ◆ *The bus driver set her down at the corner.* **3.** To put into some group; classify; consider. ◆ *When he heard the man speak, he set him down as a fool.* **4.** To explain; think a reason for. ◆ *The teacher set down the boy's poor English to his foreign birth.*

**set fire to** *v. phr.* To cause to burn; start a fire in. ◆ *The sparks set fire to the oily rags.*

**set foot** *v. phr.* To step; walk; go.—Used with a negative. ◆ *She would not let him set foot across her threshold.*

**set forth** *v., formal* **1.** To explain exactly or clearly. ◆ *The President set forth his plans in a television talk.* **2.** To start to go somewhere; begin a trip. ◆ *The troop set forth on their ten-mile hike early.*

**set free** *v. phr.* To liberate. ◆ *The trapper set all the small animals free before the snowstorm hit.*

**set in** *v.* To begin; start; develop. ◆ *He did not keep the cut clean and infection set in.* ◆ *The wind set in from the east.*

**set in one's ways** *adj. phr.* Stubborn; opinionated; unchangeable. ◆ *My grandfather is so old and set in his ways that he'll eat nothing new.*

**set off** *v.* **1.** To decorate through contrast; balance by difference. ◆ *A small gold pin set off her plain dark dress.* **2.** To balance; make somewhat equal. ◆ *Her great wealth, as he thought, set off her plain face.* **3a.** To begin to go. ◆ *They set off for the West in a covered wagon.* **3b.** To cause to begin. ◆ *An atomic explosion is created by setting off a chain reaction in the atom.* **3c.** To cause to explode. ◆ *On July 4 we set off firecrackers in many places.*

**set of new threads** *n. phr.* New men's suit. ◆ *"Nice set of new threads!" Ed said, when he saw Dave in his new tailor-made outfit.*

**set one's hand to the plow** See PUT ONE'S HAND TO THE PLOW.

**set one's heart on** *v. phr.* To want very much. ◆ *He set his heart on that bike.*

**set one's house in order** See PUT ONE'S HOUSE IN ORDER.

**set one's mind at rest** *v. phr.* To relieve someone's anxieties; reassure someone. ◆ *"Let me set your mind at rest about the operation," Dr. Vanek said. "You'll be back on your feet in a week."*

**set one's mind on** *v. phr.* To be determined to; decide to. ◆ *He has set his mind on buying an old chateau in France.*

**set one's sights** *v. phr.* **1.** To want to reach; aim for. ◆ *John has set his sights higher than the job he has now.* **2.** To wish to get or win. ◆ *Owen set his sights on the championship.*

**set one's teeth on edge** *v. phr.* **1.** To have a sharp sour taste that makes you rub your teeth together. ◆ *The lemon juice set my teeth on edge.* **2.** To make one feel nervous or annoyed. ◆ *She looks so mean that her face sets my teeth on edge.*

**set out** *v.* **1.** To leave on a journey or voyage. ◆ *The Pilgrims set out for the New World.* **2.** To decide and begin to try; attempt. ◆ *George set out to improve his pitching.* **3.** To plant in the ground. ◆ *The gardener set out some tomato seedlings.*

**set right** *v. phr.* To discipline; correct; indicate the correct procedure. ◆ *"Your bookkeeping is all messed up," the accountant said. "Let me set it right for you, once and for all."*

**set sail** *v. phr.* To begin a sea voyage; start sailing. ◆ *The ship set sail for Europe.*

**set store by** *v. phr., informal* To like or value; want to keep. Used with a qualifying word between *set* and *store*. ◆ *Pat doesn't set much store by Mike's advice.*

**set the pace** *v. phr.* To decide on a rate of speed of travel or rules that are followed by others. ◆ *Louise set the pace in selling tickets for the school play.*

**set the stage for** *v. phr.* To prepare the way or situation for (an event); to make a situation ready for something to happen. ◆ *The country's economic problems set the stage for a depression.*

**set the world on fire** *v. phr., informal* To do something outstanding; act in a way that attracts much attention or makes you famous. ◆ *John works hard, but he will never set the world on fire.*

**setting-up** *adj.* Done early in the morning to make you fresh and feel strong for the day. ♦ *Tom jumped out of bed and did his setting-up exercises.*

**settle a score** *also* **wipe out an old score** *v. phr.* To hurt (someone) in return for a wrong or loss. ♦ *John settled an old score with Bob by beating him.*

**settle down** *v.* **1.** To live more quietly and sensibly; have a regular place to live and a regular job; stop acting wildly or carelessly, especially by growing up. ♦ *John will settle down after he gets a job and gets married.* **2.** To become quiet, calm, or comfortable. ♦ *Father settled down with the newspaper.*

**settle for** *v.* To be satisfied with (less) agree to; accept. ♦ *Jim wanted $200 for his old car, but he settled for $100.*

**settle on** *v. phr.* To decide which one to choose among various alternatives. ♦ *My parents have been debating what kind of a car to get and have finally settled on a BMW from Germany.*

**settle up** *v. phr.* To pay up; conclude monetary or other transactions. ♦ *"Let's settle up," Carol's attorney said, when she sued Don for a hefty sum of money after their divorce.*

**set to music** *v. phr.* To compose a musical accompaniment to verse. ♦ *Schubert and Beethoven both set to music many a famous poem by Goethe and Schiller.*

**set up** *v.* **1.** To provide the money for the necessities for. ♦ *When he was twenty-one, his father set him up in the clothing business.* **2.** To establish; start. ♦ *The government has set up many hospitals for veterans of the armed forces.* **3.** To make ready for use by putting the parts together or into their right place. ♦ *The men set up the new printing press.* **4.** To bring into being; cause. ♦ *Ocean tides are set up by the pull between earth and the moon.* **5.** To claim; pretend. ♦ *He set himself up to be a graduate of a medical school, but he was not.* **6.** To harm someone by entrapment or some other ruse. ♦ *Joe was actually innocent of the robbery, but his "trusted friends" set him up, so the police found the gun in his car.*

**setup** *n. phr.* (stress on *set*) **1.** Arrangement, management, circumstances. ♦ *Boy, you really have a wonderful setup in your office!* **2.** Financial

arrangement. ♦ *It is a fairly generous setup sending your uncle $1,000 a month.*

**set up shop** *v. phr.* To start a new business. ♦ *Mary and Jane, who design and produce new women's clothing, decided to set up shop on Michigan Avenue.*

**seventh heaven** *n. phr., literary* The pinnacle of happiness. ♦ *We were in seventh heaven when the helicopter flew us over the magnificent Grand Canyon.*

**seven twenty-four** *adj. phr.* A shop that stays open 24 hours a day, 7 days a week. ♦ *"When are you open?" Rose asked at the corner store. "We are a seven twenty-four place," the shopkeeper replied.*

**sewed up** *adj. phr., informal* Won or arranged as you wish; decided. ♦ *Dick thought he had the job sewed up, but another boy got it.*

**sexual harassment** *n. phr.* The act of constantly making unwanted advances of a sexual nature for which the offended party may seek legal redress. ♦ *The court fined Wilbur Catwallender $750,000 for sexual harassment of two of his female employees.*

**shack up with** *v. phr., slang* To move in with (someone) of the opposite sex without marrying the person. ♦ *Did you know that Ollie and Sue aren't married? They just decided to shack up for a while.*

**shadow of one's self** *or* **shadow of one's former self** *n. phr.* A person who has lost his or her former intellectual prowess fame, or position, or a person who, due to illness, has become extremely thin and weak. ♦ *We were shocked when we saw poor Al when he came out of the hospital's cancer ward. He was but a shadow of his former self.* ♦ *The aged poet started to write again after twenty years of silence, but he is a shadow of himself.*

**shaggy dog (story)** *n. phr.* A special kind of joke whose long and often convoluted introduction and development delay the effect of the punch line. ♦ *Uncle Joe only seems to bore his audiences with his long shaggy dog jokes, for when he comes to the long-awaited punch line, he gets very few laughs.*

**shake a leg** *v. phr., slang* To go fast; hurry. ♦ *Shake a leg! The bus won't wait.*

**shakedown** *n.* (stress on *shake*) **1.** A test. ♦ *Let's take the new car out and give it a shakedown.* **2.** An act of extorting money by threatening. ♦ *It was a nasty shakedown, to get $500 from the old man, promising to protect him.*

**shake down** *v. phr.* (stress on *down*) **1.** To cause to fall by shaking. ♦ *He shook some pears down from the tree.* **2.** *informal* To test, practice, get running smoothly (a ship or ship's crew). ♦ *The captain shook down his new ship on a voyage to the Mediterranean Sea.* **3.** *slang* To get money from by threats. ♦ *The gangsters shook the store owner down every month.*

**shake hands on** *v. phr.* To agree to a business transaction and seal it with a friendly handshake. ♦ *"All right," John said, "I accept your terms. Let's shake hands on it."*

**shake in one's shoes** *or* **shake in one's boots** *v. phr., informal* To be very much afraid. ♦ *The robber shook in his boots when the police knocked on his door.*

**shake off** *v., informal* To get away from when followed; get rid of; escape from. ♦ *Tom could not shake off his cold.*

**shake the dust from one's feet** *v. phr.* To depart or leave with some measure of disgust or displeasure. ♦ *Jim was so unhappy in our small, provincial town that he was glad to shake the dust from his feet and move to New York.*

**shake up** *v., informal* (stress on *up*) To bother; worry; disturb. ♦ *The notice about a cut in pay shook up everybody in the office.*

**shake-up** *n.* (stress on *shake*) A change; a reorganization. ♦ *After the scandal there was a major shake-up in the Cabinet.*

**shape up** *v. phr., informal* **1.** To begin to act or work right; get along satisfactorily. ♦ *"How is the building of the new gym coming along?" "Fine. It's shaping up very well."* **2.** To show promise. ♦ *Plans for our picnic are shaping up very well.*

**shape up or ship out** *v. phr., informal* To either improve one's disposition or behavior, or quit or leave. ♦ *When Paul neglected to carry out his part of the research work that Professor Brown had assigned him with for the fifth time, the professor cried, "Shape up, or ship out, Paul. I have lost my patience with you!"*

**sharp as a tack** *adj. phr.* **1.** Very neatly and stylishly dressed ♦ *That new boy always looks sharp as a tack in class.* **2.** Very intelligent; smart; quick-witted. ♦ *Tom is sharp as a tack; he got 100 on every test.*

**shed light on** *or* **upon** See CAST LIGHT ON; THROW LIGHT ON.

**sheepskin** *n.* Diploma. ♦ *Dr. Miller has half a dozen different sheepskins hanging on the wall of his office.*

**shell out** *v., informal* To pay or spend. ♦ *Dick had to shell out a lot of money for his new car.*

**she's joined the club** *v. phr., slang* To have become pregnant. ♦ *"Why does your sister Suzie look so pale?" Joan inquired. "She's joined the club," Mary, Sue's sister replied. "She's due in December."*

**shift for oneself** *v. phr.* To live or act independently with no help, guidance or protection from others; take care of yourself. ♦ *Mrs. McCarthy was forced to shift for herself after her husband died.*

**shine up to** *v., slang* To try to please; try to make friends with. ♦ *Smedley shines up to all the pretty girls.*

**ship comes in** All the money a person has wished for is received; wealth comes to a person. Used with a possessive. ♦ *Mr. Brown is just waiting for his ship to come in.*

**ship out** *v.* To begin a journey; leave. ♦ *The army group shipped out for the Far East today.*

**shipshape** *adj.* In perfect condition; in good order. ♦ *After we left the islands, we left the rented car shipshape for the next driver.*

**ships that pass in the night** *n. phr.* Casual acquaintances or one-time lovers, who will probably never see each other again. ♦ *Tim and Lorraine were just ships that pass in the night.*

**shirk one's duty** *v. phr.* To be negligent or irresponsible. ♦ *If you continue to shirk your duty, you can expect to be fired.*

**shit hits the fan** *v. phr. vulgar, avoidable* Indicative of grave or exciting consequences. ♦ *Just wait until the governor hears what happened—then the shit will hit the fan.*

**shit-faced** *adj. vulgar, avoidable* Very drunk. ♦ *John was too drunk to talk to the guests, he just sat there, shit-faced.*

**shit—or get off the pot** *v. phr., vulgar, avoidable* Given as advice or command meaning, " Do or a least try to do the job, or let someone else do it." ♦ *"What are the working conditions around here?" John asked Tom. "They are all straight shooters around here; the general mood can be characterized as 'shit—or get off the pot!'"*

**shoe on the other foot** The opposite is true; places are changed. ♦ *He was my captain in the army but now the shoe is on the other foot.*

**shoestring catch** *n.* A catch of a hit baseball just before it hits the ground. ♦ *The left fielder made a shoestring catch of a line drive to end the inning.*

**shoo away** *v. phr.* To frighten or chase away. ♦ *When the children gathered around the new sports car, we shooed them away.*

**shoo-in** *n., informal* Someone or something that is expected to win; a favorite; sure winner. ♦ *Chris is a shoo-in to win a scholarship.* ♦ *This horse is a shoo-in. He can't miss winning.*

**shoot ahead of** *or* **past** *or* **through** *or* **alongside of** *v. phr.* To move or drive ahead rapidly. ♦ *As we had to slow down before the tunnel, a red sports car shot ahead of us.*

**shoot for the stars** *v. phr.* To set very high expectations for oneself; aim high. ♦ *My brother John wants to be president of the United States; he is a very ambitious fellow who's shooting for the stars.*

**shoot from the hip** *v. phr., informal* **1.** To fire a gun held at the hip without aiming by aligning the barrel with one's eye. ♦ *In many Western movies the heroic sheriff defeats the villains by shooting from the hip.* **2.** To speak sincerely, frankly, and without subterfuge. ♦ *"What kind of an administrator will Mr. Brown be?" the head of the search committee asked. "He shoots straight from the hip," he was assured.*

**shoot off one's mouth** *or* **shoot off one's face** *v. phr., slang* To give opinions without knowing all the facts; talk as if you know everything. ♦ *I want to study the problem before I shoot off my face.*

**shoot one's wad** *v. phr. slang, colloquial* **1.** To spend all of one's money. ♦ *We've shot our wad for the summer and can't buy any new garden furniture.* **2.** To say everything that is on one's mind. ♦ *Joe feels a lot better now that he's shot his wad at the meeting.*

**shoot out** *v.* **1.** To fight with guns until one person or side is wounded or killed; settle a fight by shooting.—Used with *it.* ♦ *The cornered bank robbers decided to shoot it out with the police.*

**shoot questions at** *v. phr.* To interrogate rapidly and vigorously. ♦ *The attorney for the prosecution shot one question after another at the nervous witness.*

**shoot straight** *or* **shoot square** *v., informal* To act fairly; deal honestly. ♦ *You can trust that salesman; he shoots straight with his customers.* ♦ *We get along well because we always shoot square with each other.*—**straight shooter** *or* **square shooter** *n., informal Bill is a square-shooter.*—**straight-shooting** *adj.* ♦ *The boys all liked the straight-shooting coach.*

**shoot the breeze** *or* **bat the breeze** *or* **fan the breeze** *or* **shoot the bull** *v. phr., slang* To talk. ♦ *Jim shot the breeze with his neighbor while the children were playing.* ♦ *The fishermen were shooting the bull about the school of sailfish they had seen.*

**shoot the works** *v. phr., slang* **1.** To spare no expense or effort; get or give everything. ♦ *Billy shot the works when he bought his bicycle; he got a bell, a light, a basket, and chrome trimmings on it, too.* **2.** To go the limit; take a risk. ♦ *The motor of Tom's boat was dangerously hot, but he decided to shoot the works and try to win the race.*

**shoot up** *v.* **1.** To grow quickly. ♦ *Billy had always been a small boy, but when he was thirteen years old he began to shoot up.* **2.** To arise suddenly. ♦ *As we watched, flames shot up from the roof of the barn.* **3.** *informal* To shoot or shoot at recklessly; shoot and hurt badly. ♦ *The cowboys got drunk and shot up the bar room.* ♦ *The soldier was shot up very badly.* **4.** To take drugs by injection. ♦ *A heroin addict will shoot up as often as he can.*

**shop around for** *v. phr.* To make the rounds of various commercial establishments in order to find the most economical answer for one's needs. ♦ *We've been shopping around for a* *larger condominium that is affordable, and near the university.*

**shoplifter** *n.* A thief who steals things from a store. ◆ *The TV camera identified the shoplifter, who was then arrested and sentenced to jail.*

**shopworn** *adj.* A piece of merchandise that is offered below the usual price because it is slightly damaged or soiled. ◆ *Although shopworn, the jacket was perfectly usable, so he eagerly bought it.*

**shore leave** *n.* Permission given to a man in the navy to leave his ship and go where he wants for a certain length of time. ◆ *The ship did not dock long enough for the sailors to get shore leave.*

**shore patrol** *n.* The police of a navy. ◆ *The sailors who were fighting in town were arrested by the shore patrol.*

**shore up** *v.* To add support to (something) where weakness is shown; make (something) stronger where support is needed; support. ◆ *When the flood waters weakened the bridge, it was shored up with steel beams and sandbags until it could be rebuilt.*

**short and sweet** *adj.* Brief and to the point. ◆ *Henry's note to his father was short and sweet. He wrote, "Dear Dad, please send me $5. Love, Henry."*

**shortchange** *v. phr.* To return less money to a customer in a store than is coming to him or her; cheat. ◆ *I was shortchanged by the cashier when I got seven dollars back instead of eight.*

**shortcut** *n.* A road shorter than the one that people normally take. ◆ *We can save twenty minutes if we take this shortcut over the hill.*

**short end** *n.* The worst or most unpleasant part. ◆ *The new boy got the short end of it because all the comfortable beds in the dormitory had been taken before he arrived.*

**shorthanded** *adj.* Understaffed; short on workers. ◆ *With several employees gone for the holiday weekend and two dozen people in line, the rent-a-car agency suddenly found itself terribly shorthanded.*

**short haul** *n.* A short distance; a short trip. ◆ *The Scoutmaster said that it was just a short haul to the lake.*

**short list** *or* **short-listed** *v. phr.* To place on the list of select finalists for a job.

◆ *Only three of the twenty-seven applicants were short-listed for the assistant professorial vacancy in our department.*

**short of**[1] *adj. phr.* **1.** Less or worse than. ◆ *Don't do anything short of your best.* **2.** Not having enough. ◆ *We did not buy anything because we were short of money.*

**short of**[2] *adv. phr.* Away from; at a distance from. ◆ *The day's drive still left us a hundred miles short of the ocean.*

**short of breath** *adj.* Panting and wheezing. ◆ *He ran up six flights of stairs so rapidly that he was short of breath for several minutes.*

**short-order cook** *n.* A person who prepares food that cooks quickly. ◆ *Bruce found a summer job as a short-order cook in a drive-in restaurant.*

**short shrift** *n.* Little or no attention.— Usually used with *get* or *give*. ◆ *In books about jobs, women's work is consistently given short shrift.*

**short-spoken** *adj.* Using so few words that you seem impatient or angry; speaking in a short impatient way; saying as little as possible in an unfriendly way. ◆ *Jim is always short-spoken when he is tired.*

**shot across the bow** *n. phr., naval expression* A warning shot, physical or verbal, in which the enemy is put on notice that unless they surrender, they will be fired at. ◆ *The president's speech was a shot across the bow of Syria, when he demanded that escaped Iraqi leaders not be given asylum there.*

**shot in the arm** *n. phr., informal* Something inspiring or encouraging. ◆ *We were ready to quit, but the coach's talk was a shot in the arm.*

**shot in the dark** *n. phr.* An attempt without much hope or chance of succeeding; a wild guess. ◆ *It was just a shot in the dark, but I got the right answer to the teacher's question.*

**shot through with** Full of. ◆ *His speech was shot through with praise for the president.*

**shoulder the burden** *or* **shoulder the task** *v. phr.* To undertake carrying out a duty, a task, or repaying a debt. ◆ *John is shouldering the burden of his children's education even after his divorce from Sally.* ◆ *The vice president* of the company should shoulder the task of running the place when the president is sick.

**shoulder to cry on or to lean on** *n. phr.* A sympathetic person who is willing to listen to one's complaints and troubles. ♦*When Ken left her, Donna needed a shoulder to lean on, and Bob was right there to fill the role.*

**shoulder to shoulder** *adv. phr.* **1.** One beside the other; together. ♦*The three boys were shoulder to shoulder all during the working hours.* Compare SIDE BY SIDE. **2.** Each helping the other; in agreement; together. Used with *stand.* ♦*We can win the fight if we all stand shoulder to shoulder.*

**shout down** *v.* To object loudly to; defeat by shouting. ♦*The crowd shouted down the Mayor's suggestions.*

**shout from the housetops or shout from the rooftops** *v. phr., informal* To tell everyone; broadcast, especially one's own personal business. ♦*Mr. Clark was so happy when his son was born that he shouted the news from the housetops.*

**shove down one's throat or ram down one's throat** *v. phr., informal* To force you to do or agree to (something not wanted or liked.) ♦*We didn't want Mr. Bly to speak at our banquet, but the planning committee shoved him down our throats.*

**show around** *v. phr.* To act as a host or guide to someone; to show newly arrived people or strangers what's what and where. ♦*When Gordon and Rose arrived in Hawaii for the first time, their host showed them around the islands.*

**show cause** *v. phr.* To give a reason or explanation. ♦*The judge asked the defendants to show cause why they should not be held without bail.*

**showdown** *n.* (stress on *show*) A final challenge or confrontation during which both sides have to use all of their resources. ♦*You cannot know a country's military strength until a final showdown occurs.*

**showgirl** *n.* One who works as an entertainer in a bar or nightclub, musical show, etc. ♦*Several famous Hollywood stars actually started their careers as showgirls.*

**show in or out or up or to the door** *v. phr.* To usher; conduct; accompany. ♦*"My husband will show you in," Mary said to the guests when they arrived at the door.*

**showoff** *n.* (stress on *show*) A boastful person. ♦*Jim always has to be the center of attention; he is an insufferable showoff.*

**show off** *v. phr.* (stress on *off*) **1.** To put out nicely for people to see; display; exhibit. ♦*The Science Fair gave Julia a chance to show off her shell collection.* **2.** *informal* To try to attract attention; *also,* try to attract attention to. ♦*Joe hasn't missed a chance to show off his muscles since that pretty girl moved in next door.*

**show of hands** *n. phr.* An open vote during a meeting when those who vote "yes" and those who vote "no" hold up their hands to be counted. ♦*The chairman said, "I'd like to see a show of hands if we're ready for the vote."*

**show one's colors** *v. phr.* **1.** To show what you are really like. ♦*We thought Toby was timid, but he showed his colors when he rescued the ponies from the burning barn.* **2.** To make known what you think or plan to do. ♦*Mr. Ryder is afraid that he will lose the election if he shows his colors on civil rights.*

**show one's face** *v. phr.* To be seen; appear. ♦*After cheating on the test, Chris was ashamed to show his face.*

**show one's hand** *v. phr.* To reveal or exhibit one's true and hitherto hidden purpose. ♦*Only after becoming Chancellor of Germany did Adolf Hitler really show his hand and reveal that he intended to take over other countries.*

**show one's teeth** *v. phr.* To show anger; show belligerence. ♦*He is a very mild, private person, but during a tough business negotiation he knows how to show his teeth.*

**show one's true colors** See SHOW ONE'S COLORS.

**show the white feather** *v. phr.* To show signs of cowardice. ♦*The gang beat up the new member because he showed the white feather when the police arrived.*

**show the door** *v. phr.* To ask (someone) to go away. ♦*Our neighbors invited themselves to the party and stayed until Harry showed them the door.*

**show up** v. (stress on *up*) **1.** To make known the real truth about (someone). ♦ *The man said he was a mind reader, but he was shown up as a fake.* **2.** To come or bring out; become or make easy to see. ♦ *This test shows up your weaknesses in arithmetic.* **3.** *informal* To come; appear. ♦ *We had agreed to meet at the gym, but Larry didn't show up.*

**shrug off** v. To act as if you are not interested and do not care about something; not mind; not let yourself be bothered or hurt by. ♦ *Alan shrugged off our questions; he would not tell us what had happened.*

**shudder to think** v. phr. To be afraid; hate to think about something. ♦ *The professor is so strict I shudder to think what his final exam questions will be like.*

**shuffle off this mortal coil** v. phr., *formal, chiefly British* To die *(from Shakespeare's* Hamlet*)* ♦ *"When will you leave me your estate, Father?" David inquired from his dad. "Not before I shuffle off this mortal coil," the father replied with a sour smile.*

**shut-eye** n., *slang* Sleep. ♦ *It's very late. We'd better get some shut-eye.* ♦ *I'm going to get some shut-eye before the game.*

**shut off** v. **1.** To make (something like water or electricity) stop coming. ♦ *Please shut off the hose before the grass gets too wet.* **2.** To be apart; be separated from; *also* to separate from. ♦ *Our camp is so far from the highway we feel shut off from the world when we are there.*

**shut out** v. **1.** To prevent from coming in; block. ♦ *During World War II, Malta managed to shut out most of the Italian and German bombers by throwing up an effective antiaircraft screen.* **2.** To prevent (an opposing team) from scoring throughout an entire game. ♦ *The Dodgers shut out the Reds, 5–0.*

**shut the door** See CLOSE THE DOOR.

**shut up** v. **1.** *informal* To stop talking. ♦ *Shut up and let Joe say something.* ♦ *If you'll shut up for a minute, I'll tell you our plan.* **2.** To close the doors and windows of. ♦ *We got the house shut up only minutes before the storm hit.* **3.** To close and lock for a definite period of time. ♦ *The Smiths always spend Labor Day shutting up their summer home for the year.* ♦ **4.** To confine. ♦ *That dog bites. It should be shut up.*

**shut your trap** See SHUT UP. **1.**

**shy away** or **shy off** v. To avoid; seem frightened or nervous. ♦ *The boys shied away from our questions.* ♦ *The horse shied off when Johnny tried to mount it.*

**sick and tired** adj. **1.** Feeling strong dislike for something repeated or continued too long; exasperated; annoyed. ♦ *John is sick and tired of having his studies interrupted.* ♦ *I've been studying all day, and I'm sick and tired of it.*

**sick at heart** adj. phr. Very sad; regretful; longingly desirous. ♦ *Poor Mary was sick at heart for over a year after her husband left her for a younger woman.*

**side against** v. To join or be on the side that is against; disagree with; oppose. ♦ *Bill and Joe sided against me in the argument. We sided against the plan to go by plane.*

**side by side** adv. **1.** One beside the other in a row. ♦ *Charles and John are neighbors; they live side by side on Elm Street.* **2.** Close together. ♦ *The two boys played side by side all afternoon.*

**sidekick** n. A companion; a close friend of lesser status. ♦ *Wherever you see Dr. Howell, Dr. Percy, his youthful sidekick is sure to be present as well.*

**side street** n. A street that runs into and ends at a main street. ♦ *The store is on a side street just off Main Street.*

**side with** v. To agree with; help. ♦ *Alan always sides with Johnny in an argument.* ♦ *Gerald sided with the plan to move the club.*

**sight for sore eyes** n. phr., *informal* A welcome sight. ♦ *After our long, dusty hike, the pond was a sight for sore eyes. "Jack! You're a sight for sore eyes!"*

**sight-read** v. To be able to play music without memorization by reading the sheet music and immediately playing it. ♦ *Experienced, good musicians are expected to be able to sight-read.*

**sight unseen** adv. phr. Before seeing it; before seeing her, him, or them. ♦ *Tom read an ad about a car and sent the money for it sight unseen.*

**sign in** v. To write your name on a special list or in a record book to show that you are present. ♦*Every worker must sign in when coming back to work.*

**sign off** *v.* **1.** To end a program on radio or television. ♦*That TV station always signs off after the late movie.*

**sign of the times** *n. phr.* A characteristic of the times in which one lives. ♦*It is a sad sign of the times that all the major lakes and rivers are badly polluted and fish in them are poisoned.*

**sign on** *v. phr.* **1.** To sign an agreement to become an employee. ♦*The new cowboys signed on with the wealthy rancher in Nevada.* **2.** To start a radio or television broadcast. ♦*Station WLAK signs on every morning at 6 A.M.*

**sign one's own death warrant** *v. phr.* To cause your own death or the loss of something you want very much. ♦*When Jim's fiancée saw him on a date with another girl, he signed his own death warrant.*

**sign on the dotted line** *v. phr.* To attach one's signature on an important document, such as a contract, a bill of sales, etc. ♦*The seller said to the buyer, "All you need to do is sign on the dotted line."*

**sign out** *v.* To write your name on a special list or in a record book to show that you are leaving a place. ♦*Most of the students sign out on Friday.*

**sign over** *v.* To give legally by signing your name. ♦*He signed his house over to his wife.*

**sign up** *v.* **1.** To promise to do something by signing your name; join; sign an agreement. ♦*We will not have the picnic unless more people sign up.* **2.** To write the name of (a person or thing) to be in an activity; also, to persuade (someone) to do something. ♦*Betty decided to sign up her dog for obedience training.*

**signed, sealed, and delivered** *adj. phr.* Finished; completed; in a state of completion. ♦*"How is the campus renovation plan for the governor's office coming along?" the dean of the college asked. "Signed, sealed, and delivered," his assistant answered.*

**silent majority** *n., informal* The large majority of people who, unlike the militants, do not make their political and social views known by marching and demonstrating and who, presumably, can swing an election one way or the other. ♦*Sidney Miltner is a member of the silent majority.*

**silver anniversary** *or* **wedding** *n. phr.* The twenty-fifth wedding anniversary of a couple; the twenty-fifth anniversary of a business or an association, etc. ♦*"The day after tomorrow is Mom and Dad's silver anniversary," Sue said to her brother. "I hope you have a nice present picked out."*

**simmer down** *v., informal* To become less angry or excited; become calmer. ♦*Tom got mad, but soon simmered down.*

**sing a different tune** *or* **whistle a different tune** *also* **sing a new tune** *v. phr., informal* To talk or act in the opposite way; contradict something said before. ♦*Charles said that all smokers should be expelled from the team but he sang a different tune after the coach caught him smoking.*

**sing a sad song** *v. phr., slang* To tell a sad story. ♦*Albert is an expert complainer; he always sings a sad song and gains the sympathy of people around him.*

**sing for one's supper** *v. phr., informal* To have to work for what one desires. ♦*I realized a long time ago that I had to sing for my supper if I wanted to get ahead in my profession.*

**single out** *v. phr.* To select or choose one from among many. ♦*There were a lot of pretty girls at the high school prom but Don immediately singled out Sally.*

**sing one's praises** *v. phr.* To extol or praise continuously. ♦*The audience left the concert with everyone singing the praises of the young piano virtuoso.*

**sink in** *or* **soak in** *v., informal* To be completely understood; be fully realized or felt. ♦*Everybody laughed at the joke but Joe; it took a moment for it to sink in before he laughed too.*

**sink or swim** *v. phr.* To succeed or fail by your own efforts, without help or interference from anyone else; fail if you don't work hard to succeed. ♦*When Joe was fourteen, his parents died, and he was left by himself to sink or swim.*

**sit back** *v.* **1.** To be built a distance away; stand away (as from a street). ♦*Our house sits back from the road.* **2.** To relax; rest, often while others are working; take time out. ◆ *Sit back for a minute and think about what you have done.*

**sit by** *v.* **1.** To stay near; watch and care for. ◆ *Mother sat by her sick baby all night.* **2.** To sit and watch or rest especially while others work ◆ *Don't just sit idly by while the other children are all busy.*

**sit in** *v.* (stress on *in*) **1.** To be a member; participate. ◆ *We're having a conference and we'd like you to sit in. also* **sit in on:** To be a member of; participate in. ◆ *We want you to sit in on the meeting.* **2.** To attend but not participate. Often used with *on.* ◆ *Our teacher was invited to sit in on the conference.*

**sit it out** *v. phr.* To wait until an unpleasant or taxing situation passes. ◆ *The storm knocked out the power and we have no candles, I guess we'll just have to sit it out.*

**sit on** *v.* **1.** To be a member of (a jury, board, commission), etc. ◆ *Mr. Brown sat on the jury at the trial.* **2.** *informal* To prevent from starting or doing something; squelch. ◆ *The teacher sat on Joe as soon as he began showing off.*

**sit on a bomb** *or* **bombshell** *v. phr., informal* To be in possession of anything that is potentially disastrous or dangerous. ◆ *The finance department will be sitting on a bomb unless it finds a way to cut overhead expenses.*

**sit on a volcano** *v., informal* **1.** To be in a place where trouble may start or danger may come suddenly. ◆ *The policemen who patrolled the big city slum area that summer were sitting on a volcano.*

**sit on one's hands** *v. phr., informal* To do nothing; fail or refuse to do anything. ◆ *We asked Bill for help with our project, but he sat on his hands.*

**sit out** *v.* To not take part in. ◆ *The next dance is a polka. Let's sit it out.*

**sit through** *v.* To watch or listen until (something) is finished. ◆ *The show was so boring that we could hardly sit through the first act.*

**sit tight** *v. phr., informal* To make no move *or* change; stay where you are.—Often used as a command. ◆ *The doctor said to sit tight until he arrived.*

**sitting duck** *n. phr.* Someone in a vulnerable position, who doesn't know what danger he or she is facing. ◆ *Many a widow is a sitting duck for men seeking a quick adventure.* ◆ *Unsuspecting tourists, who leave their car doors open in national parks, may be sitting ducks for thieves and robbers.*

**sit up** *v.* (stress on *up*) **1.** To move into a sitting position. ◆ *Joe sat up when he heard the knock on his bedroom door.* **2.** To stay awake instead of going to bed. ◆ *Mrs. Jones will sit up until both of her daughters get home from the dance.* **3.** *informal* To be surprised. ◆ *Janice really sat up when I told her the gossip about Tom.*

**sit-up** *n.* (stress on *sit*) A vigorous exercise in which the abdominal muscles are strengthened by locking one's feet in a fastening device and sitting up numerous times. ◆ *Do a few sit-ups if you want to reduce your waist.*

**sit up and take notice** *v. phr., informal* To be surprised into noticing something. ◆ *George's sudden success made the town sit up and take notice.*

**sit up for** *v. phr.* To wait until after the usual bedtime for someone's return. ◆ *Mrs. Smith always sits up for her two daughters, no matter how late it is.*

**sit up with** *v. phr.* To be with; particularly to keep someone ill company. ◆ *Mrs. Brown sat up with her sick husband all night in the hospital room.*

**sit well (with)** *v.* Find favor with; please. ◆ *The reduced school budget did not sit well with the teachers.*

**sit with** *v., informal* To be accepted by; affect.—Used in interrogative sentences and in negative sentences modified by *well.* ◆ *How did your story sit with your mother?*

**six of one and half-a-dozen of the other** *n,. phr.* Two things the same; not a real choice; no difference. ◆ *Which coat do you like better, the brown or the blue? It's six of one and half-a-dozen of the other.*

**sixth sense** *n. phr.* An extrasensory sense; the ability to foresee the future. ◆ *My cat has a sixth sense; she sometimes looks around at something I cannot see.* ◆ *John knew that we should not go out on Main Street on Saturday when the scaffold fell; sometimes I feel he has a sixth sense.*

**size up** v., *informal* To decide what one thinks about (something); to form an opinion about (something). ♦ *Give Joe an hour to size up the situation and he'll tell you what to do next.*

**skate on thin ice** v. phr. To take a chance; risk danger, disapproval or anger. ♦ *You'll be skating on thin ice if you ask Dad to increase your allowance again.*

**skating rink** n., *slang, citizen's band radio jargon* Slippery road. ♦ *Attention all units—there's a skating rink ahead!*

**skeleton at the feast** n. phr. A source or reminder of something sad or depressing in the midst of a celebration or a happy party. ♦ *Everyone was having a good time at Joan's wedding, except for poor Mary, whose memories of her recent divorce were a skeleton at the feast for her.*

**skeleton in the closet** n. phr. A shameful secret; someone or something kept hidden, especially by a family. ♦ *The skeleton in our family closet was Uncle Willie. No one mentioned him because he drank too much.*

**skid lid** n., *slang* A crash helmet worn by motorcyclists and race drivers. ♦ *How much did you pay for that handsome skid lid?*

**skid row** n. The poor part of a city where men live who have no jobs and drink too much liquor. ♦ *That man was once rich, but he drank and gambled too much, and ended his life living on skid row.*

**skim the surface** v. phr. To do something very superficially. ♦ *He seems knowledgeable in many different areas but his familiarity is very superficial, since he only skims the surface of everything he touches.*

**skin alive** v. phr. **1.** *informal* To scold angrily. ♦ *Mother will skin you alive when she sees your torn pants.* **2.** *informal* To spank or beat. ♦ *Dad was ready to skin us alive when he found we had ruined his saw.* **3.** *slang* To defeat. ♦ *We all did our best, but the visiting gymnastic team skinned us alive.*

**skin and bones** n. A person or animal that is very thin; someone very skinny. ♦ *Have you been dieting? You're nothing but skin and bones!*

**skin-deep** adj. Only on the surface; not having any deep or honest meaning; not really or closely connected with what it seems to belong to. ♦ *Mary's friendliness with Joan is only skin-deep.*

**skin off one's nose** n. phr., *slang* Matter of interest, concern, or trouble to you. Normally used in the negative. ♦ *Go to Jake's party if you wish. It's no skin off my nose.* ♦ *Grace didn't pay any attention to our argument. It wasn't any skin off her nose.* ♦ *You could at least say hello to our visitor. It's no skin off your nose.*

**skip it** v. phr., *informal* To forget all about it. ♦ *When Jack tried to reward him for returning his lost dog, the man said to skip it.*

**skip out** v., *informal* To leave in a hurry; especially after cheating or taking money dishonestly; sneak away; leave without permission. ♦ *The man skipped out of the hotel without paying his bill.*

**skirt around** v. phr. To avoid something. ♦ *"Let's not skirt around the facts," said the attorney to his client. "You must tell me the truth."*

**sky is the limit** There is no upper limit to something. ♦ *"Buy me the fastest racehorse in Hong Kong," Mr. Lee instructed his broker. "Spend whatever is necessary; the sky is the limit."*

**slack off** v. phr. **1.** To become less active; grow lazy. ♦ *Since construction work has been slacking off toward the end of the summer, many workers were dismissed.* **2.** To gradually reduce; taper off. ♦ *The snowstorms tend to slack off over the Great Lakes by the first of April.*

**slap in the face**[1] n. An insult; a disappointment. ♦ *We felt that it was a slap in the face when our gift was returned unopened.*

**slap in the face**[2] v. phr. To insult; embarrass; make feel bad. ♦ *John slapped our club in the face by saying that everyone in it was stupid.*

**slap one's wrist** v. phr. To receive a light punishment. ♦ *She could have been fired for contradicting the company president in public, but all she got was a slap on the wrist.*

**slap together** See THROW TOGETHER 1.

**slated for** *or* **slated to be** Going to be; planned or intended for. ♦ *People think the governor is slated to be president.*

**slave driver** n. A cruel, merciless boss or employer who makes the people under him work extremely hard for little compensation. ♦ *Mr. Catwallender is such a slave driver that nobody cares to work for him anymore.*

**sleep around** *v. phr., slang, vulgar, avoidable* To be free with one's sexual favors; to behave promiscuously. ♦ *Sue Catwallender is a nice girl but she sleeps around an awful lot with all sorts of guys.*

**sleep a wink** *v. phr.* To get a moment's sleep; enjoy a bit of sleep.—Used in negative and conditional statements and in questions. ♦ *I didn't sleep a wink all night.*

**sleep in** *v. phr.* To sleep much later than usual, such as on Saturday and Sunday when one doesn't have to go to work. ♦ *"May I talk to John?" the caller asked, "I am sorry. He is sleeping in this morning, please call back in an hour or so," John's wife, an early riser, replied.*

**sleep like a baby** See SLEEP LIKE A LOG.

**sleep like a log** *v. phr.* To sleep very deeply and soundly. ♦ *Although I am usually a light sleeper, I was so exhausted from the sixteen-hour transpacific flight that, once we got home, I slept like a log for twelve hours.*

**sleep off** *v. phr.* To sleep until the effect of too much alcohol or drugs passes. ♦ *George had too many beers last night and he is now sleeping off the effects.*

**sleep on** *v.* To postpone a decision about. ♦ *We will have to sleep on your invitation until we know whether we will be free Monday night.*

**sleep with** *v. phr.* To have a sexual affair with someone; have sex; copulate. ♦ *It has been rumored in the office that the boss sleeps with all the girls he hires.*

**slinging match** *n. phr.* A loud, angry quarrel. ♦ *The debate deteriorated into a most unseemly slinging match.*

**slip away** *v. phr.* To leave unnoticed. ♦ *The party was such a bore that we decided to quietly slip away.*

**slip me five** See GIVE ME SOME SKIN.

**slip off** *v. phr.* **1.** To slide off something. ♦ *The children climbed up the hill but when it was time to come down, they didn't walk, but slipped off the smooth, old ledges.*

**slip of the pen** *n. phr.* The mistake of writing something different from what

you should or what you planned. ♦ *That was a slip of the pen. I meant to write September, not November.* ♦ *I wish you would forget it. That was a slip of the pen.*

**slip of the tongue** *also* **slip of the lip** *n. phr.* The mistake of saying something you had not wanted or planned to say; an error of speech. ♦ *She didn't mean to tell our secret; it was a slip of the lip.*

**slip one's mind** *v. phr.* To forget something. ♦ *I meant to mail those letters but it entirely slipped my mind.*

**slip through one's fingers** *v. phr.* To escape without someone's knowing how. ♦ *Policemen surrounded the building, but the thief managed to slip through their fingers.*

**slipup** *n.* (stress on *slip*) A mistake. ♦ *"I'm sorry, sir. That was an unfortunate slipup," the barber said when he scratched the client's face.*

**slip up** *v. phr.* (stress on *up*) To make a mistake. ♦ *Someone at the bank slipped up. There are only 48 pennies in this 50¢ roll of coins.*

**slow as molasses in January** *adj. phr., informal* Extremely slow. *"Hurry up, for God's sake—you are as slow as molasses in January!" Joan cried at her sleepy husband.*

**slow burn** *n., informal* A slowly increasing feeling of anger. ♦ *Barbara's slow burn ended only when Mary explained the misunderstanding.*

**slowdown** *n.* (stress on *slow*) A period of lesser activity, usually in the economic sphere. ♦ *We all hope the current slowdown in the economy will soon be over.*

**slow down** *v. phr.* (stress on *down*) To go more slowly than usual. ♦ *The road was slippery, so Mr. Jones slowed down the car.* ♦ *Pat once could run a mile in five minutes, but now that he's older he's slowing down.*

**slow on the draw** *adj. phr.* Not very smart; having difficulty figuring things out. ♦ *Poor Eric doesn't get very good grades in physics; when it comes to problem-solving, he is rather slow on the draw.*

**slow up** *v.* **1.** To go more slowly. ♦ *The truck slowed up as it approached the toll gate.* **2.** To become less busy. ♦ *Business slows up at the stores after Christmas.*

**slug it out** *v. phr.* To have a strong verbal or physical battle with someone; to contest something most vigorously. ♦ *The two candidates for Congress were slugging it out on radio and on television.*

**smack one's lips** *v. phr.* To reveal an appetite for; show enjoyment of. ♦ *Eleanor smacked her lips over the dessert of strawberries and whipped cream.*

**small fry** *n.* **1.** Young children. ♦ *In the park, a sandbox is provided for the small fry.* **2.** Something or someone of little importance. ♦ *Large dairies ignore the competition from the small fry who make only a few hundred pounds of cheese a year.*

**small** *or* **wee hours** *n. phr.* The very early hours of the morning between 1 and 4 A.M. ♦ *My brother was in trouble for coming home in the small hours.*

**small talk** *n. phr.* General idle conversation. ♦ *At the party there was the usual kind of small talk about the cost of living increase and the war in Africa.*

**small-time** *adj., informal* Unimportant; minor; with little power or importance. ♦ *He has a job as a drummer with a small-time band.*

**smash hit** *n., informal* A very successful play, movie or opera. ♦ *The school play was a smash hit.*

**smell a rat** *v. phr., informal* To be suspicious; feel that something is wrong. ♦ *Every time Tom visits me, one of my ashtrays disappears. I'm beginning to smell a rat.*

**smell to heaven** *or* **smell to high heaven** *or* **stink to heaven** *or* **stink to high heaven** *v. phr., informal* To smell extremely foul; be very bad smelling. ♦ *"Don't you ever open the windows around here? Man, the place stinks to high heaven!" John exclaimed, as he entered his friend's badly neglected apartment.*

**smell up** *v., informal* To make a bad smell. ♦ *A skunk smelled up our yard last night.*

**smoke like a chimney** *v. phr., informal* To smoke very heavily and continuously. ♦ *"If you continue smoking like a chimney" the doctor told my uncle, "you'll wind up in the hospital with lung cancer."*

**smoke out** *v. phr.* (stress on *out*) **1.** To force out with smoke. ♦ *The boys smoked a squirrel out of a hollow tree.* ♦ *The farmer tried to smoke some gophers out of their burrows.* **2.** *informal* To find out the facts about. ♦ *It took the reporter three weeks to smoke out the whole story.*

**smoke-out** *n.* (stress on *smoke*) A successful conclusion of an act of investigative journalism revealing some long-kept secrets. ♦ *Journalist Bob Woodward was the hero of the Watergate smoke-out.*

**smoke screen** *n. phr.* A camouflage; a veil; something used to cover or hide something. ♦ *June hides her commercial interests behind a smoke screen of religious piety.*

**smoke the pipe of peace** *v. phr.* To rekindle an old friendship after a period of fights and quarrels. ♦ *John and David, who were old classmates, didn't talk to each other for a decade because of politics. Eventually they ran into each other in the street, went to a bar, and over some beers decided to smoke the pipe of peace.*

**Smokey Bear** *or* **Smokey-the-Bear** *or* **the Smokies** *n., slang, citizen's band radio jargon* A policeman; a patrol car; frequently abbreviated as *Smokey.* ♦ *Slow down, Smokey's ahead!*

**smoking gun** *n. phr.* Material proof or crucial testimony that some crime has been committed. ♦ *A DNA examination was the smoking gun that proved beyond any doubt that the accused rapist was indeed guilty.*

**smooth away** *v.* To remove; (unpleasant feelings) take away. ♦ *Mr. Jones' new job smoothed away his worry about money.*

**smooth down** *v.* To make calm; calm down. ♦ *Mrs. Smith's feelings were hurt and we couldn't smooth her down.*

**smooth over** *v.* To make something seem better or more pleasant; try to excuse. ♦ *Bill tried to smooth over his argument with Mary by making her laugh.*

**S.N.A.F.U.** *or* **snafu** *n. phrase, abbreviation slang, army slang, vulgar, avoidable* Situation normal, all fucked up. ♦ *Even President Bill Clinton called some messy situations during his eight-year tenure in the White House "snafus" on national television.*

**snail's pace** *n.* A very slow movement forward. ♦ *Time moved at a snail's pace before the holidays.*

**snake in the grass** *n. phr., informal* A person who cannot be trusted; an unfaithful traitor; rascal. ♦ *Some snake in the grass told the teacher our plans.*

**snap one's fingers at** *v. phr.* To show contempt for; show no respect for; pay no attention to; scorn; disregard. ♦ *John snapped his fingers at the sign that said "Do not enter," and he went in the door.*

**snap out of** *v., informal* To change quickly from a bad habit, mood, or feeling to a better one.—Often used with *it.* ♦ *The coach told the lazy player to snap out of it.*

**snapshot** *n.* A small photograph, unlike a professional portrait. ♦ *We took several snapshots of the scenery while driving around the island.*

**snap up** *v., informal* To take or accept eagerly. ♦ *Eggs were on sale cheap, and the shoppers snapped up the bargain.*

**sneeze at** *v., informal* To think of as not important; not take seriously.—Used with negative or limiting words and in questions. ♦ *Is a thousand dollars anything to sneeze at?* ♦ *John finished third in a race with twenty other runners. That is nothing to sneeze at.*

**snow in** *v.* To block up or trap by much snow; keep inside. ♦ *After the storm the farmer and his family were snowed in for three days.*

**snow job** *n., slang, informal* **1.** Insincere or exaggerated talk designed to gain the favors of someone. ♦ *Joe gave Sue a snow job and she believed every word of it.* **2.** The skillful display of technical vocabulary and prestige terminology in order to pass oneself off as an expert in a specialized field without really being a knowledgeable worker in that area. ♦ *That talk by Nielsen on pharmaceuticals sounded very impressive, but I will not hire him because it was essentially a snow job.*

**snow under** *v.* **1.** To cover over with snow. ♦ *The doghouse was snowed under during the blizzard.* **2.** *informal* To give so much of something that it cannot be taken care of; to weigh down by so much of something that you cannot do anything about it.—

Usually used in the passive. ♦ *The factory received so many orders that it was snowed under with work.*

**snug as a bug in a rug** *adj. phr.* Comfortable; cozy. ♦ *"Are you warm enough?" the boy's mother asked. "Yeah," he replied, "I'm snug as a bug in a rug."*

**soak up** *v.* **1.** To take up water or other liquid as a sponge does. ♦ *The rag soaked up the water that I spilled.* **2.** To use a sponge or something like a sponge to take up liquid. ♦ *John soaked up the water with the rag.* **3.** *informal* To take up into yourself in the way a sponge takes up water. ♦ *Mary was lying on the beach soaking up the sun.* ♦

**so-and-so**[1] *pronoun, informal* Someone whose name is not given. ♦ *Don't tell me what so-and-so thinks. Tell me what you think.*

**so-and-so**[2] *n., informal* A person of a special kind and usually of a very bad kind. ♦ *I wish that old so-and-so who thinks digging is easy work was right here digging now.*

**so ——— as to**—Used with an adjective or adverb before an infinitive to show a result. ♦ *Who could be so mean as to do a thing like that?* ♦ *Ruth wouldn't be so careless as to forget her pen.*

**soap opera** *n. phr.* Radio or television serialized stories of a sentimental nature, often involving sex, crime, and social intrigue. These shows often advertise soap products, hence their name. ♦ *The two longest running soap operas in the United States were* "Dallas" *and* "Knot's Landing."

**so be it** *also* **be it so** *adv. phr., formal* **1.** Let it be that way; may it be so. *So be it.* ♦ *We shall smoke the pipe of peace.* **2.** Very well; all right. ♦ *Will the company lose money by doing this? So be it, then.*

**sob story** *n.* A story that makes you feel pity or sorrow; a tale that makes you tearful. ♦ *The beggar told us a long sob story before he asked for money.*

**social butterfly** *or* **society butterfly** *n. phr.* A person, who spends an inordinate amount of time going to parties. ♦ *John will never amount to anything. He wastes his time dancing, drinking, and telling jokes, being the social butterfly that he is.*

**social climber** *n.* A person who tries to mix with rich or well-known people and be accepted by them as friends and equals. ♦*People do not like Mrs. Brown very well; she is known as a social climber.*

**sock it** *v. phr., also interj., slang, informal* To give one's utmost; everything one is capable of; to give all one is capable of. ♦*Right on, Joe, sock it to 'em!* ♦*I was watching the debate on television and more than once Bill Buckley really socked it to them.*

**so far** *also* **thus far** *adv.* Until this time or to this place. ♦*The weather has been hot so far this summer.*

**so far, so good** *informal* Until now things have gone well. ♦*So far, so good; I hope we keep on with such good luck.*

**soft drink** *n. phr.* A nonalcoholic beverage such as 7-Up, Coca-Cola, etc. ♦*She drinks no alcohol; she always orders a soft drink.*

**softhearted** *adj.* Generous; sympathetic. ♦*Street beggars tend to exploit the softhearted nature of passersby.*

**soft in the head** *adj. phr.* Not very intelligent, stupid; dumb. ♦*John is a brilliant fellow, but his younger brother, Jim, is rather soft in the head.*

**soft touch** *n.* A person with a sympathetic disposition from whom it is easy to get help, primarily money. ♦*My Uncle Herb is a soft touch; whenever I'm in need I ask him for a quick twenty bucks.*

**so help me** *interj., informal* I promise; I swear; may I be punished if I lie. ♦*I've told you the truth, so help me.*

**so it goes** Akin to the French *c'est la vie!* This exclamation means "that's life." ♦*Too bad Jim has lost his job but there are lots of people who are better qualified; well, so it goes!*

**sold on** *adj.* Approving of; well disposed toward; convinced of the value of. ♦*When Japanese cars first appeared on the market Andy was hesitant to drive one but now he is sold on them.*

**so long** *interj., informal* Good-bye.—Used when you are leaving someone or he is leaving you. ♦*So long, I will be back tomorrow.*

**so many**[1] *adj.* **1.** A limited number of; some ♦*Our school auditorium will hold only so many people.* **2.** A group

of.—Often used for emphasis. ♦*The children were all sitting very quietly in their chairs, like so many dolls.*

**so many**[2] *pron.* A limited number; some. ♦*Many people want to come to the prom; but the gymnasium will hold only so many.*

**somebody up there loves/hates me** *slang* An expression intimating that an unseen power in heaven, such as God, has been favorable or unfavorable to the one making the exclamation. ♦*Look at all the money I won! I say somebody up there sure loves me!* ♦*Look at all the money I've lost! I say somebody up there sure hates me!*

**something else** *adj., slang, informal* So good as to be beyond description; the ultimate; stupendous. ♦*Janet Hopper is really something else.*

**something else again** *n. phr.* A different kind of thing; something different. ♦*I don't care if you borrow my dictionary sometimes, but taking it without asking and keeping it is something else again.*

**something in the wind** *n. phr., informal* There is something significant or important happening or about to happen that some people can sense. ♦*I cannot prove this to you, but there is something in the wind, which tells me that the economy will soon get much stronger.*

**so much**[1] *adj.* **1.** A limited amount of; some. ♦*Sometimes students wonder if the teacher knows they have only so much time to do their lessons.* **2.** Equally or amounting to; only amounting to.—Often used for emphasis. ♦*Charley spends money as if it were so much paper.*

**so much**[2] *pron.* A limited amount; some; a price or amount that is agreed or will be agreed on. ♦*You can do only so much in a day.*

**so much**[3] *adv.* By that much; by the amount shown; even.—Used with the comparative and usually followed by the. ♦*So much the worse for you if you break the rules.*

**so much as** *adv. phr.* **1.** Even.—Usually used in negative sentences and questions. ♦*He didn't so much as thank me for returning his money that I found.*

**so much for** Enough has been said or done about.—Used to point out that you have finished with one thing or are going to take up something else. ♦ *So much for the geography of Ireland. We will now talk about the people who live there.*

**song and dance** *n.*, *informal* **1.** Foolish or uninteresting talk; dull nonsense. Usually used with *give.* ♦ *I met Nancy today and she gave me a long song and dance about her family.* **2.** A long lie or excuse, often meant to get pity. Usually used with *give.* ♦ *Billy gave the teacher a song and dance about his mother being sick as an excuse for being late.*

**sonic boom** *n.* A loud noise and vibration in the air, made when a jet plane passes the speed of sound (1087 feet per second). ♦ *Fast jet planes sometimes cause a sonic boom, which can break windows and crack the plaster in houses below them.*

**son of a bitch** *or* **sunuvabitch** *also* **S.O.B.** *n. phr.*, *vulgar*, *avoidable (but becoming more and more acceptable, especially if said with a positive or loving intonation).* Fellow, character, guy, individual. Negatively: ♦ *Get out of here you filthy, miserable sunuvabitch!* Positively: ♦ *So you won ten million dollars at the lottery, you lucky son of a bitch (or sunuvabitch)!*

**son of a gun** *n. phr.*, *slang* **1.** A bad person; a person not liked. ♦ *I don't like Charley; keep that son of a gun out of here.* **2.** A mischievous rascal; a lively guy.—Often used in a joking way. ♦ *The farmer said he would catch the son of a gun who let the cows out of the barn.* **3.** Something troublesome; a hard job. ♦ *The test today was a son of a gun.*

**sooner or later** *adv. phr.* At some unknown time in the future; sometime. ♦ *Grandpa is very slow about fixing things around the house, but he always does it sooner or later.*

**sore spot** *or* **sore point** *n.* A weak or sensitive part; a subject or thing about which someone becomes angry or upset easily. ♦ *Don't ask Uncle John why his business failed; it's a sore spot with him.*

**sort out** *v. phr.* **1.** To alphabetize; arrange in numerical order. ♦ *The secretary helped Professor Brown sort out his numerous index cards.* **2.** To clarify.

♦ *"Help me sort out these bills," she begged her husband.*

**so-so** *adj.* Fair; neither good nor bad. ♦ *The children's grades were just so-so on the test.*

**so to speak** *adv. phr.* To say it in this way. ♦ *John was, so to speak, the leader of the club, but he was officially only the club's secretary.*

**sought after** *adj.* Wanted by many buyers; searched for. ♦ *Antiques are much sought after nowadays.*

**soul-searching** See SEARCH ONE'S HEART *or* SEARCH ONE'S SOUL.

**sound bite** *n. phr.* A much-quoted statement made by a politician. ♦ *President Bush's statement "We have an old saying in the West, 'dead or alive,' referring to Osama Bin Laden, has become a famous sound bite.*

**sound effects** *n.* The noises made to imitate real sounds in a play, movie, or program. ♦ *The movie was good but the sound effects were not very true to life.*

**sound off** *v.* **1.** To say your name or count "One! Two! Three! Four!" as you march.—Used as orders in U.S. military service. ♦ *"Sound off!" said the sergeant, and the soldiers shouted, "One! Two! Three! Four!" with each step as they marched.* **2.** *informal* To tell what you know or think in a loud clear voice, especially to brag or complain. ♦ *If you don't like the way we're doing the job, sound off!*

**sound out** *v.* To try to find out how a person feels about something usually by careful questions. ♦ *Alfred sounded out his boss about a day off from his job.*

**sound sheet** *n.*, *slang*, *informal* A thin low-quality phonograph recording frequently bound into books and magazines for use as promotional or advertising material; it may have either a spoken or a musical message. ♦ *Don't throw that away; Sue is collecting sound sheets for her market research course.*

**sound truck** *n. phr.* A truck equipped with loudspeakers. ♦ *During the senatorial campaign, the streets of the big city were full of sound trucks blaring out messages.*

**souped-up** *adj.*, *informal* More powerful or faster because of changes and additions. ♦*Many teen-aged boys like to drive souped-up cars.*

**sour grapes** *n. phr., originally from one of Aesop's fables* A saying often heard when one belittles something he or she cannot get, but wants very much. ♦*"I didn't get the job I wanted, but it is a good thing, because it's not a very good company," Ted said. "Excuse me," John replied, "but it sounds to me like a case of 'sour grapes.'"*

**so what** *informal* Used as an impolite reply showing that you don't care about what another has said. ♦*Roy boasted that he was in the sixth grade, but Ted said, "So what? I am in Junior High."*

**sow one's wild oats** *v. phr.* To do bad or foolish things, especially while you are young. ♦*Mr. Jones sowed his wild oats while he was in college, but now he is a wiser and better man.*

**sow the wind and reap the whirlwind** To cause trouble and thereby receive a great deal more than one has originally bargained for.—A proverb. ♦*Joan seduced Mary's husband, and later married him. She didn't know that he had five children and three ex-wives to support. When she complained about her bad luck, her mother replied: "Sow the wind and reap the whirlwind, remember?"*

**spaced out** *adj., slang, informal* Having gaps in one's train of thought, confused, incoherent; resembling the behavior of someone who is under the influence of drugs. ♦*Joe's been acting funny lately— spaced out, you might say.*

**space probe** *n., Space English* An unmanned spacecraft other than an Earth satellite fitted with instruments which gather and transmit information about other planets in the solar system (e.g., Venus, Mars, and Jupiter) on what are called fly-by missions, i.e., without the craft landing on any of these bodies. ♦*Both the U.S.A. and Russia have sent up many a space probe during the last several decades.*

**spare me** See GIVE ME A BREAK.

**speakeasy** *n.* A bar during Prohibition where illegal alcoholic beverages were sold. ♦*Al Capone's associates met in a Chicago speakeasy to drink and discuss business.*

**speak for** *v.* **1.** To speak in favor of or in support of. ♦*At the meeting John spoke for the change in the rules.* **2.** To make a request for; to ask for. ♦*The teacher was giving away some books. Fred and Charlie spoke for the same one.* **3.** To give an impression of; be evidence that (something) is or will be said.—Used with the words *well* or *ill.* ♦*It seems that it will rain today. That speaks ill for the picnic this afternoon.* ♦*It speaks well for Mary that she always does her homework.*

**speak of the devil (and he appears)** *or* **talk of the devil** A person comes just when you are talking about him.—A proverb. ♦*We were just talking about Bill when he came in the door. Speak of the devil (and he appears).*

**speak one's mind** *v. phr.* To say openly what you think; give advice that may not be liked. ♦*John thought it was wrong to keep George out of the club and he spoke his mind about it.*

**speak out of turn** *v. phr.* To say something tactless; commit an indiscretion. ♦*You spoke out of turn in criticizing Aunt Hermione's old furniture; she considers herself quite a connoisseur on the subject.*

**speak out** *or* **speak up** *v.* **1.** To speak in a loud or clear voice. ♦*The trucker told the shy boy to speak up.* **2.** To speak in support of or against someone or something. ♦*Willie spoke up for Dan as club president.*

**speak the same language** *v. phr.* To have similar feelings, thoughts, and tastes; have a mutual understanding with another person. ♦*We both love listening to Mozart. Obviously, we speak the same language.*

**speak up** *v. phr.* **1.** To speak louder. ♦*Would you please speak up? We can't hear you in the back row.* **2.** To complain; voice one's opposition to something. ♦*If you think you are not treated properly at work, don't be shy—speak up!*

**speak volumes** *v. phr.* To tell or show much in a way other than speaking; be full of meaning. ♦*The nice present she gave you spoke volumes for what she thinks of you.*

**speak well of** *v. phr.* To approve of; praise. ♦*Everyone always speaks well of my sister because she's so kind.*

**speak with a forked tongue** *v. phr., literary* To lie; to say one thing while thinking of the opposite. ♦*I have learned not to trust Peter's promises because he speaks with a forked tongue.*

**speed trap** *n.* A place where police hide and wait to catch drivers who are going even a little faster than the speed limit. ♦*Mr. Jones was caught in a speed trap.*

**speed up** *v.* To go faster than before; *also,* to make go faster. ♦*The car speeded up when it reached the country.*

**spell out** *v.* **1.** To say or read aloud the letters of a word, one by one; spell. ♦*John could not understand the word the teacher was saying, so she spelled it out on the blackboard.* **2.** To read slowly, have trouble in understanding. ♦*The little boy spelled out the printed words.* **3.** *informal* To explain something in very simple words; explain very clearly. ♦*The class could not understand the problem, so the teacher spelled it out for them.*

**spell trouble** *v. phr.* To signify major difficulties ahead. ♦*The note we just received from the Chancellor seems to spell trouble.*

**spending money** *or* **pocket money** *n.* Money that is given to a person to spend. ♦*When the seniors went to New York City on a trip, each was given $20 in spending money.*

**spend the night** *v. phr.* To sleep somewhere. ♦*It was so late after the party that we decided to spend the night at our friends' house.*

**spent rocket** *n. phr.* A previously brilliant and productive person, who, due to old age or illness, has been unproductive for some time. ♦*Professor Riddle, who won the Pulitzer Prize twenty years ago, doesn't say or do very much these days. Poor man is a veritable spent rocket.*

**spick-and-span** *adj.* Sparkling clean; having a brand new look. ♦*She is such a good housekeeper that her kitchen is always spick-and-span.*

**spill one's guts** *v. phr.* To confess under interrogation; completely relate a story; name accomplices. ♦*After two hours of intensive interrogation the accused criminal spilled his guts, and led the police to the arrest of his fellow criminals.*

**spill the beans** *v. phr., informal* To tell a secret to someone who is not supposed to know about it. ♦*John's friends were going to have a surprise party for him, but Tom spilled the beans.*

**spin a yarn** *v. phr.* To tell a story of adventure with some exaggeration mixed in; embellish and protract such a tale. ♦*Uncle Fred, who used be a sailor, knows how to spin a fascinating yarn, but don't always believe everything he says.*

**spine-chilling** *adj.* Terrifying; causing great fear. ♦*Many children find the movie, "Frankenstein," spine-chilling.*

**spinoff** *n.* (stress on *spin*) A byproduct of something else. ♦*The television soap opera "Knot's Landing" was considered a spinoff of "Dallas," with many of the same characters featured in both.*

**spin off** *v. phr.* (stress on *off*) To bring something into existence as a byproduct of something that already exists. ♦*When Dr. Catwallender opened his medical practice, he also spun off a small dispensary beside it where patients could get their prescriptions filled.*

**spin one's wheels** *v. phr.* **1.** Said of cars stuck in snow or mud whose wheels are turning without the car moving forward. ♦*There was so much snow on the driveway that my car's wheels were spinning in it and we couldn't get going.* **2.** To exert effort in a job without making any progress. ♦*I've been working for the firm for two decades, but I feel I am merely spinning my wheels.*

**spin out** *v. phr.* **1.** To go out of control. ♦*The bus spun out on the icy road and fell into the ditch.* **2.** To make something go out of control. ♦*Tom stepped on the breaks so fast that he spun his car out of control and went off the road.*

**spirit away** *v. phr.* To hide or smuggle something out; abduct. ♦*The famous actress was spirited away by her bodyguards as soon as she emerged from the door.*

**spit** *or* **piss into the wedding cake** *v. phr., vulgar, avoidable* To spoil someone's pleasure or celebration by doing or saying something harsh or unseemly in an otherwise happy gathering; bring up depressing or unhappy subjects at a supposedly happy time. ♦ *Stuart really spit into the wedding cake when he told Burt in a bragging fashion that Lucy, Burt's bride, used to be his girlfriend.*

**spitting image** *n.* **spit and image** informal An exact likeness; a duplicate. ♦ *John is the spitting image of his grandfather.*

**spit up** *v.* To vomit a little. ♦ *The baby always spits up when he is burped.*

**split hairs** *v. phr.* To find and argue about small and unimportant differences as if the differences are important. ♦ *John is always splitting hairs; he often starts an argument about something small and unimportant.*

**split second** *n.* A very short time; less than a second. ♦ *The lightning flash lasted a split second, and then disappeared.*

**split the difference** *v. phr., informal* To settle a money disagreement by dividing the difference, each person giving up half. ♦ *Bob offered $25 for Bill's bicycle and Bill wanted $35; they split the difference.*

**split ticket** *n.* A vote for candidates from more than one party. ♦ *Mr. Jones voted a split ticket.*

**split up** *v. phr.* (stress on *up*) **1.** To separate; get a divorce. ♦ *After three years of marriage, the unhappy couple finally split up.* **2.** To separate something; divide into portions. ♦ *The brothers split up their father's fortune among themselves after his death.*

**split-up** *n.* (stress on *split*) A separation or division into two or many smaller parts. ♦ *The split-up of our company was due to the founder's untimely death.*

**spoil for** *v. phr.* To want something very badly; be belligerent or pugnacious about something. ♦ *After a few drinks it became embarrassingly evident that Hal was spoiling for a fight.*

**spoken for** *adj.* Occupied; reserved; taken; already engaged or married. ♦ *"Sorry, my boy," Mr. Jones said condescendingly, "but my daughter is already spoken for. She will marry Fred Wilcox next month."*

**sponge bath** *n.* A bath with a cloth or sponge and a little water. ♦ *During the drought the family had only sponge baths.*

**sponge on** *or* **off** *v. phr.* To exploit parasitically; depend upon for support. ♦ *He is already forty years old, but he refuses to go to work and sponges off his retired parents.*

**spoon-feed** *v.* **1.** To feed with a spoon. ♦ *Mothers spoon-feed their babies.* **2a.** To make something too easy for (a person). ♦ *Bill's mother spoon-fed him and never let him think for himself.* **2b.** To make (something) too easy for someone. ♦ *Some students want the teacher to spoon-feed the lessons.*

**sporting blood** *n.* Willingness to take risks; spirit of adventure. ♦ *The cowboy's sporting blood tempted him to try to ride the wild horse.*

**spot check** *n. phr.* A sample check or investigation. ♦ *Internal Revenue Service employees often conduct a spot check of individual returns when the figures don't add up.*

**spread it on thick** See LAY IT ON *or* LAY IT ON THICK.

**spread like wildfire** *v. phr.* To spread uncontrollably and rapidly. ♦ *Bad news has a tendency to spread like wildfire.*

**spread oneself too thin** *v. phr.* To try to do too many things at one time. ♦ *As the owner, chef, waiter, and dishwasher of his restaurant, Pierre was spreading himself too thin.*

**spring a leak** *v. phr.* **1.** To develop a hole (said of boats) through which water can enter, threatening the boat to sink. ♦ *When our small boat sprang a leak, we rapidly returned to shore to fix it.* **2.** To be threatened by some oncoming danger. ♦ *Our firm sprang a leak when the vice president suddenly died of a heart attack.*

**spring chicken** *n., slang* A young person.—Usually used with *no.* ♦ *Mr. Brown is no spring chicken, but he can still play tennis well.*

**spring on one** *v. phr.* To approach someone unexpectedly with an unpleasant idea or project. ♦ *Our firm was merely six weeks old when they sprang the news on me that I had to go to Algiers to open a new branch there.*

**spring up** *v. phr.* To arise suddenly. ♦ *Small purple flowers were springing up all over our backyard.*

**sprout wings** *v. phr.* **1.** To enter the stage after a period of development when wings appear (said of larvae that turn into butterflies). ◆ *The dragonflies suddenly sprouted wings and are flying all about in the park.* 2. To become good and virtuous (as if airborne). ◆ *Joe has helped many colleagues in need; he seems to have sprouted wings.*

**spruce up** *v., informal* To make clean or neat. ◆ *Mary spruced up the house before her company came.*

**square away** *v. phr.* 1. To arrange the sails of a ship so that the wind blows from behind. ◆ *The captain ordered the crew to square away and sail before the wind.* 2. *informal* To put right for use or action. Used in the passive or participle. ◆ *The living room was squared away for the guests.* 3. *informal* To stand ready to fight; put up your fists. ◆ *Jack and Lee squared away.*

**squared away** *adj. phr.* Looked after properly; tucked away; arranged. ◆ *My first two daughters are happily married, but my third one, Jennifer, isn't squared away yet.*

**square deal** *n. phr.* 1. Equitable or fair treatment. ◆ *We are proud to say that at this firm every employee gets a square deal.*

**square meal** *n. phr.* A full, nourishing well-balanced meal. ◆ *The refugees looked as if they hadn't had a square meal in months.*

**square off** *v. phr., informal* To stand ready for fighting with the fists. ◆ *The two boxers squared off when the bell rang.*

**square peg in a round hole** *n., informal* A person who does not fit into a job or position; someone who does not belong where he is. ◆ *Arthur is a square peg in a round hole when he is playing ball.*

**square up** *v. phr.* To liquidate debts and other obligations. ◆ *I want to square up my medical bills before I accept my new teaching assignment in Africa.*

**squeak by** *v. phr.* 1. To barely succeed. ◆ *He was so poorly prepared for his bar exam that he barely squeaked by.* 2. To clear with difficulty. ◆ *The entrance to the corridor in the old Italian castle was so narrow that I barely managed to squeak by it.*

**squeak through** *v., informal* To be successful but almost fail; win by a small

score. *Susan squeaked through the history examination.* ◆ *The football team squeaked through 7–6.*

**squeeze out of** *v. phr.* To apply pressure to someone in order to obtain what one desires. ◆ *The police were interrogating the suspect to squeeze information out of him.*

**stab in the back**[1] *v. phr., slang* To say or do something unfair that harms (a friend or someone who trusts you). ◆ *Owen stabbed his friend Max in the back by telling lies about him.*

**stab in the back**[2] *n. phr., slang* An act or a lie that hurts a friend or trusting person; a promise not kept, especially to a friend. ◆ *John stabbed his own friend in the back by stealing from his store.*

**stab in the dark** *n. phr.* A random attempt or guess at something without previous experience or knowledge of the subject. ◆ *"You're asking me who could have hidden grandpa's will," Fred said. "I really have no idea, but let me make a stab in the dark—I think my sister Hermione has it."*

**stack the cards** *v. phr.* 1. To arrange cards secretly and dishonestly for the purpose of cheating. ◆ *The gambler had stacked the cards against Bill.* 2. To arrange things unfairly for or against a person; have things so that a person has an unfair advantage or disadvantage; make sure in an unfair way that things will happen.—Used in the passive with "in one's favor" or "against one." ◆ *A tall basketball player has the cards stacked in his favor.*

**stack up against** *or* **stack up to** *v. phr.* To measure up to something similar; be comparable to something of a kindred nature. ◆ *We want to know how small American cars stack up against the German and Japanese competition.*

**stage fright** *n. phr.* The fear one feels before appearing in front of an audience. ◆ *Many famous actors and actresses admit that they often have stage fright before the curtain goes up.*

**stagestruck** *adj.* Desirous of becoming an actor or actress; enamored of the acting profession. ◆ *Milly is so stagestruck that she waits for actresses at the stage door after each performance to get their signatures.*

**stage whisper** *n. phr.* A loud whisper intended to reach other ears than those of the person(s) addressed. ♦ *Some jokes should be told in a stage whisper.*

**stake a claim** *v. phr.* **1.** To claim ownership of land by driving stakes to show boundaries. ♦ *The gold hunters staked claims in the West.* **2.** *informal* To claim a person or thing as your own by some sign. Usually used with *on.* ♦ *George staked a claim on Dianne by giving her his class ring.*

**stamping ground** *n., informal* A place where a person spends much of his time. ♦ *Pete's soda fountain is an after-school stamping ground.*

**stamp out** *v.* To destroy completely and make disappear. ♦ *In the last few years, we have nearly stamped out polio by using vaccine.*

**stand a chance** *or* **stand a show** *n. phr.* To have a possibility or opportunity; be likely to do or get something. ♦ *Fred doesn't stand a chance of being elected.*

**stand behind someone or something** *v. phr.* To firmly support morally or financially. ♦ *It is generally believed that corporate America stands behind the Republican Party.* ♦ *I stand behind what I said in court yesterday, no matter how strange it may sound.*

**standard time** *also* **slow time** *n.* Clock time that is set by law or agreement in a country or in part of a country; *especially, in the United States:* the clock time used between fall and spring, which is an hour slower than the time used in the summer.—Abbreviation **ST.** ♦ *When we go to bed Saturday night, we will set our clocks back an hour, because Sunday we will be on standard time again.*

**stand by** *v.* **1.** To be close beside or near. ♦ *Mary could not tell Jane the secret with her little brother standing by.* **2.** To be near, waiting to do something when needed. ♦ *The policeman in the patrol car radioed the station about the robbery, and then stood by for orders.* **3.** To follow or keep (one's promise). *He is a boy who always stands by his promises.* **4.** To be loyal to; support; help. *When three big boys attacked Bill, Ed stood by him.* ♦ *Some people blamed Harry when he got into trouble, but Joe stood by him.*

**stand down** *v. phr.* To stop being in a state of emergency. ♦ *After the danger had passed, the commanding general ordered the troops to stand down.*

**stand for** *v.* **1.** To be a sign of; make you think of; mean. ♦ *The letters "U.S.A." stand for "United States of America."* ♦ *The written sign "=" in an arithmetic problem stands for "equals."* **2.** To speak in favor of something, or show that you support it. ♦ *The new president stood for honest government.* **3.** *Chiefly British* To try to be elected for. ♦ *Three men from London are standing for Parliament.* **4.** *informal* To allow to happen or to be done; permit.— Usually used in the negative. ♦ *The teacher will not stand for fooling in the classroom.*

**stand in awe of** *v. phr.* To look upon with wonder; feel very respectful to. ♦ *The soldier stood in awe to his officers.*

**stand in for** *v. phr.* To substitute for someone. ♦ *The famous brain surgeon was called out of town so his assistant had to stand in for him during the operation.*

**standing ovation** *n. phr.* Loud and prolonged applause given to a performer in a theater or concert hall, during which the audience stands up out of respect and admiration. ♦ *The world-famous violinist got a standing ovation in Chicago's Symphony Center after she played all of Beethoven's violin sonatas.*

**stand in with** *v. phr., informal* To be liked by or friendly with.—Usually used with *well.* ♦ *John stands in well with the teacher.*

**stand off** *v.* (stress on *off*) **1.** To stay at a distance; stay apart. ♦ *At parties, Mr. Jones goes around talking to everyone, but Mrs. Jones is shy and stands off.* **2.** To keep (someone or something) from coming near or winning. ♦ *The other schools wanted to beat our team and win the championship, but our boys stood them all off.*

**standoffish** *adj.* Stiff; aloof; reserved in manner. ♦ *The famous chess player is hard to get to know because he is so standoffish.*

**stand on ceremony** *v. phr.* To follow strict rules of politeness; be very formal with other people. Used with a helping verb in the negative. ♦*Grandmother does not stand on ceremony when her grandchildren call.*

**stand one in good stead** *v. phr.* To be helpful or useful to. ♦*Julia knew how to typewrite, and that stood her in good stead when she looked for a job.*

**stand one's ground** *also* **hold one's ground** *v. phr.* **1.** To stay and fight instead of running away. ♦*The enemy attacked in great numbers but our men stood their ground.* **2.** To defend a belief or statement; refuse to weaken when opposed; insist you are right. ♦*John's friends said he was mistaken but he stood his ground.*

**stand one up** *v. phr.* To fail to show up at a specific place and time agreed upon for a date. ♦*Poor Ted was stood up by his fickle girlfriend, Suzie, so he had a drink and went to the movies by himself.*

**stand on one's own feet** *or* **stand on one's own two feet** *v. phr.* To depend on yourself; do things yourself; earn your own living; be independent. ♦*You should learn to stand on your own two feet.*

**stand out** *v.* **1.** To go farther out than a nearby surface; project. ♦*A mole stood out on her cheek.* **2.** To be more noticeable in some way than those around you; be higher, bigger, or better. ♦*Fred was very tall and stood out in the crowd.*

**stand pat** *v., informal* To be satisfied with things and be against a change. ♦*Bill had made up his mind on the question and when his friends tried to change his mind, he stood pat.*

**stand the gaff** *v. phr., informal* To stand rough treatment; do well in spite of great physical or mental hardship. ♦*An athlete must learn to stand the gaff.*

**stand the pace** *or* **stay the pace** *or* **stand the course** *or* **stand the pace** *v. phr.* To be able to endure difficult work, tiring living conditions, etc. ♦*We will hire John but we are a little concerned about whether he will be able to stand the pace at this factory, because we must work harder than the competition.* ♦*Many young army recruits can't stay the pace during basic training, and decide to quit.*

**stand to reason** *v. phr.* To seem very likely from the known facts. ♦*Joe is intelligent and studies hard; it stands to reason that he will pass the examination.*

**stand trial** *v. phr.* To submit to a trial by court. ♦*The case has been postponed and he may not have to stand trial until next April.*

**stand up** *v.* **1.** To be strong enough to use hard or for a long time. ♦*A rocket must be built strongly to stand up under the blast-off.* **2.** *informal* To make a date and then fail to keep it. ♦*June cried when Bill stood her up on their first date.*

**stand up and be counted** *v. phr.* To be willing to say what you think in public; let people know that you are for or against something. ♦*The equal rights movement needs people who are willing to stand up and be counted.*

**stand-up comic** *n. phr.* A performer, male or female, who entertains the audience with funny stories and jokes often making fun of recent events and politics, whether in a theater or on television. ♦*Jay Leno is one of America's best-known stand-up comics.*

**stand up for** *or informal* **stick up for** *v.* To defend against attack; fight for. ♦*John always stands up for his rights.*

**stand up to** *v.* To meet with courage. ♦*Mary stood up to the snarling dog that leaped toward her.*

**stand up with** *v., informal* To be best man or maid of honor at a wedding. ♦*A groom often chooses his brother to stand up with him.*

**stare in the face** *n. phr.* **1.** To be about to meet or to happen to (you.) ♦*Grandmother became very sick and death was staring her in the face.* **2.** To be easy to see; be plain. ♦*Are you looking for your pencil? It's on your desk, staring you in the face.*

**starry-eyed** *adj. phr.* Naïve; credulous; idealistic. ♦*"I am worried about Mary's going to New York alone," her mother said to her father., "She is just a starry-eyed romantic who may be in for a rude awakening when she confronts the realities of life in the big city."*

**Stars and Stripes** *n. phr.* The flag of the United States; a symbol of America; America herself. ♦*John is extremely* *patriotic; he is ready to do anything for the Stars and Stripes.*

**stars in one's eyes** *n. phr.* **1.** An appearance or feeling of very great happiness or expectation of happiness. ◆ *Mary gets stars in her eyes when she thinks of her boyfriend.* **2.** A belief in the possibility of quick and lasting reforms in people and life and an eagerness to make such changes. ◆ *Some inexperienced people get stars in their eyes when they think of improving the world.—*starry-eyed *adj.* Very happy and excited, perhaps with little reason; eager and self-confident about improving human nature and general conditions of life. ◆ *Young people are often starry-eyed and eager to improve the world; they do not know how hard it is.*

**start from scratch** See FROM SCRATCH.

**start in** *v., informal* **1.** To begin to do something; start. ◆ *Fred started in weeding the garden. The family started in eating supper.* **2.** To begin a career. ◆ *Bob started in as an office boy and became president.* **3.** To give a first job to. ◆ *The bank started him in as a clerk.*

**start off on the right foot** *v. phr.* To have a good start; be well liked; make a positive impression. ◆ *Jack got off on the right foot in the hospital as an intern by volunteering to help in the Emergency Room.*

**start off on the wrong foot** *v. phr.* To have a bad start to a relationship. ◆ *"I know we started off on the wrong foot, because I wanted to take you to bed right away," Jack said to Suzie, "but I really love you a lot. Could you please give me another chance?"*

**start out** *v.* **1.** To begin to go somewhere. *Bill started out for school on his bicycle.* ◆ *Art started out on a voyage around the world.* **2.** To begin a career or life. *Harry started out as an errand boy in a business office.* **3.** *informal* To give one a first job. ◆ *The garage man started Pete out as a grease rack man.*

**start something** *v. phr., informal* To make trouble; cause a quarrel or fight. ◆ *Jack likes to play tricks on the other boys to start something.*

**start the ball rolling** See GET THE BALL ROLLING.

**start up** *v.* **1.** To begin operating. ◆ *The driver started up the motor of the car.* **2.** To begin to play (music). ◆ *The conductor waved his baton, and the band started up.* **3.** To rise or stand suddenly. ◆ *When he heard the bell, he started up from his chair.*

**stash bag** *or* **stuff bag** *n., slang, informal* **1.** A small bag containing marijuana cigarettes or the ingredients for making them. ◆ *The police are holding John because they found a stash bag full of the stuff on him.* **2.** Any small bag resembling a stash bag used for small personal items such as lipstick, driver's license, etc. ◆ *Do you have any room for my keys in your stash bag?*

**state-of-the-art** *adj. phr.* The best and the latest any field of research can offer; modern; the latest; the most advanced. ◆ *State-of-the-art personal computers may cost a little more than older models, but may be worth the cost for those who need them.*

**status symbol** *n. phr.* Signs of wealth and prestige. ◆ *A new yacht or airplane might be a status symbol to a bank manager.*

**stave off** *v., literary* To keep from touching or hurting you. ◆ *They staved off starvation by eating two of the sled dogs.*

**stay in** *v. phr.* To remain at home. ◆ *The weather was so bad that we decided to stay in all day.*

**stay in touch** See IN TOUCH. Contrast OUT OF TOUCH.

**stay out** *v. phr.* To stay away from home. ◆ *Her father was very upset because Mary stayed out until 3 A.M. last night.*

**stay put** *v. phr.* To stay in place; not leave. ◆ *Harry's father told him to stay put until he came back.*

**stay the course** *or* **stay the pace** See STAND THE PACE.

**stay up late** *v. phr.* To not go to bed until very late. ◆ *Peter has to stay up late these days as he is preparing for his comprehensive exams.*

**steal a march on** *v. phr.* To get ahead of someone by doing a thing unnoticed; get an advantage over. ◆ *The army stole a march on the enemy by marching at night and attacking them in the morning.*

**steal away** See SLIP AWAY.

**steal one's thunder** *v. phr.* To do or say something, intentionally or not, that another person has planned to say or do. ♦ *Fred intended to nominate Bill for president, but John got up first and stole Fred's thunder.*

**steal the show** *v. phr.* To act or do so well in a performance that you get most of the attention and the other performers are unnoticed. ♦ *Mary was in only one scene of the play, but she stole the show from the stars.*

**steal the spotlight** *v. phr.* To attract attention away from a person or thing that people should be watching. ♦ *When the maid walked on the stage and tripped over a rug, she stole the spotlight from the leading players.*

**steal up on** *v. phr.* To stealthily approach one; sneak up on someone. ♦ *The thief stole up on his victim, snatched her purse, and ran away.*

**steamed up** *adj., informal* Excited or angry about or eager to do something. ♦ *The coach gave the team a pep talk before the game, and he got them all steamed up to win the game.*

**steer clear of** *v.* 1. To steer a safe distance from; go around without touching. ♦ *A ship steers clear of a rocky shore in stormy weather.* 2. *informal* To stay away from; keep from going near. ♦ *Fred was angry at Bill, and Bill was steering clear of him.*

**steer one straight** *v. phr.* To give someone sensible advice, helping him or her to make the right choices. ♦ *The local minister steered many gang members straight by persuading them not to do drugs and to return to school.*

**stem the tide** *v. phr.* To resist; hold back something of great pressure or strength. ♦ *The way to stem the tide of juvenile delinquency is to strengthen education and to pass a stiff gun control law.*

**step all over** See WALK OVER.

**step by step** *adv. phr.* Gradually; little by little. ♦ *Step by step everyone can learn how to use a computer, no matter how old they are.*

**step down** *v.* 1. To come down in one move from a higher position to a lower. ♦ *As soon as the train stopped, the conductor stepped down to help the passengers off.* 2. To make go slower little by little. ♦ *The train was approaching the station, so the engineer stepped it down.* 3. To leave a job as an

official or some other important position. ♦ *When the judge became ill, he had to step down.*

**step in** *v.* 1. To go inside for a quick visit. ♦ *It was a cold night, and when the policeman passed, we invited him to step in for a cup of coffee.* 2. To begin to take part in a continuing action or discussion, especially without being asked. ♦ *When the dogs began to fight, John stepped in to stop it before they were hurt.*

**step inside** *v.* To come or go inside. ♦ *Mother invited the callers to step inside.*

**step into** *v.* 1. To come or go into. ♦ *The taxi stopped, and we stepped into it.* 2. To begin to do, undertake. *When the star became sick, his understudy stepped into his part.*

**step into one's shoes** *v. phr.* To do what someone else usually does after he has stopped doing it. ♦ *When Bill's father died, Bill had to step into his father's shoes to support his mother.*

**step off** *v.* 1. To walk or march quickly. ♦ *The drum major lowered his baton and the band stepped off.* 2. *or* **pace off.** To measure by taking a series of steps in a line. ♦ *The farmer stepped off the edge of the field to see how much fencing he would need.*

**step on it** *or* **step on the gas** *v. phr.* 1. To push down on the gas pedal to make a car go faster. ♦ *Be very careful when you step on the gas. Don't go too fast.* 2. *informal* To go faster; hurry. ♦ *Step on it, or we'll be late for school.*

**step on one's toes** *or* **tread on one's toes** *v. phr.* To do something that embarrasses or offends someone else. ♦ *If you break in when other people are talking, you may step on their toes.* ♦ *Mary is pretty, and she often treads on the toes of the girls by stealing their boyfriend.*

**step out** *v. phr.* 1. To go out, particularly socially, as on a date. ♦ *Paul said to Sylvia, "You look so dressed up tonight—you must be stepping out, eh?"* 2. To leave for a short period during the work day to go to the lavatory or to get a cup of coffee. ♦ *"May I speak to Mr. Kotz?" Roy asked. "I'm sorry, sir. He just stepped out for a minute," the secretary answered.*

**step out on** *v. phr.* To be unfaithful to one's marriage partner or steady lover. ♦ *It is rumored that he has been stepping out on his wife. That's why she's so upset.*

**stepped up** *adj.* Carried on at a faster or more active rate; increased. ♦ *To fill the increase in orders, the factory had to operate at a stepped-up rate.*

**step up** *v.* **1.** To go from a lower to a higher place. ♦ *John stepped up onto the platform and began to speak.* **2.** To come towards or near; approach. ♦ *The sergeant called for volunteers and Private Jones stepped up to volunteer.* **3.** To go or to make (something) go faster or more actively. ♦ *When John found he was going to be late, he stepped up his pace.* **4.** To rise to a higher or more important position; be promoted. ♦ *This year Mary is secretary of the club, but I am sure she will step up to president next year.*

**step up to the plate** *v. phr. from baseball* To face a challenge, to shoulder a responsibility. ♦ *Eventually both the Palestinians and the Israelis will have to step up to the plate and start working in earnest on a viable peace plan.*

**sterling character** *n. phr.* A person of irreproachable character; one of the highest professional standards. ♦ *The nominee for the Supreme Court must be a sterling character in every possible way.*

**stew in one's own juice** *v. phr., informal* To suffer from something that you have caused to happen yourself. ♦ *I warned you not to steal those apples. You got caught, and you can stew in your own juice.*

**stick around** *v., informal* To stay or wait nearby. ♦ *John's father told him to stick around and they would go fishing.*

**stick by one** *v. phr.* To support; remain loyal to. ♦ *All of Peter's friends stuck by him faithfully, in spite of what has been said about him in the press.*

**stick in one's throat** *v. phr.* To be something you do not want to say; be hard to say. ♦ *Jean wanted to ask the teacher's pardon, but the words stuck in her throat.*

**stick-in-the-mud** *n., informal* An overcareful person; someone who is old-fashioned and fights change. ♦ *Mabel said her mother was a real stick-in-the-mud to make a rule that she must be home by 10 o'clock on weeknights and 11:30 Saturdays.*

**stick one's neck out** *or* **stick one's chin out** *v. phr., informal* To do something dangerous or risky. ♦ *When I was in trouble, Paul was the only one who would stick his neck out to help me.* ♦ *John is always sticking his chin out by saying something he shouldn't.*

**stick one's nose into** See NOSE INTO.

**stick out** *v.* **1a.** To stand out from a wall or other surface; project; extend. ♦ *The limb stuck out from the trunk of the tree.* **1b.** To be seen or noticed more easily or quickly than others; be noticeable. ♦ *My house is the only brick one on the street. It sticks out and you can't miss it.* **1c.** Often used in the informal phrase *stick out like a sore thumb.* ♦ *John is so shy and awkward that he sticks out like a sore thumb.* **2.** *informal* To keep on doing something until it is done no matter how long, hard, or unpleasant. ♦ *Mathematics is hard, but if you stick it out you will understand it.*

**stick out like a sore thumb** *v. phr.* To be conspicuous; be different from the rest. ♦ *When the foreign student was placed in an advanced English grammar class by mistake, it was no wonder that he stuck out like a sore thumb.*

**stick to** *v. phr.* To adhere to; obey; follow. ♦ *John stuck to his original decision to become a doctor.* ♦ *If you make a promise, stick to your word, and don't let your friends down.*

**stick together** *v.* To remain close together in a situation. ♦ *Stick together in the cave so that no one gets lost.*

**stick to one's guns** *or* **stand by one's guns** *v. phr.* To hold to an aim or an opinion even though people try to stop you or say you are wrong. ♦ *People laughed at Columbus when he said the world was round. He stuck to his guns and proved he was right.*

**stick to one's ribs** *or* **stick to the ribs** *v. phr., informal* To keep you from getting hungry again too quickly. ♦ *Doctors say you should eat a good breakfast that sticks to your ribs.*

**stick to the point** *v. phr.* To stay on course during a discussion; adhere to the topic; not talk about extraneous matters. ♦ *Stick to the point and stop telling us your life history!*

**stick up** *v., informal* (stess on *up*) To rob with a gun. ♦ *In the old West, outlaws sometimes stuck up the stagecoaches.*

**stick-up** *n., informal* (stress on *stick*) A robbery by a man with a gun. ♦ *Mr. Smith was the victim of a stick-up last night.*

**stick with** *v., informal* **1.** *or* **stay with** To continue doing; not quit. ♦ *Fred stayed with his homework until it was done.* **2.** To stay with; not leave. ♦ *Stick with me until we get out of the crowd.* **3.** To sell (someone) something poor or worthless; cheat. ♦ *Father said that the man in the store tried to stick him with a bad TV set.* **4.** To leave (someone) with (something unpleasant); force to do or keep something because others cannot or will not.—Used in the passive. ♦ *Mr. Jones bought a house that is too big and expensive, but now he's stuck with it.*

**stick with** *v. phr.* To unfairly thrust upon; encumber one with. ♦ *In the restaurant my friends stuck me with the bill although it was supposed to be Dutch treat.*

**sticky fingers** *n. phr., slang* **1.** The habit of stealing things you see and want. ♦ *Don't leave money in your locker; some of the boys have sticky fingers.*

**still life** *n. phr.* A term used by artists to describe a motionless picture of a bowl of fruit, flowers, etc. ♦ *One of van Gogh's most famous still lifes is a vase of yellow flowers.*

**still waters run deep** Quiet people probably are profound thinkers.—A proverb. ♦ *He doesn't say much, but he sure looks smart. Well, still waters run deep, isn't that true?*

**stir up** *v.* **1.** To bring (something) into being, often by great exertion or activity; cause. ♦ *It was a quiet afternoon, and John tried to stir up some excitement.* **2.** To cause (someone) to act; incite to action or movement; rouse. ♦ *The coach's pep talk stirred up the team to win.*

**stir up a hornet's nest** *v. phr.* To make many people angry; do something that many people don't like. ♦ *The principal stirred up a hornet's nest by changing the rules at school.*

**stock-in-trade** *n. phr.* The materials which one customarily deals, sells, or offers. ♦ *Imported silk blouses from the Orient are the stock-in-trade of their small shop.*

**stone-blind** *adj. phr.* **1.** Completely blind. ♦ *Poor Al is stone-blind and needs help to get across the street carefully.*

**stone-broke** *or* **dead broke** *or* **flat broke** *adj., informal* having no money; penniless. ♦ *Jill wanted to go to the movies but she was stone-broke.* ♦ *The man gambled and was soon flat broke.*

**stone-cold** *adj.* Having no warmth; completely cold.—Used to describe things that are better when warm. ♦ *The boys who got up late found their breakfast stone-cold.*

**stone-dead** *adj., informal* Showing no signs of life; completely dead. ♦ *Barry tried to revive the frozen robin but it was stone-dead.*

**stone-deaf** *adj. phr.* Completely deaf. ♦ *Sam is stone-deaf so let him read your lips if you know no sign language.*

**stone's throw** *or* **within a stone's throw** *adv. phr.* Within a very short distance. ♦ *They live across the street from us, just within a stone's throw.*

**stone wall** *or* **brick wall** *n. phr.* Something hard to overcome; an idea or belief that is hard to change. ♦ *The students ran into a brick wall when they asked the principal to put off the examination.*

**stool pigeon** *n.* A criminal who informs on his associates. ♦ *The detective was able to solve the crime mainly through information obtained from a stool pigeon.*

**stop and go** *adj. phr.* Congested; almost standing still. ♦ *Traffic on the Kennedy Expressway can be stop and go on weekends; if you want to get to O'Hare Airport on time, you had better leave an hour early.*

**stop at nothing** *v. phr.* To be unscrupulous. ♦ *Al will stop at nothing to get Nancy to go out with him.*

**stop cold** *or* **stop dead** *or* **stop in one's tracks** *v. phr., informal* To stop very quickly or with great force. ♦ *The hunter pulled the trigger and stopped the deer cold.* ♦ *When I saw Mary on the street, I was so surprised I stopped dead.* ♦ *The deer heard a noise and he stopped in his tracks.*

**stop-gap** See QUICK FIX.

**stop off** *v.* To stop at a place for a short time while going somewhere. ♦ *We stopped off after school at the soda fountain before going home.*

**stop over** *v.* To stay at a place overnight or for some other short time while on a trip elsewhere. ♦ *When we came back from California, we stopped over one night near the Grand Canyon.*

**stop short** *v. phr.* To suddenly stop. ♦ *Jake stopped short when he heard somebody yell out his name loud but there was no one in sight.*

**stop street** *n.* A street where cars must come to a full stop before crossing another street. *Johnny was late because he traveled on a stop street.*

**stop the show** *v. phr.* To elicit such a strong applause from the audience that the show is interrupted. ♦ *Pavarotti's rendition of "O sole mio" always stops the show.*

**stop up** *v. phr.* To block; close. ♦ *If you want to get rid of the leak, you must stop up the two holes you have in the ceiling.*

**storm in a teacup** *or* **storm in a spittoon** *n. phr.* An insignificant, trifling, local affair that isn't worth noticing, let alone getting involved in. ♦ *The Winnetka Ladies' Poetry Club Contest turned into a storm in teacup.* ♦ *The arm-wrestling match in the local bar became a storm in a spittoon.*

**storm off** *or* **storm out of** *v. phr.* To leave suddenly and in anger as if demonstrating one's anger and dissatisfaction. ♦ *Suzie stormed out of the room when Tom finally confessed that he wasn't seriously interested in marriage and starting a family.*

**stow away** *v.* **1.** *informal* To pack or store away. ♦ *After New Year's Day the Christmas decorations were stowed away until another season.* **2.** To hide on a ship or another kind of transportation to get a free ride. ♦ *John ran away from home and stowed away on a freighter going to Jamaica.*

**straighten out** *v.* To correct a mistake; make you realize you are wrong. ♦ *The teacher saw Jim's awkward sentence on the board and asked for volunteers to straighten it out.*

**straighten up** *v.* To put in order; make neat. ♦ *Vic had to straighten up his room before he could go swimming.*

**straight face** *n.* A face that is not laughing or smiling. ♦ *It is hard to tell when Jim is teasing you. He can tell a fib with a straight face.*

**straight from the horse's mouth** *slang* Directly from the person or place where it began; from a reliable source or a person that cannot be doubted. ♦ *They are going to be married. I got the news straight from the horse's mouth—their minister.*

**straight from the shoulder** *adv. phr., informal* In an open and honest way of speaking; without holding back anything because of fear or politeness or respect for someone's feelings; frankly. ♦ *John asked what he had done wrong. Bob told him straight from the shoulder.*

**straightlaced** *adj.* Of very strict morals and manners. ♦ *She is so straightlaced that she won't even go out with a man unless she senses that he is serious about her.*

**straight off** *adv. phr.* At once; immediately. ♦ *After school is over, you come home straight off, and don't waste time.*

**straight off the reel** *adv. phr.* Uninterruptedly; without stopping. ♦ *To play sixteen sets of tennis in one weekend straight off the reel can be too much of a good thing, leading to exhaustion.*

**straight shooters** See SHOOT STRAIGHT.

**straight ticket** *n.* A vote for all the candidates of a single party. ♦ *Uncle Fred was a loyal member of his party. He always voted the straight ticket.*

**strain at a gnat** *v. phr.* To make a big deal of facing a relatively minor challenge, especially after having dealt with bigger, more difficult issues. ♦ *"Man, you have climbed Mount Everest, and you're huffing and puffing because we're climbing a little hill?" the tour guide said to the famous explorer. "Your attitude is a classical case of straining at a gnat!"*

**strange to say** *adv. phr.* Not what you might think; surprisingly.—Used for emphasis. ♦ *Strange to say, Jerry doesn't like candy.*

**strapped for** *adj.* Broke; out of funds. ♦ *My brother is so extravagant that he is always strapped for cash.*

**straw in the wind** *n. phr.* A small sign of what may happen. ♦ *The doctor's worried face was a straw in the wind.*

**straw poll** *n. phr.* An informal survey taken in order to get an opinion. ♦ *The results of our straw poll show that most faculty members prefer to teach between 9 and 11 A.M.*

**straw that breaks the camel's back** See LAST STRAW.

**stretch a point** *or* **strain a point** *v. phr.* To permit something different or more than usual; not tell the exact truth or make an exception. ♦ *It's straining a point to call Joe a hero just because he saved the kitten from drowning in the bathtub.*

**stretched too thin** See SPREAD ONESELF TOO THIN.

**stretch of the imagination** *n. phr.* Imaginative attempt or effort. ♦ *By no stretch of the imagination can I see Al as a successful lawyer.*

**stretch one's legs** *v. phr.* To go for a walk. ♦ *After having sat all day at the computer, I decided to go and stretch my legs in the park.*

**strike a bargain** *v. phr.* To arrive at a price satisfactory to both the buyer and the seller. ♦ *After a great deal of haggling, they managed to strike a bargain.*

**strike a chord** *v. phr.* To find oneself in agreement with someone else's feelings and ideas. ♦ *John's proposal to expand the firm's foreign trade struck a chord with the vice president, who had been thinking along similar lines on his own.*

**strike a happy medium** *v. phr.* To find an answer to a problem that is half-way between two unsatisfactory answers. ♦ *Two teaspoons of sugar made the cup of coffee too sweet, and one not sweet enough. One heaping teaspoon struck a happy medium.*

**strikebreaker** *n.* One who takes the place of workers on strike or one who recruits such people. ♦ *The striking workers threw rotten eggs at the strikebreakers.*

**strike gold** *v. phr.* **1.** To find gold. ♦ *Ted struck gold near an abandoned mine in California.* **2.** To find suddenly the answer to an old puzzle. ♦ *Professor Brown's assistant struck gold when he came up with an equation that explained the irregular motions of a double star.*

**strike it rich** *v. phr., informal* **1.** To discover oil, or a large vein of minerals to be mined, or a buried treasure. ♦ *The old prospector panned gold for years before he struck it rich.* **2.** To become rich or successful suddenly or without expecting to. ♦ *John did not know that he had a rich Uncle John in Australia. John struck it rich when his uncle left his money to John.*

**strike one funny** *v. phr.* To appear or seem laughable, curious, ironic, or entertaining. ♦ *"It strikes me funny," he said, "that you should refuse my invitation to visit my chateau in France. After all, you love both red wine and old castles."*

**strike one's fancy** *v. phr.* To please one's predilections; appeal to one. ♦ *The red tie with the yellow dragon on it happened to strike my fancy, so I bought it.*

**strike** *or* **hit a sour note** *v. phr.* To spoil the mood at a gathering by hearing some bad news. ♦ *The news of Mr. Brown's sudden illness struck a sour note during our New Year's Eve party.*

**strike out** *v.* **1.** To destroy something that has been written or drawn by drawing a line or cross through it or by erasing it. ♦ *John misspelled "corollary." He struck it out and wrote it correctly.* **2.** To begin to follow a new path or a course of action that you have never tried. ♦ *The boy scouts struck out at daybreak over the mountain pass.* **3.** To put (a batter) out of play by making him miss the ball three times; *also:* To be put out of play by missing the ball three times. ♦ *The pitcher struck out three men in the game.*

**strike out at** *v. phr.* To attack someone verbally or physically. ♦ *She was so angry that she struck out at him every occasion she got.*

**strike the hour** *v. phr.* To mark or toll the hour (said of clocks or bells). ♦ *We heard the church clock strike the hour of two.*

**strike up** *v.* **1a.** To start to sing or play. ♦ *The President took his place on the platform, and the band struck up the national anthem.* **1b.** To give a signal to start (a band) playing. ♦ *When the team ran on the field, the band director struck up the band.* **2.** To bring about; begin; start. ♦ *It did not take Mary long* to strike up acquaintances in her new school.

**strike up a conversation** v. phr. To start talking to someone for the first time, as on a train, a bus, an airplane, etc. ♦ *"How did you two meet?" Aunt Matilda asked the happy couple on their twenty-fifth wedding anniversary. "You won't believe this," they said, "but we struck up a conversation on a flight from New York to Chicago."*

**strike while the iron is hot** See MAKE HAY WHILE THE SUN SHINES.

**string along** v., informal **1.** To deceive; fool; lead on dishonestly. ♦ *Mary was stringing John along for years but she didn't mean to marry him.* **2.** To follow someone's leadership; join his group. ♦ *Those of you who want to learn about wild flowers, string along with Jake.*

**string out** v. To make (something) extend over a great distance or a long stretch of time. ♦ *The city and county needed to string out the telephone poles for several miles.*

**strings attached** adv. phr. With some special proviso or condition that is a handicap. ♦ *John inherited a large fortune but with the string attached that he could not touch a penny of it before his 28th birthday.*

**stroke of luck** See RUN OF LUCK.

**strong language** n. phr. Cursing; swearing. ♦ *When Ned learned that he had been fired, he used some very strong language about his boss.*

**strung out** adj., slang, colloquial **1.** Nervous, jittery, jumpy; generally ill because of drug use or withdrawal symptoms. ♦ *The only explanation I can think of for Max's behavior is that he must be strung out.* **2.** To suffer because of a lack of something previously accustomed to, such as the love and affection of someone. ♦ *Sue is all strung out for Jim; they've just split up.*

**stubborn as a mule** See PIGHEADED.

**stuck on** slang Very much in love with; crazy about. ♦ *Judy thinks she is very pretty and very smart. She is stuck on herself.* ♦ *Lucy is stuck on the football captain.*

**stuck-up** adj., informal Acting as if other people are not as good as you are; conceited; snobbish. ♦ *Mary is very stuck-up, and will not speak to the poor children in her class.*

**stuck with** adj. phr. Left in a predicament; left having to take care of a problem caused by another. ♦ *Our neighbors vanished without a trace and we got stuck with their cat and dog.*

**stuff and nonsense** n. Foolish or empty writing or talk; nonsense. ♦ *When Jane said she was too sick to go to school, her mother answered, "Stuff and nonsense! I know there's a test today."*

**stuff one's face** v. phr. To eat an inordinate amount of food with great vigor and speed. ♦ *Tim will never be less obese if he keeps stuffing his face like this every time he sees food on the table.*

**stuff the ballot box** v. phr. To give more votes to a candidate in an election than there are people who actually voted for him. ♦ *It is a crime to stuff the ballot box.*—**ballot-stuffing** adj. phr.

**stuffed shirt** n. phr. A pretentious bore; a pompous, empty person. ♦ *I think that Howard is a terrible stuffed shirt with no sense of humor.*

**stuffed up** adj. phr. Impeded; blocked. ♦ *Our kitchen sink is all stuffed up so I have to call the plumber.*

**stumble across** v. phr. To encounter a person or thing, mostly by accident. ♦ *I gave up looking for my old hat when I accidentally stumbled across it in a dark corner of the closet.*

**subject to** adj. phr. **1.** Under the government or control of; in the power of. ♦ *The English colonies in America were subject to the English king.* **2.** Likely to get or have; liable. ♦ *John is in rather poor health and is subject to colds.* **3.** Depending on some change, happening, or need. ♦ *Agreements made by the President with other countries are subject to the approval of the Senate.*

**such as** conj. **1.** Of a kind or amount shown or named; of a kind like. ♦ *Many different pies were in the bakery such as apple, cherry, and blueberry pies.* **2.** Of the average or ordinary kind; poor; humble. ♦ *Such as the food was, there was plenty of it.*

**such as it is** Just as it appears or is presented, not being any better or worse than most others of its kind; being average or mediocre. ♦ *Jane told her parents her grades, such as they were.*

**such that** *conj.* Of a kind or amount that; so great or so little that; enough that. ♦*Jimmy made such noise that his sister told him to be quiet.*

**sucker list** *n., slang* A list of easily fooled people, especially people who are easily persuaded to buy things or give money. ♦*The crook got hold of a sucker list and started out to sell his worthless stock.*

**suck in** *v.* **1.** *informal* To pull in by taking a deep breath and tightening the muscles; flatten. ♦*"Suck in those abdominal muscles," the gym teacher said.* **2.** *slang* To make a fool of; cheat. ♦*The uneducated farmer was sucked in by a clever crook.*

**suck up to** See SHINE UP TO.

**sugarcoat the pill** See GILD THE PILL.

**sugar daddy** *n., slang, semi-vulgar, avoidable* An older, well-to-do man, who gives money and gifts to a younger woman or girls usually in exchange for sexual favors. ♦*Betty Morgan got a mink coat from her sugar daddy.*

**suit up** *v. phr.* To don a uniform or sports outfit. ♦*The veterans like to suit up for the Fourth of July parade.*

**suit yourself** *v. phr., informal* To do what one likes or prefers. ♦*"I don't care where you want to sleep," he said. "Suit yourself!"*

**sum total** *n.* The final amount; everything taken together; total. ♦*The sum total of expenses for the trip was $450.*

**sum up** *v.* To put something into a few words; shorten into a brief summary; summarize. ♦*The teacher summed up the lesson in three rules.*

**sunbelt** *n., informal* A portion of the southern United States where the winter is very mild in comparison to other states. ♦*The Simpsons left Chicago for the sunbelt because of Jeff's rheumatism.*

**sunny-side up** *adj.* Fried on one side only. ♦*Barbara likes her eggs sunny-side up.*

**sure enough** *adv.* As expected. ♦*Charles was afraid he had done badly on the test, and sure enough, his grade was failing.*

**surefire** *adj.* Without fail; effective; bringing actual results. ♦*During a campaign the only surefire way to get the sympathy of the voters is to mingle with them in person.*

**sure thing 1.** *n., informal* Something sure to happen; something about which there is no doubt. ♦*It's no fun betting on a sure thing.*—**sure thing 2.** *adv.* Of course; certainly. ♦*Sure thing, I'll be glad to do it for you.*

**surf the Web** *v. phr.* To look through information on the Internet. ♦*John can find answers for most of your questions; he can surf the Web like a professional.*

**survival of the fittest** *n. phr.* The staying alive or in action of the best prepared; often: idea that those living things best able to adjust to life survive and those unable to adjust die out. ♦*With changes in the world's climate, dinosaurs died but many smaller animals lived on. It was survival of the fittest.*

**swallow one's pride** *v. phr.* To bring your pride under control; humble yourself. ♦*After Bill lost the race, he swallowed his pride and shook hands with the winner.*

**swallow one's words 1.** To speak unclearly; fail to put enough breath into your words. ♦*Phyllis was hard to understand because she swallowed her words.* **2.** See EAT ONE'S WORDS.

**swallow up** *v. phr.* To do away with; absorb; engulf. ♦*My expenses are so great that they swallow up my modest salary.*

**swan song** *n. phr., literary* A farewell or last appearance. ♦*The famous soprano gave her swan song in* La Traviata *before she retired.*

**swat team** *n., informal* Police unit trained for especially hazardous or sensitive law-enforcement assignments; short for Special Weapons and Tactics. ♦*Joe made the SWAT team of the NYPD due to his athletic skills.*

**swear by** *v.* **1.** To use as the support or authority that what you are saying is truthful; take an oath upon. ♦*A witness swears by the Bible that he will tell the truth.* **2.** To have complete confidence in; be sure of; trust completely. ♦*We can be sure that Fred will come on time, since his friend Tom swears by him.*

**swear in *or* swear into** *v.* To have a person swear or promise to do his duty as a member or an officer of an organization, government department, or similar group.—*Swear into* is used when the name of the group is given. ♦*At the inau-*

guration, the Chief Justice of the Supreme Court swears in the new president.

**swear off** v., informal To give up something you like or you have got in the habit of using by making a promise. ♦ Mary swore off candy until she lost ten pounds.

**swear out** v. To get (a written order to do something) by swearing that a person has broken the law. ♦ The police swore out a warrant for the suspect's arrest.

**sweat blood** v. phr., slang 1. To be very much worried. ♦ The engine of the airplane stopped, and the pilot sweated blood as he glided to a safe landing. 2. To work very hard. ♦ Jim sweated blood to finish his composition on time.

**sweat out** v., informal To wait anxiously; worry while waiting. ♦ Karl was sweating out the results of the college exams.

**sweep off one's feet** v. phr. To make (someone) have feelings (as love or happiness) too strong to control; overcome with strong feeling; win sudden and complete acceptance by (someone) through the feelings. ♦ The handsome football captain swept Joan off her feet when he said so many things to her at the dance.

**sweep the city** or **country** or **nation** or **world** v. phr. To gain great attention or popularity throughout the city, country, etc. ♦ Pavarotti's unmatched tenor voice swept the world in an unprecedented manner.

**sweep under the rug** v. phr. To hide or dismiss casually (something one is ashamed of or does not know what to do about). ♦ In many places, drug abuse by school children is swept under the rug.

**sweetie pie** n., informal A person who is loved; darling; sweetheart. ♦ Arnold blushed with pleasure when Annie called him her sweetie pie.

**sweet on** adj. phr., informal In love with; very fond of. ♦ John is sweet on Alice.

**sweet talk 1.** n., informal Too much praise; flattery. ♦ Sometimes a girl's better judgment is overcome by sweet talk. **2.** v., informal To get what you want by great praise; flatter. ♦ Polly could sweet talk her husband into anything.

**sweet tooth** n. phr. A great weakness or predilection for sweets. ♦ Sue has such a sweet tooth that she hardly eats anything else but cake.

**swelled head** n., informal A feeling that you are very important or more important than you really are. ♦ When John won the race, he got a swelled head. ♦ Pretty girls shouldn't get a swelled head about it.—**swell-headed** adj. phr.

**swim against the current** or **swim against the stream** v. phr. To do the opposite of what most people want to do; go against the way things are happening; struggle upstream. ♦ The boy who tries to succeed today without an education is swimming against the stream.

**switched on** adj., slang 1. In tune with the latest fads, ideas, and fashions. ♦ I dig Sarah, she is really switched on. 2. Stimulated; as if under the influence of alcohol or drugs. ♦ How come you're talking so fast? Are you switched on or something?

**sword of Damocles** n. phr., from Greek mythology A constant threat or imminent danger. ♦ Nuclear war hangs over modern humanity's head like the sword of Damocles.

**sworn enemies** n. phr. People or groups or nations that have a long-standing dislike for each other. ♦ The Israelis and the Arabs have been sworn enemies for a long time but hopefully they will eventually sign a lasting peace accord.

**tack on** *v. phr.* To append; add. ♦*We were about to sign the contract when we discovered that the lawyer had tacked on a codicil that was not acceptable to us.*

**tag along with** *v. phr.* To accompany someone to a social activity. ♦*Don's kid brother tags along with him everywhere Don goes in spite of his young age.*

**tag end** *or* **tail end** *n., informal* The end, farthest to the rear, last in line, nearest the bottom, or least important. ♦*John was at the tail end of his class.* ♦*Mary's part in the play came at the tag end, and she got bored waiting.*

**tail between one's legs** *n. phr.* State of feeling beaten, ashamed, or very obedient, as after a scolding or a whipping. ♦*The army sent the enemy home with their tails between their legs.*

**taillight** *n.* The rear red light of a car. ♦*My father was fined $15 for driving without a taillight.*

**tail wags the dog** Said of situations in which a minor part is in control of the whole. ♦*He is just a minor employee at the firm, yet he gives everyone orders, a case of the tail wagging the dog.*

**take a back seat** *v. phr., informal* To accept a poorer or lower position; be second to something or someone else. ♦*During the war all manufacturing had to take a back seat to military needs.*

**take a bath** *v. phr., informal* To come to financial ruin. ♦*Boy, did we ever take a bath on that merger with Brown & Brown, Inc.*

**take a blast** *v. phr.* To become inebriated; to become intoxicated. ♦*I saw you taking a blast from drinking too much beer last night.*

**take a bow** *v. phr.* To stand up or come on a stage to be clapped for or praised for success. ♦*The audience shouted for the author of the play to take a bow.*

**take a break** *v. phr.* To have a brief rest period during the course of one's work. ♦*"You've worked hard. It's time to take a break," the boss said.*

**take a breather** See TAKE A BREAK.

**take a chance** *v. phr.* To accept the risk of failure or loss ♦*We will take a chance on the weather and have the party outdoors.*

**take a crack at** *v. phr.* To try doing something. ♦*It was a difficult challenge to reorganize our antiquated campus, but the resident architect decided to take a crack at it.*

**take a different tack** *v. phr.* To approach a problem differently from the mainstream or the majority of one's colleagues. ♦*Albert Einstein took a different tack to the question of space and time from that of his contemporaries, and thereby produced the Theory of Relativity.*

**take a dig at** *v. phr.* To attack verbally; offend; denigrate. ♦*If you keep taking digs at me all the time, our relationship will be a short one.*

**take a dim view of** *v. phr.* **1.** To have doubts about; feel unsure or anxious about. ♦*Tom took a dim view of his chances of passing the exam.* **2.** To be against; disapprove. ♦*The teacher took a dim view of the class's behavior.*

**take a drop** *v. phr.* **1.** To indulge in alcoholic drinks. ♦*Aunt Liz doesn't really drink; she just takes a drop every now and then.* **2.** To lose value; decrease in price. ♦*Stocks took a big drop yesterday due to the international crisis.*

**take advantage of** *v. phr.* **1.** To make good use of. ♦*The cat took advantage of the high grass to creep up on the bird.* ♦*Jim took advantage of Tracy's innocence, got her drunk, and raped her.* **2.** To treat (someone) unfairly for your own gain or help; make unfair use of.

**take after** *v.* To be like because of family relationship; to have the same looks or ways as (a parent or ancestor). ♦*She takes after her father's side of the family in looks.*

**take a fancy to** *v. phr.* To become fond of; cultivate a predilection for. ♦*Aunt Hermione has taken a fancy to antique furniture.*

**take a flop** *v. phr.* To fall heavily. ♦*I took a nasty flop on the ice-covered sidewalk.*

**take aim** *v. phr.* To get ready to hit, throw at, or shoot at by sighting carefully. ♦ *Before the hunter could take aim, the deer jumped out of sight.*

**take a hand in** *v. phr.* To assist in the direction of; participate. ♦ *The University Faculty Club decided to take a hand in helping the recent refugees.*

**take a hint** *v. phr.* To understand an allusion or a suggestion and behave accordingly. ♦ *"I don't like people who smoke," she said. "Can't you take a hint and either quit smoking or seeing me?"*

**take a joke** *v. phr.* Accept in good spirit some derision directed at oneself. ♦ *My brother has a good sense of humor when teasing others, but he cannot take a joke on himself.*

**take a load off one's feet** *v. phr.* To alleviate one's fatigue by sitting down during some taxing work. ♦ *"You've been standing there for hours, Jake,"* John said. *"Why don't you take a load off your feet?"*

**take amiss** *or* **the wrong way** *v. phr.* To become offended due to a misunderstanding. ♦ *"I hope you won't take it amiss," the boss said to Jane, "that I find you irresistibly attractive."*

**take a nap** *or* **take a snooze** *v. phr.* To sleep for a short while. ♦ *If you can take a nap even for just half an hour when working hard, you will be able to continue better than before.*

**take a new turn** *v. phr.* To start a new course; decide upon a new direction. ♦ *The company took a new turn under Jack's directorship.*

**take a nose dive** *v. phr.* To plummet; fall sharply. ♦ *The stock market took a nose dive after the news of the President's heart attack.*

**take apart** *v. phr.* To dismantle; disassemble. ♦ *Boys like taking radios and watches apart, but they seldom know how to put them back together again.*

**take a pot shot at** See POTSHOT.

**take a powder** *v. phr., slang* To leave hurriedly; run out or away; desert, flee. ♦ *All the gang except one had taken a powder when the police arrived.*

**take a punch at** *v. phr.* To try to hit (someone) with the fist; swing or strike at; attack with the fists. ♦ *Bob was very angry and suddenly he took a punch at Fred.*

**take a shine to** *v. phr., slang* To have or show a quick liking for. ♦ *He took a shine to his new teacher the very first day.*

**take a shot at** *v. phr.* To try casually; attempt to do. ♦ *"Can you handle all these new book orders?" Tom asked. "I haven't done it before," Sally replied, "but I can sure take a shot at it."*

**take a snooze** See TAKE A NAP.

**take a spill** *v. phr.* To fall down; tip over. ♦ *During the harsh winter, when the sidewalk is covered with ice, many people take a spill.*

**take a spin** *v. phr.* To go for a ride in a car, especially for pleasure. ♦ *"How about taking a spin in my new sports car?" John asked his girlfriend.*

**take at one's word** *v. phr.* To believe everything (someone) says; to act on what is said. ♦ *If you say you don't want this coat, I'll take you at your word and throw it away.*

**take a stand** *v. phr.* To assert one's point of view; declare one's position. ♦ *It is time for American society to take a stand against crime.*

**take a turn** *v. phr.* To become different; change. ♦ *Mary's fever suddenly took a bad turn.* Used with *for the better* or *for the worse.* ♦ *In the afternoon the weather took a turn for the better.*

**take a turn for the better** *v. phr.* To start improving; start to get better. ♦ *Aunt Hermione was very ill for a long time, but last week she suddenly took a turn for the better.*

**take a turn for the worse** See FOR THE WORSE.

**take away one's breath** *v. phr.* To impress one immensely either positively or negatively. ♦ *The beauty of Chicago's skyline at night took the tourist's breath away.* ♦ *The sight of the dead bodies lying in the ditch took away the breath of the peacekeeping force.*

**take-away restaurant** *or* **take-out restaurant** *n. phr.* A special kind of restaurant where the customers don't sit at tables, but must purchase the food and take it away in special plastic containers. ♦ *The best Chinese duck in our neighborhood is sold in the local take-away restaurant.*

**take back** *v.* **1.** To change or deny something offered, promised, or stated. ♦ *I take back my offer to buy the house now that I've had a good look at it.*

**2.** admit to making a wrong statement. ♦*I want you to take back the unkind things you said about Kenneth.*

**take by storm** *v. phr.* **1.** To capture by a sudden or very bold attack. ♦ *The army did not hesitate. They took the town by storm.* **2.** To win the favor or liking of; make (a group of people) like or believe you. ♦*John gave Jane so much attention that he took her by storm, and she said she would marry him.*

**take by surprise** *v. phr.* **1.** To appear in front of someone suddenly or to suddenly discover him before he discovers you; come before (someone) is ready; appear before (someone) unexpectedly. ♦ *The policeman took the burglar by surprise as he opened the window.* **2.** To fill with surprise or amazement; astonish. ♦ *When our teacher quit in the middle of the year to work for the government, it took us all by surprise.*

**take care** *v. phr.* To be careful; use wisdom or caution. ♦*Take care that you don't spill that coffee!*

**take care of** *v. phr.* **1.** To attend to; supply the needs of. ♦*She stayed home to take care of the baby.* **2.** *informal* To deal with; do what is needed with. ♦*I will take care of that letter.*

**take center stage** *v. phr.* To be the focus of attention; be the main attraction at a social event. ♦ *The president of the United States usually takes center stage at international meetings and conferences.*

**take charge** *v. phr.* To begin to lead or control; take control or responsibility; undertake the care or management (of persons or things). ♦*When Mrs. Jackson was in the hospital, her sister took charge of the Jackson children until Mrs. Jackson could care for them.*

**take cover** *v. phr.* To seek shelter or protection. ♦*The rain began so suddenly that we had to take cover in a doorway.*

**take down** *v.* **1.** To write or record (what is said). ♦*I will tell you how to get to the place; you had better take it down.* **2.** To pull to pieces; take apart. ♦*It will be a big job to take that tree down.* ♦*In the evening the campers put up a tent, and the next morning they took it down.* **3.** *informal* To reduce the pride or spirit of; humble. ♦*Bob thought he was a good wrestler, but Henry took him down.*

**take down a notch** *or* **take down a peg** *v. phr., informal* To make (someone) less proud or sure of himself. ♦ *The team was feeling proud of its record, but last week the boys were taken down a peg by a bad defeat.*

**take effect** *v. phr.* **1.** To have an unexpected or intended result; cause a change. ♦ *It was nearly an hour before the sleeping pill took effect.* **2.** To become lawfully right, or operative. ♦ *The new tax law will not take effect until January.*

**take exception to** *v. phr.* To speak against; find fault with; be displeased or angered by; criticize. ♦ *There was nothing in the speech that you could take exception to.*

**take five** *v. phr.* To take a five-minute break during some work or theatrical rehearsal. ♦ *"All right, everyone," the director cried. "Let's take five."*

**take flak** *or* **draw flak** *v. phr., from military* To draw criticism of all sorts, in random shots. ♦ *The proponent of the new theory took a lot of flak from jealous, disgruntled colleagues.* ♦ *The new sales strategy drew flak from the administration, until it was proved to be successful.*

**take for** *v.* To suppose to be; mistake for. ♦ *Do you take me for a fool?*

**take for a ride** *v. phr., slang* **1.** To take out in a car intending to murder. ♦ *The gang leader decided that the informer must be taken for a ride.* **2.** To play a trick on; fool. ♦ *The girls told Linda that a movie star was visiting the school, but she did not believe them; she thought they were taking her for a ride.* **3.** To take unfair advantage of; fool for your own gain. ♦ *His girlfriend really took him for a ride before he stopped dating her.*

**take for granted** *v. phr.* **1.** To suppose or understand to be true. ♦*A teacher cannot take it for granted that students always do their homework.* **2.** To accept or become used to (something) without noticing especially or saying anything. ♦*No girl likes to have her boyfriend take her for granted; instead, he should always try to make her like him better.*

**take French leave** *v. phr.* To leave secretly; abscond. ♦ *The party was so* *boring that we decided to take French leave.*

**take heart** *v. phr.* To be encouraged; feel braver and want to try. ◆ *The men took heart from their leader's words and went on to win the battle.*

**take heed** *v. phr., literary* To pay attention; watch or listen carefully; notice. ◆ *Take heed not to offend the dean.*

**take hold of** *v. phr.* To grasp. ◆ *The old man tried to keep himself from falling down the stairs, but there was no railing to take hold of.*

**take ill** *or* **take sick** *v.* To become sick. ◆ *Father took sick just before his birthday.*—Used in the passive with the same meaning. ◆ *The man was taken ill on the train.*

**take in** *v.* 1. To include. ◆ *The country's boundaries were changed to take in a piece of land beyond the river.* 2. To go and see; visit. ◆ *We planned to take in Niagara Falls and Yellowstone Park on our trip.* 3. To make smaller. ◆ *This waistband is too big; it must be taken in about an inch.* 4. To grasp with the mind; understand. ◆ *He didn't take in what he read because his mind was on something else.* 5a. To deceive; cheat; fool. ◆ *The teacher was taken in by the boy's innocent manner.* 5b. To accept without question; believe. ◆ *The magician did many tricks, and the children took it all in.* 6a. To receive; get. ◆ *The senior class held a dance to make money and took in over a hundred dollars.* 6b. Let come in; admit. ◆ *When her husband died, Mrs. Smith took in boarders.* 7. To see or hear with interest; pay close attention to. ◆ *When Bill told about his adventures, the other boys took it all in.*

**take in stride** *v. phr.* To meet happenings without too much surprise; accept good or bad luck and go on. ◆ *He learned to take disappointments in stride.*

**take in tow** *v. phr.* To take charge of; lead; conduct. ◆ *Brian and Kate took a group of children in tow when they went to see the circus.*

**take into account** *v. phr.* To remember and understand while judging someone or something; consider. ◆ *How much time will we need to get to the lake? You have to take the bad road into account.*

**take issue with** *v. phr.* To be openly against; speak against; disagree with. ◆ *He thought his boss was wrong but was afraid to take issue with him on the matter.*

**take it** *v. phr.* 1. To get an idea or impression; understand from what is said or done.—Usually used with *I.* ◆ *I take it from your silence that you don't want to go.* 2. *informal* To bear trouble, hard work, criticism; not give up or weaken. ◆ *Bob lost his job and his girl in the same week, and we all admired the way he took it.*

**take it all in** *v. phr.* To absorb completely; listen attentively. ◆ *Bill's piano music filled the room and we took it all in with admiration.*

**take it away** *v. phr., informal* Theatrical expression You're on; it's your turn; you're next. ◆ *And here comes that wonderful comedian, Bob Hope. The announcer said, "Take it away, Bob."*

**take it easy** *v. phr., informal* 1. *or* **go easy** *or* **take things easy** To go or act slowly, carefully, and gently. Used with *on.* ◆ *Take it easy. The roads are icy.* ◆ *"Go easy," said Billy to the other boys carrying the table down the stairs.* 2. *or* **take things easy** To avoid hard work or worry; have an easy time; live in comfort. ◆ *The doctor said that Bob would have to take things easy for awhile after he had his tonsils out.*

**take it from me** *v. phr., informal* Believe me, I know what I am talking about. ◆ *"The criminal will revisit the scene of his crime—take it from me," said the chief of detectives to the journalists.*

**take it from the top** *v. phr., informal* Musical and theatrical expression To start again from the beginning. ◆ *The conductor said, "We must try it once again. Take it from the top and watch my baton."*

**take it into one's head** *v. phr.* To get a sudden idea; decide without thinking. ◆ *The boy suddenly took it into his head to leave school and get a job.*

**take it on the chin** *v. phr., informal* 1. To be badly beaten or hurt. ◆ *Our football team really took it on the chin today. They are all bumps and bruises.* 2. To accept without complaint something bad that happens to you; accept trouble or defeat calmly. ◆ *A good* *chess player can take it on the chin when he loses.*

**take it or leave it** *v. phr., informal* To accept something without change or refuse it; decide yes or no.—Often used like a command. ♦ *He said the price of the house was $10,000, take it or leave it.*

**take it out on** *v. phr., informal* To be unpleasant or unkind to (someone) because you are angry or upset; get rid of upset feelings by being mean to. ♦ *The teacher was angry and took it out on the class.*

**take its toll** *v. phr.* To cause loss or damage. ♦ *The bombs had taken their toll on the town.*

**take kindly to** *v.* To be pleased by; like.—Usually used in negative, interrogative, and conditional sentences. ♦ *He doesn't take kindly to any suggestions about running his business.*

**take leave of one's senses** *v. phr.* To go mad; become crazy. ♦ *"Have you taken leave of your senses?" Jake cried, when he saw Andy swallow a live goldfish.*

**take liberties** *v. phr.* To act toward in too close or friendly a manner; use as you would use a close friend or something of your own. ♦ *Mary would not let any boy take liberties with her.*

**take lying down** *v. phr.* To accept something without defense or protest. ♦ *If you take such insults lying down, you will only encourage more of the same.*

**taken aback** *also* **taken back** *adj.* Unpleasantly surprised; suddenly puzzled or shocked. ♦ *When he came to pay for his dinner he was taken aback to find that he had left his wallet at home.*

**taken by** *or* **with** *v. phr.* To be impressed by; intrigued by. ♦ *Ned was much taken by the elegance of Sophie's manners.*

**take note of** *or* **take notice of** *v. phr.* **1.** To look carefully at; pay close attention to; observe well. ♦ *A detective is trained to take note of people and things.* **2.** To notice and act in response; pay attention. ♦ *Two boys were talking together in the back of the room but the teacher took no notice of them.*

**take oath** *v. phr.* To promise to tell the truth or to do some task honestly, calling on God or some person or thing as a witness. ♦ *Mary took an oath that she did not murder her husband.* ♦ *John took oath that he would fill the office of president faithfully.*

**takeoff** *n.* (stress on *take*) **1.** Departure of an airplane; the act of becoming airborne. ♦ *The nervous passenger was relieved that we had such a wonderfully smooth takeoff.* **2.** Imitation; a parody. ♦ *Vaughn Meader used to do a wonderful takeoff on President Kennedy's speech.*

**take off** *v. phr.* (stress on *off*) **1a.** To leave fast; depart suddenly; run away. ♦ *The dog took off after a rabbit.* **1b.** *informal* To go away; leave. ♦ *The six boys got into the car and took off for the movies.* **2.** To leave on a flight, begin going up. ♦ *A helicopter is able to take off and land straight up or down.* **3.** *informal* To imitate amusingly; copy another person's habitual actions or speech. ♦ *He made a career of taking off famous people for nightclub audiences.* **4.** To take (time) to be absent from work. ♦ *When his wife was sick he took off from work.*

**take off one's hat to** *v. phr.* To give honor, praise, and respect to. ♦ *He is my enemy, but I take off my hat to him for his courage.*

**take offense at** *v. phr.* To become indignant; become angry. ♦ *Why do you always take offense at everything I say?*

**take off one's hands** *v. phr.* **1.** To abdicate one's responsibility of a person or matter. ♦ *"I am herewith taking my hand off your affairs," Lou's father said. "See how you succeed on your own." ***2.** To buy; relieve someone of something. ♦ *He offered to take my old car off my hands for $350.*

**take on** *v.* **1.** To receive for carrying; be loaded with. ♦ *A big ship was at the dock taking on automobiles in crates to carry overseas for sale.* **2.** To begin to have (the look of); take (the appearance of). ♦ *Others joined the fistfight until it took on the look of a riot.* **3a.** To give a job to; hire; employ. ♦ *The factory has opened and is beginning to take on new workers.* **3b.** To accept in business or a contest. ♦ *The big man took on two opponents at once.*

**take one at one's word** *v. phr.* To naively lend credence to what one tells one. ♦ *It's a bad idea to take street vendors at their word in large, crowded cities.*

**take one out** *v. phr.* To invite one, to go out, and pay for the food and entertainment. ♦ *"My husband never takes me out anymore,"* Mrs. Smith complained to her psychiatrist. *"How about your taking him out?"* the psychiatrist replied with a smile.

**take one's breath away** *v. phr.* To surprise greatly; impress very much; leave speechless with surprise or wonder or delight; astonish. ♦ *The sunset is so beautiful it takes our breath away.*

**take one's leave** *or* **take leave of** *v. phr., formal* To say good-bye and leave. ♦ *He stayed on after most of the guests had taken their leave.*—**leave-taking** *n. The end of school in June is a time of leave-taking.*

**take one's life in one's hands** *v. phr.* To face great danger or take great risk. ♦ *Driving that car with those worn tires would be taking your life in your hands.*

**take one's medicine** *v. phr.* To accept punishment without complaining. ♦ *The boy said he was sorry he broke the window and was ready to take his medicine.*

**take one's name in vain** *v. phr.* **1.** To call upon (God) as a witness to your truth or honesty when you are lying; swear by (God) untruthfully. ♦ *You shall not take the name of the Lord your God in vain.* **2.** *informal* To talk about a person or mention his name. ♦ *"Did I hear someone taking my name in vain?"* asked Bill as he joined his friends.

**take one's pick** *v. phr.* To choose freely from a variety of available choices. ♦ *"Seymour is either a genius or a very clever liar,"* his neighbor said. *"Take your pick!"*

**take one's own sweet time** See TAKE ONE'S TIME.

**take one's time** *v. phr.* To avoid haste; act in an unhurried way. ♦ *It is better to take your time at this job than to hurry and make mistakes.*

**take one's word** *v. phr.* To believe one's promise. ♦ *Herb took Eric's word when he promised to pay up his debt.*

**take one up on something** *v. phr.* To make someone keep a promise. ♦ *I will take you up on your promise to take me to Hawaii next winter.*

**take on faith** *v. phr.* To lend credence to something due to one's confidence in the source, rather than based on evidence. ♦ *One should never take on faith what one hears about Washington politics.*

**take on oneself** *or* **take upon oneself** *v. phr.* **1.** To accept as a duty or responsibility. ♦ *He took it on himself to see that the packages were delivered.* **2.** To assume wrongfully or without permission as a right or privilege. ♦ *You should not have taken it upon yourself to accept the invitation for the whole family.*

**take on the chin** *v. phr.* To gracefully accept criticism. ♦ *It's good to be able to tell people what they do wrong, but it is equally important to be able to take it on the chin when they tell you what you have done wrong.*

**take out** *v. phr.* **1.** To ask for and fill in. ♦ *Mary and John took out a marriage license.* **2.** To aim at and shoot to kill. ♦ *The police sharpshooters took out the wanted kidnapper with a telescopic rifle.*

**take out after** *v. phr.* To start pursuing one. ♦ *The watchdog took out after the burglars.*

**take out on** *v. phr.* To vent one's sadness, frustration, or anger on someone who is usually innocent of the problem at hand. ♦ *"Why are you always taking out your frustrations on me?"* Jane asked Tom, when he slammed the door.

**take-out order** *n. phr.* An order in a restaurant that one does not eat on the premises, but takes home. ♦ *The new Chinese restaurant on the corner sells nice take-out orders.*

**take over** *v.* **1a.** To take control or possession of. ♦ *He expects to take over the business when his father retires.* **1b.** To take charge or responsibility. ♦ *The airplane pilot fainted and his co-pilot had to take over.* **2.** To borrow, imitate, or adopt. ♦ *The Japanese have taken over many European ways of life.*

**take pains** *v. phr.* To do something very carefully and thoroughly. ♦ *She always takes pains with her appearance.*

**take part** *v. phr.* To have a part or share; join. ♦ *The Swiss did not take part in the two World Wars.*

**take pity on** *also* **take pity upon** *v. phr.* To feel sympathy or pity and do something for. ♦ *The farmer took pity upon the campers, and let them stay in his barn during the rain.*

**take place** *v. phr.* To happen; occur. ♦ *The accident took place only a block from his home.*

**take potluck** *v. phr.* To share as a guest an everyday meal without special preparation. ♦ *You are welcome to stay for dinner if you will take potluck.*

**take root** *v. phr.* **1.** To form roots so as to be able to live and grow. ♦ *We hope the transplanted apple trees will take root.* **2.** To be accepted; to be adopted; to live and succeed in a new place. ♦ *The immigrants to our country took root and began to think of themselves as Native Americans.*

**take shape** *v. phr.* To grow or develop into a certain fixed form. ♦ *Plans for our vacation are beginning to take shape.* ♦ *Their new home took shape as the weeks went by.*

**take sides** *v. phr.* To join one group against another in a debate or quarrel. ♦ *Switzerland refused to take sides in the two World Wars.*

**take someone for a ride** *v. phr., informal* **1.** To cheat or swindle someone. ♦ *Poor Joe Catwallender was taken for a ride.* **2.** To kill someone after kidnapping. ♦ *The criminals took the man for a ride.*

**take steps** *v. phr.* To begin to make plans or arrangements; make preparations; give orders.—Usually used with *to* and an infinitive. ♦ *The city is taking steps to replace its streetcars with busses.*

**take stock** *v. phr.* **1.** To count exactly the items of merchandise or supplies in stock; take inventory. ♦ *The grocery store took stock every week on Monday mornings.* **2.** To study carefully a situation, or a number of possibilities or opportunities. ♦ *During the battle the commander paused to take stock of the situation.*

**take stock in** *v. phr., informal* To have faith in; trust; believe.—Usually used in the negative. ♦ *He took no stock in the idea that women were worse politicians.*

**take the bread out of one's mouth** *v. phr.* To take away or not give your rightful support, especially through selfish pleasure. ♦ *She accused her husband of drinking and gambling—taking bread out of his children's mouths.*

**take the bull by the horns** *v. phr., informal* To take definite action and not care about risks; act bravely in a difficulty. ♦ *He decided to take the bull by the horns and demand a raise in salary even though it might cost him his job.*

**take the cake** *v. phr., slang* **1.** To take the first prize; be the best; rank first. ♦ *Mr. Jones takes the cake as a storyteller.* **2.** To be the limit; to be the worst; have a lot of nerve; be a very rude, bold, or surprising action. ♦ *I let Jack borrow my baseball and he never gave it back. Doesn't that take the cake?*

**take the day off** See DAY OFF.

**take the edge off** *also* **take off the edge** *v. phr.* To lessen, weaken, soften or make dull. ♦ *Eating a candy bar before dinner has taken the edge off Becky's appetite.*

**take the fifth** *v. phr., informal* **1.** Taking refuge behind the Fifth Amendment of the Constitution of the United States which guarantees any witness the right not to incriminate himself while testifying at a trial. ♦ *Alger Hiss took the Fifth when asked whether he was a member of the Communist Party.* **2.** Not to answer any question in an informal setting. ♦ *Have you been married before?—I take the Fifth.*

**take the floor** *v. phr.* To get up and make a speech in a meeting. ♦ *The audience became very attentive the moment the president took the floor.*

**take the hair of the dog that bit you** *quasi-proverbial phrase idiom* Frequently offered as advice to someone with a hangover suggesting that the best way to get rid of a hangover is to have another drink. ♦ *"I feel awful," Jack complained to his wife. "What's the matter?" she asked. "I had too much to drink last night," he confessed. "In that case you should take the hair of the dog that bit you, and pour yourself a whiskey on the rocks," she replied, laughing.*

**take the heat** *v. phr.* **1.** To overcome pressure in a trying situation. ♦ *John makes an ideal boss. He can take the heat like nobody else.* **2.** To be held responsible for errors or mistakes committed. ♦ *Although Ted had nothing to do with the problems at the factory, he had to take the heat, as no one else came* *forth to tell the true story of what had happened.*

**take the law into one's own hands** *v. phr.* To protect one's supposed rights or punish a suspected wrongdoer without reference to a court.—An overused expression. ◆ *His farm was going to be sold for taxes, but he took the law into his own hands and drove the sheriff away with a shotgun.*

**take the lid off** *v. phr.* **1.** To let out in the open; divulge. ◆ *It's about time to take the lid off the question of how many prisoners of war are still in enemy hands.* **2.** To start to face an issue. ◆ *"The best way to deal with your divorce," the doctor said to Fran "is to take the lid off of it."*

**take the offensive** *v. phr.* To make oneself the attacking party. ◆ *After many months of preparation, the freedom fighters were ready to take the offensive.*

**take the pledge** *v. phr.* To swear to give up drinking, smoking, or using drugs. ◆ *Gary finally took the pledge and he has kept it thus far.*

**take the plunge** *v. phr.* To take a fatal or decisive step; venture. ◆ *When I asked Don when he and Melissa were going to get married, he answered that they'll take the plunge in September.*

**take the rap** *v. phr., slang* To receive punishment; to be accused and punished. ◆ *Joe took the burglary rap for his brother and went to prison for two years.*

**take the rough with the smooth** *v. phr.* Often heard as advice or an admonition given to a complainer. To accept bad news and difficulties as calmly and cheerfully as one accepts good news and good luck. ◆ *Jim, an eternal complainer, said to his wife, "I don't understand why they make me work at night, after I just got a promotion to shop manager." The wife replied, "You were lucky to get promoted while so young, so now you must take the rough with the smooth."*

**take the stand** *v. phr.* To assume one's position in the witness box during a trial. ◆ *The judge asked the defendant to take the stand.*

**take the stump** *or* **take to the stump** *v. phr.* To travel around to different places making political speeches. ◆ *The men running for president took to the stump to attract votes.*

**take the wind out of one's sails** *v. phr.* To surprise someone by doing better or by catching him in an error. ◆ *John came home boasting about the fish he had caught; it took the wind out of his sails when he found his little sister had caught a bigger one.*

**take the words out of one's mouth** *v. phr.* To say what another is just going to say; to put another's thought into words. ◆ *"Let's go to the beach tomorrow." "You took the words right out of my mouth; I was thinking of that."*

**take things easy** See TAKE IT EASY 2.

**take time off** See TIME OFF; Compare DAY OFF.

**take time out** See TIME OUT.

**take to** *v.* **1.** To go to or into; get yourself quickly to. Used in the imperative. ◆ *Take to the hills! The bandits are coming!* **2.** To begin the work or job of; make a habit of. ◆ *He took to repairing watches in his spare time.* **3.** To learn easily; do well at. ◆ *Father tried to teach John to swim, but John didn't take to it.* **4.** To like at first meeting; be pleased by or attracted to; accept quickly. ◆ *Our dog always takes to children quickly.*

**take to heart** *also* **lay to heart** *v. phr.* To be seriously affected by; to feel deeply. ◆ *He took his brother's death very much to heart.*

**take to one's heels** *also* **show a clean pair of heels** *v. phr.* To begin to run or run away. *When he heard the police coming, the thief took to his heels.*

**take to task** *v. phr.* To reprove or scold for a fault or error. ◆ *The principal took Bill to task for cheating on his test.*

**take to the cleaners** *v. phr., slang* **1.** To win all the money another person has (as in poker). ◆ *Watch out if you play poker with Joe; he'll take you to the cleaners.* **2.** To cheat a person out of his money and possessions by means of a crooked business transaction or other means of dishonest conduct. ◆ *I'll never forgive myself for becoming associated with Joe; he took me to the cleaners.*

**take turns** *v. phr.* To do something one after another instead of doing it all at the same time. ♦ *In class we should not talk all at the same time; we should take turns.*

take up *v.* **1.** To remove by taking in. ♦ *When the vacuum cleaner bag is full, it will not take up dirt from the rug.* **2.** To fill or to occupy. ♦ *The oceans take up the greater part of the earth's surface.* **3.** To gather together; collect. ♦ *We are taking up a collection to buy flowers for John because he is in the hospital.* **4.** To begin; start. ♦ *The teacher took up the lesson where she left off yesterday.* **5.** To begin to do or learn; go into as a job or hobby. ♦ *He recently took up gardening.* **6.** To pull and make tight or shorter; shorten. ♦ *The tailor took up the legs of the trousers.* **7.** To take or accept something that is offered. ♦ *I took John up on his bet.*

take up arms *v. phr., literary.* To get ready to fight; fight or make war. ♦ *The people were quick to take up arms to defend their freedom.*

take up with *v.* To begin to go around with (someone); see a lot of. ♦ *Frank has taken up with Lucy lately.*

take with a grain of salt *also* take with a pinch of salt *v. phr.* To accept or believe only in part; not accept too much. ♦ *We took Uncle George's stories of the war with a pinch of salt.*

taking pictures *v. phr., slang, citizen's band radio jargon* To use a radar-operated speed indicator in order to enforce the 55 m.p.h. speed limit. ♦ *The Smokeys are taking pictures!*

talent scout *n. phr.* A person employed by a large organization to seek out promising and gifted individuals. ♦ *Gordon has been working as a talent scout for a television program.*

talent show *n.* An entertainment in which new entertainers try to win a prize. ♦ *Mary won the talent show by her dancing.*

talk a blue streak *v. phr., informal* To talk on and on, usually very fast. ♦ *Sue is a nice girl but after one drink she talks a blue streak and won't stop.*

talk a mile a minute See TALK A BLUE STREAK.

talk back *also* answer back *v., informal* To answer rudely; reply in a disrespectful way; be fresh. ♦ *When the teacher told the boy to stop smoking, he*

talked back to her and said she couldn't make him.

talk big *v., informal* To talk boastfully; brag. ♦ *He talks big about his pitching, but he hasn't won a game.*

talk double Dutch *v. phr.* To talk in a way that cannot be understood by the listener. ♦ *I don't get a word of what you're saying, my friend; you're talking double Dutch.*

talk down *v.* **1.** To make (someone) silent by talking louder or longer. ♦ *Sue tried to give her ideas, but the other girls talked her down.* **2.** To use words or ideas that are too easy. ♦ *The speaker talked down to the students, and they were bored.*

talking book *n.* A book recorded by voice on phonograph records for blind people. ♦ *Billy, who was blind, learned history from a talking book.*

talking point *n.* Something good about a person or thing that can be talked about in selling it. ♦ *The streamlined shape of the car was one of its talking points.*

talk in circles *v. phr.* To waste time by saying words that don't mean very much. ♦ *After three hours at the negotiating table, the parties decided to call it quits because they realized that they had been talking in circles.*

talk into *v.* **1.** To get (someone) to agree to; make (someone) decide on (doing something) by talking; persuade to.— Used with a verbal noun. ♦ *Bob talked us into walking home with him.* **2.** To cause to be in or to get into by talking. ♦ *You talked us into this mess. Now get us out!*

talk of the town *n. phr.* Something that has become so popular or prominent that everyone is discussing it. ♦ *Even after three decades, Picasso's famous metal statue is still the talk of the town in Chicago.*

talk one's head off *v. phr.* To talk at length trying to put a point across without any success. ♦ *I was talking my head off this morning in the office to convince the boss that we must expand our business, but it was no use, as he turned a deaf ear to everything I had to say.*

talk out *v.* To talk all about and leave nothing out; discuss until everything is agreed on; settle. ♦ *After their quarrel,*

*Jill and John talked things out and reached full agreement.*

**talk out of** *v.* **1.** To persuade not to; make agree or decide not to.—Used with a verbal noun. ♦ *Mary's mother talked her out of quitting school.* **2.** To allow to go or get out by talking; let escape by talking. ♦ *Johnny is good at talking his way out of trouble.*

**talk out of turn** See SPEAK OUT OF TURN.

**talk over** *v.* **1.** To talk together about; try to agree about or decide by talking; discuss. ♦ *Tom talked his plan over with his father before he bought the car.* **2.** To persuade; make agree or willing; talk and change the mind of. ♦ *Fred is trying to talk Bill over to our side.*

**talk shop** *v. phr., informal* To talk about things in your work or trade. ♦ *Two chemists were talking shop, and I hardly understood a word they said.*

**talk through one's hat** *v. phr., informal* To say something without knowing or understanding the facts; talk foolishly or ignorantly. ♦ *John said that the earth is nearer the sun in summer, but the teacher said he was talking through his hat.*

**talk turkey** *v. phr., informal* To talk about something in a really businesslike way; talk with the aim of getting things done. ♦ *Charles said, "Now, let's talk turkey about the trip to Paris. The fact is, it will cost each student $850."*

**talk up** *v.* **1.** To speak in favor or support of. ♦ *Let's talk up the game and get a big crowd.*

**tall story** *or* **tale** *n. phr.* See FISH STORY.

**tamper with** *v.* **1.** To meddle with (something); handle ignorantly or foolishly. ♦ *He tampered with the insides of his computer and ruined it.* **2.** To secretly get someone to do or say wrong things, especially by giving him money, or by threatening to hurt him. ♦ *A friend of the man being tried in court tampered with a witness.*

**tan one's hide** *v. phr., informal* To give a beating to; spank hard. ♦ *Bob's father tanned his hide for staying out too late.*

**taper down** *adj. phr.* To decrease; reduce. ♦ *He has tapered down his drinking from three martinis to one beer a day.*

**taper off** *v.* **1.** To come to an end little by little; become smaller toward the end.

♦ *The river tapers off here and becomes a brook.* **2.** To stop a habit gradually; do something less and less often. ♦ *Robert gave up smoking all at once instead of tapering off.*

**tar and feather** *v.* To pour heated tar on and cover with feathers as a punishment. ♦ *In the Old West bad men were sometimes tarred and feathered and driven out of town.*

**tax trap** *n., informal* Predicament in which taxpayers in middle-income brackets are required to pay steeply progressive rates of taxation as their earnings rise with inflation but their personal exemptions remain fixed, resulting in a loss of real disposable income. ♦ *Everybody in my neighborhood has been caught in a tax trap.*

**teach a lesson** *v. phr.* To show that bad behavior can be harmful. ♦ *The burns Tommy got from playing with matches taught him a lesson.*

**team up with** *v. phr.* To join with; enter into companionship with. ♦ *My brother prefers to do business by himself rather than to team up with anybody else.*

**tear around** *v. phr.* To be constantly on the go; dash around. ♦ *No one can understand how she manages to tear around from one social event to another and yet be a good mother to her children.*

**tear down** *v.* **1.** To take all down in pieces; destroy. ♦ *The workmen tore down the old house and built a new house in its place.* **2.** To take to pieces or parts. ♦ *The mechanics had to tear down the engine, and fix it, and put it together again.* **3.** To say bad things about; criticize. ♦ *"Why do you always tear people down? Why don't you try to say nice things about them?"*

**tear into** *v. phr.* To attack vigorously, physically or verbally. ♦ *The anxious school children tore into the new Harry Potter book on sale at the bookstore.*

**tearjerker** *n.* A sentimental novel or movie that makes one cry. ♦ *Love Story, both in its novel form and as a movie, was a famous tearjerker.*

**tear oneself away** *v. phr.* To force oneself to leave; leave reluctantly. ♦ *The beaches in Hawaii are so lovely that I had to tear myself away from them in order to get back to my job in Chicago.*

**tear one's hair** v. phr. To show sorrow, anger, or defeat. ◆*Ben tore his hair when he saw the wrecked car.*

**tear one's hair out over** See PULL ONE'S HAIR OUT OVER

**tear up** v. 1. To dig a hole in; remove the surface of; remove from the surface. ◆*The city tore up the street to lay a new water pipe.* 2. To tear into pieces. ◆*John tore up his test paper so that his mother wouldn't see his low grade.*

**tee off** v. 1. To hit the golf ball from a small wooden peg or tee to begin play for each hole. ◆*We got to the golf course just in time to see the champion tee off.* 2. slang To hit a ball, especially a baseball very hard or far. ◆*He teed off on the first pitch.* 3. slang To attack vigorously. ◆*The governor teed off on his opponent's speech.* 4. slang To make (someone) angry or disgusted. ◆ *It teed me off when Bill called me a communist.*

**teetotaller** n. phr. A person who won't drink alcohol either for religious of other reasons. ◆*The Millers, who are teatotallers, have an "I am holier than you" attitude. They turn their wine-glasses upside down even at elegant parties in demonstration of their antial-coholic stance.*

**tee up** v. To set the golf ball on the tee in preparation for hitting it toward the green. ◆*Tiger Woods teed the ball up for the final hole.*

**T.G.I.F.** v. phr., informal, abbreviation "Thank God it's Friday" Said by people working a five-day week in anticipation of a free weekend. ◆*"What are you so happy about?" John asked his grinning colleague in the teachers' lounge at Central High. "T.G.I.F.," John's senior colleague replied, "or didn't you notice it was Friday?"*

**tell apart** v. phr. To see the difference between; know each of. ◆*The teacher could not tell the twins apart.*

**tell a thing or two** v. phr., informal To tell in plain or angry words; scold. ◆*When John complained about the hard work, his father told him a thing or two.*

**tell it like it is** v. phr., slang, informal To be honest, sincere; to tell the truth. ◆*Joe is the leader of our commune; he tells it like it is.*

**tell it to the marines** or **tell it to Sweeney** slang I don't believe you; stop trying to fool me. ◆*John said, "My father knows the president of the United States." Dick answered, "Tell it to the marines."*

**tell off** v. informal To speak to angrily or sharply; attack with words; scold. ◆*Mr. Black got angry and told off the boss.*

**tell on** v. To tell someone about another's wrong or naughty acts.—Used mainly by children. ◆*Andy cheated on the test and John told the teacher on Andy.*

**tempest in a teapot** n. phr. Great excitement about something not important. ◆*Bess tore her skirt a little and made a tempest in a teapot.*

**tempt fate** or **tempt the fates** v. phr. To take a chance; run a risk; gamble. ◆*You're tempting fate every time you drive that old wreck of a car.*

**ten-four?** v. phr., interrog., slang, citizen's band radio jargon Do you understand? ◆*Is that a ten-four?*

**ten gallon hat** n., informal A tall felt hat with a wide, rolled brim worn by men in the western part of the United States. ◆*Men from the southwest often wear ten gallon hats.*

**ten roger** v. phr., slang, citizen's band radio jargon I acknowledge. ◆*That's a ten roger.*

**ten to one** or **two to one** adv. or adj. phr., informal Almost certainly, nearly sure to be true; very likely to happen. ◆*Ten to one it will rain tomorrow.*

**thank one's lucky stars** v. phr., informal To be thankful for good luck; think oneself lucky. ◆*You can thank your lucky stars you didn't fall in the hole.*

**thanks to** prep. With the help of. ◆*Thanks to a good teacher, John passed the examination.* 2. Owing to; because of. ◆*Thanks to a sudden rain, the children came home with wet clothes.*

**that is that** or **that's that** informal The matter is decided; there is nothing more to be said; it is done. ◆*Jim, you will go to school this morning, and that is that.*

**that'll be the day** informal That will never happen. ◆*Joe wanted me to lend him money to take my girl to the movies. That'll be the day!*

**That makes two of us!** Informal way to say, "I am in agreement with what you are saying or doing." ♦*So you voted for Senator Aldridge? So did I—that makes two of us.*

**that's a laugh *or* that's a scream** *v. phr., informal* Said as a remark of disbelief or scorn upon hearing something outlandish. ♦*"Did you know," John asked, "how much the new department head is making, together with his wife?" "No, I don't," his colleague Tim replied. "Well, its is just about three times more than you and I make together. How about that?" "That's a scream!" Tim answered.*

**that's more like it** *adj. phr., informal* That is more acceptable, more reasonable, more what is expected ♦*"Are you going to help me with this extra work?" Tim's boss asked at 5 P.M. "If you mean tonight, I won't be able to, because I have a date," Tim replied. "Well, Tim," his boss continued, "this is an emergency." "In that case I can move my date," Tim replied with a sigh. "Splendid!" the boss exclaimed. "That's more like it!"*

**that's where it's at** *adj. phr., informal* Often heard as a comment concerning the relevance and currency of a state of affairs, meaning that the situation stands at its optimum. ♦*"Young, talented, and black, that's where it's at" was a popular expression during the early days of the civil rights movement, offering encouragement to young African-Americans.* ♦*"I want to go into the computer business," Jack's fourteen-year-old son declared. "OK," came the father's reply, "you're right. That's where it's at."*

**That takes care of that!** Informal way to say, "That concludes our business." ♦*I paid my ex-wife the last alimony check and that takes care of that!*

**That will do!** Informal expression of impatience meaning "stop," "no more." ♦*"That will do, Tom," his mother cried. "I've had just about enough of your sleeping under the table."*

**That's about the size of it!** Informal way to say, "What you said is true; the rumor or the news is true." ♦*"I am told you're leaving our firm for Japan," Fred said to Tom. "That's about the size of it," Tom replied with a grin.*

**that's my boy** See ATTA BOY!

**That's the story of my life...** Usually spoken when something goes wrong. ♦*I spent seven years writing a novel, but no publisher wants to accept it. That's the story of my life.*

**That's the ticket!** Informal way to say, "excellent; correct." ♦*"First we'll go up the Sears Tower, and then we'll take a night sightseeing tour on the lake," Fran said. "That's the ticket!" Stan, an old inhabitant of Chicago, replied.*

**That's the way the ball bounces *or* the cookie crumbles!** Nothing unusual about that. Said of unpleasant things. ♦*"Susan left me for a heavyweight boxer, and then I got drunk and wrecked my car," Bob bitterly complained. "Well, that's the way the cookie crumbles," Pam answered philosophically.*

**the bigger they are, the harder they fall** Often heard when someone in a high position is caught doing something illegal and falls from his or her position, indicating defiance of one's disliked superiors.—A proverb. ♦*When President Nixon was facing impeachment because of the Watergate scandal, and resigned the presidency of the United States, the journalist remarked, "The bigger they are, the harder they fall."*

**the brand of Cain *or* the mark of Cain** *n. phr., biblical* The stigma of murder, especially fratricide, patricide, or matricide. ♦*When the Menendez brothers killed their parents, our minister at church said, "Behold the brand of Cain haunting us to this day."*

**the business** *n., slang*—Usually used with *give* or *get*. **1.** All that you are able to do; greatest effort. ♦*Johnny gave the tryouts the business but he failed to make the team.* **2.** The most harm possible; the greatest damage or hurt. ♦*Fred got the business when Tom caught him with his bicycle.* **3.** A harsh scolding. ♦*The teacher gave Walter the business when he came to school late again.*

**the creeps** *n., informal* **1.** An uncomfortable tightening of the skin caused by fear or shock. ♦*Reading the story of a ghost gave Joe the creeps.* **2.** A strong feeling of fear or disgust. ♦*The cold, damp, lonely swamp gave John the creeps.*

**the Dark Continent** *n. phr.* Africa was referred to by this expression, especially throughout the nineteenth century. ♦ *Many great explorers, such as Dr. Livingstone, went to the Dark Continent.*

**the devil to pay** *n. phr.* A severe penalty. ♦ *If we don't finish the work by next Monday, there will be the devil to pay.*

**the edge** *n., informal* The advantage.— Usually used in the phrases *get the edge on, have the edge on.* ♦ *Mary has the edge on Jane in the beauty contest.*

**the idea** *or* **the very idea** *n. phr.*—Used in exclamations to show that you do not like something. ♦ *The very idea of Tom bringing that dirty dog into my clean house!*

**the lid** *n., slang* Something that holds back or holds out of sight. ♦ *The police blew the lid off the gambling operations.*

**the likes of** *informal* Something like or similar to; something of the same kind as. ♦ *I have never seen the likes of John.*

**the long and the short** *or* **the long and short** *n. phr.* All that needs to be said; the basic fact; point. ♦ *The money isn't there, and that's the long and short of it.*

**the lower forty-eight** *n. phr.* The contiguous continental United States of America as seen from the state of Alaska. ♦ *"We Alaskans have a state that takes up a full fourth of the lower forty-eight," my Alaskan friend said proudly.*

**the matter** *adj.* Not as it should be; wrong.—Used in questions or with negatives or *if.* ♦ *Why don't you answer me? What's the matter?*

**then again** *adv.* As an opposite possibility; another thing. ♦ *He may be here tomorrow. Then again, he may not come until next week.* ♦ *I thought you told me about the fire, but then again it could have been Bill.*

**then and there** *adv. phr.* At that very time and place in the past; right then. ♦ *He said he wanted his dime back then and there, so I had to give it to him.*

**the other day** *adv. phr.* In the recent past. ♦ *I saw an incredible parade of elephants along Michigan Avenue the other day on my way to work.*

**the picture** *n.* The way things are or were; the facts about something; the situation; what happened or happens.

♦ *Old Mr. Brown is out of the picture now and his son runs the store.*

**the pits** *n., slang* **1.** A low class, blighted and ill-maintained place, motel room or apartment. ♦ *Max, this motel is the pits; I will not sleep here!* **2.** The end of the road, the point of no return, the point of total ruin of one's health *(from the drug anticulture referring to the arm-pits as the only place that had veins for injections).* ♦ *John flunked high school this year for the third time; he will never get to college; it's the pits for him.* **3.** A very depressed state of mind. ♦ *Poor Marcy is down in the pits over her recent divorce.*

**the powers that be** *n. phr.* Constituted authority; those in power. ♦ *I have done all I can; the rest is up to the powers that be.*

**the proof of the pudding is in the eating** Whether a new invention or idea works or not must be judged from observing it in action and not in theory.—A proverb. ♦ *When Ted presented his new gasoline-conserving sports car model to the director of the factory, the director replied, "Looks nice, but the proof of the pudding is in the eating. Let's see how this will perform on the road."*

**There** *or* **here you are!** **1.** Informal way to say, "Here is what you wanted." ♦ *The doorman politely opened the door of the taxi and said, "There you are, sir!"* **2.** You have found the correct answer; you are correct. ♦ *"The reason for the violent crime rate is the all too easy availability of handguns," he said. "Yeah, there you are!" Officer Maloney replied.*

**there is more than one way to get a pig to market** *or* **flay a fox** *or* **skin a cat** There are always new and different ways to accomplish a difficult task.—A proverb. ♦ *"How did you get Tom to study so hard?" Eleanor asked. "I simply disconnected the television set," Tom's mother answered. "There's more than one way to get a pig to market."*

**there is nothing to it** Informal way to say, "It is easy." ♦ *Cooking stir-fried Chinese food is really not difficult at all; in fact, there's nothing to it.*

**There you go!** **1.** Informal way to say, "You are doing it already and you are doing it well." ♦ *"Is roller skating hard?" Freddie asked. "No," Beth replied, "let me show you how to do it. There you go!"*

**the road to hell is paved with good intentions** Often heard when one comments on good intentions having gone bad, meaning that thinking positively should be complemented by positive action.—A proverb. ♦ *"Socialism was meant to eliminate poverty in the world, yet people never suffered more than in Soviet Russia," Ivan remarked. "Indeed," Boris replied, "the road to hell is paved with good intentions."*

**the ropes** *n. plural, informal* Thorough or special knowledge of a job; how to do something; the ways of people or the world. ♦ *When you go to a new school it takes a while to learn the ropes.*

**the score** *n., slang* The truth; the real story or information; what is really happening; the way people and the world really are. ♦ *Very few people know the score in politics.*

**the three R's** *n. phr.* (W)riting, reading, and (a)rithmetic, the three basic skills of an elementary education. ♦ *Barry has completed the three R's, but otherwise he has had little formal education.*

**the ticket** *n.* Exactly what is needed.— Often used with *just.* ♦ *This airtight locker is just the ticket for storing your winter clothes.*

**the tracks** *n.* The line between the rich or fashionable part of town and the poor or unfashionable part of town. ♦ *The poor children knew they would not be welcome on the other side of the tracks.*

**the wiser** *adj.* Knowing about something which might be embarrassing of knowing.—Usually used with *nobody* or *no one.* ♦ *Mary took the teacher's book home by mistake, but early the next morning she returned it with nobody the wiser.*

**the works** *n., plural, slang* **1.** Everything that can be had or that you have; everything of this kind, all that goes with it. ♦ *When the homeless man found $100, he went into a fine restaurant and ordered the works with a steak dinner.* **2.** Rough handling or treatment; a bad beating or scolding; killing; murder.—Usually used with *get* or *give.* ♦ *The gangster told his accom-*

*plice he would give him the works if he double-crossed him.*

**thing or two** *n. phr., informal* **1.** Facts not generally known, or not known to the hearer or reader; unusual or important information. ♦ *Mary told Joan a thing or two about Betty's real feelings.* **2.** A lot; much. ♦ *Bob knows a thing or two about sailing.*

**Things are looking up!** Informal way to say that conditions are improving. ♦ *Things are looking up at our university as the governor promised a 5% salary raise.*

**think a great deal of** *or* **think a lot of** *also* **think much of** *v. phr.* To consider to be very worthy, valuable, or important; to esteem highly. ♦ *Mary thinks a great deal of Tim.* ♦ *Father didn't think much of Paul's idea of buying a goat to save lawn mowing.*

**think aloud** *or* **think out loud** *v.* To say what you are thinking. ♦ *"I wish I had more money for Christmas presents," Father thought aloud. "What did you say?" said Mother. Father answered, "I'm sorry. I wasn't talking to you. I was thinking out loud."*

**think better of** *v.* To change your mind about; to consider again and make a better decision about. ♦ *John told his mother he wanted to leave school, but later he thought better of it.*

**Think big!** *v. phr., informal* To believe in one's ability, purpose, or power to perform or succeed. ♦ *Be confident; be positive; tell yourself you are the greatest; above all, think big!*

**think city** *n. phr.* School, college, the university. ♦ *I wish tuition cost less these days. One gets broke by having to go to think city for so many years.*

**think little of** *v. phr.* Think that (something or someone) is not important or valuable. ♦ *Joan thought little of walking two miles to school.*

**think nothing of** *v. phr.* To think or consider easy, simple, or usual. ♦ *Jim thinks nothing of hiking ten miles in one day.*

**think nothing of it** *v. phr., informal*— Used as a courteous phrase in replying to thanks. *"Thank you very much for your help." "Think nothing of it."*

**think on one's feet** *v. phr.* To think quickly; answer or act without waiting;

know what to do or say right away. ♦ *Our teacher can think on his feet; he always has an answer ready when we ask him questions.*

**think out** *v.* **1.** To find out or discover by thinking; study and understand. ♦ *Andy thought out a way of climbing to the top of the pole.* **2.** To think through to the end; to understand what would come at last. ♦ *Bill wanted to quit school, but he thought out the matter and decided not to.*

**think out loud** See THINK ALOUD.

**think over** *v.* To think carefully about; consider; study. ♦ *When Charles asked Betty to marry him, she asked him for time to think it over.*

**think piece** *n., slang* **1.** The human brain. ♦ *Lou's got one powerful think piece, man.* **2.** Any provocative essay or article that, by stating a strong opinion, arouses the reader to think about it and react to it by agreeing or disagreeing. ♦ *That article by Charles Fenyvesi on Vietnamese refugees in the Washington Post sure was a think piece!*

**think tank** *n.* A company of researchers who spend their time developing ideas and concepts. ♦ *The government hired a think tank to study the country's need for coins, and was advised to stop making pennies.*

**think twice** *v.* To think again carefully; reconsider; hesitate. ♦ *The teacher advised Lou to think twice before deciding to quit school.*

**think up** *v.* To invent or discover by thinking; have a new idea of. ♦ *Mary thought up a funny game for the children to play.*

**third class** *n.* **1.** The third best or highest group; the class next after the second class. ♦ *Mary won the pie-making contest in the third class, for the youngest girls.* **2.** Mail that is printed, other than magazines and newspapers that are published regularly, and packages that are not sealed and weigh less than a pound. ♦ *The company uses third class to mail free samples of soap.* **3.** The least expensive class of travel. ♦ *I couldn't afford anything better than the third class on the ship coming home from France.*

**third degree** *n. phr.* A method of severe grilling used to extract information from an arrested suspect. ♦ *"Why give me the third degree?" he asked indignantly. "All I did was come home late because I had a drink with my friends."*

**third sex** *n., informal* Homosexual individuals who are either men or women. ♦ *Bill is rumored to belong to the third sex.*

**third world** *n.* **1.** The countries not aligned with either the former U.S.S.R.-dominated Communist bloc or the U.S.A.-dominated capitalist countries. ♦ *New Zealand made a move toward third country status when it disallowed American nuclear submarines in its harbors.* **2.** The developing nations of the world where the industrial revolution has not yet been completed. ♦ *Africa and the rest of the third world must be freed from starvation and illiteracy.*

**this and that** *also* **this, that, and the other** *n. phr.* Various things; different things; miscellaneous things. ♦ *When the old friends met they would talk about this and that.*

**this is how the cookie crumbles** *or* **that's how the cookie crumbles** *v. phr., informal* That's how things are; that's life. ♦ *It's too bad about John and Mary getting divorced, but then that's how the cookie crumbles.*

**thorn in the flesh** *or* **thorn in one's side** *n. phr.* Something that causes stubborn trouble; a constant bother; a vexation. ♦ *The new voter organization soon became the biggest thorn in the senator's side.* ♦ *The guerrilla band was a thorn in the flesh of the invaders.*

**thrash out** *v. phr.* To discuss fully; confer about something until a decision is reached. ♦ *They met to thrash out their differences concerning how to run the office.*

**three-ring circus** *n.* A scene of much confusion or activity. ♦ *It is a three-ring circus to watch that silly dog play.*

**three sheets in the wind** *or* **three sheets to the wind** *adj. phr., informal* Unsteady from too much liquor; drunk. ♦ *The sailor came down the street, three sheets in the wind.*

**thrill one to death** *or* **pieces** See TICKLE PINK.

**through and through** *adv.* Completely; entirely; whole-heartedly. ♦ *Bob was a ball player through and through.*

♦ *Mary was hurt through and through by Betty's remarks.*

**through hell and high water** See HELL AND HIGH WATER.

**through street** *n.* **1.** A street on which cars can move without stopping at intersections, but cars on streets crossing it have to stop at the intersection. ♦ *You have to be especially careful crossing a through street.* **2.** A street that is open to other streets at both ends; a street that has a passage through it, so that it is not necessary to come back to get out of it. ♦ *We thought we could get through to Main St. by going up a side street but there was a sign that said "Not a through street."*

**through the grapevine** *adv. phr.* As a matter of gossip from colleagues, acquaintances, etc. ♦ *"I heard through the grapevine that we will be down-sizing our inventory next year," Ted said. "I hope it isn't true," Fred replied.*

**through the mill** *adv. phr.* **1.** Experienced. ♦ *You could tell immediately that the new employee had been through the mill.* **2.** Through real experience of the difficulties of a certain way of life. ♦ *Poor Jerry has had three operations in one year, and now he's back in the hospital. He's really gone through the mill.*

**through thick and thin** *adv. phr.* Through all difficulties and troubles; through good times and bad times. ♦ *George stayed in college through thick and thin, because he wanted an education.*

**through train** *n. phr.* A direct train that doesn't necessitate any changes. ♦ *We'll take the through train from Chicago to New York because it's the most convenient.*

**throw a curve** *v. phr., slang, informal* **1.** To mislead or deceive someone; to lie. ♦ *John threw me a curve about the hiring.* **2.** To take someone by surprise in an unpleasant way. ♦ *Mr. Weiner's announcement threw the whole company a curve.*

**throw a monkey wrench** *or* **throw a wrench** *v. phr., informal* To cause something that is going smoothly to stop. ♦ *The game was going smoothly until you threw a monkey wrench into the works by fussing about the rules.*

**throw a party** *v. phr., informal* To hold a party; have a party. ♦ *The club is throwing a party in the high school gym Saturday night.*

**throw a punch** *v. phr.* To strike at someone with your fist; hit; punch. ♦ *Bob became so mad at Fred that he threw a punch at him.*

**throw a veil over something** *v. phr.* To conceal; hide; no longer talk about something unpleasant. ♦ *"Look, we've been divorced for more than ten years now. Why bring up such unpleasant matters?" Eugene said to Irene. "OK, I agree," she replied. "Let's throw a veil over our past differences."*

**throw away** *v.* **1.** To get rid of as unwanted or not needed; junk. ♦ *Before they moved they threw away everything they didn't want to take with them.* **2.** To waste. ♦ *The senator criticized the government for throwing away billions on the space program.* **3.** To fail to make use of. ♦ *She threw away a good chance for a better job.*

**throw caution to the winds** *also* **throw discretion to the winds** *v. phr.* To be daring; make a bold or risky move. ♦ *Fearing that the Iraqis were planning to start a war, the Americans decided to throw caution to the winds and attack the Iraqis first.*

**throw cold water on** *also* **dash cold water on** *or* **pour cold water on** *v. phr.* To discourage; say or do something to discourage. ♦ *Henry's father threw cold water on his plans to go to college by saying he could not afford it.*

**throw down the gauntlet** *v. phr.* To challenge, especially to a fight. ♦ *Another candidate for the presidency has thrown down the gauntlet.*

**throw dust into one's eye** *v. phr.* To mislead someone; give false information; delude or deceive. ♦ *There is a danger that our new business partners will try to throw dust into our eyes.*

**throw for a loss** *v. phr.* To surprise or shock (someone); upset; make worry greatly; cause trouble. ♦ *Mr. Simpson was thrown for a loss when he lost his job.*

**throw in** *v.* **1.** To give or put in as an addition; to give to or with something else. ♦ *John threw in a couple of tires when* *he sold Bill his bicycle.* **2.** To push into operating position. ♦ *Mr. Jones threw in the clutch and shifted the gears.*

**throw something in one's face** *or* **throw something in one's teeth** *v. phr.* To blame a person for (something wrong); not allow someone to forget (a mistake or failure). Used with *back.* ♦ *Bob came home late for dinner last week, and his mother keeps throwing it back in his face.*

**throw in one's lot with** *or literary* **cast in one's lot with** *v. phr.* To decide to share or take part in anything that happens to; join. ♦ *When Carl was old enough to vote, he threw in his lot with the Democrats.*

**throw in the sponge** *or* **throw up the sponge** *or* **throw in the towel** *v. phr., informal* To admit defeat; accept loss. ♦ *When Harold saw his arguments were not being accepted, he threw in the towel and left.*

**throw off** *v.* **1.** To get free from. ♦ *He was healthy enough to throw off his cold easily.* **2.** To mislead; confuse; fool. ♦ *They went by a different route to throw the hostile bandits off their track.*

**throw off the scent** *v. phr.* To mislead; confuse. ♦ *The robbers went different ways hoping to throw the sheriff's men off the scent.*

**throw off the track** *v. phr.* To divert; mislead; confuse. ♦ *The clever criminals threw the detective off the track by changing their names and faces.*

**throw oneself at someone's feet** *v. phr.* To make a public display of serving, loving, or worshipping someone. ♦ *When the new girl entered school, several boys threw themselves at her feet.*

**throw one's hat in the ring** *or* **toss one's hat in the ring** *v. phr., informal* To announce that you are going to try to be elected to an official position; become a candidate for office. ♦ *The senator threw his hat in the ring for president.*

**throw one's weight around** *v. phr., informal* To use one's influence or position in a showy or noisy manner. ♦ *Bob was stronger than the other boys, and he threw his weight around.*

**throw open 1.** To open wide with a sudden or strong movement. ♦ *He dashed in and threw open the windows.*

**2.** To remove limits from. ♦ *The Homestead Act threw open the West.* ♦ *When a hurricane and flood left many people homeless, public buildings were thrown open to shelter them.*

**throw or feed one to the wolves** *v. phr.* **1.** To turn someone into a scapegoat. ♦ *In order to explain the situation to the media, the governor blamed the mayor and threw him to the wolves.*

**throw out** *or* **toss out** *v.* **1.** To put somewhere to be destroyed because not wanted. ♦ *He didn't need the brush anymore so he threw it out.* **2.** To refuse to accept. ♦ *The inspector tossed out all the parts that didn't work.* **3.** To force to leave; dismiss. ♦ *When the employees complained too loudly, the owner threw them out.* **4.** To cause to be out in baseball by throwing the ball. ♦ *The shortstop tossed the runner out.*

**throw out of gear** *v. phr.* **1.** To separate the gears of (a car or some other machine) when you want to stop it. ♦ *When John wanted to stop, he threw the car out of gear and braked sharply.* **2.** To stop or bother (what someone is doing or planning); confuse; upset. ♦ *The whole country was thrown out of gear by the assassination of the President.*

**throw over** *v.* To give up for another; break your loyalty or attachment to. ♦ *Bob threw Mary over for a new girlfriend.*

**throw the baby out with the bath (bathwater)** *v. phr.* To reject all of something because part is faulty. ♦ *God knows that there are weaknesses in the program, but if we act too hastily we may throw the baby out with the bathwater.*

**throw the book at** *v. phr., informal* To give the most severe penalty to (someone) for breaking the law or rules. ♦ *Because it was the third time he had been caught speeding that month, the judge threw the book at him.*

**throw together** *v.* **1.** *also* **slap together** To make in a hurry and without care. ♦ *Bill and Bob threw together a cabin out of old lumber.* **2.** To put in with other people by chance. ♦ *Bill and Tom became friends when they were thrown together in the same cabin at camp.*

**throw up** *v.* **1.** *informal or slang* To vomit. ♦ *The heat made him feel sick and he* thought he would throw up. **2.** To build in a hurry. ♦ *The contractor threw up some temporary sheds to hold the new equipment.*

**throw up one's hands** *v. phr.* To give up trying; admit that you cannot succeed. ♦ *Mrs. Jones threw up her hands when the children messed up the living room for the third time.*

**throw up one's hands in horror** *v. phr.* To be horrified; feel alarmed; give up hope of straightening things out; be shocked by something terrible. ♦ *Everybody threw up their hands in horror at the destruction caused by the hurricane.*

**thrust down one's throat** *or* **push down one's throat** *v. phr.* To force one's own ideas on someone else. ♦ *It never pays in the long run to thrust one's own ideas down the throat of another.* ♦ *If you keep pushing your weird ideas about business down my throat, I will stop talking to you.*

**thumb a ride** *v. phr., informal* To get a ride by hitchhiking; hitchhike. ♦ *Not having much money, Carl decided to thumb a ride to New York.*

**thumb one's nose** *v. phr.* To look with disfavor or dislike; regard with scorn; refuse to obey. ♦ *Betty thumbed her nose at her mother's command to stay home.*

**thumb through** *v. phr.* To examine superficially; read cursorily. ♦ *I have read* War and Peace *but Fran has only thumbed through it.*

**thus and so** *also* **thus and thus** *adv. phr.* In a particular way; according to directions that have been given. ♦ *The teacher is very fussy about the way you write your report. If you don't do it thus and so, she gives you a lower mark.*

**tickle one's funny bone** *v. phr.* To amuse one; make one laugh. ♦ *It tickles my funny bone listening to Sam; he is full of the most amazing humorous anecdotes.*

**tickle pink** *v. phr., informal* To please very much; thrill; delight. Usually used in the passive participle. ♦ *Agnes was tickled pink with the great reviews about her first book of short stories.*

**tick off** *v.* **1.** To mention one after the other; list. ♦ *The teacher ticked off the assignments that Jane had to do.* **2.** To scold; rebuke. ♦ *The boss ticked off the waitress for dropping her tray.* **3.** To

anger or upset. Usually used as *ticked off.* ♦ *She was ticked off at him for breaking their dinner date again.*

**tide over** *v.* To carry past a difficulty or danger; help in bad times or in trouble. ♦ *An ice cream cone in the afternoon tided her over until supper.*

**tidy sum** *n. phr.* A large amount of money. ♦ *The Smith's big new home cost them a tidy sum.*

**tie down** *v.* To keep (someone) from going somewhere or doing something; prevent from leaving; keep in. ♦ *The navy tied the enemy down with big gunfire while the marines landed on the beach.*

**tied to one's mother's apron strings** Not independent of your mother; not able to do anything without asking your mother. ♦ *Even after he grew up he was still tied to his mother's apron strings.*

**tie in** *v.* To connect with something else; make a connection for. Used with *with.* ♦ *The teacher tied in what she said with last week's lesson.* ♦ *The detectives tied in the fingerprints on the man's gun with those found on the safe, so they knew that he was the thief.*

**tie-in** *n.* A connection; a point of meeting. ♦ *John's essay on World War II provides a perfect tie-in with his earlier work on World War I.*

**tie in knots** *v. phr.* To make (someone) very nervous or worried. ♦ *The thought of having her tooth pulled tied Joan in knots.*

**tie one on** *v. phr.* To invite someone for a drink; pay for someone's drink in a bar. ♦ *If you help me with my homework, we can go to a bar of your choice and I'll tie one on you.*

**tie one's hands** *v. phr.* To make (a person) unable to do anything.— Usually used in the passive. ♦ *Father hoped Jim would not quit school, but his hands were tied; Jim was old enough to quit if he wanted to.*

**tie one up in knots** *v. phr.* To laugh so hard that it actually hurts. ♦ *We were tied up in knots for a whole hour while listening to Bob's incredible adventures in the Sahara.*

**tie the knot** *v. phr., informal* To get married; *also* to perform a wedding ceremony. ♦ *Diane and Bill tied the knot yesterday.*

**tie up** *v. phr.* (stress on *up*) **1.** To show or stop the movement or action of; hinder; tangle. ♦ *The crash of the two trucks tied up all traffic in the center of town.* **2.** To take all the time of. ♦ *The meeting will tie the President up until noon.* **3.** To limit or prevent the use of. ♦ *His money is tied up in a trust fund and he can't take it out.* **4.** To enter into an association or partnership; join. ♦ *Our company has tied up with another firm to support the show.* **5.** To dock. ♦ *The ships tied up at New York.* **6.** To finish; complete. ♦ *We've talked long enough; let's tie up these plans and start doing things.*

**tie-up** *n.* (stress on *tie*) A congestion; a stoppage of the normal flow of traffic, business or correspondence. ♦ *There was a two-hour traffic tie-up on the highway.*

**tighten one's belt** *v. phr.* To live on less money than usual; use less food and other things. ♦ *When father lost his job we had to tighten our belts.* ♦ *When the husband lost his job, the Smiths had to do without many things, but when their savings were all spent, they had to tighten their belts another notch.*

**tighten the screws** *v. phr.* To try to make someone do something by making it more and more difficult not to do it; apply pressure. ♦ *When many students still missed class after he began giving daily quizzes, the teacher tightened the screws by failing anyone absent four times.*

**tight-lipped** *adj.* A taciturn person; one who doesn't say much. ♦ *The witness was tight-lipped about what she saw for fear of physical retaliation by the mob.*

**tight money** *n. phr.* The opposite of inflation, when money is hard to borrow from the banks. ♦ *The government decided that tight money is the way to bring down inflation.*

**tight squeeze** *n. phr.* A difficult situation; financial troubles. ♦ *The Browns aren't going out to dinner these days; they are in a tight squeeze.*

**tightwad** *n. phr.* A stingy person. ♦ *My father is such a tightwad that he won't give me an allowance.*

**Tijuana taxi** *n., slang, citizen's band radio jargon* A police car. ♦ *I've got a Tijuana taxi in sight.*

**till the cows come home** *adv. phr.* Until sunset; until the last. ♦ *The women in the country used to sit in the spinning room making yarn out of skeins of wool, usually till the cows came home.*

**till the last gun is fired** *or* **until the last gun is fired** *adv. phr.* Until the end; until everything is finished or decided. ♦ *The candidate didn't give up hope of being elected until the last gun was fired.*

**tilt at windmills** *v. phr., literary* To do battle with an imaginary foe. ♦ *John is a nice guy but when it comes to departmental meetings he wastes everybody's time by constantly tilting at windmills.*

**time after time** See TIME AND AGAIN.

**time and again** *or* **time and time again** *adv.* Many times; repeatedly; very often. ♦ *Children are forgetful and must be told time and time again how to behave.*

**time and a half** *n. phr.* Pay given to a worker at a rate half again as much as he usually gets. ♦ *Tom gets one dollar for regular pay and a dollar and a half for time and a half.*

**time and tide wait for no man** The law's of nature cannot be changed on behalf of anyone, so it is a good idea to make a decision when the time is right, otherwise you may lose your chance.—A proverb. ♦ *"Let's buy that house we always wanted now," Ted's wife suggested. "The interest rate will never be lower." "I guess you're right," Ted agreed. "It's as the saying goes, 'Time and tide wait for no man.'"*

**time is ripe** The best time has come for doing something. ♦ *The prime minister will hold elections when the time is ripe.*

**time off** *n. phr.* A period of release from work. ♦ *If I had some time off this afternoon, I would finish writing the letters I promised.*

**time of one's life** *n. phr.* A very happy or wonderful time. ♦ *John had the time of his life at the party.*

**time out** *n. phr.* Time during which a game, a lecture, a discussion or other activity is stopped for a while for some extra questions or informal discussion, or some other reason. ♦ *"Time out!"—The students said, "Could you explain that again?"*

tin ear *n. phr.* 1. A lack of sensitivity to noise. ♦ *The construction noise doesn't bother Fred; he's got a tin ear.* 2. A lack of musical ability; state of being tone deaf. ♦ *People with a tin ear make poor choir members.*

tip off *v., informal* To tell something not generally known; tell secret facts to; warn. ♦ *The thieves did not rob the bank as planned because someone tipped them off that it was being watched by the police.*

tip one's hat to one *v. phr.* To recognize someone's success and contributions by complimenting the person. ♦ *"I tip my hat to you," the Nobel Laureate for Literature said to the young man, whose first book of poetry just appeared, bringing him the Pulitzer Prize.*

tip the scales *v. phr., informal* 1. To weigh. ♦ *Martin tips the scales at 180 pounds.* 2. *or* tip the balance To have important or decisive influence; make a decision go for or against you; decide. ♦ *John's vote tipped the scales in our favor, and we won the election.*

tit for tat *n. phr.* Equal treatment in return; a fair exchange. ♦ *I told him if he did me any harm I would return tit for tat.* ♦ *They had a warm debate and the two boys gave each other tit for tat.*

to a degree *adv. phr.* 1. *Chiefly British* Very; to a large extent. ♦ *In some things I am ignorant to a degree.* 2. Somewhat; slightly; in a small way; rather. ♦ *His anger was, to a degree, a confession of defeat.*

to advantage *adv. phr.* So as to bring out the good qualities of; favorably; in a flattering way. ♦ *The jeweler's window showed the diamonds to advantage.* ♦ *The green dress showed up to advantage with her red hair.*

to a fault *adv. phr.* So very well that it is in a way bad; to the point of being rather foolish; too well; too much. ♦ *John carries generosity to a fault; he spends his money making scholarship grants to anyone who asks.*

to a large extent See IN GREAT MEASURE.

to all intents and purposes *adv. phr.* In most ways; in fact. ♦ *The president is called the head of state, but the prime minister, to all intents and purposes, is the chief executive.*

to a man *adv. phr.* Without exception; with all agreeing. ♦ *The workers voted to a man to go on strike.*

to and fro *adv. phr.* Forward and back again and again. ♦ *Busses go to and fro between the center of the city and the city limits.*

to a T *or* to a turn *adv. phr.* Just right; to perfection; exactly. ♦ *The roast was done to a turn.* ♦ *His nickname, Tiny, suited him to a T.*

to-be *adj.* That is going to be; about to become.—Used after the noun it modifies. ♦ *Bob kissed his bride-to-be.*

to be on the safe side *adv. phr.* To take extra precautions; reduce or eliminate the possibility of a mistake, an error, or even danger. ♦ *Dad always keeps his valuables in a bank's safe deposit box, just to be on the safe side.*

to be sure *adv. phr.* Without a doubt; certainly; surely. ♦ *"Didn't you say Mr. Smith would take us home?" "Oh, yes. To be sure, I did."*

to blame *adj. phr.* Having done something wrong; to be blamed; responsible. ♦ *The teacher tried to find out who was to blame in the fight.*

to boot *adv. phr.* In addition; besides; as something extra. ♦ *He not only got fifty dollars, but they bought him dinner to boot.*

to date *adv. or adj. phr.* Up to the present time; until now. ♦ *To date twenty students have been accepted into the school.*

to death *adv. phr., informal* To the limit; to the greatest degree possible.—Used for emphasis with verbs such as *scare, frighten, bore.* ♦ *Cowboy stories bore me to death, but I like mysteries.*

toe the line *or* toe the mark *v. phr.* To be very careful to do just what you are supposed to do; obey the rules and do your duties. ♦ *The new teacher will make Joe toe the line.*

to eyeball *v. phr.* 1. To stare at someone or something as if wishing to get to know one or acquire the item viewed; ogle. ♦ *"Stop eyeballing that waitress," Tom warned his friend, Ted. "Do you want to be thrown out of the bar?"* 2. To look over one's shoulder; control one's behavior. ♦ *I really hate it when my mom eyeballs me while I'm doing homework.*

together with *prep.* In addition to; in the company of; along with. ♦ *The police found a knife, together with the stolen money, hidden in a hollow tree.*

**to go** *v. phr.* To take away food one doesn't want to consume on the premises of a restaurant. ♦ *"Is this for here, or to go?" the girl at the counter asked. "To go," I replied.*

**to heel** *adj. phr.* **1.** Close behind. ♦ *The dog ran after a rabbit, but Jack brought him to heel.* **2.** Under control; to obedience. ♦ *When Peter was sixteen, he thought he could do as he pleased, but his father cut off his allowance, and Peter soon came to heel.*

**to hell with** *or* **the hell with** *prep. phr., informal*—Used to express disgusted rejection of something. ♦ *It's slop; the hell with what the cook calls it.*

**toll call** *n. phr.* A long distance telephone call for which one has to pay. ♦ *We had several toll calls on last month's telephone bill.*

**toll free** *adv. phr.* Calling an (800) telephone number with the call paid by the business whose number one has dialed. ♦ *You can call us day and night, seven days a week, toll free.*

**Tom, Dick, and Harry** *n. phr.* People in general; anyone; everyone.—Usually preceded by *every* and used to show scorn or disrespect. ♦ *The drunk told his troubles to every Tom, Dick and Harry who passed by.*

**tone down** *v.* To make softer or quieter; make less harsh or strong; moderate. ♦ *She wanted the bright colors in her house toned down.*

**tongue-in-cheek** *adj. phr.* In an ironic or insincere manner. ♦ *When the faculty complained about the poor salary increments, the university's president said that he was not a psychiatrist, thus making an inappropriate tongue-in-cheek remark.*

**tongue-lashing** *n.* A sharp scolding or criticism. ♦ *Jim's mother gave him a tongue-lashing for telling family secrets.*

**tongues wag** *informal* People speak in an excited or gossipy manner; people spread rumors. ♦ *When the bank clerk showed up in an expensive new car, tongues wagged.*

**tongue twister** *n.* A word or group of words difficult to pronounce whose meaning is irrelevant compared to the difficulty of enunciation. ♦ *"She sells sea shells by the seashore" is a popular American tongue twister.*

**to no avail** *or* **of no avail**[1] *adj. phr., formal* Having no effect; useless, unsuccessful. ♦ *Tom's practicing was of no avail. He was sick on the day of the game.*

**to no avail**[2] *adv. phr., formal* Without result; unsuccessfully. ♦ *John tried to pull the heavy cart, but to no avail.*

**too bad** *adj.* To be regretted; worthy of sorrow or regret; regrettable.—Used as a predicate. ♦ *It was too bad Bill had measles when the circus came to town.*

**too big for one's breeches** *or* **too big for one's boots** *adj. phr.* Too sure of your own importance; feeling more important than you really are. ♦ *That boy had grown too big for his breeches. I'll have to put him back in his place.*

**too ——— by half** *adj. (princ. British)* Much too; excessively. ♦ *The heroine of the story is too nice by half; she is not believable.*

**too close for comfort** *adj. phr.* Perilously near (said of bad things). ♦ *When the sniper's bullet hit the road the journalist exclaimed, "Gosh, that was too close for comfort!"*

**too many cooks spoil the broth** *or* **stew** A project is likely to go bad if managed by a multiplicity of primary movers.—A proverb. ♦ *When several people acted all at once in trying to reshape the company's investment policy, Tom spoke up and said, "Let me do this by myself! Don't you know that too many cooks spoil the broth?"*

**too many irons in the fire** See IRONS IN THE FIRE.

**to oneself**[1] *adv. phr.* **1.** Silently; in the thoughts; without making a sign that others can see; secretly. ♦ *Bill laughed to himself when John fell down.* **2.** Without telling others; in private; as a secret.—Used after *keep*. ♦ *John knew the answer to the problem, but he kept it to himself.*

**to oneself**[2] *adj. phr.* **1.** Without company; away from others; alone; deserted. ♦ *The boys went home and John was left to himself.* **2.** Following one's own beliefs or wishes; not stopped by others. ♦ *The teacher left Mary to herself to solve the problem.*

**to one's face** *adv. phr.* Directly to you; in your presence. ♦*I called him a coward to his face.*

**to one's feet** *adv. phr.* To a standing position; up. ♦*When Sally saw the bus coming, she jumped to her feet and ran out.*

**to one's heart's content** *adv. phr.* To the extent of one's wishes; one's complete satisfaction. ♦*There is a wonderful small restaurant nearby where you can eat to your heart's content.*

**to one's name** *adv. phr.* In your ownership; of your own; as part of your belongings. ♦*Ed had only one suit to his name.*

**to order** *adv. phr.* According to directions given in an order in the way and size wanted. ♦*A very big man often has his suits made to order.*

**tooth and nail** *adv. phr.* Very forcefully; vehemently; at almost any cost. ♦*John stuck to his decision to become a pianist tooth and nail, but he would have been better off choosing some other profession.*

**tooth and nail** *adv. phr.* With all weapons or ways of fighting as hard as possible; fiercely.—Used after *fight* or a similar word. ♦*The farmers fought tooth and nail to save their crops from the grasshoppers.*

**toot one's own horn** See BLOW ONE'S OWN HORN.

**top banana** *or* **top dog** *n., slang informal* The head of any business or organization; the most influential or most prestigious person in an establishment. ♦*Who's the top banana/dog in this outfit?*

**top-drawer** *adj., informal* Of the best; or most important kind. ♦*Mr. Rogers is a top-drawer executive and gets a very high salary.*

**to pieces** *adv. phr.* **1.** Into broken pieces or fragments; destroyed. ♦*The cannon shot the town to pieces.* **2.** *informal* So as not to work; into a state of not operating. ♦*After 100,000 miles the car went to pieces.* **3.** *informal* Very much; greatly; exceedingly. ♦*Joan was thrilled to pieces to see Mary.* ♦*The shooting scared Bob to pieces.*

**top off** *v.* To come or bring to a special or unexpected ending; climax. ♦*George had steak for dinner and topped it off with a fudge sundae.*

**top-of-the-line** *adj. phr.* Of the best quality; the most expensive. ♦*The Buick is a top-of-the line American automobile, comparable to the Cadillac.*

**to put it mildly** See TO SAY THE LEAST.

**to say nothing of** See NOT TO MENTION.

**to say the least** *v. phr.* To understate; express as mildly as possible. ♦*After all we did for him, his behavior toward us, to say the least, was a poor way to show his appreciation.*

**to scale** *adv. phr.* In the same proportions as in the true size; in the same shape, but not the same size. ♦*He drew the map to scale, making one inch represent fifty miles.*

**to speak of** *adj. phr., informal* Important; worth talking about; worth noticing.— Usually used in negative sentences. ♦*Judy's injuries were nothing to speak of; just a few scratches.*

**toss off** *v. phr.* **1.** To drink rapidly; drain. ♦*He tossed off two drinks and left.* **2.** To make or say easily without trying or thinking hard. ♦*She tossed off smart remarks all during dinner.*

**toss one to the sharks** See THROW ONE TO THE WOLVES.

**total terrorist** *n. phr. since 9/11/01, slang* A stern or harsh person, such as a teacher or a parent. ♦*My Dad is a total terrorist! He insists on my doing my homework before he allows me to watch television.*

**totally awesome** *adj. slang* Very good; excellent; outstanding. Having originated as "valley girl talk" in California, this affectation has become as common, as "cool." ♦*Have you seen "Shakespeare in Love" with Gwyneth Paltrow? It is totally awesome.*

**to that effect** *adj. or adv. phr.* With that meaning. ♦*She said she hated spinach, or words to that effect.*

**to the best of one's knowledge** As far as you know; to the extent of your knowledge. ♦*To the best of my knowledge she is a college graduate, but I may be mistaken.*

**to the bitter end** *adv. phr.* To the point of completion or conclusion. ♦*They knew the war would be lost, but the men fought to the bitter end.*

**to the bone** *adv., slang, informal* Thoroughly, entirely, to the core, through all layers. ♦*I am dreadfully* tired; I've worked my fingers to the bone.

**to the contrary** adv. or adj. phr. With an opposite result or effect; just the opposite; in disagreement; saying the opposite. ◆We will expect you for dinner unless we get word to the contrary.

**to the effect that** adj. phr. With the meaning or purpose; to say that. ◆He made a speech to the effect that we would all keep our jobs even if the factory were sold.

**to the eye** adv. phr. As it is seen; as a person or thing first seems; apparently. ◆That suit appears to the eye to be a good buy, but it may not be.

**to the fore** adv. or adj. phr. Into leadership; out into notice or view; forward. ◆In the progress of the war some new leaders came to the fore.

**to the full** adv. phr. Very much; fully. ◆We appreciated to the full the teacher's help.

**to the hilt** or **up to the hilt** adv. phr. To the limit; as far as possible; completely. ◆The Smith's house is mortgaged up to the hilt.

**to the letter** adv. phr. With nothing done wrong or left undone; exactly; precisely. ◆When writing a test you should follow the instructions to the letter.

**to the manner born** adj. phr. At ease with something because of lifelong familiarity with it. ◆She says her English is the best because she is to the manner born.

**to the nth degree** adv. phr. To the greatest degree possible; extremely; very much so. ◆His choice of words was exactly to the nth degree.

**to the tune of** adv. phr., informal To the amount or extent of; in the amount of. ◆When she left the race track she had profited to the tune of ten dollars.

**to the wall** adv. phr. Into a place from which there is no escape; into a trap or corner. Used after drive or a similar word. ◆John's failing the last test drove him to the wall.

**to this day** adv. phr. Up till the present; until now. ◆Although I have traveled all over the world, to this day I can't think of a nicer place to be than Hawaii.

**touch and go** adj. phr. Very dangerous or uncertain in situation. ◆Our team won

the game, all right, but it was touch and go for a while.

**touch base with** v. phr. To confer or consult with one. ◆Before we make a decision, I'd like to touch base with our financial department.

**touch down** v. phr. (stress on down) To alight; land on the ground. ◆Everyone felt relieved when the 747 jumbo jet finally touched down at Kennedy International Airport after a bumpy ride due to strong wind.

**touchdown** n. phr. (stress on touch) A goal scored during the game of American football. ◆Yale won easily over Harvard at the annual Ivy League sports contest, by scoring several unexpected touchdowns.

**touch off** v. To start something as if by lighting a fuse. ◆The president's resignation touched off a national panic.

**touch on** or **touch upon** v. To speak of or write of briefly. ◆The speaker touched on several other subjects in the course of his talk.

**touch to the quick** v. phr. To hurt someone's feelings very deeply; offend. ◆His remark about her lack of education touched her to the quick.

**touchup** n. (stress on touch) **1.** A small repair; a small amount of paint. ◆Just a small touchup here and there and your novel may be publishable. **2.** Redoing the color of one's hair. ◆My roots are showing; I need a touchup.

**touch up** v. (stress on up) **1.** To paint over (small imperfections.) ◆I want to touch up that scratch on the fender. **2.** To improve with small additions or changes. ◆He touched up the photographic negative to make a sharper print. **3.** slang To talk into lending; wheedle from. ◆He touched George up for five bucks.

**tough act to follow** n. phr. A speech, performance, or activity of such superior quality that the person next in line feels and thinks that it would be very difficult to match it in quality. ◆Sir Lawrence Olivier's performance of Hamlet was a tough act to follow in every sense.

**tough as nails** adj. phr. To be extremely unyielding in one's opinions; to be stingy. ◆"Could we get a loan from your uncle for the house?" Ted asked his wife Jean. "He is a millionaire, all right, but he is as tough as nails when it comes to finances. I'll see what I can do," she replied.

**tough cat** *n., slang* A man who is very individualistic and, as a result, highly successful with women. ♦*Joe is a real tough cat.*

**tough cookie** *n. phr.* An extremely determined, hardheaded person, or someone with whom it is unusually difficult to deal. ♦ *Marjorie is a very pretty girl, but when it comes to business she sure is one tough cookie.*

**tough it out** *v. phr.* To live through and endure a trying situation. ♦ *The tourists got lost in the desert without a compass, and they had to tough it out for three days on a single bottle of water.*

**tough luck** *n. phr.* An informal way to say that one had that coming; it serves one right. ♦*So your date didn't show up, eh? Tough luck, fellow.*

**tower of strength** *n. phr.* Someone who is strong, helpful, and sympathetic, and can always be relied on in times of trouble. ♦*John was a veritable tower of strength to our family while my father was in the war and my mother lay ill in the hospital.*

**town and gown** *n.* The residents of a college town and the students and teachers of the college. ♦ *The senator made a speech attended by both town and gown.*

**toy with an** *or* **the idea** *v. phr.* To consider an idea or an offer periodically without coming to a decision. ♦ *He was toying with the idea of accepting the company's offer of the vice presidency in Tokyo, but he was unable to decide.*

**track down** *v.* To find by or as if by following tracks or a trail. ♦ *The hunters tracked down game in the forest.*

**trade in** *v.* To give something to a seller as part payment for another thing of greater value. ♦ *The Browns traded their old car in on a new one.*

**trade-in** *n.* Something given as part payment on something better. ♦ *The dealer took our old car as a trade-in.*

**trade on** *v.* To use as a way of helping yourself. ♦ *The senator's son traded on his father's name when he ran for mayor.*

**trading stamp** *n.* One of the stamps that you get (as from a store or gas station) because you buy something there; a stamp you get with a purchase and save in special books until you have enough to take to a special store and trade for something you want. ♦*Mother always buys things in stores where they give trading stamps.*

**travel light** *v. phr.* To travel with very little luggage or with very little to carry. ♦*Plane passengers must travel light.*

**tread water** *v. phr.* To keep the head above water with the body in an upright position by moving the feet as if walking. ♦ *He kept afloat by treading water.*

**trial and error** *n.* A way of solving problems by trying different possible solutions until you find one that works. ♦*John found the short circuit by trial and error.*

**trial balloon** *n.* A hint about a plan of action that is given out to find out what people will say. ♦*John mentioned the presidency to Bill as a trial balloon to see if Bill might be interested in running.*

**trick of the trade** *n. phr., usually in plural, informal* 1. A piece of expert knowledge; a smart, quick, or skillful way of working at a trade or job. ♦*Mr. Olson spent years learning the tricks of the trade as a carpenter.* 2. A smart and sometimes tricky or dishonest way of doing something in order to succeed or win. ♦ *The champion knows all the tricks of the boxing trade; he knows many ways to hurt his opponent and to get him mixed up.*

**trick or treat** *n.* The custom of going from house to house on Halloween asking for small gifts and playing tricks on people who refuse to give. ♦ *When Mrs. Jones answered the doorbell, the children yelled "Trick or treat." Mrs. Jones gave them all some candy.*

**triple threat** *n.* A football player who is able to pass, kick, and run all very well. ♦ *The triple threat halfback was the star of the team.*

**tripped out** *adj., slang, informal* Incoherent, confused, faulty of speech, illogical; as if under the influence of drugs or alcohol. ♦ *It was hard to make sense of anything Fred said yesterday, he sounded so tripped out.*

**trip up** *v.* 1. To make (someone) unsteady on the feet; cause to miss a step, stumble, or fall. ♦ *A root tripped Billy up while he was running in the woods, and he fell and hurt his ankle.* **2.** To cause (someone) to make a mistake. ♦ *The teacher asked tricky questions in the test to trip up students who were not alert.*

**trot out** *v. phr.* To bring out for inspection; display. ♦ *Don't mention compact disks to Joe, or he'll trot out his entire collection and we'll be stuck here all night.*

**true to one's colors** *adj. phr.* Loyal to an aim, a cause, goal, or ambition. ♦ *The soldiers of George Washington were true to their colors in the American War of Independence against the British.*

**trump card** *n.* Something kept back to be used to win success if nothing else works. ♦ *Mary had several ways to get Joan to come to her party. Her trump card was that the football captain would be there.*

**trump up** *v.* (stress on *up*) To make up (something untrue); invent in the mind. ♦ *Every time Tom is late getting home he trumps up some new excuse.* ♦ *The Russians were afraid he was a spy, so they arrested him on a trumped-up charge and made him leave the country.*

**try on** *v.* To put (clothing) on to see if it fits. ♦ *The clerk told him to try the coat on.*

**try one's hand** *v. phr.* To make an inexperienced attempt (at something unfamiliar.) ♦ *I thought I would try my hand at bowling, although I had never bowled before.*

**try one's patience** *v. phr.* To irritate one; annoy one; cause someone to become impatient. ♦ *Little Tommy's constant bombarding me with "why?" "why?" "why?" and more "whys," really tried my patience.* ♦ *The constant construction noise in our high-rise apartment building is trying the patience of all the tenants.*

**try one's wings** *v. phr.* To try out a recently acquired ability. ♦ *Marjorie just had her twelfth French lesson and wants to try her wings by speaking with our visitors from Paris.*

**tryout** *n.* (stress on *try*) An audience at a theater or opera for would-be actors and singers. ♦ *The Civic Opera is holding tryouts throughout all of next week. Maybe I'll go and see if I can sing in the chorus.*

**try out** *v. phr.* (stress on *out*) **1.** To test by trial or by experimenting. ♦ *The scientists tried out thousands of chemicals before they found the right one.* **2.** To try for a place on a team or in a group. ♦ *Shirley will try out for the lead in the play.*

**tuck in** *v. phr.* To place the covers carefully around the person (usually a child) in bed. ♦ *When I was a child, my mother used to tuck me into bed every night.*

**tug-of-war** *n.* **1.** A game in which two teams pull on opposite ends of a rope, trying to pull the other team over a line marked on the ground. ♦ *The tug-of-war ended when both teams tumbled in a heap.* **2.** A contest in which two sides try to defeat each other; struggle. ♦ *The tug of war between the union men and management ended in a long strike.*

**tune in** To adjust a radio or television set to pick up a certain station. ♦ *Tom tuned in to Channel 11 to hear the news.*

**tune out** *v. phr.* To not listen to something. ♦ *"How can you work in such a noisy environment?" Jane asked Sue. "Well, I simply tune it out," she answered.*

**tune up** *v.* (stress on *up*) **1a.** To adjust (a musical instrument) to make the right sound. ♦ *Before he began to play, Harry tuned up his banjo.* **1b.** To adjust a musical instrument or a group of musical instruments to the right sound. ♦ *The orchestra came in and began to tune up for the concert.* **2.** To adjust many parts of (car engine) which must work together so that it will run properly. ♦ *He took his car to the garage to have the engine tuned up.*

**tune-up** *n.* (stress on *tune*) **1.** The adjusting or fixing of something (as a motor) to make it work safely and well. ♦ *Father says the car needs a tune-up before winter begins.* **2.** Exercise or practicing for the purpose of getting ready; a trial before something. ♦ *The team went to the practice field for their last tune-up before the game tomorrow.*

**turn a blind eye** *v. phr.* To pretend not to see; not pay attention. ♦ *The corrupt* police chief turned a blind eye to the open gambling in the town.

**turn a cold shoulder** See COLD SHOULDER.

**turn a deaf ear to** v. phr. To pretend not to hear; refuse to hear; not pay attention. ♦ The teacher turned a deaf ear to Bob's excuse.

**turn a hand** v. phr. To do anything to help.—Usually used in the negative. ♦ When we were all hurrying to get the house ready for company, Mary sat reading and wouldn't turn a hand.

**turn an honest penny** v. phr. To realize a good profit. ♦ Tom turned an honest penny in the soybean trading business.

**turn away** v. phr. To bar someone from entering a place. ♦ A huge number of people were turned away from Orchestra Hall because all tickets had been sold out.

**turncoat** n. phr. A treacherous person, who abandons one party, faith, or cause for another the moment the former side loses. ♦ Many former Nazi Party members sought refuge in the Communist Party in East Germany and elsewhere; these were the turncoats of the post-World War II era.

**turn color** v. phr. To become a different color. ♦ In the fall the leaves turn color.

**turn down** v. 1. To reduce the loudness, brightness, or force of. ♦ The theater lights were turned down. 2. To refuse to accept; reject. ♦ His request for a raise was turned down.

**turn for the worse** See FOR THE WORSE.

**turn in** v. 1. or **hand in** To give to someone; deliver to someone. ♦ I want you to turn in a good history paper. 2. To inform on; report. ♦ She turned them in to the police for breaking the street light. 3. To give in return for something. ♦ We turned our car in on a new model. 4. informal To go to bed. ♦ We were tired, so we turned in about nine o'clock.

**turn in one's grave** or **turn over in one's grave** v. phr. To be so grieved or angry that you would not rest quietly in your grave. ♦ If your grandfather could see what you're doing now, he would turn over in his grave.

**turn it up a notch** See STEP UP. 3.

**turn off** v. (stress on off) 1. To stop by turning a knob or handle or by working a switch; to cause to be off. ♦ He turned the water off. 2. To leave by turning right or left onto another way. ♦ Turn off the highway at exit 5. 3. To disgust, bore, or repel (someone) by being intellectually, emotionally, socially, or sexually unattractive. ♦ I won't date Linda Bell anymore—she just turns me off.

**turn of the screw** n. phr. An unexpected and sudden turn of events, affecting the fates of the participants. ♦ It was quite a turn of the screw when it was found out that the murder victim faked his own death to be able to collect on his life insurance.

**turn of the tide** n. phr. from Shakespeare's Julius Caesar A change in fortunes of war, politics, etc. ♦ The Battle of the Bulge in the Ardennes toward the end of World War II was a decisive turn of the tide in the favor of the Allies against Nazi Germany.

**turn on** v. 1. To start by turning a knob or handle or working a switch; cause to be on. ♦ Who turned the lights on? 2. informal To put forth or succeed with as easily as turning on water. ♦ She really turns on the charm when that new boy is around. 3. To attack. ♦ The lion tamer was afraid the lions would turn on him. 4. slang The opposite of turning someone off; to become greatly interested in an idea, person, or undertaking; to arouse the senses pleasantly. ♦ Mozart's music always turns me on. 5. Introducing someone to a new experience, or set of values. ♦ Syd turned me on to transcendental meditation, and ever since I've been feeling great!

**turn on a dime** v. phr. To be able to turn in a very narrow spot comparable to a small coin. ♦ This new sports car can turn on a dime.

**turn one's back on** v. phr. To refuse to help (someone in trouble or need.) ♦ He turned his back on his own family when they needed help.

**turn one's head** v. phr., informal To make you lose your good judgment. ♦ The first pretty girl he saw turned his head.

**turn one's nose up at** v. phr. To scorn; snub; look down at somebody or something. ♦ I don't understand why Sue has to turn her nose up at everyone who didn't go to an Ivy League college.

**turn one's stomach** v. phr., informal To make you feel sick. ♦The smell of that cigar was enough to turn your stomach.

**turn on one's heel** v. phr. To turn around suddenly. ♦When John saw Fred approaching him, he turned on his heel.

**turnout** n. (stress on turn) The number of people in attendance at a gathering. ♦This is a terrific turnout for Tim's poetry reading.

**turn out** v. (stress on out) 1. To make leave or go away. ♦His father turned him out of the house. 2. To turn inside out; empty. ♦He turned out his pockets looking for the money. 3. To make; produce. ♦The printing press turns out a thousand books an hour. 4. informal To get out of bed. ♦At camp the boys had to turn out early and go to bed early too. 5. informal To come or go out to see or do something. ♦Everybody turned out for the big parade. 6. To prove to be; be in the end; be found to be. ♦The noise turned out to be just the dog scratching at the door. 7. To make (a light) go out. ♦Please turn out the lights.

**turnover** n. (stress on turn) 1. The proportion of expenditure and income realized in a business; the volume of traffic in a business. ♦Our turnover is so great that in two short years we tripled our original investment and are expanding at a great rate. 2. Triangular baked pastry filled with some fruit. ♦John's favorite dessert is apple turnovers. 3. The number of employees coming and going in a company. ♦The boss is so strict in our office that the turnover in personnel is very large.

**turn over** v. (stress on over) 1. To roll, tip, or turn from one side to the other; overturn; upset. ♦The bike hit a rock and turned over. 2. To think about carefully; to consider. ♦He turned the problem over in his mind for three days before he did anything about it. 3. To give to someone for use or care. ♦I turned my library books over to the librarian. 4. Of an engine or motor; to start. ♦The battery is dead and the motor won't turn over. 5a. To buy and then sell to customers. ♦The store turned over $5,000 worth of skiing equipment in January. 5b. To be bought in large enough amounts; sell.

♦In a shoe store, shoes of medium width turn over quickly, because many people wear that size.

**turn over a new leaf** v. phr. To start afresh; to have a new beginning. ♦"Don't be sad, Jane," Sue said. "A divorce is not the end of the world. Just turn over a new leaf and you will soon be happy again."

**turn over in one's grave** See TURN IN ONE'S GRAVE .

**turn over in one's mind** v. phr. To carefully consider. ♦I will have to turn it over in my mind whether to accept the new job offer from Japan.

**turn tail** v. phr., informal To run away from trouble or danger. ♦When the bully saw my big brother, he turned tail and ran.

**turn the clock back** v. phr. To return to an earlier period. ♦Mother wished she could turn the clock back to the days before the children grew up and left home.

**turn the corner** v. phr. To pass an important juncture in a complicated, difficult, or dangerous situation, such as war or serious illness, with improvement in sight. ♦"We have turned the corner on Mr. Smith's condition," the heart transplant surgeon said with a happy smile. "He is off the 'dangerous' list and is now in 'serious condition' only."

**turn the other cheek** v. phr. To let someone do something to you and not to do it in return; not hit back when hit; be patient when injured or insulted by someone; not try to get even. ♦Joe turned the other cheek when he was hit with a snowball.

**turn the scales** v. phr. To affect the balance in favor of one party or group against the other. ♦It could well be that the speech he made turned the scales in their favor.

**turn the tables** v. phr. To make something happen just the opposite of how it is supposed to happen. ♦The boys turned the tables on John when they took his squirt gun away and squirted him.

**turn the tide** v. phr. To change what looks like defeat into victory. ♦We were losing the game until Jack got there. His coming turned the tide for us, and we won.

**turn the trick** *v. phr., informal* To bring about the result you want; succeed in what you plan to do. ♦ *Jerry wanted to win both the swimming and diving contests, but he couldn't quite turn the trick.*

**turn thumbs down** *v. phr.* To disapprove or reject; say no. ♦ *The company turned thumbs down on Mr. Smith's sales plan.*

**turn turtle** *v. phr.* To turn upside down. ♦ *The car skidded on the ice and turned turtle.*

**turn up** *v.* **1.** To find; discover. ♦ *The police searched the house hoping to turn up more clues.* **2.** To appear or be found suddenly or unexpectedly. ♦ *The missing boy turned up an hour later.*

**turn up like a bad penny** *v. phr.* To keep coming back; periodically recur.—A proverb. ♦ *The man, who claims that he is a homeless veteran, actually owns two cars and a home; he makes more in a month than a fully employed teacher. Wherever we look, he keeps turning up like a bad penny.*

**turn up one's nose at** *v. phr.* To refuse as not being good enough for you. ♦ *He thinks he should only get steak, and he turns up his nose at hamburger.*

**turn up one's toes** *v. phr., slang* To die. ♦ *One morning the children found that their pet mouse had turned up his toes, so they had a funeral for him.*

**twiddle one's thumbs** *v. phr.* To do nothing; be idle. ♦ *I'd rather work than stand around here twiddling my thumbs.*

**twist one around one's little finger** *also* **turn one around one's little finger** *or* **wrap one around one's finger** *v. phr.* To have complete control over; to be able to make (someone) do anything you want. ♦ *Sue can twist any of the boys around her little finger.*

**twist one's arm** *v. phr., informal* To force someone; threaten someone to make him do something. ♦ *I had to twist Tom's arm to make him accept our dinner invitation.*

**two bits** *n., slang* Twenty-five cents; a quarter of a dollar. ♦ *A haircut only cost two bits when Grandfather was young.*

**two-by-four** *n. phr.* A wood post measuring 2 × 4 inches cut to order in length, commonly used in frame house constructions to prop up the wall. ♦ *When Tim noticed the burglar in his backyard, he hit him on the head with a two-by-four.*

**two cents** *n. informal* **1.** Something not important or very small; almost nothing. ♦ *When John saw that the girl he was scolding was lame, he felt like two cents.* **2.** *or* **two cents worth** Something you want to say; opinion.— Used with a possessive. ♦ *If we want your two cents, we'll ask for it.*

**two-faced** *adj.* Insincere; disloyal; deceitful. ♦ *Don't confide too much in him as he has the reputation of being two-faced.*

**Two's company; three's a crowd** An informal way to express a situation when two people desire privacy and a third one is present.—A proverb. ♦ *Beth and Carl wanted to be alone so when Maggie joined them they said, "Two's company; three's a crowd."*

**two strikes against one** *n. phr.* Two opportunities wasted in some undertaking, so that only one chance is left. ♦ *Poor John has two strikes against him when it comes to his love for Frances: first, he is too fat, and, second, he is bald.*

**two-time** *v., slang* To go out with a second boy or girlfriend and keep it a secret from the first. ♦ *Mary cried when she found that Joe was two-timing her.*

**U.F.O.** *n. phr.* Unidentified Flying Object. ◆ *Some people think that the U.F.O.s are extraterrestrial beings of higher than human development who pay periodic visits to Earth to warn us of our self-destructive tendencies.*

**ugly duckling** *n.* An ugly or plain child who grows up to be pretty and attractive. ◆ *Mary was the ugly duckling in her family, until she grew up.*

**uh-huh** *or* **um-hum** *adv., informal* Yes.— Used only in speech or when recording dialogue. ◆ *When I asked for an appointment, the nurse said, "Um-hum, I have an opening at four o'clock on Friday."*

**Uncle Sam** *n. phr.* The nickname of the United States of America. ◆ *"Uncle Sam wants you!" is a common poster, encouraging young men and women to join the U.S. armed forces.* ◆ *"I work for Uncle Sam," said John, "so every time I move, the government moves my entire household from one country to the next. I am in the diplomatic service, you see."*

**under a cloud** *adj. phr.* **1.** Under suspicion; not trusted. ◆ *The butcher is under a cloud because the inspectors found his scales were not honest.* **2.** Depressed, sad, discouraged. ◆ *Joe has been under a cloud since his dog died.*

**under age** *adj. phr.* Too young; not old enough; below legal age. ◆ *He could not enlist in the army because he was under age.*

**under arrest** *adj. phr.* Held by the police. ◆ *The three boys were seen breaking into the school building and soon found themselves under arrest.*

**under construction** *adv. phr.* In the process of being built or repaired. ◆ *It is a good idea to take the train to work while the expressway is under construction.*

**under cover** *adv. or adj. phr.* Hidden; concealed. ◆ *The prisoners escaped under cover of darkness.*

**under fire** *adv. phr.* Being shot at or being attacked; hit by attacks or accusations; under attack. ◆ *The principal was under fire for not sending the boys home who stole the car.*

**under lock and key** *adv. phr.* Secured; locked up; well protected. ◆ *Dad keeps all his valuables under lock and key.*

**under one's belt** *adv. phr., informal* **1.** In your stomach; eaten; or absorbed. ◆ *Jones is talkative when he has a few drinks under his belt.* **2.** In your experience, memory or possession; learned or gotten successfully; gained by effort and skill. ◆ *Jim has to get a lot of algebra under his belt before the examination.*

**under one's breath** *adv. phr.* In a whisper; with a low voice. ◆ *The teacher heard the boy say something under his breath and she asked him to repeat it aloud.*

**under one's heel** *adv. phr.* In one's power or control. ◆ *If one marriage partner always wants to keep the other person under his or her heel, it is not a happy or democratic arrangement and may lead to a divorce.*

**under one's nose** *or* **under the nose of** *adv. phr., informal* In sight of; in an easily seen or noticeable place. ◆ *The thief walked out of the museum with the painting, right under the nose of the guards.*

**under one's own steam** *adv. phr., informal* By one's own efforts; without help. ◆ *We didn't think he could do it, but Bobby finished his homework under his own steam.*

**under one's spell** *adv. phr.* Unable to resist one's influence. ◆ *From the first moment they saw each other, Peter was under Nancy's spell.*

**under one's thumb** *or* **under the thumb** *adj. or adv. phr.* Obedient to you; controlled by you; under your power. ◆ *The mayor is so popular that he has the whole town under his thumb.*

**under one's wing** *adv. phr.* Under the care or protection of. ◆ *The boys stopped teasing the new student when Bill took him under his wing.*

**under orders** *adv. phr.* Not out of one's own desire or one's own free will; obligatorily; not freely. ◆ *"So you were a Nazi prison guard?" the judge asked. "Yes, your Honor," the man answered, "but I was acting under orders and not because I wished to harm anyone."*

**under protest** *adv. phr.* Against one's wish; unwillingly. ◆ *"I'll go with you all right," she said to the kidnapper, "but I want it clearly understood that I do so under protest."*

**under the circumstances** *adv. phr.* In the existing situation; in the present condition; as things are. ◆ *Under the circumstances, the pedestrian had to give the robbers their money.*

**under the counter** *adv. phr., informal* Secretly (bought or sold). ◆ *The liquor dealer was arrested for selling beer under the counter to teenagers.* ◆ *During World War II, some stores kept scarce things hidden for under-the-counter-sales to good customers.*

**under the gun** *adv, phr.* In a precarious position; under extraordinary pressure. ◆ *John feels really exhausted these days; he has been under the gun at his workplace for weeks now, due to the new director's unreasonable demands on his time and energy.*

**under the hammer** *adv. phr.* Up for sale at auction ◆ *The picture I wanted to bid on came under the hammer soon after I arrived.*

**under the sun** *adj. or adv. phr.* On earth; in the world.—Used for emphasis. ◆ *The president's assassination shocked everyone under the sun.*

**under the weather** *adv. phr.* In bad health or low spirits. ◆ *Mary called in today asking for a sick day as she is under the weather.*

**under the wire** *adv. phr.* With a narrow time limit; in the last minute. ◆ *The journalist's new lead article on Russia was due in press at 5 P.M., and he got it in at 4:57, just under the wire.*

**underway** *adv. phr.* In progress; in motion. ◆ *The yearly fund-raising campaign for the renovation of our university campus is already underway.*

**under wraps** *adv. or adj. phr.* Not allowed to be seen until the right time; not allowed to act or speak freely; in secrecy; hidden. ◆ *What the President is planning will be kept under wraps until tomorrow.*

**unknown quantity** *n.* Someone or something whose value and importance are not known, especially in a certain situation, time or place; a new and untested person or thing. ◆ *What we would find if we could fly to Mars is an unknown quantity.*

**until all hours** *adv. phr.* Until very late at night. ◆ *He is so anxious to pass his exams with flying colors that he stays up studying until all hours.*

**until hell freezes over** *adv. phr., slang* Forever, for an eternity. ◆ *He can argue until hell freezes over; nobody will believe him.*

**untimely end** *n. phr.* Premature death. ◆ *Many a young American soldier came to an untimely end during both world wars.*

**unwritten law** *n. phr.* Common rules of decency; common sense and right reason, which are not codified in writing. ◆ *When a house is on fire, one first rescues the children and the helpless, according to the unwritten law.*

**up against** *prep. phr.* Blocked or threatened by. ◆ *When she applied to medical school, the black woman wondered whether she was up against barriers of sex and race prejudice.*

**up against it** *adj. phr., informal* Faced with a great difficulty or problem; badly in need. ◆ *You will be up against it if you don't pass the test. You will probably fail arithmetic.*

**up and about** *or* **around** *adv. phr.* Recovered and able to move about; once again in good health after an illness. ◆ *My sister was ill for several weeks, but is now up and about again.*

**up and at them 1.** *adv. phr.* Actively engaged in a task as if doing combat. ◆ *"You want to know whether he will make a diligent worker?" Dick asked. "Well, I can tell you that most of the time he is up and at them like no one else I know."* **2.** *v. phr.* To become aggressively engaged in doing something. ◆ *Come on, up and at them, you guys. We still have a lot of work to get done.*

**up-and-coming** *adj. phr.* Bound toward success; upwardly mobile; progressive; ambitious. ◆ *The newly elected state senator is an up-and-coming young politician.*

**up and doing** *adj. phr.* Recovered; well; active. ◆ *Mary was bedridden with a serious illness, but she is totally cured now, up and doing.*

**up a tree** *adv. or adj. phr.* **1.** Hunted or chased into a tree; treed. ◆ *The dog* *drove the coon up a tree so the hunter could shoot him.* **2.** *informal* in trouble; having problems; in a difficulty that it is hard to escape or think of a way out of. ♦ *John's father has him up a tree in the checker game.*

**up for grabs** *adj. phr., informal* Available for anyone to try to get; ready to be competed for; there for the taking. ♦ *When the captain of the football team moved out of town, his place was up for grabs.*

**up front¹** *n., slang, informal* The managerial section of a corporation or firm. ♦ *Joe Catwallender finally made it (with the) up front.*

**up front²** *adj., slang, informal* Open, sincere, hiding nothing. ♦ *Sue was completely up front about why she didn't want to see him anymore.*

**uphill battle** *n. phr.* A heavy task fraught with difficulty and constantly recurring obstacles. ♦ *Retired lower middle-class people must fight a constant uphill battle to make ends meet on a fixed pension.* ♦ *The medical profession is fighting an uphill battle in trying to wipe out the AIDS epidemic worldwide.*

**up in arms** *adj. phr.* **1.** Equipped with guns or weapons and ready to fight. ♦ *All of the American colonies were up in arms against the British.* **2.** Very angry and wanting to fight. ♦ *The students were up in arms over the new rule against food in the dormitory.*

**up in the air** *adj. or adv. phr.* **1.** *informal* In great anger or excitement. ♦ *My father went straight up in the air when he heard I damaged the car.* **2.** *also in midair* Not settled; uncertain; undecided. ♦ *Plans for the next meeting have been left up in the air until Jane gets better.*

**up one's alley** See DOWN ONE'S ALLEY.

**up one's sleeve** *or* **in one's sleeve** *adv. phr.* **1.** Hidden in the sleeve of one's shirt or coat and ready for secret or wrongful use. ♦ *The crooked gambler hid aces up his sleeve during the card game so that he would win.* **2.** *informal* Kept secretly ready for the right time or for a time when needed. ♦ *Jimmy knew that his father had some trick up his sleeve because he was smiling to himself during the checker game.*

**upper crust** *n., informal* The richest, most famous, or important people in a certain place; the highest class. ♦ *It is a school that only the children of the upper crust can afford.*

**upper hand** *or* **whip hand** *n.* Controlling power; advantage. ♦ *The cowboy trained the wild horse so that he finally got the whip hand and tamed the horse.*

**upper story** *n.* **1.** A floor or level of a building above the first floor. ♦ *The apartment house where Gene lives is five stories high and he lives in one of the upper stories.* **2.** *slang* A person's head or brain. ♦ *Lulu has nobody home in the upper story.*

**Upsadaisy!** *or* **Upsee-daisy!** *or* **Upsy-daisy!** *adv. phr.*—A popular exclamation used when just about anything is lifted, particularly a small child raised to his or her highchair or bed. ♦ *"Upsee-daisy!" the nurse said with a smile on her face, as she lifted the baby from its bed.*

**ups and downs** *n. phr.* Vicissitudes; alternating periods between good and bad times; changes in fortune. ♦ *He is now a wealthy stock trader, but at the beginning of his career he, too, had many ups and downs.*

**upset the applecart** *or* **upset one's applecart** *v. phr., informal* To ruin a plan or what is being done, often by surprise or accident; change how things are or are being done, often unexpectedly; ruin or mix up another person's success or plan for success. ♦ *We are planning a surprise party for Bill, so don't let Mary upset the applecart by telling him before the party.*

**upside down** *adv. phr.* Overturned so that the bottom is up and the top is down. ♦ *The problem with this company is that everything is upside down; we need a new C.E.O.*

**up the creek** *or* **up the creek without a paddle** *adj. phr., informal* In trouble or difficulty and unable to do anything about it; stuck. ♦ *Father said that if the car ran out of gas in the middle of the desert, we would be up the creek without a paddle.*

**up tight** *or* **uptight** *adj., slang, informal* Worried, irritated, excessively eager or anxious. ♦ *Why are you so uptight about getting that job? The more you worry, the less you'll succeed.*

**up to** *prep.* **1.** As far, as deep, or as high as. ♦ *The water in the pond was only up to John's knees.* **2.** Close to; approaching. ♦ *The team did not play up to its best today.* **3.** As high as; not more than; as much or as many as. ♦ *Pick any number up to ten.* **4.** *or* **up till** *or* **up until**—Until; till. ♦ *Up to her fourth birthday, the baby slept in a crib.* **5.** Capable of; fit for; equal to; strong or well enough for. ♦ *We chose Harry to be captain because we thought he was up to the job.* **6.** Doing or planning secretly; ready for mischief. ♦ *What are you up to with the matches, John?* **7.** Facing as a duty; to be chosen or decided by; depending on. ♦ *It's up to you to get to school on time.*

**up-to-date** *adj.* Modern; contemporary; the latest that technology can offer. ♦ *"I want an up-to-date dictionary of American idioms," Mr. Lee said, "that has all the latest Americanisms in it."*

**up to no good** *adv. phr.* Intending to do something bad; perpetrating an illicit act. ♦ *We could tell from the look on Dennis the Menace's face that he was once again up to no good.*

**up to one** *adj. phr.* Left to someone else's discretion or decision. ♦ *"I am afraid it is not up to me to decide whether you will get a salary raise next year or not," John said to a junior colleague.*

**up to one's ears** *adv. phr.* Immersed in; covered with. ♦ *"Around final examination time," Professor Brown explained, "I am always up to my ears in work."*

**up to one's neck** *adv. phr.* Overwhelmed with; submerged in. ♦ *"During the summer season in our cottage by the lake," the Allens complained, "we are usually up to our necks in uninvited guests."*

**up to par** *or informal* **up to scratch** *or informal* **up to snuff 1.** In good or normal health or physical condition. ♦ *I have a cold and don't feel up to par.* ♦ *The boxer is training for the fight but he isn't up to scratch yet.* **2.** *or* **up to the mark** As good as usual; up to the usual level or quality. ♦ *John will have to work hard to bring his grades up to snuff.*

**up to speed** *adv. phr.* Back to the normal routine; back to normal speed. ♦ *After* the economic slowdown in the wake of 9/11/01, business is up to speed again in New York City.

**up to the chin in** *or* **in———up to the chin** *adj. phr.*, *informal* Used also with *ears*, *elbows*, *eyes* or *knees* instead of *chin*, and with a possessive instead of *the*. **1.** Having a big or important part in; guilty of; not innocent of; deeply in. ♦ *Was Tom mixed up in that trouble last night? He was up to his ears in it.* **2.** Very busy with; working hard at. ♦ *Bob is up to his neck in homework.* **3.** Having very much or many of; flooded with. ♦ *Mary was up to her knees in invitations to go to parties.*

**up to the last minute** *adv. phr.* Until the last possible moment; until the very end. ♦ *When I try to send in an important eyewitness report from the scene of a major accident, I must keep working up to the last minute.*

**up to the mark** See UP TO PAR 2.

**up-to-the-minute** See UP-TO-DATE.

**urban homesteading** *n.*, *informal* Renovation and occupation through cooperative ownership by tenants of previously abandoned city apartment buildings. ♦ *Urban homesteading is on the rise in many big American cities these days.*

**used to**[1] *adj. phr.* In the habit of or familiar with. ♦ *People get used to smoking and it is hard for them to stop.*

**used to**[2] *or* **did use to** *v. phr.* Did formerly; did in the past.—Usually used with an infinitive to tell about something past. ♦ *Uncle Henry used to have a beard, but he shaved it off.* ♦ *I don't go to that school any more, but I used to.* ♦ *We don't visit Helen as much as we used to.*

**used to be** *or* **did use to be** *v. phr.* Formerly or once was. ♦ *Dick used to be the best student in our class last year; now two other students are better than he is.*

**use every trick in the book** *v. phr.*, *informal* To avail oneself of any means at all in order to achieve one's goal, not exclusive of possibly immoral or illegal acts. ♦ *Algernon used every trick in the book to get Maxine to go out with him, but she kept refusing.*

**use one's head** *or slang* **use one's bean** *or slang* **use one's noodle** *or slang* **use**

**one's noggin** *v. phr.* To use your brain or mind; think; have common sense.— Often used as a command. ♦ *If you used your bean you wouldn't be in trouble now.* ♦ *Never point a gun at anybody, John. Use your head!*

**user-friendly** *adj. phr., computer jargon* A machine, such as a personal computer, a video recorder, a cell phone, etc., which is easy to run even by non-experts. ♦ *Word 2000 is quite a user-friendly program; anyone can learn it in less than a week.* ♦ *Some video recorders are not very user-friendly, so people often need to ask for help in programming them.*

**use up** *v. phr.* **1.** To use until nothing is left; spend or consume completely. ♦ *Don't use up all the soap. Leave me some to wash with.*

**usher in** *v. phr.* To function as the start of a period of time or an age different from the period that preceded it. ♦ *The 1960s ushered in the age of civil rights in the United States, whereas September 11, 2001 ushered in the age of the war on terrorism.*

**utility room** *n.* A room in a house or building for machinery and other things important in the daily use of the building and the work of the people in it. ♦ *There is a utility room upstairs where Mother does the laundry.*

**U-turn** *n. phr.* A 180 degree turn made on a road in a car; a road sign allowing or disallowing such a turn. ♦ *"Officer," Tim asked the policeman sitting in his car, "May I make a U-turn here?" "No," the policeman answered. "Didn't you see the 'No U-turn' sign on the corner?"*

**vanishing cream** n. A cosmetic cream for the skin that is used chiefly before face powder. ◆ *Mrs. Jones spread vanishing cream on her face before applying her face powder.*

**variety show** n. A program that includes several different kinds of entertainment (as songs, dances, comic skits and little dramas). ◆ *Jane's father was the master of ceremonies of a variety show on TV.*

**variety store** n. A store that sells many different kinds of things, especially items that are fairly small and in everyday use. ◆ *I went into a variety store and bought some paint.* ◆

**verbal diarrhea** n. phr. The inability to keep silent; overtalkativeness. ◆ *Archibald is a nice guy but he's got verbal diarrhea and he can't shut up for a single minute.*

**very well** interj., formal Agreed; all right.—Used to show agreement or approval. ◆ *Very well. You may go.* ◆ *Very well, I will do as you say.*

**vibrations** or **vibes** n. Psychic emanations radiating from an object, situation, or person. ◆ *I don't think this relationship will work out—this guy has given me bad vibes.*

**vicious circle** n. phr. A kind of circular or chain reaction in which one negative thing leads to another. ◆ *Some people take so many different kinds of medicine to cure an illness that they develop other illnesses from the medicine and are thus caught in a vicious circle.*

**Vietnam syndrome** n., informal An attitude in government circles that diplomacy may be more effective in solving local political problems in other countries than the use of military force, stemming from the failure of the U.S. military intervention in Vietnam. ◆ *The pundits of Foggy Bottom display the Vietnam syndrome these days when it comes to Iran.*

**virgin page** n. phr. An empty page with no writing on it. ◆ *In the middle of the new book there were a couple of virgin pages, probably due to a printing error.*

**visible to the naked eye** adj. phr. **1.** Perceivable without glasses, binoculars, microscope, or telescope. ◆ *The stars are distant objects, but on a clear summer night they are visible to the naked eye.* **2.** Obvious, clear-cut. ◆ *After the books were audited, it became visible to the naked eye that Carwallender embezzled the company's retirement fund.*

**visiting nurse** n. A nurse who goes from home to home taking care of sick people or giving help with other health problems. ◆ *After John returned home from the hospital, the visiting nurse came each day to change his bandages.*

**voice an opinion** v. phr. To go on record by uttering an opinion in speech, especially in public, or by writing an article in a newspaper or giving a radio or television interview. ◆ *Ms. Bevilaqua keeps voicing the opinion, both verbally and in writing, that it was a mistake to repeal Prohibition.* ◆ *Antiabortion advocates voice the opinion that a woman has no choice whether to give birth or not.*

**voice box** n. The part of the throat where the sound of your voice is made; the larynx. ◆ *Mr. Smith's voice box was taken out in an operation, and he could not talk after that.*

**voiceprint** n., technological, colloquial The graphic pattern derived from converting an individual's voice into a visible graph used by the police for identification purposes, much as fingerprints. ◆ *They have succeeded in identifying the murderer by using a voiceprint.*

**vote a straight ticket** v. phr. To not differentiate one's ballot according to individual names and posts, but to vote for all candidates for all positions of the same party. ◆ *"I never have time to study the ballot in detail," Marie said, "and so I tend to vote a straight Democratic ticket."*

**vote in** v. phr. To elevate to the status of "Law of the Land" by special or general ballot. ◆ *Congress has finally voted in the Brady Law that requires that prospective gun owners wait a special period of time before making their purchase.*

**vote one out** v. phr. To terminate one's elected office by casting a negative vote about that person (judge, congressman, etc.), mostly so that someone else might occupy the same position. ◆ *Congressman Smith was voted out last November in favor of Congresswoman Bradley.*

**wade in** *or* **wade into** *v., informal* **1.** To go busily to work. ◆ *The house was a mess after the party, but Mother waded in and soon had it clean again.* **2.** To attack. ◆ *Jack waded into the boys with his fists flying.*

**wade through** *v. phr.* To read through something long and laborious. ◆ *It took John six months to wade through Tolstoy's* War and Peace *in the original Russian.*

**wait-and-see** *adj. phr.* Caution; patient; circumspect. ◆ *The city council decided to take a wait-and-see attitude, before deciding to invest more money in a new airport.*

**wait at table** *or* **wait on table** *or* **wait table** *v. phr.* To serve food. ◆ *Mrs. Lake had to teach her new maid to wait on table properly.* ◆ *The girls earn spending money by waiting at table in the school dining rooms.*

**waiting list** *n.* A list of persons waiting to get into something (as a school). ◆ *The landlord said there were no vacant apartments available, but that he would put the Rogers' name on the waiting list.*

**waiting room** *n. phr.* The sitting area in a doctor's, lawyer's, accountant's, etc. office, or in a hospital, or other workplace, where people wait their turn. ◆ *Some doctor's offices have elegantly furnished waiting rooms with magazines, newspapers, and coffee for the patients.*

**wait on** *or* **wait upon** *v.* **1.** To serve. ◆ *The clerk in the store asked if we had been waited upon.* **2.** *formal* To visit as a courtesy or for business. ◆ *John waited upon the President with a letter of introduction.* **3.** To follow. ◆ *Success waits on hard work.*

**wait on hand and foot** *v. phr.* To serve in every possible way; do everything for (someone). ◆ *Sally is spoiled because her mother waits on her hand and foot.*

**wait out** *v. phr.* To exercise patience and refrain from acting prematurely. ◆ *"The stock market is down," John said to his broker, "What should we do?" "I suggest you do nothing right now," the broker advised. "This is a time to wait it out and see which way things turn out."*

**wait up** *v. phr.* To not go to bed until a person one is worried about comes home (said by parents and marriage partners). ◆ *She always waits up for her husband when he's out late.*

**wake-up call** *n. phr.* A stark and shocking reminder that things are not as they ought to be. ◆ *September 11, 2001 was a powerful wake-up call that airline security in the United States needed immediate and drastic overhauling.*

**walk all over** See WALK OVER.

**walk a tightrope** *v. phr.* To be in a dangerous or awkward situation where one cannot afford to make a single mistake. ◆ *"When we landed on the moon in 1969," Armstrong explained, "we were walking a tightrope till the very end."*

**walk away with** *or* **walk off with** *v.* **1.** To take and go away with; take away; often: steal. ◆ *When Father went to work, he accidentally walked off with Mother's umbrella.* ◆ **2.** To take, get, or win easily. ◆ *Jim walked away with all the honors on Class Night.* ◆ *Our team walked off with the championship.*

**walking catastrophe** *n. phr.* A terribly clumsy, awkward, or untoward person, who ruins everything he or she touches. ◆ *Poor Uncle Joe keeps getting fired from every job he ever tries; moreover, he wrecks one car after another, and is always broke. Women are avoiding him like the plague because he is a walking catastrophe.*

**walking dictionary** *n. phr.* A person highly knowledgeable in matters of language use. ◆ *If you want to know what "serendipity" means, ask my Uncle Fred. He is a professor of English and is also a walking dictionary.*

**walking encyclopedia** *n. phr.* A polymath; a person very well versed in a number of different disciplines. ◆ *My uncle is a veritable walking encyclopedia when it comes to the history of World War II.*

**walking papers** *or* **walking orders** *also* **walking ticket** *n., informal* A statement that you are fired from your job; dismissal. ♦ *The boss was not satisfied with Paul's work and gave him his walking papers.*

**walk in the park** *n. phr.* Something very easy to do or to accomplish. ♦ *"Is it difficult to surf the net?" six-year-old Tommy asked of his twelve-year-old brother. "No, not at all, it's a walk in the park."*

**walk off the job** *v. phr.* To go on strike. ♦ *The Canadian postal workers walked off the job in protest. People who want to send a letter to the United States have to rent a mailbox in Buffalo, New York, and drive to it periodically.*

**walk of life** *n. phr.* Way of living; manner in which people live. ♦ *People from every walk of life enjoy television.*

**walk on air** *v. phr., informal* To feel happy and excited. ♦ *Sue has been walking on air since she won the prize.*

**walk on eggs** *v. phr.* To act with utmost caution due to being in a precarious position. ♦ *Tom has been walking on eggs ever since he started working for a new boss in Cincinnati.*

**walk out** *v.* **1.** To go on strike. ♦ *When the company would not give them higher pay, the workers walked out.* **2.** To leave suddenly; especially to desert. ♦ *He didn't say he wasn't coming back; he just walked out.* Used informally with *on.* ♦ *The man walked out on his wife and children.*

**walk over** *or* **walk all over** *or* **step all over** *v. phr, informal* To make (someone) do whatever you wish; make selfish use of; treat like a slave; impose upon. ♦ *Jill is so friendly and helpful that people walk all over her.*

**walk the floor** *v. phr.* To walk one direction and then the other across the floor, again and again; pace. ♦ *Mrs. Black's toothache hurt so much that she got up and walked the floor.*

**walk the plank** *v. phr.* **1.** To walk off a board extended over the side of a ship and be drowned. ♦ *The pirates captured the ship and forced the crew to walk the plank.* **2.** *informal* To resign from a job because someone makes you do it. ♦ *When a new owner bought the store, the manager had to walk the plank.*

**wallflower** *n.* A girl who has to sit out dances because nobody is asking her to dance. ♦ *"I used to be a wallflower during my high school days," Valerie complained, "but my luck changed for better once I got into college."*

**wallow in misery** *v. phr.* To be a professional victim; incessantly complain about one's troubles, taking masochistic pleasure from one's bad fate. ♦ *"You must stop wallowing in your misery, Max," his psychiatrist said, "and get your act together. I am prescribing for you a mild antidepressant and 45 minutes of daily exercise."*

**wallow in the mire** *v. phr.* To indulge oneself entirely to sensual pleasures, such as drinking, sex, and drugs. ♦ *Felix inherited a lot of money from his wealthy father, so instead of working or studying, he spends all of his time wallowing in the mire.*

**walls have ears** Someone may be listening even if it is not apparent.—A proverb. ♦ *"Not so loud, please! This is confidential!" the director said to his news assistant. "Walls have ears, you know!"*

**want ad** *n.* A small advertisement on a special page in a newspaper that offers employment opportunities and merchandise. ♦ *"You want a temporary job?" he asked the recent arrival in town. "Go and look at the want ads!"*

**want to bet on it?** *or* **wanna bet?** *v. phr., informal* Often used when one wants to be sure that the other person means what he or she said, meaning, "Are you sure?" ♦ *"I am certain we will find some form of primitive life on Mars or on Europa, Jupiter's biggest moon," the science director of NASA said. "You want to bet on it?" a skeptical journalist asked, when a major probe was getting ready to be launched.*

**want to make something of it?** *v. phr., informal* A threatening response to some criticism or an insult, meaning "so what?" ♦ *"So you wear a fur coat, crocodile leather shoes, and have several gold rings in your nose. Are you a pimp or something?" Fred asked his long-lost roommate from college. "Hold it, buddy, do you want to make something of it?" Ted replied defiantly.*

**war baby** *n., informal* A person born during a war. ♦ *War babies began to increase college enrollments early in the 1960s.*

**ward off** *v. phr.* To deflect; avert. ♦ *Vitamin C is known to ward off the common cold.*

**warm one's blood** *v. phr.* To make you feel warm or excited. ♦ *When the Bakers came to visit on a cold night, Mr. Harmon offered them a drink to warm their blood.*

**warm up** *v.* (stress on *up*) **1.** To reheat cooked food. ♦ *Mr. Jones was so late that his dinner got cold; his wife had to warm it up.* **2.** To become friendly or interested. ♦ *It takes an hour or so for some children to warm up to strangers.* **3.** To get ready for a game or other event by exercising or practicing. ♦ *The coach told us to warm up before entering the pool.*

**warm-up** *n.* (stress on *warm*) A period of exercise or practice in preparation for a game or other event. ♦ *Before the television quiz program, there was a warm-up to prepare the contestants.*

**wash and wear** *adj.* Not needing to be ironed.—Refers especially to synthetic and synthetic blend fabrics. ♦ *Sally's dress is made of a wash and wear fabric.*

**washed out** *adj.* Listless in appearance; pale, wan. ♦ *Small wonder Harry looks so washed out; he has just recovered from major surgery.*

**washed up** *adj.* Ruined; finished; a failure. ♦ *Harry is looking awfully sad. I hear his business has collapsed and he is all washed up.*

**wash one's hands of** *v. phr.* To withdraw from or refuse to be responsible for. ♦ *We washed our hands of politics long ago.*

**washout** *n.* (stress on *wash*) A dismal failure. ♦ *As far as investments were concerned, Dick and his precious advice turned out to be a total washout.*

**wash out** *v. phr.* (stress on *out*) To disappear; vanish. ♦ *Do you think this stain will wash out?*

**waste away** *v.* To become more thin and weak every day. ♦ *Jane is wasting away with tuberculosis.*

**waste one's breath** *v. phr.* To speak or to argue with no result; do nothing by talking. ♦ *I know what I want. You're wasting your breath.*

**watched pot never boils** If you watch or wait for something to get done or to happen, it seems to take forever.—A proverb. ♦ *Jane was nine months pregnant and Tom hovered over her anxiously. She said, "You might as well go away and play some golf. A watched pot never boils, you know!"*

**watch every penny** See PINCH PENNIES.

**watch it** *v. phr. informal* To be careful.— Usually used as a command. ♦ *Watch it—the bottom stair is loose!*

**watch one's language** *v. phr.* To be careful of how one speaks; avoid saying impolite or vulgar things. ♦ *"You boys watch your language," Mother said, "or you won't be watching television for a whole week!"*

**watch one's step** *v. phr.* To mend one's ways; exercise prudence, tact, and care. ♦ *I have to watch my step with the new boss as he is a very proud and sensitive individual.*

**water down** *v.* To change and make weaker; weaken. ♦ *The teacher had to water down the course for a slow-learning class.*

**watered down** *adj.* Weakened; diluted. ♦ *The play was a disappointing, watered down version of Shakespeare's Othello.*

**watering hole** *or* **place** *n. phr.* A bar, pub, or nightclub where people gather to drink and socialize. ♦ *I like "The Silver Dollar"—it is my favorite watering hole in all of Sidney, Nebraska.*

**water over the dam** *or* **water under the bridge** *n. phr.* Something that happened in the past and cannot be changed. ♦ *Since the sweater is too small already, don't worry about its shrinking; that's water over the dam.*

**way off** *adj. phr.* At a great distance from a particular point (said of a discrepancy). ♦ *We were way off on our calculations; the house cost us twice as much as we had thought.*

**way the wind blows** *or* **how the wind blows** *n. phr.* The direction or course something may go; how things are; what may happen. ♦ *Most senators find out which way the wind blows in their home state before voting on bills in Congress.*

**ways and means** *n. plural* Methods of getting something done or getting money; how something can be done and paid for. ♦ *The boys were trying to think of ways and means to go camping for the weekend.*

**way to go** *adj. phr., informal* An exclamation of praise given to one who has done or achieved something out of the ordinary. ♦ *"Way to go, Charlie," his friends exclaimed, when, after beating an apparently terminal case of cancer, he not only graduated with honors, but also won the gold medal for diving in the Olympics.*

**wear and tear** *n. phr.* Deterioration through use. ♦ *After 75,000 miles there is usually a lot of wear and tear on any car.*

**wear blinders** *or* **blinkers** *v. phr.* To refuse or be unable to consider alternative ways of thinking or acting. ♦ *Anybody who disputes the importance of learning languages is wearing blinders.*

**wear down, wear off** *or* **wear away** *v.* **1.** To remove or disappear little by little through use, time, or the action of weather. ♦ *Time and weather have worn off the name on the gravestone.* **2.** To lessen; become less little by little. ♦ *John could feel the pain again as the dentist's medicine wore away.* **3.** To exhaust; tire out, win over or persuade by making tired. ♦ *Mary wore her mother down by begging so that she let Mary go to the movies.*

**wear on** *v.* **1.** To anger or annoy; tire. ♦ *Having to stay indoors all day long is tiresome for the children and wears on their mother's nerves.* **2.** To drag on; pass gradually or slowly; continue in the same old way. ♦ *As the years wore on, the man in prison grew old.*

**wear one's heart on one's sleeve** *also* **pin one's heart on one's sleeve** *v. phr.* To show your feelings openly; show everyone how you feel; not hide your feelings. ♦ *Sometimes it is better not to pin your heart on your sleeve.*

**wear out** *v.* **1a.** To use or wear until useless. ♦ *The stockings are so worn out that they can't be mended any more.* **1b.** To become useless from use or wear. ♦ *One shoe wore out before the other.* **2.** *or* **tire out** To make very tired; weaken. ♦ *When Dick got home from the long walk, he was all worn out.* ♦ *Don't wear yourself out by playing*

too hard. **3.** To make by rubbing, scraping, or washing. ♦ *The waterfall has worn out a hole in the stone beneath it.*

**wear out one's welcome** *v. phr., informal* To visit somewhere too long or come back too often so that you are not welcome any more. ♦ *The Smith children have worn out their welcome at our house because they are so loud.*

**wear the trousers** *or* **wear the pants** *v. phr., informal* To have a man's authority; be the boss of a family or household. ♦ *Mr. Wilson is henpecked by his wife; she wears the trousers in that family.*

**wear thin** *v.* **1.** To become thin from use, wearing, or the passing of time. ♦ *My old pair of pants has worn thin at the knees.* **2.** To grow less, or less interesting; decrease. ♦ *The joke began to wear thin when you heard it too many times.*

**wear well** *v.* **1.** To continue to be satisfactory, useful, or liked for a long time. ♦ *Their marriage has worn well.* **2.** To carry, accept, or treat properly or well. ♦ *Grandfather wears his years well.*

**weasel out** *v. phr.* To renege on a previous promise; not keep an obligation for some not always straight reason. ♦ *I'm so tired I think I am going to weasel my way out of going to that meeting this afternoon.*

**weasel word** *n., informal* A word which has more than one meaning and may be used to deceive others. ♦ *When the thief was being questioned by the police, he tried to fool them with weasel words.*

**weather** See FAIR-WEATHER FRIEND.

**weather eye** *n.* **1.** Eyes that can tell what the weather will be. ♦ *Grandfather's weather eye always tells him when it will rain.* **2.** Eyes ready or quick to see; careful watch.—Usually used in phrases like *keep a weather eye on, open,* or *out for.* ♦ *Mrs. Brown kept a weather eye on the children so they wouldn't hurt each other.* ♦ *Keep a weather eye out for Uncle George at the store.* ♦ *Keep a weather eye open for deer.* ♦ *The police have a weather eye out for the robbers.* Compare LOOK OUT.

**weather the storm** *v. phr.* To survive some disaster. ♦ *When Peter and Sue* started their business they had very little money, but in a year they weathered the storm.

**wee hours** The crack of dawn, or just before it, usually between 1 A.M. and 4 A.M. or 2 A.M. and 5 A.M. ♦ *He stayed up all night when they were expecting their first child; finally, a boy was born in the wee hours of the morning.*

**weed out** *v.* **1.** To remove what is unwanted, harmful, or not good enough from. ♦ *Mother weeded out the library because there were too many books.* **2.** To take (what is not wanted) from a collection or group; remove (a part) for the purpose of improving a collection or group; get rid of. ♦ *The coach is weeding out the weak players this week.*

**wee folk** *or* **little folk** *or* **little people** *n. pl.* Fairy people; brownies; elves; fairies; or goblins. ♦ *There are many stories about little people dancing in the moonlight.*

**week of Sundays** *n. phr.* A long time; seven weeks. ♦ *I haven't seen them in a week of Sundays.*

**weigh anchor** *v. phr.* To set sail; get going. ♦ *After a week in Hawaii, we weighed anchor and sailed south toward Tahiti.*

**weigh down** *also* **weight down** **1.** To make heavy; cause to go down or bend with weight; overload. ♦ *The evergreens are weighed down by the deep snow.* **2a.** To overload with care or worry; make sad or low in spirits.—Used in the passive. ♦ *The company is weighed down by debt.* **2b.** To make heavy, hard, or slow; make dull or uninteresting.—Often in the passive used with *by* or *with.* ♦ *The book is weighted down with footnotes.*

**weigh in** *v.* **1a.** To take the weight of; weigh. ♦ *The man at the airport counter weighed in our bags and took our plane tickets.* **1b.** To have yourself or something that you own weighed.—Often used with *at.* ♦ *We took our bags to the airport counter to weigh in.* **1c.** To have yourself weighed as a boxer or wrestler by a doctor before a match.—Used with *at.* ♦ *The champion weighed in at 160 pounds.* **2.** *slang* To join or interfere in a fight, argument, or discussion. ♦ *We told Jack that if we wanted him to*

weigh in with his opinion we would ask him.

**weigh on** *or* **weigh upon** *v.* **1.** To be a weight or pressure on; be heavy on. ♦ *The pack weighed heavily on the soldier's back.* **2.** To make sad or worried; trouble; disturb; upset. ♦ *John's wrongdoing weighed upon his conscience.* **3.** To be a burden to. ♦ *His guilt weighed heavily upon him.*

**weigh on one's mind** See WEIGH ON 2.

**weigh one's words** *v. phr.* To choose your words carefully; be careful to use the right words. ♦ *In a debate, a political candidate has little time to weigh his words, and may say something foolish.*

**weight of the world on one's shoulders** *or* **world on one's shoulders** *or* **world on one's back** *n. phr.* A very heavy load of worry or responsibility; very tired or worried behavior, as if carrying the world; behavior as if you are very important. ♦ *John acts as if he were carrying the world on his back because he has a paper route.*

**welcome mat** *n.* **1.** A mat for wiping your shoes on, often with the word *welcome* on it, that is placed in front of a door. ♦ *Mother bought a welcome mat for our new house.* **2.** *informal* A warm welcome; a friendly greeting.—Used in such phrases as *the welcome mat is out* and *put out the welcome mat.* ♦ *Our welcome mat is always out to our friends.*

**welcome with open arms** See WITH OPEN ARMS.

**well and good** *adj. phr.* Good; satisfactory. ♦ *If my daughter finishes high school, I will call that well and good.*—Used without a verb to show agreement or understanding. ♦ *Well and good; I will come to your house tomorrow.*

**well-heeled** *adj., slang* Wealthy; having plenty of money. ♦ *Bob's father, who is well-heeled, gave him a sports car.*

**well, I never!** See YOU DON'T SAY.

**well-off** *adj. phr.* **1.** Rich. ♦ *They may not be millionaires, but they are sufficiently well-off.* **2.** In good condition; free of problems or difficulties. ♦ *He is pleased that his business is well-off.*

**well put** *adj. phr.* Well expressed or defined. ♦ *His remarks about too much violence on television were extremely well put.*

**well-to-do** *adj.* Having or making enough money to live comfortably; prosperous. ♦*John's father owns a company and his family is well-to-do.* ♦*This is the part of town where the well-to-do live.*

**wend one's way** *v. phr.* To head in a certain direction, mostly by foot. ♦*The tired pilgrims wended their way toward Lourdes in hopes of getting cured at the holy site.* ♦*The drunken mayor of the small provincial town didn't know how to wend his way home in the dark at 4. A.M.*

**we're in business** *or* **now we're in business** *v. phr.* We have reached the state where things are in order and we can continue our negotiations, seal our agreement, etc. ♦*Once the smaller states that wanted to build a nuclear arsenal decided to quit, the American secretary of state, who has been trying to prevent such proliferation, sighed with relief, "Now we're in business!"*

**wet behind the ears** *adj. phr., informal* Not experienced; not knowing how to do something; new in a job or place. ♦*The new student is still wet behind the ears; he has not yet learned the tricks that the boys play on each other.*

**wet blanket** *n. informal* A person or thing that keeps others from enjoying life. ♦*The weatherman throws a wet blanket on picnic plans when he forecasts rain.*

**wet one's whistle** *v. phr., slang* To have a drink, especially of liquor. ♦*Uncle Willie told John to wait outside for a minute while he went in to the cafe to wet his whistle.*

**what about** *interrog.* **1.** About *or* concerning what; in connection with what. ♦*"I want to talk to you." "What about?"*

**what a drag** *adj. phr., used as an exclamation* To be extremely boring, dull, uninteresting, and tiring. ♦*"What a drag! Let's get out of this lecture!" Bob poked his friend Ted in the arm, whereupon they got up and left.*

**What a pity!** How unfortunate! What a shame! ♦*What a pity that he couldn't join us on our Hawaiian trip.*

**what a shame** See WHAT A PITY.

**what do you take me for?** *v. phr., informal, asked in indignation* What sort of an idiot do you think I am? What sort of a person do you think I am? ♦*When the comptroller at the firm found that there was a missing sum of $250,000, he confronted Ted: "Did you have anything to with this loss?" "What do you take me for?" Ted replied indignantly.*

**whatever turns you on** *n. phr., slang* It's OK with me; we can do what you want. ♦*"Do you want to listen to jazz or to Mozart?" Oliver asked his girlfriend. "It's all the same to me," she replied. "Whatever turns you on."*

**what for** *interrog.* For what reason; why? ♦*What are you running for?* ♦*Billy's mother told him to wear his hat. "What for?" he asked.*

**what gives?** *or* **what's going on?** *n. phr., informal* What is happening? What's up? What is the situation? ♦*"What gives?" Ben asked his friend Ted, after being away from the firm for a month.*

**what have you** *or* **what not** *n. phr., informal* Whatever you like or want; anything else like that. ♦*We found suits, coats, hats and what not in the closet.*

**what if** What would, or will, happen if; what is the difference if; suppose that. ♦*What if we paint it red. How will it look?*

**what of it** *or* **what about it** *interj., informal* What is wrong with it; what do you care. ♦*"John missed the bus." "What of it?"*

**what's in it for me?** *v. phr. informal* How does this deal or activity benefit me? Why should I become involved in it? ♦*"Let's buy a dinner boat and run it on Lake Michigan," the investment banker suggested to Edward, the classical concert pianist. "What's in it for me?" Edward asked. "That sort of clientele doesn't go for Mozart or Beethoven. I'd like to skip this one, if you don't mind."*

**what's the damage?** *n. phr., informal, mostly asked as a question* How much do I owe you? How much does the total bill come to? ♦*"What's the damage?" the tourist asked at the shop where he picked up a lot of presents for his children.*

**what's sauce for the goose, is sauce for the gander** What goes for the one, also goes for the other.—A proverb. ♦*If Herb gets a speeding ticket, so should*

*Erica, who was right behind him; after all, what's sauce for the goose is sauce for the gander.*

**what's the big idea** *or* **what's the idea** *informal* What is the purpose; what do you have in mind; why did you do that; what are you doing; how dare you. ♦ *I heard you are spreading false rumors about me, what's the big idea?*

**what's the scoop?** *n. phr., informal, mostly used as a question* What is the latest news? What is happening? ♦ *"What's the scoop?" Joe asked his friend Tim. "Are we getting the new contract or not?"*

**what's up** *or* **what's cooking** *also* **what's doing** *slang* What is happening or planned; what is wrong. ♦ *"What's up?" asked Bob as he joined his friends. "Are you going to the movies?"* ♦ *What's cooking? Why is the crowd in the street?* ♦ *What's doing tonight at the club?*

**what's what** *or* **what is what** *n. phr., informal* **1.** What each thing is in a group; one thing from another. ♦ *The weeds and the flowers are coming up together, and we can't tell what is what.* **2.** All that needs to be known about something; the important facts or skills. ♦ *When Bob started his new job, it took him several weeks to learn what was what.*

**what's with** *or* **what's up with** *also* **what's by** *slang* What is happening to; what is wrong; how is everything; what can you tell me about. ♦ *Mary looks worried. What's with her?*

**what's yours?** *n. phr., informal, interrogative* What can I offer you to drink? ♦ *"What's yours?" Ernest asked his guests. "Nothing alcoholic for me," Alan answered. "Booze gives me a headache."*

**what with** *prep.* Because; as a result of. ♦ *I couldn't visit you, what with the snowstorm and the cold I had.*

**wheel and deal** *v. phr., slang* To make many big plans or schemes; especially with important people in government and business; in matters of money and influence; handle money or power for your own advantage; plan important matters in a smart or skillful way and sometimes in a tricky, or not strictly honest way. ♦ *Mr. Smith made a for-*

*tune by wheeling and dealing on the stock market.*—**wheeler-dealer** *n. phr., slang* A person with power and control. ♦ *The biggest wheeler-dealer in the state has many friends in high places in business and government.*

**wheelhorse** *n. phr.* A reliable and industrious worker on whom one may depend. ♦ *Jake is such a good worker that he is the wheelhorse of our tiny firm.*

**when hell freezes over** *adv. phr., slang* Never. ♦ *I'll believe you when hell freezes over.*

**when in Rome, do as the Romans do** When one is in a strange or new place, it is a good idea to imitate the customs of the natives.—A proverb. ♦ *"I cannot get used to eating with chopsticks," Sam complained to his wife. "Well, you'd better learn to use them, since we are in China," Mary replied. "Remember the old saying 'When in Rome, do as the Romans do.'"*

**when it rains it pours** Things we wish for and that are not coming often start to come in huge quantities, much more than we needed or wanted.—A proverb. ♦ *When Ted opened his new business, hardly anyone called or sent him e-mails. After a couple of months the calls and e-mails came so fast and so many that he had to hire two secretaries to handle the traffic. He remarked, "When it rains it pours.*

**when one's ship comes home** *or* **in** *v. phr., a proverb* When one's labor and projects bear fruit; when one finally succeeds. ♦ *"I know you have been frustrated for a long time," John said to Ted, "but don't worry. You have done a lot of good work and sooner or later your ship will come home."*

**when one's ship comes in** See SHIP COME IN.

**when push comes to shove** *adv. phr.* A time when a touchy situation becomes actively hostile or a quarrel turns into a fight. ♦ *Can we count on the boss' goodwill, when push comes to shove?*

**when the cat's away, the mice will play** When one's supervisor at work is gone, things loosen up and the employees feel freer; when the parents are gone, children take liberties that they would not if the parents were home.—A proverb.

♦ *When the chief of police left town for a vacation, all the officers had a great party. The sergeant remarked: "When the cat's away, the mice will play."*

**when the chips are down** *adv. cl., informal* When the winner and loser of a bet or a game are decided; at the most important or dangerous time. ♦ *When the chips were down, the two countries decided not to have war.*

**where it's at** *adv. phr., informal* That which is important; that which is at the forefront of on-going social, personal, or scientific undertakings. ♦ *We send sophisticated machines to Mars instead of people, that's where it's at.*

**where there is muck, there is money** Dirt and industrial pollution are closely associated with money.—A proverb. ♦ *"I hate to live in Gary, Indiana," Jane complained to her husband. "There is so much air pollution here." "That's true, darling," her husband, an oil engineer, replied, "but you mustn't forget that where there is muck, there is money."*

**where there's smoke, there's fire** Where you see the effect of something, you are likely to discover its cause as well.—A proverb. ♦ *Tim has been speaking about the advantages of being single and the fact that divorce can be a blessing. Also, he has been showing up alone at parties. Maybe his marriage to Sue is on the rocks; after all, where there is smoke, there is fire.*

**where the action is** *n. phr., informal* Where the prostitutes hang out in bars, where there is gambling, legal or illegal. ♦ *"Show us where the action is," the tourists asked the taxi driver when they got into Reno, Nevada.*

**where the shoe pinches** *n. phr., informal* Where or what the discomfort or trouble is. ♦ *Johnny thinks the job is easy, but he will find out where the shoe pinches when he tries it.*

**which is which** *n. phr.* Which is one person or thing and which is the other; one from another; what the difference is between different ones; what the name of each one is. ♦ *Joe's coat and mine are so nearly alike that I can't tell which is which.*

**while ago** *adv.* At a time several minutes in the past; a few minutes ago; a short time ago.—Used with *a*. ♦ *I laid my glasses on this table a while ago; and now they're gone.*

**while away** *v.* To make time go by pleasantly or without being bored; pass or spend. ♦ *We whiled away the summer swimming and fishing.*

**while back** *adv.* At a time several weeks or months in the past.—Used with *a*. ♦ *We had a good rain a while back, but we need more now.*

**whipping boy** *n. phr.* The person who gets punished for someone else's mistake. ♦ *"I used to be the whipping boy during my early days at the company," he musingly remembered.*

**whip up** *v., informal* **1.** To make or do quickly or easily. ♦ *The reporter whipped up a story about the fire for his paper.* **2.** To make active; stir to action; excite. ♦ *The girls are trying to whip up interest for a dance Saturday night.*

**whispering campaign** *n.* The spreading of false rumors, or saying bad things, about a person or group, especially in politics or public life. ♦ *A bad man has started a whispering campaign against the mayor, saying that he isn't honest.*

**whistle a different tune** See SING A DIFFERENT TUNE.

**whistle-blower** *n. phr.* A person who betrays his or her accomplices by talking to the police. ♦ *The gang wants to kill Joe, because they found out that he is a whistle-blower and turned them in.*

**whistle for** *v., informal* To try to get (something) but fail; look for (something) that will not come. ♦ *Mary didn't even thank us for helping her, so the next time she needs help she can whistle for it.*

**whistle in the dark** *v. phr., informal* To try to stay brave and forget your fear. ♦ *Tom said he could fight the bully with one hand, but we knew that he was just whistling in the dark.*

**whistle-stop** *n.* A small town where the trains only stop on a special signal. ♦ *President Truman made excellent use of the whistle-stop during his 1948 campaign for the presidency.*

**white-collar workers** *n. phr.* Workers employed in offices and at desks as opposed to those who work as manual workers; the middle class. ♦ *It is a well-known fact that white-collar workers are less well organized than unionized manual workers.*

**white elephant** *n. phr.* Unwanted property, such as real estate, that is hard to sell. ♦ *That big house of theirs on the corner sure is a white elephant.*

**white lie** *n. phr.* An innocent social excuse. ♦ *I am too busy to go to their house for dinner tonight. I will call them and tell a little white lie about having the flu.*

**white sale** *n.* The selling, especially at lower prices, of goods or clothing usually made of white cloth. ♦ *Mother always buys many things at the January white sale to save money.*

**whitewash** *n., informal* A soothing official report that attempts to tranquilize the public. ♦ *Some people believe that the Warren Commission's report on the Kennedy assassination was a whitewash.*

**whitewash something** *v., informal* To explain a major, national scandal in soothing official terms so as to assure the public that things are under control and there is no need to panic. ♦ *Many people in the United States believe that President Kennedy's assassination was whitewashed by the Warren Commission.*

**whodunit** *n.* A detective story; a murder story; a thriller. ♦ *Agatha Christie was a true master of the whodunit.*

**whole cheese** *slang or informal* **whole show** *n., informal* The only important person; big boss. ♦ *Joe thought he was the whole cheese in the game because he owned the ball.* ♦ *You're not the whole show just because you got all A's.*

**who pays the piper calls the tune** Whoever has the means to pay for something has the power to decide what will be done and how.—A proverb. ♦ *Mr. Willoughby bought two hundred acres of undeveloped land to be converted into lots for private homes. Many people don't like his plans, but as the saying goes, "Who pays the piper calls the tune."*

**who's who** *or* **who is who** *informal* **1.** Who this one is and who that one is; who the different ones in a group of people are or what their names or positions are. ♦ *It is hard to tell who is who in the parade because everyone in the band looks alike.* **2.** Who the important people are. ♦ *John didn't recognize the champion on television. He doesn't know who is who in boxing.* ♦ *After about a year, Mr. Thompson had lived in this town long enough to know who was who.*

**why and wherefore** *n.* The answer to a question or problem. Usually used in the plural. ♦ *Father told him not to always ask the whys and wherefores when he was told to do something.*

**wide of the mark** *adv. or adj. phr.* **1.** Far from the target or the thing aimed at. ♦ *James threw a stone at the cat but it went wide of the mark.* **2.** Far from the truth; incorrect. ♦ *You were wide of the mark when you said I did it, because Bill did it.*

**wiener roast** *or* **hot dog roast** *n.* A party where frankfurters are cooked and eaten over an outdoor fire. ♦ *Mary's Girl Scout troop had a hot dog roast on their overnight hike.*

**wild card in the deck** *n. phr.* An unknown item or force that one must reckon with. ♦ *"The whereabouts of Osama Bin Laden and Saddam Hussein are the wild cards in the deck," said Mr. Rumsfeld, secretary of defense.*

**wildcat strike** *n. informal* A strike not ordered by a labor union; a strike spontaneously arranged by a group of workers. ♦ *The garbage collectors have gone on a wildcat strike, but the union is going to stop it.*

**wild goose chase** *n. phr.* An absurd and completely futile errand. ♦ *I was on a wild goose chase when I was sent to find a man who never really existed.*

**wild horses would not drag it from me** No power on earth can make me give away the secret, or to divulge it.—A proverb. ♦ *"Do you know where grandpa buried the sixteen gold bullions after the bank robbery?" Fred asked his older brother. "I do," came the answer, "but wild horses would not drag it from me."*

**will a duck swim?** *v. phr., rhetorical question* Of course; naturally; certainly. ♦ *"Will Bush run again for president?" Jack asked. "Will a duck swim?" Peter replied.*

**will not hear of** v. phr. Will not allow or consider, refuse attention to or permission for. ♦ *John's father told him he would not hear of his having a car.*

**windbag** n. Someone who talks too much; a boring person. ♦ *Uncle Joe goes on and on; he is a boring windbag.*

**windfall** n. An unexpected gift or gain of sizeable proportion. ♦ *The unexpected retroactive pay raise was a most welcome windfall.*

**window dressing** n. phr. An elaborate exterior, sometimes designed to conceal one's real motives. ♦ *All those fancy invitations turned out to be nothing but window dressing.*

**window of opportunity** n. phr. A favorable time to do something, e.g., launch a satellite, take diplomatic or military action, etc. ♦ *Our next window of opportunity to send a probe to Mars will occur when Earth and Mars will be the nearest to each other.*

**window-shop** v. phr. To walk from store to store and look at the merchandise without buying it. ♦ *When I have no money, I like to window-shop and plan on what I might get when I will be able to afford it.*

**wind up** v. 1. To tighten the spring of a machine; to make it work or run. ♦ *He doesn't have to wind up his watch because it is run by a battery.* 2. To make very excited, nervous, upset. ♦ *The excitement of her birthday party got Jane all wound up so she could not sleep.* 3. informal To bring or come to an end; finish; stop. ♦ *Before Jim knew it, he had spent all his money and he wound up broke.* 4. To put (your business or personal affairs) in order; arrange; settle. ♦ *Fred wound up his business and personal affairs before joining the Navy.*

**win hands down** v. phr. To win conclusively and without external help. ♦ *The opposition was so weak that Dan won the election hands down.*

**win in a walk** or **win in a breeze** v. phr., informal To win very easily; win without having to try hard. ♦ *Joe ran for class president and won in a walk.* ♦ *Our team won the game in a breeze.*

**winning streak** n. A series of several wins one after the other. ♦ *The team extended their winning streak to ten.*

**win out** v. phr. To win after a rather protracted struggle. ♦ *The lawsuit lasted a long time, but we finally won out.*

**win over** v. phr. To convert to one's position or point of view. ♦ *The Democrats offered him a high-level executive position and thus way won him over to their side.*

**wipeout** n. (stress on *wipe*) A total failure. ♦ *The guy is so bad at his job that he is a total wipeout.*

**wipe out** v. (stress on *out*) 1. To remove or erase by wiping or rubbing. ♦ *The teacher wiped out with an eraser what she had written on the board.* 2. informal To remove, kill, or destroy completely. ♦ *Doctors are searching for a cure that will wipe out cancer.*

**wisecrack** n. A joke or witty remark usually made at someone else's expense. ♦ *The comedians kept up a steady stream of wisecracks.*

**wise guy** n. phr., informal A person who acts as if he were smarter than other people; a person who jokes or shows off too much ♦ *Bill is a wise guy and displeases others by what he says.*

**wise up to** v. phr., slang To finally understand what is really going on after a period of ignorance. ♦ *Joe immediately quit his job when he wised up to what was really going on.*

**wishful thinking** n. phr. A human tendency to anticipate a favorable outcome of something planned or wished for. ♦ *"If only I could afford to buy that new sports car I saw yesterday," John said, "I could leave everyone behind on the highway in complete safety." "That's a lot of wishful thinking," his wife cut him short.*

**wish on** v. 1. To use as a lucky charm while making a wish. ♦ *Mary wished on a star that she could go to the dance.*

**witch-hunt** n. phr. A hysterical movement during which people are persecuted for having views (political or religious) considered different or unpopular. ♦ *During the McCarthy era many innocent Americans were accused of being Communists, as Republican patriotism deteriorated into a witch-hunt.*

**with a vengeance** adv. phr. To an extreme extent; very severely. ♦ *When tuberculosis was wiped out, people* *thought they were safe from this disease, but in certain parts of the world it came back with a vengeance.*

**with a whole skin** *also* **in a whole skin** *adv. phr.* With no injury; unhurt; safely. ♦ *The horse threw him off, but he got away in a whole skin.*

**with bated breath** *adv. phr.* With great excitement; with eager anticipation. ♦ *All day long I have been waiting with bated breath for the arrival of the express package that was promised to me yesterday.*

**with bells on** *adv. phr., informal* With enthusiasm; eager or ready and in the best of spirits for an event. ♦ *"Will you come to the farewell party I'm giving for Billy?" asked Jerry. "I'll be there with bells on," replied Ed.*

**with child** *adv. phr., literary* Going to have a baby; pregnant. ♦ *The angel told Mary she was with child.*

**with flying colors** *adv. phr.* With great or total success; victoriously. ♦ *Tom finished the race with flying colors.*

**with good grace** *adv. phr.* With pleasant and courteous behavior; politely; willingly; without complaining. ♦ *The boys had been well-coached; they took the loss of the game with good grace.*

**within an ace of** *informal or* **within an inch of** *adv. phr.* Almost but not quite; very close to; nearly. ♦ *Tim came within an ace of losing the election.* ♦ *John was within an inch of drowning before he was pulled out of the water.*

**within an inch of one's life** *adv. phr.* Until you are almost dead; near to dying. ♦ *The bear clawed the hunter within an inch of his life.*

**within bounds** *adv. or adj. phr.* **1.** Inside of the boundary lines in a game; on or inside of the playing field. ♦ *You must hit the ball inside the lines of the tennis court or it will not be within bounds.* ♦ *If you kick the football over a sideline, it will not be in bounds.* **2.** Inside of a place where one is allowed to go or be. ♦ *The soldiers are within bounds on one side of the city, but are out of bounds on the other side.* **3.** Inside of safe or proper limits; allowable. ♦ *He succeeded in keeping his temper within bounds.*

**within call** *or* **within hail** *adv. phr.* **1.** Near enough to hear each other's voices. ♦ *When the two ships were within hail,*

*their officers exchanged messages.* **2.** In a place where you can be reached by phone, radio, or TV and be called. ♦ *The soldiers were allowed to leave the base by day, but had to stay within call.*

**within reason** *adv. or adj. phr.* Within the limits of good sense; in reasonable control or check; moderate. ♦ *I want you to have a good time tonight, within reason.*

**with might and main** *adv. phr.* With full strength or complete effort. ♦ *John tried with all his might and main to solve the problem.*

**with open arms** *adv. phr.* **1.** With words or actions showing that you are glad to see someone; gladly, warmly, eagerly. ♦ *After his pioneering flight in the Friendship VII, Col. John Glenn was welcomed with open arms by the people of his hometown.*

**without a hitch** *adv. phr.* Without any trouble or obstacle; successfully. ♦ *Our trip to Europe and back went off without a hitch, except for the waiting in lines at the airports.*

**without batting an eye** *or* **without batting an eyelash** See BAT AN EYE.

**without fail** *adv. phr.* Without failing to do it or failing in the doing of it; certainly, surely. ♦ *Be here at 8 o'clock sharp, without fail.*

**without further ado** *or* **without much ado** *adv. phr.* Simply. ♦ *Once Sam was shown how to run his personal computer, he sat down and started sending and receiving e-mail messages without further ado.*

**with reference to** See IN REFERENCE TO.

**with regard to** See IN REFERENCE TO.

**with relation to** See IN RELATION TO.

**with respect to** See IN RESPECT TO.

**with the best** *or* **with the best of them** *adv. phr.* As well as anyone. ♦ *John can bowl with the best of them.*

**wolf down** *v. phr.* To eat or drink in a great hurry, mostly standing up in the kitchen. ♦ *Ted was so hungry and had so little time, that he grabbed two cold frankfurters out of his refrigerator and just wolfed them down.*

**wolf in sheep's clothing** *n. phr.* A person who pretends to be good but really is bad. ♦ *Mrs. Martin trusted the lawyer until she realized that he was a wolf in sheep's clothing.*

**word for word** *adv. phr.* In exactly the same words. ♦*Mary copied Sally's composition word for word.*

**word of mouth** *n. phr.* Communication by oral rather than written means. ♦*The merchant told us that the best customers he had were recommended to him by word of mouth.*

**words of one syllable** *n. phr.* Language that makes the meaning very clear; simple, or frank language. ♦*Mary explained the job to Ann in words of one syllable so that she would be sure to understand.*

**word to the wise** *n. phr.* A word of warning or advice which the intelligent person is expected to follow.—A proverb. ♦*I had once spoken to him about being late all the time, and thought that a word to the wise was enough.*

**work cut out** See CUT OUT 2 *adj.* 1.

**worked up** *adj.* Feeling strongly; excited; angry; worried. ♦*Mary was all worked up about the exam.*

**work in** *v.* 1. To rub in. ♦*The nurse told Mary to put some cream on her skin and to work it in gently with her fingers.* 2. To slip in; mix in; put in; ♦*When Mary was planning the show, she worked a part in for her friend Susan.*

**working girl** *n., slang* 1. *(vulgar, avoid!)* A prostitute. ♦*I didn't know Roxanne was a working girl.* 2. A girl, usually single, who supports herself by working in an honest job, such as in an office, etc. ♦*The average working girl can't afford such a fancy car.*

**work into** *v.* 1. Force into little by little. ♦*John worked his foot into the boot by pushing and pulling.* 2. Put into; mix into. ♦*Mary worked some blue into the rug she was weaving.*

**work off** *v.* To make (something) go away, especially by working. ♦*John worked off the fat around his waist by doing exercise every morning.*

**work on** *also* **work upon** *v.* 1. Have an effect on; influence. ♦*Some pills work on the nerves and make people feel more relaxed.* 2. To try to influence or convince. ♦*Senator Smith worked on the other committee members to vote for the bill.*

**work one's fingers to the bone** *v. phr.* To work very hard. ♦*"I have to work my fingers to the bone for a measly pittance of a salary," Fred complained.*

**workout** *n.* (stress on *work*) A physical exercise session. ♦*My morning workout consists of sit-ups and push-ups.*

**work out** *v. phr.* (stress on *out*) 1. To find an answer to. ♦*John worked out his math problems all by himself.* 2. To plan; develop. ♦*Mary worked out a beautiful design for a sweater.* 3. To accomplish; arrange. ♦*The engineers worked out a system for getting electricity to the factory.* 4. To be efficient; get results. ♦*If the traffic plan works out, it will be used in other cities too.* 5. To exercise. ♦*John works out in the gym two hours every day.*

**work over** *v. phr., slang* To beat someone up very roughly in order to intimidate him or extort payment, etc. ♦*Matthew was worked over by the hoodlums in the park right after midnight.*

**work through channels** *v. phr.* To go through the proper procedures and officials. ♦*At a state university everybody must work through channels to get things done.*

**work up** *v.* 1. To stir up; arouse; excite. ♦*I can't work up any interest in this book.* ♦*He worked up a sweat weeding the garden.* 2. To develop; originate. ♦*He worked up an interesting plot for a play.*

**world is one's oyster** Everything is possible for you; the world belongs to you; you can get anything you want. ♦*When John won the scholarship, he felt as though the world was his oyster.*

**world without end** *adv. phr., literary* Endlessly; forever; eternally. ♦*Each human being has to die, but mankind goes on world without end.*

**worlds apart** *adj. phr.* Completely different; in total disagreement. ♦*Jack and Al never agree on anything; they are worlds apart in their thinking.*

**worm in** *v. phr.* To insinuate oneself; penetrate gradually. ♦*By cultivating the friendship of a few of the prominent merchants, Peter hoped to worm his way into that exclusive elite of export magnates.*

**worm may turn** Even the meek will ultimately rebel if always maltreated. ♦*Sam may think that he can continue to mistreat his wife, but, knowing her, I* *think that some day the worm may turn.*

**worm out** *v. phr.* To learn through persistent questioning; draw out from. ♦ *I finally wormed out of her the reason she broke off her engagement to Larry.*

**worn threadbare** *or* **worn to a shred** *or* **worn to shreds** *adj. phr.* Thin; used; torn; said of clothes or ideas. ♦ *Jack never buys any new trousers; he likes his old ones worn to shreds.* ♦ *Professor Catwallender's ideas are outdated and worn threadbare.*

**worn to a frazzle** *adj. phr.* To be fatigued; be exhausted. ♦ *I'm worn to a frazzle cooking for all these guests.*

**worrywart** *n. phr.* A person who always worries. ♦ *"Stop being such a worrywart,"* Bob said to Alice, who was constantly weighing herself on the bathroom scale.

**worse for wear** *adj. phr.* Not as good as new; worn out; damaged by use.—Used with *the.* ♦ *Her favorite tablecloth was beginning to look the worse for wear.*—Often used with *none* to mean: as good as new. ♦ *The doll was Mary's favorite toy but it was none the worse for wear.*

**worth a cent** *adj. phr.* Worth anything; of any value.—Used in negative, interrogative, and conditional sentences. ♦ *The book was old and it was not worth a cent.*

**worth one's salt** *adj. phr.* Being a good worker, or a productive person; worth what you cost. ♦ *Mr. Brown showed that he was worth his salt as a salesman when he got the highest sales record for the year.*—Used with *not* or *hardly.* ♦ *When the basketball team did so poorly, people felt that the coach was hardly worth his salt.*

**worth one's weight in gold** *adj. phr.* Extremely useful or valuable. ♦ *Dr. Jonas Salk saved so many lives by inventing the antidote to polio that he is worth his weight in gold.* ♦ *Real Russian red caviar from the Caspian Sea is so expensive that it's almost worth its weight in gold.*

**would-be** *adj.* Aspiring. ♦ *The Broadway casting offices are always full of would-be actors.*

**would that** *or* **I would that** *or* **would God** *or* **would heaven** *literary* I wish that.—Used at the beginning of a sentence expressing a wish; followed by a verb in the subjunctive; found mostly in poetry and older literature. ♦ *Would that my mother were alive to see me married.* Syn. IF ONLY.

**wouldn't put it past one** *v. phr.* To think that someone is quite capable or likely to have done something undesirable or illegal. ♦ *The congressman is insisting that he didn't violate congressional ethics, but knowing both his expensive habits and his amorous escapades, many of us wouldn't put it past him that he might have helped himself to funds illegally.*

**wrack one's brains** *or* **beat one's brains** *v. phr.* To think very hard about a problem. ♦ *Ted has been wracking his brains on how to get the company out of debt.* ♦ *I have been beating my brains trying to do my income tax.*

**wrap one around one's finger** See TWIST ONE AROUND ONE'S LITTLE FINGER.

**wrap one's brain** *or* **wrap one's mind around something** *v. phr., slang* To understand something; gain a sympathetic insight into how something works. ♦ *I am sorry, but I just can't wrap my brain around what Stanley Fish says about Milton.* ♦ *Joe just can't wrap his mind around transformational grammar.*

**wrapped up in** *adj. phr.* Thinking only of; interested only in. ♦ *John has no time for sports because he is all wrapped up in his work.*

**wrap up** *or* **bundle up** *v. phr.* **1.** To put on warm clothes; dress warmly. ♦ *Mother told Mary to wrap up before going out into the cold.* **2.** *informal* To finish (a job). ♦ *Let's wrap up the job and go home.* **3.** *informal* To win a game. ♦ *The Mets wrapped up the baseball game in the seventh inning.*

**wreak havoc with** *v. phr.* To cause damage; ruin something. ♦ *His rebellious attitude is bound to wreak havoc at the company.*

**wringing wet** *adj.* Wet through and through; soaked; dripping. ♦ *He was wringing wet because he was caught in the rain without an umbrella.*

**write home about** *v. phr.* To become especially enthusiastic or excited about; boast about. ♦ *Joe did a good* *enough job of painting but it was nothing to write home about.*

**write off** *v. phr.* (stress on *off*) **1.** To remove (an amount) from a business record; cancel (a debt); accept as a loss. ◆ *If a customer dies when he owes the store money, the store must often write it off.* **2.** To accept (a loss or trouble) and not worry anymore about it; forget. ◆ *Jim's mistake cost him time and money, but he wrote it off to experience.* To say that (something) will fail or not be good; believe worthless. ◆ *Just because the boys on the team are young, don't write the team off.*

**write-off** *n.* (stress on *write*) A loss. ◆ *This last unfortunate business venture of ours is an obvious write-off.*

**writer's cramp** *n* . Pain in the fingers or hand caused by too much writing. ◆ *Holding your pencil too tightly for too long often gives you writer's cramp.*

**writer's block** *n. phr.* A condition of being unable to write; a period when the words just won't come. ◆ *They say that the reason for Ernest Hemingway's suicide was a severe and seemingly endless writer's block.*

**write-up** *n.* (stress on *write*) A report or story in a newspaper or magazine. ◆ *I read an interesting write-up about the President in a new magazine.*

**write up** *v.* (stress on *up*) **1.** To write the story of; describe in writing; give a full account of. ◆ *Reporters from many newspapers are here to write up the game.* ◆ *The magazine is writing up the life of the President.* **2.** To put something thought or talked about into writing; finish writing (something). ◆ *The author had an idea for a story when he saw the old house, and he wrote it up later.*

**writing** *or* **handwriting on the wall** *n. phr., literary* A warning; a message of some urgency. ◆ *"This nuclear plant is about to explode, I think," the chief engineer said. "We'd better get out of here in a hurry, the handwriting is on the wall."*

# ♦ X ♦

**x-double minus** *adj., slang, informal* Extremely poorly done, bad, inferior (said mostly about theatrical or musical performances). ♦ *Patsy gave an x-double minus performance at the audition and lost her chance for the lead role.*

**xing something out** *v. phr.* To delete words or entire sentencs from a manuscript by typing the letter xxxxxxxx many times. ♦ *I can't make out the rest of this letter; all the words have been xed out from the last paragraph.*

**X marks the spot.** An indication made on maps or documents of importance to call attention to a place or a feature of some importance. ♦ *The treasure hunter said to his companion, "Here it is; X marks the spot."*

**Xmas** *n.* abbreviation for *Christmas.* ♦ *"Merry Xmas to you" John scribbled on a card in haste.*

**x-rated** *adj., slang informal* Pertaining to movies, magazines, and literature judged pornographic and therefore off limits for minors. ♦ *My son celebrated his 21st birthday by going to an x-rated movie.*

**x-raying machine** *n., slang, citizen's band radio jargon* Speed detection device by radar used by the police. ♦ *The smokies are using the x-raying machine under the bridge!*

**x. y. or X. Y.** *n. phr.* An unnamed person. ♦ *I got a letter from an unknown person, who signed the letter as "x. y." The person said that he or she wanted to make a donation to our church, but wishes to remain nameless.*

**yak-yak** *or* **yakety-yak** *or* **yakib-yak** *n.,* *slang* Much talk about little things; talking all the time about unimportant things. ◆ *Tom sat behind two girls on the bus and he got tired of their silly yak-yak.*

**yard sale** See GARAGE SALE.

**year-round** *or* **year-around** *adj.* Usable, effective, or operating all the year. ◆ *Colorado is a year-round resort; there is fishing in the summer and skiing in the winter.*

**yellow-bellied** *adj., slang* Extremely timid, cowardly. ◆ *Joe Bennett is a yellow-bellied guy, don't send him on such a tough assignment!*

**yellow journalism** *n. phr.* Cheap and sensational newspaper writing; inflammatory language designed to stir up popular sentiment against another country. ◆ *Yellow journalism is hardly ever truly informative.*

**yellow-livered** *adj.* Cowardly. ◆ *The young boy greatly resented being called yellow-livered and started to fight right away.*

**yeoman service** *n. phr.* Help in time of need; serviceable and good assistance. ◆ *Sam was pressed into yeoman service in organizing our annual fundraiser for cerebral palsy victims.*

**yes-man** *n., informal* A person who tries to be liked by agreeing with everything said; especially, someone who always agrees with a boss or the one in charge. ◆ *John tries to get ahead on his job by being a yes-man.*

**yoo-hoo** *interj.*—Used as an informal call or shout to a person to attract his attention. ◆ *Louise opened the door and called "Yoo-hoo, Mother—are you home?"*

**you bet** *or* **you bet your boots** *or* **you bet your life** *informal* Most certainly; yes, indeed; without any doubt.—Used to declare with emphasis that a thing is really so. ◆ *Do I like to ski? You bet your life I do.* ◆ *You bet I will be at the party.* ◆ *You can bet your boots that Johnny will come home when his money is gone.*

**you bet your bottom dollar** See GAMBLE ON THAT.

**you can say that again** See YOU SAID IT.

**you can't make a silk purse out of a sow's ear** One cannot make something delicate out of something coarse or inferior.—A proverb. ◆ *Alan was asked to edit Frank's poetry, but no matter how hard he tried, the material remained unpublishable. When his wife saw his struggle, she said: "Why bother, honey? You can't make a silk purse out of a sow's ear."*

**you can take (lead) a horse to water, but you can't make him drink** One can do one's best to arrange a meeting, a conference, or bring one or several individuals to a common ground, but there is no guarantee that they will use the opportunity so afforded.—A proverb. ◆ *The president of the United States invited the two leaders of the neighboring countries at war to the White House hoping that they would sign the proposed peace agreement. When they refused to do so, the secretary of state wryly commented, "This goes to show that you can take a horse to water, but you can't make him drink."*

**you can't teach an old dog new tricks** It is very hard or almost impossible to train an older person to acquire some new skill.—A proverb. ◆ *You'll never teach your grandfather how to do his income tax on a personal computer. You can't teach an old dog new tricks.*

**you don't say** *or* **well, I never** *adj. phr., informal* Said in surprise or in astonishment, or disbelief; you're kidding; this sounds nonsensical. ◆ *"I almost beat Steffi Graff in tennis," John's daughter declared, after a visit to Germany, where she had a chance to play the famous champion for ten minutes. "You don't say!" her father replied, laughing.* ◆ *"I am a shoo-in for the Pulitzer Prize," Ted's son, a senior in high school said, when his first poem was published in the school paper. The father laughed and replied, "Well, I never..."*

**you're on** *v. phr., informal* An acceptance to an offer or an invitation. ◆ *"So you are willing to take both of us to dinner and to the opera?" John asked his* friend, Ted. "Yes, of course. I said so, didn't I? "All right, my friend, you're on!" John replied.

**you're telling me** interj., informal—Used to show that a thing is so clear that it need not be said, or just to show strong agreement. ♦ "You're late." "You're telling me!"

**your guess is as good as mine** We are both just guessing; neither one of us is really sure what the truth is.—A proverb. ♦ "Who will be the next president of the United States? George W. Bush, or a Democrat?" "I know whom I would prefer, but your guess is as good as mine."

**yours truly** adv. phr. **1.** Signing off at the end of letters. ♦ Yours truly, Tom Smith. **2.** I, the first person singular pronoun, frequently abbreviated as t.y. ♦ As t.y. has often pointed out...T.y. is not really interested in the offer.

**you said it** or **you can say that again** interj., slang—Used to show strong agreement with what another person has said. ♦ "That sure was a good show." "You said it!" ♦ "It sure is hot!" "You can say that again!"

**you scratch my back, and I'll scratch yours** When two people do reciprocal favors for one another, this saying is often used, meaning, "If you do me the favor I ask of you, I will do you the favor you ask of me."—A proverb. ♦ "You scratch my back, and I'll scratch yours," Professor Jones said to his colleague Professor Smith, when they agreed to write letters of recommendation for one another.

**you tell 'em** interj., slang—Used to agree with or encourage someone in what he is saying. ♦ The drunk was arguing with the bartenders and a man cried, "You tell 'em!"

**yum-yum** interj., informal—Used usually by or to children, to express great delight, especially in the taste of food. ♦ "Yum-Yum! That pie is good!"

**zero hour** *n.* **1.** The exact time when an attack or other military action is supposed to start. ◆*Zero hour for the bombers to take off was midnight.* **2.** The time when an important decision or change is supposed to come; the time for a dangerous action. ◆*It was zero hour and the doctor began the operation on the man.*

**zero in on** *v.* **1.** To adjust a gun so that it will exactly hit (a target); aim at. ◆*Big guns were zeroed in on the enemy fort.* ◆*American missiles have been zeroed in on certain targets, to be fired if necessary.* **2.** *slang* To give your full attention to. ◆*The Senate zeroed in on the Latin-American problems.* ◆*Let's zero in on grammar tonight.*

**zero time flat** *n. phr.* An extremely short duration; fractions of a second; often said as an exaggeration. ◆*"How soon can you get that letter typed up, Suzie?" Dean Doolittle asked his secretary. "I'll do it in zero time flat just for you," Suzie answered flirtatiously.*

**zip one's lip** See BUTTON ONE'S LIP.

**zone defense** *n.* A defense in a sport (as basketball or football) in which each player has to defend a certain area. ◆*The coach taught his team a zone defense because he thought his players weren't fast enough to defend against individual opponents.*

**zonk out** *v. phr., slang* **1.** To fall asleep very quickly. ◆*Can I talk to Joe?—Call back tomorrow, he zonked out.* **2.** To pass out from fatigue, or alcohol. ◆*You won't get a coherent word out of Joe, he has zonked out.*

**zoom in** *v. phr.* **1.** To rapidly close in on (said of airplanes and birds of prey). ◆*The fighter planes zoomed in on the enemy target.* **2.** To make a closeup of someone or something with a camera. ◆*The photographer zoomed in on the tiny colibri as it hovered over a lovely tropical flower.*